THE OXFORD HANDBOOK OF

THE ECONOMICS OF FOOD CONSUMPTION AND POLICY

THE ECONOMICS OF FOOD CONSUMPTION AND POLICY

Edited by

JAYSON L. LUSK
JUTTA ROOSEN

and

JASON F. SHOGREN

OXFORD
UNIVERSITY PRESS

OXFORD
UNIVERSITY PRESS

Great Clarendon Street, Oxford OX2 6DP

Oxford University Press is a department of the University of Oxford.
It furthers the University's objective of excellence in research, scholarship,
and education by publishing worldwide in

Oxford New York

Auckland Cape Town Dar es Salaam Hong Kong Karachi
Kuala Lumpur Madrid Melbourne Mexico City Nairobi
New Delhi Shanghai Taipei Toronto

With offices in

Argentina Austria Brazil Chile Czech Republic France Greece
Guatemala Hungary Italy Japan Poland Portugal Singapore
South Korea Switzerland Thailand Turkey Ukraine Vietnam

Oxford is a registered trade mark of Oxford University Press
in the UK and in certain other countries

Published in the United States
by Oxford University Press Inc., New York

© Oxford University Press 2011

British Library Cataloguing in Publication Data

Data available

Library of Congress Cataloging in Publication Data

Data available

Typeset by SPI Publisher Services, Pondicherry, India
Printed in Great Britain
on acid-free paper by
CPI Antony Rowe, Chippenham, Wiltshire

ISBN 978-0-19-956944-1

1 3 5 7 9 10 8 6 4 2

ACKNOWLEDGMENTS

We are grateful to have an extraordinarily talented and conscientious group of colleagues who were able and willing to undertake the task of writing the chapters that comprise this book. Many people helped review chapters of the book and provided valuable feedback to the authors.

Thanks to Sven Anders, John C. Beghin, Brian Briggeman, Stephan Brosig, Jae Bong Chang, Chanjin Chung, Keith Coble, Jay Corrigan, John Crespi, Larissa Drescher, Ellen Goddard, Shida Henneberry, Lynn Kennedy, Carl Lagerkvist, Tigran Mekonyan, Greg Poe, Timothy Richards, Matt Rousu, Christiane Schroeter, Silke Thiele, Koert van Ittersum, and Emie Yiannaka. Thanks to the editors at Oxford University Press for encouraging us to undertake this project and for helping coordinate the process.

J.L.L.
J.R.
J.F.S.

Contents

PART I THEORY AND METHODS

PART II FOOD POLICY

PART III TOPICS AND APPLICATIONS

List of Figures

LIST OF TABLES

List of Contributors

Awudu Abdulai Professor, Department of Food Economics and Consumption Studies, University of Kiel

W. L. (Vic) Adamowicz Distinguished University Professor, Department of Rural Economy, University of Alberta

Luis Miguel Albisu Unit Head, Agro-Food Economics and Natural Resources, Agro-Food Research and Technology Centre of Aragon (CITA)

Frode Alfnes Associate Professor, School of Economics and Business, Norwegian University of Life Sciences

Sven M. Anders Assistant Professor, Department of Rural Economy, University of Alberta

Fredrik Carlsson Professor, Department of Economics, University of Gothenburg

Sean B. Cash Associate Professor, Friedman School of Nutrition Science and Policy, Tufts University, Boston

Julie A. Caswell Professor and Chairperson, Department of Resource Economics, University of Massachusetts Amherst

Marco Costanigro Assistant Professor, Department of Agricultural and Resource Economics, Colorado State University

Sven-Olov Daunfeldt Associate Professor, HUI Research AB, and Lecturer, Department of Economics, Dalarna University

Andreas C. Drichoutis Lecturer, Department of Economics, University of Ioannina

Fabrice Etilé Research Fellow, Alimentation et Sciences Sociales Research Unit (ALISS), Institut National de la Recherche Agronomique (INRA), and Paris School of Economics

Jacinto F. Fabiosa Co-Director, Food and Agricultural Policy Research Institute (FAPRI), Iowa State University

John A. (Sean) Fox Professor, Department of Agricultural Economics, Kansas State University

Konstantinos Giannakas Professor and Co-Director, Center for Agricultural and Food Industrial Organization, Department of Agricultural Economics, University of Nebraska-Lincoln

Azucena Gracia Researcher, Agro-Food Economics and Natural Resources Unit, Agro-Food Research and Technology Centre of Aragon (CITA)

Roland Herrmann Professor, Institute of Agricultural Policy and Market Research, Justus-Liebig University Giessen

Sandra A. Hoffmann Senior Economist, US Department of Agriculture Economic Research Service, Washington, DC

Wallace E. Huffman C. F. Curtiss Distinguished Professor of Agriculture and Life Sciences and Professor of Economics, Iowa State University

Helen H. Jensen Professor of Economics and Head, Food and Nutrition Policy Division, Center for Agricultural and Rural Development, Iowa State University

Olof Johansson-Stenman Professor, Department of Economics, School of Business, Economics and Law, University of Gothenburg

David R. Just Associate Professor, H. Dyson School of Applied Economics and Management, Cornell University

Harry M. Kaiser Gellert Family Professor of Applied Economics and Management, H. Dyson School of Applied Economics and Management, Cornell University

Christian Kuhlgatz Research Assistant, Department of Food Economics and Consumption Studies, University of Kiel

Panagiotis Lazaridis Professor, Department of Agricultural Economics and Rural Development, Agricultural University of Athens

Maria L. Loureiro Associate Professor, Departamento de Fundamentos da Análise Económica, Universidade de Santiago de Compostela

Jayson L. Lusk Professor and Willard Sparks Endowed Chair, Department of Agricultural Economics, Oklahoma State University

Jill J. McCluskey Professor, School of Economic Sciences, Washington State University

Stéphan Marette Research Fellow at Institut National de la Recherche Agronomique (INRA) and Chair, UMR Économie Publique INRA-AgroParisTech

Thomas L. Marsh Professor, School of Economic Sciences, Washington State University

William A. Masters Professor, Friedman School of Nutrition Science and Policy, Tufts University

Pierre R. Mérel Assistant Professor, Department of Agricultural and Resource Economics, University of California-Davis

Rodolfo M. Nayga, Jr. Professor and Tyson Chair in Food Policy Economics, Department of Agricultural Economics and Agribusiness, University of Arkansas

Jonas Nordström Associate Professor, Institute of Food and Resource Economics, University of Copenhagen, and Associate Professor, Department of Economics, Lund University

Nicholas E. Piggott Professor, Department of Agricultural and Resource Economics, North Carolina State University

Kyrre Rickertsen Professor, School of Economics and Business, Norwegian University of Life Sciences

Jutta Roosen Professor and Chair for Marketing and Consumer Research, Business School, Technische Universität München

Ana Isabel Sanjuán Researcher, Agro-Food Economics and Natural Resources Unit, Agro-Food Research and Technology Centre of Aragon (CITA)

Ted C. Schroeder University Distinguished Professor, Department of Agricultural Economics, Kansas State University

Richard J. Sexton Professor, Department of Agricultural and Resource Economics, University of California-Davis

Ian Sheldon Andersons Professor of International Trade, Department of Agricultural, Environmental and Development Economics, Ohio State University

Jason F. Shogren Stroock Professor of Natural Resource Conservation and Management, Department of Economics and Finance, University of Wyoming

Hayden Stewart Agricultural Economist, US Department of Agriculture, Economic Research Service

Joffre D. Swait Professor, Alberta School of Business, University of Alberta

Johan F. M. Swinnen Director, LICOS Centre for Institutions and Economic Performance, and Professor, Department of Economics, University of Leuven

Mario F. Teisl Professor, School of Economics, and Director, School of Policy and International Affairs, University of Maine

Ramona Teuber Researcher, Institute of Agricultural Policy and Market Research, Justus-Liebig University Giessen

Linda Thunström Research AB, HUI

Glynn T. Tonsor Assistant Professor, Department of Agricultural Economics, Kansas State University

Thijs Vandemoortele LICOS Centre for Institutions and Economic Performance and Department of Economics, University of Leuven

Joachim von Braun Director, Center for Development Research (ZEF Bonn), and Professor, Department for Economic and Technological Change, Bonn University

Christoph R. Weiss Professor, Department of Economics, Vienna University of Economics and Business

Parke Wilde Associate Professor, Friedman School of Nutrition Science and Policy, Tufts University

Michael K. Wohlgenant William Neal Reynolds Distinguished Professor, Department of Agricultural and Resource Economics, North Carolina State University

INTRODUCTION

JAYSON L. LUSK, JUTTA ROOSEN,
AND JASON F. SHOGREN

Throughout their history, humans' lives have been inextricably connected with the food they eat. All humans rely on food for sustenance and survival, but food has also shaped culture and civilization. Although much time was spent battling hunger and malnutrition, humans' proclivity for new and exotic goods such as spices or cane sugar made our ancestors willing to leave their homes seeking to trade with those in faraway lands. Given the historical importance of food and its link to culture, it is perhaps not surprising that food and agriculture are among the most regulated and romanticized industries in the modern world.

Historically, the challenge for humans has been to secure a sufficient supply of food to stave off hunger and starvation. As a result, much of the research on food and agriculture in the past century has focused on issues related to production efficiency, food supply, and farm profitability. While the problem of food availability has not been completely eradicated, people living in today's developed countries are as likely to suffer from problems of *over*consumption as from hunger or malnutrition. Today's food consumers not only have access to more food than ever before, they can also choose between a much wider variety and quality of foods than ever in the past; so much so that some psychologists claim consumers suffer from "choice overload."

As a result of these changes, farmers, agribusiness, policymakers, and academics have increasingly turned their attention away from the farm and toward the food consumer and to issues related to food consumption. Many recent developments have triggered greater interest in the economics of food consumption around the globe. Growing concerns about rising food prices and nutrition and have spurred speculation about the causes and consequences of expensive food. At the same time, consumer and environmental groups are demanding more from the food production system—sustainability, naturalness, reduced environmental impacts, and less use of genetic modification, growth hormones, pesticides, and so on. Technologies that have the potential to increase productivity and lower food prices are being spurned by some consumers and governments. Agricultural policies, which historically served to support farm incomes, are now being used to promote environmental objectives, protect consumers from unwanted food technologies, and identify origin of production. Perhaps at no time in the past has the food production system been confronted with such a confluence of challenges, and many, though not all, of the developments are a result of changes in consumer demand for food—demand for alternative production practices, increasing demand from developing countries, demand for new food products, demand for better nutrition, etc.

Although research on food demand and consumption has been active for several decades (e.g., see Unnevehr et al. 2010 for a historical account), there are presently few resources to which someone can turn as a basic reference on the economics of food consumption and policy that covers specificities of theories and methods related to the study of food consumers and covers issues in food demand and policy. This book is meant to fill that gap. Our hope is that it will serve as a useful reference guide to graduate students and academics working in the field of food economics and policy who are interested in the consumer end of the supply chain, and also to people employed in food and agricultural industries, special interest and activist groups, and policymakers.

The book is divided into three main parts: I, Theory and Methods; II, Food Policy; and III, Topics and Applications. The first section of the book contains eleven chapters covering the core theoretical and methodological approaches that are used in studying the economics of food consumption and policy. The focus of the chapters is on the application of the theories and methods to food consumption. There is no single unified theory of consumer demand. Rather, the literature consists of several competing and complementary theories, which are covered in Chapters 1 through 6. The chapters show how food consumers can be conceptualized as choosing quantities of goods (Chapter 1) or purchasing inputs from the market to produce goods and services of value (Chapter 2). Chapters 3 through 6 extend these foundational models to cases where consumers are uncertain about the quality or safety of food (Chapter 3), are less than perfectly rational (Chapter 4), and choose which good to buy given a good's characteristics (Chapters 5 and 6). While each of these chapters also discuss empirical implementation of the conceptual models, Chapters 7 and 8 delve more deeply into consumer research methods, focusing specifically on stated preference and experimental methods to determine product valuations of non-market goods or attributes. Chapters 9 through 11 cover topics related to the integration of models of consumer preference into market-level models involving interactions with firms and policymakers. Chapters 9 and 10 conceptualize consumer decision-making in light of the surge in product differentiation by firms. Chapter 11 provides a framework for assessing the economic effects of changes in consumer demand and food policy interventions on market prices and the welfare of food producers and consumers.

The second section of the book focuses specifically on policy issues related to food consumption. Several chapters in this section focus on the theory and conceptual issues relevant in food markets, such as product bans and labels, labeling, standards, political economy, and scientific uncertainty. Other chapters home in on policy issues of particular interest to the consumer end of the food supply chain such as food safety, nutrition, food security, and development.

The final section of the book turns attention to particular issues and topics related to the economics of food consumption and policy. These chapters are largely empirical and descriptive in nature, and are meant to serve as introductions to current topics. Several chapters discuss general trends in food consumption such as globalization, rising food prices, changes in away-from-home food consumption, and changes in food variety. The last section also contains chapters dealing with more specific food quality and food safety dimensions and with topics of emerging interest related to advertising, meat, environment, and ethics.

References

Unnevehr, L., J. Eales, H. Jensen, J. L. Lusk, J. McCluskey, and J. Kinsey. 2010. "Food and Consumer Economics." *American Journal of Agricultural Economics* 92: 506–21.

PART I

THEORY AND METHODS

CHAPTER 1

....

CONSTRAINED UTILITY MAXIMIZATION AND DEMAND SYSTEM ESTIMATION

....

NICHOLAS E. PIGGOTT AND
THOMAS L. MARSH

1 INTRODUCTION

....

The purpose of this chapter is to present an overview of constrained utility maximization and demand system analysis, targeting the applied economist examining issues of food demand. For completeness dual representations of the constrained utility maximization approach are presented, illustrating theoretical consistency between ordinary and inverse demand systems. An application of US food demand (food at home (FAH), food away from home (FAFH), and alcoholic beverages (ABs)) and relevant hypothesis tests are illustrated for both ordinary demand systems (quantity formation) and inverse demand systems (price formation). A comprehensive literature exists on the economics and econometrics of consumer demand analysis. Nonetheless, the central importance of the consumer to food markets continues to confront agricultural economists today. For example, demand systems are applied to estimate elasticities used in models for policy analysis (i.e., equilibrium displacement models, trade models), predict and forecast, test structural change, calculate welfare effects from price changes, and assess market effects from advertising, information, and food recalls. Consequently, the presentation of this chapter strives to strike a balance between theoretical rigor, empirical application, and implementation, which are important for quality research outcomes and effective policy recommendations.

The chapter is organized in the following manner. First, we provide an overview of the literature on consumer and demand system analysis with emphasis on complete food demand systems.[1] Second, we precent theoretical foundations, including the axioms of choice, constrained utility maximization, properties, and general demand restrictions. Third, we discuss dual functions, including the expenditure function, the indirect utility function, and the distance function. The first three dual approaches are standard tools of the applied demand system analyst. The distance function approach is less prevalent in the literature, but provides a theoretically consistent means to derive inverse demand relationships and to study consumer price formation. Fourth, we introduce welfare effects and integrability along with separability and aggregation. Fifth, we provide a review of functional forms. Sixth, we cover econometric issues that include estimation, inference and hypothesis testing, specification tests, and other empirical issues. Seventh, we provide an empirical example that focuses on FAH, FAFH, and ABs. Models of the almost ideal demand and inverse almost ideal demand systems are estimated and reported as well as some additional hypothesis tests and inferences regarding model performance. Finally, we provide concluding remarks.

1.1   Literature Review

This section highlights historical and broad contributions to neoclassical consumer demand analysis with focus on food and agricultural economics. More specific and targeted contributions are noted in the sections that follow.

The development of the linear expenditure model by Stone (1954) is often credited as one of the seminal papers in the demand system literature. This was followed by Barten's (1967) fundamental matrix equation, which was an important step in formalizing economic restrictions of consumer theory into a unified demand systems approach. Gorman's (1953, 1959, 1981) seminal work on preferences, separability, and aggregation laid a cornerstone for consumer demand theory. Barten (1977) reviewed some of the earlier demand system specification and estimation issues, while Pollak and Wales (1980, 1981, 1992) provided results on conditional demand models and incorporating demographic variables into demand systems. Deaton (1986) surveyed standard econometric issues of demand system estimation. Current demand system literature has focused on the rank of demand systems and functional specifications (see LaFrance and Pope 2008, 2009).[2]

---

[1] See LaFrance and Hanemann (1989) for development of incomplete demand systems. LaFrance (2001) provides a household production modeling framework for the applied economic analysis of consumption.

[2] Gorman (1981) demonstrated that in the case of exactly aggregable demand systems, integrability implies the matrix of Engle curve coefficients is at most rank 3. Full rank systems are those with rank equal to the columns of the coefficient matrix (Lewbel 1990). Barnett and Serletis (2008) provide a good discussion of demand system rank with examples.

Demand systems approaches have been pervasive in the agricultural economics literature, especially when examining the impact of prices, income, and other factors on food demand. For example, a significant amount of effort has been expended explaining changes in US food consumption and in particular identifying whether there has been structural change in demand. An incomplete list of such studies includes Chavas (1983), Moschini and Meilke (1984, 1989), Wohlgenant (1985), Dahlgran (1987), Eales and Unnevehr (1988, 1993), and Chalfant and Alston (1998). In addition, Holt and Goodwin (1997) investigated habit formation using US meat expenditures. Meanwhile, Capps and Love (2002) considered the use of electronic scanner data on fruit juices and drinks. Dhar, Chavas, and Gould (2003) explored branded products in the soft drink market using scanner data. Piggott (2003) examined US food demand using generalized PIGLOG models. A recent paper on the economic and econometric structure of food demand and nutrition is provided by LaFrance (2008).

Issues of advertising, health, and food safety effects on consumer demand have been examined using ordinary demand system approaches. Huang (1996) estimated nutrient elasticities in food demand. Brester and Schroeder (1995) examined the impacts of brand and generic advertising on meat demand in the US, while Piggott et al. (1996) investigated the impacts of advertising on meat demand in Australia. Kinnucan et al. (1997) investigated the effects of health and generic advertising on US meat demand. Piggott and Marsh (2004) examined the impact of public food safety information on meat demand. Marsh, Schroeder, and Mintert (2004) reported on the effect of product recalls on meat demand.

Relative to ordinary demand system approaches, which assume prices are fixed, inverse demand systems, which assume quantities are fixed, have received much less attention. Huang (1988) studied an inverse demand system for composite foods. Price formation has been previously studied for meat demand (Eales and Unnevehr 1994; Holt and Goodwin 1997; Holt 2002) and fish (Barten and Bettendorf 1989; Holt and Bishop 2002; Kristofersson and Rickertsen 2004, 2007). Alternatively, Moschini and Rizzi (2007) specified and estimated a system of mixed demand systems that allow adjustment of prices for some goods and of quantities for other goods to clear the market.[3]

Commonly used books on consumer demand analysis include (but are not limited to) Shephard (1970), Phlips (1974), Deaton and Muellbauer (1980b), Johnson, Hassan, and Green (1984), Theil and Clements (1987), Cornes (1992), Varian (1992), and Pollak and Wales (1992). These books provide a historical reference and neoclassical concepts of consumer demand with methods and applications to demand system analysis and duality theory. Other useful texts and readings include Chipman et al. (1971), Blackorby, Primont, and Russell (1978), Deaton (1981, 1986), Lancaster (1991), and Slottje (2009).

[3] Samuelson (1965) first analyzed mixed demand systems.

2   PREFERENCES AND UTILITY MAXIMIZATION

In empirical analysis the existence of demand functions is often assumed with the anticipation that the law of demand and other properties may hold. Fortunately, microeconomic theory provides a set of fundamental assumptions on individual consumer preferences, often called the axioms of choice, which establish a theoretically consistent framework for demand system analysis. From the axioms of choice the existence of a utility function can be deduced, providing a convenient means to represent consumers' behavior. Furthermore, existence and properties of demand functions can be derived from constrained maximization with origins in the fundamental axioms on individual preferences.[4]

2.1   Axioms of Choice

Let X be a set of consumption bundles defined mathematically as a subset of a finite n-dimensional Euclidean space. The symbol $\succsim$ is used to mean "at least as preferred as" whereas $\succ$ is used to mean "strictly preferred to." Superscripts on vectors, for example, $\mathbf{x}^1$, will be used to distinguish different vectors. The axioms of choice are

> *Axiom 1.* Reflexivity. For any bundle $\mathbf{x} \in X$, $\mathbf{x} \succsim \mathbf{x}$.
> *Axiom 2.* Completeness. For any two bundles $\mathbf{x}^1 \in X$ and $\mathbf{x}^2 \in X$, either $\mathbf{x}^1 \succsim \mathbf{x}^2$ or $\mathbf{x}^2 \succsim \mathbf{x}^1$.
> *Axiom 3.* Transitivity. Let $\mathbf{x}^1, \mathbf{x}^2, \mathbf{x}^3 \in X$. If $\mathbf{x}^1 \succsim \mathbf{x}^2$ and $\mathbf{x}^2 \succsim \mathbf{x}^3$, then $\mathbf{x}^1 \succsim \mathbf{x}^3$.
> *Axiom 4.* Closure. For all $x \in X$, sets $\left\{ \mathbf{x}^1 \in X : \mathbf{x}^1 \succsim \mathbf{x} \right\}$ and $\left\{ \mathbf{x}^1 \in X : \mathbf{x} \succsim \mathbf{x}^1 \right\}$ are closed.

The first axiom states that each bundle is as preferred as itself. The second axiom allows any two bundles to be compared. Axioms 1–4 are sufficient to allow representation of the preference ordering by a continuous, real-valued utility function $u(\mathbf{x})$.[5]

> *Axiom 5.* Non-satiation. The utility function $u(\mathbf{x})$ is non-decreasing in each of its arguments and for all $\mathbf{x}$ in the choice set is increasing in at least one of its arguments.
> *Axiom 6.* Convexity. If $\mathbf{x}^2 \succsim \mathbf{x}^1$, then for $0 \leq \lambda \leq 1$, $\lambda \mathbf{x}^2 + (1 - \lambda)\mathbf{x}^1 \succ \mathbf{x}^1$.

This axiom is a formal representation that indifference curves are convex to the origin, stating that the linear combination of $\mathbf{x}^1$ and $\mathbf{x}^2$ is as preferred as $\mathbf{x}^1$. From axioms 1–6 the utility function is non-decreasing, quasi-concave, and unique up to a strictly monotone function.[6]

---

[4] See Deaton and Muellbauer (1980b) and Cornes (1992) for additional introductory readings and references.

[5] See Blackorby, Primont, and Russell (1978).

[6] See Blackorby, Primont, and Russell (1978). Strict convexity rules out linear segments of indifference surfaces and facilitates the assumption of a second-order differentiable utility function in the optimization process. This assumption is useful in the application of duality theory.

The axioms of choice not only provide the logical and mathematical foundation for neoclassical consumer choice theory, but also provide means to justify constrained utility maximization. So should someone ask how an economist defends the use of a utility function, one answer is that it is equivalent to ranking preferences for bundles of goods.

2.2   The Primal Problem

The constrained utility maximization problem is represented by $\max_{x}\{u(\mathbf{x})\,st\,\mathbf{p}'\mathbf{x} = m\}$ where u is a continuous, non-decreasing, and quasi-concave utility function, $\mathbf{x} = (x_1, \ldots, x_n)' > 0$ is a $(n \times 1)$ non-negative vector of goods, $\mathbf{p} = (p_1, \ldots, p_n)' > 0$ is a $(n \times 1)$ vector of given prices, and m is total fixed expenditure. The Lagrangian of the primal problem is $L = u(\mathbf{x}) + \lambda\left(m - \sum_{i=1}^{n} p_i x_i\right)$ with the first-order conditions yielding a system of $n+1$ partial differential equations $\frac{\partial L}{\partial x_i} = \frac{\partial u}{\partial x_i} - \lambda p_i = 0, i = 1, \ldots, n$ and $\frac{\partial L}{\partial \lambda} = m - \sum_{i=1}^{n} p_i x_i = 0$. Applying the Implicit Function Theorem, the utility-maximizing quantities demanded are $\mathbf{x} = \mathbf{x}(\mathbf{p}, m)$, which are the uncompensated (i.e., Marshallian) demand functions.[7] The Hotelling–Wold Identity $\frac{p_\ell}{m} = \frac{\partial u}{\partial x_\ell} / \sum_{j=1}^{n} x_j \frac{\partial u}{\partial x_j}$ provides the uncompensated system of inverse demand equations.

This set of demand functions satisfies the properties of homogeneity, aggregation, symmetry, and negativity (often termed the general demand restrictions). Both the derivative and elasticity form of these properties are provided ahead. Elasticity expressions are, for example, defined as $\varepsilon_{im} = \frac{\partial x_i}{\partial m} \frac{m}{x_i}$, which represents the total expenditure elasticity of demand for good i, and $\varepsilon_{ij} = \frac{\partial x_i}{\partial p_j} \frac{p_j}{x_i}$, which represents the price elasticity of demand for good i and price j. The ith share equation is $w_i = \frac{p_i x_i}{m}$. Applying Euler's Theorem (see Intriligator 1971; Silberberg 1978) with homogeneity of degree 0 in $\mathbf{p}$ and m gives rise to

$$0 = \sum_{j=1}^{n} \frac{\partial x_i}{\partial p_j} p_j + \frac{\partial x_i}{\partial m} m \Leftrightarrow \sum_{j=1}^{n} \varepsilon_{ij} + \varepsilon_{im} = 0.$$

Differentiating the budget constraint with respect to m yields Engle aggregation

$$\sum_{i=1}^{n} p_i \frac{\partial x_i(p, m)}{\partial m} = 1 \Leftrightarrow \sum_{i=1}^{n} w_i \varepsilon_{im} = 1.$$

Differentiating the budget constraint with respect to p_j yields Cournot aggregation

$$\sum_{i=1}^{n} p_i \frac{\partial x_i(p, m)}{\partial p_j} = - q_j \Leftrightarrow \sum_{i=1}^{n} w_i \varepsilon_{ij} = - w_j.$$

---

[7] If one does not assume an interior solution, then the first-order conditions can be derived by using the Kuhn–Tucker conditions (see Intriligator 1971).

From Young's Theorem, Slutsky symmetry can be derived as

$$\frac{\partial x_i}{\partial p_j} + x_j \frac{\partial x_i}{\partial m} = \frac{\partial x_j}{\partial p_i} + x_i \frac{\partial x_j}{\partial m}, i \neq j \Leftrightarrow w_i \varepsilon_{ij} + w_i w_j \varepsilon_{im} = w_j \varepsilon_{ji} + w_i w_j \varepsilon_{jm}, i \neq j.$$

From the Slutsky equation the standard price and income effects can be generated.[8] Compensated effects (and elasticities) can be derived from the substitution matrix as $\frac{\partial x_i^h}{\partial p_j} = \frac{\partial x_i}{\partial p_j} + x_j \frac{\partial x_i}{\partial m} \Leftrightarrow \varepsilon_{ij}^h = \varepsilon_{ij} + w_j \varepsilon_{im}$, which is useful in classifying goods into substitutes ($\varepsilon_{ij}^h > 0, i \neq j$) and complements ($\varepsilon_{ij}^h < 0, i \neq j$). The matrix of compensated (i.e., Hicksian) demand functions is negative semi-definite, implying for each own-price effect the negativity condition of

$$\frac{\partial x_i^h}{\partial p_i} < 0, i = 1, \ldots, n.$$

Barten (1964, 1977) provides detailed derivations of general demand restrictions, including Barten's fundamental matrix equation, which concisely summarizes the above information. A set of parameters estimated from a demand system satisfying each of these restrictions is then fully consistent with the concept of constrained utility maximization.

3   DUAL FUNCTIONS

Duality involves transforming consumer preferences represented in one variable (e.g., quantity space for the utility function) to another variable, which can be more convenient for some theoretical or empirical problems. For example, in the expenditure function, preferences appear in price space as opposed to quantity space for the direct utility function. Below we provide an overview of the expenditure, indirect utility, and distance functions along with theoretical properties.[9]

3.1   Expenditure Function

The expenditure function is defined as the minimum expenditure of attaining utility level u at price $\mathbf{p}$. The dual expression can be defined as $e(\mathbf{p}, u) = \min_x \{\mathbf{p}'\mathbf{x} \; s.t. \; u(\mathbf{x}) = u\}$. The expenditure function is non-decreasing in $\mathbf{p}$, increasing in u, homogeneous of degree 1 in $\mathbf{p}$, and concave in $\mathbf{p}$. From Shephard's Lemma the compensated (i.e., Hicksian)

---

[8] Note that Engle aggregation, homogeneity, and symmetry imply Cournot aggregation, and are not independent relationships.

[9] See Blackorby, Primont, and Russell (1978) for a more rigorous presentation of duality theory and Deaton and Muellbauer (1980b), Varian (1992), and Cornes (1992) for additional introductory readings. Refer to Lusk et al. (2002) for some insights on the empirical properties of duality theory.

demand function arises from $\frac{\partial e(\mathbf{p}, u)}{\partial p_j} = x_j^h(\mathbf{p}, u)$. The compensated demand functions are homogeneous of degree 0 in prices and satisfy the negativity condition.

3.2   Indirect Utility Function

The consumer's indirect utility function can be defined as

$$v(\mathbf{p}, m) = \max_x \{u(\mathbf{x}) \; s.t. \; \mathbf{p}'\mathbf{x} = m\} = u(\mathbf{x}(\mathbf{p}, m))$$

The indirect utility function is non-increasing in $\mathbf{p}$, non-decreasing in m, homogeneous of degree 0 in $\mathbf{p}$ and m, and quasi-convex in $\mathbf{p}$. From Roy's Identity the uncompensated demand functions arise

$$\left(\frac{\partial v(\mathbf{p}, m)}{\partial p_j}\right) \Big/ \left(\frac{\partial v(\mathbf{p}, m)}{\partial m}\right) = -x_j$$

As above, the general demand restrictions of homogeneity, adding up, symmetry, and negativity hold. Alternatively, the uncompensated demand function can be obtained by the dual identity $x_j(\mathbf{p}, m) = x_j^h(\mathbf{p}, v(\mathbf{p}, m))$.

3.3   Distance Function

A less familiar dual function is the distance function from which inverse demand systems can be derived.[10] This is important in food demand analysis when quantities are predetermined. The standard consumer distance function can be defined by

$$d(\mathbf{x}, u) = \sup_{\tilde{d}} \left\{ \tilde{d} > 0 | (\mathbf{x}/\tilde{d}) \in S(u), \forall u \in \mathbf{R}^1_+ \right\}.$$

Here, u is a (1×1) scalar level of utility, $\mathbf{x} = (x_1, \ldots, x_n)'$ is a $(n \times 1)$ vector of predetermined goods, and $S(u)$ is the set of all vectors of goods $\mathbf{x} \in \mathbf{R}^n_+$ that can produce the utility level $u \in \mathbf{R}^1_+$. The underlying behavioral assumption is that the distance function represents a rescaling of all goods consistent with a target utility level u. Intuitively, d is the maximum value by which one could divide $\mathbf{x}$ and still realize u. The value d places $\mathbf{x}/d$ on the boundary of $S(u)$ and on a ray through $\mathbf{x}$.

Compensated inverse demand equations may be obtained by applying Gorman's Lemma $\frac{\partial d(\mathbf{x}, u)}{\partial \mathbf{x}} = \tilde{\mathbf{p}}^h(\mathbf{x}, u)$, where $m = \sum_{i=1}^n p_i x_i$ and $\tilde{\mathbf{p}} = (\tilde{p}_1, \ldots, \tilde{p}_n)$ is a $(n \times 1)$ vector

---

[10] An even less familiar concept is the benefit function. Luenberger (1992) introduced the benefit function and Chambers, Chung, and Färe (1996) demonstrated that the benefit function is equivalent to a directional distance function. As pointed out by Luenberger (1992), the consumer distance function and the benefit function are distinctly different specifications. McLaren and Wong (2009) use the benefit function to specify and estimate price-dependent or inverse demand models.

of expenditure normalized prices or $\tilde{p}_i = p_i/m$.[11] The properties of a distance function are that it is homogeneous of degree 1, non-decreasing, and concave in quantities $\mathbf{x}$, as well as non-increasing and quasi-concave in utility u (Shephard 1970; Cornes 1992). The Antonelli matrix $\frac{\partial^2 d(\mathbf{x},u)}{\partial \mathbf{x} \partial \mathbf{x}'}$ is negative semi-definite. Because the distance function is homogeneous of degree 1 in quantities, it follows that the compensated inverse demand function is homogeneous of degree 0 in quantities. Uncompensated inverse demand functions can be obtained by applying the dual identity $\tilde{\mathbf{p}}(\mathbf{x}) = \tilde{\mathbf{p}}^h(\mathbf{x}, u(\mathbf{x}))$.

The uncompensated price flexibilities are $f_{i\ell} = \frac{\partial \ln p_i(\mathbf{x};\mathbf{c})}{\partial \ln x_\ell}$. The compensated flexibilities $f_{i\ell}^h = \frac{\partial \ln p_i(\mathbf{x},u)}{\partial \ln x_\ell}$ can be recovered using the expression $f_{i\ell}^h = f_{i\ell} - f_i w_j$. Scale flexibilities $f_i = \frac{\partial \ln p_i(\lambda \mathbf{x})}{\partial \ln \lambda}$ can be derived by $\frac{\partial \ln p_i(\lambda \tilde{\mathbf{x}})}{\partial \ln \lambda} = \sum_{j=1}^n f_{ij}$ for any scalar λ (Anderson 1980). Conceptual and empirical properties exist between flexibilities and elasticities, which are discussed further in Huang (1994) and Lusk et al. (2002).

4   AGGREGATION AND SEPARABILITY

Consumers at any given time allocate resources between many goods (e.g., between foods or food groups, food/non-food goods, durable/non-durable goods, or current/future goods). It is important to find ways in which the consumer problem can be simplified, either by aggregation, so that whole categories can be dealt with as single units, or by separation, so that the problem can be dealt with in smaller, more manageable units, making it empirically tractable (Deaton and Muellbauer 1980b). Below we provide a brief introduction of aggregation and separability issues to set the stage for the empirical analysis later in this chapter.[12]

4.1   Aggregation

Aggregation can be thought of as the transition from the microeconomics of individual consumer behavior to the analysis of market demand. It is important to know what useful properties, if any, of the disaggregated model survive the aggregation process. Generally speaking, the aggregate demand function will possess no interesting properties other than homogeneity and continuity (Varian 1992: 155).

However, functional forms exist that can yield aggregate demand functions that are useful in economic analysis. Two forms of aggregation are exact linear aggregation and exact non-linear aggregation. An important role of aggregation theory is to provide

---

[11] If $\mathbf{x}$ is a bundle for which $u(\mathbf{x}) = u$ then $d(\mathbf{x}, u) = 1$, and the share form of the expression above is given by $\frac{\partial \ln d(\mathbf{x},u)}{\partial \ln \mathbf{x}} = \mathbf{w}(\mathbf{x}, u)$.

[12] See Blackorby, Davidson, and Schworm (1991) for a more rigorous presentation and Deaton and Muellbauer (1980b) and Cornes (1992) for additional readings.

necessary conditions under which it is possible to treat aggregate consumer behavior as if it were the outcome of the decisions of a single utility maximizing consumer.

Consider the aggregate demand function $x_i = x_i(\mathbf{p}, M) \equiv \sum_{h=1}^{H} x_{ih}(\mathbf{p}, m_h) = x_i(\mathbf{p}, m_1, \ldots, m_H)$, where there are $h = 1, \ldots, H$ consumers. Aggregate demand exists (theoretically) with an income for each consumer. In empirical work total income or the mean income level are more available but data may not be accessible for the income of each individual. Linear aggregation of income $M = \sum_{h=1}^{H} m_h \left(\Leftrightarrow \bar{M} = \frac{1}{H}\sum_{h=1}^{H} m_h\right)$ implies linearity of income for consumer demand. More formally $x_i(\mathbf{p}, M) \equiv \sum_{h=1}^{H} x_{ih}(\mathbf{p}, m_h)$ with $M = \sum_{h=1}^{H} m_h$ if and only if $\frac{\partial x_{ih}}{\partial m_h} = \beta_i(\mathbf{p}) \forall h, i$. That is, this occurs if and only if the demand function is a linear function of income

$$x_i(\mathbf{p}, M) = \sum_{h=1}^{H} [\beta_i(\mathbf{p}) m_h + a_{ih}(\mathbf{p})] = \beta_i(\mathbf{p}) M + \alpha_i(\mathbf{p})$$

In effect, under exact linear aggregation, Engle curves are linear and the same slope for each individual. These restrictive conditions are not appealing for most empirical work.

Exact non-linear aggregation, wherein Engle curves are not necessarily linear, generalizes the above specification (see Deaton 1986). It requires only that demand for goods depends on prices and a representative level of expenditure, M, which itself can be a function of the distribution of expenditures and of prices. In this case, the market pattern of demand can be thought of as deriving from the behavior of a single representative individual endowed with total expenditure M and prices $\mathbf{p}$. A particularly relevant case for the applied economist occurs when the representative expenditure level is independent of prices and only depends on the distribution of expenditures. This case is known as the price-independent generalized linearity (PIGL). The logarithmic form is known as the PIGLOG, where the microexpenditure function is expressed as

$$\ln e(u, \mathbf{p}) = (1 - u)\ln a(\mathbf{p}) + u \ln b(\mathbf{p})$$

for function of prices $a(\mathbf{p})$ and $b(\mathbf{p})$. This gives rise to the almost ideal demand system, which is non-linear in expenditure, and is pervasive in the food demand literature. We illustrate this further as an application in the empirical section of this chapter. For recent extensions and further discussion of these issues, see Slottje (2009).

4.2 Separability

Separability is relevant because it has the potential to reduce the dimensionality of the consumer demand problem and allow a researcher to examine one aspect of a problem in relative isolation from others. For example, meat is often assumed separable from other foods. There are several historical forms of separability in the economic literature, including Hicksian separability and functional separability. Here we focus on functional separability.[13]

Alternative forms of separability inherit characteristics from the structure of the utility function. Consider, first, the concept of additive separability (Houthakker 1960). The utility function that is additively separable is expressed as $u(x) = {}_f(x_1) + \ldots + {}_f(x_n)$. This implies functional independence of the marginal utility of good i from the consumption of any other good, or

$$\frac{\partial u}{\partial x_i} = \frac{\partial f_i}{\partial x_i} \Rightarrow \frac{\partial^2 u}{\partial x_i \partial x_j} = \frac{\partial^2 f_i}{\partial x_i \partial x_j} = 0.$$

Is the additivity assumption ever defensible? Some argue it is for broad aggregates such as food, housing, or clothing, as opposed to individual commodities. However, most agree that the restrictive nature implied for the underlying preference structure limits its usefulness for food demand analysis.

A more general concept is weak separability, which has been applied in many empirical food demand studies. Suppose there exists a partition of m groups of goods (with n_m goods in group m), and consider two groups q and r (say, beverages and meats, respectively). Formally, weak separability arises when $u(x_{11}, \ldots, x_{1n_1}, x_{21}, \ldots, x_{2n_2}, \ldots, x_{m1}, \ldots, x_{mn_m}) = F(f_1(x_{11}, \ldots, x_{1n_1}), \ldots, f_m(x_{m1}, \ldots, x_{mn_m}))$ if and only if $\frac{\partial}{\partial x_{qk}}\left[\left(\frac{\partial u}{\partial x_{ri}}\right) / \left(\frac{\partial u}{\partial x_{rj}}\right)\right] = 0 \quad \forall r, i, j, k, q (q \neq r)$ and where $k \in \{1, \ldots, n_q\}$ and $i, j \in \{1, \ldots, n_r\}$. In other words, under weak separability, the ratio of marginal utilities from goods within one group (say, meats) is independent relative to the change in consumption of a good in another group (say, beverages). Goldman and Uzawa (1964) demonstrated that a direct result of weak separability is that price effects from outside a particular group of goods are translated through income effects. Alternative forms of separability that may be of interest to the applied economist are implicit and asymmetric separability.[14]

5 INTEGRABILITY AND WELFARE EFFECTS

The problem of integrability is summarized by the question "If $\mathbf{x}(\mathbf{p}, m)$ satisfies the general demand restrictions, can one integrate $\mathbf{x}(\mathbf{p}, m)$ back and recover the utility function?" As demonstrated above, in mathematical terminology, the first-order

---

[13] Hicksian separability occurs if prices of a group of goods change proportionately, then the corresponding group of goods can be aggregated into a single composite commodity having a single price for purposes of analyzing consumer demand. However, if prices of a group of goods do not change proportionately, then an alternative approach such as weak separability is needed.

[14] See Blackorby, Primont, and Russell (1978) and Moschini, Moro, and Green (1994) for more details related to weak and other forms of separability. To read more on two-stage budgeting and separability, see Deaton and Muellbauer (1980b).

conditions form a system of partial differential equations (PDEs). A necessary condition for a local solution to the system of PDEs is symmetry of cross-partial derivatives (i.e., satisfy mathematical integrability and path independence). Hence, economic integrability requires mathematical integrability (i.e., Slutsky symmetry) plus Engle aggregation, homogeneity, and curvature properties of $x = h^m(\mathbf{p}, m)$. Therefore, recovering a utility, indirect utility, or expenditure function requires economic integrability (Hurwicz and Uzawa 1971; Silberberg 1978).

Integrability not only allows recovery of preference structure, but also provides the means to measure exact welfare changes.[15] Two standard measures of exact welfare are equivalent and compensating variation. Consider a consumer with an initial price vector and budget at $(\mathbf{p}^0, m^0)$. The idea is to obtain a measure of the welfare change implied by the move from $(\mathbf{p}^0, m^0)$ to $(\mathbf{p}^1, m^1)$. The equivalent variation associated with the move from $(\mathbf{p}^0, m^0)$ to $(\mathbf{p}^1, m^1)$ is defined as that amount of income that, if given to the consumer, would have exactly the same effect on his/her welfare as the move from $(\mathbf{p}^0, m^0)$ to $(\mathbf{p}^1, m^1)$. The equivalent variation can be represented by $EV^{01} = E(\mathbf{p}^0, u^1) - E(\mathbf{p}^1, u^1)$. For a single price change it can be represented by $EV^{01} = \int_{p_j^1}^{p_j^0} x_j^h(\mathbf{p}, u^1) dp_j$.

Compensating variation provides an answer to the following question: How much income would have to be taken away from the consumer in order to negate the effect of moving from $(\mathbf{p}^0, m^0)$ to $(\mathbf{p}^1, m^1)$? The compensating variation can be represented by $CV^{01} = E(\mathbf{p}^0, u^0) - E(\mathbf{p}^1, u^0)$. For a single price change it can be represented by $CV^{01} = \int_{p_j^1}^{p_j^0} x_j^h(\mathbf{p}, u^0) dp_j$. Approaches to estimate the magnitude and precision of welfare changes for single or multiple price changes are discussed in Vartia (1983) and Breslaw and Smith (1995).[16] See Just, Hueth, and Schmitz (2004) for further reading on applied welfare economics.

6   FUNCTIONAL FORMS AND EXAMPLES

Popular functional forms of ordinary demand systems include the translog model of Christensen, Jorgenson, and Lau (1975), the almost ideal (AI) demand system of Deaton and Muellbauer (1980a, b), and the normalized quadratic model (Diewert and Wales 1988). Differential demand systems were developed by Barten (1964) and Theil (1965), who provide alternative specifications of the Rotterdam model. Barnett (1979) provided theoretical foundations for the Rotterdam model. Several generalizations of these models include the AI translog model of Lewbel (1989), the generalized translog (Pollak and Wales 1980), the generalized AI (Bollino 1987), the globally flexible AI (Chalfant 1987), the generalized AI translog (Bollino and Violi 1990), the quadratic

---

[15] See Diewert (2009) for exact index methods to approximate cost of living and welfare changes.

[16] Kim (1997) provided information to estimate welfare impacts from quantity measurements. Holt and Bishop (2002) apply this approach to price formation of fish.

AI (Banks, Blundell, and Lewbel 1997), and the nested PIGLOG (Piggott 2003). LaFrance and Pope (2009) derived a generalized quadratic expenditure system. Functional forms of inverse demand systems include the inverse linear expenditure model, the inverse almost ideal (IAI) demand model of Eales and Unnevehr (1994), and inverse normalized quadratic model of Holt and Bishop (2002).

For illustrative purposes we include two duality examples. The first example uses the Cobb–Douglas functional form, which is a globally regular function with rank 1.[17] The second example uses the AI demand function, which is a locally flexible function of rank 2. Note that with the Cobb–Douglas specification, it is straightforward to derive the inverse uncompensated demand function directly from the uncompensated demand function. However, as shown below with the AI functional form, solving for the inverse demand function directly from the demand function is not always possible, further motivating the usefulness of duality relationships.

6.1   Duality Example I: The Cobb–Douglas Functional Form

A simple example demonstrating the dual relationships is the Cobb–Douglas functional form. Consider the utility function $u(\mathbf{x}) = \left(x_1^{\alpha_1} x_2^{\alpha_2} \right)$ with two goods where $\alpha_1 + \alpha_2 = 1$. Following standard relationships the following dual functions can be derived: (a) the indirect utility function $v(\mathbf{p}, M) = \left(\alpha_1 \frac{M}{p_1} \right)^{\alpha_1} \left(\alpha_2 \frac{M}{p_2} \right)^{\alpha_2}$ and (b) the expenditure function $e(\mathbf{p}, u) = \left(u \left(\frac{p_1}{\alpha_1} \right)^{\alpha_1} \left(\frac{p_2}{\alpha_2} \right)^{\alpha_2} \right)$. The distance function is $d(\mathbf{x}, u) = \left(\frac{(x_1)^{\alpha_1}(x_2)^{\alpha_2}}{u} \right)$. Further, and considering good 1 for convenience, applying Roy's Identity to the indirect utility function yields the uncompensated demand function $x_1^m = \alpha_1 \frac{M}{p_1}$. This demand system is homothetic with Engle curves through the origin and of rank 1.[18] The compensated demand function $x_1^h = \left(u \frac{p_1}{p_2} \frac{\alpha_2}{\alpha_1} \right)^{\alpha_1 - 1}$ (from Shephard's Lemma), uncompensated inverse demand function $p_1^m = \frac{\alpha_1 M}{(x_1)}$ (by the Hotelling–Wold Identity), and compensated inverse demand function $\tilde{p}_1^h = \frac{\alpha_1}{u} \left(\frac{(x_1)}{(x_2)} \right)^{\alpha_1 - 1}$ (from Gorman's Lemma). From the Hotelling–Wold Identity the uncompensated inverse share equation is given by $w_1^{im} = \left[\alpha_1 \left(\frac{x_i}{(x_i - c_i)} \right) \right] / \left[\sum_{j=1}^n \left[\alpha_1 \left(\frac{x_j}{(x_j - c_j)} \right) \right] \right]$ while the uncompensated share equation $w_1^m = \frac{p_1 c_1}{M} + \alpha_1 \frac{M^*}{M}$.[19]

---

[17]   See Barnett and Serletis (2008) for discussion of global regularity versus flexible functional forms (arbitrary second-order approximation) and rank.

[18]   This is a rank 1 demand system because it is comprised of a single term that is a function of price. See Barnett and Serletis (2008).

[19]   This uncompensated inverse share expression is identical to equation (6) in Moschini and Vissa (1992) and derived in Marsh and Piggott (2010).

6.2   Duality Example II: The Almost Ideal Demand Function

Following Deaton and Meullbauer (1980a) the expenditure functions can be defined as $\ln e(\mathbf{p}, u) = (1 - u) \ln a(\mathbf{p}) + u \ln b(\mathbf{p})$. Applying Shephard's Lemma and substituting the indirect utility function yields the share expression $w_i = \alpha_i + \sum_{j=1}^{n} \gamma_{ij}$ $\ln p_j + \beta_i \ln (m/P)$ where $\ln P = \alpha_0 + \sum_{j=1}^{n} \alpha_j \ln p_j + \frac{1}{2} \sum_{i=1}^{n} \sum_{j=1}^{n} \gamma_{ij} \ln p_i \ln p_j$. This demand system is logarithmic in expenditure with two terms containing price functions and is of rank 2. Necessary demand conditions that lead to parameter restrictions are: $\sum_{i=1}^{n} \alpha_i = 1$, $\sum_{j=1}^{n} \gamma_{ij} = 0$, $\sum_{i=1}^{n} \beta_i = 0$ adding up; $\sum_{i=1}^{n} \gamma_{ij} = 0$ homogeneity; and $\gamma_{ij} = \gamma_{ji}$ symmetry.

Following Eales and Unnevehr (1994) the logarithmic distance function may be specified as $\ln d(\mathbf{x}, u) = (1 - u) \ln a(\mathbf{x}) + u \ln b(\mathbf{x})$. The IAI expenditure system is obtained by substituting in the equations $\ln a(\mathbf{x}) = \tilde{\alpha}_0 + \sum_{j=1}^{n} \tilde{\alpha}_j \ln x_j + \frac{1}{2} \sum_{i=1}^{n} \sum_{j=1}^{n} \tilde{\gamma}_{ij} \ln x_i \ln x_j$ and $\ln b(\mathbf{x}) = \tilde{\beta}_0 \prod_{i=1}^{n} x_i + \ln a(\mathbf{x})$. Applying Gorman's Lemma and substituting in the direct utility function $u(\mathbf{x}) = \ln a(\mathbf{x})/(\ln a(\mathbf{x}) - \ln b(\mathbf{x}))$, which is obtained by inverting the distance function at $d(\mathbf{x}, u) = 1$. The share form of the inverse demand function is $w_i = \tilde{\alpha}_i + \sum_{j=1}^{n} \tilde{\gamma}_{ij} \ln x_j + \tilde{\beta}_i \ln Q$ where $\ln Q = \tilde{\alpha}_0 + \sum_{j=1}^{n} \tilde{\alpha}_j \ln x_j + \frac{1}{2} \sum_{i=1}^{n} \sum_{j=1}^{n} \tilde{\gamma}_{ij} \ln x_i \ln x_j$. Necessary demand conditions lead to parameter restrictions of the distance function specification as follows: $\sum_{i=1}^{n} \tilde{\alpha}_i = 1$, $\sum_{j=1}^{n} \tilde{\gamma}_{ij} = 0$, $\sum_{i=1}^{n} \tilde{\beta}_i = 0$ adding up; $\sum_{i=1}^{n} \tilde{\gamma}_{ij} = 0$ homogeneity; and $\tilde{\gamma}_{ij} = \tilde{\gamma}_{ji}$ symmetry.

7   ECONOMETRIC METHODS

There is an extensive literature on the empirical estimation of consumer demand models. Working (1926) provided a seminal paper entitled "What Do Statistical Demand Curves Show?" Stone's empirical application of the linear expenditure system arrived in 1954. Deaton (1986) provided an extensive review of demand system models and estimation issues. Lafrance (2008) provided a recent example of aggregate food demand analysis. A more current focus has been on microeconometric analysis, the analysis of individual-level data, which is now more available to the applied economist and is briefly discussed below (see Cameron and Trivedi 2005).

Consider a system with $i = 1, \ldots, N$ goods and $t = 1, \ldots, T$ time-series observations; this yields NT total observations. For estimation purposes, the demand system can be represented at time t by the non-linear specification $w_t = f_t(\beta, x_t) + \varepsilon_t$ where w_t is a vector of share equations, f is a differentiable non-linear function of unknown parameters β structuring the consumer's model, x_t is a vector of explanatory exogenous variables, and ε_t a vector of unknown residuals. Classical assumptions on the residual of the regression model are that $E(\varepsilon_t | x_t) = 0$ and $E(\varepsilon_t \varepsilon_t' | x_t) = \Omega$ is a finite contemporaneous correlation matrix. Here, the expected value of the residuals is 0 with constant variance exhibiting independence over time and correlation across equations. Standard estimators of this model, which are contingent on the properties of the residuals (and the maintained assumptions of the demand model), are least squares, maximum likelihood, and generalized method of moments. For example, the iterative seemingly unrelated regression model is commonly applied in the presence of contemporaneous correlation across equations. However, across competing estimators, trade-offs exist between less restrictive model assumptions and performance properties of the estimators. General discussion about, and specific references for, finite-sample (e.g., bias and efficiency) properties and large-sample (consistency and asymptotic efficiency) properties and distributions of these estimators can be found in Davidson and MacKinnon (1993), Mittelhammer (1996), Mittelhammer, Judge, and Miller (2000), and Greene (2008). In the share form of the system, the adding up constraint induces singularity in the covariance matrix Ω of the residual ε. This is addressed by omitting one of the goods from the estimation process, leaving $N-1$ goods and $(N-1) \times T$ remaining observations. Parameter estimates from the omitted equation are recovered through general demand restrictions.

Important econometric issues arise in estimation of demand systems, including identification, residual violations, and simultaneity. Working (1926) initially addressed issues of identification of demand and supply models. Hsiao (1983) provided a review of identification issues with insightful examples. Davidson and MacKinnon (1993) provided another good source for background on identification.

In empirical applications, contingent on the data-generating process, the residuals of the model could exhibit heteroskedastic disturbances, autoregressive disturbances, or combinations of these processes, which typically reduces efficiency (but does not affect consistency) of the estimator. Berndt and Savin (1975) developed the approach to estimation and hypothesis testing in singular equation systems with autoregressive disturbances. Given that the form of heteroskedasticity is known, then feasible least squares, iterated seemingly unrelated regression, maximum likelihood, and generalized methods of moments remain standard tools to consistently estimate systems of equations. White's heteroskedastic robust consistent covariance estimator and the Newey–White autoregressive–heteroskedastic consistent covariance estimator are often applied in practice if the form of heteroskedasticity is unknown (Greene 2008). For time-series data, unit root processes are feasible and require specific attention in demand system estimation (see Greene 2008). Balcombe (2004) applied cointegration methods to demand system analysis.

Simultaneity, on the other hand, in the regression model can arise and create bias and inconsistent parameter estimates, and the usual tests for these parameters are not appropriate (Judge et al. 1985; Thurman 1987). Here the model $w_t = f_t(\beta, x_t) + \varepsilon_t$ contains x_t, which is a vector of explanatory predetermined and endogenous variables. Hausman–Wu tests provide a general form of specification testing for endogeneity (Judge et al. 1985). In this situation, instrumental variable approaches are common estimators (Deaton 1986), as well as limited or full information maximum likelihood and generalized method of moments. Tests for weak instruments and overidentification restrictions are also standard tools and discussed in Greene (2008).

Hypothesis testing related to model parameters and specification is a crucial part of demand systems analysis. The standard Wald, Lagrange multiplier, and likelihood ratio test approaches for individual and joint hypotheses (e.g., symmetry) are covered in Engle (1984), as well as Mittelhammer (1996), Mittelhammer, Judge, and Miller (2000), Greene (2008), and Davidson and MacKinnon (1993). Bewley (1986) and Moschini, Moro, and Green (1994) provide adjusted likelihood ratio test approaches designed for tests in systems estimation. These hypothesis testing procedures can also be used to compare nested models by parameter restrictions. However, comparing performance of non-nested models is often of interest in practice. Non-nested hypothesis testing arises when, for example, competing models are not nested in the sense that one model cannot be made a special case of another by parameter restrictions. An introduction to non-nested testing is included in Davidson and MacKinnon (1993). Vuong (1989) provided a generalized likelihood test for non-nested models useful for testing between competing specifications of demand systems.

Other empirical research focused on hypothesis testing is relevant to the applied economist. McGuirk et al. (1995) provided an overview of system misspecification testing and structural change related to meat demand. Moschini, Moro, and Green (1994), Eales and Unnevehr (1988), and Eales and Wessells (1999) test for separability in food products. Useful non-parametric tests for normality and independence are described in Mittelhammer (1996, ch. 10).

The availability of more disaggregate data has refocused some traditional issues and introduced other econometric issues into the forefront of demand system estimation. For example, Dhar, Chavas, and Gould (2003) examined brand-level scanner data and tested for simultaneity and separability. Furthermore, missing observations that are latent in nature remain pervasive in disaggregate data often adding an additional layer of censoring complexity to systems estimators (Yen and Lin 2006). Spatial processes have recently received attention in systems estimation of disaggregate data. These topics are rich areas of future research.

8   Empirical Application

This section highlights how different approaches and methods can impact results in practice. That is, researchers' empirical application of demand systems is fraught with auxiliary hypotheses of specification choices that can impact results. This reality of empirical work is unavoidable and presents significant challenges to researchers. Space limitation precludes a thorough and complete analysis of all of the challenges involved. We limit our attention to examination of a single data set that involves annual US food-at-home (FAH), food-away-from-home (FAFH), and alcoholic beverages (AB) consumption over the period 1978–2007. This offers the novel opportunity to explore price formation for FAH, FAFH, and AB, which has not been published as far as we are aware. Furthermore, we investigate an important modeling choice involving food demand that confronts agricultural economists. Specifically, we investigate whether a system of inverse demands, where prices are a function of quantities providing an alternative and fully dual approach to ordinary demand system, is a more appropriate way to model food demand consistently with the idea that food quantities are exogenous (supply is inelastic) and it is price that must adjust to establish a market clearing equilibrium. The possibility of demand models that specify prices as a function of quantities is motivated by the perishability of the many foods now consumed and the increasing prevalence of consumption of food away from home which tends to be freshly prepared with a limited shelf life. To evaluate this question we employ a novel straightforward example of estimating the IAI demand system (Eales and Unnevehr 1994) and the AI demand system (Deaton and Muellbauer 1980a) using the same data set and then proceed to make comparisons of each of the models' statistical performance based on econometric criteria and also qualitative assessments of the estimated economic effects in an effort to identify definitively an empirically preferred approach.

8.1   The Inverse Almost Ideal (IAI) Demand System

The share form of the IAI demand system can be expressed as

$$w_i = \alpha_i + \sum_{j=1}^{n} \gamma_{ij} \ln x_j + \beta_i \ln Q$$

where

$$\ln Q = \alpha_0 + \sum_{j=1}^{n} \alpha_j \ln x_j + \frac{1}{2} \sum_{i=1}^{n} \sum_{j=1}^{n} \gamma_{ij} \ln x_i \ln x_j$$

and variables w_i = expenditure share of food $i (w_i = \frac{p_i x_i}{M})$, x_i = quantity demanded of food i, p_i = price of food i, and parameters are to be estimated as $\alpha_0, \alpha_i, \gamma_{ij}$, and β_i (Eales and Unnevehr 1994). Necessary demand conditions that lead to parameter restrictions of the distance function specification are as follows:

$$\sum_{i=1}^{n} \alpha_i = 1, \ \sum_{j=1}^{n} \gamma_{ij} = 0, \ \sum_{i=1}^{n} \beta_i = 0 \text{ adding up}$$

$$\sum_{i=1}^{n} \gamma_{ij} = 0 \text{ homogeneity}$$

$$\tilde{\gamma}_{ij} = \tilde{\gamma}_{ji} \text{ symmetry}$$

Price and scale flexibilities are defined by

$$\frac{\partial \ln p_i(\mathbf{x})}{\partial \ln x_\ell} = \frac{1}{w_i}\left[\gamma_{i\ell} + \beta_i\left(\alpha_\ell + \sum_{j=1}^{n}\gamma_{j\ell}\ln(x_j)\right)\right] - \delta_{i\ell}$$

$$\frac{\partial \ln p_i(\lambda\tilde{\mathbf{x}})}{\partial \ln \lambda} = -1 + \beta_i/w_i,$$

where the last equality simplifies due to imposition of general demand restrictions with reference vector $\tilde{\mathbf{x}}$

8.2   The Almost Ideal (AI) Demand System

The share form of AI demand function can be derived as

$$w_i = \alpha_i + \sum_{j=1}^{n}\gamma_{ij}\ln p_j + \beta_i \ln P$$

where

$$\ln P = \alpha_0 + \sum_{j=1}^{n}\alpha_j \ln p_j + \frac{1}{2}\sum_{i=1}^{n}\sum_{j=1}^{n}\gamma_{ij}\ln p_i \ln p_j,$$

and w_i= expenditure share of food i($w_i = \frac{p_i x_i}{M}$), p_i=price of food i, x_i=quantity demanded of food i, and parameters are to be estimated as $\alpha_0, \alpha_i, \gamma_{ij}$, and β_i (Deaton and Muellbauer 1980a). Necessary demand conditions that lead to parameter restrictions of the expenditure function specification are as follows:

$$\sum_{i=1}^{n}\alpha_i = 1, \quad \sum_{j=1}^{n}\gamma_{ij} = 0, \quad \sum_{i=1}^{n}\beta_i = 0 \quad \text{adding up}$$

$$\sum_{i=1}^{n}\gamma_{ij} = 0 \text{ homogeneity}$$

$$\gamma_{ij} = \gamma_{ji} \text{ symmetry.}$$

Price and expenditures elasticities are defined by

$$\frac{\partial \ln q_i(\mathbf{p})}{\partial \ln p_\ell} = \frac{1}{w_i}\left[\gamma_{i\ell} - \beta_i\left(\alpha_\ell + \sum_{j=1}^{n}\gamma_{j\ell}\ln(p_j)\right)\right] - \delta_{i\ell}$$

$$\frac{\partial \ln q_i(\mathbf{p})}{\partial \ln M} = -1 + \beta_i / w_i$$

8.3   Empirical Results

The IAI and AI models are applied to aggregate annual time-series data for food demand in the United States over the period 1978–2007 (thirty years). Expenditures on food are maintained to be weakly separable from expenditure on all other goods. The annual consumer expenditure data are from the United States Department of Agriculture measuring FAFH, FAH, and AB. Per capita expenditure series were derived by dividing expenditures by US population data from the Census Bureau. Per capita consumption series were then constructed by dividing the expenditure data by the appropriate price index, which is from the Bureau of Labor Statistics.

The summary statistics are shown in Table 1.1, which reveals that US consumers, over the past thirty years, spent an average of $2,665 per person annually on food. These expenditures were allocated on average as follows: 39.4 percent on FAFH, 48.5 percent on FAH, and 12 percent on AB. However, these average expenditure shares mask an important trend that FAFH expenditures have become more prominent, while FAH expenditures have been declining, with expenditures on AB remaining relatively stable. These trends are made clear in Figure 1.1, which reveals that if these trends continue then FAFH will soon account for the largest component of US consumers' food budget. Piggott (2003) makes the point that there has been an abundant literature investigating factors responsible for these changes and the growing importance of FAFH. A large part of

Table 1.1 Summary statistics of annual data, 1978–2007 (30 observations)

Variables	Average	Standard deviation	Minimum	Maximum
FAFH expenditure ($/capita)	1,073.770	400.830	430.870	1,840.180
FAH expenditure($/capita)	1,271.880	333.359	687.507	1,932.630
Alcoholic beverages ($/capita)	319.555	102.139	162.691	538.209
Total expenditures ($/capita)	2,665.200	834.276	1,281.070	4,311.020
FAFH price index	139.385	38.271	68.300	206.659
FAH price index	138.178	36.560	73.800	201.245
Alcoholic beverages price index	141.944	39.409	74.100	207.026
Share FAFH	0.394	0.031	0.336	0.428
Share FAH	0.485	0.028	0.447	0.537
Share alcoholic beverages	0.120	0.006	0.110	0.128

Sources: Food expenditures are from Economic Research Service, US Department of Agriculture, <http://www.ers.usda.gov/briefing/CPIFoodAndExpenditures/Data/table1.htm>; price data are from US Bureau of Labor Statistics <http://data.bls.gov/PDQ/outside.jsp?survey=cu>; population data are from US Census Bureau <http://www.census.gov/popest/archives/1990s/popclockest.txt>, <http://www.census.gov/popest/states/NST-ann-est2007.html>.

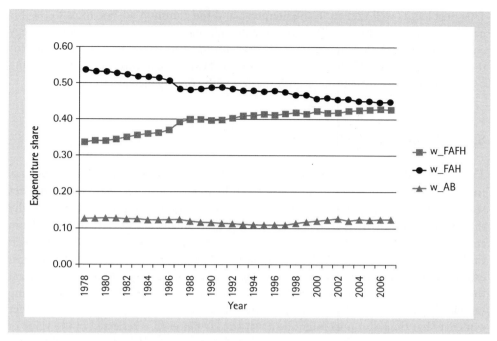

FIGURE 1 US expenditure shares of FAH, FAFH, and AB, 1978–2007

this literature has been concerned with utilizing cross-sectional data such as panel data and assessing the impact of household demographics and change in the workforce participation etc. A viable alternative approach following Piggott (2003) is to employ aggregate time-series data applied to theoretical consistent complete demand systems. Of particular interest in this chapter is to examine the empirical question of whether a system of inverse demands, where prices are a function of quantities providing an alternative and fully dual approach to the ordinary demand system, is a more appropriate way to model food demand consistently with the idea that food quantities are exogenous (supply is inelastic) and it is price that must adjust to establish a market clearing equilibrium.

8.4   Some Estimation Issues

The IAI and AI models are estimated as separable complete systems of equations including FAFH, FAH, and AB using iterated non-linear estimation techniques in SAS (proc model and ITSUR). Because of the singular nature of the share system, one of the equations must be deleted in estimation (AB). General demand restrictions of homogeneity, symmetry, and aggregation are imposed and treated as maintained hypotheses. Both the IAI and AI models include the difficult-to-estimate α_0 parameter, which can cause convergence issues owing to difficulties in identifying values of this parameter.

This problem is well known in the literature and the common ad-hoc fix is to set this parameter to zero. In an effort to estimate this parameter, an estimation strategy employed was first to estimate each model with $\alpha_0=0$ to generate starting values for the unrestricted model, where α_0 is unrestricted. This strategy was successful, allowing us to identify and estimate α_0 in both models with convergence at 1.0E-5.

8.5   Parameter Estimates

The estimated parameters for the IAI and AI models are reported in Table 1.2. Inspecting the statistical significance of individual parameter estimates provides some insight into the potential relative goodness of fit of each model. It is noteworthy that in both models the parameter α_0 was not individually statistically different from zero at the 5 percent level, providing some support to previous work that has imposed this parameter to zero to facilitate estimation. The IAI model has five of the eight estimated parameters being individually statistically significantly different from zero at the 5 percent level compared with only two parameters in the AI model being individually statistically significantly different from zero at the 5 percent level. Further evidence that the IAI model might be a statistically better fit is reflected in the value of the maximized log-likelihood values of 272.6 for the IAI model compared with 208.7 for the AI model. Finally, the individual R^2 for the estimated FAH and FAFH are 0.97 in the IAI model, compared with the lesser 0.74 and 0.83 respectively for the AI model. Thus, based on a larger number of individually statistically significant parameters, a larger maximized likelihood value, and larger R^2 for each equation, the estimated

Table 1.2 Estimated coefficients for the inverse almost ideal (IAI) and almost ideal (AI) models

	IAI model	AI model
α_0	−470.037 (412.500)	43.949 (28.693)
α_{FAH}	62.906 (36.271)	20.992 (13.062)
α_{FAFH}	−54.617 (29.956)	−20.166 (13.264)
β_{FAH}	0.134* (0.042)	0.502* (0.067)
β_{FAFH}	−0.117* (0.041)	−0.504* (0.052)
$\gamma_{FAH,FAH}$	−8.214* (2.452)	10.444 (6.095)
$\gamma_{FAH,FAFH}$	7.229* (1.940)	−10.454 (6.118)
$\gamma_{FAFH,FAFH}$	−6.282* (1.611)	10.443 (6.181)
LL	272.622	208.663
R^2_{FAH}	0.977	0.737
R^2_{FAFH}	0.972	0.829

Notes: Figures in parentheses are the estimated standard errors.
* denotes a coefficient that is statistically significantly different from zero at 5% level. LL is the maximized likelihood value.

parameter results suggest that the IAI might be a more statistically appropriate model compared with the AI model in explaining expenditure shares over the period 1978–2007.

8.6   Flexibility and Elasticity Estimates

Another criterion for evaluating competing models is to compare estimated economic effects (flexibilities and elasticities) and their reasonableness with prior beliefs and their consistency with theory. Table 1.3 provides a comparison of the estimated flexibilities and elasticities for the IAI model and the AI model. For the IAI model all of the uncompensated own-price flexibilities are negative, as are the scale flexibilities. A 1 percent increase in the quantity of FAH consumed is associated with a 0.379 percent decline in the price of FAH. Interestingly, a 1 percent increase in the quantity of FAFH consumed is associated with a 0.687 percent decline in the price of FAFH, revealing a much more elastic response compared with FAH. A 1 percent increase in the quantity of AB is associated with a 0.311 percent decline in the price of AB. Scale

Table 1.3 Estimated flexibilities for the IAI model and elasticities for the AI model

	Flexibilities IAI model				Elasticities AI model		
			Uncompensated				
	P_{FAH}	P_{FAFH}	P_{AB}		Q_{FAH}	Q_{FAFH}	Q_{AB}
Q_{FAH}	−0.379	−0.252	−0.028	P_{FAH}	−1.296	−0.786	−0.197
Q_{FAFH}	−0.403	−0.687	−0.152	P_{FAFH}	0.301	−0.464	0.204
Q_{AB}	−0.265	−0.558	−0.311	P_{AB}	−0.145	0.311	−1.176
			Compensated				
	P_{FAH}	P_{FAFH}	P_{AB}		Q_{FAH}	Q_{FAFH}	Q_{AB}
Q_{FAH}	−0.118	0.067	0.051	P_{FAH}	−0.400	0.323	0.077
Q_{FAFH}	0.088	−0.085	−0.003	P_{FAFH}	0.283	−0.482	0.199
Q_{AB}	0.182	−0.008	−0.174	P_{AB}	0.253	0.801	−1.054
			Scale or expenditure				
		Scale				Expenditure	
	P_{FAH}	P_{FAFH}	P_{AB}		Q_{FAH}	Q_{FAFH}	Q_{AB}
	−0.659	−1.243	−1.134		2.279	−0.040	1.011
			Measures of consistency with theory (percent compensated < 0)				
	P_{FAH}	P_{FAFH}	P_{AB}		Q_{FAH}	Q_{FAFH}	Q_{AB}
	70.0	66.7	100.0		86.7	90.0	100.0
			Percent NSD				
	66.7				86.7		

Notes: Reported estimates are the respective means from flexibilities and elasticities calculated over the sample. Measures of consistency with theory involve checking the negativity of uncompensated and compensated flexibilities at every data point and the negative semi-definiteness (NSD) of the substitution matrix.

flexibilities indicate that scale of consumption increases of 1 percent would lead to declines in FAH price of 0.659 percent, FAFH price of 1.2 percent, and AB price of 1.134 percent. These flexibilities seem reasonable and plausible. Checking their consistency with underlying theory reveals that the compensated own-price flexibilities of FAH and FAFH are only consistent with the negativity condition at 70 and 66.7 percent of observations, respectively. Furthermore, the Antonelli substitution effects were found to be consistent with negative semi-definiteness at 66.7 percent of observations (failing during the period at the beginning of the sample, 1978–88).

For the AI model all of uncompensated own-price elasticities are negative and two of the expenditure elasticities (FAH and AB) are positive, with the other (FAFH) being borderline negative. A 1 percent increase in the price of FAH is associated with a 1.296 percent decline in the quantity demanded of FAH. Interestingly, a 1 percent increase in the price of FAFH is associated with a 0.464 percent decline in the quantity demanded for FAFH, revealing a much more inelastic demand response. A 1 percent increase in the price of AB is associated with a 1.176 percent decline in the quantity demanded of AB. Expenditure elasticities convey that FAH is a luxury good (2.279), FAFH is borderline inferior (−0.04), and AB is a borderline luxury good (1.011). Checking their consistency with underlying theory reveals that the compensated own-price flexibilities of FAH and FAFH are consistent with the negativity condition at 86.7 and 90 percent of observations, respectively. Furthermore, the Hicksian substitution effects were found to be consistent with negative semi-definiteness at 86.7 percent of observations (failing during the period at the beginning of the sample 1978–81). In sum, both models' estimated effects seem mostly plausible, with the caveat that neither model is fully consistent with theory owing to problems being consistent with negativity of flexibilities and elasticities (FAH and FAFH) as well as the magnitudes of expenditure elasticities—with the AI model being inconsistently slightly less than the IAI model.

8.7   In-Sample Non-Nested Tests

Since the IAI and AI models have the same set of dependent variables, it is possible to test whether the IAI model rejects the AI model using a non-nested test framework developed by Vuong (1989). Testing the IAI model against the AI model, if the null hypothesis is true the average value of the log-likelihood should be zero and the test statistic should be close to zero. Alternatively, if the test statistic is positive and statistically significantly different from zero ($Z_{0.05} = 1.96$), then the IAI model rejects the AI model. We calculated the Vuong test with the IAI against the AI and the test statistic was found to be 8.725 (Table 1.4), providing strong statistical support for the IAI model with the AI being rejected. This result echoes the other statistical results favoring the in-sample performance of the IAI model over the AI model.

Table 1.4 Statistical inferences for the IAI model versus the AI model, non-nested test (Vuong statistic = 8.725) (out-of-sample one-period-ahead forecasting performance)

Criteria	IAI model	AI model
$tr(\Omega)$	0.00170	0.01478
$|\Omega|$	7.07E-08	5.05E-06

Note: See Piggott (2003: 11) for methods used in calculating Ω.

8.8   Out-of-Sample Non-Nested Tests

Since both the IAI and AI models have the same set of dependent variables, it is also possible to evaluate each model's respective out-of-sample forecast accuracy. Owing to the small sample on hand, and to conserve degrees of freedom, each model is evaluated on its ability to make *one*-period-ahead forecasts using the approach of Piggott (2003). This approach leads to two different statistics being calculated that utilize all of the information contained in the forecast error vector generated by the one-period-ahead forecast errors at each observation. The first statistic, $tr(\Omega)$, which is the trace of the estimated covariance of one-period-ahead forecast errors, is equivalent to the sum of squared forecast errors (SSFE) for the two equations estimated. Table 1.4 reveals, based on this criterion, that the IAI model (0.00170) outperformed the AI model (0.01478) with markedly smaller one-period-ahead forecast errors. The second statistic, $|\Omega|$, which is the determinant of the covariance of forecast errors, is favorably impacted if there is correlation between forecast errors. Table 1.4 reveals, based on this criterion, that the IAI model (7.07E-08) once again outperformed the AI model (5.05E-06) with smaller one-period-ahead forecast errors. Thus, there appears to be further support for the IAI model over the AI model based on the criterion of out-of-sample one-period-ahead forecast prediction performance.

9   CONCLUSION

The constrained utility maximization model provides the basis for ordinary demand system estimation and has been the mainstay for food demand analysis in the agricultural economics literature. Duality theory provides alternative approaches to both ordinary and inverse demand system approaches. In particular, the distance function approach allows applied researchers the opportunity to specify inverse demand systems to study consumer price formation. An overview of the literature was presented with the intention of balancing theoretical concepts and empirical application.

We provide a straightforward illustrative example of US food demand (food at home, food away from home, and alcoholic beverages) using aggregate annual time-series data in the United States over the period 1978–2007. Applying a standard AI demand model and IAI demand model, we find that the price formation model dominates the quantity formation model in both in- and out-of-sample testing. A plausible explanation is motivated by the perishability properties of the many foods now consumed and the increasing prevalence of consumption of food away from home, which tends to be freshly prepared with a limited shelf life. This result calls for a more complete examination of the less commonly employed inverse demand systems in agricultural economics to establish its performance compared to the mainstay ordinary demand systems over a broader range of empirical applications to food demands and more general functional forms. Rationalizing this empirical question of the auxiliary hypothesis of specification choices as to whether an ordinary or inverse demand system is most appropriate for a particular application is left for future work, with the question of inverse models being more appropriate for demand analysis remaining open for further careful scrutiny.

REFERENCES

Alston, J. M., J. A. Chalfant, and N. E. Piggott. 2001. "Incorporating Demand Shifters in the Almost Ideal Demand System." *Economic Letters* 70: 73–8.

Anderson, R. W. 1980. "Some Theory for Inverse Demand for Applied Demand Analysis." *European Economic Review* 14: 281–90.

Balcombe, K. G. 2004. "Retesting Symmetry and Homogeneity in a Cointegrated Demand System with Bootstrapping: The Case of Meat Demand in Greece." *Empirical Economics* 29: 451–62.

Banks, J., R. Blundell, and A. Lewbel. 1997. "Quadratic Engle Curves and Consumer Demand." *Review of Economics and Statistics* 79: 527–39.

Barnett, W. A. 1979. "Theoretical Foundations for the Rotterdam Model." *Review of Economic Studies* 46: 109–30.

——and L. J. Bettendorf. 1989. "Price Formation of Fish: An Application of an Inverse Demand System." *European Economic Review* 33: 1509–25.

——and A. Serletis. 2008. "Consumer Preferences and Demand Systems." *Journal of Econometrics* 147: 210–24.

Barten, A. P. 1964. "Consumer Demand Functions under Conditions of Almost Additive Preferences." *Econometrica* 32: 1–38.

——1967. "Evidence on the Slutsky Conditions for Demand Equations." *Review of Economics and Statistics* 49: 77–84.

——1977. "The System of Consumer Demand Functions Approach: A Review." *Econometrica* 45: 23–51.

——and L. Bettendorf. 1989. "Price Formation of Fish: An Application of an Inverse Demand System." *European Economic Review* 33: 1509–25.

Berndt, E. R., and N. E. Savin. 1975. "Evaluation and Hypothesis Testing in Singular Equation Systems with Autoregressive Disturbances." *Econometrica* 32: 937–57.

Bewley, R. 1986. *Allocation Models: Specification, Estimation, and Applications*. Cambridge, MA: Ballinger.

Blackorby, C., R. Davidson, and W. Schworm. 1991. "Implicit Separability: Characterization and Implications for Consumer Demands." *Journal of Economic Theory* 55: 364–99.

——, D. Primont, and R. Russell. 1978. *Duality, Separability, and Functional Structure: Theory and Economic Applications*. New York: North-Holland.

Bollino, C. A. 1987. "GAIDS: A Generalized Version of the Almost Ideal Demand System." *Economic Letters* 23: 199–202.

—— and R. Violi. 1990. "GAITL: A Generalized Version of the Almost Ideal and Translog Demand System." *Economic Letters* 33: 127–9.

Breslaw, J. A., and J. B. Smith. 1995. "A Simple and Efficient Method to Estimate the Magnitude and Precision of Welfare Changes." *Journal of Econometrics* 10: 313–27.

Brester, G. W., and T. C. Schroeder. 1995. "The Impacts of Brand and Generic Advertising on Meat Demand." *American Journal of Agricultural Economics* 77: 69–79.

Cameron, A. C., and P. K. Trivedi. 2005. *Microeconometrics: Methods and Applications*. New York: Cambridge University Press.

Capps, O., and H. A. Love. 2002. "Econometric Considerations in the Use of Electronic Scanner Data to Conduct Consumer Demand Analysis." *American Journal of Agricultural Economics* 84: 807–16.

Chalfant, J. A. 1987. "A Globally Flexible, Almost Ideal Demand System." *Journal of Business and Economic Statistics* 5: 233–42.

—— and J. M. Alston. 1998. "Accounting for Changes in Taste." *Journal of Political Economy* 96: 391–410.

Chambers, R. G., Y. Chung, and R. Färe. 1996. "Benefit and Distance Functions." *Journal of Economic Theory* 70: 407–19.

Chavas, J. P. 1983. "Structural Change in the Demand for Meat." *American Journal of Agricultural Economics* 65: 148–53.

Chipman, J. S., L. Hurwicz, M. K. Richter, and H. F. Sonnenschein, eds. 1971. *Preferences, Utility and Demand*. New York: Harcourt Brace Jovanovich.

Christensen, L. R., D. W. Jorgenson, and L. J. Lau. 1975. "Transcendental Logarithmic Utility Functions." *American Economic Review* 653 (June), 367–83.

Cornes, R. 1992. *Duality and Modern Economics*. New York: Cambridge University Press.

Dahlgran, R. A. 1987. "Complete Flexibility Systems and the Stationarity of U.S. Meat Demand." *Western Journal of Agricultural Economics* 12: 152–63.

Davidson, R., and J. G. MacKinnon. 1993. *Estimation and Inference in Econometrics*. New York: Oxford University Press.

Deaton, A. S., ed. 1981. *Essays in the Theory and Measurement of Consumer Behavior: In Honour of Sir Richard Stone*. New York: Cambridge University Press.

—— 1986. "Demand Analysis." In Z. Griliches and M. D. Intriligator, eds, *Handbook of Econometrics*, 3. New York: North-Holland.

—— and J. Muellbauer. 1980a. "An Almost Ideal Demand System." *American Economic Review* 70 (June), 312–26.

————. 1980b. *Economics and Consumer Behavior*. New York: Cambridge University Press.

Dhar, T., J. P. Chavas, and B. W. Gould. 2003. "An Empirical Assessment of Endogeneity Issues in Demand Analysis for Differentiated Products." *American Journal of Agricultural Economics* 85: 605–17.

Diewert, W. E. 2009. "Cost of Living Indexes and Exact Index Numbers." In Slottje (2009).

—— and T. J. Wales. 1988. "Normalized Quadratic Demand Systems of Consumer Demand Functions." *Journal of Business and Economic Statistics* 6: 303–12.

Eales, J. S., and L. J. Unnevehr. 1988. "Demand for Beef and Chicken Products: Separability and Structural Change." *American Journal of Agricultural Economics* 70: 521–32.

——. 1993. "Simultaneity and Structural Change in U.S. Meat Demand." *American Journal of Agricultural Economics* 75: 259–68.

——. 1994. "The Inverse Almost Ideal Demand System." *European Economic Review* 38: 101–15.

—— and C. Wessells. 1999. "Testing Separability of Japanese Demand for Meat and Fish within Differential Demand Systems." *Journal and Agricultural and Resource Economics* 24/1: 114–26.

Engle, R. F. 1984. "Wald, Likelihood Ratio, and Lagrange Multiplier Tests in Econometrics." Z. Griliches and M. D. Intriligator, eds, *Handbook of Econometrics*, 2. New York: North-Holland.

Goldman, S. M., and H. Uzawa. 1964. "A Note on Separability in Demand Analysis." *Econometrica* 32/3 (July), 387–98.

Gorman, W. M. 1953. "Community Preference Fields." *Econometrica* 21: 63–80.

—— 1959. "Separable Utility and Aggregation." *Review of Economic Studies* 35: 469–81.

—— 1981. "Some Engle Curves." In Deaton (1981).

Greene, W. 2008. *Econometric Analysis*, 6th edn. New York: Prentice Hall.

Holt, M. T. 2002. "Inverse Demand Systems and Choice of Functional Form." *European Economic Review* 46: 117–42.

—— and R. C. Bishop. 2002. "A Semiflexible Normalized Inverse Demand System: An Application to the Price Formation of Fish." *Empirical Economics* 27: 23–47.

—— and B. K. Goodwin. 1997. "Generalized Habit Formulation in an Inverse Almost Ideal Demand System: An Application to Meat Expenditures in the U.S." *Empirical Economics* 22: 293–320.

Houthakker, H. S. 1960. "Additive Preferences." *Econometrica* 28: 244–57.

Hsiao, C. 1983. "Identification." In R. F. Engle and D. McFadden, eds, *Handbook of Econometrics*, 1. New York: North-Holland.

Huang, K. S. 1988. "An Inverse Demand System for U.S. Composite Foods." *American Journal of Agricultural Economics* 70: 902–9.

—— 1994. "A Further Look at Flexibilities and Elasticities." *American Journal of Agricultural Economics* 76: 313–17.

—— 1996. "Nutrient Elasticities in a Complete Food Demand System." *American Journal of Agricultural Economics* 78: 21–9.

Hurwicz, L., and H. Uzawa. 1971. "On the Problem of Integrability of Demand Functions." In Chipman et al. (1971).

Intriligator, M. 1971. *Mathematical Optimization and Economic Theory*. Englewood Cliffs, NJ: Prentice Hall.

Johnson, S. R., Z. A. Hassan, and R. D. Green. 1984. *Demand Systems Estimation: Methods and Applications*. Ames: Iowa State University Press.

Judge, G. G., W. E. Griffiths, R. Carter Hill, H. Lutkepohl, and T. C. Lee. 1985. *The Theory and Practice of Econometrics*. New York: Wiley.

Just, R. E., D. L. Hueth, and A. Schmitz. 2004. *The Welfare Economics of Public Policy: A Practical Approach to Project and Policy Evaluation*. Northampton, MA: Edward Elgar.

Kim, H. Y. 1997. "Inverse Demand Systems and Welfare Measurements in Quantity Space." *Southern Economic Journal* 63: 663–79.

Kinnucan, H. W., H. Xiao, C.-J. Hsia, and J. D. Jackson. 1997. "Effects of Health Information and Generic Advertising on U.S. Meat Demand." *American Journal of Agricultural Economics* 79: 13–23.

Kristofersson, D., and K. Rickertsen. 2004. "Efficient Estimation of Hedonic Inverse Input Demand System." *American Journal of Agricultural Economics* 86: 1127–37.

——————. 2007. "Hedonic Price Models for Dynamic Markets." *Oxford Bulletin of Economics and Statistics* 69/3: 387–412.

LaFrance, J. T. 2001. "Duality for the Household: Theory and Application." In B. Gardner and G. Rausser, eds, *Handbook of Agricultural Economics*. New York: Elsevier Science.

—— 2008. "The Structure of U.S. Food Demand." *Journal of Econometrics* 147: 336–49.

—— and W. M. Hanemann. 1989. "The Dual Structure of Incomplete Demand Systems." *American Journal of Agricultural Economics* 71: 262–74.

—— and R. D. Pope. 2008. *Full Rank Rational Demand Systems*. Working Paper. Washington, DC: Washington State University.

——————. 2009. "The Generalized Quadratic Expenditure System." In Slottje (2009).

Lancaster, K. 1991. *Modern Consumer Theory*. Worcester: Billing.

Lewbel, A. 1989. "Nesting the AIDS and Translog Demand Systems." *International Economic Review* 30: 349–56.

—— 1990. "Full Rank Demand Systems." *International Economic Review* 31: 289–300.

Luenberger, D. G. 1992. "Benefit Functions and Duality." *Journal of Mathematical Economics* 21: 461–81.

Lusk, J. L., A. M. Featherstone, T. L. Marsh, and A. O. Abdulkadri. 2002. "Empirical Properties of Duality Theory." *Australian Journal of Agricultural and Resource Economics* 46 (Mar.), 45–68.

McGuirk A., P. Driscoll, J. Alwang, and H. Huang. 1995. "System Misspecification Testing and Structural Change in Demand for Meats." *Journal of Agricultural and Resource Economics* 20: 1–21.

McLaren, K. R., and K. K. G. Wong. 2009. "The Benefit Function Approach to Modeling Price-Dependent Demand Systems: An Application of Duality Theory." *American Journal of Agricultural Economics* 91/4 (Nov.), 1110–23.

Marsh, T. L., and N. Piggott. 2010. *Measuring Pre-Committed Quantities through Consumer Price Formation*. Working Paper. Washington, DC: School of Economic Sciences, Washington State University.

——, T. C. Schroeder, and J. Mintert. 2004. "Impacts of Meat Product Recalls on Consumer Demand in the USA." *Applied Economics* 36: 897–909.

Mittelhammer, R. C. 1996. *Mathematical Statistics for Economics and Business*. New York: Springer.

——, G. Judge, and D. Miller. 2000. *Econometric Foundations*. New York: Cambridge University Press.

Moschini, G., and K. D. Meilke. 1984. "Parameter Stability and the U.S. Demand for Beef." *Western Journal of Agricultural Economics* 9: 271–82.

——————. 1989. "Modeling the Pattern of Structural Change in U.S. Meat Demand." *American Journal of Agricultural Economics* 71: 253–61.

—— and P. L. Rizzi. 2007. "Deriving a Flexible Mixed Demand System: The Normalized Quadratic Model." *American Journal of Agricultural Economics* 89: 1034–45.

Moschini, G., and A. Vissa. 1992. "A Linear Inverse Demand System." *Journal of Agricultural and Resource Economics* 17/2: 294–302.

——, D. Moro, and R. D. Green. 1994. "Maintaining and Testing Separability in Demand Systems." *American Journal of Agricultural Economics* 71: 61–73.

Phlips, L. 1974. *Applied Consumption Analysis.* Amsterdam: North-Holland.

Piggott, N. 2003. "The Nested PIGLOG Model: An Application to U.S. Food Demand." *American Journal of Agricultural Economics* 85: 1–15.

—— and T. L. Marsh. 2004. "Does Food Safety Information Impact US Meat Demand?" *American Journal of Agricultural Economics* 86 (Feb.), 154–74.

——, J. A. Chalfant, J. M. Alston, and G. R. Griffith. 1996. "Demand Response to Advertising in the Australian Meat Industry." *American Journal of Agricultural Economics* 78: 268–79.

Pollak, R. A., and T. J. Wales. 1980. "Comparison of the Quadratic Expenditure System and Translog Demand System with Alternative Specifications of Demographics Effects." *Econometrica* 48/3 (Apr.), 595–612.

————. 1981. "Demographic Variables in Demand Analysis." *Econometrica* 49 (Nov.), 1533–51.

————. 1992. *Demand System Specification and Estimation.* Oxford: Oxford University Press.

Samuelson, P. A. 1965. "Using Full Duality to Show that Simultaneously Additive Direct and Indirect Utilities Implies Unitary Price Elasticity of Demand." *Econometrica* 33: 781–96.

Shephard, R. W. 1970. *The Theory of Cost and Production Functions.* Princeton: Princeton University Press.

Silberberg, E. 1978. *The Structure of Economics: A Mathematical Analysis.* New York: McGraw-Hill.

Slottje, D., ed. 2009. *Contributions to Economic Analysis: Quantifying Consumer Preferences.* New York: Elsevier Science.

Stone, R. 1954. "Linear Expenditure Systems and Demand Analysis: An Application to the Pattern of British Demand." *Economic Journal* 64: 511–27.

Theil, H. 1965. "The Information Approach to Demand Analysis." *Econometrica* 33 (Jan.), 67–87.

—— and K. W. Clements. 1987. *Applied Demand Analysis: Results from System-Wide Approaches.* Cambridge, MA: Ballinger.

Thurman, W. N. 1987. "Endogeneity Testing in a Supply and Demand Framework." *Review of Economics and Statistics* 68: 638–46.

Varian, H. R. 1992. *Microeconomic Analysis*, 3rd edn. New York: W. W. Norton.

Vartia, Y. O. 1983. "Efficient Methods of Measuring Welfare Change and Compensated Income in Terms of Ordinary Demand Functions." *Econometrica* 51: 79–98.

Vuong, Q. H. 1989. "Likelihood Ratio Tests for Model Selection and Non-Nested Hypotheses." *Econometrica* 57: 307–33.

Wohlgenant, M. K. 1985. "Estimating Cross Elasticities of Demand for Beef." *Western Journal of Agricultural Economics* 10: 322–9.

Working, E. J. 1926. "What Do Statistical Demand Curves Show?" *Quarterly Journal of Economics* 41: 212–35.

Yen, S. T., and B. H. Lin. 2006. "A Sample Selection Approach to Censored Demand Systems." *American Journal of Agricultural Economics* 88: 742–9.

CHAPTER 2

....

HOUSEHOLD PRODUCTION THEORY AND MODELS

....

WALLACE E. HUFFMAN*

1 INTRODUCTION

....

Becker (1976) is best known for modeling household decisions and resource allocation in a model where a household is both a producing and a consuming unit. Output that is produced by the household is consumed directly and not sold in the market. Becker claimed the productive household model was a major advance in understanding household behavior relative to models that treated households as purely consuming units (e.g., see Varian 1992: 94–113). Margaret Reid (1934) provided an early description of household production behavior, and her work is an important antecedent to Becker's formal modeling of the productive household. And in the early 1960s Mincer (1963) became convinced of serious misspecification of empirical household demand functions for food, transportation services, and domestic services; the opportunity cost of the homemaker's or traveler's time and household non-labor- (or full-)income were omitted variables. He also showed that using cash income as an explanatory variable was inappropriate because it reflected a variety of household decisions, including a decision on how many hours to work for pay. Food economic studies over the past four decades have largely overlooked the potential of household production theory and models in demand analysis.

* Jessica Schuring, Abe Tegene, Sonya Huffman, and Peter Orazem made helpful comments on an earlier draft. Alicia Rossburg provide extensive editorial suggestions. Also, this version has benefited from an anonymous reviewer and the editors' comments. Chiho Kim, Tubagus Feridhanusetyawan, Alan McCunn, Jingfing Xu, and Matt Rousu also helped with data construction and estimation. Dale Jorgenson generously provided capital service price and quantity data for durable goods of the US household sector. The project is funded by the Iowa Agricultural Experiment Station and more recently by a cooperative agreement from the Economic Research Service (ERS), US Department of Agriculture.

This chapter first presents a brief review of empirical studies of food demand, especially linkages to household production theory and models. However, the main objectives of the chapter are: (1) to present several types of microeconomic models of household decision-making and highlight their implications for empirical food demand studies and (2) to present an empirical application of insights gained from household production theory for a household input demand system fitted to unique data on the US household sector over the post-Second World War period, 1948–96.[1] Finally, I address how future food demand studies might build a stronger bridge to the models of household behavior including a production function and resource of human time of adult household members. The chapter focuses on household production theory and models for non-agricultural households largely in developed countries.[2]

Relative to neoclassical demand functions, the models of productive household behavior that are developed in this chapter include the opportunity cost of time of adults, full-income budget constraint, and technical efficiency or technical change in household production as determinants of the demand for food and other inputs. An important dimension of these models is that time spent shopping, preparing and eating food has a cost even though there is not a direct cash outlay and that individuals who have a higher opportunity cost of time find ways to substitute toward less human time intensive means of household production.

The remainder of the chapter is organized into four major sections.

2   A BRIEF REVIEW OF DEMAND THEORY AND EMPIRICAL STUDIES OF FOOD DEMAND

Although LaFrance (2001) presents an abstract restatement of neoclassical demand theory and the theory of demand with household production, he does not present a review of the empirical food demand literature, empirical applications, or estimates of household demand systems. Looking more broadly, I uncovered two papers that make a concerted effort to incorporate household production theory into an empirical study of the demand for food. These papers are by Prochaska and Schrimper (1973) and Hamermesh (2007). Prochaska and Schrimper use cross-sectional micro- or household data to estimate the demand by households for food away from home. The authors

---

[1] In contrast to Becker's and Gronau's perspective on household decision-making, there is a sizable literature that applies game theory or bargaining theory to two-adult household decision-making, for example, see Blundell and MaCurdy (1999) and Browning, Chiappori, and Lechene (2009).

[2] For those who are interested in a conceptual model of agricultural household decision-making where decisions are made on inputs for farm production and for household production, see Huffman and Orazem (2007: 2286–92), or agricultural household models that incorporate a time constraint and multiple job holding of household members, see Huffman (1991; 2001: 344–7) and Strauss (1986a). Empirical studies of food demand by agricultural households include Strauss (1986b) and Pitt and Rosenzweig (1986).

include a measure of the opportunity cost of time of the homemaker or opportunity wage and a comprehensive measure of household income, computed as the annual value of the homemaker's time endowment evaluated at the market wage plus household non-labor income. They found that an increase in the homemakers' opportunity cost of time and comprehensive household income significantly increased the demand for food away from home. They also show that significant specification bias would have occurred in the estimated coefficients of the included variables if the opportunity cost of time had been excluded or ignored.[3]

A recent study by Hamermesh (2007) builds on household production theory in his empirical study of demand for food at home and away from home and time allocated to eating by married couples in 1985 and 2003. Key explanatory variables are husband's and wife's wage rates and a household's non-labor income. He finds that a higher wage rate for the husband and wife increases the demand for food away from home significantly. Although the estimated effect of the husband's and wife's wage rates on the demand for food at home is negative, only the estimated coefficient for wife's wage is significantly different from zero. In the 1985 data, he found that non-labor income has a significant positive effect on the demand for food at home but a negative effect on the demand for food away from home. However, in the 2003 data, income effects are reduced and much weaker than in the 1985 data.

Other food demand studies that incorporate household production theory are by Kinsey (1983), Park and Capps (1997), Sabates, Gould, and Villarreal (2001), Keng and Lin (2005).

Although Kinsey (1983) lays out a Beckerian model of household production in a study of the demand for households' purchases of food away from home, her empirical analysis she does not follow through. For example, she claims that the wage rates of working women do not vary much and then excludes women's price of time from a household's demand for food away from home. In contrast, labor economists have made a working individual's wage the target of frequent empirical investigations, and predicted wage rates are regularly included in models explaining labor supply, demand for children, and migration (Tokle and Huffman 1991; Blundell and MaCurdy 1999; Card 1999; Huffman and Feridhanusetyawan 2007).

Keng and Lin (2005) show that as women's labor market earnings increase, their household's demand for food away from home increases. In addition, a few other studies have included the education of the household manager, a rough proxy for her opportunity cost of time, as a regressor in food demand equations. For example, Park and Capps (1997) found that the probability a household purchases ready-to-eat or ready-to-cook meals increases with the education of the household manager, but education was not included in the expenditure equation for ready-to-cook meals.

---

[3] Chen et al. (2002) did not find a statistically significant effect of an individual's wage on the demand for particular nutrients—riboflavin, fatty acids, and oleic acids—in the National Health and Nutrition Examination Survey (NHANES) data set.

In new research at the ERS, Andrews and Hamrick (2009) argue that "eating requires both income to purchase food and time to prepare and consume it." Their focus is on income effects: "food spending tends to rise with a household's income. However, the opposite is true for time devoted to preparing food." Their research does not focus on price effects. In conclusion, there is not an abundance of evidence that productive household theory has been integrated into econometric studies of food demand.

3   A Neoclassical Model of Household Decisions to Allocate Human Time and Cash Income

Early models of labor supply decisions of household members made small advances in neoclassical demand theory by adding leisure time to the list of goods that a household consumes and by adding a new type of resource constraint—adult human time endowments that were allocated between leisure and work for pay (Varian 1992: 95–113, 144–6; Blundell and MaCurdy 1999). This model provides an important benchmark by incorporating the opportunity cost of time into household decision-making, but it does not go so far as adding a household production function. To see this, assume that the household consumes and obtains utility from leisure (L) and two purchased goods—food (X_1) and non-food goods and services (X_2)—and utility can be summarized by a strictly concave utility function

$$U = U(L, X_1, X_2; \tau). \tag{1}$$

In (1) τ is a taste parameter, affecting the translation of leisure and purchased goods into utility.

The household receives a time endowment each time period, e.g., year, and it is allocated between leisure (L) and hours of work for pay (h):

$$T = L + h. \tag{2}$$

The household receives cash income (I^C) from members working for a wage (W) and from interest, dividends, and unanticipated gifts (V), and this income is allocated to purchasing X_1 and X_2 such that

$$I^C = W \cdot h + V = P_1 X_1 + P_2 X_2. \tag{3}$$

Although a household might choose to allocate all physical time to leisure and spend only V on X_1 and X_2, most households choose to forgo some leisure and to allocate this time to wage work, in order to purchase larger quantities of X_1 and X_2. Under these conditions, I can rearrange equation (2) to obtain $h = T - L$. Substitute this relationship into equation (3) and rearrange to obtain Beckerian (Becker 1976) full income (F) constraint

$$F = W \cdot T + V = W \cdot L + P_1 X_1 + P_2 X_2. \tag{4}$$

Note that full income is received from the value of the time endowment at the wage rate (W) plus non-labor income (V), and hence, it does not vary with hours of work. Moreover, full income received is spent on leisure and purchases of food and non-food goods and services.

At this interior solution, the household chooses L, X_1, and X_2 to maximize equation (1) subject to equation (4) with a Lagrange multiplier (λ), which is the marginal utility of full income. These first-order conditions for the household's decision problem are

$$L: U_L = \lambda W \tag{5a}$$

$$X_i: U_{X_i} = \lambda P_i, i = 1, 2 \tag{5b}$$

$$\lambda: W \cdot T + V - W \cdot L - P_1 X_1 - P_2 X_2 = 0 \tag{5c}$$

Equations (5a)–(5c) can be solved jointly to obtain the general form of the household's demand functions for leisure, food, and non-food goods and services:

$$L^\star = D_L(W, P_1, P_2, V, \tau) = D_L(W, P_1, P_2, F, \tau) \tag{5a}$$

$$X_i^\star = D_{X_i}(W, P_1, P_2, V, \tau) = D_{X_i}(W, P_1, P_2, F, \tau), i = 1, 2.^4 \tag{5b}-(5c)$$

Clearly, the demands for leisure, food purchases, and non-food purchases are determined by the wage rate, which is the price of leisure at an interior solution, the price of purchased food (P_1), the price of non-food purchases (P_2), income (V or F), and tastes (τ). The income effect on demand can be represented either by non-labor income (V) or as full income (F), given that W, which is the opportunity cost of time, is held constant in either case. Given the optimal choice of leisure and the time constraint (2), obtain the general form of the labor supply equation

$$h^\star = T - L^\star = S_h(W, P_1, P_2, V, \tau) = S_h(W, P_1, P_2, F, \tau). \tag{6}$$

Hence, hours of work or labor supply are determined by exactly the same set of variables as those that determine the demand for leisure, food purchases, and non-food purchases.

In this model of household demand for food (X_1), there is a major difference in cross-price effects owing to an increase in P_2, which eliminates some consumption opportunities, and W, which increases consumption opportunities. The reason for this difference is that the household starts each period with a positive time endowment for

---

[4] Although T is a determinant of demand, it is a constant that does not vary across household so it can be suppressed in the specification of the demand (and supply) functions.

each adult (T), which rises in value whenever the wage rate increases, but does not hold inventories of X_2. Hence, the Marshallian or money income constant own- and cross-price elasticities of demand for food (X_1) are

$$\partial X_1/\partial P_1 = (\partial X_1/\partial P_1)_{\bar{U}} - X_1 \partial X_1/\partial F \qquad (7a)$$

$$\partial X_1/\partial P_2 = (\partial X_1/\partial P_2)_{\bar{U}} - X_2 \partial X_1/\partial F \qquad (7b)$$

$$\partial X_1/\partial W = (\partial X_1/\partial W)_{\bar{U}} + (T-L)\partial X_1/\partial F \qquad (7c)$$

where $(\partial X_1/\partial Y)_{\bar{U}}$ is the utility constant (Hicksian) effect of a change in price $\{P_1, P_2, W\}$ on the demand for food, and $T-L$ ($= h > 0$) at an interior solution.

Another notable difference in the demand for food in this model relative to one where decisions on time use are ignored is that the opportunity cost of time, as represented by the wage rate (W), is an additional determinant of demand. A less notable difference is that V (or F) represents the pure income effect on quantity demanded in place of cash income (I). Hence, econometric food demand studies that ignore household expenditures on leisure and the price of time of household members will suffer from misspecification bias including omitted variable bias.[5]

4   MODELS OF CONSUMPTION THAT INCORPORATE HOUSEHOLD PRODUCTION THEORY

The unique feature of adding the household production function to the theory of household decision-making is that it becomes possible to bring the theory of the firm to bear on household decisions, including the demand for food and supply of labor (Becker 1976).

4.1   A   Becker-Type Model

In Becker's model household production (Michael and Becker 1973; Becker 1976), a household consumes only commodities that it produces, and the production of each commodity requires an input of human time of one or more household members and an input/good purchased in the market. To gain further insights, assume that a household consumes and obtains utility from two commodities, e.g., Z_1 is home-prepared meals, and Z_2 is a non-food commodity such as washed and ironed clothing,

---

[5] As we shall see in the next section, it is hard to justify a household utility function that is separable in leisure and other goods consumed.

or clean and organized interior of the house. Household utility is summarized by a strictly concave utility function

$$U = U(Z_1, Z_2; \tau) \tag{8}$$

where τ is a taste parameter. Each commodity Z_i is produced using a purchased input, X_i, and housework of one or more household member, t_i. For example, X_1 refers to standard food purchased at the grocery store, and X_2 might be soap, water, and utilities for heating water, or drying and ironing clothing. However, to simplify the analysis further, assume each production function is strictly concave and exhibits constant returns to scale in the two variable inputs, but there are neither fixed costs of production nor joint production between Z_1 and Z_2:

$$Z_i = G_i(X_i, t_i; \varphi_i), i = 1, 2, \tag{9a} - (9b)$$

where φ_i is a technology or efficiency parameter. The household has a time constraint. It receives a time endowment each time period, e.g., year, which is allocated between housework $(t_1 + t_2)$ and hours of work for pay (h):

$$T = t_1 + t_2 + h. \tag{10}$$

The household has a cash income constraint (I), which it receives as cash income from members working for a wage (W) and from income on financial assets (interest and dividends) and unanticipated gifts (V), and this cash income is allocated to purchasing X_1 and X_2

$$I = W \cdot h + V = P_1 X_1 + P_2 X_2. \tag{11}$$

In this model, I first examine household decision-making in the input space, i.e., to choose inputs so as to maximize utility (8), subject to the production technology, physical time, and cash income constraint. Moreover, if the household allocates physical time to work in the market at wage rate (W), the physical time (10) and cash income constraints (11) can be combined into one full-income constraint

$$F = W \cdot T + V = P_1 X_1 + W t_1 + P_2 X_2 + W \cdot t_2. \tag{12}$$

In addition, one method of incorporating the technology constraint is by substitution (9a) and (9b) into (8). The new constrained optimization with Lagrange multiplier λ (marginal utility of full income) becomes

$$\psi = U[G_1(X_1, t_1; \varphi_1), G_2(X_2, t_2; \varphi_2); \tau] + \lambda[W \cdot T + V - P_1 X_1 - W \cdot t_1 - P_2 X_2 - W \cdot t_2]. \tag{13}$$

The first-order conditions for an interior solution is

$$X_i: U_{Z_i} G_{iX_i} - \lambda P_i = 0, i = 1, 2 \tag{14a}$$

$$t_i: U_{Z_i} G_{it_i} - \lambda W = 0, i = 1, 2 \tag{14b}$$

$$\lambda: W \cdot T + V - W \cdot L - P_1 X_1 - P_2 X_2 = 0, \tag{14c}$$

where U_{Z_i} is the marginal utility of commodity Z_i, G_{iX_i} is the marginal product of input X_i in producing Z_i, and G_{it_i} is the marginal product of input t_i in producing Z_i. A notable feature of these first-order conditions in (14a) and (14b) is that for a household to maximize utility subject to its technology and resource constraints, it must produce Z_1 and Z_2 at minimum cost

$$MC_{Z_i} = W / G_{iX_i} = P_i / G_{it_i} = \pi_i(W, P_i, \phi) i, \, i = 1, 2. \tag{15}$$

$MC_{Z_i} = \pi_i(W, P_i, \phi_i)$ is the marginal cost of Z_i, which depends on the opportunity cost of time (W), the price of purchased input (P_i), and the technology or efficiency parameter (φ_i). Moreover, with fixed input prices to the household and constant returns to scale in producing the Z_is, the marginal cost of producing each Z_i is unchanged with a proportional rescaling, e.g., doubling of both variable inputs.

From equations (14a)–(14c), solve for the following general form of the implicit demand functions for the inputs in this model

$$X_i^* = D_{X_i}(P_1, P_2, W, V, \phi_1, \phi_2, \tau) = D_{X_i}(P_1, P_2, W, F, \phi_1, \phi_2, \tau), \, i = 1, 2 \tag{16a}$$

$$t_i^* = D_{t_i}(P_1, P_2, W, V, \phi_1, \phi_2, \tau) = D_{t_i}(P_1, P_2, W, F, \phi_1, \phi_2, \tau), \, i = 1, 2 \tag{16b}$$

And, hence, the general form of the demand equations for housework and supply of labor can be derived as follows:

$$t_p^* = t_1^* + t_2^* = D_{t_p}(P_1, P_2, W, V, \phi_1, \phi_2, \tau) = D_{t_p}(P_1, P_2, W, F, \phi, 1\phi_2, \tau) \tag{17a}$$

$$h^* = T - t_1^* - t_2^* = S_H(P_1, P_2, W, V, \phi_1, \phi_2, \tau) = S_H(P_1, P_2, W, F, \phi_1, \phi_2, \tau). \tag{17b}$$

Moreover, the demand for purchased inputs, such as food, housework, and labor supply, are all a function of the prices (P_is) of purchased inputs for home production (such as meat and fish; potatoes, pasta, bread; tomatoes, lettuce, cucumbers; and milk and eggs), price of housework (W), non-labor or full income (V or F), the technology or efficiency parameters (φ_1 and φ_2), and the taste parameter (τ).[6] Hence, with the household production model the education of the homemaker can be connected to the efficiency of household production (φ_i) and not be forced into an association of tastes with education. Many labor economists accept that a homemaker's education or skill may raise the productivity of household production time (Becker 1976; Michael and Becker 1973).

---

[6] In contrast, if we assume the technology of household production is represented by a joint production function, $G(Z_1, Z_2, X_1, X_2, t_p, \varphi) = 0$, with Zs as commodities (outputs); Xs and t_p as inputs, and efficiency parameter φ, where $G(\cdot, \varphi)$ is convex in outputs, decreasing in inputs, and strictly increasing in φ, then we obtain roughly the same implicit input demand functions as in (16a) and (17a) and supply function as in (17b).

Given the above results, the household's decision problem is stated in the commodity or Z-space. I now define the full-income constraint in terms of the quantity and marginal cost of the Z_is

$$F = \pi_1 Z_1 + \pi_2 Z_2. \tag{18}$$

Now, assume that the household chooses the Z_is so as to maximize utility (8) subject to the full-income constraint in (18) and obtain the following first-order conditions for an interior solution:

$$Z_i: U_{Z_i} - \lambda \pi_i = 0, \, i = 1, 2 \tag{19a}-(19b)$$

$$\lambda: F - \pi_1 Z_1 - \pi_2 Z_2 = 0. \tag{19c}$$

Equations (19a)–(19c) can be solved jointly for the implicit demand functions for the commodities (Z_is)

$$Z_i = D_{Z_i}(\pi_1, \pi_2, F, \tau), \, i = 1, 2. \tag{20}$$

Hence, the demand for Z_i is determined by the marginal cost of the two commodities, full income available for spending ($F = W \cdot T + V$), and the taste parameter (τ). Moreover, under the assumptions that the household faces fixed input prices and constant returns to scale in the production of both commodities, the iso-cost line or slope of the budget constraint of the household in commodity or Z-space is a straight line.

An example can help shed new light on insights gained by adding household production to demand theory. Consider two alternative meat dishes for dinner, one consisting of pork loin in the form of boneless pork chops cooked on the stove top and the second consisting of a pork loin baked in the stove's oven. Hence, X_i is pounds of pork loin and t_i is the amount of the cook's time required in overseeing cooking the loin. Let's assume that two pounds of loin are prepared in both cooking processes, but it takes twenty minutes of the cook's time to fry the pork chops and 1.5 hours to roast the loin, including basting the loin roast. Hence, I have defined fixed-proportions input–output technology where $X_i = a_i Z_i$ and $t_i = b_i Z_i$ so that $\pi_i = a_i P_i + b_i W$, $i = 1$, 2. Now let P_i be \$5.00 for two pounds of pork loin (either as quarter-pound cut chops or as a two pound roast).

Now first assume that the opportunity cost, or price of the cook's time, is initially the minimum wage, roughly \$8 per hour. Then the marginal cost of two pounds of fried pork chops is $\pi_1 = \$5.00 + \$2.67 = \$7.67$. In contrast, the marginal cost of two pounds of roasted pork loin is $\pi_2 = \$5.00 + \$12.00 = \$17.00$. Although the "grocery store cost of the pork loin" is identical in these two cases, the marginal cost of ready-to-eat pork loin is roughly twice as much when it comes prepared as a loin roast as compared to fried chops. Hence, when the cost of the cook's time is factored into the decision, the absolute and relative cost of cooked chops versus a cooked loin roast changes dramatically.[7]

---

[7] Although the cook may be able to engage in a secondary activity such as watching TV or monitoring children, the main point is that cooking the roast, including basting it, requires the presence of the cook.

Second, let us now assume that the price of the cook's time is three times higher or $24 per hour (which is roughly equivalent to annual full-time earnings of $48,000 per year). The marginal cost of two pounds of fried pork chops is now $\pi_1' = \$5.00 + \$8.00 = \$13.00$, and of two pounds of ready-to-eat pork loin roast is $\pi_2' = \$5.00 + \$36.00 = \$41.00$. Hence, even though the grocery store cost of the pork loin remains unchanged in our second example, the marginal cost of two pounds of cooked pork loin roast is more than three times as expensive as is two pounds of fried pork chops. Hence, the difference in the marginal cost of cooked pork loin roast compared to fried pork chops has increased significantly from the first example. Furthermore, this logic can be used to explain why wealthy households tend to consume expensive easy-to-prepare cuts of meat rather than cheap time-consuming-to-prepare ones. When the cost of the cook's time tripled, the marginal cost of the time-intensive pork loin roast increases relative to the marginal cost of the fried pork chops—from $17/6.67 = 2.55$ in the first example to $41/13 = 3.15$ in the second example. Hence, as the price of the cook's time increases, the marginal cost of cook's time-intensive pork meals increases relative to those that are less intensive in cook's time—fried pork chops. Viewed another way, as women have obtained more education and entered the labor force, which increases the opportunity cost of their time, cook's-time intensive meal preparation has become less attractive. Given that meals prepared at home are on average more nutritious than meals eaten away from home, this change has a negative impact on the production of good health (Lin, Frazão, and Guthrie 1999). See application at the end of this section.

A second factor that weighs against pork loin roasts is that the minimum size is about two pounds, which would feed a relatively large household (or a dinner party), and as average household sizes declined over the 1950s and 1960s, households are more likely to be too small to make roasting a loin economical and fried pork chops become more likely. However, frying pork chops in cooking oil, which means adding oil and calories per ounce of prepared meat, is widely recognized as a less healthful means of preparing loin than the more time-intensive oven roasting.[8] Given that women continue to be the main meal planners and preparers, these examples show how rising opportunity cost of women's time has tipped the scale toward less healthy meal preparation for household's members (Kerkhofs and Kooreman 2003; Lin, Frazão, and Guthrie 1999; Robinson and Godbey 1997).

After replacing fixed- for variable-proportions production technology, additional insights from the Becker model of household production are obtained. To do this, continue with the two-commodity–two-input model. Moreover, assume that $X = X_1 + X_2$, i.e., the purchased inputs are perfect substitutes, and continue with total time in housework allocated between t_1 and t_2. In addition, assume that commodity Z_2 is relatively time-intensive to produce, and the prices of the purchased component of

---

[8] Basting liquid for pork loin roasts consists of some vegetable oil, but also wine and spices. However, a much smaller share of the loin comes in direct contact with the oil than in fried pork chops, which reduces oil uptake.

production of each Z (P_is) is fixed to the household. Given the assumption of constant returns to scale in the production of both commodities, all of the information about production of each commodity can be represented on a unit isoquant, i.e., $Z_i = 1$. Total production involves only rescaling the information in the unit isoquant model.

Consider panel A in Figure 2.1, where the initial iso-cost line $C_0 C_0'$ with slope ($-W/$ P) is drawn tangent to the one-unit isoquant for Z_1 and Z_2 at a and b. Because I will focus on the implications of an increase in the wage rate, I will measure cost in term of units of X, which is unchanged in our example. Hence, in the initial situation, the cost of one unit of Z_1 and Z_2 is $0C_0$ in units of X. An increase in the wage rate from W to W' while minimizing cost causes a substitution effect away from time (t_i) toward the purchased input component (X_i) and the marginal cost of both Zs increases in units of X—to $0C_{11}$ for Z_1 and to $0C_{12}$ for Z_2. However, the marginal cost of Z_2, which is relatively time-intensive, rises relative to the marginal cost of Z_1.

Next, consider the effect of an increase in the wage rate (W) in commodity or Z-space. The initial budget constraint is $R_0 R_0'$ with tangency to U_0 at a and with optimal quantities of Z_1^0 and Z_2^0 in Figure 2.1, panel B. I have already shown that when the wage rate increases, the marginal cost or price of the time-intensive commodity Z_2 increases relative to the marginal cost of the less time-intensive commodity Z_1 (Figure 2.1, panel A).[9] The new relative marginal cost or price line for the Zs is $R_1 R_1'$ tangent to U_0 at point b in Figure 2.1, panel B. Given that the production of both Zs uses purchased inputs and housework, the household will experience a net increase in consumption opportunities as a result of the increase in the wage rate and a new budget constraint of $R_2 R_2'$. Hence, the increase in consumption opportunities is represented by the area $R_1 R_2 R_2' R_1'$, and the household can now move to any point between j and l on $R_2 R_2'$. Even with a pure substitution effect away from the housework-intensive commodity Z_2 as the wage increases, the consumption of Z_2 will actually increase. This occurs when the new optimum is between j and k on $R_2 R_2'$. However, if the new optimum is located between k and l on $R_2 R_2'$, the quantity demanded of Z_2 will decline. In addition, there is a high probability that the consumption of Z_1 will increase.

Becker's model of household production has been criticized because of his assumption of constant returns to scale in producing each commodity (the Zs) and the assumption of no joint production in producing the Zs, for example see Pollak and Wachter (1975). However, these assumptions are only needed to obtain a straight-line iso-cost constraint or budget constraint, which implies that household preferences and the budget constraint are independent.

Additional insights can be obtained by considering the following model of joint production. Assume the household obtains utility directly from consuming Z_1, which is produced using X_1 and t_1, as in equation (9a), but t_1 also provides utility (or disutility) directly to the household. For example, time cleaning the house or doing the laundry

---

[9] This is an application of the Lerner–Pearce Diagram from international trade theory (Lerner 1952; Deardorff 2002).

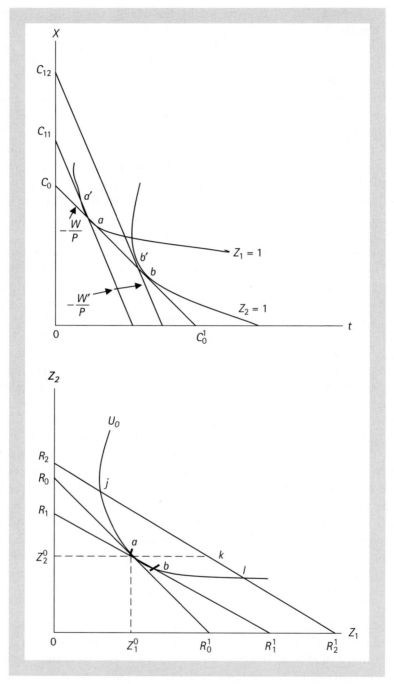

FIGURE 2.1 Becker's Variable-Input Proportions model
Top diagram: Optimal input choice: impact of wage rate increase.
Bottom diagram: Optimal commodity choice: impact of wage rate increase.

may directly lower utility but time gardening may directly raise utility, irrespective of the utility obtained from the product produced. Hence, the household's strictly concave utility function can be written as

$$U = U(Z_1, t_1; \tau). \tag{21}$$

The household's time constraint is

$$T = t_1 + h, \tag{22}$$

and the full-income budget constraint is

$$W \cdot T + V - P_1 X_1 - W \cdot t_1 = 0. \tag{23}$$

The household now chooses X_1 and t_1 so as to maximize (21) subject to the technology of producing Z_1 and the full-income constraint

$$\psi = U[G_1(X_1, t_1; \varphi_1), t_1; \tau] + \lambda[W \cdot T + V - P_1 X_1 - W \cdot t_1]. \tag{24}$$

The first-order conditions at an interior solution are

$$X_1: U_{Z_1} G_{1X_1} - \lambda P_1 = 0 \tag{25a}$$

$$t_1: U_{Z_1} G_{1t_1} + U_{t_1} - \lambda W = 0 \tag{25b}$$

$$\lambda: W \cdot T + V - P_1 X_1 - W \cdot t_1 = 0 \tag{25c}$$

where U_{t_1} represents only the direct contribution of t_1 to utility. Rearranging equations (25a) and (25b) provides important information about optimal input combinations for producing Z_1

$$G_{1t_1} / G_{1X_1} = (W - U_{t_1}/\lambda)/P_1. \tag{26}$$

First, if t_1 does not directly enter the household utility, i.e., $U_{t_1} = 0$, then obtain the standard result for producing Z_1^0 at cost minimization, or point a in Figure 2.2. If, instead, the household obtains positive utility directly from housework, e.g., the homemaker enjoys cooking or gardening, then the direct impact of housework on utility is positive, $U_{t_1} > 0$, and the optimal input combination will be at point b in Figure 2.2, which implies that more time will be devoted to cooking or gardening than when pure cost minimization reigns. In contrast, if the household obtains negative utility directly from housework, e.g., the homemaker dislikes cleaning the house and doing the laundry, then the direct effect of housework on utility is negative, $U_{t_1} < 0$, and the optimal input combination will be at point c in Figure 2.2, which implies that less time will be devoted to cleaning or doing the laundry than when cost minimization reigns. Clearly, this substitution toward more X_1 in producing Z_1^0 could include hiring a home cleaning service or taking clothing to a commercial laundry for washing and ironing.

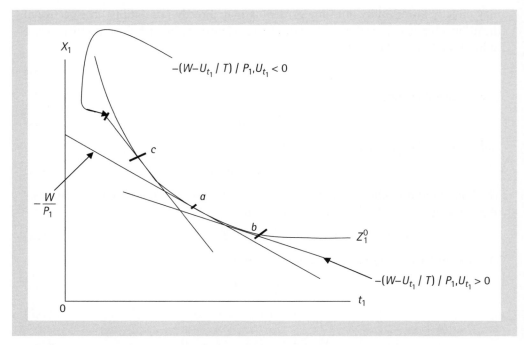

FIGURE 2.2 Effects of "joint" production on Optimal Input Proportions for commodity Z_1

4.2   A Gronau-Type Model

The most notable feature of the Gronau model of household production is that home-produced and purchased goods are perfect substitutes, but this could also be one of its shortcomings (Gronau 1977, 1986). Assume a household consumes and obtains utility from two goods, leisure (L) and a good X, say meals, which can be produced at home, denoted as X_1, or purchased in the market, denoted as X_2. In Gronau's framework, these goods are assumed to be perfect substitutes, where the household only values total X rather than individual quantities of home-produced and purchased X

$$X = X_1 + X_2. \tag{27}$$

Also, the household has a strictly concave utility function

$$U = U(L, X; \tau) \tag{28}$$

And, for simplicity, assume that the household's production function for X_1 is strictly concave in one variable input, housework (h_1):

$$X_1 = G_1(h_1; \varphi) \tag{29}$$

where φ is a technology or efficiency parameter. The household faces a time constraint, receiving an endowment T each period that is allocated to leisure (L), housework (h_1), and wage work (h_2):

$$T = L + h_1 + h_2. \tag{30}$$

The household has cash income from wage work (h_2) and non-labor income (V), which it allocates to X_2:

$$I = W \cdot h_2 + V = P_2 X_2. \tag{31}$$

Equation (30) can be solved for h_2 and substituted into equation (31) to obtain the household's full-income constraint:

$$F = W \cdot T + V = W \cdot L + W \cdot h_1 + P_2 X_2. \tag{32}$$

Equation (29) can be substituted into (27), which in turn is substituted into (28), and h_1 and X_2 can be chosen to maximize the modified utility function subject to the full-income constraint

$$\psi = U[L, G_1(h_1; \varphi) + X_2; \tau] + \lambda(W \cdot T + V - W \cdot L - W \cdot h_1 - P_2 X_2). \tag{33}$$

The first-order conditions for an interior solution are

$$L: U_L - \lambda W = 0 \tag{34a}$$

$$h_i: U_X G_{1h_1} - \lambda W = 0 \tag{34b}$$

$$X_2: U_X - \lambda P_2 = 0 \tag{34c}$$

$$\lambda: W \cdot T + V - WL - W \cdot h_1 - P_2 X_2 = 0 \tag{34d}$$

Combining equations (34b) and (34c), obtain the result that X_1 should be produced under the standard one-variable input profit-maximizing condition, $P_2 G_{1h_1} = W$, and the general form of the optimal quantity of housework demanded, t_1, and supply of X_1 is given by

$$h_1^* = D_{t_1}(W, P_2, \phi) \tag{35a}$$

$$X_1^* = G_1(h_1^*; \phi) = S_{X_1}(W, P_2, \phi). \tag{35b}$$

Conditions (34a), (34c), and (34d) can be solved jointly for the following demand functions for L^* and X_2^*:

$$L^* = D_L(W, P_2, V, \tau, \varphi) = D_L(W, P_2, F, \tau, \varphi) \tag{36a}$$

$$X_2^* = D_{X_2}(W, P_2, V, \tau, \phi) = D_{X_2}(W, P_2, F, \tau, \phi) \tag{36b}$$

Rearranging the time constraint (30) and using the information in equations (35a) and (36a), obtain the general form of the household's labor supply equation

$$h_2 = T - L^* - h_1^* = S_{h_2}(W, P, V, \tau, \varphi) = S_{h_2}(W, P, F, \tau, \varphi). \tag{37}$$

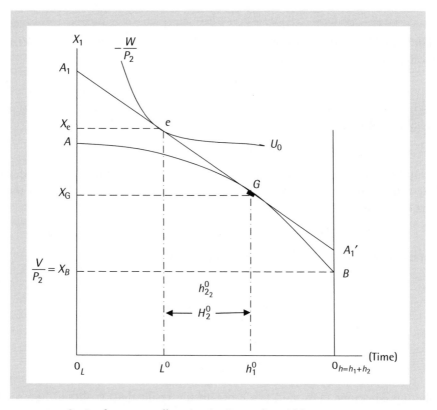

FIGURE 2.3 Optimal resource allocation in Gronau's model

Figure 2.3 displays a graphic representation of the optimal resource allocation at an interior solution for the Gronau model of household production. Units of X are on the vertical axis and units of time are on the horizontal axis, but the maximum length of this axis is T, which is reflected by the erection of a vertical line at this amount of human time. The household can purchase X_B units of X from its non-labor income (V). At point B on the vertical axis T, the household considers how best to allocate a unit of time: to produce X directly or to work for a wage and purchase the added X from earnings. The boundary of the technology and resource constraints facing the household are represented by $A_1 GB0_h$ in Figure 2.3. Moreover, Figure 2.3 is drawn such that at point B, the marginal product of housework in producing $X(G_{1h_1})$ is greater than the real wage (W/P_2), so it is optimal for the household to allocate time to housework rather than wage work along the production relationship as the segment AGB. At point G optimal housework is h_1^0. This results in the quantity $X_B - X_G$ of home-produced goods. Additional forgone leisure should be allocated to wage work since the figure for the marginal product of housework in producing X is lower than the real wage. The household's utility maximum (U_0) occurs at e, with $X_e - X_G$ of X purchased from earnings. In the figure, the optimal amount of leisure is L^0 and of wage work is $h_2^0 = L^0 - h_1^0$.

An usual prediction of this model is that if non-labor income (V) increases, the household will optimally keep the quantity of home-produced goods (X_1) unchanged, but allocate the additional income to purchase units of X in the market (X_2) and leisure (L). However, if P_2 increases, this reduces the real wage rate (W/P_2) and unambiguously increases the amount of time allocated to and quantity of home goods produced. The net impact on leisure, hours of work, and total quantity of X consumed will be determined by resulting substitution and income effects. In this model, it is also obvious that an increase in the efficiency of producing X_1 at all h, e.g., owing to better information or training in home production, will increase the amount of time allocated to and production of home goods (X_1).

4.3   Application of Household Production Theory to Health with Food as an Input

Of considerable interest is the household's production of good health, especially as it is related to obesity and associated health problems (Finkelstein, Fiebelkorn, and Wang 2003; Huffman et al. 2010). Inputs in the health production function include food, which is a source of protein, energy, vitamins, minerals, fiber; leisure time; and medical care. However, food intake also frequently yields utility directly because food texture and taste give satisfaction and eating and drinking together are a major part of satisfaction-yielding social interaction.

Let's assume a household has a strictly concave utility function

$$U = U(H, X, C, LP, LO; H_e, Z) \tag{38}$$

where utility U depends on the current health status of the household members (H); consumption of food and drink (X) and other purchased goods (C) (excluding purchased health care); and physically active leisure (LP) and other leisure time (LO). The variable H_e represents early health status, e.g., genetic potential for good/bad health or sometimes summarized by health status at birth such as birth weight (Fogel 1994). Z denotes fixed observables, such as education, gender, and race/ethnicity of adults. Current health, other purchased goods, and other leisure time (H, C, and LO) are assumed to be positive "goods," i.e., a marginal increase in any one of them directly Increases household utility (U_H, U_C, $U_{LO} > 0$) and, hence, better (current) adult health status increases household utility, as do higher consumption of other purchased goods and more time allocated to sedentary leisure, e.g., TV viewing, surfing the Web. However, time allocated to vigorous physically active leisure may directly reduce utility, i.e., adults find this activity unpleasant or uncomfortable and then $U_{LP} < 0$.

Let's assume the household's production function for adult health status is

$$H = H(LP, X, I; H_e, Z, \varphi), \tag{39}$$

where $H(\cdot)$ is a strictly concave function and I is a vector of purchased health inputs or medical care. The parameter φ summarizes unobservable factors which affect the efficiency of current production of health status, e.g., genetic predisposition for good/ bad health such as obesity. In the health production function, I expect $H_{LP}, H_I > 0$, or, holding other factors constant, additional time allocated to physically active leisure (LP) or a larger quantity of purchased health care (I) produces more good health. Although many adults may obtain disutility from vigorous physically active leisure, the fact that its marginal product in health production is positive can result in a combined direct and indirect effect on marginal utility ($U^S_{LP} = U_H H_{LP} + U_{LP} > 0$) if the positive first term on the right in this equation ($U_H H_{LP}$) outweighs a negative second term (U_{LP}).

The marginal product of food in health production (H_X) is expected to be positive for some foods (i.e., $H_X > 0$) and perhaps negative for others (i.e., $H_X < 0$). For example, fresh fruits and vegetables, which are high in fiber, vitamins, and minerals, are expected to have a positive marginal product on health output, but the marginal product might be negative for processed fruits and vegetables, which frequently contain "added sugar" and sometimes contain "added salt and fat" and less fiber and fewer vitamins and minerals than fresh produce. All meats and fish contain protein, which is essential for cell reproduction and growth, but they also contain fat. Since fats are very calorie-dense, they can contribute to excess energy intake and obesity. Also, some fats (low-density ones) detract from cardiovascular health and others (high-density ones) are neutral or positive to cardiovascular health. But some fat is needed to make fresh vegetables more palatable and to dissolve essential vitamins. Also, fat makes some other foods taste "good," which implies that the direct effect of X on utility is positive, or $U_X > 0$. If a type of food has a negative marginal product in the production of good health, the combined marginal effect of X on utility may still be positive, provided that $U^S_X = U_H H_X + UX > 0$, or the first term on the right of this equation ($U_H H_X$) is outweighed by a positive second term on the right (U_X).

Assume the household has two adults and their time constraint consists of a time endowment (T) which is allocated among work for pay (R), physically active leisure (LP), and other leisure (LO): $T = R + LP + LO$. Let P_x, P_1, P_C denote the price vectors corresponding to X, I, and C, respectively, W denotes the wage rate or opportunity cost of time of an adult, V denotes household non-labor income, then household cash income constraint $WR + V$ is spent on X, I, and C such that $WR + V = P_X X + P_I I + P_C C$. Now the household's decision is to choose LP, LO, R, X, I, and C to maximize household utility subject to staying within the human time and cash income constraints

$$\max_{LP,LO,R,X,I,C} u = U\big(H(LP, X, I; H_e, Z, \varphi), X, C, LP, LO; H_e, Z\big)$$

$$s.t. \quad P_X \cdot X + P_I \cdot I + P_C \cdot C = WR + V \tag{40}$$

$$R + LP + LO = T, R \geq 0, LP \geq 0, LO \geq 0$$

where the first constraint is the household's cash income constraint and the second constraint is the household's time constraint. The Lagrangian for the constrained utility maximization is

$$\Phi = U(H(LP, X, I; H_e, Z, \varphi), X, C, LP, LO; H_e, Z) \\ + \lambda(WR + V - P_X \cdot X - P_I \cdot I - P_C \cdot C) + \mu(T - R - LP - LO) \tag{41}$$

where λ and μ are the Lagrange multipliers, indicating the marginal utility of cash income ($WR + V$) and marginal utility of the time endowment (T), respectively.

The first-order conditions for an optimum, including Kuhn–Tucker conditions on LP and R, are

$$LP : U_H \cdot H_{LP} + U_{LP} - \mu^* \le 0 \quad (LP^* \cdot U_H \cdot H_{LP} + U_{LP} - \mu^*) = 0 \quad LP^* \ge 0$$
$$R : \lambda^* \cdot W - \mu^* \le 0 \quad R^*(\lambda^* \cdot W - \mu^*) = 0 \quad R^* \ge 0$$
$$LO : U_{Lo} = \mu^*$$
$$X : U_H \cdot H_X + U_X = \lambda^* P_X$$
$$I : U_H \cdot H_I = \lambda^* P_I$$
$$C : U_c = \lambda^* P_c$$
$$\lambda : P_x \cdot X^* + P_I \cdot I^* + P_c \cdot C^* = WR^* + V$$
$$\mu : R^* + LP^* + LO^* = T$$

where $U_H = \partial U / \partial H$, $U_{LP} = \partial U / \partial LP$, $U_C = \partial U / \partial C$, $U_{LO} = \partial U / \partial LO$, $UX = \partial U / \partial X$, $H_{LP} = \partial H / \partial LP$, and $H_X = \partial H / \partial X$ and $H_I = \partial H / \partial I$ represent partial derivatives.

These immediately above first-order conditions can be solved jointly for an interior solution (where the opportunity cost of time is W) to obtain the implicit household optimal demand function for LP, LO, X, I, and C:

$$LP^* = LP(W, P_X, P_I, P_C, V, H_e, Z, \varphi)$$
$$LO^* = LO(W, P_X, P_I, P_C, V, H_e, Z, \varphi)$$
$$X^* = X(W, P_X, P_I, P_C, V, H_e, Z, \varphi) \tag{42}$$
$$I^* = I(W, P_X, P_I, P_C, V, H_e, Z, \varphi)$$
$$C^* = C(W, P_X, P_I, P_C, V, H_e, Z, \varphi).$$

Now upon substituting the equations in (42) into the health production function (39), obtain the general form of the household's health supply (and demand) function for (current) adult health:

$$H^* = H(LP^*, X^*, I^*; H_e, Z, \varphi) = H(W, P_X, P_I, P_C, V, H_e, Z, \varphi). \tag{43}$$

A notable feature of (43) is that it contains the same set of explanatory variables as those in the system of household demand equations (42). See Chen and Huffman (2009) for application of this model to adults' decisions to participate in physical activity and to be a healthy weight (not obese).

5   AN EMPIRICAL APPLICATION: DEMAND FOR FOOD AT HOME AND OTHER HOUSEHOLD INPUTS

To illustrate more vividly the empirical implications of household production theory and models for household demand studies, I consider the demand for inputs by the US sector over the post-Second World War period. The methodology that I follow is best described as a hybrid version of Becker's and Gronau's productive household models in which there are two classes of unpaid human time—unpaid housework and leisure—and where purchased and home-produced goods are not perfect substitutes. Following Jorgenson and Stiroh (1999), Jorgenson (2001) and Jorgenson and Slesnick (2008), inputs are defined as flows, and, hence, the input from housing, household appliances, transportation equipment, and recreation equipment is capital services and not the durable goods themselves.[10]

The immediate post-Second World War period is interesting because it was a time when the war effort that had been directed to producing tanks, planes, ships, guns, and ammunition was redirected to supplying durable goods—new houses, household appliances, and cars—to the household sector and tractors and machinery for the farm sector. Moreover, major series on the services of household durable goods available from Jorgenson start in 1948. My period of analysis ends in 1996, which is almost a half-century in length, and is a date when the transition of women from housework to market work had been largely completed (Goldin 1986).

After translating durable goods into services, it is now plausible to specify a static household input demand system that is in the spirit of equations (16a) and (17a), where leisure time is one of the t_is. Over the post-Second World War period, major changes in households included less time allocated by women to preparing meals and meal clean-up at home and more meals consumed away from home. Frequently, workday lunches are purchased and eaten at school or work and weekend dinners are eaten in restaurants. When meals are at home, ready-to-eat food is frequently purchased at fast-food restaurants, grocery delis, and restaurants, and taken home to be eaten. Advances in household appliances now provide microwave ovens with timers and electric and gas ranges with thermostatically controlled burners, and ovens give temperature control with little supervision, which may lead to higher-quality home-produced meals. These appliances are technically advanced relative to the coal, wood, kerosene, and LP gas burning cooking stoves of the late 1940s (Bryant 1986).[11]

---

[10] Although capital services are proportional to the stock of consumer durables, proper aggregation requires weighting the stocks by rental prices rather than asset acquisition prices (Jorgenson, Gollop, and Fraumeni 1987). Moreover, the rental price for each asset incorporates the rate of return, the depreciation rate, and the rate of change in the acquisition price.

[11] An alternative perspective of these input demand functions is that they represent demand functions for goods and services that yield utility directly to households (Pollak and Wachter 1975).

5.1   Specific Input Groups

Nine empirical input categories are distinguished for the aggregate household sector and indexes of price and quantity are constructed for each of them. Table 2.1 contains a brief definition of all variables used in the empirical demand system. A very brief summary of some key details about the input categories is discussed here, but greater details are available in Huffman (2008). As indicated above, households' durable goods are converted into service flows, and personal consumption expenditures on non-durables are used in constructing measures of non-durable goods or inputs. Also, considerable evidence exists that unpaid housework of women and men are not perfect substitutes, ranging from child care and meal planning and preparation where women's work dominates effort to yard and car care and snow removal where men's work dominates effort (Gronau 1977; Becker 1981; Robinson and Godbey 1997; Bianchi et al. 2000; Aguiar and Hurst 2006, tables 2 and 3). Hence, men's and women's time are treated as different inputs.

Table 2.1   Definitions of variables and sample means

Variable	Definitions	Sample mean
w_1	Expenditure share for women's (unpaid) housework	0.119
w_2	Expenditure share for men's (unpaid) housework	0.069
w_3	Expenditure share for food at home	0.052
w_4	Expenditure share for purchased housework-substitute services	0.015
w_5	Expenditure share for housing services	0.048
w_6	Expenditure share for household appliance services	0.030
w_7	Expenditure share for transportation services	0.047
w_8	Expenditure share for recreation services and entertainment	0.025
w_9	Expenditure share for "other inputs" (men's and women's leisure and other consumer goods and services)	0.595
AGE < 5	Share of resident population that is less than 5 years of age	0.090
AGE ≥ 65	Share of resident population that is 65 years of age and older	0.104
Non-metro	Share of resident population living in non-metropolitan areas	0.132
Consumer patents	Stock of patents of consumer goods, trapezoid weights over 26 years	3,262.7
F/(N)	Average household full-income expenditure per person	4,369.5
P_1	Price of women's housework, or opportunity wage	0.528
P_2	Price of men's housework, or opportunity wage	0.541
P_3	Price index for food at home	0.598
P_4	Price index for purchased housework-substitute services	0.512
P_5	Price index for housing services	0.565
P_6	Price index for household appliance services	0.580
P_7	Price index for transportation services	0.611
P_8	Price index for recreation services and entertainment	0.660
P_9	Price index for "other inputs" (e.g., men's and women's leisure and other consumer goods and services)	0.552
P	Stone price or cost of living index	0.556

The choice of exactly nine input groups is subjective. This is a large enough number to provide large amounts of information about the structure of US household production and it is near the maximum number of input categories can be supported in an econometric model with the data at hand. The complete set of input categories is: (i) women's (unpaid) housework, (ii) men's (unpaid) housework, (iii) food at home, (iv) purchased housework-substitute services (e.g., domestic services, laundry and dry-cleaning services, and food away from home), (v) housing services (for owner-occupied and rental housing), (vi) services of household appliances (including imputed services from computers, furnishings owned, and household utilities), (vii) transportation services (imputed services of transportation capital owned, purchased transportation services, and fuel for transportation), (viii) recreational services and entertainment (imputed services of recreation capital owned and recreation services purchased), and (ix) other goods and services (largely men's and women's leisure) and other purchased services.[12] Hence, in this empirical framework, unpaid housework and "other" inputs, which are largely leisure time, are distinct input categories.[13]

For this study, the daily time endowment of adults is rescaled from twenty-four hours to a modified time endowment of fourteen or fifteen hours per day, by excluding time allocated to sleeping, eating, and other personal care. No evidence exists that time allocated to personal care by women and men is responsive to prices or income, or even to trend (see Robinson and Godbey 1997: 337).[14] Moreover, Ramey, and Francis (2005) and Greenwood, Seshadri, and Yorukoglu (2005) use similar modified time endowments of roughly 100 hours per week in developing national economy macro simulation/calibration models.

Each individual aged 16 and older who is not in school is assumed to allocate his/her modified time endowment among unpaid housework, labor market work, including commuting, and leisure. Housework is defined as time allocated primarily to: food preparation and clean-up; house, yard, and car care; care of clothing and linens; care of family members; and shopping and management. Thus, housework in this study is considerably broader than "core housework"—cooking, cleaning and washing dishes, doing the laundry, and cleaning and straightening the house. Labor market work includes work for pay and commuting time to work. Time allocated to leisure or free time is time allocated primarily to social organizations, entertainment, recreation, and

---

[12] Some might suggest that food away from home be treated as a separate input category, but for the early part of the study period its share was quite small. See Prochaska and Schrimper (1973) for evidence.

[13] Only one price exists for men's and one for women's time, and hence, it is not possible to include leisure time as a separate input. However, men's and women's leisure does account for more than 85 percent of the "other input" category. Jorgenson and Slesnick (2008) use a household demand system consisting of four groups (non-durables, capital services, consumer services, and leisure). In particular, they do not distinguish between unpaid housework and true leisure and label the aggregate of the two "leisure."

[14] However, technical change associated with showering/bathing—soaps, shampoos, deodorants, shaving equipment—has made it possible for steady increases in the quality of personal hygiene, with a roughly unchanged amount of time spent on personal care.

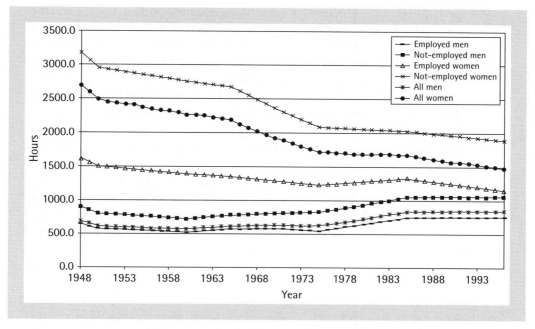

FIGURE 2.4 Average annual hours of unpaid household work of employed and not employed men and women, 16–64 years of age: 1948–96

communications.[15] However, it is defined residually for each individual as his/her allocatable time endowment less hours of housework and hours of labor market work.

The (modified) time endowment is set as follows. For women and men aged 16 to 64 who are not enrolled in school, the modified endowment is assumed to be fourteen and fifteen hours per day, respectively. The size of these modified time endowments is based on information presented in Robinson and Godbey (1997: 337) and Juster and Stafford (1991: 477), showing that women spend a little more time on sleep and personal care than men. For women and men who are 65 years of age and older, the modified time endowment is thirteen and fourteen hours, respectively. The small reduction relative to individuals 16–64 years of age reflects that additional time is spent recovering from illnesses.[16] In deriving aggregate average hours of paid work and of unpaid housework, a distinction is made between the number of employed and not employed women and men because these numbers have changed dramatically over time, which is a major factor in reallocation of adult time (see Figure 2.4 and Huffman 2008 for more details).

[15] In empirical research, Juster and Stafford (1985, 1991) also distinguish between time allocated to housework and leisure. For the purposes of my study, it is important to maintain these distinctions for the primary uses of non-market time.

[16] All computations dealing with time use assume a 365-day and fifty-two-week year.

Annual hours of unpaid housework for working and non-working women and men aged 16–64, who are not in school, and for age 65 and over were derived from benchmark data. Hours of work for pay were obtained from US Department of Labor data files.[17] Data on commuting time were derived from information reported in Robinson and Godbey (1997). Hours of women's and men's leisure are computed as the adjusted time endowment less hours of unpaid housework, and hours of work for pay, including time for commuting to work. Among men and women aged 16–64 who are not in school, women on average have slightly less leisure time than men, but for men and women, the average amount of leisure time rose over 1948 to 1975, and then decreased a little.

The price of time allocated to housework and leisure is defined as the forgone market wage following procedures in Smith and Ward (1985) where an adjustment downward occurs in the wage for the not-employed groups. An average nominal wage rate over working and not-working men (and women) is constructed as the weighted average of the average nominal wage rate for employed and not-employed men (and women), which is an index number solution to the aggregate problem. See Huffman (2008) for details.

Consumers purchase non-durable goods and services for consumption and acquire consumer durables in order to obtain a flow of services to use in household production. Capital services are proportional to the stock of assets, including computers, but aggregation requires weighting the stocks by rental prices rather than acquisition prices for assets. The rental price for each asset incorporates the rate of return, the depreciation rate, and the rate of decline in the acquisition price. The Bureau of Economic Analysis (BEA) provides data on purchases of twelve types of consumer durable goods used in the construction of service measures for household durable goods.

Input price indexes are Tornqvist indexes (Diewert 1976; Deaton and Muellbauer 1980a: 174–5). The Tornqvist index permits substitution to occur within major input categories as relative prices of subcomponents change. The overall price index for the nine-input group making full expenditures is, however, the Stone price or cost of living index (Stone 1954).

5.2   Mean Values and Long-Term Trends over the Post-Second World War Period

Mean full-income expenditure per capita over the study period is $4,369 in 1987 dollars. The mean expenditure share on women's unpaid housework is 0.119, men's unpaid housework is 0.069, food at home is 0.052, purchased housework-substitute services is 0.015, housing services is 0.030, household appliance services is 0.030, transportation

---

[17] The derived annual average hours of labor market work are consistent with the census year estimates presented by McGrattan and Rogerson (2004).

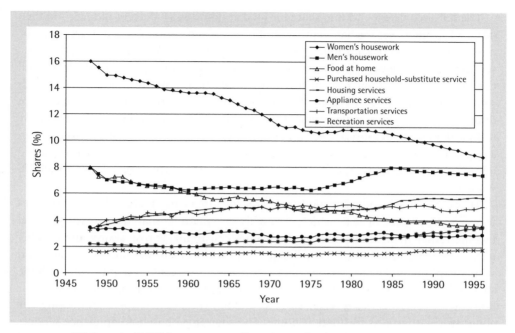

FIGURE 2.5 US household full income expenditure input shares, 1948–96

services is 0.047, recreation services and expenditures is 0.025, and "other inputs" is 0.595. Given that the other input category is dominated by leisure, the US household sector allocates a large share of full-income to leisure time, which is contrary to popular perceptions (Robinson and Godbey 1997).

Using the modified time endowment, full-income expenditures per capita in 1987 dollars were $3,668 in 1948 and $10,085 in 1996, with a mean value of $7,859. Hence, the average annual rate of growth of full-income-based consumption per capita over the sample period was 2.06 percent, slightly lower than the 2.25 percent per year growth of real per capita personal consumption expenditures in the National Income and Product Accounts (BEA). Evidence on the level and trend in eight of the nine expenditure shares (but excluding the share for "other inputs") from the aggregate data over 1948–96 are displayed in Figure 2.5.

The full-income expenditure share for women's housework is 16 percent in 1948 and displays a long-term negative trend with a slight reversal during the 1980s. The net decline over a half-century is about 7 percentage points. The share for men's housework is 8 percent in 1948 and declines slowly to 1960, as major technical advances are made in home heating equipment, and then shows almost no change from 1960 to 1975. However, it rose from 1975 to 1985, and then declined slightly. The net decline over the half-century was about 1 percentage point. Hence, during the post-Second World War period there has been a significant narrowing of the differential in the (unpaid) housework cost shares for men and women.

The full-income expenditure share for food at home was 8 percent in 1948, and then declined steadily over the half-century, ending at 3.5 percent. The expenditure share for purchased housework-substitute services (laundry and dry-cleaning services, domestic services, and food away from home) was about 1.7 percent in 1948, declined slowly until the mid-1970s, and then rose slightly, ending essentially where it started. Although some may have the conception that the expenditure share on this item has risen dramatically over the sample period, it has not changed. A major factor was the steady technical advance in fabrics used in making clothing, making them easier to care for, along with wages of domestic servants and restaurant workers, which have remained low owing to the immigration of low-skilled workers since 1980 relative to all US workers.

Turning to full-income expenditure shares for inputs, the share of housing services was only 3.5 percent in 1948, which is roughly one-tenth its share using cash personal income rather than full income as the budget constraint. It rose slowly and steadily until 1970, remained essentially unchanged from 1970 to 1980, and then rose slowly and steadily until 1996. The net change is an increase of 2.3 percentage points. Although the share of full-income expenditure allocated to food at home was larger in 1948 than for housing services, this was reversed by 1980, and in 1996 the share spent on housing was about twice as large as for food at home. The share for household appliance services rose initially, with the massive investment in new housing during the late 1940s and 1950s, displayed a slow decline to the mid-1970s, and thereafter rose very slowly. However, the net change over the half-century was negligible (see Figure 2.5). The share spent on transportation services was 3.4 percent in 1948, rose steadily until 1965, but then essentially remained unchanged until 1975. From 1975 to 1996 it rose slowly, reaching 5 percent in 1996. The share spent on recreation services and entertainment was 2 percent in 1948, had a slight negative trend until the mid-1970s, and then reversed course with a slow increase until 1996, ending the century 1.3 percentage points higher than at the beginning (see Figure 2.5).

In summary, some of the nine full-income expenditure shares show major changes over the last half-century—women's housework, food at home, and transportation services—but the others are relatively stable over time. When unpaid housework and leisure are excluded from the expenditure system, very different expenditure shares result. Deaton and Muellbauer (1980a), Jorgenson and Slesnick (1990), and Moschini (1998) also present expenditure shares using aggregate data with traditional measures of household consumption.

The relative input prices (derived as the nominal input price deflated by the Stone price or cost of living index (Stone 1954) for all nine input groups, 1948 to 1996, are displayed in Figure 2.6. They show dramatic changes over the study period.[18] A distinguishing feature of these new input prices is the dramatic change in the relative price of women's unpaid housework, which rose steadily from 1948 until 1980 by a total

---

[18] The excluded share is for the residual group labeled "other goods and services," which rose significantly over the post-Second World War period.

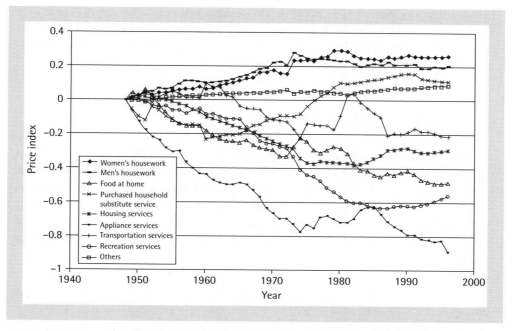

FIGURE **2.6** Prices of inputs for US households relative to the Stone cost of living index, 1948–96

of 30 percent and thereafter remained roughly unchanged. The relative price of men's unpaid housework rose about 27 percent over 1948 to 1972, then declined a little during the mid-1970s to early 1980s, and then remained largely unchanged to 1996. Hence, there was a small decline in gap between the prices of women's and men's housework over the study period.

The relative price of food at home had a strong negative trend, except for the world food crisis years in the early 1970s, declining by about 60 percent over the last half-century or a little more than 1 percent per year. The relative price of purchased housework-substitute services declined slowly over 1948 to 1967, rose slowly over 1967 to 1991, and then leveled off to 1996. The net result in the last half-century was an increase of about 10 percent (see Figure 2.5). The relative price of housing services declined steadily, cumulating into a 45 percent decline from 1948 to 1975, and then reversed its trend to increase slowly and be 10 percent higher in 1996. The relative price of household appliance services declined dramatically at a compound rate of 2.5 percent per year over 1948 to 1975, moved irregularly but trending upward over 1975 to 1985, and then declined by 35 percent to 1996. Moreover, the net decline over the half-century was a dramatic 80 percent. The relative price of transportation services moved in an irregular pattern over time and had a net decline over the whole period of 20 percent. The relative price of recreation input rose from 1948 to 1958, declined steadily from 1958 to the mid-1980s, and then rose slightly. The net decline over a half-century was, however, 20 percent. The relative price of "other inputs" rose very slowly over the half-century (see Figure 2.5). Thus, over 1948 to 1996, the data on expenditure shares and input prices show significant variation that is useful in estimating a complete household input demand system.

5.3   The Econometric Model

Among possible flexible function forms for the aggregate input demand system, I chose the almost ideal (AI) demand system by Deaton and Muellbauer (1980b) and Deaton (1986), which has cost shares as the dependent variables. In particular, the version is sometimes referred to as the linear approximation (LA) of the AI demand system (LA/AI), which has several major advantages, e.g., see Alston, Foster, and Green (1994), and has also been used by Hausman (1996) and Huffman and Johnson (2004). The econometric model is

$$w_{it} = \alpha_{i0} + \sum_{s=1}^{S} \delta_{is} D_{st} + \sum_{j=1}^{k} \gamma_{ij} \log p_{jt} + \beta_i \log [F_t / P(p_t)] + \varphi_i t + u_{it}, \qquad (44)$$

where w_{it} is the full-income expenditure share for the ith input, $i = 1, \ldots, n$, in time period $t = 1, \ldots, T$, D_{st} are translating or equivalency variables, p_{jt} is the price of the jth household input, F_t is full-income or expenditure, $P(p_t)$ is the Stone price index across the n input categories, which avoids inherent non-linearities, t is a linear time trend, and u_{it} is a random disturbance term that represents random shocks to the demand for input i in year t (Deaton and Muellbauer 1980a: 75–8; Wooldridge 2002: 251–8). The time trend is included to "detrend" the cost shares and all of the other regressors and also pick up any excluded variable that is highly correlated with trend, including gradual shift in women's skills from home production to market skills (Goldin 1986; Wooldridge 2002; Kerkhofs and Kooreman 2003; Borjas 2005).

In equation (44), the primary interest is in the αs, γs, and βs, which are key parameters of the LA/AI demand system. α_{i0} is a time-invariant unobserved effect for input i. The γs and βs are related to price and income elasticities, and symmetry, homogeneity, and adding up restrictions are imposed across the system of input demand equations (Deaton and Muellbauer 1980a: 76). Given the above restrictions and that expenditure shares sum to one, one of the share equations can be omitted in the estimation and its parameters can be recovered from the other $(n-1)$ estimated input demand equations. The ninth input category is omitted in my estimation.

The full-income expenditure elasticity of demand for the ith input is

$$\eta_{iE} = 1 + \beta_i / w_i, \, i = 1, \ldots, n. \qquad (45)$$

The Hicksian compensated own-price elasticity for the ith input is

$$\xi_{ii} = \gamma_{ii}/w_i + w_i - 1, \, i = 1, \ldots, n, \tag{46}$$

and the compensated cross-price elasticity of demand for the ith input and jth input price is

$$\xi_{ij} = \gamma_{ij}/w_i + w_j, \, i, j = 1, \ldots, n. \tag{47}$$

The specification of price elasticities in (46) and (47) has been shown in a simulation analysis by Alston, Foster, and Green (1994) to provide accurate estimates of the true price elasticities. Furthermore, the price and income elasticities that are to be calculated in this study using aggregate data are macro- rather than micro-estimates, and Rogerson and Wallenius (2007) emphasize that these macro-price and income elasticities are most appropriate for aggregate policy analysis.

Although expenditures share weighted full-income expenditure elasticities must sum to unity, any individual income elasticity of demand for an input can be positive, negative, or zero. However, for the compensated own-price elasticity of demand to be consistent with demand theory, it must be negative. Inputs are denoted as substitutes if they have a cross-price elasticity that is positive and as complements when the cross-price elasticity is negative. Given the restrictions on the demand system and letting all input prices change by 1 percent, the expenditure share weighted compensated price elasticities for the ith input is zero.

Equation (44) has two random unobserved terms (α_{i0} and u_{it}) and α_{i0} may be correlated with regressors in a demand equation and u_{it}. If the system were estimated in *level form*, this could, in principle, bias all the estimated coefficients. The additive disturbance term u_{it} in equation (44) satisfies the usual stochastic assumptions (having a zero mean, finite variance, first-order autoregressive process over time, and contemporaneous correlation across share equations). Under the hypothesis of a first-order autocorrelation and fitting a system of demand equations with cross-equation symmetry conditions, Barten (1969) emphasized that each of the equations within the system must be transformed by the same value of ρ but estimates of ρ were found to be close to one. Hence, the demand system was expressed in first-difference form for estimation. The differenced (n – 1) expenditure share equations were estimated with all restrictions imposed. In this version of the model, intercept terms become the coefficient of the linear time trend in equation (44).

The eight differenced input demand equations are configured as a stacked system of difference equations having the form of the seemingly unrelated regression (SUR) model, including contemporaneous cross-equation correlation of disturbances (Greene 2003: 340–50). The iterative feasible generalized least squares estimator is consistent, asymptotically efficient, and asymptotically equivalent to the maximum likelihood estimator (Barten 1969). The estimation is conducted using the iterative seemingly unrelated regression (ISUR) procedure in the software package Statistical Analysis System (SAS).

In addition to prices and income, the input demand system (44) contains demographic variables representing important dimensions of the structure of the population—the Ds. These translating variables are the share of the US resident civilian population that is (a) 5 years of age and younger, or pre-school age, (b) 65 years of age or older, who are retired or contemplating retirement, (c) residing in a non-metropolitan or rural area. I also allowed for the possibility of disembodied technical change to occur. Following Griliches (1990), I construct a proxy variable that is, the stock of patents of consumer goods, using trapezoidal weights (see Huffman and Evenson 2006 for a discussion of this type of weighting pattern). Also, see Huffman (2008) for more details.

5.4   The Empirical Results and their Interpretation

The nine aggregate full-income expenditure shares are the dependent variables, and they are explained econometrically by nine relative input prices: real full-income expenditures per capita; share of the population under age 5, over age 65, and living in non-metropolitan areas; and the consumer goods' patent stock and trend. The differenced versions of equation (44) is fitted to data covering forty-nine years, 1948–96, subject to symmetry and homogeneity and adding up conditions, to estimate a total of eighty-four unknown parameters of the demand system by the ISUR model.

Estimated coefficients of the LA/AI household demand system are reported in Table 2.2, and the estimated (macro) compensated price and full-income expenditure demand elasticities (equations (45)–(47)), evaluated at the sample means of the relevant variables, are reported in Table 2.3. The impacts of per capita real full-income expenditure, demographic characteristics, and own-price effects are estimated relatively precisely. The impacts of cross-price effects are estimated less precisely, but this is to be expected because they represent price effects that are of secondary importance and about which less prior information exists. Surprisingly, the coefficients of the consumer patent stock variable are non-zero, and some are significantly different from zero, which is evidence of technical change in the demand system for input in household production.

The estimated intercept terms of the first-differenced LA/AI demand system are the coefficients of the linear trend in the input demand equations (Table 2.2). Hence, a positive trend exists for the demand for women's unpaid housework, food at home, purchased housework-substitute services, housing services, appliance services, and transportation services. A negative trend exists in the demand for men's unpaid housework, recreation services and entertainment, and "other inputs."

For price and income expenditure elasticities, the associated z-values are computed for taking the respective shares as given. The Hicksian-compensated macro own-price elasticity for all nine input groups is negative, statistically significant at the 1 percent level and plausible, at -0.493 for women's unpaid housework, -0.489 for men's unpaid housework, -0.553 for food at home, -0.757 for housing services, -0.887 for appliance services, −1.087 for transportation services, −0.628 for recreation services and entertainment, and −0.338 for "other inputs." Hence, the negative and statistically significant macro own-price elasticities are supportive of an aggregate demand system being estimated that mirrors some of the properties of a microeconomic demand system.

It is an empirical question as to whether women's and men's unpaid housework are substitutes or complements. The empirical results in Table 2.3 provide evidence that women's and men's housework are complements, having a macro compensated cross-price elasticity of −0.16, which is significantly different from zero at the 5 percent level. Given the restriction on estimated coefficients that the summation across all compensated price elasticities for women's housework is zero (Deaton and Muellbauer 1980a: 43–4), the other seven input categories as a group are on average a substitute for women's housework. The average size of this compensated cross-price elasticity must be 0.09 (and cannot be zero). In fact, row 1 in Table 2.3 provides evidence that all seven of these other input categories are substitutes for women's housework.

One likely explanation for women's and men's unpaid housework being complements is that women and men perform different types of housework and that these tasks complement rather than substitute for one another (Robinson and Godbey 1997). Within married couples, housework continues to be specialized by gender. Women have continued over recent decades to perform core housework—traditionally "female" tasks like cooking and cleaning—while men perform yard, car, and external house care and maintenance. Unattached men can, however, purchase services in the market that replace women's core unpaid housework, and unattached women can purchase services in the market to replace men's unpaid housework associated with a yard, car, and exterior house care and maintenance.

Although purchased housework-substitute services and appliance services are substitutes for women's unpaid housework, as anticipated, they are also substitutes for men's unpaid housework (see Table 2.3). The respective macro cross-price elasticities between these two input categories are, in fact, much larger for men's unpaid housework than women's unpaid housework. Hence, the evidence is that this input category is a "better" substitute for men's than women's unpaid housework. Not too surprisingly, food at home and recreation services and entertainment are complements to men's housework and the other four major input categories are substitutes.

Housing and transportation services are shown to be complements to food at home, where both are inputs to produce a commodity defined as a family enjoying meals at home. Food at home, purchased housework-substitute services, and household appliance services are complements for housing. For appliance services, all of the other input groups are substitutes, except for housing services. Food at home, housing services, and transportation services are complements (and "other inputs" are substitutes) for recreation services and entertainment. However, the strongest substitute for recreation services and entertainment is the "other inputs." The compensated cross-price elasticity is one and significantly different from zero at the 1 percent level. Hence, I interpret this result to mean that a strong substitution effect exists between the "goods" component of recreation and entertainment and the "own-time" component.

The cross-price elasticities among the nine input groups imply numerous margins where "other inputs" have been substituted for women's and men's unpaid housework as the relative price of time rose in the post-Second World War period (see Figure 2.6). The results suggest that food at home and women's unpaid housework are substitutes but food at home and men's housework are complements. Purchased housework-substitute services and men's unpaid housework are shown to be strong substitutes, but purchased housework-substitute services and women's unpaid housework are weak substitutes.

The macro full-income expenditure elasticity of demand for women's housework is 0.713, for men's housework is 1.136, for food at home is 0.793, for purchased housework-substitute services is −0.420, for housing services is 0.480, for household appliance services is 0.392, for transportation services is 1.151, for recreation services and entertainment is 1.579, and for "other inputs" is 1.133. Hence, transportation services, recreation services and entertainment, and "other inputs" are luxury goods, having macro full-income expenditure elasticities greater than one. Women's unpaid housework, food at home, housing services, and household appliance services are normal inputs and have positive macro income elasticities that are less than one. Only purchased housework-substitute services are inferior, having negative macro expenditure elasticity, but this elasticity is not significantly different from zero at the 5 percent level.[19] Although the full-income expenditure elasticity for purchased housework-substitute services is essentially zero, readers can easily confuse price and income effects here. Changes in the use of this input category over the post-Second World War period is largely due to rising prices of unpaid housework and not due to rising real income.

On the whole, this set of macro full-income expenditure elasticities has considerable appeal. Looking at the post-Second World War period up to 1996, our results suggest relatively large rightward shifts in aggregate demand for normal inputs as full income has risen. This increase occurred for men's unpaid housework, household sector transportation services, recreation services and entertainment, and "other inputs." With the macro full-income expenditure elasticities of demand for both men's and women's unpaid housework being positive and their time endowment being fixed, rising non-labor income is a factor tending to make human time more scarce over time (Linder 1970; Robinson and Godbey 1997).[20]

The generally significant estimated coefficients of the consumer patent stock in the demand system supports the hypothesis of technical change in the US household sector over the post-Second World War period. The precise impact on input demand for each input category is obtained by evaluating δ_j/w_j at the sample mean of the expenditure

---

[19] However, the coefficients are estimated with restrictions so that one coefficient cannot be changed without an offsetting change in one or more other coefficients.

[20] If the wage elasticities of demand for men's and women's leisure are the same and they equal the own-price elasticity of demand for "other inputs," then the implied compensated own-wage elasticity of labor supply for women is approximately 1.98 and for men is 0.83.

Table 2.2 ISUR estimate of US household demand system for inputs: almost ideal demand system (shares) 1948–96 (asymptotic standard errors in parentheses)[a]

Variables	Women's housework (1)	Men's housework (2)	Food at home (3)	Purchased housework-substitute services (4)	Housing services (5)	Appliance services (6)	Transportation services (7)	Recreation services and entertainment (8)
Constant	0.287 (0.305)	−0.300 (0.236)	0.066 (0.264)	0.254 (0.147)	0.348 (0.129)	0.180 (0.156)	0.131 (0.236)	−0.177 (0.120)
AGE ≤5	0.424 (0.157)	0.184 (0.125)	0.118 (0.144)	−0.008 (0.087)	0.062 (0.080)	0.073 (0.093)	−0.026 (0.146)	−0.053 (0.075)
AGE ≥65	−0.360 (0.282)	−0.161 (0.223)	−0.240 (0.261)	0.229 (0.146)	0.311 (0.131)	0.025 (0.155)	−0.024 (0.243)	0.021 (0.122)
Non-metro	−0.056 (0.04)	0.007 (0.03)	−0.065 (0.04)	−0.007 (0.02)	−0.040 (0.02)	0.042 (0.03)	0.030 (0.0005)	0.034 (0.0002)
ln (Consumer patents)	0.035 (0.014)	0.032 (0.011)	0.019 (0.013)	0.002 (0.007)	−0.002 (0.006)	0.009 (0.008)	−0.021 (0.014)	0.002 (0.01)
$\ln[F/(N)]$	−0.034 (0.027)	0.009 (0.021)	−0.011 (0.023)	−0.022 (0.013)	−0.025 (0.012)	−0.018 (0.013)	0.007 (0.021)	0.014 (0.011)
$\ln P_1$	0.046 (0.014)							
$\ln P_2$	−0.028 (0.010)	0.030 (0.011)						
$\ln P_3$	0.007 (0.007)	−0.012 (0.006)	0.021 (0.008)					
$\ln P_4$	0.003 (0.006)	0.015 (0.005)	0.004 (0.004)	0.002 (0.005)				
$\ln P_5$	0.003 (0.006)	0.008 (0.006)	−0.008 (0.004)	−0.004 (0.004)	0.009 (0.007)			
$\ln P_6$	0.003 (0.005)	0.004 (0.004)	−0.001 (0.004)	0.004 (0.003)	−0.009 (0.003)	0.002 (0.004)		
$\ln P_7$	0.005 (0.005)	0.002 (0.004)	−0.003 (0.005)	−0.003 (0.003)	0.007 (0.003)	−0.001 (0.003)	−0.006 (0.006)	
$\ln P_8$	−0.002 (0.005)	−0.008 (0.005)	−0.000 (0.003)	0.008 (0.003)	−0.007 (0.004)	−0.000 (0.003)	−0.003 (0.002)	0.009 (0.004)
R^2	0.996	0.969	0.989	0.707	0.990	0.832	0.874	0.981

[a]System estimated as first-differences to induce stationarity of the time-series.

Table 2.3 Estimates of price and income elasticities: almost ideal demand system model with nine input groups, US aggregate data, 1950–96 (z-values are in parentheses)

Commodity–input groups (i)	Prices (j)									Income/ expenditure elasticity
	1	2	3	4	5	6	7	8	9	
	Compensated (e_{ij}^*)									
(1) Women's housework	−0.493 (4.29)	−0.164 (1.99)	0.110 (1.81)	0.043 (0.90)	0.070 (1.29)	0.053 (1.30)	0.085 (1.95)	0.007 (0.15)	0.289 (1.68)	0.713 (3.16)
(2) Men's housework	−0.283 (1.99)	−0.489 (3.14)	−0.116 (1.35)	0.229 (3.11)	0.166 (1.93)	0.087 (1.45)	0.077 (1.22)	−0.085 (1.21)	0.414 (1.73)	1.136 (3.75)
(3) Food at home	0.253 (1.81)	−0.154 (1.35)	−0.553 (3.71)	0.098 (1.23)	−0.109 (1.50)	0.002 (0.03)	−0.015 (0.17)	0.016 (0.24)	0.463 (1.44)	0.793 (1.81)
(4) Purchased housework-substitute services	0.330 (0.90)	1.019 (3.11)	0.328 (1.23)	−0.882 (2.79)	−0.184 (0.77)	0.295 (1.51)	−0.139 (0.75)	0.075 (0.36)	−0.841 (1.22)	−0.420 (0.51)
(5) Housing services	0.173 (1.29)	0.238 (1.93)	−0.119 (1.50)	−0.060 (0.77)	−0.757 (5.28)	−0.159 (2.56)	−0.093 (1.71)	−0.113 (1.32)	0.888 (4.16)	0.480 (1.99)
(6) Household appliance services	0.211 (1.30)	0.202 (1.45)	0.004 (0.03)	0.153 (1.51)	−0.255 (2.56)	−0.887 (7.45)	0.008 (0.08)	0.024 (0.28)	0.541 (1.51)	0.392 (0.88)
(7) Transportation services	0.217 (1.95)	0.113 (1.22)	−0.017 (0.17)	−0.046 (0.76)	−0.095 (1.71)	0.005 (0.08)	−1.087 (8.92)	−0.029 (0.56)	0.937 (3.37)	1.151 (2.63)
(8) Recreation services and entertainment	0.032 (0.15)	−0.236 (1.21)	0.034 (0.24)	0.047 (0.36)	−0.219 (1.32)	0.029 (0.28)	−0.055 (0.56)	−0.628 (3.56)	0.997 (2.64)	1.579 (3.71)
(9) "Other inputs"	0.058 (1.68)	0.048 (1.73)	0.040 (1.44)	−0.022 (1.22)	0.071 (4.16)	0.027 (1.51)	0.074 (3.37)	0.041 (2.64)	−0.338 (3.48)	1.133 (10.08)

share w_j. These results suggest that technical change in the household sector reduced the demand for women's housework relative to housing services, transportation services, and "other inputs," and increased the demand for women's unpaid housework relative to food at home and men's unpaid housework. No significant change in the demand for women's housework relative to purchased housework-substitute services, appliance services, or recreation services occurs.

The impacts of a change in the share of the population that is age 5 or less is 2.3 times larger for women's unpaid housework than for men's unpaid housework, and the impact of a change in the share of the population 65 years of age and older is 2.2 times larger on women's unpaid housework than on men's unpaid housework. Hence, the demand for women's unpaid housework is more responsive to the changing age structure of the US population than is men's housework.

6   CONCLUSIONS

Advances in household production theory and models have made almost no inroads to the study of food demand over the past fifty years. With three exceptions, food demand studies have not even adopted the slight advance in neoclassical consumer demand that occurs when one recognizes that the household has a major resource consisting of the time endowment of adult households. This means that food demand studies have continued to omit the price of time (of adult household members, especially of the homemaker) in food demand equations and to use a household's cash income rather non-labor income or full income in these equations. The tradition has been to focus on the household's cash income constraint, and how cash income is allocated to purchased goods and services, but to ignore the fact that these decisions are made jointly with adult time allocation decisions on work versus leisure. Also, the cash income constraint in traditional demand models includes labor market earnings, which results from households' decisions on time allocated to work for pay versus other activities. This means that cash income reflects a mixture of price and income effects and that estimates of the income elasticity of demand for food in these studies are invariably biased. More generally, because the price of time is omitted from these food demand equations, there are further biases in estimated price and income elasticities obtained in a demand system.

The adoption of the productive household models makes it possible to incorporate the economics of production theory into household consumption decisions. This means that commodities are in general produced at minimum cost, or the household is on the frontier of a multiple-output–multiple-input relationship. In some cases it is useful to assume that no joint production occurs in the household, but a more realistic assumption is that the household represents an institution where joint production is pervasive. For example, an adult is simultaneously preparing a meal, supervising children, and listening to the news. Moreover, with the household production model, we can associate the education of the homemakers with the efficiency of household production, and thereby free ourselves from the assumption of neoclassical models that education primarily changes tastes.

Using key concepts from household production theory, I have developed an empirical application that is a demand system for inputs used by households, and it has been fitted to data for the US household sector over the post-Second World War period. The data on expenditure shares and relative input prices show dramatic changes over time; for example, the share of women's unpaid time in consumption expenditures has fallen by 8 percentage points. The relative price of a number of inputs has changed substantially; for example, the price of household appliance services declined by 75 percent over the first twenty-five years of the study period and the price of food at home declined by 50 percent over the forty-nine-year study period. Moreover, the empirical estimate of a complete input demand system for the US household sector has provided new and interesting estimates of own-price and cross-price elasticities and full-income expenditure elasticities of demand for food at home and for eight other input groups.

The results provide estimates of the compensated own-price demand elasticities for inputs ranked from highest to lowest; these are: transportation services, appliance services, purchased services that substitute for unpaid housework, housing services, recreation services, food at home, women's unpaid housework, men's unpaid housework, and "other inputs." The results also provide evidence that food at home and women's unpaid housework are substitutes but food at home and men's unpaid housework are complements. Purchased services that substitute for unpaid housework and men's unpaid housework are shown to be strong substitutes, but purchased services and women's unpaid housework are weak substitutes. The full-income expenditure elasticities of demand for inputs ranked from highest to lowest are: recreation services, transportation services, "other inputs," men's unpaid housework, food at home, women's unpaid housework, appliance services, and purchased services that substitute for unpaid housework.

These new macro price and income elasticities show that productive household theory can be effectively applied to the measurement of inputs, to the specification of a household sector complete input demand system, and to estimation of a new type of demand system. Moreover, my results provide evidence that the compensated price elasticity of demand for food at home is relative large, and that food at home and women's housework are substitutes but food at home and men's housework are complements. Also, food at home and purchased housework-substitute services, which include food away from home, are substitutes. In addition, the compensated price elasticity of demand for services that are a substitute for unpaid housework is relatively large. Two surprising results are that the full-income expenditure elasticity of demand for food is relatively large but for services that substitute for unpaid housework, i.e., purchased housework-substitute services, is small and not significantly different from zero.

For those who are interested in recent annual data on time use, the American Time Use Survey, which was initiated by the US Department of Labor in 2003, may be a useful source of data.

This chapter has laid a foundation that can be a bridge between household production theory and future studies of the demand for food and other inputs.

REFERENCES

Aguiar, M., and E. Hurst. 2006. *Measuring Trends in Leisure: The Allocation of Time over Five Decades*. Working Paper No. 06-2. Boston: Federal Reserve Bank of Boston, Jan.

Alston, J. M., K. A. Foster, and R. D. Green. 1994. "Estimating Elasticities with the Linear Approximate Almost Ideal Demand System: Some Monte Carlo Results." *Review of Economics and Statistics* 76: 351–6.

Andrews, M., and K. Hamrick. 2009. "Shopping for, Preparing, and Eating Food: Where Does the Time Go?" *Amber Waves* 7 (Dec.), 4.

Barten, A. P. 1969. "Maximum Likelihood Estimation of a Complete System of Demand." *European Economic Review* 1 (Fall), 7–73.

BEA (Bureau of Economic Analysis). "National Income and Product Accounts." <http://www.bea.gov/bea/dn/nipaweb>.

Becker, G. S. 1976. "A Theory of the Allocation of Time." In Becker, *The Economic Approach to Human Behavior*. Chicago: University of Chicago Press.

——— 1981. *A Treatise on the Family*. Cambridge, MA: Harvard University Press.

Bianchi, S. M., M. A. Milkie, L. C. Sayer, and J. P. Robinson. 2000. "Is Anyone Doing the Housework? Trends in the Gender Division of Household Labor." *Social Forces* 79: 191–228.

Blundell, R., and T. MaCurdy. 1999. "Labor Supply: A Review of Alternative Approaches." In O. C. Ashenfelter and D. Card, eds, *Handbook of Labor Economics*, 3A. New York: Elsevier.

Borjas, G. 2005. *Modern Labor Economics*. New York: McGraw-Hill.

Browning, M., P. A. Chiappori, and V. Lechene. 2009. "Distributional Effects in Household Models: Separate Spheres and Income Pooling." *Economic Journal* 120: 786–99.

Bryant, W. K. 1986. "Technical Change and the Family: An Initial Foray." In R. Deacon and W. Huffman, eds, *Human Resources Research, 1887–1987*. Ames: College of Home Economics, Iowa State University.

Card, D. 1999. "The Casual Effect of Education on Earnings." In O. C. Ashenfelter and D. Card, eds, *Handbook of Labor Economics*, 3A. New York: Elsevier.

Chen, N. C., J. F. Shogren, P. F. Orazem, and T. D. Crocker. 2002. "Prices and Health: Identifying the Effects of Nutrition, Exercise, and Medication Choices on Blood Pressure." *American Journal of Agricultural Economics* 84: 990–1002.

Chen, Y., and W. E. Huffman. 2009. *An Economic Analysis of the Impact of Food Prices and Early Health Status on Midlife Physical Activity and Obesity in Adults*. Working Paper. Ames: Department of Economics, Iowa State University, Dec.

Deardorff, A. V. 2002. "Introduction to the Lerner Diagram." Department of Economics, University of Michigan. <http://www-personal.umich.edu/~alandear/writings/Lerner.pdf>.

Deaton, A. 1986. "Demand Systems." In Z. Griliches and M. D. Intriligator, eds, *Handbook of Econometrics*, 3. New York: North-Holland.

Deaton, A. and J. Muellbauer. 1980a. *Economics and Consumer Behavior*. London: Cambridge University Press.

———1980b. "An Almost Ideal Demand System." *American Economic Review* 70 (June), 312–26.

Diewert, E. W. 1976. "Exact and Superlative Index Numbers." *Journal of Econometrics* 4 (May), 115–45.

Finkelstein E., I. Fiebelkorn, and G. Wang. 2003. "National Medical Spending Attributable to Overweight and Obesity: How Much, and Who's Paying?" *Health Affairs* 22 (May 14), 219–26.

Fogel, R. W. 1994. "Economic Growth, Population Theory, and Physiology: The Bearing on Long-Term Processes on the Making of Economic Policy." *American Economic Review* 84: 369–95.

Goldin, C. 1986. "The Female Labor Force and American Economic Growth, 1890–1980." In S. L Engerman and R. E. Gallman, eds, *Long Term Factors in American Economic Growth*. Chicago: University of Chicago Press.

Greene, W. H. 2003. *Econometric Analysis*, 5th edn. New York: Macmillan.

Greenwood, J., A. Seshadri, and M. Yorukoglu. 2005. "Engines of Liberation." *Review of Economic Studies* 72: 109–33.

Griliches, Z. 1990. "Patent Statistics as Economic Indicators: A Survey." *Journal of Economic Literature* 28 (Dec.), 1661–1707.

Gronau, R. 1977. "Leisure, Home Production and Work: The Theory of the Allocation of Time Revisited." *Journal of Political Economy* 85: 1099–1124.

———1986. "Home Production: A Survey." In O. Ashenfelter and R. Layard, eds, *Handbook of Labor Economics*, 1. Amsterdam: Elsevier Science.

Hamermesh, D. 2007. "Time to Eat: Household Production under Increasing Income Inequality." *American Journal of Agricultural Economics* 89: 852–93.

Hausman, J. 1996. "Valuation of New Goods under Perfect and Imperfect Competition." In T. Bresnahan and R. J. Gordon, eds, *The Economics of New Goods*. Chicago: University of Chicago Press.

Huffman, S. K., and S. R. Johnson. 2004. "Impacts of Economic Reform in Poland: Incidence and Welfare Changes within a Consistent Framework." *Review of Economics and Statistics* 86 (May), 626–36.

Huffman, W. E. 1991. "Agricultural Household Models: Survey and Critique." In M. C. Hallberg, J. L. Findeis, and D. A. Lass, eds, *Multiple Job-Holding among Farm Families in North America*. Ames: Iowa State University Press.

———2001. "Human Capital: Education and Agriculture." In B. L. Gardner and G. C. Rausser, eds, *Handbook of Agricultural Economics*, IA. Amsterdam: Elsevier Science/North-Holland.

———2008. *Understanding Post-War Changes in U.S. Household Production: A Full-Income Demand-System Perspective*. Working Paper No. 06036. Ames: Department of Economics, Iowa State University, Feb. 21.

———and R. E. Evenson. 2006. "Do Formula or Competitive Grant Funds Have Greater Impacts on State Agricultural Productivity?" *American Journal of Agricultural Economics* 88: 783–98.

———and T. Feridhanusetyawan. 2007. "Migration, Fixed Costs and Location-Specific Amenities: A Hazard Rate Analysis for a Panel of Males." *American Journal of Agricultural Economics* 89 (May), 368–82.

—— and P. F. Orazem. 2007. "Agriculture and Human Capital in Economic Growth: Farmers, Schooling and Nutrition." In R. Evenson and P. Pingali, eds, *Handbook of Agricultural Economics*, 3. New York: Elsevier Science.

——, S. Huffman, K. Rickertsen, and A. Tegene. 2010. "Over-Nutrition and Changing Health Status in High Income Countries." *Forum for Health Economics and Policy* 13, art. 1.

Jorgenson, D. W. 2001. "Information Technology and the U.S. Economy." *American Economic Review* 90: 1–32.

—— and D. T. Slesnick. 1990. "Individual and Social Cost of Living Indexes." In W. E. Diewert, ed., *Price Level Measurement*. Amsterdam: Elsevier Science.

————. 2008. "Consumption and Labor Supply." *Journal of Econometrics* 147: 326–35.

—— and K. Stiroh. 1999. "Productivity Growth: Current Recovery and Long-Term Trends." *Proceedings of the American Economic Review* 89 (May), 109–15.

——, F. Gollop, and B. Fraumeni. 1987. *Productivity and U.S. Economic Growth*. Cambridge, MA: Harvard University Press.

Juster, F. T., and F. P. Stafford. 1985. *Time Goods and Wellbeing*. Ann Arbor: Survey Research Center, Institute for Social Research.

————. 1991. "The Allocation of Time: Empirical Findings, Behavioral Models, and Problems of Measurement." *Journal of Economic Literature* 29 (June), 471–522.

Keng, S. H., and C. H. Lin. 2005. "Wives' Value of Time and Food Consumed Away From Home in Taiwan." *Asian Economic Journal* 19: 319–34.

Kerkhofs, M., and P. Kooreman. 2003. "Identification and Estimation of a Class of Household Production Models." *Journal of Applied Econometrics* 18: 337–69.

Kinsey, J. 1983. "Working Wives and the Marginal Propensity to Consume Food Away From Home." *American Journal of Agricultural Economics* 65: 10–19.

LaFrance, J. T. 2001. "Duality for the Household: Theory and Applications." In B. L. Gardner and G. C. Rausser, eds, *Handbook of Agricultural Economics*, 1B. New York: North-Holland.

Lerner, A. 1952. "Factor Prices and International Trade." *Economica* 19: 1–15.

Lin, B.-H., E. Frazão, and J. Guthrie. 1999. *Away-From-Home Foods Increasingly Important to Quality of American Diet*. Agricultural Information Bulletin No. 749. Washington, DC: US Department of Agriculture, Economic Research Service, Jan.

Linder, S. B. 1970. *The Harried Leisure Class*. New York: Columbia University Press.

McGrattan, E. R., and R. Rogerson. 2004. "Changes in Hours Worked, 1950–2000." *Federal Reserve Bank of Minneapolis Quarterly Review* 28: 14–33.

Michael, R., and G. S. Becker. 1973. "On the New Theory of Consumer Behavior." *Swedish Journal of Economics* 75: 378–95.

Mincer, J. 1963. "Market Prices, Opportunity Costs, and Income Effects." In C. Christ, ed., *Measurement in Economics*. Stanford, CA: Stanford University Press.

Moschini, G. 1998. "The Semiflexible Almost Ideal Demand System." *European Economic Review* 42: 349–64.

Park, J. L., and O. Capps, Jr. 1997. "Demand for Prepared Meals by U.S. Households." *American Journal of Agricultural Economics* 79: 814–24.

Pitt, M. M., and M. R. Rosenzweig. 1986. "Agricultural Prices, Food Consumption, and the Health and Productivity of Indonesian Farmers." In I. Singh, L. Squire, and J. Strauss, eds, *Agricultural Household Models: Extensions, Applications, and Policy*. Baltimore: Johns Hopkins University Press.

Pollak, R. A., and M. L. Wachter. 1975. "The Relevance of the Household Production Function and its Implications for the Allocation of Time." *Journal of Political Economy* 83 (Apr.), 255–78.

Prochaska, F. J., and R. A. Schrimper. 1973. "Opportunity Cost of Time and Other Socioeconomic Effects on Away-From-Home Food Consumption." *American Journal of Agricultural Economics* 55: 595–603.

Ramey, V. A., and N. Francis. 2005. *A Century of Work and Leisure*. Working Paper. San Diego: University of California, June.

Reid, M. D. 1934. *The Economics of Household Production*. New York: Wiley.

Robinson, J. P., and G. Godbey. 1997. *Time for Life: The Surprising Ways Americans Use their Time*, 2nd edn. University Park: Pennsylvania State University.

Rogerson, R., and J. Wallenius. 2007. "Micro and Macro Elasticies in a Lifecycle Model with Taxes." NBER Working Paper No. 13017. Cambridge, MA: National Bureau of Economic Research, Apr.

Sabates, R., B. E. Gould, and H. J. Villarreal. 2001. "Household Composition and Food Expenditures: A Cross Country Comparison." *Food Policy* 26: 571–86.

Smith, J. P., and M. P. Ward. 1985. "Time-Series Growth in the Female Labor Force." *Journal of Labor Economics* 3 (Jan.), S59–S90.

Stone, R. 1954. "Linear Expenditure Systems and Demand Analysis: An Application to the Pattern of British Demand." *Economic Journal* 64 (Sept.), 511–27.

Strauss, J. 1986a. "The Theory and Comparative Statics of Agricultural Household Models: A General Approach." In I. Singh, L. Squire, and J. Strauss, eds, *Agricultural Household Models: Extensions, Applications, and Policy*. Baltimore: Johns Hopkins University Press.

—— 1986b. "Estimating the Determinants of Food Consumption and Caloric Availability in Rural Sierra Leone." In I. Singh, L. Squire, and J. Strauss, eds, *Agricultural Household Models: Extensions, Applications, and Policy*. Baltimore: Johns Hopkins University Press.

Tokle, J. G., and W. E. Huffman. 1991. "Local Economic Conditions and Wage Labor Decisions of Farm and Rural Nonfarm Couples." *American Journal of Agricultural Economy* 73 (Aug.), 652–70.

US Department of Commerce, Bureau of Economic Analysis. "National Accounts Data, 1929–2001." <http://www.bea.doc.gov/bea/dn1.html>.

US Department of Labor, Bureau of Labor Statistics. 2006. "American Time Use Survey." <http://www.icpsr.umich.edu/icpsrweb/ICPSR/studies/23024>.

—— "Wages, Earnings, and Benefits." <http://www.bls.gov/bls/wages.htm>.

Varian, H. R. 1992. *Microeconomic Analysis*, 3rd edn. New York: W. W. Norton.

Wooldridge, J. M. 2002. Econometric Analysis of Cross Section and Panel Data. Cambridge, MA: MIT Press.

CHAPTER 3

....

RISK PREFERENCES AND FOOD CONSUMPTION

....

JOHN A. (SEAN) FOX

1 INTRODUCTION

....

Consumers' food choices can appear to be rife with contradictions. Are risks in regard to food knowingly accepted, actively avoided, or both? Consider the Japanese, who regard fugu, a type of fish, as a prized delicacy despite the fact that it can be lethal if incorrectly prepared. Apparently, the possibility of death shortly after dinner does not deter the Japanese consumer or diminish their enjoyment of this potentially dangerous comestible. The Japanese government, on the other hand, went into overdrive following the discovery of a handful of cases of BSE-infected (mad!) cows. Despite a virtually non-existent risk to these very same fugu-eating consumers, the government instituted a policy of testing every single animal for mad cow disease.

So, how then to explain whether and how food consumption choices are connected to individual risk preferences? What are the connections between the two, and can those connections be exploited by policymakers to further public welfare, or by the food industry to enhance profits? This chapter will first examine some of the risks intrinsic to food and how those risks are perceived, or misperceived, by both consumers and the "experts." I then discuss risk preferences and examine the literature, sparse as it is, that attempts to connect those preferences to food consumption choices. The following section deals with constructed preferences—the idea that individuals might not have stable, well-defined preferences but instead that their preferences are constructed as needed and readily influenced by characteristics of the decision environment. While the debate about constructed preferences is by no means settled, the insights from that literature provide useful guidance for researchers studying food consumption choices.

2 FOOD CONSUMPTION RISKS

Many foods embody an element of risk. Renewed attention to microbial food risks in the United States can be traced to the infamous Jack-in-the-Box outbreak in 1993, which introduced *E. coli* 0157:H7 into the popular lexicon in much the same way the September 11 attacks introduced Al-Qaeda. Since then there have been several outbreaks and recalls involving the same pathogen, some of which, such as a 1996 outbreak involving unpasteurized apple juice and a 2006 outbreak linked to spinach, received widespread media attention. In 1997 an *E. coli*-related recall of 25 million pounds of ground beef led to the closure of Nebraska-based Hudson Food Company, while a similar fate befell Topps Meat Company in New Jersey in the wake of a 2007 recall involving 21 million pounds. In 2008 a recall of ground beef produced by Nebraska Beef Ltd ensnared a number of other companies including Whole Foods Market and Coleman Natural Foods (MSNBC 2009).

According to a widely cited study by the Centers for Disease Control (Mead et al. 1999), *E. coli* strains are linked to about 2,800 of 61,000 annual hospitalizations (4.5 percent) caused by *known* foodborne pathogens, and to seventy-eight of approximately 1,800 deaths (4.3 percent). The annual cost of illness and death from *E. coli* O157: H7 has been estimated at $405 million (Frenzen, Drake, and Angulo 2005). *E. coli*, however, is just one of many pathogens responsible for foodborne illness. Others, including *Salmonella* (26 percent of hospitalizations, 31 percent of deaths), *Campylobacter* (17 percent of hospitalizations), and *Listeria* (28 percent of deaths), and Norwalk-like viruses (33 percent of hospitalizations), pose a greater risk. Data on foodborne illness is imprecise, and Mead et al. estimated that *unknown* foodborne agents account for 265,000 hospitalizations and 3,200 deaths each year. Annual US deaths from foodborne pathogens are estimated at 5,000.

Food consumption may also involve risk from physical hazards such as foreign objects, bone fragments, etc., or hazards of a chemical nature such as poisons, allergens, and residues from pesticides, antibiotics, and hormones. Use of technologies such as cloning, genetic modification, and irradiation is considered hazardous by many consumer advocates. Mortality statistics suggest, however, that the most harmful consequences of food consumption are of a chronic rather than an immediate nature, and due primarily to the consumption, or overconsumption, of certain fats and other nutrients. Foremost among these delayed consequences are heart disease, cancer, diabetes, and obesity. Heron et al. (2009), using CDC data for 2006, report that of 2.4 million deaths in the United States, the leading causes were heart disease (26 percent) and cancer (23 percent), while diabetes accounted for an additional 72,000 deaths (3 percent). Diet clearly plays an important role in heart disease and diabetes, and authors such as Pollan (2008) explore in detail the consequences of the "Western diet" on those conditions. Less clear, perhaps, is the role of diet in cancer, but according to estimates by Doll and Peto (1981), 35 percent of cancer deaths can be attributed to diet, and the majority of those are avoidable (Nelson 1996).

All of which makes food consumption appear to be a risky proposition, but in relative (and absolute) terms the immediate risks from eating are actually very low. In the United States you are far more likely to be the victim of a motor vehicle accident (45,000 deaths) or a homicide (19,000 deaths) than you are to perish from foodborne pathogens. And in a population of approximately 300 million, the 5,000 deaths from foodborne illness represent an annual chance of death of less than 0.002 percent.

3   PERCEPTIONS (AND MISPERCEPTIONS) OF RISKS FROM FOOD

Risk perceptions and risk preferences (or attitudes) are inextricably linked in terms of their impact on food choices. Despite repeated assurances that the United States has the "safest food supply in the world,"[1] US consumers respond in surveys that they are concerned about food safety. For example, Brewer and Rojas (2008) reported that less than half their sample considered food to be very safe, down 10 percent from a similar study reported in 2002. Similarly, the International Food Information Council Foundation (IFICF 2009) found that only 49 percent of respondents were either somewhat or extremely confident that the US food supply is safe.

What people say and what they do, however, are often not consistent, and this would appear to be the case regarding food safety. The inconsistency is evidenced by the lack of effort on the part of consumers to inform themselves about rudimentary food safety practices, which suggest that they are not all that concerned about risks connected to food. The American Meat Institute (2009) reported that only a third of respondents were aware that a hamburger is safe to eat when the internal temperature has reached 160°F. Hartl (2004) reported that 27 percent of respondents to a mail survey in eight Midwestern states admitted to either "sometimes" or "usually" forgetting to wash their hands after handling raw meat.

Most surveys prompt respondents with the issues, and in turn find high levels of expressed concern. Knight and Warland (2004) found that US adults were equally concerned about pesticide residues, bacterial contamination (*Salmonella*), and dietary fat, with about three-quarters of respondents reporting high levels of concern. Similarly, Tucker, Whaley, and Sharp (2006) found comparable levels of perceived risk when respondents were asked about seven different food safety issues, with average responses

---

[1] See <http://www.unbossed.com/index.php?itemid=2181> for a listing of quotations by the US Department of Agriculture Food and Drug Administration officials. The "safest food" assertion has been examined in some recent studies including GAO (2008) and in an unpublished University of Regina study available at <http://www.ontraceagrifood.com/admincp/uploadedfiles/Food%20Safety%20Performance%20World%20Ranking%202008.pdf>.

on a seven-point scale ranging from 4.56 for genetically modified foods, to 5.21 and 5.33 for bacterial contamination and pesticide residues. Brewer and Rojas (2008) also reported similar levels of concern about residues and pathogens—at 3.395 and 3.396 respectively on a scale from 1 (no concern) to 5 (very strong concern). There is little doubt that bacterial pathogens constitute the most significant immediate risk, so it is somewhat curious, particularly given the tendency for people to care far more about immediate outcomes and ignore long-term risks (such as they do with heart disease), that consumers are as concerned about residues as about bacterial contamination. However, when pushed to identify the more important risk, IFICF (2009) reported that 52 percent chose "foodborne illness from bacteria" as the most important food safety issue, while 30 percent chose "chemicals in food."

Reported risk perceptions also show some correlation with demographic factors. In a review of the literature, Ellis and Tucker (2009) find that females, individuals with lower educational achievement and income, individuals with children in the household, and ethnic minorities tend to perceive higher levels of risk from food. The nature of the risk also plays a role with newer and unfamiliar hazards perceived to pose the greatest threat. Thus, BSE, SARS, and swine flu have invoked panicked reactions including school closures, export bans, use of face masks, etc., while we comfortably coexist with more familiar hazards such as the regular flu, overeating, automobiles, and swimming pools, which, statistically, pose a far greater risk to life and health.

3.1   Systematic Bias in Perceptions

A well-established empirical finding is that individual risk perceptions tend to be systematically biased (Lichtenstein et al. 1978), with the typical pattern involving overestimation of the frequency of low-probability hazards (e.g., mad cow disease, avian flu) and underestimation of more familiar, higher-probability hazards (e.g., heart disease, diabetes). Because the risk from food consumption is relatively low compared to that from other activities we would expect consumers to overestimate its risk, and that is generally the case. For example, Hartl (2004) provided subjects in a mail survey with information about the frequency of different hazards before eliciting perceptions about the risk of becoming seriously ill as a result of food poisoning. Subjects were provided with information about the annual frequency of hospital or emergency room visits per 100,000 people for six different hazards: lightning, Lyme disease, dog bites, residential fires, auto accidents, and accidental falls. Frequencies ranged from 0.13 per 100,000 for lightning up to 2,700 per 100,000 for accidental falls. The question then put to subjects was:

> How many people per 100,000 do you believe receive hospital or emergency room treatment each year <u>as a result of food poisoning</u>? (Please fill in the blank)
>
> _____yearly hospital/emergency room treatments per 100,000 people.

The distribution of responses in Figure 3.1 indicates a surprisingly wide range with 12.4 percent of the sample estimating ten or fewer hospitalizations, and 3.4 percent estimating 10,000 or more. Based on the Centers for Disease Control estimate of 325,000 annual hospitalizations for food poisoning (Mead et al. 1999), the actual frequency is around 108 per 100,000 people. Approximately 33 percent of the sample estimates were between fifty and 500 cases, which, since they fall within an order of magnitude, can be considered as reasonable estimates of the actual frequency. Of the remainder, 17 percent were below fifty, and 49 percent above 500. On balance, with a mean estimate of 2,577 cases per 100,000, and a median of 500, subjects tended to overestimate the frequency of serious foodborne illness.

Regardless of its cause, the systematic bias in risk perception has a practical consequence when consumers evaluate risk-reducing technologies. The consequence is that *reductions* in the objective level of risk will be *underestimated*, and thus undervalued, by the general public. Figure 3.2 (based on Johansson-Stenman 2008) illustrates the idea. The dashed line at a 45° angle represents unbiased risk perceptions—i.e. where the perceived risk, p, measured on the vertical axis, corresponds to the actual risk, r, on the horizontal axis. The solid line represents biased perceptions where low levels of actual risk are perceived to be higher than they are, and high levels perceived to be lower. If perceptions are biased in the manner represented by the solid line, a reduction in the objective level of risk from r_1 to r_2 will be perceived as a smaller reduction from p_1 to p_2.[2] This type of error in evaluation due to systematically biased risk perceptions may in part explain why food irradiation, a technology that virtually all scientists agree can greatly reduce the incidence of foodborne illness (GAO 2000), has not gained wider public acceptance. Many reasons have been put forward to explain why food irradiation has failed to gain a market, most of which focus on risks such as a supposed link to cancer, loss of nutrients, and worker and environmental safety concerns. Figure 3.2 illustrates another reason why acceptance of the technology has been lacking—i.e., that consumers, in addition to being concerned about the technology's risks, also discount its benefits.[3]

Systematic bias in probability assessment can be explained in a number of ways. Viscusi (1985) explained it as a logical consequence of Bayesian updating rather than a reflection of irrationality on the part of the individual. Hayes et al. (1995) offer support for the idea that individuals use prior perceptions, and their results also suggest that the weight placed on new information depends on that new information—i.e., the Bayesian

---

[2] The discussion here considers only *estimation* of probabilities as distinct from the *weighting* of probabilities. Prospect theory (Kahneman and Tversky 1979) introduced the concept of a probability weighting function according to which individuals typically overweight low probabilities and underweight high probabilities. Empirical estimation of probability weighting functions (see also Prelec 1998) typically results in inverted S-shaped functions which, if applied to Figure 3.2, would result in additional flattening of the function and an even more pronounced underestimation of the change in risk.

[3] Benefits may also be discounted as a result of "optimistic bias," whereby people consider themselves less prone than others to a given risk (Weinstein 1987; Miles, Braxton, and Frewer 1999).

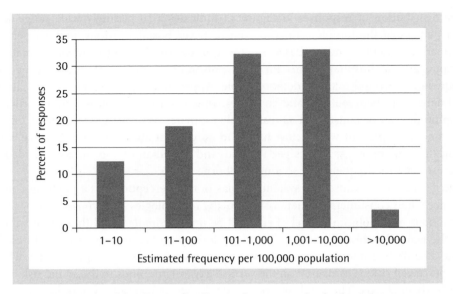

FIGURE 3.1 Estimates of the frequency of hospital treatment for food poisoning per 100,000 population

N = 653. Actual frequency is approximately 108 per 100,000.

Source: Hartl, 2004.

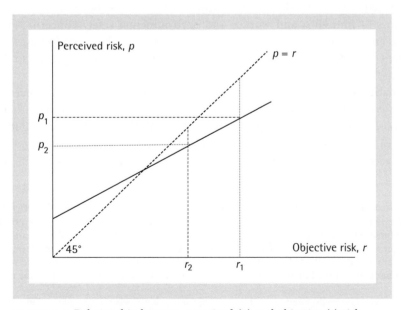

FIGURE 3.2 Relationship between perceived (p) and objective (r) risk.

updating process appeared to be non-linear. Others (e.g., Breyer 1993) mention the difficulties some individuals have in understanding probabilities—what we might call a sort of "probability dyslexia." Krupnik et al. (2002) reported that 12 percent of their respondents wrongly identified which of two people had the higher risk of death when the probabilities for each were both explicitly written as "Five in 1,000" and "Ten in 1,000" *and* represented on a grid. Difficulties with probabilities are amusingly illustrated in this anecdote from the *Salt Lake Tribune* in 2002:

> The menu at the Coffee Garden at 900 East and 900 South in Salt Lake City has included a scrumptious selection of quiche for about 10 years. The recipe calls for four fresh eggs for each quiche. A Salt Lake County Health Department inspector paid a visit recently and pointed out that research by the Food and Drug Administration indicates that one in four eggs carries salmonella bacterium, so restaurants should never use more than three eggs when preparing quiche. The manager on duty wondered aloud if simply throwing out three eggs from each dozen and using the remaining nine in four egg-quiches would serve the same purpose. The inspector wasn't sure, but she said she would research it.

3.2   The Experts versus the Public

In addition to systematic bias in assessing risk *probabilities*, the public often differs from the experts in assessing the *acceptability*, and thus the ranking, of different hazards. This is especially true in the realm of environmental risks where issues that receive the greatest regulatory attention as a consequence of their dominance in the public mindset are typically not ranked very highly by the experts. Thus, problems such as hazardous waste sites attract significant public attention and garner enormous resources aimed at remediation while posing relatively small risks (Roberts 1990; Breyer 1993). Slovic (1987) reported risk rankings for thirty activities and technologies in which nuclear power was ranked as the most risky item by two groups of lay people, while being ranked twentieth by the experts. In the context of food this divergence is evidenced in higher risk ratings among the public for technologies such as genetic modification and irradiation that food scientists generally consider safe.

Nestle (2003) characterizes two overlapping approaches to assessing the acceptability of a given risk—one from the perspective of science and the other from the perspective of values. The science-based approach focuses on the characteristics of the risk itself and on its associated benefits and costs, while a value-based approach involves psychological, cultural, and social perspectives and the balancing of a risk against scales of dread and outrage. Following Slovic (1987), Nestle describes lay people as being more concerned about, and less accepting of, risks that are perceived as unfamiliar, not well understood, uncontrollable, involuntary, and inequitable in terms of who gains and who loses. In such assessments bacterial pathogens, since most are relatively familiar, equitably distributed, and can be controlled by consumers through safe handling and cooking, provoke less dread and outrage than do the risks associated with unfamiliar exotic diseases or novel technologies. Noting that testing can never prove safety, Nestle makes the point that foods or technologies that rank highly on the scales of dread and outrage "will never appear safe enough, no matter how much effort goes into attempts to prove it harmless."

3.3   Whose Perceptions Matter?

Misperceptions and divergent assessments of risk acceptability lead to the question of whether public policy should be based only on objectively measured risks or whether it should also take into account the public's (mis)perceptions and unjustified fears. Because society cannot afford to eliminate all risks, and because choices often involve trade-offs of one risk for another, policymakers routinely make decisions where this question arises.[4] Although it doesn't deal with food risk, the question posed by Portney (1992) concerning the residents of Happyville illustrates the nature of problem. The scenario is as follows:

> You have a problem. You are Director of Environmental Protection in Happyville, a community of 1000 adults. The drinking water supply in Happyville is contaminated by a naturally occurring substance that each and every resident believes may be responsible for the above-average cancer rate observed there. So concerned are they that they insist you put in place a very expensive treatment system to remove the contaminant. Moreover, you know for a fact that each and every resident is truly willing to pay $1000 each year for the removal of the contaminant.

> The problem is this. You have asked the top ten risk assessors in the world to test the contaminant for carcinogenicity. To a person, these risk assessors—including several who work for the activist group, Campaign Against Environmental Cancer—find that the substance tests negative for carcinogenicity, even at much higher doses than those received by the residents of Happyville. These ten risk assessors tell you that while one could never prove that the substance is harmless, they would each stake their professional reputations on its being so. You have repeatedly and skillfully communicated this to the Happyville citizenry, but because of a deep-seated skepticism of all government officials, they remain completely unconvinced and truly frightened—still willing, that is, to fork over $1000 per person per year for water purification.

Viscusi (2000: 867) argued for reliance only on the objective risk: "The objective of government policy in my view should be to reduce objective risks to populations and to generate actual improvements in health rather than foster illusory increases in well-being."

---

[4] Of course, policymakers themselves may have objectives that differ from those of both the consumers and the experts. For example, in the case of Japan testing all animals for mad cow disease, it seems likely that considerations related to trade and the welfare of domestic beef producers played a role.

Others (e.g., Pollack 1998) suggest that both the objective and subjectively perceived risks should be considered. Caswell (2008) argues for the inclusion of consumer risk preferences and acceptance, and the social sensitivity of particular risks, in the prioritization and decision processes for risk management. It's a difficult question, of course, and the answer is well beyond both the scope of this chapter and the philosophical training of the author. But economists with a libertarian streak, even those sympathetic to the idea of libertarian paternalism (Sunstein and Thaler 2003), will probably be uncomfortable with Viscusi's overriding of consumer sovereignty.

In food policy, the United States and the European Union have taken different approaches to labeling requirements for new technologies. In the United States products produced through genetic engineering do not require labels if deemed not to differ substantially from products produced via traditional breeding methods. This approach would seem to be based exclusively on the scientific facts. Adherence to that same philosophy might also explain the US Department of Agriculture's refusal to allow private testing for BSE (high cost, no tangible benefit), although some might see in that decision a more sinister motive (Organic Consumers Association 2008). In contrast the European labeling requirement for GM foods is seen as reflecting the precautionary principle (see Nestle 2003), deference to consumers' fears about new technologies, and their right to be informed about the foods they eat.

4   Risk Preferences

The term "preferences," in the sense used by economists, refers to an individual's innate capacity to consistently characterize certain goods, events, characteristics, or situations as being preferred over others. The same term is often used to represent the choices people make in certain situations—i.e., their behavior—but in the sense used here it has more in common with attitudes than with behavior.[5] If this innate capacity to order is systematic and consistent, preferences can be represented by a utility function. In Figure 3.3, the utility function is $V(y)$—where the single argument, y, measured along the horizontal axis, represents money wealth. Embodied in this representation are the notions that more is better, since the function is always upward-sloping, and transitivity—if A is preferred to B, and B is preferred to C, then A must be preferred to C.

Risk preferences or attitudes are reflected in the curvature of the utility function. To illustrate, assume you are offered a gamble in which a fair coin is tossed and if the outcome is heads you win $100 and if tails you lose $100. In Figure 3.3, if we let Y_{AVG} on the horizontal axis represent your current money wealth, the two possible outcomes of

[5] For example, Curtis and Moeltner (2006) examined propensity to purchase GM foods in Romania and China. They state that "Consumer preferences are largely dependent on risk perceptions." But in this context what they mean by "preferences" is the choices consumers make—their behavior.

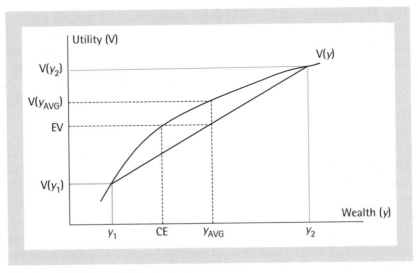

FIGURE 3.3 Risk preferences

the gamble can be represented at points y_1 and y_2 representing current money wealth minus or plus $100. The expected outcome of the gamble is a zero gain or loss represented by the point y_{AVG} itself. The question of interest is whether you prefer having this gamble to not having it. If your preferences are represented by the utility function in Figure 3.3, you would prefer *not* to have the gamble: you prefer the expected outcome (zero gain or loss) with certainty where your level of utility is $V(y_{AVG})$. Why? Because the point $V(y_{AVG})$ is above (i.e., at a higher level of utility than) the expected utility of the gamble represented by the point EV. The expected utility of the gamble is the probability weighted average of $V(y_1)$ and $V(y_2)$, which, with a fair coin, is equal to $\frac{1}{2}V(y_1) + \frac{1}{2}V(y_2)$. Thus, when the utility function is concave to the X axis, as in Figure 3.3, an individual is said to be risk-averse, and the greater the degree of concavity the more extreme the degree of risk aversion. When the function is linear, the individual is risk-neutral, being indifferent between having or not having the gamble, and when convex they are risk-seeking, preferring the gamble.

Pratt's (1964) analysis of certainty equivalents for money gambles provides the conceptual foundation for studies that examine the joint role of risk preferences and perceptions in food consumption decisions. From Pratt's work can be derived the following relationship between the value to an individual of consuming a risky food, their perception of the level of risk, and their preference for risk:

$$\Pi \approx -\frac{1}{2}\sigma^2[-U''(w)/U'(w)]$$

where Π represents value, σ^2 measures perception of the level of risk, and the expression in square brackets is the Arrow–Pratt measure of absolute risk aversion, typically denoted $r(w)$. In Pratt's representation, w represented wealth, but here we can think of it as representing the level of food safety. Thus, the value placed on a risky proposition depends on both the perception of the risk, σ^2, and the risk preference, $r(w)$. Given $U'(w) > 0$, and $U''(w) < 0$ for a risk-averse individual as represented in Figure 3.3, the risk preference, $r(w)$, is positive and thus a risk-averse individual places a negative value on consuming a risky compared to a non-risky product. For risk seekers, that value will be positive, and for individuals who are risk-neutral, with $U''(w) = 0$, it is zero.

4.1   Risk Preferences, Perceptions, and Food Consumption Choices

When we consider risk preferences in the context of food, a couple of issues come to mind that may not be well described by the money gamble scenario above. First, while outcomes in food safety could be characterized as discrete (i.e., one is either sick or not sick as a consequence of consumption), it may be more appropriate to think of them as continuous since there are degrees of severity of symptoms, and furthermore the event that gives rise to the outcome is continuous since there are varying degrees of contamination. This is not a problem, however, because the situation described in Figure 3.3 can be readily extended to cover multiple or continuous outcomes.

Another issue has to do with the argument of the function—what it is that is measured on the horizontal axis. As noted above, we may think of it as food safety (instead of money wealth), measured by the extent to which food is contaminated, and where contamination decreases as we move to the right along the X axis. The fact that there may be an upper limit on safety (zero contamination) is not a particular problem, and the representation in Figure 3.3 can still be usefully applied within a relevant range below zero contamination.[6] While risk and safety are often synonymous, risk preferences can also be defined with respect to characteristics that have nothing to do with risk of illness per se. For example, a consumer might face a choice between purchasing steak A of known tenderness or steak B of unknown tenderness, which could be better or worse than A. Examining that situation in an experimental auction, Alfnes, Rickertsen, and Ueland (2008) found that most consumers are risk-averse in that context and would prefer steak A.

The literature on the connection between risk preferences and food consumption is sparse and only a few studies have examined the joint role of risk preferences and perceptions in decision-making. An *EconLit* search found thirty-six articles with the keywords *risk* and *food* and *preference or preferences*, of which only a handful deal with

---

[6] In conflict with the law of diminishing marginal utility consumers typically place a higher value on eliminating the last unit of risk, i.e., going from 1 percent to 0 percent, than they do on reducing a higher level of risk by the same magnitude (Zeckhauser and Viscusi 1990; Hartl and Fox 2004). Policymakers, or at least those who implement policy, appear to suffer from the same affliction—what Breyer terms the problem of "the last 10 percent." The problem, of course, is that the elimination of a risk is often grossly inefficient in light of what resources could achieve elsewhere.

food consumption. Fifty-six articles were found when the words *preference or preferences* were replaced by *perception or perceptions*. This stands in contrast to the "non-food-specific" literature, where one finds three times as many articles (N = 1948) with the keywords *risk* and *preference or preferences* than with *risk* and *perception or perceptions* (N = 630). When it comes to food-related risks, economists have focused more on perceptions than on preferences (e.g., Eom 1994; Hayes et al. 1995; Wohl 1998).

Pennings, Wansink, and Meulenberg (2002) examined the roles of risk perceptions and attitudes (i.e., preferences) in the reactions of US, German, and Dutch consumers to mad cow disease (BSE). Risk attitudes and perceptions were measured using responses to questions about: (a) the extent to which consumers agreed with statements about willingness to accept risk, and (b) the level of risk they perceived to be associated with beef. Responses were scaled from 1 (strongly agree) to 9 (strongly disagree). They found that German consumers were more risk-averse than their Dutch and US counterparts, and that they also perceived a higher level of risk associated with beef. For Dutch consumers, the reaction to BSE (i.e., reducing consumption) was found to be driven primarily by risk perception, whereas for US consumers it was driven by risk attitude. For German consumers, reaction was significantly influenced by both risk attitude and perception. Based on these findings the authors suggested that the response to BSE should take into account the extent to which consumption changes are driven by attitudes or perceptions. Thus, for the United States they suggested that "tough measures are required to prevent a BSE crisis because risk attitudes drive consumption and little can be done to change consumers' risk attitudes. This means testing and slaughtering all suspected cows." For the Netherlands, on the other hand, an effective response could focus on efforts to educate consumers about the level of risk, but for Germany that approach would have to be combined with efforts to reduce or eradicate the hazard.

Schroeder et al. (2007) surveyed 4,005 consumers in the United States, Canada, Mexico, and Japan, and, like Pennings, Wansink, and Meulenberg (2002), focused on the relative influence of attitudes and perceptions on beef consumption behavior. They found that Japanese consumers were the most risk-averse, and that Japanese and Mexican consumers perceived higher levels of risk from beef than did US and Canadian consumers. They also found that risk perception had a greater impact on beef consumption than did risk attitude for consumers in the United States, Japan, and Canada. This contrasts with the Pennings et al. finding that for US consumers, behavior was driven more by risk attitude. Hence, the suggested policy response to a beef food safety event is also quite different, i.e.: "From policy and industry management perspectives, a beef food safety event in the United States and Canada can be dealt with by quickly containing the hazard and informing consumers about the low probability of adverse health effects associated with consuming the product."

Lusk and Coble (2005) investigated the link between risk preferences, risk perceptions, and willingness to consume potentially risky GM foods. Their participants (undergraduate students) were quite accepting of GM food, with over 60 percent indicating relatively strong agreement (scoring 7 or higher on a scale of 1 = strongly disagree to 9 = strongly agree) with willingness to purchase or eat GM foods. They found that both risk preferences, elicited in choices over lotteries, and risk perceptions, elicited as the average response to four Likert-type questions, were significantly correlated with acceptance. Similar to Schroeder et al. (2007), they found that risk perceptions had the relatively greater impact on behavior. In contrast, Mazzocchi et al. (2008) found that for European consumers, risk perceptions were unlikely to influence behavior, and only became important in the event of a food scare.

Lusk and Coble noted that their measure of risk preferences was elicited only in the domain of potential gains, whereas risks associated with foods are typically in the domain of losses. Risk preferences (i.e., the shape of the utility function) may differ between those domains, and a typical finding, as predicted by prospect theory, is of risk aversion for gains and risk seeking for losses.[7] They also note that risk preferences elicited in context-less gambles might not be well correlated with risk preferences in the context of food safety choices (see Hudson, Coble, and Lusk 2005). Thus, the strength of the relationship between those risk preferences and food choices may represent a lower bound; in other words, had they elicited risk preferences in the context of food safety risks the relationship between risk preferences and food choices may have been even stronger. The literature on constructed preferences points to some additional critiques of this and related studies.

5   CONSTRUCTED PREFERENCES

Establishing connections between risk preferences and food choices is challenging, not only for the obvious reason that measurement of both is subject to error, but more importantly because risk preferences are particularly sensitive to the way in which they are measured.[8] Harrison and Rutstrom (2008) review the alternative approaches to eliciting risk attitudes in the laboratory, most of which involve choices over lotteries (e.g., Holt and Laury 2002) or the stating of buying or selling prices for lotteries. Another approach involves the use of psychometric scales. Pennings and Smidts (2000) surveyed Dutch hog farmers and examined how different measures of risk attitude were related to risk-reducing market behavior such as use of futures markets. They

---

[7] A related concern has to do with the fact that risk preferences were elicited using *non-hypothetical* choices, whereas behavior with respect to the risky food was measured using responses to *hypothetical* questions. The authors noted the Laury and Holt (2005) findings that the (prospect theory) predicted pattern of risk aversions for gains/risk seeking for losses was diminished when subjects moved from a hypothetical to a non-hypothetical context in which the modal response was risk aversion for *both* losses and gains.

[8] The influence of methodology is further illustrated by Lusk et al. (2005), who found that most of the variation in consumer valuations of GM foods could be attributed to characteristics of the sample, characteristics of the food being valued, and, importantly, differences in the methods used to elicit valuations.

found that measures of risk attitude derived from lottery choices were better predictors of behavior than risk attitudes based on psychometric scales (e.g., degree of agreement with a statement such as "I like taking big financial risks").[9] Hudson, Coble, and Lusk (2005) reported results from a series of experiments with agricultural producers demonstrating a lack of consistency between risk premium measures elicited using different methods. Anderson and Mellor (2008) found that risk preferences for the same subjects were not stable across two elicitation methods—a survey with questions on hypothetical gambles and an experiment with real monetary rewards.

Results such as these suggesting that risk preferences are context-dependent provide another explanation for contradictory findings in empirical studies (e.g., Pennings, Wansink, and Meulenberg 2002; Schroeder et al. 2007) but might also cause us to question the consistency of underlying risk preferences. In fact, the literature on what is termed "constructed preferences" questions the fundamental assumption that individuals actually possess well-defined preferences.

The central idea in the constructed preference literature is that, in many situations, individuals simply do not possess or do not know their own preferences; instead preferences are constructed as needed and therefore influenced in important ways by the decision environment. The main developments in the literature are surveyed in Lichtenstein and Slovic (2006). While it is clear that we possess some fundamental preferences such as for more rather than fewer resources, those basic preferences are often insufficient, according to the theory, to guide decisions in situations when choices involve trade-offs, or conflicts among known preferences. A simple example is a choice between two food products varying in both price and quality. Our choices in those situations may not reflect what economists conceive of as an innate and fixed utility function embodying preferences for risk and wealth, but rather may reflect preferences that are constructed on the spot. Those preferences, and the manner in which they are constructed, will vary with the decision environment.

5.1   Background: Preference Reversals

The concept of constructed preferences grew largely from the phenomenon of *preference reversals*, first documented in the psychology literature in the late 1960s and early 1970s (Lichtenstein and Slovic 1971). In the context of preferences over gambles, a reversal arises when an individual indicates that they prefer gamble A over gamble B, but place a higher monetary value on gamble B. Slovic and Lichtenstein (1968) had shown that the *different attributes* of a gamble (i.e., probability of winning, amount to be won) were afforded *different weights* when individuals were asked either: (a) to

---

[9] The advantages of psychometric scales are that they are easy to implement and the questions are easy for respondents to answer. Furthermore, questions can be placed in the context of the decision environment, i.e., food safety. However, responses are not easily comparable to more familiar measures such as the Arrow–Pratt measure of risk aversion.

choose between two gambles, or (b) to provide a rating or a price for a gamble. In choosing between gambles, the probability of winning received the greater weight, whereas in the pricing task, the amount to be won was afforded the greater weight. This shifting of weights across decision tasks can lead to preference reversals, and illustrates the idea of how preferences are constructed in different ways in different decision environments.

Subsequent work has shown that preference reversals are not limited to the context of pricing or choosing between bets. Nowlis and Simonson (1997) found systematic preference reversals in experiments using consumer goods such as batteries, cameras, microwave ovens, and hotels in which lower-price, lower-quality brands were preferred more in choice than in purchase likelihood ratings. They suggested that the mechanism underlying these preference reversals was the degree of compatibility between attributes and tasks (i.e., the subject's task of either choosing between two products, rating products, expressing purchase likelihood, or expressing a willingness-to-pay or willingness-to-accept value). By that theory, attributes such as price that are readily comparable across options receive more weight in joint evaluation tasks (choice) than in tasks involving separate evaluation (rating, pricing). On the other hand, attributes that are less comparable such as brand name receive more weight in tasks in which options are evaluated separately. Their experiments provided empirical support for this hypothesis, and also demonstrated that reversals were not limited to situations in which options differed in price and brand, but also arose when the price attribute was replaced with a product feature, and when brand was replaced by country of origin.

In the context of food choices the Nowlis and Simonson hypothesis suggests that attributes such as "natural" or "locally produced" would fare better when products are evaluated separately such as with a purchase likelihood rating, whereas price will have a greater impact in comparison-based evaluations such as conjoint analysis. If this is the case, we should expect different elicitation methods to yield different results, which begs the question—which method is correct? Since choice tasks may better replicate the actions taken by consumers in the market—at least in the markets for food products where comparison-based decisions are facilitated by the options on the supermarket shelf—choice tasks such as conjoint analysis may prove more informative about consumer behavior.

5.2   Anchoring, Framing, and Priming

Ariely, Lowenstein, and Prelec (2003) showed how the valuation of experience goods was influenced to a significant degree by an irrelevant factor: the last two digits of a subject's Social Security number. This type of anchoring effect on valuations had been illustrated in the context of contingent valuation of public goods (Green et al. 1998) but Ariely et al. showed that it also applied in the context of ordinary consumer products such as wine, chocolate, and electronic equipment. They found, for example, that average valuation for a cordless computer keyboard was $56 for individuals with Social Security numbers in the top quintile, compared to $16 for subjects in the bottom quintile. They concluded "evidently, these subjects did not have, or were unable to retrieve, personal values for ordinary products."

Once initial values were established, Ariely et al. showed that subsequent *relative* valuations were as predicted by economic theory. For example, willingness-to-accept values to listen to unpleasant sounds were higher for sounds of longer durations. They termed this combination of arbitrary initial values followed by choices that are rationally consistent with earlier choices (and with economic theory) as coherent arbitrariness.[10] They also found that exposure to a market did not diminish the effect of an initial anchor that was found to persist through several rounds of market experience using a fourth price auction with no evidence of bid convergence.

The existence of an anchoring effect helps explain the reported insensitivity of contingent valuation responses to variations in the scope and scale of offered benefits. Two frequently cited studies are Kahneman (1986), who found willingness to pay to clean up all the lakes in Ontario was similar to the value placed on cleaning up the lakes in just one region, and Desvousges et al. (1993), who reported similar willingness-to-pay values to save 2,000 or 200,000 birds. Eom (1994), Hayes et al. (1995), and Hartl and Fox (2004) all report insensitivity of willingness-to-pay values to variation in the level of risk reduction. For example, Hartl and Fox found the valuation of a one-step risk reduction from ten cases to one case per 100,000 people was about half the combined valuations of two separate reductions from ten cases to three cases, and from three cases to one case, when in theory those values should be equal. Commenting on insensitivity to scope, Diamond and Hausman (1994) suggest that contingent valuation responses reflect respondent attitudes rather than an economic concept of preferences.

The context in which choices are framed can also influence results. Blake (2004) showed how consumer reaction to mad cow disease was influenced by the manner in which risks were presented. Respondents to a mail survey were presented with scenarios involving either one or twenty additional cases of BSE, or, in a third treatment, presented with both the single-case and twenty-case scenarios. When presented separately, the twenty-case scenario, as expected, provoked stronger responses than the single-case scenario: 26 percent of respondents versus 13 percent said they would stop consuming beef. When both scenarios were presented, the response to the single-case scenario was similar to when it was separately presented (12 percent said they would stop consuming), but the response to the twenty-case scenario was far stronger (with 45 percent saying they would stop consuming). When framed alongside the single-case scenario, the twenty-case scenario appears to represent a much greater risk than when presented by itself. Other work has shown how consumer choices, both in lab and in retail settings, are influenced by factors that should, in theory, be irrelevant. For

---

[10] The implication for contingent valuation studies is that they may be able to predict the slope of the demand curve but not its location.

example, Doyle et al. (1999) showed how the addition of a third alternative results in a shift of preferences among two original options. Mandel and Johnson (2002) showed how visual primes—different background "wallpaper" on a webpage—had a significant influence on hypothetical purchase choices for sofas and cars.

5.3   Economists Fight Back

Preference reversals and the existence of an individual's utility function are mutually incompatible—the existence of one precludes the other. Thus, Grether and Plott (1979) set out to refute the psychologists' findings. Their experiments, designed to control for several economic and other explanations for preference reversals such as poorly specified incentives, strategic responses, respondent confusion, etc., served only to confirm the psychologists' results. In their words, "the preference reversal phenomenon, which is inconsistent with the traditional statement of preference theory, remains."

Since then, however, economists have shown that when subjects are engaged in market arbitrage, preference reversals can be eliminated. Chu and Chu (1990) implemented a mechanism termed the "money pump," in which a subject who revealed a preference reversal was required to purchase the bet they had placed the higher value on, exchange it for the bet they said they preferred, and then sell that preferred bet for their valuation—which was lower than that of the first bet. This arbitrage exercise, which cost the subjects money, had the effect of rendering subsequent choices and valuations to be consistent with each other and thus eliminating reversals.

Going a step further, Cherry, Crocker, and Shogren (2003) demonstrated not only that arbitrage could eliminate preference reversals, but that arbitrage in a market setting could spill over and induce rationality (i.e., elimination of reversals) in a non-market setting.[11] They also found that the mechanism by which preference reversal was eliminated was through subjects reducing their valuations for high-risk lotteries, and not through changes in choice patterns among pairs of lotteries. Thus, they conclude, as have others, that reversals are driven by the mispricing of high-risk lotteries.[12] While such demonstrations of the effect of market arbitrage on preference reversals are powerful, Lichtenstein and Slovic (2006) argue, "nor can any one experiment showing the elimination of preference reversals in one situation be taken as refutation of them all."

[11] This is related to Plott's (1995) discovered preference hypothesis whereby valuations and probability assessments become more consistent and rational with repeated experience and feedback.

[12] Interestingly, Cherry, Crocker, and Shogren (2003) do not treat valuations and preferences as synonymous, but they do consider choices and preferences to be one and the same. This distinction is fundamental to their claim (p. 76) that "People adjust valuations of high-risk lotteries to achieve rationality given arbitrage; they do not alter their preferences."

5.4   Implications of Constructed Preferences for Food Consumption Studies

What are the implications, for researchers and for public policy, if preferences are not innate features of an individual's character but are constructed according to the needs of the decision environment? One implication would be that efforts to measure risk preferences and relate them to food consumption choices are a waste of time. Thus, studies such as Pennings, Wansink, and Meulenberg (2002), Lusk and Coble (2005), Schroeder et al. (2007), are, at best, measuring and including in their models a meaningless variable. More important, however, are the implications for policy recommendations from those studies: if preferences are constructed those prescriptions will be misguided. For example, the Pennings et al. assertion that "little can be done to change consumers' risk attitudes" would be incorrect, and perhaps, to take a somewhat cynical view, welfare might be well served by investments aimed at manipulating preferences. Consider also the following recommendation from Lusk and Coble: "To the extent that decisions are heavily influenced by risk preferences, consumer acceptance of GM food may not be easily changed and policies such as a ban might be preferable." This statement assumes risk preferences that are innate and fixed. Because the authors found that risk perceptions had a greater impact on behavior than risk preferences, they concluded that provision of information about risk would be an appropriate policy. However, if preferences are constructed, the exact same conclusion would apply, even if preferences were found to have a greater impact than perceptions.

Even if we reject the idea of constructed preferences, there is much that economists who investigate food consumption choices can learn from that literature. For example, the evidence that the nature of the decision task (choice versus rating versus pricing) can have a systematic impact on choices suggests that we should not expect consistency between the results of conjoint and contingent valuation approaches. In Lusk and Coble (2005), risk preferences were elicited in a *joint-evaluation*-type task in which lotteries were compared with each other side by side and the preferred option chosen, while food choices were elicited primarily in *single-evaluation*-type tasks in which subjects indicated their level of agreement or disagreement with statements about eating or purchasing GM food. Different evaluation modes—single versus joint—result in different attributes of an option receiving different weightings in the evaluation task. And while the Lusk and Coble study found a significant correlation between elicited risk preferences and preferences for genetically modified food, it is possible that that correlation would have been even stronger had the nature of the evaluation tasks coincided.

The literature also points to the important influence of default rules on choices and behavior. Default rules in contexts such as organ donation (whether one is required to opt in or opt out) or levels of retirement contribution have been shown to have significant effects (Johnson and Goldstein 2003; Sunstein and Thaler 2003). An analogy can be made with labeling where the default rule is one specifying whether or not a label is required. Different default settings may partly explain differences in views on GM foods between US and European Union consumers—a difference that might otherwise be attributed only to different preferences and risk perceptions.

6   Conclusions

There is a sound basis in theory for including both risk preferences and risk perceptions as determinants of the value consumers place on food risk reduction. Studies that omit one or the other will suffer from omitted variable bias. Most studies focus on risk perception and ignore risk preferences, while the few that attempt to measure and control for both are relatively new and have not reached consistent conclusions about the relative importance of the two factors. In one such study, Lusk and Coble (2005) found that both risk perceptions and risk preferences elicited in the lab were significantly correlated with respondents' acceptance of GM food. Going forward, it seems clear that researchers should be consistent in controlling for both factors when attempting to explain consumer behavior in the context of food risk.

But obtaining accurate measures of either risk preferences or risk perceptions is no simple matter. With perceptions, complications are introduced because of the cognitive difficulties people have with the small probabilities that characterize food-related risks and changes therein. People tend to overestimate low probabilities, and even when objective probabilities are provided, the level of risk reduction perceived by respondents in different scenarios may not coincide with that described. Situations may involve background risks, which may or may not be correlated with the risk of interest and therefore have some influence on both the respondents' perception of their exposure and their risk attitude (Lusk and Coble 2008). With food, people typically have an opportunity to self-protect (cooking, washing, peeling, etc.) and it is important to account for that opportunity in eliciting risk perception—i.e., whether the reported risk perception relates to a point before or after self-protection (Lusk 2007). Shogren and Stamland (2007) are pessimistic about individuals' ability to assess risk exposure and suggest that their survey responses reflected vague guesses rather than strongly felt perceptions.

Risk preferences or attitudes, as we have seen, are also difficult to pin down. While acknowledging that different elicitation methods produce different measures,[13] Harrison and Rutström (2008) nevertheless conclude that individual aversion to risk can be reliably measured in the laboratory. They found that most subjects behave as if they are risk-averse, and that their degree of risk aversion can be correlated with observable characteristics (gender, income, etc.). An initial challenge would be to define one best measure of risk preference, on the assumption that individuals possess an innate and

---

[13] "Evidence for different risk attitudes across procedures is, by definition, a sign of a procedural artifact" (Harrison and Rutström 2008: 50).

measurable preference for risk that guides their behavior under uncertainty. In attempting to define that "best measure," evidence that behavior under risk is correlated with biological characteristics may prove useful. For example, there is substantial evidence that women and men differ in their responses to risk. Apicella et al. (2008), and Eckel and Grossman (2008) found that risk-taking behavior in an investment game was positively correlated with testosterone levels. These findings suggest that risk preferences are associated with innate biological characteristics, and that association may guide the selection of a "best measure"—i.e., one most closely correlated with the relevant biological measures.

But even if agreement can be reached on a best measure of risk preference, it will be difficult to elicit that measure in traditional (i.e., non-laboratory) survey settings. Most food consumption studies rely on traditional survey methods—mail, phone, Internet—for data collection, and in those situations choices are, by definition, hypothetical. And, as Harrison and Rutstrom (2008) put it, "there is considerable evidence . . . that risk attitudes elicited with hypothetical responses are significantly different to risk attitudes elicited with real economic consequences." The challenge, then, is straightforward if not easy: devise methods of reliably eliciting risk preferences in surveys that are immune to hypothetical bias.

In the background are some nagging questions raised by the idea that preferences may be constructed. If they are, in fact, constructed and not innate, measured risk preferences will not be meaningful. However, as studies accumulate, we will gather evidence on this question. If preferences are constructed, we should expect inconsistent findings about how measured risk preferences are related to food decisions. Some studies will find significant correlation in the expected direction, some will find no correlation, and some will find correlation in the "wrong" direction. On the other hand, if studies consistently show, like Lusk and Coble, that measured risk preferences are significantly correlated with food choice behavior in the manner suggested by theory, that would suggest that measured risk preferences are meaningful and that their inclusion improves model performance in the sense of painting a better picture of how consumers respond to food risk.

References

Alfnes, F., K. Rickertsen, and O. Ueland. 2008. "Consumer Attitudes toward Low Stake Risk in Food Markets." *Applied Economics* 40: 3039–49.

American Meat Institute. 2009. "New Poll Reveals Knowledge Gap among Public on Meat and Poultry Handling, Cooking and Safety." Press Release. June 17. <http://www.meatami.com/ht/display/ReleaseDetails/i/50907>.

Anderson, L. R., and J. M. Mellor. 2008. *Are Risk Preferences Stable? Comparing an Experimental Measure with a Validated Survey-Based Measure.* Working Paper No. 74. Williamsburg, VA: Department of Economics, College of William and Mary.

Apicella, C. L., A. Dreber, B. Campbell, P. B. Gray, M. Hoffman, and A. C. Little. 2008. "Testosterone and Financial Risk Preferences." *Evolution and Human Behavior* 29: 384–90.

Ariely, D., G. Lowenstein, and D. Prelec. 2003. "Coherent Arbitrariness: Stable Demand Curves without Stable Preferences." *Quarterly Journal of Economics* 118: 73–105.

Blake, J. 2004. "The Effects of Future Domestic Cases of Bovine Spongiform Encephalopathy on U.S. Consumer Beef Demand." MS thesis. Kansas State University.

Brewer, M. S., and M. Rojas. 2008. "Consumer Attitudes toward Issues in Food Safety." *Journal of Food Safety* 28: 1–22.

Breyer, S. 1993. *Breaking the Vicious Circle: Toward Effective Risk Regulation*. Cambridge, MA: Harvard University Press.

Caswell, J. 2008. *Expanding the Focus of Cost–Benefit Analysis for Food Safety: A Multi-Factorial Risk Prioritization Approach*. Working Paper No. 2008–8. Amherst: Department of Resource Economics, University of Massachusetts Amherst.

Cherry, T. L., T. D. Crocker, and J. F. Shogren. 2003. "Rationality Spillovers." *Journal of Environmental Economics and Management* 45: 63–84.

Chu, Y. P., and R. L. Chu. 1990. "The Subsidence of Preference Reversals in Simplified and Marketlike Experimental Settings: A Note." *American Economic Review* 80: 902–11.

Curtis, K. R., and K. Moeltner. 2006. "Genetically Modified Food Market Participation and Consumer Risk Perceptions: A Cross-Country Comparison." *Canadian Journal of Agricultural Economics* 54: 289–310.

Desvousges, W. H., F. R. Johnson, R. W. Dunford, K. J. Boyle, S. P. Hudson, and K. N. Wilson. 1993. "Measuring Natural Resource Damages with Contingent Valuation: Tests of Validity and Reliability." In J. A. Hausman, ed., *Contingent Valuation: A Critical Assessment*. Amsterdam: Elsevier.

Diamond, P. A., and J. A. Hausman. 1994. "Contingent Valuation: Is Some Number Better Than No Number?" *Journal of Economic Perspectives* 8: 45–64.

Doll, R., and R. Peto. 1981. "The Causes of Cancer." *Journal of the National Cancer Institute* 66: 1191–308.

Doyle, J. R., D. J. O'Connor, G. M. Reynolds, and P. A. Bottomley. 1999. "The Robustness of the Asymmetrically Dominated Effect: Buying Frames, Phantom Alternatives, and In-Store Purchases." *Psychology and Marketing* 16: 225–43.

Eckel, C. C., and P. J. Grossman. 2008. "Forecasting Risk Attitudes: An Experimental Study Using Actual and Forecast Gamble Choices." *Journal of Economic Behavior and Organization* 68: 1–17.

Ellis, J. D., and M. Tucker. 2009. "Factors Influencing Consumer Perception of Food Hazards." *CAB Reviews: Perspectives in Agriculture, Veterinary Science, Nutrition and Natural Resources* 4: 1–8.

Eom, Y. S. 1994. "Pesticide Residue Risk and Food Safety Valuation: A Random Utility Approach." *American Journal of Agricultural Economics* 76: 760–71.

Frenzen, P. D., A. Drake, and F. J. Angulo. 2005. "Economic Cost of Illness Due to Escherichia Coli 0157 Infections in the United States." *Journal of Food Protection* 68: 2623–30.

GAO (United States General Accounting Office). 2000. "Food Irradiation: Available Research Indicates that Benefits Outweigh Risks." Aug. <http://www.gao.gov/archive/2000/rc00217.pdf>.

—— 2008. "Food Safety: Selected Countries' Systems Can Offer Insights into Ensuring Import Safety and Responding to Foodborne Illness." June. <http://www.gao.gov/new.items/d08794.pdf>.

Green, D., K. E. Jacowitz, D. Kahneman, and D. McFadden. 1998. "Referendum Contingent Valuation, Anchoring, and Willingness to Pay for Public Goods." *Resource and Energy Economics* 20: 85–116.

Grether, D., and C. Plott. 1979. "Economic Theory of Choice and the Preference Reversal Phenomenon." *American Economic Review* 69: 623–38.

Harrison, G. W., and E. E. Rutström. 2008. "Risk Aversion in the Laboratory." In G. W. Harrison and J. C. Cox, eds, *Research in Experimental Economics*, 12. Stamford, CT: JAI Press.

Hartl, J. 2004. "Estimating the Demand for Risk Reduction from Food-Borne Pathogens." MS thesis. Department of Agricultural Economics, Kansas State University.

—— and J. A. Fox. 2004. "Estimating the Demand for Risk Reduction from Food Borne Pathogens through Food Irradiation." *Agrarwirtschaft* 53: 309–18.

Hayes, D. J., J. F. Shogren, S. Y. Shin, and J. B. Kliebenstein. 1995. "Valuing Food Safety in Experimental Auction Markets." *American Journal of Agricultural Economics* 77: 40–53.

Heron, M., D. L. Hoyert, S. L. Murphy, J. Xu, K. D. Kochanek, and B. Tejada-Vera. 2009. *Deaths: Final Data for 2006.* National Vital Statistics Reports, 57/14. Hyattsville, MD: National Center for Health Statistics. <http://www.cdc.gov/nchs/data/nvsr/nvsr57/nvsr57_14.pdf>.

Holt, C. A., and S. K. Laury. 2002. "Risk Aversion and Incentive Effects." *American Economic Review* 92: 1644–55.

Hudson, D., K. H. Coble, and J. L. Lusk. 2005. "Consistency of Risk Aversion Measures: Results from Hypothetical and Non-Hypothetical Experiments." *Agricultural Economics* 33: 41–9.

IFICF (International Food Information Council Foundation). 2009. "2009 Food and Health Survey: Consumer Attitudes toward Food, Nutrition and Health." <http://www.ific.org/research/upload/FINAL-DRAFT-F-H-OPINION-LEADER-WEBCAST-05-20-09.pdf>.

Johansson-Stenman, O. 2008. "Mad Cows, Terrorism and Junk Food: Should Public Policy Reflect Perceived or Objective Risks?" *Journal of Health Economics* 27: 234–48.

Johnson, E. J., and D. G. Goldstein. 2003. "Do Defaults Save Lives?" *Science* 302: 1338–9.

Kahneman, D. 1986. "Comments." In R. G. Cummings, D. S. Brookshire, and W. D. Schulze, eds, *Valuing Environmental Goods*. Totowa, NJ: Rowan ' Allanheld.

—— and A. Tversky. 1979. "Prospect Theory: An Analysis of Decision under Risk." *Econometrica* 47: 263–91.

Knight, A., and R. Warland. 2004. "The Relationship between Sociodemographics and Concern about Food-Safety Issues." *Journal of Consumer Affairs* 38: 107–20.

Krupnick, A., A. Alberini, M. Cropper, N. Simon, B. O'Brien, R. Goeree, and M. Heintzelman. 2002. "Age, Health and the Willingness to Pay for Mortality Risk Reductions: A Contingent Valuation Survey of Ontario Residents." *Journal of Risk and Uncertainty* 24: 161–86.

Laury, S. K., and C. A. Holt. 2005. *Further Reflections on Prospect Theory*. Andrew Young School of Policy Studies Research Paper Series No. 06-11. Atlanta: Georgia State University. <http://ssrn.com/abstract=893614>.

Lichtenstein, S., and P. Slovic. 1971. "Reversals of Preference between Bids and Choices in Gambling Decisions." *Journal of Experimental Psychology* 89: 46–55.

—— ——. 2006. *The Construction of Preference*. New York: Cambridge University Press.

—— ——, B. Fischhoff, M. Layman, and B. Combs. 1978. "Judged Frequency of Lethal Events." *Journal of Experimental Psychology: Human Learning and Memory* 4: 551–78.

Lusk, J. L. 2007. "New Estimates of the Demand for Food Safety: Discussion." *American Journal of Agricultural Economics* 89: 1189–90.

—— and K. H. Coble. 2005. "Risk Perceptions, Risk Preference, and Acceptance of Risky Food." *American Journal of Agricultural Economics* 87: 393–405.

—— ——. 2008. "Risk Aversion in the Presence of Background Risk: Evidence from the Lab." In J. C. Cox and G. W. Harrison, eds, *Risk Aversion in Experiments*, 12. Bingley: Emerald, Research in Experimental Economics.

——, M. Jamal, L. Kurlander, M. Roucan, and L. Taulman. 2005. "A Meta-Analysis of Genetically Modified Food Valuation Studies." *Journal of Agricultural and Resource Economics* 30: 28–44.

Mandel, N., and E. J. Johnson. 2002. "When Web Pages Influence Choice: Effects of Visual Primes on Experts and Novices." *Journal of Consumer Research* 29: 235–45.

Mazzocchi, M., A. Lobb, W. B. Traill, and A. Cavicchi. 2008. "Food Scares and Trust: A European Study." *Journal of Agricultural Economics* 59: 2–24.

Mead, P. S., L. Slutsker, V. Dietz, L. F. McCaig, J. S. Bresee, C. Shapiro, P. M. Griffin, and R. V. Tauxe. 1999. "Food-Related Illness and Death in the United States." *Emerging Infectious Diseases* 5: 607–25. <http://www.cdc.gov/ncidod/eid/Vol5no5/mead.htm>.

Miles, S., D. S. Braxton, and L. J. Frewer. 1999. "Public Perceptions about Microbiological Hazards in Food." *British Food Journal* 101: 744–62.

MSNBC. 2009. "*E. Coli* Outbreaks across the U.S. that Made Headlines." <http://www.msnbc.msn.com/id/17755974>.

Nelson, N. J. 1996. "Is Chemoprevention Overrated or Underfunded?" *Journal of the National Cancer Institute* 88: 947–9.

Nestle, M. 2003. *Safe Food: Bacteria, Biotechnology and Bioterrorism.* Berkeley: University of California Press.

Nowlis, S. M., and I. Simonson. 1997. "Attribute-Task Compatibility as a Determinant of Consumer Preference Reversals." *Journal of Marketing Research* 34: 205–18.

Organic Consumers Association. 2008. "Vermont Farm Leader, Linda Faillace, on Why the USDA Will Not Allow US Beef Producer, Creekstone Farms, to Test Cows for Mad Cow Disease." Sept. <http://www.organicconsumers.org/articles/article_14873.cfm>.

Pennings, J., and A. Smidts. 2000. "Assessing the Construct Validity of Risk Attitude." *Management Science* 46: 1337–48.

——, B. Wansink, and M. Meulenberg. 2002. "A Note on Modeling Consumer Reactions to a Crisis: The Case of the Mad Cow Disease." *International Journal of Research in Marketing* 19: 91–100.

Plott, C. R. 1995. "Rational Individual Behavior in Markets and Social Choice Processes: The Discovered Preference Hypothesis." In K. Arrow, U. Colombatto, E. Perlman, and C. Schmidt, eds, *The Rational Foundations of Economic Behavior.* London: Macmillan.

Pollak, R. A. 1998. "Imagined Risks and Cost–Benefit Analysis." *American Economic Review* 88: 376–80.

Pollan, M. 2008. *In Defense of Food: An Eater's Manifesto.* New York: Penguin Press.

Portney, P. R. 1992. "Trouble in Happyville." *Journal of Policy Analysis and Management* 11: 131–2.

Pratt, J. W. 1964. "Risk Aversion in the Small and in the Large." *Econometrica* 32: 122–36.

Prelec, D. 1998. "The Probability Weighting Function." *Econometrica* 66: 497–527.

Roberts, L. 1990. "Counting on Science at EPA." *Science* 249: 616–18.

Schroeder, T. C., G. T. Tonsor, J. M. E. Pennings, and J. Mintert. 2007. "Consumer Food Safety Risk Perceptions and Attitudes: Impacts on Beef Consumption across Countries." *B. E. Journal of Economic Analysis and Policy* 7, art. 65. <http://www.bepress.com/bejeap/vol7/iss1/art65>.

Shogren, J. F., and T. Stamland. 2007. "Valuing Lives Saved from Safer Food: A Cautionary Tale Revisited." *American Journal of Agricultural Economics* 89: 1176–82.

Slovic, P. 1987. "Perception of Risk." *Science* 236: 280–5.

—— and S. Lichtenstein. 1968. "Relative Importance of Probabilities and Payoffs in Risk-Taking." *Journal of Experimental Psychology Monograph* 78: 46–55.

Sunstein, C. R., and R. H. Thaler. 2003. "Libertarian Paternalism Is Not an Oxymoron." *University of Chicago Law Review* 70: 1159–1202.

Tucker, M., S. R. Whaley, and J. S. Sharp. 2006. "Consumer Perceptions of Food-Related Risks." *International Journal of Food Science and Technology* 41: 135–46.

Viscusi, W. K. 1985. "A Bayesian Perspective on Biases in Risk Perception." *Economics Letters* 17: 59–62.

—— 2000. "Risk Equity." *Journal of Legal Studies* 29: 843–71.

Weinstein, N. 1987. "Unrealistic Optimism about Susceptibility to Health Problems: Conclusions from a Community-wide Sample." *Journal of Behavioral Medicine* 10: 481–99.

Wohl, J. B. 1998. "Consumers' Decision-Making and Risk Perceptions Regarding Foods Produced with Biotechnology." *Journal of Consumer Policy* 21: 387–404.

Zeckhauser, R. J., and W. K. Viscusi. 1990. "Risk within Reason." *Science* 248: 559–64.

CHAPTER 4

....

BEHAVIORAL ECONOMICS AND THE FOOD CONSUMER

....

DAVID R. JUST

1 INTRODUCTION

....

While many individuals spend significant amounts of time, effort, and money in attempts to modify their diet, most eating behavior occurs without much thought. People make an average of 200 to 300 decisions regarding food consumption in any given day (Wansink and Sobal 2007). Given the sheer volume of food decisions one makes and the severe time constraints that are often faced, it is no wonder that individuals might make decisions that are out of line with their health goals and desires. In order to reduce the cognitive requirements of so many decisions, individuals may rely on heuristics or decision rules to guide food consumption decisions. This has made food consumption decision-making a prime subject for the application of behavioral economic research. Within this chapter I focus on three general areas of research: food choice, food consumption volume, and the evaluation of foods.

Behavioral economics has grown in prominence in recent years as economists have sought causes for seemingly misguided or even destructive behaviors. Behavioral economics supposes that, while individuals may desire to consume some optimal bundle, they have a systematic inability to identify or choose that bundle accurately. Rather, they may rely on heuristic decision rules that have proven to work well in similar situations, or may misperceive aspects of the decision problem leading them to choices that are demonstrably suboptimal. The most prominent applications of behavioral economics have been in the field of behavioral finance (e.g., Benartzi and Thaler 1995). Behavioral economics expands the traditional rational model of behavior, drawing upon insights from psychology regarding individual perception, shifting preferences, and strategies for simplifying decision problems.

With respect to food consumption, psychologists have experimented extensively with behavior, finding many predictable behaviors that cannot be reconciled with standard economic models as they are now applied. Thus, we must find modifications to standard utility functions, models of time discounting, or models of information or perception that allow the psychological models to interact with the economic incentives. An emerging literature has tried to incorporate some psychology into economic models of food consumption. While this literature represents a starting point, much remains to be done in terms of incorporating the important elements of food behavior, and creating and using suitable individual data to calibrate these models for policy purposes.

Many have challenged the necessity for behavioral economic analysis (e.g., Mitchell 2003; or more recently, Levine 2009). I think there is no greater illustration of the importance of behavioral economic modeling than food consumption. Without behavioral economic models, traditional models suggest only three real policy levers: altering prices, providing information, and placing restrictions on what can be sold and where. Unfortunately, altering prices and information is generally ineffective in altering consumption behavior (see, e.g., Mytton et al. 2007), and can have unintended consequences. Further, restricting the market can be extremely unpopular. As I will discuss in this chapter, behavioral theory suggests a myriad other policy options that can have substantial impacts without restricting choices in any real sense. The strategy of influencing choice without restrictions or price incentives, called libertarian paternalism (Thaler and Sunstein 2003), is often much more widely appealing to both consumers and policymakers.

Traditional economic models provide only tenuous justifications for intervening in individual food behavior. Rational choice theory leaves little room for failures in willpower by assuming each observed action was the intended decision. On the other hand, behavioral theories provide a clear justification for intervention by separating individual desires from individual actions. Thus, policies may be designed that enable the individual to make decisions that are more nearly optimal in the individual's own view. Unlike price interventions, behavioral interventions of this nature are not necessarily resented by the decision maker, who is often unaware of the impacts of mechanism on their own behavior (e.g., Just et al. 2008; or more generally Johnson and Goldstein 2003). Rather, the individual believes they are better off for the intervention if the intervention encourages good behavior while not prohibiting bad behavior.

There are truly two primary literatures of behavioral economics and food consumption. One of these literatures seeks to apply general behavioral economic models to food consumption, while the other seeks to identify and incorporate known food psychological phenomena into models of economic behavior. The latter of these two introduces many new concepts to the field of behavioral economics, and provides some promising areas for future research. I seek to incorporate both approaches in this overview. The primary topics of behavioral economics related to food deal with: (1) why people choose the foods they do and when they do, (2) how people choose the volume of food they will eat, and (3) how people evaluate their experience and develop preferences for foods. I will deal with (1) to (3) in turn before providing a brief conclusion and some additional directions for future research.

2   FOOD CHOICE AND THE BATTLE
BETWEEN GOOD AND EVIL

Food decisions often involve the trade-off between current pleasure and future health benefits. Many individuals would characterize their relationship with food in terms of temptation, sin, and penance—decidedly behavioral concepts. One key question within obesity research is what drives individuals to choose unhealthy foods rather than healthy ones. Within the study of choice this could be framed as a choice between a good that is more hedonic (such as cheesecake) or utilitarian (celery). Hedonic goods are considered to be those associated with an extreme sensory experience (Hirshman and Holbrook 1982), while utilitarian goods are more functional, associated with some goal (Strahilevitz and Myers 1998). This leads individuals to view goods (or choices associated with them) in terms of moral structure—classifying objects as "wants" or "shoulds" (see Bazerman, Tenbrunsel, and Wade-Benzoni 1998).

2.1   Habits, Addiction, and Rationality

Food decisions appear to be highly habitual. Habit formation may lead individuals to hold to the status quo even when prices may change or when new health information suggests that habits have damaging effects. One prominent (non-behavioral) model of overeating suggests that individuals fully understand the consequences of their actions and have full control of them. For example, Richards, Patterson, and Tegene (2007) estimate a model that accounts for increasing obesity and overeating by using Becker and Murphy's (1988) rational addiction model. This model supposes that individuals choose to consume addictive substances with full knowledge of how it will alter their temporal preferences for the good in the future. Thus, under this model, one would never be surprised to find themselves addicted to a substance; rather it would be the expected result of a planned consumption profile. Importantly, the use of the rational addiction model leads the authors to conclude that taxes may be particularly effective in combating obesity. While the rational model may have a similar fit for data, it may have very different implications for welfare analysis and policy prescription.

Brito and Strain (1996), in studying alcoholism, note that rational addiction models fail to predict bingeing behavior. Bingeing is also common among those who overeat (Smith et al. 1998). Stress and compulsive behaviors, like bingeing, are often associated with one another. Social networks can relieve stress and reduce dependency on compulsive behavior (Fisher 1996). Similarly, Cutrona, Russel, and Rose (1986) find that social support helps control the diets of diabetics. Food acts as a substitute for social support in the short term. Thus, short periods of stress may increase consumption, introducing permanent changes in habitual behavior. The rational addiction model has also been attacked by Thaler and Shefrin (1981) for failing to account for the fact that addicted individuals report that they never planned to become addicted.

If individuals do not anticipate becoming compulsive eaters owing to their diet and exercise habits, then lower-order behaviors may truly be the culprit. In this case, policies designed to influence lower-order behaviors may be more effective than those designed to impact highly cognitive factors. Thus, policies impacting the food environment (like packaging or naming) may be more effective than those impacting price or health information (like taxes). More evidence is needed to determine the real mechanisms behind habitual overeating. This is key to determining appropriate and effective policy measures.

Bertrand and Whitmore-Schanzenbach (2009) find some evidence that increases in food consumption may be due to an increase in eating as a secondary activity. Time spent in eating as a primary activity has decreased over the last few decades. At the same time, eating while doing other things (like watching television or reading) has risen steadily. This is consistent with the notion that distractions and lower-order behaviors may be driving some of the increase in obesity (Wansink 2004).

2.2   Self-Control and Time Discounting

Several researchers have studied self-control and the ability to make the decisions one intends to. The primary behavioral economics literature on self-control models self-control problems as a result of preferences that are not consistent over time (see Gul and Pesendorfer 2004 for a review). Strotz (1955) originally proposed a model of time-inconsistent preferences, where individuals discount time in utility of consumption more heavily for the near future than the distant future, commonly called hyperbolic discounting. Time-inconsistent preferences are observed in individuals who continually procrastinate, such as those who put off starting a diet. Strotz showed that such preferences would lead individuals to choose commitment mechanisms to avoid future problems with self-control.

Within Laibson's (1997) notion of quasi-hyperbolic discounting, individuals discount consumption in the next period ($t = 1$) by some amount γ, in addition to discounting every period by δ^t so that time (and not just consumption) in the immediate term is more costly than time in the future. Optimization under such a discounting structure creates time-inconsistent preferences (i.e., incentive compatibility problems between a decision maker today and the same decision maker tomorrow). For example, an individual who desires to lose weight may compare future utility of weight loss to the forgone utility of consuming fatty foods today. If it is the case that the increase in utility from losing weight discounted by δ^t is greater than the utility lost by forgoing current consumption, then the individual would decide to go on a diet in any period $t + 1$. *However, if this same utility additionally discounted by γ is less than the utility forgone by current consumption, then the individual will not go on a diet in any period t.* Thus, the individual will, in each period, decide to put off their diet for one more period.[1] A rational individual who understands the process of procrastination and how it relates to time discounting (O'Donoghue and Rabin 2004) will look for an opportunity to pre-commit their future self to a better diet (this behavior is often observed with money savings via enrollment in an automatic withdrawal plan). To a certain extent, this may explain diet programs' use of social groups or weigh-in mechanisms that can be viewed as increasing the future cost of being overweight. The goal is to increase costs to the point that the individual's diet preferences today will match those of tomorrow.

While little work has been done directly with overeating and discounting (see Komlos, Smith, and Bogin 2004 or Borghans and Golsteyn 2006 for two recent reviews) the evidence that does exist is highly circumstantial. For example, Wilde and Ranney (2000) find that individuals receiving food stamps use a majority of their food stamp disbursement within the first few days of receiving it. While Wilde and Ranney struggle to explain such behavior with traditional economic techniques, the behavior is highly consistent with the notion of quasi-hyperbolic discounting. Here the individual may simply value trade-offs in near-term consumption too highly to consider the saving that is necessary for longer-term consumption. More recently, Scharff (2009) uses a large national data set to search for the telltale signs that obese individuals are more susceptible to hyperbolic discounting. Specifically, Schraff finds that obese women consume fewer calories when they have control of meal planning, shopping, or other influence over family food consumption. He believes this added control over meal planning and shopping can serve as a potential commitment device. Additionally, Schraff 2009 finds that health knowledge plays little role in calorie consumption, arguing that self-control issues make health knowledge of little effect.

2.3   Dual Process Models of Food Consumption

The decision between "wants" and "shoulds" is often framed as a battle between two separate decisions processes: rational thought and emotion. Epstein (1993) proposes the Cognitive-Experiential Self Theory (CEST) to describe this battle. This model supposes that there are two processes used to evaluate every stimulus: (1) an experiential system to make rapid evaluations based on affect (or emotion), and (2) the cognitive process that makes more deliberative evaluations based on rational thinking. The availability of processing resources such as time or the confluence of decisions to be made ultimately

---

[1] In fact, Tucker (2003) finds that drug abusers display more hyperbolic discounting than do non-users. This may be a useful field for future research to the extent that overeating is akin to drug addiction.

determines which process will take precedence. For example, Shiv and Fedorikhin (1999) find that individuals who were required to perform a simple task while making a food choice (between cake and fruit salad) were much more likely to choose the more hedonic item. CEST suggests that poor food behavior may result from the presence of distractions or the ultimate need to make a large number of food-related choices at once (Wansink and Sobal 2007).

This effect opens the door for a myriad of seemingly innocuous environmental factors to influence the choice of potentially sinful foods. For example, Meyers, Stunkard, and Coll (1980) find that individuals purchase significantly more ice cream when a store leaves the freezer door open. Wansink, Just, and Payne (2009) find evidence that some payment methods can distract from or draw attention to food purchases, influencing behavior. For example, individuals using debit cards to purchase food are much more likely to substitute high-calorie items for more healthy items than when using cash. This occurs despite the fact that those with the debit card spent no more than those using cash. Viewing a food significantly increases the incidence of unplanned consumption (Cornell, Rodin, and Weingarten 1989; Boon et al. 1998). It may not be surprising that visibility would affect how easily the individual might recall the pleasure associated with consuming the item. However, body chemistry also contributes. Viewing or smelling foods increases the release of dopamine in the body, which stimulates physical hunger (Volkow et al. 2002). Environmental factors also play a role in how much people eat, as will be discussed in the following section.

Loewenstein (2004) proposes including physiological factors in modeling food consumption decisions. He points out that visceral factors, the physiological processes that produce hunger, do not behave like economic notions of preferences, but rather like consumption goods. By way of example, he suggests that we can rank order visceral states like we would consumptive states. Much as I know one is usually better to consume a good than not, I know a priori that one is better off satiated than hungry. In contrast, I cannot a priori suggest one set of preferences is superior to another. In other words, I cannot guess that one is better off liking peanut butter with jam rather than honey. Loewenstein defines visceral factors as temporary and caused by distinct external factors, changing much more rapidly than tastes. These visceral factors could include triggers like the eating environment or social cues. In this model, visceral factors serve as referee in the battle between utilitarian and hedonic consumption patterns of CEST. In a "hot" state one overestimates the duration of a craving. In a "cold" state one underestimates the influence that visceral factors may have. If people tend to underestimate the impact of visceral factors, this will drive a wedge between the true value of consumption to an individual, and the *ex ante* perceived value one will obtain.

Using a mathematical model of time-discounted utility where each consumption good is associated with some random visceral factors, Loewenstein outlines several propositions governing consumption behavior:

1. The discrepancy between actual and perceived value of a good increases with intensity of associated visceral factors.
2. Visceral factors occurring in the distant future create little discrepancy between planned and perceived value.
3. Simultaneously increasing the current and future visceral factor will increase the relative actual value of the good now.
4. Current visceral factors can have a mild effect on future consumption even when those factors will not be operative in the future.
5. People underestimate the effect of visceral factors on their own behavior.
6. As time passes, individuals will forget the effect visceral factors played (they will view past behavior as strange).

Each of these propositions appears to be very well supported by the empirical food psychology literature in general. Behavioral economists have also found evidence that individuals have a difficult time predicting the utility they will obtain from consuming an item (Loewenstein, O'Donoghue, and Rabin 2003). While under most circumstances it is simple to predict whether a good will raise or lower one's utility level, the magnitude of the change may be more difficult to predict. This may be particularly applicable to food choices when placed under the stress of hunger.

Mancino (2003) and Mancino and Kinsey (2004) combine Loewenstein's model and the common household production model in an application to a survey of American food consumption. Their model shows that a high level of hunger, the visceral factor associated with food consumption, can lead to very different behavior. As individuals become busier (and time constraints begin to bind), more convenient food becomes a substitute for leisure time. Also, as one becomes busier, one may consume less often, allowing hunger to get out of control, leading to overconsumption. They suggest that the busier lifestyle has created an atmosphere where increased hunger leads individuals to periodically ignore health information, causing an increase in obesity.

2.3   References and Defaults

Kahneman and Tversky's (1979) model of loss aversion, called prospect theory, and its subsequent use in Thaler's (1980) mental accounting framework have become the foundation for much of behavioral economics. Prospect theory was originally proposed to describe choice under risk, but has since found application and support in riskless settings (e.g., Kahneman, Knetsch, and Thaler 1991). Prospect theory is built on several findings from economic experiments with two findings of primary importance in the food demand context: (1) individuals evaluate outcomes in relation to reference points—defining anything better than the reference point as a gain, and anything worse as a loss; (2) individuals display a much larger marginal utility of pain from loss and marginal utility of pleasure from gain—by about a 2 to 1 margin (see, e.g., Tversky and Kahneman 1992). Thus, for riskless consumption, prospect theory can be characterized by a utility function that is kinked at the reference amount of consumption, with a slope that is about twice as large below the reference point as above. The reference point itself may depend on habits or how the choice is framed. Thus, if one always orders the bacon cheeseburger, they may consider the cheeseburger without bacon to be a loss. Food marketers may be able to frame food decisions by manipulating the bundle offered as the standard or regular offering. For example, if the regular burger includes bacon, the cheeseburger may be viewed as a loss, where if the regular excludes bacon, the bacon cheeseburger may be seen as a gain.

Tversky and Kahneman (1991) have developed the theory of loss aversion for the multidimensional consumer problem. Here loss aversion implies kinked indifference curves, so that trading off a loss in one good requires a substantial gain in another good. Hu, Adamowicz, and Veeman (2006) find substantial impacts of reference points on preferences for genetically modified or non-genetically modified bread. Thus, those who believed genetically modified ingredients were normally present in bread were less averse to consuming genetically modified bread than otherwise.

In accordance with the popular notion of food as sinful or virtuous, food can often present a temptation to act counter to one's own best interest. Gul and Pesendorfer (2001) propose that individuals have preferences over the presence of temptations. Thus, choosing the salad option may yield lower utility to the consumer if tempting items like chocolate cake also appear on the menu. Their theory of temptation aversion supposes that consumers compare choices to whatever tempting options may be available. The more tempting items became a reference point for judging utility of the consumer. Thus, those items that may be cognitively better choices may lose their appeal when more choices are presented. This may have implications for the growth in the number of food products, or the boom in convenient dessert options. Temptation aversion is supported by food psychology research suggesting that a greater variety of foods leads to greater consumption (e.g., Miller et al. 2000).

Individuals may use mental tricks to resist temptation, like exaggerating the consequences of giving in to temptation. New York City recently required chain restaurants to display calorie content for food menu items, in hopes that the health information would improve diets. Both laboratory and field experiments show little impact of the new information, except on those who are dieting. Those dieting tend to consume *more* calories when the information is present (Downs, Loewenstein, and Wisdom 2009). Further, providing entering customers with the per meal recommended consumption of calories had little effect overall, though it increased the calorie consumption of dieters. Apparently dieters are pleasantly surprised by the low calorie content and feel more at ease in purchasing more than they otherwise would. Information has been found to have perverse effects in several settings. For example, people eating at an Italian restaurant knew that dipping bread in olive oil would increase the fat content relative to spreading butter on the bread. However, they were unaware that those who used butter tended to overcompensate by eating 23 percent more bread during the course of the meal (Wansink and Linder 2003).

One popular behavioral policy mechanism is the setting of defaults. In situations where a choice may be made passively on a one-time basis, a policymaker can often influence individual choice by setting a default option that one must opt out of if they wish. In this case, the default becomes a point of reference, and the individual's utility for consuming the good depends on whether it has default status or not. Default choices have been shown to lead people to donate organs (Johnson and Goldstein 2003), make investments (e.g., Choi et al. 2003), and select insurance plans they would not otherwise have considered (Kahneman, Knetsch, and Thaler 1991).

Unfortunately, food choices are made hundreds of times a day (Wansink and Sobal 2007), and usually require some active (though potentially habitual) decision-making. Thus, defaults may not work very well. Price and Just (2009) show this using data from school lunches. Schools may either set a default that a school lunch will not include a vegetable unless the child requests one, or that the school lunch includes the vegetable unless the child opts out. While the default has a predictably large impact on the number of children taking vegetables, the number consuming vegetables increases by only around 1 percent while the amount of food wastage increases by more than 40 percent. Although more difficult to implement, Wansink, Just, and Payne (2009) show that much stronger effects on behavior can be obtained in everyday food settings by introducing behavioral interrupts, or by creating inconsequential differences in how foods may be purchased (e.g., payment methods). Such mechanisms can lead to better eating while maintaining the perception that choices were not influenced by the policymaker.

2.4   Mental Accounting and Food

Thaler (1980, 2004) partially based his theory of mental accounting on the prospect theory model of decision-making. Mental accounting supposes behavior is determined by three components: (1) transaction utility; (2) the categorization of income for spending purposes; and (3) the frequency with which accounts are balanced. Transaction utility refers to whether the individual feels they received more or less than they paid for. Just and Wansink (2011) find that individuals show a strong reaction to transaction utility when patronizing an all-you-can-eat pizza buffet. In this case, doubling the price of the meal increased consumption by about one slice (25 percent) on average. Further, they find evidence that those who disliked the food actually consumed more. Apparently it takes more bad pizza to get your money's worth than good. This illustrates one way in which pricing can have unintuitive impacts on consumption.

Additionally, individuals tend to categorize their income into mental accounts, marking it for future spending. Thaler proposes that individuals use mental accounts as a type of self-control device, to enforce forward-looking good behavior on themselves (for example, limiting the amount of money one will spend on a single occasion of dining out). However, he notes that the device is an imperfect heuristic that can be short-circuited by certain situations. Income sources seen as one-time events are viewed as more frivolous (such as tax refunds) and are subsequently earmarked for more frivolous consumption (like plasma televisions). The idea that money is not fungible but is set aside for a specific purpose is engrained in our vocabulary early on with phrases like "lunch money." The idea of earmarking funds and mental accounts may partially explain why several studies have found that among food stamp recipients, coupons that can only be used for food purchases are more effective at raising food expenditures than an equal benefit amount given as cash even when both coupons and cash are used on food (Fox, Hamilton, and Lin 2004). This is contrary to rational economic theory, which predicts that cash and coupons would have the same effect so long as the budget for food exceeds the amount given.

Mental accounting builds on the notion of framing (Tversky and Kahneman 1981) embodied in the prospect theory model. A policymaker can lead individuals to alternative choices by manipulating the phrasing or the comparisons of outcomes. For example, Tversky and Kahneman pose two identical questions regarding health policies, though one mentions the number of people who will die under a particular policy and the other mentions the number of people who will be saved. Such simple turns of phrase can have a big impact on individual evaluations. Food demand for snack foods is generally price inelastic (Kuchler, Tegene, and Harris 2005 find price elasticities for snack products ranging from −0.2 to −0.5 using retail scanner data). However, French et al. (1997) find that within a vending machine, lowering the prices on only the low-fat foods by 50 percent increased the purchase of low-fat snacks by more than 20 percent. This result falls within the upper range of previous estimates of price responsiveness for snack foods. Such a result may not be possible without having regular-priced foods with which to compare.

3   NOT ONLY WHAT, BUT HOW MUCH

As with food choice, psychologists have found that environmental factors can have very large impacts on consumption volume, most often without the individual being aware of the effect (see Wansink 2004 for a complete review of the consumption volume literature). Environmental factors affect consumption volume through two primary mechanisms. First, some factors may work to set a suggested consumption quantity—or consumption norm. Second, some environmental factors may inhibit consumption monitoring accuracy, leading the individual to consume more than they wish to.

Environmental factors are often discussed in terms of the eating environment and the food environment. The eating environment consists of the set of objects surrounding the individual while they eat excluding the presentation of the food itself. This may include factors such as the lighting, the people present, a television, or a book. The food environment includes those items immediate to the serving of the food. This may include packaging, plates and dishes, or serving spoons. Both the food and eating environments may be important drivers of food marketing behavior. Given the control restaurants and food manufacturers have over these factors, there is likely some level of interaction between marketer profit motive and consumer response to environment (Just and Payne 2009). This is an area of research that deserves some attention by economists.

3.1   The Eating Environment, Social Norms, and Distractions

The people one chooses to eat with form one of the most important factors within the eating environment. In general, people tend to eat amounts that are similar to others when eating in a group (de Castro 1994; Birch and Fisher 2000). Thus, social norms may be very important in determining food behaviors (see Akerlof 1980 for an economic model of social norms). Alternatively, individuals may also alter what they eat owing to the distraction of conversation. Social gatherings tend to extend the length of meals, leading to greater consumption volume (Bell and Pliner 2003)—the larger the gathering, the more food is eaten (de Castro and Brewer 1992). When eating with an unfamiliar group, like on a first date or in a job interview, individuals may eat less (Mori, Chaiken, and Pliner 1987; Chaiken and Pliner 1990; Stroebele and de Castro 2004). Alluding to the strength of social norms, social gatherings tend to decrease the variance of consumption (Clendennen, Herman, and Polivy 1994). There is some evidence that obese people are more subject to such social effects (Herman, Olmsted, and Polivy 1983).

Distractions in the eating environment reduce an individual's ability to monitor how much they eat, leading them to consume more than they would otherwise. A distraction may take the form of reading (Tuomisto et al. 1998), watching television (Poothullil 2002), or other similar activities. A primary factor in consumption volume is whether an individual was paying attention to how much he or she ate (Polivy et al. 1986; Arkes 1991). More often, food consumption will be determined using simple rules of thumb (e.g., I will eat one bowlfull), which may have unintended consequences in unfamiliar settings.

3.2   The Food Environment and Food Marketing

Factors within the food environment are particularly relevant to economic models of consumption because they can often be controlled by manufacturers. It is possible to overcome monitoring problems to a degree by introducing food or food packaging that makes monitoring easier. For example, individually wrapping items tends to reduce consumption (Wansink 2004). Introducing more intermediate packaging in containers of chips or other items bought in large quantities draws attention to the consumption volume, making it easier for the individual to determine an appropriate stopping point. A related phenomenon reduces the amount people eat by introducing very small inconvenience in consumption. Even placing candies a couple steps from one's desk can significantly reduce the volume of consumption (by five to six chocolates a day; see Painter, Wansink, and Hieggelke 2002). There is some evidence that obese individuals may be more responsive to small amounts of required effort (e.g., Schachter, Friedman, and Handler 1974).

Foods placed where one can see them induces salience, serving as a constant reminder of a pleasurable experience. Salience may also be generated internally through craving or imagining the food. Internally generated salience leads to greater consumption volume than externally generated salience. For example, individuals who happen to walk by a cookie dish, and impulsively decide to eat, report eating fewer cookies than those who deliberately seek out the cookies (Wansink 1994). Salience can be manipulated by food marketers through pictorial depictions (so-called "food porn") and descriptions of food. Those asked to describe the last time they consumed soup tended to consume more than twice as much soup within the next two weeks than did a control group that was not asked (Wansink and Deshpande 1994).

Offering a greater variety of a particular food will lead to increased consumption volume (Rolls, Rowe, et al. 1981; Rolls 1986; Miller et al. 2000). In fact, increasing the perception of variety, holding actual variety constant, significantly increases consumption volume. For example, increasing the number of colors of M&M candies in a bowl from seven to ten increases consumption volume by 43 percent (Kahn and Wansink 2004). This, despite the fact that all M&M candies taste identical. Similarly, presenting subjects with Jellybeans that are mixed rather than sorted by color increased consumption by 69 percent (Kahn and Wansink 2004).

One popular explanation for the increase in obesity in the United States is the dramatically increased portion sizes (Young and Nestle 2002; Rolls 2003). In short, people eat more when they are presented with larger packages or portions of food (Nisbett 1968; Edelman et al. 1986; Wansink 1996; Rolls, Morris, and Roe 2002; Diliberti et al. 2004; Rolls, Roe, et al. 2004). This can be a substantial effect, increasing consumption up to 45 percent for a doubling of the portions (Wansink 1996). This result holds even if the food itself tastes poor (Wansink and Kim 2004). The package or portion size works to create a consumption norm, and individuals tend to judge their level of satiety based on their consumption in relation to this norm, much like a reference point. Those eating more owing to large package sizes more severely underestimate their own consumption (Wansink 1996). Wansink and Chandon (2006) find that, in general, the larger the meal, the more the individual underestimates the amount of food they have eaten. This underestimation of calories is not related to body size. As opposed to the visual cues, individuals do not appear to make decisions about when to stop eating based directly on the number of calories they have consumed (Rolls, Castellanos, et al. 1998; Rolls, Bell, and Waugh 2000; Rolls, Morris, and Roe 2002). Thus, one may be just as likely to finish an entire bowl of high-calorie dense soup as they are to finish a visually identical bowl of low-calorie dense soup.

Lastly, the shape and size of serving containers, such as bowls, plates, and glasses, can significantly affect the volume of consumption. While the common wisdom that larger serving containers leads to greater amounts served and greater consumption is true (Wansink, Painter, and van Ittersum 2006), the relationship in general is a little more complex. The height of a glass seems to matter more in consumption than its width (Piaget, 1969; Raghubir and Krishna 1999; Krider, Raghubir, and Krishna 2001). Portion sizes and dish size and shape suggest a normative consumption volume to the individual consumer. These norms can be highly effective in suggesting individual behavior.

4   TASTE AND PREFERENCE

Much work has been done to determine how individuals form perceptions of taste. An individual's evaluation of taste appears to depend upon appearance (Tuorila et al. 1998), name (Wansink, Shimizu, and Payne 2009), price (Just and Wansink 2011), brand (Cardello and Sawyer 1992), or information and descriptions given by others (Tuorila et al. 1998). Careful experimentation has revealed that those predisposed to think an item will taste good will give *ex post* evaluations that are on average better than those by individuals who expected an item to taste poor (Cardello and Sawyer 1992; Tuorila et al. 1998).

Much like confirmation bias (Mynatt, Doherty, and Tweney 1977), individuals tend to reaffirm their prior beliefs regarding the taste of a new food. Cardello and Sawyer (1992) told groups of subjects that they would be sampling a brand of juice from a new tropical fruit. Several groups were told that others had tried the juice previously and had either "liked it very much," "disliked it very much," or "neither liked nor disliked it," depending on treatment group. Groups told that others had disliked the juice expected not to like it, and on average did not like it themselves. Those with low expectations tended to revise them upward, and those with high expectations tended to revise them downward. However, these revisions did not eliminate the effect of the expectations implanted by researchers. Subjects' expectations about the overall experience biased their *ex post* analysis of taste sensations (like sweetness) that had not been mentioned in the pre-taste information. Thus, individual utility of consumption may have more to do with individual perceptions of the attributes of the good rather than the actual expressed attributes.

The food environment can have a similar impact on taste. When food is either presented on nicer serving plates, or given positive descriptive names, the individual will evaluate the food to have tasted better. For example, Wansink, van Ittersum, and Painter (2005) find that customers ordering the "Succulent Italian Seafood Filet" rated it as much tastier than did customers ordering the "Seafood Filet," though the dishes were identical. Such presentation cues can have spillover effects upon consumption and evaluation of other foods as well. Those consuming a complementary glass of wine labeled "New from California" ate 12 percent more of their accompanying meal and rated it more highly than those receiving a glass of the same wine from a bottle labeled "New from North Dakota" (Wansink, Payne, and North 2007).

Ex post evaluations of an eating experience can also be influenced by the number of choices available. Iyengar and Lepper (2000) conducted a series of experiments to test the impact of the number of choices on consumer experience. For example, in one experiment shoppers at a gourmet grocery encountered a table where they could sample various jams—either six varieties or twenty-four varieties. While a greater percentage of shoppers stopped when the larger number of varieties was present (60 percent versus 40 percent), those sampling from the larger choice set were much less likely eventually to purchase the jam (3 percent versus 30 percent). In a similar experiment, participants in the larger choice set treatment reported a lower taste rating of the chocolates they had chosen, and a greater feeling of regret regarding their choice. Boatwright and Nunes (2001) use a natural experiment in which the number of products in a supermarket was cut dramatically, leading to an 11 percent increase in sales. While general support has been found for the impact of choice on *ex post* taste evaluation (e.g., Chernev 2003), there has been substantial debate about whether consumers prefer less choice *ex ante* or are more likely to purchase given less choice (see Arunachalam et al. 2009).

5   CONCLUSION

Behavioral economic relationships are important both for their ability to describe individual motivations more credibly, but also for the variation in policy options they suggest relative to more traditional economic relationships. For example, in addressing an increase in obesity, traditional economic tools suggest imposing taxes or subsidies on various foods, perhaps banning some foods, or providing more accurate information. Alternatively, behavioral tools broaden the scope of economic policy to include the environmental cues, packaging, placement, and types of information or other issues that frame the food consumption decision. Importantly, because individuals appear to be unaware of the influence of environmental cues, these policy tools provide the opportunity to make the individual better off in their own estimation, without creating the type of resistance that is common with a sin tax.

Most of the economic consequences of food behavior have yet to be analyzed. To date the literature focuses almost entirely on the individual decision, and not on how the decision process influences the structure of food offerings and marketing. Food marketers focus substantial resources researching the impact of packaging, marketing, and content of their products. Individual decision makers are unaware of these behavioral relationships, but owing to research and experimentation, marketers may behave as if they are aware of the underlying relationships. Future research is needed to understand exactly how firms' profit motives interact with individual behavior. This is a complex issue that will require behavioral work to extend beyond the laboratory. The government already regulates the types of health claim that can be made, yet we understand little of how they are interpreted by the individual consumers. Further, we know that package sizes influence consumption volume, but what about propensity to purchase in the first place? By isolating the motivations and objectives of firms and food consumers, behavioral research has an opportunity to make substantial contributions to the regulation and functioning of the food marketplace.

References

Akerlof, G. A. 1980. "A Theory of Social Custom, of Which Unemployment May Be One Consequence." *Quarterly Journal of Economics* 94/4: 749–75.

Arkes, H. R. 1991. "Costs and Benefits of Judgment Errors: Implications for Debiasing." *Psychological Bulletin* 110/3: 489–98.

Arunachalam, B., S. R. Henneberry, J. L. Lusk, and F. B. Norwood. 2009. "An Empirical Investigation into the Excessive-Choice Effect." *American Journal of Agricultural Economics* 91/3: 810–25.

Bazerman, M. H., A. E. Tenbrunsel, and K. Wade-Benzoni. 1998. "Negotiating with Yourself and Losing: Understanding and Managing Conflicting Internal Preferences." *Academy of Management Review* 23/2: 225–41.

Becker, G. S., and K. M. Murphy 1988. "A Theory of Rational Addiction." *Journal of Political Economy* 96/4: 675–700.

Bell, R., and P. L. Pliner. 2003. "Time to Eat: The Relationship between the Number of People Eating and Meal Duration in Three Lunch Settings." *Appetite* 41/2: 215–18.

Benartzi, S., and R. H. Thaler. 1995. "Myopic Loss Aversion and the Equity Premium Puzzle." *Quarterly Journal of Economics* 110/1: 73–92.

Bertrand, M., and D. Whitmore-Schanzenback. 2009. "Time Use and Food Consumption." *American Economic Review* 99/2: 170–6.

Birch, L. L., and J. O. Fisher. 2000. "Mother's Child-Feeding Practices Influence Daughters' Eating and Weight." *American Journal of Clinical Nutrition* 71/5: 1054–61.

Boatwright, P., and J. C. Nunes. 2001. "Reducing Assortment: An Attribute-Based Approach." *Journal of Marketing* 65/3: 50–63.

Boon, B., W. Stroebe, H. Schut, and A. Jansen. 1998. "Food for Thought: Cognitive Regulation of Food Intake." *British Journal of Health Psychology* 3/1: 27–40.

Borghans, L., and B. H. H. Golsteyn. 2006. "Time Discounting and the Body Mass Index: Evidence from the Netherlands." *Economics and Human Biology* 4/1: 39–61.

Brito, D. L., and C. K. Strain. 1996. "A Model of the Consumption of Alcohol." In L. Green and J. H. Kagel, eds, *Substance Use and Abuse, Advances in Behavioral Economics*, 3. Norwood, NJ: Ablex.

Cardello, A. V., and F. M. Sawyer. 1992. "Effects of Disconfirmed Consumer Expectations on Food Acceptability." *Journal of Sensory Studies* 7/4: 253–77.

Chaiken, S., and P. Pliner. 1990. "Eating, Social Motives, and Self Presentation in Women and Men." *Journal of Experimental Social Psychology* 26/3: 240–54.

Chernev, A. 2003. "When More Is Less and Less Is More: The Role of Ideal Point Availability and Assortment in Consumer Choice." *Journal of Consumer Research* 30/2: 170–83.

Choi, J. J., D. Laibson, B. C. Madrian, and A. Metrick. 2003. "Optimal Defaults." *American Economic Review* 93/2: 180–5.

Clendennen, V., C. P. Herman, and J. Polivy. 1994. "Social Facilitation of Eating among Friends and Strangers." *Appetite* 23/1: 1–13.

Cornell, C. E., J. Rodin, and H. Weingarten. 1989. "Stimulus-Induced Eating When Satiated." *Physiology and Behavior* 45: 695–704.

Cutrona, C. E., D. W. Russel, and J. Rose. 1986. "Social Support and Adaptation to Stress by the Elderly." *Journal of Psychology and Aging* 1/1: 47–54.

deCastro, J. M. 1994. "Family and Friends Produce Greater Social Facilitation of Food Intake than Other Companions." *Physiology and Behavior* 56/3: 445–55.

——and E. Brewer. 1992. "The Amount Eaten in Meals by Humans Is a Power Function of the Number of People Present." *Physiology and Behavior* 51/1: 121–5.

Diliberti, N., P. L. Bordi, M. T. Conklin, L. S. Roe, and B. J. Rolls. 2004. "Increased Portion Size Leads to Increased Energy Intake in a Restaurant Meal." *Obesity Research* 12/3: 562–8.

Downs, J. S., G. Loewenstein, and J. Wisdom. 2009. "Strategies for Promoting Healthier Food Choices." *American Economic Review* 99/2: 159–64.

Edelman, B., D. Engell, P. Bronstein, and E. Hirsch. 1986. "Environmental Effects on the Intake of Overweight and Normal-Weight Men." *Appetite* 7/1: 71–83.

Epstein, S. 1993. "Emotion and Self-Theory." In M. Lewis and J. M. Haviland, eds, *Handbook of Emotions*. New York: Guilford.

Fisher, E. B., Jr. 1996. "A Behavioral-Economic Perspective on the Influence of Social Support on Cigarette Smoking." In L. Green and J. H. Kagel, eds, *Substance Use and Abuse, Advances in Behavioral Economics*, 3. Norwood, NJ: Ablex.

Fox, M. K., W. Hamilton, and B.-H. Lin, eds. 2004. *Effects of Food Assistance and Nutrition Programs on Nutrition and Health*, 3: *Literature Review*. Food Assistance and Nutrition Research Report No. 19-3. Washington, DC: Economic Research Service, US Department of Agriculture.

French, S. A., R. W. Jeffery, M. Story, P. Hannan, and M. P. Snyder. 1997. "A Pricing Strategy to Promote Low-Fat Snack Choices through Vending Machines." *American Journal of Public Health* 87: 849–51.

Gul, F., and W. Pesendorfer. 2001. "Temptation and Self-Control." *Econometrica* 69/6: 1403–36.

————. 2004. "Self-Control, Revealed Preference and Consumption Choice." *Review of Economic Dynamics* 7/2: 243–64.

Herman, C. P., M. P. Olmsted, and J. Polivy. 1983. "Obesity, Externality, and Susceptibility to Social Influence: An Integrated Analysis." *Journal of Personality and Social Psychology* 45: 926–34.

Hirshman, E. C., and M. B. Holbrook. 1982. "Hedonic Consumption: Emerging Concepts, Methods and Propositions." *Journal of Marketing* 46/3: 92–101.

Hu, W., W. L. Adamowicz, and M. M. Veeman. 2006. "Labeling Context and Reference Point Effects in Models of Food Attribute Demand." *American Journal of Agricultural Economics* 88/4: 1034–49.

Iyengar, S. S., and M. R. Lepper. 2000. "When Choice Is Demotivating: Can One Desire Too Much of a Good Thing?" *Journal of Personality and Social Psychology* 79/6: 995–1006.

Johnson, E. J., and D. G. Goldstein. 2003. "Do Defaults Save Lives?" *Science* 302/1338: 1338–9.

Just, D. R., and C. Payne. 2009. "Obesity: Can Behavioral Economics Help?" *Annals of Behavioral Medicine* 38/S1: 47–55.

—— and B. Wansink. 2011. "The Flat-Rate Pricing Paradox: Conflicting Effects of 'All-You-Can-Eat' Buffet Pricing." *Review of Economics and Statistics* 93/1: 193–200.

—— ——, L. Mancino, and J. Guthrie. 2008. *Behavioral Economic Concepts to Encourage Healthy Eating in School Cafeterias: Experiments and Lessons from College Students.* Economic Research Report No. 68. Washington, DC: Economic Research Service, US Department of Agriculture, Dec.

Kahn, B. E., and B. Wansink. 2004. "The Influence of Assortment Structure on Perceived Variety and Consumption Quantities." *Journal of Consumer Research* 30/4: 519–33.

Kahneman, D., and A. Tversky. 1979. "Prospect Theory: An Analysis of Decision under Risk." *Econometrica* 47/2: 263–91.

——, J. L. Knetsch, and R. Thaler. 1991. "Anomalies: The Endowment Effect, Loss Aversion and the Status Quo Bias." *Journal of Economic Perspectives* 5/1: 193–206.

Komlos, J., P. K. Smith, and B. Bogin. 2004. "Obesity and the Rate of Time Preference: Is There a Connection?" *Journal of Biosocial Science* 36/2: 209–19.

Krider, R. E., P. Raghubir, and A. Krishna. 2001. "Pizzas: π or Square? Psychological Biases in Area Comparisons." *Marketing Science* 20/4: 405–25.

Kuchler, F., A. Tegene, and J. M. Harris. 2005. "Taxing Snack Foods: Manipulating Diet Quality or Financing Information Programs?" *Review of Agricultural Economics* 27/1: 4–20.

Laibson, D. 1997. "Golden Eggs and Hyperbolic Discounting." *Quarterly Journal of Economics* 112/2: 443–77.

Levine, D. K. 2009. "Is Behavioral Economics Doomed? The Ordinary versus the Extraordinary." Max Weber Lecture, European University Institute, Florence, June 8.

Loewenstein, G. 2004. "Out of Control: Visceral Influences of Behavior." In C. F. Camerer, G. Loewenstein, and M. Rabin, eds, *Advances in Behavioral Economics*. Princeton: Princeton University Press.

—— T. O'Donoghue, and M. Rabin. 2003. "Projection Bias in Predicting Future Utility." *Quarterly Journal of Economics* 118/4: 1209–48.

Mancino, L. 2003. "Americans' Food Choices: The Interaction of Information, Intentions and Convenience." Ph.D. diss. University of Minnesota.

—— and J. Kinsey. 2004. "Diet Quality and Calories Consumed: The Impact of Being Hungrier, Busier, and Eating Out." Working Paper No. 04–02. St Paul: Food Industry Center, University of Minnesota.

Meyers, A. W., A. J. Stunkard, and M. Coll. 1980. "Food Accessibility and Food Choice: A Test of Schachter's Externality Hypothesis." *Archives of General Psychology* 37/10: 1133–5.

Miller, D. L., E. A. Bell, C. L. Pelkman, J. C. Peters, and B. J. Rolls. 2000. "Effects of Dietary Fat, Nutrition Labels, and Repeated Consumption on Sensor-Specific Satiety." *Physiology and Behavior* 71/1–2: 153–8.

Mitchell, G. 2003. "Tendencies versus Boundaries: Levels of Generality in Behavioral Law and Economics." *Vanderbilt Law Review* 56/6: 1781–1812.

Mori, D., S. Chaiken, and P. Pliner. 1987. "'Eating Lightly' and the Self-Presentation of Femininity." *Journal of Personality and Social Psychology* 53/4: 693–702.

Mynatt, C. R., M. E. Doherty, and R. D. Tweney. 1977. "Confirmation Bias in a Simulated Research Environment: An Experimental Study of Scientific Inference." *Quarterly Journal of Experimental Psychology* 29/1: 85–95.

Mytton, O., A. Gray, M. Rayner, and H. Rutter. 2007. "Could Targeted Food Taxes Improve Health?" *Journal of Epidemiology and Community Health* 61/8: 689–94.

Nisbett, R. E. 1968. "Determinants of Food Intake in Obesity." *Science* 159/3820: 1254–5.

O'Donoghue, T., and M. Rabin. 2004. "Doing it Now or Later." In C. F. Camerer, G. Loewenstein, and M. Rabin, eds, *Advances in Behavioral Economics*. Princeton: Princeton University Press.

Painter, J. E., B. Wansink, and J. B. Hieggelke. 2002. "How Visibility and Convenience Influence Candy Consumption." *Appetite* 38/3: 237–8.

Piaget, J. 1969. *The Mechanisms of Perception*. London: Routledge & Kegan Paul.

Polivy, J., C. P. Herman, R. Hackett, and I. Kuleshnyk. 1986. "The Effects of Self-Attention and Public Attention on Eating in Restrained and Unrestrained Subjects." *Journal of Personality and Social Psychology* 50/6: 1203–24.

Poothullil, J. M. 2002. "Role of Oral Sensory Signals in Determining Meal Size in Lean Women." *Nutrition Review* 44/3: 93–101.

Price, J. P., and D. R. Just. 2009. "Active versus Passive Defaults: Evidence from School Lunchrooms." Working Paper. Provo, UT: Department of Economics, Brigham Young University.

Raghubir, P., and A. Krishna. 1999. "Vital Dimensions in Volume Perception: Can the Eye Fool the Stomach?" *Journal of Marketing Research* 36/3: 313–26.

Richards, T. J., P. M. Patterson, and A. Tegene. 2007. "Obesity and Nutrient Consumption: A Rational Addiction?" *Contemporary Economic Policy* 25/3: 309–24.

Rolls, B. J. 1986. "Sensory-Specific Satiety." *Nutrition Reviews* 44: 93–101.

—— 2003. "The Supersizing of America: Portion Size and the Obesity Epidemic." *Nutrition Today* 38/2: 645–9.

——, E. A. Bell, and B. A. Waugh. 2000. "Increasing the Volume of a Food by Incorporating Air Affects Satiety in Men." *American Journal of Clinical Nutrition* 72: 361–8.

——, V. H. Castellanos, J. C. Halford, A. Kilars, D. Panyam, et al. 1998. "Volume of Food Consumed Affects Satiety in Men." *American Journal of Clinical Nutrition* 67: 1170–7.

——, E. L. Morris, and L. S. Roe. 2002. "Portion Size of Food Affects Energy Intake in Normal-Weight and Overweight Men and Women." *American Journal of Clinical Nutrition* 76/6: 1207–13.

——, L. S. Roe, T. V. E. Kral, J. S. Meengs, and D. E. Wall. 2004. "Increasing the Portion Size of a Packaged Snack Increases Energy Intake in Men and Women." *Appetite* 42/1: 63–9.

——, E. A. Rowe, E. T. Rolls, B. Kingston, A. Megson, and R. Gunary. 1981. "Variety in a Meal Enhances Food Intake in Man." *Physiology and Behavior* 26/2: 215–21.

Schacter, S., L. N. Friedman, and J. Handler. 1974. "Who Eats with Chopsticks?" In S. Schachter and J. Rodin, eds, *Obese Humans and Rats*. Potomac, MD: Laurence Erlbaum.

Scharff, R. L. 2009. "Obesity and Hyperbolic Discounting: Evidence and Implications." *Journal of Consumer Policy* 32/1: 3–21.

Shiv, B., and A. Fedorikhin. 1999. "Heart and Mind in Conflict: Interplay of Affect and Cognition in Consumer Decision Making." *Journal of Consumer Research* 26/3: 278–82.

Smith, D. E., M. D. Marcus, C. E. Lewis, M. Fitzgibbon, and P. Schreiner. 1998. "Prevalence of Binge Eating Disorder, Obesity, and Depression in a Biracial Cohort of Young Adults." *Annals of Behavioral Medicine* 20/3: 227–32.

Strahilevitz, M. A., and J. G. Myers. 1998. "Donations to Charity as Purchase Incentives: How Well They Work May Depend on What You Are Trying to Sell." *Journal of Consumer Research* 24/4: 434–46.

Stroebele, N., and J. M. deCastro. 2004. "The Effect of Ambience on Food Intake and Food Choice." *Nutrition* 20/9: 821–38.

Strotz, R. H. 1955. "Myopia and Inconsistency in Dynamic Utility Maximization." *Review of Economic Studies* 23/3: 165–80.

Thaler, R. H. 1980. "Toward a Positive Theory of Consumer Choice." *Journal of Economic Behavior and Organization* 1/1: 39–60.

——and H. M. Shefrin. 1981. "An Economic Theory of Self Control." *Journal of Political Economy* 89/2: 392–406.

——and C. R. Sunstein. 2003. "Libertarian Paternalism." *American Economic Review* 93/2: 175–9.

Tucker, J. A. 2003. "Contributions of Behavioral Economics for Understanding and Resolving Substance Use Disorders." In P. Rosenquist, J. Bloqvist, A. Koski-Jännes, and L. Öjesjö, eds, *Addiction and Life Course*. Helsinki: Nordic Council for Alcohol and Drug Research.

Tuomisto, T., M. T. Tuomisto, M. Hetherington, and R. Lappalainen. 1998. "Reasons for Initiation and Cessation of Eating in Obese Men and Women and the Affective Consequences of Eating in Everyday Situations." *Appetite* 30/2: 211–22.

Tuorila, H. M., H. L. Meiselman, A. V. Cardello, and L. L. Lecher. 1998. "Effect of Expectations and the Definition of Product Category on the Acceptance of Unfamiliar Foods." *Food Quality and Preference* 9/6: 421–30.

Tversky, A., and D. Kahneman. 1981. "The Framing of Decisions and the Psychology of Choice." *Science* 211/4481: 453–8.

————. 1991. "Loss Aversion in Riskless Choice: A Reference-Dependent Model." *Quarterly Journal of Economics* 106/4: 1039–61.

————. 1992. "Advances in Prospect Theory: Cumulative Representation of Uncertainty." *Journal of Risk and Uncertainty* 5/4: 297–323.

Volkow, N. D., G. J. Wang, J. S. Fowler, J. Logan, M. Jayne, D. Franceschi, C. Wong, S. J. Gatley, A. N. Gifford, Y. S. Ding, and N. Pappas. 2002. "'Non-Hedonic' Food Motivation in Humans Involves Dopamine in the Dorsal Striatum and Methylphenidate Amplifies this Effect." *Synapse* 44/3: 175–80.

Wansink, B. 1994. "Antecedents and Mediators of Eating Bouts." *Family and Consumer Sciences Research Journal* 23/2: 166–82.

——1996. "Can Package Size Accelerate Consumption Volume?" *Journal of Marketing* 60/3: 1–14.

——2004. "Environmental Factors that Increase the Food Intake and Consumption Volume of Unknowing Consumers." *Annual Review of Nutrition* 24/1: 455–79.

——and P. Chandon. 2006. "Meal Size, Not Body Size, Explains Errors in Estimating the Calorie Content of Meals." *Annals of Internal Medicine* 145: 326–32.

——and R. Deshpande. 1994. "'Out of Sight Out of Mind': The Impact of Household Stockpiling on Usage Rates." *Marketing Letters* 5/1: 91–100.

——and J. Kim. 2004. "Bad Popcorn in Big Buckets: Portion Size Can Influence Intake as Much as Taste." *Journal of Nutrition Education Behavior* 37/5: 242–5.

——and L. R. Linder. 2003. "Interactions between Forms of Fat Consumption and Restaurant Bread Consumption." *International Journal of Obesity* 27/7: 866–8.

——and J. Sobal. 2007. "Mindless Eating: The 200 Daily Food Decisions We Overlook." *Environment and Behavior* 39/1: 106–23.

——K. van Ittersum, and J. E. Painter. 2005. "How Descriptive Food Names Bias Sensory Perceptions in Restaurants." *Food Quality and Preference* 16/5: 393–400.

Wansink, B., D. R. Just, and C. R. Payne. 2009. *Constrained Volition and Everyday Defaults*. Working Paper. Ithaca, NY: Applied Economics and Management, Cornell University.

——, J. E. Painter, and K. van Ittersum. 2006. "Ice Cream Illusions: Bowl Size, Spoon Size, and Serving Size." *American Journal of Preventative Medicine* 145/5: 240–3.

——, C. R. Payne, and J. North. 2007. "Fine as North Dakota Wine: Sensory Expectations and the Intake of Companion Foods." *Physiology and Behavior* 90/5: 712–16.

——, M. Shimizu, and C. R. Payne. 2009. *The Impact of Names and Icons on Preschooler's Intake of Fruits and Vegetables*. Working Paper. Ithaca, NY: Department of Applied Economics and Management, Cornell University.

Wilde, P. E., and C. K. Ranney. 2000. "The Monthly Food Stamp Cycle: Shopping Frequency and Food Intake Decisions in an Endogenous Switching Regression Framework." *American Journal of Agricultural Economics* 82: 200–13.

Young, L. R., and M. Nestle. 2002. "The Contribution of Expanding Portions Size to the US Obesity Epidemic." *American Journal of Public Health* 92/2: 246–9.

CHAPTER 5

....

DISCRETE CHOICE THEORY
AND MODELING

....

W. L. (VIC) ADAMOWICZ
AND JOFFRE D. SWAIT

1 INTRODUCTION

....

Empirical models of food demand have traditionally been estimated using aggregate time series data. Demand systems versions of these models were commonly based on forms of the almost ideal demand system framework (Deaton and Muellbauer 1980) and employed variation over time periods (and, at times, spatial variation) to provide estimates of price and income elasticities. While these became very popular models for food demand analysis in the 1980s and 1990s, emphasis in recent years has changed to employing disaggregate data and to assessing demand using discrete choice models.

Disaggregate demand analysis, or microeconometric analysis, has its roots in McFadden's research on individual travel decisions that began in the early 1970s (McFadden 2001). Employing individual-level data provided richness about decision-making that was masked in aggregate time-series data. Aggregation assumptions and assumptions regarding representative consumers or homogeneity of preferences could be relaxed. Consumer responses to prices and non-price characteristics (attributes) were incorporated in a single framework. Researchers could examine the effects of brands or brand loyalty as well as brand- or product-specific advertising. Disaggregation to the level of individual choices, however, required a different form of analysis—one that examined not the quantity purchased or the expenditure share, but the assessment of factors affecting *choices*.

Discrete analysis of food choices can be grouped into two main areas: analysis that focuses on the consumer to assess preferences and welfare, and analysis that focuses on assessing consumer behavior to provide marketing or sales strategies. Both share the underpinnings of consumer demand theory and discrete choice econometrics, but they emphasize different features of the process.

Much of the food demand literature employing discrete choice analysis has focused on novel traits or food attributes with the objective of measuring the welfare effects or willingness to pay for these traits. Examples include the numerous studies examining credence attributes—including genetic modification and food choices (e.g., Hu, Adamowicz, and Veeman 2006; Carlsson, Frykblom, and Lagerkvist 2007a); preferences for organic food products (e.g., Krystallis, Fotopoulos, and Zotos 2006; Gracia and de Magistris 2008); and preferences over methods of production and animal welfare (Lagerkvist, Carlsson, and Viske 2006; Carlsson, Frykblom, and Lagerkvist 2007b; Liljenstolpe 2008). Attributes describing food safety or health risk (e.g., McCluskey et al. 2005; Loureiro and Umberger 2007) and country-of-origin labels (e.g., Ehmke, Lusk, and Tyner 2008 provides a review of this literature; see Volinskiy et al. 2009 for an example) have also been analyzed in these types of study. In this strand of the literature researchers use discrete choice models to analyze individual choices of food options characterized by various attributes including the credence attributes, risk characteristics, and other features of food. The papers in this area often employ stated preference methods (choice experiments or contingent valuation) that provide consumers with product descriptions, or they analyze the results of experiments in which consumers make actual purchases in controlled settings (e.g., Lusk and Schroeder 2004; Volinskiy et al. 2009). The results provide measures of the marginal value of attributes, including the marginal value of the credence good or novel trait under investigation (see Carlsson, Chapter 7 in this volume).

Other studies frame the issue as one of understanding consumer behavior in order to assess marketing actions, e.g., impacts of advertising or other strategies that affect returns to firms. This area of literature tends to employ scanner panel data—data collected by scanners in retail outlets—to assess consumer demand. Individual-level choices of food products are usually examined in the context of store-level variables (products available, prices, and advertising signals). Alternatively, household-level data from home scanning of purchases can be employed. A classic example of this type of approach is Erdem and Keane (1996), in which a dynamic discrete choice model is estimated from scanner panel data in order to assess marketing mix strategies—specifically advertising effort. Other examples of scanner data analysis of food products include Erdem, Imai, and Keane (2003), in which demand for ketchup brands are explored, and Keane (1997), who also examines ketchup brands but focuses on dynamic elements of consumer behavior.

Scanner data has also been used to assess consumer preferences and welfare. Gould and Dong (2000) examine cheese demand using scanner data and Richards (2000) investigates fruit demand using scanner data and incorporates both discrete and continuous components of demand. In an interesting recent application, Richards, Patterson, and Tegene (2007) use Homescan™ data to assess the possible addictive properties of components of snack foods.

As the short review of the literature presented above illustrates, discrete choice models of food demand have been estimated from a variety of data sources: choice experiments (or hypothetical choice data), experimental economic data (experimental auctions), and scanner panel data. Data fusion (combining data sources) has also been employed in disaggregate analysis of grocery items (Swait and Andrews 2003), but we do not know of applications that specifically examine food products. While each data format brings its own challenges and advantages, the conceptual framework underpinning discrete choices remains the same. We examine that framework in this chapter.

Before turning to the conceptual framework, it is useful to reflect on the relatively unique properties of disaggregate food choices and the corresponding issues for discrete choice demand analysis. First, disaggregate food demand is characterized by a large number of differentiated products (especially at the "SKU" or "stock-keeping unit" level). Each of these products usually comprises a relatively small part of a consumer's budget. This implies that there are large numbers of substitutes for any given product and/or the structure of the choice set that the consumer chooses from can be large, individual-specific, and dynamic. Furthermore, food products are often chosen routinely, and may be strongly influenced by habits, implying the importance of dynamics in choice. Food product choice may be highly sensitive to information (e.g., product warnings, information on nutrition, etc.) and choice may change rapidly in the face of new information or information cascades (Bikhchandani, Hirshleifer, and Welch 2008). Finally, food demand will be characterized by a significant degree of heterogeneity in preferences as well as learning, habit formation, and/or variety seeking. Food demand will also likely reflect aspects of reference dependence (on attributes and/or prices). Discrete choice models offer the opportunity to investigate these interesting aspects of choice behavior.

2   ECONOMIC THEORY FOR DISCRETE CHOICE MODELS

....

Hanemann (1984) provides a conceptual model that underpins discrete choice analysis. In this framework, the consumer is assumed to maximize utility from the product category (e.g., yogurt varieties; ketchup brands) and a numeraire good. Let $\mathbf{q}$ be a J-dimensional vector that contains the quantities of the product category and let ω be the numeraire good. Each good is also characterized by a k-dimensional vector of attributes or product characteristics (x). Let Y be income. The consumer maximizes utility (1) subject to a budget constraint (2) and a non-negativity constraint (3):

$$\underset{\mathbf{q},\omega}{\text{Max}}\ \ U(\mathbf{q}(x),\omega). \tag{1}$$

$$\text{Subject to}\ \sum_{j=1}^{J}\mathbf{p}_{j}q(x)_{j}+\omega = Y \tag{2}$$

$$\mathbf{q}\,(x),\, \omega \geq 0. \tag{3}$$

Hanemann (1984) incorporates the discrete choice nature of the problem by assuming that consumers choose a non-negative quantity of ω and one of the elements of $\mathbf{q}$ (e.g., q_i) in their choice decisions. That is, they choose which (and how much) of the products to choose, and the amount of the numeraire good in the decision problem. Adding constraint (4) operationalizes this assumption.

$$\mathbf{q}^i \cdot q_j = 0 \; \forall \mathbf{i} \neq \mathbf{j}. \tag{4}$$

In most discrete choice analysis, the assumption of product choice (e.g., which of the J q's to choose) is then directly modeled within an indirect utility framework. That is, conditional on choosing product j, the price and characteristics of q_j (and the numeraire good) are substituted into the utility function to create a conditional indirect utility function. For example, conditional on choosing the first good, the utility function takes the form

$$V(p, x, Y) = U(1, 0, 0, 0 \ldots; x_1, , 0, 0, 0; Y - p_1) \tag{5}$$

where the "1" in the first element of the utility function indicates that one unit of the first good is chosen,[1] and associated with that good is the k-vector of attributes x_1. Since income minus the amount spent on good 1 is equal to the amount spent on the numeraire good (based on the budget constraint), the term $Y - p_1$ represents the quantity of the numeraire good. Note that this formulation assumes "weak complementarity" in that if a good is not chosen (e.g., good 2 in equation 5), then a quality change in good 2 does not affect utility (Bockstael and McConnell 2007). Incorporating randomness by assuming that there are elements that researchers do not observe but are known to the consumer results in an expression of the conditional indirect utility function of the form

$$V(p, x, Y; \varepsilon) = U(1, 0, 0, 0 \ldots; x_1, 0, 0, 0, \ldots; Y - p_1; \varepsilon) \tag{6}$$

or more succinctly, the conditional indirect utility associated with good 1 is written as

$$V_1(p, x, M, \varepsilon) = V_1(M_1 - p_1, x_1, \varepsilon_1). \tag{7}$$

More generally, the conditional indirect utility for good i is:

$$V_i(p, x, M, \varepsilon) = V_i(M_1 - p_i, x_i, \varepsilon_i). \tag{8}$$

This leads to the traditional random utility model that is more fully described in Section 3. The expression in equation (8) is generalized to provide conditional indirect utility functions for all products under consideration (the choice set). Comparisons

---

[1] Note that this could be generalized to some quantity of the good j; Hanemann (1984) examines this more general case. It is convenient, however, to examine the case with a single unit being purchased and that is often the context in applied research.

between these conditional indirect utility functions, assuming specific functional forms for V_i and distributions for ε_i, form the basis for the discrete choice model.

Before turning to detailed analysis of the discrete choice model, it is worth noting that this approach hinges on the assumption that only one product is chosen (e.g., it assumes that making "no purchase" or choosing multiple products is not possible). The issue of including non-choice can be examined by assuming that there is a threshold over commodities (and attributes) below which the consumer chooses none of the products available (see Bunch 2007). The case of multiple products being chosen has been the focus of the branch of the literature referred to as Kuhn–Tucker models or generalized corner solution models (Phaneuf 1999; Phaneuf, Kling, and Herriges 2000).

3   MODELING DISCRETE CHOICES

In this section, we consider the operationalization of models based on the theoretical microeconomic model just presented. We start from the indirect utility function in (8), which already includes a stochastic utility component, and discuss the Random Utility (RU) framework for modeling discrete choices. A number of specific model formulations are presented, gradually extending the basic discrete modeling framework to make it more behaviorally and theoretically appealing. We limit ourselves to the problem of choosing one good among the J goods contained in a universal choice set M (say, the market). Empirically, this is not a major limitation, but it behooves us to be aware that many decisions involve the choice of a portfolio of goods from among J alternatives. Finally, note that from this point forward, for simplicity we use the terms "utility" and "indirect utility" interchangeably.

As a general introduction to the components of the RU framework, consider the following symbolic representation of the choice process:

$$i_n^* \leftarrow \underset{j \in C_n}{\Delta_n} \left\{ U = V(X, Z_n; \beta) + \varepsilon\left(\tilde{X}, Z_n; \theta\right) \right\} \tag{9}$$

where C_n ($\subseteq M$) is the choice set for the nth decision maker, and contains the J_n goods that are feasible for this individual; $V()$ is a $J_n \times 1$ vector of systematic indirect utility measures, functions of known-to-the-analyst $J_n x K$ product attributes X, sociodemographic characteristics Z, and (to be estimated) a $K x 1$ vector β of weights associated with the attributes (marginal utilities); $\varepsilon()$ is a $J_n x 1$ vector of stochastic indirect utility measures, possibly functions of $J_n x \tilde{K}$ product attributes $\tilde{X}$ (which may overlap with X), characteristics Z, and associated parametric weights θ. Jointly, the sum of V and ε constitute the total utility measure U describing the attractiveness of products; we refer to this combination as the *evaluation rule*. Operating on the total utility measures for the goods in C_n (while wholly ignoring goods outside this set) with decision rule Δ_n, the decision maker arrives at his or her final choice i_n^*. Based on a sample of choices, with corresponding information on X, $\tilde{X}$, Z, C_n, and a pre-specification of Δ_n as well as the statistical properties of $\varepsilon()$, we are able to recuperate population estimates of both β and θ via methods such as maximum likelihood.

3.1   The Workhorse of Discrete Choice Models: Multinomial Logit

Expression (9) is a very general depiction of RU's perspective on the choice process. To arrive at operational models we need to be far more specific. To begin with, we shall make the following assumptions with respect to the choice process and our abstraction of it via expression (9):

1. *Evaluation rule.* We assume that systematic utility is a linear-in-parameters, thus compensatory, combination of attributes X and weights β. (Here, we include in the "attributes" any sociodemographic effects and interactions of attributes and sociodemographics. This is done to simplify the presentation.)
2. *Stochastic utility.* We further assume that the ε's are IID Gumbel (or Type I Extreme Value)-distributed. The identical cumulative distribution functions (CDFs) are given by $F_i(\varepsilon)=\exp(-\exp(-\mu\varepsilon))$, $-\infty<\varepsilon<\infty$, where the scalar $\mu>0$ is called the scale of the distribution. Therefore, μ is the only element in θ.
3. *Decision rule.* In consonance with the theoretical microeconomic model of decision-making presented earlier, we assume that the chosen alternative is selected because it has maximum utility among the alternatives in the choice set.

Thus, the total utility associated with an alternative $j \in C_n$ is

$$U_{jn} = \beta'X_{jn}+\varepsilon_{jn}. \tag{10}$$

Applying the utility maximization decision rule, the probability that alternative j is chosen is given by

$$P_{jn} = \Pr\{U_{jn} > U_{j'n}, \; \forall j' \in C_n, j' \neq j\} = \Pr\{U_{jn} > \max(U_{j'n}), \; \forall j' \in C_n, j' \neq j\}. \tag{11}$$

Let $U_{j'n}^* = \max(U_{j'n})$, $\forall j' \in C_n, j' \neq j$. It is a property of the Gumbel distribution to be closed under the maximum operator, so it is the case that under the assumption that the εs are IID Gumbel with scale μ, the random variable U_{jn}^* (a utility measure, of course) is also Gumbel-distributed with systematic component equal to

$$V_{jn}^* = \frac{1}{\mu}\ln\left(\sum_{\substack{j' \in C_n \\ j' \neq j}} \exp(\mu V_{j'n})\right), \tag{12}$$

and a stochastic component ε_{jn}^{*} with the same scale μ as the original utilities (see Ben-Akiva and Lerman 1985: 104–5). Thus, the complex probability statement in (11) is reduced to a stochastic binary comparison between alternative j and the best of the rest:

$$P_{jn} = \Pr\left\{U_{jn} > \max(U_{j'n}), \ \forall j' \in C_n, j' \neq j\right\} = \Pr\left\{U_{jn} > U_{jn}^{*}\right\} = \Pr\left\{V_{jn} + \varepsilon_{jn} > V_{jn}^{*} + \varepsilon_{jn}^{*}\right\}$$
$$= \Pr\left\{\varepsilon_{jn}^{*} - \varepsilon_{jn} < V_{jn} - V_{jn}^{*}\right\}$$

The probability of choosing j is therefore simply the CDF of the random variable $(\varepsilon_{jn}^{*} - \varepsilon_{jn})$, evaluated at $(V_{jn} - V_{jn}^{*})$. Because both ε_{jn}^{*} and ε_{jn} are IID Gumbel variates with scale μ, their difference is logistic-distributed (again, see Ben-Akiva and Lerman 1985: 104–5). Therefore,

$$P_{jn} = \frac{1}{1 + \exp(-\mu(V_{jn} - V_{jn}^{*}))} = \frac{\exp(\mu V_{jn})}{\exp(\mu V_{jn}) + \exp(\mu V_{jn}^{*})} \tag{13}$$

$$P_{jn} = \frac{\exp(\mu V_{jn})}{\exp(\mu V_{jn}) + \sum_{\substack{j' \in C_n \\ j' \neq j}} \exp(\mu V_{j'n})} \tag{14}$$

$$\therefore P_{jn} = \frac{\exp(\mu V_{jn})}{\sum_{k \in C_n} \exp(\mu V_{kn})} = \frac{\exp(\mu \beta' X_{jn})}{\sum_{k \in C_n} \exp(\mu \beta' X_{kn})}. \tag{15}$$

This is the Multinomial Logit (MNL) model of discrete choice.

An important general observation to make about the MNL model is that choice probabilities are determined by indirect utility differences, *not* absolute utilities, as is illustrated in (13). This turns out to be an observation of singular importance, and determines most of the identification restrictions (see below) that apply to the MNL model in particular, but to all discrete choice models in general. For example, this implies that any variable that does not vary over alternatives cannot directly affect choice unless it is interacted with an alternative specific variable.

Parameter estimates for the MNL are usually obtained via maximum likelihood methods. Let δ_{jn} be the dependent variable for $\forall j \in C_n$, an indicator that is equal to one for the chosen alternative and zero otherwise. For a random sample of N choices, the log likelihood function is given by

$$\ln L = \sum_{n=1}^{N} \sum_{j \in C_n} \delta_{jn} \ln P_{jn}. \tag{16}$$

Maximization of (16) with respect to β and μ, subject to the identification restrictions discussed below, yields estimates of these parameters and a corresponding asymptotic parameter covariance matrix, the diagonal of which contains the standard error estimates (see Ben-Akiva and Lerman 1985; Louviere, Hensher, and Swait 2000; Swait 2006 for details on hypothesis testing).

Let us now address the identification conditions that pertain to the MNL model.

1. *Latent scale origin.* As is evident from (16), the choice model constitutes a highly non-linear link between the observed choices and the underlying latent utility scale U. Because U is unobservable, it is necessary that we establish an arbitrary origin (or zero point) for the scale. This is generally accomplished by setting the alternative-specific constant (or intercept) for one of the alternatives to zero. It doesn't matter which alternative is selected, as long as it's the same one for all choice sets (i.e., observations). The other goods are positioned on the scale relative to this origin. There are two implications of this normalization decision: (a) only $(J-1)$ alternative-specific constant can be estimated; and (b) any sociodemographic variable included in V needs to also have a base normalizing alternative (e.g., when one is estimating a gender effect as a shift to the alternative's intercept).

2. *Latent scale units.* The variance of ε_{jn} is equal to $\sigma_{jn}^2 = \pi^2/6\mu^2$, $\forall j \in C_n$, which implicitly defines the units of the latent scale U. Note how the scale of the Gumbel distribution is inversely related to its variance; this means that as scale increases, variance decreases. Because these variances are equal across the various goods, this implies that the individual utilities are homoskedastic, in exact analogy to the classical Ordinary Least Squares (OLS) model.

3. *Confounding of β and μ.* Note that in (15), the scale μ always shows up in product form with the vector β. That is, one is only able to estimate the product $(\mu\beta)$. Therefore, identification of the marginal utilities can only be done up to scale, requiring that we normalize μ, say, to a convenient constant (say, unity).[2] This normalization is data-set-specific since scale is not estimable within a data set without the use of exogenous information (more on this topic later); it also implies that comparisons of marginal utilities across different data sets must be done with care (e.g., Swait and Louviere 1993; Swait 2006).

Restrictions (1) and (2) are common to all choice model forms since they arise owing to the latency of the utility scale. Restriction (3) will arise in all model forms in which the systematic utility function is linear-in-the-parameters, and may hold more generally even with non-linear utility functions. Researchers need to be aware of this latter restriction because of its many implications for the comparison of marginal utilities across different data sources.

3.2   Specification of the Systematic Utility

The first main task undertaken by the discrete choice analyst is the specification of the systematic utility function V. While to some extent the importance of specifying the right set of independent variables is self-evident from both the theoretical and practical

---

[2] An alternative and equivalent normalization (from the point of view of model identification) is to fix one of the elements of β to a constant. For example, a willingness-to-pay normalization would fix the price coefficient to -1 and scale μ would then be estimable. Usually, however, the normalization via scale is employed in empirical work.

perspectives, we want to address two topics in particular: (a) functional form and (b) taste heterogeneity.

Most choice models presented in the literature do indeed simply present systematic utilities that are linear-in-the-parameter (LIP) combinations of certain problem context variables like price, quality attributes, and sociodemographic intercept shifts and interactions with the other categories of variables. LIP specifications are capable of approximating behavior that arises from highly non-linear utility functions, though it is possible to develop inherently non-linear representations of V. More recent literature, however, has demonstrated that another direction to take in the development of V is to include effects such as reference-dependence, a phenomenon arising as a prediction from prospect theory (Kahneman and Tversky 1979), which states that losses with respect to a reference alternative or condition loom larger than gains with respect to the same. This phenomenon is testable, as demonstrated by Hu, Adamowicz, and Veeman (2006) in the context of choice of bread with genetically modified ingredients using a specification in which utility is modeled as $V = \beta(X-r)$ where r is a reference point assumed to be exogenously provided or determined. Similarly, Swait (2001a) introduces the concept of attribute cutoffs into the specification of a constrained utility function. This specification results in non-compensatory decision rules. The cutoffs are elicited from respondents along with their choices, and are shown to be an important source of heterogeneity across decision makers. These are only two examples of introducing behaviorally plausible process characterizations into the systematic utility function; we believe this is a fruitful area for future research because of the richness it can bring to the analysis of discrete choice processes.

For economists, there exist some interesting implications about the use of income Y in discrete choice models. From expression (7), income enters the indirect utility function in difference form, like: $\lambda(Y-p_j)$. Thus, Y and p_j will have a common marginal utility λ (the marginal value of income). The utility functions of alternatives j and k both contain the constant term λY, since the income of the decision maker is not affected by the alternative. Now, remember that in choice models it is utility differences that determine probabilities of choice. The relative attractiveness of good j over k will be described by the difference (U_j-U_k), from which it is obvious that the terms λY cancel out; i.e., income disappears from the specification. This effect is a direct result of the functional form of model (7). It is possible to make ad hoc extensions to (7) by including non-linear representations of the impact of income, but to maintain at least some consistency with the theoretical model, the terms involving income should involve the differences ($Y-p_j$), as in $\ldots\ldots +\lambda_1(Y-p_j) + \lambda_2(Y-p_j)^2 \ldots$, or $\lambda_3 \, ln(Y-p_j)$, as a second example. Another means of preserving income in the specification is to interact it with product attributes, but this is a solution whose appeal varies from one literature to another.

3.3   Heterogeneity in Preferences

In the basic formulation of the MNL model, it has been assumed that the taste vector β is homogeneous across individuals. Clearly, the analyst can specify known sources of taste heterogeneity in V through the judicious use of decision maker characteristics, and this is to be highly recommended. But to go the next step it may be necessary to consider the inclusion of unobservable sources of taste differences. A vast literature on the representation of stochastic taste heterogeneity in choice models has arisen since 1990 (see the partial review in Swait 2006), but two general types of model have appeared. We discuss each of these approaches below.

3.3.1   *Latent Classes*

In a latent class model an unknown number (say, S) of discrete classes (or consumer segments) is assumed to exist in a population. Each class is characterized by a taste vector β_s and scale μ_s. The analyst's task is to estimate S, β_s, and μ_s. This type of model has been particularly prominent in the marketing literature, since the discrete classes have natural interpretation as market segments (see Kamakura and Russell 1989; Swait 1994).

The latent class model can be specified as follows (Swait 1994):

$$P_{in} = \sum_{s=1}^{S} P_{in|s} W_{ns} \tag{17}$$

$$P_{in} = \sum_{s=1}^{S} \left(\frac{e^{\mu_s \beta_s X_{in}}}{\sum_{j \in C_n} e^{\mu_s \beta_s X_{jn}}} \right) \left(\frac{e^{\alpha \gamma_s Z_n}}{\sum_{k=1}^{S} e^{\alpha \gamma_k Z_n}} \right) \tag{18}$$

The first term in (18) is an MNL choice model conditional on segment s membership, while the second model is a classification model, specifically a polytomous MNL model (a polytomous model uses the same predictors for all alternatives, to wit, the segments, but has different marginal impacts for each alternative). Normalization conditions necessary for this model are that all scales must be unity ($\mu_1 = \ldots = \mu_S = \alpha = 1$), and that one of the γ's (say, γ_S) must be equal to zero. Identification restrictions that apply to MNL models must also be respected in this formulation. The resulting model provides a number of classes (distinct in their preference parameters) and a model explaining the probability of class membership. We employ this model in the example presented below.

3.3.2   *Continuous Representations of Heterogeneity*

In continuous representations of heterogeneity, parametric models of underlying taste distributions are used to develop variants of core choice models such as the MNL. Perhaps the best known of these is the Mixed Logit model, due to McFadden and Train (2000). In its usual form, the Mixed Logit assumes that the individual taste vectors are draws from a multivariate normal density. Simulated Maximum Likelihood Estimation or Bayesian methods are then used to estimate both the taste mean vector and taste covariance matrix (see Train 2003). The preference parameters over the sample of observations or individuals in the Mixed Logit model are assumed to follow a particular distribution specified by the researcher. A common formulation is:

$$\beta_n = \bar{\beta} + \tau_n, \quad \tau_n \sim \text{MVN}(0, \Omega), \tag{19}$$

where the distribution of βs over the sample is distributed multivariate normal with a mean of $\bar{\beta}$ and covariance over the preference parameters of Ω (see Swait 2006).

The choice probabilities in the Mixed Logit model can be estimated using the assumptions of the distributions of τ_n (e.g., normal) and ε_{jn} (e.g., type I extreme value) to generate an expression for the probability of choice as

$$P_{in} = \int_{\tau} \left(\frac{\exp\left(V_{in|\beta_n}\right)}{\sum_{j \in C_{rn}} \exp\left(V_{jn|\beta_n}\right)} \right) \varphi_K(\tau | 0, \Omega) d\tau \tag{20}$$

where $\varphi_K(\tau | 0, \Omega)$ is a K-dimensional multivariate normal probability density function with mean zero and covariance Ω. This expression can be used in a simulation method to estimate the Mixed Logit parameters (Train 2003). This formulation of the Mixed Logit assumes that the scale parameter is equal to unity (see Swait 2006 for additional details). Many applications of this type of model can be found in the economics, transportation, and marketing literatures.

The reader is cautioned that choice model identification conditions are somewhat more complex than mentioned before with both approaches to taste heterogeneity representation. Walker (2002) is a good source for understanding identification for the Mixed Logit model. See also Swait (2006) for a discussion of the potential confounds between scale μ and stochastic taste vectors.

3.4 Dealing with Heteroskedasticity

As noted above, the MNL model assumes homoskedastic (equal variances) stochastic utilities. In the OLS model, when this condition does not hold empirically, parameter estimates are consistent but not efficient. Not so in the non-linear MNL (and any other choice model form), as discussed in Yatchew and Griliches (1985): heteroskedasticity results in biased parameter estimates. Therefore, heteroskedasticity becomes of much greater concern in the discrete choice context.

A simple extension of the basic MNL model can be used to deal with this potential problem. As shown by Swait and Adamowicz (2001; also Swait 2006), if we assume that the stochastic utilities U_{jn} are independently Gumbel-distributed with scales μ_{jn}, one can derive this straightforward generalization of the MNL:

$$P_{jn} = \frac{\exp(\mu_{jn} V_{jn})}{\sum_{k \in C_n} \exp(\mu_{jn} V_{kn})}, \tag{21}$$

termed the Heteroskedastic MNL (HMNL) model. Since the scales must be non-negative, an implementation of (21) will generally use a functional form such as

$$\mu_{jn} = \exp(\theta' \tilde{X}). \tag{22}$$

Included in $\tilde{X}$ are possibly alternative-specific constants and characteristics, as well as sociodemographics. We note that exogenous information is generally quite important in aiding identification of these alternative-specific scales. Also, it is not necessary that both alternative-specific and decision maker information be always used; the specification of (22) is driven by the choice context and the conceptual framework underlying the decision problem. While research on sources of heteroskedasticity in choice models is an active area of investigation, the literature already presents several examples including brand (Swait and Erdem 2007), decision context complexity (Swait and Adamowicz 2001), and variable range in a stated choice experiment (Dellaert, Brazell, and Louviere 1999). In any given decision context, the analyst should consider as potential sources of heteroskedasticity variables that describe how people's ability to discriminate between alternatives is affected by each source. For example, brands might be a source of heteroskedasticity because those brands that have proven reliable in the past may have smaller variances for their stochastic utilities compared to new or untried brands. Such reasoning is a fruitful means of generating candidate variables for modeling the scale function. The reader is referred to Bhat (1995) for a different choice model—the Heteroskedastic Extreme Value, or HEV—which also deals with heteroskedastic utilities.

3.5   Dealing with Stochastic Dependence between Alternatives

Perhaps one of the best-known facts about the MNL model is that it has the Independence of Irrelevant Alternatives (IIA) property. This property states that the relative likelihood of choosing one alternative compared to another can be determined solely by comparing the two alternatives; all other alternatives are irrelevant to the determination. That the MNL model has this property can be ascertained by showing that the odds of choosing alternative j over k is

$$\frac{P_{jn}}{P_{kn}} = \exp(V_{jn} - V_{kn}), \quad j, k \in C_n \tag{23}$$

Clearly, the attractiveness of alternative $a \neq j$, k does not affect this comparison. The MNL model also implies that cross-price elasticities (elasticities of probabilities of choosing alternative j with respect to a change in the prices of alternative k, $k \neq j$) are equal. That the MNL model displays IIA is a direct consequence of the assumption that the stochastic utilities are probabilistically independent: any model that makes this assumption of independence, no matter what the underlying density functions may be, will necessarily have the IIA property. The issue for the analyst, then, is whether the IIA property holds or not in a given empirical context, and what to do about it if it is present.

Because independence between stochastic utilities creates IIA, the general "cure" for it is to develop model forms that allow for covariances to exist between the utilities of pairs of alternatives. The models we have considered thus far have had diagonal covariance matrices: the MNL has $V_{MNL}(\varepsilon) = (\pi^2/6\mu^2) \cdot I_J$, where I_J is the $J \times J$ identity matrix, while the HMNL has $V(\varepsilon) = \text{Diag}(\pi^2/6\mu_1^2 \ldots \pi^2/6\mu_J^2)$. Thus, both model forms allow for no covariances between alternatives.

The Multinomial Probit (MNP) choice model allows for a more general depiction of the stochastic dependence between alternatives. It assumes that the ε's are multivariate normally distributed with mean vector $\underline{0}$ and covariance matrix Σ. However, this generality is somewhat ephemeral: because choice probabilities are determined by utility differences, only at most the $(J-1) \times (J-1)$ sub-matrix of Σ is actually identifiable. In addition, just as μ must be normalized to some constant to identify the taste vector in an MNL model, one of the elements of this sub-matrix must also be normalized. As shown in Bunch (1991), an important source on the topic of identifying MNP models, at most $[J(J-1)/2-1]$ elements of Σ are identifiable. These models have proven to be somewhat difficult to work with in practice.

Another family of models that circumvents IIA is termed the GEV (Generalized Extreme Value) class of choice models (McFadden 1978). The specific member that has seen widest application is the Nested MNL model (see Ben-Akiva and Lerman 1977; Williams 1977; Daly and Zachary 1978; McFadden 1978), and its generalization, the Tree Extreme Value (TEV) model (McFadden 1981; Daly 1987; see Swait 2006 for a small but important correction to Daly). Intuitively, these models *ex ante* cluster the alternatives in M into some finite number of mutually exclusive, collectively exhaustive "clusters" or "nests." The alternatives within a nest are correlated with one another, as captured through a certain parameter, and have zero correlation with all alternatives without the nest. An example of a 3-cluster Nested MNL is shown in Figure 5.1: the clusters are denoted by the *construct* alternatives C_1, C_2, and C_3, each of which contains two *elemental* alternatives. The six elemental alternatives constitute all the goods in M, and each belongs to one and only one cluster. Associated with the *Root* node of the tree is the overall scale μ, which corresponds to the scale in the standard MNL model; with each cluster is associated another parameter, μ_1, here assumed to be equal for all clusters (this need not always be the case). The correlation between the stochastic utility components of alternatives i and j is given by

$$\rho_{ij} = \begin{cases} 1 - (\mu/\mu_1)^2 & \text{if } C_{(i)} = C_{(j)} \\ 0 & \text{otherwise} \end{cases} \tag{24}$$

,

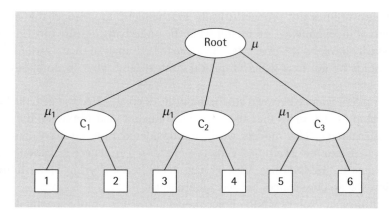

FIGURE 5.1 Example of a 3-cluster Nested Logit model

where $C_{(i)}$ is the nest that contains alternative i. This expression is valid for any Nested Logit model, as long as we remember that the scale ratio within the square root operator always involves the ratio of the scale of the root divided by the scale of the nest. Within each nest, conditional choice probabilities are given by an MNL model; the probability of each nest turns out also to be given by an MNL model, but with utility equal to the attractiveness of the set of alternatives within the nest (see below). TEV models differ from Nested MNL models in that the tree depictions tend to be deeper and not necessarily symmetrical.

To be concrete, suppose the alternatives in M are subdivided into K subsets C_k. Such a two-level Nested MNL model is given by these expressions (see derivation in Swait 2006):

$$P_{in} = P_{in|C_{(i)}} Q(C_{(i)}), i \in n, \tag{25}$$

$$P_{in|C_{(i)}} = \exp(\mu_1 V_i) \Big/ \sum_{j \in C_{(i)}} \exp(\mu_1 V_j) \tag{26}$$

$$Q(C_{(i)}) = \exp(\mu I_{(i)}) \Big/ \sum_{k=1}^{K} \exp(\mu I_k) \tag{27}$$

$$I_k = \frac{1}{\mu_1} \ln \left(\sum_{j \in C_k} \exp(\mu_1 V_j) \right), k = 1, \ldots, K, \tag{28}$$

where I_k is termed the "inclusive value" or "logsum" for the kth nest (note the similarity with expression 12), and $I_{(i)}$ is the inclusive value of the cluster containing alternative i, other quantities as previously defined. The inclusive value or logsum variable has an interesting interpretation: it is the expectation of the maximum utility among a set of independent and identically distributed Gumbel variates. Thus, in the Nested Logit model the attractiveness of a nest is given by this expectation (see expression 28).

Harking back to expression (24), it is clear that for a valid correlation to be generated by the Nested MNL model, it must be the case that $\mu_1 \geq \mu$ (for more general trees than used for model 25, the requirement is that scales grow monotonically with node depth in the tree). If this condition does not hold empirically, then the model is said to be inconsistent with utility-maximizing behavior. Empirically this is a worrisome result for economists since it compromises welfare analysis; in the interests of full disclosure, however, it should be pointed out that from the perspective of predicting choice probabilities, models violating such conditions still predict valid probabilities between 0 and 1, which sum to unity. See Hensher, Rose, and Green (2005) for alternative generalizations of the Nested MNL.

Any Nested Logit or TEV model can be represented through a tree-like depiction of the correlations between elementary alternatives. That is, there can be no cycles in the diagram for one of these models. As noted before, both these models are exemplars of the GEV class of discrete choice models. All members of this class reduce to the MNL model under specific conditions of the scales (e.g., in the Nested Logit model above, when $\mu_1 = \mu$). Another shared characteristic of GEV models is that choice probabilities are always expressed as a product of conditional probabilities (see 25).[3]

Recently, new GEV models have been reported in the literature (e.g., Koppelman and Wen 2000; Wen and Koppelman 2001; Swait 2003), many of which generalize the depiction of stochastic interdependence to networks, rather than simply trees. Swait (2001b), however, introduces an alternative behavioral explanation (to shared unobserved attributes) for interdependence—the GenL model is based on constructs representing choice set generation (see also Section 3.5).

A third method of modeling stochastic interdependence between alternatives is to utilize error components within a standard model such as the MNL. McFadden and Train (2000) showed that the Mixed Logit model is capable of approximating arbitrarily closely any discrete choice model, through the judicious addition of stochastic effects to utility functions. A Nested MNL model, for example, can be mimicked in this manner by the addition of independent stochastic effects to subgroups (nests) of alternatives, inducing thereby correlations between alternatives within a nest. An example of such a model will be developed in our empirical section.

3.6   Some Additional Considerations

In the above presentation of a rather wide array of choice model forms, two assumptions have been kept constant throughout: (a) the decision rule assumed to link utilities to choice is utility maximization; (b) the individual decision maker's choice set $C_n \subseteq M$

---

[3] Generally, derivations of the Nested MNL model are based on dissimilarity parameters θ_1, defined as the inverse of the scale parameters μ_1 used in our presentation. We have preferred to use scale parameters to maintain consistency with the MNL model.

has been assumed known to the analyst. We discuss some implications and potential relaxation of these assumptions in this section.

Utility maximization is, to economists, generally an uncontroversial and theoretically consistent (even satisfying) assumption to impose on discrete choice models. In other disciplines such as psychology and marketing, however, this assumption is much less appealing because of empirical evidence that decision makers often do not seek the best possible outcome in choice situations: rather, they are prone to use shortcuts (called heuristics) like satisficing, have multiple conflicting objectives, are affected by the environment, operate under constraints (e.g., time, effort, ability), and make mistakes in processing information (see, e.g., Simon 1955; Payne, Bettman, and Johnson 1993; de Palma, Myers, and Papageorgiou 1994; Dhar 1997a, b). In fact, from within the economics discipline itself, Heiner (1983) proposed that these very factors serve as the underlying motivation for decision makers' development of simplified rules for choosing among goods in ways that may not resemble utility maximization in the least. His argument seems particularly compelling where food choice is concerned, owing to its strongly routinized—though essential—nature. While little empirical work in discrete choice exists that relaxes the assumption of utility maximization, there is a growing realization that modeling of alternative decision rules is a necessary area of research. Relevant references on this topic are Swait (2001a), Elrod, Johnson, and White (2004), Gilbride and Allenby (2004), and Swait (2009).

The "elephant in the living room" of choice modeling (i.e., the important topic that is collectively ignored by the room's occupants) is a topic termed "choice set formation." This moniker refers to the fact that part of the specification of every discrete choice is the set of goods that are actually, or actively, compared when the chosen good is selected. Thus, the "choice set" is the set of goods that have a structurally non-zero probability of being selected. This set is not necessarily equal to M, the universal or market set, because individual constraints (e.g., income), poor inventory management at the store, prior consumer experience with a brand, etc., might remove a given alternative from evaluation and comparison at the moment of truth.

Misspecification of the true choice set is likely to have severe deleterious impacts on parameter estimates: both Swait (1984) and Swait and Ben-Akiva (1986) show that taste parameter estimates are biased by choice set misrepresentation. Both alternative-specific constants and attributes can be impacted. The addition of irrelevant alternatives, as well as the omission of relevant alternatives, introduces bias: the first by decreasing marginal utility estimates owing to the artificial introduction of irrelevant comparisons between alternatives, the second by omitting relevant comparisons in the determination of relative attractiveness.

To our knowledge, the most extensive simulation study of the impact of choice set heterogeneity is Andrews, Ainslie, and Currim (2008), who conduct an analysis of various misspecifications of the Mixed Logit model for scanner panel data. They say, "there is also evidence that the choice set component should be the first component included in the model specification" (Andrews, Ainslie, and Currim 2008: 94). They go on to recommend that analysts consider adding to the basic specification of the Mixed

Logit in the following order: first, choice set heterogeneity (i.e., choice set formation modeling), then taste heterogeneity, then state dependence (dynamics are of concern in their context since they dealt with scanner data). Their simulation studies indicate that this order is best because taste heterogeneity and state dependence can be biased by the presence of choice set heterogeneity.

Despite this knowledge, the fact is that the almost universal practice in choice modeling is to assign M (i.e., all goods existing in the market) as the choice set for all observations. Most often, this can constitute an egregious misspecification of the choice set. As a first means to tackle this issue, we have formulated all the models presented above in terms of a pre-specified choice set C_n. By this we mean to imply that it is quite possible (and highly recommended) for the analyst to make significant efforts in the a priori determination of decision maker restrictions to M to define C_n. For example, in the case of survey data, analysts should elicit from consumers information that will help eliminate alternatives from M for each individual. To be concrete, brand, quality, and price cutoffs can be directly elicited from consumers to guide construction of choice sets (Swait 2001a). Application of good sense should not be ignored: e.g., perhaps the allocation of a milk-based food item to the choice set of a lactose-allergic individual should generate second thoughts for the analyst.

Beyond the deterministic a priori specification of each observation's choice set just discussed, it is possible to consider explicit modeling of the choice set formation process. Manski (1977) suggested the modeling of choice as a two-stage process, choice set formation followed by conditional choice within the true set: probabilistically,

$$P_j = \sum_{C \in \Gamma} P_{j|C} Q(C) \tag{29}$$

where $Q(C)$ is the choice set formation model, specifically the probability that set C is the true choice set, Γ is the set of all possible choice sets (which contains $2^J - 1$ non-empty sets formed from J alternatives), and $P_{j|C}$ is the conditional choice model given set C. Because of the large number of possible choice sets in Γ, this is a very difficult problem to tackle empirically, particularly for J much greater than ten goods. This has, no doubt, contributed to the paucity of empirical applications that involve choice set formation. Nonetheless, some work exists in this area: Swait (1984) and Swait and Ben-Akiva (1987a, b) present different strategies for attacking this challenging aspect of discrete choice modeling; more recently, Swait (2001b) introduced a GEV variant of the MNL that defines construct nodes on the basis of choice sets that allows for partial enumeration of Γ. Other authors who have reported models of choice set formation include Andrews and Srinivasan (1995), Ben-Akiva and Boccara (1995), Chiang, Chib, and Narasimhan (1999), and Chang, Lusk, and Norwood (2009).

Despite these comments about the importance of considering heterogeneity in decision rules and choice sets, it should still be recognized that the empirical experience with extant choice models is relatively positive: the MNL model and its variants have shown themselves to be empirically robust formulations.[4] While this observation is not intended to discourage further research for improving representation of alternative decision rules and choice set formation in discrete choice models, this robustness of discrete choice models should serve as a comfort to both academic researchers and practitioners.

A final topic to conclude this section is that of aggregation of alternatives. In our presentation of discrete choice models, we have presented the alternative goods as being the *elemental* products or services (e.g., specific SKUs of ketchup). Sometimes, however, it is desirable to conduct analyses at some level of aggregation. For example, rather than deal with the sixty-four individual yogurt SKUs generally available for sale in a store chain, the objective might be satisfactorily addressed by working with an aggregate representation of the alternatives, say, at the brand level. Thus, instead of having choice sets with up to sixty-four goods, one would estimate models based on choice sets with four alternatives, each representing all the SKUs for a given brand. Some aggregation issues arise, of course, but particularly with respect to the aggregation of independent variables, which generally become limited to those that are common to all SKUs within the aggregation unit (e.g., for brand, one is limited to consumer loyalty measures, promotional activity, price). Prices are expressed as unit prices (money per unit weight), and are then aggregated over SKUs within the aggregation unit. Andrews and Currim (2005) do an extensive study of potential biases introduced by alternative means of performing aggregation of elemental alternatives.

A second issue with respect to aggregation of alternatives is the need to introduce a size correction factor to the aggregate utility functions. As demonstrated in Ben-Akiva and Lerman (1985, sect. 9.2), it is necessary to add the term $\ln(\psi(\Lambda_j;\gamma))$ to the utility of aggregate alternative j, where ψ is a "size" function of size variables Λ_j and parameters γ. An important note: in the aggregate utility function, the coefficient of $\ln(\psi(\Lambda_j;\gamma))$ must be constrained to unity. Also, the introduction of the size function into the aggregate utility function creates a non-linear utility function, which means that a special estimator has to be written for such a model since most estimation software assumes a linear-in-parameters specification. An example of a size variable that might be used in a scanner panel aggregated analysis might be the number of SKUs offered by a brand, and/or the number of shelf facings occupied by the SKUs of a brand.

In summary, the aggregation of alternatives creates some interesting problems for the analyst and is a specialized topic in itself. The authoritative source on this topic is still Ben-Akiva and Lerman (1985, ch. 9); in general, the transportation demand literature is the most advanced in this area, owing to that discipline's interest in the problem of predicting destination choice.

---

[4] For example, Provencher and Bishop (2004) indicate that a "simple" Logit Model outperforms both random parameter and latent class models in out-of-sample predictions in a recreational fishing site choice example.

4   KETCHUP DEMAND ANALYSIS USING SCANNER PANEL DATA

To illustrate the estimation and selection of discrete choice models it is helpful to work in an empirical context. We shall employ single-source scanner panel data provided by AC Nielsen, originating in the supermarkets of Springfield, Missouri. Individual household purchases of ketchup among twenty-two different SKUs are recorded from January 1985 through the end of December 1989. Information available about the SKUs included brand (4), price paid, size (ounces), formulae (five types), packaging type (three types), end-aisle display, and newspaper insert promotional activities at the weekly level. We specify the utility of a given ketchup SKU as a function of these attributes and promotional activities (see Fader and Hardie 1996), as well as a number of individual characteristics that describe habit-proneness to certain aspects of the product. To allow for intertemporal effects we include dummy variables that indicate whether SKU j is (a) the same as the SKU last purchased, (b) of the same brand as the SKU last purchased, (c) of the same size as the SKU last purchased, (d) of the same package type as last purchased, and (e) of the same formula as the SKU last purchased.

Each household is represented within the data set by multiple purchase occasions, from as few as one to as many as thirty-plus purchase occasions. At each purchase occasion the choice set is given by the twenty-two alternatives, implying that we are unable to add exogenous information to improve our choice set specification (see prior discussion on choice set formation). This lack of information on choice set formation is one of the most serious shortcomings of scanner panel data: not even inventory management/stockout information is usually available in these sources. Inevitably, one lives within the shortcomings of one's data sources.

The data set contains 3,242 households, making a total of 17,504 choices over the stated period. These numbers make for a total of 385,088 cases. The average number of purchases per household is 5.4 SKUs of ketchup.

The first model we discuss is a simple MNL model, presented in Table 5.1.[5] With nineteen parameters in the utility function this model displays an overall goodness of fit of $\rho^2 = 0.30$. This measure is often called McFadden's rho-squared and is defined as $\rho^2 = 1 - (L(C)/L(0))$, where L(C) is the log likelihood at the model at convergence, while L(0) is the corresponding quantity when choice is random (in the MNL model, this condition occurs when $\beta = 0$). Rho-squared varies between zero and one, like R^2, but a model with ρ^2 on the order of 0.3 is doing quite well. The Akaike Information Criterion

---

[5] One of the concerns with revealed preference data of this type is the potential for endogeneity, particularly arising from the correlation of unobservables with attributes in the utility function. For example, Besanko, Gupta, and Jain (1998) appear to use these same data for ketchup choices and explore the potential for endogeneity of price as it may be correlated with unobservable quality characteristics. Other researchers have developed methods to attempt to address endogeneity issues associated with choice models of this type (Berry, Levinsohn, and Pakes 1995; Murdock 2006).

Table 5.1 Ketchup Scanner Panel models (22 SKUs) (asymptotic t-stats)

	MNL	Heteroskedastic MNL	Error Components MNL	Error Components Heteroskedastic MNL
Utility function				
Brand 1	−0.3731 (−1.87)	−0.6723 (−5.85)	−0.3092 (−1.39)	−0.9275 (−8.23)
Brand 2	0.1343 (0.69)	−0.4721 (−4.03)	0.4558 (2.02)	−0.6124 (−5.31)
Brand 3	−1.1551 (−5.72)	−0.7872 (−6.79)	−1.4266 (−5.5)	−1.3686 (−10.15)
Brand 4	-0-	-0-	-0-	-0-
$x =$ (Size-32)/32	0.6482 (8.52)	0.2716 (9.87)	0.6290 (7.86)	0.2479 (7.66)
x^2	−1.8664 (−15.92)	−0.5342 (−12.49)	−1.9227 (−16.06)	−0.5966 (−12.73)
Formula 1	1.9569 (8.85)	0.6111 (8.3)	2.0033 (9.05)	0.6759 (9.13)
Formula 2	1.3992 (5.28)	0.5920 (7.36)	1.3495 (5.00)	0.4796 (5.66)
Formula 3	0.7280 (2.07)	0.1506 (1.63)	0.6372 (1.68)	0.1571 (1.30)
Formula 4	0.8704 (3.05)	0.4390 (5.5)	0.8755 (3.03)	0.3672 (4.25)
Formula 5	-0-	-0-	-0-	-0-
Package 1	−7.4853 (−7.24)	5.0371 (17.21)	−7.8794 (−7.53)	5.1544 (17.39)
Package 2	−7.1497 (−6.94)	5.1116 (17.43)	−7.5123 (−7.2)	5.2785 (17.62)
Package 3	-0-	-0-	-0-	-0-
Price paid ($/unit)	−0.3677 (−27.36)	−0.1253 (−15.83)	−0.3679 (−27.31)	−0.1201 (−15.93)
Display	2.6537 (92.09)	0.8652 (22.14)	2.6639 (91.54)	0.8311 (22.22)
Insert	2.6429 (99.37)	0.8829 (22.44)	2.6609 (99.05)	0.8472 (22.57)
LastSKU	2.4251 (183.91)	0.9480 (22.49)	2.4276 (183.44)	0.9040 (22.56)
LastBrand	−0.3333 (−7.28)	−1.9167 (−16.33)	−0.6219 (−9.86)	−2.0222 (−16.37)
LastSize	0.0350 (0.78)	−2.2859 (−16.14)	0.0528 (1.15)	−2.3459 (−16.33)
LastForm	1.0718 (10.37)	0.7282 (10.65)	0.9884 (8.96)	0.6801 (9.87)
LastPak	−0.1916 (−4.23)	−0.5532 (−7.56)	−0.1984 (−4.18)	−0.5124 (−7.05)
Error components				
Var(Brand 1)	-0-	-0-	0.3680 (1.30)	0.1490 (4.00)
Var(Brand 2)	-0-	-0-	1.3910 (4.30)	0.1640 (5.60)
Var(Brand 3)	-0-	-0-	0.7260 (2.70)	0.1780 (3.70)
Ln(scale)				
Brand 1	-0-	0.2480 (6.31)	-0-	0.2812 (7.23)
Brand 2	-0-	0.2221 (5.80)	-0-	0.2564 (6.77)
Brand 3	-0-	0.1791 (4.32)	-0-	0.2542 (6.04)
LastBrand	-0-	0.5350 (35.26)	-0-	0.5577 (35.44)
LastSize	-0-	0.7350 (51.87)	-0-	0.7532 (52.33)
LastForm	-0-	−0.0487 (−3.14)	-0-	−0.0585 (−3.75)
LastPak	-0-	0.1724 (10.37)	-0-	0.1650 (9.83)
Goodness of fit				
Households (no.)	3,242			
Choices (no.)	17,504			
Cases (no.)	38,5088			
LL(0)	−54,105.6			
LL(Conv)	−37,846.2	−35,715	−37,779.6	−35,586.6
Parameters (no.)	19	26	22	29
Rho-squared	0.3005	0.3399	0.3017	0.3423
AIC Rho-squared	0.3002	0.3394	0.3013	0.3417

(AIC) rho-squared measure penalizes models with larger numbers of parameters by being defined as AIC $\rho^2 = 1 - [L(C) - K]/L(0)$, where K is the number of parameters in the model. Owing to the large number of observations available for this exercise, the standard errors of the marginal utilities are small, leading to large t-statistics for most effects of interest. The effect of price is negative, as expected, and there is a marginally increasing utility attached to sizes up to 38 ounces, beyond which the utility of bigger containers decreases. Formulae 1–4 are preferred to base formula 5; package types 1 and 2 are significantly less desirable than the base type 3, all else equal. Display and insert activities positively increase SKUs utility, in about equal measure. A very strong habit persistence with respect to the last SKU purchased is exhibited in the MNL model, with some persistence with respect to formula. The last brand effect, however, indicates that there is a tendency to vary brand across time, as there is of packaging type.

The Heteroskedastic MNL model (expressions 17–18) is the next model in Table 5.1. The utility function is identical to that used in the MNL model, while the scale function (inversely related to the variance of stochastic utility) is parameterized as a function of brand and habit persistence in terms of brand, size, formula, and package type. The hypothesis underlying this specification of the scale function is that brand perception differences, as well as prior expectations and experiences with specific sizes, brands, formulae, and packaging, would impact the size and role of the stochastic utility vis-à-vis the systematic utility sources. Thus, for example, it might be expected that prior experience with a certain size of ketchup should decrease the variance of assessments of stochastic utility sources of total utility. This effect is irrespective of the LastSize effect in the utility function. So, the HMNL in Table 5.1 allows heteroskedasticity to vary as a function of brand and a complex interaction of prior consumer experience with brand and different aspects of the product.

The HMNL has a log likelihood of -35715.0, compared to -37846.2 with the MNL model. Since the latter is nested within the HMNL, we employ the likelihood ratio to test the hypothesis that the data is adequately described by the simpler MNL model. The chi-squared statistic is 4264.4 with 7 degrees of freedom, so we strongly reject the MNL model at the 95 percent confidence level.

Examination of the scale function components of the HMNL model gives a very consistent and simple message: both brand perceptions and prior experience with brand, size, and formulae lead to increases in scale (hence, decreases in variance) of the stochastic utilities, implying in turn that evaluations between products are more strongly based on systematic utility comparisons. Experience with formulae, on the other hand, had a negative (though small relative) impact on scale, leading to small increases in variance. In terms of choice behavior, the interpretation of these results is that brand perceptions and prior experience greatly reduce the role of unobserved attributes in the evaluative process compared to those factors included in the systematic utility function.

As an example of how to introduce stochastic interdependence between alternatives, we could estimate one or more Nested MNL models. Instead, we have decided to add brand-based error components to the utility functions and estimate a random coefficients MNL model. Specifically, we hypothesize that alternatives that share a given brand contain common unobserved attributes that lead to correlations between their utilities. Accordingly, we add to each utility function a stochastic term specific to the corresponding brand; all utilities sharing a common stochastic variable will have covariances proportional to the variance of the shared variate. As shown in Table 5.1, we introduced a different independent normal variate for each brand, with brand 4 having no explicit effect. This specification is equivalent to creating a Nested Logit model wherein the construct nodes are the brands.

The third model in Table 5.1 presents the direct extension of the MNL model to a Brand-Based Error Components model. The addition of the three variances implied by the latter model leads to a substantial improvement in the log likelihood function, with a chi-squared statistic of 133.2 with 3 degrees of freedom; clearly we reject the hypothesis that there is no brand-based interdependence between the stochastic elements of the utility functions. The error components illustrate the degree of heterogeneity across the sample. For example, the preferences for brand 2, relative to brand 4, are normally distributed with mean 0.456 and standard deviation $(1.39)^{1/2}$. The coefficients in Table 5.1 can also be used to construct marginal welfare measures (willingness to pay for an additional unit of the attribute) by taking the ratio of a continuous attribute and -1 times the price coefficient, or by taking the ratio of a dummy variable coefficient and -1 times the price coefficient to describe the willingness to pay for that category relative to the base category. In the MNL model in Table 5.1, for example, brand 3 is worth $(1.155/.368 = \$3.14)$ less than the base category. These coefficients can also be used to develop non-marginal welfare measures. See Carlsson, Chapter 7 in this volume, for additional information on this topic.

In addition to welfare measures, a common use of discrete choice models is the calculation of market shares and the sensitivity of market shares to changes in prices and attributes. Market shares can be calculated as the predicted probabilities evaluated over the sample of individuals. In addition, elasticities with respect to own price and cross-prices can be calculated for every alternative (see Louviere, Hensher, and Swait 2000 or Hensher, Rose, and Green 2005 for additional details on calculation of elasticities). The elasticities provide information on the sensitivity of market share to price changes. As an illustration consider Figure 5.2, in which the percentage change in market share for SKU 7 in our sample is depicted as a function of the percentage change in price. This relationship is presented for the four different models in Table 5.1. Note that there is relatively little difference between the four models. In fact the MNL and Error Components MNL model relationship is essentially identical (the lines lie on top of each other in Figure 5.2). The heteroskedastic models imply slightly less sensitivity to price changes, probably because the scale component of the heteroskedastic models includes some form of loyalty to the SKU. In all cases the models imply a fairly inelastic situation, a 20 percent change in prices yields less than a 5 percent change in market share for this SKU.

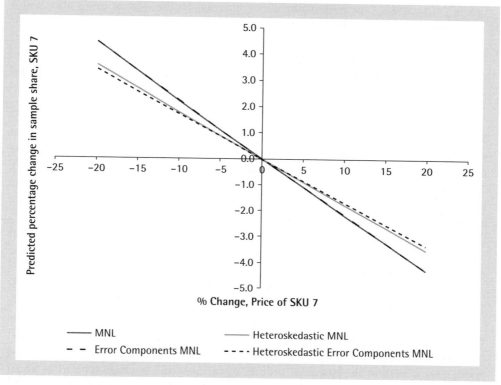

FIGURE 5.2 In-sample prediction of change in market share as a function of price: an illustration using SKU 7 in the Ketchup data

The final model presented in Table 5.1 adds heteroskedasticity to the Brand-Based Error Components model. Together, the scale function and the error components achieve a very large improvement over the humble MNL model: the chi-squared statistic is 4,519.2 with 10 degrees of freedom. This is something to write home about, to be sure! And it will be noted that the vast majority of this improvement is due to the addition of heteroskedasticity to the model, not error components. The reader should peruse the various models in Table 5.1 and analyze the differences in marginal utility estimates as heteroskedasticity versus error components are being introduced. The various models potentially imply quite different policy impacts since price slopes are quite different, and the signs of different packaging types differ substantially.

While *one data set doth not generality make*, it stands to reason that first concentrating one's interest on the modeling of the variances in the covariance matrix will be more rewarding than focusing first on the off-diagonal covariances. As a general modeling strategy for handling discrete choice data, it seems advisable to

1. $\bar{V}$. First specify the systematic utility function to the best of one's ability and knowledge. Do not include stochastic taste heterogeneity at this stage, though known sources of heterogeneity (Z_n) should be included.
2. Diag(Σ). Next, specify sources of heteroskedasticity;
3. OffDiag(Σ). Specify sources of correlations between alternatives that help describe non-IIA behavior.
4. V_n. Finally, introduce stochastic taste heterogeneity at this stage.

Such a sequence, it seems to us, has the best chance of minimizing misattributions of effects to spurious components of the random utility framework (e.g., attributing heteroskedasticity to taste heterogeneity; see Swait 2006 for a discussion of this issue).

In this example we also construct a latent class model (see Section 3.3 above). For the ketchup example, we shall employ no predictors in the classification model. We are able to do this only because there are multiple purchases observed per household (i.e., these data have a panel structure). If there were only one observation per household, it would be mandatory to have exogenous information to allow identification of the classification probabilities.

Finally, the classes will be defined in terms of taste heterogeneity along the dimensions of brand, price, size, promotional activity, and consumer loyalty and experience. Owing to the fact that product characteristics vary over only twenty-two SKUs (excluding price, of course), and these characteristics remain fixed during the period of observation (a situation common with scanner panel data for consumer packaged goods), we constrain the marginal utilities of formula and package type to be equal across latent classes. Normally, all coefficients are allowed to vary in latent class models.

Table 5.2 shows a summary of the fit statistics for the latent class models, varying S from one to four classes. (A non-panel estimator was employed to obtain these results.) The reason this is done is because the statistical properties of maximum likelihood estimators are not defined for discrete parameters, such as the unknown number of classes, S. Hence, it is customary to utilize a multiplicity of information criteria measures like the AIC, AIC3, and BIC to select S (see notes of Table 5.2 for

Table 5.2 Comparative goodness–of–fit measures, Ketchup Scanner Panel Latent Class models

Classes	−2*LogLik	AIC[a]	AIC3[b]	BIC[c]	Negentropy[d]
1	75,692.4	75,730.4	75,749.4	75,846.0	1
2	74,368.6	74,434.6	74,467.6	74,635.3	0.38543
3	74,052.2	74,142.3	74,187.3	74,416.1	0.3809
4	73,674.2	73,792.1	73,851.1	74,151.1	0.34813

[a]AIC = −2*LogLik + 2K_s, K_s = no. of parameters for s-class model.
[b]AIC3 = −2*LogLik + 3K_s.
[c]BIC = −2*LogLik + (Ln N)K_s, N = no. of observations.
[d]Negentropy = $1 - \dfrac{\sum_{n=1}^{N}\sum_{l=1}^{s}[-W_{nl} \quad \ln \quad W_{nl}]}{N \quad \ln \quad s}$,
S = no. of segments, W_{nl} = probability of n being in segment s.

definitions of these measures). Another measure of interest is negentropy, a measure varying from 0 to 1, which indicates how well discriminated or separated the classes seem to be (the higher the measure, the more discriminating the corresponding class structure in that individuals are more unambiguously assigned to a single class). On the basis of this last measure, it was decided to maintain the three-class solution as most appropriate, though in terms of the other measures the four-class solution shows promise.

The three-class solution is shown in Table 5.3. The smallest class has a size of about 21 percent of the sample, followed by a class with about 32 percent, and the largest class

Table 5.3 Latent Class model for Ketchup Scanner Panel (asymptotic t–stats)

	Class 1	Class 2	Class 3
Utility function			
Brand 1	0.3223 (1.28)	−0.7359 (−2.11)	26.6522 (116.07)
Brand 2	0.5421 (2.20)	−0.3054 (−0.91)	27.8709 (0.00)
Brand 3	−1.1055 (−4.10)	−0.9625 (−2.77)	−12.0705 (−0.00)
Brand 4	-0-	-0-	-0-
$x = (Size-32)/32$	2.4813 (7.40)	0.4161 (3.43)	−0.1181 (−0.43)
x^2	−21.4753 (−18.41)	−0.7269 (−3.73)	−1.1662 (−2.30)
Formula 1	1.9172 (8.49)	1.9172	1.9172
Formula 2	1.1122 (3.90)	1.1122	1.1122
Formula 3	0.8563 (1.72)	0.8563	0.8563
Formula 4	0.6302 (2.06)	0.6302	0.6302
Formula 5	-0-	-0-	-0-
Package 1	−1.2239 (−0.88)	−1.2239	−1.2239
Package 2	−0.9753 (−0.71)	−0.9753	−0.9753
Package 3	-0-	-0-	-0-
Price paid ($/unit)	−0.5405 (−16.32)	−0.0360 (−1.51)	−1.0954 (−13.17)
Display	3.1313 (49.68)	1.7645 (22.61)	3.6291 (29.18)
Insert	2.9156 (52.89)	1.5660 (21.29)	3.9879 (32.23)
LastSKU	1.5310 (39.89)	2.9601 (122.01)	3.0451 (50.24)
LastBrand	−0.8105 (−8.77)	0.3160 (3.40)	0.8073 (2.90)
LastSize	−0.2149 (−0.23)	−0.8679 (−9.83)	−1.0311 (−6.61)
LastForm	0.3902 (2.02)	2.0662 (6.07)	0.8129 (2.32)
LastPak	0.8022 (1.02)	0.2604 (2.59)	−0.8321 (−4.89)
Classification function			
Class size (MNL coefficient)	0.8313 (8.04)	0.4247 (3.85)	-0-
Class size	0.48	0.32	0.21
Goodness of fit			
Households (no.)	3,242		
Choices (no.)	17,504		
Cases (no.)	38,5088		
LL(0)	−54,105.6		
LL(Conv)	−37,026.1		
Parameters (no.)	45		
Rho-squared	0.3157		
AIC Rho-squared	0.3148		

constituting about 48 percent of the sample. This indicates that the classes are of a robust consistency: small class sizes imply little support for the corresponding taste parameter vectors, so will generally be accompanied by taste vectors with large standard errors (low t-stats). Class 3 seems to be the most highly price sensitive (−1.0954), followed by class 1, with a price sensitivity of about half that magnitude (−0.5405), while class 2 shows itself to be insensitive to price (note that these comparisons are under the maintained hypothesis of equal error variances across the classes). Class 3 shows a very strong preference for brands 1 and 2, and attaches an extremely negative utility to brand 3, all else equal. In addition to comparing coefficients, the researcher can examine ratios of coefficients and the price coefficient to compare implicit marginal willingness to pay amounts over the classes. A number of such interesting distinctions can be discerned from Table 5.3.

The acid test, however, is not how interesting the interpretation of the latent classes might be. Rather, it is whether the addition of taste heterogeneity to the MNL model produces a competitive specification to the models presented in Table 5.1. Certainly, comparing the three-class MNL model from Table 5.3 to the one-class MNL in Table 5.1 shows that the former model is vastly superior to the latter: taste heterogeneity seems to add a tremendous amount of power to explaining the observed choices. However, comparison of the three-class MNL model (forty-five parameters, LL = −37026.1) to the Heteroskedastic MNL (twenty-six parameters, LL = −35715.0) clearly demonstrates that parameterization of the sources of scale variation leads to a much, much enhanced capability to explain observed behavior. These latter two models are not nested within one another, so a likelihood ratio test is not appropriate to select between them. A nonnested test like Ben-Akiva and Swait (1986) is called for: it makes use of the difference in AIC ρ^2 to choose between non-nested models. In the present comparison, this difference is (0.0246); the probability of this magnitude of difference with twenty-two alternatives is less than or equal to 3.5×10^{-10}. Thus, the probability that the three-class latent class model is superior to the Heteroskedastic MNL is negligible.

5   DISCRETE CHOICE ANALYSIS
OF FOOD DEMAND

This chapter has provided an overview of the methods employed in discrete choice models relevant to food demand analysis. To conclude, we provide a brief description of some interesting extensions and future research issues in the area of discrete choice analysis and food demand.

Time plays a significant role in food demand. Consumers learn about new products and attributes (e.g., nutrition) and their tastes likely change over time. They are influenced by memories and they are also influenced by the ease of simply purchasing the same product repeatedly if it "satisfies" a component in the food basket. Choice sets also change over time. While there has been some examination of the role of time in food choice, there are relatively few studies of habit formation, variety seeking, and related phenomena involving foods. Notable exceptions include Keane (1997) and Richards, Patterson, and Tegene (2007), who use scanner panel data to directly assess habits and intertemporal issues. A number of challenging issues arise including preference evolution and propensities for variety seeking versus consistency in consumption. Several econometric models have been formulated (Chintagunta 1999; Swait et al. 2004) and improved access to scanner data will facilitate analysis of these intertemporal choice phenomena.

Most analysis of food demand assumes that a single decision maker is making a choice independently from a set of products described by exogenous attributes. However, in reality, food choices by an individual are likely influenced (or even specified) by others (family members, peers). Positional externalities may play a role in food choices (wine, restaurants, etc.) just as they appear to play such a role in choices of housing, cars, etc. (Frank 2008). Within households, food choices may be the result of bargaining processes among the household members. In addition, attributes of food may not be exogenous. Endogeneity may exist in disaggregate data (Train 2003; Petrin and Train 2010) when there are omitted variables that induce a correlation between the error term and utility (e.g., a missing attribute is embedded in the error term and the consumer assumes that higher prices imply higher levels of this attribute). There has been relatively little analysis of peer effects or endogeneity in the area of discrete choice analysis of food demand (for applications in other literatures, see Brock and Durlauf 2001; Murdock 2006; Petrin and Train 2010; and see Manski 2000 for an overview of social interactions effects in economics).

The determination and evolution of choice sets in the food demand area is a challenging problem but also an avenue for interesting research. One line of research may be in the econometric assessment of choice sets. In the literature, a number of methods of assessing choice set structure have been developed ranging from the use of latent class models to infer choice set structure (Swait 1994) to the use of econometric methods to identify the choice set structure that best fits the data (Swait and Ben-Akiva 1987a; Swait 2001a; von Haefen 2008). Another fascinating area of research is the consumer psychology assessment of choice sets. Research in this area suggests that large choice sets leave consumers dissatisfied (e.g., Iyengar and Lepper 2000; Schwartz 2004; Arunachalam et al. 2009) and that the proliferation of products (notable in the food area!) may be welfare-decreasing. This is in direct contradiction to the economic notion that larger choice sets are always welfare-enhancing. A richer theory that includes the "costs of thinking" (Shugan 1980) in consumer choices may emerge.

While the size and structure of choice sets is known to affect measures of preferences and elasticities, some researchers are suggesting that the composition of the choice set affects preferences in unusual ways. Wilcox et al. (2009) suggest that when a healthy food option is available in a choice set, the consumers are more likely to choose the least healthy option—implying that the *presence* of the healthy option meets a goal of the consumer and then the least healthy option is chosen. This effect of choice set structure on food choice has not received a great deal of attention in the literature, in which most analyses assume that the presence of healthy options in a choice set will reduce the likelihood of choice of the least healthy option.

Finally, the issue of whether consumer preferences are compensatory or non-compensatory has, for some time, been a topic of investigation in various areas of discrete choice analysis, including food choices. Econometric models that assess whether preferences are compensatory or not and incorporate these effects into the model are emerging. These include Swait's cutoffs model (Swait 2001b), Elrod, Johnson, and White (2004), and Gilbride and Allenby (2004). Hu, Adamowicz, and Veeman (2006) assess reference-dependence in the context of food choice—allowing for a type of non-compensatory preference. There are likely several econometric avenues for the incorporation of these features into demand analysis.

The analysis of disaggregate choice data of food demand is likely to increase our understanding of this essential aspect of human existence. However, as with any methodology, discrete choice analysis also presents analysts with a number of unique challenges, among which model identification and interpretation are of particular concern. Thus, we recommend that analysts follow the disciplined approach to model specification that we outlined in this chapter. To reiterate, though the common practice in modeling discrete choices is to introduce taste heterogeneity into a specification immediately, we recommend that the analyst first concern herself with specification of the systematic component using best theory and current knowledge, along with known sources of heterogeneity; next, model the scale (variance) of the error terms; subsequently, introduce components to capture correlation across alternatives; then, finally, introduce stochastic taste heterogeneity. Such a sequence has two benefits: owing to the latent nature of the utility variable, this order minimizes the risk of misattribution of effects by following what we believe is the natural hierarchy of importance within the Random Utility framework; it also encourages the use of exogenous information in the formulation of constructs such as scales and covariances, improving one's capacity to tease apart possible confounding factors arising in discrete data.

REFERENCES

Andrews, R., and I. Currim. 2005. "An Experimental Investigation of Scanner Data Preparation Strategies for Consumer Choice Models." *International Journal of Research in Marketing* 22/3: 319–31.

——and T. C. Srinivasan. 1995. "Studying Consideration Effects in Empirical Choice Models Using Scanner Panel Data." *Journal of Marketing Research* 32/1: 30–41.

——, A. Ainslie, and I. Currim. 2008. "On the Recoverability of Choice Behaviors with Random Coefficient Choice Models in the Context of Limited Data and Unobserved Effects." *Management Science* 54/1: 83–99.

Arunachalam, B., S. R. Henneberry, J. L. Lusk, and F. B. Norwood. 2009. "An Empirical Investigation into the Excessive-Choice Effect." *American Journal of Agricultural Economics* 91/3: 810–25.

Ben-Akiva, M. 1985. *Discrete Choice Analysis: Theory and Application to Travel Demand.* Cambridge, MA: MIT Press.

——and B. Boccara. 1995. "Discrete Choice Models with Latent Choice Sets." *International Journal of Research in Marketing* 12/1: 9–24.

——and S. Lerman. 1977. "Disaggregate Travel and Mobility Choice Models and Measures of Accessibility." Paper presented at the Third International Conference on Behavioural Travel Modelling, Tanunda, South Australia, Apr. 2–7.

——and J. Swait. 1986. "The Akaike Likelihood Ratio Index." *Transportation Science* 20/2: 133–6.

Berry, S., J. Levinsohn, and A. Pakes. 1995. "Automobile Prices in Market Equilibrium." *Econometrica* 63/4: 841–90.

Besanko, D., S. Gupta, and D. C. Jain. 1998. "Logit Demand Estimation under Competitive Pricing Behavior: An Equilibrium Framework." *Management Science* 44/11: 1533–47.

Bhat, C. R. 1995. "A Heteroskedastic Extreme Value Model of Intercity Mode Choice." *Transportation Research Part B* 29/6: 471–83.

Bikhchandani, S., D. Hirshleifer, and I. Welch. 2008. "Information Cascades." In S. N. Durlauf and L. E. Blume, eds, *The New Palgrave Dictionary of Economics*, 2nd edn. New York: Palgrave Macmillan. <http://www.dictionaryofeconomics.com/article?id=pde 2008_I000103>.

Bockstael, N. E., and K. E. McConnell. 2007. *Environmental and Resource Valuation with Revealed Preferences.* Dordrecht: Springer.

Brock, W. A., and S. N. Durlauf. 2001. "Discrete Choice with Social Interactions." *Review of Economic Studies* 68/2: 235–60.

Bunch, D. 1991. "Estimability in the Multinomial Probit Model." *Transportation Research Part B* 25/1: 1–12.

——2007. *Theory-Based Functional Forms for Analysis of Disaggregated Scanner Panel Data.* Working Paper. Davis: Graduate School of Management University of California, Davis.

Carlsson, F., P. Frykblom, and C. J. Lagerkvist. 2007a. "Consumer Benefits of Labels and Bans on GM Foods: Choice Experiments with Swedish Consumers." *American Journal of Agricultural Economics* 89/1: 152–61.

————————. 2007b. "Consumer Willingness to Pay for Farm Animal Welfare: Mobile Abattoirs versus Transportation to Slaughter." *European Review of Agricultural Economics* 34/3: 321–44.

Chang, J. B., J. L. Lusk, and F. B. Norwood. 2009. "How Closely Do Hypothetical Surveys and Laboratory Experiments Predict Field Behavior?" *American Journal of Agricultural Economics* 91/2: 518–34.

Chiang, J., Chib, S., and Narasimhan, C. 1999. "Markov Chain Monte Carlo and Model of Consideration Set and Parameter Heterogeneity." *Journal of Econometrics* 89/1–2: 223–48.

Chintagunta, P. 1999. "Variety Seeking, Purchase Timing and the 'Lightning Bolt' Brand Choice Model." *Management Science* 45/4: 486–98.

Daly, A. 1987. "Estimating 'Tree' Logit Models." *Transportation Research Part B* 21/4: 251–67.

——and S. Zachary. 1978. "Improved Multiple Choice Models." In D. A. Hensher and Q. Dalvi, eds, *Determinants of Travel Choice*. Westmead: Saxon House.

Deaton, A., and J. Muellbauer. 1980. "An Almost Ideal Demand System." *American Economic Review* 70/3: 312–26.

Dellaert, B., J. Brazell, and J. J. Louviere. 1999. "The Effect of Attribute Variation on Consumer Choice Consistency." *Marketing Letters* 10/2: 139–47.

de Palma, A., G. M. Myers, and Y. Y. Papageorgiou. 1994. "Rational Choice under an Imperfect Ability to Choose." *American Economic Review* 84/3: 419–40.

Dhar, R. 1997a. "Consumer Preference for a No-Choice Option." *Journal of Consumer Research* 24/2: 215–31.

——1997b. "Context and Task Effects on Choice Deferral." *Marketing Letters* 8/1: 119–30.

Ehmke, M. T., J. L. Lusk, and W. Tyner. 2008. "Measuring the Relative Importance of Preferences for Country of Origin in China, France, Niger, and the United States." *Agricultural Economics* 38/3: 277–85.

Elrod, T., R. Johnson, and J. White. 2004. "A New Integrated Model of Noncompensatory and Compensatory Decision Strategies." *Organizational Behavior and Human Decision Processes* 95/1: 1–19.

Erdem, T., and M. Keane. 1996. "Decision Making under Uncertainty: Capturing Dynamic Brand Choice Processes in Turbulent Consumer Goods Markets." *Marketing Science* 15/1: 1–20.

——, S. Imai, and M. Keane. 2003. "Brand and Quantity Choice Dynamics under Price Uncertainty." *Quantitative Marketing and Economics* 1/1: 5–64.

Fader, P., and B. Hardie. 1996. "Modeling Consumer Choice among SKUs." *Journal of Marketing Research* 33/4: 442–52.

Frank, R. H. 2008. "Should Public Policy Respond to Positional Externalities?" *Journal of Public Economics* 92/8–9: 1777–86.

Gilbride, T., and G. Allenby. 2004. "A Choice Model with Conjunctive, Disjunctive, and Compensatory Screening Rules." *Marketing Science* 23/3: 391–406.

Gould, B. W., and D. Dong. 2000. "The Decision of When to Buy a Frequently Purchased Good: A Multi-Period Probit Model." *Journal of Agricultural and Resource Economics* 25/2: 636–52.

Gracia, A., and T. de Magistris. 2008. "The Demand for Organic Foods in the South of Italy: A Discrete Choice Model." *Food Policy* 33/5: 386–96.

Hanemann, W. M. 1984. "Discrete/Continuous Models of Consumer Demand." *Econometrica* 52/3: 541–61.

Heiner, R. A. 1983. "The Origin of Predictable Behavior." *American Economic Review* 73/4: 560–95.

Hensher, D., J. M. Rose, and W. H. Greene. 2005. *Applied Choice Analysis: A Primer*. Cambridge: Cambridge University Press.

Hu, W. Y., W. L. Adamowicz, and M. M. Veeman. 2006. "Labeling Context and Reference Point Effects in Models of Food Attribute Demand." *American Journal of Agricultural Economics* 88/4: 1034–49.

Iyengar, S. S., and M. R. Lepper. 2000. "When Choice Is Demotivating: Can One Desire Too Much of a Good Thing?" *Journal of Personality and Social Psychology* 79/6: 995–1006.

Kahneman, D., and A. Tversky. 1979. "Prospect Theory: An Analysis of Decision under Risk." *Econometrica* 47/2: 263–91.

Kamakura, W., and G. Russell. 1989. "A Probabilistic Choice Model for Market Segmentation and Elasticity Structure." *Journal of Marketing Research* 26/4: 379–90.

Keane, M. 1997. "Modeling Heterogeneity and State Dependence in Consumer Choice Behavior." *Journal of Business and Economic Statistics* 15/3: 310–27.

Koppelman, F., and C. Wen. 2000. "The Paired Combinatorial Logit Model: Properties, Estimation and Application." *Transportation Research Part B* 34/2: 75–89.

Krystallis, A., C. Fotopoulos, and Y. Zotos. 2006. "Organic Consumers' Profile and their Willingness to Pay (WTP) for Selected Organic Food Products in Greece." *Journal of International Consumer Marketing* 19/1: 81–106.

Lagerkvist, C., F. Carlsson, and D. Viske. 2006. "Swedish Consumer Preferences for Animal Welfare and Biotech: A Choice Experiment." *AgBioForum* 9/1: 51–8.

Liljenstolpe, C. 2008. "Evaluating Animal Welfare with Choice Experiments: An Application to Swedish Pig Production." *Agribusiness* 24/1: 67–84.

Loureiro, M., and W. Umberger. 2007. "A Choice Experiment Model for Beef: What US Consumer Responses Tell Us about Relative Preferences for Food Safety, Country-of-Origin Labeling and Traceability." *Food Policy* 32/4: 496–514.

Louviere, J. J., D. Hensher, and J. Swait. 2000. *Stated Choice Methods: Analysis and Applications in Marketing, Transportation and Environmental Valuation*. Cambridge: Cambridge University Press.

Lusk, J. L., and T. C. Schroeder. 2004. "Are Choice Experiments Incentive Compatible? A Test with Quality Differentiated Beef Steaks." *American Journal of Agricultural Economics* 86/2: 467–82.

McCluskey, J. J., K. M. Grimsrud, H. Ouchi, and T. I. Wahl. 2005. "Bovine Spongiform Encephalopathy in Japan: Consumers' Food Safety Perceptions and Willingness to Pay for Tested Beef." *Australian Journal of Agricultural and Resource Economics* 49/2: 197–209.

McFadden, D. 1978. "Modelling the Choice of Residential Location." In A. Karlquist, L. Lundqvist, F. Snickers, and J. W. Weibull, eds, *Spatial Interaction Theory and Residential Location*. Amsterdam: North-Holland.

——1981. "Econometric Models of Probabilistic Choice." In C. Manski and D. McFadden, eds, *Structural Analysis of Discrete Data*. Cambridge, MA: MIT Press.

——2001. "Economic Choices." *American Economic Review* 91/3: 351–78.

——and K. Train. 2000. "Mixed MNL Models for Discrete Response." *Journal of Applied Econometrics* 15/5: 447–70.

Manski, C. 1977. "The Structure of Random Utility Models." *Theory and Decision* 8/3: 229–54.

——2000. "Economic Analysis of Social Interactions." *Journal of Economic Perspectives* 14/3: 115–36.

Murdock, J. 2006. "Handling Unobserved Site Characteristics in Random Utility Models of Recreation Demand." *Journal of Environmental Economics and Management* 51/1: 1–25.

Payne, J. W., J. R. Bettman, and E. J. Johnson. 1993. *The Adaptive Decision Maker*. New York: Cambridge University Press.

Petrin, A., and Train, K. 2010. "A Control Function Approach to Endogeneity in Consumer Choice Models." *Journal of Marketing Research* 47/1: 3–13.

Phaneuf, D. 1999. "A Dual Approach to Modeling Corner Solutions in Recreation Demand." *Journal of Environmental Economics and Management* 37/1: 85–105.

——, C. Kling, and J. Herriges. 2000. "Estimation and Welfare Calculations in a Generalized Corner Solution Model with an Application to Recreation Demand." *Review of Economics and Statistics* 82/1: 83–92.

Provencher, B., and R. C. Bishop. 2004. "Does Accounting for Preference Heterogeneity Improve the Forecasting of a Random Utility Model? A Case Study." *Journal of Environmental Economics and Management* 48/1: 793–810.

Richards, T. J. 2000. "A Discrete/Continuous Model of Fruit Promotion, Advertising, and Response Segmentation." *Agribusiness* 16/2: 179–96.

——, P. M. Patterson, and A. Tegene. 2007. "Obesity and Nutrient Consumption: A Rational Addiction?" *Contemporary Economic Policy* 25/3: 309–24.

Schwartz, B. 2004. *The Paradox of Choice: Why More Is Less.* New York: Ecco.

Shugan, S. 1980. "The Cost of Thinking." *Journal of Consumer Research* 7/2: 99–111.

Simon, H. A. 1955. "A Behavioral Model of Rational Choice." *Quarterly Journal of Economics* 69/1: 99–118.

Swait, J. 1984. "Probabilistic Choice Set Formation in Transportation Demand Models." Ph.D. thesis. Massachusetts Institute of Technology.

——1994. "A Structural Equation Model of Latent Segmentation and Product Choice for Cross-Sectional Revealed Preference Choice Data." *Journal of Retailing and Consumer Services* 1/2: 77–89.

——2001a. "A Non-Compensatory Choice Model Incorporating Attribute Cutoffs." *Transportation Research Part B* 35/10: 903–28.

——2001b. "Choice Set Generation within the Generalized Extreme Value Family of Discrete Choice Models." *Transportation Research Part B* 35/7: 643–66.

——2003. "Flexible Covariance Structures for Categorical Dependent Variables through Finite Mixtures of Generalized Extreme Value Models." *Journal of Business and Economic Statistics* 21/1: 80–7.

——2006. "Advanced Choice Models." In B. Kanninen, ed., *Valuing Environmental Amenities Using Choice Experiments: A Common Sense Guide to Theory and Practice.* Dordrecht: Springer.

——2009. "Choice Models Based on Mixed Discrete/Continuous PDFs." *Transportation Research Part B* 43/7: 766–83.

——and Adamowicz, W. 2001. "The Influence of Task Complexity on Consumer Choice: A Latent Class Model of Decision Strategy Switching." *Journal of Consumer Research* 28/1: 135–48.

——and Andrews, R. 2003. "Enhancing Scanner Panel Models with Choice Experiments." *Marketing Science* 22/4: 442–60.

——and Ben-Akiva, M. 1986. "Analysis of the Effects of Captivity on Travel Time and Cost Elasticities." In *Behavioural Research for Transport Policy: The 1985 International Conference on Travel Behaviour: 16–19 April 1985, Noordwijk, the Netherlands.* Utrecht: VNU Science Press.

————1987a. "Incorporating Random Constraints in Discrete Models of Choice Set Generation." *Transportation Research Part B* 21/2: 91–102.

————1987b. "Empirical Test of a Constrained Choice Discrete Model: Mode Choice in São Paulo, Brazil." *Transportation Research Part B* 21/2: 103–15.

——and T. Erdem. 2007. "Brand Effects on Choice and Choice Set Formation under Uncertainty." *Marketing Science* 26/5: 679–97.

——and J. Louviere. 1993. "The Role of the Scale Parameter in the Estimation and Comparison of Multinomial Logit Models." *Journal of Marketing Research* 30/3: 305–14.

——, W. L. Adamowicz, and M. van Bueren. 2004. "Choice and Temporal Welfare Impacts: Incorporating History into Discrete Choice Models." *Journal of Environmental Economics and Management* 47/1: 94–116.

Train, K. 2003. *Discrete Choice Methods with Simulation.* Cambridge: Cambridge University Press.

Volinskiy, D., W. L. Adamowicz, M. Veeman, and L. Srivastava. 2009. "Does Choice Context Affect the Results from Incentive-Compatible Experiments? The Case of Non-GM and Country-of-Origin Premia in Canola Oil." *Canadian Journal of Agricultural Economics* 57/2: 205–21.

von Haefen, R. H. 2008. "Latent Consideration Sets and Continuous Demand System Models." *Environmental and Resource Economics* 41/3: 363–79.

Walker, J. 2002. "The Mixed Logit (or Logit Kernel) Model: Dispelling Misconceptions of Identification." *Transportation Research Record* 1805: 86–98.

Wen, C., and F. Koppelman. 2001. "The Generalized Nested Logit Model." *Transportation Research Part B* 35/7: 627–41.

Wilcox, K., B. Vallen, L. Block, and G. J. Fitzsimons. 2009. "Vicarious Goal Fulfillment: When the Mere Presence of a Healthy Option Leads to an Ironically Indulgent Decision." *Journal of Consumer Research* 36/3: 380–93.

Williams, H. C. W. L. 1977. "On the Formation of Travel Demand Models and Economic Evaluation Measures of User Benefit." *Environment and Planning A* 9/3: 285–344.

Yatchew, A., and Z. Griliches. 1985. "Specification Error in Probit Models." *Review of Economics and Statistics* 67/1: 134–9.

CHAPTER 6

....

HEDONIC PRICE ANALYSIS
IN FOOD MARKETS

....

MARCO COSTANIGRO AND JILL J. McCLUSKEY

1 INTRODUCTION

....

A transformation has been occurring in modern food markets. Consumer expectations for quality are increasing and, at the same time, consumers demand increasingly customized products. One can think about the common habit of ordering an espresso drink. Coffee used to come with two options: cream and sugar. Now there are thousands of combinations, and consumers are willing to pay for them. Many simple commodity markets have evolved into highly differentiated product markets in order to fulfill heterogeneous consumer preferences for product attributes (Barkema and Drabenstott 1995). Customization contributes to consumer welfare because it enables each consumer to select an attribute bundle that comes as close as possible to matching her preferences. In addition to a larger number of product attributes, greater variety within each one of them increases the likelihood that she might obtain exactly the option that maximizes her utility. This customization of purchases has implications for economic theory and estimation, especially how researchers analyze markets. Approaches that perform well for examining food commodities have often limited applicability and usefulness when studying differentiated food products.

Traditional demand theory is based on the premise that a product generates utility. Hence, utility theory has been used to analyze consumers' choice and consumption of a good based on price and a budget constraint. In economic models of demand for differentiated products, consumer utility is derived from the summation of utilities associated with each individual attribute embedded in the product (Lancaster 1966; McFadden 1973; Rosen 1974; Berry, Levinsohn, and Pakes 1995).

Even though the origin of the study of differentiated products, and specifically hedonic methods, is often traced to the work of Waugh (1928) and the field of agricultural and food economics, the discipline has impacted numerous fields of economics. Important developments in the theory and empirics of hedonics have come from the consumer price index literature (see Triplett 2006 for a summary), real estate economics, non-market valuation of environmental amenities (see Freeman 1993; Taylor 2003), and hedonic modeling of labor markets (see Viscusi 1993). Many of the findings in these areas of application have obvious implications for performing hedonic studies on food products. In this chapter we present the basic theory of hedonic modeling, its empirical application and relevance, and the principal limitations and challenges.

2   HEDONIC THEORY

Hedonic price analysis is based on the hypothesis that consumers' utility is not generated by the purchased product itself, but rather by the qualities and characteristics it contains. Differentiated goods are therefore treated as bundles of various quality attributes which differentiate them from other related goods, and the observed equilibrium market price is a function of the (implicit) prices of each quality attribute. This idea is formally presented in Lancaster (1966), but the earliest hedonic-type models can be traced back to the contributions of early agricultural economists. Based on the observation that vegetable lots in Boston produce markets showed considerable variations in price, Waugh (1928) regressed the price of asparagus on color, size of stalks, and uniformity of spears to determine which quality traits significantly influenced prices. Similarly, Court (1939) analyzed the characteristics influencing automobile prices. In the 1960s the relationship between product characteristics and prices was examined in order to separate the effect of changes in product quality from inflation (Adelman and Griliches 1961; Griliches 1971).

Early contributions to the formal theory of hedonic pricing theory include Court (1941), Tinbergen (1951), and Rosen (1974), who is often referenced as the seminal contribution. Even though the principal original contribution of the latter article relates to hedonic demand estimation, Rosen (1974) formalized how the hedonic price function, mapping multiple product attributes into price space, can be obtained from the market behavior of profit-maximizing firms and utility-maximizing consumers. Our presentation of the theoretical framework closely follows his work. Other useful presentations of hedonic price theory in an environmental economics context include Freeman (1993) and Taylor (2003).

2.1   The Hedonic Model

Consider a row vector of K product characteristics identifying the ith product, $z_i = (z_1, \ldots, z_k)$, and assume that there are a significantly large number of differentiated products to ensure that a "spectrum of products" exists, allowing for marginal analysis. In the remainder of this chapter, we use the subscript k to indicate or emphasize an attribute, and i to indicate a product. Vectors appear in bold, and subscripts are omitted when the context is not ambiguous. Each differentiated product is offered at a posted market price depending on its vector of attributes, so that market prices can be represented by the (unknown to the researcher) *hedonic price function* $p(z_1, \ldots, z_k)$. The key assumptions of Rosen's development of the hedonic model are largely collinear to those of perfect competition: all consumers are aware of all the available versions of a differentiated product, switching from one product to another is costless, and a large number of producers and consumers with no market power buy and sell the differentiated product. Even though we adopt these assumptions in the following exposition, we emphasize that the existence of a hedonic price function taking the form $p(z)$ arises from consumers' preferences for product attributes, and does not hinge on the assumption of perfect competition (Bajari and Benkard 2005). Indeed, modified versions to account for firms' market power or non-continuous product space have been developed (see Pakes 2003; Bajari and Benkard 2005).

The utility a consumer obtains from consuming good $z = (z_1, \ldots, z_k)$ is represented by $U = U(x, z_1, \ldots, z_k; \alpha)$, where x is a composite good normalized to have a unit price, and α is a taste parameter. Maximizing utility subject to the budget constraint $y = x + p(z)$, where y is income, results in the first-order condition $\frac{\partial p}{\partial z_k} = p_{z_k} = \frac{U_{z_k}}{U_x}$, $k = 1, \ldots, K$. This set of conditions implies that utility is maximized when a consumer is indifferent between switching to a product with an extra unit of any attribute and paying the associated implicit price p_{z_k}, or using the money to purchase the composite good. The second-order conditions will be satisfied with the usual assumptions on utility and if $p(z)$ is not too concave. The *bid function* $\theta = \theta(z_1, \ldots, z_k; u, y, \alpha)$ captures the amount that a consumer is willing to pay for the vector of characteristics z as a function of a fixed level of utility u, income, and consumer's taste. This function is made to satisfy the relationship

$$U(y - \theta, z_1, \ldots, z_k; \alpha) = u, \tag{1}$$

thereby defining a family of indifference surfaces relating the levels of product characteristics and their valuation in terms of forgone money (in the form of the amount of consumption of the composite good $y - \theta$). Differentiation shows that the bid functions are increasing in z_k, i.e., $\theta_{z_k} = \frac{U_{z_k}}{U_x} > 0$ for all consumers, yet they may differ across consumer with different income or tastes.

Consider now the producers' decisions, which is symmetric to the consumer's problem. Following again Rosen's notation, let $M(z)$ represent the number of goods produced with product characteristics z, and $C(M, z; \beta)$ indicate the cost function, where the parameters $\boldsymbol{\beta}$ differentiate firms based on the factor prices they face and their production technology. Assume that the cost function is increasing and convex in M and $\mathbf{z}$. Each firm maximizes profits $\pi = Mp(\mathbf{z}) - C(M, \mathbf{z}; \boldsymbol{\beta})$ by optimizing with respect to the choices of M and $\mathbf{z}$. At the optimum, the marginal revenue from an additional unit of $\mathbf{z}$ is equal to its marginal cost of production, $p(\mathbf{z}) = C_M$, and the marginal revenue from increasing any product attribute is equal to the (per unit) marginal cost of adding it to the bundle: $p_{z_k}(z) = \frac{C_{z_k}}{M}$. Analogous to the consumer's bid function, the seller's *offer function* $\phi = \phi(z_1, \ldots, z_k; \pi, \boldsymbol{\beta})$ indicates the price that a firm characterized by the vector $\boldsymbol{\beta}$ is willing to accept for selling the differentiated good $\mathbf{z}$ and maintain the (fixed) profit π. This function defines a family of producer indifference surfaces in price characteristics space (given that M is optimally chosen), and satisfies the necessary relationships

$$\pi = M\phi - C(M, z_1, \ldots, z_k; \boldsymbol{\beta}) \text{ and}$$
$$C_M(M, z_1, \ldots, z_k; \boldsymbol{\beta}) = \phi. \tag{2}$$

Given convexity of the cost function in characteristic space, the per unit marginal implicit costs of increasing each characteristic, $\phi_{z_k} = \frac{C_{z_k}}{M}$, $k = 1, \ldots, K$, is positive. Therefore, all firms' offer functions are increasing in the levels of $\mathbf{z}$, but may differ depending on technology and factor prices.

Since there are many consumers and supply is atomistic, consumers and producers take the price function $p(\mathbf{z})$ as given. Thus, using asterisks to indicate optima, a consumer's utility is maximized when $\theta(\mathbf{z}^*; u^*, y, \boldsymbol{\alpha}) = p(z^*)$ and $\theta_{z_k} = p_{z_k}(\mathbf{z}^*)$, $k = 1, \ldots, K$, i.e., when the bid functions are tangent to the hedonic price function in all the dimensions of $\mathbf{z}$. Analogously, maximum profit and an optimal mix of attributes imply that and $p(\mathbf{z}^*) = \phi(z_1^*, \ldots, z_k^*; \pi^*, \boldsymbol{\beta})$ and $p_{z_k}(\mathbf{z}^*) = \phi(z_1^*, \ldots, z_k^*; \pi^*, \boldsymbol{\beta})$, $k = 1, \ldots, K$,

When the conditions $\theta_{z_k}(\mathbf{z}^*) = \phi_{z_k}(\mathbf{z}^*) = p_{z_k}(\mathbf{z}^*)$, $k = 1, \ldots, K$, and $p(\mathbf{z}^*) = \theta(\mathbf{z}^*; u^*, y, \boldsymbol{\alpha}) = \phi(z_1^*, \ldots, z_k^*; \pi^*, \boldsymbol{\beta})$ hold for at least one consumer and a producer, a sale occurs. In other words, observing a market transaction for the product $\mathbf{z}_i$ at price $p(\mathbf{z}_i)$, the pair $\{p(\mathbf{z}_i), \mathbf{z}_i\}$ implies that the marginal bid of the buyer and the marginal offer of the seller are exactly matched, and equal the implicit marginal hedonic price function determined by the market in all the dimensions of the vector $\mathbf{z}$. This is depicted in Figure 6.1, which shows tangencies between two producer–consumer pairs (assuming strictly concave bid and convex offer functions), and is similar to Rosen's (1974) and Taylor's (2003) representations.

The figure also portrays how the hedonic price function is found by tracing the locus of tangency points between the buyer's bid and the seller's offer curve, and $p(z_i)$ represents a joint envelope of a family of value functions. Given a stable distribution of preferences and technology in the population of consumers and firms participating in a market (i.e., in cross-sectional data), the hedonic price function can be represented as being solely a function of product attributes:

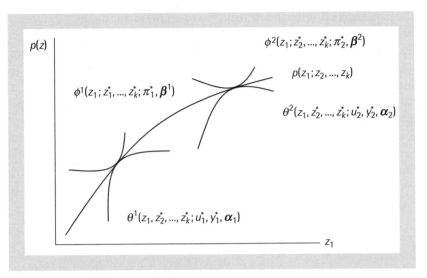

FIGURE 6.1 Hedonic price equilibrium

$$p(\mathbf{z}) = p(z_1, z_2, z_3, \dots, z_k) \tag{3}$$

Thus, once product attributes and prices are observed, forming the data set $\{p(\mathbf{z}_i), \mathbf{z}_i\}$, $i = 1, \dots, N$, a researcher can empirically determine the shape of the hedonic price function $\hat{p}(\mathbf{z})$ and recover marginal implicit prices for each attribute $\hat{p}_{z_k}(\mathbf{z})$, $k = 1, \dots, K$. This task is often referred to as the "first stage" of hedonic regression. Figure 6.1 portrays an application in which the hedonic price function is concave in z_1 and thus the implicit price of the attribute z_1 (the market price of adding an extra unit of z_1 to the bundle) diminishes as z_1 grows larger. This need not always be the case and the hedonic price function can take virtually any shape. Indeed, the principal empirical challenge (which we discuss in Section 3) of the first-stage regression stems from the lack of guidance from hedonic theory in choosing a functional form. What can perhaps be inferred from the setup of the model is that, given a population of heterogeneous consumers and firms, the hedonic price functions and its derivatives are likely non-linear in $\mathbf{z}$, and therefore implicit marginal prices $\frac{\partial p(\mathbf{z})}{\partial z_k} = \hat{p}_{z_k}(\mathbf{z})$ are a function of the vector of attributes embedded in a product.

As mentioned before, if one observes the bundle of characteristics that is actually chosen by a given consumer, then the set of implicit prices $\hat{p}_{z_k}(\mathbf{z}^*)$, $k = 1, \dots, K$ (evaluated at the chosen level of attributes), represents his/her willingness to pay for each z_k, as implied by the consumer optimality conditions. Taylor (2003: 263) shows how, based on this general idea, the estimated hedonic price function can be used to perform some limited welfare computations. We emphasize, nevertheless, that marginal implicit price functions should not be directly interpreted as general measures of consumers' willingness to pay for product attributes. Since both cost and willingness to pay factors determine the implicit prices, their interpretation is closer to that of an equilibrium market price. To provide an example, it is incorrect to infer that, because a particular attribute has the largest implicit price, it is the attribute that consumers value the most. High implicit prices may very well be due to elevated costs of production, and it is possible that only a small fraction of consumers actually purchase bundles containing that expensive attribute.

The *second stage* of hedonic regression refers to the estimation of the aggregated demand for (and supply of) individual product attributes, which allows for classical welfare analysis and comparison of alternative policies. Food-related examples include laws regulating the availability of product attributes or mandating their minimum or maximum levels (e.g., trans-fat oils, fat content, etc.). Unfortunately, the estimation of hedonic demand and supply functions is complicated by several empirical challenges, notably identification of demand and supply parameters and endogeneity of the second-stage regressors. Even though the debate over the empirical issues of hedonic demand estimation has evolved in a joint discussion, here we try to separate the two principal issues for the sake of exposition.

As in all demand studies, simply observing all the pairs of (implicit) prices and quantity purchased $\left\{ p_{z_k}(\mathbf{z}^*), \mathbf{z}^* \right\}$, $k = 1, \ldots, K$, does not allow identifying the demand or supply schedules for each attribute. To estimate demand, we need variables that are known to shift demand (but not supply), and are not included in the first-stage regression. Along these lines, Rosen suggested that, once estimated implicit marginal price functions are used to calculate attributes' prices at the level purchased by each consumer, aggregate inverse demand (D) and supply (S) for the kth attribute could be recovered by regressing $\hat{p}_{z_k}(\mathbf{z}^*)$ against $\mathbf{y}_1$, a vector of product attributes and a vector of sociodemographic consumer characteristics (the empirical counterpart of $\boldsymbol{\alpha}$), or a vector of producers' characteristics, $\mathbf{y}_2$, yielding (asterisks omitted from now on):

$$\hat{p}_{z_k}(\mathbf{z}) = D(\mathbf{z}, \mathbf{y}_1) \tag{4}$$

$$\hat{p}_{z_k}(\mathbf{z}) = S(\mathbf{z}, \mathbf{y}_2). \tag{5}$$

One pitfall of this approach, which was pointed out by Brown and Rosen (1982), is that if the $\hat{p}_{z_i}(\mathbf{z})$ are linear combinations of $\mathbf{z}$ (say, $\mathbf{Z}(\mathbf{Z}'\mathbf{Z})^{-1}\mathbf{Z}'\mathbf{p}$ from a first-stage linear regression in which $\mathbf{Z}$ is NxK and $\mathbf{p}$ is $Nx1$), equations (4) and (5) are still not identified. As Brown and Rosen wrote, "Any new information that they [the estimated implicit prices] may provide can only come from a priori restrictions placed on the functional form of the hedonic price function" (1982: 766).

Indeed, to overcome the difficulty, some authors (e.g., Quigley 1982) imposed additional identifying structure on the hedonic model via specific assumptions on the functional form of consumers' utility. Palmquist (1984) and Epple (1987) took another avenue by proposing the use of data from multiple markets as a source of identifying information. The logic is that, if the equilibrium hedonic price functions differ across markets but tastes can be controlled for, hedonic functions estimated for multiple markets allow obtaining several $\{p_{z_k}(\mathbf{z}), \mathbf{z}\}$ pairs for each "type" of consumer.

After a long hiatus in the debate over identification, Ekeland, Heckman, and Nesheim (2002, 2004) and Bajari and Benkard (2005) revived the discussion. Bajari and Benkard (2005) identified demand by assuming that the parametric form of utility is known, but leave the distribution of utility parameters across consumers unrestricted. Ekeland, Heckman, and Nesheim (2002) proposed a promising approach that exploits the recent advances in non-parametric methods and availability of computing power. Their method is based on extracting, rather than assuming, the identifying information embedded in the shape of the hedonic price function via non-parametric estimation.

The second major problem of hedonic demand and supply estimation relates to the endogeneity of the second-stage regressors. Brown and Rosen (1982) and Bartik (1987) noted that, since marginal implicit prices usually depend on the level of product attributes, consumers' choices of the pairs $\{p_{z_k}(\mathbf{z}), \mathbf{z}\}$ are simultaneous and perhaps correlated with unobserved taste variables (and thus the error term), biasing second-stage estimates. Some authors refer to this issue as the "sorting" problem. Consistent estimation of the demand and supply parameters can in theory be achieved via traditional two-stage least squares techniques, yet appropriate instruments for the endogenous regressors need to be available. In the words of Bartik, "The practical problem for empirical hedonic research [i.e., estimating hedonic demand parameters] is finding instruments whose exogeneity can be defended with some plausibility" (1987: 87).

Owing to the novelty and complexity of the recent non-parametric approaches to identification and the difficulties of finding good instruments or multi-market data sets, empirical estimation of second-stage hedonic demand models has been limited, especially in food markets. An exception is Nerlove (1995), who noted that in certain circumstances prices can be considered exogenous, and thus demand is identified and estimable in a single stage if data on quantity purchased of each differentiated good is available. He considered the wine market in Sweden, the argument being that Sweden represents a very small fraction of the world market, has no domestic production, and wine prices are controlled by the government, which simply adds a percentage markup to import prices. To offer here a rather simplified version of his model, Nerlove considers a whole class of closely related (but differentiated) commodities, and the representative consumer chooses a spectrum of quantities $\mathbf{Q}(\mathbf{z}_i)$, $i = 1, \ldots, N$, to consume[1] based on their income and preferences. The empirical model arising from utility maximization takes the form

---

[1] In Nerlove's article, consumers' preferences are represented by an index function mapping characteristics into valuations of quality, $\mathbf{A}(\mathbf{z})$, their exogenously determined prices $\mathbf{P}(\mathbf{z})$, and all the other available goods, $\mathbf{x}$. The utility function is represented as $U[V[\mathbf{A}(\mathbf{z}), \mathbf{Q}(\mathbf{z})], \mathbf{x}]$. Given the separability assumptions implied by the commas and an overall utility function homothetic in V versus other goods, the relative prices of the other goods will not influence choices between the varieties, allowing one to keep the focus on the trade-offs between attribute contents and their prices. From utility maximization Nerlove derives a spectrum of demand functions, which takes the form $\mathbf{Q}(\mathbf{z}) = \phi[\mathbf{P}(\mathbf{z}), \mathbf{y}_1 a(\mathbf{z})]$. Here, $\mathbf{y}_1$

$$\mathbf{Q(z)} = R[p(\mathbf{z}), \mathbf{z}, \mathbf{y}_1], \tag{6}$$

The empirical usefulness is that, *when supply is completely elastic and prices are exogenous*, one can estimate demand for each bundle or variety by regressing the quantities of each product against its unit price, the measures of quality attributes characterizing the variety, and consumers' characteristics.

Obviously, under this specification the coefficients associated with the quality characteristics $\mathbf{z}$ do not capture the implicit prices calculated in Rosen's traditional setting. Rather, they measure the difference in quantity consumed that can be linked to the presence of an extra unity of a specific product attribute, holding price constant. Implicit prices, the market price for a marginal increase in one attribute holding quantity constant, can nevertheless be recovered from (6) via the implicit function theorem as $p_{z_k} = \frac{R_{z_k}}{R_p}$. In summary, the method applies to settings in which consumers' choices do not affect prices and supply is virtually unlimited (see Durham, Pardoe, and Vega 2004 for an application to wine choices in restaurants).

Even when estimation of demand and supply of attributes is not possible because of the rather cogent technical and data requirements, simple estimation of the hedonic price function provides a wealth of information. Indeed, a wide array of empirical results are owed to first-stage regression (e.g., mass appraisal of real estate prices based on house characteristics, the computation of price indices separating the price effect of quality improvements from inflation, the estimation of the market value of environmental amenities or the reputation of firms).

2.2   Hedonic Modeling of Food Products

As discussed in the previous section, agricultural economists have long utilized the hedonic price relationship, and the hedonic price technique has been utilized to estimate the implicit prices of attributes for numerous food products, creating a rather vast literature. Again, most studies are limited to the (first-stage) estimation of the hedonic price functions. Examples include estimating the implicit price of apple size and grades (Tronstad, Huthoefer, and Monke 1992; Carew 2000); tuna qualities (McConnell and Strand 2000); nutritional and convenience factors in breakfast cereals (Stanley and Tschirhart 1991); chemical composition of wheat (Espinosa and Goodwin 1991); the value of leaner cuts (Unnevehr and Bard 1993) and package size and brand name in beef (Ward, Lusk, and Dutton 2008) and pork (Parcell and Schroeder 2007); and the price premium for organic tomatoes (Huang and Lin 2007) or veal labeled with specific geographical indication of origin (Loureiro and McCluskey 2000).

A large literature of hedonic models has been developed for wine, largely because of the considerable product differentiation in the industry. Combris, Lecocq, and Visser (1997) showed that objective characteristics (such as expert rating score and vintage)

---

represents consumers' characteristics, which include income, and the quality index $A(z)$ (the consumers' preferences) is represented by a common function of the elements of $\mathbf{z}$, $a(\mathbf{z})$.

are statistically significant in the hedonic price equation, while sensory variables (such as tannins content and other measurable chemicals) are not. This is not to say that quality has nothing to do with wine prices. Many researchers (Oczkowski 1994; Landon and Smith 1997; Schamel and Anderson 2003) have found that expert quality ratings are significant explanatory variables. Possible explanations for the insignificance of sensory cues are the consumers' difficulty with isolating the effect of each chemical on the final flavor and smell and that only a small percentage of wine purchasers are connoisseurs. In summary, expert ratings act as a quality signal to the consumer.

Since consumers cannot assess wine quality until after consumption, but they are aware that a large range in quality and prices exists, the applications of the hedonic method to the wine market offers an excellent framework to study reputation effects. Numerous studies (e.g., Schamel and Anderson 2003; Steiner 2004; Costanigro, McCluskey, and Mittelhammer 2007; Carew and Florkowski 2010) have found that certain regions of production command a *ceteris paribus* premium, which captures production costs differentials, comparative advantages due to *terroir*, and the value of the collective reputation of a production district. Landon and Smith (1998) used a hedonic model to explicitly model reputations as consumers' expectations on quality, and separated firm (winery) and regional reputations. Extending this line of research, Costanigro, McCluskey, and Goemans (2010) used a hedonic wine model to study how names and reputations nest within each other, and showed that reputation price premiums tend to migrate from aggregate (regional) names to specific (firm) ones as product prices increase.

To summarize, first-stage estimates of implicit prices of food attributes are useful on several accounts. First, producers aware of their own production costs can use implicit prices to devise marketing strategies and optimal mix of attributes. Furthermore, the hedonic approach is an effective tool in isolating the premium for "credence attributes" such as organic certification, geographical indications, or other socially responsible characteristics (e.g., dolphin-friendly tuna, fair trade coffee) that consumers cannot verify even after purchase. The added policy and regulatory interest of such studies originates from the producers' incentives when credence attributes have high implicit prices. In the absence of regulations, some producers may make a false claim and pocket the premium at zero production cost. Similarly, production districts with positive price premiums will want to prevent other producers from unduly using their name (e.g., the "Champagne" wine case), or their own members from lowering quality to save on production costs and free-ride on collective reputation (see Winfree and McCluskey 2005). Within this framework, hedonic models can be used to quantify the long-term effects of exogenous shocks on quality, or implementation of regulatory policies.

3   HEDONIC EMPIRICAL ISSUES

The relationship between prices and attributes is left unspecified by hedonic theory. Even the additive separability of the product attributes in the hedonic price function, a common tenet of most empirical hedonic applications, is an econometric assumption rather than a result derived from theory. It is generally accepted that the appropriate econometric model and functional form should be chosen by the researcher based on the specific application and the available data.

Owing to this lack of theoretical structure, a survey of the work accomplished since the early days of hedonic modeling encompasses the whole armamentarium of econometric models and methods familiar to applied economists, including parametric, semi-parametric, and non-parametric approaches. Our objective is to describe briefly each econometric model within the hedonic context and provide the reader with an understanding of the implications and trade-offs inherent to the choice of each alternative. The focus is kept on the first stage of hedonic regression.

3.1   Parametric and Semi-Parametric Models

In its most basic specification the estimated hedonic function takes the following linear form:

$$P_i = \alpha_0 + \sum_{k=1}^{K} \alpha_k z_{ki} + \varepsilon_i; \tag{7}$$

while additivity and linearity in parameters are common assumptions of parametric models, the chosen functional forms vary widely and often include non-linear transformations of the dependent variable, the regressors, or interaction. Ekeland, Heckman, and Nesheim (2002, 2004) emphasize that, since the curvature of the hedonic function is determined by the curvature of heterogeneous firm profit functions and consumers' utility functions, hedonic and implicit price functions can be expected to be non-linear. Regarding the parametric distribution of product prices little can be said a priori, but many authors note that non-negativity and right-skewness are features consistent with the log-normal distribution.[2] A logarithmic transformation of the dependent variable in (7) therefore yields

$$\ln (P_i) = \alpha_0 + \sum_{k=1}^{K} \alpha_k z_{ki} + \varepsilon_i \tag{8}$$

where ε is distributed $N(0, \sigma^2)$ if prices are indeed log-normally distributed. A survey of the literature will reveal that the log-linear model is by far the most commonly used specification in applied hedonic models and it is considered to be the "canonical" functional form in certain applications (Aldy and Viscusi 2008). Despite this

---

[2] If $y = \exp (X\beta + \varepsilon)$ and ε is distributed $N(0, \sigma^2)$, then y is log-normally distributed with mean $\exp (X\beta + 0.5\sigma^2)$ and variance $\exp (2X\beta) \left[e^{2\sigma^2} - e^{\sigma^2} \right]$. Taking the log transformation yields the linearized regression model $\ln (y) = X\beta + \varepsilon$; see Mittelhammer, Judge, and Miller (2000: 209).

popularity, it is not uncommon for empirical tests to reject the log-linear model in favor of alternative specifications (e.g., Halvorsen and Pollakowski 1981; Landon and Smith 1998), and generally the adoption of a specific functional form on a priori grounds is not justified.

Specification searches can be implemented by estimating several alternative functional forms. After their parallel estimation, alternative econometric models are measured against a series of specification (e.g., the Ramsey Regression Equation Specification Error Test (RESET) test by Ramsey 1969) and other diagnostic tests assessing homoskedasticity (Breush–Pagan; Goldfeld–Quandt) or normality (Shapiro–Wilk, Jarque–Bera), to choose the "best" model (see Landon and Smith 1998 for an example). Out-of sample forecasting performance should also be an important choice criterion for selecting an appropriate specification, as evaluation of within-sample performance alone can produce overfitted models and non-robust results. This can be accomplished by setting aside a small subsample (say, 10 percent of the available observations) for model validation purposes (for example, Fletcher, Mangan, and Raeburn 2004 consider mean forecasting error and mean percent forecasting error).

The single-parameter Box–Cox transformation of the dependent variable (Box and Cox 1964) has seen many applications in the hedonic literature (e.g., Stanley and Tschirhart 1991; McCluskey and Rausser 2003). The model takes the form

$$p_i^\theta = \alpha_0 + \sum_{k=1}^{K} \alpha_k z_{ki} + \varepsilon_i \tag{9}$$

where $p_i^\theta = \frac{(p_i^\theta - 1)}{\theta}$ for $\theta \neq 0$, and $p_i^\theta = \ln(p)$ for $\theta = 0$. Estimation involves simultaneously finding the transformation of the dependent variable, $\hat{\theta}$, and other model parameters maximizing a likelihood function[3] derived from a normality assumption. Thus, Box–Cox procedures simultaneously pursue normalization of the dependent variable (and the error term) and best possible fit. While the procedure was originally designed as a way of imposing approximate normality on a non-normally distributed random variable, in the hedonic context it is often used to determine the appropriate choice of functional form. For example, a failure to reject the null hypothesis that $\theta = 0$ results in the adoption of a log-linear model. Even though this practice is widespread and generally accepted, we point out that normalization was a historical necessity when the only available tool was least squares estimation (which is sensitive to the outliers typical of skewed distributions). Nowadays, a variety of estimation methods robust to outliers are available, and the need for normalization seems less cogent.

Halvorsen and Pollakowski (1981) extended the use of this approach to create the quadratic Box–Cox functional form, a nesting approach in which an extremely flexible

---

[3] Note that the use of Box–Cox transformation is one of the rare instances in which a fully parametric hedonic model is specified and estimated via maximum likelihood.

functional form allows deriving many specifications as special cases. The model takes the form

$$P_i^{\theta} = \alpha_0 + \sum_{k=1}^{K} \alpha_k z_{ki}^{\lambda} + \frac{1}{2} \sum_{k=1}^{K} \sum_{j=1}^{K} \gamma_{kj} z_{ki}^{\lambda} z_{ki}^{\lambda} + \varepsilon_i \tag{10}$$

where $\gamma_{kj} = \gamma_{jk}$ and θ and λ are Box–Cox transformations. Many alternative functional forms, including the translog (Christensen, Jorgenson, and Lau 1973), log-linear, double log, and quadratic, can be compared by testing the restrictions imposed on (7) by each functional form. Modern software packages often allow estimating a value of λ_k specific to each attribute. When this is done, interaction terms can usually be omitted.

While current econometric software makes it relatively simple to estimate such models, their cost may be prohibitive in terms of degrees of freedom, convergence issues, induced collinearity, and, most importantly, the overall interpretability of the model (this point was stressed by Cassel and Mendelssohn 1985). In addition to the obvious relationship between dependent and independent variables and the resulting implicit price function, the implications of choosing one functional form over another can also be analyzed by considering the implied hedonic contours. Hedonic contour graphs portray the possible combinations of any two attributes yielding the same product price, holding the other attributes constant (see Triplett 2006: 175).

3.2   Heteroskedasticity

Heteroskedastic errors are widespread in hedonic applications, and specific patterns of heteroskedasticity may be typical of a specific good or group of products. Often, the variance of the error term increases with the magnitude of the predicted prices,[4] yielding the heteroskedastic process $\sigma_i^2 = \sigma^2(\hat{p}_{ik})$, where σ^2 is a constant (see Faux and Perry 1999 in a valuation of irrigation water for an example). One possible explanation for this increase in the variance of prices about the conditional mean is provided by Rosen's (1981) article "The Economics of Superstars." In other instances, the variance may be related to a product attribute (or more), taking the form $\sigma_i^2 = \sigma(z_{ik})$. To provide an example, building-age-related heteroskedasticity is common in real estate hedonic models (Goodman and Thibodeau 1998).

Under heteroskedasticity, the OLS estimator is inefficient and the standard estimator of the variance–covariance matrix is biased. The hedonic literature has dealt with the problem adopting the classical textbook remedies: one can either rely on the consistency of the OLS estimator while correcting the estimates of the coefficients' standard errors (White 1980) or adopt a weighted least squares approach to transform the data. It is worth reminding that the second approach implies knowing or discovering the

---

[4] Note that if y is log-normally distributed, estimating $\mathbf{y} = \mathbf{X\beta} + \boldsymbol{\varepsilon}$ will produce this kind of heteroskedasticity.

correct structure of heteroskedasticity at the risk of biasing the coefficient estimates, and researchers should keep in mind the Hippocratic precept "First, do no harm" when dealing with this problem.

Since heteroskedasticity can be induced by misspecification, certain data transformations may stabilize the variance. It is important to discriminate between induced heteroskedasticity and "true" heteroskedasticity as the two problems call for different remedial action. Thursby (1982) shows that the combined use of the RESET and Goldfeld–Quandt provide a way to distinguish the two.[5] Early work by Zarembka (1974) suggested that, since data transformations may stabilize the variance or induce heteroskedasticity, the Box–Cox procedure is not robust to heteroskedastic errors, biasing results toward variance-stabilizing transformations. Lahiri and Egy (1981) showed that, if z is a variable related to the pattern of heteroskedasticity according to $\sigma_i^2 = \sigma^2(z_i^\delta)$, δ and θ can be jointly estimated, and separate transformations for misspecification and heteroskedasticity can be implemented.

3.3   Collinearity

A common feature of hedonic regression is a large number of explanatory variables. Since most hedonic research uses observational data, some degree of collinearity is unavoidable, causing potentially noisy estimates. If the implicit prices are of minor interest per se, as when building hedonic price indices, collinearity is of limited concern. If instead valuing product attributes is the primary objective of the analysis, remedial action should be considered. The fact that coefficients in hedonic regression can often be bounded, at a minimum in term of their signs, inspired the Bayesian approach (e.g., Atkinson and Crocker 1987; Gilley and Pace 1995), yet non-frequentist methods have seen limited application so far in the hedonic literature.

A more common approach is reducing the dimensionality of the data matrix with the use of multivariate analysis techniques such as principal components (Asher 1992), or factor analysis (Rosiers, Thériault, and Villeneuve 2000). One caveat associated with the adoption of such techniques is that the resulting data constructs may lack a clear economic interpretation, which defeats the purpose of the modeling exercise when the primary objective is a study of implicit price functions. If a particular subset of coefficients is of interest, a possible approach is applying dimensionality-reducing techniques to all variables *but* the ones of direct interest.

---

[5] Since the RESET test is insensitive to heteroskedasticity, a significant RESET test implies misspecification, while heteroskedasticity is signaled by an insignificant RESET and a significant GQ test.

3.4   Specification Search Example: A Hedonic Price Equation for Wine

An example of a semi-parametric model of a hedonic price function for red wine is offered in this section. This example is based on a standard specification search performed in Costanigro, McCluskey, and Mittelhammer (2007). The section then proceeds to show price-dependent market segmentation in the wine market. The data set is composed of 13,024 observations derived from ten years (1991–2000) of ratings scores reported in the *Wine Spectator* magazine for California and Washington red wines. The variables include the price of the wine adjusted to 2000 values by a consumer price index (CPI) for alcohol, score obtained in expert sensory evaluation by the *Wine Spectator's* experts, the number of cases produced, and the years of aging before commercialization. Descriptive statistics for these variables are reported in Table 6.1. Indicator variables were used to denote regions of production, wine varieties, and the presence of label information. Table 6.2 presents the variables with a brief description.

A series of possible transformations of the dependent variable were considered and evaluated on the basis of variance stabilization, normality of the residuals, and misspecification. The Goldfeld–Quandt test was used to detect heteroskedasticity proportional to predicted values and the RESET test for misspecification (second, third, and fourth power). For the normality of the residuals, we employed three different tests: Anderson–Darling, Komolgorov–Smirnov and Ryan–Joiner. Results of the tests are presented in Table 6.3. The inverse square transformation performed the best. The specifications of the independent variables were also determined by screening possible transformations of the non-binary variables and examining excluded-variable residual plots. The following hedonic price function was estimated via OLS:

Table 6.1 Descriptive statistics of quantitative explanatory variables

State	variable	Mean	Median	Minimum	Maximum
California[a]	Price[b]	31.1	22	3	2,000
	Cases	6,719	1,467	16	950,000
	Score	86.1	87	60	99
	Age	2.8	3	1	9
Washington[c]	Price[b]	23.3	20	5	144
	Cases	6,720	1,000	45	550,000
	Score	86.8	87	67	96
	Age	2.8	3	1	7

[a] 11,774 observations.
[b] Adjusted to year 2000 by a CPI index for alcohol.
[c] 1,250 observations.

Table 6.2 Descriptions of the abbreviation used for the explanatory variables

Predictor	short description
Score	Rating score from the wine spectator
Scscore	Score centered by subtracting its mean
Scscore^2	Scscore squared
Age	Years of aging before commercialization
Agesc	Age centered by subtracting its mean
Agesc^2	Agesc squared
Cases	Number of cases produced
Lncas	Natural log of hundreds of cases produced
Napa	Region of production
Bay area	
Sonoma	
South coast	
Carneros	
Sierra foothills	
Mendocino	
Washington	
Non-varietal	Grape variety
Pinot Noir	
Cabernet	
Merlot	
Syrah	
Reserve	"Reserve" was reported on the label
Vineyard	Specific name of the vineyard on the label
Estate	"Estate" produced wine
91,..., 99	Vintage
Wa	Washington state wines

$$Price_i^{-0.5} = \beta_0 + \beta_0^w + (\beta_1)(Score_i) + (\beta_2)(Score_i)^2 + (\beta_3)(Age_i) + (\beta_4)(Age_i)^2$$
$$+ (\beta_5)LN(Cases_i) + \sum_{k=1}^{5}(\beta_{5+k})(Variety_i) + \sum_{k=1}^{9}(\beta_{10+k})(Vintage_i)$$
$$+ \sum_{k=1}^{3}(\beta_{19+k})(Label_i) + \sum_{k=1}^{7}(\beta_{22+k})(Region_i) + \varepsilon_i \tag{11}$$

Variables interacting Washington state with other attributes were also estimated but are not reported owing to their statistical insignificance. As Table 6.3 shows, formal testing still detected a moderate degree of heteroskedasticity (and misspecification),[6] but the possible gains in estimation efficiency that might be achieved by adjusting the estimator for an appropriate heteroskedastic process are muted by the consistency of

---

[6] It should be noticed that the power of a test is increasing in sample size. In the limit, if the sample is large enough, a formal test will reject virtually *any* hypothesis stated in the form of strict equality.

Table 6.3 Test statistics result for several specifications of the dependent variable

Transformation of dependent variable	Normality			Specification			Heteroskedasticity
	Anderson–A-squared	Ryan–Joiner R	Komolgorov–Smirnov D	Reset (2) F-value	Reset (3) F-value	Reset (4) F-value	Goldfeld–Quandt GQ
−2	552.548	0.879	0.155	1237.100	692.730	469.090	20.497
	0.000	0.000	0.000	0.000	0.000	0.000	0.000
−1.5	295.709	0.938	0.114	713.450	436.320	294.860	9.029
	0.000	0.000	0.000	0.000	0.000	0.000	0.000
−1	106.373	0.979	0.066	228.520	172.030	116.840	3.923
	0.000	0.000	0.000	0.000	0.000	0.000	0.000
−0.5	18.584	0.997	0.025	1.236	26.907	19.097	1.618
	0.000	0.000	0.000	0.266	0.000	0.000	0.000
Box–Cox (−0.36)	14.972	0.997	0.023	9.3751	23.5	***	1.2214
	0.000	0.000	0.000	0.002	0.000	0.000	0.000
Natural log	62.396	0.974	0.048	187.000	101.960	69.217	1.807
	0.000	0.000	0.000	0.000	0.000	0.000	0.000
0.5	581.245	0.804	0.140	543.330	276.400	184.920	8.911
	0.000	0.000	0.000	0.000	0.000	0.000	0.000
Linear	2,200.000	0.490	0.285	465.850	242.590	168.760	92.490
	0.000	0.000	0.000	0.000	0.000	0.000	0.000
1.5	3,400.000	0.305	0.385	264.230	147.330	101.640	777.130
	0.000	0.000	0.000	0.000	0.000	0.000	0.000
2	3,800.000	0.233	0.421	147.590	82.081	59.130	12,204.150
	0.000	0.000	0.000	0.000	0.000	0.000	0.000

Note: Probability values are displayed below statistical test values.

the OLS estimator and the large sample size on which the estimators are based.[7] As a matter of caution the covariance matrix of the parameters was estimated using White's consistent heteroskedasticity-robust estimator.

Estimated coefficients of the model in (11) are reported in Table 6.4. The large t-statistics suggest that collinearity does not represent an issue in this sample. In interpreting the results, it is important to note that owing to the transformation of

Table 6.4 Hedonic price estimation for red wine

Variable	coefficient	t
Constant	21.999	104.7
Scscore	−0.620	−61.29
Scscore^2	−0.022	−16.47
Agesc	−1.302	−23.69
Agesc^2	0.108	2.63
Lncas	1.004	41.75
Napa[a]	−5.483	−36.77
Bay area[a]	−3.437	−17.34
Sonoma[a]	−4.053	−28.31
South coast[a]	−3.222	−20.46
Carneros[a]	−4.291	−23.74
Sierra foothills[a]	−2.327	−10.3
Mendocino[a]	−2.406	−12.64
Wa[a]	−0.652	−0.95
Non-varietal[b]	−4.319	−27.29
Pinot Noir[b]	−3.252	−32.16
Cabernet[b]	−2.479	−24.4
Merlot[b]	−2.200	−21.79
Syrah[b]	−0.582	−4.26
Reserve[c]	−1.105	−10.89
Vineyard[c]	−0.858	−11.46
Estate[c]	−0.601	−2.88
91[d]	5.353	31.78
92[d]	5.339	31.38
93[d]	4.372	27.24
94[d]	4.097	27.8
95[d]	3.311	23.24
96[d]	2.397	17.75
97[d]	1.749	13.07
98[d]	0.393	2.77
99[d]	0.668	5.02

[a] Omitted dummy variable: generic California.
[b] Omitted dummy variable: Zinfandel.
[c] Omitted dummy variable: no additional label information.
[d] Omitted variable: year 2000.

[7] There is also the mitigating issue of the need to discover the correct heteroskedastic structure of the error process.

the dependent variable, coefficients with a negative sign signify a positive marginal implicit price. Empirical results conformed to a priori expectations: for all estimated models, price is increasing in aging and rating score over the range of the data and decreasing in the number of cases produced. Confirming previously published results, regional appellations command price premiums relative to a generic California wine, with Napa Valley bringing the largest premium. The coefficients associated with the variety variables capture the difference in price relative to Zinfandel grapes, and the coefficients for vintages refer to price differences relative to the excluded year 2000. This empirical example was a first step in understanding the Washington and California red wine markets.

3.5   Some Considerations on the Retransformation Problem

In hedonic modeling, non-linear transformations of the dependent variable induce implicit price functions that depend on the price of the differentiated product, which in turn is a function of the levels of all attributes. If we consider a deterministic model in the form $h(p) = \mathbf{z}\boldsymbol{\beta}$, where $h(p)$ represents a non-linear transformation, the implicit price functions can be recovered as $\frac{\partial p}{\partial z_k} = \frac{\partial [h^{-1}(\mathbf{Z}\boldsymbol{\beta})]}{\partial z_k} = \frac{\partial h^{-1}(p)}{\partial p} \frac{\partial \mathbf{z}\boldsymbol{\beta}}{\partial z_k}$, where $\frac{\partial h^{-1}(p)}{\partial p}$ is a function of p in virtue of the non-linearity of h. In many applications, this is a desirable feature. For example, when estimating a hedonic model of wine prices, we might expect the implicit price of one extra year of cellaring to be proportional to the total price of the product. One down side is that once a transformation of the dependent variable is adopted, it is applied indiscriminately to the implicit price function of all attributes. An additional problem is that the original units of measure are lost, and applied economists and policymakers alike are interested in the dollar value of goods and product attributes, not log dollars or inverse square root dollars. To restore the original units of measure, inverse transformations (e.g., exponentiation after the natural log) are often applied[8] on predicted values and estimated coefficients to restore the original units of measure. While this is legitimate within the deterministic model presented before, Jensen's inequality implies that generally[9] $E(y|x) \neq h^{-1}(E(h(y)|x))$ and $\frac{\partial E(y|x)}{\partial x} \neq \frac{\partial h^{-1}[E(h(y)|x)]}{\partial x}$.

The issue of retransformation has been largely ignored in hedonic modeling, but has been analyzed within the context of log-linearization of multiplicative models (e.g., Cobb–Douglas in production models and gravity equations in international trade), but

---

[8] Koenker (2005: 47), discussing this practice, writes, "You can do it, but it would be wrong," citing a Nixon dictum.

[9] If $h(p)$ is strictly convex, then $E[h(p)] > h[E(p)]$; if $h(p)$ is strictly concave, then $E[h(p)] < h[E(p)]$. Thus, exponentiation after the logarithmic transformation will tend to underestimate the conditional mean.

the implications straightforwardly extend to hedonic models. While early results by Goldberger (1968) on log-normal distributions suggested that only estimates of the intercept are affected by retransformation bias, which could be easily eliminated, more recent work by Silva and Tenreyro (2006: 664) show that, in the presence of an unknown form of heteroskedasticity, "the nonlinear transformation of the dependent variable changes the properties of the error term in a nontrivial way" and therefore "it is not possible to recover information about the conditional expectation of y from the conditional mean of $\ln(y)$."

Manning (1998) presents a broader treatment of the issue within the context of models of health care expenditure, where, much like in hedonics, non-linear transformations are implemented to deal with a heavily right-skewed dependent variable. Modifying the notation to highlight our application to hedonic modeling, the author first considers the familiar log-linear model $\ln(p) = z\boldsymbol{\beta} + \epsilon$; with $E(\varepsilon) = 0$, $E(\epsilon|z) = 0$, and non-constant variance $E(\varepsilon^2) \neq c$ to show that:

$$E(p|\mathbf{z}) = e^{z\boldsymbol{\beta}} E(e^{\varepsilon}) = e^{z\boldsymbol{\beta}} \int e^{\varepsilon} dF(\varepsilon) \neq e^{z\boldsymbol{\beta}}; \qquad (12)$$

where $F(\varepsilon)$ is the cumulative distribution of ε. If the assumption that ε is distributed N $(0, \sigma^2(Z))$ is made, implying that prices are log-normally distributed but the variance is proportional to one or more of the explanatory variables, the conditional expectation of the original variable can be recovered as

$$E(p|\mathbf{z}) = e^{z\boldsymbol{\beta} + 0.5\sigma^2(\mathbf{z})} \qquad (13)$$

and

$$\frac{\partial E(p|z_k)}{\partial z_k} = E(p|\mathbf{z}) \left[\boldsymbol{\beta}_k + 0.5 \frac{\partial \sigma^2(\mathbf{z})}{\partial z_k} \right] \qquad (14)$$

Substitution of $\sigma^2(\mathbf{Z})$ with σ^2 in equations (13) and (14) produces Goldberger's (1968) results regarding bias correction adjustment and unbiasedness of retransformed estimates of the slope parameters under homoskedasticity. For the general case of a Box–Cox transformation and unknown price distribution to recover $E(p|\mathbf{z})$ the integral $\int [1 + \theta(\mathbf{z}\boldsymbol{\beta} + \varepsilon)]^{\frac{1}{\theta}} dF(\varepsilon)$ needs to be evaluated. In Manning's words, "The price of using a log (or any other) transform of the dependent variable is that the analyst must also learn about the nature of the error structure" (1998: 293). A possible approach to avoid the retransformation problem is estimating the hedonic price function at multiple conditional quantiles (Koenker and Basset 1978), leaving the dependent variable in its linear form. In this way, implicit prices can be immediately recovered from the estimated coefficient, and are allowed to vary across (predicted) prices. This method has been used in Costanigro, McCluskey, and Goemans (2010), but its general applicability to multiple hedonic settings is the object of ongoing work.

3.6   Non-Parametric and Hybrid Models

Consider the following econometric model:

$$p = \mathbf{g}(\mathbf{z}) + \varepsilon, \tag{15}$$

where no assumptions are made regarding the probability density function of ε, and $g(\mathbf{z})$ is left unspecified. The appealing feature of the hedonic model in (15) is that the analyst only needs to identify the product attributes appearing in $\mathbf{Z}$, leaving the determination of the functional dependency of prices and attributes to be completely data-driven.

Kernel regression estimators, of which Nadaraya–Watson is a popular example, are able to estimate $E(p|z)$ in this "assumption-free" environment by evaluating $\hat{g}(\mathbf{z})$ in a series of piecewise estimation using only data in the proximity (i.e., with similar values in the covariates) of a given point of evaluation $(p_0, \mathbf{z}_0)$. The general idea[10] is that, if Kernel density estimators can be used to estimate the joint and marginal density functions $f(p, \mathbf{z})$ and $f(\mathbf{z})$, then one can reconstruct the shape of the conditional density function $E(p|z) = g(z) = \int_{-\infty}^{\infty} p \left[\frac{f(p,z)}{f(z)} \right] dp$.

For each point of evaluation, a non-parametric estimate of $g(\mathbf{z}_0)$ can be represented as a weighted function of the dependent variable:

$$\hat{P}_0 = \hat{g}(\mathbf{z}_0) = \sum_{i=1}^{N} w_i(\mathbf{z}_0; \mathbf{z}_i; h) p_i, \tag{16}$$

where $w_i(\mathbf{z}_0; \mathbf{z}_i; h)$ emphasizes that the weight assigned by the Kernel function to each observation is proportional to some measure[11] of distance between each set of covariates in the pairs (z_{0k}, z_{ik}). The parameter h, named bandwidth, determines the size of the data neighborhoods, and is either set by the researcher or determined by some pre- or post-data optimality criterion. For each point of evaluation, data points falling outside of the neighborhood receive a zero weight. The whole surface of the conditional density is reconstructed by estimating $\hat{g}(\mathbf{z})$ at multiple points of evaluation, thereby accommodating for virtually any functional relationship between regressand and regressors.

The cost of eliminating all structure and assumptions from the econometric model is that non-parametric estimates tend to be noisy and imprecise. In the hedonic context, the problem is exacerbated by the large number of regressors and the so-called curse of dimensionality (Bellman 1961): for a given point of evaluation $(p_0, \mathbf{z}_0)$ and a fixed choice of the bandwidth parameter h, increasing the number of regressors reduces the number of observations close to a point of evaluation, making the data sparse and the

---

[10] Kernel regression and the Nadaraya–Watson estimator are presented in detail in most graduate-level econometric books. See, e.g., Mittelhammer, Judge, and Miller (2000: 613).

[11] Common choices are the Epanechnikov and the Tricube Kernel functions.

estimates imprecise. Thus, large and "dense" data sets are necessary to achieve acceptably precise estimates.

While Nadaraya–Watson-type estimators have seen few applications in the hedonic literature, applied economists have used a number of strategies to conjugate the appealing features of non-parametric methods and the necessity of introducing some structure in the econometric model. One approach is the joint use of variable bandwidth algorithms that include more data when the design matrix becomes sparse, such as the locally weighted scatterplot smoothing (LOESS) (Cleveland and Devlin 1988), and the adoption of polynomial expansions accommodating for the possible curvature of $g(\mathbf{z})$ when a sparse design matrix induces larger—potentially "not local"—neighborhoods of data (see Trevor Hastie and Loader 1993). For the case of a linear (first-order) approximation to $g(\mathbf{z}_0)$, the local polynomial estimator (Fan and Gijbels 1996: 58) solves the minimization problem:

$$\underset{\hat{\boldsymbol{\alpha}}, \hat{\boldsymbol{\beta}}}{\operatorname{argmin}} \quad \left\{ \sum_{i=1}^{n} [p_i - \hat{\boldsymbol{\alpha}}_{(z_0)} - (\mathbf{z}_i - \mathbf{z}_0)\hat{\boldsymbol{\alpha}}, \hat{\boldsymbol{\beta}}_{(z_0)}]^2 K[(\mathbf{z}_i - \mathbf{z}_0)/h] \right\} \qquad (17)$$

where K represents a Kernel weighting function of choice.[12] It should be noted that Nadaraya–Watson-type estimators can be conceptualized as zero-order polynomial expansions, in which only the intercept $\hat{\boldsymbol{\alpha}}_{(z_0)}$ in (17) is estimated. In addition, to allow for some curvature, the local linear regressor of (17) makes implicit prices immediately available, as the estimate of $\frac{\partial E(p|z_0)}{\partial z_k}$ can be found in the kth entry of $\hat{\boldsymbol{\beta}}_{(z_0)}$. Estimation is implemented via a series of weighted OLS regressions; one at each point of evaluation, where the weights are determined by the Kernel function and each row of $\mathbf{z}$ is transformed according to $\mathbf{z}_i^* = [\mathbf{z}_i - \mathbf{z}_0]$. Applications of Local Polynomial Regression to hedonic modeling are becoming increasingly common, and include Bin (2004), Martins-Filho and Bin (2005), Bajari and Benkard (2005), Bontempsa, Simioni, and Surry (2008), and Costanigro, Mittelhammer, and McCluskey (2009).

Another way of imposing some structure to the econometric model is estimating hybrid functions (e.g., Anglin and Gencay 1996; Bontemps, Simioni, and Surry 2008) in which a set of attributes ($\mathbf{x}$) enter the econometric model parametrically while other attributes ($\mathbf{z}$) are estimated non-parametrically, thereby obtaining the econometric model

$$\mathbf{p} = \mathbf{x}\boldsymbol{\beta} + g(\mathbf{z}) + \boldsymbol{\varepsilon}; \qquad (18)$$

where $\mathbf{x}$ may include a transformed variable. Qualitative regressors, which complicate non-parametric estimation,[13] and control variables of minor economic interest are

---

[12] Note that Nadaraya–Watson-type estimators can be conceptualized as zero-order polynomial expansions, in which only the intercept $\hat{\boldsymbol{\alpha}}_{(z_0)}$ is estimated.

[13] (Racine and Li 2004) present a method to include ordered and unordered qualitative regressors in the non-parametric part of the model. See Parmeter, Henderson, and Kumbhakar (2007) for an application to hedonic modeling.

generally included in the parametric part, while the non-parametric approach is reserved for the subset of variables of principal economic interest.

The back-fitting approach (Friedman and Stuetzle 1981; Hastie and Tibshirani 1990) adds even more structure to the model, estimating hybrid models in which the functional form of a set of variables is left unspecified, but an assumption of additivity is made:

$$p = \mathbf{x}\boldsymbol{\beta} + \sum_{j-1}^{J} g_j(\mathbf{z}_j) + \varepsilon \tag{19}$$

Estimation of each $g_j(\mathbf{z}_j)$. is accomplished iteratively in a series of non-parametric regressions on excluded-variable residuals (see Bin 2004 and Martins-Filho and Bin 2005 for an application to hedonic models).

Because of their computationally intensive nature, non-parametric methods were rarely employed in the early years of the hedonic literature, but are now becoming increasingly common in the face of their generally superior predictive performance and the increase in computing power available to applied economists. Recent theoretical contributions in hedonic modeling (Ekeland, Heckman, and Nesheim 2002; Bajari and Benkard 2005) show that the non-linearity of implicit price functions can also serve as a base for the identification of the second stage of hedonic regression in single markets data suggest that the trend will continue.

3.7 Aggregation and Market Segmentation

Since the hedonic model assumes the market is in equilibrium and there is perfect information, products with similar vectors of attributes should share similar implicit price functions. If price differences arise, perfectly informed buyers will purchase only the cheaper products, until the equilibrium is re-established. Therefore, diverging implicit price functions, when encountered, provide some evidence for the existence of market segments.

The debate over the relevance of market segmentation in hedonic modeling originated in the real estate literature with Straszheim (1974), who noted that implicit price functions changed across San Francisco districts and segmenting the hedonic regression accordingly increased the overall explanatory power of the hedonic model. When submarkets exist, he noted, estimating a single aggregate hedonic function will generally produce biased estimates. According to Freeman (1993: 368), a fundamental condition for the existence of different price functions is that "the structure of demand, the structure of supply, or both, must differ across segments." This stems from the fact that the hedonic price function is a double envelope of bid (demand) and offer (supply) functions. Furthermore, some form of obstacle to mobility must impede sellers from arbitraging and buyers from migrating to cheaper markets.

While segmenting factors in markets for differentiated products include the three major dimensions of space, time, and product characteristics, the literature on market segmentation largely focused on geographical and spatial factors, owing to the original context of modeling real estate prices. To provide a few examples within this vast stream of literature, Straszheim (1974) considered political boundaries, Goodman and Thibodeau (1998) differences in school district performance and ethnic composition across districts. Along similar lines, the work of environmental economists quantifying how vicinity to amenities (e.g., Tyrväinen and Miettinen 2000) or nuisance factors (e.g., Bontemps, Simioni, and Surry 2008) influences property values is also a (sometimes implicit) exercise in identifying submarkets. In food markets, spatial market segmentation often arises from differences in consumer preferences across countries (consider, for example, the different valuation of the "organic" attribute across countries observed by Baker et al. 2004).

Temporal differences in equilibrium prices are at the core of the hedonic price indexing literature (see Triplett 2006 for a general survey), where the hedonic framework is used to measure changes in prices across time periods holding constant product attributes. In other hedonic studies, price indices are routinely used to control for such temporal variations.

Market segmentation induced by product characteristics generally arises from the bundled nature of differentiated products. One possibility is that certain combinations of attributes may not be produced or available for purchase. If the attribute space is not a convex set, researchers may run the risk of extrapolating their results. More importantly, Pakes (2003) notes that, when (proprietary) attributes exist as a result of product innovation, market power will distort the implicit price function of *all* the attributes bundled with the improved product.

Costanigro, Mittelhammer, and McCluskey (2009) consider use-based market segments, noting that

> as the vectors of attribute levels characterizing two goods increasingly diverge, it is more likely that consumers purchase the goods for different purposes. That is, the more two products are differentiated, the less they are fungible in the same or similar use. Further, the costs associated with assembling a given bundle of attributes in the same product will change as the vector of attributes changes.

Even though their application is the wine market, the concept applies more generally. Consider the automotive industry: SUVs and sports cars are both vehicles, but they are generally used for different purposes. Many product attributes may be similar across these types of vehicle, yet the structure of the buyers' preferences, the number of competing firms, and their cost structure will change.

Once a reason for suspecting market segmentation is identified, an empirical strategy to ultimately estimate separate hedonic functions is needed. The most immediate approach is to isolate a number of data partitions (i.e., the market segments) for which a unique hedonic function can be estimated. In some cases the presence of one or more product attributes unambiguously identifies a market segment, and the categorization process is rather trivial (e.g., estimate separate regressions for offices, apartments, and detached houses).

When the transition from one market segment to another is gradual and a clear-cut rule for isolating market segments does not exist, the empirical task is more challenging. Such complications often arise when multiple concurring factors generate the market segments, or when a gradual transition in segmenting factors generates partially overlapping market segments. One approach is to apply data clustering algorithms (Ward and K-means are frequent choices) to the original data or to factor scores and principal components (e.g., Bourassa et al. 1999; Watkins 1999), thereby identifying market segments on the basis of similarities in attribute levels. For this method to produce desirable results, the researcher needs to know which attributes to include in the clustering step (i.e., the segmenting factors), and a direct, *constant* (i.e., no threshold or qualitative effects) relationship between changes in attribute levels and changes in implicit price functions needs to hold. Costanigro, Mittelhammer, and McCluskey (2009) pointed out that these conditions rarely hold, and proposed a multi-step process in which the hedonic function is first estimated locally (i.e., non-parametrically) and then using a clustering algorithm to isolate data partitions with similar implicit price functions. The remaining drawback, common to all clustering approaches, is that the classes of products identified by each data partition may not be immediately clear to the researcher.

A second approach is making market segmentation an explicit part of the hedonic model. In certain cases, segmenting factors can be included as extra product attributes (e.g., positive and negative externalities in environmental studies), and varying implicit price functions can be accommodated via appropriate interaction terms between attributes and segmenting factors. When more than one segmenting factor exists, or segmenting factors are not known to the researcher, latent class (Aitkin and Rubin 1985) and mixture models (Heckman and Singer 1984) are appropriate, even though these methods have seen little application in the hedonic context. The principal drawback of these likelihood-based techniques is their heavy parameterization: the researcher needs to commit to a density function describing the price distribution, and one describing the genesis of submarkets.

4   Conclusions

Increasingly food products are heterogeneous and have multiple characteristics. This is a relatively recent phenomenon and is in contrast to the food commodities that were purchased by previous generations of consumers. The mass customization of purchases changes how researchers can most effectively study food markets. Work is needed to determine how to analyze, both conceptually and empirically, the increased differentiation and variety that exists in today's food markets.

Many interesting new topics of research are emerging in this area of inquiry. Not only will agricultural economists need to combine information about consumer preferences that are present in different sources of data, they will also need to turn to other disciplines to better understand markets. This includes insights from sensory scientists about factors that affect taste and eating quality, and concepts from marketing and psychology to investigate how values, culture, identity, and social norms affect markets.

From an empirical point of view, the increasing globalization of the world food markets offers the opportunity to use spatial statistical techniques to investigate to what extent multiple markets overlap and interact in determining food prices. The use of spatial information helps to control for omitted variables correlated with space. Such variables in food markets could include location of production origin (especially important for products that rely on collective reputations such as wine), preferences for organic foods and other socially responsible food attributes, and the general availability of variety.

In this chapter we discussed theoretical and empirical issues related to both hedonic theory and product characteristics models. There are many empirical issues to address and potential problems to overcome with both approaches. This is a fruitful area of research with increased customization of products and the increasing availability of large data sets, including scanner data from the food industry.

REFERENCES

Adelman, I., and Z. Griliches. 1961. "On an Index of Quality Change." *Journal of the American Statistical Association* 56: 535–48.

Aitkin, M., and D. B. Rubin. 1985. "Estimation and Hypothesis Testing in Finite Mixture Models." *Journal of the Royal Statistical Society*, ser. B: *Methodological* 47: 67–75.

Aldy, J. E., and W. K. Viscusi. 2008. "Adjusting the Value of a Statistical Life for Age and Cohort Effects." *Review of Economics and Statistics* 90/3: 573–81.

Anderson, S. 2008. "Product Differentiation." In S. N. Durlauf and L. E. Blume, eds, *The New Palgrave Dictionary of Economics*. Basingstoke: Palgrave Macmillan.

Anglin, P. M., and R. Gençay. 1996. "Semiparametric Estimation of a Hedonic Price Function." *Journal of Applied Econometrics* 11: 633–48.

Asher, C. C. 1992. "Hedonic Analysis of Reliability and Safety for New Automobiles." *Journal of Consumer Affairs* 26/2: 377.

Atkinson, S. E., and T. D. Crocker. 1987. "A Bayesian Approach to Assessing the Robustness of Hedonic Property Value Studies." *Journal of Applied Econometrics* 2/1: 27–45.

Bajari, P., and C. L. Benkard. 2005. "Demand Estimation with Heterogeneous Consumers and Unobserved Product Characteristics: A Hedonic Approach." *Journal of Political Economy* 113/6: 1239–76.

Baker, S., K. E. Thompson, J. Engelken, and K. Huntley. 2004. "Mapping the Values Driving Organic Food Choice: Germany versus the UK." *European Journal of Marketing* 38/8: 995–1012.

Barkema, A., and M. Drabenstott. 1995. "The Many Paths of Vertical Coordination: Structural Implications for the U.S. Food System." *Agribusiness* 11: 483–92.

Bartik, T. J. 1987. "The Estimation of Demand Parameters in Hedonic Price Models." *Journal of Political Economy* 95/1 (Feb.), 81–8.

Bellman, R. 1961. *Adaptive Control Processes: A Guided Tour*. Princeton: Princeton University Press.

Berry, S. T., J. Levinsohn, and A. Pakes. 1995. "Automobile Prices in Market Equilibrium." *Econometrica* 64: 841–90.

Bin, O. 2004. "A Prediction Comparison of Housing Sales Prices by Parametric versus Semi-Parametric Regressions." *Journal of Housing Economics* 13: 68–84.

Bontemps, C., M. Simioni, and Y. Surry. 2008. "Semiparametric Hedonic Price Models: Assessing the Effects of Agricultural Nonpoint Source Pollution." *Journal of Applied Econometrics* 23/6: 825–42.

Bourassa, S. C., F. Hamelink, M. Hoesli, and B. D. MacGregor. 1999. "Defining Housing Submarkets." *Journal of Housing Economics* 8: 160–83.

Box, G. E. P., and D. R. Cox. 1964. "An Analysis of Transformations." *Journal of the Royal Statistical Society*, ser. B: *Methodological* 26/2: 211–52.

Brown, J. N., and H. S. Rosen. 1982. "On the Estimation of Structural Hedonic Price Models." *Econometrica* 50/3: 765–8.

Carew, R. 2000. "A Hedonic Analysis of Apple Prices and Product Quality Characteristics in British Colombia." *Canadian Journal of Agricultural Economics* 48: 241–57.

—— and W. J. Florkowski. 2010. "The Importance of Geographic Wine Appellations: Hedonic Pricing of Burgundy Wines in the British Columbia Wine Market." *Canadian Journal of Agricultural Economics* 58/1: 93–108.

Cassel, E., and R. Mendelsohn. 1985. "The Choice of Functional Forms for Hedonic Price Equations: Comment." *Journal of Urban Economics* 18/2: 135–42.

Christensen, L. R., D. W. Jorgenson, and L. J. Lau. 1973. "Transcendental Logarithmic Production Frontiers." *Review of Economics and Statistics* 55/1: 28–45.

Cleveland, W. S., S. J. Delvin, and E. Grosse. 1988. "Regression by Local Fitting." *Journal of Econometrics* 37: 87–114.

Combris, P., S. Lecocq, and M. Visser. 1997. "Estimation of a Hedonic Price Equation for Bordeaux Wine: Does Quality Matter?" *Economic Journal* 107: 390–403.

Costanigro, M., J. McCluskey, and C. Goemans. 2010. "The Economics of Nested Names: Name Specificity, Reputation and Price Premia." *American Journal of Agricultural Economics* 92/5 (Oct. 1), 1339–50.

—— ——, and R. C. Mittelhammer. 2007. "Segmenting the Wine Market Based on Price: Hedonic Regression When Different Prices Mean Different Products." *Journal of Agricultural Economics* 58/3: 454–66.

——, R. C. Mittelhammer, and J. J. McCluskey. 2009. "Let the Market Be Your Guide: Estimating Equilibria in Differentiated Product Markets with Class-Membership Uncertainty." *Journal of Applied Econometrics* 24: 1117–35.

Court, A. T. 1939. "Hedonic Price Indexes with Automotive Examples." In *The Dynamics of Automobile Demand*. New York: General Motors.

Court, L. M. 1941. "Entrepreneurial and Consumer Demand Theories for Commodities Spectra." *Econometrica* 9: 135–62.

Durham, C. A., I. Pardoe, and E. Vega. 2004. "A Methodology for Evaluating How Product Characteristics Impact Choice in Retail Settings with Many Zero Observations: An Application to Restaurant Wine Purchase." *Journal of Agricultural and Resource Economics* 29/1: 112–31.

Ekeland, I., J. J. Heckman, and L. Nesheim. 2002. "Identifying Hedonic Models." *American Economic Review* 92/2: 304–9.

—— ——. 2004. "Identification and Estimation of Hedonic Models." *Journal of Political Economy* 112/S1: S60–S109.

Epple, D. 1987. "Hedonic Prices and Implicit Markets: Estimating Demand and Supply Functions for Differentiated Products." *Journal of Political Economy* 95/1: 59–80.

Espinosa, J. A., and B. K. Goodwin. 1991. "Hedonic Price Estimation for Kansas Wheat Characteristics." *Western Journal of Agricultural Economics* 16: 72–85.

Fan, J., and I. Gijbels. 1996. *Local Polynomial Modelling and its Applications*, 1st edn. London: Chapman and Hall/CRC, Mar. 1.

Faux, J., and G. M. Perry. 1999. "Estimating Irrigation Water Value Using Hedonic Price Analysis: A Case Study in Malheur County, Oregon." *Land Economics* 75/3: 440–52.

Fletcher, M., J. Mangan, and E. Raeburn. 2004. "Comparing Hedonic Models for Estimating and Forecasting House Prices." *Property Management* 22/3: 189–200.

Freeman, A. M. 1993. *The Measurement of Environmental and Resource Values: Theory and Methods*. Washington, DC: Resources for the Future.

Friedman, J. H., and W. Stuetzle. 1981. "Projection Pursuit Regression." *Journal of the American Statistical Association* 76: 817.

Gilley, O. W., and R. K. Pace. 1995. "Improving Hedonic Estimation with an Inequality Restricted." *Review of Economics and Statistics* 77/4: 609.

Goldberger, A. S. 1968. "The Interpretation and Estimation of Cobb–Douglas Functions." *Econometrica* 36/3–4: 464–72.

Goodman, A. C., and T. G. Thibodeau. 1998. "Dwelling Age Heteroskedasticity in Repeat Sales House Price Equations." *Real Estate Economics* 26/1: 151–71.

Griliches, Z., ed. 1971. *Price Indexes and Quality Change*. Cambridge, MA: Harvard University Press.

Halvorsen, R., and H. O. Pollakowski. 1981. "Choice of Functional Form for Hedonic Price Equations." *Journal of Urban Economics* 10/1: 37–49.

Hastie, T., and C. Loader. 1993. "Local Regression: Automatic Kernel Carpentry: Rejoinder." *Statististical Science* 8/2: 139–43.

—— and R. J. Tibshirani. 1990. *Generalized Additive Regression*. London: Chapman Hall.

Heckman, J., and B. Singer. 1984. "A Method for Minimizing the Impact of Distributional Assumptions in Econometric Models for Duration Data." *Econometrica* 52/2: 271–320.

Huang, C. L., and B.-H. Lin. 2007. "A Hedonic Analysis of Fresh Tomato Prices among Regional Markets." *Review of Agricultural Economics* 29/4: 783–800.

Koenker, R. 2005. *Quantile Regression*. Cambridge: Cambridge University Press.

—— and G. Bassett. 1978. "Regression Quantiles." *Econometrica* 46/1 (Jan.), 33–50.

Lahiri, K., and D. Egy. 1981. "Joint Estimation and Testing for Functional Form and Heteroskedasticity." *Journal of Econometrics* 15/2: 299–307.

Lancaster, K. 1966. "A New Approach to Consumer Theory." *Journal of Political Economy* 74: 132–57.

Landon, S., and C. E. Smith. 1997. "The Use of Quality and Reputation Indicators by the Consumers: The Case of Bordeaux Wine." *Journal of Consumer Policy* 20: 289–323.

—— ——. 1998. "Quality Expectations, Reputation, and Price." *Southern Economic Journal* 64/3: 628–47.

Loureiro, M. L., and J. J. McCluskey. 2000. "Assessing Consumer Response to Protected Geographical Identification Labeling." *Agribusiness* 16/3: 309–20.

McCluskey, J. J., and G. C. Rausser. 2003. "Stigmatized Asset Value: Is It Temporary or Long-Term?" *Review of Economics and Statistics* 85/2: 276–85.

McConnell, K. E., and I. E. Strand. 2000. "Hedonic Prices for Fish: Tuna Prices in Hawaii." *American Journal of Agricultural Economics* 82/1: 133–44.

Manning, W. G. 1998. "The Logged Dependent Variable, Heteroskedasticity, and the Retransformation Problem." *Journal of Health Economics* 17/3: 283–95.

Martins-Filho, C., and O. Bin. 2005. "Estimation of Hedonic Price Functions via Additive Nonparametric Regression." *Empirical Economics* 30/1: 93–114.

Mittelhammer, R. C., G. G. Judge, and D. J. Miller. 2000. *Econometric Foundations.* Cambridge: Cambridge University Press.

Nerlove, M. 1995. "Hedonic Price Functions and the Measurement of Preferences: The Case of Swedish Wine Consumers." *European Economic Review* 39: 1697–1716.

Oczkowski, E. 1994. "Hedonic Wine Price Function for Australian Premium Table Wine." *Australian Journal of Agricultural Economics* 38: 93–110.

Pakes, A. 2003. "A Reconsideration of Hedonic Price Indexes with an Application to PCs." *American Economic Review* 93/5: 1578–96.

Palmquist, R. B. 1984. "Estimating the Demand for the Characteristics of Housing." *Review of Economics and Statistics* 66/3 (Aug.), 394–404.

Parcell, J. L., and T. C. Schroeder. 2007. "Hedonic Retail Beef and Pork Product Prices." *Journal of Agricultural and Applied Economics* 39: 29–46.

Parmeter, C. F., D. J. Henderson, and S. C. Kumbhakar. 2007. "Nonparametric Estimation of a Hedonic Price Function." *Journal of Applied Econometrics* 22/3: 695–9.

Quigley, J. M. 1982. "Nonlinear Budget Constraints and Consumer Demand: An Application to Public Programs for Residential Housing." *Journal of Urban Economics* 12/2 (Sept.), 177–201.

Racine, J., and Q. Li. 2004. "Nonparametric Estimation of Regression Functions with both Categorical and Continuous Data." *Journal of Econometrics* 119/1: 99–130.

Ramsey, J. B. 1969. "Tests for Specification Errors in Classical Linear Least-Squares Regression Analysis." *Journal of the Royal Statistical Society*, ser. B: *Methodological* 31/2: 350–71.

Rosen, S. 1974. "Hedonic Prices and Implicit Markets: Product Differentiation in Pure Competition." *Journal of Political Economy* 82: 34–55.

—— 1981. "The Economics of Superstars." *American Economic Review* 71/5 (Dec.), 845–58.

Rosiers, F. D., M. Thériault, and P. Villeneuve. 2000. "Sorting Out Access and Neighbourhood Factors in Hedonic Price Modelling." *Journal of Property Investment and Finance* 18/3: 291–315.

Santos Silva, J. M. C., and S. Tenreyro. 2006. "The Log of Gravity." *Review of Economics and Statistics* 88/4: 641–58.

Schamel, G., and K. Anderson. 2003. "Wine Quality and Varietal, Regional and Winery Reputations: Hedonic Prices for Australia and New Zealand." *Economic Record* 79: 357–69.

Stanley, L. R., and J. Tschirhart. 1991. "Hedonic Prices for a Nondurable Good: The Case of Breakfast Cereals." *Review of Economics and Statistics* 73/3: 537–41.

Steiner, B. 2004. "French Wines on the Decline? Econometric Evidence from Britain." *Journal of Agricultural Economics* 55/2: 267–88.

Straszheim, M. 1974. "Hedonic Estimation of Housing Market Prices: A Further Comment." *Review of Economics and Statistics* 56/3: 404–6.

Taylor, L. O. 2003. "The Hedonic Method." In P. A. Champ, K. J. Boyle, and T. C. Brown, eds, *A Primer on Non-Market Valuation.* Boston: Kluwer Academic Publishers.

Thursby, J. G. 1982. "Misspecification, Heteroscedasticity, and the Chow and Goldfeld–Quandt Tests." *Review of Economics and Statistics* 64/2: 314–21.

Triplett, J. 2006. *Handbook on Hedonic Indexes and Quality Adjustments in Price Indexes.* Paris: OECD.

Tronstad, R., L. S. Huthoefer, and E. Monke. 1992. "Market Windows and Hedonic Price Analyses: An Application to the Apple Industry." *Journal of Agricultural and Resource Economics* 17: 314–22.

Tyrvainen, L., and A. Miettinen. 2000. "Property Prices and Urban Forest Amenities." *Journal of Environmental Economics and Management* 39: 205–23.

Unnevehr, L. J., and S. Bard. 1993. "Beef Quality: Will Consumers Pay for Less Fat?" *Journal of Agricultural and Resource Economics* 18/2: 288–95.

Viscusi, W. K. 1993. "The Value of Risks to Life and Health." *Journal of Economic Literature* 31/4 (Dec.), 1912–46.

Ward, C. E., J. L. Lusk, and J. M. Dutton. 2008. "Implicit Value of Retail Beef Product Attributes." *Journal of Agricultural and Resource Economics* 33/3: 364–81.

Watkins, K. 1999. "Property Valuation and the Structure of Urban Housing Markets." *Journal of Property Investment and Finance* 17: 157–75.

Waugh, F. 1928. "Quality Factors and Vegetable Prices." *Journal of Farm Economics* 10: 185–96.

White, H. 1980. "A Heteroskedasticity-Consistent Covariance Matrix Estimator and a Direct Test for Heteroskedasticity." *Econometrica* 48/4: 817–38.

Winfree, J. A., and J. J. McCluskey. 2005. "Collective Reputation and Quality." *American Journal of Agricultural Economics* 87/1 (Feb.), 206–13.

Zarembka, P. 1974. *Transformation of Variables in Econometrics.* Gottingen: Ibero-Amerika Institut für Wirtschaftsforschung, University of Gottingen.

CHAPTER 7

....

NON-MARKET VALUATION: STATED PREFERENCE METHODS

....

FREDRIK CARLSSON

1 INTRODUCTION

....

Stated preference methods assess the value of goods and characteristics of goods by using individuals' stated behavior in a hypothetical setting. The method includes a number of different approaches such as conjoint analysis, contingent valuation, and choice experiments. There are two broad areas within food economics where stated preference methods are, and should be, used. The first relates to the public good aspects of the production and consumption of food. The second pertains to the demand and willingness to pay (WTP) for particular alternatives of food, or particular characteristics of food products. The main reasons for using a stated preference method instead of revealed preference methods such as actual market data are: (1) there are public good aspects (e.g., people care about other people's consumption), (2) the difficulty of disentangling preferences for different characteristics of goods using market data, and (3) not all levels of the characteristics exist in the market today. Stated preference methods have been used extensively in the area of food economics. Examples of study areas are preferences for genetically modified food products (e.g., Loureiro and Hine 2002; Lusk, Roosen, and Fox 2003; Lusk, Jamal, et al. 2005; Carlsson, Frykblom, and Lagerkvist 2007a); animal welfare (e.g., Carlsson, Frykblom, and Lagerkvist 2007b; Liljenstolpe 2008); and food safety (e.g., Hamilton, Sunding, and Zilberman 2003; Canavari, Novella, and Scarpa 2005).

The most established stated preference method is the contingent valuation method (CVM) method. In CVM studies, respondents are asked whether or not they would be willing to pay a certain amount of money for realizing a change in the level of a good, where most often the good is a public or quasi-public good (see, e.g., Mitchell and

Carson 1989; Bateman and Willis 1999). However, in this chapter I shall focus the discussion on the choice experiment method, or stated choice method. In a choice experiment, individuals are given a hypothetical setting and asked to choose their preferred alternative among several alternatives in a choice set, and are usually asked to perform a sequence of such choices. Each alternative is described by a number of attributes or characteristics, and the levels of the attributes vary between choice sets. The reasons for focusing on the choice experiment method here is that it is a generalization of CVM, and that it is the stated preference method that is most extensively used in food economics. Most studies look at the influence of various characteristics of the food product on consumer behavior, and in that case choice experiments are more suitable. The major exception where CVM is used, and perhaps is more suitable, is in the case of bans on certain characteristics, for example genetically modified food products and labeling (see, e.g., Hamilton, Sunding, and Zilberman 2003).

The purpose of this chapter is to give a detailed description of the steps involved in designing a choice experiment and analyzing the responses. However, the econometric analysis is covered in detail by Adamowicz and Swait (Chapter 5 in this volume). I shall also discuss a number of behavioral aspects of stated preference surveys, with an emphasis on hypothetical bias.

2   An Economic Model of Behavior and Estimation Issues

2.1   The Economic Model

In this section I briefly present the underlying economic model that is used to analyze discrete choices. A more detailed discussion can be found in Adamowicz and Swait (Chapter 5 in this volume). Although most stated preference studies only deal with the discrete choice between several alternatives, the underlying economic model can actually deal with both the decision about which good to choose and how much to consume of the chosen good. Hanemann (1984) calls this a discrete/continuous choice. For example, a consumer decides first which type of meat to buy, and then how many kilograms to buy. However, the model I present here is only dealing with the discrete choice. Suppose that an individual k is faced with a choice between N mutually exclusive alternatives. Each alternative is described with a vector of attributes, a_i, the price of each alternative is p_i, and the exogenous income is Y. We assume that the individual wishes to maximize utility by choosing one of the available alternatives. Given a number of restrictions (see Adamowicz and Swait, Chapter 5 in this volume) the maximization problem can be expressed as

$$V_k[a, p, Y_k] = \max[V_{1k}(a_1, Y_k - p_1), \ldots, V_{Nk}(a_N, Y_k - p_N)], \tag{1}$$

where V_k is the indirect utility function. Thus, the individual chooses alternative i if and only if

$$V_{ik}(a_i, Y_k - p_i) > V_{jk}(a_j, Y_k - p_j); \forall j \neq i \tag{2}$$

In order to make the model operational, there are two additional things that have to be done. The first is to make an assumption about the functional form of the utility function. The second is to allow for unobservable (for the researcher) effects that could be due to unobserved characteristics of the individual, attributes that are not included, measurement error, and/or heterogeneity of preferences (Hanemann and Kanninen 1999). In order to allow for these effects, the Random Utility approach (McFadden 1974) is used to link the deterministic model with a statistical model of human behavior. We simply introduce an additive error term, so the conditional utility function is written as

$$V_{ik}(a_i, Y_k - p_i) + \varepsilon_{ik}. \tag{3}$$

Alternative i is chosen if and only if

$$V_{ik}(a_i, Y_k - p_i) + \varepsilon_{ik} > V_{jk}(a_j, Y_k - p_j) + \varepsilon_{jk}; \forall j \neq i \tag{4}$$

Since the utility functions have a random element, we can rewrite the above condition in probability terms:

$$P[\delta_i = 1] = P\lfloor V_{ik}(a_i, Y_k - p_i) + \varepsilon_{ki} > V_{jk}(a_j, Y_k - p_j) + \varepsilon_{jk}; \forall j \neq i \rfloor \tag{5}$$

A thorough discussion of different specifications of the error terms are discussed in Adamowicz and Swait (Chapter 5 in this volume). What we shall discuss in more detail here is a number of estimation issues.

2.2   Estimation Issues

The first issue is the functional form of the utility function. The most common assumption is a utility function that is linear in the parameters. This is not as restrictive as it seems since a linear in parameters function can allow for non-linear effects of attributes and interaction terms with observable socioeconomic characteristics. One important property of discrete choice models is that only the differences in utility between alternatives affect the choice probabilities, not the absolute levels of utility. This means that not all parameters of the utility function can be estimated. For example, if there is no difference in the levels of an attribute between the alternatives, then the parameter for that attribute cannot be estimated. In other words, there must be a difference between the alternatives in order to estimate the parameter. Note that in a choice experiment the levels of an attribute could be equal in one or several of the choice sets. This would not mean that we could not estimate the parameter; i.e., there need not be a difference in all of the choice sets.

The property that there must be a difference between the alternatives also has implications for the possibility of including alternative-specific constants. An alternative-specific constant would capture the average effect on utility of attributes or factors that are not included. However, since only differences in utility matter, only differences in alternative-specific constants matter. A standard way of accounting for this is to normalize one of the constants to zero. In that case, the other constants would be interpreted as relative to the normalized constant.

The fact that only utility difference matters also has implications for how socioeconomic characteristics can enter the model. Socioeconomic characteristics are supposed to capture taste variation. One way of including them is to normalize the parameter of one of the alternatives to zero, just as in the case of the constant. The parameters that are estimated should then be interpreted as relative to the normalized parameter. Another interpretation of this approach is to see the socioeconomic characteristics as interacting with the alternative-specific constants. Finally, these characteristics could be made to interact with the attributes of the alternatives.

Note that it is not necessary to include alternative-specific constants. In particular, if the choice experiment has a generic design, it would actually not be reasonable to include constants.[1] If we include constants in that case and they are significant, that would indicate that there is something else affecting respondents' choices that we have not been able to capture. With an alternative-specific design, constants should in general be included.

That only the difference in utility matters also has some important implications for how income should enter the utility function. The most common assumption is that utility is a linear function of income, so that the utility of alternative i is

$$V_{ik} = f(\beta, a_i) + \lambda(Y_k - p_i) + \varepsilon_{ik}, \tag{6}$$

where a_i is the vector of attributes of alternative i, β is the corresponding parameter vector, and λ is the marginal utility of income. Since only the differences in utility affect the choice probabilities, income would not be included as an explanatory variable. The marginal utility of income, λ, is still estimable since each alternative implies a certain cost. If we want to include income, there are two alternatives. The first is to specify another functional form of the utility function, for example a quadratic income term. The second is to include the income variable by interacting the variable with another characteristic or alternative-specific constant. The reason for choosing the simple functional form where income enters linearly has mainly to do with calculation of welfare measures, which we will come back to.

In the literature, it has become increasingly common to allow also for unobserved heterogeneity through Mixed Logit and Latent-Class models (see, e.g., Train (2003);

---

[1] In a generic experiment, the alternatives are simply labeled A, B, C or 1, 2, 3. In an alternative specific experiment the alternative could be brand names, shops, different national parks.

Adamowicz and Swait, Chapter 5 in this volume). In a Mixed Logit model, the researcher has to decide which parameters should be random and which fixed, and the distribution of the random parameters. The choice of distribution is not a straightforward task. In principle, any distribution could be used, but in previous applications the most common ones have been the normal and the log-normal distribution. Other distributions that have been applied are the uniform, triangular, and Raleigh distributions. However, before we make the choice about the distribution we must also determine which parameters should be randomly distributed and which parameters should be fixed. This choice can depend on several factors. For example, in many choice experiments it has been common to assume that the cost parameter is fixed. One reason for this is that the distribution of the marginal willingness to pay (MWTP) is then the distribution of the attribute. The other alternative would, of course, be to assume that *only* the parameter of the cost attribute is randomly distributed. This has been called a random marginal utility model (see von Haefen 2003). An alternative is to use a test procedure suggested by McFadden and Train (2000). With this test, artificial variables are constructed from a standard logit estimation

$$z_{it} = \left(a_{it} - \sum_{j \in C} a_{jt} P_{jt} \right)^2, \tag{7}$$

where P_{jt} is the conditional logit probability for alternative j in choice situation t. The logit model is then re-estimated with these artificial variables, and the test of whether a coefficient should be fixed or not is based on the significance of the coefficient of the artificial variable (see McFadden and Train 2000 for details).

Suppose now that we have determined the set of coefficients that should be randomly distributed. The next step is to specify a particular distribution for each of the random parameters. One might consider several aspects. For example, we might want to impose certain restrictions. The most natural one might be that all respondents should have the same sign of the coefficients. Of the previously discussed distributions, it is only the log-normal distribution that has this property. For example, if we assume that the cost coefficient is log-normally distributed, we ensure that all individuals have a non-positive price coefficient.[2] In this case, the log-normal coefficients have the following form:

$$\beta_k = \pm \exp(b_k + v_{ik}), \tag{8}$$

where the sign of coefficient β_k is determined by the researcher according to expectations, b_k is constant and the same for all individuals, and v_{ik} is normally distributed across individuals with mean and variance equal to 0 and σ_k, respectively. This means

---

[2] If we want to estimate a model with a log-normally distributed coefficient and our expectation is that the sign of the coefficient is negative, we must estimate the model with the negative value of the corresponding variable. The reason is that the log-normal distribution by definition will force the coefficient to be positive.

that the coefficient has the following properties: (a) median $= \exp(b_k)$; (b) mean $= \exp(b_k + \sigma_k/2)$; and (c) standard deviation $= \exp(b_k + \sigma_k^2/2)(\exp(\sigma_k^2) - 1)^{0.5}$. While the log-normal distribution seems like a reasonable assumption, there may be some problems with applying this distribution. First, this is the distribution that causes the most problems with convergence in model estimation. One reason for this is most likely that it puts a restriction on the preferences in terms of all respondents having the same sign of the coefficient. Another problem with the log-normal distribution is that the estimated welfare measures could be extremely high since values of the cost attribute close to zero are possible (see, e.g., Revelt and Train 1998). Therefore, the most common distribution assumption has been normal distribution, i.e., that the coefficient for the k-attribute is given by $\beta_k \sim N[b_k, w_k]$. However, there is an increasing interest in other distributions, in particular, distributions where marginal WTP can be constrained to be non-negative (Hensher and Greene 2003). One such distribution is a triangular distribution where the standard deviation parameter is constrained to be equal to the mean of the parameter.

There has recently been discussion in the literature over whether the random parameter model implies restrictive assumptions about the scale parameter, i.e., the standard deviation of the error term of the utility function (Train and Weeks 2005; Louviere 2006; Scarpa, Thiene, and Train 2008). For example, it has been almost standard to assume that the cost coefficient is fixed since this facilitates estimation and since the distribution of the MWTP is the distribution of the corresponding attribute. This implies an assumption that the scale parameter is the same for all respondents, which is questionable. As discussed by Train and Weeks (2005), there are, however, two problems with allowing the price coefficient to be randomly distributed. First, the distribution of the marginal WTP of the attribute could be intractable; for example, there could be a normal distribution of the attribute coefficient and a log-normal distribution of the cost coefficient. Second, uncorrelated utility coefficients could translate into marginal WTPs that are correlated. Therefore, Train and Weeks (2005) suggest a modeling strategy where the model is parameterized in terms of WTP instead of utility.[3] This means that assumptions about the distribution of WTP are made. However, whether this specification of the model results in different WTPs than the standard model formulation is an empirical question (Scarpa 2008).

3   WELFARE MEASURES

The main purpose of a choice experiment is often to estimate the welfare effects of changes in the attributes. In order to obtain these, researchers have generally assumed a simple functional form for the utility function by imposing a constant marginal utility

---

[3] This is similar to the approach in contingent valuation where the WTP distribution is analyzed directly (Cameron 1988), but they extend it to multinomial choices and random coefficients.

of income, as described above. Again remember that we focus on purely discrete choices; this means that in some cases the welfare measures have to be interpreted with care. For example, in the case of a food product choice experiment, the welfare measures are per package or per kilogram, depending on what has been defined in the survey. Two types of welfare measure are commonly reported: (1) marginal WTP and (2) total WTP (Hanemann 1999; Louviere, Hensher, and Swait 2000).

3.1   Marginal Willingness to Pay

The simplest welfare measure that can be obtained from a choice experiment is marginal WTP (MWTP); this is the marginal rate of substitution between the attribute and money. Let us assume a simple linear utility function

$$v_{ik} = \beta a_i + \lambda(Y_k - p_i) + \varepsilon_{ik}. \tag{9}$$

The marginal rate of substitution between any of the attributes and money is then simply the ratio of the coefficient of the attribute and the marginal utility of income, found by totally differentiating (9) and rearranging:

$$MRS_k = \frac{dY_k}{da_i} = -\frac{\partial v_{ik}/\partial a_i}{\partial v_{ik}/\partial Y_k} = -\frac{\beta_i}{\lambda} = MWTP. \tag{10}$$

MWTP shows how much money an individual is willing to sacrifice for a marginal change in the attribute. However, in many instances the attributes are not continuous; for example, the attribute could be a dummy variable indicating if the attribute is present or not. In that case, the ratio of the attribute coefficient and the marginal utility of money is strictly not a MWTP since we cannot talk about a marginal change of the discrete attribute. The interpretation of this WTP measure is instead the amount of money a respondent is willing to pay for a change in the attribute levels from, say, zero to one.

I shall now discuss two extensions of the estimation of MWTP. The first is non-linear utility functions. It is straightforward to allow for a non-linear utility function, but then the MWTP would have to be evaluated at a certain level of the attribute. Suppose we include a quadratic term of attribute $a1^2$, so that the utility function is

$$v_{ik} = \beta_1 a_1 + \beta_2 a_1^2 + \beta_3 a_2 + \lambda(Y_k - p_i) + \varepsilon_{ik}. \tag{11}$$

The marginal WTP for attribute a_i is then

$$MWTP = -\frac{\partial v_{ik}/\partial a_1}{\partial v_{ik}/\partial Y} = -\frac{\beta_1 + 2\beta_2 a_1}{\lambda} \tag{12}$$

The MWTP thus depends on the level of the attribute, and we would have to decide at what values to calculate the WTP.

The second extension is to allow for observed heterogeneity in WTP. This can be done by interacting the attributes of the choice experiment with a set of socioeconomic characteristics. This way we would obtain the MWTP for different groups of people with a certain set of socioeconomic characteristics.[4] Of particular interest is perhaps the assumption of a constant marginal utility of money. Morey, Sharma, and Karlström (2003) suggest a simple approach where the utility is a piecewise linear spline function of income. For example, we could divide the sample into three groups: low-income, medium-income, and high-income respondents. For each of these groups we estimate a separate coefficient of marginal utility. This allows us to estimate separate MWTP expressions for each of these groups.

3.2 Total Willingness to Pay

With total WTP we mean willingness to pay to go from one alternative to another, or willingness to pay for a change in several attributes, or willingness to pay for one alternative compared with all other alternatives. The best examples in the case of food products are perhaps evaluation of bans or labels, or introduction of a new product. This is perhaps the best example of when CVM method is more suitable. If we are primarily interested in the total WTP for a particular scenario or for, say, a ban, then it is advisable to conduct a CVM survey instead of a choice experiment. However, in many cases we could be interested in obtaining both total WTP and MWTP.

When we discuss total WTP, it is useful to distinguish between generic and alternative-specific experiments. In a generic experiment, the alternatives are simply labeled A, B, C, or 1, 2, 3. In an alternative-specific experiment the alternative could be brand names, shops, different national parks. With an alternative-specific experiment, the choice between the alternatives potentially implies something more than a trade-off between the attributes we present. This will be revealed through the inclusion of alternative-specific constants. This in turn means that if a respondent is forced to make a choice between alternatives, she is not only sacrificing the attribute levels of the non-chosen alternatives, she is also potentially sacrificing other aspects as measured by the alternative-specific constants. If the experiment is generic, this is not an issue, and strictly we would not need to include alternative-specific constants in a generic experiment.

However, let us begin with the alternative-specific case. We assume a simple linear utility function

$$V_{ik} = \beta a_i + \lambda(Y_k - p_i) + \varepsilon_{ik}, \tag{13}$$

---

[4] Note that in many choice experiments, the socioeconomic characteristics are interacted with the alternative-specific constants. In that case they will not affect the *marginal* WTP.

where the attribute vector includes an alternative-specific constant. Since marginal utility of income is constant, the ordinary and compensated demand functions coincide. The compensating variation (CV) is in general obtained by solving the equality

$$V_k(a^0, p^0, Y_k) = V_k(a^1, p^1, Y_k - CV), \tag{14}$$

where a^0 is the attribute vector before and a^1 is the attribute vector after the change, and V is the unconditional utility function. The unconditional utility function can be written as

$$V_k[a, p, Y_k] = \mu Y_k + \max[\beta a_1 - p_1 + \varepsilon_1, \ldots, \beta a_N - p_N + \varepsilon_N], \tag{15}$$

where N is the number of alternatives. Inserting this into the equality for the compensating variation we have:

$$\begin{aligned} \lambda Y_k + \max[\beta a_1^0 - p_1^0 + \varepsilon_1^0, \ldots, \beta a_N^0 - p_N^0 + \varepsilon_N^0] = \\ \lambda(Y_k - CV) + \max[\beta a_1^1 - p_1^1 + \varepsilon_1^1, \ldots, \beta a_N^1 - p_N^1 + \varepsilon_N^1] \end{aligned}. \tag{16}$$

Solving for the compensating variation,

$$CV = \frac{1}{\lambda}\{\max[\beta a_1^0 - p_1^0 + \varepsilon_1^0, \ldots, \beta a_N^0 - p_N^0 + \varepsilon_N^0] - \max[\beta a_1^1 - p_1^1 + \varepsilon_1^1, \ldots, \beta a_N^1 - p_N^1 + \varepsilon_N^1]\}. \tag{17}$$

Thus, the compensating variation is the difference between the utility after the change and that before the change, normalized by the marginal utility of income. However, since we do not know what choice the individual would make, we have the expected indirect utility in the expression. What remains is to find expressions for the expected value of the maximum indirect utility of the alternatives. In order to do this, we need to make an assumption about the error terms (see, e.g., Small and Rosen 1981; Hanemann 1984). If the error terms have an extreme value distribution, the expected value of the maximum value is the so-called log-sum value (or the inclusive value):

$$\max[\beta a_1^0 - p_1^0 + \varepsilon_1^0, \ldots, \beta a_N^0 - p_N^0 + \varepsilon_N^0] = \ln \sum_{i=1}^{N} e^{v_i} \tag{18}$$

Therefore, the compensating variation is

$$CV = \frac{1}{\lambda}\left\{\ln \sum_{i \in S_{mo}} e^{v_i} - \ln \sum_{i \in S_m} e^{v_i}\right\}. \tag{19}$$

Thus, the compensating variation is the difference in expected utility before and after the change, normalized by the marginal utility of income, where the expected utility is obtained using the log-sum formula.

For a generic experiment it does not make sense to think of a choice between several alternatives. Instead, the total WTP for a generic experiment is simply the sum of willingness to pay for each attribute change. Suppose we conduct a generic choice experiment with four attributes, including the cost attribute. We estimate the following utility function:

$$V_{ik} = \beta_1 a_1 + \beta_2 a_2 + \beta_3 a_3 + \lambda(Y_k - p_i) + \varepsilon_{ik}. \tag{20}$$

Based on the estimated model we wish to calculate the WTP for a change in all three attributes: Δa_1, Δa_2, and Δa_3. The total WTP would then be

$$WTP = -\frac{\beta_1 \Delta a_1 + \beta_2 \Delta a_2 + \beta_3 \Delta a_3}{\lambda}. \tag{21}$$

However, a generic choice experiment could also include an opt-out alternative, for example a no-purchase option. In that case, an alternative-specific constant for the opt-out should be included in the model. Let us denote the opt-out with the subscript 0. The utility function would then be

$$v_{ik} = \beta_1 a_1 + \beta_2 a_2 + \beta_3 a_3 + \lambda(Y_k - p_i) + \varepsilon_{ik}; i \neq 0$$

$$v_{0k} = \alpha_0 + \lambda Y + \varepsilon_{0k} \tag{22}$$

Whether or not to include the opt-out constant in the WTP depends on what we want to measure. If we want to know the WTP for a subject that is currently not choosing the opt-out, we would calculate the WTP as

$$WTP = -\frac{\beta_1 \Delta a_1 + \beta_2 \Delta a_2 + \beta_3 \Delta a_3}{\lambda}. \tag{23}$$

If we want to know the WTP of a particular attribute combination for a subject that is currently choosing the opt-out, the WTP would be

$$WTP = -\frac{-\alpha_0 + \beta_1 a_1 + \beta_2 a_2 + \beta_3 a_3}{\lambda}. \tag{24}$$

This measure is thus the price that would make someone indifferent to buying.

4   DESIGN OF STATED PREFERENCE SURVEY

The actual design of a stated preference survey is in many respects the most crucial part of the whole exercise. If the study is not well designed, it does not matter what econometrics you apply or how well the interviews are done; the results will still be useless. I shall discuss three important parts of the design of a stated preference survey: (1) definition of attributes and attribute levels, (2) experimental design, and (3) survey context, behavioral aspects, and validity tests.

4.1   Definition of Attributes and Levels

The first step in the development of a choice experiment is to conduct a series of focus group studies aimed at selecting the relevant attributes. The focus group studies could be in terms of verbal protocols, group discussion, and actual surveys; see, e.g., Layton and Brown (1998) for a discussion of how to use focus groups for pretesting the question format and attributes. A starting point involves studying the attributes and attribute levels used in previous studies and their importance in the choice decisions. Additionally, the selection of attributes should be guided by the attributes that are expected to affect respondents' choices, as well as those attributes that are policy-relevant. This information forms the base for which attributes and relevant attribute levels should be included in the first round of focus group studies.

The task in a focus group is to determine the number of attributes and attribute levels. As a first step, the focus group studies should provide information about credible minimum and maximum attribute levels. Additionally, it is important to identify possible interaction effect between the attributes, for example if the preference for a particular attribute depends on the levels of another attribute. If we want to calculate welfare measures, it is necessary to include a monetary attribute such as a price or a cost. In such a case, the focus group studies will indicate the best way to present a monetary attribute. Credibility plays a crucial role; the researcher must ensure that the attributes selected and their levels can be combined in a credible manner. Hence, proper restrictions may have to be imposed (see, e.g., Layton and Brown 1998).

The focus group sessions should shed some light on the best way to introduce and explain the task of making a succession of choices from a series of choice sets. As Layton and Brown (1998) explain, choosing repeatedly is not necessarily a behavior that could be regarded as obvious for all goods. When it comes to recreational choices, for example, it is clear that choosing a site in a choice set does not preclude choosing another site given different circumstances. Furthermore, it must be made clear to the respondent that the choices are independent. This is particularly important when repeated choices are a natural part of the decision, such as with food purchases. However, in the case of public goods, such repeated choices might require further justification in the experiment, and in particular, it must be made clear that the choices are independent of each other.

A general problem with applying a stated preference survey is the choice between the amount of information given and obtained, and the complexity of the task. The ultimate goal is to obtained high-quality information about people's preferences. This means that we should ask a sufficient number of well-designed questions, but not ask so many questions that the quality of the responses decreases. To what extent the survey is difficult or not will clearly depend on the context and the subject pool. I shall discuss a number of these issues in Section 4.3, but I think one should not overstate the problem of complexity. Most respondents can handle a fair number of attributes, and make a number of choice tasks. Many experiments that obtain plausible results included four to eight attributes, and four to sixteen choice tasks.

4.2   Statistical Design

The statistical design has to do with the construction of the actual choice sets that respondents will face, or, in other words, how attribute levels will be combined. The reason why we have to care at all about this is that for most, if not all, choice experiments it is impossible to let all respondents answer all possible choice sets since the number of choice sets becomes too large. It is therefore necessary to reduce the number of choice sets that is included in the final design. However, this is not the only reason why we have to care about the statistical design.

There are a number of aspects that one should consider when performing the statistical design. The most important aspect is, of course, to assure that the effects that one wishes to estimate are identified, i.e., that the variation of the attribute levels allows us to estimate the parameters of the utility function. In practice we have to specify in advance which effects we want to be able to estimate. Since the design determines what effects are estimable, this is clearly one very important part of the design, and a part that is often overlooked. One common assumption is to estimate so-called main effects; this means that we assume that there are no interaction effects between the attributes. To make this important point more concrete, suppose we have an experiment with two non-monetary attributes and a cost attribute. With a main effects design we would then rule out that the preferences of one attribute depend on the levels of the other attribute.

The objective of an optimal statistical design is to extract the maximum amount of information from the respondents, subject to the number of attributes, attribute levels, and other characteristics of the survey such as cost and length of the survey. The central question is then how to select the attribute levels to be included in the stated preference experiment in order to extract maximum information from each individual. However, note that the following discussion will take the number of attribute levels and the actual levels as given. As we have seen, the choices regarding these two aspects are, of course, also important, not least with respect to what we can learn from the responses. For binary attributes, this is not really an issue. This could, for example, be an attribute describing whether genetically modified fodder has been used or not. For attributes with several levels, and in particular for continuous attributes such as the cost attribute, the choice of number of levels and the levels themselves is more important. The necessary number of levels for a continuous attribute depends on what we want to be able to estimate. For example, if we want to be able to estimate non-linear effects, we need to include more than two levels. On the other hand, if we only want to estimate a main effect, strictly what is needed is two levels. At the same time, it is not advisable, in my opinion, to include only two levels of a cost attribute. It is a risky strategy, since if the chosen levels are such that the respondent only cares about the cost (or totally disregards the cost), the responses will not provide much information.

A number of design principles have been discussed in the literature. The statistical aspect of the design has to do with the construction of the combinations and the variance–covariance matrix of the estimator. The purpose, from a statistical point of view, of the design is to minimize the "size" of the covariance matrix of the estimator, implying precise estimates of the parameters. One common measure of efficiency, which relates to the covariance matrix, is D-efficiency

$$D - \textit{efficiency} = [\Omega^{1/K}]^{-1}, \tag{25}$$

where K is the number of parameters to estimate and Ω is the covariance matrix of the parameter estimates. Although there are several other criteria of efficiency such as A- and G-efficiency, which are all highly correlated, the main reason for choosing D-efficiency is that it is less computationally burdensome (see, e.g., Kuhfeld, Tobias, and Garratt 1994). Huber and Zwerina (1996) identify four principles for an efficient design of a choice experiment based on a non-linear model: (1) level balance, (2) orthogonality (the variation in attribute levels is uncorrelated), (3) minimal overlap, and (4) utility balance. A design that satisfies these principles has a maximum D-efficiency. The level balance criterion requires that the levels of each attribute occur with equal frequency in the design. A design has minimal overlap when an attribute level does not repeat itself in a choice set. Utility balance requires that the utility of each alternative in a choice set is equal.

In order to understand these principles and to show different design strategies that can be applied, I shall work with a small design example. Suppose we have three attributes: one with two levels and two with three levels: $x_1 = \{0, 1\}$, $x_2 = \{0, 1, 2, 3\}$, $x_3 = \{0, 1, 2, 3\}$. The choice experiment is a binary choice experiment, i.e., each choice set consists of two alternatives. The total number of possible combinations, called the full factorial design, is $2^1 \times 4^2 = 32$. Note that this is the number of combinations for one alternative. In practice it would be possible to include all these combinations, but let us suppose that we wish to reduce the number of possible alternatives. We can then use an econometric package such as SAS or SPSS, or a special design program such as Ngene, to generate a fractional factorial design. A fractional design is a subset of the full factorial design. Suppose that for this particular problem we seek to generate a main effects fractional factorial design with eight combinations and that we do this by maximizing the D-efficiency (D-optimality), assuming that we have a linear design problem (I shall explain later on what I mean by this). This would result in the fractional design shown in Table 7.1.

This design fulfills two criteria: it is orthogonal and it has level balance. However, we have not designed the choice sets yet. All we have so far is a fractional design. A number of approaches can be used to create the choice sets, and I shall discuss only a few. One simple approach is to use a cyclical design (Bunch, Louviere, and Andersson 1996). A cyclical design is a simple extension of the orthogonal approach. First, each of the

Table 7.1 An orthogonal main effects design

Combination	x_1	x_2	x_3
1	1	3	3
2	1	2	2
3	1	1	1
4	1	0	0
5	0	3	0
6	0	2	1
7	0	1	3
8	0	0	2

Table 7.2 A cyclical design

Choice set	Alternative 1			Alternative 2		
	x_1	x_2	x_3	x_1	x_2	x_3
1	1	3	3	0	0	0
2	1	2	2	0	3	3
3	1	1	1	0	2	2
4	1	0	0	0	1	1
5	0	3	0	1	0	1
6	0	2	1	1	3	2
7	0	1	3	1	2	0
8	0	0	2	1	1	3

combinations in the orthogonal design is allocated to a choice set, and represents the first alternative in that set (so there are now eight choice sets). Attributes of the additional alternatives are then constructed by cyclically adding alternatives into the choice set based on the attribute levels. The attribute level in the new alternative is the next-higher attribute level to the one applied in the previous alternative, and if the highest level is attained, the attribute level is set to its lowest level. By construction, this design has level balance, orthogonality, and minimal overlap. The cyclical design for this example is presented in Table 7.2. Let us look at choice set number 4; here the attribute x_1 is equal to one for the first alternative. The level of attribute x_1 for alternative 2 is thus zero, since the attribute is a two-level attribute. Attribute x_2 is equal to zero for alternative 1. This means that attribute x_2 is equal to one in alternative 2. Finally, attribute x_3 is also zero in the first alternative, and is thus equal to one in alternative 2.

An alternative is to create the choice sets simultaneously (see, e.g., Louviere 1988). Creating the choice sets simultaneously means that the design is selected from the collective factorial. The collective factorial is an L^{AC} factorial, where C is the number of alternatives and each alternative has A attributes with L levels, so in our case with two alternatives the collective factorial is $2^{2(alternatives)^{*}1(attributes)} \times 4^{2(alternatives)^{*}2(attributes)}$.

Therefore, when we create the full factorial we specify, in our case, six attributes, instead of three. This design strategy is also very simple. One problem with this simultaneously design approach is that both the full and the fractional factorial can become very large. For our small design this is, however, not a problem.

A third alternative is to use a random design principle (see, e.g., Lusk and Norwood 2005). With this approach we would just randomly draw design combinations and combine them into choice sets. The set of design combinations that we draw from could be the full factorial design or a fractional factorial design such as the one presented in Table 7.1. Since it is difficult practically to let each individual face a unique combination of randomly drawn choice sets, it is often necessary to create a number of questionnaire versions that each contains a particular set of choice sets.

One thing that should be mentioned about designs is that often a final design is split into different versions, in particular if the number of alternatives and attributes is large; this is called blocking the design. The blocking could be done by random drawing or by applying exactly the same criteria again, i.e., orthogonality, level balance, and minimum overlap.

So far I have only touched upon the statistical aspects of the design, but have not talked at all about the fourth criterion of an optimal design: utility balance. The design I have used so far does not consider utility balance when generating the design. The reason for this is that for linear models utility balance does not matter for statistical efficiency. However, for non-linear discrete choice models it turns out that utility balance does matter for statistical efficiency, since the covariance matrix depends on the true parameters in the utility function. A series of papers have shown that designs that take utility balance into consideration produce lower standard errors than the orthogonal designs; see, e.g., Huber and Zwerina (1996), Zwerina, Huber, and Kuhfeld (1996), Sandor and Wedel (2001), Kanninen (2002), and Carlsson and Martinsson (2003). In order to illustrate their design approach it is necessary to return to the Multinomial Logit model. McFadden (1974) showed that the maximum likelihood estimator for the Conditional Logit model is consistent and asymptotically normally distributed with the mean equal to β and a covariance matrix given by

$$\Omega = (Z'PZ)^{-1} = [\sum_{n=1}^{N}\sum_{j=1}^{J_m} z'_{jn}P_{jn}z_{jn}]^{-1}, \tag{26}$$

where $z_{jn} = x_{jn} - \sum_{i=1}^{J_n} x_{in}P_{in}$.

This covariance matrix, which is the main component in the D-optimal criteria, depends on the true parameters in the utility function, since the choice probabilities, P_{in}, depend on these parameters.

The utility balance aspect of the design problem closely resembles the problem of optimal design of the bid vector for closed-ended compensating variation surveys. A good statistical design is a function of the parameter vector, but we conduct the experiment to find the parameter. Thus, this is a Catch-22 problem. One solution is to do some sort of sequential design, where a number of pilot studies are conducted before the main study. This, of course, is costly and not without problems. However, it is important to understand that, irrespective of the choice of statistical design, information regarding respondents' preferences for the attributes is needed. For example, if the attribute levels are assigned in such a way that the choice depends only on the level of a certain attribute in the choice set, not much information is extracted. Another example would be choice sets where one alternative completely dominates the rest. In order to avoid situations of these types, some prior information is needed, relating not to the difference between the design strategies, but to the way in which the information is entered into the creation of the design.

However, there has also been criticism of utility-balanced design principles; see, e.g., Kanninen (2002) and Louviere et al. (2008). Think of the extreme case where two alternatives are almost identical in utility terms, which means that it is a difficult choice to make if we really try to assess and compare their utility. It also means that the choice we make is not that important to us, since the utility loss is small if we choose the "wrong" alternative. Consequently, there is a high risk that the responses to such a choice would be almost random and would thus not provide us with much information. Thus, there is a clear potential drawback to utility-balanced designs. On the other hand, we could argue that asking respondents to make choices between dominating or almost dominating alternatives would also give us very little information about their preferences. Consequently, the second alternative is also not very appealing (and, of course, no one has argued that one should strive for dominating alternatives).

One alternative approach would be to eliminate beforehand choice sets that are strictly dominating and, more importantly, choice sets that contain alternatives that are highly dominating although not strictly dominating. This begs the question, what is a highly dominating alternative? There is, of course, no simple rule. One strategy could be to collect prior information about the parameters of the utility function and then use this prior information to compute choice probabilities and, for example in the case of a binary experiment, exclude all choice sets where the choice probability is higher than 0.9 for an alternative. Clearly, the choice of cutoff point is arbitrary and this approach would still require an actual estimation of priors on the parameters of the utility function.

A final problem with the design has to do with how the levels of the attributes can be combined in practice. Some attributes might be correlated, but at the same time, we have to remember that one purpose of the statistical design is to get rid of the correlation, and the real world correlation is an argument for using stated preference data instead of revealed preference data.

4.3   Survey Context, Behavioral Aspects, and Validity Tests

In the previous section, I addressed optimal design of a choice experiment from a statistical perspective. However, in empirical applications there may be other issues to consider in order to extract the maximum amount of information from respondents. The first issue is the context of the choice experiment. Most stated preferences surveys relating to food products put the respondent in a situation where he or she can choose to buy only one alternative, most often in a specific quantity. With this setting, the respondent cannot express any preference for the consumption choices of others, since his or her choices will not affect the choice sets of the others. An example where respondents might care about the choices and consumption of others is genetically modified (GM) food products. A consumer may prefer GM-free products owing to what Antle (1999) calls extrinsic, or public good, quality. Thus, the consumer cares about the production process even if it does not affect product quality, for example owing to animal, environmental, ethical, or religious reasons. This in turn implies that a consumer might prefer a ban rather than mandatory labeling (Carlsson, Frykblom, and Lagerkvist 2007a). In order to measure this type of preference, the choice experiment would need to be framed somewhat differently. One alternative is to put the respondent in a situation where he or she can choose to buy only one alternative, but explain that the choice restricts the alternatives available for others as well. Another alternative is to frame the experiment such that the respondent is to choose between different "states of the world."

One issue to consider in the development of the questionnaire is whether to include a base case scenario or an opt-out alternative. This is particularly important if the purpose of the experiment is to calculate welfare measures. If we do not allow individuals to opt for a status quo alternative, this may distort the welfare measure for non-marginal changes. This decision should, however, be guided by whether or not the current situation and/or non-participation is a relevant alternative. A non-participation decision can be econometrically analyzed by, for example, a Nested Logit model with participants and non-participants in different branches (see, e.g., Blamey et al. 2000). A simpler alternative is to model non-participation as an alternative where the levels of the attributes are set to the current attribute levels.

Another issue is whether to present the alternatives in the choice sets in a generic (alternatives A, B, C) or alternative-specific form (Coca Cola, Pepsi, etc.). Blamey et al. (2000) discuss advantages of these two approaches and compare them in an empirical study. An advantage of using alternative-specific labels is familiarity with the context and hence the cognitive burden is reduced. However, the risk is that the respondent may not consider trade-offs between attributes. This approach is preferred when the emphasis is on valuation of the labeled alternatives. An advantage of the generic model is that the respondent is less inclined to consider only the label and thereby will focus more on the attributes. Therefore, this approach is preferred when the emphasis is on the marginal rates of substitution between attributes.

Many decisions regarding food consumption affect several members of the household, and presumably many decisions are made jointly. Surprisingly few stated preference studies have looked at the household valuation of products and public goods (see, e.g., Arora and Allenby 1999; Dosman and Adamowicz 2006; Bateman and Munro 2009; Beharry-Borg, Hensher, and Scarpa 2009). Even if the survey is not designed to investigate household decision-making, it is necessary to describe in the scenario the intended setting; for example, are the decisions made for the household or not? However, stated preference surveys could also be used to explore the relationship between individual and household decision-making. Beharry-Borg, Hensher, and Scarpa (2009) present an analytical framework for analyzing joint and separate decisions made by couples. The advantages of using a survey, instead of real purchase data, is that we can obtain data for both individual and joint choices by interviewing couples both individually and jointly.

There are a number of aspects of respondent behavior that affect the design of the survey and the choice of internal validity tests. The broadest issue is perhaps task complexity. This is determined by factors such as the number of choice sets presented to the individual, the number of alternatives in each choice set, the number of attributes describing those alternatives, and the correlation between attributes for each alternative (Swait and Adamowicz 1996). In complex cases, respondents may simply answer carelessly or use some simplified lexicographic decision rule. This could also arise, for example, if the levels of the attributes are not sufficiently differentiated to ensure trade-offs. In practice, it is difficult to separate this behavior from preferences that are genuinely lexicographic, in which case the respondents have a ranking of the attributes but the choice of an alternative is based solely on the level of their most important attribute. Genuine lexicographic preferences in a choice experiment are not a problem, although they provide us with little information in the analysis compared to the other respondents. However, if a respondent chooses to use a lexicographic strategy because of its simplicity, systematic errors are introduced, which may bias the results. One strategy for distinguishing between different types of lexicographic behavior is to use debriefing questions, where respondents are asked to give reasons why they, for example, focused on only one or two of the attributes in the choice experiment (DeShazo and Fermo 2002; Hensher, Rose, and Greene 2005).

A number of studies find that task complexity affects decisions (Bradley 1988; Adamowicz et al. 1998; DeShazo and Fermo 2002). Mazotta and Opaluch (1995) and Swait and Adamowicz (1996) analyze task complexity by assuming it affects the variance term of the model. The results of both papers indicate that task complexity does in fact affect variance, i.e., an increased complexity increases the noise associated with the choices. Task complexity can also arise when the amount of effort demanded when choosing the preferred alternative in a choice set may be so high that it exceeds the ability of respondents to select their preferred option. The number of attributes in a choice experiment is studied by Mazotta and Opaluch (1995) and they find that including more than four or five attributes in a choice set may lead to severe detriment to the quality of the data collected owing to the task complexity. Another aspect of complexity is the number of choice sets. Hensher, Stopher, and Louviere (2001) and Carlsson and Martinsson (2008) find no evidence of any substantial or significant effect on respondent behavior of the number of choice sets. However, Hensher (2006) found that the number of choice sets had a statistically significant impact on the valuation of travel time savings. Finally, a relatively recent stream of papers look at the extent to which respondents attend to all the attributes presented. A simplifying strategy when faced with a complex survey could be to focus on only some of the attributes, although there are, of course, other reasons why a respondent would ignore some attributes, such as that they actually do not care about the attribute or as a way of protesting against the survey (by ignoring the cost attribute). A number of studies have found evidence of subjects ignoring attributes to a relatively large extent, although the effect on WTP estimates is less clear (see, e.g., Hensher, Rose, and Greene 2005; Campbell, Hutchinson, and Scarpa 2008; Scarpa, Thiene, and Hensher 2010).

One interesting aspect of choice experiments is the possibility of building in internal and external consistency tests. By internal consistency tests I mean within-subject tests, and by external consistency tests I mean between-subject tests. There are both advantages and disadvantages to internal and external tests. For example, with an internal test we do not have to control for potential differences in the samples, but at the same time internal tests could be seen as a weaker form of test since they could be perceived as simple "rationality" tests of the respondent. However, as we shall see, some of these tests are still better suited to internal tests. I shall look briefly at two validity tests: transitivity and stability of preferences.

In order to test for transitive preferences, we have to construct such a test. For example, in the case of a pairwise choice experiment we have to include three specific choice sets: (1) Alt. 1 versus Alt. 2, (2) Alt. 2 versus Alt. 3, and (3) Alt. 1 versus Alt. 3. For example if the respondent chooses Alt. 1 in the first choice set and Alt. 2 in the second choice set, then Alt. 1 must be chosen in the third choice if the respondent has transitive preferences. Carlsson and Martinsson (2001) conducted tests of transitivity and they did not find any strong indications of violations.

The standard assumption in stated preference surveys is that the utility function of each individual is stable throughout the experiment. The complexity of the exercise might cause violations of this assumption, arising from learning and fatigue effects: "learning" in the sense of learning the preferences (Plott 1996) or learning the institutional setup (Bateman et al. 2008). The issue of learning and stability of preferences is not as simple as it seems. There is a lot of evidence that people's preferences are formed through repeated interactions (List 2003). If we conduct a stated preference survey on a good involving attributes that are not that familiar to the respondent, there is a risk that the preferences are not really formed before the survey situation. A test of the stability of the preferences could then reveal that the preferences are not stable. It is then not obvious that this is related to problems with the method itself; instead it could be that preferences are indeed constructed as the respondent goes through the survey. However, there is a potential counteracting effect to learning, and that is coherent arbitrariness (Ariely, Loewenstein, and Prelec 2008). This means that individuals' choices are often internally coherent, but at the same time they can be strongly anchored to some initial starting point. This is equivalent to starting point bias in stated preference surveys (Herriges and Shogren 1996; Ladenburg and Olsen 2008). The empirical evidence on stability of preferences is mixed. Johnson, Matthews, and Bingham (2000) test for stability by comparing responses to the same choice sets included both at the beginning and at the end of the experiment. They find a strong indication of instability of preferences. However, there is a potential problem of confounding effects of the sequencing of the choice sets and the stability of the preferences. An alternative approach, without the confounding effect, is applied in Carlsson and Martinsson (2001) in a choice experiment on donations to environmental projects. In their exercise, half of the respondents received the choice sets in the order {A,B} and the other half in the order {B,A}. A test for stability was then performed by comparing the preferences obtained for the choices in subset A, when it was given in the sequence {A,B}, with the preferences obtained when the choices in subset A were given in the sequence {B,A}. This could then be formally tested in a likelihood ratio test between the pooled model of the choices in subset A and the separate groups. A similar test could be performed for subset B. By using this method Carlsson and Martinsson (2001) found only a minor problem with instability of preferences. Layton and Brown (2000) conducted a similar test of stability in a choice experiment on policies for mitigating impacts of global climate change; they did not reject the hypothesis of stable preferences. Bryan et al. (2000) compared responses in the same way, but with the objective of testing for reliability, and found that 57 percent of the respondents did not change their responses when given the same choice set in a two-part choice experiment. Furthermore, in an identical follow-up experiment two weeks after the original experiment, 54 percent of the respondents made the same choices on at least eleven out of twelve choice situations.

5   HYPOTHETICAL BIAS

One important issue is whether individuals actually would do what they state they would do if it were for real. There has been an extensive discussion about the possibility of eliciting preferences, both for private and for public goods, with stated preference methods and the extent of hypothetical bias. With hypothetical bias we mean the bias introduced by asking a hypothetical question and not confronting the respondent with a real situation. I shall begin this section with a discussion about the incentive properties of different choice formats, then I shall look at the empirical evidence on hypothetical bias, and finally at methods for reducing hypothetical bias.

In assessing this bias, it is important to distinguish between private and public goods, as well as between goods with essentially no non-use values and goods with a non-negligible proportion of non-use values. As we shall see, there are reasons to believe that there are particular problems with measuring non-use values in hypothetical surveys. This is not, of course, saying that non-use values should not be measured; rather, that there are some inherent problems with measuring these values. The reason for this is that non-use values are to varying extents motivated by "purchase of moral satisfaction" (Kahneman and Knetsch 1992) and "warm glow" (Andreoni 1989), and that they often involve an "important perceived ethical dimension" (Johansson-Stenman and Svedsäter 2008). Note that we are not saying that non-use values are a result of stated preference surveys, but that it is particularly difficult to measure non-use values.

5.1   Incentives for Truthful Revelation of Preferences

I shall begin by outlining the discussion and arguments made by Carson et al. (1999) and Carson and Groves (2007). It is important to be aware of their assumptions and what aspects of individual behavior they are not investigating. The basic premise behind their work is the assumption that individuals behave strategically when responding to a survey. Furthermore, they start from the assumption of a so-called consequential survey, which is defined as one that is perceived by the respondent as something that may potentially influence agency decisions, as well as one where the respondent cares about the outcome. This means that they rule out purely hypothetical surveys. Indeed, they argue that economics has essentially nothing to say about purely hypothetical surveys. Do note that one core result of their research is that the probability that the survey is consequential does not affect the incentive properties; the only thing that is required is that this probability is positive. Finally, the incentive properties for any type of stated preference question also depends on (1) the type of good, i.e., is it a private or a public good? and (2) the payment mechanism, i.e., is the payment coercive or voluntary?

The result of Carson and Groves (2007) is essentially negative: most question formats that we use are not incentive-compatible. They argue that essentially the only incentive-compatible format is a binary discrete choice, and this in turn is only incentive-compatible for the cases of (1) a new public good with coercive payments, (2) the choice between two public goods, and (3) a change in an existing private or quasi-public good. I shall not go through all the results of their research; instead I shall focus on an understanding of the intuition of their results and the implications of them. The best way to understand this is to work with a simple example, which is not intended to cover all the different possibilities covered by Carson and Groves. I shall assume that the survey is consequential. Suppose we wish to value a public good that can be described by a set of attributes. The utility of a particular attribute combination is $V(p, q_i, Y)$. Suppose that an individual is confronted with a binary choice between two levels of a public good: q_0 and q_1, and that the initial level of the public good is the status quo. The new level of the public good is associated with a bid level of t_k. The respondent is asked to say yes or no to the bid and the new level of the public good. Given no uncertainty and assuming that the proposed bid is the actual cost, the optimal outcomes are

$$\text{Nochange: } V(p, q_0, Y) > V(p, q_1, Y - t_k)$$
$$\text{Nochange: } V(p, q_0, Y) < V(p, q_1, Y - t_k) \tag{27}$$

The question is whether this mechanism is incentive-compatible. In order to make this as simple as possible, suppose that the actual cost the respondent would face is equal to the bid and that the respondent believes this.[5] Furthermore, assume that there are no other effects on the utility of the outcome and of the responses in the survey than those described. So the respondent does not care about anything other than the attributes of the good, although this, of course, could involve non-use values. What is ruled out is, for example, a utility of the act of responding in the survey. For example, the respondent does not receive any utility from pleasing the interviewer, nor receives any utility from feeling good by responding in a certain perhaps ethical way. We shall come back to these issues later on. Given these restrictions, would a respondent gain anything from not telling the truth? The answer is no. Suppose that the respondent prefers no change, then the best response for that individual is no, and vice versa. The easiest way to understand this is perhaps to think: what would the person gain from not answering truthfully? Let us take the case of a respondent who prefers no change. What would that person gain from answering yes to the valuation question? By answering yes the probability that the public good is provided increases, but the respondent does not want that, at least not given the cost. Of course, this argument critically depends on all the assumptions we have discussed.[6]

Let us now look at a simple choice experiment. Suppose we ask respondents to choose between three alternatives, with the following utilities:

$$V_1(p, q_1, Y - t_1) \tag{28}$$

$$V_2(p, q_2, Y - t_2)$$

$$V_3(p, q_3, Y - t_3)$$

Let us assume that $V_1 > V_2 > V_3$ for a particular respondent. The question is, will this respondent always choose alternative 1? The answer is no. This can be seen as a voting situation between three candidates where the winner is the candidate that receives the highest number of votes. From the literature we now that this type of situation can create voting cycles and paradoxes. For example, suppose that it is only a small fraction of the population that prefers alternative 1, and that is common knowledge. A respondent who prefers this alternative would then have incentives to choose alternative 2 instead, since that would increase the probability that alternative 2 wins

---

[5] We know that, in reality, the bid a respondent faces is not necessarily equal to the cost, and we cannot know that the respondent believes that the bid is equal to the actual cost even if we tell them that.

[6] What if, for example, the respondent does not interpret the proposed bid as the actual cost he or she would face? Then the situation would differ. The respondent would make a similar evaluation as before, but instead it would be based on expectation about the cost. Consequently, not even the binary question format would be incentive-compatible in this case, at least not for all respondents.

over alternative 3. This is the basic reasoning behind why choice experiments are not incentive-compatible for a public good.

The incentives are similar for a private good. The main difference is that it is possible that more than one alternative is provided. This does not change the result to any large extent unless all but one alternative are provided. In an actual experiment, respondents would not know the number of alternatives that will be provided. Carson and Groves (2007) argue that this will result in respondents choosing alternatives that are the most preferred, or close to the most preferred, as long as they believe many alternatives will be provided, the difference in utility between the alternatives is small, or they have little information about other respondents' preferences. Carson and Groves further argue that this is mainly a problem when we want to estimate the total WTP. If the main interest is MWTP, or marginal trade-offs between attributes in general, this is less problematic. The reason is that the scale parameter cancels out when we make marginal comparisons.

The above discussion is, of course, very simplified. Three things are worth mentioning, though none of them changes the basic results of incentive compatibility or incompatibility. On the other hand, the things we shall discuss will perhaps put the issue of incentive compatibility into perspective. The first aspect has to do with uncertainty. For example, what if the respondent is uncertain about whether the proposed bid in a closed-ended question is the cost he or she would face? As mentioned, that would clearly affect the properties, since the respondent would use the expected cost as the basis for the decisions and not the proposed bid. In the case of a choice experiment, the situation is even more complex. Here the respondent also needs information about others' preferences and how they would choose. Alpizar, Carlsson, and Martinsson (2003) discuss in detail how uncertainty about others' preferences affects the behavior of the respondents in a choice experiment. Three straightforward and important conclusions can be drawn from their analysis. First, introducing imperfect information does not ensure that the degree of strategic behavior is reduced. It may well be the case that respondents form such expectations so that they act strategically even if they would not have done so with perfect information. Second, using a generic (no labels) presentation of the alternatives instead of an alternative-specific (labels) form probably reduces the risk of strategic behavior since it increases the complexity of forming expectations regarding other respondents' preferences. Third, it is generally advisable to introduce uncertainty explicitly into the choice experiment. This can be done by saying that there is uncertainty regarding individuals' preferences for the alternatives and the attributes.

The second aspect that needs to be mentioned when discussing incentive compatibility is that there can be other effects on the respondent's utility than those specified in the scenario. Perhaps the most classical example is to please the interviewer. By giving a certain answer that one thinks is the one the interviewer wants, the respondent is better off. Similarly, by acting in a certain way, for example expressing environmentally friendly preferences or certain ethical preferences, the respondent is better off. This is also, of course, the underlying reason for actual behavior. However, the survey situation could be seen as a cheap way of "purchasing moral satisfaction" (Kahneman and Knetsch 1992) or receiving a "warm glow" (Andreoni 1989). The fact that the survey is perceived as a consequential survey does not change this fact. Values of this type are more likely to occur for goods with non-use values, but at the same time the very reasons why we conduct stated preferences is that the goods have non-use values. There are, of course, other reasons for conducting stated preference surveys, but if we want to measure non-use values, stated preferences is the only alternative.

5.2   The Empirical Evidence

There is a vast literature testing the performance of stated preference methods with respect to how well they mimic real behavior. As we have discussed, it is important to distinguish between tests involving private goods, such as choice of mode of transport, and tests involving public goods, such as environmental goods. In transportation economics there have been a number of tests of the external validity of stated preference methods. These tests largely concern choice experiments or similar methods such as conjoint analysis and different ranking and rating formats. The validity tests are either comparative studies with both hypothetical choice/ranking data and revealed preference data (e.g., Benjamin and Sen 1982) or comparisons of predicted market shares from hypothetical choice/ranking studies with observed market shares (e.g., Wardman 1988). The evidence from a large proportion of studies is that choice experiments generally pass external tests of validity. However, as we have discussed, it is not obvious that these results carry over to hypothetical experiments on non-market goods.

Marketable private goods have been used frequently to test for external validity of the contingent valuation method, and some of these studies have indicated that individuals overstate their WTP in a hypothetical setting (see, e.g., Bishop and Heberlein 1979; Cummings, Harrison, and Rutström 1995; Frykblom 1997). Some previous studies on donations to environmental projects using the contingent valuation method have also indicated overstatement of hypothetical WTP (see, e.g., Seip and Strand (1992); Brown et al. (1996); and see List and Gallet (2001) for a meta-analysis on hypothetical bias). Another way to test external validity is to compare the results of CVM studies with revealed preference studies. Carson et al. (1996) performed a meta-analysis, including eighty-three studies, allowing 616 comparisons, and they found that CVM estimates of WTP were slightly lower than their revealed preference counterparts, with a mean ratio between CVM and revealed preferences of 0.89.

There are a number of cases where laboratory and natural field experiments can be used as an alternative to stated preference surveys. The main application is within food economics, where both stated preference and experiments have been used to elicit preferences for food attributes and the effects of information on consumer choices. A number of studies compare results from lab experiments with stated preference surveys on the same topic. Most of these are done with the purpose of testing for hypothetical bias. The results are clearly mixed for choice experiments. Carlsson and Martinsson (2001) failed to reject a hypothesis of equal marginal WTP in a real and a hypothetical setting (both conducted in a lab), while Johansson-Stenman and Svedsäter (2008) did reject the equality of marginal WTPs. Lusk and Schroeder (2004) found that hypothetical choices overestimate total WTP, but did not reject the equality of marginal WTPs for changes in individual attributes.

There are also studies that compare lab experiments, stated preference surveys, and behavior outside the lab. Shogren et al. (1999) conducted a hypothetical mail survey and a lab experiment concerning irradiated food, and compared the results with actual store purchases. They found that both the survey and the lab experiment resulted in a larger market share prediction of irradiated chicken than the grocery store prediction. Chang, Lusk, and Norwood (2009) found that both a stated preference survey and an actual lab experiment predicted actual retail sales fairly well, although the non-hypothetical experiment performed better than the hypothetical choice experiment. The most interesting finding is perhaps the one in Lusk, Pruitt, and Norwood (2006), where they compared a framed field experiment with actual retail sales. They found that the results of the framed field experiment predicted consumer behavior in the store, although there is some evidence of more pro-social behavior in the framed field experiment.

What is the interpretation of these results? I think there are two important take-home messages. First, we should be careful when comparing results obtained from either a laboratory experiment or a stated preference survey with actual behavior. Clearly, this difference cannot be explained only by hypothetical bias in the strictest sense, since both actual lab experiments and stated preference survey results have some problems with predicting actual retail behavior. Second, although the results are mixed, actual lab experiments seem to perform better than stated preference experiments. As discussed by Levitt and List (2007), there are a number of factors that can explain the behavioral differences between the laboratory and the real world: scrutiny, context, stakes, selection of subjects, and restrictions on time horizons and choice sets. Some of these are, of course, important explanations for the difference between even lab experiments and retail sales. There are at least three important differences. The first is the degree of scrutiny: in both the lab and the survey situation, subjects/respondents know that they are taking part in a study where someone is interested in their behavior. The second is the choice set restriction: in the lab and the survey, the choice sets are clearly defined and restricted, while in a store the choice sets are larger and perhaps less clear. The third is the context in which the choices are made, i.e., the store versus the lab. There is a vast literature comparing behavior in the lab and the field showing that these could be important factors explaining the difference. The degree of anonymity in experiments is one potential measure of scrutiny, and a number of experiments show that the extent of pro-social behavior increases, the less anonymous the decisions are (see, e.g., List et al. 2004; Soetevent 2005). The effects of choice set restrictions can also be important. For example, Bardsley (2008) and List (2007) find that subjects' behavior in traditional dictator games changes when they are faced with the possibility of taking money from the recipient's endowment. Consequently, when comparing behavior in a survey situation and in an actual situation, many of these factors could also be different, and explain the potential differences. This is particularly important for tests of external validity.

5.3 Methods for Reducing Hypothetical Bias

A number of measures to reduce and/or correct for hypothetical bias have been suggested in the literature. In this section I shall look at three approaches: (1) using follow-up certainty questions, (2) using cheap talk and consequential scripts, and (3) using time-to-think protocol.

   With a follow-up certainty question respondents are asked to rate how certain they are that they would actually pay. Usually a ten-point Likert scale is used (10 = very certain and 1 = very uncertain). Then only certain responses are used to estimate WTP.[7] A series of studies have shown that using only certain responses results in a hypothetical WTP that is insignificantly different from actual WTP (see, e.g., Champ et al. 1997; Champ and Bishop 2001; Vossler et al. 2003; Blumenschein et al. 2008). While this method indeed seems to reduce hypothetical bias, the major problem is that there does not seem to be any consistency in the threshold. Sometimes a threshold of eight works best and sometimes, for example, a threshold of ten. It is not evident how respondent uncertainty responses can be implemented in a choice experiment, and few studies have used this approach. Lundhede et al. (2009) designed two experiments where respondents were asked to assess how certain they were of their response after each choice set. However, using various recoding approaches, they did not find any significant or consistent effects on WTP.

   Cheap talk scripts were initially suggested by Cummings and Taylor (1999), and they are an attempt to bring down the hypothetical bias by thoroughly describing and discussing the propensity of respondents to exaggerate stated WTP. The success of cheap talk scripts has varied. Using private goods, classroom experiments, or closely controlled field settings, the use of cheap talk has proven to be potentially successful (Cummings and Taylor 1999; List 2001). Similarly, short cheap talk scripts have also been effective in reducing marginal WTP in choice experiments (Carlsson, Frykblom, and Lagerkvist 2005). Mixed results have been found when incorporating a public good with private good attributes (Aadland and Caplan 2003, 2006), and one possible explanation for the difference is that the length and structure of the cheap talk script matters. A somewhat different approach that can be called a consequential script has

[7] In some early applications the certainty information was used to recode yes responses as no responses. This means that *by definition* the estimated mean WTP will be lower compared with no recoding.

been suggested by Bulte et al. (2005). With this script the respondents are told explicitly that the results from the study could have an actual effect and that they should consider this when answering. This type of script seems to have a similar effect on WTP as a cheap talk script. However, whether the effect of this script was desirable or not would partly depend on the incentive properties of the valuation question. Furthermore, this script is perhaps less likely to reduce effects such as purchase of moral satisfaction and warm glow.

Finally, giving respondents time to consider their responses has been shown in a number of studies to result in more consistent responses and lower WTP (Whittington et al. 1992; Cook et al. 2007). There are two potential effects of giving respondents time to think: they may consider the budget constraint more carefully and the focus on the issues is reduced, and the influence of the interviewer is reduced. Both these effects are likely to reduce WTP, and hence the hypothetical bias.

6 DISCUSSION

This chapter has provided an overview of stated preference methods for food demand analysis, with a focus on the choice experiment method. To conclude, I provide a brief discussion of some issues for ongoing and future research.

I shall actually start where I ended. Hypothetical bias remains one of the most important problems with stated preference methods, although one sometimes get the sense that people not working with stated preference methods are exaggerating the problem. There is some more recent work on implementation of methods to reduce hypothetical bias. One suggestion is to use a so-called oath script. In an incentive-compatible second-price auction, Jacquemet et al. (2009) asked bidders to swear on their honor to give honest answers prior to participating. They found that in treatments with an oath script, responses were more sincere than in treatments without an oath script. Another recent suggestion is to use a third-person perception approach, or inferred valuation. With this approach, subjects are asked what they believe an average person would do (Carlsson, Daruvala, and Jaldell 2008; Lusk and Norwood 2009a, b). Lusk and Norwood (2009a) found that predictions of others' voting were similar to actual voting behavior. Lusk and Norwood (2009b) found that for goods with high normative consequences, own stated WTP was higher than the predicted WTP of others. Carlsson, Daruvala, and Jaldell (2008) found that subjects stated a lower WTP when asked about others' behavior than when asked about their own WTP. For these two approaches, more empirical evidence is clearly needed, and it remains to be seen if they can be implemented in a traditional stated preference survey.

Another area for future research is the role of context dependence that we have also discussed in this chapter. It is clear that context matters in the survey situation, but at the same time context also matters in other situations, such as contributions to public goods and donations (see, e.g., Landry et al. 2006; Alpizar, Carlsson, and

Johansson-Stenman 2008a). One interesting question is whether context is more or less important in hypothetical contexts (see, e.g., Hanemann 1994; Bertrand and Mullainathan 2001; Alpizar, Carlsson, and Johansson-Stenman 2008b). Furthermore, the analytical tools in stated preferences are highly suitable for analyzing and incorporating context dependence (Swait et al. 2002). An excellent example of such a study is one by Hu, Adamowicz, and Veeman (2006), where the effect of labels and reference points on food demand is studied. However, more empirical studies are clearly needed.

Finally, surprisingly few stated preference studies consider the social context. Within the area of food economics, the social context is likely to be very important in many circumstances, in particular since many decisions are made within the household, where the decision maker is not one single individual. Stated preference methods are actually highly suitable for analyzing household decisions and relating household decisions to individual preferences since it is possible to conduct surveys at both the household level and the individual level.

REFERENCES

Aadland, D., and A. Caplan. 2003. "Willingness to Pay for Curbside Recycling with Detection and Mitigation of Hypothetical Bias." *American Journal Agricultural Economics*, 85/2: 492–502.

——. 2006. "Cheap Talk Revisited: New Evidence from CVM." *Journal Economic Behavior and Organization* 60/4: 562–78.

Adamowicz, W., P. Boxall, M. Williams, and J. Louviere. 1998. "Stated Preferences Approaches to Measuring Passive Use Values." *American Journal of Agricultural Economics* 80/1: 64–75.

Alpizar, F., F. Carlsson, and O. Johansson-Stenman. 2008a. "Anonymity, Reciprocity, and Conformity: Evidence from Voluntary Contributions to a National Park in Costa Rica." *Journal of Public Economics* 92/5–6: 1047–60.

Alpizar, F., F. Carlsson, and O. Johansson-Stenman. 2008b. "***Does Context Matter More for Hypothetical than for Actual Contributions? Evidence from a Natural Field Experiment." *Experimental Economics* 11/3: 299–314.

——, and P. Martinsson. 2003. "Using Choice Experiments for Non-Market Valuation." *Economic Issues* 8/1: 83–110.

Andreoni, J. 1989. "Giving with Impure Altruism: Applications to Charity and Ricardian Equivalence." *Journal of Political Economy* 97/6: 1447–58.

Antle, J. M. 1999. "The New Economics for Agriculture." *American Journal of Agricultural Economics* 81/5: 993–1010.

Ariely, D., G. Loewenstein, and D. Prelec. 2008. *"Coherent Arbitrariness": Stable Demand Curves without Stable Preferences.* Working Paper. Cambridge, MA: Massachusetts Institute of Technology.

Arora, N., and G. Allenby. 1999. "Measuring the Influence of Individual Preference Structures in Group Decision Making." *Journal of Marketing Research* 36/4: 476–87.

Bardsley, N. 2008. "Dictator Game Giving: Altruism or Artifact?" *Experimental Economics* 11/2: 122–33.

Bateman, I., and A. Munro. 2009. "Household versus Individual Valuation: What's the Difference?" *Environmental and Resource Economics* 43/1: 119–35.

—— and K. Willis. 1999. *Valuing Environmental Preferences.* Oxford: Oxford University Press.

——, D. Burgess, G. Hutchinson, and D. Matthews. 2008. "Learning Design Contingent Valuation (LDCV): NOAA Guidelines, Preference Learning and Coherent Arbitrariness." *Journal of Environmental Economics and Management* 55/2: 127–41.

Beharry-Borg, N., D. Hensher, and R. Scarpa. 2009. "An Analytical Framework for Joint vs Separate Decisions by Couples in Choice Experiments: The Case of Coastal Water Quality in Tobago." *Environmental and Resource Economics* 45/1: 95–117.

Benjamin, J., and L. Sen. 1982. "Comparison of the Predictive Ability of Four Multiattribute Approaches to Attitudinal Measurement." *Transportation Research Record* 890: 1–6.

Bertrand, M., and S. Mullainathan. 2001. "Do People Mean What They Say? Implications for Subjective Survey Data." *American Economic Review* 91/2: 67–72.

Bishop, R., and T. Heberlein. 1979. "Measuring Values of Extra-Market Goods: Are Indirect Measures of Value Biased?" *American Journal Agricultural Economics* 61/5: 926–30.

Blamey, R., J. Bennett, J. Louviere, M. Morrison, and J. Rolfe. 2000. "A Test of Policy Labels in Environmental Choice Modeling Studies." *Ecological Economics* 32/2: 269–86.

Blumenschein, K., G. Blomquist, M. Johannesson, N. Horn, and P. Freeman. 2008. "Eliciting Willingness to Pay without Bias: Evidence from a Field Experiment." *Economic Journal* 118/525: 114–37.

Bradley, M. 1988. "Realism and Adaptation in Designing Hypothetical Travel Choice Concepts." *Journal of Transport Economics and Policy* 22/1: 121–37.

Brown, T., P. Champ, R. Bishop, and D. McCollum. 1996. "Which Response Format Reveals the Truth about Donations to a Public Good?" *Land Economics* 72/2: 152–66.

Bryan, S., L. Gold, R. Sheldon, and M. Buxton. 2000. "Preference Measurement Using Conjoint Methods: An Empirical Investigation of Reliability." *Health Economics* 9/5: 385–95.

Bulte, E., S. Gerking, J. List, and A. de Zeeuw. 2005. "The Effect of Varying the Causes of Environmental Problems on Stated Values: Evidence from a Field Study." *Journal of Environmental Economics and Management* 49/2: 330–42.

Bunch, D., J. Louviere, and D. Andersson. 1996. *A Comparison of Experimental Design Strategies for Choice-Based Conjoint Analysis with Generic-Attribute Multinomial Logit Models.* Working Paper. Davis: Graduate School of Management, University of California, Davis.

Cameron, T. 1988. "A New Paradigm for Valuing Non-Market Goods using Referendum Data: Maximum Likelihood Estimation by Censored Logistic Regression." *Journal of Environmental Economics and Management* 15/3: 355–79.

Campbell, D., G. Hutchinson, and R. Scarpa. 2008. "Incorporating Discontinuous Preferences into the Analysis of Discrete Choice Experiments." *Environmental and Resource Economics* 41/3: 101–17.

Canavari, M., G. Nocella, and R. Scarpa. 2005. "Stated Willingness-to-Pay for Organic Fruit and Pesticide Ban: An Evaluation Using Both Web-Based and Face-to-Face Interviewing." *Journal of Food Products Marketing* 11/3: 107–34.

Carlsson, F., and P. Martinsson. 2001. "Do Hypothetical and Actual Marginal Willingness to Pay Differ in Choice Experiments? Application to the Valuation of the Environment." *Journal of Environmental Economics and Management* 41/2: 179–92.

Carlsson, F., and P. Martinsson. 2003. "Design Techniques for Stated Preference Methods in Health Economics." *Health Economics* 12/4: 281–94.

————. 2008. "How Much Is Too Much? An Investigation of the Effect of the Number of Choice Sets, Starting Point and the Choice of Bid Vectors in Choice Experiments." *Environmental and Resource Economics* 40/2: 165–76.

———, D. Daruvala, and H. Jaldell. 2008. *Do You Do What You Say or Do You Do What You Say Others Do?* Working Papers in Economics No. 309. Gothenburg: Department of Economics, University of Gothenburg.

———, P. Frykblom, and C. J. Lagerkvist. 2005. "Using Cheap-Talk as a Test of Validity in Choice Experiments." *Economics Letters* 89/2: 147–52.

Carlsson, F., P. Frykblom, and C. J. Lagerkvist. 2007a. "***Consumer Benefits of Labels and Bans on GM Foods: Choice Experiments with Swedish Consumers." *American Journal of Agricultural Economics* 89/1: 152–61.

Carlsson, F., P. Frykblom, and C. J. Lagerkvist. 2007b. "***Consumer Willingness to Pay for Farm Animal Welfare: Transportation of Farm Animals to Slaughter versus the Use of Mobile Abattoirs." *European Review of Agricultural Economics* 34/3: 321–44.

Carson, R., and T. Groves. 2007. "Incentive and Informational Properties of Preference Questions." *Environmental and Resource Economics* 37/1: 181–210.

———, N. Flores, K. Martin, and J. Wright. 1996. "Contingent Valuation and Revealed Preference Methodologies: Comparing the Estimates for Quasi-Public Goods." *Land Economics* 72/1: 80–99.

———, R. Groves, and M. Machina. 1999. "Incentive and Informational Properties of Preference Questions." Paper presented at the European Association of Environmental and Resource Economists Ninth Annual Conference, Oslo.

Champ, P., and R. Bishop. 2001. "Donation Payment Mechanisms and Contingent Valuation: An Empirical Study of Hypothetical Bias." *Environmental and Resource Economics* 19/4: 383–402.

———, R. Bishop, T. Brown, and D. McCollum. 1997. "Using Donation Mechanisms to Value Nonuse Benefits from Public Goods." *Journal of Environmental Economics and Management* 33/2: 151–62.

Chang, J. B., J. Lusk, and F. B. Norwood. 2009. "How Closely Do Hypothetical Surveys and Laboratory Experiments Predict Field Behavior?" *American Journal of Agricultural Economics* 91/2: 518–34.

Cook, J., D. Whittington, D. Canh, F. R. Johnson, and A. Nyamete. 2007. "Reliability of Stated Preferences for Cholera and Typhoid Vaccines with Time to Think in Hue, Vietnam." *Economic Inquiry* 45/1: 100–14.

Cummings, R., and L. Taylor. 1999. "Unbiased Value Estimates for Environmental Goods: A Cheap Talk Design for the Contingent Valuation Method." *American Economic Review* 89/3: 649–65.

———, G. Harrison, and E. Rutström. 1995. "Home-Grown Values and Hypothetical Surveys: Is the Dichotomous Choice Approach Incentive Compatible?" *American Economic Review* 85/1: 260–6.

DeShazo, J. R., and G. Fermo. 2002. "Designing Choice Sets for Stated Preference Methods: The Effects of Complexity on Choice Consistency." *Journal of Environmental Economics and Management* 44/1: 123–43.

Dosman, D., and W. Adamowicz. 2006. "Combining Stated and Revealed Preference Data to Construct an Empirical Examination of Intra-Household Bargaining." *Review of the Economics of the Household* 4/1: 15–34.

Frykblom, P. 1997. "Hypothetical Question Modes and Real Willingness to Pay." *Journal Environmental Economics and Management* 34/3: 275–87.

Hamilton, S. F., D. L. Sunding, and D. Zilberman. 2003. "Public Goods and the Value of Product Quality Regulations: The Case of Food Safety." *Journal of Public Economics* 87/3–4: 799–817.

Hanemann, M. 1984. "Discrete/Continuous Models of Consumer Demand." *Econometrica* 52/3: 541–61.

—— 1994. "Valuing the Environment through Contingent Valuation." *Journal of Economic Perspectives* 8/5: 19–43.

—— 1999. "Welfare Analysis with Discrete Choice Models." In J. Herriges and C. Kling, eds, *Valuing Recreation and the Environment*. Cheltenham: Edward Elgar.

—— and B. Kanninen. 1999. "The Statistical Analysis of Discrete-Response CV Data." In I. Bateman and K. Willies, eds, *Valuing Environmental Preferences*. Oxford: Oxford University Press.

Hensher, D. 2006. "Revealing Differences in Willingness to Pay Due to Dimensionality of Stated Choice Designs: An Initial Assessment." *Environmental and Resource Economics* 34/1: 7–44.

—— and W. Greene. 2003. "The Mixed Logit: The State of Practice." *Transportation* 30/2: 133–76.

——, J. Rose, and W. Greene. 2005. "The Implications on Willingness to Pay of Respondents Ignoring Specific Attributes." *Transportation* 32/3: 203–22.

——, P. Stopher, and J. Louviere. 2001. "An Exploratory Analysis of the Effect of Number of Choice Sets in Designed Choice Experiments: An Airline Choice Application." *Journal of Air Transport Management* 7/6: 373–9.

Herriges, J., and J. Shogren. 1996. "Starting Point Bias in Dichotomous Choice Valuation with Follow-Up Questioning." *Journal of Environmental Economics and Management* 30/1: 112–31.

Hu, W., W. Adamowicz, and M. Veeman. 2006. "Labeling Context and Reference Point Effects in Models of Food Attribute Demand." *American Journal of Agricultural Economics* 88/4: 1034–49.

Huber, J., and K. Zwerina. 1996. "The Importance of Utility Balance in Efficient Choice Designs." *Journal of Marketing Research* 33/3: 307–17.

Jacquemet, N., R.-V. Joule, S. Luchini, and J. F. Shogren. 2009. *Preference Elicitation under Oath*. Working Papers No. 43. Paris: Centre d'Économie de la Sorbonne.

Johansson-Stenman, O., and H. Svedsäter. 2008. "Measuring Hypothetical Bias in Choice Experiments: The Importance of Cognitive Consistency." *B. E. Journal of Economic Analysis and Policy* 8, art. 41.

Johnson, R., W. Matthews, and M. Bingham. 2000. "Evaluating Welfare-Theoretic Consistency in Multiple Response Stated-Preference Surveys." Working Paper T-0003. Durham, NC: Triangle Economic Research.

Kahneman, D., and J. Knetsch. 1992. "Valuing Public Goods: The Purchase of Moral Satisfaction." *Journal of Environmental Economics and Management* 22/1: 57–70.

Kanninen, B. 2002. "Optimal Design for Multinomial Choice Experiments." *Journal of Marketing Research* 39/2: 214–17.

Kuhfeld, W., R. Tobias, and M. Garratt. 1994. "Efficient Experimental Design with Marketing Research Applications." *Journal of Marketing Research* 31/4: 545–57.

Ladenburg, J., and S. Olsen. 2008. "Gender Specific Starting Point Bias in Choice Experiments: Evidence from an Empirical Study." *Journal of Environmental Economics and Management* 56/3: 275–85.

Landry, C., A. Lange, J. List, M. Price, and N. Rupp. 2006. "Toward an Understanding of the Economics of Charity: Evidence from a Field Experiment." *Quarterly Journal of Economics* 121/2: 747–82.

Layton, D., and G. Brown. 1998. "Application of Stated Preference Methods to a Public Good: Issues for Discussion." Paper presented at the NOAA Workshop on the Application of Stated Preference Methods to Resource Compensation, Washington, DC, June 1–2.

————. 2000. "Heterogeneous Preferences Regarding Global Climate Change." *Review of Economics and Statistics* 82/4: 616–24.

Levitt, S. D., and J. A. List. 2007. "What Do Laboratory Experiments Measuring Social Preferences Reveal about the Real World?" *Journal of Economic Perspectives* 21/2: 153–74.

Liljenstolpe, C. 2008. "Evaluating Animal Welfare with Choice Experiments: An Application to Swedish Pig Production." *Agribusiness* 24/1: 67–84.

List, J. 2001. "Do Explicit Warnings Eliminate the Hypothetical Bias in Elicitation Procedures? Evidence from Field Auction Experiments." *American Economic Review* 91/5: 1498–1507.

———— 2003. "Does Market Experience Eliminate Market Anomalies?" *Quarterly Journal of Economics* 118/1: 41–72.

———— 2007. "On the Interpretation of Giving in Dictator Games." *Journal of Political Economy* 115/3: 482–93.

———— and C. Gallet. 2001. "What Experimental Protocol Influence Disparities between Actual and Hypothetical Stated Values?" *Environmental and Resource Economics* 20/3: 241–54.

————, R. Berrens, A. Bohara, and J. Kerkvliet. 2004. "Examining the Role of Social Isolation on Stated Preferences." *American Economic Review* 94/3: 741–52.

Loureiro, M., and S. Hine. 2002. "Discovering Niche Markets: A Comparison of Consumer Willingness to Pay for Local (Colorado-Grown), Organic, and GMO-Free Products." *Journal of Agricultural and Applied Economics* 34/3: 477–87.

Louviere, J. 1988. *Analyzing Decision Making: Metric Conjoint Analysis*. Newbury Park, CA: Sage.

———— 2006. "What You Don't Know Might Hurt You: Some Unresolved Issues in the Design and Analysis of Discrete Choice Experiments." *Environmental and Resource Economics* 34/1: 173–88.

————, D. Hensher, and J. Swait. 2000. *Stated Choice Methods: Analysis and Application*. Cambridge: Cambridge University Press.

————, T. Islam, N. Wasi, D. Street, and L. Burgess. 2008. "Designing Discrete Choice Experiments: Do Optimal Designs Come at a Price." *Journal of Consumer Research* 35 (Aug.), 360–75.

Lundhede, T., S. Olsen, J. Jacobsen, and B. J. Thorsen. 2009. "Handling Respondent Uncertainty in Choice Experiments: Evaluating Recoding Approaches against Explicit Modeling of Uncertainty." *Journal of Choice Modelling* 2/2: 118–47.

Lusk, J., and B. Norwood. 2005. "Effect of Experimental Design on Choice-Based Conjoint Valuation Estimates." *American Journal of Agricultural Economics* 87/3: 771–85.

————. 2009a. "An Inferred Valuation Method." *Land Economics* 85/3: 500–14.

————. 2009b. "Bridging the Gap between Laboratory Experiments and Naturally Occurring Markets: An Inferred Valuation Method." *Journal of Environmental Economics and Management* 58/2: 236–50.

——and T. Schroeder. 2004. "Are Choice Experiments Incentive Compatible? A Test with Quality Differentiated Beef Steaks." *American Journal Agricultural Economics* 86/2: 467–82.

——, M. Jamal, L. Kurlander, M. Roucan, and L. Taulman. 2005. "A Meta Analysis of Genetically Modified Food Valuation Studies." *Journal of Agricultural and Resource Economics* 30/1: 28–44.

——, J. R. Pruitt, and B. Norwood. 2006. "External Validity of a Framed Field Experiment." *Economics Letters* 93/2: 285–90.

——, J. Roosen, and J. A. Fox. 2003. "Demand for Beef from Cattle Administered Growth Hormones or Fed Genetically Modified Corn: A Comparison of Consumers in France, Germany, the United Kingdom, and the United States." *American Journal Agricultural Economics* 85/1: 16–29.

McFadden, D. 1974. "Conditional Logit Analysis of Qualitative Choice Behavior." In P. Zarembka, ed., *Frontiers in Econometrics*. New York: Academic Press.

——and K. Train. 2000. "Mixed MNL Models for Discrete Response." *Journal of Applied Econometrics* 15/5: 447–70.

Mazotta, M., and J. Opaluch. 1995. "Decision Making when Choices Are Complex: A Test of Heiner's Hypothesis." *Land Economics* 71/4: 500–15.

Mitchell, R., and R. Carson. 1989. *Using Surveys to Value Public Goods: The Contingent Valuation Method*. Washington, DC: Resources for the Future.

Morey, E., V. Sharma, and A. Karlström. 2003. "A Simple Method of Incorporating Income Effects into Logit and Nested-Logit Models: Theory and Application." *American Journal of Agricultural Economics* 85/1: 248–53.

Plott, C. 1996. "Rational Individual Behavior in Markets and Social Choice Processes: The Discovered Preference Hypothesis." In K. Arrow, E. Colombatto, M. Perleman, and C. Schmidt, eds, *Rational Foundations of Economic Behavior*. London: Macmillan.

Revelt, D., and K. Train. 1998. "Mixed Logit with Repeated Choices: Households' Choices of Appliance Efficiency Level." *Review of Economics and Statistics* 80/4: 647–57.

Sandor, Z., and M. Wedel. 2001. "Designing Conjoint Choice Experiments Using Managers Prior Beliefs." *Journal of Marketing Research* 38/4: 430–44.

Scarpa R., M. Thiene, and D. Hensher. 2010. "Monitoring Choice Task Attribute Attendance in Non-Market Valuation of Multiple Park Management Services: Does it Matter?" *Land Economics* 86/4: 817–39.

————, and K. Train. 2008. "Utility in WTP space: A Tool to Address Confounding Random Scale Effects in Destination Choice to the Alps." *American Journal of Agricultural Economics* 90/5: 994–1010.

Seip, K., and J. Strand. 1992. "Willingness to Pay for Environmental Goods in Norway: A Contingent Valuation Study with Real Payments." *Environmental and Resource Economics* 2/1: 91–106.

Shogren, J. F., J. A. Fox, D. J. Hayes, and J. Roosen. 1999. "Observed for Food Safety in Retail, Survey, and Auction Markets." *American Journal of Agricultural Economics* 81/5: 1192–9.

Small, K., and S. Rosen. 1981. "Applied Welfare Economics with Discrete Choice Econometrics." *Econometrica* 49/1: 105–30.

Soetevent, A. R. 2005. "Anonymity in Giving in a Natural Context: An Economic Field Experiment in Thirty Churches." *Journal of Public Economics* 89/11–12: 2301–23.

Swait, J., and W. Adamowicz. 1996. *The Effect of Choice Environment and Task Demands on Consumer Behavior: Discriminating between Contribution and Confusion.* Working Paper. Edmonton: Department of Rural Economy, University of Alberta.

————, M. Hanemann, A. Diederich, J. Krosnick, D. Layton, W. Provencher, D. Schkade, and R. Tourangeau. 2002. "Context Dependence and Aggregation in Disaggregate Choice Analysis." *Marketing Letters* 13/3: 195–205.

Train, K. 2003. *Discrete Choice Methods with Simulation.* New York: Cambridge University Press.

——and M. Weeks. 2005. "Discrete Choice Models in Preference Space and Willingness-to-Pay Space." In A. Alberini and R. Scarpa, eds, *Applications of Simulation Methods in Environmental Resource Economics.* Dordrecht: Springer.

von Haefen, R. 2003. "Incorporating Observed Choices into the Construction of Welfare Measures from Random Utility Models." *Journal of Environmental Economics and Management* 45/2: 145–64.

Vossler, C., R. Ethier, G. Poe, L. Gregory, and M. Welsh. 2003. "Payment Certainty in Discrete Choice Contingent Valuation Responses: Results from a Field Validity Test." *Southern Economic Journal* 69/4: 886–902.

Wardman, M. 1988. "A Comparison of Revealed and Stated Preference Models of Travel Behaviour." *Journal of Transport Economics and Policy* 22/1: 71–91.

Whittington, D., V. K. Smith, A. Okorafor, A. Okore, J. L. Liu, and A. McPhail. 1992. "Giving Respondents Time to Think in Contingent Valuation Studies: A Developing Country Application." *Journal of Environmental Economics and Management* 22/3: 205–25.

Zwerina, K., J. Huber, and W. Kuhfeld. 1996. *A General Method for Constructing Efficient Choice Designs.* Working Paper. Durham, NC: Fuqua School of Business, Duke University.

CHAPTER 8

....

NON-MARKET VALUATION:
EXPERIMENTAL METHODS

....

FRODE ALFNES AND KYRRE RICKERTSEN*

1 INTRODUCTION

....

> As a method of research, controlled experimentation is universally used among scientists. They conduct experiments on a small scale to discover facts from which overall conclusions may be reached. In the gradual evolution of marketing research from an art to a science, some practitioners have endeavored to employ experimental methods where possible.
>
> (Applebaum and Spears 1950: 505)

In experimental valuation studies, participants make either consequential bids or choices with real products and real money. Test marketing is the earliest variant of such experiments. In test marketing, new products or marketing strategies are tested in a few stores or regions to expose problems that otherwise would go undetected until full-scale introduction of the product or strategy. It has primarily been used to investigate the effects of marketing mix strategies on the market shares of branded products. The results of test marketing seldom end up in scientific journals, but there are some exceptions. The first scientific article describing a test marketing experiment is Ginzberg (1936). He describes an experiment conducted by a mail order company that distributed two versions of its catalog with different prices. Applebaum and Spears (1950) give a thorough discussion of the early test marketing methodology, and Hawkins (1957) describes a handful of the early experiments. Test marketing techniques have developed and are now a part of the toolbox used in the final stage of product

* The Research Council of Norway, Grant nos. 178300/I10 and 199564/O10, provided financial support to the writing of this chapter. We are grateful for useful comments from our editor Jayson L. Lusk and one anonymous referee.

development of new, branded, low-priced, and frequently purchased consumer products.[1]

During the last two decades and independent of the marketing literature, a second wave of experimental studies has been undertaken by applied economists with an interest in food consumption and marketing. Their focus has mainly been on willingness to pay (WTP), whereas the marketing literature has mostly concentrated on market shares. We address the second wave in this chapter.

When high-quality market data are available, they are usually to be preferred. However, such data cannot always be used to answer the questions of interest. As discussed in Louviere, Hensher, and Swait (2000: 21), there are several reasons why alternatives to market data may be preferred. If you want to investigate the WTP or potential market share for a new product, or a product with new features, there are often no relevant market data. If relevant market data do exist, there may be limited variability or a high degree of multicollinearity in the data. For example, competitors may match each other's prices, leading to constant relative prices over time. New variables may also explain future product choices. For example, until new labeling requirements are introduced, we cannot use market data to predict the effects of these requirements. Finally, available market data often do not include any background information on consumers, so it is difficult to explain why they made their choices.

Alternatives to market data are stated preference and experimental data.[2] Stated preference data are collected by using surveys with non-consequential questions. Stated preference studies can be designed to avoid several of the problems in market data. The researcher can ask about new and non-existent products or product attributes, vary all variables independently, and control most aspects of the study, including information, alternative products, and the sample. The main reason for the interest in experimental data is that they are generated using real economic incentives. In experimental markets using incentive-compatible mechanisms, participants have real economic incentives to reveal their preferences truthfully. We are thus avoiding the problem that participants are more willing to spend their money in hypothetical than in real settings. This is a problem that has been found to be both product- and context-specific (List and Shogren 1998). For a meta-analysis of the hypothetical bias problem, see List and Gallet (2001).

---

[1] Silk and Urban (1978) point out several problems associated with test marketing: it is time-consuming and costly, researchers do not have control over changes in external factors, ideas are exposed to competitors, and it is difficult to gather information on the motivation for behavior. As an alternative to test marketing, they recommend simulated test marketing. Clancy, Krieg, and Wolf (2006) provide a review of current simulated test marketing methodology. Simulated test marketing has become a big industry with tests of about 6,000 concepts and repositions each year. The methods used are mainly attitude, preference, and purchase intent questions combined with exposure to advertising. The results are calibrated on data from previous product launches in the same product category. However, some of the providers also use choice-based experiments as discussed later in this chapter.

[2] One could argue that experimental economists are creating markets that did not previously exist, so experimental data are really hypothetical market data.

A second reason for the increased interest in experimental data is the rapid development of new food products. In the peak year of 1995, manufacturers introduced 16,900 food and beverage products in the United States (Nestle 2002: 25). With this stream of new food products, the probability of failure in the market is high, and experimental studies of marketing strategies may reduce the risk of market failure for a new product.

A third reason for this interest is that several new and controversial technologies have been developed and adopted in food production. Such technologies include the use of hormones in livestock production, the use of genetically modified (GM) plants, and irradiation of foods to avoid microbiological hazards. In an environment where some consumers oppose a given technology while others support it, policymakers have to regulate their use. WTP estimates from experimental studies are used in cost–benefit analyses that are performed as a part of this decision process.

A fourth reason is an ambition to test and further develop economic theories and valuation techniques. Important examples of theoretical investigations of consumer theory include the willingness-to-pay willingness-to-accept divergence (e.g., Shogren, Shin, et al. 1994; Plott and Zeiler 2005), preference reversals (e.g., List 2002), coherent arbitrariness (Ariely, Loewenstein, and Prelec 2003), and behavior under risk and uncertainty (e.g., Hayes et al. 1995). The use of experimental economics in understanding and testing consumer behavior in general is beyond the scope of this chapter but is discussed in, for example, Davis and Holt (1993), Kagel and Roth (1995), and Lusk and Shogren (2007).

For further reading, Davis and Holt (1993) and Kagel and Roth (1995) provide good introductions to experimental economics. A more detailed examination of many of the auction topics covered in this chapter is found in Lusk and Shogren (2007). Louviere, Hensher, and Swait (2000) and Hensher, Rose, and Greene (2005) are good references for many design issues in attribute-based choice experiments. Street and Burgess (2007) and Kuhfeld (2010) are good references for state-of-the-art methods for creating fractional factorial design for choice experiments.

The outline of this chapter is as follows. Different incentive-compatible valuation mechanisms used to evaluate food attributes are described and compared in Sections 2.1 to 2.6. Section 3.1 discusses the relationships between laboratory and field experiments. Valuation mechanisms can be implemented in different ways, and Section 3.2 examines the effects of differences in the implementation and suggested procedural refinements of the valuation mechanisms. Section 3.3 assesses the validity of laboratory results outside the laboratory. Some empirical results that illustrate the usefulness of experimental markets are briefly discussed in Section 4. The chapter concludes with our suggestions for a "best practice" implementation of valuation experiments in food economics and marketing in Section 5.

2   Incentive-Compatible Valuation Mechanisms

In an incentive compatible auction, each participant's weakly dominant strategy is to submit a bid that is equal to his or her valuation of the offered product. Incentive-compatible auction mechanisms commonly used in valuation studies are Vickrey-style sealed-bid auctions with endogenously determined market prices and the Becker–DeGroot–Marschak (BDM) mechanism. In addition to these mechanisms, several choice-based methods are incentive-compatible. As discussed below, each mechanism has its pros and cons, and the choice of mechanism depends on the situation. Some features of the mechanisms are summarized in Table 8.1, which is a revised and expanded version of Lusk and Shogren (2007, table 5.1).

2.1   Sealed-Bid Auctions with Endogenously Determined Market Price

In a second-price sealed-bid auction, also referred to as a Vickrey auction (Vickrey 1961), the participants submit sealed bids and one unit of the good is sold to the highest bidder for a price that is equal to the second-highest bid. Second-price sealed-bid auctions have frequently been used in food valuation studies (e.g., Buhr et al. 1993; Noussair, Robin, and Ruffieux 2002; Alfnes and Rickertsen 2003).

Strategically equivalent to the Vickrey auction is the nth-price auction, also known as the uniform-price auction. In an nth-price sealed-bid auction, the participants submit sealed bids and $n - 1$ units of the good are sold to the $n - 1$ highest bidders for a uniform price equal to the nth-highest bid. The second-price auction is an nth-price auction where $n = 2$.

There are two arguments for choosing an n that is close to half the number of participants in the auction. First, the price will be closer to the mean WTP than in a second-price auction. This may engage low-value bidders, who may view a second-price auction as non-consequential since they do not expect to win the auction.[3] However, a high n may disengage high-value bidders, who believe that they will never lose. The empirical results in Lusk, Alexander, and Rousu (2007) are in line with these arguments. They found that a median-price auction tends to provide the highest punishment from non-truthful bidding when one jointly considers low-, medium-, and high-value bidders.

---

[3] This is particularly true in a multiple-trial second-price auction with posted prices as discussed below.

Table 8.1 Some incentive-compatible mechanisms

Elicitation mechanism	Participant procedure	Market price	Rule	No. of winners
English auction	Sequentially offer ascending bids	Last offered bid	Highest bidder pays market price	1
Second-price auction	Simultaneously submit sealed bids	Second-highest bid	Highest bidder pays market price	1
nth-price auction	Simultaneously submit sealed bids	nth-highest bid	$n - 1$ highest bidders pay market price	$n - 1$
Random nth-price auction	Simultaneously submit sealed bids	Randomly drawn nth-highest bid	$n - 1$ highest bidders pay market price	$n - 1$
Becker–DeGroot–Marschak	Simultaneously submit sealed bids	Randomly drawn price	Participant pays market price if bid exceeds market price	Individually determined
Real choice	Choose alternatives in multiple scenarios	Randomly drawn binding scenario	Everybody pays market price	All participants
Incentive-compatible conjoint ranking mechanism	Rank alternatives in multiple scenarios	Randomly drawn binding scenario	Everybody pays market price	All participants
Open-ended choice experiment	Simultaneously submit quantities	Randomly drawn price	Everybody pays market price for submitted quantities	All participants
Multiple price list	Accept/reject stated prices	Randomly drawn price	Participants pay market price if it is accepted	Individually determined
Real dichotomous choice experiment	Accept/reject	Given price	Participants pay market price if it is accepted	Individually determined
Quantity trade-off experiment	Accept/reject	No price	Participants complete trade if it is accepted	Individually determined

Second, some participants may view an auction as a competition that they would like to win. In a second-price auction, there is only one winning bid, whereas there are $n - 1$ winning bids in an nth-price auction. The increased number of winners may reduce the utility from winning.

A potential problem with using the nth-price auction is that it can be difficult to obtain several identical items of a heterogeneous food product. Yue, Alfnes, and Jensen (2009) circumvent this problem in their nth-price auction by letting the participants investigate and bid on at least as many items as there are participants in each session, and then letting each participant draw his or her unique item as binding. Studies using the nth-price auction include Hoffman et al. (1993), who used a fifth-price auction; Knetsch, Tang, and Thaler (2001), who used a ninth-price auction; and Yue, Alfnes, and Jensen (2009), who used a fourth-price auction.

An extension of the *n*th-price auction is the random *n*th-price auction that was used in Shogren, Fox, et al. (1994) and formally introduced by Shogren, Margolis, et al. (2001). In a random *n*th-price auction, the monitor randomly draws a number *n* (between 2 and the number of participants) after the participants have submitted their sealed bids. Then, as in the non-random *n*th-price auction, *n* − 1 units of the good are sold to the *n* − 1 highest bidders for a price equal to the *n*th-highest bid. A random drawing of *n* should engage all participants. However, it further complicates an unfamiliar market mechanism, and the whole experiment may look more like a lottery for some participants. Studies using the random *n*th-price auction include List and Shogren (2002), Huffman (2003), and Rousu et al. (2004).

Either an endowment or a full bidding approach is used in sealed-bid auctions. In the endowment approach, the auction participants are endowed with one product and bid on an upgrade to another product. The difference in value between the two products is estimated by the bid. In the full bidding approach, the participants bid on two or more products simultaneously. One product is chosen randomly and sold to the highest bidder(s). The other products are not sold. The difference in value between any two products is estimated by the difference in the bids. The endowment approach goes back to work by Shogren and Hayes and colleagues in the early 1990s (e.g., Hayes et al. 1995), and the full bidding approach to work by Hoffman et al. (1993). Corrigan and Rousu (2006b) find that endowing auction participants with a good leads them to submit higher bids for the subsequent units of the same good, and recommend the full bidding approach. For a discussion of the pros and cons of the two approaches, see Lusk and Shogren (2007: 65–8) and Alfnes (2009).

Most experimental auctions are conducted with repeated bidding and bids that are truncated at zero. Owing to this truncation, usually double-hurdle or Tobit panel models are used to investigate treatment and socioeconomic effects on the bids. Lusk and Shogren (2007: 95–112) provide a discussion on the estimation of these models.

2.2   Becker–DeGroot–Marschak (BDM) Mechanism

In the BDM mechanism (Becker, DeGroot, and Marschak 1964), each participant submits a sealed bid for a product. Afterwards, a sales price is randomly drawn from a distribution of prices in an interval from zero to a price that is higher than the anticipated maximum bid.[4] If a participant's bid is higher than the randomly drawn price, the participant purchases one unit of the product and pays a price that is equal to the drawn price. Because the bidders do not compete against one another, the BDM mechanism is not an auction. However, it is strategically equivalent to incentive-compatible auctions (e.g., Noussair, Robin, and Ruffieux 2004a).

---

[4] The limits of the distribution are typically not revealed to the participants to avoid anchoring.

The main advantage of the BDM mechanism is that it can be conducted with only one participant. Therefore, it is often preferred in studies conducted at the point of purchase, such as grocery stores, or other places where it is difficult to run a full-scale auction with an endogenously determined market price. Studies using the BDM mechanism include Lusk, Fox, et al. (2001), Lusk and Fox (2003), Wertenbroch and Skiera (2002), and Nunes and Boatwright (2004). The econometric models used to estimate treatment and socioeconomic effects on the bids are similar to those used for the sealed-bid auctions.

2.3 Price List Experiments

Cummings, Harrison, and Rutström (1995) used a real dichotomous choice (RDC) method where they asked a set of consumers if they would buy a commodity at a given price. If the respondents answered yes, they were required to buy the product for the given price, and if they answered no, no sales were completed. Since it is in a respondent's best interest to say yes if and only if the price is lower than his WTP for the product, the RDC method is incentive-compatible.

An extension of the RDC is the multiple price list (MPL) format used by Kahneman, Knetsch, and Thaler (1990).[5] In their MPL experiment, each participant was given a list with the following statement: "At a price of $8.75 I will buy_____ I will not buy_____," with values ranging from $0.25 to $8.75. For each value, the participant was asked to check either "I will buy" or "I will not buy." At the end, the monitor selected one row from the list at random, and the participant's choice for that row was implemented. This procedure is easy to implement and explain.[6] However, Andersen et al. (2006) discuss three possible disadvantages. First, only interval and not point valuations are elicited. Second, participants can give answers reflecting inconsistent preferences. Third, participants may be drawn to the middle of the ordered table irrespective of their true WTP.

Corrigan et al. (2009) introduced an extension of the price list format, which they called an open-ended choice experiment, where each participant was asked how many units he or she wanted to purchase at different prices. They included one existing product offered at a constant price and a novel product presented with a price list. For

---

[5] In the contingent valuation literature, the hypothetical version of the MPL is usually referred to as the payment card method.

[6] For the MPL to be incentive-compatible, it is important that the answers given do not affect the prices presented in subsequent choice situations. Hence, the non-hypothetical version of the double-bounded dichotomous-choice (DC) method (e.g., Shogren, Fox, et al. 1999; Nayga, Woodward, and Aiew 2006) is not incentive-compatible. In the double-bounded DC method each respondent is asked a second DC question, which depends on the response to the first question. If the first response is yes, the second price is some amount greater than the first bid, while if the first response is no, the second price is some amount smaller. In this case, someone with a small positive surplus from the first question has incentives to answer no to get a second question with a lower price.

each price on the price list, the participants were asked to indicate the quantity demanded for the two products. At the end of the experiment, one of the prices was randomly chosen, and the participants had to buy the quantities of the two products that they had indicated. By using the quantities chosen, Corrigan et al. (2009) calculated the aggregate demand and corresponding own-price elasticity for the novel product. For storable commodities, this procedure has a problem in common with test marketing experiments. Consumers tend to stock up on storable products when the price is low and both the calculated aggregate demand and own-price elasticity may be difficult to interpret. To solve this problem in test marketing, Hawkins (1957: 437) recommended that "the test should not be concluded until the normal continuing rate of purchase has been established," which could take several months.

2.4   Real Choice Experiments

Choice-based consumer experiments conducted in a laboratory with posted prices and real sales were introduced by Pessemier (1959, 1960). In these early experiments, each participant was told how much money he had available to spend, shown samples of merchandise, and asked to make simulated shopping trips at normal shopping speed, choosing the items that would maximize their value of the mix of merchandise and money.[7] After each experiment one respondent was randomly selected to get the actual items and change called for by the selections made during one of his shopping trips.

During the last two decades, there has been a rapid development in the design and analysis of stated choice experiments. In these experiments researchers can evaluate the impacts of several attributes simultaneously. A real choice (RC) experiment is a straightforward extension of a stated choice experiment by including real economic incentives. As in stated choice experiments, participants are asked to make choices in a series of choice scenarios. In each scenario, two or more products are presented with given prices. By varying product attributes between the choice scenarios according to an experimental design, the marginal utility parameters for the various attributes, the marginal rate of substitution between different attributes, and the relative impact of socioeconomic characteristics on the valuation of the different attributes can be estimated using discrete choice methods. To induce real economic incentives, one of the choice scenarios is randomly drawn as binding, and the choices made in that scenario are implemented. The participants pay the price and receive the product

---

[7] In Pessemier (1959) the participants had to state their preferred brand of toothpaste and cigarettes before they went on simulated shopping trips for these two products. For each of ten trips, the prices of the preferred brands were increased. Thus, the participants were faced with deciding whether they would continue to purchase their preferred brands or switch to some other brands. See also McConnell (1968) for a slightly different design where the value of the least-preferred alternative was increased by adding pennies. As with the price list format, it is important that the choices made in real choice experiments with multiple choice sets do not affect the prices in the later choice sets.

chosen in the binding scenario. For heterogeneous products, one can let the participants buy the product they evaluate by including at least as many choice sets as
participants, and letting each participant choose a unique choice set (Alfnes et al. 2006).

A major advantage of RC experiments is that the choice tasks are similar to the
choices consumers face every day in grocery stores. A weakness compared with the
auction methods is that the WTP is not directly observable, but must be estimated
based on the choices. Usually this estimation is done by using the choices of all
participants. Hence, the estimated WTP for each participant is affected by the
responses of other participants and sensitive to the model specification. For example,
if one participant does not consider price when making his or her choices, the
estimated WTP for the other participants will be affected.

Recent examples of RC experiments in food marketing research include Lusk and
Schroeder (2004), Ding, Grewal, and Liechty (2005), Alfnes et al. (2006), and Olesen
et al. (2010). Lusk and Schroeder (2004) let all their products be available in each choice
set and only varied the prices between the choice sets, while Alfnes et al. (2006) used a
fractional factorial design to vary several product attributes between the choice sets.

In an RC experiment, the participants choose their preferred product and the
ranking of the other products is unknown. To obtain the complete ranking of products,
Lusk, Fields, and Prevatt (2008) suggested an incentive-compatible conjoint ranking
mechanism (ICCRM) that was also used by Chang, Lusk, and Norwood (2009). Each
participant was asked to rank different bundles of the product and cash. One of the
options was a cash-only option. To make the mechanism incentive-compatible, a
spinning wheel divided into a number of slices of differing size was used. The product
ranked first was given the largest slice, the second-ranked product was given the
second-largest slice, and so on. After the ranking was completed, the wheel was spun
and the participant purchased the product indicated by a fixed pointer on the wheel.
An easier method for making the ICCRM incentive-compatible is to randomly select
two or more of the products after the ranking and make the participants buy the one
given the best rank.[8] The ICCRM will give a full ranking of products, but the
mechanism does not resemble the choices that consumers face in stores.

2.5   Some Other Valuation Mechanisms

In an English auction, the auctioneer announces an opening price and the bids are
successively raised until only one participant remains. The last participant wins the
object, paying the final bid. The English auction has been extensively tested and found
to perform well in the experimental economic literature (e.g., Davis and Holt 1993), but

---

[8] Suggested by our editor Jayson Lusk.

has been used in relatively few food evaluation studies. One exception is Lusk, Feldkamp, and Schroeder (2004).[9]

Several studies have used mechanisms that involve real choices between products in either an experimental store or a retail setting. Maynard et al. (2004) gave each participant a budget of US$20 and a unique price schedule, and let the participants choose between different beef products. The participants could choose to purchase as many units as they wanted within their budget. This method resembles Corrigan et al. (2009) open-ended choice experiment, but the latter placed no restrictions on the amount of money the participants had to spend during the experiment and, furthermore, let the participants indicate the quantity demanded at several price combinations.

Three variations of choice experiments adding money to some of the offered products are described in McConnell (1968), Lusk, Norwood, and Pruitt (2006), and Nayga, Woodward, and Aiew (2006). McConnell (1968) asked the participants to make repeated choices as he increased the money added to the least preferred product, while Nayga, Woodward, and Aiew (2006) used a double-bounded choice experiment where they endowed the participants with the perceived inferior product and a random amount of cash. Next, the participants were asked whether they wanted to exchange the endowed product and cash for the perceived superior product. Lusk, Norwood, and Pruitt (2006) let participants choose between three types of pork chops with different attributes. The perceived inferior products were offered with coupons that could be used to pay for grocery purchases. One potential problem with letting participants choose between gifts is that some participants may view this task differently from the choice between products.

In several experiments, the participants have been endowed with a base product to investigate how much of an alternative product it takes to make the participants switch to the alternative product. These experiments measure trade-offs in quantity rather than price. Examples of such quantity trade-off experiments (QTOE) include Masters and Sanogo (2002) and Marette, Roosen, and Blanchemanche (2008). Masters and Sanogo (2002) conducted a QTOE in a market in Mali. They gave mothers accompanied by children under 2 years of age a 400 gram can of a well-known brand of infant food. Next, they offered the mothers various quantities of a lesser-known brand of infant food to measure how much was needed to make the mothers switch to this

---

[9] There are many variations on the English auction. In the format most commonly used by auction theorists, the price rises continuously while participants gradually quit the auction (Klemperer 2004: 11). In this format, the participant with the highest valuation will win and pay a price equal to the second-highest bid, as in a second-price auction. Except for the highest bidder, the English auction is incentive-compatible, i.e., it is each participant's weakly dominant strategy to bid his true WTP. However, the English auction format typically used in auction houses may give little information about the participants' values. To illustrate, let us assume five bidders A, B, C, D, and E with values 50, 60, 70, 80, and 90, respectively. Assume that A starts the auction with a bid of 40, E rises to 80, and the auction stops. The information we end up with is that A has a WTP between 40 and 80, B, C, and D have a WTP between zero and 80, and E's WTP is above 80. We may also note that Dutch as well as first-price auctions are not incentive-compatible. These auction mechanisms are not incentive-compatible because the price paid by the winner is his own bid, i.e., the price is not independent of the winner's bid.

brand. A similar procedure was used by Marette, Roosen, and Blanchemanche (2008) in a study of consumers' reactions to product information concerning the level of omega 3 fatty acids and methyl mercury in canned sardines and tuna. During their choice procedure, the participants had to choose between an endowment of six cans of sardines or tuna and a variable number of cans with the other type of fish.[10]

2.6   Empirical Comparisons of the Mechanisms

On a theoretical basis, the sealed-bid auctions and the BDM mechanism result in identical bids and bid differences. However, many studies find that there are differences in practice with respect to the bids in experiments using induced as well as home-grown values. Unfortunately, it is impossible to test whether bids equal home-grown values, which are private values that are neither controlled nor known a priori by the experimenter. This is in contrast with induced values that are controlled by the experimenter. Most induced-value experiments find that sealed-bid auctions produce more accurate WTP estimates than the BDM mechanism. In an induced-value experiment, Noussair, Robin, and Ruffieux (2004b) found that the second-price auction generated initial average bids closer to the induced values and, moreover, led to more rapid convergence of the bids to the induced values. They concluded that the Vickrey auction is more effective as a WTP elicitation device than the BDM mechanism. They also concluded that the second-price auction generated bids closer to true values than the BDM mechanism all along the demand curve. These results are supported by the induced-value experiments reported in Lusk and Rousu (2006), who compared the second-price auction, the random nth-price auction, and the BDM mechanism. They found that, on average, the two auction formats were significantly more accurate than the BDM mechanism.

In an induced-value experiment, Shogren et al. (2001) studied disengagement and found that bidders with private values below the expected market price tended to submit lower bids than their true values in a second-price auction. In contrast, a random nth-price auction induced sincere bidding also by these participants. However, the random nth-price auction did not generate more truthful bids from bidders with bids close to the market clearing price. For these bidders, the second-price auction performed better.

Some people have negative WTP for new products such as GM foods. Parkhurst, Shogren, and Dickinson (2004) investigated the effects of allowing for negative bids in induced-value experiments. They found that the negative bids in a second-price

---

[10] As with the MPL, it is important that the choices the respondents make do not determine whether they will get a better offer or not. As discussed by Masters and Sanogo (2002: 982), their design failed in this respect and choices were therefore not incentive-compatible. Marette, Roosen, and Blanchemanche (2008) used a predetermined order of twelve choice sets on a single sheet of paper, and the choices the respondents made did not affect the subsequent choice sets.

auction were biased, while the negative bids in a random nth-price auction were imprecise.

Several studies have compared home-grown values across mechanisms, and the results are mixed. Shogren, Fox, et al. (1994) compared the second-price to a random nth-price auction for irradiated pork sandwiches and found no significant differences in mean values. Knetsch, Tang, and Thaler (2001) found significantly higher bids for coffee mugs in a second- than in a ninth-price auction. Lusk, Feldkamp, and Schroeder (2004) compared the second-price auction, the random nth-price auction, the BDM mechanism, and the English auction. They found that first-round second-price auction bids were similar to the bids produced by the other mechanisms. However, bids in later rounds of the second-price auction were significantly higher. Furthermore, the random nth-price auction yielded lower bids than the BDM mechanism and the English auction.

Lusk and Schroeder (2006) compared WTP values found by auctions and real choice experiments and found that the WTP is lower in auctions than in choice experiments. This result may be explained by consumers using posted prices as quality indicators, or viewing the auction as a way of buying products cheaply. The explicit focus on prices in the bidding process may also play a role.

The above discussion demonstrates some of the trade-offs between the mechanisms. First, auctions seem to perform better than the BDM mechanism in induced-value experiments. However, the BDM mechanism may be implemented on an individual basis, and is easy to use in a field setting like a grocery store. Second, the choices in RC experiments resemble real choices in a grocery store, and the different varieties of choice experiments seem to work well in many situations. However, RC experiments do not give independent individual-specific WTP estimates. Third, the second-price auction seems to perform best for high-value bidders, while the random nth-price auction seems to perform best for low-value bidders. Although it is impossible to make any clear recommendations concerning the choice of n in sealed-bid auctions, most recent studies seem to use an n that is higher than 2.

3   INTERNAL AND EXTERNAL VALIDITY OF BIDS AND CHOICES

In choosing between laboratory and field experiments, there is often a trade-off between a rich context in a field experiment and a high degree of control in a laboratory experiment, i.e., a trade-off between the pursuit of internal and external validity. Following Roe and Just (2009), internal validity relates to the ability to demonstrate that observed correlations are causal, and external validity relates to the ability to generalize the relationships found in the experiment to other settings such as the food market.

3.1   Laboratory versus Field Experiments

It has been common in the marketing literature to define laboratory experiments as those conducted in a controlled setting and field experiments as those conducted in an actual marketplace, such as grocery stores or restaurants (e.g., McDaniel and Gates 2009). In laboratory settings, researchers have a high degree of control over factors that influence choices or bids, while in field settings it is difficult to control external factors. On the other hand, in field settings the decisions are made in a context in which the participants are used to making similar decisions.

With their background in experimental economics, Harrison and List (2004) propose a refined categorization. They define laboratory experiments as experiments that employ a standard subject pool of students, an abstract framing, and an imposed set of rules. Field experiments recruit subjects in the field rather than in the classroom, use field goods rather than induced valuations, and have a field context rather than abstract terminology in instructions. Following Harrison and List (2004), field experiments can be divided into three categories: artifactual field experiments are identical to conventional laboratory experiments but with a non-student subject pool; framed field experiments are identical to artifactual field experiments but with field context in the commodity, task, or information set that the subjects use; natural field experiments are identical to framed field experiments except that the subjects do not know that they are participants in an experiment.

Most of the experiments discussed in this chapter use real products, a growing fraction of recent experiments use non-student participants, and a small but growing number of experiments are conducted at the point of purchase, i.e., they are framed field experiments.

3.2   Internal Validity

The mechanisms discussed in this chapter provide incentives for the participants to make bids that are consistent with their WTP. However, several anomalies have been reported in laboratory experiments. We shall briefly discuss some of these results and provide some plausible explanations for this lack of internal validity.

3.2.1   Training

Mechanisms used to elicit values may be unfamiliar to the participants. Some mechanisms may also be similar to mechanisms with which the participants are familiar, so subtle but important differences may go unnoticed. Plott and Zeiler (2005) discuss the importance of practice and training before actual bids are made. In a BDM experiment investigating the gap between willingness to pay and willingness to accept, they found that the gap disappeared when the participants were provided with (1) a detailed explanation of the mechanism and how to arrive at valuations, (2) paid practice using the mechanism, and (3) anonymity so participants are not concerned with how they are viewed by the other participants or the experimenter.

3.2.2   Bid Affiliation and Posted Prices

Induced-value experiments have shown that it takes several rounds of auctions before behavior conforms to the theoretical predictions of WTP bidding (e.g., Noussair, Robin, and Ruffieux 2004b). To let participants understand the auction mechanism and discover their "true" home-grown values for the non-familiar good, auctions with multiple trials have been commonly used in studies of home-grown values (e.g., Hoffman et al. 1993; Shogren, Shin, et al. 1994; Fox, Shogren, et al. 1998; Alfnes and Rickertsen 2003). In multiple-trial auctions for non-familiar goods, it is a common observation that bids increase over the trials.[11] Increasing bids are likely because some participants may try to buy at a low price even when they are told that the optimal strategy is to bid their true WTP. Repeated rounds with price feedback send strong signals to these participants that bidding low, in the hope of buying at a low price, is not an optimal strategy. However, the price feedback may also send signals regarding unknown characteristics of the good and thereby cause bid affiliation, i.e., bids in later rounds may be affiliated with posted prices from earlier rounds (Lusk and Shogren 2007: 82). In this case, mechanisms that are demand-revealing in induced-value settings may not be demand-revealing in settings with home-grown values (Harrison, Harstad, and Rutström 2004). If the participants are uncertain about the quality of a product, they may infer information about the value of the product by observing other participants' bids so they can revise their own bids in subsequent rounds. Hence, they are not basing their bids solely on the values they had when they entered the auction.

Empirical evidence suggests that bid affiliation is a problem. Examining panel data on bidding behavior in over forty second-price auctions, List and Shogren (1999) found some bid affiliation for novel but not familiar products. However, the influence of affiliation on the median bids was small. Furthermore, Lusk and Shogren (2007: 80–92) point to a series of results in the literature and argue that bid affiliation is a minor problem in home-grown value experiments. Corrigan and Rousu (2006a) developed an experiment to test explicitly for the effect of affiliation by using so-called confederate bidders who were instructed to place bids that were much higher than the other participants' WTP. Contrary to List and Shogren (1999) and Lusk and Shogren (2007), they found that for familiar items such as candy bars and coffee mugs, high posted prices lead to increased bids in subsequent rounds. Even though the very high bids of the confederate bidders introduced a hypothetical element into the auction, the results clearly demonstrate that bid affiliation is potentially a problem. Their conclusion is also supported by Harrison, Harstad, and Rutström (2004), who analyzed the

---

[11] One exception is Knetsch, Tang, and Thaler (2001) using a ninth-price auction, where the bids decreased.

data used in the seminal paper of Hoffman et al. (1993) and found statistical evidence of bid affiliation.

The interrelationship between auction mechanism and panel size is likely to affect the posted prices, and thereby the bids through bid affiliation. If there are many participants and few winners, the posted prices will be high. If there are few participants and relatively many winners, the posted prices will be low. Alfnes, Rickertsen, and Ueland (2008) argue that the use of an nth-price auction will reduce the affiliation problem by reducing the likelihood of price feedback that is much higher than the average bids, such as those found in Corrigan and Rousu (2006a). Finally, a statistically significant positive effect of panel size on the bids in a fourth-price auction is reported in Umberger and Feuz (2004).

There is no agreement in the literature on how to handle bid affiliation. Lusk and Shogren (2007) argue that it is a minor problem, while Harrison, Harstad, and Rutström (2004) conclude that one-shot auctions should be used. The latter recommend training participants in the auction mechanism by using another good such as chocolate. However, given the effects of incidental prices and coherent arbitrariness, as discussed below, the use of a different training product or procedure may not alleviate the problem. Most recent papers seem to use an nth-price auction with a relatively low number of rounds, but more than one.

3.2.3   Field Substitutes and Outside Options

Most food products presented in experimental markets have field substitutes. In food experiments, these field substitutes will typically be food items that can be purchased in the grocery store. As pointed out by Harrison, Harstad, and Rutström (2004), no rational consumer will purchase a product in an experimental market that costs more than the price of the good in the market. In induced-value auctions, this leads to bids truncated at the external price of the good (Cherry et al. 2004). In home-grown value experiments, the field substitutes to the product offered in the experiment may be a different product. As pointed out by Alfnes (2009), somebody that does not buy fish in an experimental fish market may end up buying chicken, pork, or beef for dinner that day instead of going to the fish market to buy fish. Hence, the real outside option affecting the optimal bids or choices in a fish experiment may be the consumer surplus from purchasing a non-fish alternative in the market. Alfnes (2009) set up a theoretical model for optimal bidding in a Vickrey auction with outside options and concluded that the effect of outside options on the optimal bidding strategies for food products is a problem for the bid levels, but not for the bid differences. Bernard and He (2010) examined the influence of field prices on bids by conducting auctions before and after the large food price increases in 2007. They found that bids were capped at given field prices and were significantly higher in sessions conducted after store prices increased. Percentage premiums, however, were not significantly different across sessions, and they concluded that the full bidding approach could still be used as long as bid differences are the focus, rather than bid levels.

3.2.4   Anchors, Coherent Arbitrariness, Incidental Prices, and Relative Bids

Empirical evidence suggests that participants use numbers that are presented to them as a part of the experiment as anchors for their stated WTP. Drichoutis, Lazaridis, and Nayga (2008) found that provision of reference price information, such as the field price of sandwiches, significantly affected the bids. Other examples of similar anchors include the distribution of prices in a price list experiment, the limits of the price distribution if revealed to the participants in a BDM mechanism experiment, bids in training sessions, posted prices in repeated auctions, and prices in the first choice sets in choice experiments.

Arbitrary numbers presented to the participants may also serve as arbitrary anchors and affect the bids. For example, Nunes and Boatwright (2004), who investigated the effect of incidental prices on participants' bids in experimental auctions, found that exposing the participants to prices of goods that were completely unrelated to the goods in the auction had a substantial effect on the bids. Similar conclusions are supported by Ariely, Loewenstein, and Prelec (2003), who demonstrated how consumers' absolute valuations of ordinary products are affected by anchors such as the participants' social security numbers. In one experiment, they asked participants to write down their social security numbers before they started the experiment. Participants with a high number bid more than participants with a low number in the following auction. However, consumers' relative valuations of different products appeared to be coherent, i.e., as if supported by demand curves derived from stable preferences.

The presence of random anchors has two implications. First, training participants by using a good other than the good of interest may be no better than using the good itself. Second, relative WTP estimates derived using the full bidding approach are likely to be more stable than the bids themselves. In the full bidding approach, it is likely that random anchors affect the bids for all the goods in a similar way. The results in Umberger and Feuz (2004) confirm that experimental auctions succeed in determining the relative WTP values for close substitutes, while the actual bids are influenced by the experimental design. In situations with many zero bids, many observations will be lost by using relative bids, and bid differences may be used. In line with this reasoning, Hoffman et al. (1993) claimed that the most reliable estimates from experimental auctions are bid differences. Furthermore, Alfnes and Rickertsen (2003) found that bid differences calculated from bids that are increasing across trials are stable. Finally, the results in Lusk, Feldkamp, and Schroeder (2004) indicate that bid differences are uninfluenced by the number of goods included in the auction.

3.3   External Validity

The validity of experimental results for actual retail behavior is important. The external validity of an experiment deals with the ability to generalize the results to other settings, treatments, measures, subjects, and occasions. External validity is increasingly the focus of experimental studies, and several articles have recently discussed why laboratory and field behavior may differ (e.g., Harrison and List 2004; List 2006; Levitt and List 2007). Low external validity of laboratory results can be caused by factors including (1) unfamiliar environment, (2) the nature of the decision task, (3) the participants not being representative, (4) the available information and attention given to information, (5) the presence of researchers that scrutinize participants' behavior, and (6) high bids that do not necessarily imply repeated purchases. Further research is needed to identify particular boundary variables and crucial differences between laboratory and field settings affecting the external validity of experiments.

3.3.1   *Nature of the Environment*

Most economic experiments take place in a laboratory or a classroom. However, a laboratory may be an abstract and unfamiliar environment for many participants, who may behave differently than they would in a retail setting (Levitt and List 2007). Furthermore, the participants do not take part in the experiment because they need to buy food, and the time and place of the experiment are decided by the researcher. In line with these arguments, Corrigan and Rousu (2008) found that consumers who intended to purchase bananas on the day of the experiment gave WTP values that were closer to the perceived field price of bananas than those who did not intend to purchase bananas that day. Hence, even regular buyers of the product may behave as non-buyers in an experiment. This can especially be a problem with highly perishable products that must be consumed within a short period of time after the experiment. Valuation studies conducted in a store setting may solve these problems. However, there are limited possibilities to train participants or collect background information in stores.

3.3.2   *Nature of Decision Tasks*

The decision tasks in an experimental market and a grocery store are typically quite different. The experiment usually includes only a small number of products, and the participants are usually only allowed to buy one unit of one product and no units of the other products. In an auction, the participants are asked to state the highest amount they are willing to pay for a product, instead of choosing among pre-priced products. In the choice-based experiments, the price of the products is varied within the experiment. Furthermore, some design features used in experimental markets may resemble lotteries. For example, most experiments involve random draws.

3.3.3   *Representative Samples*

Self-selected student samples are frequently used to keep the costs of experiments down. Such convenient samples are likely to be non-representative of consumers in the food market. Student samples typically have lower age, lower income, and more education than the general population. The biases introduced by using student samples are likely to be product-specific, and have rarely been investigated. One exception is Depositario et al. (2009), who used a fifth-price auction to investigate the WTP for golden rice among student and non-student participants in the Philippines. The mean bid of the non-student group was about 15 percent higher than the mean bid of the student group, and the difference was significant at the 5 percent level of significance.

Non-student samples may also be unrepresentative. Participants from one region may not be representative of the whole market. For example, Sawyer, Worthing, and Sendak (1979: 64) question the possibility of extrapolating their result for maple syrup collected in Massachusetts to "subjects outside the maple producing region of the Northeast and Great Lakes." Alfnes and Rickertsen (2007) try to mitigate the problem with lack of geographic representativeness by using a national stated choice survey to extrapolate the experimental results to other areas.[12] Samples recruited from the general population may also be non-representative in other ways. In many families, one person has the main responsibility for food purchases, and this person should take part in the experiment. For many food products, the top 10 percent of users by volume buy almost all the units sold of the product, and their preferences may differ significantly from the general population.

3.3.4   Information

In grocery stores, consumers make many choices based on habits. They do not usually read the product description and often pay little attention to the price of the product. In experimental markets, consumers are usually exposed to various types of explicit information, included either in a PowerPoint presentation or on a sheet of paper that is given to them. Furthermore, the price usually plays a very prominent role in the experiment. In auctions, consumers must state their reservation price, and in the various choice-based methods, the prices are varied through the experiment. Finally, smaller sample sizes are required for within-sample than between-sample tests, and therefore within-sample tests are popular among researchers. However, the within-sample design draws attention to the treatment in the experiments, and has repeatedly been found to give larger effects than the between-sample design (e.g., Johansson-Stenman and Svedsäter 2008).

3.3.5   Presence of Researchers

In a typical laboratory experiment, the participants are well aware that they are part of an experiment and that someone will examine their behavior. This scrutiny is likely to affect participants' behavior. The participants may try to behave as they think the experimenter wants them to behave, or may try to give a socially desirable impression of themselves (e.g., Sawyer 1975; Levitt and List 2007; Lusk and Norwood 2009). Social desirability bias is most likely to be a problem in studies examining product attributes

---

[12] The method used in Alfnes and Rickertsen (2007) may also be seen as a method for calibrating the survey results to get WTP estimates that are consistent with experimental markets. The article includes a review of other studies estimating similar calibration functions for survey results. See Alfnes, Yue, and Jensen (2010) for an example of how auctions can be used to alter the behavior in surveys so they give results similar to experimental markets.

with a social dimension such as environmentally friendly, animal-friendly, fair trade, or locally produced.

3.3.6   Repeated Purchase

Many studies find a relatively high price premium for new food products; however, a high premium does not necessarily result in repeated purchase of the food. Shogren, List, and Hayes (2000) discuss the origins of the high price premium. They investigated two possible explanations. First, experimental auctions are non-familiar for the participants, and the novelty of the experimental experience could result in high bids. Second, the novelty of a food product could result in high bids. Many participants may be willing to pay a premium for testing a new product, and the bid will reflect the consumption value of the good as well as the information value of learning how the product fits into their preferences.[13] For a theoretical discussion of the role of the information value in experimental auctions of new products, see Alfnes (2007).

3.3.7   Empirical Results on External Validity

Some studies have investigated the external validity of experimental methods. Brookshire, Coursey, and Schulze (1987) could not reject that the valuation of strawberries was identical in the laboratory and in door-to-door sales. Shogren et al. (1999) compared valuations elicited by a hypothetical mail survey and a non-hypothetical laboratory valuation with grocery store purchases of irradiated chicken. Their results concerning the external validity of the valuation exercises were mixed. Chang, Lusk, and Norwood (2009) used a hypothetical choice experiment, an RC experiment, and the ICCRM to predict retail market shares for different goods. Their results suggested that the non-hypothetical methods outperformed the hypothetical experiment while the ICCRM performed slightly better than RC. Also Ding, Grewal, and Liechty (2005) found that elicitation mechanisms, which properly aligned incentives, predicted behavior better than non-incentive aligned mechanisms.

Some further evidence of external validity with respect to existing products can be found in Lusk and Shogren (2007: 261). Studies conducted by industry providers are not usually published in scientific journals (Clancy, Krieg, and Wolf 2006).

4   EMPIRICAL RESULTS

This section briefly reviews some empirical results that illustrate the usefulness of experimental markets. Detailed discussions of the valuations of specific attributes in different food products are provided in other chapters of this book, and case studies

---

[13] By studying three goods that varied in familiarity, candy bars, mangoes, and irradiated meat, and doing four consecutive auctions over two weeks, Shogren, List, and Hayes (2000) concluded that the main explanation for the high price premium in their experiment was the value of preference learning.

further illustrating the applications of experimental auctions are provided in Lusk and Shogren (2007).

Food marketing issues such as packing technologies (e.g., Menkhaus et al. 1992; Hoffman et al. 1993), the use of insecticides (Roosen et al. 1998), the use of different types of feed (Alfnes et al. 2006), and grading for tenderness (Lusk, Fox, et al. 2001; Alfnes, Rickertsen, and Ueland 2008) have been analyzed. A general conclusion is that there are segments of consumers with different preferences and WTP. Sometimes little or no difference between the WTP for the old and new product is found; however, usually some increases in the mean WTP for the improved product are reported. Typically, studies dealing with attribute-based food marketing limit themselves to calculating the consumers' WTP for new products without addressing the bigger issue about the profitability of introducing them.

Some production technologies such as genetic modification are highly controversial (e.g., Lusk, Daniel, et al. 2001; Noussair, Robin, and Ruffieux 2002, 2004a; Huffman 2003; Lusk, House, et al. 2004), as are hormone treatment in livestock production (e.g., Buhr et al. 1993; Fox, Hayes, et al. 1994; Alfnes and Rickertsen 2003; Bernard and Bernard 2009), irradiation (e.g., Fox, Shogren, et al. 1998; Shogren, Fox, et al. 1999; Shogren, List, and Hayes 2000), and use of antibiotics in feed (Lusk, Norwood, and Pruitt 2006). Controversial technologies have frequently been studied, and the results suggest that the average US participant views irradiation favorably, whereas there is substantial opposition, especially in European countries, toward genetic modification, use of antibiotics in feed, and hormone treatment. Furthermore, the preferences concerning these products are highly heterogeneous, again demonstrating the importance of market segmentation.

Labels and brands are used by food producers to highlight product attributes. Examples of experimental studies of high-value brand names are Lange et al. (2002) and Combris, Lange, and Issanchou (2006), who assessed the effect of product labeling information on the WTP for five brut non-vintage champagnes. They found that the participants were unable to discriminate between the champagnes after blind tasting, while significant differences in WTP appeared when the labels were disclosed. These results led the authors to conclude that it may be more profitable for the big champagne houses to invest in marketing than in quality improvements.

As discussed above, GM foods are controversial, and are required to be labeled as such in many countries. The effects of GM labeling may be complex, as illustrated by Noussair, Robin, and Ruffieux (2002), who studied the WTP for GM cornflakes. They found that when participants observed the products with the labels as seen in the supermarket, labels with information concerning the content of GM corn had no effect on the WTP. However, when the list of ingredients was presented on large overheads, the average WTP for the GM cornflakes was reduced by 27 percent, suggesting that consumers do not automatically react to information provided by labels. Labeling a product as GMO-free or not hormone-treated may also stigmatize the products not having such labels, as discussed by Kanter, Messer, and Kaiser (2009). They found that the introduction of hormone-free and organic milk reduced US consumers' willingness to purchase conventional milk.

Several studies have focused on the effects of scientifically balanced information, and moderate effects are usually reported (e.g., Fox, Hayes, et al. 1994; Roosen et al. 1998; Noussair, Robin, and Ruffieux 2004a; Lusk, House, et al. 2004). However, the effects of information depend on the content as well as the source of the information. Substantial effects of information with either an environmental group perspective or an agricultural biotechnology industry perspective are reported (e.g., Huffman 2003; Rousu et al. 2004, 2007). Furthermore, Fox, Hayes, and Shogren (2002) found that the effects of negative information dominate the effects of positive information.

It is quite common to let participants taste the product in evaluation experiments. Significant effects of tasting are frequently found (e.g., Melton et al. 1996; Alfnes and Rickertsen 2003), and several studies have reported a strong correlation between taste scores and WTP (e.g., Lange et al. 2002; Kanter, Messer, and Kaiser 2009).

5   CONCLUSIONS

Some recommendations concerning the implementation of valuation experiments in food economics and marketing emerge from the previous sections. These recommendations are "best practice" advices, and we acknowledge that some of the advices may be controversial. Furthermore, a researcher may sometimes end up adopting second-best practice. Our recommendations are as follows.

1. *Do not deceive participants or lie to them.* Any information about the valuation mechanism and products should be true. Lies can affect behavior in experiments, and can have negative externalities on future experiments and other experimentalists. That does not mean that you have to reveal everything, but what you say should be true.

2. *Use representative consumers.* The researcher has to decide whether to use a sample of students or representative consumers, and to what extent the participants should be screened based on their consumption of the good. If the objective of the experiment is to test theory or compare mechanisms, student samples are usually satisfactory. However, students differ from other consumers. They are typically younger, have less money, are frequently without children, and so on. These differences are likely to result in different preferences concerning sensory qualities of food, different attitudes toward technology, environment, and animal welfare, and different sensitivity to price changes. We also recommend using a minimum consumption constraint to screen the participants. There is little point in including vegetarians in an experiment about beef quality. Including participants that consume the relevant product class once or twice a month will usually work.

3. *Make sure the participants understand the mechanism.* Theoretically incentive-compatible mechanisms are only incentive-compatible in practice when the participants understand how their choices or bids affect their outcomes in

the experiment. Therefore, use mechanisms that are easy to understand, and avoid design elements that may make the experiment look like a lottery. Furthermore, clearly inform the participants about their best strategy. This is especially important in mechanisms that are not choice-based. Finally, train the participants using exactly the same mechanism and the same number of goods as in the main experiment.

4. *Calculate relative WTP values.* According to microeconomic theory, only relative prices matter. Furthermore, given that anchoring and treatment effects affect the relative values of the included goods identically, they will cancel out. In experimental auctions, zero bids may make it difficult to calculate all the relative WTP values, and WTP difference may be used as a second-best option. This recommendation also implies that testing of value elicitation procedures should include tests of the relative valuations.

5. *Use a context free of scrutiny.* People act differently when they feel they are being observed, and it is important to create an environment where the participants feel relaxed and not scrutinized. The participants should be assigned a random number to identify themselves within the experiment, the forms should be completed in a room that allows for some privacy, and the choices made by the participants should be private, as far as possible.

6. *Use mechanisms with strong real economic incentives.* There are differences with respect to the strength of the incentives among the incentive-compatible mechanisms. For example, in a second-price auction with fifteen participants, a majority of the participants may sometimes change their bids substantially both upward and downward without affecting the outcome of the auction. In a median-price auction, relatively small changes may affect the outcome for many participants.

7. *Collect background information.* For producers, policymakers, and researchers it may be useful to have information about the WTP in different segments of the population. The background information should include socioeconomics, knowledge, attitudes, and purchase behavior.

8. *Let participants taste unfamiliar products.* If consumers prefer the taste of a new food product compared with the competing products in the same price range, then they are likely to adopt it. Tasting will also reduce any sensory uncertainty that may result in either lower WTP owing to risk aversion or higher WTP owing to people wanting to taste the new product. As a consequence, tasting is likely to improve the long-run external validity of the results of the experiment.

9. *Treat all products equally.* There is a large and growing literature on treatment and framing effects in economic as well as sensory experiments. To mitigate these effects, all alternatives should be treated equally. Equal treatment includes rotating the order in which products are presented between sessions, allowing participants to taste either all or none of the products, using the full bidding format in experimental auctions, and using a fractional factorial design with product ordering as one of the attributes in choice-based experiments.

10. *Delete participants with a non-response to all alternatives.* Non-response to all alternatives implies that the participant bids zero for all products or chooses none of the alternatives in all choice scenarios. Participants with non-response to all the alternatives do not reveal anything about their relative valuations of the products included in the experiment. There may be several reasons for non-responses, including the possibility that the participant has already bought a similar product, finds it inconvenient to bring anything from the experiment, does not trust the people who run the experiment, or does not like any of the products.

11. *Let participants evaluate multiple items of heterogeneous products.* Unprocessed food products such as fish, meat, and vegetables frequently differ greatly in appearance. To avoid deception, the evaluated and sold products should be identical. This can be implemented for heterogeneous products by letting the participants bid on as many items as there are participants, and then letting each participant draw one item as binding. In choice experiments, there should be as many choice sets as there are participants, so each participant can draw a unique binding choice set.

REFERENCES

Alfnes, F. 2007. "Willingness to Pay versus Expected Consumption Value in Vickrey Auctions for New Experience Goods." *American Journal of Agricultural Economics* 89: 921–31.

—— 2009. "Valuing Product Attributes in Vickrey Auctions when Market Substitutes are Available." *European Review of Agricultural Economics* 36: 133–49.

—— and K. Rickertsen. 2003. "European Consumers' Willingness to Pay for U.S. Beef in Experimental Auction Markets." *American Journal of Agricultural Economics* 85: 396–405.

————. 2007. "Extrapolating Experimental-Auction Results Using a Stated Choice Survey." *European Review of Agricultural Economics* 34: 345–63.

——, A. G. Guttormsen, G. Steine, and K. Kolstad. 2006. "Consumers' Willingness to Pay for the Color of Salmon: A Choice Experiment with Real Economic Incentives." *American Journal of Agricultural Economics* 88: 1050–61.

——, K. Rickertsen, and Ø. Ueland. 2008. Consumer Attitudes toward Low Stake Risk in Food Markets." *Applied Economics* 40: 3039–49.

——, C. Yue, and H. H. Jensen. 2010. "Cognitive Dissonance as a Means of Reducing Hypothetical Bias." *European Review of Agricultural Economics* 37: 147–63.

Andersen, S., G. W. Harrison, M. I. Lau, and E. E. Rutström. 2006. "Elicitation Using Multiple Price List Formats." *Experimental Economics* 9: 383–405.

Applebaum, W., and R. F. Spears. 1950. "Controlled Experimentation in Marketing Research." *Journal of Marketing* 14: 505–17.

Ariely, D., G. Loewenstein, and D. Prelec. 2003. "'Coherent Arbitrariness': Stable Demand Curves without Stable Preferences." *Quarterly Journal of Economics* 118: 73–105.

Becker, G. M., M. H. DeGroot, and J. Marschak. 1964. "Measuring Utility by a Single-Response Sequential Method." *Behavioral Science* 9: 226–32.

Bernard, J. C., and D. J. Bernard. 2009. "What Is It About Organic Milk? An Experimental Analysis." *American Journal of Agricultural Economics* 91: 826–36.

—— and N. He. 2010. "Confounded by the Field: Bidding in Food Auctions when Field Prices Are Increasing." *Agricultural and Resource Economics Review* 39: 275–87.

Brookshire, D. S., D. L. Coursey, and W. D. Schulze. 1987. "The External Validity of Experimental Economics Techniques: Analysis of Demand Behavior." *Economic Inquiry* 25: 239–50.

Buhr, B. L., D. J. Hayes, J. F. Shogren, and J. B. Kliebenstein. 1993. "Valuing Ambiguity: The Case of Genetically Engineered Growth Enhancers." *Journal of Agricultural and Resource Economics* 18: 175–84.

Chang, J. B., J. L. Lusk, and F. B. Norwood. 2009. "How Closely Do Hypothetical Surveys and Laboratory Experiments Predict Field Behavior?" *American Journal of Agricultural Economics* 91: 518–34.

Cherry, T. L., P. Frykblom, J. F. Shogren, J. A. List, and M. B. Sullivan. 2004. "Laboratory Testbeds and Non-Market Valuation: The Case of Bidding Behavior in a Second-Price Auction with an Outside Option." *Environmental and Resource Economics* 29: 285–94.

Clancy, K. J., P. C. Krieg, and M. M. Wolf. 2006. *Market New Products Successfully: Using Simulated Test Market Technology*. Lanham, MD: Lexington Books.

Combris, P., C. Lange, and S. Issanchou. 2006. "Assessing the Effect of Information on the Reservation Price for Champagne: What Are Consumers Actually Paying for?" *Journal of Wine Economics* 1: 75–88.

Corrigan, J. R., and M. C. Rousu. 2006a. "Posted Prices and Bid Affiliation: Evidence from Experimental Auctions." *American Journal of Agricultural Economics* 88: 1078–90.

—— ——. 2006b. "The Effect of Initial Endowments in Experimental Auctions." *American Journal of Agricultural Economics* 88: 448–57.

—— ——. 2008. "Testing Whether Field Auction Experiments Are Demand Revealing in Practice." *Journal of Agricultural and Resource Economics* 33: 290–301.

——, D. P. T. Depositario, R. M. Nayga, Jr., X. Wu, and T. P. Laude. 2009. "Comparing Open-Ended Choice Experiments and Experimental Auctions: An Application to Golden Rice." *American Journal of Agricultural Economics* 91: 837–53.

Cummings, R. G., G. W. Harrison, and E. E. Rutström. 1995. "Homegrown Values and Hypothetical Surveys: Is the Dichotomous Choice Approach Incentive-Compatible?" *American Economic Review* 85: 260–6.

Davis, D. D., and C. A. Holt. 1993. *Experimental Economics*. Princeton: Princeton University Press.

Depositario, D. P. T., R. M. Nayga, Jr., X. Wu, and T. P. Laude. 2009. "Should Students Be Used as Subjects in Experimental Auctions?" *Economic Letters* 102: 122–4.

Ding, M., R. Grewal, and J. Liechty. 2005. "Incentive-Aligned Conjoint Analysis." *Journal of Marketing Research* 42: 67–82.

Drichoutis, A. C., P. Lazaridis, and R. M. Nayga, Jr. 2008. "The Role of Reference Prices in Experimental Auctions." *Economics Letters* 99: 446–8.

Fox, J. A., D. J. Hayes, J. B. Kliebenstein, and J. F. Shogren. 1994. "Consumer Acceptability of Milk from Cows Treated with Bovine Somatotropin." *Journal of Dairy Science* 77: 703–7.

——, J. F. Shogren, D. J. Hayes, and J. B. Kliebenstein. 1998. "CVM-X: Calibrating Contingent Values with Experimental Auction Markets." *American Journal of Agricultural Economics* 80: 455–65.

——, D. J. Hayes, and J. F. Shogren. 2002. "Consumer Preferences for Food Irradiation: How Favorable and Unfavorable Descriptions Affect Preferences for Irradiated Pork in Experimental Auctions." *Journal of Risk and Uncertainty* 24: 75–95.

Ginzberg, E. 1936. "Customary Prices." *American Economic Review* 2: 296.

Harrison, G. W., and J. A. List. 2004. "Field Experiments." *Journal of Economic Literature* 42: 1009–55.

——, R. M. Harstad, and E. E. Rutström. 2004. "Experimental Methods and Elicitation of Values." *Experimental Economics* 7: 123–40.

Hawkins, E. R. 1957. "Methods for Estimating Demand." *Journal of Marketing* 21: 428–38.

Hayes, D. J., J. F. Shogren, S. Y. Shin, and J. B. Kliebenstein. 1995. "Valuing Food Safety in Experimental Auction Markets." *American Journal of Agricultural Economics* 77: 40–53.

Hensher, D. A., J. M. Rose, and W. H. Greene. 2005. *Applied Choice Analysis: A Primer.* Cambridge: Cambridge University Press.

Hoffman, E., D. J. Menkhaus, D. Chakravarti, R. A. Field, and G. D. Whipple. 1993. "Using Laboratory Experimental Auctions in Marketing Research: A Case Study of New Packaging for Fresh Beef." *Marketing Science* 12/3: 318–38.

Huffman, W. E. 2003. "Consumers' Acceptance of (and Resistance to) Genetically Modified Foods in High-Income Countries: Effects of Labels and Information in an Uncertain Environment." *American Journal of Agricultural Economics* 85: 1112–18.

Johansson-Stenman, O., and H. Svedsäter. 2008. "Measuring Hypothetical Bias in Choice Experiments: The Importance of Cognitive Consistency." *B. E. Journal of Economic Analysis and Policy*, 8/1: *Topics*, art. 41.

Kagel, J. H., and A. E. Roth. 1995. *Handbook of Experimental Economics.* Princeton: Princeton University Press.

Kahneman, D., J. L. Knetsch, and R. H. Thaler. 1990. "Experimental Tests of the Endowment Effect and the Coase Theorem." *Journal of Political Economy* 98: 1325–48.

Kanter, C., K. D. Messer, and H. M. Kaiser. 2009. "Does Production Labeling Stigmatize Conventional Milk?" *American Journal of Agricultural Economics* 91: 1097–1109.

Klemperer, P. 2004. *Auctions: Theory and Practice.* Princeton: Princeton University Press.

Knetsch, J. L., F. F. Tang, and R. H. Thaler. 2001. "The Endowment Effect and Repeated Market Trials: Is the Vickrey Auction Demand Revealing?" *Experimental Economics* 4: 257–69.

Kuhfeld, W. F. 2010. *Marketing Research Methods in SAS: Experimental Design, Choice, Conjoint, and Graphical Techniques.* SAS 9.2 edn, MR-2010. Cary, NC: SAS Institute Inc. <http://support.sas.com/techsup/technote/mr2010.pdf>.

Lange, C., C. Martin, C. Chabanet, P. Combris, and S. Issanchou. 2002. "Impact of the Information Provided to Consumers on their Willingness to Pay for Champagne: Comparison with Hedonic Scores." *Food Quality and Preference* 13: 597–608.

Levitt, S. D., and J. A. List. 2007. "What Do Laboratory Experiments Measuring Social Preferences Reveal about the Real World?" *Journal of Economic Perspectives* 21/2: 153–74.

List, J. A. 2002. "Preference Reversals of a Different Kind: The 'More Is Less' Phenomenon." *American Economic Review* 92: 1636–43.

—— 2006. "The Behavioralist Meets the Market: Measuring Social Preferences and Reputation Effect in Actual Transactions." *Journal of Political Economy* 114: 1–37.

—— and C. A. Gallet. 2001. "What Experimental Protocol Influence Disparities between Actual and Hypothetical Stated Values?" *Environmental and Resource Economics* 20: 241–54.

List, J. A. and J. F. Shogren. 1998. "Calibration of the Difference between Actual and Hypothetical Valuations in a Field Experiment." *Journal of Economic Behavior and Organization* 37: 193–205.

——— . 1999. "Price Information and Bidding Behavior in Repeated Second-Price Auctions." *American Journal of Agricultural Economics* 81: 942–9.

——— . 2002. "Calibration of Willingness-to-Accept." *Journal of Environmental Economics and Management* 43: 219–33.

Louviere, J. L., D. A. Hensher, and J. D. Swait. 2000. *Stated Choice Methods*. Cambridge: Cambridge University Press.

Lusk, J. L., and J. A. Fox. 2003. "Value Elicitation in Retail and Laboratory Environments." *Economic Letters* 79: 27–34.

—— and F. B. Norwood. 2009. "Bridging the Gap between Laboratory Experiments and Naturally Occurring Markets: An Inferred Valuation Method." *Journal of Environmental Economics and Management* 58: 236–50.

—— and M. Rousu. 2006. "Market Price Endogeneity and Accuracy of Value Elicitation Mechanisms." In J. A. List, ed., *Using Experimental Methods in Environmental and Resource Economics*. Cheltenham: Edward Elgar.

—— and T. C. Schroeder. 2004. "Are Choice Experiments Incentive Compatible? A Test with Quality Differentiated Beef Steaks." *American Journal of Agricultural Economics* 86: 467–82.

——— . 2006. "Auction Bids and Shopping Choices." *Advances in Economic Analysis and Policy* 6/1, art. 4.

—— and J. F. Shogren. 2007. *Experimental Auctions: Methods and Applications in Economic and Marketing Research*. Cambridge: Cambridge University Press.

——, M. S. Daniel, D. R. Mark, and C. L. Lusk. 2001. "Alternative Calibration and Auction Institutions for Predicting Consumer Willingness to Pay for Nongenetically Modified Corn Chips." *Journal of Agricultural and Resource Economics* 26: 40–57.

——, J. A. Fox, T. C. Schroeder, J. Mintert, and M. Koohmaraie. 2001. "In-Store Valuation of Steak Tenderness." *American Journal of Agricultural Economics* 83: 539–50.

——, T. Feldkamp, and T. C. Schroeder. 2004. "Experimental Auction Procedure: Impact on Valuation of Quality Differentiated Goods." *American Journal of Agricultural Economics* 86: 389–405.

——, L. O. House, C. Valli, S. R. Jaeger, M. Moore, J. L. Morrow, and W. B. Traill. 2004. "Effects of Information about Benefits of Biotechnology on Consumer Acceptance of Genetically Modified Food: Evidence from Experimental Auctions in the United States, England, and France." *European Review of Agricultural Economics* 31: 179–204.

——, F. B. Norwood, and J. R. Pruitt. 2006. "Consumer Demand for a Ban on Antibiotic Drug Use in Pork Production." *American Journal of Agricultural Economics* 88: 1015–33.

——, C. Alexander, and M. C. Rousu. 2007. "Designing Experimental Auctions for Marketing Research: The Effect of Values, Distributions, and Mechanisms on Incentives for Truthful Bidding." *Review of Marketing Science* 5, art. 3.

——, D. Fields, and W. Prevatt. 2008. "An Incentive Compatible Conjoint Ranking Mechanism." *American Journal of Agricultural Economics* 90: 497–8.

McConnell, J. D. 1968. "The Development of Brand Loyalty: An Experimental Study." *Journal of Marketing Research* 5: 13–19.

McDaniel, C., and R. Gates. 2009. *Marketing Research*, 8th edn. Hoboken, NJ: Wiley.

Marette, S., J. Roosen, and S. Blanchemanche. 2008. "Taxes and Subsidies to Change Eating Habits when Information Is Not Enough: An Application to Fish Consumption." *Journal of Regulatory Economics* 34: 119–43.

Masters, W. A., and D. Sanogo. 2002. "Welfare Gains from Quality Certification of Infant Foods: Results from a Market Experiment in Mali." *American Journal of Agricultural Economics* 84: 974–89.

Maynard, L. J., J. G. Hartell, A. L. Meyer, and J. Hao. 2004. "An Experimental Approach to Valuing New Differentiated Products." *Agricultural Economics* 31: 317–25.

Melton, B. E., W. E. Huffman, J. F. Shogren, and J. A. Fox. 1996. "Consumer Preferences for Fresh Food Items with Multiple Quality Attributes: Evidence from an Experimental Auction of Pork Chops." *American Journal of Agricultural Economics* 78: 916–23.

Menkhaus, D. J., G. W. Borden, G. D. Whipple, E. Hoffman, and R. A. Field. 1992. "An Empirical Application of Laboratory Experimental Auctions in Marketing Research." *Journal of Agricultural and Resource Economics* 17: 44–55.

Nayga, R. M., Jr., R. Woodward, and W. Aiew. 2006. "Willingness to Pay for Reduced Risk of Foodborne Illness: A Nonhypothetical Field Experiment." *Canadian Journal of Agricultural Economics* 54: 461–75.

Nestle, M. 2002. *Food Politics: How the Food Industry Influences Nutrition and Health.* Berkeley: University of California Press.

Noussair, C., S. Robin, and B. Ruffieux. 2002. "Do Consumers Not Care about Biotech Foods or Do They Just Not Read the Labels?" *Economic Letters* 75: 47–53.

——————. 2004a. "Do Consumers Really Refuse to Buy Genetically Modified Food?" *Economic Journal* 114: 102–20.

——————. 2004b. "Revealing Consumers' Willingness-to-Pay: A Comparison of the BDM Mechanism and the Vickrey Auction." *Journal of Economic Psychology* 25: 725–41.

Nunes, J. C., and P. Boatwright. 2004. "Incidental Prices and their Effect on Willingness to Pay." *Journal of Marketing Research* 41: 457–66.

Olesen, I., F. Alfnes, M. B. Røra, and K. Kolstad. 2010. "Eliciting Consumers' Willingness to Pay for Organic and Welfare-Labelled Salmon in a Non-Hypothetical Choice Experiment." *Livestock Science* 127: 218–26.

Parkhurst, G. M., J. F. Shogren, and D. L. Dickinson. 2004. "Negative Values in Vickrey Auctions." *American Journal of Agricultural Economics* 86: 222–35.

Pessemier, E. A. 1959. "A New Way to Determine Buying Decisions." *Journal of Marketing* 24: 41–6.

—— 1960. "An Experimental Method for Estimating Demand." *Journal of Business* 33: 373–83.

Plott, C., and K. Zeiler. 2005. "The Willingness to Pay–Willingness to Accept Gap, the 'Endowment Effect': Subject Misconceptions, and Experimental Procedures for Eliciting Valuations." *American Economic Review* 95: 530–45.

Roe, B. E., and D. R. Just. 2009. "Internal and External Validity in Economics Research: Tradeoffs between Experiments, Field Experiments, Natural Experiments, and Field Data." *American Journal of Agricultural Economics* 91: 1266–71.

Roosen, J., J. A. Fox, D. A. Hennessy, and A. Schreiber. 1998. "Consumers' Valuation of Insecticide Use Restrictions: An Application to Apples." *Journal of Agricultural and Resource Economics* 23: 367–84.

Rousu, M. C., W. E. Huffman, J. F. Shogren, and A. Tegene. 2004. "Estimating Public Value of Conflicting Information: The Case of Genetically Modified Foods." *Land Economics* 80: 125–35.

Rousu, M. C., W. E. Huffman, J. F. Shogren, and A. Tegene. 2007. "Effects and Value of Verifiable Information in a Controversial Market: Evidence from Lab Auctions of Genetically Modified Food." *Economic Inquiry* 45: 409–32.

Sawyer, A. G. 1975. "Demand Artifacts in Laboratory Experiments in Consumer Research." *Journal of Marketing Research* 1: 20–30.

——, P. M. Worthing, and P. E. Sendak. 1979. "The Role of Laboratory Experiments to Test Marketing Strategies." *Journal of Marketing Strategies* 43: 60–7.

Shogren, J. F., J. A. Fox, D. J. Hayes, and J. B. Kliebenstein. 1994. "Bid Sensitivity and the Structure of the Vickrey Auction." *American Journal of Agricultural Economics* 76: 1089–95.

——, S. Y. Shin, D. J. Hayes, and J. B. Kliebenstein. 1994. "Resolving Differences in Willingness to Pay and Willingness to Accept." *American Economic Review* 84: 255–70.

——, J. A., Fox, D. J. Hayes and J. Roosen. 1999. "Observed Choices for Food Safety in Retail, Survey, and Auction Markets." *American Journal of Agricultural Economics* 81: 1192–9.

——, J. A. List, and D. J. Hayes. 2000. "Preference Learning in Consecutive Experimental Auctions." *American Journal of Agricultural Economics* 82: 1016–21.

——, M. Margolis, C. Koo, and J. A. List. 2001. "A Random nth-Price Auction." *Journal of Economic Behavior and Organization* 46: 409–21.

Silk, A. J., and G. L. Urban. 1978. "Pre-Test-Market Evaluation of New Packaged Goods: A Model and Measurement Methodology." *Journal of Marketing Research* 15: 171–91.

Street, D. J., and L. Burgess. 2007. *The Construction of Optimal Stated Choice Experiments: Theory and Methods.* Hoboken, NJ: Wiley.

Umberger, W. J., and D. M. Feuz. 2004. "The Usefulness of Experimental Auctions in Determining Consumers' Willingness-to-Pay for Quality-Differentiated Products." *Review of Agricultural Economics* 26: 170–85.

Vickrey, W. 1961. "Counterspeculation, Auctions, and Competitive Sealed Tenders." *Journal of Finance* 16: 8–37.

Wertenbroch, K., and B. Skiera. 2002. "Measuring Consumers' Willingness to Pay at the Point of Purchase." *Journal of Marketing Research* 39: 228–41.

Yue, C., F. Alfnes, and H. H. Jensen. 2009. "Discounting Spotted Apples: Investigating Consumers' Willingness to Accept Cosmetic Damage in an Organic Product." *Journal of Agricultural and Applied Economics* 41: 29–46.

CHAPTER 9

CONSUMER DEMAND IN VERTICALLY DIFFERENTIATED MARKETS

KONSTANTINOS GIANNAKAS

1 INTRODUCTION

Product differentiation has been one of the most notable features of the increasingly industrialized agri-food system. The aggressive attempts of agribusiness firms to satisfy consumer demands for increased variety and/or higher-quality food products have been driven, at least in part, by changes in consumer preferences and incomes; technological progress facilitating the development of new products and processes; the global competition among major food supplies for dominance in the world market; as well as the reduced government support to agriculture that has made the market/consumer orientation of food production necessary for the competitiveness and profitability of food suppliers.

Important examples of differentiated food products attracting the spotlight lately include the organic and genetically modified (GM) food products (products with ingredients whose DNA has been modified through genetic engineering), as well as products like cage-free eggs, rBSt-free milk, dolphin-safe tuna, fair-trade products (like cocoa, sugar, bananas, and coffee), functional foods and nutraceuticals (like "vitamin-enriched" milk, "calcium-enriched" juices, and omega 3 eggs), and origin-labeled food products. All these products are close but imperfect substitutes to their conventional counterparts and are expected to occupy our *carte du jour* increasingly, most being viewed as higher-quality goods.

With food quality and variety being at the epicenter of consumer interests, a meaningful distinction of differentiated products is that between vertically and horizontally differentiated ones. Vertically differentiated products are those that are uniformly quality- (and, thus, utility-)ranked by consumers so that, if these products were offered at the same price, all consumers would prefer the same (higher-quality) product. While consumers agree in their quality ranking of the different products, they differ in their valuation of the perceived quality differences (and, thus, they differ in their willingness to pay (WTP) for such quality differences). Horizontally differentiated products, on the other hand, are those close but imperfect substitutes that are not uniformly utility-ranked by consumers. If these products were offered at the same price, they would all enjoy a positive market share.

The focus of this chapter is on the analysis of consumer demand in markets for vertically differentiated products—markets where quality is the main differentiating attribute of the goods involved. While the chapter will discuss the pioneering and most popular approaches to the analysis of consumer demand in markets for vertically differentiated products, this is not purported to be a literature review on the topic. The objective, instead, is to provide an overview of the analysis of consumer demand in vertically differentiated markets, the standard assumptions employed in the literature, and the relevance and ramifications of some key assumptions for the analysis of food product markets.

The chapter will present a general model of vertical product differentiation and will derive the consumer demands for, and market shares of, the different products, as well as measures of consumer surplus for the different consumer groups involved. The discussion will then focus on alternative model formulations derived through different assumptions employed in the analysis. While the assumptions employed have little effect on the consumer demands, market shares, and the measures of consumer welfare, they can have important ramifications for the equilibrium variety and the structure of different supply channels. The final part of the chapter will discuss some important issues that can be addressed using this methodological framework and will present a general analysis of two vertically differentiated food product markets.

1.1   Key Studies on Vertical Product Differentiation

Key studies in the area of vertical product differentiation are those by Mussa and Rosen (1978) that analyze quality decisions of a monopoly, by Gabszewicz and Thisse (1979, 1980) that focus on the price competition between brand-producing firms (i.e., firms producing differentiated products), and by Shaked and Sutton (1982, 1983) that show how brand-producing firms can reduce the intensity of price competition by maximizing the quality differences between their products, and introduce the finiteness property in the analysis of markets for vertically differentiated products.[1] Based on the

[1] For meaningful extensions of these pioneering studies of vertical product differentiation, see Gal-Or (1983), Bonanno (1986), Anderson, de Palma, and Thisse (1992), Choi and Chin (1992), Donnenfeld and Weber (1992, 1995), Motta (1993), Boom (1995), Wathy (1996), Lehmann-Grube (1997), Lahmandi-Ayed (2000), and Wang and Yang (2001). Important applications of these vertical product differentiation models to agri-food system issues can be found in Bureau, Marette, and Schiavina (1998), Bontems,

finiteness property, depending on the degree of consumer heterogeneity and whether the costs for quality improvement are fixed or variable[2] (which affects the relationship between the consumer WTP for quality and the unit variable costs of quality provision), these markets can be characterized by the presence of a small number of brand-producing firms—a natural oligopoly. Both the so-called principle of maximum differentiation and the finiteness property have been fundamental, key findings of the literature on vertical product differentiation (Tirole 1988; Beath and Katsoulakos 1991).

It is important to note that most of the literature on vertically differentiated products has focused on consumer demand for products supplied by brand-producing firms that decide on the price and the level of quality of their own brand. While this framework is certainly relevant when analyzing consumer attitudes toward many processed-food products supplied by different food manufacturers (like different brands of cereals or ketchup, for instance), it does not lend itself to the analysis of the differentiated food products discussed earlier (i.e., organic, GM, fair-trade, US-grown, rBST-free, etc.). A reason is that each of these important differentiated food products is typically supplied by a large number of firms—some by oligopolies, others by dominant firms and competitive fringes, others by perfectly competitive agricultural producers. In addition, the quality characteristics of the different choices (i.e., what constitutes an organic product, a GM product, a fair-trade, or a US-grown product) are usually determined by third parties (e.g., the government) and are, therefore, exogenous to the firms supplying these products. In such cases, the firms' quality choice is whether to produce organic, conventional, or GM products, rBST-free or conventional milk, cage-free or conventional eggs, fair-trade of conventional sugar, etc.

Finally, while there aren't many consumers who would consider conventional products superior to their fair-trade, organic, dolphin-safe, rBST-free, . . . counterparts, not all consumers are willing to pay a premium to purchase the "superior" product—some consumers are just indifferent to the fair-trade, organic, dolphin-safe, rBST-free, . . . attribute of a product. To the extent that this segment of indifferent consumers is present, it needs to be taken into account in the analysis of consumer demand for these products.

The model that will be presented in this chapter captures these important idiosyncrasies of the food product markets; it accounts for the existence of consumers who are indifferent between the high- and low-quality products (do not care about the vertically differentiating attribute of the high-quality product) and allows for the analysis of virtually any market structure of the supply channels of interest (and not just the brand-producing monopolies considered in the literature). It turns out that these two components of the analysis are closely related. In addition to enhancing the empirical relevance of the analysis, explicit consideration of the indifferent consumers adds

---

Monier-Dilhan, and Requillart (1999), Crespi and Marette (2001, 2002), Lapan and Moschini (2004), Zago and Pick (2004), Lavoie (2005), Roe and Sheldon (2007), and Moschini, Menapace, and Pick (2008).

[2] These costs will be (a) fixed when quality improvement is the outcome of R & D, and (b) variable when quality improvement is the result of using more costly inputs in the production process.

considerable flexibility to the market analysis of the different-quality products by relaxing the finiteness property (Lahmandi-Ayed 2007) and enabling the analysis of any relevant market structure.

The essence of the general model presented here has been developed by Giannakas and Fulton, and various adaptations of this have been utilized to analyze consumer demand for genetically modified products (Giannakas and Fulton 2002; Fulton and Giannakas 2004; Lusk et al. 2005; Sobolevsky, Moschini, and Lapan 2005; Berwald, Carter, and Gruere 2006; Veyssiere 2007; Lapan and Moschini 2007; Gruere, Carter, and Farzin 2008; and Giannakas and Yiannaka 2008[3]), organic products (Giannakas 2002; Giannakas and Yiannaka 2006; and Tribl and Salhofer 2008), and country-of-origin labeled products (Plastina, Giannakas, and Pick 2011). In addition to capturing important idiosyncrasies of the agri-food system, the general model presented below nests the essence of most other popular models of consumer demand for vertically differentiated products.

2   THE CONSUMER DEMAND IN VERTICALLY DIFFERENTIATED MARKETS

2.1   Standard Assumptions in the Literature

As mentioned previously, vertically differentiated products are those close but imperfect substitutes that are uniformly quality- (and utility-)ranked by consumers.[4] Even though consumers agree on their utility ranking of the different products, they differ in their valuation of the perceived quality differences (and, thus, in their WTP for these differences).

In addition to differing in their intensity of preference for the different products, it is generally assumed that (1) consumers are uniformly distributed with respect to their preference for the different products (with a density of 1); (2) they have unit demands—i.e., consume one unit of either the high-quality product, the low-quality product, or another substitute product (the option of "the other substitute product" is often either eliminated or substituted by the option of not buying any of the (high- or low-quality) products); and (3) the purchasing decision is a small share of the total budget.

---

[3] In analyzing the market and welfare effects of the introduction of second-generation, consumer-oriented GM products into the food system, Giannakas and Yiannaka (2008) developed a model that allows for both vertical and horizontal differentiation of the products available to consumers.

[4] It should be noted that the nature of product differentiation in a market is not always steady. For instance, Giannakas and Yiannaka (2008) show how the introduction of second-generation, consumer-oriented GM products in a market can change the nature of product differentiation between the GM products and their conventional and organic counterparts from vertical to horizontal differentiation. Drivas and Giannakas (2010) show how product innovation activity in a mixed oligopoly can change the nature of the relationship between the products supplied by different firms from horizontal to vertical product differentiation.

While most of the literature has employed the aforementioned assumptions, the analysis of consumer behavior in markets for vertically differentiated products can be easily modified to account for consumer heterogeneity based on incomes (rather than preferences; see Gabszewicz and Thisse 1979; and Shaked and Sutton 1983), and alternative distributions of the consumer-differentiating attribute (see Bonnisseau and Lahmandi-Ayed 2007).

2.2 Model Setup

Consider a consumer who has the choice between a high-quality product (e.g., organic or rBST-free milk), a low-quality product (e.g., conventional milk), and a substitute product (e.g., fruit juice). Assuming that the consumer spends a small fraction of total expenditures on these goods, her utility function can be written as

$$U_h = U - p_h + h\alpha \quad \text{if a unit of the high–quality product is consumed}$$

$$U_l = U - p_l + l\alpha \quad \text{if a unit of the low–quality product is consumed} \qquad (1)$$

$$U_s = U \qquad\qquad \text{if a unit of the substitute product is consumed}$$

where U_h is the utility associated with consuming one unit of the high-quality product, U_l is the utility associated with consuming one unit of the low-quality product, and U_s is the utility associated with the unit consumption of the substitute product. In essence, U_s represents a reservation level of utility which, for simplicity and tractability, is assumed to equal a base level of utility U. As mentioned earlier, in many studies this reservation level of utility is set equal to zero, making the third option one in which the consumer buys neither the high- nor the low-quality product.

The price of the high-quality product is p_h, the price of its low-quality counterpart is p_l, and the parameters h and l are utility enhancement factors associated with the consumption of the high- and low-quality products, respectively. The characteristic α differs by consumer and captures heterogeneous consumer preferences for high- and low-quality products. To capture the existence of consumers who are indifferent to (place no value on) the differentiating attribute of the high-quality product (organic production process or absence of growth hormones in our example), the characteristic α takes values between zero and one, while, for simplicity and tractability, consumers are assumed to be uniformly distributed between the polar values of α.

In this context, the terms $h\alpha$ and $l\alpha$ give the utility differences associated with the consumption of the high- and the low-quality products, respectively, while $U + h\alpha$ and $U + l\alpha$ represent the consumer WTP for a unit of these products.[5] To capture the

---

[5] Note that subtracting the relevant equilibrium prices from these WTP values provides an estimate of the consumer surplus associated with the consumption of these products. Equation (1) can be seen then as providing measures of the consumer surplus associated with the different choices faced by the consumers.

consumer preference for the high-quality product, h is assumed greater than l with $(h - l)\alpha$ reflecting the valuation of the perceived quality difference between the two products of the consumer with differentiating attribute α. The greater is α, the greater the consumer valuation of the quality difference between the high- and the low-quality products, and the greater the WTP for this quality difference.

Finally, to allow for positive market shares of the two vertically differentiated products, we assume that the low-quality product is priced below its high-quality counterpart with the price difference $p_h - p_l$ being less than the valuation of the quality difference between the two products for all consumers, and the price ratio p_h/p_l being greater than h/l (see equations (4) and (5) below).

2.3   Derivation of Market Shares and Consumer Demands for the Different Products

The consumption choice of an individual consumer is determined by the relationship between the utilities derived from the different products. Figure 9.1 graphs the U_h, U_l, and U_s utility curves and depicts the consumption decisions when the prices and preference parameters are such that all products (i.e., the high-quality product, the low-quality product, and the substitute product) enjoy positive market shares.

More specifically, the consumer with differentiating attribute

$$\alpha_l: \ U_l = U_h \Rightarrow \alpha_l = \frac{p_h - p_l}{h - l} \tag{2}$$

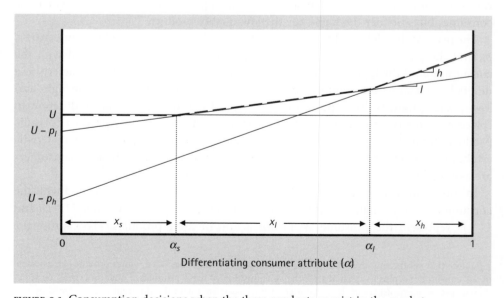

FIGURE 9.1 Consumption decisions when the three products coexist in the market

is indifferent between consuming a unit of the high- and the low-quality products: the utility associated with the consumption of these products is the same. Similarly, the consumer with differentiating characteristic

$$\alpha_s: \quad U_l = U_s \Rightarrow \alpha_s = \frac{p_l}{l} \tag{3}$$

is indifferent between consuming a unit of the low-quality product and a unit of the substitute. Consumers with strong preference for quality (i.e., consumers with $\alpha \in (\alpha_l, 1]$) prefer the high-quality product, consumers with $\alpha \in (\alpha_s, \alpha_l]$ prefer the low-quality product, while consumers with $\alpha \in [0, \alpha_s]$ consume the substitute product.

When consumers are uniformly distributed between the polar values of α, $1 - \alpha_l$ determines the share of the high-quality product in total consumption, x_h. The consumption share of the low-quality product, x_l, is given by $\alpha_l - \alpha_s$. Normalizing the mass of consumers at unity, x_h and x_l give the consumer demands for the high- and low-quality products, respectively. Mathematically, x_h and x_l can be written as

$$x_h = \frac{h - l - p_h + p_l}{h - l} \tag{4}$$

$$x_l = \frac{l p_h - h p_l}{l(h - l)}. \tag{5}$$

From equations (4) and (5) follows that the demand for the high- (low-)quality product falls with an increase in its price and/or a decrease (increase) in the strength of the consumer preference for quality,[6] and rises as the price of the low- (high-)quality product increases. If p_l were greater than p_h, the utility curve U_l would lie underneath U_h for all consumers ($\forall \alpha$), the low-quality product would be driven out of the market, and the demand for the high-quality product would be

$$x_h = 1 - \alpha'_s = \frac{h - p_h}{h} \quad \text{where } \alpha'_s : U_h = U_s. \tag{6}$$

On the other hand, if the price premium of the high-quality product, $p_h - p_l$, exceeded the valuation of the quality difference between the two products for all consumers, $h - l$, the utility curve U_h would lie underneath U_l for all consumers ($\forall \alpha$), and it would be the high-quality product priced out of the market. The demand for the low-quality product would then be

$$x_l = 1 - \alpha_s = \frac{l - p_l}{l} \tag{7}$$

Figure 9.2 graphs the inverse demand curves for the low- and high-quality products (shown as D_l and D_h, respectively) in the familiar price–quantity space when the prices

---

[6] Recall that an increase in the consumer preference for quality can occur owing to an increase in h and/or a reduction in l.

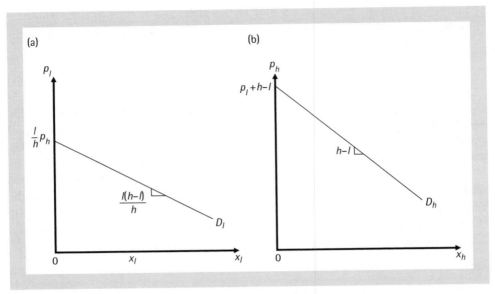

FIGURE 9.2 Consumer demands when the different products coexist in the market
(a) Low-quality product market
(b) High-quality product market

and preference parameters are such that the different products coexist in the market. The inverse demand curves (derived from equations (4) and (5)) are given by

$$p_l = \frac{l}{h}\left[p_h - (h-l)x_l\right] \tag{8}$$

$$p_h = p_l + h - l - (h-l)x_h \tag{9}$$

and further illustrate the interdependence between the markets for the two products: the price and preference parameters associated with the consumption of a product are direct arguments in the demand for its substitute.

2.4   Derivation of the Surpluses of the Different Consumer Groups

In addition to depicting the decisions of different consumers in the same utility space, Figure 9.1 also enables us to derive measures of the surplus of consumers of the high-quality product, the low-quality product, and the substitute in this same utility space. As mentioned earlier, the expressions for U_h, U_l, and U_s in equation (1) are direct measures of the consumer surplus associated with the consumption of the different products of the consumer with differentiating attribute α. In this context, the consumer surplus associated with the consumption of a product is given by the summation of the surpluses of the consumers that find it optimal to consume this product. Thus, the surplus of the consumers of the high-quality product is given by

$$CS^h = \int_{\alpha_l}^1 U_h d\alpha = \left(U - p_h + h\alpha_l + \frac{1}{2} hx_h \right) x_h \tag{10}$$

and the surplus of the consumers of the low quality product is

$$CS^l = \int_{\alpha_s}^{\alpha_l} U_l d\alpha = \left(U + \frac{1}{2} lx_l \right) x_l \tag{11}$$

Aggregate consumer surplus is given by the area underneath the effective utility curve shown by the kinked dashed line in Figure 9.1 and equals

$$CS = \int_0^{\alpha_s} U_s d\alpha + \int_{\alpha_s}^{\alpha_l} U_l d\alpha + \int_{\alpha_l}^1 U_h d\alpha =$$

$$= \frac{U p_l}{l} + \left(U + \frac{1}{2} lx_l \right) x_l + \left(U - p_h + h\alpha_l + \frac{1}{2} hx_h \right) x_h \tag{12}$$

.

In addition to enabling the derivation of theory-consistent measures of consumer surplus, this framework of analysis allows for the determination and illustration of the effects of different prices or/and preference parameters on the equilibrium quantities and market shares of *all* substitutes and the welfare of *all* consumers. For instance, a higher preference parameter associated with the consumption of the low-quality product would cause a leftward rotation of the utility curve U_l through the point $U - p_l$ in Figure 9.3. This change in U_l would attract to the low-quality product consumers that would otherwise prefer the high-quality product (those with $\alpha \in (\alpha_l, \alpha_l')$) and the substitute product (consumers with $\alpha \in (\alpha_s', \alpha_s]$) resulting in increased x_l and reduced x_h and x_s. Consumer welfare would be increased in this case by the shaded area in Figure 9.3 that equals $\Delta CS = \int_{\alpha_s'}^{\alpha_s} \left(U_l' - U_s \right) d\alpha + \int_{\alpha_s}^{\alpha_l} \left(U_l' - U_l \right) d\alpha + \int_{\alpha_l}^{\alpha_l'} \left(U_l' - U_h \right) d\alpha.$[7]

---

[7] It should be pointed out that, for simplicity of exposition, Figure 9.3 is drawn on the assumption that the change in the preference parameter l has no effect on the prices of the low- and high-quality products. This will be the case in markets with constant marginal costs and perfectly competitive structure. As will become apparent in Section 9.4, however, when either of the two conditions is not satisfied, a change in l will change both p_l and p_h and, through them, it will change the utility curves U_l and U_h and the surplus of the relevant consumer groups.

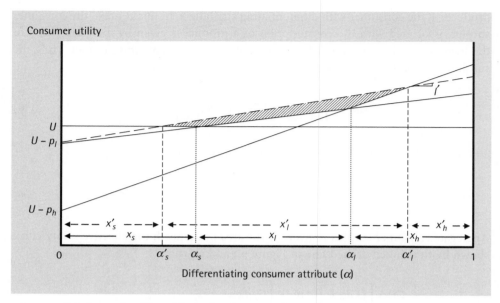

FIGURE 9.3 Market and welfare effects of a change in the preference parameter *l*

3   IMPORTANT VARIATIONS OF THE MODEL

As mentioned earlier, the model presented in the previous section can be easily modified to reflect the cases where (a) consumers have the choice of not buying any of the vertically differentiated products (by setting $U = 0$ in equation (1)), and (b) consumers have to buy either the high- or the low-quality product (by eliminating the option of the other "substitute product" from equation (1)). The ramifications of such changes to the expressions for demands/market shares and consumer surpluses are straightforward. In particular, setting $U = 0$ would affect only the expressions for the surpluses of the different consumer groups in equations (10)–(12), while requiring consumers to purchase either the high- or the low-quality product would increase the consumer demand for the low-quality product by the demand for the substitute (i.e., x_l would be increased to $x_l = \alpha_l = \frac{p_h - p_l}{h - l}$) and would reduce the surplus of the consumers with $\alpha \in [0, \alpha_s]$ by $\Delta CS = \int_0^{\alpha_s} (U_s - U_l)\, d\alpha = \frac{p_l^2}{2l}$.

The model can also be reinterpreted to reflect the cases that have been the main focus of the literature on vertical product differentiation, like (i) cases where all consumers value the vertically differentiating product attribute (i.e., there are no indifferent consumers), (ii) cases where the quality of a product is endogenous to its supplier(s), and (iii) cases where consumers differ in their incomes and not in their preferences for the vertically differentiated products.

3.1 No Indifferent Consumers

To capture case (i) where all consumers value the differentiating attribute of the vertically differentiated products (i.e., there are no indifferent consumers) commonly considered in the literature, we need to change our assumption that the differentiating attribute $\alpha \in [0,1]$ and have α take values between $\underline{a}$ and $\bar{\alpha}$ (i.e., $\alpha \in [\underline{a}, \bar{\alpha}]$) with $\underline{a} > 0$ and $\bar{\alpha} - \underline{a} = 1$. It should be noted that this modification does not affect our results on consumer demands, market shares, and consumer surpluses derived in the previous section of this chapter.[8]

3.2 Quality Characteristics Endogenous to Brand-Producing Firms

Consider next case (ii) where the level of quality and quality characteristics of the products are endogenous to the firms producing them (as opposed to having these quality characteristics determined by a third party, as is the case with fair-trade, origin-labeled, cage-free, GM, and organic products whose attributes—the characteristics that these products should have to be considered as fair-trade, origin-labeled, etc.—are exogenous to the firms). To enable the analysis of quality and price decisions by the brand-producing firms, we simply need to reinterpret the preference parameters h and l associated with the consumption of the high- and low-quality products in equation (1) as quality parameters, indices of product quality that are chosen optimally, within some relevant range, by the brand-producing firms. Predictably, allowing for endogenous determination of the quality characteristics of the different substitute products does not affect the expressions for the consumer demands, market shares, and consumer surpluses derived in Section 2.

Before considering the next variation of our model, it is important to point out that, even though the modifications required for cases (i) and (ii) do not affect the derivation of the consumer demands, market shares, and consumer surpluses, they could affect the equilibrium product variety and number of firms in the market. The reason is that the lack of indifferent consumers is a *necessary* condition for the finiteness property (leading markets for vertically differentiated products supplied by brand-producing firms to natural oligopolies) to hold.

3.3 Consumer Heterogeneity Based on Incomes

Finally, the model can be easily modified to capture case (iii) where consumers differ in their incomes and not in their preferences for the vertically differentiated products.

---

[8] For the derivation of the demands for the high- and the low-quality products when there are no indifferent consumers and $U = 0$, see Tirole (1988: 96).

Specifically, to capture this different source of consumer heterogeneity we just need to reinterpret the differentiating attribute α to be the inverse of the marginal rate of substitution between income and quality and have it, this way, reflect differences in consumer incomes (with higher αs corresponding to lower marginal utility of income and, thus, to wealthier consumers; see Tirole 1988). Similarly to the other variations of our model examined above, the different source of consumer heterogeneity does not affect the consumer demands, market shares, and consumer surpluses presented in the previous section of this chapter.

4   Uses of the Model

In addition to enabling the depiction and analysis of the decisions and welfare of the different consumer groups in the same utility space, the methodological framework presented earlier can be used to study relevant issues pertaining to the analysis of product markets, like (a) equilibrium prices, quantities, and market shares of different substitute products as well as the equilibrium product variety and welfare of the relevant interest groups under alternative market structures when the quality attributes of the products are exogenous to their suppliers, (b) equilibrium prices, quantities, and market shares of the different products, welfare of the interest groups, and the equilibrium variety and quality in the market when the product quality is endogenous to the suppliers of these products, and (c) the effects of government policies (like subsidies, taxes, quality standards, grades, labeling, etc.) and firm strategies (like product and process innovation, certification, advertising) on prices, quantities, market shares, variety, quality, and the welfare of the interest groups involved.

In fact, as long as the model formulation is internally consistent (by accounting for potential restrictions imposed by the finiteness property when analyzing competition between brand-producing firms, for instance), a set of demands for vertically differentiated products (similar to those derived in Section 2 or those that could be derived under the different formulations and assumptions presented in Section 3) can be utilized for most, if not all, relevant analyses involving consumers.[9]

The following example[10] helps illustrate how the consumer demands for the vertically differentiated products derived in Section 2 (equations (8) and (9)) can be used for a typical product market analysis. In particular, consider the equilibrium conditions in the markets for the low- and the high-quality products when the relevant substitutes coexist in the market. Figure 9.4 graphs the inverse demand curves for the low- and

---

[9] For interesting attempts to simulate and empiricize the Giannakas and Fulton framework of analysis, see Fulton and Giannakas (2004), Lusk et al. (2005), and Plastina, Giannakas, and Pick (2011).

[10] This example draws on my research for the FoodIMA project (EU Food Industry Dynamics and Methodological Advances), financed by the European Union's Sixth Framework Programme (SSPE-CT-2006-044283).

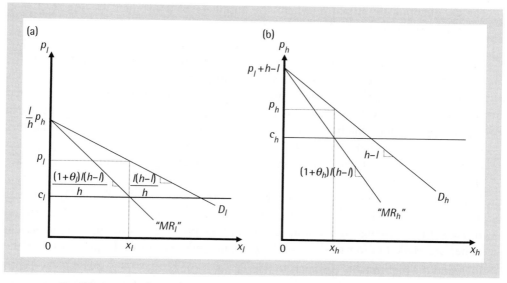

FIGURE 9.4 Equilibrium conditions in the markets for low- and high-quality products
(a) Low-quality market
(b) High-quality market

high-quality products and depicts the equilibrium conditions in the two markets in the familiar price–quantity space.

The equilibrium prices and quantities of the low- and the high-quality products can be expressed as

$$p_l = \frac{l\theta_l[\theta_h(h - l) + c_h] + h(1 + \theta_h)c_l}{(1 + \theta_l + \theta_h)h + \theta_l\theta_h(h - l)} \tag{13}$$

$$p_h = \frac{h\{(1 + \theta_l)[\theta_h(h - l) + c_h] + \theta_h c_l\}}{(1 + \theta_l + \theta_h)h + \theta_l\theta_h(h - l)} \tag{14}$$

$$x_l = \frac{h\{l[\theta_h(h - l) + c_h] - [h + (h - l)\theta_h]c_l\}}{l(h - l)[(1 + \theta_l + \theta_h)h + \theta_l\theta_h(h - l)]} \tag{15}$$

$$x_h = \frac{h[(1 + \theta_l)(h - l) + c_l] - [h + (h - l)\theta_l]c_h}{(h - l)[(1 + \theta_l + \theta_h)h + \theta_l\theta_h(h - l)]} \tag{16}$$

where θ_l and θ_h are conjectural variation elasticities capturing the degree of market power in the markets for the low- and the high-quality products, respectively, and c_l and c_h are the marginal costs faced by the suppliers of these products. The market power parameters θ take values between zero and one and capture the degree of suppliers' market power: the greater are the θs, the greater is the market power in the markets for the low- and the high-quality products. A value of $\theta = 1$ corresponds to a monopoly while a value of $\theta = 0$ reflects a perfectly competitive market structure (or an oligopolistic structure where the suppliers of a product are involved in a Bertrand price competition).

The production costs of the low- and the high-quality products reflect (i) the production, processing, and marketing costs along the two supply channels, (ii) the costs associated with the segregation and labeling, where relevant, of the two products (with the majority of these costs being incurred in the high-quality supply chain), and (iii) the market power at previous stages of the supply chain (i.e., the market power of input suppliers, food manufacturers, wholesalers, etc.). The greater are the production, processing, and/or marketing costs, and/or the greater are the labeling and segregation costs, and/or the greater is the market power upstream a supply channel, the greater are the costs of a product.

It is interesting to note that, since the prices of the low- and high-quality products are "strategic complements" (i.e., a change in the price of a product causes the price of its substitute to change in the same direction; see equations (8) and (9)), an increase in either the market power or the supplier costs in a market causes the prices of *both* the low- and the high-quality products to rise, i.e., $\frac{\partial p_i}{\partial \theta_i} > 0, \frac{\partial p_j}{\partial \theta_i} > 0, \frac{\partial p_i}{\partial c_i} > 0$ and $\frac{\partial p_j}{\partial c_i} > 0$ with $i, j \in \{l, h\}$ and $i \neq j$. While increased market power and costs in the low- (high-)quality market cause both p_l and p_h to rise, they increase the price of the low- (high-)quality product by more, i.e., $\frac{\partial p_i}{\partial \theta_i} > \frac{\partial p_j}{\partial \theta_i}$ and $\frac{\partial p_i}{\partial c_i} > \frac{\partial p_j}{\partial c_i}$. Consequently, the greater is the supplier power in a market and/or the greater are the costs of a product, the lower is the equilibrium quantity of this product and the greater is the equilibrium quantity of its substitute, i.e., $\frac{\partial x_i}{\partial \theta_i} < 0, \frac{\partial x_i}{\partial c_i} < 0, \frac{\partial x_j}{\partial \theta_i} > 0$, and $\frac{\partial x_j}{\partial c_i} > 0$.

Once the equilibrium prices and quantities have been determined, we can derive the supplier profits as

$$\Pi_l = (p_l - c_l)x_l = \frac{h\theta_l \{l[\theta_h(h-l) + c_h] - [h + (h-l)\theta_h]c_l\}^2}{l(h-l)[(1+\theta_l+\theta_h)h + \theta_l\theta_h(h-l)]^2} \tag{17}$$

$$\Pi_h = (p_h - c_h)x_h = \frac{\theta_h \{h[(1+\theta_l)(h-l) + c_l] - [h + (h-l)\theta_l]c_h\}^2}{(h-l)[(1+\theta_l+\theta_h)h + \theta_l\theta_h(h-l)]^2} \tag{18}$$

and, by substituting these equilibrium prices and quantities in equations (10)–(12), the equilibrium surplus of the different consumer groups involved. This framework could then be used to analyze the impacts of any relevant government policy, firm strategy, and/or change in consumer behavior on prices, quantities/market shares, variety, and the welfare of the interest groups involved.

Finally, the framework developed above can also be used to analyze the case of brand-producing firms that are involved in a price or quantity competition and, unlike the firms considered in the previous example, can also affect the quality characteristics of the product they supply. By definition, the brand-producing firms are the sole suppliers (i.e., monopolists) of their (high- or low-quality) product, which makes the consumer demands D_h and D_l in Figure 9.4 "their" demand curves and $\theta_h = \theta_l = 1$.

In such a case, the resulting prices, quantities, and profits will depend on the nature of the strategic interaction between the two brand-producing firms (i.e., whether they compete in prices or quantities, whether they make their decisions simultaneously or sequentially, whether they have complete and/or perfect information, etc.) and will be functions of the parameters h and l (which, as pointed out in Section 3.2, capture the level of quality of the high- and low-quality products when this quality level is endogenous to the suppliers of these products). Using backward induction, the two firms can then choose their equilibrium qualities (simultaneously or sequentially, with complete or incomplete information, etc.) determining, this way, the degree of differentiation of these products as well as the equilibrium prices, quantities, consumer welfare, and firm profits (for a simple example of price and quality competition between brand-producing firms, see Tirole 1988: 296).

5 CONCLUSIONS

This chapter provided an overview of the theory and models of consumer demand in markets for vertically differentiated products. After a discussion of the key assumptions employed in the literature, I presented a general, empirically relevant model of vertical product differentiation that captures important idiosyncrasies of the markets for food products and nests the essence of all popular formulations appearing in the literature. Using this general model, I derived the consumer demands for, and the market shares of, different quality products, identified the exact conditions under which different combinations of the products will be supplied to the market, and derived theory-consistent measures of the surplus of the different consumer groups involved.

Finally, the chapter focused on the different applications of the methodological framework and provided an example of a general market analysis that allows for the explicit consideration of any relevant structure of the markets for vertically differentiated, high- and low-quality products. In addition to providing a basis for the systematic analysis of consumer demand for vertically differentiated products, the methodological frameworks presented in this chapter could provide a valuable theoretical grounding to the empirical analyses of the increasingly relevant markets for vertically differentiated food products.

REFERENCES

Anderson, S. P., A. de Palma, and J.-F. Thisse. 1992. *Discrete Choice Theory of Product Differentiation*. Cambridge, MA: MIT Press.

Beath, J., and Y. Katsoulakos. 1991. *The Economic Theory of Product Differentiation*. Cambridge: Cambridge University Press.

Berwald, D., C. A. Carter, and G. P. Gruere. 2006. "Rejecting New Technology: The Case of Genetically Modified Wheat." *American Journal of Agricultural Economics* 88/2: 432–47.

Bonanno, G. 1986. "Vertical Differentiation with Cournot Competition." *Economic Notes* 15/2: 68–91.

Bonnisseau, J.-M., and R. Lahmandi-Ayed. 2007. "Vertical Differentiation with Non-Uniform Consumers' Distribution." *International Journal of Economic Theory* 3/3: 179–90.

Bontems, P., S. Monier-Dilhan, and V. Requillart. 1999. "Strategic Effects of Private Labels." *European Review of Agricultural Economics* 26/2: 147–65.

Boom, A. 1995. "Asymmetric International Minimum Quality Standards and Vertical Differentiation." *Journal of Industrial Economics* 43/1: 101–19.

Bureau, J.-C., S. Marette, and A. Schiavina. 1998. "Non-Tariff Trade Barriers and Consumers' Information: The Case of the EU–US Trade Dispute over Beef." *European Review of Agricultural Economics* 25/4: 437–62.

Choi, C. J., and H. S. Chin. 1992. "A Comment on a Model of Vertical Product Differentiation." *Journal of Industrial Economics* 40/2: 229–31.

Crespi, J. M., and S. Marette. 2001. "How Should Food Safety Certification Be Financed?" *American Journal of Agricultural Economics* 83/4: 852–61.

————. 2002. "Generic Advertising and Product Differentiation." *American Journal of Agricultural Economics* 84/3: 691–701.

Donnenfeld, S., and S. Weber. 1992. "Vertical Product Differentiation with Entry." *International Journal of Industrial Organization* 10/3: 449–72.

————. 1995. "Limit Qualities and Entry Deterrence." *Rand Journal of Economics* 26/1: 113–30.

Drivas, K., and K. Giannakas. 2010. "The Effect of Cooperatives on Quality-Enhancing Innovation." *Journal of Agricultural Economics* 61/2: 295–317.

Fulton, M. E., and K. Giannakas. 2004. "Inserting GM Products into the Food Chain: The Market and Welfare Effects of Different Labeling and Regulatory Regimes." *American Journal of Agricultural Economics* 86/1: 42–60.

Gabszewicz, J. J., and J.-F. Thisse. 1979. "Price Competition, Quality and Income Disparities." *Journal of Economic Theory* 20/3: 340–59.

————. 1980. "Entry (and Exit) in a Differentiated Industry." *Journal of Economic Theory* 22/2: 327–38.

Gal-Or, E. 1983. "Quality and Quantity Competition." *Bell Journal of Economics* 14/2: 590–600.

Giannakas, K. 2002. "Information Asymmetries and Consumption Decisions in Organic Food Product Markets." *Canadian Journal of Agricultural Economics* 50/1: 35–50.

—— and M. E. Fulton. 2002. "Consumption Effects of Genetic Modification: What if Consumers Are Right?" *Agricultural Economics* 27: 97–109.

—— and A. Yiannaka. 2006. "Agricultural Biotechnology and Organic Agriculture: National Organic Standards and Labeling of GM Products." *AgBioForum* 9/2: 84–93.

————. 2008. "Market and Welfare Effects of the Second-Generation, Consumer-Oriented GM Products." *American Journal of Agricultural Economics* 90/1: 152–71.

Gruere, G. P., C. A. Carter, and Y. H. Farzin. 2008. "What Labelling Policy for Consumer Choice? The Case of Genetically Modified Food in Canada and Europe." *Canadian Journal of Economics* 41/4: 1472–97.

Lahmandi-Ayed, R. 2000. "Natural Oligopolies: A Vertical Differentiation Model." *International Economic Review* 41/4: 971–87.

——— 2007. "Finiteness Property with Vertical and Horizontal Differentiation: Does it Really Matter?" *Economic Theory* 33: 531–48.

Lapan, H. E., and G. Moschini. 2004. "Innovation and Trade with Endogenous Market Failure: The Case of Genetically Modified Products." *American Journal of Agricultural Economics* 86/3: 634–48.

——— ———. 2007. "Grading, Minimum Quality Standards, and GM Labeling." *American Journal of Agricultural Economics* 89/3: 769–83.

Lavoie, N. 2005. "Price Discrimination in the Context of Vertical Differentiation: An Application to Canadian Wheat Exports." *American Journal of Agricultural Economics* 87/4: 835–54.

Lehmann-Grube, U. 1997. "Strategic Choice of Quality when Quality Is Costly: The Persistence of the High-Quality Advantage." *Rand Journal of Economics* 28/2: 372–84.

Lusk, J. L., W. B. Trail, L. O. House, C. Valli, S. R. Jaeger, M. Moore, and B. Morrow. 2005. "Consumer Welfare Effects of Introducing and Labeling Genetically Modified Food." *Economics Letters* 88/3: 382–8.

Moschini, G., L. Menapace, and D. Pick. 2008. "Geographical Indications and the Competitive Provision of Quality in Agricultural Markets." *American Journal of Agricultural Economics* 90/3: 794–812.

Motta, M. 1993. "Endogenous Quality Choice: Price vs. Quantity Competition." *Journal of Industrial Economics* 41/2: 113–31.

Mussa, M., and S. Rosen. 1978. "Monopoly and Product Quality." *Journal of Economic Theory* 18/2: 301–17.

Plastina, A. S., K. Giannakas, and D. Pick. 2011. "Market and Welfare Effects of Mandatory Country-of-Origin-Labeling in the US Specialty Crops Sector." *Southern Economic Journal* 77/4: 1044–69.

Roe, B., and I. Sheldon. 2007. "Credence Good Labeling: The Efficiency and Distributional Implications of Several Policy Approaches." *American Journal of Agricultural Economics* 89/4: 1020–33.

Shaked, A., and J. Sutton. 1982. "Relaxing Price Competition through Product Differentiation." *Review of Economic Studies* 49/1: 3–13.

——— ———. 1983. "Natural Oligopolies." *Econometrica* 51/5: 1469–83.

Sobolevsky, A., G. Moschini, and H. Lapan. 2005. "Genetically Modified Crop Innovations and Product Differentiation: Trade and Welfare Effects in the Soybean Complex." *American Journal of Agricultural Economics* 87/3: 621–44.

Tirole, J. 1988. *The Theory of Industrial Organization.* Cambridge, MA: MIT Press.

Tribl, C., and K. Salhofer. 2008. *Promoting Organic Food: Information Policy versus Production Subsidy.* Working Paper. Vienna: Federal Institute of Agricultural Economics.

Veyssiere, L. 2007. "Strategic Response to GMOs by GM-Free Countries." *European Review of Agricultural Economics* 34/3: 365–92.

Wang, X. H., and B. Z. Yang. 2001. "Mixed Strategy Equilibria in a Quality Differentiation Model." *International Journal of Industrial Organization* 19/1–2: 213–26.

Wathy, X. 1996. "Quality Choice in Models of Vertical Differentiation." *Journal of Industrial Economics* 44/3: 345–53.

Zago, A. M., and D. Pick. 2004. "Labeling Policies in Food Markets: Private Incentives, Public Intervention, and Welfare Effects." *Journal of Agricultural and Resource Economics* 29/1: 150–65.

CHAPTER 10

....

MODELS OF HORIZONTAL PRODUCT DIFFERENTIATION IN FOOD MARKETS

....

PIERRE R. MÉREL AND RICHARD J. SEXTON

1 INTRODUCTION

....

Modern food marketing emphasizes differentiated products. Characteristics important in today's food markets include a product's taste, appearance, convenience, brand appeal, and healthfulness, but also broader dimensions including characteristics of the production process, such as use of chemicals, sustainability, confinement conditions of animals, and implications of production and consumption of the product for the environment.

Two important broad categories of product differentiation are horizontal and vertical differentiation. In both cases, consumers purchase only one product or brand out of a product category. With horizontal differentiation, consumers do not agree on a preference ranking among products in the category, whereas with vertical differentiation they share the same ordinal ranking but differ in the intensity of their preference for the higher-ranked products. Both forms of product differentiation are relevant to food markets. Examples that would fit vertical differentiation include organic versus conventionally grown produce, prime versus choice beef, and a national brand versus a private-label brand of the same product. Examples of horizontal differentiation might include competing national brands of the same product, sugar content of breakfast cereals, fat content of fluid milk, and, very importantly, geographic locations of sellers.

Horizontal and vertical differentiation models are appropriate choices of modeling framework for narrowly defined product categories, where the basic postulate, that in a given time period each consumer will purchase only one product in the category, is appropriate. When broader product categories are being considered, consumers' preferences for variety are a paramount consideration. Thus, neither model would be appropriate to study behavior in a broad product category such as meat. Although the various meats may well substitute for one another in consumers' budgets, most consumers purchase more than one meat product in a given shopping period. A vertical differentiation model may, however, be appropriate if the analysis involves choice of range-free versus conventionally raised chicken or choice among organic, natural, or conventional beef. Horizontal differentiation would be an appropriate framework to study, for example, the choice of retail store or restaurant where meat products were purchased or the choice of fat content (marbling) for a given meat cut.

Together horizontal and vertical differentiation models are known as location or address models, and another defining characteristic of them is that competition is localized. In the event that several products or brands are available in the relevant category, a given product/brand competes directly only with those products located "close" to it in the product-characteristic space. By way of contrast, models of non-localized competition in the tradition of Chamberlin (1933) feature competition by a given brand/product against the rest of the market, with no particular pattern of substitution specified among specific products in the group. In such models, and in stark contrast to horizontal and vertical differentiation models, consumers may purchase all products in the category.[1]

This chapter focuses on models of horizontal differentiation; vertical differentiation is discussed in Chapter 9 in this volume, by Giannakas. We also focus on conceptual models; empirical models relevant to horizontal differentiation are covered in Chapters 5 and 6 of this volume, by Adamowicz and Swait, and Costanigro and McCluskey, respectively. The essential element of horizontal differentiation is that products are located at different points in product-characteristic space, and heterogeneous consumers each have an "ideal" characteristics bundle, which, if it could be consumed in the form of an actual product, would yield her the highest utility. Accordingly, a consumer prefers to consume a product with characteristics close to her ideal, but can be persuaded to "travel" to consume products located away from her ideal point if given a sufficient price incentive to do so. From the perspective of the underlying economics, the decision of a consumer to travel from her preferred breakfast cereal sugar (sweetness) content of, say, 9 grams per cup (General Mills' Honey Nut Cheerios) to consume Kellogg's Corn Pops (14 grams/cup) because she has a coupon for Corn Pops is fundamentally no different from her decision to travel to a cross-town grocer because products she wishes to purchase are on sale there. Thus, the concept of horizontal differentiation based upon the defining characteristic(s) of a product is closely related

---

[1] This approach is exemplified by Dixit and Stiglitz (1977), who posited a separable utility function for each consumer, with utility for the product category under study specified in constant elasticity of substitution (CES) form, implying a taste for variety itself.

to the pioneering work by Lancaster (1966) on the characteristics approach to studying consumer demand.[2]

In the next section we present a very general framework to modeling markets with differentiated products. We illustrate the limitations to this approach and argue that a solution, under the appropriate circumstances, is to impose more structure on the model, for example by assuming either horizontal or vertical differentiation. The first and best-known model of horizontal differentiation is the Hotelling (1929) model. Many extensions and generalizations of this model have been made since Hotelling's original contribution. In the short run the locations of firms and products is fixed, and analysis involves price and market share determination. In the long run firms are free to choose the location of their products and new firms may enter.

We present a somewhat generalized version of Hotelling's original model in Section 3, and derive the short-run equilibrium and key comparative statics. Section 4 then considers further extensions and generalizations of the short-run model, and Section 5 discusses applications of the model to food markets. Section 6 addresses the question of firms' optimal location in the product space. This decision is typically studied sequentially in two stages; the second stage (which is studied first) is the pricing game (the focus of Section 3), with the first stage being the location decision, which is made in rational anticipation of the manner in which location will affect the subsequent price competition. Section 7 then considers entry and the generalization of the Hotelling model due to Salop (1979), usually known as the circular city, which is most often used to study entry into a horizontally differentiated market. In Sections 3–7, firms are differentiated based upon a single characteristic:—they compete on a line or the circumference of a circle. Section 8 considers horizontal product differentiation based upon multiple product characteristics. Section 9 offers a brief conclusion.

2 A General Framework for Differentiated Markets

When firms produce differentiated products, each product has its own demand, but demands, of course, are interrelated, and it is the nature of this interrelationship that is crucial to understanding behavior in the market. A basic approach is to bypass a model of consumer behavior and begin with demand specifications at the market level.[3] To

---

[2] Lancaster's theory relies upon two fundamental propositions: (1) goods possess objective characteristics and (2) consumers' preferences are defined over bundles of characteristics rather than bundles of goods. In this setting, goods can be viewed as purchased inputs into a consumption technology that converts them into characteristics.

[3] However, it would also be straightforward to begin with a common, separable utility function for consumers such as in Dixit and Stiglitz (1977) and derive the market demands by aggregating individual demands implied by the utility specification.

illustrate this approach, assume n differentiated products in a market category, and $m \leq n$ firms that operate in the category, each selling at least one brand. Demand at the market level for each brand can be expressed as $q_i = f_i(p_1, \ldots, p_n)$, $i = 1, \ldots, n$, where q_i is sales and p_i is the price for brand or product i.

Price represents the intuitive choice of strategy variable for firms with differentiated products. Assume that each firm produces one brand, so $n = m$. Then we can represent the optimization problem for firm i as follows:

$$\max_{p_i} \quad \Pi_i(p_1, \ldots, p_n) = f_i(p_1, \ldots, p_n)p_i - c_i(f_i(p_1, \ldots, p_n)), \quad i = 1, \ldots, n, \quad (1)$$

where c_i denotes the ith seller's cost function.

The first-order condition (FOC) to this problem is the following:

$$q_i + \left(p_i - \frac{\partial c_i}{\partial q_i} \right) \left[\frac{\partial q_i}{\partial p_i} + \sum_{j \neq i} \frac{\partial p_j}{\partial p_i} \frac{\partial q_i}{\partial p_j} \right] = 0, \quad i = 1, \ldots, n. \quad (2)$$

Equation (2) expresses the intuitive condition that at its optimum a firm in a differentiated-product industry balances the increase in net revenue from raising its price by one unit, namely q_i, with the loss of its profit margin, $p_i - \frac{\partial c_i}{\partial q_i}$, on all sales sacrificed as a consequence of its price increase. The reduction in sales is represented by the term in square brackets. It includes the direct effect of i's price increase on its own sales and the indirect effects due to competitors' "reactions" to firm i's price change. These effects are represented in the summation and each consists of the product of two derivatives. The $\frac{\partial p_j}{\partial p_i}$ term is the so-called "conjectural variation" that measures how rival firm j "reacts" to the price change by firm i, and $\frac{\partial q_i}{\partial p_j}$ is the standard cross-price effect that measures how this reaction impacts firm i's sales.

Products within the same category would normally be substitutes, so $\frac{\partial q_i}{\partial p_j} > 0$. As to the conjectural variations, the Nash conjecture is $\frac{\partial p_j}{\partial p_i} = 0$, in which case the summation term in (2) vanishes. However, various forms of collusive or quasi-collusive behavior would be represented by $\frac{\partial p_j}{\partial p_i} > 0$, in which case the summation offsets the negative own-price effect, causing the firm's optimal price to be higher than under Nash behavior, ceteris paribus.

Suppose now that a firm controls more than one brand. The FOC for the price, p_a, of any single brand a under the firm's control must then include a term to account for the impact of changing p_a on the sales of the firm's other brand(s), say, b. This effect, $\frac{\partial q_b}{\partial p_a}$, will normally be positive because competing brands are substitutes, and in the FOC it will be multiplied by the profit margin for brand b. Introduction of this effect into the FOC means, ceteris paribus, that the optimal price for brand a is higher when its seller controls other brands in the category. Thus, mergers among sellers of differentiated brands increase prices in the category unless efficiency gains, i.e., reductions in the cost c_i from the merger, are large enough to offset this price impact.

The n demand functions and the n first-order conditions in (2) comprise a system of equations that describe the equilibrium in the differentiated-product market. Because the model was not built from the foundation of consumer utility maximization, it offers no guidance in terms of specification of the n demand functions. This limitation is surmounted by basing the demands on a non-address specification of utility, such as the CES function used by Dixit and Stiglitz (1977). Such formulations, however, yield no predictions about the interactions among the n products in the category, including the factors that determine the strength or weakness of substitution among the various products or brands in the category. The model involves an $n \times n$ matrix of own- and cross-price effects, and, depending upon what one assumes about the form of competition, possibly also a $n \times n$ matrix of conjectural variation terms, meaning the model quickly becomes intractable as a foundation for theoretical work, where more structure is needed to achieve simplification and sharper predictions. The choices the analyst makes in imposing this structure are crucial because they determine, in essence *ex ante*, the nature of the interaction among the products in the category under investigation.

3 A Generalized Hotelling Model

Hotelling's spatial competition model, first introduced in his 1929 article "Stability in Competition," constitutes the canonical model of horizontal differentiation. Hotelling's original model involves duopoly price competition for the patronage of consumers with inelastic demands—each is assumed to purchase one unit—who are distributed uniformly on a line with respect to their preferences for the differentiating attribute of the product. Without loss of generality, the length of the segment and the total number of consumers can each be normalized to one, allowing demands to be represented conveniently in market share form.[4] Duopoly sellers of the good are located at each end of the segment and denoted a and b, respectively; optimal location on the segment is studied in Section 6. The two goods are the same except for their location with respect to the differentiating attribute. The cost of producing the good is constant and equal to c for each seller. Consumers purchase exactly one unit from the firm who offers them the lowest total price, defined as the mill price set by the firm plus the consumer's costs of "traveling" to the firm's location, or more generally, the consumer's disutility from not consuming his ideal product variety. Transportation costs are linear per unit of distance and denoted by γ, so that the total price faced by a consumer located at x is $P_a + \gamma x$ if she purchases from seller a, and $P_b + \gamma(1 - x)$ if she purchases from seller b.

---

[4] The line segment can accommodate two product attributes if we define locations in terms of the ratio of the attributes contained by a product. For example, suppose ready-to-eat breakfast cereals are differentiated by nutrient content (measured as an index) and sugar content per serving. Then a minimum and maximum nutrient-to-sugar ratio can be defined and normalized to 0 and 1, respectively, and products located accordingly along that line.

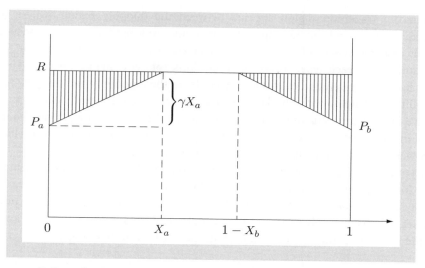

FIGURE 10.1 Delivered prices and surplus on the Hotelling line
X_i denotes the market radius of seller i. In the case depicted, consumers located between X_a
and $1 - X_b$ do not purchase the differentiated good.

The extreme form of inelasticity in Hotelling's initial model was questioned by
Lerner and Singer (1937), who introduced a reservation price $R > c$ to the otherwise
unitary consumer demands, so that each consumer purchases one unit of the good as
long as her total price does not exceed R. Salop (1979) provided a formal justification for
the reservation price based upon the presence of an outside good that can be purchased
at a fixed price in lieu of the good produced by the spatially differentiated sellers. For a
consumer located at $x \in [0, 1]$, the surplus from purchasing variety i can then be defined
as $R - P_i - \gamma |x - x_i|$, where x_i denotes the location of seller i. Figure 10.1 depicts
consumers' delivered prices (inclusive of transportation costs) and the resulting surplus
in the case where consumers located near the market center do not purchase from
either seller.

The importance of product differentiation in this generalized Hotelling model with
reservation price is determined by the magnitude of the market length times transport
cost per unit distance relative to the reservation price net of production cost—a ratio,
$\kappa = \frac{\gamma}{R - c}$, we call the "normalized transportation cost."[5] The presence of the outside
good adds a participation constraint to the sellers' pricing decisions, and this affects the
nature of competition significantly relative to the original Hotelling specification. First,
a local-monopoly equilibrium arises for sufficiently large values of the normalized
transportation cost. In this case, the market areas of the two sellers are disjoint, each
seller sets price independently of the price charged by the other seller, and consumers
located at the center of the segment are not served (the case depicted in Figure 10.1).

---

[5] This normalization was formally introduced by Hinloopen and van Marrewijk (1999).

Second, a transition region appears between the duopoly region (where sellers compete in prices and the participation constraint is not binding for any consumer—the only case that arises in Hotelling's original model) and the monopoly region. In this transition region, each seller sets price at the "kink" of her demand function. The kink occurs because the demand curves facing a seller in the monopoly and duopoly regions have different slopes, with the latter being steeper because a price decrease is less effective at attracting customers in this region, as the price-cutting firm's boundary moves in the direction of consumers with higher transportation costs to its location and lower transportation costs to the rival firm's location.

This transition region prevails for a comparatively wide range of intermediate values of κ. Comparative static results are generally reversed in this range relative to the duopoly competition region (Salop 1979). Of particular importance is that the price set by either seller is inversely related to the magnitude of consumers' transportation costs (i.e., the extent of product differentiation in the market) in this range.

3.1 Derivation of the Price Equilibrium

Denote by $Q_a(P_a, P_b; R, \gamma)$ the quantity demanded from seller a under prices P_a and P_b. Given our assumption about the reservation price of consumers, prices P_a and P_b must be lower than R in order to attract any buyer at all. Further, it is never optimal for, say, seller a to charge a price strictly lower than $P_b - \gamma$, because all consumers already purchase from seller a if $P_a = P_b - \gamma$. Similarly, it is not optimal for seller a to charge a price greater than $P_b + \gamma$, because then all consumers purchase from seller b. Given these restrictions, the demand function facing seller a has the form[6]

$$Q_a(P_a, P_b; R, \gamma) = \begin{cases} \dfrac{P_b - P_a + \gamma}{2\gamma} & \text{if } P_b - \gamma \leq P_a \leq \min(\gamma + P_b, 2R - \gamma - P_b) \\ \dfrac{R - P_a}{\gamma} & \text{if } 2R - \gamma - P_b < P_a \leq \min(R, \gamma + P_b) \end{cases} \qquad (3)$$

Function Q_a is depicted in Figure 10.2 and is kinked for values of P_b such that $\gamma + P_b > R$. Demand on the segment $[P_b - \gamma, \min(\gamma + P_b, 2R - \gamma - P_b)]$ depends on the price charged by the other seller and corresponds to the duopoly or competitive demand, where $x = \frac{P_b - P_a + \gamma}{2\gamma}$ identifies the location of the consumer who is indifferent regarding purchasing from seller a or seller b. On the segment $(2R - \gamma - P_b, \min(R, \gamma + P_b)]$ demand only depends on P_a, market radius is $\frac{R - P_a}{\gamma}$ and corresponds to the monopoly demand. Demand in the monopoly portion has twice the slope as demand in the competitive portion.

Given this formulation, three types of equilibria may arise. Duopoly competition arises for values of (γ, R, c) such that $0 < \kappa \leq \frac{2}{3}$. The Nash equilibrium is unique and

---

[6] This demand function is derived, for instance, in Mérel and Sexton (2009).

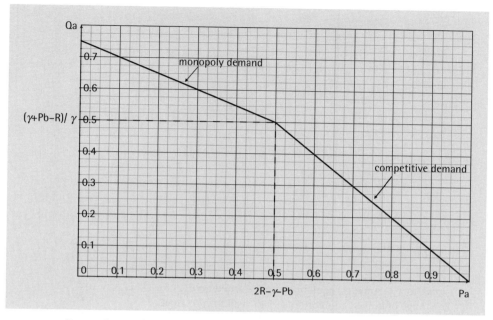

FIGURE 10.2 Demand curve facing each seller in the case of unit demands and linear transport costs
Parameters values are set at $\gamma = 1$, $R = 1$ and $P_b = 0.5$.

symmetric and characterized by $\bar{P}_a = \bar{P}_b = c + \gamma$. The market is covered and the indifferent consumer is located at $\bar{x} = \frac{1}{2}$. For $0 \le \kappa \le \frac{1}{2}$, the demand facing each seller consists only of the competitive segment and is therefore not kinked.

Each firm sets price at the kink of its demand function, and multiple "kinked" equilibria arise for values of (γ, R, c) such that $\frac{2}{3} < \kappa \le 1$. The existence of multiple equilibria in this range of normalized transportation cost was first noted by Economides (1984), and their properties are characterized in Mérel and Sexton (2010). Most applied studies will want to avoid the complexity of dealing with multiple equilibria, and the convenient simplification is to focus upon the symmetric equilibrium, which is $\bar{P}_a = \bar{P}_b = R - \frac{\gamma}{2}$.[7] The market is covered under all of the equilibria in this range, but the participation constraint of the indifferent consumer binds. In the symmetric equilibrium the indifferent consumer is located at at the midpoint, $\bar{x} = \frac{1}{2}$.

When $\kappa > 1$, the desired market radii of the two firms do not overlap—each firm, thus, is a monopolist—and each sets price independently of the other. The equilibrium price is found by choosing price to maximize profit, taking into account that the market radius served, X_i, $i = a, b$, is determined by the marginal consumer's participation

---

[7] The analysis in Mérel and Sexton (2010) provides justification for this simplifying assumption. First, all of the asymmetric equilibria are located "close" to the symmetric equilibrium, and, second, introducing even a small amount of price responsiveness (elasticity) to individual consumers' demands removes the kink in the aggregated demands facing sellers, eliminating the asymmetric equilibria.

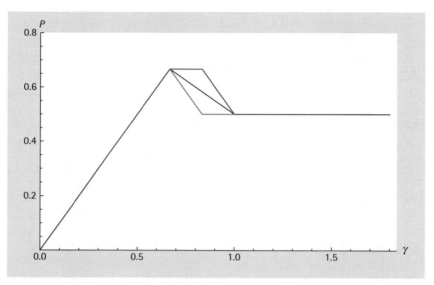

FIGURE 10.3 Symmetric equilibrium price schedule $\bar{P}(\gamma)$ for $(R, c) = (1, 0)$
The range of kinked equilibrium prices is also represented.

constraint: $P_i + \gamma X_i = R$. The optimum prices are $\bar{P}_a = \bar{P}_b = \frac{R+c}{2}$, and they do not
depend on the transportation cost. Firms serve a market area of size $\frac{R-c}{2\gamma}$. Consumers
located in the middle of the product space do not purchase the product.

A convenient monetary normalization is to set the intrinsic value of the product,
R, net of production costs to one: $R - c = 1$. The equilibrium price schedule is depicted
in Figure 10.3 as a function of the normalized transportation cost, which is just $\kappa = \gamma$ in
light of the monetary normalization. When $\kappa = 0$, the firms are not differentiated from
consumers' perspectives, and Bertrand's paradox applies, i.e., $P_a = P_b = c$. This
replicates the outcome of a market where sellers are located at a single point in product
space. As κ increases in the range $\left(0, \frac{2}{3}\right]$, product differentiation enables firms to set
prices in excess of marginal cost and earn a positive profit margin that is increasing in
κ. Indeed, for $\frac{1}{2} < \kappa < 1$, the price under duopoly competition is greater than the
monopoly price. Setting price at the kink in demand and maintaining market
coverage is optimal for the sellers for values of the normalized transport cost κ in the
range $\left(\frac{2}{3}, 1\right]$. However, for $\kappa > 1$, it is no longer optimal for the sellers to maintain
market coverage, and each sets price as an isolated monopolist. Although neither seller
faces competition, each faces an elastic demand with $\frac{\partial Q_i}{\partial P_i} = -\frac{1}{\gamma}$, $i = a, b$. The optimal
price, in consideration of this demand response to price, is lower than the price in the
kinked-equilibrium range.

What explains the non-monotonicity of equilibrium price as a function of the degree
of product differentiation? In general, two factors determine firms' prices in any market
model: responsiveness of consumers' demands to price and the intensity of competition among sellers. In the generalized Hotelling model, only the competition effect

matters for $0 \leq \kappa < \frac{2}{3}$ because no consumer's reservation price binds in this range, the market is covered, and total demand is perfectly inelastic. Thus, as κ increases, the market becomes more differentiated, price competition is less intense, and the equilibrium prices increase. However, when $\kappa = \frac{2}{3}$, the total price paid by the indifferent consumer is $c + \frac{2}{3}(R - c) + \frac{1}{2} \times \frac{2}{3}(R - c) = R$, i.e., her participation constraint binds. Any price increase from this point will cause the market no longer to be covered, i.e., total demand is no longer perfectly price-inelastic. Stated alternatively, holding prices constant, any increase in κ will cause the market not to be covered. Sellers' profit margins are high in this range of κ, and there is a mutual incentive between them to maintain market coverage, i.e., to set price at the kink of their demand curves. This means that an increase in κ will cause a reduction in price by one or both sellers so as to maintain market coverage. Under the symmetric equilibrium, each reduces price, hence the non-monotonic price schedule.

3.2 Comparative Statics

Given the closed-form solutions for the equilibrium prices, comparative statics are straightforward to derive. Prices are increasing in γ and c in the competitive range and R does not affect price because it doesn't bind for any consumer. In the kinked-equilibrium range, the symmetric price is increasing in R and decreasing in γ. Transportation cost does not affect price in the monopoly range, but it does influence the market area that is covered.

The unusual comparative statics in the kinked-equilibrium range have received little attention but are prospectively important because they lead to conclusions and policy implications that belie the conventional wisdom. For example, entry can harm consumers if it moves the market from monopoly to the kinked-equilibrium transition region (Cowan and Yin 2008), because prices are higher in this region than under monopoly. Or policies, such as improved roads, that would normally be considered as pro-consumer can actually be harmful to consumers in markets characterized by kinked equilibria, or if the investments integrate monopoly markets but result in a kinked equilibrium.[8]

The outcome of the pricing game analyzed here also shows that in spatially differentiated markets, even though firms may compete in a Bertrand–Nash fashion, they are able to capture positive rents in the short run. This provides an explanation why Bertrand's paradox may not hold in real markets. As long as they charge mill prices, however, firms do not capture all surplus, and thus the outcome of a price game with fixed locations may not be socially optimal. It will be, in the inelastic demand case with

---

[8] This point is made by Mérel, Sexton, and Suzuki (2009) in an oligopsony framework, where the analysis focuses on the potential of transportation cost improvements to improve the welfare of smallholders in a developing-economy context.

sellers located at the endpoints of the unit-length market, as long as all customers who should be served are indeed served. Given the valuation R, the unit cost c, and the linear travel cost γ, all customers located within a distance $X^* = \min\left(\frac{1}{2}, \frac{R-c}{\gamma}\right)$ of either seller should be served. If $\kappa \leq 1$, the analysis of Section 3.2 showed that all customers will be served, and they should since then $X^* = \frac{1}{2}$. But for $\kappa > 1$, the market outcome will be inefficient: customers located near the middle of the market will be excluded when they should be served. (In fact all customers should be served until κ reaches 2.) Therefore, even with inelastic demands, there are instances where the market outcome will be inefficient.

4 EXTENSIONS TO THE BASE MODEL

The effort invested by various authors in extending the basic Hotelling model is testimony to its importance. The price competition studied in Section 3 is often a precursor to analysis of firm location or entry decisions, so it is of considerable interest to know how relaxation of some of the core assumptions in the base model affects these equilibria. It is also interesting to ask if the unusual comparative static properties of the kinked equilibria survive under various extensions to the basic model. Several facets of the base model present themselves for possible extension and generalization. We limit our attention to five of the more important: (1) inelastic consumer demand, (2) linear transportation cost, (3) location of consumers and sellers on a line of finite length, (4) Nash seller conjectures, and (5) FOB (non-discriminatory) pricing strategies.

4.1 Elastic Demands

Inelastic consumer demand subject to a reservation price is a good approximation of individual demands for durable goods, but it is less appropriate for most foods because consumers are likely to vary their purchases based upon prices they face. As noted, inelastic demand plays a fundamental role in determining prices because in the duopoly competition range where reservation prices do not bind for any consumer the only brake on firms' pricing is the competition between them, which explains why the duopoly price can be greater than the monopoly price, as this competition weakens with increasing values of κ. It also plays an important role in models with entry (see Section 7) because inelastic demands imply high short-run prices, *ceteris paribus*, which in turn create more opportunities for entry. Thus, whether entry is excessive or deficient from a societal perspective in models of horizontal differentiation depends upon the elasticity of individual consumer demands (Gu and Wenzel 2009a).

A first approach to introducing more price responsiveness to demand is to retain the unit demand assumption but allow reservation prices to vary among consumers

(Boeckem 1994). The more common and general approach, however, has been to allow each consumer's demand to exhibit price responsiveness. Rath and Zhao (2001) assumed linear consumer demands, Peitz (2002) worked with unit-elastic (constant revenue) demands, Gu and Wenzel (2009a) utilized constant elasticity demands, while Mérel and Sexton (2010) introduced power demands of the form $q(p) = (R - p)^{\varepsilon}$, with p denoting the price inclusive of any transportation cost. Gu and Wenzel (2009b) work with continuous demands derived from a quasi-linear utility function.

Elastic consumer demand functions eliminate the kink in firms' demand functions, which, in turn, eliminates the multiplicity of equilibria that arise when firms price at the kink of their demands in the inelastic case. However, the key comparative static result that price is inversely related to the degree of product differentiation when sellers compete in the vicinity of the local monopoly region is robust to generalization to elastic demands, meaning that the properties of the symmetric kinked equilibrium are quite general and not restricted to the case of firms pricing at the kink points of their demand curves (Mérel and Sexton 2010). Furthermore, the parameter space that supports these equilibria may be quite large.[9]

4.2 Non-Linear Transportation Costs

The realism of the linear transportation cost assumption depends upon the product context. If the product space is geographic, then linearity is quite reasonable, as shipping rates may be a fixed rate per unit distance traveled. In a geographic space context a realistic alternative to linearity would be strictly concave costs as a function of distance traveled, reflecting the economies that are often inherent in long-distance hauls. However, the literature has focused almost exclusively on substituting quadratic transportation costs in place of the linear function. Such a strictly convex relationship is sensible when working in product-characteristic space because it reflects an increasing rate of disutility on consumers' parts, when they consume products with a characteristic that deviates increasingly from their ideal (Neven 1985).

Quadratic transportation costs also play a crucial role for existence of a price equilibrium. When firms are located within the market segment, no price equilibrium may exist with linear transportation costs, but an equilibrium always exists for quadratic transportation costs. See Section 6 for further discussion on this issue in the context of location-then-price games. Quadratic transportation costs do not, however, eliminate the kink in firms' demand functions when consumers have inelastic demands (Mérel and Sexton 2010), meaning that the three regions of competition described in the preceding section are present, as are the multiplicity of price equilibria at the kink point.

---

[9] Mérel and Sexton (2010) demonstrate this point for demand functions of the form $q(p) = (1 - p)^{\varepsilon}$, where the size of the transition region (the analog to the kinked-equilibrium region of the unit demand case) relative to the duopoly competition region ranges from 0.3 to 1.0, depending upon the value of ε.

A second modeling decision regarding transportation costs must be made if the model includes elastic consumer demands, namely whether the transportation cost is incurred once per trip or on each unit purchased. A rationale exists for either choice. If the analysis concerns consumers traveling in geographic space to visit stores, then a one-time cost makes considerable sense because the main aspects of the cost, including the value of the consumer's time, are borne only once.[10] However, if a shipping charge is based on weight or volume shipped, the cost is incurred on each unit purchased. If the transportation cost is a disutility cost from travel in product-characteristic space, it is clearly borne on each unit purchased.[11]

4.3 The Market Space

A key generalization of the linear market space is the circular market due to Salop (1979), where firms locate along the rim of a circle. Salop wished to analyze long-run equilibrium under monopolistic competition, and for this purpose Hotelling's linear city is not satisfactory. Although it is possible to consider entry in Hotelling's framework, there is an inherent asymmetry created among firms when entry occurs—e.g., as soon as a third firm is added, one firm necessarily faces a competitor on both sides of the market, whereas the other two do not.[12] This problem is avoided when firms locate on the rim of the circle, although retaining symmetric locations in the face of entry implies that all firms "relocate" when an entrant joins the market.

Apart from this extension, Salop's model retains the other key features of the generalized Hotelling model presented in Section 3, meaning that for a fixed number of firms, each firm's demand typically exhibits a monopoly region, a competitive region, and a kink where those two regions intersect. The free-entry equilibrium is studied in detail in Section 7.

An alternative one-dimensional framework known as the spokes model has been proposed recently by Chen and Riordan (2007). The idea is to allow $N \geq 2$ "spokes," each of length $\frac{1}{2}$, to extend in any direction from the midpoint of Hotelling's line. Consumers are distributed uniformly on the network of spokes, and each firm produces a single product or brand located at the endpoint of a spoke. Several features distinguish the spokes model from the circle model. By creating a new spoke with customers located on it, entry has a market-expanding effect. Competition is

---

[10] Authors who have taken this approach include Stahl (1987), Anderson, Palma, and Thisse (1992), Rath and Zhao (2001), and Gu and Wenzel (2009a).

[11] Although a rationale can be made for either choice, model simplification is undoubtedly the driving factor for authors who assume the costs are independent of quantity. In essence the generality gained by assuming elastic demands comes at a cost in terms of a restrictive assumption on transportation costs.

[12] This aspect is illustrated in a model by Faminow and Benson (1990), who study competition among three firms on a finite line, one located at each endpoint and the third at the midpoint.

non-localized, enabling the spokes model to merge features of spatial and non-spatial models of monopolistic competition. Further, entry does not require the relocation of incumbent firms to retain symmetry.

4.4 Non-Nash Conjectures

We introduced the possibility of non-Nash price conjectures in Section 2, and models with this property have been explored in the spatial competition literature as well.[13] In the duopoly context, the impact of the reaction of a competitor, say firm b, to the price change of firm a is in terms of a's perception of how its market radius (equivalently its demand in the inelastic-demand case) is affected by a price change. For market radius $X = \frac{P_b - P_a + \gamma}{2\gamma}$ we have

$$\frac{\partial X}{\partial P_a} = \frac{1}{2\gamma} \left(\frac{\partial P_b}{\partial P_a} - 1 \right). \tag{4}$$

Under Bertrand–Nash conjectures, $\frac{\partial P_b}{\partial P_a} = 0$, and the analysis in Section 3 applies.[14] A main alternative conjecture that has been considered is $\frac{\partial P_b}{\partial P_a} = 1$, which is known as Löschian competition, and is equivalent to cartel behavior in the general oligopoly literature. Under Löschian competition, $\frac{\partial X}{\partial P_a} = 0$, i.e., the firm acts as if its market radius is fixed. In the model of Section 3, Löschian competition results in $P_a = P_b = R - \frac{\gamma}{2}$. This is the price that causes the participation constraint for consumers at the midpoint of the market to bind and is identical to the symmetric kinked-equilibrium price. Thus, for all values of the normalized transportation cost that support duopoly competition, firms with Löschian conjectures charge a higher price than a spatial monopolist. Capozza and Order (1977) confirm these relative prices for the case of linear consumer demands. The result most likely holds very generally because the spatial monopolist perceives two brakes on its pricing—the elasticity, if any, of individual consumer demands and the elasticity of aggregate demand due to market area being a function of the monopolist's price. The Löschian duopolist perceives only the first source of demand elasticity.

Other conjectures can also be considered. Normally, they would lie in the interval between the Bertrand–Nash and Löschian conjectures, i.e., $0 < \frac{\partial P_b}{\partial P_a} < 1$.[15] In general price charged is an increasing function of the conjecture because the greater the conjectured

---

[13] Key examples include Greenhut, Hwang, and Ohta (1975), Capozza and Order (1977), and Greenhut, Norman, and Hung (1987).

[14] Bertrand-Nash competition is often also called Hotelling-Smithies competition in the literature on spatial competition.

[15] Another specific conjecture that has received some attention in the spatial literature is known as Greenhut–Ohta competition, wherein firms assume that total price at the market boundary is fixed. Suppose, for example, that firm a decreases price. The only way the border price remains unchanged is if firm b responds by increasing its price. Thus, Greenhut–Ohta competition is even more "accommodating," and prices are lower, than under Bertrand–Nash competition.

price response by the rival firm, the smaller is the change in market area that the price-changing firm anticipates as a consequence of its action, and the less elastic the aggregate demand it perceives that it faces. Of course, all non-Nash conjectures suffer from the key limitation that at the "equilibrium point" each firm wishes to change its price unilaterally. For this reason, more recent analyses have focused on Bertrand–Nash behavior.

4.5 Discriminatory Pricing

FOB or mill pricing is non-discriminatory; differences among consumers in the total price paid exactly reflect differences in the costs of doing business with them. However, spatial markets often present opportunities to price-discriminate. Consider the base Hotelling model from Section 3. A price-discriminating spatial monopolist could charge each consumer a delivered price equal to R, and serve a market area, X_d, determined by the condition $R = c + \gamma X_d$, that is, $X_d = \frac{R-c}{\gamma}$. In this case the discriminating spatial monopolist serves twice the market area served by a non-discriminating monopolist, earns more profit, and achieves the socially efficient outcome, albeit at consumers' expense. This example illustrates a case of uniform delivered (UD) pricing, wherein each consumer faces the same delivered price, R, and the seller nominally absorbs all transportation costs. UD pricing is the most commonly practiced alternative to FOB pricing in a geographic pricing context (Greenhut 1981).

Spatial price discrimination is most intuitive in the context of geographic space and sellers who provide delivery of a product. In a general product-characteristic context, price discrimination implies sellers offering some or all possible varieties of the product, instead of a single variety, and charging prices for this "product line" that do not reflect fully the cost differentials among the varieties. Consider cheese content of pizza, for example. Consumers are horizontally differentiated for this attribute because some want a lot of cheese, but others want less owing to calories, dislike of cheese, etc. Under FOB pricing, a seller would offer only one amount of cheese per pizza and consumers would incur a disutility cost of "traveling" to consume that amount. A price-discriminating pizza seller would provide any amount of cheese over a range, in essence allowing consumers to "have it your way." Under UD pricing, extra cheese is "free."

Extension to include elastic consumer demands generally leaves intact a monopolist's incentive to price-discriminate. Most demand functions are more elastic at higher prices, meaning that more distant consumers, facing higher total prices under FOB pricing, have more elastic demands than their counterparts located closer to the seller. Thus, by absorbing some portion of the freight charges, the spatial monopolist achieves third-degree price discrimination. The optimal rate of freight absorption depends upon the convexity of consumer demand. For example, it is 50 percent for linear demand and more than 50 percent for strictly concave demands. UD pricing is optimal only for the case of perfectly inelastic demands, as in the base Hotelling model. Price discrimination based upon partial or full absorption of freight charges cannot be undermined by consumer arbitrage, but freight charges in excess of the actual transportation costs invite resales from consumers located near the seller to distant consumers.

Whereas competitive pressures undermine attempts to price-discriminate in the non-spatial world, competitive pressure may actually induce firms to price-discriminate in horizontally differentiated competition. The reason is that competition under horizontal differentiation occurs at the market boundaries; therefore, discriminating against consumers located in the proximity of the firm and in favor of distant consumers by absorbing some or all of the transportation costs enables the firm to charge a lower delivered price in the vicinity of the market boundary and, thus, compete more effectively for customers in this region.

5 APPLICATIONS

We discuss briefly applications of the Hotelling model to various food and agricultural industry problems. We consider first the applications to mixed duopoly competition involving a cooperative and investor-owned firm (IOF) by Fulton and Giannakas (2001) and Mérel, Saitone, and Sexton (2009). Fulton and Giannakas (2001) study competition between a consumer cooperative and an IOF. Utility from consumption differs according to whether a consumer purchases the product from the co-op or the IOF. Each consumer obtains a base utility, U, from consuming the product. Consumers are distributed uniformly according to a characteristic $\alpha \in [0, 1]$ which captures heterogeneous consumer preferences for the products supplied by the co-op and IOF. Utility from consuming a unit of product from the cooperative is $U - p_c + \lambda \alpha$ and utility from consuming a unit from the IOF is $U - p_i + \mu(1 - \alpha)$. Thus, utility is enhanced by unique factors, λ for the co-op and μ for the IOF, in a way that depends upon the consumer's characteristic α. The difference $\lambda - \mu$ can be interpreted as the degree of community preference for the co-op relative to the IOF, and can be made endogenous in a broader model and made a function of the cooperative's behavior. The co-op that maximizes member welfare always sets $p_c = c_c$, where c_c denotes the co-op's marginal cost of providing the product. Its reaction function is, thus, flat.

Fulton and Giannakas (2001) also study a co-op that maximizes profits, although that objective is difficult to interpret in the context of a consumer cooperative. It does make sense if the co-op is a marketing firm whose members have produced the product being sold. This is the approach taken by Mérel, Saitone, and Sexton (2009). The co-op and IOF compete to sell a branded product to consumers located on Hotelling's line. The authors study the implications of alternative co-op membership policies for the market's performance. A cooperative that has closed membership charges a higher price for its branded product than the competing IOF, and consequently has lower market share. An open-membership co-op forces the IOF to compete more aggressively to procure the farm product, and, thus, the open-membership co-op has a "yardstick of competition" effect on the market, although rents from its branded product are dissipated by the free entry into the cooperative.

The Hotelling model has been applied recently to studies of generic and brand advertising. The topic is important because many agricultural industries require mandatory contributions to fund generic advertising programs. Some producers, however, have complained that such programs are detrimental to their efforts to create product differentiation through advertising their own branded products (Crespi and Marette 2002). This issue has been studied recently in papers by Isariyawongse, Kudo, and Tremblay (2007, 2009), who adopt the standard Hotelling model with duopoly sellers. In Isariyawongse et al. (2007) the firms' locations are a function of their (persuasive) brand advertising and also possibly the amount of generic advertising,[16] while in Isariyawongse et al. (2009) the firms' net prices are a function of their informative advertising (which reduces consumers' search costs). The game evolves in three stages. Stage 3 is the standard Hotelling price competition,[17] and stage 2 involves advertising expenditures by each firm. A tax rate to finance generic advertising is set in stage 1.

The authors are concerned primarily with the question of generic advertising's effect on the individual firms' incentives to advertise and their profits. They consider two scenarios: (1) generic advertising expands the market but has no effect on firms' differentiation, and (2) generic advertising expands the market but decreases horizontal differentiation. If generic advertising has only a market-expanding effect, it has a positive effect on firms' advertising expenditures under either the persuasive or informative interpretation. However, its effect is indeterminate under the second scenario.

Xia and Sexton (2009) investigated price setting for fluid milk, based upon its fat content. Although fat content of fluid milk is a classic case of horizontal differentiation, fluid milk departs from the standard paradigm because there is a clear ranking by cost of the various fluid milk products, with skim milk cheapest to produce, followed by 1 percent, 2 percent, and whole milk because butterfat is the most expensive ingredient in raw milk. Further, a retailer sells all four fluid milk products, not just one, as in the prototype model.

Xia and Sexton (2009) were interested in how the differential-cost dimension of the horizontally differentiated milk products would affect pricing under alternative market structures including perfect competition, oligopoly, and monopoly. The monopoly case in particular features interesting comparative static results. For example, in the covered-market case, the price of skim milk is decreasing in the butterfat cost of milk,

---

[16] In particular, if we denote by θ_1 the location of the "left-side firm," then $\partial\theta_1/\partial B_1 < 0$, where B_1 is firm 1's expenditure on brand advertising. The same idea applies for firm 2, except that $\partial\theta_2/\partial B_2 > 0$. Thus, brand advertising creates product differentiation by moving firms away from the center of the product space.

[17] Equilibrium in the pricing stage is assumed to exist, although, given the model structure, existence of a price equilibrium is a severe problem. The next section of this paper discusses the existence-of-price-equilibrium issue in detail.

even though skim milk contains no butterfat. The 2 percent milk price is also decreasing in butterfat cost.[18]

6 THE FIRST STAGE OF HOTELLING'S LOCATION-THEN-PRICE GAME

Section 3 demonstrated that in spatial markets firms are able to extract positive rents and may make socially inefficient decisions even when they compete in a Bertand–Nash fashion. More insights into the potential inefficiency of horizontally differentiated markets are gained when one considers (1) the outcome of the location game and (2) entry decisions. This is the focus of the next two sections.

The interest in determining the outcome of the location stage of the Hotelling game (the ultimate purpose of Hotelling himself) mostly resides in the ability to determine whether spatial markets can reproduce the socially optimal degree of product differentiation. With inelastic demands, under the condition that all customers should be served, the socially optimal location of the two sellers minimizes the aggregate travel costs and corresponds to the first and third quartiles of the market length. A very prolific branch of the spatial differentiation literature has therefore been investigating the conditions under which the Hotelling-type game results in excess or deficient product differentiation. Unfortunately, no general principle of excess or deficient differentiation arises.

Hotelling's seminal article introduced the much debated principle of minimum differentiation: firms tend to locate close to one another at the market center. When extended to product differentiation along one characteristic, this result meant that two competing firms would choose products that closely resemble each other, and therefore Hotelling's result is sometimes referred to as "product clustering." However, despite its intuitive attractiveness, this principle turns out to be erroneous. In a seminal contribution, d'Aspremont, Gabszewic, and Thisse (1979) demonstrated that, although firms have an incentive to move from the endpoints of the market toward the center, once they reach the market quartiles, there is no solution to the second-stage price subgame. These authors then showed that if one trades the linear travel cost assumption for quadratic costs of the form $C(x) = \gamma x^2$, where x denotes the distance traveled, a price equilibrium exists for all locations pairs, and firms choose to locate at the endpoints of the market. Hence the opposite principle of maximum differentiation results.[19]

---

[18] This result is due to relative costs. If butterfat costs rise, whole milk becomes more expensive relative to its directly "competing" product, 2 percent milk. It is optimal to increase the price of whole milk, but if the market remains covered, this means that the price of 2 percent milk must decrease. The same principle applies to pricing of 1 percent and skim milk.

[19] Under quadratic costs, sellers will locate outside the market segment if they are allowed to do so (Tabuchi and Thisse 1995), a result remindful of major shopping centers being located on the periphery of cities.

More insights into the solution to the location problem on a horizontal line were provided by Economides (1984), who introduced a reasonably low consumer reservation price to the original Hotelling setting. But it was not until recently that the complete characterization of the set of symmetric location equilibria was derived by Hinloopen and van Marrewijk (1999), although for the specific case of linear disutility or travel cost. Interestingly, just as the price game was characterized by the coexistence of several price competition regimes, the varieties game also features several regimes, again dictated by the importance of transportation cost relative to the net value of output.

The assumptions of the model are as in Section 3. We consider a linear market of length one. Unless specified otherwise, consumers are located uniformly on the line and have unit demands for one of two varieties, subject to a reservation price R. They incur the travel costs $C(\,|\,x - x_i\,|\,)$, where x denotes the consumer's location and x_i the location of seller i. For simplicity, we set production costs c to zero.

6.1 The Undercutting Strategy and the Non-Existence of the Price Equilibrium

We focus on symmetric equilibria. D'Aspremont, Gabszewicz, and Thisse (1979) show that there does not exist a pure strategy equilibrium in the price subgame, for linear transportation costs, when sellers are located inside the market quartiles. The non-existence of equilibrium is traced to the fact that for such locations, starting from the candidate Nash equilibrium in prices, each firm has an incentive to undercut the other firm. Undercutting consists of quoting a *delivered* price that is slightly below that of the rival firm. In the absence of a reservation price, this means capturing the entire market. In the presence of a low enough reservation price, this implies capturing the rival's entire clientele, virtually driving her out of business.[20] The possibility of undercutting the rival firm implies that the profit function of each seller fails to be quasi-concave. This results in reaction functions that are discontinuous and may no longer intersect. While d'Aspremont et al. (1979) characterize the non-existence of equilibrium in the instance where there is no reservation price ($R \to \infty$;), it carries on to the case where the reservation price is finite, for locations close enough to the market center. Indeed,

---

[20] Obviously, there cannot be a price equilibrium where the two sellers undercut each other at the same time. The delivered price of seller a at a given location cannot be lower and higher than that of seller B at the same time. There cannot be a price equilibrium where one firm undercuts the rival firm either. To see why, suppose this were the case. If the undercutting firm's price were zero, it could increase its price by ε, still undercutting the other firm's price, and would then be earning positive profits. So, if there is to be an equilibrium with undercutting at all, the undercutting firm must be charging a positive price. The rival firm, which by definition is earning zero profits, could then decrease its own delivered price to the level of the delivered price of the undercutting firm, and start earning positive profits. So any equilibrium must lie in the portion where firms' profit functions are quadratic (the initial candidate Nash equilibrium).

no matter how small the reservation price of consumers, there always exists a set of locations in the vicinity of the market center for which a price equilibrium in pure strategies does not exist. A consequence of this fact is that the outcome of the location game must be defined as the pair of locations at which each seller maximizes second-stage profits, given the location of the other seller, over the subset of locations for which a second-stage price equilibrium exists. Said differently, when choosing where to locate, each seller is assumed to rule out locations for which there is no pure strategy equilibrium in the price subgame.

One way to remedy the non-existence of equilibrium in the price subgame for some location pairs is to modify the travel cost specification. D'Aspremont, Gabszewicz, and Thisse (1979) showed that if travel costs are assumed to be quadratic, a price equilibrium always exists for any location pair. As a result, quadratic costs have indeed been a popular assumption in the related literature (see, e.g., Economides 1989). Economides (1986) investigates the price equilibrium existence region for power travel costs of the form $C(x) = x^{\alpha}$, $\alpha > 0$, with infinite reservation price. (The market length is normalized to one.) With linear travel costs ($\alpha = 1$), an equilibrium exists whenever sellers are located outside the market quartiles. As α increases, the range of symmetric locations for which an equilibrium exists expands, reaching the entire possible spectrum for $\alpha = 2$, that is, for exactly quadratic costs.[21]

Another branch of literature has investigated the possibility that firms compete in mixed strategies in the price subgame (Osborne and Pitchik 1987; Anderson 1988). Osborne and Pitchik (1987) find that in the original Hotelling (1929) model, there is a unique subgame perfect equilibrium in which the location choices of the two firms are pure. Firms locate at a distance of 0.27 from the market endpoints, that is, slightly within the market quartiles. At this equilibrium, the support of the second-stage equilibrium price strategy is the union of two short intervals, with most of the probability weight in the upper interval, reminiscent of occasional sales by the firms.

6.2 Outcome of the Location Game with Linear Travel Costs and Finite Reservation Price

Economides (1984) first recognized that introducing a relatively low reservation price into Hotelling's model would ensure the existence of equilibrium in the price subgame for a larger range of products (that is, for a larger range of location pairs) than when the reservation price is infinite. Hence, assuming a relatively low reservation price for consumers, he analyzed the outcome of the location-then-price game and concluded

---

[21] Egli (2007) investigates the related case where consumers have heterogeneous travel costs, these costs being restricted to be either linear or quadratic. The reservation price is high enough so that all consumers buy from either seller. He finds that a price equilibrium exists for all possible location pairs if and only if the share of consumers with linear costs is less than one half.

that in such instances sellers have a tendency to move away from each other to the point where they constitute local monopolies. That is, they choose location so as to avoid any form of price competition with the rival firm. Generally, for low reservation price there will therefore be a continuum of equilibrium locations, as long as the market is large enough to host two local monopolies with disjoint market radii. This result came in sharp contrast to Hotelling's principle of minimum differentiation, as did d'Aspremont, Gabszewicz, and Thisse (1979)'s result for quadratic travel costs.[22] As argued by Hinloopen and van Marrewijk (1999), Economides (1984)'s analysis holds for values of the normalized transportation cost κ larger than 2. This is because when sellers are isolated monopolists, the length of their market is exactly equal to $\frac{R}{\gamma}$, so that they do not overlap if and only if $\frac{R}{\gamma} \leq \frac{1}{2}$, that is, $\kappa \geq 2$.

Hinloopen and van Marrewijk (1999) completed the characterization of the solution to the two-stage game for intermediate values of the normalized travel costs ($0 < \kappa \leq 2$) and introduced the principle of "almost intermediate product differentiation." More specifically, these authors identified two subregions that closely parallel the "competitive" and "kinked-equilibrium" regions identified above for the price subgame where sellers are located at the endpoints of the market line. For both regions, the entire market segment is served, including sellers' "hinterlands."

Firms' locations on the unit segment are denoted h_i, for $i \in \{a, b\}$. For values of the reservation price just higher than those considered in Economides (1984), corresponding to values of the normalized transportation cost κ in the range $\left[\frac{4}{3}, 2\right]$, Hinloopen and van Marrewijk (1999) find that sellers will locate exactly at the market quartiles. This location outcome is insensitive to marginal changes in the market parameters (the transportation cost γ or the reservation price R), and the second-stage equilibrium price is equal to $R - \frac{\gamma}{4}$. It is therefore increasing in the reservation price R, and decreasing in the transport cost γ. Hinloopen and van Marrewijk (1999) call this Nash equilibrium a type II equilibrium because the first-stage profit function of each seller $\prod_i\left(h_i, h_j^*\right)$ has the shape of a "tent with a sharp ridge." More precisely, it is non-differentiable at its maximum h_i^*, just as the profit function of a seller in the above "kinked equilibrium" was maximized at its kink.[23] The authors call the outcome of the second-stage price game when $\kappa \in \left[\frac{4}{3}, 2\right]$ a "touching equilibrium with full supply," and it is conceptually similar to the kinked equilibrium of Section 3.

---

[22] Note that these two violations of Hotelling's principle are conceptually different. In the case of quadratic costs with no reservation price, firms still compete in price, even though they may be far apart. This is not the case when the reservation price is low so that firms constitute separate monopolies.

[23] In the price game with fixed location, the profit functions have both prices as arguments, while in the first stage of the location-then-price game, they have locations as arguments. Interestingly, the non-differentiability of the profit function at the optimizing price in a kinked equilibrium directly translates into the non-differentiability of the profit function at the optimizing location in the location game in the type II equilibrium.

In contrast, for higher values of the reservation price (or lower values of the transportation cost), the symmetric Nash equilibrium occurs at a point where each seller's profit function $\prod_i \left(h_i, h_j^* \right)$ is differentiable, and Hinloopen and van Marrewijk (1999) call this equilibrium "type I". In a type I equilibrium, sellers locate within the market quartiles, approaching the center of the market as travel costs decrease or the reservation price increases. The second-stage equilibrium price is equal to $\frac{\gamma}{2}$ and corresponds to what Hinloopen and van Marrewijk (1999) call a "competitive equilibrium with full supply," conceptually similar to the competitive regime introduced in Section 3. As sellers move toward the market center with decreasing κ, competition intensifies between them and the equilibrium price decreases. The limit of this somewhat rehabilitated "principle of minimum differentiation" is attained when the normalized transportation cost hits the critical value of $\kappa = \frac{8}{7}$. At this point sellers are located at exactly $\frac{3}{8}$ of the market endpoints, that is, halfway between the quartiles and the midpoint of the market segment. They are thus separated by a fourth of the market length, and that is the closest to one another they will get, at least if one is to focus on pure strategy equilibria.

Overall, except for the case noted by Economides (1984) where sellers constitute local monopolies, the equilibrium distance between competing sellers is always between a fourth and a half of the market length, hence the principle of "almost intermediate product differentiation." For lower values of κ, the non-existence problem in the second stage prevents the existence of a solution in the first stage, because the relocation tendencies of each firm are toward the inner portion of the market where the price equilibrium in pure strategies does not exist. This problem did not happen for higher values of κ, because even though a price equilibrium did not exist for a certain range of location pairs, relocation tendencies were away from such locations.

When normalized travel costs κ are low enough that all customers should be served, the socially optimal location of the two sellers is at the market quartiles, in order to minimize total transportation costs. The distribution of surplus between sellers and customers in the second stage has no relevance for social surplus maximization. Were we to introduce elastic demands, the analysis of the optimality of the location decisions of firms would need to be refined, because the pricing outcome in the second stage is then suboptimal. Optimality would require marginal cost pricing (here $p = 0$).

The work of Hinloopen and van Marrewijk (1999) completed the analysis of spatial duopoly under the assumption of Nash conjectures, finite reservation price, and linear travel costs. But are their results robust to the introduction of alternate travel cost specifications? In particular, following Neven (1985), who argues that quadratic costs are better suited for models of variety choice, would such travel costs lead to similar location outcomes? As already noted, with linear costs and sufficiently large reservation price, no location equilibrium exists because relocation tendencies push sellers toward the center of the market segment where there is no pure strategy price equilibrium. In contrast, with quadratic costs the symmetric equilibrium locations are at the endpoints.

Economides (1986) investigates the outcome of the location-then-price game on a Hotelling line with no reservation price for a class of transportation costs of the form $C(x) = x^\alpha, \alpha \geq 1$. He concludes that neither Hotelling's principle of minimum differentiation, nor the alternative principle of maximum differentiation (sellers locating at the market boundaries), is robust to the travel cost specification. If $\alpha < \frac{5}{3}$, the pure strategy equilibrium (when it exists) is strictly within the market segment, and for low values of α is within the market quartiles (insufficient differentiation). As expected, for convex enough cost specifications, excess product differentiation obtains. Therefore, depending on the structure of consumer preferences, the outcome of the game could display either excess or deficient product differentiation. This lack of robustness of the differentiation outcome was later confirmed by Anderson (1988), who assumes that consumers have linear-quadratic transport costs of the form $C(x) = \alpha x + \beta x^2$, and Egli (2007), who investigates the case where some consumers have linear costs while some others have quadratic costs. Not surprisingly, the degree of product differentiation observed in equilibrium is positively related to the overall convexity of the travel costs.

6.3 Relaxation of the Uniform Distribution Assumption

Another branch of the literature on location choice is concerned with the rigid assumption that consumers are uniformly distributed over the market segment. This is a relevant concern for horizontally differentiated food markets, as consumer tastes may be clustered around specific loci in product-characteristic space, rather than evenly distributed.

Anderson and Goeree (1997) investigate conditions on the consumer density $f(x)$ defined on a support $[x_1, x_2]$ under which a unique two-firm location-then-price equilibrium exists, for the case of quadratic transportation costs and in the absence of a consumer reservation price. Firms are allowed to locate outside the density boundaries. The authors show that for an equilibrium to exist and be unique, it suffices that the (symmetric) density function $f(x)$ be log-concave on $[x_1, x_2]$ (that is, that $\log(f)$ be a concave function), and that the function $H(x) = \frac{F(x)(1 - F(x))}{f(x)}$, where F denotes the cumulative distribution function of f, be strictly pseudo-concave.[24] The condition that H be strictly pseudo-concave is not very stringent and is satisfied for a whole array of commonly used density functions. In essence, it amounts to ensuring that the density function f be not "too concave." If it is, then the uniqueness of equilibrium is lost, and asymmetric equilibria can obtain. If f is "very concave," then the symmetric equilibrium may no longer exist, and only asymmetric equilibria obtain. This extends the result obtained by Tabuchi and Thisse (1995) for the special case of a symmetric triangular density.

---

[24] A function is strictly pseudo-concave if it is quasi-concave with at most one stationary point.

7 ENTRY, PRODUCT VARIETY

The issue of excess variety (too many products) or deficient variety (too few products) in a differentiated market, under free entry and scale economies, has interested economists at least since the first monopolistic competition model of Chamberlin (1933). The spatial competition literature, with its attendant interpretation as horizontal differentiation along one characteristic, has also developed models that provide insights into the potential inefficiency of market outcomes in differentiated markets with free entry. But just as the excess capacity result of Chamberlin (1933) proved not to be robust to model specification,[25] the outcomes of entry models in the spatial differentiation literature seem to depend crucially on the specification of consumer preferences. Here we present results from the spatially differentiated circular market developed by Salop (1979), a model that can be thought of as an extension of Hotelling's city to accommodate entry decisions by identical firms.

The change from a finite line to a circle allows us to abstract from boundary effects. Entry decisions are investigated focusing on symmetric equilibria where the distance between any two firms is constant, firms can relocate costlessly around the circle until profits are zero, and firms all charge the same mill price in equilibrium. Salop (1979) calls such an equilibrium a symmetric zero-profit Nash equilibrium (SZPE). The analysis requires the addition of a fixed production cost to firms' technologies. All potential firms have the same cost structure.[26]

Salop (1979) derives the number of varieties offered in equilibrium as a function of the market parameters. Since the unit demand assumption (subject to a reservation price) is maintained, the market outcome can easily be compared to the socially optimal number of varieties. Given the fixed cost, this socially optimal number of varieties is finite.

7.1 Characteristics of the SZPE

Consumers have unit demands subject to reservation price R and face linear transportation costs. Marginal costs are denoted c and the fixed cost F. As in the linear city model of Section 3, the perceived demand curve of any firm around the market circle consists of two portions: the monopoly demand (for high prices) and the competitive demand (for low prices).[27] There is a kink at the price separating those regimes, the

[25] For a discussion on this point, see, e.g., Lancaster (1990).

[26] If the fixed cost is zero and firms have identical, constant marginal costs of production, the socially optimal outcome, which is also obtained as the free-entry equilibrium, is that a firm establishes at each location, so that no travel costs are incurred any more. Conceptually, this replicates the outcome of a spot market with a homogeneous product.

[27] For even lower prices, a firm undercuts the neighboring firms and the quantity demanded increases discontinuously.

monopoly demand being flatter than the competitive demand curve. Denoting by P the price charged by the typical firm, by $\bar{P}$ the price charged by the two neighboring firms, and n the total number of firms around the circle, each firm's perceived demand in equilibrium is of the form

$$\begin{cases} Q^m = \dfrac{2}{\gamma}(R - P) \\[2mm] Q^c = \dfrac{1}{\gamma}\left(\bar{P} + \dfrac{\gamma}{n} - P\right) \end{cases}.$$

Therefore, the slope of demand in the monopoly region is twice as steep as in the competitive region, the same as for the generalized Hotelling model of Section 3.

In a SZPE, the endogenous variables (n^*, P^*) must be such that each firm maximizes profit at P^* given that the other $n^* - 1$ firms set price at P^*, and in addition each firm makes zero profit. Four regimes may arise. Simple derivations show the following:

1. If the average cost curve $AC(Q) = c + \frac{F}{Q}$ lies above the monopoly demand line $P(Q) = R - \frac{\gamma}{2}Q$, then no firm enters the market.
2. If $AC(Q)$ happens to be tangent to the monopoly demand $P(Q) = R - \frac{\gamma}{2}Q$, the equilibrium is monopolistic. Each firm sets price independently of each other and the market is generally not covered. The monopoly equilibrium configuration happens only under the restrictive condition that $R - c = \sqrt{2\gamma F}$. The equilibrium price is then $P_m = R - \sqrt{\frac{\gamma F}{2}} = c + \sqrt{\frac{\gamma F}{2}}$. The maximum number of firms is $n_m = \sqrt{\frac{\gamma}{2F}}$. (With n_m firms the market is "just" covered.)
3. For $R - c \in \left(\sqrt{2\gamma F}, \frac{3}{2}\sqrt{\gamma F}\right)$, a kinked equilibrium arises. The equilibrium price is then $P_k = R - \frac{\gamma}{2n_k}$ and the equilibrium number of firms n_k solves the equation[28]

$$Fn_k + \frac{\gamma}{2n_k} = R - c.$$

4. For $R - c \geq \frac{3}{2}\sqrt{\gamma F}$, the competitive equilibrium configuration occurs. This equilibrium corresponds to the "monopolistically competitive equilibrium" of Chamberlin (1933).[29] The equilibrium number of firms is then $n_c = \sqrt{\frac{\gamma}{F}}$ and the equilibrium price is $P_c = c + \sqrt{\gamma F}$.

Note that in Salop's model the existence of equilibrium is not threatened by the undercutting strategy, even though transportation costs are linear. The reason is that for such a strategy to be profitable to a firm, the undercutting price $\bar{P} - \frac{\gamma}{n}$ must be no

---

[28] We note a mistake in Salop (1979)'s article in his equations (20) and (21). The equilibrium price, using his notation, should read $p_k = v - \frac{c}{2n}$. The mistake also appears in Greenhut, Norman, and Hung (1987: 86).

[29] We refrain from using the term "monopoly" in this chapter to avoid confusion with the monopoly equilibrium configuration.

lower than marginal costs, a condition that is not satisfied for any of the equilibrium configurations identified above.

7.2 Comparative Statics

In the monopolistic competition model of Chamberlin (1933), the equilibrium product variety (number of firms) is inversely related to the extent of economies of scale and the substitutability between potential varieties. The number of firms increases (and so does the equilibrium price) as the scale economies decrease and as the elasticity of substitution between varieties decreases. In competitive equilibrium in the Salop model, interpreting the travel cost γ as a measure of the substitutability between product varieties, these relationships are preserved.

In light of the analysis of Section 3, it is not surprising that the kinked equilibrium in Salop's model displays perverse comparative static properties compared to the Chamberlinian competitive equilibrium. In the long run where firms are allowed to enter and exit the market, an increase in either marginal or fixed costs lowers equilibrium prices. This is due to the exit of firms, which allows remaining firms to exploit scale economies. Social welfare (in this case also equal to consumer welfare) rises. An increase in the reservation price R raises price and variety. Price rises by more than the increase in R, as scale economies are lost. Interestingly enough, consumer welfare decreases. Interpreting the increase in valuation as the outcome of advertising, this result points to the perverse effect of advertising when the equilibrium occurs at the kink of firms' demand. (Although, as pointed out by Salop 1979, if advertising is costly and raises either m or F, the cost increase itself will have a positive effect on consumer welfare!)

Finally, increases in the travel costs γ decrease equilibrium price. The number of firms n_k decreases, also the opposite of what would happen in the competitive equilibrium configuration.

7.3 Optimal Variety

Salop's model can be used to assess the social optimality of the above-described long-run equilibria. In particular, we can compare the equilibrium number of firms with the socially optimal variety. (As long as the fixed cost is positive, the socially optimal number of firms is finite.) Here, it is assumed that the parameters of the model are such that the entire market should be served.

Given the assumption that consumers are uniformly distributed along the unit circle, for an n-firm industry the average consumer travels a distance of $\frac{1}{4n}$. Aggregate social welfare is then defined as the net consumer valuation $R - c$, minus the average transport cost $\frac{\gamma}{4n}$, minus the sum of all fixed costs nF, as

$$W(n) = R - c - \frac{\gamma}{4n} - nF.$$

(Remember that the number of consumers is normalized to one.) This leads to the socially optimal number of brands, $n_w = \frac{1}{2}\sqrt{\frac{\gamma}{F}}$. Thus, we have

$$n_w < n_m < n_k < n_c$$

and it is clear that the spatial competition equilibrium displays excess variety. This is reminiscent of Chamberlin's excess capacity result, although it is driven by different assumptions. While Chamberlin's result arises from the fact that firms produce at an output below their minimum efficient scale, with no consideration to consumers' taste for variety, in Salop's model the optimum is achieved when the change in the net surplus of the average consumer from an additional brand—a surplus that positively depends on the number of firms—equals the fixed cost of adding this new brand. Unfortunately, Salop's ranking is not robust and depends crucially on the distribution of consumers and their preferences (in this case, the travel cost function). However, Salop (1979) indicates that for a uniform consumer distribution, "any utility function that is concave in distance will yield excess variety." Gu and Wenzel (2009a) also argue that Salop's result depends crucially on the assumption of unit demands, and show that the excess entry result is not robust to generalization to constant-elasticity demands.

8 HIGHER DIMENSIONS OF PRODUCT DIFFERENTIATION

Restricting firms' and consumers' locations to a single dimension is an important limitation of a Hotelling model. Many products, including food, are differentiated in multiple dimensions. An advantageous entry strategy may involve introducing a whole new dimension to the characteristic space (Caplin and Nalebuff 1991). Thus, it is important to consider extending the analysis to multiple dimensions of product differentiation. This literature has benefited from very general results regarding existence of price equilibria due to Caplin and Nalebuff (1991) in product markets characterized by multiple dimensions of differentiation.[30]

A basic extension relevant to either geographic or product-characteristic space is to extend competition to two dimensions. Tabuchi (1994) considers duopoly competition on a finite plane, with a uniform rectangular distribution of consumers, inelastic demands with no reservation price, FOB pricing, Nash conjectures, and quadratic transportation costs, with consumers required to travel along a rectangular grid. Let

---

[30] Caplin and Nalebuff (1991) define conditions on individual demand and on aggregation of demand that suffice to avoid the discontinuities in payoff functions that cause non-existence of pure-strategy equilibria, as in the case of Hotelling's original model or when firms adopt uniform-delivered prices.

firm a be located at (x_a, y_a) and firm b be located at (x_b, y_b). Then a consumer located at (x, y) is indifferent between the two sellers if

$$P_a + (x_a - x)^2 + (y_a - y)^2 = P_b + (x_b - x)^2 + (y_b - y)^2. \tag{5}$$

The locus of indifferent consumers is a straight line that is perpendicular to the line connecting the two firms' locations, a property that converts the two-dimensional uniform distribution of consumers to a one-dimensional non-uniform distribution. Tabuchi (1994) derives the interesting result in the two-stage location-pricing game that, for a rectangular market, firms operate at the opposite midpoints of the short side of the rectangle. Thus, the principle of maximum differentiation that obtains in the one-dimensional analog of this model (see Section 6), which would involve locations at opposite corners in two dimensions, does not hold. Instead there is maximum differentiation in one of the dimensions, but minimum differentiation in the other.

Irmen and Thisse (1998) asked whether Tabuchi's result on maximum differentiation in one dimension and minimum differentiation in the other would hold for $n > 2$ dimensions of differentiation, again for the case of duopoly competition with quadratic transportation costs and inelastic consumer demands. These authors introduce a "salience coefficient" into consumers' utility functions such that the loss in utility in departing from the consumer's ideal location, $\mathbf{z} = (z_1, \ldots, z_n)$, depends upon the salience of the attribute to the consumer. Thus, we have indirect utility for consuming firm a's product of the form

$$V_a(\mathbf{z}) = S - P_a - \sum_{k=1}^{n} t_k(z_k - a_k)^2, \tag{6}$$

where t_k is the salience factor of product characteristic k and a_k is the attribute of characteristic k supplied by firm a's product. Thus, characteristics have different weights but the weights are the same across consumers. Indifferent consumers are defined by the usual condition of equality of indirect utilities from patronizing either seller, but the set of indifferent consumers now comprises a $(n-1)$ dimensional hyperplane.

Tabuchi's result suggests that differentiation in one product dimension is sufficient to limit price competition, enabling the firms to choose minimum differentiation in the second product dimension. Irmen and Thisse (1998) demonstrate that this intuition extends to the $n > 2$ case, as long as the most salient product characteristic is sufficiently dominant relative to the others, enabling them to claim that Hotelling (1929) was "almost right" concerning his claim of minimum differentiation in the unidimensional differentiation case. The two firms choose midpoint locations (minimum differentiation) for all except the most salient product characteristic, and choose maximum differentiation for it. Since firms compete over the marginal consumer, limiting the dimensions of product differentiation limits the mass of indifferent consumers, making each firm's demand less elastic in its own price, and thereby yielding a higher equilibrium price, than if differentiation occured in multiple dimensions. This result may help explain various behaviors in the food sector. For example, fast-food restaurants often agglomerate in geographic space while differentiating themselves in menu offerings. Various packaged foods and soft drinks differentiate in caloric (sweetener) content but are very similar in other product dimensions.

A quite different approach to introducing multiple dimensions of differentiation is to combine spatial and non-spatial differentiation. This is the focus of work by de Palma et al. (1985), Anderson and de Palma (1988), Anderson, de Palma, and Thisse (1989b), and Anderson, de Palma, and Thisse (1989a), who adapted the stochastic utility formulation of the logit model due to McFadden (1973) to characterize utilities of consumers located along Hotelling's line. To see how these models work, assume the framework of the generalized Hotelling model from Section 3, in which case the indirect utility of a consumer located at point x of purchasing a unit from firm i located at x_i is $v_i(x) = R - P_i - \gamma |x - x_i|$. This utility specification is augmented in the following way: $u_i(x) = v_i(x) + \mu \varepsilon_i$, where ε_i is a random variable distributed with zero mean and unit variance, and μ is a positive constant that measures the degree of heterogeneity in consumers' tastes. Intuitively, this random component represents sellers' uncertainty regarding consumers' preferences.

Firms' demands are now probabilistic, with the probability $Pr_i(x)$ that a consumer located at x will purchase from seller i written as $Pr[u_i(x) > u_j(x)]$ for the case of a single competing firm j. If we assume that the ε_i are identically and independently Weibull-distributed, then $Pr_i(x)$ is given by the logit model (McFadden 1973)[31]

$$Pr_i(x) = \frac{e^{(R - P_i - \gamma |x - x_i|)/\mu}}{\sum_{k=1}^{2} e^{(R - P_k - \gamma |x - x_k|)/\mu}}. \tag{7}$$

This extension brings a couple of nice benefits. First, it creates overlapping geographic market areas, which seems consistent with reality in many settings. Second, it avoids the discontinuities in demands and payoffs that create the problems of non-existence of price equilibrium for the FOB pricing and uniform-delivered pricing cases. Let $0 < x_i < \frac{1}{2}$ define firm i's location on Hotelling's line and assume $x_i < x_j$. Further, following de Palma et al. (1985), let $P_i = P_j = P$. Then firm i's demand is defined by three probability functions, a constant (high) probability that it will attract consumers in its hinterland region, a monotone function defining the probability it will obtain a consumer located at point x in the interior region between x_i and x_j, and a constant (low) probability it will attract consumers in j's hinterland region. These probabilities vary in an intuitive way as functions of γ (the importance of the spatial dimension of differentiation), μ (the importance of the non-spatial dimension), and $|x_i - x_j|$ (in the two hinterland regions) or $(x_i - x)$ in the interior region. Obviously, a firm's chances of obtaining customers in its rival's hinterland region are increasing (decreasing) in $\mu(\gamma)$.

For μ large enough relative to γ, de Palma et al. (1985) establish minimum differentiation, i.e., firms agglomerate in the middle of the market as a Nash equilibrium to the location game. The benefits of centralized location outweigh the costs of more intense price competition in these cases because of the role of μ in moderating the price competition.

---

[31] Ch. 5 in this volume, by Adamowicz and Swait, develops logit demand models in detail.

9 CONCLUSION

Product differentiation is certainly one of the salient characteristics of today's food markets in developed economies. Whether corporate giants or small farmer cooperatives, producers are increasingly differentiating their products and adding more dimensions and attributes to them, be it nutritional profile, environmental stewardship, fair labor practices, or the absence of genetically modified products. We believe that the concept of horizontal differentiation, where consumers have a preferred variety and are heterogeneous in this respect, is suitable to the characterization of many interesting problems in food marketing.

If a market is best described as being horizontally differentiated, two attendant questions arise: from an economic standpoint, will the market supply an excessive or deficient *number* of varieties, and will these varieties be *too close* or *too far apart* on the characteristics spectrum? Since the seminal work of Hotelling (1929), research in theoretical industrial economics has sought to answer these questions. It is well known that Chamberlin (1933)'s excess capacity result is contingent upon how demand is modeled, and there may have been hope that more "structural" models borrowed from the spatial competition literature would provide a definite answer to them. Sadly, to date no general enough principle of minimum or maximum differentiation has surfaced, and results regarding excess variety also lack robustness. This lack of robustness also applies to the study of equilibrium price in spatially differentiated markets. Simple comparative statics of the equilibrium price were shown to be ambiguous, and opposite to conventional wisdom for intermediate degrees of product differentiation.

One thing the prolific literature in the line of Hotelling has accomplished, however, is to point out the conditions under which minimum, maximum, or intermediate differentiation may obtain, and similarly regarding the equilibrium number of varieties. This sensitivity of results to model specification makes it imperative that the analyst make careful choices (e.g., magnitude of reservation price, linear or quadratic disutility, form of demand function, number of dimensions of differentiation) that are descriptive of the intended application.

REFERENCES

Anderson, S. P. 1988. "Equilibrium Existence in the Linear Model of Spatial Competition." *Economica* 55: 479–91.

——and A. de Palma. 1988. "Spatial Price Discrimination with Heterogeneous Products." *Review of Economic Studies* 55: 573–92.

——and J. K. Goeree. 1997. "Location, Location, Location." *Journal of Economic Theory* 77: 102–27.

——, A. de Palma, and J.-F. Thisse. 1989a. "Demand for Differentiated Products, Discrete Choice Models and the Characteristics Approach." *Review of Economic Studies* 56: 21–35.

Anderson, S. P., A. de Palma, and J.-F. Thisse. 1989b. "Spatial Price Policies Reconsidered." *Journal of Industrial Economics* 38: 1–18.

——————.1992. *Discrete Choice Theory of Product Differentiation*. Cambridge, MA: MIT Press.

Boeckem, S. 1994. "A Generalized Model of Horizontal Product Differentiation." *Journal of Industrial Economics* 42/3: 287–98.

Caplin, A., and B. Nalebuff. 1991. "Aggregation and Imperfect Competition: On the Existence of Equilibrium." *Econometrica* 59: 25–59.

Capozza, D., and R. V. Order. 1977. "Pricing under Spatial Competition and Spatial Monopoly." *Econometrica* 45/6: 1329–38.

Chamberlin, E. H. 1933. *The Theory of Monopolistic Competition*. Cambridge, MA: Harvard University Press.

Chen, Y., and M. H. Riordan. 2007. "Price and Variety in the Spokes Model." *Economic Journal* 117: 897–921.

Cowan, S., and X. Yin. 2008. "Competition Can Harm Consumers." *Australian Economic Papers* 47/3: 264–71.

Crespi, J., and S. Marette. 2002. "Generic Advertising and Product Differentiation." *American Journal of Agricultural Economics* 84/3: 691–701.

d'Aspremont, C., J. J. Gabszewicz, and J.-F. Thisse. 1979. "On Hotelling's 'Stability in Competition'." *Econometrica* 47/5: 1145–50.

de Palma, A., V. Ginsburgh, Y. Y. Papageorgiou, and J.-F. Thisse. 1985. "Principle of Minimum Differentiation Holds under Sufficient Heterogeneity." *Econometrica* 53: 767–81.

Dixit, A. K., and J. E. Stiglitz. 1977. "Monopolistic Competition and Optimum Product Diversity." *American Economic Review* 67: 297–308.

Economides, N. S. 1984. "The Principle of Minimum Differentiation Revisited." *European Economic Review* 24: 345–68.

——1986. "Minimal and Maximal Product Differentiation in Hotelling's Duopoly." *Economics Letters* 21: 67–71.

——1989. "Symmetric Equilibrium Existence and Optimality in Differentiated Product Markets." *Journal of Economic Theory* 47/1: 178–94.

Egli, A. 2007. "Hotelling's Beach with Linear and Quadratic Transportation Costs: Existence of Pure Strategy Equilibria." *Australian Economic Papers* 46/1: 39–51.

Faminow, M., and B. Benson. 1990. "Integration of Spatial Markets." *American Journal of Agricultural Economics* 72/1: 49–62.

Fulton, M., and C. Giannakas. 2001. "Organizational Commitment in a Mixed Oligopoly: Agricultural Cooperatives and Investor-Owned Firms." *American Journal of Agricultural Economics* 83/5: 1258–65.

Greenhut, M. 1981. "Spatial Pricing in the U.S.A., West Germany, and Japan." *Economica* 48: 79–86.

——, M. Hwang, and H. Ohta. 1975. "Observations on the Shape and Relevance of the Spatial Demand Function." *Econometrica* 43/4: 669–82.

——, G. Norman, and C.-S. Hung. 1987. *The Economics of Imperfect Competition: A Spatial Approach*. Cambridge: Cambridge University Press.

Gu, Y., and T. Wenzel. 2009a. "A Note on the Excess Entry Theorem in Spatial Models with Elastic Demand." *International Journal of Industrial Organization* 27/5: 567–71.

——————.2009b. *Product Variety, Price Elasticity of Demand and Fixed Cost in Spatial Models*. Ruhr Economic Papers No. 92. Bochum: Ruhr Graduate School of Economics.

Hinloopen, J., and C. van Marrewijk. 1999. "On the Limits and Possibilities of the Principle of Minimum Differentiation." *International Journal of Industrial Organization* 17: 735–50.

Hotelling, H. 1929. "Stability in Competition." *Economic Journal* 39/153: 41–57.

Irmen, A., and J.-F. Thisse. 1998. "Competition in Multi-Characteristics Space: Hotelling Was Almost Right." *Journal of Economic Theory* 78: 76–102.

Isariyawongse, K., Y. Kudo, and V. J. Tremblay. 2007. "Generic and Brand Advertising in Markets with Product Differentiation." *Journal of Agricultural and Food Industrial Organization* 5, art. 6.

———. 2009. "Generic Advertising in Markets with Informative Brand Advertising." *Journal of Agricultural and Food Industrial Organization* 7, art. 1.

Lancaster, K. J. 1966. "A New Approach to Consumer Theory." *Journal of Political Economy* 74/2: 132–57.

——— 1990. "The Economics of Product Variety: A Survey." *Marketing Science* 9/3: 189–206.

Lerner, A. P., and H. W. Singer. 1937. "Some Notes on Duopoly and Spatial Competition." *Journal of Political Economy* 45: 145–86.

McFadden, D. 1973. "Conditional Logit Analysis of Qualitative Choice Behavior." In P. Zarembka, ed., *Frontiers of Econometrics*. New York: Academic Press.

Mérel, P. R., and R. J. Sexton. 2010. "*Kinked-Demand Equilibria and Weak Duopoly in the Hotelling Model of Horizontal Differentiation.*" *The B.E. Journal of Theoretical Economics* 10/1.

———, T. L. Saitone, and R. J. Sexton. 2009. "Cooperatives and Quality-Differentiated Markets: Strengths, Weaknesses, and Modeling Approaches." *Journal of Rural Cooperation* 37/4: 201–25.

———, R. J. Sexton, and A. Suzuki. 2009. "Optimal Investment in Transportation Infrastructure when Middlemen Have Market Power: A Developing-Country Analysis." *American Journal of Agricultural Economics* 91/2: 462–76.

Neven, D. 1985. "Two Stage (Perfect) Equilibrium in Hotelling's Model." *Journal of Industrial Economics* 33/3: 317–25.

Osborne, M. J., and C. Pitchik. 1987. "Equilibrium in Hotelling's Model of Spatial Competition." *Econometrica* 55/4: 911–22.

Peitz, M. 2002. "Price Equilibrium in Address Models of Product Differentiation: Unit-Elastic Demands." *Economic Theory* 20: 849–60.

Rath, K. P., and G. Zhao. 2001. "Two Stage Equilibrium and Product Choice with Elastic Demand." *International Journal of Industrial Organization* 19: 1441–55.

Salop, S. C. 1979. "Monopolistic Competition with Outside Goods." *Bell Journal of Economics* 10/1: 141–56.

Stahl, K. 1987. "Theories of Urban Business Location." In E. S. Mills, ed., *Handbook of Regional and Urban Economics*, 2: *Urban Economics*. Amsterdam: North-Holland.

Tabuchi, T. 1994. "Two-Stage Two-Dimensional Competition between Two Firms." *Regional Science and Urban Economics* 24: 207–27.

——— and J.-F. Thisse. 1995. "Asymmetric Equilibria in Spatial Competition." *International Journal of Industrial Organization* 13: 213–27.

Xia, T., and R. J. Sexton. 2009. "Retail Prices for Milk by Fat Content: A New Theory and Empirical Test of Retailer Pricing Behavior." *Journal of Agricultural and Resource Economics* 34/2: 256–75.

CHAPTER 11

....

CONSUMER DEMAND AND WELFARE IN EQUILIBRIUM DISPLACEMENT MODELS

....

MICHAEL K. WOHLGENANT[*]

1 INTRODUCTION
....

Equilibrium Displacement Models (EDMs) have a prominent place in applied economic analysis. The class of models defined as EDMs is technically a set of comparative static results expressed in elasticity form. One major advantage of such models is that they allow the researcher to focus on the important partial elasticities, quantity, and expenditure shares to gauge and calculate the relative importance of various supply/demand shifters on market equilibrium outcomes. Moreover, the researcher may use estimates of elasticities from previous research in the analysis without having to re-estimate all the equations going into the economic analysis. In contrast to a strictly econometric approach, the researcher often does not need to be concerned about functional form (if equilibrium changes are deemed small) and can focus on the policy applications of the model.

In the following sections, I review the basic elements of the model, discuss different applications of the models in the literature that show the utility of the approach, and then turn at last to issues related to statistical precision and approximation errors.

1.1 Conceptual Basis for EDM

EDMs are essentially logarithmic differential equations characterizing comparative statics of a system of equations describing movement from one equilibrium to another

* Special thanks are given to Jayson Lusk for extensive comments on an earlier draft that led to substantial improvements in the chapter. However, any remaining errors are the author's.

resulting from a change in one or more of the parameters of the equation system. Intriligator (1978) indicates that the technique of comparative statics can be combined with econometric results and current values of the variables to obtain quantitative estimates of comparative static results. Intriligator (1978: 495–6) states:

> Such [comparative static] results summarize the interaction between elements of the model, specifically the effect of changes in coefficients of the system and in exogenous and lagged endogenous variables on equilibrium values of all endogenous variables. They provide insight into the quantitative importance of influences contained in the model. They are also useful for purpose of forecasting and policy evaluation.

Consider a set of reduced-form equations derived from a set of supply and demand functions with m endogenous variables (i.e., prices and quantities), and with n exogenous supply and demand shift variables. Let a function $f : \mathbb{R}^n \to \mathbb{R}^m$ be differentiable at $x \in \mathbb{R}^n$. The derivative $f'(x)$ is an m $\times$ n matrix and therefore defines a linear function $L : \mathbb{R}^n \to \mathbb{R}^m$. By definition, this linear function is the differential of f at x, which can be written as follows:

$$dy = L(dx) = f'(x)dx \tag{1}$$

where dx is an arbitrary vector in $\mathbb{R}^n$ and dy is the vector in $\mathbb{R}^m$. This means that dx and dy may be viewed as variables (Binmore 1983: 214).

Because dx and dy are variables, we can introduce the new variables $d\log(x) = \hat{x}^{-1}dx$ and $d\log(y) = \hat{y}^{-1}dy$ where $\hat{x}$ and $\hat{y}$ are matrices with diagonal elements x_i and y_i; and $d\log(x)$ and $d\log(y)$ are vectors with elements $[d\log(x_i)]$ and $[d\log(y_j)]$, respectively. This specification assumes that x and y have strictly positive components, $x_i > 0$ and $y_i > 0$. Such an assumption seems reasonable in many applications with aggregate data where quantities, prices, and exogenous variables like income are strictly positive amounts. With these new variables, equation (1) can be represented as follows:

$$d\log(y) = \hat{y}^{-1}f'(x)\hat{x}\,d\log(x) \tag{2}$$

The interpretation now of the matrix of comparative statics, $\hat{y}^{-1}f'(x)\hat{x}$, is an m $\times$ n matrix of elasticities of y_i with respect to x_j. When using equation (2) in applications, discrete approximations are often necessary. In particular, equation (2) is often replaced by

$$\Delta\log(y) \cong \hat{y}^{-1}f'(x)\hat{x}\Delta\log(x) \tag{3}$$

The interpretation is that if $\Delta\log(x)$ is small and $\Delta\log(y) = \hat{y}^{-1}f'(x+\Delta x)\hat{x} - \hat{y}^{-1}f(x)\hat{x}$ is a small change induced by $\Delta\log(x)$, then equation (3) may be used to compute $\Delta\log(y)$. Such an approximation can be rationalized as a first-order Taylor's series approximation at x. A better approximation, of course, may be obtained by including the second-order terms in the approximation as well as the first-order terms. However, for many applications, the first-order approximation will suffice (Binmore 1983).

The expression in (3) will be exact in the case where the function f is a vector of constant elasticity functions. When f is a vector of linear functions, the vector functions in (3), $\Delta log (y)$ and $\Delta log (x)$, would be replaced by the vectors $\hat{y}^{-1}\Delta y$ and $\hat{x}^{-1}\Delta x$ (Alston and Wohlgenant 1990; Zhao, Mullen, and Griffith 1997).

1.2   History of EDM

The EDM is rooted in the concept of elasticity, first expressed in quantitative terms by Allen (1938) and Hicks (1957) with respect to the expression for the industry-derived demand for a factor. Buse (1958) first introduced the concept of total elasticity to agricultural economics. A significant paper by Muth (1964) was the first to express the reduced form for a system of supply and demand functions for a single product with two factors of production and exogenous supply/demand shifters in relative changes. Gardner (1975) used the Muth framework to develop implications for shifts in industry supply and demand on price spreads for food. Perrin and Scobie (1981) applied the Muth framework to systems of supply and demand functions in nutrient effects of food policies in developing countries. Sumner and Wohlgenant (1985) extended the Muth framework to include linkages with trade in the final product and the agricultural product. Other applications to trade include Gardner (1987), Duffy and Wohlgenant (1991), Brown (1995), Kinnucan and Christian (1997), and Wohlgenant (1999b). Perrin (1980) and Mullen, Wohlgenant, and Farris (1988) extended the EDM to include joint products. Lemieux and Wohlgenant (1989) used the EDM to evaluate the welfare effects of introducing a new technology, including effects of changes in quality in demand and effects with respect to length of run. Wohlgenant (1993) extended the Muth model to multi-stage industries with exogenous shifts in retail demand as well as exogenous shifts in farm supply and the marketing sector. Piggott, Piggott, and Wright (1995) used the EDM to evaluate cross-commodity generic advertising between beef, lamb, and pork in Australia. Kinnucan (1996) also considered evaluation of returns to advertising in interrelated markets. Kinnucan (1999), Kinnucan, Xiao, and Yu (2000), and Cranfield (2002) extended the EDM model with advertising to accommodate trade. Alston, Norton, and Pardey (1995) extended the basic EDM to include multiple countries/regions and multiple goods. Gotsch and Wohlgenant (2001) extended the EDM to account for dynamics present in perennial crops. Davis and Espinosa (1998) and Zhao, Mullen, and Griffith (2000) extended the EDM to incorporate stochastic components so that distributions of outputs rather than just point estimates of relative changes can be developed.

There are numerous applications other than the ones mentioned above, but these papers indicate the main developments of the EDM. In the following sections the major forms of the EDM and implications for consumer demand and welfare are highlighted.

2 THE EDM AND MEASURES OF CONSUMER WELFARE

2.1 The Basic EDM

The simplest EDM is one that describes equilibrium displacement for a single good in one market. Let E denote relative change (e.g., $EQ = \Delta Q/Q \cong \Delta \log(Q)$) so that

$$EQ_D = \eta EP - \eta \delta \qquad (4)$$

$$EQ_S = \varepsilon EP - \varepsilon k \qquad (5)$$

$$EQ_D = EQ_S \qquad (6)$$

where EQ_D is the relative change in demand, EQ_S is the relative change in supply, EP is the relative change in market equilibrium price, η is the price elasticity of demand for Q, ε is the price elasticity of supply for Q, δ is the relative change in demand ($\delta > 0$ denotes vertical, upward shift in demand), and k is the relative change in supply ($k > 0$ denotes vertical, upward shift in supply). The first equation represents the relative change in demand from a change in price and any exogenous shift in the demand curve. The second equation represents the relative change in supply from a change in price and any exogenous shift in the supply curve. The third equation is the market equilibrium condition. For given values of δ and k, the equilibrium relative changes in market price (EP) and market quantity (EQ) are as follows:

$$EP = \frac{\varepsilon k - \eta \delta}{\varepsilon - \eta} \qquad (7)$$

$$EP = \frac{-\eta\varepsilon(\delta - k)}{\varepsilon - \eta} \qquad (8)$$

In this simplest case of linear demand and supply functions with parallel demand and supply shifts, the change in consumer's surplus and producer's surplus can be determined geometrically with the aid of Figure 11.1 (Lemieux and Wohlgenant 1989; Alston, Norton, and Pardey 1995). Demand is shown to increase from D to D' owing to, say, effect of generic advertising on consumer demand, and supply increases from S to S' owing to, say, an improvement in technology allowing producers to produce the same output at lower cost. The algebraic formulae for the change in consumer's surplus and change in producer's surplus can be shown to equal

$$\Delta CS = AREA(ABP_1F) = -(\Delta P - \delta P_0)(Q_0 + 0.5\Delta Q) =$$

$$-P_0 Q_0 (EP - \delta)(1 + 0.5EQ) \qquad (9)$$

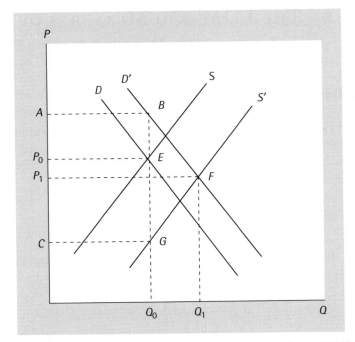

FIGURE 11.1 Welfare measurement with parallel supply–demand shifts

$$\Delta PS = Area(P_1 FCG) = (\Delta P - kP_0)(Q_0 + 0.5\Delta Q) =$$

$$P_0 Q_0 (EP - k)(1 + 0.5EQ) \tag{10}$$

represents the (vertical) exogenous change in supply; and where $\Delta P = EP \cdot P_0$ and $\Delta Q = EQ \cdot Q_0$.

The above formulae assume that the demand and supply curves are linear or can be approximated by linear functions in the neighborhood of the two market equilibrium points. Alternatively, one could assume constant elasticity functions for demand and supply so that EP and EQ would become $\Delta \log P$ and $\Delta \log Q$, respectively, instead of $\frac{\Delta P}{P_0}$ and $\frac{\Delta Q}{Q_0}$. The same formulae for relative change in price and quantity, equations (7) and (8), give exact answers when the demand and supply elasticities, and demand and supply shift parameters, are constants. The formulae for change in consumer's and producer's surplus can be shown to equal

$$\Delta CS = \int_{P_1}^{x} A(P_1 e^{-\delta})^{\eta} dP - \int_{P_0}^{x} AP_0 \, dP = -(1+\eta)^{-1} P_0 Q_0 (e^{(1+\eta)EP - \eta\delta} - 1) \tag{11}$$

$$\Delta PS = \int_0^{P_1} B(P_1 e^{-k})^\varepsilon \, dP - \int_0^{P_0} BP_0 \, dP = (1+\varepsilon)^{-1} P_0 Q_0 (e^{(1+\varepsilon)EP-\varepsilon k} - 1) \tag{12}$$

where the initial demand and supply functions are $Q_0 = AP_0$ and $Q_0 = BP_0$, respectively. The new demand and supply functions are $Q_1 = A(P_1 e^{-\delta})^\eta$ and $Q_1 = B(P_1 e^{-k})^\varepsilon$. The advantage of these formulae is that they can be used for sensitivity analysis of functional form and for type of demand/supply shift. The formulae in equations (9) and (10) are strictly for only parallel shifts in demand and supply, while the formulae in (11) and (12) are for proportional shifts in demand and supply.[1]

The above framework has been applied to a range of questions relating to shifts in supply from introduction of new technologies. Norton and Davis (1981) review applications of this basic model for evaluating rates of return to agricultural research. Alston, Norton, and Pardey (1995) provide an updated review of studies of this genre, including applications in the presence of trade in the agricultural product.

The literature in agricultural economics on incorporating demand shifts into the analysis has been quite limited. Unnevehr (1986) was one of the first to account for demand changes resulting from quality changes. She estimated the effects of changes in quality using hedonics and then represented these effects on the market for rice by a parallel shift in demand, which is appropriate when measuring change in consumer's surplus with equation (9). Lemieux and Wohlgenant (1989), in evaluating the effects on consumer's surplus from introduction of porcine somatotropin (PST), also assumed a parallel shift in demand and measured the combined effects of PST on demand and supply shifts. The demand shift parameter δ in this study was measured as consumer's willingness to pay for 10 percent leaner pork. Mullen and Alston (1994) take the same approach as Lemieux and Wohlgenant (1989) in measuring the impact of leaner lamb meat on demand by Australians for lamb meat. In two recent applications of the EDM, Lusk and Anderson (2004) and Weaber and Lusk (2010) use models with demand and supply shift variables to evaluate country-of-origin labeling and improvements in beef tenderness by genetic marker selection, respectively. Weaber and Lusk (2010) are notable in that they show how to model experimental data estimates of willingness to pay on demand shifts.

[1] The formula for change in producer's surplus with a proportional supply shift and constant elasticity of supply is presented in Zhao, Mullen, and Griffith (1997). Because the integrals in (11) diverge as $x \to \infty$ when η is constant and less than one in absolute value, they are best regarded as applying only for a limited range of variation in prices (Allen 1938: 201). The formula in equation (11) is obtained using the indirect utility function derived from the constant-elasticity demand function following the approach of Hausman (1981). Details on the derivation can be found in Wohlgenant and Zhao (2010).

2.2   Welfare Measurement Issue

The concept of consumer's surplus used in applications of the EDM is broadly consistent with the concept of compensating variation (Currie, Murphy, and Schmitz 1971). Compensating variation (CV) asks how much should a consumer be compensated, in response to a price change, in order for the consumer to reach the original indifference curve. Equivalent variation (EV) asks how much the consumer should be compensated to reach the new indifference curve. CV and EV can be applied using Hicksian demand curves. For specific agricultural commodities with small budget shares and/or small income elasticities, the income effect will be small so the error in use of consumer's surplus as an approximation to a change in CV or EV will be small (Willig 1976). For applications where the budget shares and/or income elasticities are not small (e.g., developing countries), if information is available with respect to the Slutsky equation in elasticity form, $\eta = \eta^c - w\eta_I$, (η^c is compensated or Hicksian own-price elasticity of demand, w is the expenditure share of the good relative to total consumer expenditure, and η_I is the income elasticity), then the expenditure share and income elasticity can be used to obtain the elasticity of demand for the Hicksian demand curve, which in turn could be used to approximate the change in consumer's surplus (Alston, Norton, and Pardey 1995, ch. 2). Irvine and Sims (1998) argue that better approximations can be obtained from taking a second-order Taylor's series approximation of the expenditure function and using the Slutsky equation to obtain Hicksian demand elasticities to approximate changes in CV.

Hausman (1981) suggests that whatever functional form we use, if our goal is to calculate CV or EV we should derive the expenditure function from the (assumed) demand function and then use the exact expenditure function to calculate CV or EV. He shows that there is an approximation error in using the standard measure of change in consumer's surplus applied to the Marshallian demand curve. He recommends deriving the indirect utility function through integration of the particular demand function assumed, and then using the expenditure function derived from the indirect utility function to calculate CV or EV. Hausman (1981) presents formulae for single price changes for linear and log-linear demand functions.

Similar issues arise in the case of functional forms in supply. Martin and Alston (1997) show that changes in producer's surplus due to new technology are not only sensitive to whether the supply shift is parallel or pivotal, but may not accurately represent the change in profit. This is especially the case with use of pivotal supply functions used to represent change in producer's surplus, which understates the change in profit. The problem is not easy to solve because how technology affects the market supply curve is not known in general and because there is no unique set of formulae available to capture the alternative representations of supply shifts. Similar to Irvine and Sims (1998), they recommend using change in profit from the profit function instead of change in producer's surplus, while representing technical change through scaling of the prices to incorporate the specific type of technical change modeled.

2.3   The EDM with Multiple Products

The EDM can be extended to include more than one market. One modification would be to expand the number of demand and supply functions. Consider, for example, the case of two goods, Q_x and Q_y (Gardner 1987):

$$EQ_x = \eta_x EP_x + \eta_{xy} EP_y \tag{13a}$$

$$EQ_x = \varepsilon_x (EP_x - EV_x) + \varepsilon_{xy}(EP_y - EV_y) \tag{13b}$$

$$EQ_y = \eta_{yx} EP_x + \eta_y EP_y \tag{13c}$$

$$EQ_y = \varepsilon_{yx}(EP_x - EV_x) + \varepsilon_y (EP_y - EV_y) \tag{13d}$$

where equations (13a) and (13b) represent demand and supply for good x, and equations (13c) and (13d) represent demand and supply for good y. V_x and V_y represent price wedges between consumer and producer prices such as excise taxes. These four equations can be solved simultaneously for EQ_x, EQ_y, EP_x, and EP_y for given values of EV_x and EV_y.

In this case, because of the interdependence between goods x and y, a change in either V_x or V_y will cause prices and quantities of both goods to change. Therefore, the change in consumer's surplus from such changes cannot be evaluated using the simple formulae in (9) or (10) or in (11) or (12). Gardner (1987) suggests taking a second-order Taylor's series approximation of the expenditure function to obtain:[2]

$$\Delta CS = -\sum_i Q_{i0} \Delta P_i + \frac{1}{2} \sum_i \sum_j \frac{\partial h_i}{\partial P_j} \Delta P_i \Delta P_j \tag{14a}$$

where i and j index the good in question, $\frac{\partial h_i}{\partial P_j}$ is the slope of the Hicksian demand function for good i with respect to price j, and the zero subscript denotes initial equilibrium value of quantity. Using the generalized Slutsky equation in elasticity form, $\eta_{ij} = \eta_{ij} - w_j \eta_i$, and the definitions $\Delta P_i = EP_i \cdot P_{i0}$, $\frac{\partial h_i}{\partial P_j} = \eta_{ij} \frac{Q_{i0}}{P_{j0}}$, $w_j = \frac{P_{j0} Q_{j0}}{I}$, and I equals income, equation (14a) can be shown to equal

$$\Delta CS = \sum_i P_{i0} Q_{i0} \left(-EP_i + \frac{1}{2} \sum_j \eta_{ij}^c EP_i EP_j \right) \tag{14b}$$

where $\eta_{ij} = \eta_{ij} + w_j \eta_i$.[3]

---

[2] This approach to calculating change in CV was first proposed by Hicks (1946: 330–3, Additional Note A).

[3] Alternatively, one could use the general equilibrium approach to estimation of welfare effects, which requires general equilibrium demand and supply curves, i.e., demand and supply curves that take into account the effects of price changes in the market in the question of related markets and, in turn, their impact on the demand and supply curves of the market in question (Thurman and Wohlgenant 1989). Such an approach requires, however, that there is only a shock in the market under analysis and in no other related markets. Another approach is to evaluate changes in welfare using the multiple integral

The modeling approach of Gardner (1987) is actually more general than it appears. First, it can easily be extended to more than two products. Second, it can be used to model any form of demand and/or supply shifts, despite the apparent specialized form of shifts modeled as price wedges.

To see how Gardner's framework can be extended to demand shifts with multiple products, consider an extended form of equations (13a) and (13c):

$$EQ_x = \eta_x EP_x + \eta_{xy} EP_y + \eta_{xN_x} EN_x + \eta_{xN_y} EN_y$$

$$EQ_y = \eta_{yx} EP_x + \eta_y EP_y + \eta_{yN_x} EN_x + \eta_{yN_y} EN_y$$

where the demand shift variables EN_x and EN_y could represent, for example, generic advertising for beef and pork (see, e.g., Wohlgenant 1993). Solve this system of equations for EP_x and EP_y to obtain the inverse demand system in log differential form:

$$EP_x = \varphi_x EQ_x + \varphi_{xy} EQ_y + \varphi_{xN_x} EN_x + \varphi_{xN_y} EN_y$$

$$EP_y = \varphi_{yx} EQ_x + \varphi_y EQ_y + \varphi_{yN_x} EN_x + \varphi_{yN_y} EN_y$$

where
$$\varphi_x = \frac{\eta_y}{(\eta_x\eta_y - \eta_{xy}\eta_{yx})}, \varphi_{xy} = \frac{-\eta_{xy}}{(\eta_x\eta_y - \eta_{xy}\eta_{yx})}, \varphi_{xN_x} = \frac{-(\eta_y\eta_x N_x - \eta_{xy}\eta_y N_x)}{(\eta_x\eta_y - \eta_{xy}\eta_{yx})},$$

$$\varphi_{xN_y} = \frac{-(\eta_y\eta_x N_y - \eta_{xy}\eta_y N_y)}{(\eta_x\eta_y - \eta_{xy}\eta_{yx})}, \varphi_{yx} = \frac{-\eta_{yx}}{(\eta_x\eta_y - \eta_{xy}\eta_{yx})}, \varphi_y = \frac{-\eta_x}{(\eta_x\eta_y - \eta_{xy}\eta_{yx})}, \varphi_{yN_x} = \frac{-(\eta_x\eta_x N_x - \eta_{yx}\eta_y N_x)}{(\eta_x\eta_y - \eta_{xy}\eta_{yx})}$$

and $\varphi_{yN_y} = \frac{-(\eta_x\eta_x N_y - \eta_{yx}\eta_y N_y)}{(\eta_x\eta_y - \eta_{xy}\eta_{yx})}$. Define $\delta_x = \varphi_{xN_x} EN_x + \pi_{xN_y} EN_y$ and $\delta_y = \varphi_{yN_x} EN_x + \varphi_{yN_y} EN_y$. Given this specification, the above equations can now be solved back for EQ_x and EQ_y to obtain

$$EQ_x = \eta_x(EP_x - \delta_x) + \eta_{xy}(EP_y - \delta_y)$$

$$EQ_y = \eta_{yx}(EP_x - \delta_x) + \eta_y(EP_y - \delta_y).$$

Therefore, equations (13a)–(13d) can be expressed with horizontal demand shift variables redefined as vertical demand shift variables:

$$EQ_x = \eta_x E\tilde{P}_x + \eta_{xy} E\tilde{P}_y \tag{13a'}$$

$$EQ_x = \varepsilon_x EP_x + \varepsilon_{xy} EP_y \tag{13b'}$$

$$EQ_y = \eta_{yx} E\tilde{P}_x + \eta_y E\tilde{P}_y \tag{13c'}$$

$$EQ_y = \varepsilon_{yx} EP_x + \varepsilon_y EP_y \tag{13d'}$$

approach through integration of areas under Hicksian demand functions for changes in consumer's surplus and integration of areas under supply functions for changes in producer's surplus (Just, Hueth, and Schmitz 1982).

where $E\tilde{P}_x = EP_x - \delta_x, E\tilde{P}_y = EP_y - \delta_y,$ $EV_x = 0$, and $EV_y = 0$. Note that the above approach to incorporating demand shifts is quite general and includes as a special case the simple formulation of dividing the negative of the demand shift elasticity by the own-price elasticity (i.e., $\delta = \frac{-\eta_{iN}}{\eta} EN$) when x and y are assumed to be independent in demand.[4] In addition to the above modifications, (14b) can be re-expressed as

$$\Delta CS = \sum_i P_{i0} Q_{i0} \left(-E\tilde{P}_i + \frac{1}{2} \sum_j \eta_{ij}^c E\tilde{P}_i E\tilde{P}_j \right) \tag{14c}$$

In a similar fashion, prices could be rescaled so that supply shifts could be incorporated into the analysis by defining supply-inducing prices such that EP_x and EP_y in (13b')and (13d')would be replaced by $E\tilde{P}_x = EP_x - EV_x$, and $E\tilde{P}_x = EP_x - EV_{x,}$, respectively. Change in producer's surplus could then be evaluated using a second-order Taylor's series expansion of the profit function (Martin and Alston 1997).

Gardner (1987) used the framework (13a)–(13d) to derive policy implications for changes in consumer's and producer's surplus, and deadweight loss from subsidies in agriculture. Perrin and Scobie (1981), after adding demand and shift variables, have used the same framework to estimate the economic effects from shifts in demand, shifts in supply, and market price wedges to achieve certain nutritional goals for countries as a whole. In addition to supply and demand functions and price wedges characterized by an EDM, they also include a set of relationships showing the impact of changes in quantities consumed on calorie consumption, $C = k'EQ$, where EC is the proportionate change in calories consumed, k is an $n \times 1$ vector of fractions of the amount of calories provided by each commodity, and EQ is the $n \times 1$ vector of relative changes in quantities from the type of market intervention. They do not compute welfare changes from the interventions, but instead compute Treasury costs associated with each of the interventions.

3 THE SINGLE-PRODUCT TWO-FACTOR EDM

3.1 Muth EDM

In many applications, the industry in question consists of vertically related markets. For example, beef is produced from cattle, labor, and other inputs. In such an instance, we would need to take into account the market for the product (beef) and interrelated input markets for the factors of production (e.g., cattle and labor).

Muth (1964) was the first economist to develop a comprehensive analysis of a vertically connected industry. Muth's model is a two-factor model of a competitive industry consisting of six equations:

---

[4] In particular, when $\eta_{xy} = 0$, $\eta_{yx} = 0$, and $\eta_{yN_x} = 0$, then $\delta_x = -\frac{\eta_{xN_x}}{\eta_x}$ and $\delta_y = -\frac{\eta_{yN_y}}{\eta_y}$.

$$Q = D(P, N) \quad (product\ demand\ function)$$

$$Q = f(A,\ B,\ T) \quad (production\ function)$$

$$P_A = f_A(A,\ B,\ T)P \quad (input\ demand\ function\ for\ A)$$

$$P_B = f_B(A,\ B,\ T)P \quad (input\ demand\ function\ for\ B)$$

$$A = g(P_A,\ C_A) \quad (input\ supply\ function\ for\ A)$$

$$B = h(P_B,\ C_B) \quad (input\ supply\ function\ for\ A)$$

where N is a product demand shifter, T is a production function shifter (e.g., technical change), f_A, f_B are partial derivatives of f (i.e., marginal products of A and B), and C_A and C_B are supply shifters of input supply functions for A and B, respectively. In this model, market intermediary behavior is represented by the production function and the two equations by imposing the profit maximization condition that input prices equal value marginal products. Consistent with long-run equilibrium conditions in a competitive industry, the production function is assumed to exhibit constant-returns-to-scale. Under ordinary conditions of a downward-sloping demand curve for the product and upward-sloping supply curves of the two factors of production, the six equations can be solved for the six endogenous variables in terms of the exogenous demand, production function, and input supply curve shifters. Equilibrium displacement can then be characterized through totally differentiating the six equations, converting to elasticities, and solving for the total log differentials of the six endogenous variables.

Wohlgenant (1982) has shown that intermediary behavior in the Muth model can be characterized using duality theory, given the product demand function and the input supply functions. Because the industry production function must exhibit constant-returns-to-scale in order to be compatible with long-run competitive equilibrium, the industry cost function must have the form $C = uc(P_A, P_B)Q$, where $uc(P_A, P_B)$ is the unit (total) cost function. Moreover, we know that when all firms are identical and in long-run equilibrium, the output market condition is price equals marginal cost equals average cost, or equivalently minimum unit cost, $P = uc(P_A, P_B)$. Finally, applying Shephard's lemma to the industry total cost function yields conditional factor demand functions, $A = uc_A(P_A, P_B)Q$, $B = uc_B(P_A, P_B)Q$, where $uc_A(P_A, P_B)$ and $uc_B(P_A, P_B)$ denote functions that are partial derivatives of $uc(P_A, P_B)$ with respect to P_A and P_B, respectively.

The six-equation system of Muth's can now be replaced with the following system:

$$Q = D(P, N) \quad (product\ demand\ function) \tag{15a}$$

$$P = uc(P_A, P_B) \quad (inverse\ product\ supply\ function) \tag{15b}$$

$$A = uc_A(P_A, P_B)Q \quad \textit{(conditional demand for A)} \tag{15c}$$

$$B = uc_B(P_A, P_B)Q \quad \textit{(conditional demand for B)} \tag{15d}$$

$$A = g(P_A, C_A) \quad \textit{(input supply function for A)} \tag{15e}$$

$$B = h(P_B, C_B) \quad \textit{(input supply function for B)} \tag{15f}$$

In contrast to the direct specification of the industry model by Muth (1964), market intermediary behavior in the dual representation consists of the output market condition that output price equals minimum average cost, (15b), and, given the profit-maximizing output determined at the market level by output demand, (15a), input quantities are determined via the two output-constant input demand functions (15c) and (15d). The dual approach leads to precisely the same results as the primal approach. The modeling approach is applicable to any market situation where the market activities involve an intermediate production process and can easily be generalized to n inputs (Wohlgenant 1982).

Totally differentiating equations (15a)–(15f) and converting to elasticities we obtain

$$EQ = \eta EP + \eta_N EN \tag{15a'}$$

$$EP = S_A EP_A + S_B EP_B \tag{15b'}$$

$$EA = \eta_{AA} EP_A + \eta_{AB} EP_B + EQ \tag{15c'}$$

$$EB = \eta_{BA} EP_A + \eta_{BB} EP_B + EQ \tag{15d'}$$

$$EA = \varepsilon_A EP_A + \varepsilon_{AC} EC_A \tag{15e'}$$

$$EB = \varepsilon_B EP_B + \varepsilon_{BC} EC_B \tag{15f'}$$

where $S_A = \frac{P_A A}{PQ}$ is the value share of input A and $S_B = \frac{P_B B}{PQ}$ is the value share of input B. The conditional input demand functions are homogeneous of degree zero in prices implying $\eta_{AA} + \eta_{AB} = 0$ and $\eta_{BA} + \eta_{BB} = 0$. Also, Allen (1938) shows that $\eta_{ij} = \sigma_{ij} S_j$, σ_{ij} equaling the Allen elasticity of substitution (AES) between inputs i and j. Using the homogeneity conditions and the definition of the AES in this application, it is not hard to show that $\eta_{AA} = -S_B \sigma$, $\eta_{AB} = S_B \sigma$, $\eta_{BA} = S_A \sigma$, $\eta_{BB} = -S_A \sigma$, where $\sigma = \sigma_{AB}$ is the simple elasticity of substitution between the two factors. Therefore, equations (15c') and (15d') can be written as follows:

$$EA = -S_B \sigma EP_A + S_B \sigma EP_B + EQ \tag{15c''}$$

$$EB = S_A \sigma EP_A + -S_A \sigma EP_B + EQ \tag{15d''}$$

In addition to the above specifications, technical change parameters are also included in equations (15c^{\prime\prime})-(15d^{\prime\prime}) to obtain:

$$EA = -S_B\sigma EP_A + S_B\sigma EP_B + EQ - \tau_A \tag{15c'''}$$

$$EB = S_A\sigma EP_A + -S_A\sigma EP_B + EQ - \tau_B \tag{15d'''}$$

where τ_A and τ_B denote proportional changes in technology. Alston, Norton, and Pardey (1995) use this specification to model Hicks neutral ($\tau_A = \tau_B$), Hicks B-saving ($\tau_{\downarrow}A = 0$), and Hicks A-saving ($\tau_{\downarrow}B = 0$).[5]

The final modification of the Muth EDM is to redefine demand and supply shifts as vertical demand and supply shifts. This is done by defining the shift in output demand as a vertical shift in the price direction so that $\delta = -\frac{\eta_N}{\eta} EN$, and similarly for the input supply shifters: $\gamma_A = -\frac{\varepsilon_{AC}}{\varepsilon_A} ECA$, $\gamma_B = -\frac{\varepsilon_{BC}}{\varepsilon_B} ECB$.

The six-equation system consisting of (15a'), (15b'), (15c'''), (15d'''), (15e'), and (15f') can now be written in matrix notation as follows:

$$\begin{bmatrix} 1 & -\eta & 0 & 0 & 0 & 0 \\ 0 & 1 & 0 & 0 & -S_A & -S_B \\ -1 & 0 & 1 & 0 & S_B\sigma & -S_B\sigma \\ -1 & 0 & 0 & 1 & -S_A\sigma & S_A\sigma \\ 0 & 0 & 1 & 0 & -\varepsilon_A & 0 \\ 0 & 0 & 0 & 1 & 0 & -\varepsilon_B \end{bmatrix} \begin{bmatrix} EQ \\ EP \\ EA \\ EB \\ EP_A \\ EP_B \end{bmatrix} = \begin{bmatrix} -\eta & 0 & 0 & 0 & 0 & 0 \\ 0 & 0 & 0 & 0 & 0 & 0 \\ 0 & -1 & 0 & 0 & 0 & 0 \\ 0 & 0 & 0 & -1 & 0 & 0 \\ 0 & 0 & 0 & 0 & -\varepsilon_A & 0 \\ 0 & 0 & 0 & 0 & 0 & -\varepsilon_B \end{bmatrix} \begin{bmatrix} \delta \\ \tau_A \\ \tau_B \\ \gamma_A \\ \gamma_B \end{bmatrix} \tag{16}$$

or, in matrix notation $AEy = BEx$, the solution of which is $Ey = A^{-1}BEx$. An extension of the Muth model to the n input case is derived by Wohlgenant (1982).[6]

Analytical solutions to the matrix equation (16) can be derived using Cramer's rule. For example, the solutions for the two factor prices are as follows:[7]

$$EP_A = \frac{[-(\varepsilon_B+\sigma)\eta\delta - (\varepsilon_B + S_A\sigma - S_B\eta)(\tau_A - \varepsilon_A\gamma_A) - S_B(\eta+\sigma)(\tau_B - \varepsilon_B\gamma_B)]}{[\varepsilon_A\varepsilon_B + (S_A\varepsilon_A + S_B\varepsilon_B)\sigma - \eta(S_A\varepsilon_B + S_B\varepsilon_A + \sigma)]} \tag{17a}$$

$$EP_B = \frac{[-(\varepsilon_A+\sigma)\eta\delta - (\varepsilon_A + S_B\sigma - S_A\eta)(\tau_B - \varepsilon_B\gamma_B) - S_A(\eta+\sigma)(\tau_A - \varepsilon_A\gamma_A)]}{[\varepsilon_A\varepsilon_B + (S_A\varepsilon_A + S_B\varepsilon_B)\sigma - \eta(S_A\varepsilon_B + S_B\varepsilon_A + \sigma)]} \tag{17b}$$

The denominators of both (17a) and (17b) are the same and positive when supply elasticities are positive and the demand elasticity is negative. An exogenous increase in demand increases both prices, a vertical increase in supply of factor A (respectively

---

[5] The approach of Alston, Norton, and Pardey (1995) differs from that of Muth (1964), who defines biased technical change holding output constant yielding different shift parameters for biased technical change and neutral technical change.

[6] Wohlgenant (1982) also derived results for the three-input case which may be more appropriate for applications than the two-input model of Gardner's.

[7] An easy and intuitive way to obtain the solutions for the reduced-form variables is first to obtain derived demand functions for each factor by substituting (15b') into (15a') and the result into (15c''') and (15d''') to obtain $EA = (-S_B\sigma + S_A\eta)EP_A + S_B(\sigma+\eta)EP_B - \eta\delta - \tau_A$ and $EB = S_A(\sigma+\eta)EP_A + (-S_A\sigma + S_B\eta)EP_B - \eta\delta - \tau_B$. These two derived demand functions can then be solved simultaneously with (15e') and (15f') to obtain (17a) and (17b).

factor B) increases price of factor A (respectively factor B), a vertical increase in supply of factor B (respectively factor A) decreases (increases) the price of factor A (respectively factor B) as $\sigma < -\eta$ (respectively $> -\eta$). The effects of technical change are just the opposite of effects of shifts in supply. Given the reduced-form solutions for EP_A and EP_B, reduced-form solutions for EQ, EP, EA, and EB can easily be obtained by substituting (17a) and (17b) into (15a'), (15b'), (15e'), and (15f').

In addition to the set of reduced-form equations derived from (16) which can be used to give quantitative predictions for given shifts in demand, input supplies, and technical change, welfare effects on consumers can be computed with either equation (9) or equation (11) depending upon whether we assume linear or log-linear approximation functional forms yield better approximations. Likewise, equations of the form given by (10) or (12) would be applicable to computing changes in producer's surplus for factors A and B.[8]

The matrix equation (16) can also be used to derive the Allen–Hicks formula for the industry-derived demand elasticity for a given factor of production. For example, the elasticity of derived demand for A would be obtained by first eliminating the fifth equation characterizing supply of factor A and then solving the remaining set of five equations for $\frac{EA}{EP_A}$ to obtain

$$\frac{EA}{EP_A} = \frac{\eta\sigma + \varepsilon_B(S_A\eta - S_B\sigma)}{\varepsilon_B + S_A\sigma - S_B\eta}$$

which is Hicks's (1957) well-known formula for derived demand. Note that as $\varepsilon_B \to \infty$ the formula reduces to

$$\frac{EA}{EP_A} = -S_B\sigma + S_A\eta \tag{18}$$

which is Allen's (1938) formula for derived demand.

3.2   Applications of Muth EDM to Vertical Industries

Gardner (1975) applied the Muth model to analysis of the retail–farm price ratio and the farm value share of the retail dollar, which he defined as different measures of the farm–retail price spread for food. His model is based on the reduced-form solutions for EP, EP_A, EA, and EQ from the system of equations in (16). His analysis yielded predictions of the total effects of retail demand shifters, farm supply shifters, and marketing input supply shifters on the retail–farm price

---

[8] Because of the zero profit restriction on the market intermediary there is no surplus to compute. Change in total surplus in this case consists of the sum of change in consumer's surplus and producer's surplus for factors A and B. When the market intermediary earns rents from imperfect competition, change in profit accruing to the intermediary should be included in the calculations. See Wohlgenant (2010) for an example of this type of calculation.

ratio $E(P/P_\downarrow A) = EP - EP_\downarrow A)$ and the farm value share of the retail dollar $((ES_{\downarrow A} = EP_\downarrow A + EA - EP - EQ)$. His analysis highlights the critical role of σ in specifying and estimating price relationships between farm and retail prices.

Wohlgenant (1989) extended Gardner's model to the case of a non-constant-returns-to-scale production function, and applied Gardner's model to estimation of reduced-form retail and farm prices for a set of eight US agricultural raw materials. His results confirmed Gardner's intuition on the importance of the elasticity of substitution and also showed that use of the traditional methodology of estimating retail–farm price linkages would greatly underestimate derived demand elasticities for agricultural raw materials at the farm level. In this context, the basic framework for specifying retail––farm price linkages is the two-equation system

$$EP = \Pi_{PN}EN + \Pi_{PA}EA + \Pi_{PP_B}EP_B$$

$$EP_A = \Pi_{P_A N}EN + \Pi_{P_A A}EA + \Pi_{P_A P_B}EP_B$$

where the following qualitative and quantitative restrictions are shown to hold:

$$\Pi_{PN} > 0, > \Pi_{PA} < 0, \Pi_{PP_B}?$$

$$\Pi_{P_A N} > 0, \Pi_{P_A A} < 0, \Pi_{P_A P_B}?$$

$$\Pi_{PA} = -S_P\Pi_{P_A A}$$

If constant-returns-to-scale holds, we also have the restrictions

$$\Pi_{PN} = -\Pi_{PA}$$

$$\Pi_{P_A N} = -\Pi_{P_A A}$$

These reduced-form parameters are related to the underlying partial elasticities of demand and supply as follows:[9] $\Pi_{PN} = -\frac{\varepsilon_{AP_A}}{D}, \Pi_{PA} = \frac{\varepsilon_{QP_A}}{D}, \Pi_{PP_B} = \frac{\varepsilon_{AP_A}\varepsilon_{QP_B} - \varepsilon_{QP_A}\varepsilon_{AP_B}}{D}$, $\Pi_{P_A N} = \frac{\varepsilon_{AP}}{D}, \Pi_{P_A A} = \frac{-\varepsilon_{QP}+\eta}{D}, \Pi_{P_A P_B} = \frac{-\varepsilon_{AP}\varepsilon_{QP_B}+\varepsilon_{QP}\varepsilon_{AP_B}-\eta\varepsilon_{AP_B}}{D}$, and $D = -\varepsilon_{QP}\varepsilon_{AP_A} + \eta\varepsilon_{AP_A} + \varepsilon_{AP}\varepsilon_{QP_A}$. The parameters ε_{QP}, ε_{QP_A}, ε_{QP_B} represent elasticities of output supply with respect to output price, price of factor A, and price of factor B; the parameters ε_{AP}, ε_{AP_A}, ε_{AP_B} represent elasticities of demand for factor A with respect to output price, price of factor A, and price of factor B. Note that the above restrictions associated with constant-returns-to-scale mean that when these conditions hold, the EDM results for EP and EP_A reduce to those of the Muth model in (16) for the case of a perfectly elastic supply curve for factor B.

Wohlgenant (1989) found empirically overall that all the above results hold, including the restriction of constant-returns-to-scale, further underscoring the importance of

---

[9] The assumption is made that Π_{PN} and $\Pi_{P_A N}$ are elasticities with respect to a 1 percent horizontal shift in the retail demand function. This specification is valid when $EN_i = \sum_{j\neq i}\eta_{ij}EP_j + \eta_i EI + EPOP$, where η_{ij} is the cross-price elasticity of good i with respect to price of good j, P_j is the price of the jth good, I is per capita income (or per capita total expenditure), and POP is population (Wohlgenant 1989).

the basic Muth EDM in applications. With the restriction of constant-returns-to-scale holding, Allen's formula for derived demand, (18), now is equal to $\prod_{p^{A^{A-1}}}$. Therefore, with estimates of own-price elasticities of demand for the retail products, it becomes possible to derive estimates of elasticities of substitution between the farm input and marketing input in each industry through the expression

$$\sigma = \frac{\frac{-E_{AP_A}+S_A\eta}{S_B}}{S_B} = -\Pi_{P_AA}-1 + S_A\eta$$

With this equation, Wohlgenant (1989) computed elasticities of substitution for six different food commodities: beef and veal (0.72), pork (0.35), poultry (0.11), eggs (0.25), dairy (0.96), and fresh vegetables (0.54). The elasticities of substitution were found to be statistically significant in all cases except for poultry. Brester and Wohlgenant (1993) show retail demand elasticities estimated from disappearance data (as was the case in the Wohlgenant 1989 study) are biased upward, so the estimates of σ can be regarded as lower-bound estimates. Therefore, empirical evidence supports the hypothesis that input substitution is both economically and statistically significant for a range of food commodities.

Holloway (1991), Wohlgenant (1999a), and Wohlgenant and Piggott (2003) extended the basic Muth model when applied to price spreads to allow for market power in the retail market for food. Wohlgenant (1999a), following Caplin and Nalebuff (1991), shows that for consistent aggregation to the industry level, the output price equation becomes $P = \theta\, uc(P_A, P_B)$, where $\theta \geq 1$ is the representative firm's markup over unit costs. The basic Muth EDM can be modified to account for imperfect competition by replacing (15b) with this new specification for output price determination.[10] Holloway (1991) uses the same data set as Wohlgenant (1989) and tests for market power. Overall, his findings are consistent with price-taking behavior, further confirming the importance of the basic Muth EDM.

A considerable literature has developed on the distributional effects of research benefits beginning with Freebairn, Davis, and Edwards (1982). Alston and Scobie (1983), in commenting on Freebairn, Davis, and Edwards (1982), used the Muth model to show that the distribution of research benefits is sensitive to the degree of substitutability between the farm and marketing inputs. Mullen, Alston, and Wohlgenant (1989) showed that significant input substitution between raw wool and other inputs in producing wool tops would produce greater marginal returns to wool growers than off-farm research on wool.

Wohlgenant (1993) extended this framework to incorporate shifts in demand through use of check-off funds for generic advertising versus on-farm and off-farm research. Producers as a group will maximize industry profit when the marginal returns from advertising are equal to the marginal returns from on-farm research and the

---

[10] Holloway (1991) explicitly models imperfect competition by including a fixed-cost component in the price equation to impose long-run equilibrium on the model. Such a modification, although theoretically appealing, does not add to the analytical derivation of the EDM and is therefore ignored.

marginal returns from off-farm research. Because the marginal returns from on-farm research equal the difference between the reduction in marginal revenue (due to a reduction in output price) plus the marginal benefit from research (due to a reduction in marginal costs of production), the differences in returns from advertising relative to on-farm and off-farm research can be characterized in terms of the determinants of $EP_A - \gamma_A$. Using the reduced-form equation (17a) as well as simplifying by assuming factor B is unspecialized to the industry (and therefore has an infinite elasticity of supply), the reduced-form expression for marginal net returns to producers equals[11]

$$EP_A - \gamma_A = \frac{[-\eta\delta - (S_B\sigma - S_A\eta)\gamma_A - S_B(\eta + \sigma)\gamma_B]}{(\varepsilon_A + S_B\sigma - S_A\eta)}.$$

The above relationship shows the determinants of returns to producers from allocating funds between advertising, on-farm research, and off-farm research. Of particular significance is the role played by the elasticity of substitution between the raw material (A) and other inputs (B) used in producing the final product. An increase in σ increases the relative returns from on-farm research relative to advertising and off-farm research, *ceteris paribus*. With respect to the price elasticity of demand, the formula also indicates that it is profitable for the industry to allocate more funds to advertising compared to both on-farm and off-farm research the more inelastic demand. Wohlgenant (1993) showed that the distribution of gains from advertising and research in the US beef and pork industries is quite sensitive to the degree of substitutability. Coupled with empirical results showing economically significant input substitution, this would indicate that industry groups have an incentive to consider reallocation of funds away from advertising and off-farm research to on-farm research.[12]

Incorporating market power into the basic Muth model and retracing the steps leading to the above formula, we find that the effect of θ on allocation of funds between advertising and research is now

$$EP_A - \gamma_A = \frac{[-\eta\delta - \theta(S_B\sigma - S_A\eta)\gamma_A - \theta S_B(\eta + \sigma)\gamma_B]}{(\varepsilon_A + \theta S_B\sigma - \theta S_A\eta)}.$$

As the formula shows, there is even more of an incentive to shift funding toward on-farm research if there is significant market power in the marketing sector. Simulations by Wohlgenant and Piggott (2003), however, show that relative marginal returns are more sensitive to input substitution than to market power. The results underscore the importance of accounting for non-zero substitution between the farm input and the marketing input, even in the presence of market power.

---

[11] In order to focus on the determinants of marginal returns from industry funds allocated to advertising, on-farm research, and off-farm research, the technical change parameters τ_A and τ_B have been set equal to zero.

[12] The caveat needs to be offered that the welfare effects were calculated assuming equal efficiency in allocation of funds across different uses of check-off funds, and the results are sensitive the type of supply shift for on-farm research. See Chung and Kaiser (1999) and Wohlgenant (1999c) for further discussion.

3.3   Modeling International Trade with the EDM

Sumner and Wohlgenant (1985) applied the Muth model to analysis of an increase in the federal cigarette excise tax on the US tobacco industry. Their model extended the Muth model by including trade in tobacco and trade in cigarettes. The model was also unique in that policy response by the US Department of Agriculture was treated endogenously in the model, allowing for different scenarios regarding how the Secretary of Agriculture would respond to the tax increase with regard to tobacco quota. The results underscore the importance of accounting for the trade linkages. The effect on producers' returns and tobacco price were significant. On the other hand, the incidence of the tax increase was mainly on consumers even in the case of a fixed quota.

Alston, Norton, and Pardey (1995, ch. 4) developed a detailed model for the case where there are multiple regions. Their approach is one in which they specify separate supply and demand functions for each commodity, and a market-clearing condition of the form

$$EQ_{id} = \eta_i EP_i - \eta \delta_i$$

$$EQ_{is} = \varepsilon_i EP_i - \varepsilon k_i$$

$$\sum_i \left(\frac{Q_{is}}{\sum_j Q_{js}} \right) EQ_{is} = \sum_i \left(\frac{Q_{id}}{\sum_j Q_{jd}} \right) EQ_{id}$$

$$EP_i = EP_w \quad \forall i$$

where P_w is the world price. In contrast to the Sumner and Wohlgenant (1985) model, this model requires data on all countries producing and consuming the product. Change in consumer's surplus and change in producer's surplus could be computed using equations (9) and (10) or (11) and (12) for each country, assuming small changes in prices resulting from shifts in supplies. The model can be modified in various ways to reflect institutional realities in the world market for a given good. For example, if the law of one price is assumed to hold (aside from transport cost differences and tariffs), each country's price could be related to the world price with a set of auxiliary price relationships to reflect these realities in the way showed by Gardner (1987) above in (13b) and (13d), e.g., $EP_i = EP_w + EV_i$, where P_w denotes the world price of the good in question and V_i is the price wedge between the ith country's price and the world price. The utility of this modeling approach is illustrated by Wohlgenant (1999b) in modeling the effect of trade liberalization in sugar where the price wedges were used to represent the effects of bounded tariffs on world sugar trade.

3.4   Joint Products and the EDM

The Muth model has been extended to include joint products in the intermediate product stage. Perrin (1980) extended the original Muth model by including a joint product production function and conditions for profit maximization into the model. Mullen, Wohlgenant, and Farris (1988) used duality theory to formulate the model. They assume a production function for two products that is separable in outputs and inputs, i.e., $g(Q_x, Q_y) = f(A, B)$. In addition to (15a)–(15f), the model with joint products includes specifications for constrained output supplies for both products and market equilibrium conditions. With two factors and two products there are a total of eight equations describing equilibrium for the eight variables $(Q_x, P_x, Q_y, P_y, A, P_A, B, P_B)$:

$$Q_x = D(P_x, N_x) \quad (\textit{product x demand function}) \tag{19a}$$

$$Q_y = D(P_y, N_y) \quad (\textit{product y demand function}) \tag{19b}$$

$$Q_x = S_x(P_x, P_y)f(A, B) \quad (\textit{constraint product x supply}) \tag{19c}$$

$$Q_y = S_y(P_x, P_y)f(A, B) \quad (\textit{constraint product y supply}) \tag{19d}$$

$$A = uc_A(P_A, P_B)g(Q_x, Q_y) \quad (\textit{conditional demand for A}) \tag{19e}$$

$$B = uc_B(P_A, P_B)g(Q_x, Q_y) \quad (\textit{conditional demand for B}) \tag{19f}$$

$$A = g(P_A, C_A) \quad (\textit{input supply function for A}) \tag{19g}$$

$$B = h(P_B, C_B) \quad (\textit{input supply function for B}) \tag{19h}$$

where long-run equilibrium requires $P_x Q_x + P_y Q_y = P_A A + P_B B$ and f and g are homogeneous of degree 1 functions. Differentiating (19a)–(19h) yields the following set of equations for this extended EDM:

$$EQ_x = \eta_x EP_x + \eta_x \delta_x \tag{19a'}$$

$$EQ_y = \eta_y EP_y + \eta_y \delta_y \tag{19b'}$$

$$EQ_x = \mu S_y EP_x - \mu S_y EP_y + S_A EA + S_B EB \tag{19c'}$$

$$EQ_y = -\mu S_x EP_x + \mu S_x EP_y + S_A EA + S_B EB \tag{19d'}$$

$$EA = -\sigma S_B EP_A + \sigma S_B EP_B + S_x EQ_x + S_y EQ_y - \tau_A \tag{19e'}$$

$$EB = \sigma S_A EP_A - \sigma S_A EP_B + S_x EQ_x + S_y EQ_y - \tau_B \tag{19f'}$$

$$EA = \varepsilon_A EP_A - \varepsilon_A \gamma_A \tag{19g'}$$

$$EB = \varepsilon_B EP_B - \varepsilon_B \gamma_B \tag{19h'}$$

where now vertical relative changes in demand are indexed by commodities x and y; μ is the elasticity of product transformation between commodities x and y; S_x and S_y are quantity shares of commodities x and y in total revenue $P_x Q_x + P_y Q_y$; and γ_A and γ_B are vertical relative changes in supplies of the two factors A and B. The above eight equations can be arranged in matrix notation, and log differentials of the eight endogenous variables $(EQ_x, EP_x, EQ_y, EP_y, EA, EP_A, EB, EP_B)$can be solved for the reduced-form parameters and six exogenous variables $(\delta_{\downarrow x}, \delta_{\downarrow y}, \gamma_{\downarrow A}, \gamma_{\downarrow B}, \tau_{\downarrow A}, \tau_{\downarrow B})$. The model assumes independence between the two outputs in demand, but it is possible to extend the model to include cross-price effects as in (13a) and (13c) above.[13]

3.5 Modeling Effects of Advertising

One of the most extensive applications of modeling demand shifts with the EDM is the effect of generic advertising on producer's surplus. Wohlgenant (1993) discusses some of the conceptual issues in quantifying the effects of advertising. Piggott, Piggott, and Wright (1995) show how commodity interrelationships with advertising can be modeled in the EDM framework. Kinnucan (1999) and Cranfield (2002) extend the EDM with advertising to incorporate trade. Cranfield (2002) shows that advertising intensity, AI (advertising expenditures as a share of total revenue), incorporating trade in both the product and factor market for A under constant-returns-to-scale, is

$$AI = \frac{\beta}{[(1 + k_R) + ((1 + k_F)\varepsilon_A + \sigma S_B - k_F\xi) - S_A(\eta + k_R e)](\psi + \rho)}$$

where β is the own-advertising elasticity of the final good, k_R is the share of trade in demand for the final good (exports > 0, imports < 0), k_F is the share of trade in demand for the farm input (factor A where exports > 0, imports < 0), ξ is the own-price trade elasticity for the farm input ($\xi > 0$ for export supply elasticity), e is the own-price trade elasticity for the final good ($e < 0$ for import demand elasticity), ψ is the unit cost of advertising, and ρ is the rate of return of alternative investments other than advertising.

Cranfield (2002) shows that the above expression for AI includes a number of extant formulae for single markets, including Dorfman and Steiner (1954) for fixed supplies and no trade, Nerlove and Waugh (1961) for supply response but no trade, and Kinnucan (1999) with supply response and trade; for two market levels, the AI formula includes as special cases no trade in either market (Wohlgenant 1993), no trade at the farm level (Cranfield 2002), and no trade at the retail level (Kinnucan, Xiao, and Yu 2000).

---

[13] Such a modification, however, may change the way in which demand shift parameters are modeled as the extension of (13a)–(13d) to (13a′)–(13d′) indicates. Moreover, it is important now to recognize that the multiple product version of change in consumer's surplus, equation (14c), should be used instead of (9) or (11) separately for each product.

3.6   Modeling Dynamics in the EDM

Dynamic response in supply and/or demand can easily be accommodated in the EDM framework. However, accommodating dynamics in measuring welfare changes is more challenging. Just, Hueth, and Schmitz (1982) show that one way to incorporate dynamics is to use demand and supply elasticities for different lengths of run when calculating changes in welfare for producers and consumers. Lemieux and Wohlgenant (1989) take this approach to estimating the effects of introducing porcine somatotropin in the pork industry. For each length of run (short run, intermediate-length run, and long run), different elasticities are calculated and the standard formulae (e.g., equations (9) and (10)) are used to estimate welfare effects.

Gotsch and Wohlgenant (2001) evaluate the effects of adoption and production of new cocoa cultivars on welfare. Their analysis incorporates perennial crop supply response with dynamics on the supply curve. Dynamics are modeled by shifting the supply curve for each time period based on the effects earlier adoption and planting decisions are likely to have on net present value of producer returns. Price, quantity, and welfare effects are then calculated for each time period and net present value analysis is used to estimate welfare effects. For each time period, the formulae for estimating changes in producer's surplus with both parallel and pivotal supply shifts are used and the standard formula for changes in consumer's surplus (i.e., equation (9)) is used.[14]

Weaber and Lusk (2010) evaluate the effects of a genetic improvement program in the cattle industry using net present discounted value of returns from the program on supply response over a five-year period. The approach is similar to Lemieux and Wohlgenant (1989) but with explicit attention given to discounting future net returns in calculation of change in producer's surplus in the cattle and beef industries.

4   PRECISION IN EDM VALUES

An important question when using the EDM to generate results for changes in prices, quantities, and surplus values is how sensitive are the results to alternative plausible values of the partial elasticities of the demand/supply equations. Sensitivity analysis is one approach that could be used and may be all that is needed if the researcher is only concerned about a subset of parameters. However, if there is any degree of uncertainty about the parameters (which there usually is), it is probably better to take a unified

---

[14] The formula for pivotal change in supply when the supply curve is linear is shown in Chung and Kaiser (1999).

approach such as that developed by Davis and Espinosa (1998) or Zhao, Griffiths, et al. (2000).

Davis and Espinosa (1998) and Zhao, Griffiths, et al. (2000) propose Bayesian approaches. This approach begins with specifying a reduced-form equation for each endogenous variable such as

$$E\hat{y}_j = \Pi_j(\hat{\beta}, \hat{\gamma})Ex \tag{22}$$

where $\hat{\beta}$ and $\hat{\gamma}$ are vectors of structural parameters, i.e., partial elasticities of underlying supply/demand functions, $E\hat{y}_j$ is the predicted value of the relative change in endogenous variable j, and Ex is the vector of values of relative changes in the predetermined variables. Let the multivariate distribution of $\hat{\beta}$ and $\hat{\gamma}$ be $f(\hat{\beta}, \hat{\gamma})$. If the elements of $\hat{\beta}$ and $\hat{\gamma}$ are all independent (an assumption frequently made because of different sources for elasticities), the joint distribution can be denoted as

$$f(\hat{\beta}, \hat{\gamma}) = \Pi_i f_i(\hat{\beta}) \Pi_j f_j(\hat{\gamma}) \tag{23}$$

where f_i and f_j are marginal density functions.

Davis and Espinosa (1998) propose generating empirical distributions for the reduced-form parameters by following three steps:

(1) Assume a distribution for each element of $\hat{\beta}$ and $\hat{\gamma}$.
(2) Select parameter values to characterize distributions assumed in (1).
(3) Draw a large number of observations from these distributions to generate empirical distributions for $\Pi_j(\hat{\beta}, \hat{\gamma})$.

Davis and Espinosa (1998) point out that the procedure, while analogous to a Monte Carlo simulation procedure, is more general in that the researcher's subjective values of parameters can be incorporated into the procedure, thus allowing for more information to be used in the simulations performed.

Davis and Espinosa (1998) suggest using Chebychev intervals and maximum p-values. In the spirit of Bayesian analysis, Zhao, Mullen, and Griffith (2000) instead recommend using empirical distributions and estimated proportions with, say, 95 percent confidence intervals. Their recommendation regarding results is to follow the rule: reject H_0: $P(E\hat{y}_j > C) < .025$ or $P(E\hat{y}_j < C) < .025$; do not reject H_0 otherwise. This approach has been taken by Zhao, Griffiths, et al. (2000) in evaluating returns to technical change in the Australian wool industry, to estimating optimal advertising investment in the Canadian beef industry (Cranfield 2002), to evaluating distribution of gains from advertising versus research (Wohlgenant and Piggott 2003), to estimating optimal advertising investment in the US beef and pork industries (Piggott 2003), and to estimating returns from advertising and research in the Australian grape and wine industries (Zhao, Anderson, and Wittwer 2003).

5   Effects of Approximation Error of Functional Form on EDM

The EDM is appropriate when changes in both exogenous and endogenous variables are small. When such changes are small enough, functional form does not matter, so estimates of partial elasticities and shares can be used as parameters for the reduced-form relationships. Using $\Delta \log (y)$ and $\Delta \log (x)$ will give exact changes when the functional forms are of constant-elasticity form, but these changes should be replaced by $\hat{y}^{-1}\Delta y$ and $\hat{x}^{-1}\Delta x$ when all the functions are linear (Alston and Wohlgenant 1990; Zhao, Mullen, and Griffith 1997). The problem is that we rarely know what the functions are, or they are more complicated than either log-linear or linear.

Zhao, Mullen, and Griffith (1997) extend the earlier work of Alston and Wohlgenant (1990) to evaluate errors in the EDM when second-order Taylor's series expansions of the functions are performed. They evaluate specifically the effects on the EDM and welfare measures for the simple EDM when there is only a shift in supply. If a linear approximation to demand and supply is used combined with a parallel shift in supply, Zhao, Mullen, and Griffiths (1997) show that EP will be overstated for price decreases and understated for price increases; they show that the bias in EQ is not always positive but depends on relative supply and demand elasticities; and they show that it is almost always true that ΔCS will be overestimated for a downward shift in supply. Zhao, Mullen, and Griffith (1997) obtain similar results for the errors when assuming the original functions are log-linear with a pivotal supply shift. The main difference between these results is that the errors from assuming log-linear approximations are much larger than from assuming linear approximations. In all instances, the errors are smaller, the smaller is the shift in supply.

It is possible to obtain exact error bounds on the EDM when assuming a demand shift instead of a supply shift. Consider the case first where the demand and supply functions are assumed to be linear and there is a parallel shift in demand. Taking a second-order Taylor's series expansion of the demand and supply functions for given δ and solving the equations for equilibrium price and quantity changes gives

$$EP - EP^* = [2Q_0(\varepsilon - \eta)]^{-1}\left[P_0 S''(k_2)(EP)^2 - P_0 D''(k_1)(EP - \delta)^2\right] = 0(\delta^2) \qquad (24)$$

and

$$EQ - EQ^* = [2Q_0(\varepsilon - \eta)]^{-1}P_0{}^2\left[\eta S''(k_2)(EP)^2 - \varepsilon D''(k_1)(EP - \delta)^2\right] = 0(\delta^2) \qquad (25)$$

where $EP_0 \leq k_1 \leq EP_1, EP_0 \leq k_2 \leq EP_1$, and the second-order derivatives are denoted as ($''$). Errors of both $EP - EP^*$ and $EQ - EQ^*$ are of second-order magnitude so long as the percentage shift in demand δ is small with infinitesimal order $0(\delta^2)$ as $\delta \rightarrow 0$ (cf., Zhao, Mullen, and Griffith 1997).

If $S'' < 0$ and $D'' > 0$, then it is the case that $|EP - EP^*| < 0$ and $|EQ - EQ^*| \geq\leq 0$.

For a price increase, as we would expect from an increase in demand without a supply shift, (9) implies we should expect the error in predicting the change in consumer's surplus to be positive and to be of second-order importance, provided $|EQ - EQ^*|$ is small (which we would expect by the arguments of Zhao, Mullen, and Griffith 1997). The same arguments would apply *a fortiori* for errors in approximation of $EP - EP^*$, $EQ - EQ^*$, and ΔCS for constant elasticity demand and supply functions with a proportional demand shift.[15]

6 CONCLUSIONS

The scope and value of the EDM methodology in consumer demand and welfare analysis is extensive. I have chosen what I consider to be the main developments and applications in the literature to date, although because of space constraints I have not been able to do justice to the full range of applications of the EDM. An additional example of embellishments on existing approaches includes Holloway's (1989) analysis in which a third level in the vertical market structure is added to the standard Muth model. More recently, Harrington and Dubman (2008) have combined the EDM for the demand side with mathematical programming models on the supply side to model agricultural policy.

From my perspective, a major limitation of the EDM framework is that it is strictly only valid for small changes. If large changes are considered, then one is implicitly assuming either linear functional forms or constant elasticity functional forms. More work along the lines of Zhao, Mullen, and Griffith (1997) in characterizing the magnitude of errors in the EDM framework is desirable. Even when it is not possible to overcome the problems of dependency on functional form, it would be wise to perform sensitivity analysis by developing results for both linear and constant-elasticity functional forms. The main effects of these embellishments are on how one computes changes in consumer's and producer's surplus. Formulae for accommodating those types of formulae are provided in this chapter.

In conclusion, based on the discussion in this chapter, it should be clear that the applications of the EDM are many and that its usefulness will not diminish any time soon. While modifications and extensions will likely be made, its real value lies in the fact that the researcher is forced to focus on the economics rather than solely on the technique.

---

[15] These results are not shown to save space. These can be inferred from the results of Zhao, Mullen, and Griffith (1997) in light of the forms shown in (24) and (25), which are the same except for the shift parameter occurring in the demand function and not the supply function. The case where shifts occur in both demand and supply is more complicated to analyze and is beyond the scope of this chapter.

REFERENCES

Allen, R. G. D. 1938. *Mathematical Analysis for Economists*. New York: St Martin's Press.

Alston, J. M., and G. M. Scobie. 1983. "Distribution of Research Gains in Multistage Production Systems: Comment." *American Journal of Agricultural Economics* 65: 353–6.

——and M. K. Wohlgenant. 1990. "Measuring Research Benefits Using Linear Elasticity Equilibrium Displacement Models." In J. D. Mullen and J. M. Alston, eds, *The Returns to the Australian Wool Industry from Investment in R & D (Appendix 2)*. Rural and Resource Economics Report No. 10. Sydney: New South Wales Agricultural and Fisheries.

——, G. W. Norton, and P. G. Pardey. 1995. *Science under Scarcity: Principles and Practice for Agricultural Research Evaluation and Priority Setting*. Ithaca, NY: Cornell University Press.

Binmore, K. G. 1983. *Calculus*. Cambridge: Cambridge University Press.

Brester, G. W., and M. K. Wohlgenant. 1993. "Correcting for Measurement Error in Food Demand Estimation." *Review of Economics and Statistics* 75: 352–6.

Brown, A. B. 1995. "Cigarette Taxes and Smoking Restrictions: Impacts and Policy Implications." *American Journal of Agricultural Economics* 77: 946–51.

Buse, R. C. 1958. "Total Elasticities: A Predictive Device." *Journal of Farm Economics* 40: 881–981.

Caplin, A., and B. Nalebuff. 1991. "Aggregation and Imperfect Competition: On the Existence of Equilibrium." *Econometrica* 59: 25–59.

Chung, C., and H. Kaiser. 1999. "Distribution of Gains from Research and Promotion in Multi-Stage Production Systems: The Case of the U.S. Beef and Pork Industries: Comment." *American Journal of Agricultural Economics* 81: 593–7.

Cranfield, J. A. L. 2002. "Optimal Advertising with Traded Raw and Final Goods: The Case of Variable Proportions Technology." *Journal of Agricultural and Resource Economics* 27: 204–21.

Currie, J. M., J. A. Murphy, and A. Schmitz. 1971. "The Concept of Economic Surplus and its Use in Economic Analysis." *Economic Journal* 324: 741–99.

Davis, G. C., and M. C. Espinosa. 1998. "A Unified Approach to Sensitivity Analysis in Equilibrium Displacement Models." *American Journal of Agricultural Economics* 80: 868–79.

Dorfman, R., and P. Steiner. 1954. "Optimal Advertising and Optimal Quality." *American Economic Review* 44: 826–36.

Duffy, P. A., and M. K. Wohlgenant. 1991. "Effects of an Export Subsidy on the U.S. Cotton Industry." *Southern Journal of Agricultural Economics* 3: 1–7.

Freebairn, J. W., J. S. Davis, and G. W. Edwards. 1982. "Distribution of Research Gains in Multistage Production Systems." *American Journal of Agricultural Economics* 64: 39–46.

Gardner, B. L. 1975. "The Farm-Retail Price Spread in a Competitive Food Industry." *American Journal of Agricultural Economics* 57: 399–409.

——1987. "Income Distribution through Multimarket Commodity Programs." In Gardner, *The Economics of Agricultural Policies*. New York: Macmillan.

Gotsch, N., and M. K. Wohlgenant. 2001. "A Welfare Analysis of Biological Technical Change under Different Supply Shift Assumptions: The Case of Cocoa in Malaysia." *Canadian Journal of Agricultural Economics* 49: 87–104.

Harrington, D. H., and R. Dubman. 2008. *Equilibrium Displacement Mathematical Programming Models: Methodology and a Model of the Agricultural Sector*. Technical Bulletin No. 1918. Washington, DC: Economic Research Service, US Department of Agriculture.

Hausman, J. A. 1981. "Exact Consumer's Surplus and Deadweight Loss." *American Economic Review* 71: 662–766.

Hicks, J. R. 1946. *Value and Capital*, 2nd edn. London: Oxford University Press.

——1957. *The Theory of Wages*. Gloucester, MA: Peter Smith.

Holloway, G. J. 1989. "Distribution of Research Gains in Multistage Production System: Further Results." *American Journal of Agricultural Economics* 71: 338–43.

——1991. "The Farm-Retail Price Spread in an Imperfectly Competitive Food Industry." *American Journal of Agricultural Economics* 73: 979–89.

Intriligator, M. D. 1978. *Econometric Models, Techniques, and Applications*. Englewood Cliffs, NJ: Prentice-Hall.

Irvine, I. J., and W. A. Sims. 1998. "Measuring Consumer Surplus with Unknown Hicksian Demands." *American Economic Review* 88: 314–22.

Just, R. E., D. L. Hueth, and A. Schmitz. 1982. *Applied Welfare Economics*. Englewood Cliffs, NJ: Prentice-Hall.

Kinnucan, H. W. 1996. "A Note on Measuring Returns to Generic Advertising in Interrelated Markets." *Journal of Agricultural Economics* 47: 261–7.

——1999. "Advertising Traded Goods." *Journal of Agricultural and Resource Economics* 24: 38–56.

——and J. E. Christian. 1997. "A Method for Measuring Returns to Nonprice Export Promotion with Application to Almonds." *Journal of Agricultural and Resource Economics* 22: 120–32.

——, H. Xiao, and S. Yu. 2000. "Related Effectiveness of USDA's Nonprice Export Promotion Instruments." *Journal of Agricultural and Resource Economics* 25: 559–77.

Lemieux, C. M., and M. K. Wohlgenant. 1989. "Ex Ante Evaluation of the Economic Impact of Agricultural Biotechnology: The Case of Porcine Somatotropin." *American Journal of Agricultural Economics* 71: 903–14.

Lusk, J. L., and J. D. Anderson. 2004. "Effects of Country-of-Origin Labeling on Meat Producers and Consumers." *Journal of Agricultural and Resource Economics* 29: 185–205.

Martin, W., and J. M. Alston. 1997. "Producer Surplus without Apology? Evaluating Investments in R & D." *Economic Record* 71: 146–58.

Mullen, J. D., and J. M. Alston. 1994. "The Impact of the Australian Lamb Industry of Producing Larger Leaner Lamb." *Review of Marketing and Agricultural Economics* 62: 43–60.

————, and M. K. Wohlgenant. 1989. "The Impact of Farm and Processing Research on the Australian Wool Industry." *Australian Journal of Agricultural Economics* 33: 32–47.

——, M. K. Wohlgenant, and D. E. Farris. 1988. "Input Substitution and the Distribution of Surplus Gains from Lower U.S. Beef Processing Costs." *American Journal of Agricultural Economics* 70: 245–54.

Muth, R. F. 1964. "The Derived Demand for a Productive Factor and the Industry Supply Curve." *Oxford Economic Papers* 16: 221–34.

Nerlove, M., and F. Waugh. 1961. "Advertising without Supply Control: Some Implications of a Study of the Advertising of Oranges." *Journal of Farm Economics* 41: 813–37.

Norton, G. W., and J. S. Davis. 1981. "Evaluating Returns to Agricultural Research." *American Journal of Agricultural Economics* 63: 685–9.

Perrin, R. K. 1980. "The Impact of Component Pricing of Soybeans and Milk." *American Journal of Agricultural Economics* 62: 445–55.

——and G. M. Scobie. 1981. "Market Intervention Policies for Increasing the Consumption of Nutrients by Low Income Households." *American Journal of Agricultural Economics* 63: 73–82.

Piggott, N. E. 2003. "Measures of Precision for Estimating Welfare Effects for Producers from Generic Advertising." *Agribusiness* 19: 379–91.

Piggott, R. R., N. E. Piggott, and V. E. Wright. 1995. "Approximating Farm-Level Returns to Incremental Advertising Expenditure: Methods and an Application to the Australian Meat Industry." *American Journal of Agricultural Economics* 77: 497–511.

Sumner, D. A., and M. K. Wohlgenant. 1985. "Effects of an Increase in the Federal Excise Tax on Cigarettes." *American Journal of Agricultural Economics* 67: 235–42.

Thurman, W. N., and M. K. Wohlgenant. 1989. "Consistent Estimation of General Equilibrium Welfare Effects." *American Journal of Agricultural Economics* 71: 1041–5.

Unnevehr, L. J. 1986. "Consumer Demand for Rice Grain Quality and Returns to Research for Quality Improvement in Southeast Asia." *American Journal of Agricultural Economics* 68: 634–41.

Weaber, R. L., and J. L. Lusk. 2010. "The Economic Value of Improvement in Beef Tenderness by Genetic Marker Selection." *American Journal of Agricultural Economics* 92/5: 1456–71.

Willig, R. O. 1976. "Consumer's Surplus without Apology." *American Economic Review* 66: 589–97.

Wohlgenant, M. K. 1982. *The Retail–Farm Price Ratio in a Competitive Food Industry with Several Marketing Inputs*. Faculty Working Paper No. 12. Raleigh: North Carolina State University.

——1989. "Demand for Farm Output in a Complete System of Demand Equations." *American Journal of Agricultural Economics* 71: 241–52.

——1993. "Distribution of Gains for Research and Promotion in Multi-Stage Production Systems: The Case of the U.S. Beef and Pork Industries." *American Journal of Agricultural Economics* 75: 642–51.

——1999a. "Product Heterogeneity and the Relationship between Retail and Farm Prices." *European Journal of Agricultural Economics* 26: 219–27.

——1999b. *Effects of Trade Liberalization on the World Sugar Market*. Rome: Food and Agriculture Organization of the United Nations.

——1999c. "Distribution of Gains from Research and Promotion in Multi-Stage Production Systems: The Case of the U.S. Beef and Pork Industries: Reply." *American Journal of Agricultural Economics* 81: 598–600.

——2010. "Modeling the Effects of Restricting Packer-Owned Livestock in the U.S. Swine Industry." *American Journal of Agricultural Economics* 92: 654–66.

——and N. E. Piggott. 2003. "Distribution of Gains from Research and Promotion in the Presence of Market Power." *Agribusiness* 19: 301–14.

——and X. Zhao. 2010. "Simple Formulas for Economic Surplus Calculations." Unpublished paper. Raleigh: North Carolina State University.

Zhao, X., J. D. Mullen, and G. R. Griffith. 1997. "Functional Forms, Exogenous Shifts, and Economic Surplus Changes." *American Journal of Agricultural Economics* 79: 1243–51.

——, W. Griffiths, G. R. Griffith, and J. D. Mullen. 2000. "Probability Distributions for Economic Surplus Changes: The Case of Technical Change in the Australian Wool Industry." *Australian Journal of Agricultural and Resource Economics* 44: 83–106.

——, J. D. Mullen, and G. R. Griffith 2000. "A Unified Approach to Sensitivity Analysis in Equilibrium Displacement Models: Comment." *American Journal of Agricultural Economics* 82: 236–40.

—— K. Anderson, and G. Wittwer. 2003. "Who Gains from Australian Wine Promotion and R & D?" *Australian Journal of Agricultural and Resource Economics* 47: 181–209.

PART II

FOOD POLICY

CHAPTER 12

FOOD SECURITY POLICY IN DEVELOPED COUNTRIES

PARKE WILDE

1 INTRODUCTION

The need for food security policy in developed countries is a paradox. A defining feature of economic development is a level of economic prosperity that reduces the prevalence of food insecurity and hunger. If food insecurity and hunger are sufficiently widespread in a particular country, do we still call the country "developed"? If a country is developed, is it fruitful to describe its social welfare problems in terms of "food security"? Developed countries have taken several approaches to these questions, giving different levels of emphasis to food security as an organizing framework for discussing national social welfare statistics and safety net policies.

One list of developed countries, accepted for purposes of this chapter, is the twenty-eight members of the Organization for Economic Cooperation and Development excluding Turkey and Mexico (OECD-28). This list includes the United States, European countries, Canada, Australia, New Zealand, South Korea, and Japan.

By some standards, these countries no longer have a food security problem. In the annual report of the United Nations Food and Agriculture Organization (FAO) entitled *The State of Food Insecurity in the World* or the US Department of Agriculture's (USDA's) annual global *Food Security Assessment*, based on national food supplies, the developed countries are essentially food-secure (FAO 2008; Rosen et al. 2008). Likewise, using anthropometric indicators, such as the prevalence of low weight-for-age, the problem of food insecurity is negligible in the developed countries (WHO 2009). When Nobel Laureate Robert Fogel discusses hunger in Europe and America, he does so as an economic historian describing a condition from which these countries escaped in the nineteenth and early twentieth centuries (Fogel 2004).

By other standards, food security policy in developed countries remains a topic of active research and lively debate. Survey measures of food insecurity and hunger provide evidence of continuing problems in low-income populations, even within developed countries that have adequate national food supplies, high rates of obesity, and low rates of childhood stunting and wasting due to malnutrition. Especially following the three-year period 2007–9, which witnessed rapid food price increases, financial crisis, and severe economic recession, it seems too early to relegate food security policy in developed countries to the history books.

Public attention to domestic food insecurity and hunger in national policy discussions is greatest in the United States, though food insecurity has been measured in national surveys in several other countries, including Canada, Australia, and New Zealand. In other OECD-28 countries, discussion of food insecurity and hunger is usually embedded within larger concerns about material deprivation, income inequality, and poverty. For example, in *Growing Unequal?*, a high-profile 2008 OECD report on income distribution and poverty in developed countries, basic needs for food have a low profile within a broad typology of material deprivation: housing, consumer durables, appreciation of one's own personal conditions (a sense of ability to make ends meet), capacity to afford basic leisure and social activities, characteristics of the social environment, and basic needs such as clothing and food (OECD 2008). Similarly, research in Australia and Japan finds that survey respondents rank food deprivation as just one element of an array of deprivation issues of concern (Saunders and Abe 2008).

The concept of food insecurity may be more central in the US literature, because poverty is more widespread. Among eleven rich countries, the United States ranked first according to a relative poverty line commonly used in other developed countries. The United Kingdom and the United States ranked first and second according to an absolute poverty line more similar to the US official poverty standard (Smeeding 2006). Moreover, US social insurance and cash assistance safety net support is smaller in scale, while food assistance programs are larger. Hence, the concept of food security may have greater policy relevance in the United States.

This chapter reviews food security measurement and its connection to policy responses in developed countries. Because national food supply data and anthropometric indicators of undernutrition offer little variation in developed countries, the focus is on survey-based methods, sometimes called "third generation" measures of food security (Barrett 2002; Coates et al. 2006). Although US examples get heavier emphasis, the principles of survey-based food insecurity measurement and policy application have general relevance. Examples are drawn from across a range of developed countries whenever possible.

2   MEASURING FOOD INSECURITY AND HUNGER

2.1   Definitions

Early definitions of food security emphasized the adequacy of food supplies. More recently, the FAO definition has evolved to focus on individuals and households, and broadened to include several criteria beyond food supplies:

> Food security exists when all people, at all times, have physical, social and economic access to sufficient, safe and nutritious food which meets their dietary needs and food preferences for an active and healthy life. Household food security is the application of this concept to the family level, with individuals within households as the focus of concern. (FAO 2003)

Food insecurity is the absence of food security.

US government publications refer to food security similarly, though more tersely, as "access by all people at all times to enough food for an active, healthy life" (Nord, Andrews, and Carlson 2008). An expanded definition, used by the Center for National Statistics (CNSTAT), with origins in a 1990 report from the Life Sciences Research Office (LSRO), stipulates in addition that it must be possible to acquire food in "socially acceptable ways" (Wunderlich and Norwood 2006). Though no definition wins unanimous agreement, Coates et al. (2006) distinguish four "domains" that one commonly sees in definitions of food insecurity: (1) uncertainty and worry, (2) inadequate quality, (3) insufficient quantity, and (4) social unacceptability.

The word "hunger" has two accepted meanings. In its first meaning, hunger is a physiological experience. LSRO in 1990 defined hunger as "the uneasy or painful sensation caused by a lack of food" (Wunderlich and Norwood 2006). A speaker intends this meaning when saying, late in the afternoon, "I feel hunger. Let us make dinner." In its second meaning, hunger is a social problem: "a situation in which someone cannot obtain an adequate amount of food" (quoted in Holben 2005). The 1990 LSRO definition describes hunger in its second sense as "the recurrent and involuntary lack of food." A speaker intends this meaning when saying, "I am concerned about the paradox of hunger in developed countries." The literature on food insecurity and hunger measurement has noted both meanings explicitly, whether writing about the United States (Eisinger 1998; Radimer, Olson, and Campbell 1990; Holben 2005; Wunderlich and Norwood 2006) or about low-income countries overseas (Sanchez et al. 2005).

The relationship between food insecurity and hunger definitions is debated. In one strand of the literature, food insecurity is qualitatively similar to but milder than hunger. People who do not qualify as hungry might nevertheless be classified as food-insecure if they were uncertain of getting enough at all times or if they acquired food in socially unacceptable ways. In another strand of the literature, the physiological experience of hunger is a potential consequence of food insecurity (Anderson 1990, quoted in Wunderlich and Norwood 2006). In 2006 CNSTAT argued that official statistics in the United States should restrict the term "hunger" to the physiological definition (not the social problem), and the individual level (not the household), and should treat hunger as a potential consequence of food insecurity (not a severe range of food insecurity). The CNSTAT report stated that this narrow definition of hunger is widely understood by the public and reflects "a consensus in U.S. society" (Wunderlich and Norwood 2006). However, recent empirical evidence suggests that many US survey respondents understand hunger more broadly (Nord, Finberg, and McLaughlin 2009).

2.2   Individual Survey Questions

In the 1980s the US government began adding a single question about food sufficiency to national surveys:

> Which of these statements best describes the food eaten in your household—enough of the kinds of food we want to eat, enough but not always the kinds of food we want to eat, sometimes not enough to eat, or often not enough to eat? (Wunderlich and Norwood 2006)

Beginning with a 1995 national nutrition survey, Australian research has used a question: "In the last 12 months were there any times that you ran out of food and you couldn't afford to buy more?" (Marks et al. 2001). On some Australian surveys, a follow-up question asked: "When this happened, did you go without food?" Recent Australian research has used the label "food insecurity" to describe the experience of running out, and the label "severe food insecurity" to describe the experience of going without food (Temple 2008). A 1997 national nutrition survey in New Zealand included several food security questions, including whether respondents "can afford to eat properly" and whether "food runs out because of lack of money" (Russell, Parnell, and Wilson 1999; Radimer 2002).

In some developed countries, such questions focus on distinctive culturally relevant aspects of food insecurity. The New Zealand survey asked whether "I [the respondent] feel stressed because I can't provide the food I want for social occasions." Although the OECD report *Growing Unequal?* did not have a uniform food security measure for comparable reporting across the developed countries, it did find a number of sentinel questions about constrained food choice. For the European countries, constrained food choice meant not being able to "afford to eat meat or chicken every second day if wished." For Japan, it meant not being able to "afford to eat a fruit each day if wished."

An advantage of individual survey questions is easy explanation of the results using the same terminology that was used in the survey questions themselves. A disadvantage is that each question can address only some of the domains of the definition of food security. Also, it is difficult to compare results across surveys that asked different questions.

2.3   Multiple-Question Survey Instruments

In the late 1980s and early 1990s, research efforts at Cornell University and the Food Research and Action Center developed multiple-question instruments for measuring food insecurity and hunger (Radimer 2002; Wunderlich and Norwood 2006). Variants of these questions were used in developing the US government's official food security measurement program.

Beginning in 1995, US statistics on food insecurity and hunger have been compiled from a battery of eighteen survey items. Ten of the questions are asked of all households, whether or not they have children:

1. "We worried whether our food would run out before we got money to buy more." Was that often, sometimes, or never true for you in the last 12 months?
2. "The food that we bought just didn't last and we didn't have money to get more." Was that often, sometimes, or never true for you in the last 12 months?
3. "We couldn't afford to eat balanced meals." Was that often, sometimes, or never true for you in the last 12 months?
4. In the last 12 months, did you or other adults in the household ever cut the size of your meals or skip meals because there wasn't enough money for food? (Yes/No)
5. (If yes to Question 4) How often did this happen—almost every month, some months but not every month, or in only 1 or 2 months?
6. In the last 12 months, did you ever eat less than you felt you should because there wasn't enough money for food? (Yes/No)
7. In the last 12 months, were you ever hungry, but didn't eat, because you couldn't afford enough food? (Yes/No)
8. In the last 12 months, did you lose weight because you didn't have enough money for food? (Yes/No)
9. In the last 12 months did you or other adults in your household ever not eat for a whole day because there wasn't enough money for food? (Yes/No)
10. (If yes to Question 9) How often did this happen—almost every month, some months but not every month, or in only 1 or 2 months?

Another eight questions are asked only of households with children, because they refer to symptoms of hardship for children in the household.

11. "We relied on only a few kinds of low-cost food to feed our children because we were running out of money to buy food." Was that often, sometimes, or never true for you in the last 12 months?
12. "We couldn't feed our children a balanced meal, because we couldn't afford that." Was that often, sometimes, or never true for you in the last 12 months?
13. "The children were not eating enough because we just couldn't afford enough food." Was that often, sometimes, or never true for you in the last 12 months?

14. In the last 12 months, did you ever cut the size of any of the children's meals because there wasn't enough money for food? (Yes/No)

15. In the last 12 months, were the children ever hungry but you just couldn't afford more food? (Yes/No)

16. In the last 12 months, did any of the children ever skip a meal because there wasn't enough money for food? (Yes/No)

17. (If yes to Question 16) How often did this happen—almost every month, some months but not every month, or in only 1 or 2 months?

18. In the last 12 months did any of the children ever not eat for a whole day because there wasn't enough money for food? (Yes/No)

All of the survey items are stated in the context of economic constraints. For example, the questions about going hungry make clear that the reason must be lack of "enough money for food," not hunger due to a calorie-restricted diet or insufficient time to eat at work.

Outside of the United States, the same eighteen questions are now used on national surveys in Canada (Office of Nutrition Policy and Promotion 2007), and they have been used in small-scale local surveys in other developed countries. The Food and Nutrition Technical Assistance (FANTA) program of the US Agency for International Development has developed a shorter multiple-question instrument (Coates, Swindale, and Bilinsky 2007). It has been adopted mainly in developing countries, but it provides an important alternative for future work in developed countries also. The instrument has a parallel structure for nine pairs of questions about symptoms of food-related hardship. For each symptom, one question asks whether the hardship occurred in the last four weeks. If so, the second question asks about frequency (rarely/sometimes/ often).

An advantage of the multiple-question approach is that it can in principle address all the dimensions of the definition of food insecurity. A disadvantage is increased respondent burden. Also, an array of ten or eighteen response frequencies is too cumbersome for many policy applications, so in practice the results must be condensed to a smaller number of food security measures for major communication and policy uses.

2.4   Basic Algorithms for Determining Food Security Status

The most important statistics from multiple-question food security instruments are computed using basic, practical algorithms with varying levels of complexity. For example, for food security in a twelve-month period, from the questions above, official US food security statistics are generated as follows. First, each question is converted into a binary indicator. An item is considered to be affirmed if the response is "yes" for yes/no questions, if the response is "sometimes" or "often" for frequency questions, and if the response is "almost every month" or "some months but not every month" for questions that ask in how many months a symptom occurred. Second, a raw score is computed as the sum of affirmative responses, ranging from 0–10 for households without children and 0–18 for households with children. Third, because the meaning of the raw score is inherently different for a ten-item instrument or an eighteen-item instrument, different raw score thresholds are used for households with and without children. In the official approach used from 1995 through 2003, a household was classified as

- food-secure if the raw score is 0–2;
- food-insecure without hunger if the raw score is 3–5 for households without children or 3–7 for household with children; and
- food-insecure with hunger if the raw score is 6–10 for households without children or 8–18 for households with children.

Bavier questioned the particular threshold for using the label "with hunger." He noted that a substantial fraction of households classified as food-insecure with hunger nevertheless failed to affirm a survey question using the word "hunger" (Bavier 2004; Wunderlich and Norwood 2006). Beginning with official statistics for 2005, following the CNSTAT position on hunger definition discussed above, the labels for the latter two categories were changed, respectively, to "low food security" and "very low food security."

Canadian food security statistics use the same eighteen-item instrument, but a different basic algorithm for classification. Separate raw scores and food security status determinations are based on the ten adult-referenced items and the eight child-referenced items. Based on the combination of results for adults and children, the household is classified as secure, food-insecure (moderate), or food-insecure (severe). The thresholds differ in the Canadian and US algorithms, so some households that would be classified as food-secure in the United States are classified as food-insecure in Canada.

For the FANTA nine-item instrument, a scoring system assigns points for each item based on the frequency with which a symptom of hardship occurred, for a total score of 0–27 points. However, the food security classification cannot be determined from the total points. Instead, the basic algorithm employs a table of thresholds that depends on the particular frequency response for each of the nine items. For example, "A food secure household experiences none of the food insecurity (access) conditions, or just experiences worry, but rarely." The food security classification has four levels: food-secure, mildly food-insecure, moderately food-insecure, and severely food-insecure.

The basic algorithms have the intended advantage of generating simple prevalence estimates for a small number of food security status categories from a longer set of survey questions. There are also several disadvantages: (1) substantial information from survey questions about frequency of occurrence is sometimes discarded when questions are converted to binary indicators; (2) the names of status categories are only loosely related to the language of the questions in the instrument, and subject to political debate and policy reversals; and (3) terminology for status classifications differs across survey instruments, across households with and without children, and across reference periods, to an extent that seems difficult to reconcile.

From an empirical perspective, prevalence estimates for food security categories can be used to monitor trends over time using the same survey instrument. However, a reader cannot trust a food security or food insecurity category label to have the same real meaning as the formal definitions given earlier. Instead, to understand the meaning of survey-based food security prevalence estimates, the reader must absorb the full set of survey questions and learn the classification algorithm. This circumstance reduces the intended advantages of simplicity in the basic algorithms.

2.5   Item Response Theory Methods

In part to address some of these difficulties, much of the research literature on food security measurement employs item response theory (IRT) or scaling methods. If a survey instrument has multiple items on multiple topics, one could think of the basic algorithms above as a way of summarizing multivariate results in a smaller number of useful prevalence statistics for food security categories. More ambitiously, the IRT or scaling approach supposes that there exists a single unobserved latent variable, or a small number of latent variables, which influence the responses to individual survey questions. In IRT, one could think of the survey questions as semi-opaque windows on the more fundamental food security phenomenon—like trying to locate the sun through the stained-glass window panes in a church, where no one pane gives a satisfactory view on its own.

In the food security literature, the IRT models have been motivated by several goals:

- The IRT models could in principle be used to help choose the thresholds or boundaries for classifying households into food security categories in a more basic algorithm discussed above (Ohls, Radbill, and Schirm 2001).
- The IRT models might be used to make thresholds comparable when different questions are asked of demographic groups, such as households with and without children (Wilde 2004a).
- IRT models might illuminate food insecurity as a unitary continuous phenomenon that is more fundamental than the discrete hardships represented by the individual survey items (Wunderlich and Norwood 2006).
- IRT models might assess the scaling properties of the survey items, to help demonstrate their validity as a measure of food insecurity (Wunderlich and Norwood 2006).
- IRT models might be used to assign a continuous scale score to individual households, for use in further multivariate analysis or even for clinical assessment in the field.

In the IRT literature, the actual survey responses are called manifest variables, $X_1 \ldots X_T$, where T is the number of survey items. Here, to conserve notation, we address binary indicators of affirmative response, although this case can be generalized. A continuous latent variable or vector of latent variables describing food insecurity is ϕ. As a mnemonic device, suggested in the CNSTAT report, the Greek letter phi stands for food *in*security.

Conditional on ϕ, the probabilities of affirmative responses to the items are independent:

$$P\{X_1, X_2, \ldots, X_T \,|\, \phi\} = P\{X_1 \,|\, \phi\}P\{X_2 \,|\, \phi\} \ldots P\{X_T \,|\, \phi\}. \tag{1}$$

A household with more severe food insecurity (a higher value of ϕ) can have a higher probability of affirming each item, of course. This assumption says only that, holding constant ϕ, the items are independent. In US food security measurement, some items (such as cutting or skipping meals in several months) clearly depend on other items (such as ever cutting or skipping meals), which violates this conditional independence assumption.

The specific IRT model depends on the functional form for each conditional probability. The two most studied models are linear factor analysis and the Rasch model.

2.6 Linear Factor Analysis

Linear factor analysis is similar to the linear probability model for a binary outcome. In a linear factor analysis model with, for example, four latent factors:

$$P\{X_t \,|\, \phi\} = \beta_{t0} + \beta_{t1}\phi_1 + \beta_{t2}\phi_2 + \beta_{t3}\phi_3 + \beta_{t4}\phi4. \tag{2}$$

In a technical report for the first official US food security survey in 1995, linear factor analysis led designers to drop two candidate questions about coping strategies so that the remaining questions could be scaled using a single latent food insecurity variable (Hamilton et al. 1997). Since then, food security survey instruments have usually excluded questions about the fourth domain in the definition of food security discussed above, related to acquiring food in socially acceptable ways. A later factor analysis found that the remaining questions still suggest two latent variables, related to food insecurity for adults and children in the household (Froelich 2002; Wunderlich and Norwood 2006), but most research nevertheless treats food insecurity as a unidimensional phenomenon.

Whelan, Nolan, and Maître (2008) included the question about food deprivation available in European survey data (being able to afford meals with meat, chicken, or fish) in an analysis of symptoms of material deprivation more broadly. Factor analysis suggested that three latent variables best explained the variation in the item responses. One latent variable most closely influenced the survey questions' responses about food deprivation and other consumption variables. As with other European research, food security is embedded within a larger research interest in material deprivation, not treated as a stand-alone latent variable.

2.7 The Rasch Model

A Rasch model has a logistic functional form:

$$P\{X_t \mid \phi\} = \exp\{\phi - \beta_t\}/[1 + \exp\{\phi - \beta_t\}]. \tag{3}$$

Equivalently, one could say the log odds for an affirmative response to item t equals $\phi - \beta_t$. The coefficient β_t is called the item severity calibration. The probability of an affirmative response to item t increases as food insecurity increases and decreases as the item severity calibration increases.

The Rasch model is a special case of the logistic regression model with fixed effects (Chamberlain 1980; Wooldridge 2002). As with all fixed effects logit models, the maximum likelihood estimator for food insecurity scores and item calibrations jointly is inconsistent, because the number of parameters to be estimated increases as the sample size increases. Although such joint maximum likelihood has been used in the food security literature, it is not really correct to treat the latent food security scores as parameters to be estimated by maximum likelihood when there are just a fixed small number of items.

One alternative estimation approach, marginal maximum likelihood, generates consistent estimates, but it requires strong parametric assumptions about the distribution of the food insecurity score, in addition to the assumptions already reviewed for the Rasch model (Wunderlich and Norwood 2006). Another estimation approach, conditional maximum likelihood, requires no additional distributional assumptions beyond the basic assumptions of the Rasch model. However, much as fixed effects are swept away in well-known linear fixed effects models, conditional maximum likelihood can only consistently estimate the Rasch model's item calibration parameters, not the latent food insecurity scores for individual households.

The Rasch model has been cited in motivating the basic algorithm used in US food security measurement, based on the raw score of affirmative responses (Wunderlich and Norwood 2006). A property of the Rasch model, which distinguishes it from other IRT models, is that the estimated food insecurity score increases monotonically with the raw score. Hence, setting raw score thresholds for food security categories, as the US approach does, could be seen as a way of categorizing households according to ranges of their estimated value of ϕ in the Rasch model. If the assumptions of the Rasch model were true, they would provide justification for the basic algorithm used in US measurement.

However, the Rasch model, like other IRT models, requires the conditional independence assumption in equation (1). Holding constant the food insecurity score ϕ, if different household characteristics can be used to predict the conditional probability of affirmative response for different items, then the resulting circumstance is called differential item function (DIF), a violation of assumption (1). Opsomer, Jensen, and Pan (2003) found evidence of DIF in US food security measurement. Ohls, Radbill, and Schirm (2001) also did, but argued that it was inconsequential. Wilde (2004a) showed that households with and without children have systematically different response patterns to food security items, even holding constant their raw score. At a given level of food insecurity, households with children are comparatively more likely to worry about running out of food, while households without children are comparatively more likely to report a lack of balanced meals. DIF across households with and without children is relevant, because these two groups get different question sets in the US measurement approach, so a failure of the Rasch model's assumptions makes it more difficult to explain the basic algorithm's different thresholds for determining food security status in the two household types.

Noting a number of empirical concerns about the Rasch model, the CNSTAT committee recommended that more flexible IRT models with more parameters be explored (Wunderlich and Norwood 2006). Such models might exploit some of the information that is discarded when survey questions are converted to binary indicators, and they could in principle use a more general functional form that resolves concerns about DIF and other failures of statistical assumptions in the Rasch model.

However, these alternatives also present problems of their own. They cannot be estimated by conditional maximum likelihood, so consistent estimation would require stronger assumptions about the distribution of food insecurity in a marginal maximum likelihood approach. In more complex models, thresholds for food security categories cannot be based on the raw score, so the basic algorithm would have to treat different questions differently, as in the FANTA and Canadian approaches. Experts would have to decide which response patterns merit each category label. In explaining food security statistics to non-technical policy-relevant constituencies, it would become more difficult to describe how households are categorized and to justify controversial category labels. To date, no major food security effort has used these more complex IRT models.

It may be that IRT models are less promising in food security applications than was once thought. Although the CNSTAT report endorsed IRT models and recommended exploration of more complex modes in this family, it also said, "despite the appeal of latent variable models as ways of organizing independent indicators of an underlying latent variable, there is a clear sense that one gets out of a latent variable model no more than what one puts into it" (Wunderlich and Norwood 2006). Latent variable models are heavily used in other fields, such as educational testing, where they are better motivated. One cannot use simple sentinel questions in educational testing, because test takers would learn the right answer over time. In food security measurement, as Richard Bavier has argued, "Neither of the two unifying phenomena that underlie the food security concept—increasingly severe disruption of normal food intake and increasingly severe economic distress—are latent traits" (Bavier 2004).

If latent variable models do not prove fruitful, an alternative is to focus on the manifest variables themselves, estimating the frequency of occurrence for specific symptoms of food-related hardship and reporting the results in the same language that was used in the survey questions. For example, especially since the change of US terminology for hunger, the best national estimates of hunger prevalence have been the simple frequency tabulations of responses to the single survey items about adults or children going hungry.

2.8   Empirical Evidence on Food Insecurity

Because different measurement approaches and survey questions have been used in different countries, while the countries have different levels of food insecurity, it is challenging to compare the empirical evidence on food security in the available cross-country data. As an initial effort, Table 12.1 arrays eight selected developed countries in columns, in descending order of the prevalence of inability to afford food, according to a single survey question (in Table 12.1, row 4) from the Pew Global Attitudes Project (2003). The rows in Table 12.1 report different measures of food deprivation, in approximate increasing order of severity. In the absence of a formal IRT model, the best insight into the severity of the measures comes from comparisons in response frequencies within the same country (such as the United States).

Poland has the highest prevalence of inability to afford food, according to the Pew Global Attitudes question (37 percent). The United States has the second-highest level (15 percent). Japan (4 percent) and Germany (3 percent) had the lowest levels. In Germany and Japan, but not in the United States and United Kingdom, rates of inability to afford food have been falling (improving) between the mid-1970s and 2002.

Cross-item comparisons within the United States indicate that the single Pew Global Attitudes question refers to a type of hardship that is slightly milder than the definition of food insecurity in the US official measurement approach. In the United States, based on the official multiple-item approach, 11.1 percent of households were food-insecure in 2007, and 4.1 percent had very low food security, the condition formerly known as food-insecurity with hunger. Meanwhile, 3.3 percent of US households affirmed the individual survey item about adults going hungry and not eating in 2007. Using the consistent US algorithm for classifying households, the rate of food insecurity was substantially lower in Canada (7.3 percent) than in the United States (11.1 percent).

3   Policy Responses to Food Insecurity

Countries address food security through general economic policies and through more specific food assistance programs. General economic policies include, for example, anti-poverty programs and interventions to support the low-wage labor market. Specific food assistance programs include a wide array of public sector and charitable responses to food insecurity and hunger.

3.1   General Economic Policies

Lower household income strongly predicts lower household food security. In Canada, where 9.2 percent of the population is classified as food-insecure using the multiple-question approach described above, 48 percent of the lowest-income households are food-insecure, in contrast with just 5 percent of upper-middle-income households (Office of Nutrition Policy and Promotion 2007). A similar gradient exists in the United States (Nord, Andrews, and Carlson 2008) and, one expects, the other developed countries.

Hence, a leading candidate explanation for the difference in food security across developed countries in Table 12.1 is differences in poverty rates and the anti-poverty social safety net. To investigate further, one must decide whether to use a relative or absolute measure of poverty. Over the second half of the twentieth century, European countries closed a large gap and caught up with the United States in terms of overall economic productivity per unit labor (Gordon 2007). Yet, at purchasing-power parity, European mean incomes after taxes and transfers are only 75 percent of those in the United States, largely because of fewer mean per capita annual hours worked. There is an active debate over how to interpret this transatlantic income difference. For example, Europeans would appear to have a lower standard of living if the lower European labor supply reflects involuntary unemployment, but not if the lower labor supply reflects additional voluntary leisure.

The United States stands out for its particularly high poverty rate using a relative poverty measure based on income after taxes and transfers, attributable to the combination of high median income and a high degree of economic inequality. Higher average income after taxes and transfers is generally associated with lower absolute poverty rates, holding constant the dispersion or inequality in income, while higher average income after taxes and transfers has a more complex relationship with relative poverty rates, because the poverty line is pegged to a percentage of median income. A leading contributor to the comparatively high US poverty rate in the cross-national comparisons is the effect of taxes and transfers that reduce poverty in other developed countries. Although the United States has the first- or second-highest poverty level in Smeeding's study of eleven developed countries based on income after taxes and transfers (Smeeding 2006), it has below-average poverty based on income before taxes and transfers. In Smeeding's analysis:

> In 2000, the United States spent less than 3 percent of GDP on cash and near-cash assistance for the nonelderly (families with children and the disabled). This amount is less than half the share of GDP spent for this purpose by Canada, Ireland

Table 12.1 Food security and economic conditions in eight selected members of the OECD–28 developed countries (%)

	Selected countries (in approximate descending order of inability to afford food, if reported)							
	Poland	USA	UK	Canada	France	Japan	Germany	Australia
Food security condition (in approximate order of severity)								
Worried food would run out before got money to buy more, 2007		15.4						
Could not afford to eat a fruit each day if wished (OECD)						10.5	10.1	
Could not afford meat/chicken every 2nd day if wished (OECD)			6.1					
Unable to afford food, past year, 2002 (Pew Global Attitudes)	37.0	15.0	11.0	10.0	8.0	4.0	3.0	
Unable to afford food, past year, 1974–5 (Pew Global Attitudes)		14.0	8.0	6.0	6.0	14.0	7.0	
Food-insecure, past year, 2007, Canadian classification				9.2				
Food-insecure, past year, 2007, US classification		11.1		7.3				
Food-insecure (ran out of food and couldn't afford more), Australia								5.0
Severe food insecurity (went without food), Australia								2
Very low food security, past year, 2007, US classification		4.1						
Respondent hungry but didn't eat, 2007		3.3						
Economic condition								
Relative poverty rate, 2002 (OECD)	14.6	17.1	8.3	12.0	7.1	14.9	11.0	12.4
Relative poverty rate, ~2000, after taxes and transfers (Smeeding 2006)		17.0	12.4	11.4			8.3	
Absolute poverty rate, ~2000, after taxes and transfers (Smeeding 2006)		8.7	12.4	6.9			7.6	
Food spending share of total income (USDA/ERS)	30.7	9.7	16.4	11.7	15.3	14.9	13.1	15.1

or the United Kingdom; less than a third of spending in Austria, Germany, the Netherlands or Belgium; and less than a quarter of the amount spent in Finland or Sweden. These differences are primarily long term and secular, not related to the business cycle. (Smeeding 2006)

The US Food Stamp Program, recently renamed the Supplemental Nutrition Assistance Program (SNAP), is included among the transfer programs in Smeeding's analysis.

3.2   Government Food Assistance Programs

In the United States, where food assistance has a major role in the social safety net, the federal government spent $60 billion on fifteen programs in fiscal year 2008 (Oliveira 2008). The Food Stamp Program/SNAP provided targeted benefits for food and non-alcoholic beverages from authorized grocery retailers through Electronic Benefit Transfer cards similar to debit cards. It served 28.4 million people per month on average during fiscal year 2008 at a total cost of $37.5 billion. Program eligibility depends largely on having income below 130 percent of the federal poverty standard, so the program is counter-cyclical, and caseloads have recently risen to record levels during the current recession. The primary purpose of the program is to prevent hunger and promote food security.

The Special Supplemental Food Program for Women, Infants and Children (WIC) provided nutrition counseling, services, and a package of particular high-nutrient foods and infant formula to about 8.7 million people per month, at a cost of $6.2 billion in fiscal year 2008. Only pregnant and post-partum women, infants, and children are eligible. Eligibility requires household income below 185 percent of the federal poverty standard, plus evidence of nutrition risk broadly defined. The National School Lunch Program served 30.9 million lunches, and the smaller and newer School Breakfast served 10.6 million breakfasts on average each school day in fiscal year 2008, at a cost of $11.7 billion. A free meal requires income below 130 percent of the federal poverty standard, though all federal school meals are subsidized to some extent. The Child and Adult Care Food Program served meals in centers and home day care settings, costing $2.4 billion (Oliveira 2008). These programs have primary nutrition goals, but anti-hunger effects are acknowledged as important secondary purposes.

The European policy response to poverty gives less emphasis to food in particular: "there have been few food-oriented interventions and those that have been undertaken, such as the school meals scheme, EU free beef and 'meals on wheels,' have not attracted significant public resources" (Friel and Conlon 2004). In the United Kingdom some programs to encourage healthy food consumption have an income-targeted component. For example, Healthy Start, a modified version of an earlier Welfare Food Programme, somewhat similar to the US WIC program, provides supplemental milk, fresh fruit or vegetables, or infant formula to pregnant teenagers and women who participate in other means-tested safety net programs (Dowler 2008). Similarly, in

Canada there are some food-specific programs, such as a subsidy for food transportation to remote northern areas, but social safety net programs do not generally focus on food in particular (Nord and Hopwood 2008).

Research that seeks to measure the effect of food assistance programs on food security outcomes has generally been thwarted by strong self-selection effects. For example, in the United States the prevalence of food insecurity with hunger (12.3 percent of all low-income households in 2004) was much higher among Food Stamp Program/SNAP participant households (18.6 percent in 2004) than among low-income non-participant households (10.1 percent in 2004) (Wilde 2007). As one would expect, evidence suggests that the prevalence of food insecurity falls as total income (including food stamp benefits plus cash income) increases. Yet, holding constant total income in an effort to measure the distinct impact of targeted in-kind benefits, participants continue to have higher rates of food insecurity (Wilde, Troy, and Rogers 2008). A large literature with observational data has employed a wide variety of econometric approaches to control for self-selection, but, in most cases, the authors continue to find unexpected results and caution against drawing causal inferences from their research (Wilde 2007). A recent exception is an instrumental variables analysis by Yen et al. (2008), which does find the expected relationship between food stamp participation and reduced risk of food insecurity. There has been some discussion of random-assignment research designs in food assistance impact measurement, but ethical research design requires that no arm of the study gets less than the current standard of care or the benefits to which they are entitled by law, and it is not clear if this approach is feasible.

These research difficulties do not imply that government food assistance programs are ineffective. Among other merits, such programs clearly provide valuable resources to low-income populations. These research difficulties do indicate the hurdles to using survey-based food security outcomes as program evaluation tools. The early literature on multiple-question food security surveys had high hopes that the new measures could be used to evaluate and improve government food assistance programs (Eisinger 1998). For some years, the US federal government included food security outcomes among the criteria for evaluating the Food Stamp Program/SNAP under the official performance assessment process. More recently, progress reports have omitted quantitative food security measures without giving a reason (Wilde 2004b). The CNSTAT report on food security recommended that trends in food security prevalence not be used on their own as an indicator for program assessment (Wunderlich and Norwood 2006).

3.3   Charitable Food Programs

Private sector charitable programs are another high-profile component of developed countries' response to food insecurity and hunger. In the United States a 2003 report estimated there were 5,300 emergency food kitchens and 32,700 food pantries, which rely heavily on private donations and volunteer labor. The food itself comes from direct donations and from distribution through about 400 food banks, the wholesalers of the emergency food system (Ohls et al. 2002). Food banks, which also rely heavily on private donations, but which generally use a more professional staffing structure and paid employees, receive food through purchases, donations from individuals, donations from food companies, and federal commodities. Originally, the federal commodities were largely acquired through USDA price support mechanisms, but more recently the majority are purchased through appropriations to the Emergency Food Assistance Program. Feeding America, formerly known as America's Second Harvest, the principal national network of food banks, distributed more than 2 billion pounds of food per year in recent years.

The European Federation of Food Banks similarly distributes about 0.6 billion pounds of food per year through a network of more than 26,000 charitable organizations. About half of the food is commodities from the European Union and half is charitable donations from the food industry and individuals.

Food insecurity has been found to be widespread among users of charitable food. In the United States between 34 and 45 percent of clients of food pantries and emergency kitchens were food-insecure in USDA's 2003 national study (Briefel et al. 2003). In Canada, among food pantry users in metropolitan Toronto in 1996–7, almost 70 percent were classified as food-insecure with hunger, using the methodology available at the time (Tarasuk and Beaton 1999).

The emergency food system is considered by policymakers and its many thousands of professional and volunteer workers to be an important bulwark against food insecurity and hunger. With a close connection to faith-based charitable work (Ohls et al. 2002), many of the system's supporters articulate a religious and ethical motivation for feeding the poor. A respectful counter-current has inquired whether the charitable efforts could either reduce the incentive to participate in more formal government-sponsored food assistance or undermine the political support for such programs by alleviating public perceptions of the need for them (Riches 1997; Poppendieck 1998; Winne 2008). Some empirical research suggests that low-income people who participate in the emergency food system are in fact also more likely to receive government program benefits (Bhattarai, Duffy, and Raymond 2005).

4   FOOD INSECURITY AND ITS COVARIATES

In addition to its strong association with low income, food insecurity is associated with a wide variety of other variables that reflect hardship: poor physical and mental health, depressive symptoms in adolescents, and academic and social developmental delays in children, to name just a few (Jyoti, Frongillo, and Jones 2005; Wunderlich and Norwood 2006).

The developing-country literature gives particular attention to the connection between food insecurity and low nutrient intake (Abdulai and Kuhlgatz, Chapter 13 in this volume). This link to nutrient intake is sometimes studied in developed countries as well. In the United States early studies by Cristofar and Basiotis (1992) and Rose and Oliveira (1997) associated survey measures of food insufficiency with lower dietary intake. Using data from the National Health and Nutrition Examination Survey (NHANES), Lee and Frongillo (2001) reported that food-insecure elders had significantly lower intakes of energy, protein, and several micronutrients. In Canadian adolescents and adults, Kirkpatrick and Tarasuk (2008) found greater evidence of nutrient inadequacy in food-insecure households.

Another important covariate in food security research is income or poverty. For some authors, a key point is that there is cross-household variation in food insecurity beyond that which can be explained by variation in income, indicating that food insecurity is not just about income and poverty. For other authors, having the expected covariance among survey items in the multiple-question approach, and between food insecurity and external hardship variables, is taken as a validation of the multiple-question IRT model measurement approach (Frongillo 1999).

A dissenting literature sets harder-to-meet criteria for validating the survey-based measures. For example, Bhattacharya, Currie, and Haider (2004) emphasize that poverty, too, is associated with many covariates that reflect hardship. In their analysis of data from the NHANES, using a definition of food insecurity that differed from the official US approach, poverty is predictive of poor nutrition outcomes among pre-school children, but, once one controls for poverty, food insecurity makes no additional contribution to explaining variation in the nutrition outcomes. Gundersen and Kreider (2008) note that some respondents affirm more severe food security items without affirming less severe items, raising questions about the reliability of the scale. They also emphasize the possible importance of reporting errors in food program participation status as a source of difficulty in measuring the effect of food assistance on food security.

One of the most noted covariates of food insecurity is increased risk of overweight and obesity (Townsend et al. 2001; Jyoti, Frongillo, and Jones 2005; Wilde and Peterman 2006). At least two mechanisms have been proposed that might explain this phenomenon: (a) general food availability punctuated by periodic episodes of severe shortage, such as at the end of the food stamp month, could generate boom and bust cycles in food energy intake that increase susceptibility to overweight (Wilde and Ranney 2000); and (b) low cost and easy access to energy-dense foods could be combined with higher cost and lack of local access to higher-quality less energy-dense foods, such as fresh fruits and vegetables (Drewnowski and Specter 2004; Darmon, Ferguson, and Briend 2006). Some critics of food assistance programs use the association between food insecurity and obesity to belittle the problem of food insecurity, whereas most of the research literature finds it plausible that economic constraints could contribute to both food insecurity and weight issues. Still, the association between food insecurity and obesity does drive home the point that food insecurity as measured in the survey-based "third generation" approach is related not just to lack of food, but to an array of low-income conditions that includes both food shortage and food abundance of different types. This has implications for both measurement and policy. At the least, survey questions such as the official US instrument's question about losing weight no longer seem in step with the current empirical literature.

5   CONCLUSION

Food security measurement and policy in developed countries are at a point of transition. The "third generation" of definitions and measurement approaches has centered on survey questions about symptoms of food-related hardship, usually combined into multiple-question scales using IRT methods. These survey questions address many, though frequently not all, of the dimensions of the widely accepted contemporary definition of household food insecurity. However, there has not yet been convergence in methodology across the developed countries. European sources generally address food security issues within a broader framework of material deprivation and social exclusion, whereas US sources, and to some degree Canadian and Australian sources, treat food security as its own topic. Hopes for greater convergence in the future have been complicated by uncertainty even in the US literature about how the measurement tools should be modified and improved. Motivation can be found in the US literature for developing yet more complex IRT models or, alternatively, retreating and focusing on simpler sentinel questions that can be interpreted individually. Though the specific scaling methodology used in developing the US measure cannot be recommended for wider adoption, it would be valuable for more OECD-28 countries to consider adopting multiple survey questions similar to those used in the United States and Canada. Even in countries without major expenditures on in-kind food assistance programs, similar survey tools would facilitate cross-country comparisons and illuminate an important dimension of social well-being.

Food security policy, similarly, has come to a turning point. Food security is not fully explained by household income, but household income remains one of its most reliable covariates. Early hopes have been dashed that food security can be used as the yardstick by which food assistance programs are judged. Across the developed countries, there remains a diversity of food security policies, with the United States emphasizing food assistance and food charities as the primary direct responses, while other developed countries associate food security with symptoms of material deprivation and social exclusion for which the primary response is the income-based social safety net more broadly.

REFERENCES

Anderson, S. A. 1990. "Core Indicators of Nutritional State for Difficult-to-Sample Populations." *Journal of Nutrition* 120/11S: 1559–600.

Barrett, C. B. 2002. "Food Security and Food Assistance Programs." In B. Gardner and G. Rausser, eds, *Handbook of Agricultural Economics*, 2. St Louis, MO: Elsevier Science.

Bavier, R. 2004. *Critique Presented at the First Meeting of the Panel to Review the USDA's Measurement of Food Insecurity and Hunger*. Washington, DC: Center for National Statistics.

Bhattacharya, J., J. Currie, and S. Haider. 2004. "Poverty, Food Insecurity, and Nutritional Outcomes in Children and Adults." *Journal of Health Economics* 23: 839–62.

Bhattarai, G. R., P. A. Duffy, and J. Raymond. 2005. "Use of Food Pantries and Food Stamps in Low-Income Households in the United States." *Journal of Consumer Affairs* 39/2: 276–98.

Briefel, R., J. Jacobson, N. Clusen, T. Zavitsky, M. Satake, B. Dawson, and R. Cohen. 2003. *The Emergency Food Assistance System: Findings from the Client Survey*. Food Assistance and Nutrition Research Report No. 32. Washington, DC: Mathematica Policy Research for US Department of Agriculture Economic Research Service.

Chamberlain, G. 1980. "Analysis of Covariance with Qualitative Data." *Review of Economic Studies* 47: 225–38.

Coates, J., E. Frongillo, R. Houser, B. Rogers, P. Webb, and P. Wilde. 2006. "Commonalities in the Experience of Household Food Insecurity across Cultures: What Are Measures Missing?" *Journal of Nutrition* 136: 1438S–1448S.

——, A. Swindale, and P. Bilinsky. 2007. *Household Food Insecurity Access Scale (HFIAS) for Measurement of Food Access: Indicator Guide*. Washington, DC: Food and Nutrition Technical Assistance Project (FANTA), Academy for Educational Development.

Cristofar, S. P., and P. P. Basiotis. 1992. "Dietary Intakes and Selected Characteristics of Women Ages 19–50 Years and their Children Ages 1–5 Years by Reported Perception of Food Sufficiency." *Journal of Nutrition Education* 24: 53–8.

Darmon, N., E. L. Ferguson, and A. Briend. 2006. "Impact of a Cost Constraint on Nutritionally Adequate Food Choices for French Women: An Analysis by Linear Programming." *Journal of Nutrition Education and Behavior* 38: 82–90.

Dowler, E. 2008. "Policy Initiatives to Address Low-Income Households' Nutritional Needs in the UK." *Proceedings of the Nutrition Society* 67: 289–300.

Drewnowski, A., and S. E. Specter. 2004. "Poverty and Obesity: The Role of Energy Density and Energy Costs." *American Journal of Clinical Nutrition* 79: 6–16.

Eisinger, P. K. 1998. *Toward an End to Hunger in America*. Washington, DC: Brookings Institution Press.

FAO (Food and Agriculture Organization). 2003. *Trade Reforms and Food Security: Conceptualizing the Linkages*. Rome: Food and Agriculture Organization of the United Nations.

—— 2008. *The State of Food Insecurity in the World, 2008*. Rome: Food and Agriculture Organization of the United Nations.

Fogel, R. W. 2004. *The Escape from Hunger and Premature Death, 1700–2100: Europe, America, and the Third World*. New York: Cambridge University Press.

Friel, S., and C. Conlon. 2004. *Food Poverty and Policy*. Dublin: Combat Poverty Agency.

Froelich, A. G. 2002. *Dimensionality of the USDA Food Security Index*. Ames: Department of Statistics, Iowa State University.

Frongillo, E. A. 1999. "Validation of Measures of Food Insecurity and Hunger." *Journal of Nutrition* 129: 506S–509S.

Gordon, R. J. 2007. "Issues in the Comparison of Welfare between Europe and the United States." Paper presented to Bureau of European Policy Advisers, "Change, Innovation and Distribution." Brussels.

Gundersen, C., and B. Kreider 2008. "Food Stamps and Food Insecurity: What Can Be Learned in the Presence of Nonclassical Measurement Error?" *Journal of Human Resources* 43/2: 352–82.

Hamilton, W. L., J. T. Cook, W. W. Thompson, L. F. Buron, E. A. Frongillo, C. M. Olson, and C. A. Wehler. 1997. *Household Food Security in the United States in 1995: Technical Report of the Food Security Measurement Project*. Alexandria, VA: Food and Nutrition Service, US Department of Agriculture.

Holben, D. H. 2005. *The Concept of Hunger*. Background paper for the Panel to Review the US Department of Agriculture's Measurement of Food Insecurity and Hunger. Washington, DC: Center for National Statistics.

Jyoti, D. F., E. A. Frongillo, and S. J. Jones. 2005. "Food Insecurity Affects School Children's Academic Performance, Weight Gain, and Social Skills." *Journal of Nutrition* 135: 2831–9.

Kirkpatrick, S. I., and V. Tarasuk. 2008. "Food Insecurity Is Associated with Nutrient Inadequacies among Canadian Adults and Adolescents." *Journal of Nutrition* 138: 604–12.

Lee, J. S., and E. A. Frongillo. 2001. "Nutritional and Health Consequences Are Associated with Food Insecurity among US Elderly Persons." *Journal of Nutrition* 131: 1503–9.

Marks, G. C., I. Rutishauser, K. Webb, and P. Picton. 2001. *Key Food and Nutrition Data for Australia 1990–1999*. Herston: Australian Food and Nutrition Monitoring Unit.

Nord, M., and H. Hopwood. 2008. *A Comparison of Household Food Security in Canada and the United States*. Economic Research Report No. 67. Washington, DC: Economic Research Service, US Department of Agriculture.

——, M. Andrews, and S. Carlson. 2008. *Household Food Security in the United States, 2007*. Economic Research Report No. 66. Washington, DC: Economic Research Service, US Department of Agriculture.

——, M. Finberg, and J. McLaughlin. 2009. "What Should the Government Mean by Hunger?" *Journal of Hunger and Environmental Nutrition* 4: 20–47.

OECD (Organization for Economic Cooperation and Development). 2008. *Growing Unequal? Income Distribution and Poverty in OECD Countries*. Paris: OECD.

Office of Nutrition Policy and Promotion. 2007. *Income-Related Household Food Security in Canada*. Ottawa: Health Canada.

Ohls, J., L. Radbill, and A. Schirm. 2001. *Household Food Security in the United States, 1995–1997: Technical Issues and Statistical Report*. Alexandria, VA: Food and Nutrition Service, US Department of Agriculture.

——, F. Saleem-Ismail, R. Cohen, and B. Cox. 2002. *The Emergency Food Assistance System: Findings from the Provider Survey, 2: Final Report*. Food Assistance and Nutrition Research Report No. 16-2. Washington, DC: Mathematica Policy Research for US Department of Agriculture Economic Research Service.

Oliveira, V. 2008. *The Food Assistance Landscape*. Economic Information Bulletin No. 6-6. Washington, DC: Economic Research Service, US Department of Agriculture.

Opsomer, J. D., H. H. Jensen, and S. Pan. 2003. "An Evaluation of the U.S. Department of Agriculture Food Security Measure with Generalized Linear Mixed Models." *Journal of Nutrition* 133: 421–7.

Pew Global Attitudes Project. 2003. "Most of the World Still Does Without." <http://pewglobal.org/commentary/display.php?AnalysisID=75>.

Poppendieck, J. 1998. *Sweet Charity? Emergency Food and the End of Entitlement*. New York: Penguin.

Radimer, K. L. 2002. "Measurement of Household Food Security in the USA and Other Industrialised Countries." *Public Health Nutrition* 5: 859–64.

——, C. M. Olson, and C. C. Campbell. 1990. "Development of Indicators to Assess Hunger." *Journal of Nutrition* 120: 1544–8.

Riches, G. 1997. "Hunger, Food Security and Welfare Policies: Issues and Debates in First World Societies." *Proceedings of the Nutrition Society* 56: 63–74.

Rose, D., and V. Oliveira. 1997. "Nutrient Intakes of Individuals from Food Insufficient Households in the United States." *American Journal of Public Health* 87: 1956–61.

Rosen, S., S. Shapouri, K. Quanbeck, and B. Meade. 2008. *Food Security Assessment, 2007.* GFA-19. Washington, DC: Economic Research Service, US Department of Agriculture.

Russell, D., W. Parnell, and N. Wilson. 1999. *NZ Food: NZ People Key Results of the 1997 National Nutrition Survey*. Wellington: Ministry of Health.

Sanchez, P., M. S. Swaminathan, P. Dobie, and N. Yuksel. 2005. *Halving Hunger: It Can Be Done*. London: UN Millennium Project Task Force on Hunger.

Saunders, P., and A. Abe. 2008. "Comparing Monetary and Non-Monetary Indicators of Household Well-Being in Australia and Japan." Paper prepared for the 30th General Conference of the International Association for Research in Income and Wealth, Portorož, Slovenia, Aug. 24–30.

Smeeding, T. 2006. "Poor People in Rich Nations: The United States in Comparative Perspective." *Journal of Economic Perspectives* 20/1: 69–90.

Tarasuk, V. S., and G. H. Beaton. 1999. "Household Food Insecurity and Hunger among Families Using Food Banks." *Canadian Journal of Public Health* 90/2: 109–13.

Temple, J. 2008. "Severe and Moderate Forms of Food Insecurity in Australia: Are They Distinguishable?" *Australian Journal of Social Issues* 43/4: 649–68.

Townsend, M., J. Peerson, B. Love, C. Achterberg, and S. Murphy. 2001. "Food Insecurity Is Positively Related to Overweight in Women." *Journal of Nutrition* 131: 1738–45.

Whelan, C. T., B. Nolan, and B. Maître (2008). *Measuring Material Deprivation in the Enlarged EU*. Working Paper No. 249. Dublin: Economic and Social Research Institute.

WHO (World Health Organization). 2009. "Global Database on Child Growth and Malnutrition." <http://www.who.int/nutgrowthdb/en>.

Wilde, P. 2004a. "Differential Response Patterns Affect Food-Security Prevalence Estimates for Households with and without Children." *Journal of Nutrition* 134: 1910–15.

—— 2004b. *The Uses and Purposes of the USDA Food Security and Hunger Measure*. Workshop on the Measurement of Food Insecurity and Hunger, Panel to Review the US Department of Agriculture's Measurement of Food Insecurity and Hunger. Washington, DC: National Research Council.

—— 2007. "Measuring the Effect of Food Stamps on Food Insecurity and Hunger: Research and Policy Considerations." *Journal of Nutrition* 37: 307–10.

—— and J. Peterman. 2006. "Individual Weight Change Is Associated with Household Food Security Status." *Journal of Nutrition* 136: 1395–1400.

—— and C. Ranney. 2000. "The Monthly Food Stamp Cycle: Shopping Frequency and Food Intake Decisions in an Endogenous Switching Regression Framework." *American Journal of Agricultural Economics* 82/1: 200–13.

——, L. Troy, and B. Rogers. 2008. *Household Food Security and Tradeoffs in the Food Budget of Food Stamp Program Participants: An Engel Function Approach.* Contractor and Cooperator Report No. 38. Washington, DC: Economic Research Service, US Department of Agriculture.

Winne, M. 2008. *Closing the Food Gap: Resetting the Table in the Land of Plenty.* Boston: Beacon Press.

Wooldridge, J. M. (2002). *Econometric Analysis of Cross Section and Panel Data.* Boston: MIT Press.

Wunderlich, G. S., and J. L. Norwood, eds. 2006. *Food Insecurity and Hunger in the United States: An Assessment of the Measure.* Washington, DC: National Academies Press.

Yen, S. T., M. Andrews, Z. Chen, and D. B. Eastwood. 2008. "Food Stamp Program Participation and Food Insecurity: An Instrumental Variables Approach." *American Journal of Agricultural Economics* 90/1: 117–32.

CHAPTER 13

....

FOOD SECURITY POLICY IN DEVELOPING COUNTRIES

....

AWUDU ABDULAI AND CHRISTIAN KUHLGATZ

1   INTRODUCTION

....

Recent food price hikes and the global economic crisis left their mark, as the number of hungry and malnourished people increased worldwide, particularly in developing countries. Evidence shows that about 902 million people in the developing world were malnourished in 2008, reflecting an increase of about 65 million since 2000–2 (FAO 2009). The impact of the declines in household income from the global economic downturn has been compounded by the relatively high food prices in many developing countries, resulting in further increases in the number of undernourished households in these countries. Preliminary estimates for 2009 indicate that the cutbacks in food expenditure have resulted in the number of undernourished rising above 1 billion people in developing countries (FAO 2009). This development makes it increasingly difficult to achieve the first millennium development goal (MDG) of halving the number of hungry people by 2015. Fanzo et al. (2010) identify lack of political will at both global and national levels as the major cause of the growing divergence from this important MDG. Although food insecurity had attracted little attention in the media and political agendas of developed countries during the last decades, the situation changed in 2008 as riots over higher food prices occurred throughout the developing world (Falcon and Naylor 2005; Fanzo et al. 2010). The rising numbers of food-insecure persons and the clearly established linkages between food security, national security, and global security have contributed to renewing international interest in food security policies of developing countries.[1]

---

[1] Global security is affected in cases where civil unrest threatens regimes within highly insecure regions, and thereby further destabilizes the whole region and weakens political allies. An additional

Food security involves ensuring both an adequate supply of food and access of the population to that supply, mostly through generating adequate levels of effective demand via income growth or transfers. Food security in developing countries therefore tends to be influenced by both micro and macro factors that include adoption of new technologies, support for institutions available to farmers, and food price policy, as well as monetary, fiscal, and exchange rate policies that affect overall economic growth and income distribution. The policies that are normally associated with food security usually involve structural changes in relative prices, the general economic environment, as well as other measures such as targeted food subsidies, improving technologies, and institutions available to farmers and consumers (Weber et al. 1988).[2]

Policymakers are often confronted with the dilemma of higher food prices to induce increased food production and the food security of low-income consumers, as higher prices impose a heavy cost on this group of consumers. A variety of short- and long-term policy options have been used by governments to promote food security in the developing world. Some measures affect food availability on local markets, others the individuals' entitlements to obtain food, while others tend to influence food utilization, i.e., how many nutrients an individual obtains from a given supply of food.

This chapter reviews the concept of food security and the various approaches developing countries have used to promote food security in their countries. A simple microeconomic model of food security is developed and used to discuss the operational issues on food security strategies. As argued by Mellor (1978), an employment program, or an income transfer program for the poor to improve their food security status, will be inefficient in assisting them unless provision is made for an enlarged supply of basic food commodities. Thus, policies geared at improving food security should include both income generation and food production measures. The discussion in this chapter therefore involves both direct and indirect policy interventions that are used to ensure food security in developing countries.

The chapter is organized as follows. The next section presents a simple microeconomic model of food security that explains individuals' demand for food ingredients as well as the different channels through which they become food-insecure. Sections 3 and 4 examine the food security policies of developing countries as they relate to the theoretical model derived in Section 2. Specifically, Section 3 discusses the food market intervention policies, while Section 4 focuses on the indirect food security measures normally employed to attain a sustainable social and economic environment over the long term. The final section sums up the main conclusions.

---

threat to global security is that increasing food insecurity and global inequality may raise terrorist motivation (Falcon and Naylor 2005).

[2] Sen (1999) points out that hunger relates not only to food production and agricultural expansion, but also to the functioning of the entire economy and the operation of the political and social arrangements that can, directly or indirectly, influence people's ability to acquire food and to achieve health and nourishment.

2   MICROECONOMIC FOOD SECURITY MODEL

Food security exists when all people, at all times, have access to sufficient safe and nutritious food to meet their dietary needs and food preferences for an active and healthy life (FAO 2003). Thus, both quality and quantity of diet are important components of food security. Diet quality measures the ability of foods to supply protein of high biological value and adequate supplies of micronutrients such as minerals, trace elements, and vitamins, whereas diet quantity refers to the availability and consumption of total food energy. In general, where the quantity of food is reduced, so is the intake of micronutrients (Abdulai and Aubert 2004). Access to non-food inputs such as clean water, sanitation, and health care has recently been included in the broader definition of food security (FAO 2009).

The complexity of the food security concept makes it difficult for an effective analysis of a policy's effectiveness. Notwithstanding this task, an attempt is made in a simple microeconomic food security model to show how various policy instruments affect the different dimensions of food security. The model is a version of Becker's (1965) model with the modifications proposed by Barrett (2002). To the extent that food security involves both hunger and malnutrition, we incorporate the ingredients of Lancaster's (1971) product characteristics approach to capture individuals' preferences for product attributes. As noted by Barrett (2002), five key elements that a useful food security model needs to incorporate include: (1) the physiological needs of individuals, (2) irreversibilities like death and permanent impairments, (3) behavioral dynamics, (4) uncertainty and risk, and (5) complementarities and trade-offs between food and other variables such as care giving and education. These elements are incorporated in the model below.

2.1   Model Definition

The most important elements of the model are that individuals are assumed to maximize utility derived from the consumption of goods and services (c) and health status (h). Total consumed product characteristics (x) are obtained through the consumption of c. Product characteristics include ingested metabolizable ingredients (d), which affect the individual's health status (h), and characteristics that are directly valued by the individual (e), such as taste, texture, and social acceptance. Individuals face a time constraint in producing goods and services within a production function. The health status of an individual is determined by a health production function. Given these assumptions, each individual is assumed to maximize a time-separable utility function of the form

$$U_t = E_t \sum_{\tau=t}^{T} \gamma^{\tau-t} U(e_\tau, h_\tau, m_\tau) \quad \gamma \in [0, 1] \tag{1}$$

where E_t is the expectations operator given the information set at time t, γ is the subjective discount factor, T is the number of periods, and m is leisure. Utility is non-negative and strictly increasing in the individual's health status (h), which is a vector of non-negative health dimensions such as physical and cognitive capabilities. In addition, utility is generated by the consumption of product attributes that the individual values (e), and by investing time in leisure. As indicated above, each individual faces the following constraints in maximizing the utility function:

$$x_t = A c_t \tag{2}$$
$$h_{t+1} = \Theta(h_t, d_t, l_t, z_t, \varphi^h) \tag{3}$$
$$p^c(c_t + s_t) = p_t^y y_t + b_t + g_t \tag{4}$$
$$b_t = \Psi(a_t) \tag{5}$$
$$a_{t+1} = \delta a_t + s_t + \varphi^a \quad \delta \in [0, 1] \tag{6}$$
$$\Omega(y_t, l_t, h_t, a_t | \varphi^p) = 0 \tag{7}$$
$$l_t + m_t = L \tag{8}$$
$$c_t, l_t, m_t, a_t \geq 0 \tag{9}$$

Overall consumed product characteristics (x) are obtained through the consumption of commodities and services (c) according to the linear consumption production technology denoted as matrix A in equation (2).[3] A health production function is formulated in equation (3), where the main determinants of health are chemical ingredients of ingested food, labor activity (l), other variables influencing health (z), and health shocks (φ^h).

The budget constraint formulated in equation (4) shows the relationship between the value of goods purchased for consumption and stocks and household total income, where s represents a vector of stockpiled goods, c is as defined earlier, p^c is a vector of prices of consumption goods; p^y represents the vector of prices for the household's own produce, including wage labor, and production inputs (vector y of netputs). This full-income relation ensures that the value of consumption does not exceed the sum of net income, the value of borrowings (b), and the value of non-labor income (g), such as rents and transfers received by the individual. A borrowing constraint is formulated in equation (5), so that the amount of borrowed money b cannot exceed the willingness to lend that is captured by the function $\Psi(\cdot)$, which increases in asset stocks (a). Equation (6) represents the law of motion for asset stocks, with δ as the depreciation factor and current stock-building quantities and asset shocks (φ^a) as explanatory variables. In equation (7), the production technology is captured as the function $\Omega(\cdot)$, which is

[3] For simplicity, we assume that food is linearly interrelated with metabolizable nutrients (as does Lancaster 1971).

determined by netput quantities, labor activity, health status, asset stocks, and production shocks (φ^p). Household human resources constraint is expressed in equation (8), where the total time endowment L is allocated between leisure m and hours of work for pay l. Non-negativity constraints for labor activity, consumption quantities, and assets are formulated in equation (9).

2.2   Food Security: Nutrient Provision and Food Safety

Modeling product characteristics has two advantages. First, miscellaneous positive and negative effects of food ingredients on human organisms are exactly captured. This allows a more realistic description of complex human metabolism. For example, the effects of vitamin A deficiency (food attribute) on sight (health dimension) can be explicitly modeled, and clearly differs from the effects of iodine deficiency (food attribute), which causes—among others—impairment of intelligence (health dimension).[4] The incorporation of health dimensions takes into account the fact that impairments in different parts of the human body are likely to affect labor productivity differently in equation (7), and may also be differently valued by the individual.

Second, food insecurity can be modeled in greater detail by analyzing the extent to which health dimensions are impaired by nutrient deficiency (or unhealthy food ingredients). Formally, for every health dimension k in vector h, there are three possible degrees of nutrition levels (NS), captured as thresholds for every element in d:

1. "healthy nutrient threshold" $NS_{k,t}^1(l_t, z_t, \varphi^h)$: the minimum nutrient requirement (upper limit for unhealthy ingredients and overconsumption) to maintain proper functioning of the health dimension;
2. "non-permanent impairment nutrient threshold" $NS_{k,t}^2(l_t, z_t, \varphi^h)$: the minimum nutrient requirement to prevent permanent impairment; and
3. "survival nutrient threshold" $NS_{k,t}^3(l_t, z_t, \varphi^h)$: the minimum nutrient requirement for survival.

Nutrient requirements increase in current labor activity level (l_t), and change with other health-influencing factors (z_t) such as age, gender, pregnancy status, and stature. Furthermore, negative health shocks (φ^h), involving illnesses such as diarrhea and measles or worm infections, lead to less nutrient absorption and higher nutrient requirements (WHO 1982). Thus, lack of nutrients that support the immune system, e.g., vitamin A, may trigger a vicious cycle by causing higher vulnerability to illnesses, which in turn raises required nutrient intake. This approach is also able to explicitly model hunger, which is defined as the "physiological sensation associated with insufficient food intake" (American Dietetic Association 1990). Along an individual's health

---

[4] Detailed impacts of vitamin A and iodine deficiencies on health status are documented in WHO (1982) and Hetzel (1983), respectively.

dimension "energy requirement," a decline below the NS^1_t threshold implies lack of caloric intake, resulting in the negatively perceived health output hunger.

For the human organism as a whole, formal degrees of healthy (NS^1_t), non-impairment (NS^2_t), and survival (NS^3_t) nutrient states are determined by nutrient thresholds of those health dimensions that impose the tightest constraints on food ingredients (highest minimum nutrient requirements/lowest upper limit for unhealthy ingredients). If at some time t^d, any element in the vector of ingested food d falls below the required NS^3_t level, at least one vital function of the organism breaks down and the individual dies, which is formally expressed as $h = 0$, $\forall t > t^D$.

The analysis of nutrient requirements and food ingredients given above has been rather deterministic. However, food security as an *ex ante* concept of exposure to undernutrition or malnutrition requires the incorporation of decisions under uncertainty. These include health shocks, shocks to asset stocks (φ^a), and production shocks (φ^p), as well as uncertainty regarding prices and transfers. In addition, imprecise knowledge on nutrient requirements and food ingredients is likely to drive risk-averse individuals even further away from consumption bundles in proximity to nutrition state thresholds.

Risk is incorporated in the model by assuming that individuals make consumption decisions conditional on a subjective joint density function $\Phi(\cdot)$ over exogenous variables (Barrett 2002). Given this density function and control variables x_t, s_t, and l_t, food security can be defined as the marginal probability at time t of exceeding any of the three nutrition states in time $t + s$ (where $s \geq 0$):

1. "healthy food security":

$$FS^1_t = \Pr\left(d_{t+s} \geq NS^1_{t+s} \forall d \in N \land d_{t+s} \leq NS^1_{t+s} \forall d \in UN\right)$$

2. "non-permanent impairment food security":

$$FS^2_t = \Pr\left(d_{t+s} \geq NS^2_{t+s} \forall d \in N \land d_{t+s} \leq NS^2_{t+s} \forall d \in UN\right)$$

3. "survival food security":

$$FS^3_t = \Pr\left(d_{t+s} \geq NS^3_{t+s} \forall d \in N \land d_{t+s} \leq NS^3_{t+s} \forall d \in UN\right)$$

where N is the set of nutrients and UN is the set of unhealthy ingredients. To distinguish "food-secure" from "food-insecure" individuals, a threshold that allows a classification according to the three food security probabilities outlined above needs to be defined. In case of the current period ($s = 0$), food security degrees are binary variables that are directly or indirectly observable. Given the formal model of hunger above, it can be easily seen that the aim of decreasing hunger is positively correlated to that of increasing food security, but only as far as an individual's energy requirement represents one of the constrained health dimensions.

Even if nutrients themselves do not give any direct utility, they indirectly influence food consumption decisions owing to their effects on physical well-being. In cases where individuals cannot afford consumption bundles that simultaneously provide enough amounts of different nutrients (e.g., iron and vitamin A), the consumption decision definitely transforms into a trade-off between the various health conditions related to those nutrients (e.g., physical and cognitive incapability due to iron deficiency versus inability to see due to vitamin A deficiency).[5] Given that the individual is aware of this mechanism, consumption decision is likely to be influenced by the personal valuation of the affected health dimensions (equation (1)) and their expected contribution to the individual's labor productivity (equation (7)).

In some settings, temporary nutrient deficiencies may be accepted by individuals in order to help other family members improve their nutrition, thus ensuring future income generation opportunities, or just for deriving utility from non-nutrition characteristics. As is evident from Table 13.1, nutrition deficiency—e.g., of iodine and vitamin A—is widespread in both developing and developed countries. Remarkable differences between the regions, for example, exceptionally low malnutrition rates in America, a high prevalence of inadequate iodine nutrition in the eastern Mediterranean, and a prevalent vitamin A deficiency in pre-school-age children of Southeast Asia and Africa, justify different food policy approaches to improve food security in the different regions.

Table 13.1 Malnutrition in different world regions

Region	Inadequate iodine nutrition: millions of affected persons (percentage)[a]	Vitamin A deficiency: millions of affected persons (percentage)[b]	
		Pre-school-age children	Pregnant women
Africa	312.9 (41.5)	56.4 (44.4)	4.18 (13.5)
Americas	98.6 (11)	8.68 (15.6)	0.23 (2.0)
SouthEast Asia	503.6 (30)	91.5 (49.9)	6.69 (17.3)
Europe	459.7 (52)	5.81 (19.7)	0.72 (11.6)
Eastern Mediterranean	259.3 (47.2)	13.2 (20.4)	2.42 (16.1)
Western Pacific	374.7 (21.2)	14.3 (12.9)	4.9 (21.5)
Total	2008.8 (30.6)	190 (33.3)	19.1 (15.3)

[a] Estimates for iodine nutrition are based on surveys from 1994 to 2006.
[b] Vitamin A deficiency indicator is a serum retinol threshold of $<0.70\,\mu$mol/l. WHO estimates for vitamin A deficiency are based on surveys from 1995 to 2005.
Source: De Benoist et al. (2008); WHO (2009).

---

[5] The impacts of iron deficiency on cognitive function and work capacity are reviewed in Pollitt (1993) and Haas and Brownlie (2001), respectively.

2.3   Analyzing Food Security Policies

The microeconomic model presented above illustrates the various dimensions of food security as expressed by the three components of nutrition availability, nutrition access, and food utilization, and can be employed to show how government policies affect the food security status of individuals.

Nutrition availability may be improved by the supply of sufficient foodstuffs at the local markets to ensure that food meant for consumption and storage (i.e., food in c_t and s_t) is not in limited supply. Besides ensuring higher productivity and output levels, major food security policies in this area generally include improving market integration through infrastructure, private trade supportive policies, state trading, as well as public buffer stocks (Abdulai 2000). Governments in developing countries therefore invest in research and development (R & D), farm infrastructure (irrigation and soil-conservation technologies) and extension services, and early warning systems, or subsidize farm inputs to shift the individual's production function $\Omega(\,\cdot\,)$ for food upward or decrease food supply fluctuations (φ^p). Public investment programs in storage facilities such as rat-proof granaries that reduce asset shocks (φ^a) and depreciation (δ) are direct policies that tend to influence private assets. An indirect but significant policy for preventing negative asset shocks is the provision of institutions for a stable legal environment. This is particularly important because the occurrence of food insecurity itself may negatively affect regional security since food-insecure households are more likely to act against the law in order to improve their access to food (Falcon and Naylor 2005). Privately stored food (a_t), which can be employed to overcome food shortfalls, also contributes to the household's (future) nutrition availability.

Given that nutrient availability remains a chronic problem in developing countries and crisis-prone regions, the issue of improving food availability continues to attract attention in these countries. This is in contrast to the discussion of food security in the developed world, where food production and availability are generally at higher levels, markets are well integrated, and the institutions are stable over time, contributing to lower levels of food insecurity. Moreover, measures for improving farm productivity are not that relevant for achieving food security in developed countries, given that relatively small proportions of the populace are engaged in farming. As argued by Coates et al. (2006), food insecurity in developed countries mostly arises from short-comings in food access, which partly explains why relatively more attention is given to examining and explaining this complex concept in research work related to the food sector (see also Wilde, Chapter 12 in this volume).

Nutrition access is solely derived from equation (4), i.e., food buyers are dependent on food prices as well as food availability, and on any of the right-hand-side elements that determine their purchasing power. Government policies related to food availability (c_t and s_t) have been discussed above. Policies that help in lowering and/or stabilizing consumers' food prices (p^c) and/or stabilizing producers' food prices (p^y) have been generally employed to improve nutrition access in developing countries. In particular, improving the non-farm earnings of individuals is a way of enhancing their "entitle-ment" over an adequate amount of food (Sen 1999).[6] Policies that have been generally used to address non-farm earnings possibilities include education policies to enhance the human capital of individuals, promoting credit institutions to improve access to credit, as well as policies that foster market integration through trade incentives and better infrastructure, which provide both extended rural–urban linkages and spatial income diversification (Abdulai and Delgado 1999).

Public work programs are employed to stabilize income shocks, while supplementary feeding programs normally target vulnerable groups (e.g., pregnant women, children) that need special diets (with the targeting criterion in z_t). Market failures in financial markets have also been addressed to enhance borrowing conditions (b_t) and provide better insurance and hedging possibilities that help stabilize income (φ^p). Commodity and cash transfers (g_t) are measures that are mainly used in the framework of food safety nets, emergency food aid, schooling services, and input starter packs, as well as providing incentives for schooling or health services.

Finally, food utilization is incorporated through the consumption technology A in equation (2) and through φ^h in equation (3), which includes health shocks that reduce the nutrient absorption capability of an individual's organism. The former can be influenced by policies altering the overall food quality, e.g., through micronutrient fortification and better access to clean water, or by individual nutrition education programs on food preparation. The latter is commonly handled by enhancing sanita-tion conditions, health education programs, and better access to medical treatment (e.g., placement of and access to medical facilities, and trade and distribution of medicine).

3   FOOD MARKET POLICIES IN
DEVELOPING COUNTRIES

....

Given that food constitutes a substantial share of the expenditure of both rural and urban populations, developing countries tend to employ diverse policy measures to influence agricultural prices.[7] These policies, which normally have direct impacts on food prices and food availability, are discussed below.

---

[6] According to Sen (1999), a family's entitlement depends on, among other things, distinct influences such as ownership over productive resources as well as wealth that commands a price in the market, production possibilities and their use, as well as the ability to sell and buy goods and the determination of relative prices of different products.

[7] On average, households in low-income countries spent 53 percent of their expenditure on food in 1996; the corresponding figures for middle-income and high-income countries were 35 and 17 percent, respectively (Seale, Regmi, and Bernstein 2003).

3.1   Price and Trade Regulation Policies

In this section, we briefly discuss the main price and trade regulation policies that are commonly used in developing countries with the goal of improving food security.

The rationale behind government-administered consumer prices for staple food (issue prices) is either to improve food access through lower market prices for consumers, or to stabilize consumption in times of upward price shocks by imposing price ceilings. The majority of developing countries have historically maintained low food prices to help urban consumers and to foster industrialization through lower wages. In pursuing these objectives, two paths of food price subsidies have generally been followed. These include universal price subsidies that benefit net food buyers, and limited access subsidies, where rationed quantities are granted at concessional prices. Universal price subsidies have generally been criticized as inefficient since all individuals profit from general food subsidies. The greater share of rationed food grains has generally been distributed to the politically vocal and well-organized groups, which include the urban population, government employees, and industrial workers.[8] While these beneficiaries have normally supported the cheap price policies, escalating fiscal expenditures for food subsidies and occasional political pressure from multinational donors have compelled most developing countries to liberalize food markets over time.

Discrimination against the agricultural sector through non-compensated cheap food price policies has been continually criticized because of its negative impact on farm households' welfare and farm investments, thus harming the current and future food security of most rural households (e.g., Schultz 1964). To encourage domestic food supply and improve local food availability, some governments of developing countries have offered producers higher than market prices, determined producer price floors, or subsidized farm inputs. Higher procurement prices have the ability to lift food-insecure farmers above the food security threshold, while price floors are designed to prevent farmers just above the food security threshold from falling into insecurity through declines in farm incomes. In particular, Asian countries with rice as the main staple food have effectively employed price stabilization policy as a food security tool (Timmer and Dawe 2007).

An issue that usually accompanies procurement price increases is the extent to which these higher prices are passed on to domestic consumers. If no sufficient compensation is given to consumers, rising food expenditures tend to impair the food security of net food buyers such as the urban population and rural workers not engaged in food production. This negative impact may be low in the case of foods that have small relevance to dietary requirements and contribute less to households' expenditure. For example, while Kenyan consumers have had to face higher retail prices for sugar, price increases in staple foods, such as rice in Asia or wheat in

---

[8] For example, India's public distribution system has been found to favor the population in urban districts considerably (Gulati, Sharma, and Kahkonen 1996).

northern Africa and the Middle East, have commonly not been fully passed on to consumers.

Efficient price stabilization policies should normally incorporate factors that affect a country's specific price and production risks, e.g., if it is landlocked or prone to droughts and floods. Given that decision makers are usually subjected to rent-seeking activities of special-interest groups, it is not surprising that the procurement and issue prices that are chosen tend to be suboptimal (Dixit and Josling 1997; Rashid, Cummings, and Gulati 2007).

Trade restriction regimes have commonly been employed in the form of quotas and tariffs. Import and export trade restrictions for the food sector have historically been implemented to reduce dependency on foreign imports. Current import restrictions such as quotas and tariffs generally offer net-food-importing countries the opportunity to respond to world market price fluctuations.

For example, developing countries recently had to deal with the sharp increases in world food prices, particularly for staple cereal foods (see Figure 13.1). These price increases resulted in food crises in some regions, as the number of undernourished persons increased significantly (see Table 13.2). The trend of a declining proportion of undernourished people in the developing world has been reversed in the late 2000s. In Latin America and the Caribbean, where absolute numbers of undernourished persons had previously been reduced, the number of malnourished people increased

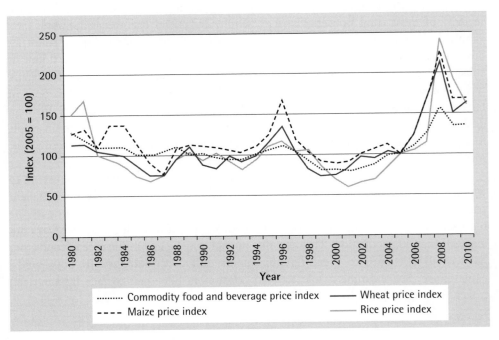

FIGURE 13.1 Food price indices, 1980–2010

Source: IMF (2009).

Table 13.2 Prevalence of undernourished people by region

Region	Millions of undernourished (% share in total population)				
	1990–92	2000–02	2004–2006	2008[a]	2009[a]
Asia and Pacific	585.7 (20)	552.1 (16)	566.2 (16)	581.0 (16)	642 (18)
Latin America and Caribbean	52.6 (12)	49.4 (9)	45.3 (8)	46.7 (8)	53 (9)
Near East and North Africa	19.1 (6)	31.6 (8)	33.8 (8)	37.2 (8)	42 (9)
Sub-Saharan Africa	168.8 (34)	205.5 (32)	212.3 (30)	237.0 (31)	265 (34)
Developing world	826.2 (20)	838.0 (17)	857.7 (16)	902.0 (17)	1002 (18)

Source: FAO (2009).

[a]Figures on proportion of undernourished in 2008 and 2009 are calculated using data from FAO (2009) and UN (2009). FAO estimates for 2009 are preliminary.

significantly. Declining global food prices in 2009 could not prevent a further increase in the number of undernourished, which indicates massive income losses due to the global economic recession (FAO 2009). These estimates only capture part of the food-insecure population since food insecurity also includes people who are not currently suffering from malnourishment but are at risk of falling below the healthy nutrient state thresholds (NS) in future periods (Barrett 2002).

The food price increases resulted in some countries re-examining their liberalized agricultural trade policies and intervening by imposing food price controls and trade restriction policies. For instance, Argentina, China, India, Russia, and Thailand restricted food exports in the wake of the price increases, while food-importing countries reduced their tariffs and taxes on food and agricultural imports to improve domestic food supply (Wodon and Zaman 2008). Timmer and Dawe (2007) argue that such measures helped in stabilizing domestic rice prices in Bangladesh and as such circumvented high levels of inefficient public procurement.

Some authors have argued that tightening export restrictions tends to discourage local food production and also intensifies the burden on the food-importing countries. For example, von Braun (2008) points out that the elimination of export bans could reduce international grain price fluctuation and reduce price levels by 30 percent.

3.2 State Engagement in Storage and Trade

This section discusses the specific consequences arising from state and parastatal agencies that are legal monopolies or act as competitors in stockholding, national food trade, and/or international food trade.

Government engagement in holding strategic food reserves may be justified on food security grounds and probably market failures in domestic private stockholding. Two strategic objectives of public buffer stocks can be derived from these justifications: (1) to reduce year-to-year domestic harvest fluctuations, in which government stocks are mostly substitutes for international trade flows, and (2) to smooth consumption in the presence of significant seasonality in agricultural markets (Siamwalla 1988). Available evidence reveals that public buffer stocks are in most cases more expensive than procuring food from international markets. If prices of public grain reserves are stickier than prices on the open markets, public storage authorities have to cope with large consumer switches between publicly provided food and food from the open market (Krishna and Chibber 1983). Thus, measures to prevent supply gaps at all times require inefficiently large precautionary food inventories, with large opportunity costs.

Although grain price fluctuations have not increased since the 1970s and the traditionally thin international rice market has considerably expanded and become more stable since the 1990s, the significant impact of a few key players, such as China, the United States, and European Union, on the world market has raised new doubts on the reliability of international trade (Calpe 2004; Byerlee, Jayne, and Myers 2006). During liberalization periods, public buffer stocks have in some countries proved to be hardly dispensable. To be effective, modern public grain reserves generally require a well-informed, as well as professional, management with good analytical capacities. The empirical evidence suggests that mismanagement and decisions based on wrong production estimates have led to catastrophic outcomes in the past (e.g., Charman and Hodge 2007). Although advanced information technology may provide more efficient tools for data handling, public buffer stock authorities need to deal with decreased information spillovers they obtained from the former public and now privatized state trading enterprises. In markets where private stockholders do not have significant market power, probably a more efficient way to achieve consumption smoothing during the marketing season is to subsidize private grain storage (Siamwalla 1988).

The objectives of state trading enterprises (STEs) usually include pursuing cheap food policies, supporting farm gate prices, stabilizing domestic prices through food transport between regions, subsidizing lower-income groups, and in some cases providing farms with needed inputs. Direct participation of the state in agricultural markets is mostly a means to support and complement administered pricing policies. The operation of STEs can be economically justified in the presence of market failures. Rashid, Cummings, and Gulati (2007) discuss four commonly accepted types of market failure in this context; (1) weak infrastructure and limited flow of information, (2) risk mitigation for technology diffusion, (3) thinness and volatility of international markets, and (4) inability to participate in international markets, e.g., due to low foreign exchange reserves. They demonstrate for six Asian countries (Bangladesh, India, Indonesia, Pakistan, the Philippines, and Vietnam) that all of these justifications of STEs have become less persuasive over time. This stems from the fact that other implemented policy measures, such as public work programs for building road infrastructure, investment in agricultural research and prospective macro policies, as well as exogenous developments such as reduced price volatility in international rice markets and advances in information technology, have substantially reduced the market failures that costly STEs were initially meant to circumvent. In contrast, private traders have become more and more effective in coping with food crises.

STEs have commonly operated at significantly higher unit costs than the private sector (e.g., Rashid, Cummings, and Gulati 2007). This inefficiency partly stems from services to remote areas that may not be adequately covered by private traders and hence may have to rely on safety net support in a privatization scenario. A major political incentive to further operate STEs is the flexibility to enact political mandates promptly without parliamentary scrutiny (Dixit and Josling 1997). With this quick and direct government response tool, governments have, however, been tempted to solve food crises with unforeseen and immense food transport activities. Such STE actions, as well as abruptly adjusted preferential arrangements for STEs, have the potential to seriously discourage private traders from participating in food trade. For example, the reduction of food import tariffs for STEs during the food crises in 2004 in Madagascar resulted in a dramatic breakdown of commercial food imports, which substantially worsened the food supply situation at local markets (Dorosh 2008).

On the other hand, domestic food distribution systems have shown to be prone to fundamental design errors. For instance, the shift in India's Public Distribution System from universal food rations to targeted food rations has reduced the access of poor households to public food rations, probably because private ration shop owners store fewer public food rations owing to less expected demand (Kochar 2005).

3.3   Agricultural Market Liberalization

Given the drawbacks mentioned in the above sections and the disappointing results of expensive regulation policies on food security in the 1960s and 1970s, many developing countries have made efforts to liberalize their agricultural markets. Support for trade liberalization is based on conventional welfare analysis, which shows that price controls undermine the functioning of prices as indicators of scarcity and, thus, result in welfare losses. Regulatory limits on trade, privately held stocks, and food processing furthermore discourage private investments and prevent private actors from pursuing their optimal strategies.

However, Timmer and Dawe (2007) point out that price stabilization policy can help ensure food security when access to credits and insurances is incomplete. Myers (2006) also asserts that when the theoretical welfare model is extended by allowing for discontinuous jumps in the utility function at low nutrition levels, welfare gains can be obtained through price stabilization policies. These gains can be of considerable magnitude, especially for the poor with nutrition intake close to the food security threshold. Nevertheless, the inability of these policies to overcome the fundamental problems of market failures, their obstruction of efficient private entrepreneurs' engagement, and excessive rent-seeking behavior have usually made them an increasingly expensive instrument.

Kherallah et al. (2000) show that the market reforms undertaken by developing countries have largely contributed to food security in these countries, although some of them found themselves stuck in the transition process. For example, private traders in Bangladesh were able to stabilize food markets after the government had fully liberalized the markets for the major crops in the early 1990s (del Ninno, Dorosh, and Subbarao 2007). However, considerable threat to food security was observed in cases where producer subsidies were withdrawn without efforts to diversify the incomes of affected producers, and particularly in remote areas where market forces could not fill the gap left by the STEs. This was the case in Malawi at the end of the 1980s, where the abolition of agricultural input subsidies and the closure of many markets of the state marketing board resulted in a national food crisis (Harrigan 2008). On realizing the emergencies that emerge through liberalization, governments have commonly stopped or reversed further transition, so that regulation and government agencies still play a significant role in agricultural markets in many developing countries.

3.4   Public Safety Nets for Food Access

With public actions in food markets on the retreat, the role of the state is increasingly seen as the provider of public insurance, i.e., safety nets for food access and health, and public goods, such as physical infrastructure. This section focuses on public insurance schemes through safety nets. The shift toward approaches that aim at helping households meet their individual nutrition demand also marks a significant shift from supply-side policies to food access policies. Two common instruments for public insurance in developing countries are supplementary feeding and public works programs. Supplementary feeding programs have been widely used in developing countries with significant focus on infants, children, and pregnant or lactating mothers as target groups. They are commonly operated in cooperation with NGOs, and a large share of the employed food comes from international sources, like food aid (Barrett 2002). Intervention designs range from controlled feeding at health facilities, over home-visiting physicians who supervise nutrient intake, to take-home rations.

In a comprehensive meta-analysis, Dewey and Adu-Afarwuah (2008) investigate the effects of a multitude of complementary feeding interventions for children on diverse health outcomes in developing countries. To avoid bias in comparing treatment and control groups, the authors mostly included interventions with randomized treatment assignment, or non-randomized interventions with a low risk of confounding effects. They found that child growth can be considerably improved when programs are employed in a well-controlled environment. Findings on child morbidity have mainly been inconsistent; in three out of ten studies, the morbidity rates even increased in the intervention group. Possible explanations for such adverse effects are reductions in breastfeeding in the intervention groups or unhygienic preparation and storage of supplements at home (Dewey and Adu-Afarwuah 2008). The results of feeding interventions on children's behavioral development are mixed, with two out of four studies reporting significant improvements in the infants' ability to walk by 12 months. Feeding interventions mostly enhanced the children's micronutrient status for iron and vitamin A. These findings suggest that feeding interventions can be effective, but this largely depends on how the local context, particularly household behavior, is taken into account. To be effective, large-scale feeding intervention programs thus need a carefully thought-out design, which may involve considerable costs in implementing.

Given the general insufficiencies of physical infrastructure and fluctuating rates of unemployment and underemployment in developing countries, labor-intensive public work programs have been increasingly considered as a promising instrument with few opportunity costs (Dev 1995). For example, the government of Ethiopia has committed to spend 80 percent of their food assistance resources on food for work projects (FDRE 1996). Public work schemes have been used in South Asia since ancient times to ensure food entitlements, and have proved to be relatively successful (Clay 1986; Dev 1995).

Two food-security-related purposes are pursued through the establishment of public work programs. The first, short-run purpose is to smooth food consumption by providing a cash or in-kind wage. The particular domain of public work provision is during the slack season and in the face of covariate shocks like droughts and floods, where market demand for unskilled labor usually breaks down (Barrett 2007). When rightly timed, these programs have the ability to overcome market failures in the financial market. The second is the construction and maintenance of assets that foster future economic growth. The created assets usually include road and social infrastructure, reforestation, or on-farm improvements such as irrigation, water, and soil conservation. Most of these assets have public good characteristics, and are therefore not sufficiently provided by market forces to meet the social optimum. The rationale for building on-farm assets is to overcome market failures that hinder farmers from investing. The choice of what to construct is not trivial, and many top-down planning approaches that did not incorporate local advisers have often resulted in poorly developed infrastructure (Holden, Barrett, and Hagos 2006).

An indirect effect of public work on food access is its potential to drive up market wages because of (1) its characteristic as a reservation wage, and (2) productivity gains through the built assets that increase labor demand (Abdulai, Barrett, and Hoddinott 2005). The design of public work programs is knowledge-intensive and requires proper adjustments to the local economic environment. This requires setting a wage rate high enough to ensure adequate nutrition for the participants but low enough to minimize inclusion errors (attracting food-secure people) and crowding out workers of regular jobs. It is, however, important to mention that if the increase in demand for food accompanying the additional employment of low-income people is not met by an increased food supply, the employment-based increase in real income will be substantially reduced by higher prices (Mellor 1978).

3.5   Measures to Optimize Food Utilization

Some developing countries have employed food fortification measures with micronutrients such as iodine, vitamin A, iron, and zinc to optimize food utilization. The advantage of these measures is that they can improve nutrition status without necessarily altering food access. While in most cases nutrient requirements can be met with foodstuffs accessible on local markets, it has been found that enrichment with iron is often the only option to meet the requirements of infants, given the high costs of iron-rich food (Dewey and Adu-Afarwuah 2008).

Common approaches in developing countries are the fortification of salt with iodine; wheat flour with iron, vitamin B_1 and B_2, and niacin; milk and margarine with vitamin A and D; and sugar with vitamin A. Fortified food is also often provided in supplementary feeding programs, like the nutrient supplementation of the large-scale Mexican Progresa program (Rivera et al. 2004). In general, micronutrient fortification has proven to be a cost-effective instrument that has the ability to reach large shares of the population at very low costs, as shown by iodized salt, which costs about 5 cents per person per year (Barrett 2002).

Nutrition education programs are an alternative method to micronutrient fortification, and attempt to achieve a more balanced nutrient intake by improving food consumption patterns. This is an especially promising approach when aimed at persons who are responsible for the preparation of food for other household members. In their systematic review on developing countries, Dewey and Adu-Afarwuah (2008) concluded that the impact of nutrition education interventions for mothers had rather modest impacts on child weight and growth. However, while child morbidity was not affected in two studies, an efficacy trial in Brazil reported significant decreases in diarrhea and respiratory infections.

4   POLICIES INFLUENCING THE ECONOMIC ENVIRONMENT

In addition to the direct policy interventions discussed above, governments normally employ a wide array of measures to influence food production and availability in order to enhance food security in their countries. These measures are discussed below.

4.1   Public Investment in the Agricultural Sector

The need for public investment in agricultural development stems from the atomistic nature of the sector, whereby small-scale farmers lack the means to undertake long-term investment. Public investment in land-augmenting infrastructure such as irrigation, rural electricity, and transport networks, and in supply-shifting factors such as agricultural research and extension services, can enhance the incentive content of prices facing farmers (Rao 1989; Abdulai and Huffman 2000). Available evidence shows that public investment in agriculture—along with infrastructure spending—generally yields the highest returns in terms of poverty reduction and economic growth (Fan, Yu, and Saurkar 2008; Minten and Barrett 2008; Fan and Zhang 2008). Despite this potential, public expenditure for the sector has declined over the last decades (see Table 13.3).

With public agricultural expenditure per agricultural GDP ratios of below 10 percent in the developing world, support for the agricultural sector appears to lag far behind that of developed countries, which have ratios of over 20 percent (Fan, Yu, and Saurkar 2008). The difference is even greater for public spending in agricultural R & D, which was 0.37 percent for low-income countries, 0.67 percent for middle-income countries, and 2.35 percent for high-income countries (Asenso-Okyere and Davis 2009). Only China, India, and Brazil appear to have extensive research programs in all R & D areas, including gene manipulation technology (Pingali and Raney 2005). In the face of the food crisis, African countries have begun to reiterate their commitment, agreed upon in the Comprehensive African Agricultural Development Plan, to increase their public investment in agriculture to an annual 10 percent share of their national budgets (on average below 5 percent in the years 2000 and 2002).

The view that public investment in agricultural infrastructure is induced by price increases was heavily criticized by Rao (1989). He argued that evidence pertaining to public investment in land-augmenting or supply-shifting factors does not support the argument that agricultural prices play a powerful role in promoting or retarding agricultural growth. Similarly to arguments advanced by the World Bank (2007), Rao (1989) concludes that the weak political power of the rural population and the discriminatory trade and macroeconomic policies of developing countries are among the reasons for the chronic underfunding of agricultural R & D.

Although extension services have proven to be effective, as shown by the median rate of return of 58 percent, they have been increasingly scaled down by many developing

Table 13.3 Public agriculture expenditures as a percentage of agricultural GDP

Region	1980	1990	2000	2002
Africa	7.4 (2.29)	5.44 (1.37)	5.71 (1.2)	6.72 (1.47)
Asia	9.44 (2.96)	8.51 (1.71)	9.54 (1.35)	10.57 (1.23)
Latin America	19.51 (1.66)	6.79 (0.78)	11.1 (0.64)	11.57 (0.6)
Total	10.76 (2.23)	8.04 (1.24)	9.34 (1.03)	10.32 (1.09)

Values in parentheses are unweighted shares that are reported because the weighted averages commonly calculated at regional and global levels may bias toward large countries.

Source: Fan, Yu, and Saurkar (2008), using data from International Monetary Fund, *Government Financial Statistics Yearbook*.

countries (Alston et al. 2000). Instruments that have been employed to enhance access to farm inputs include universal input price subsidies, concessional credit arrangements with STEs, non-recurring subsidized input packages, and targeted distribution of inputs after natural disasters. An example of a universal free distribution of farm inputs is the Malawian Starter Pack intervention, which emerged as a response to growing soil degradation and successfully addressed the food insecurity of the rural poor (Harrigan 2008).[9] As is the case for food, such input price subsidies are not targeted toward the food-insecure and tend to become a persistent expenditure item, once introduced. These measures therefore need to be carefully targeted to limit leakages.

4.2   Financial Sector in Rural and Peri-Urban Regions

Throughout the developing world, poor households lack access to formal financial markets. While informal insurance and credit arrangements can at least partly fill this gap for idiosyncratic shocks, this is typically not the case when covariate risks affect the whole community.[10] What follows is depletion, erosion, and dis-saving of physical and human capital as well as the destructive exploitation of the environment.

Owing to their inability to save money, obtain loans, or buy insurance, poor households find it difficult to cope with income shocks, which tend to affect their food security status in different ways. First, the household can afford less food, and may therefore fall into food insecurity. Second, as a response to the risky environment, the household can make precautionary savings. This *ex ante* measure to mitigate shocks prevents individuals from investing in income-generating activities, thus reducing their ability to improve their future food security status (Zeller et al. 1997). Third, liquidity constraints favor engagement in economic activities with immediate profits, which usually yield low returns, and hinder adoption of new technologies (Abdulai and Huffman 2005; Barrett 2007; Abdulai, Monnin, and Gerber 2008).

To enhance the functioning of financial markets, developing countries have implemented government lending projects that involve state-owned banks providing loans at subsidized interest rates. The results of these approaches have rather been disappointing. Reasons for these disappointing outcomes include corruption and administrative targeting that excluded large parts of poor households (Armendáriz de Aghion and Morduch 2005). Some governments of developing countries have played an indirect but significant role in the revolution of microfinance, with a focus on microcredits and

---

[9] Later, the Starter Pack intervention was scaled down to a targeted anti-poverty program, which, however, could not adequately handle an upcoming food crisis (Harrigan 2008).

[10] Problems in informal markets include significant market power of the best-informed credit lenders, credit rationing due to high default rates, and the importance of social networks for credit access, which discriminates against those with few contacts and ethnic minorities (Zeller et al. 1997; Barrett 2007).

microsavings. For example, the Grameen Bank started as a special project from the state-owned Bangladesh Bank, and has received loans at concessional rates from that bank. State-owned banks in Indonesia (Bank Rakyat Indonesia) and Thailand (Bank of Agriculture and Agricultural Cooperatives) have also established innovative microfinance programs with a wide range of small-scale customers.

4.3   Transportation and Communication Infrastructure

Improved infrastructure in developing countries affects food security in a number of ways. These include: (1) reduction in search costs and transportation costs of market participants; (2) increase in agricultural productivity as a result of better access to inputs, credits, services, and information; (3) improved access to health services; (4) improvement in human capital as a result of better access to education and health services; (5) better job opportunities. In spite of the empirical evidence on the positive impact of transportation and communication infrastructure on economic and agricultural growth, public expenditure devoted to infrastructure remains quite low in developing countries (Antle 1983; Easterly and Levine 1997; World Bank 2004).

At the macro level, Torero, Chowdhury, and Bedi (2006) have found a significant positive effect of telecommunications penetration in developing countries on economic growth. An analysis of the garment industry of China, India, Pakistan, and Bangladesh based on firm-level survey data also revealed that better telephone services can increase income through higher wage rates, firm profitability, and growth (Dollar, Hallward-Driemeier, and Mengistae 2005). Gabre-Madhin (2001) analyzed the Ethiopian grain market and argues that, given considerable information deficiencies among traders and brokers, the use of information technology can considerably increase interspatial trade flows. Meanwhile, the Ethiopian government supported the 2008 established Ethiopian Commodity Exchange, which uses radio, television, cellular phone technology, and electronic price display boards to spread agricultural commodity prices countrywide. In addition, information asymmetries arising from poor measurement of traded items and lack of trustworthiness have been addressed with warehouse receipt systems, in which food commodities are properly weighed and stored.

4.4   Health Care, Sanitation, and Water Access

Given that many parts of the developing world still face serious problems in the health sector, such as unequal access to medical treatment, lack of sanitation facilities, and scarce and contaminated water, many governments have engaged in providing public health services to reduce the risk of infection and cope with health shocks (Gwatkin et al. 2007). It is encouraging to note that, at the macro level, public spending on health care in developing and transition countries has been effective in improving the health of the poor population (Gupta, Verhoefen, and Tiongson 2003). Thus, public spending has added overall to private and informal health provisions, as well as international health projects. In detail, sanitation, hygiene, water supply, and water quality interventions have mostly been found to be effective in fighting diseases and mortality (Esrey et al. 1991; Fewtrell et al. 2005).

In addition to providing public health services, developing countries have engaged in providing water and sanitation infrastructure. This is because increased water supply through these public goods can improve an individual's food security by ensuring better hygiene conditions and also freeing time that would otherwise be used for water collection (Esrey et al. 1991; Hutton and Haller 2004). While laying water pipes is the most costly intervention for improving water supply, it provides daily access to treated water (Hutton and Haller 2004). Water provided by other interventions, such as building wells or spring protection, is, on the other hand, vulnerable to becoming contaminated when transported or stored at home. Given that measures to improve microbial safety immediately before consumption are very effective in reducing diarrheal infection, water treatment at the point of use is proposed as an effective measure in fighting waterborne illnesses (Fewtrell et al. 2005).

5   CONCLUSIONS

In this chapter, we have argued that food security remains a major concern in the developing countries, and that national governments have employed various policies to address food security concerns of their citizens. Given the broad definition of food security, these policies usually involve direct interventions involving structural changes in relative prices and targeted food subsidies, as well as indirect measures such as improving agricultural infrastructure and the general economic environment, and providing farmers with new farm technologies to increase food production. To the extent that ensuring food security also involves measures that stimulate adequate levels of effective demand through "entitlements," governments have also employed income diversification strategies and cash transfers to achieve food security goals. However, these income support measures for the poor are only efficient when provision is made for an enlarged supply of basic food commodities. This underlines the significance of investing in the agricultural sector to boost food production.

The discussion in this chapter has shown that over time the food policies of developing countries have largely moved from direct state interventions that attempted to circumvent food market failures to a more liberalized market approach, where the state entrusts private entities with the task of adequate provision of food, but still invests in safety nets and public goods to overcome market failures. With the reduction of state activities, significant linkages between governments and private enterprises, NGOs, multilateral organizations, research institutions, and donor countries have been established to improve food security in developing countries. The discussion in the chapter also clearly revealed that despite the evidence that public investment in agriculture—along with infrastructure spending—generally yields the highest returns in terms of poverty reduction and economic growth, public expenditure for the sector has declined over the last decades. Governments therefore need to increase public investment in agriculture to promote productivity and overall economic growth.

The voluminous literature on food security in developing countries referred to in this chapter shows the efforts several policy analysts have put into research to examine policy options and their impacts on food security. However, a number of important questions still remain unaddressed. For example, in analyzing the effects of stabilization schemes on food prices, an important issue that crops up is that of determining the adjustments that do the least damage to economic growth and equitable distribution of income in the society. As pointed out by Timmer (1989), addressing such issues normally requires general equilibrium analyses, with dynamic investment functions linked to the impact on expectations of instability in food prices, in credit markets, and in the budgetary behavior of government. Most food security analyses remain partial and highly intuitive. Despite this limitation, there is a general consensus that our understanding of the food security policies of developing countries has been significantly enhanced by the carefully conducted theoretical and empirical analyses over the last two decades.

References

Abdulai, A. 2000. "Spatial Price Transmission and Asymmetry in the Ghanaian Maize Market." *Journal of Development Economics* 63/2: 327–49.

——— and D. Aubert. 2004. "A Cross-Section Analysis of Household Demand for Food and Nutrients in Tanzania." *Agricultural Economics* 31/1: 67–79.

——— and C. Delgado. 1999. "Determinants of Nonfarm Earnings of Farm-Based Husbands and Wives in Northern Ghana." *American Journal of Agricultural Economics* 81/1: 117–30.

——— and W. Huffman. 2000. "Structural Adjustment and Efficiency of Rice Farmers in Northern Ghana." *Economic Development and Cultural Change* 48/3: 503–21.

——— ———. 2005. "The Diffusion of New Agricultural Technologies: The Case of Crossbred-Cow Technology in Tanzania." *American Journal of Agricultural Economics* 87/3: 645–59.

———, C. B. Barrett, and J. Hoddinott. 2005. "Does Food Aid Really Have Disincentive Effects?" *World Development* 33/10: 1689–1704.

———, P. Monnin, and J. Gerber. 2008. "Joint Estimation of Information Acquisition and Adoption of New Technologies under Uncertainty." *Journal of International Development* 20/4: 437–51.

Alston, J. M., M. Marra, P. Pardey, and T. J. Wyatt. 2000. "Research Returns Redux: A Meta-Analysis of the Returns to Agricultural R & D." *Australian Journal of Agricultural and Resource Economics* 44/2 (June). <http://ssrn.com/abstract=235962>.

American Dietetic Association. 1990. "Position of the American Dietetic Association: Domestic Hunger and Inadequate Access to Food." *Journal of the American Dietetic Association* 90: 1437–41.

Antle, J. M. 1983. "Infrastructure and Aggregate Agricultural Productivity: International Evidence." *Economic Development and Cultural Change* 31: 609–19.

Armendáriz de Aghion, B., and J. Morduch. 2005. *The Economics of Microfinance*. Cambridge, MA: MIT Press.

Asenso-Okyere, K., and K. Davis. 2009. *Knowledge and Innovation for Agricultural Development*. IFPRI Policy Brief No. 11. Washington, DC: International Food Policy Research Institute.

Barrett, C. B. 2002. "Food Security and Food Assistance Programs." In B. Gardner and G. Rausser, eds, *Handbook of Agricultural Economics*, 2. Amsterdam: Elsevier.

—— 2007. "Displaced Distortions: Financial Market Failures and Seemingly Inefficient Resource Allocation in Low-Income Rural Communities." In E. Bulte and R. Ruben, eds, *Development Economics between Markets and Institutions*. Wageningen: Wageningen Academic Publishers.

Becker, G. S. 1965. "A Theory of the Allocation of Time." *Economic Journal* 75/299: 493–517.

Byerlee, D., T. Jayne, and R. J. Myers. 2006. "Managing Food Price Risks and Instability in a Liberalizing Market Environment: Overview and Policy Options." *Food Policy* 31: 275–87.

Calpe, C. 2004. "International Trade in Rice, Recent Developments and Prospects." *World Rice Research Conference 2004*. Tsukuba: Food and Agriculture Organization.

Charman, A., and J. Hodge. 2007. "Food Security in the SADC Region: An Assessment of National Trade Strategy in the Context of the 2001–03 Food Crisis." In B. Guha-Khasnobis, S. S. Acharya, and B. Davis, eds, *Food Insecurity, Vulnerability and Human Rights Failure*. Basingstoke: Palgrave Macmillan.

Clay, E. J. 1986. "Rural Public Works and Food-for-Work: A Survey." *World Development* 14/10–11: 1237–52.

Coates, J., E. A. Frongillo, R. Houser, B. Rogers, P. Webb, and P. Wilde. 2006. "Commonalities in the Experience of Household Food Insecurity across Cultures: What Are Measures Missing?" *Journal of Nutrition* 136: 1438S–1448S.

de Benoist, B., E. McLean, M. Andersson, and L. Rogers. 2008. "Iodine Deficiency in 2007: Global Progress since 2003." *Food and Nutrition Bulletin* 29/3: 195–202.

del Ninno, C., P. A. Dorosh, and K. Subbarao. 2007. "Food Aid, Domestic Policy and Food Security: Contrasting Experiences from South Asia and Sub-Saharan Africa." *Food Policy* 32: 413–35.

Dev, S. M. 1995. "India's (Maharashtra) Employment Guarantee Scheme: Lessons from Long Experience." In J. von Braun, ed., *Employment for Poverty Reduction and Food Security*. Washington, DC: International Food Policy Research Institute.

Dewey, K. G., and S. Adu-Afarwuah. 2008. "Systematic Review of the Efficacy and Effectiveness of Complementary Feeding Interventions in Developing Countries." *Maternal and Child Nutrition* 4: 24–85.

Dixit, P. M., and T. Josling. 1997. *State Trading in Agriculture: An Analytical Framework*. Working Paper No. 97-4. Washington, DC: International Agricultural Trade Research Consortium.

Dollar, D., M. Hallward-Driemeier, and T. Mengistae. 2005. "Investment Climate and Firm Performance in Developing Countries." *Economic Development and Cultural Change* 54/1: 1–31.

Dorosh, P. 2008. "Food Price Stabilisation and Food Security: International Experience." *Bulletin of Indonesian Economic Studies* 44/1: 93–114.

Easterly, W., and R. Levine. 1997. "Africa's Growth Tragedy: Policies and Ethnic Divisions." *Quarterly Journal of Economics* 112/4: 1203–50.

Esrey, S. A., J. B. Potash, L. Roberts, and C. Schiff. 1991. "Effects of Improved Water Supply and Sanitation on Ascariasis, Diarrhoea, Dracunculiasis, Hookworm Infection, Schistosomiasis, and Trachoma." *Bulletin of the World Health Organization* 69: 609–21.

Falcon, W. P., and R. L. Naylor. 2005: "Rethinking Food Security for the Twenty-First Century." *American Journal of Agricultural Economics* 85/5: 1113–27.

Fan, S., and X. Zhang. 2008. "Public Expenditure, Growth and Poverty Reduction in Rural Uganda." *African Development Review* 20/3: 466–96.

——, B. Yu, and A. Saurkar. 2008. "Public Spending in Developing Countries: Trends, Determination, and Impact." In S. Fan, ed., *Public Expenditures, Growth, and Poverty*. Baltimore: Johns Hopkins University Press.

Fanzo, J., P. Pronyk, A. Dasgupta, M. Towle, V. Menon, G. Denning, A. Zycherman, R. Flor, and G. Roth. 2010. *An Evaluation of Progress toward the Millennium Development Goal One Hunger Target: A Country-Level, Food and Nutrition Security Perspective*. New York: United Nations Development Group.

FAO (Food and Agriculture Organization). 2003. *Trade Reforms and Food Security: Conceptualizing the Linkages*. Rome: Food and Agriculture Organization of the United Nations.

—— 2009. *The State of Food Insecurity in the World 2009*. Rome: Food and Agriculture Organization of the United Nations.

FDRE (Federal Democratic Republic of Ethiopia). 1996. *Food Security Strategy 1996*. Addis Ababa: Federal Democratic Republic of Ethiopia.

Fewtrell, L., R. B. Kaufmann, D. Kay, W. Enanoria, L. Haller, and J. M. Colford, Jr. 2005. "Water, Sanitation, and Hygiene Interventions to Reduce Diarrhoea in Less Developed Countries: A Systematic Review and Meta-Analysis." *The Lancet Infectious Diseases* 5: 42–52.

Gabre-Madhin, E. 2001. *Marketing Institutions, Transaction Costs, and Social Capital in the Ethiopian Grain Market*. Research Report No. 124. Washington, DC: International Food Policy Research Institute.

Gulati, A., P. Sharma, and S. Kahkonen. 1996. *The Food Corporation of India: Successes and Failures in Indian Foodgrain Marketing*. IRIS India Working Paper No. 18. College Park: Center for Institutional Reform and the Informal Sector, University of Maryland.

Gupta, S., M. Verhoefen, and E. R. Tiongson. 2003. "Public Spending on Health Care and the Poor." *Health Economics* 12: 685–96.

Gwatkin, D. R., S. Rutstein, K. Johnson, E. Suliman, A. Wagstaff, and A. Amouzou. 2007. *Socio-economic Differences in Health, Nutrition, and Population within Developing Countries: An Overview*. Washington, DC: World Bank.

Haas, J. D., and T. Brownlie. 2001. "Iron Deficiency and Reduced Work Capacity: A Critical Review of the Research to Determine a Causal Relationship." *Journal of Nutrition* 131: 676S–690S.

Harrigan, J. 2008. "Food Insecurity, Poverty and the Malawian Starter Pack: Fresh Start or False Start?" *Food Policy* 33/3: 237–49.

Hetzel, B. 1983. "Iodine Deficiency Disorders (IDD) and their Eradication." *The Lancet* 322: 1126–9.

Holden, S., C. B. Barrett, and F. Hagos. 2006. "Food-for-Work for Poverty Reduction and the Promotion of Sustainable Land Use: Can It Work?" *Environment and Development Economics* 11/1: 15–38.

Hutton, G., and L. Haller. 2004. *Evaluation of the Costs and Benefits of Water and Sanitation Improvements at the Global Level*. Geneva: World Health Organization.

IMF (International Monetary Fund). 2009. *World Economic Outlook Database*. Washington, DC: International Monetary Fund. <http://www.imf.org/external/pubs/ft/weo/2008/02/weodata/index.aspx>.

Kherallah, M., C. Delgado, E. Gabre-Madhin, N. Minot, and M. Johnson. 2000. *The Road Half Traveled: Agricultural Market Reform in Sub-Saharan Africa*. Food Policy Report. Washington, DC: International Food Policy Research Institute.

Kochar, A. 2005. "Can Targeted Food Programs Improve Nutrition? An Empirical Analysis of India's Public Distribution System." *Economic Development and Cultural Change* 54: 203–35.

Krishna, R., and A. Chibber. 1983. *Policy Modeling of a Dual Grain Market: The Case of Wheat in India*. Research Report No. 38. Washington, DC: International Food Policy Research Institute.

Lancaster, K. 1971. *Consumer Demand: A New Approach*. New York: Columbia University Press.

Mellor, J. W. 1978. "Food Price Policy and Income Distribution in Low-Income Countries." *Economic Development and Cultural Change* 27/1: 1–28.

Minten, B., and C. B. Barrett. 2008. "Agricultural Technology, Productivity, and Poverty in Madagascar." *Word Development* 36/5: 797–822.

Myers, R. J. 2006. "On the Costs of Food Price Fluctuations in Low-Income Countries." *Food Policy* 31: 288–301.

Pingali, P., and T. Raney. 2005. *From the Green Revolution to the Gene Revolution: How Will the Poor Fare?* ESA Working Paper No. 05-09. Rome: Food and Agriculture Organization of the United Nations.

Pollitt, E. 1993. "Iron Deficiency and Cognitive Function." *Annual Review of Nutrition* 13: 521–37.

Rao, J. M. 1989. "Getting Agricultural Prices Right." *Food Policy* 14/1: 28–42.

Rashid, S., R. Cummings, Jr., and A. Gulati. 2007. "Grain Marketing Parastatals in Asia: Results from Six Case Studies." *World Development* 35/11: 1872–88.

Rivera, J. A., D. Sotres-Alvarez, J.-P. Habicht, T. Shamah, and S. Villalpando. 2004. "Impact of the Mexican Program for Education, Health, and Nutrition (Progresa) on Rates of Growth and Anemia in Infants and Young Children." *Journal of the American Medical Association* 291/21: 2563–70.

Schultz, T. W. 1964. *Transforming Traditional Agriculture*. New Haven: Yale University Press.

Seale, J., A. Regmi, and J. Bernstein. 2003. *International Evidence on Food Consumption Patterns*. Technical Bulletin No. 1904. Washington, DC: Economic Research Service, United States Department of Agriculture.

Sen, A. 1999. *Development as Freedom*. Oxford: Oxford University Press.

Siamwalla, A. 1988. "Public Stock Management." In J. W. Mellor and R. Ahmed, eds, *Agricultural Price Policy for Developing Countries*. Baltimore: Johns Hopkins University Press.

Timmer, C. P. 1989. "Food Price Policy: The Rationale for Government Intervention." *Food Policy* 14/1: 17–27.

——and D. Dawe. 2007. "Managing Food Price Instability in Asia: A Macro Food Security Perspective." *Asian Economic Journal* 21: 1–18.

Torero, M., S. K. Chowdhury, and A. S. Bedi. 2006. "Telecommunications Infrastructure and Economic Growth: A Cross-Country Analysis." In M. Torero and J. von Braun, eds, *Information and Communication Technology for Development and Poverty Reduction.* Baltimore: Johns Hopkins University Press.

UN (United Nations). 2009. *World Population Prospects: The 2008 Revision.* CD-ROM edn. New York: Department of Economic and Social Affairs, Population Division, United Nations.

von Braun, J. 2008. *High Food Prices: The Proposed Policy Actions.* Keynote Address to the ECOSOC Special Meeting "The Global Food Crisis." New York: International Food Policy Research Institute.

Weber, M. T., J. M. Staatz, J. S. Holtzman, E. W. Crawford, and R. H. Bernsten. 1988. "Informing Food Security Decisions in Africa: Empirical Analysis and Policy Dialogue." *American Journal of Agricultural Economics* 70/5: 1044–52.

WHO (World Health Organization). 1982. *Control of Vitamin A Deficiency and Xerophthalmia.* Report of a joint WHO/UNICEF/USAID/Helen Keller International/IVACG meeting, Jakarta. Technical Report Series No. 672. Geneva: World Health Organization.

——2009. *Global Prevalence of Vitamin A Deficiency in Populations at Risk 1995–2005.* Geneva: World Health Organization.

Wodon, Q., and H. Zaman. 2008. *Rising Food Prices in Sub-Saharan Africa: Poverty Impact and Policy Responses.* Washington, DC: World Bank.

World Bank. 2004. *The World Development Report 2005: A Better Investment Climate for Everyone.* Washington, DC: World Bank.

——2007. *The World Development Report 2008: Agriculture for Development.* Washington, DC: World Bank.

Zeller, M., G. Schrieder, J. von Braun, and F. Heidhues. 1997. *Rural Finance for Food Security for the Poor.* Washington, DC: International Food Policy Research Institute.

CHAPTER 14

....

ECONOMIC DEVELOPMENT, GOVERNMENT POLICIES, AND FOOD CONSUMPTION

....

WILLIAM A. MASTERS

1 INTRODUCTION

....

This chapter addresses the influence of economic development and government policies on food consumption around the world. By *economic development*, I mean long-run changes in economic activity; these are heavily influenced by *government policies*, which also mediate the links from development to *food consumption* outcomes, with feedback loops from food consumption outcomes back to policymakers and the economic development process itself. The process I seek to describe is illustrated by Figure 14.1, showing how changes in food consumption might be driven by an underlying process of economic development and policy change. An improvement (or worsening) in any part of this engine of growth might influence its performance, as each gear is enmeshed with the others.

The interacting influence of economic development and government policies on food consumption outcomes is obvious to any observer (e.g., Manzel and D'Alusio 2008). Even comparing regions with similar physical climate, South Americans are known for their grass-fed beef and southeastern Africans for their white maize porridge. Both preferences owe something to people's income level and employment options, which are generally more limited in southern Africa, but also to government interventions that have long kept grazing land for cattle relatively abundant in South America, and made processed white maize relatively cheap in southern Africa. These kinds of forces help explain differences across countries and also changes over time, and may point to opportunities for policy change to mediate more effectively between the forces of economic development and people's food consumption outcomes.

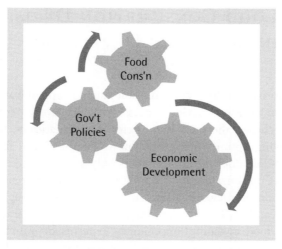

FIGURE 14.1 Food consumption changes as an outcome of economic development policies

My task in this chapter is to analyze the interacting influences illustrated in Figure 14.1, in a unified framework that could help explain the diversities and similarities we observe around the world. The facts I seek to explain are summarized elsewhere in this Handbook. Most notably, the chapter by Fabiosa (Chapter 23) describes how consumption patterns have been "trading up" over time and converging across countries, as part of economic globalization, while Albisu, Gracia, and Sanjuán (Chapter 30) describe these changes in terms of demographic change. Focusing on recent events, von Braun (Chapter 24) shows how price spikes in a shared world market are experienced very differently by different countries, owing to differences in initial conditions and policy responses. Finally, government efforts to protect food consumers from income and price shocks are described in the chapters by Wilde (Chapter 12) and Abdulai and Kuhlgatz (Chapter 13), addressing more and less affluent countries respectively.

To help make sense of the diverse literature and disparate facts about food consumption changes and differences across countries, the first section of this chapter offers a series of thought experiments about individual decision-making in economic development. How might a hypothetical person or household, armed only with native intelligence and ability to learn from others, respond to changes in circumstances? Pursuing that question reveals what standard economic models can—and can't—explain about changes in food consumption during economic development, including the puzzle of why governments act as they do. Readers who are very familiar with economics will recognize the approach, and might appreciate the novelty of how it is presented—or might choose to skip that part of the chapter and move directly to the evidence presented on food prices as influenced by government policies, and on households' actual food consumption choices.

2   FOOD CONSUMPTION DECISIONS
IN ECONOMIC DEVELOPMENT

The economics approach to food consumption aims to explain our diverse choices in terms of a common decision-making process, by which every person has compared their options and chosen the ones they prefer. Mathematically, this choice can be represented as having optimized some unknown mathematical function, subject to various constraints. Such optimization models only approximate the actual decision-making process, and optimization itself is only a metaphor for what people actually do, but the optimization framework allows us to construct thought experiments of surprising subtlety and explanatory power. In this section we trace the major steps needed to explain food consumption changes in terms of individual optimization. Each step is represented graphically, to communicate ideas that could also be presented using calculus (Varian 2009) or more generally using real analysis (Mas-Colell, Whinston, and Green 1995).

2.1   Food Consumption Decisions as Optimal Choices

The basic thought experiment used in economics to explain food consumption is shown in Figure 14.2, adapted from similar diagrams in Norton, Alwang, and Masters (2010) and many other textbooks. The axes shows quantities consumed. They are labeled with food on the horizontal axis and other goods on the vertical axis, but

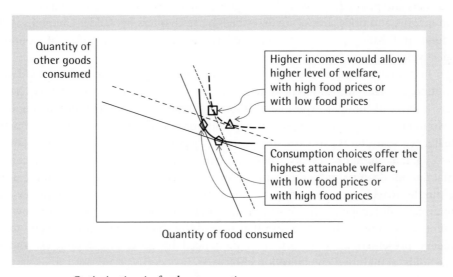

FIGURE 14.2 Optimization in food consumption

every step of the following thought experiments would be identical if we relabeled these axes with anything that people want or need. By definition, however, quantities should be recorded so that more is better, and any undesirable "bads" should be recorded as their inverse. Any unit of measure can be used. As it happens, the data presented at the end of this chapter are expressed first for all foods in calories per person per day, and then for cereal grains in millions of metric tons per region per year.

To begin, consider what is even possible for a person to obtain. Their income, purchasing power, or other entitlements can be represented graphically as straight lines, showing the combinations of food and other goods that could possibly be acquired at a given rate of barter exchange between them. Consumption below or to the left of each line would be possible, but by definition goods are recorded so that consumption above or to the right is preferable, and the dashed lines represent a preferred level of entitlement. The slope (rise/run) of this income constraint is the quantity of other goods that can be exchanged for a unit of food, which in price terms would be the price of food divided by the price of other goods, so that the steeper lines represent more expensive food. For now, both income and prices are simply accounting constraints, drawn arbitrarily on Figure 14.2; their causes will be addressed below.

Consumer choices are captured in Figure 14.2 by the shape of the two curves, with each curve defined as all combinations of the two goods that would be equally satisfactory. By definition, the dashed curve offers a higher level of "welfare." Optimization enters here: a mathematical consequence of consumers having chosen what they prefer is that, around any observed consumption choice, these indifference curves must be flat or convex as shown on Figure 14.2. This shape arises because, after consumers have chosen their preferred quantities, any further substitution of one good for the other must offer diminishing marginal benefits—hence their indifference curves must be increasingly flat to the right of any chosen point, and increasingly steep to the left of it. Other curvature is possible elsewhere along the indifference curve, but an optimizing consumer would exploit all such opportunities for increasing marginal benefits until diminishing returns has set in.

Our first thought experiment using Figure 14.2 asks how optimizing people will adjust to a change in their income constraint, as might occur during economic development or as a result of policy change. If we were to observe them consuming at the diamond- or square-shaped points, for example, how would they react if food became cheaper and more abundant? Intuitively we might expect them to consume more food—and to prefer the lower price—and Figure 14.2 shows that is usually but not always optimal. The reduction in food prices flattens the income constraint, so optimizing consumers at any given welfare level will choose to consume more food and less of other goods. But the change in food prices will also change their income level, shown for example as a shift between the solid and the dashed curves. Most people are food buyers, so that the reduction in food price raises the income they have left to buy other things. They might move from the diamond to the triangle, with an increase in consumption of both goods. But farmers might be food sellers, so the price reduction would lower their income. Such people might move from the square to the pentagon, and actually reduce food intake. Our thought experiment tells us that adjustments involve both a substitution effect at a given level of welfare, and an income effect from a shift in welfare levels, both of which must be taken into account to explain food consumption.

The framework illustrated in Figure 14.2 is built from the assumption that consumers have a known product available to buy at the prices shown. This begs the question of how markets arise to provide known goods at fixed prices. The growth of markets is a result as well as a cause of economic development; it may occur spontaneously between buyers and sellers when product characteristics are known (e.g., Fafchamps and Minten 2001), but, as shown by Akerlof (1970), products of unknown quality may remain off the market entirely until collective action provides quality assurance (e.g., Masters and Sanogo 2002).

The framework of Figure 14.2 also begs the question of what determines incomes, which we will address below. But even before that, thinking about consumption as an optimization decision provides immediate insight into observed dietary patterns and changes. The economics approach suggests that otherwise identical people will choose different foods if they have different incomes and face different prices—and that their diets will become more similar if their incomes and prices converge. This view helps to explain differences in food culture and dietary habits, as consequences as much as as causes of differences in food consumption choices. Note that "convergence" here does not mean uniformity: as documented by Ruel (2003) for low-income countries, and by Thiele and Weiss (2003) for a high-income country, many people exhibit a strong preference for dietary diversity, so that economic convergence unleashes ever greater variety in the diet at each place and time as people become able to acquire more foods that were previously unaffordable.

2.2 Constraints on Food Consumption: Incomes, Prices, and Market Participation

To take the analysis one step further, we ask what determines prices and the consumers' income level. The optimization approach to this question is shown in Figure 14.3, by which prices and incomes depend fundamentally on the physical production possibilities available at a particular place and time. That production possibilities frontier defines the limit of what can be created by a farm household, village, country, or other decision-making group, given their resources, technology, and environment. Here, the key implication of optimization is that, around any observed production choice, these production possibility frontiers are bowed outward, with diminishing marginal returns in production as resources are shifted from food to other goods. As with the indifference curves, opportunities for increasing marginal returns may arise but will be exploited by optimizing producers, so observed points arise where there are diminishing returns. In this case, the location and curvature of the frontier has been

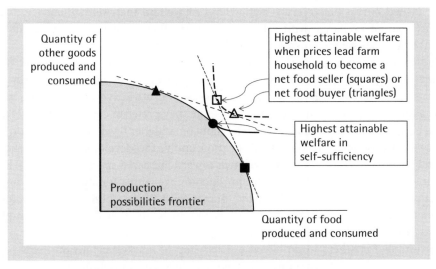

FIGURE 14.3 A household model of the gains from specialization

drawn to explain the dashed lines from the previous figure, as the highest possible income and welfare attainable at any given relative prices.

One thought experiment we can conduct with this model is to compare optimal choices at the given relative prices, along the dashed lines, with the choices that would be available if this decision maker were required to be self-sufficient. The highest welfare level attainable in self-sufficiency is shown by the solid indifference curve. The solid dot shows the point of self-sufficiency, where production equals consumption. Relative prices in self-sufficiency are given by the slope of the production possibilities frontier and the solid indifference curve at that point.

An astonishing fact about the results of Figure 14.3 is that accepting market prices would be preferred to the price seen with self-sufficiency *at all market prices*, no matter what is bought or sold. Market prices are shown by the slope of the dashed lines, whose rise over run is the quantity of other goods that can be traded for a unit of food. If the market places a higher value on food than would hold in self-sufficiency, then the dashed line is relatively steep and the household can raise its welfare by becoming a net food seller. They would specialize in producing food (at the solid triangle), some of which they would sell to buy more non-food items (at the open triangle). The diagram has been drawn so that the exact same level of welfare can be attained in the opposite case, when the market price of food is low so that this same household would respond by becoming a net food buyer, producing more of the other goods (as the solid square) for sale to consume more food (at the open square). The fact that the two dashed lines happen to reach the same dashed curve and hence the same welfare level is a coincidence: the general conclusion is that *any* dashed line will allow the household to reach *some* dashed curve that offers a higher level of welfare than self-sufficiency, simply because market exchange with a larger group of other people helps overcome each producer and consumer's own local diminishing returns.

The optimization framework provides remarkable insight into how economic development and government policies can lift food consumption through the growth of markets, as otherwise self-sufficient households find attractive opportunities to sell some goods they produce in exchange for others they prefer to consume. Each of these market opportunities is valuable in itself, allowing a higher level of consumption for a given set of productive resources. More profoundly, the development of markets in general permits an endless sequence of steps toward increased specialization, and hence sustained growth in consumption and production over time. Ridley (2010) argues that specialization for trade is the distinctive human trait that accounts for our biological success relative to other species. Once production is uncoupled from consumption, people can save and invest in specialized efforts to serve others, which in turn creates opportunities for others to do likewise. Each step of market expansion helps people overcome the diminishing returns that each individual, household, village, or other group would otherwise face, and allows each individual or group to benefit from and contribute to the lives of an ever larger number of others.

Figure 14.3 is a geometric demonstration that explains why households, villages, and countries choose to trade with people elsewhere, rather than remain self-sufficient. It is not a demonstration of economic development as such, because households are not actually "initially" self-sufficient: there is ample archaeological evidence that, in reality, even the earliest known human settlements engaged in trade (Dillian and White 2010). What changes over time and differs across households is the *extent* of access to markets, as new opportunities for profitable trade are developed over time and attract a larger and larger fraction of total activity. In today's highest-income countries, the same goods change hands so often that the annual volume of trade far exceeds the annual value of production. The ratio is smaller in lower-income countries, and among the world's poorest people most production is destined for home consumption as illustrated in Figure 14.3.

A household's degree of market access depends strongly on their spatial location, and is closely tied to their consumption and production levels (e.g., Kanbur and Venables 2005; Minten and Stifel 2008). A common explanation is that limited market participation causes low productivity, but it is equally possible that low productivity forces households into greater self-sufficiency. Both directions of causality could coexist, but they have very different implications for development policy (Barrett 2008). Rios, Shively, and Masters (2009) test the two hypotheses using a large sample of households from Guatemala, Vietnam, and Tanzania, and find that increases in farm productivity drive higher market participation much more consistently than the other way around. This result is independent of what products are sold: some farmers turn out to have relatively high productivity in food production and are net food sellers, whereas others have high productivity in other things and are net food buyers.

2.3   Constraints on Market Participation: Productivity and the Gains from Specialization

The link between productivity and gains from specialization is illustrated in Figure 14.4. The thought experiment shown here demonstrates how, relative to the exact same "initial" point of self-sufficiency as Figure 14.3, a more constrained production possibilities frontier (shown as the dark curve) makes for limited market exchange opportunities and a lower welfare level, with lower quantities of both food and other goods consumed at the same market prices as Figure 14.3.

   Development policies can help households lift the production constraints illustrated in Figure 14.4, principally through R & D and technology dissemination, to help farmers do more with the resources they have. As documented by Alston et al. (2000), the payoff to these projects is typically much larger than the returns on other investments, indicating persistent underspending on that kind of public good. Why might governments underinvest in productivity enhancement? One explanation is that those gains are widely spread over many years and many people, so that beneficiaries remain unaware, unable or unwilling to organize politically in pursuit of this kind of public action. As discussed later in this chapter in the context of food price policy, governments tend to choose interventions that deliver concentrated benefits to influential groups, while spreading costs in ways that avoid provoking resistance. McMillan and Masters (2003) show how many but not all African governments have chosen both low R & D levels and price policies that limit economic growth, which is consistent with more recent evidence from price policies around the world presented in Section 2 of this chapter.

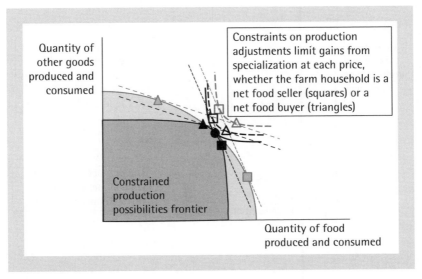

FIGURE 14.4 The household model with constrained production possibililties

2.4   Consequences of Market Participation: Food Prices and Consumption Choices

Figure 14.5 shows how higher food prices influence farm households, in the same framework as Figure 14.3 and 14.4. For a farmer who already faces high enough food prices to justify producing (at the solid square) more food than she consumes (at the open square), a further increase in food prices raises food production and allows more consumption of both goods along a higher welfare level. In contrast, a farmer who faces relatively low food prices and therefore specializes in producing other things (at the solid triangle), which she sells to buy more food (at the open triangle), the increase in food prices sharply lowers food consumption and welfare to the lower of the two dashed curves.

The main point of the thought experiment in Figure 14.5 is to emphasize that a rise in food prices increases food production among both buyers and sellers—but those farm households who are net food buyers suffer surprisingly large losses in welfare, because they not only pay more for food but also are forced to be more self-sufficient, removing their earlier gains from trade.

2.5   Investment and Scale Effects

In my analysis so far, food consumption has been explained solely by prices and productivity. A crucial extension is to consider the effect of additional investment which might allow food producers to overcome diminishing returns. Figure 14.6

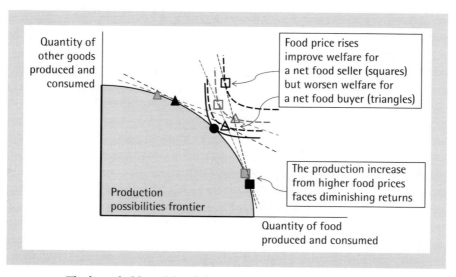

FIGURE 14.5 The household model with higher food prices

provides a general illustration of production response from increments of investment in additional inputs. The solid line shows the output level achievable at each level of input use. Starting from zero, output might remain low until a critical mass of investment is achieved, above which output offers increasing returns to additional size. The dashed lines show net income levels: as before, the line's rise over run in quantity terms is fixed by market prices, as the price of inputs divided by the price of the output. At a high enough price ratio (the steepest dashed line), inputs do not produce enough output to justify their use in production, so quantities chosen are zero. It is only when relative prices improve, as shown by a flatter dashed line, that it becomes worthwhile for production to begin with a jump from zero to the minimum size of operation shown by the solid square. Further price changes lead to diminishing returns, for example up to the open square, but notice that other indivisible investments might lead to a second threshold of size and eventual jump up to the solid triangle. This is the same process by which optimization leads to production and consumption being observed only in regions of diminishing returns, but in Figure 14.6 the unobserved regions are shown explicitly in between the dot and the solid square, and then in between the open square and the solid triangle.

Figure 14.6 illustrates how investment levels and the exploitation of scale economies depend on technological opportunities that offer increasing returns, combined with relative-price changes that make it worthwhile to invest in them. The most common source of increasing returns is machinery, buildings, and equipment, whose through-put often rises with volume while costs rise with surface area. The result is the two-thirds rule of engineering, by which costs rise by (roughly) two-thirds of capacity. As materials improve to hold things together, there is no intrinsic limit to these cost reductions. The two-thirds rule could lead to ever larger production units, except that

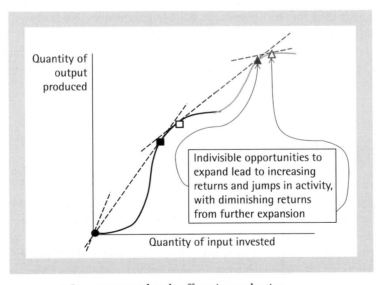

FIGURE 14.6 Investment and scale effects in production

actual production costs depend on much more than the cost of machines, buildings, and equipment.

For food production, increased farmland or farm animals can be added at a roughly constant cost for each additional unit, but more remote acreage imposes additional transport costs and crowding imposes additional costs of congestion. Furthermore, additional workers can be added at roughly constant cost of labor, but only if they are self-motivated. As documented by Allen and Lueck (2003), for example, the transaction and supervision costs of employing hired workers in most field crop operations ensure that self-motivated family members can operate farms at lower unit costs than employees. The vast majority of farming observed in the world is family-operated. The exceptional cases of successful employee-operated, investor-owned agriculture occur principally where production costs involve a lot of industrial-type processing, as in a tea or sugar plantation, or where labor supervision costs are kept low by spatial concentration and non-seasonality, such as confined animal operations or some horticultural production.

The relationships illustrated by Figure 14.6 provide a striking explanation for why we observe roughly similar farm sizes within regions, and very different farm sizes across them. For example, one place might have farm sizes shown by the squares, while another will have larger farm sizes shown by the triangles. This leads to one more thought experiment: would moving from the squares to the triangles be desirable? It turns out that larger farm sizes offer higher incomes only when the appropriate technology is available and relative prices justify its use, as shown by the dashed line being as flat or flatter than the long light-colored segment, and the dashed curve turning up in its light-colored segment. In any given region, acreage per farm is similar because farmers' optimization has already occurred, adjusting farm sizes to provide a farm family's workers with just enough income to justify staying on the farm—as opposed to migrating for work elsewhere. Allowing farm sizes to adjust in this way has been an important feature of successful development policies (Tomich, Kilby, and Johnston 1995), accommodating the rise and then fall in each country's number of farm families that is associated with population growth and structural transformation (Timmer 2009).

2.6   Supply, Demand, and Government Policies

So far I have taken market prices as given, but in practice they are variables that depend on production, consumption, and government choices. My final thought experiment captures the role of government in Figure 14.7, which has the same horizontal axis as Figures 14.2–14.5 but has the price of food relative to other things on the vertical axis. The upward-sloping line shows quantity produced at each price ("supply"), and the downward-sloping line shows quantity consumed at each price ("demand"). Both curves are drawn squiggly to emphasize that their shape is arbitrary, as supply moves

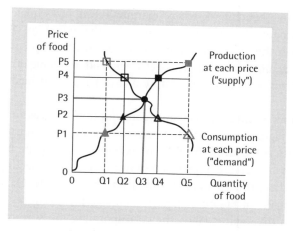

<small>FIGURE 14.7</small> Supply, demand, and policies

along the production possibilities frontiers and demand moves along and between the indifference curves of Figures 14.2–14.5. Here, the only consequence of optimization is that the production curve is flat or upward-sloping, which follows from Figures 14.5 and 14.6. From Figure 14.2, it follows that the consumption curve is generally down-ward-sloping but could slope up if the income effect of higher prices outweighs the substitution effect between goods.

The interaction between supply and demand shown in Figure 14.7 is far from straightforward. Even if each individual producer and consumer is optimizing, the result of their interactions cannot generally be considered an optimum. Only under the very restrictive conditions of a perfectly competitive market would sellers increase supply until buyers exhaust demand at that price, such as quantity Q3 at price P3 in Figure 14.7. Real-life food markets often fall short of the perfectly competitive bench-mark, for reasons such as a gap in the information available to buyers and sellers, or fixed costs and scale effects that offer incumbent buyers or sellers an entry barrier against potential competitors. Such market failures limit the extent of the market, leaving unexploited opportunities for trades whose marginal benefits would exceed their costs. A classic example that affects many food markets involves information gaps as described by Akerlof (1970), who showed that even high-quality goods cannot be sold if buyers do not trust sellers. Food markets are also affected by scale effects and barriers to entry, often because consumption and production occur at the household scale, while transport and processing can be done at lower cost in larger-scale enter-prises so that a multitude of consumers and of farm households are served by a handful of suppliers and middlemen whose pricing decisions depend on the threat of entry by competitors. Production and consumption decisions may also affect third parties through non-market mechanisms such as disease transmission or environmental pollution. In all of these cases, government interventions could improve consumption by overcoming the market failure, helping buyers and sellers move closer to the perfectly competitive benchmark where marginal costs just equal marginal benefits. A central determinant of consumer well-being is the extent to which governments actually accomplish this task, offsetting market failures to help consumers specialize and trade with each other. In practice, governments often pursue other goals, and their active "policy failures" may limit consumption as much as their inactivity in the face of "market failure."

To trace the link between prices and consumption choices, one useful thought experiment using Figure 14.7 is simply to retrace the steps taken earlier using Figures 14.2–14.6. When prices rise from P1 to P2, for example, we re-create the triangles shown in Figure 14.4, with an increase in production from Q1 to Q2, a decline in consumption from Q5 to Q4, and a shrinkage in net buying from Q5–Q1 to Q4–Q2. As we know from the indifference curves of Figure 14.4, such a change must reduce welfare. How does that loss appear in this figure? Here, the corresponding measure of welfare effects is known as economic surplus, whose change is defined as the area between the two price levels traced from zero out to the supply curve (for change in economic surplus from production, also known as "producer surplus"), or to the demand curve (for change in economic surplus from consumption, or "consumer surplus"). The slopes of the supply and demand curves ensure that the loss due to reduced consumption from the vertical axis out to the hollow triangles is larger than from the gain from increased production out to the solid triangles.

The thought experiment just conducted simply retraces the logic of Figure 14.4. The losses from restricting trade become larger as quantities approach self-sufficiency, and are largest when production equals consumption at Q3, the solid dot where price is P3. At prices above P3, production would be larger than consumption, so we would observe net selling. To limit visual clutter we have drawn the resulting squares at previously labeled quantities: at P4 and P5 consumption falls to Q2 and Q1, while production rises to Q4 and Q5. These could correspond to the squares in Figure 14.4, except that the new supply–demand diagrams lack any mechanism to show whether the increased income from more production is spent on consumption of this as opposed to other goods. In Figure 14.4 a higher price of food caused that particular food seller to consume more of it, as the income effect from greater sales outweighed the substitution effect from higher prices. The accounting for income effects was achieved through the income constraint, which ensured that all earnings from the sale of one thing was spent on the other. Figure 14.7 has no such general equilibrium feedback. The resulting partial-equilibrium economic surplus measures can be useful when the product in question accounts for a small share of total income, even though a complete accounting for income effects would be needed to obtain exact measurements of welfare changes.

The main advantage of Figure 14.7 over previous diagrams is that, by separating production from consumption, we gain insight into the role of government. Our final thought experiment considers why national governments, as opposed to individual consumers and producers, often forgo the gains from specialization and trade in favor of greater self-sufficiency. Why might governments reduce total economic surplus by restricting trade?

Figure 14.7 reveals who gains and who loses from trade restrictions. If foreigners offered to sell food at P1, the highest level of welfare would be reached by producing Q1, consuming Q5, and using free trade to import the difference. Restricting these imports would raise local prices (for example, to P2), which would generate a small increase in economic surplus from more production (from Q1 to Q2) at the cost of a much larger decrease in economic surplus from less consumption (from Q5 to Q4). An exactly symmetrical experience arises with exports. If foreigners offer to buy at P5, restricting exports would reduce the price (for example, to P4) and generate an increase in local consumption (again, from Q1 to Q2) at the cost of a decrease in production (from Q5 to Q4).

Restricting trade in either direction makes it profitable to undertake those trades that are permitted: in the case of imports, the remaining quantity traded (Q4–Q2) can be bought from foreigners at P1 and sold to locals at P2, for a profit of P2–P1 on every unit imported. Likewise for exports, the profit is P5–P4 on every unit exported. That profit can be taken by government through an import tariff or export tax, or it can be given to political favorites as rents on an import quota or export license. But the larger effect of trade restrictions is to transfer economic surplus between producers and consumers. In the case of import restriction, the economic surplus gain from increased production (which is P2–P1 out to the supply curve) will benefit producers in proportion to their market share, while the burden of economic surplus loss (P2–P1 out to the demand curve) is borne by consumers in proportion to consumption. Likewise for export restrictions, the large cost from reduced production (P5–P4 out to the supply curve) is shared among producers, while consumers benefit in proportion to how much they use.

To explain policy choices in terms of individuals' decision-making, our thought experiment compares people's incentives to pursue public policy goals as opposed to their own private activity. So far, my analysis has placed equal weight on each dollar earned or spent by individual producers, consumers, or traders. If economic interests were all equally influential in politics, political bodies would choose free trade in private goods, while using taxes and regulations to provide public goods such as quality assurance, infrastructure, or productivity enhancements in order to maximize national income. But political organization could be easier for some interests than others, leading real-life governments to favor those interest groups over the nation as a whole.

Paarlberg (2010) provides a broad overview of food policy choices in the development process. To explain how some groups can consistently gain disproportionate influence, Downs (1957) emphasized the threshold cost of becoming informed and engaged in political action, which would lead individuals to remain "rationally ignorant" and inactive about interests that are low-priority for them. Olson (1965) emphasized marginal costs and benefits, which give individuals a greater incentive to be "free riders" about interests that they share with a larger group. Both rational ignorance and free-ridership limit the power of widely spread interests, allowing smaller but highly motivated interest groups to have disproportionate political influence.

Changes in food consumption during economic development offer an extreme example of asymmetry in how concentrated or diffuse a given economic interest can be. In a poor country with limited specialization, food production is spread among a majority of the population, many of whom are actually net food buyers. A minority of the population have non-farm jobs, but still spend a relatively large fraction of their income buying the food they need, and a few of them also buy non-food agricultural products for processing or export. Our thought experiment predicts that, in this setting, political processes will favor the buyers' interest in low prices for agricultural products, using export restrictions and other interventions to transfer funds from production to consumption despite the resulting damage to the economy as a whole. From that point forward, if economic development proceeds despite these interventions, then a shrinking fraction of the population will become increasingly specialized farmers. Each farmer will produce an ever larger quantity of a few products, while food expenditure becomes an ever smaller share of consumers' budgets. Our thought experiment predicts that governments will then switch sides to favor high farm prices. Anderson (1995) provides a more complete analysis of this switch, but some back-of-the-envelope arithmetic illustrates how economic development changes farmers' political leverage: a typical high-income country has one food producer for every twenty consumers, so a dollar of transfer to each producer costs each consumer only 5 cents. Import restrictions and other measures can readily transfer to each farmer an amount equal to the country's per capita national income, at a modest cost to each consumer. As transfers grow, they eventually become so costly as to push the issue higher on policymakers' agenda, but some transfer of this type is to be expected when producers are highly motivated to invest heavily in political activity on this one issue, while consumers remain unaware of the transfer or have other concerns of greater political relevance.

The thought experiments presented in Section 1 of this chapter trace the implications of individuals' optimization to generate a surprisingly rich set of predictions about how food consumption is linked to economic development and government policies. Individuals may not always make optimal choices, but to the extent that they do, we find that reaching the highest available level of consumption requires specialization for the market. Those opportunities are constrained not only by market prices, but also by production possibilities in each potential area of specialization. Governments can act to expand households' opportunities, but they face strong political pressures to restrict trade and also to underinvest in productivity enhancement, in part because political processes favor actions that produce narrowly targeted gains at the expense of diffuse losses. Aggregate improvements in total consumption depend on social institutions that help government promote specialization and market development through the provision of public goods and other collective actions. Many such opportunities are detailed elsewhere in this Handbook in areas such as food safety and quality certification, or broader interventions in public health, infrastructure, research, and education where public investments can enhance economic productivity. Trade restrictions are unlikely to accomplish that result, but our thought experiments suggest they are likely to be widespread in the direction of helping consumption at the expense of production in poor countries, and vice versa in rich ones.

3   EMPIRICAL EVIDENCE ON PRICE POLICY AND MARKET OUTCOMES IN ECONOMIC DEVELOPMENT

Having established a framework for interpretation, I now turn to some of the available data, starting with government interventions that drive food prices along the lines of Figure 14.7, and then considering aggregate production and consumption choices along the lines of Figures 14.2–14.6, so as to form a more complete picture of the interrelationships sketched in Figure 14.1.

3.1   Food Policy in Economic Development

By far the largest and most comprehensive effort to measure the price effects of government intervention in food markets is provided in the online data set of Anderson and Valenzuela (2009), from a World Bank project involving over a hundred researchers writing case studies for sixty-eight countries over more than forty years, covering a total of seventy-seven major food products and agricultural commodities. The resulting data set provides over 25,000 pairs of prices, such as P1–P2 or P4–P5 in Figure 14.7, along with the appropriate quantities such as Q1–Q2 and Q4–Q5. The resulting estimate of total economic surplus transfers is provided in Figure 14.8, for five-year averages over all available years, after conversion of local currencies into constant US dollars in purchasing-power parity terms. As predicted, the world's high-income countries (in dark bars) consistently intervene to favor production over consumption, while lower-income countries (in white bars) at first did the reverse but switched in the 1990s as their incomes grew.

Interestingly, total transfers in industrialized countries have declined since the 1990s, suggesting that the magnitude of transfer had become large enough for the issue to generate counter-pressures among consumers and taxpayers, as well as among government officials concerned with aggregate national income. The institutional structures through which farm supports have been disciplined include the inclusion of agriculture in international treaties such as the World Trade Organization, North American Free Trade Agreement, or the European Union, as well as unilateral moves through national policymaking processes.

Masters and Garcia (2010) use the individual observations underlying Figure 14.8 in a series of econometric tests, finding strong support for many but not all of the hypotheses about government intervention found in the literature. Most importantly, the data are clearly consistent with the rational ignorance hypothesis of Downs (1957), as interventions have indeed been larger in markets where the benefits are concentrated among a few while costs are dispersed among many. Overall, the link to economic development is illustrated in Figure 14.9, which shows a smoothed regression line

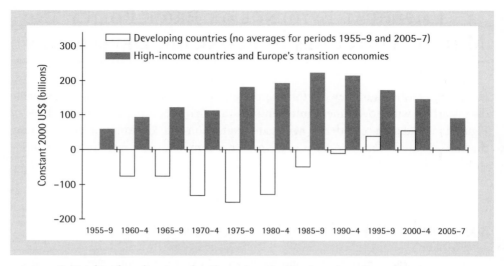

FIGURE 14.8 Total trade policy transfers through agricultural markets, by region

Source: Author's adaption, from data in Anderson, K., ed. (2009).

through all 2,520 individual observations for the price effect of government intervention in a particular commodity market, country, and year, as a function of the average per capita annual income in that country and year. The regression line shows the mean level of intervention at each income level, surrounded by its 95 percent confidence interval, for all farm products on the left panel, and then separately for imported and exported products on the right panel.

In the left panel of Figure 14.9 there is an interesting non-linearity, as poor countries subsidize consumption at the expense of production at a moderate rate up to about US $5,000 per year of per capita income, after which increased income is associated with a sharp rise in production subsidies at the expense of consumption. One source of non-linearity is the absence of any upper bound on the subsidies whose average level can easily reach +100 percent (a doubling of producer revenue), whereas government's ability to tax production is limited by the ability of low-income farmers to withdraw into self-sufficiency if their market participation is too heavily taxed.

The right panel of Figure 14.9 contrasts imports with exports, revealing that even in poor countries there are consistent import restrictions that favor producers over consumers (e.g., a rise from P1 to P2 in Figure 14.6), but these are more than offset by export restrictions that have the opposite effect (e.g., a fall from P5 to P4). The statistical tests in Masters and Garcia (2010) associate some of this anti-trade bias with a revenue-seeking effect, by which developing-country governments with fewer alternative sources of revenue use both import tariffs and export taxes to help fund the public sector, while more developed countries can tax a wider range of recorded activity using income or property and sales taxes, or value-added taxes.

In summary, observed patterns of price intervention are consistent with the predictions of our analytical framework, as government interventions tend to create

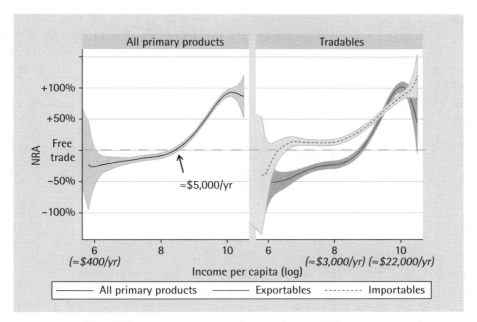

FIGURE 14.9 Tariff-equivalent trade policy transfers as a function of per capita income
Each row shows data from 66 countries in each year from 1961 to 2005 (N = 2,520), smoothed
with confidence intervals using Stata's lpolyci at bandwidth 1 and degree 4. Income per capita is
expressed in US$ at 2000 PPP prices.

Source: Adapted from Masters and Garcia (2010).

concentrated benefits that mobilize supporters, at the expense of diffuse costs that
provoke little resistance. At some point the costs become so politically conspicuous that
they can no longer be ignored, and support levels no longer rise with economic
development. In poorer countries the same mechanism leads to taxation of production
to benefit consumption, supplemented by a revenue motive due to limited ability to
enforce other kinds of taxes.

3.2   Food Consumption and Production in Economic Development

Having tested our framework against government choices that drive prices, I turn now
to evidence on the resulting quantities consumed and produced. A wide variety of data
sources could be exploited, many of which are used in other chapters of this Handbook.
For this section, I focus on just one kind of data, namely Food Balance Sheet (FBS)
estimates of the Food and Agriculture Organization (FAO). The FAO Food Balance
Sheets attempt the heroic task of reconciling national statistics from every country in
the world, to produce national, regional, and global estimates of quantities produced,

traded, and consumed for every possible food commodity. Jacobs and Sumner (2002) provide an independent review of FBS data: the underlying observations are of very limited accuracy and the results should be viewed with a wide margin of error, but no other data source even comes close to the comprehensive coverage attempted by the FBS.

In Table 14.1 I show the first and last available years of FBS data, summarizing food consumption in terms of total energy intake per capita per day, by type of food, for the world as a whole and for selected low-income regions. Although food quantities are poorly measured and their conversion to calories is rough at best, the resulting picture is quite clear. Total calorie consumption has risen sharply in all regions but especially in Southeast Asia and in China, whose per capita energy intake is now estimated to exceed the world average. On average South Asians continue to consume fewer total calories than Africans. In the poorest regions most calories continue to be sourced from cereal grains, with energy from animal products remaining under 10 percent. Starchy roots are of continued importance mainly in Africa, having fallen sharply in importance for the Chinese. Use of vegetable oils has risen quickly everywhere, and they are generally larger as a source of dietary energy than fruits and vegetables combined, or sugars and sweeteners. For the world as a whole, alcoholic beverages are about as large a source of calories as vegetables.

Table 14.2 offers the same data broken down by energy in the form of carbohydrates, protein, or fats. Again the breakdown is a rough approximation but quite striking in so far as the protein share of global diets has changed relatively little. The principal change has been increased consumption of fats. The main sources of protein are still cereal grains, and the main source of fats is oilseeds and other crops, although animal sources now exceed 20 percent of protein consumed even in Africa, and consumption of animal fats had been low but is now high in China and Southeast Asia.

Table 14.1 FAO FBS estimates of per capita food consumption by source and region, 1961 and 2007 (%)

	World		South Asia		Africa		Southeast Asia		China	
	1961	2007	1961	2007	1961	2007	1961	2007	1961	2007
Cereals	49	46	64	60	50	50	65	59	57	49
Animal products	15	17	6	9	8	8	6	11	4	21
Starchy roots	8	5	1	2	16	14	10	4	20	5
Vegetable oils	5	10	4	8	6	8	4	7	2	8
Vegetables	2	3	1	2	2	2	1	2	4	6
Fruits	2	3	2	3	4	4	3	3	0	2
Sugars/sweeteners	9	8	9	8	5	6	5	7	2	3
Alcoholic beverages	2	3	0	0	2	2	0	1	1	3
All other sources	7	5	12	8	8	7	6	6	10	3
Total (kcal/day)	2,195	2,796	1,990	2,370	2,027	2,455	1,803	2,586	1,469	2,981

Source: Calculated from FAOStat (2010).

Table 14.2 FAO estimates of food consumption by macronutrient category, 1961 and 2007 (%)

Macronutrient category (% of total energy, kcal/day)	World		South Asia		Africa		Southeast Asia		China	
	1961	2007	1961	2007	1961	2007	1961	2007	1961	2007
Carbohydrate	70	64	77	72	72	71	79	71	80	61
Protein	11	11	10	10	10	10	8	10	11	12
Fats	19	25	13	19	17	19	13	19	9	27
Total energy	2,195	2,796	1,990	2,370	2,027	2,455	1,803	2,586	1,469	2,981
Protein by source										
Cereals	44	42	58	57	52	52	61	50	48	40
Other vegetables	25	21	28	22	29	27	18	18	45	23
Animals	31	38	14	21	9	21	21	32	8	38
Fats by source										
Cereals	11	6	21	10	18	16	15	9	20	7
Other vegetables	38	49	52	59	56	61	58	53	53	36
Animals	51	44	28	31	26	24	27	38	27	57

Source: Calculated from FAOStat (2010), Food Balance Sheet.

Table 14.3 FAO Food Balance Sheet estimates for cereals by region, 1961–9 and 2000–7 (%)

	World		South Asia		Africa		Southeast Asia		China	
	1960s	2000s	1960s	2000s	1960s	2000s	1960s	2000s	1960s	2000s
Production (mmt/yr)	929	1,967	115.8	266.5	58.9	117.0	49.8	127.0	148.3	356.0
Food use	47	47	82	89	71	107	64	71	57	58
Feed use	38	37	2	7	10	21	4	19	17	33
Stock accumulation	1	−1	0	0	3	1	3	4	1	−7
Net imports	n.a.	n.a.	8	1	9	41	−1	5	4	0
Waste etc.	16	14	10	9	20	20	14	26	15	3

Note: n.a. = not applicable.
Source: Calculated from FAOStat (2010).

Table 14.3 focuses just on cereal grains, which are sufficiently homogeneous in nutrient density that we can compare production, consumption, and net trade data in quantity terms. To smooth out annual fluctuations, the data shown here are period averages for the 1960s (actually 1961–9) and the 2000s (actually 2000–7). Total cereals output has more than doubled in all regions shown except Africa, which almost doubled. In developing countries, most of the cereals produced are estimated to have been consumed as food, but for the world as a whole only 47 percent is consumed as food and the rest is used as animal feed, as seed, or is counted by the FAO as lost in storage, transport, processing, or marketing. Loss percentages vary widely across regions, which could reflect underlying differences but might also reflect measurement errors. Trade flows make up the difference between production and use, but trade volumes are a small fraction of total production for all regions except Africa, which is uniquely reliant on cereal imports for its sustenance: Africa is thought to consume more than its total production, thanks to a flow of imports that was even larger than South Asia's in the 1960s and now brings in more than 40 percent as much cereal grain as local production. In these data the Africa region includes North Africa, but even Sub-Saharan Africa is a huge net importer of cereal grains.

4   CONCLUSIONS

This chapter summarizes the economics approach to explaining food consumption decisions during economic development, focusing particularly on the role of local food production, market exchange, and government interventions that influence food prices. Food cultures clearly differ widely across countries and over time. These differences reveal consistent patterns of change in food consumption associated with economic development, and strong regularities in government interventions as well. My analysis focuses on these patterns, aiming to sketch an underlying structure that can help explain at least some of the differences and similarities in food consumption choices observed around the world, and help readers assess the likely impacts of alternative government interventions.

The economics approach explains individual decisions as the result of optimization, which generates a number of remarkable predictions that I explore in a series of thought experiments about consumption, production, and market exchange. My first result is that consumption levels are highest when individuals exploit opportunities for trade with others, as specialization and investment lead to greater purchasing power and access to a larger quantity of more diverse foods. The resulting market outcomes cannot themselves be characterized as an optimum, however, except under the extreme conditions of perfectly competitive markets. Real markets may fall short of the perfectly competitive benchmark for many reasons, such as limited information, transaction costs, entry barriers, and other causes of market failure. Government interventions can improve consumption by overcoming these constraints to make markets work more effectively, but policymaking processes are subject to constraints of their own. Most notably, I find that governments often restrict trade and underinvest in productive public goods, which I explain in part by asymmetries in political influence between those who benefit from and those who pay the cost of these choices. Despite these limitations, most of the world has seen marked expansion in food consumption and living standards, continuing the long history of nutritional change documented by Fogel (2004).

References

Akerlof, G. A. 1970. "The Market for 'Lemons': Quality Uncertainty and the Market Mechanism." *Quarterly Journal of Economics* 84/3: 488–500.

Allen, D. W., and D. Lueck. 2003. *The Nature of the Farm: Contracts, Risk, and Organization in Agriculture.* Cambridge, MA: MIT Press.

Alston, J. M., M. C. Marra, P. G. Pardey, and T. J. Wyatt. 2000. "Research Returns Redux: A Meta-Analysis of the Returns to Agricultural R & D." *Australian Journal of Agricultural and Resource Economics* 44/2: 185–215.

Anderson, K. 1995. "Lobbying Incentives and the Pattern of Protection in Rich and Poor Countries." *Economic Development and Cultural Change* 43/2 (Jan.), 401–23.

—— ed. 2009. *Distortions to Agricultural Incentives: A Global Perspective.* London: Palgrave Macmillan; Washington, DC: World Bank.

—— and E. Valenzuela. 2009. *Estimates of Global Distortions to Agricultural Incentives, 1955 to 2007.* Washington, DC: World Bank. Database at <http://www.worldbank.org/agdistortions>.

Barrett, C. B. 2008. "Smallholder Market Participation: Concepts and Evidence from Eastern and Southern Africa." *Food Policy* 33/4: 299–317.

Dillian, C. D., and C. L. White. 2010. *Trade and Exchange: Archaeological Studies from History and Prehistory.* New York: Springer.

Downs, A. 1957. "An Economic Theory of Political Action in a Democracy." *Journal of Political Economy* 65/2: 135–50.

Fafchamps, M., and B. Minten. 2001. "Property Rights in a Flea Market Economy." *Economic Development and Cultural Change* 49/2: 229–67.

FAOStat. 2010. *Food Balance Sheet.* June 2. <http://faostat.fao.org>.

Fogel, R. W. 2004. *The Escape from Hunger and Premature Death, 1700–2100.* New York: Cambridge University Press.

Jacobs, K. L., and D. A. Sumner. 2002. "The Food Balance Sheets of the Food and Agriculture Organization: A Review of Potential Ways to Broaden the Appropriate Uses of the Data." <http://faostat.fao.org/abcdq/docs/FBS_Review.pdf>.

Kanbur, R., and A. F. Venables, eds. 2005. *Spatial Inequality and Development.* New York: Oxford University Press.

McMillan, M. S., and W. A. Masters. 2003. "An African Growth Trap: Production Technology and the Time-Consistency of Agricultural Taxation, R & D and Investment." *Review of Development Economics* 7/2: 179–91.

Manzel, P., and F. D'Alusio. 2008. *Hungry Planet: What the World Eats.* Berkeley: Tricycle Press.

Mas-Colell, A., M. Whinston, and J. Green. 1995. *Microeconomic Theory.* New York: Oxford University Press.

Masters, W. A., and A. F. Garcia. 2010. "Agricultural Price Distortion and Stabilization." In K. Anderson, ed., *ThePolitical Economy of Agricultural Price Distortions.* New York: Cambridge University Press.

—— and D. Sanogo. 2002. "Welfare Gains from Quality Certification of Infant Foods: Results from a Market Experiment in Mali." *American Journal of Agricultural Economics* 84/4: 974–89.

Minten, B., and D. C. Stifel. 2008. "Isolation and Agricultural Productivity." *Agricultural Economics* 39/1: 1–15.

Norton, G., J. Alwang, and W. A. Masters. 2010. *Economics of Agricultural Development: World Food Systems and Resource Use*, 2nd edn. New York: Routledge.

Olson, M. 1965. *The Logic of Collective Action*. Cambridge, MA: Harvard University Press.

Paarlberg, R. 2010. *Food Politics*. New York: Oxford University Press.

Ridley, M. 2010. *The Rational Optimist: How Prosperity Evolves*. New York: Harper.

Rios, A. R., G. E. Shively, and W. A. Masters. 2009. "Farm Productivity and Household Market Participation: Evidence from LSMS Data." Paper presented at the International Association of Agricultural Economists' Conference, Beijing, Aug. 16–22. <http://purl.umn.edu/51031>.

Ruel, M. T. 2003. "Operationalizing Dietary Diversity: A Review of Measurement Issues and Research Priorities." *Journal of Nutrition* 133/11: 3911S–3926S.

Thiele, S., and C. Weiss. 2003. "Consumer Demand for Food Diversity: Evidence for Germany." *Food Policy* 28/2: 99–115.

Timmer, C. P. 2009. *A World without Agriculture: The Structural Transformation in Historical Perspective*. Washington, DC: AEI Press.

Tomich, T. P., P. Kilby, and B. F. Johnston. 1995. *Transforming Agrarian Economies: Opportunities Seized, Opportunities Missed*. Ithaca, NY: Cornell University Press.

Varian, H. R. 2009. *Intermediate Microeconomics: A Modern Approach*, 8th edn. New York: Norton.

CHAPTER 15

FOOD STANDARDS AND INTERNATIONAL TRADE

IAN SHELDON

1 INTRODUCTION

In the post-war period, the distribution of goods within national markets and across borders has become increasingly affected by the proliferation of standards and technical regulations (Maskus and Wilson 2001; Essaji 2008), with increased regulatory intensity being particularly noticeable in the food and agricultural sector over the past two decades (Roberts 1999; Josling, Roberts, and Orden 2004; Henson and Jaffee 2008; Maertens and Swinnen 2008).[1] Based on data for the two-digit Harmonized System (HS), Essaji finds that six of the ten sectors with the highest intensity of technical regulations (TR) cover food and agricultural products.[2]

The proliferation of standards and technical regulations in the food and agricultural sectors, as well as the wider manufacturing sector, is typically regarded as the response of policymakers to consumer demands for improved product safety, increased environmental protection, and greater product information (Roberts 1999; Maskus and Wilson 2001; Essaji 2008; Wilson 2008).[3] Roberts (1999: 337) argues that standards and technical regulations "have as their *prima facie* objective the correction of market inefficiencies stemming from externalities associated with the production, distribution,

---

[1] Following Wilson (2008) the language "standards" and "standards and technical regulations" is used interchangeably in this chapter. Roberts (1999: 337) defines a standard as a "technical specification or set of specifications related to characteristics of a product or its manufacturing process."

[2] In descending order of TR-intensity (with the two-digit HS code list in parentheses), the specific sectors are: cereals (10); fish, crustaceans, and other aquatic vertebrates (03); edible preparations of meat, fish, and crustaceans (16); edible vegetables, roots, and tubers (07); prepared vegetables, fruit, nuts, and other plant parts (2); prepared cereals and flours (19) (Essaji 2008).

[3] See Antle (2001) for an extensive discussion of this in the context of food safety.

and consumption of these products. These externalities may be regional, national, transnational, or global."

The key to this description is the role of technical regulations and standards in solving market failures. Josling, Roberts, and Orden (2004) suggest that standards in the food and agricultural sector can be classified under two broad categories: (1) provision of public goods such as control of pesticide use in agricultural production; and (2) reduction of transactions costs associated with information asymmetries between producers and consumers concerning food product characteristics, e.g., the extent of pesticide residues in a product that consumers are unable to ascertain either before or after its consumption.

While the theory of optimal intervention prescribes that market distortions should be targeted at source (Bhagwati 1984), there is acknowledgment that they may also provide protection for domestic producers and are, therefore, subject to "regulatory capture" (Roberts 1999; Fischer and Serra 2000; Sturm 2006; Essaji 2008; Swinnen and Vandemoortele 2009). Given the potential for standards and technical regulations to distort international trade, a key outcome from the formation of the World Trade Organization (WTO) in 1994 was the Agreement on the Application of Sanitary and Phytosanitary Measures, and the revised Agreement on Technical Barriers to Trade. The objective of these agreements is to ensure that standards and technical regulations, while potentially meeting legitimate economic objectives, are not disguised restrictions on international trade.[4]

Although the main focus of this chapter is not the intricacies of trade law and food standards, it is interesting to note that between 1995 and 2002, WTO members filed thirty-two requests for formal consultations related to food regulation trade barriers under the WTO's dispute settlement process (Josling, Roberts, and Orden 2004). These covered a wide range of sectors and technical regulations, and involved both developed and developing countries as petitioners and respondents. Perhaps the most analyzed Panel and Appellate Board rulings were those involving the US complaint against the European Community's use of measures concerning the use of hormones in meat and meat products (Roberts 1998), and India, Malaysia, Pakistan, and Thailand's complaint against the US prohibition of imports of certain shrimp and shrimp products (Charnowitz 2002). More recently, the introduction of genetically modified (GM) crops and the European Union (EU) requirement for labeling of food products containing genetically modified organisms (GMOs) has attracted a good deal of attention from the popular media, non-governmental organizations, as well as economists (Sheldon 2002, 2004).[5]

---

[4] See Josling (2008) for a detailed discussion of the institutional environment for food standards and international trade.

[5] In 2006 the WTO ruled on a complaint by the United States concerning the EU regulation on GM crops. It found that the EU failed its WTO obligations by not lifting its moratorium on the approval of GM crops and delaying the approval of new crops. In addition, the WTO ruled against the marketing and import bans put in place by six EU member states (Sheldon 2007).

The tension between the notion that standards and technical regulations are, on the one hand, consumer-driven but, on the other, may provide protection to domestic producers characterizes much of their economic analysis. For example, early theoretical work by Casella (1996) examines standards in the context of provision of public goods. Given that demand for public goods will depend on economic primitives such as factor endowments, consumer preferences, and technology, necessarily provision will differ between countries depending on their stage of development. Using a simple model, Casella shows that with international trade, standards of developed and developing countries will converge over time, if demand is a function of the level of income. The implication of this result is that if trade itself eventually results in countries establishing similar standards for the provision of public goods, there is no need for such standards to be harmonized as a precondition for trade liberalization.

In contrast to this benign view of standards, there has been considerable discussion of the problems of regulatory compliance faced by developing countries in accessing developed-country markets, given the latter typically have higher levels of regulatory intensity than the former (Jaffee and Henson 2004; World Bank 2005; Essaji 2008). Testing the hypothesis of "standards as barriers" has been a dominant feature of the limited amount of empirical research on the impact of food safety regulations on trade flows of specific food and agricultural commodities (e.g., Calvin and Krissoff 1998; Paarlberg and Lee 1998; Otsuki, Wilson, and Sewadeh 2001; Wilson and Otsuki 2004; Peterson and Orden 2005; and Anders and Caswell 2009). A common finding of these empirical studies is that more stringent standards imposed by developed countries act as barriers to trade.[6]

What is somewhat surprising about the extant literature on food standards and international trade is the lack of any extensive theoretical underpinnings for what has essentially been either descriptive or empirical analysis. The objective of this chapter, therefore, is to explore in more detail two different aspects of international trade and standards based on resolution of *either* a public goods *or* an asymmetric information problem. In the next section, a general equilibrium setting is developed, drawing extensively on existing work in the trade and environmental economics literature. This analysis is designed to capture some key stylized facts and basic hypotheses concerning North–South trade where standards and technical regulations are targeted at negative externalities in food production. In the following section, a partial equilibrium setting is developed, drawing on recent work by the current author examining the role of labeling standards in maximizing the gains from international economic integration. Finally, the discussion in the chapter is summarized, and some conclusions are drawn concerning potential future research on food standards and international trade.

---

[6] See also the survey of this literature in Wilson (2008).

2   NORTH–SOUTH TRADE AND
FOOD STANDARDS

....

As noted above, standards are often justified as a means of solving specific market failures such as externalities. However, it is typically claimed that developing countries are hampered in their ability to meet such standards owing to a lack of necessary human capital and poor governance (Maskus and Wilson 2001; Essaji 2008). Essaji also presents empirical evidence to support the hypothesis that the capacity to satisfy standards is correlated with real GDP per capita, developing countries specializing away from industries with heavier regulatory burdens.[7] It is interesting, therefore, to see how far one gets with a general a model of North–South trade with standards that captures these stylized facts.

In order to do this, a model of trade and standards in the presence of environmental externalities originally due to Copeland and Taylor (1994, 1995) is adapted. Assume there is a bloc of countries representing the developed North, and a bloc representing the developing South, producing along a continuum of consumption goods, $z \in [0, 1]$, with one primary input, effective labor l.[8] Part of this continuum consists of food consumption goods, the remainder being other non-food goods. Assume that a public bad b is produced jointly with each consumption good z in the continuum. In the case of food production, pesticide runoff will be a public bad if there are health risks associated with drinking-water contamination (Segerson 1990). The output y of any good z in the continuum is a function of combining both effective labor l and the bad b via the following constant returns to scale Cobb–Douglas technology:

$$y(l, b; z) = \begin{cases} l^{1-\alpha(z)} b^{\alpha(z)} & \text{if } b \leq \lambda l \\ 0 & \text{if } b > \lambda l \end{cases} \tag{1}$$

where $\lambda > 0$, $\alpha(z)$ varies across goods, and $\alpha(z) \in [\bar{\alpha}, \hat{\alpha}]$, with $0 < \bar{\alpha} < \hat{\alpha} < 1$.[9] The interpretation of (1) is that effective labor l and the bad b can be substituted for one another in production of any good z, but there are limits to these substitution possibilities, i.e., any point above the production ray $b = \lambda l$ is not feasible for any given labor input l. This follows from the bad b being a by-product of production (Copeland and Taylor 1995).

On the consumption side, consumers in the North and South have identical utility functions, consumption goods z and the public bad b being separable in utility; and given homothetic preferences, the share of spending on each consumption good z

---

[7] Essaji combines a measure of human resource capacity and capacity to implement testing and certification procedures to generate an index of a country's capacity to meet technical regulations.

[8] This model is essentially an adaptation of Dornbusch, Fischer, and Samuleson's (1977) Ricardian model with a continuum of consumption goods. See also Copeland and Taylor (2003, 2004) for a Heckscher–Ohlin-type setting with two goods and two factors of production.

[9] Derivation of the technology in (1) can be found in Copeland and Taylor (1994, appendix).

in the continuum is a constant. The utility function of a representative consumer is given as

$$U = \int_0^1 f(z)\ln[x(z)]dz - \frac{\beta D^\gamma}{\gamma},$$ (2)

where $x(z)$ is consumption of z, $f(z)$ is the budget share for each good in the continuum, and the sum of budget shares is $\int_0^1 f(z)dz = 1$; D is aggregate production of the public bad; β measures the representative consumer's disutility associated with the public bad; and $\gamma \geq 1$, implying consumers' willingness to pay for a reduction in the level of the public bad is non-decreasing in its aggregate level.

Without government regulation, firms have no incentive to abate the public bad, always choosing a point along the production ray $b = \lambda l$. However, if it is assumed that a public standard s is set for an allowable level of the public bad, and firms abate a small amount of the public bad, there will be an interior solution.[10] In enforcing the standard, it is assumed that the government imposes a per unit compliance cost c_b on firms that utilize the public bad in production, the compliance cost consisting of certification and monitoring costs. It should be noted that while the per unit compliance cost has similar effects to a per unit tax on pollution, there is no presumption, as in Copeland and Taylor (1994, 1995), that c_b is set optimally.

Given a return on a unit of effective labor w_e, and the per unit compliance cost c_b, cost minimization for any good in the continuum z implies that

$$\frac{w_e}{c_b} = \frac{1 - \alpha(z)}{\alpha(z)} \frac{b}{l}.$$ (3)

Expression (3) indicates that the share in production costs of the compliance cost is a constant $\alpha(z)$, so that goods in the continuum can be ordered in terms of their intensity in generating the public bad, $\alpha'(z) > 0$.[11]

Suppose the technology in (1) is available to firms in both North and South, and each has the same endowment of workers L, but the supply of effective labor is greater in the North than the South, $A(h)L > A(h^*)L$, where h is the human capital/worker, and $h > h^*$ (* denoting the South). Given that the return to effective labor is higher in the North than the South, income per capita in the North exceeds that in the South, and if demand for the public good is income-elastic, then the North will set a higher standard s and higher per unit compliance costs c_b will be charged to cover the costs of monitoring and enforcement.[12]

By minimizing total costs subject to the Cobb–Douglas production function in (1), the average (unit) cost function for a good z in the continuum can be written as

[10] Copeland and Taylor (1994) show that as long as $b/l < \lambda$ for all z, an interior solution exists.

[11] Both food and non-food consumption goods are assumed to be spread along this continuum in terms of their generation of the public bad. This ensures that both North and South will produce both food and non-food consumption goods in equilibrium.

[12] To keep the algebra to a minimum, compliance costs are being treated as exogenous here; however, it is possible to derive them explicitly as a function of income (see Appendix).

$$a(w_e, c_b; h, z) = \kappa(z)c_b^{\alpha(z)}[w/A(h)]^{1-\alpha(z)}, \tag{4}$$

where $\kappa(z) \equiv \alpha^{-\alpha}(1-\alpha)^{-(1-\alpha)}$ is a good-specific constant, and w is the wage rate for raw labor. For given wages and compliance costs, a good z in the continuum will be produced in the North if $a(w, c_b; h, z) \leq a^*(w^*, c_b^*; h^*, z)$, such that

$$\omega \equiv \frac{w}{w^*} \leq \frac{A}{A^*}\left(\frac{c_b^*}{c_b}\right)^{\alpha(z)/(1-\alpha(z))} \equiv T(\tilde{z}). \tag{5}$$

Conversely, a good z in the continuum is produced in the South if $\omega \geq T(\tilde{z})$. Given $c_b > c_b^*$, and $\alpha'(z) > 0$, $T(\tilde{z})$ is decreasing in z, i.e., the North's comparative advantage in producing any good z falls as compliance costs become a larger fraction of total production costs. Therefore, for any given value of relative wages ω, there will be a critical industry $\tilde{z}$ on the $T(\tilde{z})$ schedule where goods are either produced in the North on the interval $z \in [0, \tilde{z}]$, or they are produced in the South on the interval $z \in [\tilde{z}, 1]$, with the North (South) producing the goods that are least (most) intensive in their production of the public bad.

In order to determine equilibrium relative wages ω, and hence the critical industry $\tilde{z}$, it is necessary to follow the approach of Dornbusch, Fischer, and Samuelson (1977) by introducing the demand side of the economy through a balance of trade schedule. Given the assumption of homothetic preferences, first define the proportion of income spent on Northern and Southern produced goods respectively:

$$\begin{array}{l} \psi(\tilde{z}) \equiv \int_0^{\tilde{z}} f(z)dz \\ 1 - \psi(\tilde{z}) \equiv \int_{\tilde{z}}^1 f(z)dz, \end{array} \tag{6}$$

and then define the balanced trade condition as:

$$[1 - \psi(\tilde{z})]wL = \psi(\tilde{z})w^* L, \tag{7}$$

i.e., total imports of Southern goods by the North have to equal total exports of Northern goods to the South. Rearranging (7) generates a balance of trade schedule:

$$\omega = \frac{\psi(\tilde{z})}{1 - \psi(\tilde{z})} \equiv B(\tilde{z}), \tag{8}$$

$B(0) = 0$, $B(1) = \infty$, and $dB/d\tilde{z} > 0$, $B(\tilde{z})$ sloping upward to reflect the fact that as the range of goods produced in the North increases, its exports increase and its imports fall, so that the relative wages ω have to increase to balance trade. Combining both $T(\tilde{z})$ and $B(\tilde{z})$ schedules determines the equilibrium relative wage ω and critical industry $\tilde{z}$; see Figure 15.1.

Assuming that the public bad b is local, given $h > h^*$, and $s > s^*$, the equilibrium is one where the North specializes in goods that are intensive in their use of effective labor $z \in [0, \tilde{z}]$, while the South specializes in goods that are intensive in their use of the public bad $z \in [\tilde{z}, 1]$. This reflects both the North's comparative advantage in producing goods that generate less of the public bad, as well as the fact that it sets higher

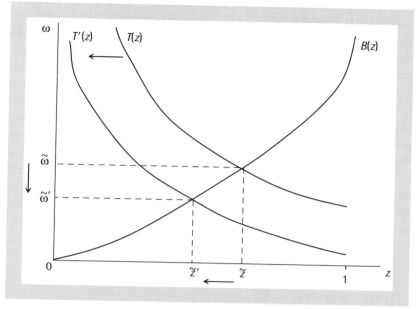

FIGURE 15.1 Equilibrium North–South trade

regulatory standards. Over time, if there is technological change in the South, h^* increasing, the $T(\tilde{z})$schedule in Figure 15.1 shifts down to the left $T'(\tilde{z})$, the South increasing its production of goods that are intensive in their use of effective labor, and at the same time raising the level of their standards s^* as their per capita income rises.[13] In the limit, though, if North and South end up with similar levels of effective labor, $h = h^*$, and therefore similar levels of standards, $s = s^*$, the pattern of trade will be indeterminate. However, if $A/A^* > 1$, then the North will be a net exporter of embodied labor services, while the South will be a net exporter of embodied public bad.

The result presented in Figure 15.1 assumes that aggregate damage D from the public bad is only local in its effects, food standards being benign in that their level simply reflects the relative development of the North versus the South. Suppose, however, that the public bad produced in the South is assumed to have potential effects in the North. For example, while the local public bad in the South is pesticide runoff, consumers in the North may also be concerned about the potential for pesticide residues on food consumption goods imported from the South (Wilson and Otsuki 2004).[14] As a result, consumers in the North demand that standards s also be applied to imported goods

[13] The argument that standards for pesticide use in the South will eventually rise as their per capita income rises draws on the notion that demand for environmental quality is a normal good. Support for this argument is based on what is termed the environmental Kuznets curve, which hypothesizes an inverse U-shaped relationship between per capita incomes and environmental quality (Copeland and Taylor 2004).

[14] Higher standards in the North may also be due to the fact that they have higher-quality institutions in place to enforce standards, and/or a different organization and structure of their media affecting consumer perceptions of risk (Swinnen and Vandemoortele 2009).

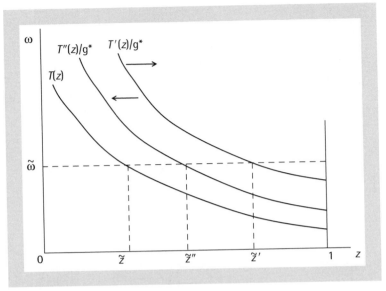

FIGURE 15.2 Standards as barriers or catalysts to trade

from the South. These standards can either be supplied publicly, or they could be private standards established, for example, by coalitions of food retailers in the North (Henson 2008).[15]

Following Dornbusch, Fischer, and Samuelson (1977), the additional compliance costs due to application of the higher Northern standard s on the range of goods imported by the North are modeled as iceberg transport costs, g^*.[16] This implies that only a fraction $g^*(z)$ of any commodity z actually arrives, the relationship between unit costs in the North and South being rewritten as $a(w, c_b; h, z) \leq [a^*(w^*, c_b^*; h^*, z)]/g^*$. This results in a new schedule, $T'(\tilde{z})/g^*$, in Figure 15.2, such that for a given relative wage ω, there will be a set of non-traded goods in the range$(\tilde{z} - \tilde{z}')$.[17] In other words the North continues to produce and export goods in the range $z \in [0, \tilde{z}]$, for which it has a comparative advantage, but it also produces goods in the range $(\tilde{z} - \tilde{z}')$ as it is cheaper than importing those goods, although it cannot export these goods to the

---

[15] Owing to the way in which the model is set up, firms producing consumption goods have no private incentive to reduce production of the public bad. However, if retailers of final goods in the North are allowed for, they do have an incentive to establish private standards as a means of mitigating reputational and commercial risks (Fulponi 2007; Henson and Jaffee 2008; Maertens and Swinnen 2008). See also Casella (2001) for analysis of private coalitions and standards setting, and McCluskey and Winfree (2009) for analysis of the incentives for firms to pre-empt public with private standards.

[16] See Wilson (2008) for a discussion of the empirical evidence on the impact of standards on compliance costs. Alternatively, Maertens and Swinnen (2008) suggest it is the costs of non-compliance that are potentially high.

[17] If the North also faced iceberg transport costs g in exporting to the South, its unit cost function would also be adjusted, and the range of non-trade goods would become wider. See Dornbusch, Fischer, and Samuelson (1977) for how to solve out for the equilibrium relative wage in the presence of non-traded goods.

South as they can still be produced more efficiently in the South. The South also produces non-traded goods in the range $(\tilde{z} - \tilde{z}')$, but its exports are reduced to the range $z \in [\tilde{z}', 1]$. This result also provides a motive for firms in the North to lobby for higher standards to be imposed on imports from the South, thereby allowing them to produce the range of non-traded goods that they otherwise would not produce.

Introducing iceberg transport costs into the model can be interpreted as broadly capturing the "standards as barriers" hypothesis, illustrating the concerns developing countries have about proliferation of food standards and technical regulations in developed countries (both public and private), and why calls for harmonization of standards by the North are often regarded with suspicion by developing countries.[18]

Recently, however, several authors have put forward the hypothesis that, rather than barriers, higher food standards in developed countries may be a "catalyst to trade" (Henson and Jaffee 2008; Maertens and Swinnen 2008; Anders and Caswell 2009).[19] Henson and Jaffee argue that being forced to comply with higher standards provides an incentive to firms and regulators in developing countries to invest in their ability to meet such standards. For example, they appeal to Porter and van der Linde's (1995) argument that there will be regulatory-induced innovation at the firm level,[20] while Maertens and Swinnen argue that higher standards may stimulate increased vertical coordination in developing country food supply chains. Crudely, the "standards as catalysts" hypothesis is represented in Figure 15.2 by the shift in the $T'(\tilde{z})/g^*$ schedule to $T''(\tilde{z})/g^*$ as an increase in effective labor h^* in the South offsets the costs of complying with higher standards in the North. An alternative motivation for the increase in h^* is that multinational firms based in the North invest in the South in order to ensure public/private standards in the North can be complied with.[21]

3 TRADE, FOOD STANDARDS, AND LABELING

The model outlined in the previous section ignores not only the possibility that goods may be explicitly differentiated in terms of quality, e.g., organically produced, dolphin-safe, free-range, GMO-free, etc., but also that consumers may be unable to verify any

[18] See Bhagwati (1996) for a good discussion of the issue of harmonization of standards.

[19] Swann, Temple, and Shurmer (1996) provide econometric support for the hypothesis that idiosyncratic national standards can promote domestic product quality, and thereby increase exports.

[20] While Anders and Caswell's (2009) analysis of the impact of US food safety standards on imports of seafood provides some early empirical support for the "standards as catalyst" hypothesis, it should be noted that the hypothesis of regulatory-induced innovation has been strongly criticized by Palmer, Oates, and Portney (1995).

[21] Formally, the type of model presented in this section does not account for the possibility that international economic integration may result in developing countries having greater access to technology that would allow them to better comply with higher standards in developed countries (Copeland and Taylor 1994). There is, however, empirical evidence that private standards are being applied in developing countries by multinational food retailers (Reardon and Berdegue 2002).

claims made about quality. Goods that suffer such *ex post* information asymmetries are a simplified version of credence goods (Darby and Karni 1973; Dulleck and Kerschbamer 2006). Labeling in combination with a standard is one method for addressing the credence good problem, requiring a number of regulatory choices concerning the labeling regime: compulsoriness (*mandatory* or *voluntary*), explicitness (*discrete* or *continuous*), and exclusiveness where only government labeling is available (*exclusive*), or private firms may also certify (*non-exclusive*).[22]

Drawing on Roe and Sheldon (2007) and Sheldon and Roe (2009a, b), a model of vertical product differentiation can be used to analyze the efficiency and distributional implications of these regulatory choices under both autarky and international economic integration.[23] Assume initially that there is perfect information about quality and that consumers in a representative country have a unit demand for a quality-differentiated good, the quality level being defined as $u \in [\underline{u}, \infty]$, where the lower bound to quality, $\underline{u} > 0$, meets a minimum quality standard perfectly enforced by government.[24] Consumer utility U is defined as

$$U = u(y - p), \tag{9}$$

where y is income, and p is the price of the differentiated good, $(y - p)$ being expenditure on a Hicksian composite commodity, utility derived from the latter increasing in u. If a consumer decides not to buy the differentiated good, $u = 0$; hence, the good is always purchased unless its price exceeds income. Consumers derive the same surplus from a good of a particular quality, but differ in their ability to pay. Incomes are uniformly distributed on the interval $[a, b]$, $a > 0$, where $n\ (b - a)$ is a measure of the size of the representative economy.

Firms produce a single differentiated good, with all firms sharing the same production technology characterized by zero variable production costs and a fixed, quality-dependent cost, $F(u)$, which is sunk by the firm after entry into the market.[25] It is assumed that

$$F(u) = \varepsilon + \alpha(u - \underline{u})^2, \tag{10}$$

where ε and α are strictly positive constants. Sunk costs are convex and strictly increasing in quality, a sunk cost of $\varepsilon > 0$ being necessary to achieve even the minimum quality level $\underline{u}$.

---

[22] See Teisl and Roe (1998) for a complete typology of labeling regimes. See also Segerson (1999) and Crespi and Marette (2001) for discussion of mandatory versus voluntary labeling regimes.

[23] The underlying model was first introduced by Gabszewicz and Thisse (1979, 1980) and Shaked and Sutton (1982, 1983) and later extended by Boom (1995). Other models of quality and trade include Flam and Helpman (1987), Motta (1992), and Murphy and Shleifer (1997).

[24] A separate literature already exists focusing specifically on minimum-quality standards, e.g., Ronnen (1991), Boom (1995), Scarpa (1998), and Lutz (2000).

[25] This cost function is a simple way of capturing the burden of quality improvement falling on fixed costs such as R & D expenditures, as opposed to variable production costs, although the assumption of zero variable production costs can be relaxed without altering the main results.

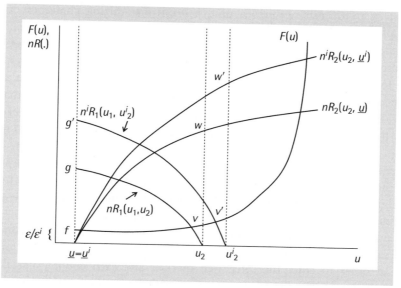

FIGURE 15.3 Autarky and trade

    The choices of firms are characterized by the following game: at stage 1, each firm decides to enter or not enter the market, incurring sunk costs ε upon entry; at stage 2, firms that have entered simultaneously choose their good's quality level, incurring the additional fixed costs for producing the chosen quality; at stage 3, firms simultaneously set good prices in a Bertrand–Nash equilibrium. If the parameters of the income distribution are $4a > b > 2a$, then exactly two firms enter the market, so long as fixed costs plus labeling costs are not prohibitively high, and each entrant has a positive market share in equilibrium, i.e., a natural duopoly. This restriction on income dispersion also ensures that each consumer either purchases one unit of the differentiated good or is indifferent between purchasing the lowest quality and purchasing none, i.e., a "covered" market. This result, the so-called "finiteness property," ensures that equilibrium market structure is endogenous (Shaked and Sutton 1982, 1983).

    The autarky equilibrium for a representative economy is described in Figure 15.3. Firms' fixed costs $F(u)$ and revenue $nR(.)$ are plotted on the vertical axis against quality u, firm 1 and firm 2's revenue functions being $nR_1(u_1,u_2)$ and $nR_2(u_2,\underline{u})$ respectively. The revenue function of firm 1 satisfies the following property: $\partial nR_1(.)/\partial u_1 < 0$, i.e., as firm 1 raises quality, its revenue falls as it faces intensified price competition from firm 2, their products becoming closer substitutes. At the same time firm 1 bears higher fixed costs as it raises quality, thereby lowering its profits. Consequently, to maximize its profits, the optimal quality choice of firm 1 is always to choose minimum quality $\underline{u}$, irrespective of the quality choice of firm 2. The revenue function of firm 2 satisfies the following properties: $\partial nR_2(.)/\partial u_2 > 0$ and $\partial^2 nR_2(.)/\partial u_2^2 < 0$, i.e., firm 2's revenue is increasing in its own quality, but at a diminishing rate, which, in combination with convex fixed costs, ensures a unique profit-maximizing choice of quality u_2 by firm 2.[26]

To understand the equilibrium, suppose firm 1, the low-quality firm, chooses $\underline{u}$. If firm 2 also sets its quality at this level, Bertrand price competition drives both firms' revenue to zero, given the assumption of zero variable production costs. In addition, owing to sunk costs ε both firms would incur a loss. Consequently, the optimal choice of firm 2, the high-quality firm, is to increase quality to u_2 in order to maximize profits given by the vertical distance $(w-v)$ between their revenue and fixed costs. At the same time, this reduces price competition with the low-quality firm, allowing the latter to maximize its profits given by the vertical distance $(g-f)$ between their revenue and fixed costs. If the low-quality firm were to increase its quality from the minimum $\underline{u}$ to $u_1 = u_2$, Bertrand price competition again results in both firms incurring a loss. Hence, in a covered market, the equilibrium choice of qualities is the pair $\underline{u}$ and u_2.

Now suppose that two North–North economies integrate, each of the same size n, with the same uniform distributions of income. Firms must incur some additional sunk costs ε^i in order to enter the integrated market, and each country has the same minimum quality standard $\underline{u}^i$ prior to integration. Owing to the fact that each economy supports only two firms under autarky, the integrated equilibrium supports only two firms, i.e., two firms will exit, although the direction of trade is indeterminate.[27] In Figure 15.3, given an increase in the population size to n^i, the high-quality firm's revenue function rotates upward to $n^i R_2(u_2, \underline{u}^i)$, resulting in an increase in the quality of good 2 to u_2^i, and an increase in the high-quality firm's profits to the vertical distance $(w'-v')$ between their revenue and fixed costs. Given u_2^i, the low-quality firm's revenue function shifts out and rotates upward to $n^i R_1(u_1, u_2^i)$, their profits increasing to the vertical distance $(g'-f)$ between their revenue and fixed costs, the quality of good 1 remaining the same at the minimum $\underline{u} = \underline{u}^i$. As a result, in the integrated equilibrium, while the prices and profits of both firms increase owing to increased vertical product differentiation, gains from economic integration come from increased quality.[28]

Now consider North and South economies, each having incomes uniformly distributed over the range $[a_k, b_k]$, and $4a_k > b_k > 2a_k$, where subscript k refers to either North (N) or South (S). In addition, assume that $a_N > a_S$, $b_N > b_S$, and, $b_N < 2b_S$, $a_N < 2a_S$, and that the same technology is available in North and South.[29] Under autarky, both North and South will be able to sustain two firms in equilibrium selling distinct

---

[26] Explicit derivation of the revenue functions can be found in Roe and Sheldon (2007).

[27] This is not uncommon in models where firms are essentially "footloose," i.e., firms can produce anywhere in the integrated market. To pin down which country trades which good, we would need additional structure; for example, in a Ricardian-type setting, differences in unit production costs would ensure that a firm in one country has a comparative advantage in producing the high-quality good, the firm located in the other country having a comparative advantage in producing the minimum-quality good, i.e., intra-industry trade in vertically differentiated products.

[28] See Roe and Sheldon (2007) for a proof that aggregate welfare increases with quality.

[29] The existence of footloose firms in this model is sufficient to ensure that technology available in the North will also be available in the South.

qualities. Also assume that the North sets and enforces a higher minimum quality standard than the South, such that $\bar{u}_N = \underline{u} + \sigma$ with $\sigma > 0$, and $\bar{u}S = \underline{u}$. Consequently, in the North, given the higher minimum quality standard, the high-quality firm, in order to escape the pressure of price competition, will also produce and sell a higher-quality good in equilibrium, resulting in the low- and high-quality goods in the North under autarky being of higher quality than their counterparts in the South. This result is consistent with the earlier observation that demand for higher quality is income-elastic, and hence correlated with the level of economic development.

Now allow the North and South to integrate, assuming as before that firms must incur some additional sunk costs ε^i in order to enter the integrated market. In addition, assume that North and South accept each other's minimum quality standard. It turns out that only three firms survive in the integrated equilibrium owing to increased price competition.[30] As a result, there is an increase in the average quality of goods consumed, the lowest-quality good exiting the market, with consumers in the South now being able to purchase the minimum-quality good produced in the North.[31] There may also be intra-industry trade, if the medium-quality good is produced in the South, and the minimum- and high-quality goods are produced in the North although this is not guaranteed.

With imperfect information, all communication of quality has to occur through a label administered and verified by a separate certifier(s), who could be either a public agency or a combination of public agency and private firm.[32] Public and private certifiers are assumed to monitor and communicate perfectly the quality of individual firms *ex ante* for a fee paid by the firms.[33] The fixed cost of certifying and labeling the good is given as

$$I^j(u) = I^j \text{ for } u > \underline{u}$$
$$= 0 \text{ otherwise} , \tag{11}$$

---

[30] See Sheldon and Roe (2009a, b) for a detailed proof of this result.

[31] The North and South could harmonize their minimum-quality standard to that of the North, in which case, the South's minimum-quality good would be driven from the market by executive fiat. However, there will still be intensified price competition between the three remaining goods. Alternatively, if the North and South harmonize to the minimum-quality standard of the South, as long as the cost of labeling the higher minimum quality is not too high, the lower minimum-quality good is still likely to be driven from the market.

[32] There are several papers in the agricultural economics literature addressing labeling and regulation in credence good markets, e.g., Marette, Crespi, and Schiavina (1999); Marette, Bureau, and Gozlan (2000); Giannakas and Fulton (2002); Fulton and Giannakas (2004); and Zago and Pick (2004). None, however, address the issue of labeling in an international trade context, and all are based on the Mussa and Rosen (1978) model of vertical differentiation where the number of goods in equilibrium is imposed exogenously as part of the analysis.

[33] The assumption of perfect monitoring, while strict, allows the market to be converted from one of credence goods to one of search goods. If monitoring were noisy, deduction of equilibrium would require a repeated game structure as in McCluskey (2000). Because monitoring is assumed to be perfect, repeating the current game would not change the resulting equilibrium.

where $j \in \{t, d\}$ and t and d stand for continuous and discrete labeling, respectively. Continuous labels communicate the exact level of quality while discrete labels merely communicate if quality meets or exceeds a particular quality threshold. Firms claiming quality meeting the minimum-quality standard are never charged a fee, $I^j(\underline{u}) = 0$, because a firm has no incentive to produce a higher-quality good and market it as the minimum quality. Both private and public certifiers are assumed to provide labeling at the same cost, there exist no economies of size, and such costs are the same throughout the integrated economy. However, if labeling of quality above the minimum is mandatory, firms have to meet any government-set labeling regulations through public certification before incurring any additional costs of private certification. It is also assumed that discrete certification is less costly, $I^t(u) \geq I^d(u) \; \forall \, u > \underline{u}$, and that there are no variable costs of labeling.[34]

First consider the case where quality is opaque to the consumer and no labeling program exists. In both North–North and North–South integrated economies, the sunk cost of entry, ε^i, combined with the three-stage game, supports the entry of only a single firm into the integrated market, while the opaqueness of quality and lack of labeling leads to production of the minimum-quality standard $\underline{u}$. The resulting price and profit levels are the simple monopoly outcome, with the poorest consumers being unable to buy even the minimum-quality good.

Second, suppose it is mandatory that any firm claiming equality higher than the minimum has to participate in an exclusive, continuous labeling program. The only difference from the perfect-information case is the addition of the cost of continuous labeling, plus firms have to incur the additional sunk costs, ε^t, of entering the integrated market. As long as two firms enter the North–North market, or three firms enter the North–South market, the outcome is identical to the perfect-information market with respect to prices, qualities, and profits for the low-quality firm. Only the profits of the high-quality firm in the North–North case, and the profits of the medium- and high-quality firms in the North–South case, are different because of labeling costs. Hence, continuous labeling does not distort firm choices so long as it is not too expensive. Consumers experience no change in welfare compared to the perfect-information case so long as two qualities are produced in the North–North case and three qualities in the North–South case, as labeling leaves price and quality unchanged in equilibrium, i.e., the gains from economic integration are still realized.

In contrast, suppose firms claiming higher than minimum environmental quality are mandated to implement a single, harmonized, discrete standard u_2^g, firms being forbidden from certifying and communicating any other standard.[35] Focusing on the

---

[34] Monitoring a discrete standard is likely to be cheaper as it merely requires checking that processes meet or exceed a given threshold, i.e., going over a checklist, while continuous labeling may require additional monitoring equipment to calibrate and report exact performance. Allowing for variable costs of labeling would be similar to allowing for variable costs of production.

[35] Harmonization implies that when two countries integrate economically, an agreed standard applies in both countries (Leebron 1996; Lutz 2000).

North–North case, if the harmonized standard u_2^g is set lower than u_2^i, the two qualities are closer together and price competition becomes more intense between the two firms: u'^g_2 in Figure 15.4. This bodes well for consumers who purchase the low-quality good, who now pay a lower price, but consumers of the high-quality good would rather have the higher quality and pay the higher price. In addition, the more intense price competition reduces the profits of the low-quality firm to $(g'-f)$, and the high-quality firm to $(w'-v')$.

If the standard u_2^g is higher than u_2^i, price competition is relaxed u''^g_2 in Figure 15.4. This harms consumers of the low-quality good, who now pay a higher price. Consumers of the high-quality good welcome the increase, as they value the quality increase more than they are harmed by the price increase. The relaxed price competition inflates the low-quality firm's profits to $(g'-f'')$. The high-quality firm also charges a higher price, but the convex, fixed cost of producing quality comes to dominate and drive the high-quality firm's profits down to $(w''-v'')$. Therefore, the high-quality firm suffers regardless of the direction of the harmonized labeling standard's deviation from the perfect-information quality choice. Of course, if the standard is set too high, the high-quality firm does not enter the integrated market at all.

Under North–South economic integration, assume one harmonized labeling standard is set, $u^g = u^k$. The impact of the labeling standard depends on its location relative to what would be optimal for the firms choosing qualities u_2^i and u_3^i. First, if $u^g \leq u_2^i$, the highest-quality good is forced from the market, and it may force the medium-quality good out of the market as well if u^g is set too low, thereby intensifying price competition too much between the medium- and minimum-quality goods. Second, if

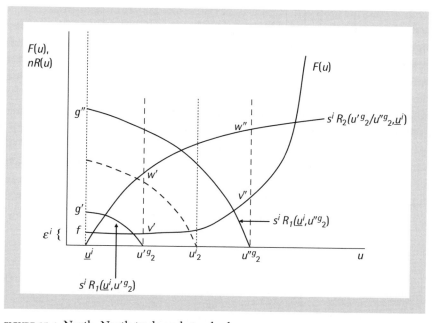

FIGURE 15.4 North–North trade and standards

$u_2^i \leq u^g \leq u_3^i$, either the medium- or the highest-quality good will be driven from the market, depending on the location of the harmonized public standard between the medium-quality and the high-quality goods. Essentially, if the standard is set not too far from the optimal level of quality, $u_2^i(u_3^i)$, the high-quality (medium-quality) good will be driven from the market, as only one good can survive at that level of quality. This will, of course, diminish competition between the remaining goods, because whether the medium- or high-quality good survives, it is the case that $\bar{u}_N \leq u_2^i \leq u^g \leq u_3^i$. Finally, $u_3^i \leq u^g$, the medium-quality good will be forced from the market as it will be unprofitable for two firms to compete at a standard set higher than that preferred by the high-quality firm.

It is important to recognize that allowing for private labeling schemes affects the results of harmonized mandatory, discrete labeling.[36] In the case of North–North integration, high-quality firms may also pay a private certifier to certify and label another quality level beyond that mandated by the regulator. That is, if the regulatory authorities choose a harmonized standard the firm deems too low, the firm may hire a private certifier to verify and communicate a higher quality. Alternatively, if the regulatory authorities choose a harmonized standard the firm deems too high, the firm may hire a private certifier to verify and communicate a lower quality—though the regulatory authorities will communicate to the public that the firm fails the harmonized standard.

The high-quality firm compares the profits it gains from selling a good at its preferred level of quality to the additional labeling costs it pays the private certifier. If the harmonized standard is "close enough" to the high-quality firm's desired quality level, the firm will not pay the additional cost of a second, private, certification. However, if the harmonized standard deviates too far from firm-preferred quality levels, the harmonized standard is disregarded and replaced by a standard chosen by the high-quality firm. Consequently, once the regulatory authorities allow private certification and labeling of credence goods, the benefits of North–North economic integration are more likely to be achieved, even if the harmonized standard does not coincide with the high-quality firm's optimal choice.

Similarly with North–South integration, firms will compare the profits they gain from selling a good at their preferred level of quality to the additional labeling costs they pay the private certifier. If the harmonized standard is "close enough" to the medium-quality and/or the high-quality firm's desired quality levels, neither firm will pay the additional cost of additional private certification. However, if the harmonized standard deviates too far from firm-preferred quality levels, the harmonized standard is disregarded and replaced by a standard chosen by the medium-quality and/or the high-

[36] For example, the Marine Stewardship Council was formed in 1996 as a partnership between the World Wildlife Fund and Unilever, a corporation with significant market share in the boxed frozen-fish sector, its objective being to provide a mechanism for labeling seafood products harvested from a sustainable source (Wessells, Johnston, and Donath 1999).

quality firm(s).[37] Therefore, if the regulatory authorities allow private certification and labeling of credence goods, the benefits of North–South economic integration are more likely to be achieved, even if the harmonized standard does not coincide with the medium-quality firm's and/or the high-quality firm's optimal choice.

The possibility of private certification also has important implications for the debate about increased economic integration, especially the so-called "race to the bottom" in standards (Bagwell and Staiger 2001). In the absence of any credence good regulations, only the minimum-quality good is produced in equilibrium, and de facto, standards never leave the bottom. In contrast, once there is mandatory discrete labeling, as long as additional private certification is permitted, there will be no race to the bottom as firms have a private incentive to produce higher than minimum-quality goods in equilibrium, i.e., even if the regulatory authorities "harmonize down" standards in a race to the bottom, private certification ensures that the full gains of economic integration will be realized.

The results may also be sensitive to the assumption that on integration, economies harmonize their labeling regulations, when in fact they may mutually recognize each other's existing labeling regimes.[38] It turns out that this does not matter in the case of mandatory, exclusive continuous labeling, because there is no divergence between countries' standards, i.e., no standards are set as labeling is continuous. However, mutual recognition of standards can affect the results in the case of mandatory, exclusive, discrete labeling. Specifically, for North–North economic integration, if one standard is close to what is optimal for the high-quality firm, mutual recognition of standards may ensure that a high-quality firm will enter the integrated market. Likewise, in the North–South case, if one standard is closer to what is optimal for the medium-quality firm, and one is closer to what is optimal for the high-quality firm, then under mutual recognition, either one or both firms will have an incentive to enter the integrated market. However, if there is little divergence between the standards of the integrating countries, and assuming no private certification is allowed, then the previous results for mandatory discrete labeling will hold even with mutual recognition, i.e., the high-quality firm may be driven out in the North–North case if the standards are set too low, while either the medium-quality and/or the high-quality firm may be driven out in the North–South case if the standards are set either too low or too high. The key point is that, compared to harmonization of standards, mutual recognition by countries of each other's labeling regimes may increase the probability that the benefits of integration will be achieved.

[37] It might be questioned whether firms based in the South will be in a position to hire private certifiers. If firms are footloose, it is always possible that a firm from the North will produce in the South and utilize private certification. There is also some evidence for private certification in developing countries (Cashore et al. 2006).

[38] In contrast to harmonization, mutual recognition implies that a country-of-origin principle is applied, i.e., a standard applied in one country is recognized in the other country. Likewise, any standard set in the latter country is recognized in the former country (Leebron 1996; Lutz 2000). See Wilson (2008) for a useful discussion of mutual recognition versus harmonization of standards.

4   CONCLUSIONS

Given the proliferation of food standards and technical regulations in the past two decades, the focus of this chapter has been on the interaction between such standards and international trade. Specifically, this interaction was set in the context of the tension between food standards as a response to market failures and the potential for protection to domestic producers. The analytical results presented reinforce an observation made by Wilson (2008): food standards are not like tariffs if their objective is to take care of market failures, however, it is important that not only are they applied in a non-discriminatory manner, but also any agreement between countries about standards has to ensure that the benefits of economic integration are realized, without undermining the resolution of market failures.

First, based on production of local public bad(s), a Ricardian-type model of international trade was presented showing that, compared to developing countries (the South), if developed countries (the North) have more effective labor and higher standards, the North specializes in producing and exporting food consumption goods intensive in their use of effective labor, while the South specializes in producing and exporting food and consumption goods intensive in their use of the public bad. With an increase in effective labor in the South, their standards converge on those of the North, reinforcing Casella's (1996) original argument that harmonization of standards as a precondition for trade liberalization is unnecessary. However, if the public bad produced in the South has the potential to impose damage on consumers in the North, exports of food consumption goods from the South are likely to face higher standards (public or private) imposed in the North. Treating higher standards on Southern exports as iceberg transport costs results in a range of non-traded goods: the hypothesis of "standards as barriers" is one that has support in much of the empirical work on food standards and trade. However, the hypothesis of "standards as catalysts" can also be nested in the model as an increase in effective labor, allowing the South to better comply with higher Northern standards.

Second, a model of vertical product differentiation was used to analyze the problem of trade in food consumption goods with credence characteristics. With perfect information, minimum- and high-quality goods are supplied in equilibrium, maximizing the benefits of both North–North and North–South economic integration. With asymmetric information, whether or not high-quality goods are supplied in equilibrium is contingent on the labeling regime for both North–North and North–South economic integration: with no labeling, only minimum quality is supplied; with continuous labeling, the perfect-information equilibrium is replicated; while with harmonized, exclusive, discrete labeling, supply of high-quality goods is dependent on the choice of public standards relative to the optimal choice of firms, i.e., regulators run the risk of driving out high-quality goods if the harmonized standard is set too high or too low. However, the benefits of economic integration are more likely to be achieved if private certification of labeling claims is allowed to coexist with public certification. In addition, if North–North and North–South agree to mutual recognition of each other's standards, the benefits of economic integration are more likely to be achieved.

In conclusion, these models are pretty robust in terms of their analysis of public standards, providing a theoretical basis for the extensive empirical work that supports the hypothesis of "standards as barriers." However, there is need for considerably more rigorous modeling of two issues that have received increasing attention, and which are now being included in empirical analysis. First, standards set by private coalitions need to be much more thoroughly embedded into models where, by assumption, firms typically have no real incentive to reduce their production of public bad(s), and where no explicit account is taken of the vertical nature of the food production system. Second, the rather ad hoc hypothesis of "standards as catalysts," for which there is so far very limited empirical support, also requires an underlying dynamic theory of why developing countries innovate in the face of higher standards in developed countries.

APPENDIX

Supposing the public bad is purely local, it is possible to derive what would be the optimal level of production of the public bad if the policymaker were to maximize the representative consumer's indirect utility subject to per capita income. Writing the indirect utility function as

$$V = \int_0^1 f(z)\ln[x(z)]dz - \int_0^1 f(z)\ln[p(z)]dz + \ln\left(\frac{I}{L}\right) - \frac{\beta D^\gamma}{\gamma}, \qquad (A1)$$

where $p(z)$ is the continuum of prices for the consumption goods z, and the first-order condition for the level of the public bad is $V_p dp/dD + V_I dI/dD + V_D = 0$. Assuming North and South are too small to influence world goods prices, $dp/dD = 0$, the first-order condition can be rearranged as $dI/dD = -V_D/V_I$, the latter part of the expression measuring marginal damage incurred by the representative consumer. If the government acts optimally, the compliance costs faced by producers should be set equal to aggregate marginal damage, i.e., $c_b = -L.V_D/V_I = \beta D^{\gamma-1} I$, the level of compliance costs, and by implication the standard s, varying positively in income I.

REFERENCES

Anders, S. M., and J. A. Caswell. 2009. "Standards as Barriers versus Standards as Catalysts: Assessing the Impact of HACCP Implementation on U.S. Seafood Imports." *American Journal of Agricultural Economics* 91/2: 310–21.

Antle, J. M. 2001. "Economic Analysis of Food Safety." In B. Gardner and G. Rausser, eds, *Handbook of Agricultural Economics*. Amsterdam: Elsevier.

Bagwell, K., and R. W. Staiger. 2001. "The WTO as a Mechanism for Securing Market Access Property Rights: Implications for Global Labor and Environmental Issues." *Journal of Economic Perspectives* 15/2: 69–88.

Bhagwati, J. N. 1984. "The Generalized Theory of Distortions and Welfare." In Bhagwati, ed., *International Trade: Selected Readings*. Cambridge, MA: MIT Press.

——1996. "The Demands to Reduce Domestic Diversity among Trading Nations." In J. N. Bhagwati and R. E. Hudec, eds, *Fair Trade and Harmonization: Prerequisites for Free Trade?* Cambridge, MA: MIT Press.

Boom, A. 1995. "Asymmetric International Minimum Quality Standards and Vertical Differentiation." *Journal of Industrial Economics* 43/1: 101–19.

Calvin, L., and B. Krissoff. 1998. "Technical Barriers to Trade: A Case Study of Phytosanitary Barriers and U.S.–Japanese Apple Trade." *Journal of Agricultural and Resource Economics* 23/2: 351–66.

Casella, A. 1996. "Free Trade and Evolving Standards." In J. N. Bhagwati and R. E. Hudec, eds, *Harmonization and Free Trade*. Cambridge, MA: MIT Press.

——2001. "Product Standards and International Trade: Harmonization through Private Coalitions." *Kyklos* 54/2–3: 243–64.

Cashore, B., F. Gale, E. Meidinger, and D. Newsom. 2006. *Confronting Sustainability: Forest Certification in Developing Countries and Transitioning Countries*. New Haven: Yale School of Forestry and Environmental Studies.

Charnowitz, S. 2002. "The Law of Environmental 'PPMs' in the WTO: Debunking the Myth of Illegality." *Yale Journal of International Law* 27/1: 59–110.

Copeland, B. R., and M. S. Taylor. 1994. "North–South Trade and the Environment." *Quarterly Journal of Economics* 109/3: 755–87.

————. 1995. "Trade and Transboundary Pollution." *American Economic Review* 85/4: 716–37.

————. 2003. *Trade and the Environment: Theory and Evidence*. Princeton: Princeton University Press.

————. 2004. "Trade, Growth and the Environment." *Journal of Economic Literature* 42/1: 7–71.

Crespi, J. M., and S. Marette. 2001. "How Should Food Safety Certification Be Financed?" *American Journal of Agricultural Economics* 83/4: 852–61.

Darby, M. R., and E. Karni. 1973. "Free Competition and the Optimal Amount of Fraud." *Journal of Law and Economics* 16/1: 67–88.

Dornbusch, R., S. Fischer, and P. A. Samuelson. 1977. "Comparative Advantage, Trade, Payments in a Ricardian Model with a Continuum of Goods." *American Economic Review* 67/5: 823–39.

Dulleck, U., and R. Kerschbamer. 2006. "On Doctors, Mechanics and Computer Specialists: The Economics of Credence Goods." *Journal of Economic Literature* 44/1: 5–42.

Essaji, E. 2008. "Technical Regulations and Specialization in International Trade." *Journal of International Economics* 76/2: 166–76.

Fischer, R., and P. Serra. 2000. "Standards and Protection." *Journal of International Economics* 52/2: 377–400.

Flam, H., and E. Helpman. 1987. "Vertical Product Differentiation and North–South Trade." *American Economic Review* 77/5: 810–22.

Fulponi, L. 2007. "The Globalization of Private Standards and the Agri-Food System." In J. F. M. Swinnen, ed., *Global Supply Chains, Standards and the Poor*. Wallingford: CABI.

Fulton, M., and K. Giannakas. 2004. "Inserting GM Products into the Food Chain: The Market and Welfare Effects of Different Labeling and Regulatory Regimes." *American Journal of Agricultural Economics* 86/1: 42–60.

Gabszewicz, J. J., and J. F. Thisse. 1979. "Price Competition, Quality and Income Disparities." *Journal of Economic Theory* 20/3: 340–59.

————. 1980. "Entry (and Exit) in a Differentiated Industry." *Journal of Economic Theory* 22/2: 327–38.

Giannakas, K., and M. Fulton. 2002. "Consumption Effects of Genetic Modification: What If Consumers Are Right?" *Agricultural Economics* 27/2: 97–109.

Henson, S. 2008. "The Role of Public and Private Standards in Regulating International Food Markets." *Journal of International Agricultural Trade and Development* 4/1: 63–81.

——and S. Jaffee. 2008. "Understanding Developing Country Strategic Responses to the Enhancement of Food Safety Standards." *World Economy* 31/3: 548–68.

Jaffee, S., and S. Henson. 2004. "Food Exports from Developing Countries: The Challenges Posed by Standards." In M. A. Aksoy and J. C. Beghin, eds, *Global Agricultural Trade and Developing Countries*. Oxford: Oxford University Press.

Josling, T. 2008. "The Institutional Framework for Food Regulation and Trade." *Journal of International Agricultural Trade and Development* 4/1: 1–15.

——, D. Roberts, and D. Orden. 2004. *Food Regulation and Trade*. Washington, DC: Institute for International Economics.

Leebron, D. W. 1996. "Lying Down with Procrustes: An Analysis of Harmonization Claims." In J. N. Bhagwati and R. E. Hudec, eds, *Fair Trade and Harmonization: Prerequisites for Free Trade?* Cambridge, MA: MIT Press.

Lutz, S. H. 2000. "Trade Effects of Minimum Quality Standards with and without Deterred Entry." *Journal of Economic Integration* 15/2: 314–44.

McCluskey, J. J. 2000. "A Game Theoretic Approach to Organic Foods: An Analysis of Asymmetric Information and Policy." *Agricultural and Resource Economics Review* 29/1: 1–9.

——and J. A. Winfree. 2009. "Pre-empting Public Regulation with Private Food Quality Standards." *European Review of Agricultural Economics* 36/4: 525–40.

Maertens, M., and J. F. M. Swinnen. 2008. "Standards as Barriers and Catalysts for Trade, Growth and Poverty Reduction." *Journal of International Agricultural Trade and Development* 4/1: 47–61.

Marette, S., J.-C. Bureau, and E. Gozlan. 2000. "Product Safety Provision and Consumers' Information." *Australian Economic Papers* 39/4: 426–41.

——, J. M. Crespi, and A. Schiavina. 1999. "The Role of Common Labeling in a Context of Asymmetric Information." *European Review of Agricultural Economics* 26/2: 167–78.

Maskus, K. E., and J. S. Wilson. 2001. "A Review of Past Attempts and the New Policy Context." In Maskus and Wilson, eds, *Quantifying the Impact of Technical Barriers to Trade*. Ann Arbor: University of Michigan Press.

Motta, M. 1992. "Sunk Costs and Trade Liberalization." *Economic Journal* 102/412: 578–87.

Murphy, K. M., and A. Shleifer. 1997. "Quality and Trade." *Journal of Development Economics* 53/1: 1–145.

Mussa, M., and S. Rosen. 1978. "Monopoly and Product Quality." *Journal of Economic Theory* 18/2: 301–17.

Otsuki, T., J. S. Wilson, and M. Sewadeh. 2001. "Saving Two in a Billion: Quantifying the Trade Effect of European Food Safety Standards on African Exports." *Food Policy* 26/5: 495–514.

Paarlberg, P. L., and J. G. Lee. 1998. "Import Restrictions in the Presence of a Health Risk: An Illustration Using FMD." *American Journal of Agricultural Economics* 80/1: 175–83.

Palmer, K., W. E. Oates, and P. R. Portney. 1995. "Tightening Environmental Standards: The Benefit–Cost or the No-Cost Paradigm?" *Journal of Economic Perspectives* 9/4: 119–32.

Peterson, E. B., and D. Orden. 2005. "Effects of Tariffs and Sanitary Barriers on High- and Low-Value Poultry Trade." *Journal of Agricultural and Resource Economics* 30/1: 109–27.

Porter, M. E., and C. van der Linde. 1995. "Toward a New Conception of the Environment– Competitiveness Relationship." *Journal of Economic Perspectives* 9/4: 97–118.

Reardon, T., and J. A. Berdegue. 2002. "The Rapid Rise of Supermarkets in Latin America: Challenges and Opportunities for Development." *Development Policy Review* 20/4: 371–88.

Roberts, D. 1998. "Preliminary Assessment of the Effects of the WTO Agreement on Sanitary and Phytosanitary Trade Regulation." *Journal of International Economic Law* 1/3: 377–405.

—— 1999. "Analyzing Technical Barriers to Trade in Agricultural Markets." *Agribusiness: An International Journal* 15/3: 335–54.

Roe, B., and I. M. Sheldon. 2007. "Credence Good Labeling: The Efficiency and Distributional Implications of Several Policy Approaches." *American Journal of Agricultural Economics* 89/4: 1020–33.

Ronnen, U. 1991. "Minimum Quality Standards, Fixed Costs, and Competition." *Rand Journal of Economics* 22/4: 490–504.

Scarpa, C. 1998. "Minimum Quality Standards with More Than Two Firms." *International Journal of Industrial Organization* 16/5: 665–76.

Segerson, K. 1990. "Liability for Groundwater Contamination from Pesticides." *Journal of Environmental Economics and Management* 19/3: 227–43.

—— 1999. "Mandatory versus Voluntary Approaches to Food Safety." *Agribusiness: An International Journal* 15/1: 53–70.

Shaked, A., and J. Sutton. 1982. "Relaxing Price Competition through Product Differentiation." *Review of Economic Studies* 49/1: 3–13.

—— ——. 1983. "Natural Oligopolies." *Econometrica* 51/5: 1469–83.

Sheldon, I. M. 2002. "Regulation of Biotechnology: Will We Ever Freely Trade GMOs?" *European Review of Agricultural Economics* 29/1: 155–76.

—— 2004. "Europe's Regulation of Agricultural Biotechnology: Precaution or Protection?" *Journal of Agricultural and Food Industrial Organization* 2/2, art. 4. <http://www.bepress. com/jafio/vol2/iss2/art4/ > .

—— 2007. "Food Principles: Likely Impact of the 2006 WTO Ruling on the Regulatory Environment for GM Crops?" *Brown Journal of World Affairs* 14/1: 121–34.

—— and B. Roe. 2009a. "Vertical Product Differentiation and Credence Goods: Mandatory Labeling and Gains from International Integration." *EconoQuantum* 5/1: 9–33.

—— ——. 2009b. "Public vs. Private Eco-Labeling of Environmental Credence Goods: Maximizing the Gains from International Integration." *Journal of Food and Agricultural Industrial Organization* 7/2, art. 4. <http://www.bepress.com/jafio/vol7/iss2/art4/ > .

Sturm, D. M. 2006. "Product Standards, Trade Disputes, and Protectionism." *Canadian Journal of Economics* 39/2: 564–81.

Swann, P., P. Temple, and M. Shurmer. 1996. "Standards and Trade Experience: The UK Experience." *Economic Journal* 106/438: 1297–313.

Swinnen, J. F. M., and T. Vandemoortele. 2009. *Trade, Development, and the Political Economy of Public Quality Standards*. Licos Discussion Paper 236/2009. University of Leuven: LICOS Centre for Institutions and Economic Performance. <http://www.econ.kuleuven.be/licos/DP/DP2009/DP236.pdf>.

Teisl, M. F., and B. Roe. 1998. "The Economics of Labeling: An Overview of Issues for Health and Environmental Disclosure." *Agricultural and Resource Economics Review* 27/2: 140–50.

Wessels, C. R., R. J. Johnston, and H. Donath. 1999. "Assessing Consumer Preferences for Eco-Labeled Seafood: The Influence of Species, Certifier, and Household Attributes." *American Journal of Agricultural Economics* 81/5: 1084–9.

Wilson, J. S. 2008. "Standards and Developing Country Exports: A Review of Selected Studies and Suggestions for Future Research." *Journal of International Agricultural Trade and Development* 4/1: 35–45.

——and T. Otsuki. 2004. "To Spray or Not to Spray: Pesticides, Banana Exports, and Food Safety." *Food Policy* 29/2: 131–46.

World Bank. 2005. *Challenges and Opportunities Associated with International Agro-Food Standards*. Washington, DC: World Bank.

Zago, A. M., and D. Pick. 2004. "Labeling Policies in Food Markets: Private Incentives, Public Intervention, and Welfare Effects." *Journal of Agricultural and Resource Economics* 29/1: 150–65.

CHAPTER 16

....

THE POLITICAL ECONOMY
OF FOOD STANDARDS

....

JOHAN F. M. SWINNEN AND THIJS VANDEMOORTELE[*]

1   INTRODUCTION

....

Food standards are an increasingly important factor in the present global food system. Food standards address a large variety of issues in food consumption and production such as nutrition (e.g., low fat), food safety (e.g., pesticide residues), food quality (e.g., minimum size requirements), environmental (e.g., low carbon dioxide emission), and social concerns (e.g., no child labor).

There exists an extensive theoretical literature on the economics of quality regulation and standards. While not specifically focusing on food standards, the analyses in this literature can be readily applied to any kind of (food) standard. Initially, the main focus of this literature was on the competition and welfare effects of minimum quality standards. The welfare analysis of these minimum quality standards, e.g., by Ronnen (1991), Crampes and Hollander (1995), and Valletti (2000), was mainly performed in a framework of vertical differentiation in quality, such as was introduced in the economics literature by Spence (1976), Mussa and Rosen (1978), and Tirole (1988). Others also studied the welfare impacts of minimum quality standards, although not in a vertical differentiation framework, e.g., Leland (1979) and Bockstael (1984).

In the more recent theoretical work involving standards the focus has shifted to the analysis of the relation between trade and standards. While minimum quality standards were previously the predominant subject of analysis, other types of standards

* The authors gratefully acknowledge the valuable comments and suggestions from Jayson Lusk and an anonymous reviewer. We thank Jill McCluskey for support and encouragement on this project. This research was financially supported by Research Foundation—Flanders (FWO) and the K. U. Leuven Excellence and Methusalem Funds.

such as labeling standards (e.g., Fulton and Giannakas 2004; Roe and Sheldon 2007) or environmental standards (e.g., Schleich 1999) became apparent. The prevailing conclusion that emerges from this literature on the relation between standards and trade is that standards are protectionist in nature. For example, in the theoretical analyses of Schleich (1999), Fischer and Serra (2000), Anderson, Damania, and Jackson (2004), and Sturm (2006) standards are found to be non-tariff barriers to trade that protect domestic producers. Several authors have dealt with the effects of standards as barriers to trade, e.g., Barrett (1994), Sykes (1995), Thilmany and Barrett (1997), Barrett and Yang (2001) and Baltzer (2010). Only some authors have argued that standards are not necessarily protectionist instruments, e.g., Tian (2003), Swinnen and Vandemoortele (2009, 2011) and Marette and Beghin (2010).

Although this literature deals with the welfare and trade effects of (food) standards, little of this literature is concerned with how (public) food standards are set by governments. However, this is an important question that merits serious analysis. The general literature on minimum quality standards shows that welfare may increase or decrease with the implementation of a minimum quality standard, and that different groups in society, e.g., consumers, low-quality producers and high-quality producers, may be affected differently. Recent literature has integrated these insights in an open economy model to analyze why food standards are set at a certain level. A political economy perspective that allows for interest groups trying to influence the government is essential to understand the determination of the public standard. It also has important implications for the welfare effects of standards, whether they are suboptimal or not, and for the possible trade-protectionist nature of standards. Only recently has some work been done on the political economy of public standards to explain why standards are set at a certain level, and how this affects trade (Anderson, Damania, and Jackson 2004; Swinnen and Vandemoortele 2008, 2009, 2011).

The political economy of regulation has a long tradition, starting with the seminal work of George Stigler, who analyzed the demand for regulation by economic interest groups and their potential use of public resources and power to improve their economic status (Stigler 1971). Extensive research has been done on the subject of lobbying, for example by Bhagwati (1982) and Becker (1983). Krueger (1974) developed a model of competitive rent seeking and focused on the negative welfare implications of rent seeking, as applied to trade policy. Much of the applied work on political economy and lobbying is in the domain of trade policy regulation. In important contributions from Hillman and Ursprung (1988) and Magee, Brock, and Young (1989), competing political parties promise to implement trade polices if elected, and lobby groups contribute resources to the political party that promises them the highest welfare for the purpose of increasing the probability that their favorite party is elected (see Hillman 1989 for a review of the literature). In another approach that we shall follow in this chapter, an incumbent government seeks to maximize its political support that consists of the lobby contributions (welfare) of certain interest groups and the (deadweight loss of) welfare in society; see e.g., Hillman (1982) and Grossman and Helpman (1994, 1995).

In this chapter we review the emerging literature on public food regulation by developing a general conceptual framework of the political economy of public food standards. We use this general framework to explain key insights from the literature and indicate how specific applications of the framework have yielded additional conclusions.

While we focus on public food standards, we cannot ignore private standards, which are increasingly important in food markets. Therefore, we present a discussion on the relation between public and private food standards at the end of this chapter.

The structure of this chapter is as follows. In Section 2 we provide an overview of different interest groups who may have varying interests in public food standards, and how these different interests can be captured in a political economy model. In Section 3 we discuss the political equilibrium of this model and some factors that may influence this equilibrium. In Section 4 we present the relation between this political equilibrium and development, and the impact of perceptions and media. Section 5 discusses how various types of food standards can be incorporated in this general framework, and whether food *safety* standards are different from other types of standards. Section 6 analyzes the relation between trade and the political economy of public standards, and their possible (producer-)protectionist nature. Section 7 provides an overview of the relation between public and private food standards, and Section 8 concludes this chapter.

2   INTEREST GROUPS AND PUBLIC FOOD STANDARDS

....

Food standards may have varying impacts on different actors in food markets. Consequently these different groups have opposing or coinciding interests with respect to food standards. In this section we discuss the interests of the different groups who may have an impact on the political process of setting a public food standard, and how these interests can be modeled in the framework of a small open economy.

2.1   Producers

The first interest group consists of the producers in the domestic food sector. The general term "producers" may capture farmers who produce the initial food product, but may equally represent companies that produce farm inputs, processors of farm outputs, or retailers who sell the final food product to consumers.[1] How the cost of a

---

[1] For example, a food standard that regulates maximum pesticide residue levels in food has implications both for pesticide producers and for farmers who apply the pesticide. Additionally, such a standard may have implications for food processors who have to label their product according to the standard.

regulation is translated into price changes within the supply chain depends on the market power of the different actors and their specific relationships.[2] To refrain from vertical organization issues in the food supply chain, we use the general notion of "producers" and represent producers by one single interest group.

We assume that production is a function of a sector-specific input factor that is available in inelastic supply. All profits made in the import-competing sector accrue to this specific factor. The unit cost function $g = g(q, s)$ depends on output produced (q) and the level of standards in that sector (s). A higher s refers to a more stringent standard.

Food standards typically involve some costs for producers. Food standards may affect production costs and/or entail implementation costs, because a standard, in general, imposes some production constraints or obligations. In fact, all standards can be defined as a prohibition to use a cheaper technology. Examples are the prohibition of an existing technology (e.g., child labor) or of a technology that has not yet been used but that could potentially lower costs (e.g., genetic modification (GM) technology). Also, traceability standards can be interpreted as a prohibition of cheaper production systems that do not allow tracing the production. This implies that the unit costs increase with higher standards $\left(\frac{\partial g}{\partial s} > 0\right)$ for $s > 0$.

The model assumes a small open economy where domestic firms are price takers and domestic prices of imported goods equal world prices. Assume that when the country imposes a standard, the production costs of the imported goods also rise as the standard is also imposed on imported goods—and is equally enforced. This leads to a price increase, henceforth called the "marginal price effect" of a standard $\left(\frac{\partial p}{\partial s} > 0\right)$. More specifically, the unit cost function of foreign (f) producers is $g^f\left(q^f, s\right)$ where q^f is foreign production. The world price p then equals the unit costs of the foreign producers and we have $p(s) = g^f\left(q^f, s\right)$, and $\frac{\partial p}{\partial s} = \frac{\partial g^f}{\partial s}$.

Subsequently, domestic producers may gain (because of the marginal price effect) or lose (because of the marginal unit cost increase) from (a change in) the standard. Producer profits are equal to

$$\Pi_p(s) = \max_q \left\{ q \cdot (p(s) - g(q, s)) \right\}$$

and by the envelope theorem the marginal effect on producer's profits $\Pi_p(s)$ of a standard is equal to

$$\frac{\partial \Pi_p}{\partial s} = q \cdot \left(\frac{\partial p}{\partial s} - \frac{\partial g}{\partial s} \right).$$

Producers' profits decrease with an increase of the standard when the marginal unit cost increase $\frac{\partial g}{\partial s}$ is larger than the marginal price effect $\frac{\partial p}{\partial s}$. When the marginal unit cost increase is smaller than the marginal price effect, producers gain from an increase of

---

[2] For example, to cover their labeling expenses, processors may either try to pay less for their inputs to farmers, or ask for higher prices from consumers.

the standard. Therefore, producers have an incentive to (try to) influence the standard setting by the government, but the direction of this influence is not predetermined and depends on the relative effects. Producers have larger incentives to lobby when the difference (in absolute value) between these two marginal effects is larger.

2.2 Consumers

The second interest group involved in this political economy model are the consumers of the good on which a standard is or may be applied. Consumers may value food standards for a variety of reasons. Swinnen and Vandemoortele (2009) discern three main reasons; namely, food safety, food quality, and social or environmental motives. In general, a standard that guarantees one or more of these features of the product affects utility as it reduces or solves informational asymmetries (Leland 1979). Therefore, a standard induces consumption of the product, *ceteris paribus*, because a reduction of information asymmetries generates a higher willingness to pay for that product. For example, consumers who perceive health problems with certain (potential) ingredients or production processes may increase consumption if they are guaranteed the absence of those elements. To model this, we assume a utility function of a representative consumer:

$$U = U(c, s) \tag{1}$$

where c is consumption of the good and s is the standard imposed on this good. We assume that utility is increasing and concave in consumption $\left(\frac{\partial U}{\partial c} > 0, \frac{\partial^2 U}{\partial c^2} < 0\right)$ and increasing in the standard $\left(\frac{\partial U}{\partial s} > 0\right)$. The representative consumer maximizes utility such that $\frac{\partial U}{\partial c} = p$. This first-order condition determines the demand function that identifies consumption $c(p, s)$ as a function of the price and the standard.

Subsequently, consumers may gain (because of the marginal utility effect) or lose (because of the marginal price effect) from (a change in) the standard. Consumer surplus $\Pi_c(s)$ is defined as

$$\Pi_c(s) = U(c, s) - p(s) \cdot c(p, s)$$

and by the envelope theorem the marginal effect on consumer surplus $\Pi_c(s)$ of a standard is equal to

$$\frac{\partial \Pi_c}{\partial s} = \frac{\partial U}{\partial s} - \frac{\partial p}{\partial s} c.$$

Consumer surplus increases with the standard if the marginal utility effect $\frac{\partial U}{\partial s}$ is larger than the marginal increase in cost of consumption $\frac{\partial p}{\partial s} c$. Vice versa, if the marginal increase in the cost of consumption outweighs the beneficial marginal utility effect, consumer surplus decreases with the standard. In both cases consumers have an incentive to try to influence the government's standard-setting behavior.

For now, we keep this exposition as general as possible and continue our analysis with the general definition of consumer utility as put forward under definition (1), but it is clear that the analysis can be readily applied to different specifications of the utility function, as we do in Section 5.

2.3   Other Interest Groups

In addition to consumers and producers, there are often other interest groups involved in the decision-making process on food standards. For example, when the standard affects certain externalities, non-governmental organizations (NGOs) may also have an interest in the implementation of a standard that affects this externality. Depending on the type of externalities affected, such as social externalities (e.g., child labor) or environmental externalities (e.g., carbon dioxide emissions), different NGOs can be involved in the lobby game.

Likewise, governments of countries other than the standard-imposing country may have an interest in influencing the standard-setting process in the standard-imposing country. For example, if an exporting country has low food standards and its producers experience difficulties in meeting the standard imposed by an importing country, the government of the exporting country has an incentive to influence the importing country's government to decrease the level of the standard. For example the US government influenced European Union (EU) decision-making on the REACH chemical regulation.[3] This directive regulates how chemicals should be tested on safety, and dictates that manufacturers should bear the burden of this testing. Because it was argued that REACH would be too costly for the US chemical industry, the US government worked to influence the EU legislation.

3   THE POLITICAL ECONOMY OF PUBLIC FOOD STANDARDS

Consider a government that maximizes its own objective function which, following the protection-for-sale approach of Grossman and Helpman (1994), consists of a weighted sum of contributions from interest groups and social welfare. Similar to Grossman and Helpman (1994), we restrict the set of policies available to politicians and only allow them to implement a public standard.

We assume that all interest groups affected by the standard are politically organized and that they lobby simultaneously. This assumption differs from Grossman and

---

[3] REACH stands for "Registration, Evaluation, and Authorization of Chemicals."

Helpman (1994), Anderson, Damania, and Jackson (2004), and Cadot, de Melo, and Olarreaga (2004). For example, we believe it is not realistic to assume that consumers are not organized—or do not effectively lobby—on issues related to food standards. There is substantive evidence that consumers lobby governments on issues of public food standards. In reality, consumer lobbying occurs not only through consumer organizations but also through political parties representing consumer interests.

The "truthful"[4] contribution schedule of interest group j is equal to the function $C_j(s) = \max\{0; \Pi_j(s) - b_j\}$, in which the constant b_j represents the share of surplus income $\Pi_j(s)$ the interest group does not want to invest in lobbying the government. One could also interpret this constant b_j as a minimum threshold, a level of profits or surplus below which the interest groups believe the return from lobbying is less than its cost. The government's objective function is a weighted sum of the contributions of interest groups (weighted by α_j) and overall social welfare, where α_j represents the relative lobbying strength of interest group j:

$$V(s) = \sum_j \alpha_j C_j(s) + W(s) \tag{2}$$

where we define welfare $W(s)$ as the sum of surplus incomes of the interest groups, i.e., as

$$W(s) \equiv \sum_j \Pi_j(s) \tag{3}$$

The government chooses the level of the standard to maximize its objective function (2). Each possible level of this standard corresponds to a certain level of interest group surplus, and hence also to a certain level of contributions. This is driven by the functional form and the truthfulness of the contribution schedules that show that the government will receive higher contributions from interest groups if the imposed standard creates higher surplus. Conversely, the government receives lower contributions if the standard decreases interest group surplus. Therefore, maximizing these contributions from producers (consumers) by choosing the level of standard is equivalent to maximizing their income surplus. The government will thus choose the level of standards such that it maximizes the weighted sum of the income surpluses of the interest groups, and social welfare.[5] The politically optimal standard, s^*, is therefore determined by the following first-order condition, subject to $s^* \geq 0$:

---

[4] The common-agency literature (e.g., Bernheim and Whinston 1986) states that a truthful contribution schedule reflects the true preferences of the interest group. In this particular political economy model, this implies that lobby groups set their lobbying contributions in accordance with their expected surplus income and how this is marginally affected by the standard. We refer to Swinnen and Vandemoortele (2011) for a proof of the truthfulness of the contribution schedules in this model.

[5] This objective function implies that a government has no particular interest in the standard other than how it affects the interest groups' surplus incomes and contributions. However, governments may value standards for additional reasons. For example, a higher standard may require a larger bureaucracy to govern this standard, leading to higher budgets for and control by the government. We abstract from

$$\sum_{j} \alpha_j \frac{\partial \Pi_j(s^*)}{\partial s} + \frac{\partial W(s^*)}{\partial s} = 0. \tag{4}$$

Optimality condition (4) implicitly defines s^* as a function of several variables, such as lobbying strength, consumer preferences, and cost increases of (domestic and foreign) producers.[6]

First, it is obvious from condition (4) that a change in the political weights α_j, capturing exogenous differences in the political weight of a lobby group, affects s^*. When the political weight of a lobby group increases exogenously, it implies that its contributions are more effective in influencing the decisions of the government. However, the sign of the effect on s^* depends on the relative benefits of s^* for the interest groups. More specifically, an increase in α_j leads to a higher standard s^*, if and only if interest group j gains from increasing the standard beyond s^*. In this case the government will set the optimal standard at a higher level if α_j increases, and vice versa.

Second, an exogenous change in the preferences of consumers for standards will affect the politically optimal standard s^*. A shift in consumer preferences affects the marginal utility of a standard. Higher consumer preferences, for example, for food safety or quality, lead to higher consumer surplus and higher contributions in favor of public food standards, which lead to higher public standards, and vice versa.

Third, the marginal cost increase caused by a food standard, for both domestic and foreign producers, will affect the politically optimal standard. A higher marginal unit cost increase for domestic producers implies lower marginal benefits of standards for domestic producers, *ceteris paribus*. This leads to lower standards as producers will contribute less for public food standards.

A higher marginal unit cost increase for foreign producers may increase or decrease the politically optimal standard, depending on other factors. On the one hand, the resulting higher marginal price effect results in lower marginal consumer benefits and contributions. On the other hand, it increases the marginal profits and contributions of domestic producers. The size of these effects and the net effect depends on the relation between domestic production and consumption and on the functional form of the various functions. As a result, standards may move in either direction with changes in the marginal cost increase for foreign producers, depending on the relative benefits and the political weights of the different lobby groups.

Finally, an important general implication from this discussion is that either consumers or producers may lobby in favor of or against standards, and that the political equilibrium may be affected by various factors.

---

these additional objectives in order to focus the analysis on the relation between the politically optimal standard and the standard's impact on interest groups.

[6] Formal derivations how these variables affect the politically optimal food standard are in Swinnen and Vandemoortele (2011).

4   DEVELOPMENT AND THE POLITICAL ECONOMY OF PUBLIC FOOD STANDARDS

These results can be used to explain the empirically observed positive relationship between standards and economic development. It is often argued that this relationship simply reflects consumer preferences. While the model confirms that (income-related) preference variations play a role, it also suggests a more complex set of causal factors that affect the relationship between development and the political economy of public standards. The analysis suggests several reasons for the wide variety in standards across the world, and in particular between developing ("poor") and developed ("rich") countries.

First and most obvious, lower income levels are typically associated with lower consumer preferences for food standards. Because the effect on consumer surplus of a public standard is then lower, consumer contributions are lower in developing nations than in rich countries and this results in a lower politically optimal standard level in poor countries.

This is consistent with international survey evidence on consumer preferences for GM standards. Rich-country consumers are generally more opposed to GM than poor-country consumers. Consumers in rich countries have less to gain from biotech-induced farm productivity improvements compared to developing-country consumers, who have much to gain from cheaper food (McCluskey et al. 2003). This argument is also consistent with empirical observations that consumers from developed countries have generally higher preferences for other applications of biotechnology, such as medical applications (Hossain et al. 2003; Savadori et al. 2004; Costa-Font, Gil, and Traill 2008), that have more (potential) benefits for richer consumers.

Second, studies find that the quality of institutions (including institutions for enforcement of contracts and public regulations) is positively correlated with development (North 1990). Lower quality of institutions implies that enforcement and control costs of standards (i.e., the increase in unit costs with higher standards) are higher. These higher enforcement costs lead to lower politically optimal standards.

Third and related to this, while poor countries, with low wages and less urban pressure on land use, may have a cost advantage in the production of raw materials, better institutions in rich countries lower the marginal increase in unit production costs caused by standards. A lower marginal increase in unit production costs could result from higher education and skills of producers, better public infrastructure, easier access to finance, etc. These factors induce higher public standards.

In combination, the factors we discussed above are likely to induce a shift of the political equilibrium from low standards to high standards with development. If we define a "coalition" as both groups having the same preferences, i.e., either $s = 0$ (anti) or $s > 0$ (pro), then in extreme cases the variations in the mechanisms identified here may result in a "pro-standard coalition" of consumers and producers in rich countries.

In rich countries, in addition to consumers, producers may also support standards as they enhance their competitive position against imports as compliance may be less costly for domestic producers compared to importers. In contrast, an "anti-standard coalition" may be present in poor countries as, in addition to producers, consumers may also oppose standards since they may be more concerned with prices than standards.

4.1 Perceptions and the Media

So far, we have assumed that consumers have rational expectations and unbiased perceptions of standards. However, studies claim that perceptions of the public may differ significantly from expert opinions on a diversity of issues (e.g., Flynn, Slovic, and Mertz 1993; Savadori et al. 2004). For example, Ansell and Vogel (2006) argue that the public has exaggerated negative perceptions about food safety issues, and therefore values food safety standards higher than what is scientifically justified. If so, biased perceptions may play an important role in the political economy of public standards (Swinnen and Vandemoortele 2009).[7]

Several studies find that consumer perceptions are functions of the level of consumer trust in government regulators, attitudes toward scientific discovery, and media coverage (Loureiro 2003; Curtis, McCluskey, and Wahl 2004; Kalaitzandonakes, Marks, and Vickner 2004).

For example, a reason for the differences in perceptions across countries explored by Curtis, McCluskey, and Swinnen (2008) is the different organization and structure of the media in rich versus poor countries. Mass media is the main source of information for consumers to form attitudes regarding many issues, including genetically modified foods (GMFs) (Hoban and Kendall 1993; Shepherd et al. 1998).

Commercial media are more likely to highlight potential risks associated with biotechnology in their reporting (McCluskey and Swinnen 2004). The increased cost of media information in developing countries leads to lower media consumption and to a proportionately stronger reduction in risk reporting.

In addition, government control of the media is stronger in poor countries. This may lead to a more positive coverage of new technologies such as biotechnology, which in turn may contribute to more favorable perceptions of GMFs and biotechnology among consumers in these less developed countries (LDCs).

The public is most negative toward GMFs in most of the developed countries, especially in the EU and Japan. The United States is an exception as consumers are largely ambivalent about GMFs. In LDCs consumer attitudes toward GMFs are less

---

[7] Consumer perceptions can be incorporated in the formal analysis by rewriting the representative consumer's utility as $U = U(c, \lambda s)$ where λ is the variable that measures the bias in consumer perceptions. λ is equal to one if the consumer's perceptions of the standard's effects are unbiased. See also n. 9.

negative and in many cases positive (see Curtis, McCluskey, and Swinnen 2008 for a review of the evidence). Therefore, the media structure and information provision is likely to induce a more pro-standard attitude in rich countries than in poor, as increased access to media will increase attention to risks and negative implications of low standards.

A related element is how the rural/urban population structure affects perceptions. McCluskey et al. (2003) find that people associated with agriculture are much more in favor of GMFs than urban consumers.[8] It is likely that consumers who are associated with agriculture have a better idea of the amount of pesticides used on non-GMFs than urban consumers, and hence of the benefits from GMFs (such as pesticide-resistant crops). As developing countries have a higher proportion of rural residents, this may contribute to explain the differences in preferences.

Hence, both perception factors may reinforce the effects of consumer preferences and quality of institutions in inducing a positive relationship between standards and development.

5   DIFFERENT TYPES OF FOOD STANDARDS

The utility function defined under (1) is very general. However, depending on the type of standard under analysis, a more specific and detailed structure of the consumers' utility function may be appropriate. In a political economy framework similar to the one presented above, Swinnen and Vandemoortele (2009) distinguish between three types of standards in their theoretical analysis: food safety standards, food quality standards, and social and environmental standards. Along the lines of this categorization, three examples that are consistent with our general framework are explained here.

5.1   Food Safety Standards and Risk

The first category of standards is food safety standards. In the analysis of Brom (2000), this is the type of standards that matters to all consumers. The main purpose of food safety standards is to provide consumers with safe food. Examples of such standards are the limitation of pesticide residues on vegetables, or more generally the prohibition of dangerous substances in any food.

If the standard under consideration is a food safety standard, the incorporation of risk into the utility function might be appropriate (Swinnen and Vandemoortele 2009). A possible specification of the utility function is

---

[8] Unpublished research of Scott Rozelle and Jikun Huang confirms this result for China.

$$U(c, s) = Eu(c, s) = [1 - \rho(s)]u(c) - \rho(s)d(c)$$

where $Eu(c, s)$ is the expected utility of consumption c and the standard s. This modeling of expected utility in relation to product (safety) characteristics is based on the literature on product warranties (see, e.g., Cooper and Ross 1985; Emons 1988; Elbasha and Riggs 2003). The good may or may not contain the product characteristics desired by the consumer. If the product characteristics are satisfactory, utility of consumption is $u(c)$, which is increasing and concave in c ($u'(\cdot) > 0$, $u''(\cdot) < 0$). However, if the good does not have the desired characteristics, i.e., the good proves to be unsafe, consumers incur a disutility of consumption $d(c)$, which is increasing and convex in c ($d'(\cdot) > 0$, $d''(\cdot) > 0$). The probability of the latter outcome is $\rho(s)$ and is decreasing and convex in the standard ($\rho'(\cdot) < 0, \rho''(\cdot) > 0$).[9]

5.2   Food Quality Standards and Product Differentiation

The second category is food quality standards. These standards ensure certain product quality characteristics to the consumers. These product characteristics do not include safety, but rather concern consumer preferences about other aspects of nutritional quality, taste, color, size, etc. These standards may be linked to personal lifestyle choices (e.g., vegetarians). If the standard under analysis is a food quality standard, a vertical differentiation framework, in which consumers are heterogeneous in their willingness to pay for a (quality) standard, might be more appropriate (Swinnen and Vandemoortele 2011). This modeling of standards is the standard approach in the literature on minimum quality standards (see, e.g., Ronnen 1991; Jeanneret and Verdier 1996; Valletti 2000). Consumers are assumed to consume at most one unit of the good, and their preferences can be described by the following individual indirect utility function (see Tirole 1988):

$$u_i = \begin{cases} \phi_i(\varepsilon + s) - p & \text{if he buys the good with standard } s \text{ at price } p \\ 0 & \text{if he does not buy} \end{cases}$$

where ϕ_i is the preference parameter. Consumers with higher ϕ_i are more willing to pay for a product with a public standard s and the non-standard-related value ε of the product. φ_i is uniformly distributed over the interval $[\phi - 1, \phi]$ with $\phi \geq 1$ and $i \in \{1, \ldots, N\}$. Consumers with $\phi_i < p/(\varepsilon + s)$ will not consume this product, which implies that the market will be "uncovered."[10] The aggregate demand function, with N consumers, is then:

---

[9] Biased consumer perceptions can be incorporated in this utility specification by defining λ as a measure for the bias in consumer risk perception. The expected utility of consumption is then rewritten as $Eu(c, s) = [1 - \lambda\rho(s)]u(c) - \lambda\rho(s)d(c)$.

[10] This specification supposes that a standard leads to a vertical quality improvement, i.e., all consumers prefer higher standards. Yet, consumers differ in their willingness to pay for higher

$$c(p, s) = N(\phi - p/(\varepsilon + s)).$$

5.3   Social and Environmental Food Standards and Externalities

The third category covers public standards that aim at regulating social and environmental issues and is linked with the ethical values of a society. Examples include the prohibition of using child labor and the limitation of carbon dioxide emission in the production process. A possible extension of this general consumer framework is to include consumption and/or production externalities, as done by, for example, Fischer and Serra (2000), Anderson, Damania, and Jackson (2004), Besley and Ghatak (2007), and Swinnen and Vandemoortele (2008, 2009). In this case, the general welfare function as defined in (3) is extended to include externalities. These externalities can be either positive or negative, and can relate to consumption and/or production externalities. A possible specification is the following:

$$W = \sum_j \Pi_j(s) + E(x, s) \tag{5}$$

where $E(x, s)$ is the externality, and x can be either domestic consumption, domestic production, or total domestic and foreign production, depending on the type of externality. A standard decreases a negative externality (in absolute value) and increases a positive externality, such that $\frac{\partial E(x,s)}{\partial s} > 0$.

5.4   Are Food Safety Standards Different from Other Types of Food Standards?

An important result of the analysis of Swinnen and Vandemoortele (2009) is that, in an environment with only public standards, food safety standards will be set at higher levels than public food quality standards because the utility effect of safety standards (i.e., the marginal effect of standards on consumer welfare) is stronger, *ceteris paribus*.[11]

standards, and hence also in their willingness to contribute to the government. The individual willingness to pay for a standard is represented by the individual consumer surplus or utility. Hence, aggregate consumer surplus is a consistent measure for the total willingness to pay (and to contribute) for a certain level of the standard. Using aggregate consumer surplus as the consumers' surplus income in the consumers' contribution schedule ensures, therefore, the truthfulness of this schedule. Accordingly, while this specification assumes consumer heterogeneity, consumers can still be represented by one single interest group.

[11] To make a theoretical comparison possible, Swinnen and Vandemoortele (2009) analyze the three types of standards in the "risk specification," combined with elements of the "externality specification."

The relative importance of social and environmental standards compared to food safety and food quality standards depends on the specifics of the standards (which determine their marginal effects on consumer welfare), and cannot be ranked unambiguously.

A second result is that the relative importance of the various food standards does not imply that the most important are also necessarily the most important trade barriers—or protectionist instruments. The general relationship between food standards and protectionism is complex and depends not just on the nature of the standards but also on the interaction between the standard and differences in implementation costs, production costs (comparative advantage), and standard enforcement between domestic and foreign producers, as presented in the next section.

6   Trade and the Political Economy of Public Food Standards

An important aspect of public standards that has attracted a lot of attention is their potential use as instruments of "protection in disguise" (Vogel 1995). In fact, most studies on (the political economy of) standards in open economy models consider standards as protectionist instruments (Fischer and Serra 2000; Anderson, Damania, and Jackson 2004; Sturm 2006).

To analyze this issue it is important to first clarify some key elements in the relationship between trade and standards. For this purpose, we assume that there are only two interest groups; namely, consumers and producers $(j = p, c)$. Standards can be set to benefit (or "protect") producer or consumer interests. Hence, first it is important to define "protectionism" as producer protectionism (as it is usually understood) or consumer protection. Second, as with tariffs and trade restrictions, standards may either harm or benefit producers. Hence, unlike other studies suggest, there is no *ex ante* reason to see standards as producer protectionism. Third, while almost all standards affect trade, there is no simple relation between "trade distortions" and "producer protection."

The rest of this section is organized as follows. We first identify the key factors that characterize the relationship between trade and standards and its effects. Then we identify under which conditions standards reduce trade, i.e., act as "trade barriers" or enhance trade, i.e., act as "trade catalysts." Next we identify when there is

---

The authors argue that the disutility $d(c)$ of consuming goods with inferior food safety characteristics is larger than the disutility of consuming goods with inferior food quality characteristics. This is consistent with the result of Lusk and Briggeman (2009) that consumers assess food safety as the most important food value compared to other values related to food quality such as nutrition and taste.

"overstandardization" and "understandardization"; and finally we combine all these insights to evaluate the validity of the "standards-as-(producer-)protection" argument.

6.1   Comparative Advantage and Compliance with Standards

Trade and politically optimal standards are interrelated in several ways. First, trade affects the net impact of standards on producers and consumers as reflected in expression (4) and hence the political contributions and their relative influence. For a given level of consumption, with larger imports and lower domestic production, the effect of standards on aggregate producer profits will be smaller and hence producer contributions lower, and the lower will be producer influence on policy. In the extreme case when there is no domestic production, only consumer interests affect government policy. Formally, in this case the first term in equation (4) drops out, and the political equilibrium condition equals the optimality condition for consumers. Vice versa, for a given level of domestic production more imports and higher consumption levels imply that the effects on total consumer surplus will be larger and therefore consumer contributions and their influence on policy higher.

Second, standards may affect the comparative advantage in production between domestic and foreign producers, as standards may affect the relative production costs of foreign and domestic producers differently. This is the argument used by Anderson, Damania, and Jackson (2004) to argue why EU producers lobby against GMOs: they argue producers in countries such as the United States and Brazil have a comparative production cost advantage in the use of GM technology and therefore it would be rational for EU producers to support (rather than oppose) cost-increasing standards to ban GMOs. This argument makes assumptions on the nature of the supply functions and the technology, which may not hold in general. Standards will increase production cost advantages when they reinforce scale economies (reflected in a downward pivot of the supply function) but not when they have a scale-neutral impact or when they have scale diseconomies (causing an upward pivot of the supply function). Differences in these effects will induce differences in reactions to standards by domestic producers. However, the effects are conditional. Producers will oppose standards more (or support them less) if they have a comparative disadvantage and standards reinforce this, compared to when standards are scale-neutral. The opposite holds when standards reduce the comparative disadvantage vis-à-vis foreign producers.[12]

Notice that, although these factors do relate standards and trade, they do not say anything about standards being trade-distorting or protectionist measures.

---

[12] Similarly, producers would support more (or oppose less) if they had a comparative advantage and standards reinforce this—and vice versa. However, our model focuses on the import case.

6.2   Standards as Catalysts or Barriers to Trade?

An important implication of this model is that standards (almost) always affect trade. Only in very special circumstances do standards not affect trade. This is when the effect on domestic production exactly offsets the effect on consumption.

When standards reduce trade, they are "trade barriers." However, when imports increase, standards work as "catalysts to trade" (Maertens and Swinnen 2007). This will be the case when the marginal consumption gain (loss) from the standard is larger (smaller) than the marginal gain (loss) from the standard in domestic production. Moreover, as we shall discuss next, whether trade flows increase or decrease upon introduction of a standard in itself does not automatically relate to (or is not necessarily equivalent to) producer protectionism.

6.3   Over- and Understandardization

To assess whether public standards reduce welfare (i.e., are set at suboptimal levels) Swinnen and Vandemoortele (2011) use the same framework to identify optimal policy as is used in evaluating tariffs in traditional trade theory; that is, by comparing it to the socially optimal trade policy. The political equilibrium is said to be welfare-reducing (suboptimal) when the politically optimal tariff t^* differs from the socially optimal tariff $t^{\#}$. In a small open economy, this analysis leads to the well-known result that the socially optimal tariff level is zero and free trade is optimal, i.e., a positive tariff that constrains trade is harmful to social welfare.

Similarly, we compare the politically optimal standard s^* with the socially optimal standard $s^{\#}$ in a small open economy. To determine $s^{\#}$ we maximize the welfare function as defined in equation (3). The socially optimal standard $s^{\#}$ is determined by[13]

$$\sum_{j} \frac{\partial \Pi_j(s^{\#})}{\partial s} = 0. \tag{6}$$

It is clear from comparing conditions (4) and (6) that the politically optimal standard s^* will only equal the socially optimal standard $s^{\#}$ when all α_j are equal in the political equilibrium, and/or when all $\frac{\partial \Pi_j}{\partial s}$ equal zero at $s^{\#}$. Notice that $s^{\#} > 0$ is possible. In this case trade flows may change from the imposition of the standard, but this change is socially optimal, i.e., it increases domestic welfare.

Consider the case where the only interest groups are producers and consumers $(j = p, c)$. If the above condition is not fulfilled, i.e., if α_p and α_c are different in the government's objective function, the political and social outcomes will be

---

[13] This first-order condition is subject to $s^{\#} \geq 0$; otherwise $s^{\#} = 0$.

different.[14] Again, however, the diversion between the two optima may be in either direction. Hence, "overstandardization" ($s^* > s^\#$) or "understandardization" ($s^* < s^\#$) may result.

If $\alpha_p > \alpha_c$, this will result in overstandardization ($s^* > s^\#$) when producers' profits increase with a higher standard $\left(\frac{\partial \Pi_p}{\partial s} > 0\right)$ at $s^\#$ and in understandardization otherwise. The resulting overstandardization creates higher profits for producers than in the social optimum. Hence, this overstandardization distorts trade to the advantage of the domestic sector. Inversely with $\frac{\partial \Pi_p}{\partial s} < 0$ at $s^\#$, the resulting understandardization (given that $s^\# > 0$) reduces the negative effect of the standard on producers' profits. Hence, domestic producers benefit from this understandardization such that it serves as protection in disguise.

In a similar fashion, $\alpha_c > \alpha_p$ results in overstandardization when $\frac{\partial \Pi_c}{\partial s} > 0$ and in understandardization when $\frac{\partial \Pi_c}{\partial s} < 0$ at $s^\#$. Whether these suboptimal standards are "protectionist" or not depends on the impact of standards on producers. However, at $s^\#$, $\frac{\partial \Pi_p}{\partial s}$ and $\frac{\partial \Pi_c}{\partial s}$ always have opposite signs (except for the trivial case where both equal zero and $s^* = s^\#$). Hence, when overstandardization results $\left(\frac{\partial \Pi_c}{\partial s} > 0\right)$, producers always lose from overstandardization with respect to their situation in the social optimum as $\frac{\partial \Pi_p}{\partial s} < 0$ at $s^\#$. The politically optimal standard s^* is then, although suboptimal, not "protectionist." Vice versa, producers will be hurt by understandardization $\left(\frac{\partial \Pi_c}{\partial s} < 0\right)$ as $\frac{\partial \Pi_p}{\partial s} > 0$ at $s^\#$, with $s^\# > 0$. In both cases the suboptimal standards result in trade distortions that do not protect domestic producers.

7   PRIVATE AND PUBLIC FOOD STANDARDS

So far we have focused solely on public food standards set by governments. However, it is well documented that private food standards, introduced by private companies, are increasingly important (Henson 2004). Firms have the possibility of introducing private standards in the same domains in which the government imposes public standards, such as food safety, food quality, and social and environmental aspects of food production. Producers have thus not only the option of lobbying the government with the goal of influencing decision-making on public standards but also of introducing their own private standards, or doing both. Not surprisingly, extending the model to integrate this joint decision-making by private companies significantly complicates the analysis. In fact, formally developing such an integrated model and deriving its results requires a full chapter in itself (see, e.g., Vandemoortele 2011). We shall therefore limit ourselves here to a discussion of the issues determining the relation between public and private food standards.

---

[14] We do not discuss the case with different lobby weights where $\frac{\partial \Pi_p}{\partial s} = \frac{\partial \Pi_c}{\partial s} = 0$ at $s^\#$, implying that $s^\#$ is optimal for both lobby groups. In that case neither consumers nor producers have incentives to lobby for a different standard, and $s^* = s^\#$.

First, the sequence in which the standard setting of private and public actors takes place is important. When both types of standards are set simultaneously, producers face a simultaneous decision problem. They have to decide whether to invest in a private standard, whether to lobby with respect to a public standard, or whether to do both. Other cases of sequencing are when firms can set private standards before the government introduces its regulation on public standards, or vice versa that public standards are introduced first.

Second, costs of implementing standards may differ between public and private standards. McCluskey (2007) distinguishes between the mechanism of implementing the standard and the standard itself. She assumes that private standards are from the company's point more flexible in response to changes in technology and consumer preferences than public standards. Hence, adopting a private standard instead of a public standard may be advantageous to companies, as they can choose the private standard that least increases implementation costs. Under the assumption that private companies can impose their private standards first, McCluskey (2007) shows that firms can minimize the negative effect on revenues of standards by pre-empting the public standard setting of governments by imposing their own private standards.

Third, another aspect is the differential impact of private versus public standards on foreign producers, which also implies that the price effect of standards will differ between public and private standards. In the case of public standards, importers will have to satisfy the standards. However, foreign importers do not necessarily comply with private standards set by domestic companies. A special case would be when private standards set by domestic companies become de facto public standards (such as the case with GlobalGAP standards in the EU fruit and vegetable retail sector). In this case importers may have to follow the same (private) standards as domestic companies. However, in other cases foreign companies may not abide by private standards of domestic companies. Depending on market conditions, this may induce domestic companies to lobby for public standards rather than to impose private ones.

Fourth, consumers' utility may be affected differently by public and private standards. For example, private standards may be perceived as more or less credible than their public counterparts. However, this credibility affects the effect of a standard on consumer utility. Hence, the optimal private and public standards would be different.

Finally, there is the important issue of enforceability of standards. One factor is that private companies may not be able to enforce some standards if there are potential free-rider problems at the sectoral level with some producers trying to benefit from not adhering to the standards. Another factor is that the standard's credibility and thus the effect on consumer utility may be affected by the consumer's perception of the enforcement of the standard setting, and whether it differs between private and public standards. This attitude can relate to the quality of the institutions of a country and its perception on the objectives and constraints of those involved in implementing and controlling standards in the private and the public sector. Moreover, enforcement of standards on imported goods may be different between private and public standards, as different mechanisms and actors will ensure enforcement.

8 CONCLUSIONS

....

In this chapter we presented insights from the emerging literature on the political economy of public food standards. The chapter first identified the different interest groups that may be affected by public food standards and what their specific interests are. We then used a formal conceptual framework of the political economy of public standards to derive the politically optimal public standard and to analyze how different factors influence this political equilibrium. The political weights of the respective groups, the standards' relative benefits and costs for the different interest groups, consumer quality preferences, and implementation costs of domestic and foreign producers all affect the politically optimal standard.

The observed positive relationship between public food standards and economic development results from a combination of these effects. Higher income levels lead to more stringent standards not only because of higher consumer preferences for quality, but also because of less costly enforcement of standards and lower production costs related to standards for domestic producers. In combination these factors may result in a pro-standard coalition of consumers and producers in rich countries and an anti-standard coalition in poor countries.

If consumer perceptions of the effects of public food standards are biased, this will obviously have an impact on the politically optimal standards. Both (the structure of) the media, the level of development of a country, and consumers' professional activities or geographic location may influence these perceptions.

The nature of food standards is likely to affect the level of standards. Food safety standards are likely to be set at higher levels than public food quality standards because food safety standards have a relatively stronger marginal impact on consumer welfare.

Furthermore, there is an important relationship between trade and standards. Trade affects the net impact of standards on domestic producers and consumers and hence their political contributions. Standards may also affect the comparative production cost advantage between countries, which may lead to either higher or lower standards. In this way, standards may serve as protection in disguise, or not. Standards may be "barriers" to trade but also "catalysts" to trade, and both "under-" or "overstandardization" may occur, depending on a variety of factors. These findings imply that the effects of specific standards should be analyzed carefully before categorizing them as protectionist instruments.

Finally, in an environment where both private and public standards are present, public decision-making becomes more complicated because of several interactions between private and public standards. Four factors play a role in the equilibrium set of standards: the sequencing of the private and public decision-making on standards, their respective implementation costs, their respective impact on imports, and their respective enforcement. Each of these factors will affect the equilibrium choices of private and public standard setting.

References

Anderson, K., R. Damania, and L. A. Jackson. 2004. *Trade, Standards, and the Political Economy of Genetically Modified Food.* World Bank Policy Research Working Paper No. 3395. Washington, DC: World Bank.

Ansell, C., and D. Vogel. 2006. *What's the Beef?* Cambridge, MA: MIT Press.

Baltzer, K. 2010. *Minimum Quality Standards and International Trade.* FOI Working Papers No. 2010/15. University of Copenhagen: Institute of Food and Resource Economics.

Barrett, C. B., and Y. Yang. 2001. "Rational Incompatibility with International Product Standards." *Journal of International Economics* 54: 171–91.

Barrett, S. 1994. "Strategic Environmental Policy and International Trade." *Journal of Public Economics* 54: 325–38.

Becker, G. 1983. "A Theory of Competition among Pressure Groups for Political Influence." *Quarterly Journal of Economics* 98: 371–400.

Bernheim, B. D., and M. D. Whinston. 1986. "Menu Auctions, Resource Allocation, and Economic Influence." *Quarterly Journal of Economics* 101/1: 1–31.

Besley, T., and M. Ghatak. 2007. "Retailing Public Goods: The Economics of Corporate Social Responsibility." *Journal of Public Economics* 91/9: 1645–63.

Bhagwati, J. N. 1982. "Directly Unproductive Profit-Seeking Activities." *Journal of Political Economy* 90: 988–1002.

Bockstael, N. 1984. "The Welfare Implications of Minimum Quality Standards." *American Journal of Agricultural Economics* 66: 466–71.

Brom, F. W. A. 2000. "Food, Consumer Concerns, and Trust: Food Ethics for a Globalizing Market." *Journal of Agriculture and Environmental Ethics* 12: 127–39.

Cadot, O., J. de Melo, and M. Olarreaga. 2004. "Lobbying, Counterlobbying, and the Structure of Tariff Protection in Poor and Rich Countries." *World Bank Economic Review* 18/3: 345–66.

Cooper, R., and W. Ross. 1985. "Product Warranties and Double Moral Hazard." *Rand Journal of Economics* 16/1: 103–13.

Costa-Font, M., J. M. Gil, and W. B. Traill. 2008. "Consumer Acceptance, Valuation of and Attitudes towards Genetically Modified Food: Review and Implications for Food Policy." *Food Policy* 33: 99–111.

Crampes, C., and A. Hollander. 1995. "Duopoly and Quality Standards." *European Economic Review* 39: 71–82.

Curtis, K. R., J. J. McCluskey, and J. F. M. Swinnen. 2008. "Differences in Global Risk Perceptions of Biotechnology and the Political Economy of the Media." *International Journal of Global Environmental Issues* 8/1-2: 79–89.

————, and T. I. Wahl. 2004. "Consumer Acceptance of Genetically Modified Food Products in the Developing World." *AgBioForum* 7/1-2: 69–74.

Elbasha, E. H., and T. L. Riggs. 2003. "The Effects of Information on Producer and Consumer Incentives to Undertake Food Safety Efforts: A Theoretical Model and Policy Implications." *Agribusiness* 19/1: 29–42.

Emons, W. 1988. "Warranties, Moral Hazard, and the Lemons Problem." *Journal of Economic Theory* 46: 16–33.

Fischer, R., and P. Serra. 2000. "Standards and Protection." *Journal of International Economics* 52: 377–400.

Flynn, J., P. Slovic, and C. K. Mertz. 1993. "Decidedly Different: Expert and Public Views of Risks from a Radioactive Waste Repository." *Risk Analysis* 13/6: 643–8.

Fulton, M., and K. Giannakas. 2004. "Inserting GM Products into the Food Chain: The Market and Welfare Effects of Different Labeling and Regulatory Regimes." *American Journal of Agricultural Economics* 86/1: 42–60.

Grossman, G. M., and E. Helpman. 1994. "Protection for Sale." *American Economic Review* 84/4: 833–50.

————. 1995. "Trade Wars and Trade Talks." *Journal of Political Economy* 103/4: 675–708.

Henson, S. 2004. "National Laws, Regulations, and Institutional Capabilities for Standards Development." Paper presented at the World Bank training seminar on Standards and Trade, Washington, DC.

Hillman, A. L. 1982. "Declining Industries and Political-Support Protectionist Motives." *American Economic Review* 72/5: 1180–7.

——1989. *The Political Economy of Protection*. Chur: Harwood.

——and H. W. Ursprung. 1988. "Domestic Politics, Foreign Interests, and International Trade Policy." *American Economic Review* 78/4: 729–45.

Hoban, T. J., and P. A. Kendall. 1993. *Consumer Attitudes about Food Biotechnology*. Raleigh: North Carolina Cooperative Extension Service.

Hossain, F., B. Onyango, B. Schilling, W. Hallman, and A. Adelaja. 2003. "Product Attributes, Consumer Benefits and Public Approval of Genetically Modified Foods." *International Journal of Consumer Studies* 27: 353–65.

Jeanneret, M., and T. Verdier. 1996. "Standardization and Protection in a Vertical Differentiation Model." *European Journal of Political Economy* 12: 253–71.

Kalaitzandonakes, N., L. A. Marks, and S. S. Vickner. 2004. "Media Coverage of Biotech Foods, and Influence on Consumer Choice." *American Journal of Agricultural Economics* 86/5: 1238–46.

Krueger, A. O. 1974. "The Political Economy of the Rent-Seeking Society." *American Economic Review* 64/3: 291–303.

Leland, H. E. 1979. "Quacks, Lemons, and Licensing: A Theory of Minimum Quality Standards." *Journal of Political Economy* 87/6: 1328–46.

Loureiro, M. L. 2003. "GMO Food Labelling in the EU: Tracing 'the Seeds of Dispute.'" *EuroChoices* 2/1: 18–22.

Lusk, J. L., and B. C. Briggeman. 2009. "Food Values." *American Journal of Agricultural Economics* 91/1: 184–96.

McCluskey, J. J. 2007. "Public and Private Food Quality Standards: Recent Trends and Strategic Incentives." In J. F. M. Swinnen, ed., *Global Supply Chains, Standards, and the Poor*. Wallingford: CABI.

——and J. F. M. Swinnen. 2004. "Political Economy of the Media and Consumer Perceptions of Biotechnology." *American Journal of Agricultural Economics* 86/5: 1230–7.

——, K. M. Grimsrud, H. Ouchi, and T. I. Wahl. 2003. "Consumer Response to Genetically Modified Food Products in Japan." *Agriculture and Resource Economics Review* 32/2: 222–31.

Maertens, M., and J. F. M. Swinnen. 2007. "Standards as Barriers and Catalysts for Trade, Growth and Poverty Reduction." *Journal of International Agricultural Trade and Development* 4/1: 47–62.

Magee, S. P., W. A. Brock, and L. Young. 1989. *Black Hole Tariffs and Endogenous Policy Theory: Political Economy in General Equilibrium*. Cambridge: Cambridge University Press.

Marette, S., and J. C. Beghin. 2010. "Are Standards Always Protectionist?" *Review of International Economics* 18/1: 179–92.

Mussa, M., and S. Rosen. 1978. "Monopoly and Product Quality." *Journal of Economic Theory* 18: 301–17.

North, D. C. 1990. *Institutions, Institutional Change and Economic Performance*. New York: Cambridge University Press.

Roe, B., and I. Sheldon. 2007. "Credence Good Labeling: The Efficiency and Distributional Implications of Several Policy Approaches." *American Journal of Agricultural Economics* 89/4: 1020–33.

Ronnen, U. 1991. "Minimum Quality Standards, Fixed Costs, and Competition." *RAND Journal of Economics* 22/4: 490–504.

Savadori, L., S. Savio, E. Nocotra, R. Rumiati, M. Finucane, and P. Slovic. 2004. "Expert and Public Perception of Risk from Biotechnology." *Risk Analysis* 24: 1289–99.

Schleich, T. 1999. "Environmental Quality with Endogenous Domestic and Trade Policies." *European Journal of Political Economy* 15: 53–71.

Shepherd, R., D. Hedderley, C. Howard, and L. J. Frewer. 1998. "Methodological Approaches to Assessing Risk Perception Associated with Food-Related Risks." *Risk Analysis* 18: 95–102.

Spence, M. 1976. "Product Differentiation and Welfare." *American Economic Review* 66: 407–14.

Stigler, G. J. 1971. "The Theory of Economic Regulation." *Bell Journal of Economics and Management Science* 3: 3–18.

Sturm, D. M. 2006. "Product Standards, Trade Disputes, and Protectionism." *Canadian Journal of Economics* 39/2: 564–81.

Swinnen, J. F. M., and T. Vandemoortele. 2008. "The Political Economy of Nutrition and Health Standards in Food Markets." *Review of Agricultural Economics* 30/3: 460–8.

———, 2009. "Are Food Safety Standards Different from Other Food Standards? A Political Economy Perspective." *European Review of Agricultural Economics* 36/4: 507–23.

———, 2011. "Trade and the Political Economy of Food Standards." *Journal of Agricultural Economics* 62/2: 259–80.

Sykes, A. O. 1995. *Product Standards for Internationally Integrated Goods Markets*. Washington, DC: Brookings Institution.

Thilmany, D. D., and C. B. Barrett. 1997. "Regulatory Barriers in an Integrating World Food Market." *Review of Agricultural Economics* 19/1: 91–107.

Tian, H. 2003. "Eco-Labelling Scheme, Environmental Protection, and Protectionism." *Canadian Journal of Economics* 36/3: 608–33.

Tirole, J. 1988. *The Theory of Industrial Organization*. Cambridge, MA: MIT Press.

Valletti, T. M. 2000. "Minimum Quality Standards under Cournot Competition." *Journal of Regulatory Economics* 18/3: 235–45.

Vandemoortele, T. 2011. "Political and Economic Theory of Standards." Ph.D. diss. University of Leuven.

Vogel, D. 1995. *Trading Up: Consumer and Environmental Regulation in a Global Economy*. Cambridge, MA: Harvard University Press.

CHAPTER 17

HEALTH INVESTMENTS UNDER RISK AND AMBIGUITY

OLOF JOHANSSON-STENMAN[*]

1 INTRODUCTION

It is obvious that food-related public health investments, and regulations more generally, have to deal with uncertainty. For example, how should we deal with genetically engineered food and various chemical food additives? On the one hand, these new technologies offer potentially very large productivity improvements, with corresponding potential welfare improvements. This is not least important in developing countries, where about 1 billion of the world's population live on less than 1 dollar per day (Collier 2007) and about the same number of people are malnourished (FAO 2008); see also Abdulai and Kuhlgatz (Chapter 13 in this volume) on issues related to food security in developing countries. On the other hand, there are, of course, various risks associated with these technologies. Somehow we must deal with both the potential benefits and the risks. The question of the present chapter is how, in principle, this should be done. In other words, we are intrinsically concerned with the normative *ought*-question concerning how a public decision maker should behave rather than the descriptive *is*-question corresponding to how such a decision maker behaves, or is expected to behave, under uncertainty.

While uncertainty has been incorporated into mainstream economic theory for a long time (e.g., Arrow 1971; Drèze and Modigliani 1972; Dreze 1987), there are many problems with applying the conventional approach in practice. In particular, there is a

* I am grateful to Nicholas Treich, Johan Stennek, an anonymous referee, and the editor Jutta Roosen for very constructive comments. Financial support from the Swedish Research Council is gratefully acknowledged.

fair amount of evidence that people often deviate systematically from von Neumann and Morgenstern's (1944) expected utility (EU) theory. Indeed, by now there are a large number of competing non-EU models, of which prospect theory (Kahneman and Tversky 1979; Tversky and Kahneman 1992; Schmidt, Starmer, and Sugden 2008) constitutes the most prominent example.[1] However, whether there are any direct implications of these alternative theories for normative conclusions, in the sense of how a social decision maker ought to act, is less clear. It appears reasonable to view much of the behavior reflecting deviations from expected utility as indications of what Kahneman, Wakker, and Sarin (1997) and Kahneman and Thaler (2006) denote *decision* utility, simply reflecting choice, as opposed to *experienced* utility, reflecting well-being. Consequently, one can argue that many of the observed deviations from EU theory have no direct implications for how a social decision maker should act.

However, the conventional von Neumann and Morgenstern (1944) approach to EU theory assumes that the probability distribution is known, whereas this is rarely the case in reality, where there are instead often largely diverging views even among the experts. One can argue, and it is indeed often argued, that this fact makes the conventional EU approach unsuitable for social decision-making under uncertainty.

Still, according to *subjective* expected utility (SEU) theory, as famously expressed and axiomatized already by Savage (1954),[2] rational decision makers should form their own subjective probability distributions and behave *as if* these probabilities were the objective ones. For example, suppose your decision regarding what kind of margarine to buy depends in part on how healthy (and unhealthy) the different kinds are. In making this judgment you will obviously have to rely on external experts, and typically also on secondary sources of these opinions as expressed, for example, by media and friends. If you read another article claiming that type A margarine is better for you than type B, you would perhaps update your judgment somewhat in favor of type A margarine, etc.

Note that SEU theory doesn't say much about how these subjective probabilities are formed. Indeed, one individual may generally trust medical experts with respect to food recommendations, another may agree with a particular type of alternative medicine school, while a third may be largely guided by religious beliefs. Obviously, these three individuals may arrive at very different subjective probabilities regarding the health consequences of different kinds of food. SEU theory doesn't say that one individual's subjective probabilities are "better" than others, nor does it say that they are equally good. SEU theory is simply silent on these issues.

However, SEU theory does imply restrictions on the structure of these expected utilities for each individual. Notably, it implies that compound lotteries should be

---

[1] See Starmer (2000) for an overview of non-expected utility theory, Fox (Ch. 3 in this volume) for an overview of risk preferences and food consumption, and Just (Ch. 4 in this volume) for a more general discussion of behavioral economics and the food consumer.

[2] See Ramsey (1931) and de Finetti (1937) for earlier contributions to SEU theory that Savage (1954) incorporated into the von Neumann and Morgenstern (1944) framework.

evaluated at their resulting net probabilities. For example, suppose that 100 experts are judging whether or not a certain food is unhealthy or not. For analytical simplicity, assume that you know that precisely one of them is right and that you consider them equally likely to be right, i.e., you believe that each has a 1 percent probability of being right. One of them believes that the food is unhealthy with a probability of 90 percent, while all others believe that the food is unhealthy with a probability of 1 percent. The net probability that the food is unhealthy in this compound lottery is then equal to $0.01 \cdot 90\% + 0.99 \cdot 1\% = 0.9\% + 0.99\% = 1.89\%.$[3]

However, while this kind of reasoning may seem plausible, much experimental and empirical evidence suggests otherwise. In fact, it seems that people typically have a particular aversion to unknown risks and hence place more weight on the judgments of more pessimistic experts. If we denote the uncertainty with respect to the true probability *ambiguity*, it seems, in other words, that people often tend to be *ambiguity-averse* (Camerer and Weber 1992). An ambiguity-averse individual would then behave as if, in the above example, the resulting probability that the food is unhealthy is higher than 1.89 percent.

Ambiguity aversion has been shown to be economically relevant and to persist in many different experimental settings and samples (Sarin and Weber 1993; Gilboa 2004) including business owners and managers who are supposedly familiar with decisions under uncertainty (Chesson and Viscusi 2003). Additionally, it is often found that people are willing to spend substantial amounts of money to avoid ambiguous processes in favour of processes that are equivalent in terms of SEU theory (Becker and Brownson 1964; Chow and Sarin 2001). There is also evidence in terms of conventional empirical studies, in particular from the financial sector, that the observed pattern cannot be explained by conventional theory, but is consistent with theories incorporating ambiguity aversion (see Camerer and Weber 1992; Mukerji and Tallon 2001; Chen and Epstein 2002; Gilboa 2004).

With respect to food safety, Shogren (2005) compared the monetary equivalents for risk elimination under non-ambiguous and ambiguous probability scenarios, respectively, in a survey about the foodborne pathogen *Salmonella*. He found a higher mean willingness to pay for a given probability reduction under the ambiguous scenario, although the difference is not large enough to be statistically significant. Other health-related studies include Ritov and Baron (1990), who, based on a hypothetical experiment, found reluctance to vaccination under missing information about side effects of the vaccine; and Riddel and Shaw (2006), who, based on survey evidence from Nevada residents, found a large effect of ambiguity on attitudes toward risks related to nuclear

---

[3] Moreover, SEU theory implies that the individual would update the subjective probabilities in a Bayesian way when new information becomes available. For example, if the ninety-nine more optimistic experts change their minds so that they now believe that the food is unhealthy with a probability of 2 percent, then the new resulting probability that the food is unhealthy is equal to $0.01 \cdot 90\% + 0.99 \cdot 2\% = 0.9\% + 1.98\% = 2.88\%.$

waste transport. Theoretically, Treich (2010) shows that ambiguity aversion tends to increase the value of a statistical life.

This chapter deals with the question of how a public decision maker should think about issues of known and unknown risks. In doing this, a simple baseline model is used throughout the chapter, where a public decision maker can invest in order to decrease the health risk. Since the investment is risky, the question concerns how much to invest. While I shall model a simple investment that decreases the health damage and that can be bought at a given per unit price, one can interpret the investment much more broadly as any public measure that has positive expected health consequences and that is associated with some social costs (see, e.g., Lichtenberg and Zilberman 1988; Lichtenberg, Zilberman, and Bogen 1989; Cropper 1992). For example, the food industry faces a large number of detailed regulations including labeling and food safety standards motivated ultimately by health reasons. Strengthening these regulations is in most cases costly (see, e.g., Chapters 19 by Marette and Roosen and 21 by Hoffmann in this volume). This is so whether the costs eventually fall on the food company owners as lower profits or on the consumers as higher prices.

The optimal investment levels are then derived and compared for a number of different decision rules, starting with the simplest ones and then gradually adding more complexities. Section 2 discusses three decision rules: the best guess, the maximin, and the expected value decision rules. The best guess decision rule simply implies maximization of the relevant decision variable, here consumption, for the most likely outcome of the risky variable. The maximin decision rule implies that we are making the outcome as good as possible for the worst-case scenario, whereas with the expected value decision rule we maximize the expected value of consumption, implying that we take all possible outcomes and their associated probabilities into account.

Section 3 presents the St Petersburg paradox, which clearly shows that the expected value decision rule cannot be universally applied. Section 4 introduces a non-linear utility function to the model, meaning that we can handle risk aversion and also resolve the St Petersburg paradox. The optimal investment rules are then derived for different utility specifications. Section 5 presents the optimal investment rules for a special case of a state-dependent expected utility model, namely when consumption and the absence of damage are imperfect substitutes.

Whereas Sections 2–5 handle the probabilities as exogenously given, Sections 6–8 in contrast deal with the problem when the decision maker does not know the objective probabilities. Section 6 presents yet another paradox, the Ellsberg paradox, which illustrates that most people do not seem to apply SEU theory as their universal decision rule when the probabilities are not known. Section 7 deals with the problem of unknown probabilities by adding probability distributions of the probabilities. Decision rules for three different models that allow for ambiguity aversion (in addition to risk aversion), i.e., that put a larger weight on the more pessimistic probability distributions, are then derived and discussed. Section 8 returns to the more fundamental question regarding whether models of ambiguity aversion can be justified for normative analysis or whether we should after all stick to SEU models. Section 9 concludes the chapter.

2 Best Guess, Maximin, and Expected Value Decision Rules

In order to be able to focus clearly on how to deal with uncertainty, the basic model will throughout the chapter be kept very simple and deal with the choice of a single health investment level, I. For the same simplicity reason, the model will deal with a representative individual in a static framework, implying that distributional, discounting, and timing issues are ignored and that no meaningful distinction can be made between income and wealth. Strategic interaction between agents will also be ignored, such that all decision rules are conducted in games against nature.

2.1 The Basic Model

Consider a representative individual who faces the budget

$$C = Y - I - D, \tag{1}$$

where C is consumption, Y is gross income, I is health investments, and D is damage costs related to imperfect food safety. This formulation implies that consumption and the absence of health damage are perfect substitutes, which is not a central assumption here but will be central when introducing risk aversion. The damage costs, in turn, are written as

$$D = D_0 f(I), \tag{2}$$

where $f'(I) < 0, f''(I) > 0$ and $f(0) = 1, f(\infty) = 0$. D_0 is a stochastic variable with n possible outcomes, $D_0^1, \ldots, D_0^n$ occurring with (objective) probabilities $p^1, \ldots, p^n$, respectively. Thus, the damage cost equals D_0 if no investment is made and the larger the investment, the lower the cost; yet the damage cost will always be positive irrespective of the investment. This pattern appears fairly realistic for most potential food safety investments in practice. The following exponential function constitutes an example of a functional form of f that is consistent with this pattern:

$$f(I) = \exp(-\alpha I). \tag{3}$$

The problem of the decision maker is to choose the investment level I before knowing which value of D_0 will materialize. What should the decision maker then do?

2.2 The Best Guess Decision Rule

Perhaps the most straightforward alternative for a decision maker is to go for the most likely outcome and then invest optimally given that this outcome will occur. Suppose that the most likely outcome is given by D_0^L. This clearly implies that

$$C = Y - I - D_0^L f(I), \tag{4}$$

which is maximized for

$$\frac{\partial C}{\partial I} = -1 - D_0^L f'(I) = 0, \tag{5}$$

so that

$$f'(I) = -1/D_0^L. \tag{6}$$

We can then, in principle, solve for I by using the inverse function of f'. Since I shall do this repeatedly for different cases in this chapter, I shall go through this procedure in detail. Consider first the general case where

$$f'(I) = A, \tag{7}$$

where A is a constant. Then we can, implicitly, solve for I such that

$$I = g(A), \tag{8}$$

where g is the inverse function of f'. Since $f'(I) < 0$, we know that $g'(A) > 0$. Moreover, since A has a monotonic relation with $-1/A$, we can alternatively write

$$I = h(-1/A) = h(-1/f'(I)), \tag{9}$$

where $h'(-1/A) > 0$. In the case here, where $A = -1/D_0^L$, we then have

$$I = h(D_0^L), \tag{10}$$

where $h' > 0$. Thus, we have, not surprisingly, found that the larger the most likely damage costs (in absence of any investments), the larger the optimal investments.

In the special case where f has the specific exponential function form mentioned above in (3), we have

$$I = \frac{1}{\alpha} \ln\left(\alpha D_0^L\right). \tag{11}$$

An obvious advantage with this approach is that it is cognitively straightforward and computationally undemanding, which is presumably the reason it is often used, including in scientific contexts. For example, in the literature dealing with how much to invest in order to decrease the negative effects of global warming, the optimization is in most cases made based on the assumption of a known temperature increase for a given emission trajectory and known costs for a given temperature increase, whereas both relations are highly uncertain; see, e.g., Stern (2007).

Yet, an equally obvious drawback with this decision rule is that it completely ignores the outcomes of the (perhaps only slightly) less likely alternatives. For example, suppose that there are two possible outcomes, *I* and *II*, where the initial damage in *I* is zero while it is very large in *II*, and where we assume that the probability that *I* occurs is 55 percent and that *II* occurs is 45 percent. Then it does hardly seem reasonable to optimize based on the assumption that *I* will occur.

Thus, although the above decision rule might be a way in which we often solve problems in practice, since it is cognitively quite straightforward and computationally undemanding, it is difficult to justify as a general principle.

2.3 The Maximin Decision Rule

An alternative decision rule, which is equally straightforward as the one above, is the maximin decision rule, meaning that we make the outcome as good as possible for the worst-case scenario. This means that we maximize consumption for the case where the initial damage D_0 is greatest among the possible alternatives, i.e., irrespective of the probabilities. Thus, the decision maker chooses an optimal investment for the case where high damage occurs. We would then maximize

$$C = Y - I - D_0^{Max} f(I),\tag{12}$$

implying that

$$f'(I) = -1/D_0^{Max}\tag{13}$$

Using (9) where $A = -1/D_0^{Max}$, we then have

$$I = h(D_0^{Max}).\tag{14}$$

By comparing (10) and (14), it clearly follows that the optimal investment is larger by using the maximin decision rule than when using the best guess decision rule. This is also true, of course, if we use the specific functional form according to (3), in which case we obtain that

$$I = \frac{1}{\alpha}\ln\left(\alpha D_0^{Max}\right).\tag{15}$$

This alternative can be seen as the application of some precautionary principle, interpreted loosely.

However, while it may make perfect sense to apply some kind of precautionary measures (e.g., Gollier, Jullien, and Treich 2000; Eeckhoudt, Gollier, and Schlesinger 2005), it is difficult to defend the maximin criterion as a general principle. For example, according to Bostrom (2002), the probability that an asteroid larger than 1 kilometer in diameter will hit Earth in a single year is approximately 1/500,000, and the probability that it will affect a single country or part of a country is, of course, correspondingly smaller. Suppose that the worst outcome for a particular food-related prospect is that the area will be hit by a large asteroid. Clearly, it does not make sense to base the optimization regarding which investments to make on the assumption that the area will be hit by an asteroid next year.

More generally, it appears difficult to base a general decision rule on only a subset of the possible outcomes. I therefore next turn to a decision rule that takes all possible outcomes into account.

2.4 The Expected Value Decision Rule

An alternative to the above decision rules is instead to maximize the expected consumption, which is equivalent to minimizing the expected costs in terms of I and D together, meaning that we would use the information about all possible outcomes. Then we would maximize

$$E(C) = \sum_{i=1}^{n} p^i \big(Y - I - D_0^i f(I) \big), \tag{16}$$

implying that

$$f'(I) = -\frac{1}{\sum_{i=1}^{n} p^i D_0^i} = -\frac{1}{E(D_0)}, \tag{17}$$

so that the optimal investment, using (9), is given by

$$I = h\Big(\sum_{i=1}^{n} p^i D_0^i \Big) = h(E(D_0)). \tag{18}$$

Thus, the optimal investment is larger than in the best guess scenario but lower than when using the maximin decision rule. This is again true, of course, if we use the specific functional form according to (3), in which case we obtain that

$$I = \frac{1}{\alpha} \ln \Big(\alpha \sum_{i=1}^{n} p^i D_0^i \Big) = \frac{1}{\alpha} \ln(\alpha E(D_0)). \tag{19}$$

Note in particular that the optimum conditions are independent of the initial income Y and hence also of uncertainty regarding the income level.

3 THE ST PETERSBURG PARADOX

So far, the principle of maximizing the expected value appears easier to defend than the alternative ones. However, this principle is also difficult to defend generally, as has been known for some hundred years. The most well-known example that clearly shows the limitations of simply maximizing the expected value, or expected consumption in our case, is obtained from the so-called St Petersburg paradox.

Consider a lottery where a fair coin is flipped repeatedly until it comes up tails. The total number of flips, n, determines the prize, which equals 2^n. For example, if the coin comes up tails the first time, the prize is $2^1 = 2$, and then the lottery ends. If instead it comes up heads the first three times and then comes up tails, the prize is $2^4 = 16$, and then the lottery ends, etc. Now, what is the value of this lottery? The expected dollar value is simply given by

$$\sum_{i=1}^{\infty} p(\text{total number of flips} = i) \cdot 2^i = 0.5 \cdot 2 + 0.5^2 \cdot 2^2 + 0.5^3 \cdot 2^3 \ldots = 1 + 1 + 1 \ldots, \quad (20)$$

and is thus clearly infinite. Yet, most people are not willing to pay very much for participating in such a lottery, and moreover one cannot credibly argue that rational people *should*. This shows clearly that the maximizing expected value decision rule does not constitute a reasonable universal decision rule either. Alternatively expressed, risk neutrality, which is implicitly assumed in the expected value decision rule, is generally not a valid assumption.

A solution to the St Petersburg paradox had already been proposed by Daniel Bernoulli in 1738, who assumed that people maximize *utility* rather than *money*, and that utility is concave in money, in turn implying risk aversion. Bernoulli assumed a logarithmic utility function, but the essential assumption is that the utility function is concave in income (or wealth). How much, then, would a utility-maximizing individual be willing to pay for participating in such a lottery? Consider an individual with (a cardinal) utility function $U = \ln Y$, where Y is income. An individual who maximizes expected utility would then at most be willing to pay CV for the lottery, such that

$$\ln(Y) = \sum_{i=1}^{\infty} 0.5^i \cdot \ln(Y - CV + 2^i). \quad (21)$$

While this maximum willingness to pay is not possible to find analytically,[4] it is straightforward to obtain it numerically. It is easy, moreover, to show that the maximum willingness to pay increases monotonically with the initial income Y. For example, when Y is US$10 million, the maximum willingness to pay is still less than $40. Thus, simply introducing a logarithmic utility function can explain the St Petersburg paradox. It is also worth mentioning that the degree of concavity implicitly

---

[4] Yet, it is easy to solve analytically for the case where utility is a function of the payoff only, i.e., for the case where there is no asset integration with other sources of income. Suppose the individual either gets X certainty, or participates in the lottery, then we have that

$\ln X = \sum_{i=1}^{\infty} 0.5^i \ln 2^i = \sum_{i=1}^{\infty} i \ 0.5^i \ln 2 \ = \ln 2 \sum_{i=1}^{\infty} i \ 0.5^i = 2 \ln 2 = \ln 4.$

Hence, the individual would be indifferent between receiving $4 for sure and participating in the lottery. However, it should be pointed out that such a model is inconsistent with the conventional model where different sources of income are dealt with in the same way; see, e.g., Rabin (2000), Rabin and Thaler (2001), and Johansson-Stenman (2010). Yet, as these authors also point out, there is ample empirical evidence that people do not perfectly integrate gamble gains with other sources of income or wealth.

assumed by using a logarithmic utility function is not at all extreme, but rather, if anything, on the low side.[5]

The example with the St Petersburg paradox thus shows that introducing a concave utility function, i.e., introducing risk aversion, can have a very large impact on optimal behavior. Risk aversion is also the standard explanation behind why it can be fully rational for consumers to buy insurances despite the fact that they know that the insurance companies are making profits, and hence that their own expected value must be negative on average. Hence, it appears worthwhile to explore the implications of risk aversion for the optimal investment decision in the basic model considered in this chapter, which is the task of the next two sections.

4 EXPECTED UTILITY

Let us make the same assumptions as above, but introduce a strictly concave utility function such that utility $U = u(C)$, where $u'(C) > 0$ and $u''(C) < 0$. Before dealing with the risky case, consider the benchmark case with certainty. In this case we obtain

$$U = u(Y - I - D_0 f(I)).\tag{22}$$

Thus, as before, we assume (for analytical simplicity) that consumption and absence of health damage are perfect substitutes, which, of course, is a strong assumption and which will be relaxed in Section 5. The first-order condition corresponding to (22) is given by

$$u'(Y - I - D_0 f(I))(D_0 f'(I) + 1) = 0,\tag{23}$$

so that

$$f'(I) = -1/D_0.\tag{24}$$

Using again the inverse function technique based on (9), we obtain

$$I = h(D_0).\tag{25}$$

Intuitively, when there is no uncertainty involved, maximization of $U = u(Y - I - D_0 f(I))$ is equivalent to maximizing net consumption $Y - I - D_0 f(I)$.

---

[5] A logarithmic utility function implies a constant relative risk aversion parameter, defined by $-C u''(C)/u'(C)$, equal to unity. Many studies estimate this parameter. For example, Blundell, Browning, and Meghir (1994) and Attanasio and Browning (1995) estimate the relative risk aversion parameter based on consumption decisions over the lifecycle and find in most of their estimates the relative risk aversion parameter to be in the order of magnitude of 1 or slightly above. Vissing-Jørgensen (2002) estimates this parameter based on observed behavior in risky decisions and finds that the relative risk aversion parameter differs between stockholders (approximately 2.5 to 3) and bondholders (approximately 1 to 1.2).

4.1 Optimal Safety Investment under Risk Aversion

Consider now again the case where D_0 is stochastic, as in the previous section, so that expected utility is given by

$$EU = \sum_{i=1}^{n} p^i u\left(Y - I - D_0^i f(I)\right). \tag{26}$$

It can then be shown (see Appendix) that we can write the optimal investment level as

$$I = h\left(E(D_0)\left(1 + \mathrm{cov}\left[\frac{D_0}{E(D_0)}, \frac{u'(C)}{E(u'(C))}\right]\right)\right) \tag{27}$$

Thus, the optimal investment level exceeds the level implied by the expected value maximization if and only if the normalized covariance between the damage in the absence of any investments, D_0, and the marginal utility of consumption, $u'(c)$, is positive.[6] And from (22), it is easy to see that it is. This result may seem surprising. Indeed, taking risk aversion into account typically tends to decrease the size of a given risky investment (see, e.g., Rothschild and Stiglitz 1970, 1971).

Why, then, does risk aversion here increase, and not decrease, the optimal investment? The reason is that risk aversion, as the name suggests, implies a willingness to pay for reducing the risk, i.e., the variation in terms of the outcome (here consumption). And a higher investment here implies a lower expected *ex post* variation of consumption (in addition to the expected damage), which is contrary to the typical investment decision where an increase in a risky investment tends to increase the overall risk.[7] In the special case where f is given by (3), we similarly obtain

$$I = \frac{1}{\alpha}\ln\left(\alpha E(D_0)\left(1 + \mathrm{cov}\left[\frac{D_0}{E(D_0)}, \frac{u'(C)}{E(u'(C))}\right]\right)\right) \tag{28}$$

4.2 Optimal Safety Investment When Income Is Uncertain

In reality, both health damage and income are uncertain. Let us for simplicity start with the case with no uncertainty about health costs. From (25), we then have that $I = h(D_0)$, implying that the optimal investment level is independent of the income *level*. But what about *variation* in income? Let Y be a stochastic variable with m different values, $Y^1, \ldots, Y^m$, so that expected utility is given by

---

[6] Note that the covariance expression is, of course, in itself a function of I, but the comparison of the optimal investment with the previous cases is still equally valid.

[7] See also Howarth (2003) and Brekke and Johansson-Stenman (2008) for discussions of similar mechanisms when discussing optimal social discount rates regarding investments in order to combat global warming.

$$EU = \sum\nolimits_{i=1}^{m} p^i u\left(Y^i - I - D_0 f(I)\right). \tag{29}$$

It can then be shown (see Appendix) that we here too can write the optimal investment level as

$$I = h(D_0). \tag{30}$$

Intuitively, the maximization of u is always independent of Y, and hence also independent of variations of Y.

Consider next the case where both D_0 and Y are stochastic, so that expected utility is given by

$$EU = \sum\nolimits_{i=1}^{n} \sum\nolimits_{j=1}^{m} p^{ij} u\left(Y^j - I - D_0^i f(I)\right) = \sum\nolimits_{i=1}^{n} \sum\nolimits_{j=1}^{m} p^{ij} u\left(C^{ij}\right), \tag{31}$$

where p^{ij} is the probability that the damage in the absence of investments is equal to D_0^i and that the income is equal to Y^j, and hence that the resulting consumption is given by C^{ij}. It can then be shown (see Appendix) that we can write the optimal investment level as in (27), i.e.,

$$I = h\left(E(D_0)\left(1 + \mathrm{cov}\left[\frac{D_0}{E(D_0)}, \frac{u'(C)}{E(u'(C))}\right]\right)\right). \tag{32}$$

However, here we cannot a priori determine whether the normalized covariance expression is positive or negative. Clearly, if the distributions of Y and D_0 are sufficiently positively correlated, then the overall tendency may be that utility is greater when the damage is greater, in turn implying that the covariance between damage and the marginal utility of consumption becomes negative. One may, for example, think of cases where the expected damage is proportional to the consumption of a certain good, which in turn is highly income-elastic. Yet, in the benchmark case where damage and marginal utility of consumption are independently distributed, and hence uncorrelated, which perhaps is a reasonable starting point for many food-related health risks, we know that the covariance is larger than zero, and hence that the riskiness (in health damage) tends to increase the investment compared to the expected value case.

5 STATE-DEPENDENT EXPECTED UTILITY: WHEN CONSUMPTION AND ABSENCE OF DAMAGE ARE IMPERFECT SUBSTITUTES

So far, we have assumed that private consumption and absence of damage are perfect substitutes, implying, for example, that the marginal willingness to pay for reducing the damage further is independent of the income level. This is clearly a very restrictive assumption. In order to analyze the optimal investment level more generally, I shall here consider the case where private consumption and absence of damage are imperfect substitutes. Let us make the same assumptions as above, but relax the assumption of perfect substitutability, such that utility $U = u(C, -D)$, where $\frac{\partial u}{\partial(-D)} > 0$ and $\frac{\partial^2 u}{\partial(-D)^2} < 0$ and where, as before, $\frac{\partial u}{\partial C} > 0$ and $\frac{\partial^2 u}{\partial C^2} < 0$; also assume that u is strictly quasi-concave. This formulation implies that under risk, we have a case of a state-dependent EU model, since the value of the damage will generally depend on the consumption levels (see, e.g., Karni 1985, 2009a for overviews of state-dependent EU theory).

Before dealing with the risky case, however, consider the benchmark case with certainty, in which we obtain $U = u(Y - I, -D_0 f(I))$, implying the first-order condition, with respect to I, $\frac{\partial u}{\partial C} + D_0 \frac{\partial u}{\partial(-D)} f'(I) = 0$, which can be rewritten as $f'(I) = -\frac{\partial u}{\partial C} / \left(\frac{\partial u}{\partial(-D)} D_0 \right)$, implying from (9) that

$$I = h\left(D_0 \frac{\partial u}{\partial(-D)} / \frac{\partial u}{\partial C} \right) = h(D_0 MRS_{-D,C}), \tag{33}$$

where $MRS_{-D,C} = \frac{\partial u}{\partial(-D)} / \frac{\partial u}{\partial C}$ is the marginal willingness to pay, in terms of private consumption, for reducing the damage. In the special case where f is given by (3), we similarly obtain

$$I = \frac{1}{\alpha} \ln(\alpha D_0 MRS_{-D,C}). \tag{34}$$

5.1 Optimal Safety Investment under Risk Aversion

When we introduce uncertainty in damage, D, expected utility is given by

$$EU = \sum_{i=1}^{n} p^i u\left(Y - I, -D_0^i f(I) \right). \tag{35}$$

The optimal investment level can then be written as (see Appendix):

$$I = h\left(E(D_0) \frac{E(\partial u(C,-D)/\partial(-D))}{E(\partial u(C,-D)/\partial C)} \left(1 + \text{cov}\left[\frac{D_0}{E(D_0)}, \frac{\partial u(C,-D)/\partial(-D)}{E(\partial u(C,-D)/\partial(-D))} \right] \right) \right). \tag{36}$$

In order to interpret this result, let us compare (36) with (33). The factor $MRS_{-D,C} = -\frac{\partial u}{\partial D} / \frac{\partial u}{\partial C}$ in (33) here corresponds to the factor $E\left(\frac{\partial u(C,-D)}{\partial(-D)} \right) / E\left(\frac{\partial u(C,-D)}{\partial C} \right)$. However, we also have the covariance expression associated with the insurance value of the investment. Note that the normalized covariance is not between D_0 and the marginal utility of consumption, but between D_0 and the marginal utility of reduced damage. Still, since $\frac{\partial u}{\partial(-D)} > 0$ and $\frac{\partial^2 u}{\partial(-D)^2} < 0$, we have that the normalized covariance expression is positive and hence contributes to a larger investment level. When f is given by (3), we correspondingly obtain

$$I = \frac{1}{\alpha}\ln\left(\alpha E(D_0)\frac{E(\partial u(C,-D)/\partial(-D))}{E(\partial u(C,-D)/\partial C)}\left(1+\mathrm{cov}\left[\frac{D_0}{E(D_0)},\frac{\partial u(C,-D)/\partial(-D)}{E(\partial u(C,-D)/\partial(-D))}\right]\right)\right).$$

(37)

5.2 When Both Damage and Income Are Stochastic

Consider finally the case where both D_0 and Y are stochastic, so that expected utility is given by

$$EU = \sum_{i=1}^{n}\sum_{j=1}^{m}p^{ij}u\left(Y^j - I, -D_0^i f(I)\right).$$

(38)

The optimal investment level can then be written as (see Appendix):

$$I = h\left(E(D_0)\frac{E(\partial u(C,-D)/\partial(-D))}{E(\partial u(C,-D)/\partial C)}\left(1+\mathrm{cov}\left[\frac{D_0}{E(D_0)},\frac{\partial u(C,-D)/\partial(-D)}{E(\partial u(C,-D)/\partial(-D))}\right]\right)\right).$$

(39)

Hence, here too we obtain an identical algebraic expression when we also allow for income variations, i.e., (39) is identical to (36), and (37) will also continue to hold for the special case where f is given by (3). Yet, the values are, of course, likely to differ, depending in particular on how the health damage covaries with income.

6 THE ELLSBERG PARADOX

The above analysis based on the EU decision rule has introduced considerable sophistication beyond the simple EU decision rule, and this increased complexity has made it possible to explain phenomena such as the St Petersburg paradox. Yet, as mentioned in the introduction, there is nevertheless considerable evidence that people's choices under uncertainty tend to be inconsistent with the implications of EU theory, including SEU utility theory. A well-known example is given by the so-called Ellsberg (1961) paradox, as follows. Suppose you have an urn containing 30 red balls and 60 balls that are either black or yellow; the balls are well mixed. You do not know (but you may, of course, have a subjective guess) the relative shares of black and of yellow balls. Consider now the choice between Gamble A and Gamble B:

Gamble A	Gamble B
You receive $100 if you draw a red ball	You receive $100 if you draw a black ball

Consider next the choice between Gamble C and Gamble D:

Gamble C	Gamble D
You receive $100 if you draw a red or yellow ball	You receive $100 if you draw a black or yellow ball

It turns out in surveys as well as real-money experiments that most people prefer A to B and D to C (e.g., Becker and Brownson 1964; Slovic and Tversky 1974; Einhorn and Hogarth 1986; Curley and Yates 1989). However, this violates SEU theory. To see this, note that if you prefer A to B, your subjective probability that the ball is red must be larger than that the ball is black. But if this is true, then the probability that the ball is either red or yellow must be larger than the probability that the ball is either black or yellow. Therefore, preferring A to B and D to C implies a contradiction.

Why, then, do most people seem to prefer A to B and D to C? A plausible explanation goes as follows. In Gamble A, the individual knows that the probability that the ball is red is 20/60 = 1/3. In Gamble B, the individual does not know the objective probability that the ball is black; it can be either lower or higher than 1/3 and take any value from 0 to 2/3. If the individual is a bit "pessimistic," he/she might conjecture that it is lower than 1/3, and hence go for A.

In Gamble C, the individual does not know the probability that the ball is either red or yellow; it can be anything from 1/3 to 1. In Gamble D, in contrast, the probability that the ball is either black or yellow is known and equals 40/60 = 2/3. In this case, an individual who is a bit pessimistic regarding the probabilities in Gamble C will go for Gamble D.

Note that choosing A over B and D over C, *if taken separately*, is not inconsistent with SEU theory. Rather, both choices may seem perfectly reasonable in an SEU perspective. Indeed, if a firm (or an individual) offers you a gamble, it is reasonable to suspect that the firm does so for a reason, which is presumably that the expected profit for the firm, which knows the objective probabilities, is positive if you accept the offer. Thus, if a firm invites you to sell Gamble A and instead obtain Gamble B, it would make perfect sense to believe that the objective probability that the ball is black is lower than 1/3, and hence you should turn down the offer. Similarly, if a firm invites you to sell Gamble D and instead obtain Gamble C, it would be reasonable to expect that the objective probability that the ball is yellow is lower than 1/3 and therefore that the objective probability that the ball is either red or yellow is lower than 2/3. Hence, you should turn down this offer too. The violation of SEU theory is thus related to *both* choosing A over B and D over C, and not to each of these choices separately.

In the next section, I shall consider alternative theoretical formalizations that are consistent with the behavior in the above example, i.e., that have the power to explain the Ellsberg paradox. These formalizations have in common that they share some kind of ambiguity aversion, meaning, somewhat loosely, an attitude or preference for known risks over unknown risks.

7 Decision Models Based on Ambiguity Aversion

This section describes three different ways of formalizing ambiguity aversion. In order to make comparisons with the previously described decision rules based, for example, on expected value and on expected utility maximization, I shall stick to the same basic assumptions as before in our highly stylized model. As before, there are n possible outcomes, $D_0^1, \ldots, D_0^n$. However, now we do not know the "true" probability distributions. Instead, there are k possible probability distributions that the decision maker has to consider. Without loss of generality, we can order the probability distributions, such that the implied expected utility derived from them is in an increasing order $P^1, \ldots, P^k$, where $P^j = \{p^{j1}, \ldots, p^{jn}\}$ and where consequently

$$\sum_{i=1}^{n} p^{1i} u\big(Y - I - D_0^i f(I)\big) < \ldots < \sum_{i=1}^{n} p^{ki} u\big(Y - I - D_0^i f(I)\big). \qquad (40)$$

Moreover, the decision maker does not necessarily consider all probability distributions to be equally likely. The decision maker's subjective probability, obtained with the help of experts and other information, that probability distribution P^j is the correct one is given by q^j, etc. Then how should the decision maker proceed?

7.1 The Gilboa and Schmeidler's Maximin Expected Utility Approach

The maximin EU approach by Gilboa and Schmeidler (1989)[8] simply implies that the decision maker should only take into account the beliefs of the most pessimistic probability distribution, P^1, in the sense that this distribution is associated with the lowest expected utility of the k different probability distributions.

Thus, the objective function of the decision maker, W, which without loss of generality we can denote *welfare*, is given by the maximization of the expected utility as reflected by the most pessimistic beliefs regarding the probability distributions

$$W = EU(P^1) = \sum_{i=1}^{n} p^{1i} u\big(Y - I - D_0^i f(I)\big). \qquad (41)$$

This expression, of course, looks exactly the same as (31), with the only difference that the previously "objective" probabilities are here replaced by the most pessimistic one of the alternatives. Let us use the short notation $SE^1(D_0)$ for the expected value of D_0 associated with the most pessimistic probability distribution, and

---

[8] See also Schmeidler (1989) for a model that under some conditions is very similar to the one considered here.

$$SE^1(u'(C)) = \sum_i p^{1i} u'(C^i) \qquad (42)$$

for the expected marginal utility of consumption based on the most pessimistic probability distribution. We can then write the optimal investment as

$$I = h\left(SE^1(D_0)\left(1 + \text{cov}^1\left[\frac{D_0}{SE^1(D_0)}, \frac{u'(C)}{SE^1(u'(C))} \right] \right) \right), \qquad (43)$$

where $\text{cov}^1\left[\frac{D_0}{SE^1(D_0)}, \frac{u'(C)}{SE^1(u'(C))} \right]$ is the normalized covariance based on the most pessimistic probability distribution, i.e., probability distribution no. 1, between the marginal utility of consumption and D_0. We can, of course, again use the functional form according to (3) and obtain

$$I = \frac{1}{\alpha}\ln\left(\alpha SE^1(D_0)\left(1 + \text{cov}^1\left[\frac{D_0}{SE^1(D_0)}, \frac{u'(C)}{SE^1(u'(C))} \right] \right) \right). \qquad (44)$$

Thus, this approach implies a maximin decision rule with respect to the expected utilities of different experts, or to probability distributions more generally. As such, it is clearly less extreme than the maximin decision rule in terms of outcomes that were presented in Section 2.3. The two decision rules will coincide in the case where the most pessimistic expert perceives that the most pessimistic outcome will occur with probability 1. On the other hand, it tends to imply a higher optimal investment level than one based on SEU maximization.[9] Still, it may be questioned on the grounds that it only takes into account the most pessimistic probability distribution and that it hence ignores all other probability distributions.

To see that this kind of ambiguity aversion can indeed explain the Ellsberg paradox outlined in the previous section, assume that an individual who does not know the distributions of the black and the yellow balls quite reasonably considers all combinations possible. Then it cannot be ruled out that 60 balls are black and that 0 are yellow, that 10 are black and 50 yellow, that 0 are black and 60 yellow, etc.

Consider now the choice between Gamble A and Gamble B above. In Gamble A, the objective probability that the ball is red is 20/60 = 1/3, whereas in Gamble B, the objective probability that the ball is black is unknown and can be anything from 0 to 2/3. Applying the decision rule by Gilboa and Schmeidler, the individual will then

---

[9] I write "tends to" since this has not been shown formally. Indeed, in the related problem of determining the optimal investment in a risky asset (which is not linked to safety improvement as here), Gollier (2011) shows that one can generally not say that the optimal investment is lower under ambiguity aversion compared to the standard expected utility case (for the same underlying utility function). Yet, he derives sufficient conditions for when this is the case. My conjecture in the present case is that it is presumably possible to construct an example where ambiguity aversion decreases the optimal investment level (although this problem is harder than in the case considered by Gollier, since the investment here affects the safety level as well). Nevertheless, I do not consider this possibility to be economically important, and my conjecture is that for all reasonable functional forms of the utility functions one may think of, the introduction of ambiguity aversion of the Gilboa and Schmeidler type increases the optimal investment level.

consider the most pessimistic of the possible probabilities that the ball is black, which is 0. Hence, the individual will go for A, since 1/3 is clearly larger than 0.

Consider, similarly, the choice between Gambles C and D. In Gamble C, the probability that the ball is either red or yellow is not known and can be anything from 1/3 to 1. Applying the Gilboa and Schmeidler decision rule then again implies that the action is based on the most pessimistic probability, which is that the probability that the ball is either red or yellow is 1/3. In Gamble D, the probability that the ball is either black or yellow is known and equal to 2/3, which is clearly higher than 1/3. Hence, the individual would choose D. Taken together, an individual who uses the decision rule by Gilboa and Schmeidler would act consistently with the choice of most people, as discussed in the previous section, and hence choose A over B and D over C.

This example also illustrates that the decision rule by Gilboa and Schmeidler implies a rather extreme ambiguity aversion, and it appears that also less extreme ambiguity aversion may be able to explain the Ellsberg paradox. In the following two subsections, we shall therefore consider decision rules with potentially less extreme ambiguity aversion.

7.2 Klibanoff, Marinacci, and Mukerji's Smooth Ambiguity Approach

The "smooth ambiguity" approach presented by Klibanoff, Marinacci, and Mukerji (2005) implies a generalization of the approach by Gilboa and Schmeidler (1989).[10] It is "smooth" in the sense that it introduces *degrees* of ambiguity aversion, in contrast to the maximin approach by Gilboa and Schmeidler (1989), and as such it implies smooth indifference curves. Instead of only focusing on the most pessimistic probability distribution, the smooth ambiguity approach can be seen as a weighted aggregation of all probability distribution. The objective function based on smooth ambiguity aversion can be written

$$W = \sum_{j} \psi\left(EU(P^{j})\right) q^{j} = \sum_{j} \psi\left(\sum_{i=1}^{n} p^{ji} u\left(Y - I - D_{0}^{i} f(I)\right)\right) q^{j}, \qquad (45)$$

where q^{j} reflects the probabilistic weight attached to the probabilistic scenario j (sometimes denoted second-order probabilities) and the function ψ reflects ambiguity aversion. The larger the degree of ambiguity aversion, as reflected by the curvature of ψ, the larger the differences in weights attached to pessimistic and optimistic probability distributions. This means that in the most ambiguity-averse case, the smooth ambiguity approach converges to the maximin EU approach by Gilboa and Schmeidler (1989), whereas in the case of no-ambiguity aversion, it converges to the conventional subjective EU approach.

[10] For simplicity, we consider a discrete version of their model, whereas they use continuous probability distributions. See also Klibanoff, Marinacci, and Mukerji (2009) for an extension of this model to an intertemporal context.

Before deriving the optimal investment for this case, I shall derive the optimal investment for the benchmark case of no-ambiguity aversion where then $\psi'(EU(P^j))$ is a constant for all probability distributions. In order to do this, I shall proceed as before by differentiating the objective functions with respect to I, setting this expression to zero and solving for I.

Let us use the short notation

$$SE^G(u'(C)) = \sum_j \sum_i q^j p^{ji} u'(C^i) \tag{46}$$

for the decision maker's subjective expected marginal utility of consumption when taking all information into account, i.e., both the uncertainty with respect to the probability distributions and the uncertainty within each probability distribution, but without any different weighting through the ψ-function. The optimal investment can then be written (see Appendix)

$$I = h\left(SE^G(D_0)\left(1 + \text{cov}^G\left[\frac{D_0}{SE^G(D_0)}, \frac{u'(C)}{SE^G(u'(C))}\right]\right)\right). \tag{47}$$

Note that this expression is almost identical to (32). The only difference is that (47) is based on subjective probabilities, where the overall problem can be seen as a compound lottery (i.e., involving probabilities of probabilities), whereas (32) is based on objective probabilities and a simple lottery.

With this benchmark case at hand, let us now return to the more general derivation of the optimal investment level. Using the short notations

$$SE^G(\psi'(EU)u'(C)) = \sum_j \sum_i q^j p^{ji} \psi'(EU(P^j)) u'(C^i) \tag{48}$$

for the decision maker's subjective expected marginal welfare of consumption (i.e., how a unit of consumption contributes to welfare, W), we can write the optimal investment as (see Appendix)

$$I = h\left(SE^G(D_0)\left(1 + \text{cov}^G\left[\frac{D_0}{SE^G(D_0)}, \frac{\psi'(EU)u'(C)}{SE^G(\psi'(EU)u'(C))}\right]\right)\right). \tag{49}$$

By comparing (49) to (47), it can be observed that the only difference is that the normalized covariance expression is here between the initial damage and the marginal *welfare* of consumption, instead of between the initial damage and the marginal *utility* of consumption. We can alternatively rewrite (49) as

$$I = h\left\{ SE^G(D_0)\left(1 + \text{cov}^G\left[\frac{D_0}{SE^G(D_0)}, \frac{u'(C)}{SE^G(u'(C))}\right]\right)\right.$$
$$\left.\left(\text{cov}^G\left[\frac{D_0}{SE^G(D_0)}, \frac{\psi'(EU)u'(C)}{SE^G(\psi'(EU)u'(C))} - \frac{u'(C)}{SE^G(u'(C))}\right]\right)\right\} \tag{50}$$

Hence, the optimal investment level is higher than that based on the subjective EU approach, corresponding to the expression on the first line of (50), if $\psi'(EU)u'(C)$

covaries more positively with D_0 than does $u'(C)$. Since ψ is a concave transformation, this tends, of course, to be the case (although not strictly shown, and the caveat in footnote 9 applies here too). Using again the functional form of f according to (3), we obtain

$$
\begin{aligned}
I = \frac{1}{\alpha}\ln\bigg\{ &\alpha SE^G(D_0)\left(1+\text{cov}^G\left[\frac{D_0}{SE^G(D_0)},\frac{u'(C)}{SE^G(u'(C))}\right]\right) \\
&\left(\text{cov}^G\left[\frac{D_0}{SE^G(D_0)},\frac{\psi'(EU)u'(C)}{SE^G(\psi'(EU)u'(C))}-\frac{u'(C)}{SE^G(u'(C))}\right]\right)\bigg\}
\end{aligned}
\tag{51}
$$

7.3 Gajdos, Hayashi, Tallon, and Vergnaud's Ambiguity Approach

An even more recent approach to how one may make ambiguity aversion instrumental is the approach of Gajdos et al. (2008). They provide an axiomatic analysis suggesting a functional form where welfare (in the sense of objective function) consists of a weighted average of, on one hand, the lowest expected utility of the different probability distributions, i.e., the objective function in the model by Gilboa and Schmeidler (1989), and, on the other hand, the subjective expected utility taking all probability distributions into account, as follows:

$$
\begin{aligned}
W &= \phi EU(P^1) + (1-\phi)\sum_j q^j EU(P^j) \\
&= \phi\sum_{i=1}^n p^{1i}u\big(Y-I-D_0^i f(I)\big) + (1-\phi)\sum_j q^j\sum_{i=1}^n p^{ji}u\big(Y-I-D_0^i f(I)\big)
\end{aligned}
\tag{52}
$$

Thus, (52) corresponds to Gilboa and Schmeidler's maximin approach when $\phi=1$ and to the SEU model when $\phi=0$. By using (42) and (46), we can then write the optimal investment as (see Appendix)

$$
\begin{aligned}
I = h\bigg\{ &\frac{\phi SE^1(u'(C))\Omega^{1G}+(1-\phi)SE^G(u'(C))}{\phi SE^1(u'(C))+(1-\phi)SE^G(u'(C))} \\
&SE^G(D_0)\left(1+\text{cov}^G\left[\frac{D_0}{SE^G(D_0)},\frac{u'(C)}{SE^G(u'(C))}\right]\right)\bigg\}
\end{aligned}
\tag{53}
$$

where

$$
\Omega^{1G} = \frac{SE^1(D_0)\left(1+\text{cov}^1\left[\frac{D_0}{SE^1(D_0)},\frac{u'(C)}{SE^1(u'(C))}\right]\right)}{SE^G(D_0)\left(1+\text{cov}^G\left[\frac{D_0}{SE^G(D_0)},\frac{u'(C)}{SE^G(u'(C))}\right]\right)}.
$$

.

Hence, the expression inside the h-function consists of two factors. The second one, on the second line, constitutes in itself the expression that would result if the public decision makers were subjective expected utility maximizers. The first factor, on the first line, is clearly larger than one if and only if Ω^{1G} exceeds one. And since, again, superscript 1 denotes the most pessimistic probability distribution, in expected utility terms it is reasonable to believe that $SE^1(D_0) > SE^G(D_0)$. There is, moreover, no reason to believe that the corresponding covariance expression is larger based on the decision maker's subjective probability distributions (based on all existing feasible probability distributions) than based on the most pessimistic one. (Yet, the same qualification as before applies here too; see footnote 9.) How much larger the optimal investment is compared to the baseline SEU-maximizing case depends not only on Ω^{1G}, and hence on the factors that it consists of, but also on ϕ. This is logical, since the larger the ϕ, the larger the weight put on the most pessimistic probability distribution. As for the approach of Klibanoff, Marinacci, and Mukerji (2005), the optimal investment level here tends to be smaller than that based on the maximin approach by Gilboa and Schmeidler (1989). There is no reason to expect that either of the investment levels implied by the approaches of Klibanoff, Marinacci, and Mukerji (2005) and Gajdos et al. (2008) would exceed the other. Let us for completeness again use the functional form of f according to (3) and obtain

$$
\begin{aligned}
I = \frac{1}{\alpha}\ln\Bigg\{ &\alpha\frac{\phi SE^1(u'(C))\Omega^{1G} + (1-\phi)SE^G(u'(C))}{\phi SE^1(u'(C)) + (1-\phi)SE^G(u'(C))} \\
&SE^G(D_0)\left(1 + \mathrm{cov}^G\left[\frac{D_0}{SE^G(D_0)}, \frac{u'(C)}{SE^G(u'(C))}\right]\right)\Bigg\}.
\end{aligned}
\tag{54}
$$

Finally, by comparing (49) and (53), we obtain that the investment level implied by Klibanoff, Marinacci, and Mukerji (2005) exceeds the one by Gajdos, Hayashi, Tallon, and Vergnaud (2008) if

$$
\begin{aligned}
\mathrm{cov}^G&\left[\frac{D_0}{SE^G(D_0)}, \frac{\psi'(EU)u'(C)}{SE^G(\psi'(EU)u'(C))} - \frac{u'(C)}{SE^G(u'(C))}\right] \\
&> \frac{\phi SE^1(u'(C))\Omega^{1G} + (1-\phi)SE^G(u'(C))}{\phi SE^1(u'(C)) + (1-\phi)SE^G(u'(C))},
\end{aligned}
\tag{55}
$$

and vice versa. Thus, this tends to be the case the larger the degree of curvature imposed through the ψ-function and the smaller the ϕ, which follows intuition.

8 Reflections: Should Policymakers Really Be Ambiguity-Averse?

As mentioned above, there is evidence that people, at least sometimes, tend to be ambiguity-averse. A related issue is whether public policy tends to reflect ambiguity aversion as well. There are some indications that it does. For example, Viscusi (1998) argues that policymakers are too stringent when they face ambiguous risks; he exemplifies with the higher regulation of synthetic risks compared to more familiar but often more severe carcinogens. Viscusi and Hamilton argue that "These biases, in effect, institutionalise ambiguity aversion biases" (Viscusi and Hamilton 1999: 1013). Similarly, Sunstein (2000, 2005) argues that, in the presence of divergent risk scenarios, policymakers focus too much on the worst-case scenario and do not sufficiently account for the low probabilities involved.

Thus, that people tend to be ambiguity-averse is well documented, and, as indicated above, there is also some evidence that actual policy tends to reflect some ambiguity aversion. Moreover, as illustrated in the previous section, there are also a couple of recent models that operationalize ambiguity aversion and hence make it possible to incorporate such aspects into the decision rules; see, e.g., Karni (2009b) and Chambers and Melkonyan (2010) for recent papers on regulation under ambiguity aversion.

Yet, to conclude from this that the decision maker's regulation policy ought to reflect ambiguity aversion would be to derive an *ought* from an *is*. Still, one may perhaps argue that the principle of consumer sovereignty implies that if people are ambiguity-averse, then it should be reflected by a corresponding ambiguity aversion in policymaking. While this kind of reasoning has some appeal, it is not difficult to come up with counter-arguments.

The most obvious one draws on the fact that consumer sovereignty may not be the ultimate social goal in itself. Indeed, one may, following, e.g., Broome (1999), Ng (1999), O'Donoghue and Rabin (2006), and Johansson-Stenman (2008), assume that what matters intrinsically is well-being rather than choice. Or, using the terminology of Kahneman, Wakker, and Sarin (1997), we are intrinsically interested in *experienced* utility rather than *decision* utility.

Hence, if the ultimate goal is to maximize social well-being, and it is believed that respecting people's preferences, as revealed by their choices, is an effective way of obtaining this goal, then it follows that it is indeed a good idea for policymakers to respect the principle of consumer sovereignty. However, this is then contingent on the assumption that people do know, and act in accordance with, what is best for them (in terms of their well-being). This assumption, as a general reliable rule, has been questioned in recent behavioral economics literature. In particular, it has been argued that people tend to have self-control problems that imply time inconsistency, and that they make short-sighted decisions that they end up regretting, and hence fail to act in accordance with their own will. As a result, policy measures based on different kinds of paternalism have been proposed. For example, Gruber and Köszegi (2002) argue in favor of cigarette taxation, not in order to internalize *externalities* (which they argue are rather limited anyway), but in order to internalize what they denote *internalities*, i.e., in order to help them act in accordance with their own ultimate will and interest. Similarly, O'Donoghue and Rabin (2006) argue in favor of "fat taxes" and other "sin taxes." For good overviews of such arguments more generally, see Camerer et al. (2003) and Thaler and Sunstein (2008). See also Sugden (2004) and Bernheim and Rangel (2007, 2009) for different arguments and alternative choice-based approaches when people make mistakes. Regardless of how one feels about such paternalistic policies, it is not easy to argue in favor of time-inconsistent public policy in order to mimic the time inconsistencies of citizens.

The question here is whether ambiguity aversion should be seen as a genuine preference that the decision maker ought to reflect just as much as it should reflect other values of its citizens, or whether it should be seen as an internally inconsistent decision rule similar in nature to time inconsistency or loss aversion, and as such be seen as a kind of irrationality that the decision maker has no reason to mimic. My own view, following, e.g., Savage (1972), Drezé (1987), and Al-Najjar and Weinstein (2009a, b), is basically in line with the latter. I believe it is difficult to find good arguments in normative analysis against the axioms underlying subjective expected utility theory, including Savage's (1954) Sure-Thing Principle,[11] which is typically sacrificed in alternative axiomatically motivated models of ambiguity aversion (e.g., Gilboa and Schmeidler 1989; Gajdos et al. 2008). Likewise, I find it difficult to argue that compound lotteries should be evaluated fundamentally differently than the resulting simple lotteries. As expressed by Al-Najjar and Weinstein (2009b: 364), "The formal models in the ambiguity aversion literature rely on taste to fit observed behaviour, offering no substantive insights into *why* decision makers cannot form probability judgments."

Yet, the literature on ambiguity aversion is rapidly increasing, and there are certainly several highly intelligent and prominent authors who disagree with my view. For example, Gilboa, Postlewaite, and Schmeidler (2009: 285) argue that it is sometimes "more rational not to behave in accordance with a Bayesian prior than to do so,"[12] and

---

[11] Suppose that a decision maker knows that two mutually exclusive events A and B will occur with probabilities p_A and $1-p_A$, respectively, where p_A may be unknown. The Sure-Thing Principle then says that if the decision maker would take a certain action if he/she knew that A would occur, and also if he/she knew that B would occur, then he/she would take the action also in an uncertain case when p_A is completely unknown. In the words of Savage (1954): "A businessman contemplates buying a certain piece of property. He considers the outcome of the next presidential election relevant. So, to clarify the matter to himself, he asks whether he would buy if he knew that the Democratic candidate were going to win, and decides that he would. Similarly, he considers whether he would buy if he knew that the Republican candidate were going to win, and again finds that he would. Seeing that he would buy in either event, he decides that he should buy, even though he does not know which event obtains, or will obtain, as we would ordinarily say." Yet, one may argue that the Sure-Thing Principle has less intuitive appeal when lotteries constitute the events.

[12] "Bayesian" refers here to a person who behaves according to SEU theory, and not as the term is typically used in statistics, where it simply reflects a person who updates the probability judgments according to Bayes's rule.

that this is in particular the case when there is no, or very limited, information available to form a prior in an SEU assessment. They then ask the natural question, "What would then be the rational thing to do, in the absence of additional information?", to which they answer, "Our main point is that there may not be any decision that is perfectly rational" (2009: 287). However, such an answer is not very helpful when contemplating how a public decision maker ought to act. Gilboa and Schmeidler (2001: 17–18) provide an alternative definition of rationality: "an action, or sequence of actions, is rational for a decision maker if, when the decision maker is confronted with an analysis of the decisions involved, but with no additional information, she does not regret her choices." Whether ambiguity aversion is consistent with such a definition of rationality is debated. For example, Gilboa and Schmeidler (2001) argue that it is, while Al-Najjar and Weinstein (2009) argue that it is not. Personally, I find the definition in itself to be somewhat problematic since it implies, or at least seems to imply, that the same action may be considered rational for an individual with low cognitive capacity and irrational for an individual with high cognitive capacity.

Nevertheless, I do have some caveats. First, choice situations under ambiguity may induce fear to a larger extent, and it appears just as reasonable to deal with this kind of fear as with other kinds of negative welfare effects, as recently argued also by Treich (2010). More generally, people may experience feelings (e.g., feelings of regret; cf., Loomes and Sugden 1982) through the decision processes per se. In principle, though, one can describe the different states of the world to which the SEU theory applies in a comprehensive way that includes such feelings.[13] Second, such feelings of fear and other feelings may induce indirect welfare effects through consumer adaptations, and such effects should presumably be considered too (see Johansson-Stenman 2008).

Third, a decision maker may use a decision rule with ambiguity aversion in order to trade off other unavoidable shortcomings. For example, suppose that a decision maker is aware of seemingly unavoidable time inconsistency in the decision-making process. Then, conditional on such time inconsistency, ambiguity aversion may under some conditions work as a commitment and help combat the negative welfare implications of the time inconsistency (cf., Siniscalchi 2009a, b). This is similar in nature to the finding by Benabou and Tirole (2002) that it can be "rational" for a time-inconsistent individual to be overoptimistic with respect to own abilities.

Fourth, and perhaps most importantly, real decisions about risk at a social level will always have to simplify reality. Such simplifications are not always innocuous. More specifically, in situations where there are several risks involved, at different levels, formal analysis will almost always (have to) ignore some of the risks. This means

---

[13] One might perhaps object that it appears unnatural to write (cardinal) utility as a function of feelings, since utility per se is often seen to reflect subjective well-being as reflected by emotions. Yet, utility reflects everything that is in the person's interest and not only the emotions associated with the process. Moreover, it is common to write utility functions in terms of some sub-utility function, e.g., in terms of private consumption, and such sub-utility functions are presumably also related to subjective well-being.

that for actually applied decision rules, it is implicitly assumed for many sub-problems that the most likely outcome will occur, and the most likely outcome tends to be where nothing bad happens. Now, if this is a systematic pattern, the net effect tends to be that the overall social risk will be biased downward. One could therefore argue that ambiguity aversion is a way to correct for neglect of some risks involved in more complex risky problems.

9 CONCLUSION

This chapter has analyzed the basic question of how a public decision maker should think when faced with issues of known and unknown risks by means of a simple baseline model where the decision maker can invest in order to decrease the health risk. Since the investment is risky, the question concerns how much to invest. Optimal investment levels have been derived and compared for a number of decision rules, namely the best guess, the maximin, the expected value, and the expected utility rules. Three different rules that incorporate ambiguity aversion into the expected utility model were also analyzed. Overall, taking risk aversion into account through the expected utility approach tends to increase the optimal investment compared to when using the simple expected value approach. Similarly, ambiguity aversion tends to increase the optimal investment beyond what corresponds to subjective utility maximization.

Finally, it was discussed whether it makes sense to incorporate ambiguity aversion into public policy decision rules. It was concluded that this is doubtful, since it may be argued that the empirical evidence that people tend to be ambiguity-averse is a reflection of inconsistencies and irrationality rather than of their true preferences that are linked to their well-being. However, it is worth pointing out again some examples of what SEU theory does not say. It does not say that we should trust expert judgments (or for that matter that we should not trust them). Moreover, it does not say that policy should not be largely motivated by very unlikely catastrophic outcomes. Indeed, my personal view is that this part of the probability distribution is actually the most important one when it comes to actions related to global warming, and it can certainly not be ruled out that this may be the case also for some food-risk-related issues.

Yet, some caveats were also presented. In particular it was argued that when dealing with complex social phenomena that include several sub-problems, one will for practical reasons have to ignore some of the risks involved. This is an important problem that deserves more attention, and one practical way of doing this is to incorporate some kind of ambiguity aversion as a way of adjusting for this kind of ignorance of some risks. Whether ambiguity aversion in terms of the models presented above, and similar ones, is a good way of correcting for such risk neglects is an open question for future research.

Appendix

Derivation of Equation (27)

The first-order condition associated with (26) is given by

$$\sum_{i=1}^{n} p^i u' \left(Y - I - D_0^i f(I) \right) \left(-1 - D_0^i f'(I) \right) = 0. \tag{A1}$$

Solving for $f'(I)$ implies that

$$f'(I) = -\frac{\sum_{i=1}^{n} p^i u' \left(C^i \right)}{\sum_{i=1}^{n} p^i u'(C^i) D_0^i}, \tag{A2}$$

where $u' \left(C^i \right) = u' \left(Y - I - D_0^i f(I) \right)$. Then we have

$$I = h \left(\frac{\sum_{i=1}^{n} p^i u' \left(C^i \right) D_0^i}{\sum_{i=1}^{n} p^i u'(C^i)} \right) = h \left(\frac{E(D_0 u'(C))}{E(u'(C))} \right). \tag{A3}$$

Since, by definition, we have that $E(D_0 u'(C)) = E(D_0)E(u'(C)) + \mathrm{cov}[D_0, u'(C)]$, it follows that

$$\begin{aligned} \frac{E(D_0 u'(C))}{E(u'(C))} &= E(D_0) + \frac{\mathrm{cov}[D_0, u'(C)]}{E(u'(C))} \\ &= E(D_0) \left(1 + \mathrm{cov} \left[\frac{D_0}{E(D_0)}, \frac{u'(C)}{E(u'(C))} \right] \right) \end{aligned} \tag{A4}$$

Substituting (A4) into (A3) gives (27).

Derivation of Equation (30)

The first-order condition associated with (29) is given by

$$\sum_{i=1}^{n} p^i u' \left(Y^i - I - D_0 f(I) \right) \left(-1 - D_0 f'(I) \right) = 0, \tag{A5}$$

in turn implying that

$$f'(I) = -\frac{\sum_{i=1}^{n} p^i u' \left(C^i \right)}{\sum_{i=1}^{n} p^i u'(C^i) D_0} = -\frac{1}{D_0}. \tag{A6}$$

Using (9) finally implies (30).

Derivation of Equation (32)

The first-order condition associated with (31) is given by

$$\sum_{i=1}^{n}\sum_{j=1}^{m}p^{ij}u'\left(Y^{j}-I-D_{0}^{i}f(I)\right)\left(-1-D_{0}^{i}f'(I)\right)=0. \tag{A7}$$

Solving for $f'(I)$ implies that

$$f'(I)=-\frac{\sum_{i=1}^{n}\sum_{j=1}^{m}p^{ij}u'\left(C^{ij}\right)}{\sum_{i=1}^{n}\sum_{j=1}^{m}p^{ij}u'(C^{ij})D_{0}^{i}}, \tag{A8}$$

where $u'\left(C^{ij}\right)=u'\left(Y^{j}-I-D_{0}^{i}f(I)\right)$. Then, using (9) we have that

$$I=h\left(\frac{\sum_{i=1}^{n}\sum_{j=1}^{m}p^{ij}u'\left(C^{ij}\right)D_{0}^{i}}{\sum_{i=1}^{n}\sum_{j=1}^{m}p^{ij}u'(C^{ij})}\right)=h\left(\frac{E(D_{0}u'(C))}{E(u'(C))}\right). \tag{A9}$$

However, the second way of writing this expression is identical to (A3). Hence, we can here too write the optimal investment as in (27).

Derivation of Equation (36)

The first-order condition associated with (35) is given by

$$\sum_{i=1}^{n}p^{i}\left(\frac{\partial u(C,-D^{i})}{\partial C}+\frac{\partial u(C,-D^{i})}{\partial(-D^{i})}D_{0}^{i}f'(I)\right)=0, \tag{A10}$$

in turn implying that

$$f'(I)=-\frac{\sum_{i=1}^{n}p^{i}\partial u(C,-D^{i})/\partial C}{\sum_{i=1}^{n}p^{i}\,\partial u(C,-D^{i})/\partial(-D^{i})D_{0}^{i}}, \tag{A11}$$

so that, using (9), we have

$$I=h\left(\frac{\sum_{i=1}^{n}p^{i}\,\partial u(C,-D^{i})/\partial(-D^{i})D_{0}^{i}}{\sum_{i=1}^{n}p^{i}\partial u(C,-D^{i})/\partial C}\right) \tag{A12}$$

Multiplying and dividing by the same expression, we can rewrite this as

$$I=h\left(\frac{\sum_{i=1}^{n}p^{i}\,\partial u(C,-D^{i})/\partial(-D^{i})D_{0}^{i}}{\sum_{i=1}^{n}p^{i}\partial u(C,-D^{i})/\partial(-D^{i})}\frac{\sum_{i=1}^{n}p^{i}\partial u(C,-D^{i})/\partial(-D^{i})}{\sum_{i=1}^{n}p^{i}\partial u(C,-D^{i})/\partial C}\right). \tag{A13}$$

By using the definitions of expected value, we can rewrite (A13) as

$$I=h\left(\frac{E\left(\partial u(C,-D)/\partial(-D^{i})\,D_{0}\right)}{E\left(\partial u(C,-D)/\partial(-D)\right)}\frac{E\left(\partial u(C,-D)/\partial(-D^{i})\right)}{E\left(\partial u(C,-D)/\partial C\right)}\right). \tag{A14}$$

We can then rewrite the first ratio in the parentheses in (A14) by a covariance expression as follows:

$$\frac{E(D_0 \partial u(C,-D)/\partial(-D))}{E(\partial u(C,-D)/\partial(-D))} = E(D_0)\left(1 + \text{cov}\left[\frac{D_0}{E(D_0)}, \frac{\partial u(C,-D)/\partial(-D)}{E(\partial u(C,-D)/\partial(-D))}\right]\right). \quad (A15)$$

Substituting (A15) into (A14) implies (36).

Derivation of Equation (39)

The first-order condition associated with (38) is given by

$$\sum_{i=1}^{n}\sum_{j=1}^{m} p^{ij}\left(\frac{\partial u(C^j,-D^i)}{\partial C^j} + \frac{\partial u(C^j,-D^i)}{\partial(-D^i)} D_0^i f'(I)\right) = 0. \quad (A16)$$

Solving for $f'(I)$ implies that

$$f'(I) = -\frac{\sum_{i=1}^{n}\sum_{j=1}^{m} p^{ij}\, \partial u(C^j,-D^i)/\partial C^j}{\sum_{i=1}^{n}\sum_{j=1}^{m} p^{ij}\, \partial u(C^j,-D^i)/(-D^i)D_0^i}. \quad (A17)$$

Then, using (9), we have

$$I = h\left(\frac{\sum_{i=1}^{n}\sum_{j=1}^{m} p^{ij}\, \partial u(C^j,-D^i)/(-D^i)D_0^i}{\sum_{i=1}^{n}\sum_{j=1}^{m} p^{ij}\, \partial u(C^j,-D^i)/\partial C^j}\right)$$

$$= h\left(\frac{E(\partial u(C,-D)/\partial(-D))D_0}{E(\partial u(C,-D)/\partial(-D))} \frac{E(\partial u(C,-D)/\partial(-D))}{E(\partial u(C,-D)/\partial C)}\right). \quad (A18)$$

By then using (A15), we obtain (39).

Derivation of Equation (47)

By differentiating (45) with respect to I, we obtain

$$\sum_{j}\psi'(EU(P^j))\left(\sum_{i}p^{ji}u'(C^i)(1+D_0^i f'(I))\right)q^j = 0, \quad (A19)$$

so

$$f'(I) = -\frac{\sum_{j}\sum_{i}q^j p^{ji}\psi'(EU(P^j))u'(C^i)}{\sum_{j}\sum_{i}q^j p^{ji}\psi'(EU(P^j))u'(C^i)D_0^i}, \quad (A20)$$

Since ψ' is constant, we can rewrite (A20) as

$$f'(I) = -\frac{\sum_{j}\sum_{i}q^j p^{ji}u'(C^i)}{\sum_{j}\sum_{i}q^j p^{ji}u'(C^i)D_0^i}. \quad (A21)$$

Let us use the short notation

$$SE^G(u'(C)D_0) = \sum_j \sum_i q^j p^{ji} u'(C^i) D_0^i \qquad (A22)$$

for the decision maker's subjective expected value of the product of the marginal utility of consumption and D_0. In other words, $SE^G(u'(C)D_0)$ reflects a weighted mean value of the initial damage, where the weights are given by the marginal utility of consumption. Substituting (46) and (A22) into (A21) then implies

$$f'(I) = -\frac{SE^G(u'(C))}{SE^G(u'(C)D_0)}. \qquad (A23)$$

Using again (9), we obtain

$$I = h\left(\frac{SE^G(u'(C)D_0)}{SE^G(u'(C))}\right), \qquad (A24)$$

where we can substitute

$$SE^G(u'(C)D_0) = SE^G(D_0)\left(1 + cov^G\left[\frac{D_0}{SE^G(D_0)}, \frac{u'(C)}{SE^G(u'(C))}\right]\right), \qquad (A25)$$

and obtain (47).

Derivation of Equation (49)

Let us use the short notation

$$SE^G(\psi'(EU)u'(C)D_0) = \sum_j \sum_i q^j p^{ji} \psi'(EU(P^j)) u'(C^i) D_0^i \qquad (A26)$$

for the decision maker's subjective expected value of the product of the marginal welfare of consumption and initial damage D_0. Thus, $SE^G(\psi'(EU)u'(C)D_0)$ reflects a weighted mean value of the initial damage, where the weights are given by the marginal welfare of consumption. Substituting (48) and (A26) into the first-order condition (A21), we obtain

$$f'(I) = -\frac{SE^G(\psi'(EU)u'(C))}{SE^G(\psi'(EU)u'(C)D_0)}. \qquad (A27)$$

Then, using (9), we obtain

$$I = h\left(\frac{SE^G(\psi'(EU)u'(C)D_0)}{SE^G(\psi'(EU)u'(C))}\right). \qquad (A28)$$

Using finally that

$$
\begin{aligned}
&SE^G(\psi'(EU)u'(C)D_0) \\
&= SE^G(D_0)\left(1+\text{cov}^G\left[\frac{D_0}{SE^G(D_0)},\frac{\psi'(EU)u'(C)}{SE^G(\psi'(EU)u'(C))}\right]\right),
\end{aligned}
\tag{A29}
$$

and substituting (A29) together with (46) into (A28), we obtain (49).

Derivation of Equation (53)

The first-order condition for an optimal investment level corresponding to (52) is given by

$$
\phi\sum_{i=1}^n p^{1i}u'\left(C^i\right)\left(1+D_0^i f'(I)\right)+(1-\phi)\sum_j\sum_{i=1}^n q^j p^{ji}u'\left(C^i\right)\left(1+D_0^i f'(I)\right)=0, \tag{A30}
$$

implying

$$
f'(I)=-\frac{\phi\sum_{i=1}^n p^{1i}u'\left(C^i\right)+(1-\phi)\sum_j\sum_{i=1}^n q^j p^{ji}u'\left(C^i\right)}{\phi\sum_{i=1}^n p^{1i}u'(C^i)D_0^i+(1-\phi)\sum_j\sum_{i=1}^n q^j p^{ji}u'(C^i)D_0^i}, \tag{A31}
$$

and, using (9),

$$
I=h\left(\frac{\phi\sum_{i=1}^n p^{1i}u'\left(C^i\right)D_0^i+(1-\phi)\sum_j\sum_{i=1}^n q^j p^{ji}u'\left(C^i\right)D_0^i}{\phi\sum_{i=1}^n p^{1i}u'(C^i)+(1-\phi)\sum_j\sum_{i=1}^n q^j p^{ji}u'(C^i)}\right). \tag{A32}
$$

Let us use the short notation

$$
SE^1(u'(C)D_0)=\sum_i p^{1i}u'\left(C^i\right)D_0 \tag{A33}
$$

for the expected value of the product of the marginal utility of consumption and initial damage associated with the most pessimistic probability distribution. Substituting (42), (46), (A25), and (A33) into (A32) then implies

$$
I=h\left(\frac{\phi SE^1(u'(C)D_0)+(1-\phi)SE^G(u'(C)D_0)}{\phi SE^1(u'(C))+(1-\phi)SE^G(u'(C))}\right). \tag{A34}
$$

By next using that

$$
SE^1(u'(C)D_0)=SE^1(D_0)\left(1+\text{cov}^1\left[\frac{D_0}{SE^1(D_0)},\frac{u'(C)}{SE^1(u'(C))}\right]\right) \tag{A35}
$$

and substituting (A22) into (A34), we obtain (53).

References

Al-Najjar, N. I., and J. Weinstein. 2009a. "The Ambiguity Aversion Literature: A Critical Assessment." *Economics and Philosophy* 25: 249–84.

———. 2009b. "Rejoinder: 'The Ambiguity Aversion Literature: A Critical Assessment.'" *Economics and Philosophy* 25: 357–69.

Arrow, K. J. 1971. *Essays in the Theory of Risk Bearing*. Chicago: Markham.

Attanasio, O. P., and M. Browning. 1995. "Consumption Over the Life Cycle and Over the Business Cycle." *American Economic Review* 85: 1118–37.

Becker, S., and F. O. Brownson. 1964. "What Price Ambiguity? Or the Role of Ambiguity in Decision Making." *Journal of Political Economy* 72: 62–73.

Benabou, R., and J. Tirole. 2002. "Self-Confidence and Personal Motivation." *Quarterly Journal of Economics* 117: 871–915.

Bernheim, D., and A. Rangel. 2007. "Toward Choice-Theoretic Foundations for Behavioral Welfare Economics." *American Economic Review: Papers and Proceedings* 464–70.

———. 2009. "Beyond Revealed Preference: Choice-Theoretic Foundations for Behavioral Welfare Economics." *Quarterly Journal of Economics* 124: 51–104.

Bernoulli, D. 1738. "Specimen Theoriae Novae de Mensura Sortis." *Commentarii Academiae Scientiatatum Imperalas Petropolitanae* 5: 175–92. Trans. as "Exposition of a New Theory on the Measurement of Risk." *Econometrica* 22 (1954), 23–6.

Blundell, R., M. Browning, and C. Meghir. 1994."Consumer Demand and the Life-Cycle Allocation of Household Expenditures." *Review of Economic Studies* 61: 57–80.

Bostrom, N. 2002. "Existential Risks: Analyzing Human Extinction Scenarios and Related Hazards." *Journal of Evolution and Technology* 9/1.

Brekke, K. A., and O. Johansson-Stenman. 2008. "The Behavioural Economics of Climate Change." *Oxford Review of Economic Policy* 24: 280–97.

Broome, J. 1999. *Ethics out of Economics*. Cambridge: Cambridge University Press.

Camerer, C., and M. Weber. 1992. "Recent Developments in Modelling Preferences: Uncertainty and Ambiguity." *Journal of Risk and Uncertainty* 5: 325–70.

———, S. Issacharoff, G. Loewenstein, T. O'Donoghue, and M. Rabin. 2003. "Regulation for Conservatives: Behavioral Economics and the Case for 'Asymmetric Paternalism.'" *University of PennsylvaniaLaw Review* 151: 1211–54.

Chambers, R. G., and T. A. Melkonyan. 2010. "Regulatory Policy Design in an Uncertain World." *Journal of Public Economic Theory* 12/6: 1081–1107.

Chen, Z., and L. G. Epstein. 2002. "Ambiguity, Risk, and Asset Returns in Continuous Time." *Econometrica* 70: 1403–43.

Chesson, H. W., and W. K. Viscusi. 2003. "Commonalities in Time and Ambiguity Aversion for Long-Term Risks." *Theory and Decision* 54: 57–71.

Chow, C. C., and R. K. Sarin. 2001. "Comparative Ignorance and the Ellsberg Paradox." *Journal of Risk and Uncertainty* 22: 129–39.

Collier, P. 2007. *The Bottom Billion*. Oxford: Oxford University Press.

Cropper, M. L. 1992. "The Determinants of Pesticide Regulation: A Statistical Analysis of EPA Decision Making." *Journal of Political Economy* 100: 175–97.

Curley, S. E., and F. J. Yates. 1989. "An Empirical Evaluation of Descriptive Models of Ambiguity Reactions in Choice Situations." *Journal of Mathematical Psychology* 33: 397–427.

De Finetti, B. 1937. "La Prévision: Ses lois logiques, ses sources subjectives." *Annales de l'Institut Henri Poincaré* 7: 1–68. Trans. H. E. Kyburg in H. E. Kyburg and H. E. Smokler, eds, *Studies in Subjective Probabilities*. New York: Wiley, 1964.

Drèze, J. H. 1987. *Essays on Economic Decisions under Uncertainty*. New York: Cambridge University Press.

——and F. Modigliani. 1972. "Consumption Decisions under Uncertainty." *Journal of Economic Theory* 5: 308–35.

Eeckhoudt, L., C. Gollier, and H. Schlesinger. 2005. *Economic and Financial Decisions under Risk*. Princeton: Princeton University Press.

Einhorn, H. J., and R. M. Hogarth. 1986. "Decision Making under Ambiguity." *Journal of Business* 59: S225–S250.

Ellsberg, D. 1961. "Risk, Ambiguity, and the Savage Axioms." *Quarterly Journal of Economics* 75: 643–69.

FAO (Food and Agriculture Organization). 2008. *The State of Food Insecurity in the World 2008*. Rome: Food and Agriculture Organization.

Gajdos, T., T. Hayashi, J.-M. Tallon, and J.-C. Vergnaud. 2008. "Attitude toward Imprecise Information." *Journal of Economic Theory* 140: 27–65.

Gilboa, I., ed. 2004. *Uncertainty in Economic Theory: Essays in Honor of David Schmeidler's 65th Birthday*. London: Routledge.

——and D. Schmeidler. 1989. "Maxmin Expected Utility with a Non-Unique Prior." *Journal of Mathematical Economics* 18: 141–53.

————. 2001. *A Theory of Case-Based Decisions*. Cambridge: Cambridge University Press.

——, A. Postlewaite, and D. Schmeidler. 2009. "Is It Always Rational to Satisfy Savage's Axioms?" *Economics and Philosophy* 25: 285–96.

Gollier, C. Forthcoming. "Does Ambiguity Aversion Reinforce Risk Aversion? Applications to Portfolio Choices and Asset Pricing." *Review of Economic Studies*.

——, B. Jullien, and N. Treich. 2000. "Scientific Progress and Irreversibility: An Economic Interpretation of the 'Precautionary Principle.'" *Journal of Public Economics* 75: 229–53.

Gruber, J., and B. Köszegi. 2002. "Is Addiction 'Rational'? Theory and Evidence." *Quarterly Journal of Economics* 116: 1261–1303.

Howarth, R. B. 2003. "Discounting and Uncertainty in Climate Change Policy Analysis." *Land Economics* 79: 369–81.

Johansson-Stenman, O. 2008. "Mad Cows, Terrorism and Junk Food: Should Public Policy Reflect Subjective or Objective Risks?" *Journal of Health Economics* 27: 234–48.

——2010. "Risk Aversion and Expected Utility of Consumption over Time." *Games and Economic Behavior* 68: 208–19.

Kahneman, D., and R. Thaler. 2006. "Anomalies: Utility Maximisation and Experienced Utility." *Journal of Economic Perspectives* 20: 221–34.

——and A. Tversky. 1979. "Prospect Theory: An Analysis of Decision under Risk." *Econometrica* 47: 263–91.

——, P. Wakker, and R. Sarin. 1997. "Back to Bentham? Explorations of Experienced Utility." *Quarterly Journal of Economics* 112: 375–405.

Karni, E. 1985. *Decision Making under Uncertainty: The Case of State Dependent Preferences*. Cambridge, MA: Harvard University Press.

——2009a. "State-Dependent Utility." In P. Anand, P. K. Pattanaik, and C. Puppe, eds, *Handbook of Rational and Social Choice*. Oxford: Oxford University Press.

Karni, E. 2009b. "A Reformulation of the Maxmin Expected Utility Model with Application to Agency Theory." *Journal of Mathematical Economics* 45: 97–112.

Klibanoff, P., M. Marinacci, and S. Mukerji. 2005. "A Smooth Model of Decision Making under Ambiguity." *Econometrica* 73: 1849–92.

—————. 2009. "Recursive Smooth Ambiguity Preferences." *Journal of Economic Theory* 144: 930–76.

Lichtenberg, E., and D. Zilberman. 1988. "Efficient Regulation of Environmental Health Risks." *Quarterly Journal of Economics* 103: 167–78.

—————, and K. Bogen. 1989. "Regulating Environmental Health Risks under Uncertainty: Groundwater Contamination in California." *Journal of Environmental Economics and Management* 17: 22–4.

Loomes, G., and R. Sugden. 1982. "Regret Theory: An Alternative Theory of Rational Choice under Uncertainty." *Economic Journal* 92: 805–24.

Mukerji, S., and J.-M. Tallon. 2001. "Ambiguity Aversion and Incompleteness of Financial Markets." *Review of Economic Studies* 68: 883–904.

Ng, Y.-K. 1999. "Utility, Informed Preference, or Happiness: Following Harsanyi's Argument to its Logical Conclusion." *Social Choice and Welfare* 16: 197–216.

O'Donoghue, T., and M. Rabin. 2006. "Optimal Sin Taxes." *Journal Public Economics* 90: 1825–49.

Rabin, M. 2000. "Risk Aversion and Expected Utility Theory: A Calibration Theorem." *Econometrica* 68: 1281–92.

——and R. H. Thaler. 2001. "Anomalies: Risk Aversion." *Journal of Economic Perspectives* 15: 219–32.

Ramsey, F. P. 1931. "Truth and Probability." In R. B. Braithwaite and F. Plumpton, eds, *The Foundations of Mathematics and Other Logical Essays*. London: Kegan Paul, Trench, Trubner.

Riddel, M., and W. D. Shaw. 2006. "A Theoretically-Consistent Empirical Model of Non-Expected Utility: An Application to Nuclear-Waste Transport." *Journal of Risk and Uncertainty* 32: 131–50.

Ritov, I., and J. Baron. 1990. "Reluctance to Vaccinate: Omission Bias and Ambiguity." *Journal of Behavioral Decision Making* 3: 263–77.

Rothschild, M., and J. E. Stiglitz. 1970a. "Increasing Risk: I. A Definition." *Journal of Economic Theory* 2/3: 225–43.

—————. 1970b. "Increasing Risk II: Its Economic Consequences." *Journal of Economic Theory* 3/1: 66–84.

Sarin, R. K., and M. Weber. 1993. "Effects of Ambiguity in Market Experiments." *Management Science* 39: 602–15.

Savage, L. J. 1954. *The Foundations of Statistics*. New York: Wiley.

——1972. *The Foundations of Statistics*, rev., enlarged. New York: Dover.

Schmeidler, D. 1989. "Subjective Probability and Expected Utility without Additivity." *Econometrica* 57: 571–87.

Schmidt, U., C. Starmer, and R. Sugden. 2008. "Third-Generation Prospect Theory." *Journal of Risk and Uncertainty* 36: 203–23.

Shogren, J. F. 2005. "Economics of Diet and Health: Research Challenges." *Food Economics: Acta Agriculturae Scandinavica C* 2/3–4: 117–27.

Siniscalchi, M. 2009a. "Two Out of Three Ain't Bad: A Comment on 'The Ambiguity Aversion Literature: A Critical Assessment.'" *Economics and Philosophy* 25: 335–56.

—— 2009b. *Dynamic Choice under Ambiguity*. Technical Report No. 1430, CMS-EMS Discussion Paper. Evanston, Ill.: Northwestern University.

Slovic, P., and A. Tversky. 1974. "Who Accepts Savage's Axiom?" *Behavioral Science* 19: 368–73.

Starmer, C. 2000. "Developments in Non-Expected Utility Theory: The Hunt for a Descriptive Theory of Choice under Risk." *Journal of Economic Literature* 38: 332–82.

Stern, N. 2007. *The Economics of Climate Change: The Stern Review*. Cambridge: Cambridge University Press.

Sugden, R. 2004. "The Opportunity Criterion: Consumer Sovereignty without the Assumption of Coherent Preferences." *American Economic Review* 94: 1014–33.

Sunstein, C. R. 2000. "Cognition and Cost–Benefit Analysis." In M. D. Adler and E. A. Posner, eds, *Cost–Benefit Analysis: Legal, Economic and Philosophical Perspectives*. Chicago: University of Chicago Press.

—— 2005. *Laws of Fear: Beyond the Precautionary Principle*. Cambridge: Cambridge University Press.

Thaler, R. H., and C. R. Sunstein. 2008. *Nudge: Improving Decisions about Health, Wealth, and Happiness*. New Haven: Yale University Press.

Treich, N. 2010. "The Value of a Statistical Life under Ambiguity Aversion." *Journal of Environmental Economics and Management* 59: 15–26.

Tversky, A., and D. Kahneman. 1992. "Advances in Prospect Theory: Cumulative Representation of Uncertainty." *Journal of Risk and Uncertainty* 5: 297–323.

Viscusi, W. K. 1998. *Rational Risk Policy*. New York: Oxford University Press.

—— and J. T. Hamilton. 1999. "Are Risk Regulators Rational? Evidence from Hazardous Waste Cleanup Decisions." *American Economic Review* 89: 210–27.

Vissing-Jørgensen, A. 2002. "Limited Asset Market Participation and the Elasticity of Intertemporal Substitution." *Journal of Political Economy* 4: 825–53.

von Neumann, J., and O. Morgenstern. 1944. *Theory of Games and Economic Behavior*. Princeton: Princeton University Press.

CHAPTER 18

PRIVATE VERSUS THIRD PARTY VERSUS GOVERNMENT LABELING

JULIE A. CASWELL AND SVEN M. ANDERS

1 PRIVATE VERSUS THIRD PARTY VERSUS GOVERNMENT LABELING

Labeling is a means of changing the amount or kind of product information that is available in the market. It can be analyzed and evaluated by asking who wants to change information availability and why, and what impact those changes have on market performance and for whom. Major leverage in answering these questions has come from viewing products as sets of attributes (e.g., taste, color, food safety, nutritional content, and production methods) and recognizing that buyers' perception of product quality depends on their information about and experience with these product attributes. Labeling can significantly change the information environment, purchasing behavior, and markets for quality themselves. This potential to influence markets underlies the current great interest in food labeling among companies, non-governmental organizations (NGOs), governments, and consumers.

This chapter focuses on understanding the relative merits of private, third party, and government labeling systems that differ in who sets the standards and who certifies that the product deserves to carry the label. In practice there are no clear demarcations between private, third party, and government labeling. There are many hybrid schemes, and innovation in labeling program design is ongoing. To analyze different types of labeling we focus first briefly on economic and marketing tools for under-standing relationships between information, product quality, and labeling. We turn to incentives and rationales for labeling to be private, third party, or government-based and considerations for evaluating the performance of labeling systems. We then present a survey of the evidence to date on the performance impacts of different labeling schemes. We conclude with a discussion of key issues for the future of food labeling, food labeling policy, and performance.

2   ECONOMIC AND MARKETING TOOLS FOR UNDERSTANDING LABELING

The role of information in determining the operation of markets has been a major focus of economic and marketing research in recent decades. The impact of labeling has similarly received significant attention. Here we summarize key insights from this work that are relevant to the comparison of different types of food labeling.

2.1   Economic Tools for Understanding the Operation of Markets for Quality

The level of information and who has access to it are major determinants of how markets perform because information on price and quality drives the purchase of products by consumers. When consumers (or buyers in general) have perfect information, they are able to select products that best match their preferences or choose not to purchase if products do not meet their needs. When information is imperfect or lacking, market failures of several varieties may occur. Consumers may fail to buy products that meet their preferences because they are unaware of, cannot be assured of, or are deceived about the quality of the product.

The inability of consumers to identify and purchase products that fit their preferences causes failures in markets for quality. Akerlof (1970) described an example of such a failure with his "lemons" problem in the market for used cars. A lack of credible quality signals creates incentive for sellers to misrepresent the true quality of their products and lowers buyers' willingness to pay for high quality. Ultimately, the asymmetry of information between buyers and sellers will lead the market for higher quality to collapse.

Akerlof's work, and analysis that has built on it, have proven powerful in understanding information and markets for quality because it so clearly explains the relationship between credible information and the existence of markets for quality. Good information supports not only markets for high-quality products but, more generally, markets for diverse levels of quality where different combinations of price and quality can be matched to consumer preferences and willingness to pay. Akerlof also focused on mechanisms, including prevention of fraud, certification, and labeling, that can support credible signaling of quality and, therefore, markets for quality.

Two further economic tools are essential for understanding food labeling. The first tool is the recognition that the information environment for product quality varies not only in the amount of information available but also in its timing. Akerlof's work focuses on an experience good: the quality of the used car can only be evaluated by the buyer after purchase and use. Other products will be search goods, where the quality can be evaluated prior to purchase, while still others are credence goods, where the buyer cannot effectively evaluate quality even after purchase and use (Nelson 1970, 1974; Darby and Karni 1973). The second further tool is viewing products as bundles of attributes based on Lancaster's (1971) alternative characterization of consumer demand, where consumers are seen as demanding the attributes of products rather than the product itself. Their overall evaluation of product quality and willingness to pay is based on the bundle of attributes offered by the product.

Putting these economic tools together, labeling influences markets because it affects the amount and types of information available and can mitigate failures in markets for quality that result from consumers having no, lacking, or asymmetric information. Food labeling influences the information environment and markets for quality through conveying information about the search, experience, or credence attributes of food products.

2.2   Marketing Tools for Understanding the Operation of Markets for Quality

Marketing is focused on communication and the means by which the design, production quality, packaging, and all other attributes of the product are combined successfully to signal quality levels to consumers. Useful tools for evaluating food labeling emerge from the marketing-based quality perception framework. This framework distinguishes between the effects on the quality level perceived by consumers of a product's intrinsic quality attributes and the extrinsic quality indicators and cues that may be used to signal quality (Steenkamp 1989; Steenkamp and van Trijp 1996). Together these intrinsic and extrinsic aspects create a differentiated attribute space for products.

Figure 18.1 shows the attribute space for food products (Caswell 2006). A product's quality is determined by its set of intrinsic quality attributes. The major intrinsic quality attribute categories for food are safety, nutrition, sensory, value/function, and process. Consumers value these attributes and as a bundle they determine the buyers' perception of quality and willingness to pay. The intrinsic quality attributes may be signaled to buyers through, and their quality perceptions are influenced by, extrinsic quality indicators and cues the product carries such as certification, labeling, price, and brand name.

Much discussion of labeling and certification for food products has made use of a distinction between product and process attributes of products. This approach has

Intrinsic quality attributes	Extrinsic quality indicators and cues
1. Food safety attributes Foodborne pathogens Heavy metals and toxins Pesticide or drug residues Soil and water contaminants Food additives, preservatives Physical hazards Spoilage and botulism Irradiation and fumigation Other **2. Nutrition attributes** Calories Fat and cholesterol content Sodium and minerals Carbohydrates and fiber content Protein Vitamins Other **3. Sensory/organoleptic attributes** Taste and tenderness Color Appearance/blemishes Freshness Softness Smell/aroma Other **4. Value/function attributes** Compositional integrity Size Style Preparation/convenience Package materials Keepability Other **5. Process attributes** Animal welfare Authenticity of process/place of origin Legality of production practices Traceability Biotechnology/biochemistry Organic/environmental impact Worker safety Other	**1. Test/measurement indicators** Quality management systems Certification Records Traceability Quality signaling/labeling Minimum quality standards Occupational licensing Other **2. Cues** Price Brand name Manufacturer name Store name Packaging Advertising Country of origin Distribution outlet Warranty Reputation Past purchase experience Other information provided

↔

FIGURE 18.1 Attribute space for food products

Source: Adapted from Caswell (2006).

defined product attributes as those internal to the product and process attributes as somehow external to the product. We do not use this distinction because we do not view it as particularly helpful. For example, how a food is processed (e.g., organic) may affect internal attributes (e.g., pesticide residues), meaning that many process attributes are unlikely to be only external to the final product. Adopting the approach of treating the entire range of product attributes as intrinsic, as is done in Figure 18.1, facilitates analysis of multifaceted labeling and certification programs that can address multiple product attributes. More generally, a marketing approach highlights the opportunities for companies arising from coordinated use of intrinsic quality attributes and extrinsic quality indicators and cues to signal quality to consumers.

2.3   How Labeling Schemes Work

Labeling schemes work by altering the information environment for buyers. Labeling can improve the information environment for any type of intrinsic quality attribute regardless of whether it is search, experience, or credence. The scope for enhanced information is usually largest with credence attributes where information is least available to buyers (Golan, Kuchler, and Mitchell 2001). For example, it can assure that a product was produced organically. Labeling can also improve information availability for experience attributes. For example, labeling could assure buyers about the cooking characteristics of a food product by setting and communicating standards for the product. Effective labeling can transform credence and experience attributes into search attributes (Caswell and Mojduszka 1996). The information environment for attributes that are already search can also be improved through labeling, for example if the labeling program lowers the cost of searching for information.

The final market-level impacts of labeling for consumers are connected to changes throughout the supply chain. Product labeling and other forms of quality signaling are systems with a clear hierarchy. They require setting of a quality standard, verifying or certifying that a product conforms to the standard along the supply chain, and then labeling. Thus, labeling schemes are inextricably linked to quality assurance systems. These systems for final-product marketing are in turn a subset of all quality assurance and certification systems in use throughout the supply chain to control business-to-business as well as business-to-consumer transactions. While our primary focus is on consumer labeling, we also discuss business-to-business systems as part of the overall quality assurance and signaling landscape for food products.

Table 18.1 presents a typology that captures the main elements in labeling schemes including who owns (and sets) the labeling standard, who certifies that products (and/or processes) meet the standard and are eligible for a label, and whether the scheme is voluntary or mandatory. The typology is arranged to move from private to third party to government schemes. Types I through V are voluntary, while Type VI is mandatory. Type I involves private standard setting, certification, and labeling by either the

Table 18.1 A labeling typology

Type	Owner of labeling standard	Primary means of label certification	Labeling approach	Description
I	Private, first or second party	First or second party	Voluntary	Product or process attribute claims on labels by individual companies based on self-declared standards, with self-certification by buyer or seller
II	Private, collective third party	First or second party	Voluntary	Product or process attribute claims on labels by companies based on collective self-declared standards, with self-certification by buyer or seller
III	Private, collective third party	Third party	Voluntary	Product or process attribute claims on labels by companies based on collective self-declared standards, with third party certification
IV	Independent third party	Third party	Voluntary	Product or process attribute claims on labels by companies based on standards set by independent body (e.g., non-governmental organization, private certification body), with third party certification
V	Government	Government or third party	Voluntary	Product or process attribute claims on labels by companies based on government standard, with government or third party certification
VI	Government	Government	Mandatory	Product or process attribute claims on labels by companies based on government standard, with government certification

Note: First party = product seller; second party = product buyer; third party = not the buyer, seller, or government (e.g., private collectives of companies; independent entities such as non-governmental organizations or private certification bodies). Government = local, regional, national, or multi-country government entities.

product seller (first party) or the buyer (second party). In Types II and III the standards are private but set by a collective of companies, with first, second, or third party certification. We label these collectives as third party recognizing that they are not independent third parties. In Type IV independent third parties (NGOs or private certification bodies) set and certify label claims. In Types V and VI governments set standards with government or third party certification. We now turn to rationales and incentives for private, third party, and government labeling; criteria for judging label performance; and evidence to date on label performance.

3   INCENTIVES AND RATIONALES FOR LABELING SCHEMES

Interest in labeling in food markets has grown based on private incentives, initiatives of independent bodies (e.g., NGOs and certification organizations), and government rationales for labeling. Private parties seek to differentiate their products using credible labeling. Third party certification bodies have stepped forward to serve this need, while NGOs have developed third party labeling schemes largely to encourage specific production practices. Many governments use information as an alternative regulatory strategy. Informed consumer choices may achieve policy objectives more effectively or in a more politically acceptable manner than direct regulation of production practices or food products themselves. This mix of forces explains the great diversity in labeling approaches seen in different product markets and across countries.

3.1   Private Incentives for Labeling

There are multiple incentives for Type I voluntary labeling by private first and second parties. First and foremost, successful labeling allows companies to differentiate their products and potentially influence consumer preferences. These are profit-driven or market-defending incentives for companies to label their products. Labeling can reduce imperfect and asymmetric information, supporting market differentiation through matching consumers with willingness to pay for particular attributes with products offering those attributes (Golan, Kuchler, and Mitchell 2001; Roe and Sheldon 2007). Labeling coupled with underlying certification systems can convey assurances about the quality of a very wide range of attributes. Market failures can be market opportunities as creation of standards, certification, and quality signaling (labeling) systems can successfully differentiate products in the market.

A second, related incentive for labeling programs stems from the paradigm shift in the development of more complex vertical relationships in food marketing. Quality signaling and consumer labeling can be used in conjunction with standards and certification to provide quality assurance along the supply chain, again supporting value creation and market shares.

Overall behind this interest in quality signaling is the growing influence of consumer perceptions, concerns, and demand; changing regulatory environments; and increased retail concentration (Henson 2008). Recent market developments have seen a significant shift in the locus of standard setting and certification activities from individual companies (first and second parties) to third parties. The initial adoption of private retail food standards was primarily driven by competition among retailers to differentiate themselves and establish a reputation with their customer base. At the same time, integration of many food supply chains and globalization created potentially increased risks from uncertain quality, particularly safety, in supply chains. Setting their own standards and certifying suppliers allows multinational companies to protect their reputations and brands, while reducing liability. The range of attributes of interest in quality competition has continued to increase, for example focusing on environmental footprints, labor and social standards, and animal welfare (Hatanaka, Bain, and Busch 2005).

3.2   Incentives for Development of Third Party Labeling

The period of very active development of Type I labeling by first and second parties has been followed by a move toward greater convergence of private food standards into Type II and III systems (private, collective third party), particularly by retailers (Fulponi 2006) but also by consortia of retailers, processors, and others. In addition, Type IV labeling by independent third parties has grown, particularly by NGOs and private certification bodies.

In Type II and III voluntary labeling, common standards are set by private, collective third parties. This convergence to common standards can have several benefits. These standards free companies from continuous updating of their own standards. The benefit is reinforced when buyers move from second to third party auditing, allowing them to source product flexibly from suppliers who hold certification to the standard without new audits to individual standards. These standards may also simplify operations and reduce barriers to entry/continuation of certification for suppliers who are subject to fewer standards and certification audits. On the negative side from a company perspective, common private third party standards reduce the scope for differentiation from competitors. Indeed, successful common retail standards (e.g., GlobalGAP 2009) are frequently primarily used in business-to-business transactions within the supply chain and not at the consumer level (Henson and Reardon 2005).

Concern about the rise of private, collective third party systems has focused on the potential that they may be used as a means for concentrated and powerful retailers or processors to further implement their own private global food management systems. Certification while voluntary may be required for participation in high-value supply chains, with the systems having a "pay to play nature" where the fee structures for certification may extract surplus (profits) from market participants. Stated in economic terms, fees may be used as a form of price discrimination that exploits producers' willingness to pay to participate in particular supply chains. Concern has additionally focused on whether Type II and III systems place unreasonable burdens on exporters in developing countries.

Type IV labeling by independent third parties (NGOs and private certification bodies) is also on the rise. NGO labeling schemes are typically designed with two goals in mind. The first is to set standards for particular production and marketing practices that the NGO supports along supply chains. The second is to create or support a consumer market for these practices in order to encourage companies to follow them. NGOs can both shape and give voice to consumer and societal demands. For example, the Marine Stewardship Council sets standards for sustainable fisheries practices, while certification and labeling at the consumer level establishes a market mechanism to reward companies that follow these practices with sales that may be at a premium price. NGOs may also be concerned with establishing fairness in supply chains, for example through fair trade standards. Independent certification bodies establish Type IV labeling schemes as a business opportunity, to play a role as a neutral and fair party in the supply chain, or to promote particular products or processes.

3.3   Policy Rationales for Government Labeling

The major incentives for Type V voluntary and VI mandatory labeling by governments are to correct or mitigate market failures or imperfections. In the case of market failure, demand for particular quality attributes is societal rather than consumer-driven. For example, governments may set and enforce standards when a private market for safety fails to exist or underperforms because consumers are not fully aware of the health implications of the products they purchase or do not personally experience the full cost of product choice and use. In cases of public goods (e.g., prevention of public health risks from *E. coli*), the private sector usually undersupplies quality. In cases of significant risks, governments may use direct, mandatory regulation to improve social welfare. Labeling may be used when direct regulation is constrained (e.g., for tobacco products) or as a complement to direct regulation (e.g., labeling of safe use practices for meat products).

In the case of market imperfections, particularly imperfect information, governments seek to play an active role in information provision through voluntary and mandatory labeling programs and through systems to prevent and punish fraud and deception. Whether a country chooses to use mandatory or voluntary programs is strongly influenced by whether it believes there is a market imperfection (or at the extreme a market failure) in providing information and how it views its responsibility to address the problem. Governments may take four main approaches to consumer labeling (Caswell 2006):

- *Need-to-know.* Governments may judge that the public needs to know some information (e.g., nutritional quality, environmental sustainability) in making a purchase decision or safely using a product. In this case, labeling will usually be mandatory.
- *Right-to-know.* Governments may judge that the public has a right to know other information before buying a product. This information is frequently about attributes that are not safety-related but are other attributes that consumers

care about. In this case, labeling will also usually be mandatory ensuring that a defined minimum level of information is provided.

- *Want-to-know.* Governments may judge that the public wants to know other information about products or production processes. The regulator may actively oversee the provision of this information when it believes doing so will increase market efficiency (e.g., certified organic). A frequent means of doing so is by setting standards or defining minimum requirements that are the basis for voluntary labeling.
- *Fraud protection.* At base, governments are always responsible for protecting consumers against market deception and fraud in claims made for products.

Governments may view the benefits and costs of regulation and of labeling differently and choose different types of level accordingly, as occurred in the cases of hormones in beef and the labeling of biotechnology/genetically modified organisms (Bureau, Marette, and Schiavina 1998; Caswell 2000; Gruere, Carter, and Farzin 2009). In other areas, consensus is developing, for example that nutritional labeling is "need-to-know" and should be mandatory. As a further example, governments now largely treat eco-labeling as a "want-to-know" or "fraud protection" situation by establishing government-based voluntary standards or monitoring first, second, or third party claims. In the United States, voluntary federal organic standards serve "want-to-know" and "fraud protection" goals.

Governments do not only focus on consumer information in choosing labeling programs. Labeling may also serve other purposes including influencing product design, assuring the public that monitoring is being done, defining public values, and forming a basis for educational programs (Caswell and Padberg 1992). The programs may also be designed to promote market development or other societal goals. For example, state-level labeling programs such as Washington apples can be geared toward promoting local industry but may face problems of free-riding on the jointly held reputation of the product by low-quality producers (McCluskey and Loureiro 2005). Similarly, organic standards and labeling can support market development. In the European Union, regulations establishing protected designations of origin and protected geographical indications are based on consumer information, industry and rural development, cultural heritage, and fraud protection objectives (Giovannucci et al. 2009).

While labeling programs may correct or mitigate market failures or imperfections, they may also create them. Private parties, NGOs, or others may seek rents through the establishment of government labeling programs that misrepresent (inflate) quality or disadvantage rival products or supply chains. In an era of reduced traditional barriers to trade, labeling can be used by governments as a non-tariff trade barrier. A currently controversial labeling program in this respect is country-of-origin labeling (Anders and Caswell 2009b).

4   Performance Considerations for Evaluating Labeling Systems

Multiple incentives have resulted in a very diverse set of private, third party, and government labeling schemes. The performance of labeling systems may be evaluated from private, group, and government perspectives based on measuring benefits and costs and their incidence. From an overall societal viewpoint, the question is what levels of labeling and division of underlying standard setting and labeling responsibilities between private companies, third parties, and government best reaches performance objectives. This division of labor is particularly important to consider as labeling systems continue to develop rapidly and because scarce resources, both private and governmental, force decision makers to search for the most effective options—including the possible conclusion that labeling has more costs than benefits or that other regulatory approaches are more beneficial. Moreover, the trade-offs between the different objectives that stakeholders (private and public) have for adopting and implementing standards need to be understood. We discuss performance considerations in four groups.

4.1   Informing and Serving Consumer Choice

The central function of labeling schemes is to deliver information to consumers. Labeling can correct for absent, asymmetric, or incomplete information, allowing consumers to identify and purchase products that best meet their needs. This matching of consumers to products in turn supports markets for diverse levels of quality. Of course, labeling can also be used to persuade consumers that particular product attributes are important and should be considered in the purchase decision.

Setting a baseline for "improvements" in consumer decision-making is important to evaluating the performance of all six types of labeling scheme. Teisl, Bockstael, and Levy (2001) argue that a clear metric is whether consumers are better matched to the products that meet their needs. For example, Type I (private, voluntary) nutrition labeling by supermarkets may allow some consumers to select low-fat, nutritionally sound products, while others use it to find the products with the most fat—both should be considered improvements. On the other hand, the benefits measures in the regulatory impact analysis for the Type VI (government, mandatory) nutrition labeling in the United States counts consumer moves toward more nutritious products and related improvements in health outcomes as benefits but not better matching of other consumers to less nutritious products (USFDA 1991). Similarly, companies will evaluate the effectiveness of Types I to III (private and private, collective) labeling based on whether consumers purchase more of their products based on the standards being met and quality signaling through labeling. For Type IV labeling, NGOs will also judge effectiveness by increased sales of labeled (e.g., eco-labeled) products and support for preferred, underlying production standards. From their different perspectives, each of these approaches to measuring the labeling effect is legitimate.

The growth of labeling schemes has led to concern that label proliferation threatens to diminish the expected welfare benefits from increased information (Gracia, Loureiro, and Nayga 2007). Such proliferation may increase search costs for consumers and transaction costs for supply chain stakeholders. At the same time, consumers may benefit from having competing standards in the market that provide variety in certification and label choices. Labeling benefits can be reduced or the overall welfare effect may even be negative if the competing certifications are difficult to understand, verify, or trust.

The presence or absence of fraud and deception is important to the evaluation of all six types of labeling schemes. Problems may occur in setting standards, certification, or labeling. In monitoring claims, governments must take a position on the degree of freedom to give the market in choosing attributes to label. For example, is any claim that can be supported non-deceptive even if the attribute has no real influence on quality? Governments must have a regulatory philosophy, set guidelines, or directly regulate labeling schemes to address this issue.

4.2   Business-to-Business Communication and Value Chain Development

A second major function of labeling schemes is to coordinate business-to-business activities and develop value chains. This marketing support may be primarily dependent on standard setting and certification activities, with labeling being the tip of the iceberg (Bureau, Marette, and Schiavina 1998). In some cases the process may not employ retail labeling at all (e.g., GlobalGAP). However, consumer-level labeling creates incentives for production of particular quality levels that reach back through the entire supply chain (Jahn, Schramm, and Spiller 2005).

As with consumer information, the performance considerations and metrics depend upon the viewpoint. For Type I labeling, the performance of the labeling scheme is judged by first and second parties based on private benefits (e.g., differentiation, coordination) and costs (e.g., standard setting, standard monitoring, and labeling). For Types II and III labeling (private, collective third party), benefits are judged by the participants again based on benefits and costs of participation. These benefits and costs may be viewed differently by different participants. The same labeling scheme that is viewed as streamlining and efficient in producing quality by major retailers may be viewed as oppressive and arbitrary by some suppliers. Type IV labeling players (NGOs and independent certifying bodies) focus on either attainment of market awareness, participation, and volume goals, or other organizational goals.

Type V labeling schemes (government, voluntary) may also focus on value chain development. A prominent example is the European Union's systems of protected designations of origin and protected geographical indications (Giovannucci et al. 2009). Market development is a central objective of these schemes.

In this area of performance evaluation, too, governments must have a regulatory philosophy for overseeing business-to-business activities and value chain development through labeling schemes. For example, governments may monitor and regulate Types I to IV labeling schemes to assure transparency and lack of fraud, and that they are fairly operated and not functioning as a platform for implicit or explicit collusion (e.g., quantity restrictions, quality restrictions, price setting, exclusionary practices). This may be particularly important with the rise of powerful third party labeling schemes. The costs of loss of credibility in terms of market reputation and share can create strong incentives for certification systems to police themselves (McCluskey and Loureiro 2005). When governments themselves become active in chain development through Type V labeling, their activities should be monitored with the same performance goals in mind.

4.3   Additional Group and Societal Goals

Labeling may be pursued by third parties and governments for additional group or public policy goals focused on welfare considerations. Several examples will serve to illustrate the breadth of these additional goals. NGOs have established standards in Type IV labeling schemes with the intent of providing incentives for environmental (eco-labeling) and economic (fair trade) sustainability (Crespi and Marette 2005). Governments have established voluntary Type V systems of geographical identification for foods to support rural development and for retention of cultural heritage (Marette, Clemens, and Babcock 2007). Governments have mandated nutrition labeling schemes (Type VI) as a measure to address the obesity problem and reduce the burdens of health care costs (Teisl, Bockstael, and Levy 2001).

In general, Types II through IV labeling (third party in standards and/or certification) provide a higher degree of independence between the labeler and the party seeking labeling. Souza Monteiro and Anders (2010) identify certifier independence and objectiveness as attributes of crucial importance to the credibility of certification schemes.

For governments, the choice of labeling strategies is part of a larger decision process in which they determine which risks or attributes require intervention and the level of intervention into markets. Governments also have obligations to comply with international trade agreements in designing labeling schemes. Voluntary labeling programs (Type V) as well as co-regulation (García Martínez et al. 2007) hybrids of Types II through IV may be viewed as a relatively mild and cost-effective form of market intervention that leaves choice to consumers and provides incentives to supply chains.

4.4 Who Controls the Process of Labeling Scheme Development?

A final performance consideration is who controls the process of developing labeling schemes and whether there is or needs to be any overall coherence in this process. Is there a means of assuring over time that private, third party, and government labeling schemes develop by incorporating best practices for standard setting, certification, and labeling?

The development of labeling, with underlying standards and certification, may result in a healthy competition to determine who can best provide and communicate quality assurance to consumers and in the supply chain. The process can address problems of imperfect information and facilitate markets for quality attributes, especially for credence attributes. It can use market mechanisms to reward desirable practices through product differentiation and potential price premiums as buyers in the supply chain and consumers can better identify and trust in higher-quality products. It can be used by governments, consumer groups, NGOs, and private parties to provide incentives for positive developments on both the supply and demand sides of the market.

However, there is potential for labeling to work poorly or incompletely in facilitating markets for quality. Labeling, and related standards and certification, may impose requirements on the production chain that do not actually improve delivered quality because requirements are not well targeted. They may provide false signals of quality through either poor design or fraud, making it more difficult for buyers to locate products that meet their needs. They may be used strategically by companies, groups of companies, countries, or other parties to disadvantage competing products or to extract payments. A labeling approach may not be appropriate at all for attributes with public good characteristics or significant risks to entire sectors and/or populations. Given the potential up and down sides of labeling development, a key question is the performance of private versus third party versus government labeling.

5 Economic Evidence on the Impacts of Different Types of Food Labeling

Labeling systems, food standards, and certification of attributes are developing simultaneously on several fronts. The academic interest in the economic mechanisms of food labeling has grown accordingly. The discussion of labeling and certification in food industries has long been dominated by Type VI mandatory labeling standards. As a complementary regulatory tool to push behavioral change among consumers, mandatory labeling has often also induced important changes and innovation across food markets that contribute to the achievement of specific policy objectives (Teisl and Roe 1998).

As consumers have learned to understand and use complex label information, demand and willingness to pay for information on how and where a food was produced and who produced it have contributed to the growth of Types I through IV private and third party labeling. Labeling of food quality attributes that goes well beyond mandatory minimum requirements poses growing regulatory challenges in preserving and communicating food quality, especially safety, along globalized supply chains.

Several streams of academic work have resulted in numerous theoretical papers and empirical studies that advance understanding of the economics of food labeling. However, comparative analyses of the impact of different types of labeling scheme on consumer choices and firm behavior are few and the relative merits of different types of labeling are under debate. Also, to date economists have presented limited evidence on the merits of various mechanisms that exist to assure the credibility and trustworthiness of competing food labels—apart from a long-running discussion over the effectiveness of voluntary versus mandatory food labeling (Caswell 1998). Here we first explore evidence on the impact of Type VI mandatory labeling, then turn to evidence on voluntary labeling schemes (Types I through V).

5.1   Evidence on the Impact of Type VI Mandatory Labeling

Governments may or should intervene to regulate the production and/or consumption of goods in cases where market failure, socially unacceptable outcomes, or evidence of unfair competition exists. Golan, Kuchler, and Mitchell (2001) state that mandatory labeling can be an appropriate regulatory tool under circumstances where consumer preferences are heterogeneous. Mandatory labeling should occur only when no other political consensus on regulation exists. The respective information has to be clear and concise, and should enhance food quality, and regulatory costs and benefits should both be borne by the consumer. Motivated by poor consumer fraud protection and unfair competition, mandatory food labeling in the United States has been dominated by efforts to improve consumer nutrition information to achieve specific nutrition policy objectives.

Following the seminal work on the economics of product attributes and information by Nelson (1970, 1974) and Darby and Karni (1973), the labeling literature has applied various qualitative and quantitative methods to investigate consumers' label use and response patterns. For credence attributes, labeling and the provision of information rest on the ability to mitigate search cost and transform "hidden" information into searchable attributes (Caswell and Mojduszka 1996). The existing labeling literature on credence food attributes certainly supports this case, although experts agree that information deficits and demands are affected by a multitude of environmental, socioeconomic, and psychological factors.

The 1990 US Nutrition Labeling and Education Act (NLEA), which mandated nutrition labeling, has received the greatest research attention (Drichoutis, Lazaridis, and Nayga 2005). It was passed in response to rising food-related chronic diseases and a proliferation of voluntary nutrition labeling. Several studies indicate that the NLEA affected consumer behavior (Variyam 2008). However, the literature is in disaccord as to whether mandatory labeling has led to lasting nutritional improvements among US consumers. Lin, Lee, and Yen (2004) argue in favor of a lasting impact on consumers' use of nutrition information and Mathios (2000) for an increase in the general degree of information made available by food manufacturers. Mojduszka and Caswell (2000) find that nutrition quality signaling was flawed prior to passage of the NLEA, and Kim, Nayga, and Capps (2000) find a positive impact of label usage on nutrition and diet quality in the US population. However, Variyam (2008) argues that previous findings on the impact of label use on intake of selected nutrients (e.g., fat, sodium) need to be viewed with caution when evaluating future benefits and costs of nutrition labeling policies.

The public discussion of diet health issues has generally viewed the NLEA as a success (Crespi and Marette 2005). Yet, much of this success has been attributed to its focus on educating consumers on how to read labels. Kiesel and Villas-Boas (2007) emphasize that ignoring differential influences and interdependencies in the effects of media sources on consumer behavior can potentially bias the results of benefit–cost analysis of labeling policies. Analysis of issues surrounding food regulation in the United States (e.g., Nestle 2000) may offer additional explanations for the largely mixed results on the success of food labeling policies found in the literature (Golan, Kuchler, and Mitchell 2001).

Golan, Kuchler, and Krissoff (2007) conclude that the primary effects of mandatory labeling of foods may be on product reformulation to avoid unfavorable disclosures. The recent labeling requirement for trans fats in the United States is a case in point (Unnevehr and Jagmanaite 2008). While label users directly benefit from the additional information, the welfare of non-users also increases as product quality improves owing to reformulation induced by regulation (Caswell and Padberg 1992). However, anticipated benefits of mandatory labeling may largely depend on the strategic behavior of firms in response to the regulation and consumers' understanding and use of labeling information provided to them (Variyam and Cawley 2006).

The costs of mandatory labeling can roughly be divided into government and industry costs. The governmental costs of mandatory regulation are borne by taxpayers, and industry costs will be reflected in product pricing to consumers. A "fair" distribution of labeling cost will largely depend on consumers' willingness to pay (WTP) for information. This calls into question whether tax mechanisms to recoup the cost of mandatory labeling are optimal and non-distorting (Crespi and Marette 2005).

The choice of mandatory labeling may rely in part on whether the private market will voluntarily provide quality attributes and labeling about them. This in turn depends on the underlying demand for the attributes themselves. There are a relatively large number of studies of consumer WTP for numerous credence attributes. These range from nutritional labeling (Prathiraja and Ariyawardana 2003), organic foods (Kalaitzandonakes, Marks, and Vickner 2004), and animal welfare (Lusk, Norwood, and Pruitt 2006), to the geographical origin of food stuffs (Loureiro and Umberger 2005). Results range from substantial price premiums and distinct consumer segments to avoidance behavior or insignificant effects. Drichoutis, Lazaridis, and Nayga (2005) point out that few existing WTP studies sufficiently address differences in benefit–cost considerations among consumer segments. The authors conclude that more WTP studies are needed to elicit differences in labeling benefit–cost ratios across a variety of food products, types of information, and markets.

From a firm's point of view, mandated information on food packages would only be optimal if the information generates more revenue. Mandatory labeling will only help to improve a firm's communication or signaling efforts if the labeling is conducted credibly and allows consumers to verify the claims made. This in turn will limit the ability of competitors to misuse labeling as a purely competitive tool (Teisl and Roe 1998). Changes in mandatory labeling rules, if seen through the Akerlof (1970) "lemons" model, can create new market opportunities and competition between companies as uncertainty, resulting information asymmetries, and quality deterioration are overcome. Mojduszka and Caswell (2000) argue that in the United States weak private incentives to disclose nutritional information voluntarily resulted in unreliable and inconsistent signals to consumers prior to passage of mandatory nutritional labeling.

Teisl and Roe (1998) argue that if market inefficiencies are the central reason why firms are not providing information to consumers, then mandatory product labeling is less justifiable as benefit–cost ratios for such interventions are often unknown a priori. Also, the political economy of the relationship between the food industry and government regulators has to be considered. Recent efforts to implement mandatory country-of-origin labeling for fresh meats, seafood products, and several other foods in the United States has been met with criticism. Proposals for Type VI mandatory labeling based on arguments that consumers have the right to know where their food comes from have sparked a discussion over the justification for such regulation and its benefit–cost effect (Lusk and Anderson 2004). Golan, Kuchler, and Mitchell (2001) state that in such instances economic theory supports alternative approaches that may be more effective in improving welfare outcomes.

5.2   Evidence on the Impact of Types I–V Voluntary Labeling

A paradigm shift has occurred in food labeling as many agri-food supply chains have become more international in scope forcing budget-constrained regulators to cede more responsibility for food quality to privately owned and operated food standards. Historically, public intervention in food markets was motivated by objectives to assure food safety and prevent threats to life and health, food adulteration, and consumer deception (Gardner 2003). Over the last two decades, the increasing complexity of many globalized food supply chains has frequently overstrained national agencies assigned with regulatory oversight of food quality, particularly safety. At the same time, many governments have increased their involvement in Type V government voluntary labeling programs in order to pursue diverse public policy goals.

The rapid integration of international agri-food supply chains may expose consumers and food producers to growing quality uncertainties often associated with imports of perishable food products. Information deficiencies and asymmetries on credence attributes important to consumers have forced retailers to assume greater responsibility individually or collectively in the provision of food safety and minimum quality to consumers both domestically and internationally (Fulponi 2006).

As an example, the 1990 Food Safety Act in the United Kingdom requires retailers to act as stewards for consumer food safety and quality by implementing stricter control mechanisms for upstream production and processing along supply chains (Hobbs and Kerr 1992; Hobbs, Fearne, and Spriggs 2002). In response to market pressures and to mitigate potential liabilities and protect brand reputation, retailers across Europe and in North America have developed growing numbers of food quality and safety labeling and certification requirements to force suppliers to provide various means of independently monitored quality assurance (Hayes and Jensen 2003).

Voluntary standards increasingly exceed regulatory standard requirements, putting private standards and retail chains in an even stronger role in shaping food production and management systems. As suppliers and producers require voluntary firm accreditation and product certification to enter more lucrative retail markets, voluntary certification systems start to show elements of mandatory standards (Fulponi 2006). In addition, the provision of Types I through III private voluntary labeling information at the store shelf has emerged as a competitive instrument by which retailers differentiate themselves from the competition (Berning, Chouinard, and McCluskey 2008). Type IV labeling by NGOs and private certification bodies is also competing in this market.

As a consequence, the interaction and balance between public and private standards is changing (Deaton 2004; Fulponi 2006). Given scarcer regulatory resources there is growing interest in issues of regulatory cooperation and co-regulation (García Martínez et al. 2007). Initially driven by retailers' efforts to rebuild shattered reputation and trust after the food safety scandals of the 1990s, private retail food standards have rapidly emerged in numbers and scope (Henson and Hooker 2001). Fulponi (2006) estimates that voluntary food standards account for roughly 70 percent of total retail sales across major European food markets. The development of Types II through IV third party approaches has led to a greater convergence of standards and requirements with possible efficiencies as well as potential for exercise of market power.

A significant literature has developed over the last two decades focusing on the conceptual understanding and empirical measurement of the economic forces behind the development of private and independent voluntary labeling and certification systems for credence attribute claims (Roe and Sheldon 2007). Growth in these

Types I through IV labeling schemes is based on consumer interest in credence attribute labeling and on retailer, processor, and supplier interest in differentiation based on these attributes. The attributes labeled range from local, organic, and fair trade to free-range, shade-grown, and animal welfare friendly, among others.

Not surprisingly, the growing consumer interest in more knowledge of credence product attributes and production practices has led to more research on the underlying attitudes, perceptions, and preferences of consumers. A multitude of empirical studies have explored the economic impacts and viability of labeling systems taking an attribute demand approach and using mostly stated and revealed preference methods (Lusk, Norwood, and Pruitt 2006). Greater consumer interest in methods used in agri-food production and processing have resulted in greater research interest in process-based food attributes such as organic (Cranfield, Deaton, and Shellikeri 2009) and the role of GM technology in food production (Gruere, Carter, and Farzin 2009). In response to the increasing globalization of food supply, several consumer segments seek foods labeled as "local" (Thilmany, Bond, and Bond 2008) or are willing to pay for labels showing certified geographical origin, believing origin to be linked to unique product quality (Anders and Caswell 2009b). In addition to their private demand, consumers may be willing to pay for environmental and welfare-related credence attributes as a voluntary contribution to public goods based on altruistic motives. The specific relationship between private and public attributes combined in environmental product labeling has been addressed in a growing eco-labeling literature, much of which is focused on the "tragedy of the commons" associated with unregulated fisheries (Brecard et al. 2009; Caswell and Anders 2009). Rising concerns over the linkage between diet and health and other verifiable intrinsic food attributes have resulted in greater diversity of "easy-to-understand" front-of-package nutritional labeling (Wansink, Sonka, and Hasler 2004; Grunert et al. 2010).

Aside from WTP estimates, the literature has largely neglected to investigate benefit–cost considerations for credence attribute labeling that could speak to the relative effectiveness of different types of private and independent voluntary labeling (Types I through IV). In cases where voluntary labeling of credence attributes can alter product offerings and/or production methods over time (e.g., animal welfare practices, dolphin-friendly tuna), the distribution of consumer and producer welfare effects matters as the preferences of certain consumers may restrict future choices and production practices for an entire population (Tonsor, Olynk, and Wolf 2009). Similarly, there is very little empirical analysis of what thresholds are appropriate to justify government-established (Type V) voluntary labeling systems and how different countries may view this choice. For example, why is organic labeling a popular form of Type V labeling across countries but fair trade is not? Similarly, why is geographical indications labeling important in the European Union but not in the United States? The political economy of Type V labeling is ripe for analysis.

5.3   Credibility of Third Party Certification

Certification and quality signaling systems are dependent on their credibility and the trust that buyers in the supply chain or consumers place in them (Hatanaka, Bain, and Busch 2005). The economic literature agrees that objective and verifiable information about food attributes, especially credence attributes, plays an essential role in improving market efficiency and welfare for both consumers and stakeholders along food supply chains. Distrust and opportunistic behavior may occur in situations where the seller has a significant information advantage over the buyer regarding true product characteristics. In this context, credence attributes and goods differ significantly from those for experience attributes because experience can rarely alleviate the underlying informational problem. Roe and Sheldon (2007) state that if labeling signals are not credible or are biased, verifying quality may be difficult and consumers can only base their purchase decision on subjective beliefs, allowing moral hazard in credence goods markets.

Similarly, if certification procedures are not rigorously performed, credence quality claims may become questionable. In a market environment where asymmetric information prevails, reputation may take a critical role in overcoming information gaps (McCluskey and Loureiro 2005). However, reputation may be an insufficient signal in cases of credence attributes where the truthfulness of a claim remains unobservable even *ex post* in transactions between businesses or with consumers. Because certification is costly and not always entirely verifiable, incentives may persist to minimize effort in verifying quality attributes and to behave opportunistically in the food chain (Souza Monteiro and Anders 2010). In this context Giannakas (2002: 3) points out that "The assumption of perfectly functioning certification [systems] is [still] implicitly or even explicitly present in most economic studies of markets for credence goods." Caswell, Bredahl, and Hooker (1998) state that independent certification of product claims using third party certification may act as a catalyst in business transactions by reducing information asymmetries and transaction costs along agri-food chains. Thus, third party certification can mitigate risks of market failure and fraud in markets for credence goods (Deaton 2004).

Third party certification is seen as a mechanism that facilitates coordination and information exchange in an increasingly complex food system. Henson and Reardon (2005) and Fulponi (2006) provide empirical analyses of the impact and use of third party certification to mitigate uncertainties and reduce information asymmetries for credence attribute information between producers and retailers. The certifying organization's certificates will be accepted as credible signals in the marketplace only if it succeeds in establishing a positive reputation and trust between business partners. Jahn, Schramm, and Spiller (2005) quote the financial auditing literature as a rich source of evidence on the importance of integrity for the assessment of the quality of certification. Tirole (1986) offers important insight into the importance of an "independent" third party in economic transactions by showing that collusion between a firm and a "dependent" third party certifier may significantly hinder the process of information revelation. Lizzeri (1999) and Hvide (2004) further substantiated this finding using game-theoretical approaches to show that certifier independence and stringency of standard enforcement are essential conditions for the credibility and functioning of markets for third party certification services. Carriquiry and Babcock (2007) show that firm reputation and brand value have a significant effect on the level of investment in quality certification as a means of asset value protection. Tighter oversight of private certification systems may be necessary in some cases to assure that less powerful players in supply chains retain some of the benefits of the systems (Jahn, Schramm, and Spiller 2005).

Previous research has primarily focused on the motivations of firms to adopt food standards (Carriquiry and Babcock 2007) and on evaluating generic "ISO 9001" standards (Calisir, Bayraktar, and Beskese 2001). The empirical evidence on the efficiency and effectiveness of private voluntary certification schemes remains limited. This seems particularly the case for the rapidly growing Type III sector-specific and retailer-driven quality assurance schemes, such as GlobalGAP, the BRC Global Standard, and the International Food Standard systems (Trienekens and Zuurbier 2008). Actual evaluation of the reliability of third party certification systems is very rare. One example is Albersmeier et al. (2009), who evaluated auditing quality in a German quality assurance system, finding several areas for concern.

Third party certifiers have grown in importance as a fundamental pillar of the international food system (Hatanaka, Bain, and Busch 2005). A number of issues regarding the performance of third party certification of labeling claims warrant research attention from policy, industrial organization, and trade perspectives. First is evaluation of the efficiency of private and voluntary, especially third party, systems of standard setting, verification, and assurance versus a traditional system of mandatory governmental standards.

Second, the potential welfare implications of Types II and III private, third party certification of credence attribute claims will be especially relevant in cases where the certifier possesses market power. The increasing influence of large-scale private governance systems such as GlobalGAP in food markets has received limited attention in the economic literature, particularly from a comparative point of view. The decision to obtain (or not) certification for products or services from an internationally prevalent standard such as GlobalGAP may entail considerable consequences for market access. This is particularly important for producer groups in developing countries. The ability to penetrate premium markets may directly impact firm profits because the cost of certification is not negligible, as is attested by a growing literature on the economic effects of food standards on producers in developing countries (Henson and Jaffee 2008; Anders and Caswell 2009a). Third, the choice of standard and the process of attribute certification has become a strategic decision for many agri-food producers and processors (Carriquiry and Babcock 2007), increasing the need for comparative analysis of this choice. Finally, the role of third party certifiers in vertical food supply chains needs closer investigation as to the degree to which their contribution to value-added may be masked by adverse and rent-seeking behavior where the assumption of third party certifiers' independence is violated.

5.4   Summary of Evidence on the Relative Merits of Private, Third Party, and Government Labeling

There are several theoretical and conceptual contributions that focus on the relative merits of private versus third party versus government labeling systems. These contributions discuss the circumstances under which each type of approach is likely to be more appropriate, including the presence of market failures and imperfections, the importance of the attribute being communicated, the strength of market incentives to produce and communicate quality, and other objectives such as supporting particular production practices or locations. Overall, the conceptual understanding of the relative merits of the systems seems well developed.

We may also have substantial evidence of the relative merits of different labeling systems from our ongoing, worldwide experiment in the development of these systems, if one believes that private parties, independent parties, and governments will over time sort out which types of labeling system best meet performance goals in different situations. However, there is a marked lack of literature that analyzes different food labeling systems and regulatory approaches in a comparative, empirical manner using economic benefit–cost measures to identify best practices. This research would focus on effects on consumer choice, market development, and other performance objectives from the perspectives of private, NGO, and public parties. This type of analysis is necessary to address division-of-labor issues focused on which private, third party, government, and hybrid approaches should be used to affect the delivery of information to consumers and the performance of markets.

6   ISSUES FOR THE FUTURE OF LABELING

We noted in beginning this chapter that labeling is a means of changing the amount or kind of product information that is available in the market. Private, third party, and government labeling schemes pursue similar objectives (e.g., inform consumers and influence demand, develop markets, promote particular production practices) but with different objective functions. The different schemes operate simultaneously and are constantly under development.

Starting from a consumer perspective, the major issue for the future is how well and reliably different labeling schemes will deliver information on verified quality that they need when they want it in formats that are useful and do not overtax their processing skills and level of interest. From a private company perspective, the major issues are choosing labeling schemes that will effectively set standards, verify quality, and communicate quality allowing for differentiation, efficient operation, liability and reputation protection, and market advantage. Outsourcing to Types II and III schemes that are private, collective, and third party is an increasingly popular approach to assure credible labeling for a broad range of quality attributes. From a Type IV NGO or independent certification body perspective, the major issue is defining standards and labels that will gain enough traction in the market to affect outcomes such as sustainability, fair trade, or a broader range of quality attributes.

Governments face several major issues because they both oversee Types I through IV and operate Types V and VI labeling schemes. Most fundamentally, governments must judge when more direct forms of regulation are needed instead of, or to complement, labeling approaches in cases of market failures (e.g., public goods associated with food safety) or significant market imperfections due to information problems. If labeling is an appropriate approach, governments then squarely face the question of the division of labor in information provision: to what extent can market processes be relied on to deliver quality assurance and communication and to what extent are government labeling programs called for based on public policy objectives? Within Types V and VI schemes, governments must determine which types of attribute labeling are need-to-know and right-to-know, indicating mandatory labeling, and which are want-to-know, indicating voluntary labeling programs. They must also manage these issues in an environment of limited resources and in which, under international trade agreements, other countries scrutinize and potentially challenge choices made based on discriminatory impacts.

A key consideration for those developing Types I through IV private and third party schemes is whether government approaches to quality and quality assurance will shift in the future in ways that support the expansion or constriction of certification and quality signaling systems. In retrospect, will the current period be seen as one when government oversight was at its least stringent—in other words, a relative free-for-all? Will governments find that these systems have problems and drawbacks that require more active oversight?

Alternatively, governments may decide that private systems are yielding desirable market performance and, rather than constraining these systems, they may give them further leeway in the future. It is important to note that companies and other market players (e.g., small-scale producers) may prefer, and even lobby for, a more activist government approach if the private system becomes unruly or disadvantages them. From an economic perspective, participants in certification and quality signaling schemes must recognize that property rights in these systems are not fixed—nor are the private benefits and costs. Detailed understanding of the structures and competitive forces in individual food industries is crucial knowledge for regulators to determine whether oversight is adequate and for industry stakeholders to understand directions in which this oversight might go. Comparative analysis of the relative merits of private versus third party versus government labeling is much needed from both market and policy perspectives.

REFERENCES

Akerlof, G. 1970. "The Market for 'Lemons': Qualitative Uncertainty and the Market Mechanism." *Quarterly Journal of Economics* 84: 488–500.

Albersmeier, F., H. Schulze, G. Jahn, and A. Spiller. 2009. "The Reliability of Third-Party Certification in the Food Chain: From Checklists to Risk-Oriented Auditing." *Food Control* 20/10: 927–35.

Anders, S., and J. A. Caswell. 2009a. "Standards-as-Barriers versus Standards-as-Catalysts: Assessing the Impact of HACCP Implementation on U.S. Seafood Imports." *American Journal of Agricultural Economics* 91/2: 310–21.

————. 2009b. "The Benefits and Costs of Proliferation of Geographical Labeling for Developing Countries." *Estey Centre Journal of International Law and Trade Policy* 10/1: 77–93.

Berning, J. P., H. H. Chouinard, and J. McCluskey. 2008. "Consumer Preferences for Detailed versus Summary Formats of Nutrition Information on Grocery Store Shelf Labels." *Journal of Agricultural and Food Industrial Organization* 6/1, art. 6. <http://www.bepress.com/jafio/vol6/iss1/art6/>.

Brecard, D., B. Hlaimi, L. Sterenn, Y. Perraudeau, and F. Salladarre. 2009. "Determinants of Demand for Green Products: An Application to Eco-Label Demand for Fish in Europe." *Ecological Economics* 69/1: 115–25.

Bureau, J. C., S. Marette, and A. Schiavina. 1998. "Non-Tariff Trade Barriers and Consumers' Information: The Case of EU–US Trade Dispute on Beef." *European Review of Agricultural Economics* 25/4: 437–62.

Calisir, F., C. A. Bayraktar, and B. Beskese. 2001. "Implementing the ISO 9001 Standards in Turkey: A Study of Large Companies' Satisfaction with ISO 9001." *Total Quality Management* 12/4: 429–38.

Carriquiry, M. A., and B. A. Babcock. 2007. "Reputations, Market Structure and the Choice of Quality Assurance Systems in the Food Industry." *American Journal of Agricultural Economics* 89/1: 12–23.

Caswell, J. A. 1998. "How Labeling of Safety and Process Attributes Affects Markets for Food." *Agricultural and Resource Economics Review* 27/2: 151–8.

——— 2000. "An Evaluation of Risk Analysis as Applied to Agricultural Biotechnology (With a Case Study of GMO Labeling)." *Agribusiness* 16/1: 115–23.

——— 2006. "Quality Assurance, Information Tracking, and Consumer Labeling." *Marine Pollution Bulletin* 53/10–12: 650–6.

——— and S. M. Anders. 2009. "The Economics of Market Information Related to Certification and Standards in Fisheries." Paper prepared for the Organization for Economic Cooperation and Development (Agriculture and Fisheries)/Food and Agriculture Organization, Round Table on Eco-Labelling and Certification in the Fisheries Sector, The Hague, Apr. 22–3.

——— and E. M. Mojduszka. 1996. "Using Informational Labeling to Influence the Market for Quality in Food Products." *American Journal of Agricultural Economics* 78/5: 1248–53.

——— and D. L. Padberg. 1992. "Toward a More Comprehensive Theory of Food Labels." *American Journal of Agricultural Economics* 74/2: 460–8.

———, M. E. Bredahl, and N. H. Hooker. 1998. "How Quality Management Metasystems Are Affecting the Food Industry." *Review of Agricultural Economics* 20/2: 547–57.

Cranfield, J., B. J. Deaton, and S. Shellikeri. 2009. "Evaluating Consumer Preferences for Organic Food Production Standards." *Canadian Journal of Agricultural Economics* 57: 99–117.

Crespi, J. M., and S. Marette. 2005. "Eco-Labeling Economics: Is Public Involvement Necessary?" In S. Krarup and C. S. Russell, eds, *Environment, Information, and Consumer Behavior*. Cheltenham: Edward Elgar.

Darby, M. R., and E. Karni. 1973. "Free Competition and the Optimal Amount of Fraud." *Journal of Law and Economics* 16: 67–88.

Deaton, B. J. 2004. "A Theoretical Framework for Examining the Role of Third-Party Certifiers." *Food Control* 15: 615–19.

Drichoutis, A. C., P. Lazaridis, and R. M. Nayga, Jr. 2005. "Nutrition Knowledge and Consumer Use of Nutritional Food Labels." *European Review of Agricultural Economics* 32/1: 93–118.

Fulponi, L. 2006. "Private Voluntary Standards in the Food System: The Perspective of Major Food Retailers in OECD Countries." *Food Policy* 31: 1–13.

García Martínez, M., A. Fearne, J. A. Caswell, and S. Henson. 2007. "Co-regulation as a Possible Model for Food Safety Governance: Opportunities for Public–Private Partnerships." *Food Policy* 32/3: 299–314.

Gardner, B. 2003. "U.S. Food Quality Standards: Fix for Market Failure or Costly Anachronism?" *American Journal of Agricultural Economics* 85/3: 725–30.

Giannakas, K. 2002. "Information Asymmetries and Consumption Decisions in Organic Food Product Markets." *Canadian Journal of Agricultural Economics* 50/1: 35–50.

Giovannucci, D., T. Josling, W. Kerr, B. O'Connor, and M. T. Yeung. 2009. *Guide to Geographical Indications: Linking Products and their Origins*. Geneva: International Trade Centre.

GlobalGAP (Global Partnership for Good Agricultural Practice). 2009. *GlobalGAP Standards*. <http://www.globalgap.org/cms/front_content.php?idcat=3>.

Golan, E., F. Kuchler, and B. Krissoff. 2007. "Do Food Labels Make a Difference? . . . Sometimes." *Amber Waves*. United States Department of Agriculture, Economic Research Service. Nov. <http://yy9g.info/AmberWaves/November07/Features/FoodLabels.htm>.

——, and L. Mitchell. 2001. *Economics of Food Labeling*. Agricultural Economic Report No. 793. Washington, DC: Economic Research Service, US Department of Agriculture.

Gracia, A., M. Loureiro, and R. M. Nayga, Jr. 2007. "Do Consumers Perceive Benefits from the Implementation of a EU Mandatory Nutritional Labeling Program?" *Food Policy* 32/2: 160–74.

Gruere, G. P., C. A. Carter, and H. Y. Farzin. 2009. "Explaining International Differences in Genetically Modified Food Labeling Policies." *Review of International Economics* 17/3: 393–408.

Grunert, K. G., L. Fernández-Celemín, J. M. Wills, S. Storcksdieck, and L. Nureeva. 2010. "Use and Understanding of Nutrition Information on Food Labels in Six European Countries." *Journal of Public Health* 18/3: 261–77. <http://www.springerlink.com/content/k3851qt081155215/fulltext.pdf>.

Hatanaka, M., C. Bain, and L. Busch. 2005. "Third-Party Certification in the Global Agrifood System." *Food Policy* 30/3: 354–69.

Hayes, D. J., and H. H. Jensen. 2003. *Lessons from the Danish Ban on Feed-Grade Antibiotics*. Staff General Research Papers No. 11284. Ames: Department of Economics, Iowa State University.

Henson, S. 2008. "The Role of Public and Private Standards in Regulating International Food Markets." *Journal of International Agricultural Trade and Development* 4/1: 63–81.

—— and N. H. Hooker. 2001. "Private Sector Management of Food Safety: Public Regulation and the Role of Private Controls." *International Food and Agribusiness Management Review* 4: 7–17.

—— and S. Jaffee. 2008. "Understanding Developing Country Strategic Responses to the Enhancement of Food Safety Standards." *World Economy* 31/4: 548–68.

—— and T. Reardon. 2005. "Private Agri-Food Standards: Implications for Food Policy and the Agri-Food System." *Food Policy* 30/3: 241–53.

Hobbs, J. E., and W. A. Kerr. 1992. "The Cost of Monitoring Food Safety and Vertical Coordination in Agribusiness: What Can Be Learned from the British Food Safety Act 1990?" *Agribusiness* 8/6: 575–84.

——, A. Fearne, and J. Spriggs. 2002. "Incentive Structures for Food Safety and Quality Assurance: An International Comparison." *Food Control* 13/2: 77–81.

Hvide, H. K. 2004. *A Theory of Certification with an Application to the Market of Auditing Services*. Discussion Papers No. 2004/10. Berthgen: Department of Finance and Management Science, Norwegian School of Economics and Business Administration.

Jahn, G., M. Schramm, and A. Spiller. 2005. "The Reliability of Certification: Quality Labels as a Consumer Policy Tool." *Journal of Consumer Policy* 28: 53–73.

Kalaitzandonakes, N., L. A. Marks, and S. S. Vickner. 2004. "Media Coverage of Biotech Foods and Influence on Consumer Choice." *American Journal of Agricultural Economics* 86/5: 1238–46.

Kiesel, K., and S. B. Villas-Boas. 2007. "Got Organic Milk? Consumer Valuations of Milk Labels after the Implementation of the USDA Organic Seal." *Journal of Agricultural and Food Industrial Organization* 5: 1–38.

Kim, S.-Y., R. M. Nayga, Jr., and O. Capps, Jr. 2000. "The Effect of Food Label Use on Nutrient Intakes: An Endogenous Switching Regression Analysis." *Journal of Agricultural and Resource Economics* 25/1: 215–31.

Lancaster, K. J. 1971. "A New Approach to Consumer Theory." *Journal of Political Economy* 74: 132–57.

Lin, C. T., J. Y. Lee, and S. T. Yen. 2004. "Do Dietary Intakes Affect Search for Nutrient Information on Food Labels?" *Social Science and Medicine* 59: 1955–67.

Lizzeri, A. 1999. "Information Revelation and Certification of Intermediaries." *Rand Journal of Economics* 30/2: 214–31.

Loureiro, M. L., and W. Umberger. 2005. "Assessing Consumer Preferences for Country-of-Origin Labeling." *Journal of Agricultural and Applied Economics* 37/1: 49–63.

Lusk, J. L., and J. D. Anderson. 2004. "Effects of Country-of-Origin Labeling on Meat Producers and Consumers." *Journal of Agricultural and Resource Economics* 29/2: 185–205.

——, F. B. Norwood, and J. R. Pruitt. 2006. "Consumer Demand for a Ban on Antibiotic Drug Use in Pork Production." *American Journal of Agricultural Economics* 88: 1015–33.

McCluskey, J. J., and M. L. Loureiro. 2005. "Reputation and Production Standards." *Journal of Agricultural and Resource Economics* 30/1: 1–11.

Marette, S., R. Clemens, and B. A. Babcock. 2007. *The Recent International and Regulatory Decisions about Geographical Indications*. Working Paper No. 07-MWP 10. Ames: Midwest Agribusiness Trade Research and Information Center, Iowa State University.

Mathios, A. D. 2000. "The Impact of Mandatory Disclosure Laws on Product Choices: An Analysis of the Salad Dressing Market." *Journal of Law and Economics* 42: 651–76.

Mojduszka, E. M., and J. A. Caswell. 2000. "A Test of Nutritional Quality Signaling in Food Markets prior to Implementation of Mandatory Labeling." *American Journal of Agricultural Economics* 82/2: 298–309.

Nelson, P. 1970. "Information and Consumer Behavior." *Journal of Political Economy* 78: 311–29.

—— 1974. "Advertising as Information." *Journal of Political Economy* 81: 729–54.

Nestle, M. 2000. *Food Politics: How the Food Industry Influences Nutrition and Health.* Berkeley: University of California Press.

Prathiraja, P. H. K., and A. Ariyawardana. 2003. "Impact of Nutritional Labeling on Consumer Buying Behavior." *Sri Lankan Journal of Agricultural Economics* 5/1: 35–46.

Roe, B., and I. Sheldon. 2007. "Credence Good Labeling: The Efficiency and Distributional Implications of Several Policy Approaches." *American Journal of Agricultural Economics* 89/4: 1020–33.

Souza Monteiro, D., and S. Anders. 2010. "Third-Party Certification, Food Standards and Quality Assurance in Supply Chains." *Journal on Chain and Network Science* 9/2: 83–8.

Steenkamp, J.-B. E. M. 1989. *Product Quality: An Investigation into the Concept and How It Is Perceived by Consumers.* Assen: Van Gorcum.

—— and H. C. M. Trijp. 1996. "Quality Guidance: A Consumer-Based Approach to Food Quality Improvement Using Partial Least Squares." *European Review of Agricultural Economics* 23/2: 195–215.

Teisl, M. F., and B. Roe. 1998. "The Economics of Labeling: An Overview of Issues for Health and Environmental Disclosure." *Agricultural and Resource Economics Review* 27/2: 140–50.

——, N. E. Bockstael, and A. Levy. 2001. "Measuring the Welfare Effects of Nutrition Information." *American Journal of Agricultural Economics* 83/1: 133–49.

Thilmany, D., C. A. Bond, and J. K. Bond. 2008. "Going Local: Exploring Consumer Behavior and Motivations for Direct Food Purchases." *American Journal of Agricultural Economics* 90/5: 1303–9.

Tirole, J. 1986. "Hierarchies and Bureaucracies: On the Role of Collusion in Organisations." *Journal of Law, Economics and Organization* 2/2: 181–214.

Tonsor, G. T., N. Olynk, and C. Wolf. 2009. "Consumer Preferences for Animal Welfare Attributes: The Case of Gestation Crates." *Journal of Agricultural and Applied Economics* 41/3: 713–30.

Trienekens, J., and P. Zuurbier. 2008. "Quality and Safety Standards in the Food Industry, Developments and Challenges." *International Journal of Production Economics* 113/1: 107–22.

Unnevehr, L. J., and E. Jagmanaite. 2008. "Getting Rid of Trans Fats in the US Diet: Policies, Incentives and Progress." *Food Policy* 33/6: 497–503.

USFDA (United States Food and Drug Administration). 1991. "Regulatory Impact Analysis of the Proposed Rules to Amend the Food Labeling Regulations." *Federal Register* 56/229 (Nov. 27): 60856–77.

Variyam, J. N. 2008. "Do Nutrition Labels Improve Dietary Outcomes?" *Health Economics* 17/6: 695–708.

—— and J. Cawley. 2006. *Nutrition Labels and Obesity.* Working Paper No. 11956. Cambridge, MA: National Bureau of Economic Research.

Wansink, B., S. T. Sonka, and C. M. Hasler. 2004. "Front-Label Health Claims: When Less Is More." *Food Policy* 29/6: 659–67.

CHAPTER 19

··

BANS AND LABELS WITH CONTROVERSIAL FOOD TECHNOLOGIES

··

STÉPHAN MARETTE AND JUTTA ROOSEN

1 INTRODUCTION

··

In the last couple of decades, many controversies around food technologies and/or innovations have gained momentum, mainly through wide media coverage. Faced with the issues surrounding government authorization for genetically modified organisms (GMOs), nanotechnologies, and meat from cloned animals, public authorities have intervened to guarantee transparency to consumers and to assure "satisfactory" products with acceptable quality and safety levels. However, the impact of such interventions is not simple and often leads to numerous criticisms by civil society, along with much hesitation on the part of the regulator. Public authorities are often torn between the impetus to promote food innovations that may be controversial, the need to favor product diversity and consumer freedom of choice, and a sufficient level of consumer protection when a controversy emerges.

Clarifying these trade-offs would help the debates. We argue that there are economic considerations in any discussion of public policy on controversies, and although the issues are complicated, there is already much guidance that can be given. From a policy perspective, this chapter seeks to address the following questions: What is a controversy, and what are the markets concerned by such a problem? We shall address why controversies have become so prominent in many food markets. Moreover, we clarify how to approach the question of an optimal policy by studying when a regulator should promote labels compared to other tools such as standards or a ban.

For the controversial food issues of our times, this chapter presents some of the main contributions in both the empirical and theoretical literature, so as to provide economists, citizens, or policymakers with resources and help to inform their decisions. We discuss methods of quantifying the welfare impact of a ban or label on the controversial good. The chapter concludes with a discussion of the implications for public policy.

2   FOOD WITH CONTROVERSIAL CHARACTERISTICS

Food controversies arise from the presence or absence of specific characteristics related to the production or market process. They are characterized by disagreements among different groups of consumers or discrepancies between consumers and regulatory agencies, and their intensity varies across countries. We do not claim to be exhaustive when we list issues linked to a product such as animal welfare, animal cloning, nanotechnologies, recombinant bovine somatotropin (rBST), antibiotics, GMOs, pesticide residues, child labor standards, or carbon emissions.

Food products possess a multitude of characteristics, and the controversial characteristics often concern the production process. Indeed, some need not be directly reflected in the physical characteristics of a commodity; they rather reflect processes or conditions of production that, in and of themselves, impart value to some consumers. These characteristics are generally classified as credence "goods" (see Darby and Karni 1973) since they are difficult to observe before or after purchase for consumers and require public intervention to guarantee their existence on the market.

In terms of consumer preferences, a controversial characteristic may be characterized by a proportion of vocal, reluctant, and/or highly concerned consumers with a high willingness to pay (WTP) for avoiding the characteristic versus a proportion of relatively or completely indifferent consumers with a WTP equal (or close) to zero for avoiding the characteristic. In other words, within a country there is considerable disagreement on one or several characteristics that are relevant and on the extent to which they may legitimately be the subject of stringent regulation. The highly concerned consumers will try to impose the highest possible standards, including a complete ban on the controversial product/characteristic. Conversely, a proportion of indifferent consumers will try to minimize the "problem" deemed artificial and will plead either for a vast range of affordable choices among differentiated products or for ignoring altogether the concerns considered "irrational." There is also disagreement between concerned (or vocal) consumers who focus on quality or purity of goods and producers who claim that cost is the key driver of consumer purchase behavior.

In this chapter, we do not address other controversial issues related to North–South trade or the production of food or energy (e.g., biofuel, ethanol, etc.) on agricultural land. These issues differ from the themes discussed in this chapter since they mostly involve distributional questions intermediated by market access and regulation. They are not directly related to the question of controversial technology studied here.

However, the example of GMOs shows that a distinction is never clear-cut and that many of these questions are often complex and interrelated.

Often the range of the controversy is not limited to the question "What type of product do consumers want?" Very often societal questions are involved, expressed by consumer and environmental activist groups that pose the question not only for the optimal degree of consumer protection but also in relation to the question "What is the world we want to live in?" Such a broad view raised by active and reluctant consumers often muddles the debate rather than focusing disagreements such that they can be tackled by regulation.

In this regard, it is important to recognize that a single controversy implies several economic issues, which makes the exchange of arguments among opponents and proponents often non-fruitful. The economic questions underlying many controversies concern one or several of the following aspects: namely, public good characteristics, such as the environmental impact of a technology; private good characteristics, such as health and safety issues; questions of equity, such as the impact of a new technology on small firms; and/or questions of the freedom of choice for consumers, related to the ability to differentiate among products using the technology or not.

To structure our discussion we focus on two types of controversy, one implying mostly ethical concerns, the second regarding acceptance of individual risk.

First, there are disagreements on ethical and cultural attributes. A growing number of consumers are concerned about the possible adverse effects of their purchases on natural resources in other countries. Other consumers are ethically sensitive to distributional impacts, for example, the monopoly power of firms that may threaten food security in the long term. New technologies like genetic modification or nanotechnologies provide patents that reinforce market power. However, it may be paradoxical to reject new technologies for ethical or cultural reasons when, at the same time, they are admitted for non-food products such as medicines. There is also growing public pressure for the imposition of more environment-friendly practices such as labels regarding carbon emissions in the fight against global warming, or to protect the "common resources of humanity" such as the tropical rainforest and the stock of marine resources.

Second, controversies may also concern physical characteristics such as food or environmental safety and the "acceptable" level of risk. It is widely recognized that it is seldom possible or economically sensible to achieve zero risk with respect to food safety. However, there is no agreement on what constitutes justifiable risk or "acceptable risk." Some consumers prefer to emphasize risk elimination (e.g., sterilization of mineral waters, ban on cheese made from unpasteurized milk, use of food irradiation, etc.). Others emphasize the possibility of risk control (inspections, hazard analysis and critical control points (HACCPs), etc.), which avoids altering effects on the product, and point to the inconsistency of seeking to achieve zero risk in one area while tolerating high risk in others (Hayes et al. 1995). Regarding environmental safety, the risks of alterations of the "natural" capital are often raised by environmentalists for GMOs or nanotechnology. Although the risk-based approach allows for a "scientific" definition of risks or uncertainty, many studies show that risk complicates the issue because of possibly diverging risk perceptions of experts and laypersons (Rowe and Wright 2001).

Ambiguous information and scientific uncertainty may even exacerbate controversies. Powell (1997) highlights the difficulties of obtaining reliable scientific assessments of hazards in food, because of genetic mutations, for example, or combinations of pathogens with uncertain effects, or the influence of exogenous and unforeseeable factors on micro-organisms. Another issue is the impact of multiple exposure, for example to pesticide residues in consumer products (National Research Council 2008). The difficulty of properly measuring carbon emissions linked to a product can lead to confusion or suspicion among consumers. The standards accepted by scientists do not always have an indisputable scientific foundation: some have had to be revised at various times and scientific "certainty" is sometimes fragile, especially with regard to the long-term properties of products as, for instance, carcinogenic impacts. Controlling short-term risks does not mean that long-term risks or uncertainties do not exist. Environmental and consumer groups endorse the inclusion of the "precautionary principle," which would allow exceptions to regulations in case that scientific proof does not go far enough. However, industries often advocate that the precautionary principle is not an operative tool for regulation and simply an indirect way of avoiding painful and up-front regulatory decisions.

Consumer research has made significant contributions to the perception of risks posed by technologies in general (Slovic 1987) and in the food domain (Fife-Shaw and Rowe 1996). Newer research has highlighted the role of trust in regulation and risk communication (Frewer and Miles 2001). Ignoring consumers' values may result in an absence of their support for the introduction of new food technologies. New media, especially the Internet, can provide a considerable sounding board for the detractors of new technologies. One thorny problem for economists is related to the "vague" opinions underlined by the media and vocal consumer groups versus consumers' actual purchases. For instance, Kalaitzandonakes, Marks, and Vickner (2004) have examined consumer responses to biotech media coverage. Consumers could choose between food products that were labeled as containing GMO ingredients and unlabeled ones containing only conventional ingredients. Even if media coverage of biotechnology was substantial and relatively negative, Kalaitzandonakes et al. found that consumers did not respond to the media coverage and did not change their purchases.

Another issue with controversies is that social deliberation and agreement is not likely to take place. For instance, at the beginning of the GMO debate, it was thought that the problem was linked to lack of information and that rational choice and risk analysis would lead to an agreement that GMOs are acceptable. However, studies have shown that opposition or support for the technology is not related to knowledge and that opposing consumers are likely to remain opposed to the technology even after being informed (Christoph, Bruhn, and Roosen 2008; Marette, Roosen, Bieberstein, et al. 2009). This opposition is often driven by a strong preference for "natural food" emphasized by many consumers (Rozin et al. 2004), even if the term "natural" is hard to characterize precisely. Hence, it is important to think about regulatory approaches when controversies cannot be resolved.

The GMO example shows that it is particularly important to turn to lab, field, or natural experiments for studying consumer behavior beyond political opinions or media coverage. Experimental methods are particularly tailored to the analysis of controversial goods, since they capture heterogeneity in consumers' preferences (see Lusk and Shogren 2007). However, one needs to recognize that experiments on consumer choice focus on the private decisions of consumers and may not completely consider public good aspects. There were numerous studies for eliciting WTP for avoiding GMOs (see surveys on WTP linked to GMOs by Lusk, Jamal, et al. 2005; Costa-Font, Gil, and Traill 2008). Noussair, Robin, and Ruffieux (2002) show that a majority of French consumers are indifferent to GMOs, in comparison with non-GMOs, a view that contradicts the current regulatory practice that seems largely influenced by the vocal minority of reluctant consumers and environmental activist groups. Huffman et al. (2003, 2007) show sensitivity of WTP to the source of information (NGOs, multinationals, or public health authorities). Lusk, Roosen, and Fox (2003) and Lusk, House, et al. (2005) directly compared WTP between the United States and some European countries and show a larger level of reluctance to accept GMOs among European consumers compared to the US consumers, although there was significant heterogeneity in preferences in both locations. These studies on GMO reluctance pave the way for studies on technologies like cloning or nanotechnologies (see Bieberstein et al. 2009).

To complete the analysis, we focus on a few other controversies and their economic consequences; namely, hormone use in meat and milk, animal welfare, and food irradiation.[1] This brief study of these three topics can be completed by reading Chapter 32, by Schroeder and Tonsor, and Chapter 35, by Loureiro, in this volume.

First, there are controversies linked to hormone use for meat and milk production. rBST is used in a number of countries, including the United States, to increase milk yields. The dispute over growth hormones relates to the consideration that should be given to arguments other than "objective" medical risk when sanitary regulations are being defined. The most sensitive issue comes from the use of growth hormones in beef (see Bureau, Marette, and Schiavina 1998). The dispute between the European Union (EU) and the United States on the use of growth hormones in cattle has been going on for twenty years. The EU's refusal to authorize the use of such substances has the effect of limiting imports from countries where they are used. The dispute was settled on appeal in 1998 in the World Trade Organization (WTO). The Appellate Body concluded that the EU import prohibition on meat and meat products derived from cattle to which specified hormones had been administered was inconsistent with the

---

[1] Note that for meat, which is concerned in these three controversies, the use of antibiotics is also controversial although it is not addressed in detail in this chapter because of lack of space. Lusk, Norwood, and Pruitt (2006) elicit a high WTP for pork without antibiotics, mainly because of risks of resistance to antibiotics (see also Hayes and Jensen 2003).

requirements of the Sanitary and Phyto-sanitary Agreement. The ban on hormone-treated beef in Europe inspired a lab experiment to study consumer preferences. Alfnes and Rickertsen (2003) show that most participants in Norway preferred domestic to imported beef. Hormone-treated beef received the lowest mean bid, but 28 percent of the participants were indifferent or preferred US hormone-treated to US hormone-free beef.

The hormone case also highlights, as does the GMO case, the issues involved in supranational regulation. The resolution of controversies takes place not in democratically justified institutions but in supranational administrations such as the EU Commission or the WTO. This may exacerbate the impression of consumers that regulatory choices are only to a limited extent based on their preferences.

Second, animal welfare regulations, introduced under pressure from animal rights activists, may have important consequences for markets. In some cases, products that do not comply with certain rules may be prohibited. Lagerkvist, Carlsson, and Viske (2006), via a choice experiment, and Napolitano et al. (2008), via a lab experiment, measure WTP for animal welfare (including the use of hormones). Napolitano et al. (2008) show that information about high standards of animal welfare significantly influence consumers' WTP if paired with products presenting a good eating quality. Lagerkvist et al. (2006) compare consumer preferences for immunocastration versus surgical castration and no castration in pork production. Results suggest that consumers place a higher value on pork from immunocastrated pigs than pork from surgically castrated pigs. They show the complexity of measuring WTP for quality, when animal welfare potentially encompasses many characteristics deemed as quality dimensions. Multiple quality dimension also comes up as an issue of food safety, where Shogren (2003) has shown that consumers' WTP for single food safety attributes needs to be interpreted relatively to other characteristics not measured in the study (Goldberg and Roosen 2007). The definition of animal welfare is also very sensitive for poultry, where regulation could have a very considerable impact on the competitiveness of poultry and egg producers. The size of cages or the animal density limitation could cause a substantial rise in production costs. Meaningful regulation is also challenged by effective ways to communicate to consumers via possible alternatives such as "free-range," "cage-free," "organic," or "natural" eggs/chicken.

Third, irradiated food is directly related to food safety and fears linked to new technologies. Since the 1990s, the World Health Organization has concluded that irradiated food presents no toxicological risk and is very efficient for improving food safety. Consumers in some countries, however, remain opposed to irradiation, which is little used in Europe or in the United States as a result (see Fox, Hayes, and Shogren 2002 for experimental results from the United States). This example shows that, despite scientific considerations, even very subjective quality considerations can have an indirect effect on trade. The issue of food safety gained momentum during the 2006 *E. coli* 0157:H7 bacteria outbreak in spinach in the Midwest of the United States. The industry tried to develop *ex ante* tools (based on "plant" inspections) for promoting safety such as the California Leafy Greens Marketing Agreement from February 2007, where all participants must adhere to established good agricultural practices. After this outbreak, the *Wall Street Journal* (2006) was highly supportive of mandatory irradiation for the full sanitization of fruit and vegetables in the United States and hammered "irrational leftist" groups for their reluctance about irradiation, impeding an up-front regulation.

These examples suggest that controversies may sometimes have large impacts on food markets. In this context, regulation is beneficial in thwarting both market failures and controversial muddles, even if there is a major risk of useless and costly regulation.

3   BANS OR LABELS: ADVANTAGES AND LIMITS OF THESE REGULATORY TOOLS

Public intervention is useful to alleviate market failures that often lead to the absence of qualities and suboptimal choices by firms. Many controversial characteristics are credence characteristics generally impossible for consumers to detect before or after purchasing (Darby and Karni 1973). They differ from experience characteristics, where quality is revealed after purchasing.

Because of a lack of information and regulation, consumers' WTP is insufficient to cover the production costs linked to high quality, which leads to the absence of exchange (Akerlof 1970), while the trade would have taken place in a situation of perfect information. If the consumer's WTP is lower than the production cost of high-quality goods, only low-quality goods that are less costly to produce are traded and the high quality is excluded from the market. To compensate for these problems, sellers may signal products' quality and consumers may use middlemen, who are better informed, pointing out the quality of the goods presented to them. These actions soon find their limits if there are many producers, preventing effective traceability of the producers' efforts or in a context of scientific uncertainty, which makes simple and clear communication difficult to accomplish. In this context, regulation can restore credibility and guarantee trade, but regulation can also transmit essential information to consumers and citizens.

We may group the various tools of intervention and market regulation into three main categories: a ban, a norms and standards approach, and labeling.

We briefly detail a simple demand approach with different types of consumer. The characterization of preferences largely follows Polinsky and Rogerson (1983). Turning first to consumer preferences, demand of each consumer $i = \{1, \ldots, N\}$ is derived from a quasi-linear utility function that consists of the quadratic preference for the market good of interest and is additive in the numeraire:

$$U_i(q_i, w_i) = aq_i - \bar{b}q_i^2/2 - Ir_iq_i + w_i, \tag{1}$$

where the term $aq_i - \bar{b}q_i^2/2$ is the immediate satisfaction of consumer i from consuming a quantity q_i of the good and w_i is the numeraire good consumed by i. For simplicity $a, \bar{b}$ are the same for the N consumers. The effects of externalities and information are captured by the term $-Ir_iq_i$. The parameter I represents the knowledge and/or externality regarding the specific characteristic brought by the product with the new technology. If consumers are not aware of the specific characteristic or if there is an unaccounted externality linked to the specific characteristic, then $I = 0$. Conversely, $I = 1$ means that consumers are aware of the specific characteristic and can unambiguously identify the product with the new controversial technology. They internalize the externality and reduce consumption. The perceived damage associated with the consumption of the good with the specific characteristic is denoted $-r_iq_i$.[2]

Maximization of (1) under the budget constraint $pq_i + w_i = y_i$, where y_i denotes the income of person i, leads to the following inverse demand function, $p = a - \bar{b}q_i - I \times r_i$. The corresponding demand for the consumer i is $q_i(p) = Max[0, (a - p - I \times r_i)/\bar{b}]$. We assume that a proportion $\beta = N_1/N$ of consumers are completely indifferent to the specific characteristic, with $r_i = 0$ for every $i = 1, \ldots, N_1$. The proportion $(1-\beta) = 1 - N_1/N$ of reluctant consumers associates a damage per unit consumed equal to r across all this subgroup. In this case, it is possible to divide the previous aggregate demand in two subgroup demands, with $Q_1^D(p) = \sum_{i=1}^{N_1} q_i(p) = Max[0, N_1(a - p)/\bar{b}]$ for the consumers indifferent to the negative characteristic, and $Q_2^D(p, I) = \sum_{i=1}^{(N-N_1)} q_i(p) = Max[0, (N - N_1)[a - p - I \times r]/\bar{b}]$ for the concerned consumers. With $b = \bar{b}/N$, $N_1 = \beta N$, and $(N-N_1) = (1-\beta)N$, the respective inverse demands are given by (2). The (inverse) demand functions for the two subgroups become:

$$\begin{cases} p_1^D(Q) = Max[0, a - (b/\beta)Q] & \text{indifferent consumers} \\ p_2^D(Q, I) = Max[0, a - Ir - [b/(1-\beta)]Q] & \text{concerned consumers} \end{cases} \quad (2)$$

The supply side with a perfectly competitive industry with price-taking firms is defined by $p_B^S(Q) = d + D.Q$ for the regular (old) product without the controversial characteristic and $p_N^S(Q) = c + C.Q$ for the new but controversial product, with $c < d, C < D$. We consider a situation where technological development leads to a cost-saving "new" product that is adopted by producers and is being sold in the marketplace. The cost savings of this technology causes the product price to fall.

Figure 19.1 shows demand defined by (2) and supply. The price p is located on the vertical axis and the quantity Q is shown along the horizontal axis.

---

[2] The case where consumers attach a positive value to the characteristic is completely symmetric. It can be captured by a negative value of r.

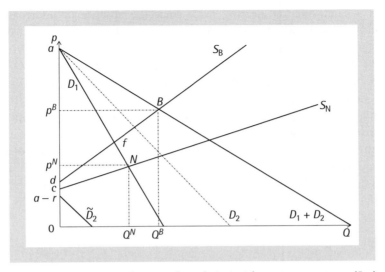

FIGURE 19.1 Ban versus absence of regulation with aware consumers ($I=1$)

It is first assumed that reluctant consumers are well informed about the presence or the absence of controversial products with $I = 1$ in equations (1) and (2). The case where consumers are not aware of the fact that the product they now consume possesses a controversial attribute ($I=0$) is presented at the end of this section.

3.1 The Absence of Regulation

Under the absence of both regulation and label, the supply of new and controversial products $p_N^S(Q) = c + C.Q$ is represented by S_N in Figure 19.1. As the new technology is more efficient with $c < d, C < D$, the old technology is driven out of the market because no firm would be able to supply the regular product competitively given the absence of a label signaling the difference between the old and the new technology. For simplicity, it is assumed that private and credible labels are not available for being voluntarily selected by producers. On the demand side, the proportion β of consumers is completely indifferent since these consumers are not concerned by the additional characteristic brought by the new technology. This subgroup has an overall demand D_1.

The proportion $(1 - \beta)$ of reluctant consumers is concerned by controversial products (for instance for safety/environmental, ethical, social reasons). Their maximum WTP under the absence of the new technology would be a, with a demand D_2 represented by the dashed line. Their WTP for a given quantity decreases by r for products with the controversial characteristic (with a parallel demand shift from D_2 to $\tilde{D}_2$ because of the stable slope in (2)). Therefore, the demand by highly concerned consumers is $\tilde{D}_2$ with a maximum WTP equal to $a-r$ (represented on the Y axis).

There is a single market clearing price since the absence of information about the product characteristic makes it impossible to distinguish the two qualities and to segment the market. Market clearing leads to the equilibrium price $p^N = (bc + aC\beta)/(b + C\beta)$ such that demand $p_1^D(Q)$ equalizes supply $p_N^S(Q) = c + C.Q$ and determines equilibrium quantity $Q^N = (a - c)\beta/(b + C\beta)$ (see point N). Reluctant consumers do not buy the product since, c, the minimum price with a strictly positive supply, is higher than the maximum WTP, $a-r$, of reluctant consumers (one extension would consist in presenting the alternative case where reluctant consumers purchase the new good with $a-r>c$). Producer surplus corresponds to area cNp^N and is equal to $PS^N = C(a - c)^2\beta^2/[2(b + C\beta)^2]$. The surplus of indifferent consumers corresponds to area $p^N Na$ and is equal to $CS^N = b(a - c)^2\beta/[2(b + C\beta)^2]$. Total welfare summing all surpluses is given by area cNa and is equal to $W^N = PS^N + CS^N = (a - c)^2\beta/[2(b + C\beta)]$.

3.2   The Ban

A ban on products with a controversial characteristic satisfies the proportion of vocal, reluctant, and/or highly concerned consumers with a high WTP for avoiding the characteristic, but it frustrates the proportion of rather indifferent consumers with a WTP equal (or close) to zero for avoiding the characteristic.

Given a ban on the new technology, the supply shifts to S_B (represented by the regular-products supply, $p_B^S(Q) = d + D.Q$) that is higher than S_N, because not using the new, controversial technology leads to higher cost of production. On the other hand, a ban does not change the demand of indifferent consumers, which remains at D_1. The proportion of reluctant consumers regains confidence owing to the absence of the controversial technology. Their maximum WTP under the absence of the new technology is a. The demand by highly concerned consumers is now D_2, leading to overall demand equal to $D_1 + D_2$. There is a single equilibrium price $p^B = (bd + a D)/(b + D)$ with a market clearing equilibrium quantity $Q^B = (a - d)/(b + D)$ (see point B). Reluctant consumers purchase products since the new technology is forbidden. Producer surplus corresponds to area dBp^B and is equal to $PS^B = D(a - d)^2/[2(b + D)^2]$. The surplus of consumers corresponds to area $p^B Ba$ and is equal to $CS^B = b(a - d)^2/[2(b + D)^2]$. Total welfare is the sum of consumer and producer surplus and given by area dBa, which is equal to $W^B = (a - d)^2/[2(b + D)]$.

Figure 19.1 depicts the changes in welfare when shifting from no regulation to a ban. Two opposite effects can be identified. The first one is caused by imperfect information for the proportion $(1-\beta)$ of concerned consumers who are reluctant to accept the new technology. Since these consumers cannot differentiate between the two types of good, they decrease their demand at any given price and they are driven out of the market. The ban increases their demand and their surplus since they are buying products. The second effect of a ban is linked to the price-increasing effect coming from the supply shift. The effect of a ban, i.e., the comparison between the welfare cNa with no regulation and the welfare dBa under a ban of the new technology is ambiguous and depends on the per unit damage, r, and the proportion of reluctant consumers $(1-\beta)$. If area $cNfd$ is larger than area afB, the decrease in price is large enough for the absence of regulation to be beneficial to the country. Alternatively, if area $cNfd$ is lower than area afB, the ban is socially beneficial since the absence of regulation would involve a relatively large decrease in demand (via the per unit damage r) and in the surplus by the proportion $(1-\beta)$ of concerned domestic consumers.

3.3   The Standard

Unlike the previous instrument, consisting in banning the product, a minimum-quality standard only bans low-quality levels (Marette 2007). This case is outside our framework presented in equation (1) since a complete study requires a continuum of quality/safety choices that could be made by firms. We briefly present economic mechanisms related to the standard.

Norms and standards that impose on producers a minimum level of quality/safety can take many forms, such as obligations to achieve a particular result as regards pesticide residue in products or specifications on processes, for example, food irradiation to combat pathogenic bacteria ($E.\ Coli$ O157:H7, salmonella, . . .). Standards also concern the authorization procedures for new products such as GMOs and cloned meat.

By guaranteeing a minimum level of quality and safety to consumers, standards make trade easier if safer products lead to a WTP of consumers that is sufficiently high and allows prices to cover the safety costs of firms. In other words, a standard may ward off Akerlof's (1970) market failure problem by increasing average quality. In our model, a standard could lower the damage r in equation (2), allowing purchase by reluctant consumers with $\tilde{D}_2$ (see Figure 19.1) when $a-r$ becomes higher than c. However, standards have the drawback of reducing both the diversity of products, by eliminating qualities below the standard, and competition, by limiting entry to the market for firms (see Marette and Beghin 2010). Furthermore, as regards the innocuousness of food products, it is seldom possible to reach a zero-risk level, which may generate continued controversies, particularly in times of a food safety crisis. From standards that reduce the diversity of products, we now turn to the label that maintains diversity.

3.4   The Label

Information and labeling policies are more favorable to product diversity because they allow the presence of various qualities bought by consumers in full knowledge of the facts. These policies concern quality labels like private labels or organic labels. Labels

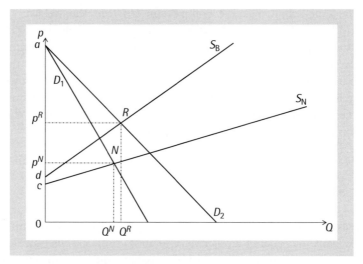

FIGURE **19.2** A mandatory label

are sometimes mandatory, as in the case of informative messages on the dangers of alcohol during pregnancy. These labeling policies aim to give consumers a sense of responsibility while guaranteeing their freedom of choice.

Figure 19.2 presents a situation under a mandatory label indicating the presence or absence of the controversial characteristic. For simplicity, it is assumed that the label fully transmits the relevant information so that it is fully understood by all consumers. To simplify further, it is assumed that labeling is costless, an assumption that can easily be relaxed. For a complete analysis, the additional labeling costs for firms and regulators should be subtracted from the surpluses introduced in Figure 19.2.

Labeling makes it possible to segment the market into two varieties: one that contains the controversial characteristic that is disliked by some consumers, and the "traditional" variety that is free of the characteristic. It is assumed that the segmentation is perfect and that no arbitraging between the two segments can occur. With labeling, there are two prices clearing the market since the label makes it possible to identify the presence or absence of the controversial characteristic by segmenting the market. The proportion $(1-\beta)$ of reluctant consumers may now turn to the product produced without the negative characteristic, so that the demand is D_2 with a maximum WTP equal to a as for D_1.

Exactly as under the absence of regulation (since the label is not costly and reluctant consumers do not choose controversial goods), the first equilibrium price is p^N with controversial products bought by the proportion β of indifferent consumers searching for the lowest price (see analytical expressions above). The profits of producers correspond to area cNp^N (see analytical expressions above). The surplus of indifferent consumers corresponds to area pNa. The label allows the existence of the second equilibrium price $p^R = [bd + a\,D(1 - \beta)]/[b + D(1 - \beta)]$, where the classic product is bought by the proportion $(1-\beta)$ of reluctant consumers who avoid the new technologies. The concerned consumers' surplus is $p^R Ra$, defined by $CS^R = b(a-d)^2(1-\beta)/[2[b+D(1-\beta)]^2]$, and the producer's profits are dRp^R, defined by $PS^R = D(a-d)^2(1-\beta)^2/[2[b+D(1-\beta)]^2]$. Taking into account both segments, overall welfare is $(cNa + dRa)$, defined by $W^1 = (a-c)^2\beta/[2(b+C\beta)] + (a-d)^2(1-\beta)/[2[b+D(1-\beta)]]$, which is the maximum possible welfare. In other words, if the label is clear and if its cost is relatively low, labeling policy leads to the highest welfare. However, a relatively high cost of labeling leads the regulator to turn to the social choice between ban and no regulation described in Figure 19.1, since the label is not socially optimal.[3]

One of the main limits of a labeling policy lies in the low memorization capacity of consumers and possible confusion as soon as the information given is technical or complex. With the previous model, the difficulty in recognizing, understanding, and/or memorizing a label means that only a proportion $\omega(1 - \beta)$ avoids the new product and chooses the regular product because of a perfect understanding, while a proportion $(1 - \omega)(1 - \beta)$ does not buy any product (as in Figure 19.1) since these consumers do not interpret the label as a signal of regular products. Wansink, Sonka, and Hasler (2004) underline the limitations of labels to convey complex information. Furthermore, a tendency toward the proliferation of labels is observed, with, in particular, the multiplication of claims about health, environment, or social characteristics, which may limit the impact of labels for consumers. Label proliferation swells the risk of muddle among consumers or citizens and the difficulty in recalling information (Roosen et al. 2009). In general, it is possible to distinguish three types of confusion: brand and label similarity, information (over)load, and/or ambiguous information (Mitchell, Walsh, and Yamin 2005).

An example of confusion is linked to the proliferation of green and sustainability claims, which makes it hard to remain clear on their different meanings. We mention just a few of the better-known labels: the German Blue Angel, the Nordic Swan, dozens of organic certification labels, "dolphin-safe," "California clean," "bird-friendly," "shade-grown," "Green Seal," and the mandatory information about miles per gallon for cars. In fact, the Eco-Labels Center, a US-based consumer advocacy group, lists over 200 US eco-labels across various products on its website (Eco-Labels Center 2008). Among these 200 or so eco-labels that were monitored, many make imprecise claims that do not help consumers clarify their opinions. These "poor" and imprecise labels often tarnish the credibility of well-defined labels that follow diligent procedures of meaningful product and process definition.

Information about product characteristics can be provided in the form of "negative" labeling, which marks a product as containing characteristics that are not desired by some consumers. On the other hand, "positive" labeling highlights in an affirmative way compliance with a production standard. There may be important differences

---

[3] Labeling costs can be borne by consumers, producers, or taxpayers depending on the type of fee selected for financing the cost of the label (see Crespi and Marette 2001).

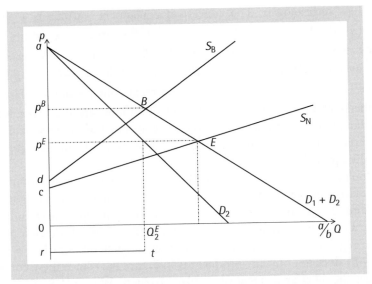

FIGURE 19.3 Ban versus absence of regulation with unaware consumers ($I=0$)

between the two approaches since consumers may react differently to a negative signal compared to a positive one. A negative label may create artificial "awareness" for indifferent consumers, who begin to get nervous when a new label is offered (Hu, Veeman, and Adamowicz 2005). In addition, the regulatory and labeling costs have to be borne by producers whether or not they use the controversial technology, which has implications for market outcome and competition. Crespi and Marette (2003) show that there is no a priori rule since regulatory costs may be imposed on producers either with or without the controversial technology in order to minimize market distortions.

To complete our analysis of regulatory issues in controversies, we turn to the case where reluctant consumers are not aware of the fact that the product they consume possesses a controversial attribute, corresponding to the case $I=0$ (for example, some people may be unaware that some foods are irradiated or contain genetically modified ingredients). For a situation where consumers are completely ignorant about the new technology, the demand curve remains unchanged, but welfare changes owing to ignorance (Foster and Just 1989; Teisl, Bockstael, and Levy 2001).

Figure 19.3 showing the absence of regulation differs from Figure 19.1 because D_2 does not depend on damage like $\tilde{D}_2$ in Figure 19.1. In other words, the use of the controversial technology does not impact the demand of concerned consumers (in equation (2) the demand is $p_2(Q, 0)$). In Figure 19.3, there is a single equilibrium price p^E with a market clearing equilibrium quantity Q^E. The cost of ignorance linked to non-internalized damage for reluctant consumers should be accounted for in the welfare calculations. For the proportion $(1-\beta)$ of concerned/reluctant consumers, the cost of ignorance is defined by $r(1 - \beta)Q^E = rQ_2^E$ and represented by area $ort\,Q_2^E$, where Q_2^E is consumption by these concerned consumers at price p^E. Adding the usual consumer surplus (area $p^E Ea$) and producer surplus (area cEp^E) to the cost of ignorance (area $ortQ_2^E$) yields an overall welfare represented by area $cEa - 0rtQ_2^E$ in the absence of intervention.

In this context, regulation is necessary to thwart the absence of damage internalization by consumers. In Figure 19.3, imposing a ban eliminates products with the controversial characteristic and leads to equilibrium B, which is equivalent to that of Figure 19.1. The externalized damage disappears because of the ban, but, as discussed above, new costs would arise out of making the new technology non-accessible. The arbitrage between the label and the ban is equivalent to that described in relation to Figure 19.2, since the cost of ignorance linked to the damage disappears.

To sum up the results linked to Figures 19.1, 19.2, and 19.3, labels improve welfare compared to a ban since diversity and freedom of choice are beneficial to society. However, prohibitive labeling costs and a high risk of muddle among consumers regarding the significance of labeling may lead to a ban as the socially optimal choice. There is no clear theoretical conclusion about the optimal instrument to select. Hence, empirical welfare estimates obtained by combining calibrated equilibrium models and results from experiments or surveys are valuable in informing regulators' choices between bans, standards and norms, and labels. The empirical evaluation of the trade-offs involved is a crucial step toward rigorous and convincing cost–benefit analysis.

4   COST–BENEFIT ANALYSIS FOR CLARIFYING DEBATES

The previous analysis does not give any definitive conclusion on the optimal use of a label or a ban.[4] However, the framework of Figures 19.1 and 19.2 can be used to integrate results from lab experiments or surveys eliciting WTP for controversial goods. For each controversial characteristic, it is relatively easy to run an experiment or a survey to calculate surplus measures (Rousu et al. 2004). This is clearly a case-by-case (or a "controversy-by-controversy") approach. We briefly present one method for calibrating and quantifying the impact of regulatory instruments on welfare by using WTP estimates. For the cloned-beef controversy, Lusk and Marette (2010) compare three methodologies, including the following one for estimating welfare with WTP elicited by surveys or experiments.

The integration of experimental economic results into calibrated models of market supply and demand helps in assessing the impacts of *ex ante* regulatory measures, that is to say, before the effective implementation of ban or labeling policies. The

---

[4] The discussion can be extended to a minimum quality or safety standard that is less drastic than a ban since products with a higher quality or safety than the standard are allowed.

experimental results from the lab or the field are a basis to anticipate consumers' reactions (including imagined risks underlined by Pollak 1998). Calibrated models of partial equilibrium help anticipate the price adjustments on markets and achieve quantified analyses computing welfare and directly usable by the public decision maker.

The calibration of the initial situation or baseline scenario aims at representing an existing situation that may vary across countries. For instance, as GMOs are banned in Europe, the calibration of the initial situation would be given by equilibrium B in Figure 19.1 (when the product is not allowed because of a ban preceding the introduction of a new technology). Based on equilibrium B, the demand and supply equations on the domestic market are represented by linear approximations with the corresponding elasticity at the point of approximation. By inversing equation (2), the overall demand without information (with $I = 0$) is defined by $Q = Q_1^D(p) + Q_2^D(p, 0) = (a - p)/b$. With the observed quantity $\hat{Q}$ sold over a period, the average price $\hat{p}$ observed over the period, and the direct price elasticity $\hat{\varepsilon}$ $(= (dQ/dP)(P/Q))$ obtained from econometric estimates, the calibration leads to estimated values for demand equal to $1/\tilde{b} = -\hat{\varepsilon}\hat{Q}/\hat{p}$, $\tilde{a} = \tilde{b}\hat{Q} + \hat{p}$. Elasticities can be estimated or found in the literature.

The relative variations of WTP observed in the experiment or survey focusing on the controversial characteristic may serve to determine the demand shift between D_2 and $\tilde{D}_2$ shown in Figures 19.1 and 19.2 (see Marette, Roosen, and Blanchemanche 2008; Marette, Roosen, Blanchemanche, and Verger 2008). For instance, with the GMOs example, it is possible to forecast the impact of the introduction of GMOs when a ban is lifted by introducing results from experiments. The demand variation is based on the lab experiment via the relative variation of WTP defined by $\delta = [E(WTP^{hh}) - E(WTP^h)]/E(WTP^h)$, where $E(.)$ denotes the expected value of the WTP for subjects of the experiment who significantly change their WTP after they learn of the characteristic of the controversial product (namely $WTP^{hh} \neq WTP^h$). The parameter h denotes the situation before the information was revealed and hh denotes the situation afterward. The relative change δ isolates the relative WTP for the controversial characteristic independently from the initial endowment or the initial value of the product offered during the experiment/survey. With the model calibrated for an initial price p^B in Figure 19.1 (when the product is not allowed because of a ban preceding the introduction of a new technology), the value of the parallel demand shift is $r = -\delta p^B$, consistently with the stable slope in (2). In other words, the relative variation δ combined to the equilibrium price p^B allows the integration of experimental results for a market context. The welfare described above and the effects presented in Figures 19.1–19.3 can be quantified for a specific controversy linked to a particular good.

These methods may be mobilized for cost–benefit analyses enlightening decision makers on the consequences of various public choices. Various extensions can be introduced to refine the analysis. For instance, the supply chain could be also taken into account in the welfare analysis by detailing the supply function at different levels (Hennessy, Roosen, and Jensen 2003). Quantity variations linked to a specific regulation maybe also be taken into account in the welfare analysis. Disdier and Marette (2010) show how to take into account the coefficient measuring the forgone trade linked to standards in a gravity equation to determine the relative variations of both price and quantity in a partial equilibrium model used for welfare analysis (with a model similar to the one introduced with equation (1)).

Cost–benefit analysis can be used to enable public authorities to make decisions concerning national regulations. This could be used in the case of nanotechnologies where industries try to avoid debate because of experience with the introduction of GMOs (Manach 2009). When a controversy emerges, we recommend that the method combining market data, costs in the supply chain, and experimental or survey results should be used systematically by focusing on the impact of instruments such as labels and bans. This cost–benefit analysis could be conducted after risk assessment and before the legislative process. Being up-front with consumers' reluctance by using a transparent cost–benefit analysis could help streamline arguments. Even though society does not accept all risks in the same way, and even though social choices cannot be reduced to the equalization of marginal costs and benefits, cost–benefit analysis is an important stage in the framing of regulations (Arrow et al. 1996).

5   CONCLUSION

Ignoring consumer values may result in a falling away of their support for the introduction of new technologies. Taming an "irrational" controversy is a difficult task because of the complexity of risks and benefits given different weights in different parts of the population. The literature presented in this chapter provides some clues about consumers' reluctance toward new technologies in the food domain and the nature of controversies.

Future work should propose complete cost–benefit analysis using experiments and careful calibration of scenarios for new possible controversies linked to rising issues like nanotechnologies in food or the environment, animal cloning, or the carbon footprint of food. Presenting a transparent cost–benefit analysis to society may streamline controversial debate by presenting the consequences of regulatory choices such as labels or a ban on some products. With regard to such issues, accompanied by scientific uncertainty (see Chapter 17 in this volume by Johansson-Stenman), the appropriate handling of information within an experimental context can be crucial to the results. In addition, economists must acknowledge the limitations of institutions and limits to the rationality of individual consumers. While it is unlikely to come up with a perfect policy that overcomes these limits, a careful cost–benefit analysis should lead to a more rational policy analysis.

When a controversy begins, we recommend that the method that combines market data, costs in the supply chain, and experimental or survey results should be used systematically to focus on the welfare impact of instruments such as labels and bans.

Such a cost–benefit analysis revealed to citizens is better than doing nothing, which sometimes stokes the idea of conspiracy. It may also help to encourage rational discussion on the pros and cons of the technology by developing a means of precisely pinning down the arguments. The results of this survey point out the importance of developing economic analyses using WTP estimates based on experiment and survey results leading to welfare measures for helping the decision maker and facilitating political decisions. However, it should not be forgotten that the arguments involved in most controversies are complex and are often hidden in strategic turmoil.

REFERENCES

Akerlof, G. 1970. "The Market for 'Lemons': Qualitative Uncertainty and the Market Mechanism." *Quarterly Journal of Economics* 84: 488–500.

Alfnes, F., and K. Rickertsen. 2003. "European Consumers' Willingness to Pay for U.S. Beef in Experimental Auction Markets." *American Journal of Agricultural Economics* 85: 396–409.

Arrow, K. J., M. L. Cropper, G. C. Eads, R. W. Hahn, L. B. Lave, R. G. Noll, P. R. Portney, M. Russell, R. Schmalensee, V. K. Smith, and R. N. Stavins. 1996. "Is There a Role for Benefit–Cost Analysis in Environmental, Health, and Safety Regulation?" *Science* 272 (12 Apr.), 222–3.

Bieberstein A., J. Roosen, S. Marette, S. Blanchemanche, and F. Vandermoere. 2009. *Impacts of Information Choice and Cheap Talk on Consumer Willingness-to-Pay for Nanotechnologies in Food.* Working Paper. Paris: INRA-Met@risk.

Bureau, J. C., S. Marette, and A. Schiavina. 1998. "Non-Tariff Trade Barriers and Consumers' Information: The Case of EU–US Trade Dispute on Beef." *European Review of Agricultural Economics* 25/4: 437–62.

Christoph, I. B., M. Bruhn, and J. Roosen. 2008. "Knowledge, Attitudes towards and Acceptability of Genetically Modified Products in Germany." *Appetite* 51: 58–68.

Costa-Font, M., J. M. Gil, and W. B. Traill. 2008. "Consumer Acceptance, Valuation of and Attitudes towards Genetically Modified Food: Review and Implications for Food Policy." *Food Policy* 33: 99–111.

Crespi, J., and S. Marette. 2001. "How Should Food Safety Certification Be Financed?" *American Journal of Agricultural Economics* 83/4: 852–61.

—— ——. 2003. "'Does Contain' vs. 'Does Not Contain': Does It Matter Which GMO Label Is Used?" *European Journal of Law and Economics* 16/3: 327–44.

Darby, M., and E. Karni. 1973. "Free Competition and the Optimal Amount of Fraud." *Journal of Law and Economics* 16: 67–88.

Disdier, A.-C., and S. Marette. 2010. "The Combination of Gravity and Welfare Approaches for Evaluating Non-Tariff Measures." *American Journal of Agricultural Economics* 92/3: 713–26.

Eco-Labels Center. 2008. *Greener Choices: Label Index.* Washington, DC. <http://www.greenerchoices.org/eco-labels/labelIndex.cfm>.

Fife-Shaw, C., and G. Rowe. 1996. "Public Perceptions of Everyday Food Hazards: A Psychometric Study." *Risk Analysis* 16/4: 487–500.

Foster, W., and R. Just. 1989. "Measuring Welfare Effects of Product Contamination with Consumer Uncertainty." *Journal of Environmental Economics and Management* 17: 266–83.

Fox, J., D. Hayes, and J. Shogren. 2002. "Consumer Preferences for Food Irradiation: How Favorable and Unfavorable Descriptions Affect Preferences for Irradiated Pork in Experimental Auctions." *Journal of Risk and Uncertainty* 24/1: 75–95.

Frewer, L. J., and S. Miles. 2001. "Risk Perception, Communication and Trust: How Might Consumer Confidence in the Food Supply be Maintained?" In L. Frewer, E. Risvik, and H. Schifferstein, eds, *Food, People, and Society*. Berlin: Springer.

Goldberg, I., and J. Roosen. 2007. "Scope Insensitivity in Health Risk Reduction Studies: A Comparison of Choice Experiments and the Contingent Valuation Method for Valuing Safer Food." *Journal of Risk and Uncertainty* 34/2: 123–44.

Hayes, D., and H. H. Jensen. 2003. "Lessons from the Danish Ban on Feed-Grade Antibiotics." *Choices*, 3rd quarter. <http://www.choicesmagazine.org>.

——, J. Shogren, Y. Shin, and J. Kliebenstein. 1995. "Valuing Food Safety in Experimental Auction Markets." *American Journal of Agricultural Economics* 77: 40–53.

Hennessy, D., J. Roosen, and H. H. Jensen. 2003. "Systemic Failure in the Provision of Safe Food." *Food Policy* 28: 77–96.

Hu, W., M. M. Veeman, and W. L. Adamowicz. 2005. "Labeling Genetically Modified Food: Heterogeneous Consumer Preferences and the Value of Information." *Canadian Journal of Agricultural Economics* 53: 83–102.

Huffman, W. E., M. C. Rousu, J. F. Shogren, and A. Tegene. 2003. "The Public Good Value of Information from Agribusinesses on Genetically Modified Food." *American Journal of Agricultural Economics* 85: 1309–15.

——————. 2007. "The Effects of Prior Beliefs and Learning on Consumers' Acceptance of Genetically Modified Food." *Journal of Economic Behavior and Organization* 63: 193–206.

Kalaitzandonakes, N., L. A. Marks, and S. S. Vickner. 2004. "Media Coverage of Biotech Foods, and Influence on Consumer Choice." *American Journal of Agricultural Economics* 86/5: 1238–46.

Lagerkvist, C. J., F. Carlsson, and D. Viske. 2006. "Swedish Consumer Preferences for Animal Welfare and Biotech: A Choice Experiment." *AgBioForum* 9/1: 51–8.

Lusk, J. L., and S. Marette. 2010. "Welfare Effects of Food Labels and Bans with Alternative Willingness to Pay Measures." *Applied Economic Perspectives and Policy* 32: 319–37.

—— and J. F. Shogren. 2007. *Experimental Auctions: Methods and Applications in Economic and Marketing Research*. Cambridge: Cambridge University Press.

——, L. O. House, C. Valli, S. R. Jaeger, M. Moore, B. Morrow, and W. B. Traill. 2005. "Consumer Welfare Effects of Introducing and Labeling Genetically Modified Food." *Economics Letters* 88: 382–8.

——, M. Jamal, L. Kurlander, M. Roucan, and L. Taulman. 2005. "A Meta Analysis of Genetically Modified Food Valuation Studies." *Journal of Agricultural and Resource Economics* 30: 28–44.

——, B. Norwood, and R. Pruitt. 2006. "Consumer Demand for a Ban on Subtherapeutic Antibiotic Use in Pork Production." *American Journal of Agricultural Economics* 88: 1015–33.

——, J. Roosen, and J. A. Fox. 2003. "Demand for Beef from Cattle Administered Growth Hormones or Fed Genetically Modified Corn: A Comparison of Consumers in France, Germany, the United Kingdom and the United States." *American Journal of Agricultural Economics* 85: 16–29.

Manach, J.-M. 2009. "Nanotechnologies: Le syndrome OGM?" *Le Monde*, Apr. 10. <http://www.internetactu.net/2009/04/09/nanotechnologies-et-gestion-du-risque>.

Marette, S. 2007. "Minimum Safety Standard, Consumer's Information and Competition." *Journal of Regulatory Economics* 32: 259–85.

—— and J. C. Beghin. 2010. "Are Standards Always Protectionist?" *Review of International Economics* 18: 179–92.

——, J. Roosen, A. Bieberstein, S. Blanchemanche, and F. Vandermoere. 2009. "Impact of Environmental, Societal and Health Information on Consumers' Choices for NanoFood." *Journal of Agricultural and Food Industrial Organization* 7/2, art. 11. <http://www.bepress.com/jafio/vol7/iss2/art11>.

—— ——, and S. Blanchemanche. 2008. "Taxes and Subsidies to Change Eating Habits When Information Is Not Enough: An Application to Fish Consumption." *Journal of Regulatory Economics* 34: 119–43.

—— —— ——, and P. Verger. 2008. "The Choice of Fish Species: An Experiment Measuring the Impact of Risk and Benefit Information." *Journal of Agricultural and Resource Economics* 33: 1–18.

Mitchell, V., G. Walsh, and M. Yamin. 2005. "Towards a Conceptual Model of Consumer Confusion." *Advances in Consumer Research* 32: 143–50.

Napolitano, F., C. Pacelli, A. Girolami, and A. Braghieri. 2008. "Effect of Information about Animal Welfare on Consumer Willingness to Pay for Yogurt." *Journal of Dairy Science* 91: 910–17.

National Research Council. 2008. *Phthalates and Cumulative Risk Assessment: The Task Ahead.* Washington, DC: National Academies Press.

Noussair, C., S. Robin, and B. Ruffieux. 2002. "Do Consumers Not Care about Biotech Foods or Do They Just Not Read the Labels?" *Economics Letters* 75: 47–53.

Polinsky, A. M., and W. Rogerson. 1983. "Products Liability and Consumer Misperceptions and Market Power." *Bell Journal of Economics* 14: 581–9.

Pollak, R. A. 1998. "Imagined Risks and Cost–Benefit Analysis." *American Economic Review* 88/2: 376–9.

Powell, M. 1997. *Science in Sanitary and Phytosanitary Dispute Resolution.* Discussion Paper No. 97-50. Washington, DC: Resources for the Future.

Roosen, J., S. Marette, S. Blanchemanche, and P. Verger. 2009. "Does Health Information Matter for Modifying Consumption? A Field Experiment Measuring the Impact of Risk Information on Fish Consumption." *Review of Agricultural Economics* 31: 2–20.

Rousu, M. C., W. E. Huffman, J. F. Shogren, and A. Tegene. 2004. "Estimating the Public Value of Conflicting Information: The Case of Genetically Modified Foods." *Land Economics* 80/1: 125–35.

Rowe, G., and G. Wright. 2001. "Differences in Expert and Lay Judgments of Risk: Myth or Reality." *Risk Analysis* 21/2: 341–56.

Rozin, P., M. Spranca, Z. Krieger, R. Neuhaus, D. Surillo, A. Swerdlin, and K. Wood. 2004. "Preference for Natural: Instrumental and Ideational/Moral Motivations, and the Contrast between Foods and Medicines." *Appetite* 43/2: 147–54.

Shogren, J. F. 2003. "Food-Safety Economics: Consumer Health and Welfare." In A. G. J. Velthuis, L. J. Unnevehr, H. Hogeveen, and R. B. M. Huirne, eds., *New Approaches to Food-Safety Economics.* Berlin: Springer.

Slovic, P. 1987. "Perception of Risk." *Science* 236: 280–5.

Teisl, M., N. Bockstael, and A. Levy. 2001. "Measuring the Welfare Effects of Nutrition Information." *American Journal of Agricultural Economics* 83/1: 133–49.

Wall Street Journal. 2006. "*E. Coli*'s Enablers." Dec. 18: A16. <http://www.ifsqn.com/forum/index.php/topic/5970-e-colis-enablers-wall-street-journal/>.

Wansink, B., S. Sonka, and C. Hasler. 2004. "Front-Label Health Claims: When Less Is More." *Food Policy* 29: 659–67.

CHAPTER 20

....

NUTRITIONAL LABELING

....

ANDREAS C. DRICHOUTIS, RODOLFO M. NAYGA, JR.,
AND PANAGIOTIS LAZARIDIS*

1 INTRODUCTION

....

Over the past decades diet and nutrition have emerged as very important factors in the maintenance and promotion of health, especially in light of the dramatic rise in obesity rates (particularly in developed countries; Loureiro and Nayga 2005). The World Health Organization (2006) indicated that in 2005 there were 1.6 billion overweight adults and at least 400 million obese adults in the world. By 2015 these figures are expected to rise to 2.3 billion overweight and 700 million obese adults. Some of the key causes of this epidemic are increased consumption of energy-dense foods high in saturated fats and sugars, and reduced physical activity. Hence, healthy diets and healthier food choices are becoming the target of many public programs.

Although health is generally valued by everyone, changing dietary habits toward healthier eating patterns is not a trivial task. One of the approaches being used by policymakers is nutrition education, which can be provided by several means, including provision of nutritional information on food products. Nutritional attributes of food products can be seen as both credence and search attributes (Nelson 1970; Darby and Karni 1973; Nelson 1974). However, nutritional attributes can only be transformed from a credence attribute to a search attribute once nutritional information is presented on the product (Caswell and Mojduszka 1996). Hence, it has been hypothesized that providing credible information to consumers about the nutritional content of foods will help them make healthier food choices.

There are three general types of nutritional information on food packages: nutritional labels or fact panels (the latter term is usually used in the United States, Canada, Australia and New Zealand), health claims (e.g., "Plant sterols have been shown to

* We are grateful to Mary Yannakoulia, Stathis Klonaris, Jutta Roosen, and an anonymous reviewer for helpful comments.

lower/reduce blood cholesterol. High cholesterol is a risk factor in the development of coronary heart disease"), and nutrition claims (e.g., low-energy, fat-free, high-protein, etc.). It is not trivial to differentiate fully between these terms. In fact, Hawke (2004) uses three whole pages to define them. Briefly, a nutritional label or a nutrition facts panel is a quantitative list of nutrients that can be in linear or tabular form (the fact panel is in tabular form). A nutrition claim, on the other hand, characterizes the level of nutrient in a food product. Health claims generally provide a suggestion about the health benefits of a specific food product. They can be categorized as nutrient function claims, other function claims, reduction of disease risk claims, and disease prevention claims. Health claims can also vary in form between countries.

Over the years, there has been considerable marketing and economic research on nutrition information, including a number of literature review papers. For example, Baltas (2001) reviewed studies up to 1998 and Cowburn and Stockley (2005) reviewed studies that have been published up to 2002. Drichoutis, Lazaridis, and Nayga (2006) and Grunert and Wills (2007) updated the previous literature reviews, while Pothoulaki and Chryssochoidis (2009) reviewed the related health claims literature. In many sections of this chapter, we have only included published papers after 2005 to avoid overlaps with previous published reviews. Hence, in our review we do not cover issues that relate to the determinants of label use or the effects of label use on diet as we have covered this ground in one of our previous review papers (see Drichoutis, Lazaridis, and Nayga 2006).

This chapter is organized as follows: in the next section we review the regulatory environment with respect to nutrition information in several countries. Readers are advised also to see Hawkes (2004). We then discuss the trends in label formats and the increasing number of studies that have focused on this issue in Section 3. In Section 4 we summarize some of the theoretical attempts at modeling the economics of nutrition information search. We then illustrate and address some important econometric issues (i.e., self-selection) that have been only minimally covered in the extensive empirical literature on nutritional labeling and health outcomes (Section 5). In Section 6, we discuss the literature on nutritional labeling and food away from home, which has received a lot of attention over the last five years. Section 7 mainly updates previous literature reviews on nutritional labels and nutrition/health claims, and we then conclude with future areas of research in Section 8.

2   THE REGULATORY ENVIRONMENT[1]

2.1   Nutrition Information in the United States

In the United States, the Nutritional Labeling and Education Act (NLEA) was passed by the US Congress in 1990. This law then went into effect in 1994 and gave the Food

---

[1] This section draws on Drichoutis (2008, ch. 2).

and Drug Administration (FDA) the authority to require nutritional labeling in most pre-packaged foods regulated by the Agency, excluding foods in restaurants. Before 1994 food companies in the United States were providing nutrition information on food packages on a voluntary basis. The NLEA lists very detailed requirements about the nutrition facts panels format. It requires that nutrition information be presented in a box, that headings and nutrients are separated by bars, and defines a font size of at least 8-point type, etc. All values expressed must be in terms of the stated "Serving Size" and, except for fish or game meat, must be based on the product as packaged. The nutrient information that the NLEA requires to be listed are calories, calories from fats, fats, saturated fats, cholesterol, sodium, potassium (only if a claim is made), carbohydrates, dietary fiber, proteins, vitamins, and minerals. There are several details and exemptions on the requirement of these nutrients based on the content of the nutrients to the food. Since January 2006, the nutrition facts panel has also been mandated to include information about trans fatty acids.

The NLEA also regulates nutrient content claims and health claims. Nutrient content claims such as light, low-calorie, or low-fat have standardized definitions. There are two kinds of health claim: the Significant Scientific Agreement (SSA) health claims and the qualified health claims. For qualified health claims, the evidence is not well enough established to meet the SSA standard required for the FDA to issue an authorizing regulation. Hence, qualifying language is included as part of the claim to indicate that the evidence supporting the claim is limited.

2.2   Nutrition Information in the European Union

Nutritional labeling in the European Union (EU) is generally governed by Council Directive 90/496/EEC, which was amended by Commission Directives 2003/120/EC and 2008/100/EC. The directive concerns all foodstuffs intended for supply to restaurants, hospitals, canteens, and other similar mass caterers with the exception of natural mineral waters and diet integrators/food supplements. The directive makes nutritional labeling optional unless a nutrition claim appears on the labels, or in advertising, with the exclusion of generic advertising. Where nutritional labeling is provided, information must be given in the form of either group 1 or group 2 (also known as BIG 4 and BIG 8 respectively). Group 1 contains energy value, proteins, carbohydrates, and fats, while group 2 contains energy value, proteins, carbohydrates, sugars, fats, saturated fat, dietary fiber, and sodium. Where a nutrition claim is made for sugars, saturated fat, dietary fiber, or sodium, the information to be given must be in the form of group 2. Nutrition labeling may also include the amounts of additional nutrients like starch, polyols, monounsaturated fats, polyunsaturated fats, cholesterol, or several minerals/ vitamins as listed in an annex of the regulation. All this information is to be presented together in one tabular form. They can only be presented in a linear form when space is limited.

In January 2003, the Commission consulted member states and stakeholders about the revision of the directive 90/496/EEC and the preparation of a proposal amending the voluntary provision of nutritional information to become mandatory. In November 2004, the Commission then published an impact assessment on the introduction of mandatory nutritional labeling for pre-packaged food products across the EU (European Advisory Services 2004). As part of the consultation process, a paper discussing the revision of technical issues was also published in May 2006, which paves the way for the final adoption of new mandatory rules.

Regulation for nutrition and health claims was left to the member states and many chose not to regulate them for a considerable period of time. In 2003 the Commission put forward a proposal for a Health Claims Regulation. Prior to 2003 a discussion paper was published on the Commission's website in order to gather comments and specific suggestions on these claims. The Commission received comments from more than ninety stakeholders. The European Parliament then held its first reading vote on the Commission's proposal in 2005. The EU health ministers endorsed the Commission's proposal, including the provision for nutrient profiles and the authorization procedure, during this first reading vote at the Health Council. The European Parliament second reading vote took place in May 2006, and in December 2006 a Regulation on the use of nutrition and health claims for foods was adopted by the Council and Parliament (EC 1924/2006). This Regulation laid down harmonized rules for the use of health or nutritional claims on foodstuffs based on nutrient profiles. The regulation specifies the conditions under which a nutrition claim can be made. A list of authorized health claims will be adopted progressively by the European Commission and Member States taking into account the opinions of the European Food Safety Authority (EFSA). This list will come from the approved requests that were submitted to national competent authorities and then forwarded to EFSA as well as to the Commission. The Commission carried out a consolidation process resulting in a final list of 4,637 claims after examining 44,000 submitted claims. EFSA expects to complete evaluation in 2011.

2.3   Nutrition Information in Canada

Similarly to the United States, Canada enacted nutritional labeling regulations that were passed in 2003. Nutrition labeling then became mandatory for all pre-packaged foods in December 2007. The nutrition facts table provides information on calories and thirteen nutrients: fats, saturated fats, trans fats, cholesterol, sodium, carbohydrates, dietary fiber, sugars, proteins, vitamin A, vitamin C, calcium, and iron. These labeling regulations also updated the requirements for over forty nutrient-content claims and allowed the use of five health claims on food labels or in advertisements.

Before the passage of the regulation, nutritional labeling was optional with a few exceptions. The format of the nutrition facts table was then not consistent, and if nutritional labeling was provided, information was given on only a few nutrients. Not all nutrient content claims were regulated and diet-related health claims were not allowed.

2.4   Nutrition Information in Australia and New Zealand

Nutritional labels are also now mandatory in Australia and New Zealand. The regulation mandating nutritional labeling went into effect in January 2003, in lieu of the previous voluntary system. According to the regulation, a nutrition information panel must be listed on nearly all packaged foods. These panels should list how much energy, proteins, total fats, saturated fats, carbohydrates, sugars, and sodium is in the product.

In December 2003 the Australia and New Zealand Food Regulation Ministerial Council agreed to a new policy for nutrition, health, and related claims. At present, nutrient content claims and some health maintenance claims are allowed. However, other types of health claim are prohibited.

The Food Standards Australia New Zealand (FSANZ) has initiated the development of a standard for health, nutrition, and related claims for inclusion in the Food Standards Code. This is still an open process involving extensive public consultation and close liaison with key stakeholders and expert advisers.

An external Scientific Advisory Group is responsible for the development of the Substantiation Framework for Nutrition, Health, and Related Claims. The Final Assessment Report and draft Standard were submitted to the Ministerial Council in May 2008. The Ministerial Council has requested a Review of the draft standard by the end of 2011. It is expected that this will be one of the last steps in the development of nutrition and health claims regulations in Australia and New Zealand.

2.5   Nutrition Information in the Rest of the World

Other countries that have mandatory nutritional labeling regulations include Argentina, Brazil, Paraguay, Uruguay, Israel, and Malaysia (Hawkes 2004). The issue is more diverse and complex, however, with respect to nutrition and health claims. Hawkes (2004, table 2) listed thirty-seven countries that have no specific regulations on health claims and listed only twenty-four countries that allow nutrition or other function claims. Given the increasing interest in nutrition and health, it is likely that more countries will implement mandatory rules on provision of nutrition information/labels on food products.

3   EFFECTIVENESS OF DIFFERENT LABEL FORMATS

Nutritional label formats are getting increasing attention from empirical researchers. Literature reviews in the past have revealed that consumers do not understand complex (often quantitative) information (e.g., Drichoutis, Lazaridis, and Nayga 2006) and that formats of labels have a significant impact on consumer behavior.

This does not mean that more simplistic formats are able to help consumers adequately make appropriate food choices. For example, in an experiment examining snack food consumption (Antonuk and Block 2006), non-dieters exposed to a dual-column label (i.e., information for a single serving as well as for the whole package) ate less of a candy snack (M&M's) than non-dieters exposed to a single-column label. On the other hand, dieters' eating behavior did not vary based on the label format. In Drichoutis, Nayga, and Lazaridis (2009b) consumers' ability to extract information from an EU-type format nutritional label was not related to diet quality (as measured by a Mediterranean diet index).

However, consumers on average seem to prefer detailed nutritional labels over labels containing only summary information, although they exhibit a high dispersion of preferences (Berning, Chouinard, and McCluskey 2008). Consumers are even willing to pay more for a product with more information but only if they actively search for this information (Kimura et al. 2008). This preference for more detailed information is also reflected in Gracia, Loureiro, and Nayga (2009) where consumers' willingness to pay a premium was found to be about twice as much more for a box of breakfast cookies with a nutritional label than for a box of breakfast cookies with only a "light" nutritional claim. Socioeconomic characteristics of consumers requiring more detailed information versus more simplistic nutrition claims are also quite different (Stranieri, Baldi, and Banterle 2009).

Some researchers have not shied away from recommending ways to market the health properties of products. Booth (2006) suggested showing the energy density of the foods in terms of the amount of activity required to expend the energy contained in a typical serving; for example, "Walk 30" would mean thirty minutes of walking would be required to expend the consumed energy. For foods targeting children or adolescents, popular activities could be used; for example, "Football 40." Cinar and Murtomaa (2009) suggested labeling healthy food with a simple "health-friendly" logo of teeth and heart, depicted as standing side by side. In front of these two figures, a text in green then indicates that the food is health-friendly.

Therefore, it is not a surprise that in Europe (which only regulates *what* information is to be presented and not *how* information should be presented) there has been an outburst of new front-of-pack label formats that are supported by both national and international health organizations as well as by food companies. These include the healthier choice Tick, smileys, stars, multiple traffic light,[2] wheel of health, guideline daily allowances (GDA) scores, etc. Several other variants and combinations of these formats are endorsed by various organizations and governments. Such simple label formats allow one to evaluate rapidly the nutrient content of a product although there are differences in consumer-friendliness and usage intentions in these formats (Feunekes et al. 2008). It has also been shown that the presence of a visual decision aid

---

[2] The "traffic light" label places colors next to each nutrient of a product, similar to traffic lights, which indicate low, medium, and high assessments of the nutrient. Usually foods are labeled with a panel of colored spots relating to the amount of sugar, salt, fat, and saturated fat.

(in the form of star rating[3]) at the point of purchase can improve choice for low-literacy consumers (Jae and Delvecchio 2004). In another study, eye movements were recorded while participants made healthiness ratings for different types of label formats (Jones and Richardson 2007). In this study, the traffic light label (TL) helped consumers to become attentive to the important nutrients and improved the accuracy of their healthiness ratings of nutritional labels with respect to a standard label format. In addition, consumers exhibit higher liking for front-of-pack calorie flags, especially for simpler forms of this signpost label (e.g., calories per serving or per 100 grams versus flags with references to daily needs or exercise) (van Kleef et al. 2008). Balcombe, Fraser, and di Falco (2009) have also identified a strong preference among consumers to avoid a basket of goods containing a mix of foods with any "Red" lights. However, it was unclear whether consumers were responding to the information or whether they were responding to the color scheme.

This abundance of label formats has initiated a "label war" over the last few years between TL and GDAs in the EU. Food producers in Europe, under the auspices of their confederation,[4] joined forces and endorsed the GDA format, probably to forestall the possible mandatory implementation of the TL system. On the other hand, consumer organizations and governmental departments such as the Food Standards Agency have been reported to favor the TL system. Politicians' positions differ according to their party affiliation and their closeness to either the producer or the consumer side.

Campaigns in favor of and against GDAs have also appeared.[5] Consumer organizations such as the German-based foodwatch[6] are even commissioning marketing studies in an effort to prove their arguments (i.e., in favor of TL). This "war" is not without winners since in June 2010 members of the European Parliament voted against TL and backed GDAs. The coexistence of a range of signpost labels is, of course, against consumers' interests since it may cause difficulties or confusion for shoppers using them (Malam et al. 2009).

In fact, there might be gains by mandating a standardized format rather than the current environment, in which everyone is allowed to display its newly invented format. Among consumers, label users are more likely to consider such initiatives as beneficial (Gracia, Loureiro, and Nayga 2007). Loureiro, Gracia, and Nayga (2006) and

---

[3] The form of star rating uses a predetermined number of stars (e.g., five), and the number of stars depicted with full color versus the overall number of stars shows the relative nutrient value of the product. For example, a product with three full-colored stars should be considered healthier than a product with one full-colored star.

[4] Confederation of the Food and Drink Industries of the EU (Confédération des Industries Agro-Alimentaires de l'UE).

[5] For example, the food industry's campaign for GDA food labeling (<http://www.whatsinsideguide.com> and <http://gda.ciaa.eu>). A European campaign against GDA food labeling used to be available (<http://stopgda.eu>) but the website has been taken down since members of the European Parliament voted against TL and endorsed GDAs.

[6] <http://foodwatch.de>.

Drichoutis, Lazaridis, and Nayga (2009b) have found that European consumers would value having standardized nutritional information in food products. On the other hand, mandating nutrition information creates asymmetric opportunities for firms, which then affects their strategies and survival. Moorman, Du, and Mela (2005) find that the NLEA in the United States led to an increase in small-share firm exits.

The findings from all these studies discussed above suggest that there are still a lot of inconsistencies and gaps in the literature related to nutritional labeling. Section 8 discusses some of these future areas of research.

4   ECONOMIC THEORIES OF NUTRITION INFORMATION

In his seminal paper, Stigler (1961) begins with the statement: "one should hardly have to tell academicians that information is a valuable resource: knowledge is power." This raises a question of how much power consumers will demand if they have to spend time to acquire it. According to Stigler's theory, as long as the additional cost of information search does not outweigh the additional benefits, consumers will continue to search for additional information.

Sexton's work (1979) on an economic theory of food labeling is one of the earliest we know of. In his work, Sexton distinguishes between data and information. The former is potential information and it becomes information only when it is processed by the recipient (i.e., the consumer). Sexton treats nutrition information as a shifter of demand curves in the cases of incomplete and perfect information, respectively. In cases when the consumer's demand curve does not coincide with the true demand curve under perfect information, misallocations in consumer's expenditures can result, with corresponding changes in consumer surplus and welfare. The consumer can overevaluate, underevaluate, or correctly evaluate the nutritional attributes of the product, but in either of the first two cases, consumers can suffer welfare losses.

Demand for and the provision of information can be determined by the cost–benefit trade-off. In Sexton's model, the benefit to consumers from processing information is the reduction in the expected loss from expenditure misallocations. The cost to the consumer is the cost of processing the data into useful information. An optimum level of consumer information processing is achieved when the marginal benefit of processing is equal to the marginal cost of processing.

Subsequent theoretical analysis of nutrition information has been based on Foster and Just's (1989) framework, which considers a case where an individual chooses to consume x_0 of a good with a quality subjective distribution captured by a parameter θ_0. A contamination of the good degrades the subjective distribution to θ_1 and moves the consumer to x_1. Foster and Just consider the case where the individual is not told of the contamination incident and therefore its loss is greater than simply a movement along the consumption path from x_0 to x_1 for θ_0 and θ_1, respectively. This imperfect information case is reflected in the cost of ignorance measurement.

Teisl, Bockstael, and Levy (2001) adopt this framework for nutrition information in an attempt to measure the welfare impacts of providing nutrient information on food products. Although provision of nutrition information is not a change in the quality per se, it can signify a difference in the amount of information provided. For example, a nutritional label provides information that allows individuals to update their initial (and perhaps imperfect) assessment from θ_0 to a new subjective distribution θ_1. If an individual does not observe information represented by θ_1, the cost of ignorance is given by

$$COI = CS - CV = e(p_0, \bar{U}_0, \theta_1) - \tilde{e}(p_0, \bar{U}_0, \theta_1; x_0) \qquad (1)$$

where CS is the compensating surplus measure,

$$CS = e(p_0, \bar{U}_0, \theta_0) - \tilde{e}(p_0, \bar{U}_0, \theta_1; x_0) \qquad (2)$$

CV is the compensating variation

$$CV = e(p_0, \bar{U}_0, \theta_0) - e(p_0, \bar{U}_0, \theta_1) \qquad (3)$$

p is price of the good x, $\bar{U}$ is defined as expected utility such that $\max_x \bar{U}(x, y, \theta) = \max_x E_\theta$, and $e(p, \bar{U}, \theta)$ is the expenditure function.

In another attempt at modeling label use, Drichoutis et al. (2008) and Drichoutis, Lazaridis, and Nayga (2009a) build a model of demand for nutrition information by modifying Grossman's (1972) model of the demand for health. In their model, they assume that there are three composite commodities in the market. A group of "unhealthy" food products is denoted as B, a group of "healthy" foods is denoted as G, and a group of all other commodities is denoted as Z. The utility function of a typical consumer is defined as

$$U = U(H, G, B, Z, W, E, N, R) \qquad (4)$$

where H is the stock of health, W is working time, E is time spent on health-enhancing activities (e.g., sports or exercise time in general), N is time spent on searching and acquiring nutrition information, and R is residual time.

Consumers produce health according to a health production function:

$$H = H(G, B, W, E, Ni; \delta) \qquad (5)$$

where Ni is the stock of nutrition information possessed by the individual and $H_{Ni} > 0$. In addition, it is assumed that

$$G = G(Ni; t) \text{ and } B = B(Ni; t) \qquad (6)$$

where t represents taste preferences. Nutrition information stock is endogenous and produced according to the production function

$$Ni = Ni(mN; N_k) \qquad (7)$$

where m reflects the efficiency of the consumer to derive and process information from one unit of time N spent on gathering information ($0 \leq m \leq 1$).

In the health production function (5), G and B are inputs in the production of health. As in Grossman's paper (1972), δ is the rate of depreciation of health, which is assumed to be exogenous and to vary with the age of the individual or environmental conditions.

Individuals' budget constraint is

$$P_G G + P_B B + P_z Z = wW + Y \qquad (8)$$

where consumers' market wage rate is w and Y is unearned income. P_G, P_B, and P_Z are the prices of G, B, and Z, respectively. Individuals' time constraint is

$$W + E + N + R = T \qquad (9)$$

where T is equal to the decision's period time endowment.

With this model, Drichoutis et al. (2008) and Drichoutis, Lazaridis, and Nayga (2009a) derive the demand function for nutrition information by maximizing (4) with respect to (5)–(9).

The theoretical models discussed above provide some guidance and can serve as a framework in the development of empirical models of nutritional information use.

5 LABEL USE, SELF-SELECTION, AND HEALTH OUTCOMES

In the relevant literature, label use has been employed either as a dependent or as an independent variable. This is common practice, especially in studies that aim to evaluate the effect of label use on nutrition/health knowledge and health outcomes. Self-selectivity, however, is a critical issue when the label use decision is represented as an independent variable. In what follows, we discuss three alternative methods from the extant literature that deal with self-selection, an important issue in the econometrics of nutritional labeling. In general, the literature that deals with self-selection in label use has utilized three approaches: (i) a Heckman-type approach (switching regression model), (ii) a Difference-In-Differences approach, or (iii) a propensity score matching approach.

The problem of self-selection can be illustrated as follows. Assume the following model:

$$y_i = \beta_0 + \sum_{j=1}^{k} \beta_j x_{ij} + \beta_{k+1} L + \varepsilon_i \qquad (10)$$

where y_i is the outcome variable of interest, $x_1, \ldots, x_k$ are a number of independent variables (e.g., sociodemographic and/or attitudinal variables), and L is a binary variable indicator of label use. The problem of self-selectivity arises when the label use decision is based on individual self-selection and the unobserved characteristics of label users differ systematically from those of non-label users. This subsample heterogeneity is econometrically problematic when unobserved characteristics are distributed differently across label users and non-label users. Ignoring this possibility in the estimation of equation (10) could lead to inconsistent estimates.

This issue has in general been ignored in the relevant literature. There are, however, a few studies that are notable exceptions, which took different approaches in tackling this problem.

Kim, Nayga, and Capps (2000, 2001) examined the effect of label use on the consumption of a range of nutrients and the healthy eating index (HEI). They employed a Heckman-type solution (switching regression approach) using the following three-equation system:

$$P(L=1) = \Phi\left(\gamma_0 + \sum_{j=1}^{n} \gamma_j w_{ij} + u_i\right) \tag{11}$$

$$y_{iL} = \beta_{0L} + \sum_{j=1}^{k} \beta_{jL} x_{ij} + \varepsilon_{1i} \tag{12}$$

$$y_{iN} = \beta_{0N} + \sum_{j=1}^{k} \beta_{jN} x_{ij} + \varepsilon_{2i}. \tag{13}$$

Equation (11) represents the decision whether or not to use labels (modeled as the probability of observing one of these states) given the level of characteristics w_i (γ_0 and γ_j are the associated coefficients to be estimated). Equations (12) and (13) assume that the way y_i (the health outcome variable, e.g., the HEI) is affected by the characteristics x_i is different between label users (L) and non-label users (N). Given that the error terms are correlated in the three equations and they have non-zero expected values in the last two equations, a Full Information Maximum Likelihood method was employed.

Variyam (2008) also examined the same effect but employed a different method known as Difference-in-Differences (Ashenfelter and Card 1985). In his study, Variyam exploits the quasi-experimental setup arising from the fact that nutritional labels are mandatory for most foods sold in stores but not for restaurant foods and other foods consumed away from home. The paper compared the observed outcome of a label user with the outcome that would have resulted had that person not used labels. Usually these two outcomes are not available for each observation. However, in the case examined by Variyam, there are data available for nutrient intake from food at home, where labeling is mandatory, and nutrient intake from food away from home, where consumers are not exposed to labels. This allows for the estimation of the following two-equations system:

$$y_{iH} = \beta_{0H} + \sum_{j=1}^{k} \beta_{jH} x_{ij} + \beta_{k+1H} L_i + \gamma_i + \varepsilon_{i1} \tag{14}$$

$$y_{iA} = \beta_{0A} + \sum_{j=1}^{k} \beta_{jA} x_{ij} + \beta_{k+1A} L_i + \gamma_i + \varepsilon_{i2} \tag{15}$$

Equation (14) represents nutrient intake from all types of food at home with mandatory labeling (H), and equation (15) represents nutrient intake from food away from home where labeling is not mandatory. The coefficient γ_i represents individual-level unobserved fixed effects.

Given the set of observable characteristics x_j, the coefficient β_{k+1H} is the effect of label use on nutrient intake in the presence of label use and β_{k+1A} is the effect in the absence of label use. Consequently, their difference is the net effect of label use.

A third method known as Propensity Score Matching (PSM) was used in Drichoutis, Nayga, and Lazaridis (2009a). PSM can be used with cross-sectional data when each individual is observed in one of the two situations, either as a label user or as a non-label user. In this case, the outcome that would have resulted had a label user not used labels is inferred by matching every individual in the treatment group (label users) with an individual in the non-treatment group (non-label users).[7] In essence, PSM mimics a randomized experiment. The choice of match is dictated by observable characteristics, and the mean effect of treatment can be calculated as the average difference in outcomes between the treated and the non-treated. Propensity score solves a practical problem in matching estimators that arises when the number of characteristics increases, by matching cases based on a single index that reflects the probability of participation. Rosenbaum and Rubin (1983) showed that matching on the propensity score could achieve consistent estimates of the treatment effect in the same way as matching on all characteristics. The propensity score is defined as the conditional probability of receiving a treatment (using nutritional labels) given pre-treatment (not using nutritional labels) characteristics w_i. This stage is estimated using a probability model of the form

$$P(L=1) = \Phi \left(\gamma_0 + \sum_{j=1}^{k} \gamma_j w_{ij} + u_i \right).$$

The parameter that receives most attention in the literature is the average treatment effect on the treated:

---

[7] There are, of course, several matching algorithms besides one-to-one matching.

$$t_{ATT} = E(t \mid T=1) = E[H_1 \mid T=1] - E[H_0 \mid T=1] \tag{16}$$

where H_0 and H_1 are the health outcomes of interest in the associated states $T=0$ and 1. Drichoutis, Nayga, and Lazaridis (2009a) extended the PSM to the case of multiple levels of treatment (i.e., levels of label use) by estimating several binary probability models as in Lechner (2002).

In summarizing the research findings of the above-cited studies, Kim, Nayga, and Capps (2000) found that nutritional label use decreases individuals' average daily intakes of calories from total fats and saturated fats, cholesterol, and sodium by 6.9 percent, 2.1 percent, 67.60 milligrams, and 29.58 milligrams, respectively, and increases average daily fiber intake by 7.51 grams. In another study Kim, Nayga, and Capps (2001) found that label use improves diet quality as measured by HEI, ranging from 3.5 points to 6.1 points. Variyam (2008) found that label use increases fiber and iron intakes of label users compared with non-label users. He also showed that a model that does not account for self-selection implies significant label effects for all but two of the thirteen nutrients (energy and sodium) that are listed on the label. In contrast to the previous articles that studied the effect of label use on diet quality, Drichoutis, Nayga, and Lazaridis (2009a) studied the effect of label use on body mass index (BMI). They do not find a consistent statistically significant effect of label use on BMI, and conclude that in most cases, label use does not reduce BMI.

The studies discussed above assessed the effect of label use on nutrition/health outcomes. Based on their findings, we can conclude that label use could improve dietary quality but the magnitude of these improvements is relatively small. There are a number of areas that researchers can focus on in the future related to evaluation of the impact of label use on health outcomes, and these will be discussed later in this chapter.

6   Nutritional Labeling and Food Away From Home Consumption

Even though mandatory nutritional labeling rules are in effect in the United States, Australia and New Zealand, and elsewhere, obesity rates are still rising in these countries and are a significant health concern for policymakers and health authorities. Food away from home (FAFH) (e.g., fast food), which is not included in most nutritional labeling regulations, has taken much of the blame owing partly to its increasing share of the food budget. Currently, the federal government in the United States does not require restaurants to provide nutrition information unless the restaurant makes a nutritional claim about its food. Therefore, approximately half of the country's largest chain restaurants provide no nutritional information (Wootan and Osborn 2006). However, a number of states and cities have taken some action. For example, the New York City Board of Health now requires the city's restaurant chains to show calorie information on their menus and menu board. The new regulation came into effect on March 31, 2008, and applies to any chain restaurant in New York City that has fifteen or more outlets anywhere in the United States. The city's health department has estimated that this law will reduce the number of obese individuals in New York by 150,000 over the next five years (New York City Department of Health and Mental Hygiene 2008). Other places with similar laws now include San Francisco and King County, Washington (Rutkow et al. 2008). There is also now pending legislation in the US Congress for a national mandatory nutritional labeling regulation in the FAFH sector.

The proportion of FAFH on total food expenditures is increasing globally. For example, in 2005 consumers in the United States spent close to half (49 percent) of their total food budget on FAFH compared to 26.3 percent in 1960 (Economic Research Service, USDA 2007, table 10). Similar trends are also apparent in Europe. In Spain FAFH expenditure accounts for almost one-third of total food expenditure (Mutlua and Gracia 2006). In Ireland, between 1987 and 1999/2000, food expenditure allocated to FAFH increased from 14 to 23 percent (Keelan, Newman, and Henchion 2008), while in Greece FAFH expenditure almost doubled between 1981/2 and 2004/5 from 17.4 to 33.4 percent (Lazaridis and Drichoutis 2005; Greek Household Budget Survey 2004/5). Consequently, the FAFH market has received increasing scrutiny from consumer groups and government agencies regarding the nutritional quality of the food offered in this market. Hence, this is a new area that is stimulating much research on nutrition information/labeling.

While the issue is still in its infancy in Europe, food companies in the United States and Australia are refurbishing their image by making nutrition information available in their stores, websites, and brochures. For example, McDonald's was one of the first restaurant chains in Australia that offered nutrition information on food packages (*Scientific American* 2007). In 2007 they also introduced Percent Daily Intake on food packages.

Other restaurant chains like Subway, the third-largest global operator after Yum! Brands (Taco Bell, KFC, Pizza Hut, etc.) and McDonald's, are positioning themselves as health-conscious restaurants to take advantage of the fast-growing concern on health.

Owing to increasing attention given to nutritional labeling in the FAFH sector, there is now an abundance of studies dealing with nutrition information on restaurant and away-from-home settings. The results are often contradictory. We attempt to synthesize the published research that appeared in scientific outlets after 2005 in the following paragraphs.

Bassett et al. (2008) conducted a study of 275 restaurants in New York City and randomly selected 7,318 customers of eleven fast-food chains for the survey. Their results indicate that respondents purchased an average of 827 calories, with 34 percent purchasing 1,000 calories or more. Subway was the only chain that posted calorie information at point of purchase, and the interviewees more often reported seeing caloric information than customers of other chains. Subway customers who reported seeing caloric information purchased fifty-two fewer calories than did other Subway customers. However, some consumers are still more likely to underestimate the caloric content of main dishes and choose higher-calorie side dishes, drinks, and desserts in "healthy" restaurants (e.g., Subway) than restaurants that do not make this claim (e.g., McDonald's) (Chandon and Wansink 2007).

Burton et al. (2006) report that availability of nutrition information at point of purchase in restaurants can be useful since consumers usually underestimate the levels of fats, saturated fats, and calories of restaurant items by a factor of two. In their subsequent experiments, provision of nutrition information influenced product attitudes, purchase intentions, and choice. In another study, the majority of respondents (92 percent) who reported reading nutrition information in dining halls at the University of Nebraska indicated changing their food choices after reading nutrition information (Driskell, Schake, and Detter 2008).

Howlett et al. (2009) conclude that if nutrition information was available at the point of sale, some segments of consumers, such as those highly motivated to process nutrition information, would often attempt to balance their consumption during subsequent eating occasions, especially after consuming a food item (sandwich in their experiment) unexpectedly high in calories.

In a more recent study, Bollinger, Leslie, and Sorensen (2011) examine the impact of mandatory calorie posting on consumers' purchase decisions in New York City, using detailed data from Starbucks. Starbucks stores in Boston and Philadelphia, where no mandatory calorie posting was commenced, served as the controls. The authors find that mandatory calorie posting does influence consumer behavior at Starbucks, causing average calories per transaction to decrease by 6 percent and that this effect persists even ten months after the date posting started. However, almost all of the effect was attributed to food purchases and not to changes in beverage purchases. From the industry's point of view, what is interesting is that Starbucks' revenue actually increased by 3 percent at stores located within 100 meters of an important competitor, namely Dunkin Donuts.

Generally, however, not many restaurants currently provide extensive nutrition information on food items being sold. In a study of table service restaurants in Minneapolis, only about one-third of the surveyed restaurants provided nutritional information of their standard menu, and this was only for menu items with specific health claims (Harnack 2006). Information was generally absent from children's menu.

So will consumers use nutritional information in the FAFH market if they become mandatory? Although US consumers tend to indicate an interest in having nutrition information available (Lando and Labiner-Wolfe 2007) and the vast majority of them support a law requiring nutritional labeling on restaurant menus (O'Dougherty et al. 2006), almost half of a Canadian sample of consumers indicate that they are not likely to use nutritional labels in restaurants if they become available (Krukowski et al. 2006). Consumers do indicate, however, a preference for graphical and simplistic icons on labels that will signal more healthful options in restaurant settings (Lando and

Labiner-Wolfe 2007). Perhaps this is the reason why a willingness-to-pay study for food-away-from-home products by Drichoutis, Lazaridis, and Nayga (2009c) shows higher valuation for a TL versus a US-type nutrition facts panel. Similarly, consumers in a Spanish sample valued nutritional information provided in a fact panel format (detailed format) higher than condensed information in the form of a nutrition claim (Gracia, Loureiro, and Nayga 2009).

In a review of studies that examined the effect of calorie information at restaurants and cafeterias on food choices (Harnack and French 2008), the authors found only weak and inconsistent effects (coupled with some methodological shortcomings). In another study, food choices from fast-food meals were studied across several experimental conditions where calorie information and value size pricing was varied (Harnack et al. 2008). Subjects in this study selected and consumed similar meals in terms of calorie content across experimental conditions although more than half in the calorie provision treatments stated afterwards that they noticed the listed information. Similarly, the provision of calorie and fat content information on the menus of three popular restaurants (McDonald's, Panda Express, and Denny's) did not modify food choice behavior of a US adolescent sample (Yamamoto et al. 2005).

In summary, the studies that have been conducted so far provide inconclusive and incomplete evidence about whether nutritional information will be used in restaurant settings and/or whether it will be effective in improving health outcomes.

7   AN UPDATE OF THE RELATED LITERATURE

Those working on nutrition information research would like to think that information is the ultimate tool that could change consumer behavior. However, food consumption behavior is complex and can be affected by several other factors like package size, plate shape, lighting, socializing, and variety (Wansink 2004). For example, Wansink and Cheney (2005) asked participants in an experiment to choose snacks from one of two alternative buffet tables with large and medium sizes of serving bowls, respectively. Participants served with large bowls consumed on average 56 percent (142 calories) more than those served with small bowls, and consumption was not influenced by body weight, hours since prior meal, age, or education. In another experiment, Wilcox et al. (2009) found that when a healthy food item was available in a choice set, individuals were more likely to make indulgent food choices probably because the mere presence of the healthy food option vicariously fulfilled nutrition-related goals and provided consumers with a license to indulge.

Other lab studies have shown that mood can affect consumption of hedonic foods (e.g., buttered popcorn and M&M's) with those exposed to a sad movie eating larger amounts than those exposed to a happy movie (Garg, Wansink, and Inman 2007). This effect is, however, attenuated when nutrition information is present. Even the structure of an assortment can moderate the effect of actual variety on perceived variety and in turn consumption quantities (Kahn and Wansink 2004).

Provision of health information affects product choice but not hedonic rating (Roosen et al. 2007). It has been found that taste significantly predicts both attitude toward and selection of most foods, while people seem not to use nutritional information when deciding how healthy foods are (Aikman, Min, and Graham 2006). For example, although nutritional information positively influences expectations about the product, this influence is limited by the subject's sensory experience (Behrens, Villanueva, and da Silva 2007). In another study, subjects rated wholemeal muffins more highly when information about the dietary fiber content of the product was present (Baixauli et al. 2008). Bui et al. (2008) found that among other nutrients, consumers significantly overestimated fat levels of alcoholic beverages when a fact panel was not present, and that when nutrient information was provided, future consumption intentions increased. This could suggest that a "fat-free" campaign by alcoholic beverage manufacturers could be exploited to increase consumption of certain consumer segments. There is evidence, however, that certain population groups want to see both ingredients and nutritional information displayed on alcoholic beverage packaging (Kypri et al. 2007).

Paternalistic actions (e.g., mandatory rules of nutrition information) by local and national governments, however, are not guaranteed to improve health outcomes. For example, taxing snack foods has been shown to be insufficient to induce major changes in consumers' salty snack choices (Kuchler, Tegene, and Harris 2005). However, taxes of this form could be used to generate a revenue stream that could finance nutrition education campaigns. Perhaps this is more than necessary since studies have shown that such education campaigns (e.g., consumer workshops) have a positive impact on attitude and behaviors related to nutritional label use (Lindhorst et al. 2007). In a home–school intervention (Blom-Hoffman et al. 2008), parents who received an interactive children's book with consistent messages about nutrition information demonstrated increased knowledge of the "Five a Day," and after the first and second year of the intervention their children were consuming 0.54 and 0.36 additional servings of fruit and vegetables per day compared to children of the control group (although the figures were not statistically significant). In a similar note, Todd and Variyam (2008) studied the changing pattern of nutritional label use in the United States ten years after the NLEA. They found a decrease in the use of labels, with the decrease in label use higher for individuals 20–9 years old and/or individuals with education up to high school. They suggested that this might be due to the lack of education campaigns since younger adults and new residents in the country were least likely to have benefited from the public awareness campaigns conducted just after the new labels were introduced.

It is also important to consider ethnic diversity and cultural appropriateness when developing and applying health/nutrition information programs (Rich and Thomas 2008). It has been found, for example, that Spanish-language television in the United States significantly airs more food advertisements containing nutrition information and health claims than English-language television in the United States (Abbatangelo-Gray, Byrd-Bredbenner, and Austin 2008). The results from other studies (Kozup, Burton, and Creyer 2006; Howlett, Burton, and Kozup 2008) indicate that without appropriate consumer education programs that enhance consumers' knowledge and understanding of information, it is likely that the nutrition facts panels will have limited and unintended consequences.

It is worth noting that the less-educated are more likely to rely on doctors, television, and neighbors as their source of nutrition information (McKay et al. 2006). In addition, in an era of high-speed Internet and fast information, it is not surprising that many people seek information through Internet sources. What requires policymakers' attention is the fact that as many as 80 percent of the visits and time spent on seeking health and nutrition information (at least for Canadians) on commercial websites are for information that is often inadequate and misleading (Ostry, Young, and Hughes 2008).

Compared with nutritional labels, nutrition and health claims purport to signal, in an easier (sometimes graphical) way, the nutrient content of a product and the effects of it on health. However, determining patterns of food consumption in relation to health is not an easy task. Determining the actual health value of any single foodstuff is complex and does not come cheap either (Scientific American 2007). Large-scale nutrition-related studies are necessary to establish proof of the effect of foodstuff on health. Since this is costly and the industry usually undertakes much of the associated costs (by financing research programs), it is not a surprise that nutrition studies are distorted (Lesser et al. 2007).

Before the passage of the NLEA in the United States in 1990, most health professionals and representatives of state governments supported a total ban on health claims with the argument that they blur the line between foods and drugs (Taylor and Wilkening 2008). Supporters of health claims won the battle and called for strict controls from the FDA. Today the FDA distinguishes between SSA and qualified health claims, and requires credible scientific evidence for the former and less than conclusive evidence for the latter. However, qualified health claims have to be accompanied by a disclaimer. Consumers, on the other hand, do not clearly distinguish between nutrient content claims, structure/function claims, and health claims (Williams 2005), and do not perceive significant differences between qualified and SSA health claims (Hooker and Teratanavat 2008). The same study has found that visual aids may be required to help consumers differentiate between health claims although consumers might use the visual aid to draw inferences about overall product quality rather than strength of the scientific evidence associated with the health claim. Similarly, in another study (Kapsak et al. 2008), consumers found it difficult to discriminate across health claim levels and projected the scientific validity grade of the health claims onto other product attributes.

Consumer perceptions can differ substantially between countries (Italy, Germany, the United Kingdom, and the United States for the specific study) and health benefit being claimed (e.g., cardiovascular disease, stress, infections, fatigue, overweight, and concentration) but much less by the claim type (e.g., content, structure/function, product, disease-risk reduction, or marketing claim) (van Trijp and van der Lans

2007). Many other factors can therefore influence consumers' purchase decisions with respect to health claims (Williams and Ghosh 2008). Even if the claims are accurate and truthful, a study has shown that low-fat nutrition claims can increase food intake, especially among overweight consumers, by increasing perceptions of the appropriate serving size and decreasing consumption guilt (Wansink and Chandon 2006). Another US study indicates that FDA health claims for soy-based foods influence frequency of consumption only for frequent consumers and not for infrequent or non-consumers (Rimal, Moon, and Balasubramanian 2008).

In the EU a regulation on nutrition and health claims went into effect on January 19, 2007. According to that regulation, a list of approved and rejected claims was to be established by 2010 (the target was subsequently pushed back for 2011). Some authors are skeptical if this regulation will actually make things clearer for consumer. For example, Brennan et al. (2008) analyzed the nutrient and health claims that appeared on TV advertisements in the United Kingdom for a week in March 2006 and indicated that they are not very optimistic that health-related claims in food advertising will become clearer as a result of the regulations. This is because most health claims, even though confusing, would still be permissible under the new regulation. The US health claims, on a similar note, have been seen as having limited success as a communication tool for health information and have been deemed misleading for consumers (Hasler 2008). A study that examined health claims in magazine advertisements in Australia (Jones et al. 2008) found that most of them were less than accurate, leaving considerable potential for the existence of misleading claims in food advertising. Indeed, a recent study that reviewed published papers in New Zealand and Australia concluded that there is apparent lack of consumer understanding about nutritional claims (Mhurchu and Gorton 2007). In addition, more than 5 percent of claims in New South Wales in 2003 did not comply with regulations (Williams et al. 2006).

8   CONCLUDING REMARKS AND FUTURE RESEARCH

Nutrition and health issues are undoubtedly at the forefront of many individual, government, and societal concerns. Globally, increasing obesity rates are becoming a major issue and challenge not only for individual choices but also for public policies and programs (Nayga 2008). Nutritional labeling is only one of the many possible instruments that policymakers and health authorities can use to improve dietary behavior and health outcomes. But it has become one of the most important instruments being used based on past and recent regulations as well as related legislation currently being considered in many countries; hence the need to continue research in the area of nutritional information/label use.

While the marketing and economics literature on nutritional information/label use is growing relatively fast, there are many more areas that need attention from researchers to answer definitively some of the very important questions that policymakers and health authorities need to make informed decisions. For example, we really do not definitively know yet if, indeed, reading nutritional labels can significantly change behavior, improve diets, and/or reduce obesity. Findings from some of the studies discussed above are quite inconsistent in this regard, which is not surprising considering the use of different data sets, methodologies, analyses, models, countries, etc. We also do not know what types of nutritional information and in what form or formats would provide the greatest impact on consumer behavior, dietary intake, and BMI.

Then there is the area of labeling in the FAFH market that we discussed above. This topic has attracted much scrutiny in recent years owing to the increasing share of FAFH in total food expenditures in the United States and elsewhere. Current regulations related to nutritional labeling are also focused only in the food at home market and not in the FAFH market. More research is then needed in this area that can provide information about consumers' perceptions, attitudes, and use of nutritional information in the FAFH market, not to mention the need to evaluate the effect of label use in the FAFH market on health-related outcomes.

Researchers will need more and better data to answer some of the issues raised above and throughout this chapter. Nayga (2008) discussed in detail some of these data issues that will need to be considered, including the need for more accurate dietary intake measurements, time use data, and panel/longitudinal data. He also discussed some of the important methodological and modeling issues that would also be relevant in nutritional label use research. This could include incorporating innovative methods from behavioral, experimental, and neuroeconomics among others as well as the need for multidisciplinary teams and interdisciplinary models to tackle the complex issues that have been discussed in this chapter.

Many countries spend considerable amounts of money on programs and policies related to nutrition information/labeling. Economists need to be more involved in the evaluation of these programs and policies, and in the development of robust econometric and statistical methods that can accurately measure their effectiveness in improving dietary and health behavior as well as quality of life.

References

Abbatangelo-Gray, J., C. Byrd-Bredbenner, and S. B. Austin. 2008. "Health and Nutrient Content Claims in Food Advertisements on Hispanic and Mainstream Prime-Time Television." *Journal of Nutrition Education and Behavior* 40/6: 348–54.

Aikman, S. N., K. E. Min, and D. Graham. 2006. "Food Attitudes, Eating Behavior, and the Information Underlying Food Attitudes." *Appetite* 47/1: 111–14.

Antonuk, B., and L. G. Block. 2006. "The Effect of Single Serving versus Entire Package Nutritional Information on Consumption Norms and Actual Consumption of a Snack Food." *Journal of Nutrition Education and Behavior* 38/6: 365–70.

Ashenfelter, O., and D. Card. 1985. "Using the Longitudinal Structure of Earnings to Estimate the Effect of Training Programs." *Review of Economics and Statistics* 67/4: 648–60.

Baixauli, R., A. Salvador, G. Hough, and S. M. Fiszman. 2008. "How Information about Fibre (Traditional and Resistant Starch) Influences Consumer Acceptance of Muffins." *Food Quality and Preference* 19/7: 628–35.

Balcombe, K., I. Fraser, and S. di Falco. 2009. *Traffic Lights and Food Choice: A Choice Experiment Examining the Relationship between Nutritional Food Labels and Price.* Discussion Papers No. 09/15. Canterbury: School of Economics, University of Kent.

Baltas, G. 2001. "Nutrition Labelling: Issues and Policies." *European Journal of Marketing* 35/5–6: 708–21.

Bassett, M. T., T. Dumanovsky, C. Huang, L. D. Silver, C. Young, C. Nonas, T. D. Matte, S. Chideya, and T. R. Frieden. 2008. "Purchasing Behavior and Calorie Information at Fast-Food Chains in New York City, 2007." *American Journal of Public Health* 98/8: 1457–9.

Behrens, J. H., N. D. M. Villanueva, and M. da Silva. 2007. "Effect of Nutrition and Health Claims on the Acceptability of Soyamilk Beverages." *International Journal of Food Science and Technology* 42/1: 50–6.

Berning, J. P., H. Chouinard, and J. J. McCluskey. 2008. "Consumer Preferences for Detailed versus Summary Formats of Nutrition Information on Grocery Store Shelf Labels." *Journal of Agricultural and Food Industrial Organization* 6/1, art. 6. <http://www.bepress.com/jafio/vol6/iss1/art6>.

Blom-Hoffman, J., K. R. Wilcox, L. Dunn, S. S. Leff, and T. J. Power. 2008. "Family Involvement in School-Based Health Promotion: Bringing Nutrition Information Home." *School Psychology Review* 37/4: 567–77.

Bollinger, B., P. Leslie, and A. Sorensen. 2011. "Calorie Posting in Chain Restaurants." *American Economic Journal: Economic Policy* 3/1: 91–128.

Booth, M. L. 2006. "Behavioural Food Labelling." *International Journal of Obesity* 30/12: 1800.

Brennan, R., B. Czarnecka, S. Dahl, L. Eagle, and O. Mourouti. 2008. "Regulation of Nutrition and Health Claims in Advertising." *Journal of Advertising Research* 48/1: 57–70.

Bui, M., S. Burton, E. Howlett, and J. Kozup. 2008. "What Am I Drinking? The Effects of Serving Facts Information on Alcohol Beverage Containers." *Journal of Consumer Affairs* 42/1: 81–99.

Burton, S., E. H. Creyer, J. Kees, and K. Huggins. 2006. "Attacking the Obesity Epidemic: The Potential Health Benefits of Providing Nutrition Information in Restaurants." *American Journal of Public Health* 96/9: 1669–75.

Caswell, J. A., and E. M. Mojduszka. 1996. "Using Informational Labeling to Influence the Market for Quality in Food Products." *American Journal of Agricultural Economics* 78/5: 1248–53.

Chandon, P., and B. Wansink. 2007. "The Biasing Health Halos of Fast-Food Restaurant Health Claims: Lower Calorie Estimates and Higher Side-Dish Consumption Intentions." *Journal of Consumer Research* 34/3: 301–14.

Cinar, A. B., and H. Murtomaa. 2009. "A Holistic Food Labelling Strategy for Preventing Obesity and Dental Caries." *Obesity Reviews* 10/3: 357–61.

Cowburn, G., and L. Stockley. 2005. "Consumer Understanding and Use of Nutrition Labelling: A Systematic Review." *Public Health Nutrition* 8/1: 21–8.

Darby, M. R., and E. Karni. 1973. "Free Competition and the Optimal Amount of Fraud." *Journal of Law and Economics* 16/1: 67–88.

Drichoutis, A. C. 2008. "Consumer Behaviour and Nutrition Information: Theoretical Model and Empirical Application on Food Labels." Ph.D. thesis (in Greek). Agricultural University of Athens. <http://works.bepress.com/andreas_drichoutis/36>.

———, P. Lazaridis, and R. M. Nayga, Jr. 2006. "Consumers' Use of Nutritional Labels: A Review of Research Studies and Issues." *Academy of Marketing Science Review* 9: 1–22.

——————. 2009a. "A Model of Nutrition Information Search with an Application to Food Labels." *Food Economics* 5/3: 138–51.

——————. 2009b. "On Consumers' Valuation of Nutrition Information." *Bulletin of Economic Research* 61/3: 223–47.

——————. 2009c. "Would Consumers Value Food Away From Home Products with Nutritional Labels?" *Agribusiness* 25/4: 550–75.

——————, M. Kapsokefalou, and G. M. Chryssohoidis. 2008. "A Theoretical and Empirical Investigation of Nutritional Label Use." *European Journal of Health Economics* 9/3: 293–304.

Drichoutis, A. C., R. M. Nayga, Jr., and P.Lazaridis. 2009a. "Can Nutritional Label Use Influence Body Weight Outcomes?" *Kyklos* 62/4: 500–25.

——————. 2009b. "Nutritional Label Users' Ability to Perform Nutrition Tasks as a Dietary Consumption Constraint." In A. N. Rezitis, ed., *Research Topics in Agricultural and Applied Economics*, 1. Bentham Science Publishers. <http://www.benthamscience.com/ebooks/9780199569441/index.htm>.

Driskell, J. A., M. C. Schake, and H. A. Detter. 2008. "Using Nutrition Labeling as a Potential Tool for Changing Eating Habits of University Dining Hall Patrons." *Journal of the American Dietetic Association* 108/12: 2071–6.

Economic Research Service, USDA (United States Department of Agriculture). 2007. *Food CPI and Expenditures: Food Expenditure Tables*. Washington, DC: Economic Research Service, United States Department of Agriculture.

European Advisory Services. 2004. *The Introduction of Mandatory Nutrition Labelling in the European Union*. Brussels: European Advisory Services.

Feunekes, G. I., I. A. Gortemaker, A. A. Willems, R. Lion, and M. van den Kommer. 2008. "Front-of-Pack Nutrition Labelling: Testing Effectiveness of Different Nutrition Labelling Formats Front-of-Pack in Four European Countries." *Appetite* 50/1: 57–70.

Foster, W., and R. E. Just. 1989. "Measuring Welfare Effects of Product Contamination with Consumer Uncertainty." *Journal of Environmental Economics and Management* 17 (Nov.), 266–83.

Garg, N., B. Wansink, and J. J. Inman. 2007. "The Influence of Incidental Affect on Consumers' Food Intake." *Journal of Marketing* 71/1: 194–206.

Gracia, A., M. Loureiro, and R. M. Nayga, Jr. 2007. "Do Consumers Perceive Benefits from the Implementation of a EU Mandatory Nutritional Labelling Program?" *Food Policy* 32/2: 160–74.

——————. 2009. "Consumers' Valuation of Nutritional Information: A Choice Experiment Study." *Food Quality and Preference* 20/7: 463–71.

Greek Household Budget Survey 2004/2005. Athens: National Statistical Service of Greece.

Grossman, M. 1972. "On the Concept of Health Capital and the Demand for Health." *Journal of Political Economy* 80/2: 223–55.

Grunert, K. G., and J. M. Wills. 2007. "A Review of European Research on Consumer Response to Nutrition Information on Food Labels." *Journal of Public Health* 15/5: 385–99.

Harnack, L. J. 2006. "Availability of Nutrition Information on Menus at Major Chain Table-Service Restaurants." *Journal of the American Dietetic Association* 106/7: 1012–15.

—— and S. A. French. 2008. "Effect of Point-of-Purchase Calorie Labeling on Restaurant and Cafeteria Food Choices: A Review of the Literature." *International Journal of Behavioral Nutrition and Physical Activity* 5/51 (Oct.). <http://www.ijbnpa.org/content/5/1/51>.

——————, J. M. Oakes, M. T. Story, R. W. Jeffery, and S. A. Rydell. 2008. "Effects of Calorie Labeling and Value Size Pricing on Fast Food Meal Choices: Results from an Experimental Trial." *International Journal of Behavioral Nutrition and Physical Activity* 5/63 (Dec.). <http://www.ijbnpa.org/content/5/1/63>.

Hasler, C. M. 2008. "Health Claims in the United States: An Aid to the Public or a Source of Confusion?" *Journal of Nutrition* 138: 1216S–1220S.

Hawkes, C. 2004. *Nutrition Labels and Health Claims: The Global Regulatory Environment.* Geneva: World Health Organization.

Hooker, N. H., and R. Teratanavat. 2008. "Dissecting Qualified Health Claims: Evidence from Experimental Studies." *Critical Reviews in Food Science and Nutrition* 48/2: 160–76.

Howlett, E. A., S. Burton, and J. Kozup. 2008. "How Modification of the Nutrition Facts Panel Influences Consumers at Risk for Heart Disease: The Case of Trans Fat." *Journal of Public Policy and Marketing* 27/1: 83–97.

——————, K. Bates, and K. Huggins. 2009. "Coming to a Restaurant Near You? Potential Consumer Responses to Nutrition Information Disclosure on Menus." *Journal of Consumer Research* 36/3: 494–503.

Jae, H., and D. Delvecchio. 2004. "Decision Making by Low-Literacy Consumers in the Presence of Point-of-Purchase Information." *Journal of Consumer Affairs* 38/2: 342–54.

Jones, G., and M. Richardson. 2007. "An Objective Examination of Consumer Perception of Nutrition Information Based on Healthiness Ratings and Eye Movements." *Public Health Nutrition* 10/3: 238–44.

Jones, S. C., P. Williams, L. Tapsell, and K. Andrews. 2008. "Health Claims and Food Advertising: Comparison of Marketing and Nutrition Experts' Ratings of Magazine Advertisements." *Food Australia* 60/11: 526–33.

Kahn, B. E., and B. Wansink. 2004. "The Influence of Assortment Structure on Perceived Variety and Consumption Quantities." *Journal of Consumer Research* 30/4: 519–33.

Kapsak, W. R., D. Schmidt, N. M. Childs, J. Meunier, and C. White. 2008. "Consumer Perceptions of Graded, Graphic and Text Label Presentations for Qualified Health Claims." *Critical Reviews in Food Science and Nutrition* 48/3: 248–56.

Keelan, C., C. Newman, and M. Henchion. 2008. "Quick-Service Expenditure in Ireland: Parametric vs. Semiparametric Analysis." *Applied Economics* 40/20: 2659–69.

Kim, S.-Y., R. M. Nayga, Jr., and O. Capps, Jr. 2000. "The Effect of Food Label Use on Nutrient Intakes: An Endogenous Switching Regression Analysis." *Journal of Agricultural and Resource Economics* 25/1: 215–31.

——————————. 2001. "Food Label Use, Self-Selectivity, and Diet Quality." *Journal of Consumer Affairs* 35/2: 346–63.

Kimura, A., Y. Wada, D. Tsuzuki, S. Goto, D. S. Cai, and I. Dan. 2008. "Consumer Valuation of Packaged Foods: Interactive Effects of Amount and Accessibility of Information." *Appetite* 51/3: 628–34.

Kozup, J., S. Burton, and E. H. Creyer. 2006. "The Provision of Trans Fat Information and its Interaction with Consumer Knowledge." *Journal of Consumer Affairs* 40/1: 163–76.

Krukowski, R. A., J. Harvey-Berino, J. Kolodinsky, R. T. Narsana, and T. P. DeSisto. 2006. "Consumers May Not Use or Understand Calorie Labeling in Restaurants." *Journal of the American Dietetic Association* 106/6: 917–20.

Kuchler, F., A. Tegene, and J. M. Harris. 2005. "Taxing Snack Foods: Manipulating Diet Quality or Financing Information Programs?" *Review of Agricultural Economics* 27/1: 4–20.

Kypri, K., A. McManus, P. M. Howat, B. R. Maycock, J. D. Hallett, and T. N. Chikritzhs. 2007. "Ingredient and Nutrition Information Labelling of Alcoholic Beverages: Do Consumers Want It?" *Medical Journal of Australia* 187/11–12: 669.

Lando, A. M., and J. Labiner-Wolfe. 2007. "Helping Consumers Make More Healthful Food Choices: Consumer Views on Modifying Food Labels and Providing Point-of-Purchase Nutrition Information at Quick-Service Restaurants." *Journal of Nutrition Education and Behavior* 39/3: 157–63.

Lazaridis, P., and A. C. Drichoutis. 2005. "Food Consumption Issues in the 21st Century." In P. Soldatos and S. Rozakis, eds, *The Food Industry in Europe*. Athens: Stamoulis.

Lechner, M. 2002. "Program Heterogeneity and Propensity Score Matching: An Application to the Evaluation of Active Labor Market Policies." *Review of Economics and Statistics* 84/2: 205–20.

Lesser, L. I., C. B. Ebbeling, M. Goozner, D. Wypij, and D. S. Ludwig. 2007. "Relationship between Funding Source and Conclusion among Nutrition-Related Scientific Articles." *Public Library of Science Medicine* 4/1: e5.

Lindhorst, K., L. Corby, S. Roberts, and S. Zeiler. 2007. "Rural Consumers' Attitudes towards Nutrition Labelling." *Canadian Journal of Dietetic Practice and Research* 68/3: 146–9.

Loureiro, M. L., and R. M. Nayga, Jr. 2005. "International Dimensions of Obesity and Overweight Related Problems: An Economics Perspective." *American Journal of Agricultural Economics* 87/5: 1147–53.

——, A. Gracia, and R. M. Nayga, Jr. 2006. "Do Consumers Value Nutritional Labels?" *European Review of Agricultural Economics* 33/2: 249–68.

McKay, D. L., R. F. Houser, J. B. Blumberg, and J. P. Goldberg. 2006. "Nutrition Information Sources Vary with Education Level in a Population of Older Adults." *Journal of the American Dietetic Association* 106/7: 1108–11.

Malam, S., S. Clegg, S. Kirwan, S. McGinigal, M. Raats, J. Barnett, V. Senior, C. Hodgkins, and M. Dean. 2009. *Comprehension and Use of UK Nutrition Signpost Labelling Schemes.* London: British Market Research Bureau.

Mhurchu, C. N., and D. Gorton. 2007. "Nutrition Labels and Claims in New Zealand and Australia: A Review of Use and Understanding." *Australian and New Zealand Journal of Public Health* 31/2: 105–12.

Moorman, C., R. Du, and C. F. Mela. 2005. "The Effect of Standardized Information on Firm Survival and Marketing Strategies." *Marketing Science* 24/2: 263–74.

Mutlua, S., and A. Gracia. 2006. "Spanish Food Expenditure Away From Home (FAFH): By Type of Meal." *Applied Economics* 38: 1037–47.

Nayga, R. M., Jr. 2008. "Nutrition, Obesity, and Health: Policies and Economic Research Challenges." *European Review of Agricultural Economics* 35/3: 281–302.

Nelson, P. 1970. "Information and Consumer Behavior." *Journal of Political Economy* 78/2: 311–29.

——1974. "Advertising as Information." *Journal of Political Economy* 82/4: 729–54.

New York City Department of Health and Mental Hygiene. 2008. "Board of Health Votes to Require Chain Restaurants to Display Calorie Information in New York City." Jan. 22. <http://www.nyc.gov/html/doh/html/pr2008/pr008-08.shtml>.

O'Dougherty, M., L. I. Harnack, S. A. French, M. Story, J. M. Oakes, and R. W. Jeffery. 2006. "Nutrition Labeling and Value Size Pricing at Fastfood Restaurants: A Consumer Perspective." *American Journal of Health Promotion* 20/4: 247–50.

Ostry, A., M. L. Young, and M. Hughes. 2008. "The Quality of Nutritional Information Available on Popular Websites: A Content Analysis." *Health Education Research* 23/4: 648–55.

Pothoulaki, M., and G. Chryssochoidis. 2009. "Health Claims: Consumers' Matters." *Journal of Functional Foods* 1/2: 222–8.

Rich, S. S., and C. R. Thomas. 2008. "Body Mass Index, Disordered Eating Behavior, and Acquisition of Health Information: Examining Ethnicity and Weight-Related Issues in a College Population." *Journal of American College Health* 56/6: 623–8.

Rimal, A., W. Moon, and S. K. Balasubramanian. 2008. "Soyfood Consumption: Effects of Perceived Product Attributes and the Food and Drug Administration Allowed Health Claims." *British Food Journal* 110/6–7: 607–21.

Roosen, J., S. Marette, S. Blanchemanche, and P. Verger. 2007. "The Effect of Product Health Information on Liking and Choice." *Food Quality and Preference* 18/5: 759–70.

Rosenbaum, P. R., and D. B. Rubin. 1983. "The Central Role of the Propensity Score in Observational Studies for Causal Effects." *Biometrika* 70/1: 41–56.

Rutkow, L., J. S. Vernick, J. G. Hodge, and S. P. Teret. 2008. "Preemption and the Obesity Epidemic: State and Local Menu Labeling Laws and the Nutrition Labeling and Education Act." *Journal of Law Medicine and Ethics* 36/4: 772–89.

Scientific American. 2007. "Take Nutrition Claims with a Grain of Salt." 297/3. <http://www.scientificamerican.com/article.cfm?id=take-nutrition-claims-with-grain-of-salt>.

Sexton, R. J. 1979. *A Theory on Information and its Application to the Effect of Labeling on Food Products.* Staff Paper No. P79-35. St Paul: Department of Agricultural and Applied Economics, University of Minnesota, Oct.

Stigler, G. J. 1961. "The Economics of Information." *Journal of Political Economy* 69/3: 213–25.

Stranieri, S., L. Baldi, and A. Banterle. 2009. "Do Nutrition Claims Matter to Consumers? An Empirical Analysis Considering European Requirements." *Journal of Agricultural Economics* 61/1: 15–33.

Taylor, C. L., and V. L. Wilkening. 2008. "How the Nutrition Food Label Was Developed, Part 2: The Purpose and Promise of Nutrition Claims." *Journal of the American Dietetic Association* 108/4: 618–23.

Teisl, M. F., N. E. Bockstael, and A. S. Levy. 2001. "Measuring the Welfare Effects of Nutrition Information." *American Journal of Agricultural Economics* 83/1: 133–49.

Todd, J. E., and J. N. Variyam. 2008. *The Decline in Consumer Use of Food Nutrition Labels, 1995–2006.* Economic Research Report No. 63. Washington, DC: Economic Research Service, US Department of Agriculture.

van Kleef, E., H. van Trijp, F. Paeps, and L. Fernández-Celemín. 2008. "Consumer Preferences for Front-of-Pack Calories Labelling." *Public Health Nutrition* 11/2: 203–13.

van Trijp, H. C. M., and I. A. van der Lans. 2007. "Consumer Perceptions of Nutrition and Health Claims." *Appetite* 48/3: 305–24.

Variyam, J. N. 2008. "Do Nutrition Labels Improve Dietary Outcomes?" *Health Economics* 17/6: 695–708.

Wansink, B. 2004. "Environmental Factors that Increase the Food Intake and Consumption Volume of Unknowing Consumers." *Annual Review of Nutrition* 24 (July), 455–79.

——and P. Chandon. 2006. "Can 'Low-Fat' Nutrition Labels Lead to Obesity?" *Journal of Marketing Research* 43/3: 605–17.

——and M. M. Cheney. 2005. "Super Bowls: Serving Bowl Size and Food Consumption." *Journal of the American Medical Association* 293/14: 1727–8.

Wilcox, K., B. Vallen, L. Block, and G. J. Fitzsimons. 2009. "Vicarious Goal Fulfillment: When the Mere Presence of a Healthy Option Leads to an Ironically Indulgent Decision." *Journal of Consumer Research* 36/3: 380–93.

Williams, P. 2005. "Consumer Understanding and Use of Health Claims for Foods." *Nutrition Reviews* 63/7: 256–64.

——and D. Ghosh. 2008. "Health Claims and Functional Foods." *Nutrition and Dietetics* 65: S89–S93.

——, H. Yeatman, L. Ridges, A. Houston, J. Rafferty, A. Roesler, M. Sobierajski, and B. Spratt. 2006. "Nutrition Function, Health and Related Claims on Packaged Australian Food Products: Prevalence and Compliance with Regulations." *Asia Pacific Journal of Clinical Nutrition* 15/1: 10–20.

Wootan, M. G., and M. Osborn. 2006. "Availability of Nutrition Information from Chain Restaurants in the United States." *American Journal of Preventive Medicine* 30/3: 266–8.

World Health Organization. 2006. *Obesity and Overweight*. Geneva: World Health Organization.

Yamamoto, J. A., J. B. Yamamoto, B. E. Yamamoto, and L. G. Yamamoto. 2005. "Adolescent Fast Food and Restaurant Ordering Behavior with and without Calorie and Fat Content Menu Information." *Journal of Adolescent Health* 37/5: 397–402.

CHAPTER 21

....

FOOD SAFETY POLICY

....

SANDRA A. HOFFMANN*

1 INTRODUCTION

....

Modern food safety policy came into being at the turn of the twentieth century in response to scandals in the meat packing and food processing industries (Sinclair 1906). A second generation of policy is emerging now, also driven by scandals and crises of trust, including the early 1990s' *E. coli* O157:H7 outbreak in the United States and the bovine spongiform encephalopathy (BSE) scandal of the late 1990s in the United Kingdom. Behind the current crises lie economic and technological transformations in both food and the food supply system. Institutions are rushing to catch up with the implications that these changes have for public health risks.

The first generation of food safety law was characterized by command and control forms of safety regulation. Policy was nationally focused and relied on early twentieth-century industrial management practices such as continuous line inspection, visual product inspection, and detailed specification of approved hygiene practices. At the heart of this second generation of food safety policy is an emerging global consensus on the need for a preventive, public-health-focused policy that fosters integrated management of foodborne hazards from farm to fork. This consensus calls for use of modern science-based risk management instruments that enhances efficiency by more accurately target-ing public actions and by allowing firms flexibility in how they achieve public health goals rather than relying on narrowly prescriptive command and control policies. While the broad vision for this second generation of policy is clear, much of the detail has yet to be worked out. Economists have a significant role to play in this process.

* Many thanks go to Bill Harder for his help on this chapter and to Resources for the Future (RFF) for funding his internship. I am a senior economist with the US Department of Agriculture (USDA) Economic Research Service. This work was conducted while I was a Fellow with RFF. The views expressed herein are mine and do not necessarily reflect the views of the Economic Research Service or USDA.

The aim of this chapter is to orient economists new to this issue. First, this chapter provides an overview of the scope of current food safety problems and the food safety policy reforms being adopted to address them around the world. Current efforts to modernize food safety policy are being shaped by several larger trends: globalization, use of risk analysis and cost–benefit analysis in public administration, and total quality management regimes in industry. Then, this chapter briefly examines two major roles that public economics can play in food safety policy: better informing policymakers about the social benefits and costs of their decisions and strengthening risk assessment.

2   TRENDS IN FOOD SAFETY CHALLENGES

Illness from foodborne pathogens is a significant global health concern (WHO 2002; Rocourt et al. 2003). Population-level incidence estimates, however, are uncertain due to underreporting and difficulty in attributing illness to food consumption. In the United States the Centers for Disease Control estimate that contaminated foodborne pathogens cause approximately 47.8 million illnesses, 128,000 hospitalizations, and 3,000 deaths among a population of 308.4 million each year (Scallan et al. 2011a, b). The World Health Organization believes incidence rates in Organization for Economic Cooperation and Development (OECD) countries are similar (Rocourt et al. 2003). In developing countries, where it is more difficult to separate water and foodborne illness, approximately 2.2 million people die from these causes annually (WHO 2002; Rocourt et al. 2003). Such a level of illness and mortality places a drain on productivity, effect imposing an in-kind of tax on human energy (FAO/WHO 1984).

Chemical hazards remain a concern. In 1996 the United States passed the first major pesticide legislation reform in thirty years, requiring evaluation of the cumulative impact of low-dose exposure to multiple chemicals on adult and child health and that standards be set to protect children (NRC 1993; Hamilton and Crossley 2004). The new European chemical regulatory law, REACH (Registration, Evaluation, Authorization, and Restriction of Chemical Substances), addresses similar concerns (European Council 2006).

The last three decades have also seen significant scientific transformation (Kinsey 2001). New technologies, such as genetically modified foods and, more recently, nanotechnology, often raise public concern and calls for new regulation. Consumer attitudes toward new technologies have differed considerably across countries, leading to differences in laws and the threat of trade disputes (Brom 2004).

Globalization has brought many benefits to consumers, including more varied and nutritious food supplies throughout the year, but it has also complicated management of both infectious and non-infectious foodborne hazards. In developing countries, globalization has fostered industrialization and urbanization, which has placed strains on capacity for adequate sanitation and safe food handling (Käferstein et al. 1997; WHO 2002). Higher volumes of trade in food can raise incomes in exporting countries and provide wider food choice and lower prices in importing countries. Poor sanitation in developing countries can result in contamination of food exports to developed countries, such as the 1996 *Cyclosporiasis* outbreak in the US linked to Guatemalan raspberries (Katz et al. 1999; Calvin, Flores, and Foster 2003). But trade may also spread foodborne pathogens between developed countries, as in the spread of BSE from Britain to Japan in 2001, or from developed to developing countries (McCluskey et al. 2005).

With globalized markets, weak institutional capacity in one country can influence health globally. Emerging economies, such as China, are experiencing a period of rapid industrialization and urbanization such as that of Europe and North America in the nineteenth century, and they are encountering the same kinds of problem documented by Upton Sinclair and other journalists at the turn of the last century. Recent experience with economic adulteration of pet food, milk, and toothpaste from China demonstrates the need for the institutional capacity of industry and governments in emerging economies to grow with their productive capacity (Roth et al. 2008; Gale and Hu 2009).

Current disease levels reflect past as well as current investments in controlling foodborne hazards. A failure to maintain these controls can lead to a re-emergence of problems thought to have been addressed. In 1999 Belgian animal feed was unintentionally contaminated with dioxin in polychlorinated biphenyls and distributed to approximately 2,500 farms. In the winter of 2008–9, neglect of a leaky roof led to more than 700 people being made ill by *Salmonella*-contaminated peanut products in the United States (US CDC 2009b). These incidents remind us that failure in private management and public enforcement are always possible (Covaci et al. 2008).They also remind us that without continued control, problems that are now largely contained, like *trichinae* in US pork, can re-emerge.

3   Public Sector Response

Over the past two decades, many countries and regions have taken significant steps to modernize their food safety law. These efforts have drawn on wider trends in public administration and industrial management and involve an increasing role for international institutions in global coordination.

3.1   Science-Based Public Decision Analysis

Food safety policy has a long history of using risk analysis to guide public decisions. In the United States, federal administrative agencies have been required to show a rational basis for their rule-making actions since passage of the Administrative Procedure Act in the 1940s. A study by US Food and Drug Administration (FDA) toxicologists in the mid-1950s introduced safety factors as a scientific means of establishing acceptable daily intake of food additives on the basis of acute toxicity, an approach still applied today (Lehman and Fitzhugh 1954). By the early 1980s, risk analysis in the United States was being relied on more widely to justify regulatory action, not only in food safety, but also in national environmental policy, consumer product safety, and occupational safety law. Federal agencies saw the 1980 US Supreme Court case *Industrial Union Department* v. *American Petroleum Institute*, 448 U.S. 607 (the Benzene case), as indicating that they needed to conduct scientific assessment of risk when developing health and environmental standards.

In 1981 Congress directed the FDA to contract a National Academies study on the merits of an independent institution to conduct risk assessments for all federal agencies as a means of protecting the scientific integrity of risk assessment (NRC 1983). The report characterized risk analysis as a three-part process involving risk assessment, management, and communication. Ultimately, the report did not recommend an independent risk assessment agency, but did argue that the scientific process of risk assessment needed to be protected from the more political process of risk management. The report did not break new ground. Instead, it consolidated and clarified the structure of existing risk governance practices in federal agencies. Yet its influence has extended far beyond the United States.

In the United States, the 1980s also saw the first formal requirement that cost–benefit analysis be conducted to evaluate major health and safety regulations (Smith 1984; US Office of the President 1993). This was viewed in part as a means for the Office of the President to gain greater control over the agendas of departments and agencies (Andrews 2006). In reaction, the US Environmental Protection Agency (EPA) administrator looked to risk analysis as a way to keep regulatory oversight focused on "science-based, outcome-focused analysis" (Andrews 2006). In particular, the EPA looked to comparative risk ranking to help set and justify the Agency's agenda (US EPA 1987). The rather qualitative approach to risk ranking relied on by the EPA did not live up to the hopes placed in it (Finkel and Golding 1994; Davies 1996).

Today food safety agencies in the United States and elsewhere are drawing on this experience in using much more quantitative risk ranking processes to prioritize inspection and to inform broader agency priority setting (US FDA Center for Food Safety and Nutrition 2006; FAO 2009; NRC 2009). Even more quantitative risk ranking has one critical limitation: it generally does not take into account the relative effectiveness, cost, or non-health benefits of reducing risk (Nelson and Krupnick 2005). These factors are critical to efficient use of public resources.

In the European Union (EU) and its member states, the precautionary principle has played a central role in debates over risk management policy. The precautionary principle provides norms for risk management in situations where decision makers have reasonable grounds for concern about risk to health or the environment, but there remains substantial scientific uncertainty. Under the precautionary principle, a decision maker has the option to act to protect health or the environment while seeking more complete scientific information. Article 7 of the EU's General Food Law gives risk managers the option of acting under the precautionary principle when confronted by conditions where they have reasonable concern about safety but significant scientific uncertainty. These actions must still conform to norms of non-discrimination and proportionality and are provisional until more adequate scientific information is available. The Sanitary and Phytosanitary (SPS) Agreement adopts a rather weak form of the precautionary principle by allowing nations to regulate on the basis of available scientific information when there is "insufficient" scientific information. The regulatory action must be provisional pending better information, applied in a way that is non-discriminatory and reviewed within a reasonable period of time. Substantial time has been spent in meetings of the Codex Alimentarius Commission (Codex) over the past few years debating the proposals containing precautionary principles (Neal Fortin, personal communication). The *Codex Working Principles for Risk Analysis* note that precaution is "an inherent element of risk analysis" and that risk assessment and risk management should reflect scientific uncertainty about the hazards of concern, but they do not directly invoke the precautionary principle (UN CAC 2003).

3.2   Risk-Based Process Management in Industry

In the late 1950s, NASA asked Pillsbury, a major US food processing firm, to adapt failure mode and effects analysis systems used in rocket development to the development of food products that could meet the reliability needs of manned space flight. The result was a process called hazard analysis and critical control point (HACCP) systems (Huelebak and Schlosser 2002).

HACCP provides a systematic way to identify, assess, and control points in a food production system where foodborne hazards are most likely to enter. Because firms are free to choose how best to control these critical points, HACCP is promoted as providing the flexibility to use more cost-effective technology and to adapt to changing conditions. HACCP found fairly quick acceptance among national governments and international institutions (Unnevehr and Jensen 1999). In 1993 Codex included HACCP guidelines in its *Recommended International Code of Practice*. Throughout the 1990s, US food safety agencies began shifting to HACCP as their basic regulatory approach to controlling microbial hazards (US FDA 1995, 2001; USDA FSIS 1996).

3.3   International Institutions and Food Safety: The WTO and the Sanitary and Phytosanitary Agreement

Government commitments to greater economic integration have had and will continue to have significant impact on food safety policy. The General Agreement on Trade and Tariffs (GATT), negotiated in the wake of the Second World War, has provided and continues to provide the central legal structure for international trade. Its goal is to liberalize trade through successive rounds of negotiation guided by the principles of equal treatment for trading partners, transformation of non-tariff barriers to tariffs, and negotiation to reduce tariffs over time (General Agreement on Tariffs and Trade (GATT) 1947, art. I). GATT recognizes limited exceptions to its general requirements. One of the most important is the exception for actions required to protect health (GATT 1947, art. XX).

The Uruguay Round of trade negotiations (1986–94) created a permanent institutional home for GATT within the World Trade Organization (WTO). It also resulted in adoption of the SPS Agreement (Alemanno 2007; Fortin 2009). This agreement provides a basis for distinguishing legitimate from protectionist use of safety and phytosanitary laws and encouraging their legitimate use (WHO 1997). The SPS Agreement seeks to provide greater certainty about when national sanitary and phytosanitary laws comply with GATT and to reduce their impact on trade by promoting harmonized laws (SPS Agreement, Art. 2(1)).

Like other GATT provisions, the SPS Agreement is enforced by international dispute resolution processes and, if necessary, trade sanctions levied by injured countries against offending ones. The agreement recognizes that compliance may make it more difficult for developing countries to be involved in international trade and encourages wealthier members to provide or fund technical assistance to help poorer countries develop food safety systems that comply with the SPS Agreement and to provide time extensions to poorer countries for compliance with SPS obligations (SPS Agreement, Arts 9 and 10(3)).

3.4 The Evolving Role of Codex Alimentarius

Under the SPS Agreement, standards consistent with those agreed to by Codex are presumed to be in compliance with GATT. Nations adopting other standards need to support their scientific legitimacy through risk analysis.

Codex was established in 1963 by the United Nations' Food and Agriculture Organization (FAO) and World Health Organization (WHO) to provide a forum for international technical collaboration on the development of food safety and quality standards (Josling, Roberts, and Orden 2004). Membership in Codex is open to nations that are members or associate members of the WHO and FAO, but other countries may participate as observers (UN CAC 2008). Some 175 countries, representing 98 percent of the world's population, currently participate (van der Meulen and van der Velde 2008). Post (2005) and Ansell and Vogel (2006) provide critical analyses of the influence of Codex on food safety governance worldwide.

Codex works through a system of technical subject matter and regional subcommittees. These committees work to prepare and revise draft standards through a formal procedure of iterative review by the Commission and member governments. Decisions on rules are reached by consensus as often as possible (UN CAC 2008).

Much of Codex's effort has gone into producing model standards. These include commodity standards aimed at preventing consumer fraud, quantitative standards for food additives, and quantitative tolerances for contaminants such as pesticides and veterinary drugs. The Commission has also developed a set of recommended practices referred to as codes of practice, or guidelines. These include guidelines for HACCP systems and an international food hygiene code (UN CAC 1997, 1999). Codex has adopted more than 200 standards, close to fifty hygiene and technological codes, some sixty guidelines, more than 1,000 food additives and contaminants evaluations, and more than 3,200 maximum residue limits for pesticides and veterinary drugs.

Since 1995 Codex has also developed guidelines for microbial risk assessment, biotechnology risk assessment, microbial risk management, and validation of safety control measures as well as principles for traceability and risk analysis. Borrowing from the 1983 US National Academies of Sciences' (NAS) Red Book, it outlines a four-step process for microbial risk assessment: hazard identification, exposure assessment, hazard characterization, and risk characterization (UN CAC 1999). Codex discussions have contributed significantly to the spread and development of the relatively new field of predictive microbiology. Codex principles on risk analysis also incorporate the 1983 NAS recommendation that risk assessment and risk management be separated to protect the scientific integrity of the risk assessment and avoid conflict of interest (UN CAC 2007).

3.5   European Union Reform

From 1958 to the mid-1990s, the focus of European food law was to reduce barriers to creating an integrated internal market for foods (van der Meulen and van der Velde 2008; Alemanno 2006). Uncertainty about product content, not food safety, was viewed as the major barrier to a single food market. The BSE crisis and other foodborne illness crises of the 1990s changed this perspective (van der Meulen and van der Velde 2008). The nature of BSE—a fatal neurodegenerative disease related to scrapie in sheep—and the way that crisis was handled had a significant impact on subsequent legislative reform.

At the time it was identified, the British government maintained that BSE, like scrapie, was not transmissible to other species (Prusiner 1991). By the late 1980s, transmission among cattle was traced to the presence of animal offal and bone meal in cattle feed. Britain banned this practice in 1988 and the EU banned importation of beef offal from Britain. Scientific evidence began to mount that BSE was being transmitted to humans (Krapohl 2008). Britain continued to maintain that this was not the case until March 21, 1996 (Darton 1996; van der Meulen and van der Velde 2008). The European Commission (EC) banned export of cattle and cattle products from the United Kingdom several days later.

A 1996 EU Committee of Inquiry found that the structure of EU food safety governance that allowed domination of decisions by a single member state, politicization of science, and lack of transparency contributed to the inability of the EU to respond to the crisis quickly (European Parliament 1997). Subsequent European food safety crises contributed to pressure for immediate action (van der Meulen and van der Velde 2008; Holland and Pope 2004). Recommendations for structural change followed quickly in the form of a Green Paper in April 1997 and a White Paper on food safety in January 2000 (EC 1997, 2000).

The White Paper laid out a road map for EU legislative reform guided by five central principles: clearly defined food safety responsibilities for all actors; traceability of food, feeds, and food ingredients to their sources; risk analysis as the framework for science-based policy; transparency and separation of scientific analysis from risk management; and use of the precautionary principle to guide risk management (Halkier and Holm 2006). To reduce the role of economic interests in food safety policy decisions, responsibility for risk assessment and scientific advice would lie with a new European Food (Safety) Authority and responsibility for risk management would lie with the EC. A set of eighty-four legislative and policy initiatives was outlined. The goal was to make European food law more coherent and comprehensive and to strengthen enforcement and make it more consistent across countries (van der Meulen and van der Velde 2008).

In the years that followed, most of the recommended legislation has been enacted. In January 2002 the EU General Food Law came into force. The General Food Law lays out basic principles intended to guide European food safety legislation (van der Meulen and van der Velde 2008). The system is a three-legged stool resting on an integrated farm-to-fork system of food safety responsibilities and enforcement, a modern system of monitoring and communication that allows rapid action in the case that problems arise, and protection of the integrity of scientific analysis on which policy decisions rely. The goal is to ensure "a high level of protection of human health and consumers' interest in relation to food" (EU General Food Law, Arts. 1, 5, and 9).

A core element of the new law is the ability to trace foods and share information. A centralized tracking system follows the movement of livestock from origin to slaughter (US GAO 2008). Another has been established to disseminate information about serious threats to health from food or feed to all EU member states and to notify all other European ports of entry of shipments of food refused entry at any EU port (US GAO 2008). Member states are responsible for disease surveillance and outbreak response within their country, for informing the European Centre for Disease Prevention and Control of outbreaks that may affect other member states, and for cooperating with other member states and EU-level offices in responding to multi-member country outbreaks. The public is to have access to information on the product, the nature of the risk, and the control measures taken (Holland and Pope 2004).

The final major component is a structure to ensure that scientific analysis of food safety policy is protected from political influence. Food law is to be based on risk analysis (EU General Food Law, Art. 6). The General Food Law creates the European Food Safety Agency (EFSA) as an independent entity responsible for providing scientific advice, risk assessment, and technical support for policy. It also requires member states to maintain a separation between risk assessment and management. The EC,

European Parliament, and European Council have responsibility for risk management decisions at the EU level.

Several studies have examined the European food safety policy reform movement of the 1990s from the perspectives of law, political science, public administration, and sociology, but few from an economic perspective (Alemanno 2006; Ansell and Vogel 2006; Halkier and Holm 2006; Vos and Wendler 2006). The most fundamental change in the EU system has been recognition of the central role that food safety and consumer protection play in integration of the European food market and with this adoption of risk analysis as a structure to shape and bring transparency to conflicts between the goals of integration and maintenance of diverse food cultures and other local and national values (Alemanno 2006). The EFSA has responsibility for conducting scientific assessment of new food safety policy, but national competent authorities do as well.

While both the EC and national authorities are required to take account of EFSA scientific assessment, they are not bound by it. Although many food safety issues are now covered by EU-wide regulation, not all are and, in its absence, food is deemed safe and marketable across the EU if it meets the national safety requirements. As Alemanno points out, "a claim by a domestic food authority that a certain good is safe or unsafe is likely to involve not only an assertion about science, but also about the willingness of this country to bear or not bear the level of risk considered acceptable in order to continue or reject a certain local tradition" (Alemanno 2006: 254). Of course, national decisions may also come from a desire to protect local economic interests. In the case of conflicting scientific opinion, it will be up to the European Court to determine the balance between local, national, and Europe-wide interests. It remains to be seen what balance is ultimately worked out between national and EU concerns.

4   NATIONAL RESPONSES

National governments of many OECD nations have undertaken major food safety legislative reform since the 1990s (Ansell and Vogel 2006; Halkier and Holm 2006). Within the EU, individual countries have passed laws to come into conformance with the General Food Law and to respond to the BSE crisis (Table 21.1) (Vos and Wendler 2006). Table 21.1 summarizes some of the national efforts to modernize food safety law by EU member states. Legislative and administrative reforms in Australia, Canada, and New Zealand (Table 21.2) have been driven largely by a desire to enhance the efficiency of public administration by eliminating overlapping authorities, focusing resources on high-risk areas, and reducing inconsistencies in enforcement (US GAO 2008). Although each country has its own motivation for modernization of food safety law, the presence of international forums and the driver of harmonization goals under GATT result in actions in one country influencing those in others.

Table 21.1 Elements of national food safety policy in Europe

Denmark	• Farm-to-fork risk management system • Risk classification of food establishments are the basis for inspections • Risk management conducted by Ministry of Food, Agriculture, and Fisheries • Risk assessments conducted by Technical University of Denmark
Ireland	• Oversight responsibility lies with Food Safety Authority (FSA) • Risk assessments, profiles, scientific advice with FSA committee of experts • Food safety rules for import/export of animal products enforced by Department of Agriculture and Food • Requirements in food establishments and on imports enforced by Health and Safety Executive
Sweden	• Import controls and rules governing meat packers and food processors under National Food Administration (NFA) • Production overseen by National Fisheries Board and Board of Agriculture • Marketing and small producers overseen by municipalities • Risk assessment and management conducted by different NFA departments • Outside scientific advisers play significant role in NFA • Studying idea of single agency rather than tripartite responsibilities
United Kingdom	• Farm-to-table food safety authority lies with Food Standards Agency (FSA) • GFL food and feed law implemented by FSA • Emphasis on public health and consumers • Risk management lies with an agency • Risk assessment with agency committees

Sources: House of Commons (1999); HM Treasury (2003); Slorach (2008); interview with Derrick Jones, chief economist, FSA, 2009.

4.1   US Reform Efforts

In many respects, the United States ushered in the current generation of food safety policy reform. Both the FDA and the US Department of Agriculture (USDA) began reorienting their food processing rules around HACCP in the early 1990s. In general, industry and consumer groups have supported HACCP, though both consumer groups and the GAO have insisted on the need to tie HACCP to performance standards (Holland and Pope 2004). During the past decade, the United States struggled to find the political will to take legislative action to rationalize a fragmented and sometimes underfunded system of multi-agency control. At the same time, US administrative agencies implemented reforms very similar to those embodied in Codex principles and the EU's General Food Law.

HACCP was one of the first of many steps the United States took toward more risk-based food safety management. Throughout the 1990s and the following decade, substantial technical and policy expertise in food safety was directed at adapting risk analysis methods and frameworks to microbiological hazards in foods. Much of the

Table 21.2 Elements of national reforms outside the European Union

Joint Australian–New Zealand reforms	• Joint food standard system under Food Safety Australia/New Zealand (FSANZ) • Farm-to-table food safety regulation • Risk assessment and management separated • Food standards code, technical analysis, and developing standards administered by FSANZ • Final authority over standards and balance in objectives of public health, efficient food provision, and minimal regulatory burden in hands of Food Regulation Ministerial Council
Canada	• Food safety responsibilities under Canadian Food Inspection Agency (CFIA) • Disease surveillance under Public Health Agency, participates in outbreak response • Food safety standards set by Health Canada • Enforcing standards, inspections, and quarantine under CFIA • Effectiveness of CFIA enforcement evaluated by Health Canada • Import inspection under Border Services Agency • No mandatory traceability of food generally • Focus moving toward preventive measures, risk-based inspection, product traceability
Japan	• Risk-based import control • Most imports inspected randomly • All lots of high-risk imports inspected • Priorities for monitoring imports revised annually • Random inspections free • Importers pay for enhanced inspections and violation
New Zealand	• Food safety administration not isolated from promotion of agriculture • Risk-based approach to inspection of imports • Moving toward importer verification and away from border inspection

Sources: FSANZ (2009); NZFSA (2008); Slorach (2008); WHO/FAO (2006); CAC (2007); FAO (2007a,b); Government of Canada (2009); GAO (2008).

scientific effort focused on developing microbiological risk assessment (USDA FSIS 1998; IoM 2002; WHO/FAO 2002, 2004). In the United States, responsibility for risk assessment and risk management is generally within a single agency, but assigned to different work groups or offices. Communication between risk assessors and risk managers, particularly while planning the risk assessment, help ensure that risk assessment endpoints are appropriate for risk management purposes. In recent years, both the FDA and USDA have been using risk profiling to focus inspection resources and increase their effectiveness (US FDA 2007; USDA FSIS 2008). In addition, the FDA has been looking toward more risk-based approaches to managing import safety. The United States has also invested in improvements in disease monitoring with an eye to risk-based targeting—most importantly FoodNet, a nationwide active surveillance system, and PulseNet, which uses genetic fingerprinting in tracing the source of outbreaks as well as efforts to develop more reliable methods to attribute foodborne illness to foods or sources of contamination (US CDC 2009a,c).

Given the central role US scientists and technical experts have played in developing FAO/WHO guidance, along with the integration of Codex guidelines into the SPS agreement, it is likely that the US will continue to move toward adopting international norms. The United States clearly sees international cooperation on food safety not only as a way to protect its trade interests, but also as essential to protecting the safety of its food supply. For example, the US, Australia, New Zealand, and Canada are all actively involved in international consultation on technical and policy aspects of food safety both through Codex and through multilateral forums (NZFSA 2007; US FDA 2009d).

For much of the 2000s, the United States moved toward a farm-to-fork approach to food safety, but on a more case-by-case basis than in Europe, and often in response to highly visible failures to assure food safety. For example, outbreaks of shiga-toxin *E. coli* in leafy greens in 2006 pushed produce growers and regulators to develop better control systems (Hitti 2007). Draft FDA guidance on produce safety took a supply chain approach, but was voluntary (US FDA 2009a, b, c). The United States banned feeding offal to cattle, and regulates pesticide use on farms and non-medical use of antibiotics in livestock production (Hoffmann and Harder 2010). Yet on the whole, farmers, particularly smaller farmers, have resisted on-farm regulation. In the past, conventional wisdom has been that because each state has two senators, providing rural, agricultural states with votes disproportional to their population, it is unlikely that a regulatory approach to the farm portion of farm-to-table food safety policy will be adopted.

One of the basic structural problems in US food safety regulation is that responsibility is fragmented across as many as fifteen agencies (US GAO 2009). Primary responsibilities rests with four: the USDA (meat, poultry, and processed egg products), the EPA (setting pesticide tolerances), the US Department of Commerce (seafood), and the FDA (all other foods including food additives and economic adulteration) (US GAO 2005). The US Centers for Disease Control, together with state public health authorities, are responsible for disease surveillance. Local public health authorities and state offices of public health are jointly responsible for regulating food hygiene in local food service and retail establishments, local authorities look to the FDA model food hygiene codes for guidance when drafting local ordinances.

Similar fragmentation drove food safety reform in the European Union and its member states, particularly the United Kingdom. Despite a recent string of foodborne illness outbreaks and highly publicized failures of import controls, the political will to consolidate seems to be lacking in the United States. In part, difficulties with the formation of the Department of Homeland Security raised questions about the effectiveness of such consolidation (Hall 2004).

In January 2011 the Food Safety Modernization Act (FSMA) was signed into law (US Congress 2011). The Act represents the most significant change in the US FDA's food safety authority since passage of the Food, Drug and Cosmetics Act of 1938. It does not affect other US federal agencies with food safety responsibilities. The Act embodies many elements viewed as part of a preventive, risk-based farm-to-fork approach to managing food safety. Under the Act, all FDA-regulated food facilities will be required to develop HACCP plans for the first time. FDA is also required to establish science-based standards for safe production and harvesting of fruits and vegetables. The Act was only passed once it included an exemption to the produce regulations for small farms that sell locally. The Act establishes mandatory facility inspection frequency based on risk and gives FDA access to firm-level records needed to document implementation of HACCP plans.

The FSMA extends preventive approaches to food imports as well. Importers are required to verify that their foreign suppliers have adequate preventive controls in place to assure their product is safe. Because of the breadth of their jurisdiction, FDA has had a greater problem assuring foreign producers meet US food safety standards than USDA has. The new Act allows FDA to look to third party certification to confirm this. FDA is also required to establish a voluntary program of expedited review and entry for importers importing food from certified facilities.

The FSMA also enhances FDA's capacity to respond rapidly to failures in food safety management. The Act gives FDA mandatory recall authority, the power to suspend facility registration, and expanded power to keep food suspected of being adulterated or misbranded out of the market. These provisions provide FDA with powers similar to those exercised by USDA under US meat inspection law. The Act also directs FDA to establish a traceability system for domestic and imported foods.

A series of high-level reviews of US federal food safety programs have recommended changes more far-reaching than those embodied in the FSMA (NRC 1998, 2003, 2010). The US Government Accountability Office continues to highlight problems arising from food safety authority being split across multiple agencies (US GAO 2011). It seems doubtful at this stage that further legislative action will be taken, but the federal agencies with food safety responsibility are working to improve coordination. They are likely to look to these reports as guidance as they continue to modernize food safety management under existing statutory authority.

5   ECONOMIC ANALYSIS OF FOOD SAFETY POLICY

Economists play multiple roles in informing food safety policy. Most commonly, they are called on to assess the costs and benefits of proposed policies. Most OECD countries now require some form of economic analysis of major policies. Ideally, economists also play a role in the design of policy innovations. They also have the capacity to play a greater role in improving the accuracy of risk assessment. Economic research that increases our understanding of how food safety risks are generated in food production, processing, marketing, and preparation, and how industrial structure influences these processes, can support this work. Research into consumer perceptions of and attitudes toward risk, their willingness to pay to reduce risks, and the economic burden of foodborne disease supports it as well.

5.1   Theoretical Foundations

Choice of products in a market is generally a choice among bundles of non-separable attributes (Lancaster 1971). Safety is only one of many attributes of food, and consumer preferences for safety are typically modeled using a multi-attribute utility function that recognizes possible trade-offs among attributes. Hence, a product is modeled as a set of attributes—e.g., ground beef as a bundle of fat content, freshness, price, and safety.

On the supply side, food can be modeled as a quality-differentiated product in which safety is only one of several attributes produced (Chambers 1988). Safety, like its counterparts, has a shadow price. The degree to which the cost of producing safety is separable from the cost of producing other product attributes is an empirical question, but as a general rule, suppliers must invest resources to produce safety. Antle (2001) provides an excellent overview of theoretical literature on both supply and demand applicable to food safety economics.

Supply and demand analysis is complicated by the fact that safety attributes are not usually directly observable by consumers, and often are either not observable to suppliers or observable by them only at a cost. Even where information relevant to product safety is available to one firm in the supply chain, there is a cost associated with communicating that information to downstream firms and consumers. Labeling and other information approaches to food safety policy (see Chapter 18 in this volume, by Caswell and Anders) are an attempt to deal with the resulting information asymmetries between consumers and suppliers. Traceability requirements, like those in the EU, are designed to address information asymmetry in the supply chain, increasing the speed of response to safety failures and strengthen market and liability incentives for precaution (Pouliot and Sumner 2008). Firms may also invest in obscuring information about product quality and safety by using colorants, additives, and processes that preserve attributes, such as meat color, that consumers look to as signals of safety.

5.2   Benefits Assessment

Reduction in consumer health risks is usually the primary benefit of food safety policies. Willingness to pay for reductions in risk of illness or death is generally viewed as the most complete and correct welfare-theoretic measure of these benefits, but as a practical matter, cost of illness is more widely used in regulatory analysis (for a brief discussion, see Antle 2001: 1096–7). Harrington and Portney (1987) show that willingness to pay can be decomposed into the cost of medical treatment, lost productivity, and a change in consumer utility. Because cost-of-illness estimates generally include only the cost of treatment and lost productivity, they are usually a lower bound on the benefits of preventing morbidity. Berger et al. (1987) show that cost-of-illness measures may not be a lower bound on willingness to pay for actions that reduce the probability of both morbidity and mortality. Many foodborne pathogens result in both illnesses and deaths. Kenkel (1994) demonstrates how cost-of-illness measures can significantly bias cost–benefit estimates. Chapter 5 in this volume, provides a more detailed examination of the economics literature on benefits estimation. Kuchler and Golan (1999) provide a critical review of alternative methods of valuing health risks and their use in food safety policy. The proceedings of a 2001 US Economic Research Service conference include a comprehensive discussion of the issues involved in choice of valuation metric from a US regulatory perspective (Kuchler 2001).

The public health literature often uses health adjusted life year (HALY) measures as an alternative to either cost of illness or willingness to pay. These measures are widely accepted in Europe and used in the WHO's Global Burden of Disease estimates (WHO 2008). Their use in US regulatory analysis was recently permitted by the US Office of Management and Budget (OMB) under the Bush administration (US OMB 2003). HALYs are indices of the impact of illness on physical well-being and function. They were developed to provide a common metric for the severity of health outcomes for use in evaluating the cost-effectiveness of alternative medical treatments.

HALYs must be monetized for cost–benefit analysis. This has been controversial as HALY measures are not consistent with the utility-theoretic foundations of welfare economics (Hammitt 2002, 2003; see also Krupnick 2004; Dickie and List 2006). A recent US National Academies of Sciences report recommended against monetizing HALYs (NRC 2006).

HALYs measure the impacts of illness on quality of life in terms of effects on normal activities, and qualitative attributes like pain or anxiety. They do not measure consumer preferences over reducing the risk of future health states. This leads to HALY measures placing greater weight on reducing chronic disease rather than mortality, particularly mortality in the elderly. In an empirical assessment of US diesel fuel regulation, Hubbel (2006) shows that this conceptual difference between HALY and willingness-to-pay metrics can change the outcome of regulatory analysis, notably for policies involving more chronic disease than mortality. This could be of significance for food safety analysis comparing the benefits of interventions to reduce pathogens such as *Campylobacter*, associated with significant chronic morbidity, and pathogens like *Toxoplasma gondii*, which has a higher mortality rate. It would be of even greater importance in comparing the relative merits of reducing exposure to chemical residues and pathogens.

Empirical research estimating the benefits of food safety policy has used multiple methods, including hedonic estimates of demand for safety from market data, stated preference surveys, and experimental auctions (see, e.g., Shogren et al. 1999; Marks, Kalaitzandonakes, and Vickner 2003). Van Ravenswaay (1995), Antle (2001), and Golan et al. (2005) provide reviews of the empirical literature, focusing on the United States. European valuation studies have been published related to BSE (Latouche, Rainelli, and Vermersch 1998), GM foods in Italy (Boccaletti and Moro 2000), organic foods in Denmark (Wier et al. 2002), and *Salmonella* in chicken (Sundström and Andersson 2009). Mørkbak, Christensen, and Gyrd-Hansen (2008) provide a comprehensive review of stated preference studies of meat safety and quality.

Meta-analysis, a means of statistically analyzing and combining the results of multiple studies, has been used widely in assessing the benefits of environmental policy

(Bergstrom and Taylor 2006; Nelson and Kennedy 2009). Florax, Travisi, and Nijkamp (2005) conducted a meta-analysis of research on willingness to pay to reduce health risks from pesticide exposure through food and other pathways. Lusk et al. (2005) conducted a meta-analysis consumer willingness to pay to avoid genetically modified foods. Hammitt and Haninger (2007) used meta-analysis to look at the sensitivity of willingness to pay for avoiding foodborne illness to duration and severity of illness. These studies all have a US focus.

In the US, federal agencies have relied most often on cost-of-illness estimates. OMB now asks federal agencies to also use QALY estimates in their regulatory impact analysis. Batz et al. (2011) provide cost-of-illness and QALY estimates for fourteen leading foodborne pathogens in the US. Similar efforts are underway in New Zealand, Australia, Canada, and probably in other OECD countries.

5.3   Cost Assessment

Governments of most OECD countries provide guidance on conducting regulatory cost analysis (see, e.g., US EPA 2000 or HM Treasury 2003). While there is some variation, these generally follow basic principles of applied welfare economics. US EPA guidelines decompose total social cost of regulation into three components: direct compliance costs, indirect costs to consumers and producers, and the social costs of market adjustment. Direct costs of compliance might include fixed costs, such as the capital costs of additional equipment and employee training or variable costs such as changes in production procedures and input quality. Indirect costs are social welfare losses that can occur if compliance costs are large enough to lead to increased consumer prices and changes in the consumer/producer surplus. Finally, social adjustment costs might arise if regulatory standards result in firm closure or relocation. For example, banning the use of harmful pesticides might lead to regional shifts in agricultural production, disruptions in production, and unemployment.

Unnevehr and Jensen (2005) use the EPA guidance framework to structure a review of US empirical literature on the cost of compliance with regulation of pesticide and microbial hazards in food. The broad lessons they draw from this literature illustrate some of the kinds of policy insights that can be drawn from cost assessment. First, the distribution of costs of compliance is likely to be more important than the impact on consumer prices. Most studies found little impact on the cost of food because there are many alternative sources of supply. But because supply can shift to different size or vintage of plants, different regions, or even different countries, social adjustment costs in terms of changes in employment or income may be significant. Second, studies did find meaningful long-term incentive impacts on investment in new technology, plant, equipment, and human capital. Unnevehr and Jensen emphasize the importance of these types of incentives on the nature of productivity growth in the food sector. Third, studies support the theoretical position that incentive-based measures generally provide the most cost-effective means of achieving public health goals. And fourth, a "risk-based systems approach" can provide a better way of understanding costs through the entire supply chain.

Antle (2001) builds on Chambers's (1988) model of quality-differentiated production to develop a theoretical foundation for empirical estimation of the direct costs of complying with food safety policy. Two fundamental modeling issues arise: first, whether, in representing production of the safety attributes of food, output can be fully separated from input demand (input–output separability); and second, whether it is possible to represent production of safety and other attributes through separate production functions with separate inputs (non-jointness of input use). Antle (2001) notes that usually neither will be possible in the case of food safety production. He argues that, in part because of this, analysis of the cost of food safety policy typically uses a non-separable, joint cost function rather than the primal problem of profit maximization subject to a non-separable, non-joint production function.

Antle (2001) and Unnevehr and Jensen (2005) emphasize the degree to which both theoretical modeling and empirical analysis of the costs imposed by food safety policy vary by type of policy and industrial structure. Antle (2001) presents alternative theoretical models for process controls, inspection, input and product testing, labeling, and traceability. Unnevehr and Jensen (2005) focus on differences between pesticide regulation and regulation of microbial hazards. Both papers emphasize the importance of dynamic as well as static analysis and of focusing on the impact of food safety policy on industrial structure. Both also note the difficulty of empirically distinguishing between technological and managerial innovation made in response to market incentives and government policy.

Many empirical methods are used to estimate costs of compliance. Antle (2001) emphasizes the extent to which either firm-level cost accounting (US FDA 1994; USDA FSIS 1995; Cato and Lima dos Santos 1999; Colatore and Caswell 1999) or firm-level economic-engineering modeling of production processes have been used (see Duewer and Nelson 1991; Jensen and Unnevehr 1999; Narrod et al. 1999). Because these are detailed, usually firm-specific approaches, they are usually used to develop a model of a representative plant. Antle (2001) maintains, however, that because this modeling approach is costly, the number of plants modeled is usually small; as a result, firm heterogeneity is usually not captured. Therefore, studies using this firm-level approach may be unrepresentative at the industry level. He argues that although econometric models of costs at either the plant or industry levels do not provide the process detail of accounting or economic engineering models, they do provide a better basis for estimating behavioral response of plants and market segments to regulation.

Ultimately, the results of such empirical studies are used in broader analysis of the social cost of regulation. The scope of this analysis may vary from partial equilibrium analysis of the impacts on a limited market sector where the impact of regulation on prices or average costs is small (see, e.g., Lichtenberg, Parker, and Zilberman 1988; Roosen and Hennessy 2001) to general equilibrium analysis for policies expected to have broad economy-wide effects owing to significant changes in product, input prices, or plant closure (see, e.g., Golan et al. 2005). More frequently, impacts will spread beyond the directly affected market, but will not be economy-wide. In these cases, multi-market analysis will usually be used (see, e.g., Unnevehr, Gomez, and Garcia 1998; Onal, Unnevehr, and Bekric 2000).

5.4 Integrating Economics and Risk Assessment

Risk analysis is intended to provide decision makers with a clear, fact-based understanding of how actions affect physical risks. It helps decision makers reach better decisions by providing a workable model of how real-world systems are likely to respond to proposed policy changes. This is an inherently interdisciplinary task. In practice, risk analysis has often only been interdisciplinary in limited ways. Disciplinary divides and institutional structures have created barriers to fully interdisciplinary risk analysis. In 1983 the US NAS Red Book described the institutional structure of risk analysis in the United States as having three phases: scientific risk assessment, risk management, and risk communication. In practice in the United States, economics has been seen primarily as part of risk management focusing on valuation of the costs and benefits of outcomes modeled by risk assessors (Williams and Thompson 2004). There is as yet little recognition of the contribution economics can make to improving risk modeling (Hoffmann forthcoming). In Europe, the institutional separation of risk assessment and risk management mandated by the European Union's General Food Law is likely to isolate economics even further from risk assessment.

Past discussions about the interaction between economic analysis and risk assessment have primarily focused on the difficulties the separation creates in valuing policy benefits. These discussions frequently look at how lack of communication between risk assessors and risk managers has resulted in risk assessment providing outcome measures that were difficult to use in economic analysis of policy impacts (NRC 1983, 2009; Dockins et al. 2004). There has been much less discussion about how separation of economic analysis from risk assessment weakens risk assessment.

Risks are generated by human interaction with the biological and physical world. Yet risk assessment typically focuses on modeling only the biological and physical sides of this risk generation process. Hoffmann (forthcoming) discusses ways in which broader use of fully integrated modeling of physical, biological, and socioeconomic systems could enhance the accuracy and relevance of risk assessment.

Sometimes the behavioral factors that affect risk are directly related to the policy. For example, if the policy affects the price of the food through which people are being exposed, people are likely to substitute away from this food to other foods. This will reduce the risk being focused on, but may increase other risks. More often, the behavioral factors influencing risk will be unrelated to the policy under consideration. For example, labor market trends may lead to greater consumption of food outside the home, changing patterns of exposure to foodborne pathogens and toxins. Similarly, shifts in the relative costs of production across industry sectors may lead to change in the distribution of return on investment in safety.

The kind of integrated biophysical-economic modeling that may help improve risk assessment of food safety policy is already being done in many areas of natural resource and environmental policy (Hoffmann forthcoming). For example, there is a long history of use of bioeconomic modeling in fisheries management as well as in forestry, integrated pest management, and wildlife management. Fairly simple models of both fish populations and fish markets have provided highly useful predictions of alternative fisheries policy. Sanchirico and Wilen (2007) review recent efforts to integrate models of the spatial ecology of marine subpopulations and models of human predation. The key to these efforts is their attempt to capture the salient characteristics of both population dynamics and human economic activity in a single optimization model.

Integrated physical-economic modeling has also played a critical role in assessing climate change policy (Energy Modeling Forum 2009). These large simulation models are usually made up of linked mathematical submodels of physical, biological, and economic systems with explicit mathematical linkages between the submodels, much as a multi-regional Computable General Equilibrium model will have economy-wide models of individual regions linked by trade, financial, and labor flows. Some climate models, for example, the US Department of Energy's MiniCam model, have done a great deal to create a truly integrated biophysical-economic model (McCracken et al. 1999; Sands, Jung, and Jo 2002).

Because modeling always involves judgments about which linkages are important and which simplifications matter and which do not, it will take time to develop sound judgments on how best to conduct integrated modeling in the food safety arena. The art of integrated assessment is for all involved to understand each other's models well enough to be able to identify and model critical interactions. Efforts to conduct such analysis are beginning and are likely to grow with the increased emphasis on farm-to-table, integrated risk management (Havelaar et al. 2006).

6   CONCLUSION

Food production and marketing is undergoing a level of change and innovation around the world that is reminiscent of that experienced at the turn of the last century. Markets are more vertically integrated, more concentrated, and more global than at any time in the past. Advances in communication and shipping have facilitated these and other changes. Consumers are demanding and getting new products, ready-to-eat produce, and summer produce in the winter. Novel technologies lower price, increase supply, and promise other benefits. But many of these changes also pose new challenges to maintaining the safety of the food supply. Globalized supply chains transport food-borne hazards as well as food. It also means that each country's investment in public institutions has impacts far beyond its own borders.

It is clear that conventional approaches to food safety policy that have been in place since the turn of the last century are not adequate to meet these new food safety challenges. This chapter has reviewed a rather coherent set of policy reforms that are being adopted worldwide to modernize food safety policy. It is recognized that in a world of globalized markets, global coordination of these efforts is a necessity, not only to avoid trade disputes, but also to assure the safety of the food supply. A broad consensus of the vision for this new structure for food safety policy is emerging, in part, through international negotiations over the SPS Agreement and international technical consultations sponsored by the WHO/FAO Codex. The vision is for a preventive system that manages foodborne hazard from farm to fork. This system relies on risk management practices developed in the public sector to guide environmental and health and safety policy and in the private sector to reduce risk of failure in process engineering. As a broad concept, there is also recognition that the food system has grown complex and extensive enough that safety can no longer be managed solely through reliance on command and control regulation and government inspection. There is also a desire to rely more heavily on performance standards and other approaches that allow firms flexibility in how they achieve public health goals.

These efforts are still in the early stages of development. Economics has many contributions to make because of the complexity of the management problem and the systems. To the extent that there is commitment to integrating management from farm to fork, economists are in a unique position to study and model the supply chain relationships. They are also in a position to provide needed insight into the design of incentive mechanisms and non-governmental safety assurance instruments. Economists also have a central role to play in modeling the risks, costs, and benefits of public programs. But, as in many areas of health and safety policy where science and engineering dominate policy debates, it will be a challenge for economists to make certain that their insights are heard and their relevance understood. Interdisciplinary research and modeling is central this effort.

REFERENCES

Alemanno, A. 2006. "Food Safety and the Single European Market." In Ansell and Vogel (2006).

——2007. *Trade in Food: Regulatory and Judicial Approaches in the EC and the WTO.* London: Cameron May.

Andrews, R. N. L. 2006. "Risk-Based Decision Making: Policy, Science, and Politics." In N. Vig and M. Kraft, eds, *Environmental Policy: New Directions for the Twenty-First Century*, 6th edn. Washington, DC: CQ Press.

Ansell, C., and D. Vogel. 2006. *What's the Beef? The Contested Governance of European Food Safety.* Cambridge, MA: MIT Press.

Antle, J. M. 2001. "Economics Analysis of Food Safety." In B. Gardner and G. Rausser, eds, *Handbook of Agricultural Economics*, 1. Amsterdam: Elsevier Science.

Batz, M., Hoffmann, S., and Morris, J. G., 2011. "Ranking the Risks: The 10 Pathogen–Food Combinations with the Greatest Burden on Public Health." Discussion paper, Emerging Pathogens Institute, University of Florida.

Berger, M. C., G. C. Blomquist, D. Kenkel, and G. S. Tolley. 1987. "Valuing Changes in Health Risks: A Comparison of Alternative Measures." *Southern Economic Journal* 53: 967–84.

Bergstrom, J. C., and L. O. Taylor. 2006. "Using Meta-Analysis for Benefits Transfer: Theory and Practice." *Ecological Economics* 60/2: 351–60.

Boccaletti, S., and D. Moro. 2000. "Consumer Willingness-to-Pay for GM Food Products in Italy." *AgBioForum* 3/4: 259–67.

Brom, F. 2004. "WTO, Public Reason, and Food Public Reasoning in the 'Trade Conflict' on GM-Food." *Ethical Theory and Moral Practice* 7/4: 417–31.

Calvin, L., L. Flores, and W. Foster. 2003. *Case Study Guatemalan Raspberries and Cyclospora*. 2020 Vision Briefs 10, No. 7. Washington, DC: International Food Policy Research Institute.

Cato, J. C., and C. A. Lima dos Santos. 1999. "Cost to Upgrade Bangladesh Frozen Shrimp Processing Sector to Adequate Technical and Sanitary Standards and to Maintain a HACCP Program." In L. J. Unnevehr, ed., *The Economics of HACCP: Studies of Costs and Benefits*. St Paul, MN: Eagan Press.

Chambers, R. G. 1988. *Applied Production Analysis: A Dual Approach*. Cambridge: Cambridge University Press.

Colatore, C., and J. A. Caswell. 1999. "The Cost of HACCP Implementation in the Seafood Industry: A Case Study of Breaded Fish." In L. J. Unnevehr, ed., *The Economics of HACCP: Studies of Costs and Benefits*. St Paul, MN: Eagan Press.

Covaci, A., S. Voorspoels, P. Schepens, P. Jorens, R. Blust, and H. Neels. 2008. "The Belgian PCB/Dioxin Crisis—8 Years Later: An Overview." *Environmental Toxicology and Pharmacology* 25: 164–70.

Darton, J. 1996. "Britain Ties Deadly Brain Disease to Cow Ailment." *New York Times*, Mar. 21.

Davies, C., ed. 1996. *Comparing Environmental Risks: Tools for Setting Government Priorities*. Washington, DC: Resources for the Future.

Dickie, M., and J. List. 2006. "Economic Valuation of Health for Environmental Policy: Comparing Alternative Approaches. Introduction and Overview." *Environmental and Resource Economics* 34: 339–46.

Dockins, C., C. Griffiths, N. Owens, N. Simon, and D. Axelrad. 2004. "Linking Economics and Risk Assessment." *Journal of Toxicology and Environmental Health, Part A* 67/8–10: 611–20.

Duewer, L. A., and K. E. Nelson. 1991. *Beefpacking and Processing Plants: Computer-Assisted Cost Analysis*. Washington, DC: Economic Research Service, US Department of Agriculture.

Energy Modeling Forum and Integrated Assessment Modeling Forum. <http://emf.stanford.edu>.

European Commission. 1997. Green Paper on the General Principles of Food Law in the European Union [COM (1997) 176]. <http://eur-lex.europa.eu/LexUriServ/LexUriServ.do?uri=COM:1997:0176:FIN:EN:PDF>.

—— 2000. White Paper on Food Safety [COM (1999) 719]. <http://ec.europa.eu/dgs/health_consumer/library/pub/pub06_en.pdf>.

European Council. 2006. Regulation (EC) No. 1907/2006 of the European Parliament and of the Council of 18 December 2006 concerning the Registration, Evaluation, Authorisation and Restriction of Chemicals (REACH), establishing a European Chemicals Agency, amending Directive 1999/45/EC and repealing Council Regulation (EEC) No. 793/93 and

Commission Regulation (EC) No. 1488/94 as well as Council Directive 76/769/EEC and Commission Directives 91/155/EEC, 93/67/EEC, 93/105/EC and 2000/21/EC.

European Parliament. 1997. *Report of the Temporary Committee of Inquiry into BSE, Set Up by the Parliament in July 1996, on the Alleged Contraventions or Maladministration in the Implementation of Community Law in Relation to BSE, without Prejudice to the Jurisdiction of the Community and the National Courts of February 7, 1997.* A4-0020/97/A, PE220.533/ fin/A.

European Union General Food Law, Regulation (EC) No. 178/2002, arts. 1, 5, 6, 7, 8, 9, 14, 17, 18, 19, 20, 28, 30, and 38.

FAO (Food and Agriculture Organization). 2007a. *Biosecurity ToolKit.* Rome: FAO.

—— 2007b. *Principles and Guidelines for Conducting Microbial Risk Management (MRM).* CAC/GL-63. Rome: FAO.

—— 2009. *Risk-Based Food Inspection Manual.* Rome: FAO.

FAO/WHO (Food and Agriculture Organization/World Health Organization) 1984. *The Role of Food Safety in Health and Development.* Report of the Joint FAO/WHO Expert Committee on Food Safety, Technical Report Series 705. Geneva: WHO.

Finkel, A. M., and D. Golding, eds. 1994. *Worst Things First? The Debate over Risk-Based National Environmental Priorities.* Washington, DC: Resources for the Future.

Florax, R., C. Travisi, and P. Nijkamp. 2005. "A Meta-Analysis of the Willingness-to-Pay for Reductions in Pesticide Risk Exposure." *European Review of Agricultural Economics* 32/4: 441–67.

Fortin, N. 2009. *Food Regulation: Law, Science, Policy, and Practice.* Hoboken, NJ: Wiley.

—— 2010. Personal communication. Mr Fortin is the Director of the Institute for Food Laws and Regulations, Michigan State University, East Lansing, Michigan.

FSANZ (Food Standards Australia/New Zealand). 2009. "A Short History of FSANZ." <http://www.foodstandards.gov.au/scienceandeducation/aboutfsanz/historyoffsanz.cfm>.

Gale, F., and D. Hu. 2009. "Supply Chain Issues in China's Milk Adulteration Incident." Paper presented at the International Association of Agricultural Economists' 2009 Conference, Beijing, Aug. 16–22.

Golan, E., J. Buzby, S. Crutchfield, P. Frenzen, F. Kuchler, K. Ralston, and T. Roberts. 2005. "The Value to Consumers of Reducing Foodborne Risks." In S. Hoffmann and M. Taylor, eds, *Toward Safer Food: Perspectives on Risk and Priority Setting.* Washington, DC: Resources for the Future.

Government of Canada. 2009. "Food and Consumer Safety Action Plan." *Healthy Canadians.* <http://www.tbs-sct.gc.ca/hidb-bdih/initiative-eng.aspx?Hi=85>.

Halkier, B., and L. Holm. 2006. "Shifting Responsibilities for Food Safety in Europe: An Introduction." *Appetite* 47/2: 127–33.

Hall, M. 2004. "Ex-Official Tells of Homeland Security Failures." *USA Today.* Dec. <http:// www.usatoday.com/news/washington/2004-12-27-homeland-usat_x.htm>.

Hamilton, D., and S. Crossley. 2004. *Pesticide Residues in Food and Drinking Water.* New York: Wiley.

Hammitt, J. C. 2002. "QALYs versus WTP." *Risk Analysis* 22/5: 985–1001.

—— 2003. "Valuing Health: Quality-Adjusted Life Years or Willingness to Pay?" *Risk in Perspective* 11/1: 1–6.

—— and K. Haninger. 2007. "Willingness to Pay for Food Safety: Sensitivity to Duration and Severity of Illness." *American Journal of Agricultural Economics* 89/5: 1170–5.

Harrington, W., and P. R. Portney. 1987. "Valuing the Benefits of Health and Safety Regulation." *Journal of Urban Economics* 22/1: 101–12.

Havelaar, A. H., J. Bräunig, K. Christiansen, H. Cornu, T. Hald, M. J. J. Mangen, K. Molbak, A. Pielaat, E. Snary, A. G. J. Velthuis, and H. Wahlstrom. 2006. *Integrating Risk Assessment, Epidemiology and Economics to Support Decision Making in Food Safety.* <http://www.medvetnet.org/pdf/Reports/Report_06-001.pdf>.

Hitti, M. 2007. "FDA Sets Fresh-Produce Safety Rules." *WebMD Health News.* <http://www.webmd.com/food-recipes/food-poisoning/news/20070312/fda-sets-fresh-produce-safety-rules>.

HM Treasury. 2003. *The Green Book: Appraisal and Evaluation in Central Government.* <http://www.hm-treasury.gov.uk/data_greenbook_index.htm>.

Hoffmann, S. Forthcoming. "Overcoming Barriers to Integrating Economic Analysis into Risk Assessment." *Risk Analysis.*

——and W. Harder. 2010. "Food Safety and Risk Governance in Globalized Markets." *Health Matrix: Journal of Law-Medicine* 20: 5–54.

Holland, D., and H. Pope. 2004. *EU Food Law and Policy.* The Hague: Kluwer Law International.

Hubbel, B. 2006. "Implementing QALYs in the Analysis of Air Pollution Regulations." *Environmental and Resource Economics* 34/3: 365–84.

Huelebak, K., and W. Schlosser. 2002. "Hazard Analysis and Critical Control Point (HACCP) History and Conceptual Overview." *Risk Analysis* 22/3: 547–52.

IOM (Institute of Medicine). 2002. *Escherichia coli O157:H7 in Ground Beef: Review of a Draft Risk Assessment.* Washington, DC: National Academies Press.

——2006. *Valuing Health for Regulatory Cost-Effectiveness Analysis.* Washington, DC: National Academies Press.

Jensen, H. H., and L. J. Unnevehr. 1999. "HACCP in Pork Processing: Costs and Benefits." In L. J. Unnevehr, ed., *The Economics of HACCP: Studies of Costs and Benefits.* St Paul, MN: Eagan Press.

Josling, T., D. Roberts, and D. Orden. 2004. *Food Regulation and Trade: Toward a Safe and Open Global System.* Washington, DC: Institute for International Economics.

Käferstein, F. K., Y. Motarjemi, and D. W. Bettcher. 1997. "Foodborne Disease Control: A Transnational Challenge." *Emerging Infectious Diseases* 3/4: 503–10.

Katz, D., S. Kumar, J. Malecki, M. Lowdermilk, E. H. Koumans, and R. Hopkins. 1999. "Cyclosporiasis Associated with Imported Raspberries, Florida, 1996." *Public Health Reports* 114/5: 427–37.

Kenkel, D. 1994. "Cost of Illness Approach." In G. Tolley, D. Kenkel, and R. Fabian, eds, *Valuing Health for Policy: An Economic Approach.* Chicago: University of Chicago Press.

Kinsey, J. D. 2001. "The New Food Economy: Consumers, Farms, Pharms, and Science." *American Journal of Agricultural Economics* 83/5: 1113–30.

Krapohl, S. 2008. *Risk Regulation in the Single Market.* New York: Palgrave Macmillan.

Krupnick, A. 2004. *Valuing Health Outcomes: Policy Choices and Technical Issues.* RFF Report. Washington, DC: Resources for the Future, Mar.

Kuchler, F. 2001. *Valuing the Health Benefits of Food Safety: A Proceedings.* Miscellaneous Publication No. 1570. Washington, DC: Economic Research Service, US Department of Agriculture.

—— and E. Golan. 1999. *Assigning Values to Life: Comparing Methods for Valuing Health Risks*. Agricultural Economic Report No. 784. Washington, DC: Food and Rural Economics Division, Economic Research Service, US Department of Agriculture.

Lancaster, K. 1971. *Consumer Demand: A New Approach*. New York: Columbia University Press.

Latouche, K., P. Rainelli, and D. Vermersch. 1998. "Food Safety Issues and the BSE Scare: Some Lessons from the French Case." *Food Policy* 23/5: 347–56.

Lehman, A. J., and O. G. Fitzhugh. 1954. "100-Fold Margin of Safety." *Association of Food and Drug Officials of the United States Quarterly Bulletin* 18: 33–5.

Lichtenberg, E., D. D. Parker, and D. Zilberman. 1988. "Marginal Analysis of Welfare Costs of Environmental Policies: The Case of Pesticide Regulation." *American Journal of Agricultural Economics* 70: 867–74.

Lusk, J., M. Jamal, L. Kurlander, M. Roucan, and L. Taulman. 2005. "A Meta-Analysis of Genetically Modified Food Valuation Studies." *Journal of Agricultural and Resource Economics* 30/1: 28–44.

McCluskey, J. J., K. M. Grimsrud, H. Ouchi, and T. I. Wahl. 2005. "Bovine Spongiform Encephalopathy in Japan: Consumers' Food Safety Perceptions and Willingness to Pay for Tested Beef." *Australian Journal of Agricultural and Resource Economics* 49: 197–209.

McCracken, C. N., J. A. Edmonds, S. H. Kim, and R. D. Sands. 1999. "The Economics of the Kyoto Protocol." *Energy Journal* 20, Special Issue, 25–72.

Marks, L., N. Kalaitzandonakes, and S. S. Vickner. 2003. "Evaluating Consumer Response to GM Foods: Some Methodological Considerations." *Current Agriculture, Food and Resource Issues* 4: 80–94.

Mead, P. S., L. Slutsker, V. Dietz, L. F. McCaig, J. S. Bresee, C. Shapiro, P. M. Griffin, and R. V. Tauxe. 1999. "Food-Related Illness and Death in the United States." *Emerging Infectious Diseases* 5: 607–25.

Mørkbak, M. R., T. Christensen, and D. Gyrd-Hansen. 2008. "Valuation of Food Safety in Meat: A Review of Stated Preference Studies." *Food Economics* 5: 63–74.

Narrod, C. A., S. A. Malcolm, M. Ollinger, and T. Roberts. 1999. "Pathogen Reduction Options in Slaughterhouses and Methods for Evaluating their Economic Effectiveness." <http://ageconsearch.umn.edu/bitstream/21562/1/sp99na04.pdf>.

Nelson, J. P., and P. E. Kennedy. 2009. "The Use (and Abuse) of Meta-Analysis in Environmental and Natural Resource Economics: An Assessment." *Environmental and Resource Economics* 42: 345–77.

—— and A. J. Krupnick. 2005. "Best Things First: Rethinking Priority Setting for Food Safety Policy." In S. A. Hoffmann and M. R. Taylor, eds, *Toward Safer Food: Perspectives on Risk and Priority Setting*. Washington, DC: Resources for the Future.

NRC (National Research Council). 1983. *Risk Assessment in the Federal Government: Managing the Process*. Washington, DC: National Academies Press.

—— 1993. *Pesticides in the Diets of Infants and Children: Committee on Pesticides in the Diets of Infants and Children, Board of Agriculture and Board of Environmental Studies and Toxicology, Commission on Life Sciences*. Washington, DC: National Academies Press.

—— 1998. *Ensuring Safe Food: From Production to Consumption*. Washington, DC: National Academies Press.

—— 2003. *Scientific Criteria to Ensure Safe Food*. Washington, DC: National Academies Press.

——— 2006. *Valuing Health for Regulatory Cost-Effectiveness Analysis.* Washington, DC: National Academies Press.

——— 2009. *Letter Report on the Review of the Food Safety and Inspection Service Proposed Risk-Based Approach to and Application of Public-Health Attribution Committee for Review of the Food Safety and Inspection Service Risk-Based Approach to Public-Health Attribution.* Washington, DC: National Academies Press.

——— 2010. *Enhancing Food Safety: The Role of the Food and Drug Administration.* Washington, DC: National Academies Press.

NZFSA (New Zealand Food Safety Authority). 2007. "About Us." <http://www.foodsafety.govt.nz/about>.

——— 2010. *New Zealand's Food Safety Risk Management Framework.* Wellington: NZFSA, Jan.

Onal, H., L. J. Unnevehr, and A. Bekric. 2000. "Regional Shifts in Pork Production: Implications for Regional Competition and Food Safety." *American Journal of Agricultural Economics* 82/4: 968–78.

Post, D. L. 2005. *Food Fights: Who Shapes International Food Safety Standards and Who Uses Them?* Berkeley: University of California Press.

Pouliot, S., and D. A. Sumner. 2008. "Traceability, Liability, and Incentives for Food Safety and Quality." *American Journal of Agricultural Economics* 90/1: 15–27.

Prusiner, S. 1991. "Molecular Biology of Prion Diseases." *Science* 252: 1515–22.

Rocourt, J., G. Moy, K. Vierk, and J. Schlundt. 2003. *The Present State of Foodborne Disease in OECD Countries.* Paris: OECD Publications.

Roosen, J., and D. Hennessy. 2001. "Capturing Experts' Uncertainty in Welfare Analysis: An Application to Organophosphate Use Regulation in U.S. Apple Production." *American Journal of Agricultural Economics* 83/1: 166–82.

Roth, A. V., A. A. Tsay, M. E. Pullman, and J. V. Gray. 2008. "Unraveling the Food Supply Chain: Strategic Insights from China and the 2007 Recalls." *Journal of Supply Chain Management* 44/1: 22–39.

Sanchirico, J. N., and J. E. Wilen. 2007. "Sustainable Use of Renewable Resources: Implications of Spatial-Dynamic Ecological and Economic Processes." *International Review of Environmental and Resource Economics* 1: 367–405.

Sands, R. D., T. Y. Jung, and S. Jo. 2002. "Second Generation Model for Korea." In H. Lee and T. Y. Jung, eds, *Energy and Environment Models for Korea.* PNNL-SA-33775. <http://www.globalchange.umd.edu/models/sgm>.

Scallan, E., P. Griffin, F. Angulo, R. Tauxe, and R. M. Hoekstra. 2011a. "Foodborne Illness Acquired in the United States: Unspecified Agents." *Emerging Infectious Diseases* 17/1: 16–22.

———, R. M. Hoekstra, R. Tauxe, M. Widdowson, S. Roy, J. Jones, and P. Griffin. 2011b. "Foodborne Illness Acquired in the United States: Major Pathogens." *Emerging Infectious Diseases* 17/1: 7–15.

Shogren, J. F., J. A. Fox, D. J. Hayes, and J. Roosen. 1999. "Observed Choices for Food Safety in Retail, Survey and Auction Markets." *American Journal of Agricultural Economics* 81/5: 1192–9.

Sinclair, U. 1906. *The Jungle.* New York: Doubleday, Jabber.

Slorach, S. A. 2008. "Food Safety Risk Management in New Zealand: A Review of the New Zealand Food Safety Authority's Risk Management Framework and its Application."

<http://www.foodsafety.govt.nz/elibrary/industry/Food_Safety-Nzfsa_Been.pdf> or <http://www.foodsafety.govt.nz/about/slorach-review>.

Smith, V. K. 1984. *Environmental Policy under Reagan's Executive Order: The Role of Benefit–Cost Analysis.* Chapel Hill: University of North Carolina Press.

Sundström, K., and H. Andersson. 2009. *Swedish Consumers' Willingness to Pay for Food Safety: A Contingent Valuation Study of Salmonella Risk.* SLI Working Paper No. 2009:2. Solna: Swedish National Road and Transport Research Institute.

UN CAC (United Nations, Codex Alimentarius Commission) 1997. *Hazard Analysis and Critical Control Point (HACCP) System and Guidelines for its Application.* Annex to CAC/RCP 1-1969, Rev. 3 (1997). Rome: WHO/FAO.

—— 1999. *Recommended International Code of Practice General Principles of Food Hygiene.* CAC/RCP 1-1969, Rev. 3 (1997), Amended 1999. Rome: WHO/FAO.

—— 2003. *Report of the Twenty-Sixth Session. Appendix IV: Working Principles for Risk Analysis for Application in the Framework of the Codex Alimentarius.* Rome: WHO/FAO.

—— 2007. *Working Principles for Risk Analysis for Application by National Governments: Codex Alimentarius Commission Procedural Manual,* 17th edn. Rome: WHO/FAO.

—— 2008. *2008 Codex Alimentarius Procedural Manual,* 17th edn. Rome: WHO/FAO.

Unnevehr, L., and H. Jensen. 2005. "Industry Costs to Make Food Safe: Now and under a Risk-Based System." In S. Hoffmann and M. Taylor, eds, *Toward Safer Food: Perspectives on Risk and Priority Setting.* Washington, DC: Resources for the Future.

——, M. J. Gomez, and P. Garcia. 1998. "The Incidence of Producer Welfare Losses from Food Safety Regulation in the Meat Industry." *Review of Agricultural Economics* 20/1: 186–201.

UN WHO (World Health Organization). 1997. *Food Safety and Globalization of Trade in Food: A Challenge to the Public Health Sector.* WHO/FSF/FOS 97.8 Rev. 1. Geneva: WHO.

—— 2002. *WHO Global Strategy for Food Safety.* Geneva: WHO.

—— 2008. *The Global Burden of Disease: 2004 Update.* Geneva: WHO.

UN WHO/FAO (World Health Organization/Food and Agriculture Organization). 2002. "Risk Assessments of *Salmonella* in Eggs and Broiler Chickens." <http://www.fao.org/DOCREP/005/Y4393E/Y4393E00.htm>.

—— 2004. "Risk Assessment of *Listeria monocytogenes* in Ready to Eat Foods." <http://www.fao.org/docrep/010/y5394e/y5394e00.htm>.

—— 2006. *Food Safety Risk Analysis: A Guide for National Food Safety Authorities.* FAO Food and Nutrition Paper No. 87. Rome: WHO/FAO.

US CDC (Centers for Disease Control and Prevention). 2009a. "FoodNet: Foodborne Diseases Active Surveillance Network." <http://www.cdc.gov/FoodNet>.

—— 2009b. "Investigation Update: Outbreak of *Salmonella* Typhimurium Infections, 2008–2009." <http://www.cdc.gov/salmonella/typhimurium/update.html>.

—— 2009c. "PulseNet." <http://www.cdc.gov/pulsenet>.

US Congress. 2011. FDA Food Safety Modernization Act. Public Law No. 111-353, 111th Congress, 124 Stat. 3885 (2011).

USDA FSIS (US Department of Agriculture Food Safety and Inspection Service). 1996. "Pathogen Reduction: Hazard Analysis and Critical Control Point (HACCP) Systems. Final Rule." *Federal Register* 61/144 (July 25), 38806–989.

—— 1998. "*Salmonella* Enteritidis Risk Assessment: Shell Eggs and Egg Products." <http://www.fsis.usda.gov/ophs/risk/index.htm>.

—— 2003. "Quantitative Assessment of Relative Risk to Public Health from Foodborne *Listeria monocytogenes* among Selected Categories of Ready-to-Eat Foods." <http://www.

fda.gov/downloads/food/scienceresearch/researchareas/riskassessmentsafetyassessment/ucm197330.pdf>.

——— 2008. "Public Health Based Inspection." <http://www.fsis.usda.gov/regulations/Public_Health_Based_Inspection/index.asp> (no longer available).

US EPA (Environmental Protection Agency). 1987. *Unfinished Business: A Comparative Assessment of Environmental Problems. Overview Report.* EPA No. 230287025a. <http://yosemite.epa.gov/water/owrccatalog.nsf/9da204a4b4406ef885256ae0007a79c7/d8555a5ca86d824a85256b06007256d1!OpenDocument>.

——— 2000. *Guidelines for Preparing Economic Analyses.* EPA No. 240-R-00-003. <http://yosemite.epa.gov/EE/epa/eed.nsf/webpages/Guidelines.html/$file/Guidelines.pdf>.

US FDA (US Food and Drug Administration). 1994. "Food Safety Assurance Program: Development of Hazard Analysis Critical Control Points. Proposed Rule." *Federal Register* 59/149 (Aug. 4), 39888.

——— 1995. "Procedures for the Safe and Sanitary Processing and Importing of Fish and Fishery Products. Final Rule." *Federal Register* 60/242 (Dec. 18), 65096–202.

——— 2001. "Hazard Analysis and Critical Control Point (HACCP): Procedures for the Safe and Sanitary Processing and Importing of Juice. Final Rule" *Federal Register* 66/13 (Jan. 19), 6138–202.

——— 2007. "Food Protection Plan and Import Safety Action Plan: Statement of David Acheson, Assistant Commissioner for Food Protection, Food and Drug Administration, before the Subcommittee on Oversight and Investigations, House Committee on Energy and Commerce." <http://www.fda.gov/NewsEvents/Testimony/ucm109636.htm>.

——— 2009a. "Guidance for Industry: Guide to Minimize Microbial Food Safety Hazards of Leafy Greens. Draft Guidance." <http://www.fda.gov/Food/GuidanceComplianceRegulatoryInformation/GuidanceDocuments/ProduceandPlanProducts/ucm174200.htm>.

——— 2009b. "Guidance for Industry: Guide to Minimize Microbial Food Safety Hazards of Melons. Draft Guidance." <http://www.fda.gov/Food/GuidanceComplianceRegulatoryInformation/GuidanceDocuments/ProduceandPlanProducts/ucm174171.htm>.

——— 2009c. "Guidance for Industry: Guide to Minimize Microbial Food Safety Hazards of Tomatoes. Draft Guidance." <http://www.fda.gov/Food/GuidanceComplianceRegulatoryInformation/GuidanceDocuments/ProduceandPlanProducts/ucm173902.htm>.

——— 2009d. "Quadrilateral Food Safety Group." <http://www.fda.gov/InternationalPrograms/FDABeyondOurBordersForeignOffices/QuadtilateralandTrilateral/Quadrilateral/default.htm>.

US FDA, Center for Food Safety and Nutrition. 2006. *Managing Food Safety: A Regulator's Manual for Applying HACCP Principles to Risk-Based Retail and Food Service Inspections and Evaluating Voluntary Food Safety Management Systems.* OMB Control No. 0910-0578. <http://www.fda.gov/downloads/Food/FoodSafety/RetailFoodProtection/ManagingFoodSafetyHACCPPrinciples/Regulators/UCM078159.pdf>.

US GAO (US Government Accountability Office). 2005. *Oversight of Food Safety Activities: Federal Agencies Should Pursue Opportunities to Reduce Overlap and Better Leverage Resources.* GAO-05-213. Washington, DC: GAO.

——— 2008. *Food Safety: Selected Countries. Systems Can Offer Insights into Ensuring Import Safety and Responding to Foodborne Illness.* GAO-08-794. Washington, DC: GAO.

——— 2011. *Federal Food Safety Oversight: Food Safety Working Group Is a Positive First Step but Governmentwide Planning Is Needed to Address Fragmentation.* GAOi-11-289. Washington, DC: GAO.

US Office of the President. 1993. Executive Order 12866. Code of Federal Regulation Vol. 3, Sec. 638 (1993), reprinted at US Code Vol. 5, Sec. 601.

US OMB (US Office of Management and Budget). 2003. *Regulatory Analysis*. Circular A-4. Washington, DC: OMB.

van der Meulen, B., and M. van der Velde. 2008. *European Food Law Handbook*. Wageningen: Wageningen Academic Publishers.

van Ravenswaay, E. O. 1995. "Valuing Food Safety and Nutrition: The Research Needs." In J. Caswell, ed., *Valuing Food Safety and Nutrition*. Boulder, CO: Westview Press.

Vos, E., and F. Wendler. 2006. *Food Safety Regulation in Europe: A Comparative Institutional Analysis*. Antwerp: Intersentia.

Wier, M., L. G. Hansen, L. M. Andersen, and K. Millock. 2002. "Consumer Preferences for Organic Foods." In OECD, *Organic Agriculture: Sustainability, Markets and Policies*. Wallingford: CABI.

Williams, R. A., and K. M. Thompson. 2004. "Integrated Analysis: Combining Risk and Economic Assessments while Preserving the Separation of Powers." *Risk Analysis* 24/6: 1613–23.

CHAPTER 22

....

POLICY EVALUATION AND BENEFIT–COST ANALYSIS

....

SEAN B. CASH[*]

1 INTRODUCTION

....

At its most basic, benefit–cost analysis (BCA) is an applied moral calculus, an attempt to evaluate the wisdom of a proposal through quantified reasoning. In some quarters, it is an approach that is deemed to be immoral owing to its insistence on (often) comparing monetized estimates of non-market social benefits with costs to taxpayers or producers. It is the conceit of the economist that such comparisons can and should be made nonetheless, and are meaningful for their ability to describe the trade-offs faced by both individuals and society. Moreover, attempts to quantify the non-market benefits of policies may be the best way to ensure that these benefits are not forgotten when contemplating a commitment of scare resources. In the context of policy decisions regarding food consumption, some of these benefits might include lives otherwise lost to contaminated food, the health benefits of improved nutrition, or concern for the welfare of food animals.

Zerbe and Bellas (2005: 1) contend that

> The purpose of BCA is not to monetize values, but rather to provide a ranking of choices in monetary terms. In the language of BCA, the market is a *metaphor* for a mechanism for determining value. Market values, in the language of the metaphor, need not represent "mere commodities" but instead represent choices. Choices, of course, exist outside of a commodity-type market. Goods that are not purchased with money may nevertheless be ranked in monetary terms.

* I should like to thank Laras Sekarasih and Tracy Phung for research assistance, and Elizabeth Chapkovsky for editorial assistance.

In my own teaching, I have "tricked" many skeptical undergraduates into revealing monetized lower bounds for the values they place on their best friends' lives. I first ask them whether they would sell their own appendages for 1, 5, or 10 million dollars (most, thankfully, say they would not), and then whether they would allow removal of those same appendages if doing so would save the lives of their best friends (most say they would). Yet even if we choose to interpret these estimates as having primarily ordinal rather than cardinal significance, the fact that the resulting number *can* be compared directly to fiscal constraints is both a practical opportunity for the decision maker and a moral concern to many. This is particularly poignant when the benefits may be in the form of averted mortalities and morbidities associated with improved food safety or nutrition.

The methods and theory behind BCA are well documented in a variety of excellent textbooks (e.g., Stokey and Zeckhauser 1978; Gramlich 1990; Boardman et al. 2005; Zerbe and Bellas 2005), and cannot be comprehensively covered in the space available here. Moreover, many of the measurement tools available to the analyst for estimation of welfare effects of food policies are explained in great detail in the first part of this volume, and the conceptual framework behind these measurements is described in detail by Just, Hueth, and Schmitz (1982, 2004), Freeman (2003), and others. In this chapter, I seek, instead, to summarize briefly the underlying conceptual framework of BCA, and then to comment on both the recent academic and regulatory practice of policy evaluation of food consumption policies.

2   KEY CONCEPTS IN BENEFIT–COST ANALYSIS

2.1   Decision Rules for Economic Analysis of Policies

Abraham Lincoln is often quoted for his concise expression of the underlying justification for BCA: "The true rule, in determining to embrace, or reject any thing, is not whether it have *any* evil in it; but whether it have more of evil, than of good" (Lincoln 1989: 192). Less familiar, but even more remarkable, is that Lincoln proffered this decision rule as part of an 1848 speech to the US House of Representatives in which he alludes to many of the concerns that occupy practitioners of BCA to this day. These include the distribution of benefits and costs, the distinction between positive and normative analysis, the prioritization of government projects in the face of pre-set budget constraints, the value of government investment in completing markets, and the disconnect between "statistical" valuations of projects and political valuations of the same, to name a few.

A good starting point for economic consideration of whether a policy should be accepted is the familiar concept of *Pareto optimality*, defined as a state in which it is impossible to make some individuals better off without making others worse off. More formally, "a feasible allocation $(x_1, \ldots, x_I, y_1, \ldots, y_J)$ is Pareto optimal (or Pareto efficient) if there is no other feasible allocation $(x'_1, \ldots, x'_I, y'_1, \ldots, y'_J)$ such that

$u_i(x'_i) \geq u_i(x_i)$ for all $i=1,\ldots,I$ and $u_i(x'_i) > u_i(x_i)$ for some i" (Mas Colell, Whinston, and Green 1995: 313). A simple and uncontroversial normative rule for policy evaluation is, therefore, one of accepting all *Pareto improvements*. That is to say, a policy is welfare-enhancing and should be adopted if somebody can be made better off without making others worse off.

The applicability of this *Pareto criterion* is obviously limited by the rarity of situations in which no parties are made worse off by a public program. The scope of this rule, however, broadens somewhat when we consider scenarios in which those who experience utility gains from a policy make side payments to the losers to compensate them for their losses. Gramlich (1990: 31) notes the 1974 Trade Readjustment Assistance Act, where assistance payments were made to industries harmed by the Act's tariff reductions, as an example of a program with explicit provisions for such compensation. In practice, however, the transaction costs involved in administering complex payment schemes may often be prohibitive, even in those cases when all losers could be fully compensated.

From a net welfare point of view, the applicability of the Pareto criterion can be broadened further by considering situations in which gains may be potentially realized through redistribution, regardless of whether such compensation payments are actually made. This *potential Pareto criterion* or *compensation principle* was noted in the same year in articles by Hicks (1939) and Kaldor (1939). It is commonly expressed as the *Kaldor–Hicks rule* that a program "has positive net benefits if the gainers *could* compensate the losers and still be better off" (Gramlich 1990: 32). (In actuality, this formulation is the test proposed by Kaldor; the Hicksian test asks instead if the losers could bribe the winners to forgo the benefits of a policy.) Subsequent criticisms have noted that this simple rule can be confounded by issues of reversibility (Scitovsky 1941) and intransitivity of rankings of second-best policies (Gorman 1955, summarized adeptly in Just, Hueth, and Schmitz 1982: 37–40).

When the value of these gains and losses are measurable (in monetary or other terms), a universally satisfactory redistribution is theoretically possible whenever the net gains are positive. We can therefore restate the Kaldor–Hicks rule as a *simple benefit–cost criterion*: If the benefits of a project are greater than the costs, we should support that project. When faced with several possible projects, we can apply what Stokey and Zeckhauser (1978: 137) call the *fundamental rule* of BCA: "In any choice situation, select the alternative that produces the greatest net benefit." As extensions, they note that the appropriate scale of any project is the scale that maximizes net benefits, and that when faced with multiple projects that may be adopted and a budget constraint, we should adopt the combination that maximizes the net social benefits subject to that constraint. These rules imply an equimarginal solution to the question of how much government intervention is ideal: "regulate until the incremental benefits from regulation are just offset by the incremental costs" (Arrow et al. 1996: 221).

The focus on potential compensation criteria in BCA is appealing to practitioners, in part, because it allows for the evaluation of policies to proceed even in the absence of clear guidelines about how the gains and losses *should* be distributed in society.

Efficiency requires only that the social welfare pie be as large as possible, regardless of who gets a slice. Moreover, as long as redistribution is possible, it would appear to be immoral to choose policies that do not maximize the amount of pie available to society. In reality, distributive consequences are of great political and social import. Accordingly, much has been written on both who should have standing in BCA and how distributional weights can be incorporated to bring equity concerns into BCA (see Stokey and Zeckhauser 1978: 155–8 and Zerbe and Bellas 2005: 40–60 for examples). An alternative approach suggested by Bergstrom (n.d.) is that perhaps BCA should be considered only as a first step in a policy analysis; passing a potential compensation test tells us that "*some* increase in the amount of the public good is potentially Pareto improving" (n.d.: 5). A second step would then be to assess whether the distributive consequences of the policy are acceptable and in line with other social goals. Bergstrom goes on to note that when a policy fails to meet a benefit–cost test, there is no way to allocate project costs in a Pareto-improving manner. "The project can be reasonably described as "special interest legislation." To make a case in favor of a project that fails the test, one would need to argue that implementing this project . . . is likely to achieve redistributive goals that for some reason could not be more efficiently achieved through redistribution of private goods" (n.d.: 6).

2.2   A Non-Normative Role for Benefit–Cost Analysis?

There are many criticisms of BCA as a normative framework for decision-making. First and foremost is the widespread distaste of valuing non-market outcomes in monetary terms. Monetizing the value of goods such as health and environmental protection is frequently criticized as "commodification" of rights or nature, and creating markets for bads such as pollution or health risks has been likened to the selling of indulgences (Goodin 1994). Other concerns with BCA are that it does not require consideration of distributional effects or the influence that wealth has on estimates of welfare measures (Zerbe and Bellas 2005); it does not explicitly include morality as a value or constraint (Nussbaum 2000); its reliance on both price measurement and discounting techniques that are prone to error (Chichilnisky 1997); its failure to incorporate new information to refashion the stated goals of a policy proposal (Richardson 2000); concerns that the institutional incentives of regulatory agencies may lead to biased analyses; and that precautionary approaches to regulation should take precedence over those that seek to maximize expected net present value. A growing literature within economics has also critiqued the behavioral foundations of willingness-to-pay estimates (e.g., Bernheim and Rangel 2009; Sugden 2009).

Perhaps the clearest response to all of these criticisms is Gramlich's (1990: 5) contention that "Benefit cost analysis is a framework for organizing thoughts, or considerations: nothing more and nothing less." Stokey and Zeckhauser (1978: 136) describe this framework as consisting of five steps:

1. The project or projects to be analyzed are identified.
2. All the impacts, both favorable and unfavorable, present and future, on all of society are determined.
3. Values, usually in dollars, are assigned to these impacts. Favorable impacts will be registered as benefits, unfavorable ones as costs.
4. The *net benefit* (total benefit minus total cost) is calculated.
5. The choice is made.

Considerable insight into the nature of a policy decision can be gathered through a rigorous application of the first four steps, even if we are not willing to dismiss the criticisms noted above. If we do not prescribe a decision rule (such as positive net benefits) for the fifth step, we may instead choose to focus on an informative, rather than a normative, role for BCA. Arrow et al. (1996) echo this approach when they laid out their eight principles of BCA, in which they support mandatory BCA for all major regulatory decisions, yet also argue that "agencies should not be bound by strict benefit–cost tests" and that "formal benefit–cost analysis should not be viewed as either necessary or sufficient for designing sensible policy" (1996: 222).

2.3   The Measurement of Benefits and Costs

Dupuit (1844) is generally credited with first expressing the welfare-theoretic content of a demand curve in his article considering the optimum toll for a bridge. He defined as "relative utility" what later came to be known as Marshallian consumer surplus (CS), the area under the (uncompensated) demand curve and above the price. This can be interpreted as a monetized welfare measure in that it represents the maximum willingness to pay (WTP) for a good or service. Measuring the impact of price changes with Marshallian consumer surplus yields inexact welfare measures, however, in that CS does not take into account wealth effects. For exact measures, equivalent variation (EV), giving the monetary equivalent of a price change when utility is held constant, or compensating variation (CV), which corresponds to the income change necessary to compensate for a utility change, should be used.[1] This concern may not be of great practical importance. CS measures lie in between CV and EV measures. Willig (1976) derived statements of the error bounds and showed that the differences between these measures are generally small if not trivial, and will usually be smaller than the errors caused by econometric estimation of the demand functions used in a welfare analysis.

The first eleven chapters of this volume meticulously outline much of the theory and methods behind empirical estimation of consumers' WTP and willingness to accept in both market and non-market settings. In most applications, these measures would

---

[1] EV and CV measures are formally defined in most microeconomic theory textbooks. Treatments particularly relevant for BCA practitioners can be found in Freeman (2003) and Just, Hueth, and Schmitz (2003).

primarily capture the benefits of food consumption policies. Antle (2001) describes three empirical approaches to cost estimation in the specific context of food safety policies, where costs are overwhelmingly born by firms: the accounting approach, the economic engineering approach, and the econometric approach. In the accounting approach, data from small-scale studies or surveys of plants are used to construct estimates of compliance costs, such as increased labor costs or new capital requirements, without parametric estimation of an overall cost function for the facilities in question. Antle notes that this was the approach used by the Food and Drug Administration (FDA) and the Food Safety Inspection Service in preparing the regulatory impact assessments for mandatory hazard analysis and critical control points (HACCP) regulations in the mid-1990s. In the economic engineering approach, "detailed engineering data are combined with data on input costs to construct a quantitative model of the production process" (Antle 2001: 1125), which in turn is used to create an empirical cost function. Both of these methods are subject to the concern that they may not reflect the costs imposed across an industry if only a few (inadequately) "representative" firms are used to inform the models. In contrast, the econometric approach generally sacrifices the level of process detail that can be captured with the other two methods. It can, however, more readily account for firm heterogeneity by constructing cost estimates from more representative data sets, such as the Census of Manufacturers.

An important issue in aggregating partial benefits and costs estimates to calculate the net benefits of a policy proposal is that these benefits and costs generally accrue at different times. The choice of a discount rate for calculation of net present values can be very controversial when costs and benefits are not temporally coincident, as the sign of the net discounted benefits can easily be dependent on small variations in discount rate. For this reason, Arrow et al. (1996) advocate for a core set of assumptions, including the choice of a common range of discount rates to be considered, to be adopted for general policy analysis use and enhanced comparability. This also reduces the opportunity for unscrupulous analysts to cherry-pick assumptions that will yield desired prescriptions from BCA. Arrow et al. (1996) also claim that the social discount rate should not generally be the same as the rate of return on private investment, but should instead reflect "how individuals trade off current for future consumption" (1996: 222). For detailed discussion of the choice of discount rate in welfare measurement and BCA, see Nas (1996: 131–145), Freeman (2003), and Just, Hueth, and Schmitz (2004), among others.

2.4 Alternatives to Benefit–Cost Analysis

Given both the criticism of BCA noted above and the difficulties in implementing BCA in certain contexts, several alternatives have emerged. These alternatives primarily differ in the level of standardization of the outcome metric. One common variant of BCA is the partial benefit–cost analysis, which explicitly leaves some otherwise notable benefits or costs unmeasured. For example, when conducting its BCA of mandating inclusion of trans fats in nutrition labels on packaged goods, the FDA excluded "chips, microwave popcorn, and candy" from its estimation of the health benefits of likely reformulations. The agency defended this exclusion by explaining, "these products contribute a smaller proportion of trans fat intake and . . . FDA did not have enough information to make quantitative reformulation estimates for these product categories" (US FDA 2003: 41473). Even with this omission, the FDA found that the benefits greatly outweighed the costs of the proposed regulations; inclusion of these additional benefits would have presumably only increased the net benefit calculation.

Another alternative is cost-effectiveness analysis (CEA), which has become the standard for the economic evaluation of health care (Kenkel 1997). Cost-effectiveness analysis allows for comparison of policies or approaches without estimation of the benefits, and instead seeks to identify the lowest-cost means of achieving a predetermined target. This may be particularly useful when outcome goals have been set a priori outside of the BCA framework (for example, when risk tolerances are set by scientific or political standards) or when estimating the value of benefits is particularly difficult or distasteful. In health care and food safety applications, this can be particularly appealing because it allows the analyst to avoid measuring the monetary value of mortalities and morbidities. The trade-off, however, is that CEAs do not provide the analyst with any insight into whether the considered options enhance the social welfare. CEA also does not allow for consideration of qualitative differences among different levels of the targeted benefit.

Cost utility analysis (CUA) is similar to CEA in that no monetary benefit values are used, but it does allow for differences in outcome quality. The goal of a CUA is to calculate the ratio of costs to benefits, and to compare these ratios across options, but here benefits are not measured in monetary terms. In many applications, these utilities are measured instead as Quality-Adjusted Life Years (QALYs), a measure calculated as life expectancy times a health-utility index ranging from 1 (completely healthy) to 0 (death). QALYs are used commonly in health care evaluation studies, but have been used in the food safety literature as well (e.g., Mangen et al. 2007; Guevel et al. 2008). In a similar vein, several recent studies have used body weight measures to investigate the potential benefits of food pricing policies (e.g., Powell et al. 2007; Schroeter, Lusk, and Tyner 2008; see Etilé, Chapter 29 in this volume, for additional detail).

Another type of analysis is multi-criteria analysis (MCA), in which there is deliberately no attempt to express policy effects into a single unit of measure. A recent example of an MCA system is the Multi-Factorial Risk Prioritization Framework proposed by Ruzante et al. (2010). In their framework, there are four factors that are to be considered in evaluating and ranking a potential risk management decision for foodborne pathogens. The first factor is the central public health impact, measured using Disability-Adjusted Life Years (DALYs) and cost of illnesses. The second factor is consumer perception of the risk, measured in Likert-type scales. Market-level impacts and social sensitivity are also considered. The latter captures potential social preference for protecting certain classes of consumer, such as children.

3   The Practice of Benefit–Cost Analysis of Food Policies in the United States

Outside of the area of transportation planning, national requirements for widespread application of BCA are rare. A notable exception is the requirement for Regulatory Impact Analyses (RIAs) for all proposed major regulations in the United States. This section summarizes the practice of BCA as mandated for these reviews, and then briefly highlights two recent examples of BCAs conducted for US food policies.

3.1   Regulatory Review Requirements in the United States

Under Executive Orders 12291 (Reagan 1981) and 12866 (Clinton 1993), all agencies must prepare economic analyses to show "whether a regulation's benefits were likely to exceed its costs and whether alternatives to that regulation would be more effective or less costly" (Hahn and Dudley 2007). An inter-agency economic peer review process is available for agencies to receive input on their draft RIAs from economists elsewhere in government (USFDA 2003). The RIAs are then reviewed by the Office of Information and Regulatory Affairs (OIRA) at the Office of Management and Budget (OMB), which must approve all major regulations prior to their publication in the Federal Register and enactment. Summaries of these RIAs are often published in the Federal Register as part of the final rule notices.

In this context, "major" regulations would generally include many proposed food-related agency actions, which would fall under the current order's scope of (among others) those with over $100 million in expected economic impacts, those that adversely affect "the economy, productivity, competition, jobs, the environment, public health or safety, or State, local, or tribal governments or communities," and those that impact the budgets of entitlement programs recipients (Clinton 1993). OIRA clearance decisions can only be overturned by agency appeal to the OMB director or the President (Graham 2007). In addition, Congress has since required that OMB produce reports on the costs and benefits of federal regulation (Hahn and Dudley 2007).

OMB also provides formal guidance on how BCAs are to be conducted for regulatory analysis. Circular A-4 lays out the principles and best practices to be used, including specific guidance on establishing scope and baselines, evaluating alternatives, ensuring the transparency and reproducibility of results, estimation of benefits and costs, and the measurement of health and safety benefits (OMB 2003). With regard to the latter, the guidelines specifically request that health and safety rule-makings are evaluated with both CEA and BCA, i.e., that health risks and benefits must be monetized (2003: 28). The handling of discount rates is specified in OMB Circular A-94, which specifies a base case discount rate for BCAs of 7 percent (OMB 1992, as revised). Market discount rates for use in CEAs and lease purchase calculations are updated annually in an appendix.

The primary responsibility for conducting BCAs for regulatory review lies with the regulating agencies themselves. The principal agencies responsible for food consumption policies in the United States are the US Department of Agriculture (USDA) and the FDA. USDA has responsibility for food assistance programs, food safety standards and inspection, labeling of certain products, nutrition education and promotion, and agricultural production and promotion programs. The FDA, as part of the US Department of Health and Human Services, regulates the composition and labeling of packaged foods, including nutrition labeling requirements and health claims. The US Environmental Protection Agency (EPA) also has jurisdiction over food production issues with potential direct impact on consumers, such as pesticide use and genetically modified products, as well as indirect market effects influencing the price and availability of products.

At USDA, the Office of Risk Assessment and Cost–Benefit Analysis (ORACBA), under the Office of the Chief Economist, oversees the RIAs required for the regulatory review process. BCAs for RIA or internal purposes may be conducted by ORACBA staff, by analysts elsewhere in the Agency, such as in the Economic Research Service or program-specific offices, or by contracted researchers outside the Agency. In the FDA, the economics staff in the Office of Planning is in charge of regulatory review. Both agencies have their own internal guidance documents for preparing RIAs, in addition to the OMB guidelines noted above.

How good of a job do US federal agencies do in conducting BCA? Hahn and Dudley (2007) note that since the US government has been requiring some form of BCA and review for all major regulatory actions since 1981, there are ample data available to assess the quality of these analyses empirically. They focus on seventy-four RIAs conducted by the EPA between 1982 and 1999, and use a score card method based on the government's standards for economic analysis outlined in the executive orders and OMB guidelines noted above. Although they focus solely on one agency, they note that EPA is the major player in this area, accounting for more than half of both the available RIAs and the total costs of regulation (Hahn 2000). They find that the overall quality of these studies is generally low, without notable differences across the presidential administrations studied. They also identify both common methodological and presentation deficiencies in the reports, such as failure to calculate net benefits, and failure to summarize monetized benefits in executive summaries.

3.2   Recent Examples of Economic Evaluation of Food Consumption Policies

Within the limited literature discussing BCA of domestic food policies, most of the focus has been on the analysis of food safety policies such as beef irradiation and mandatory HACCP regulation. The methods and practice of economic analysis of food safety policies are nicely described in Antle (2001), and many of the legal, policy, and economic aspects of ensuring a safe food supply are covered in Hoffman and Taylor (2005). There has also been considerable policy attention to ways of influencing health outcomes by altering the behavior of food consumers with labels, price interventions, and education campaigns (some of these approaches are described in Chapter 20 in this volume, by Drichoutis, Nayga, and Lazaridis, and Chapter 29, by Etilé). In general, these attempts at influencing consumer behavior have not often been investigated through the lens of formal BCA; indeed, formal economic analysis of public health initiatives of any sort are rare (Dollahite, Kenkel, and Thompson 2008). Two recent examples of such analyses are the FDA's study of the benefits and costs of trans fat labeling of foods, and recent studies of the benefits of Expanded Food and Nutrition Education Programs.

3.2.1 Regulatory Impact Analysis of Trans Fat Labeling

On July 11, 2003, the FDA published its final rule requiring that trans fatty acids be included on a separate line in the nutritional label on packaged foods and dietary supplements (US FDA 2003). These requirements went into effect on January 1, 2006, and provide US consumers with a readily accessible tool to assess their food options on the basis of a macronutrient strongly linked to risks of coronary heart disease and diabetes. The rule publication included the final RIA. The costs quantified in the analysis included the total testing, relabeling, and reformulation costs for the estimated 154,400 product categories to be affected by the regulation, with relabeling costs being the most expensive of these three impacts. The total cost of the regulation was estimated to be between $139 million and $275 million, with a medium cost estimate of $185 million. To estimate the benefits of the proposed regulation, the analysts had to model both the likely changes in trans fat intake and the resulting changes in health states. The FDA concluded that its final trans fat labeling rule for packaged foods would save between 240 to 480 deaths per year. They used monetary values of both the extension of longevity and the savings in medical costs associated with reductions in non-fatal cases of coronary heart disease to estimate the value of these health benefits over twenty years, using a variety of estimates for the value of a statistical life year saved. When calculated with a 3 percent discount rate and a $300,000 value of a statistical life year saved, these benefits are estimated to total over $13 billion, indicating strong net welfare gains from the labeling requirement. When interpreted as a CEA, these estimates suggest a cost per life year saved of approximately $4,500.

The regulatory review process is generally seen as posing barriers to health regulation through its requirement of OMB approval of major rules, but Graham (2007) provides a compelling counter-example. He describes how the OMB, under his leadership in the OIRA, helped bring the trans fat labeling rule into being. Economists (and others) within the FDA believed that the new label requirement would help consumers overcome informational obstacles, and would encourage healthful reformulations of many products contributing to dietary health risks. The regulatory effort in the FDA had first started under the Clinton administration, but in 2001 had stalled; OMB staff members were aware of this initiative and felt it might have merit. This situation led the OMB to develop "a tool which we called the 'prompt letter.' It was intended to be a polite nudge—a suggestion that an agency give priority to a matter, or alternatively, explain to the OMB in a public reply letter why it should not be a priority" (Graham 2007: 174). The FDA responded to the prompt letter by finishing the rule-making process. Graham explains this intervention by noting that the OMB's role should not be defined by advocating against regulation, but rather "to advance the cause of 'smart regulation,' which sometimes will lead to more rather than less regulation" (Graham 2007: 174–5).

3.2.2   Expanded Food and Nutrition Education Programs

The US federal government has been funding Expanded Food and Nutrition Education Program (EFNEP) initiatives since 1969. These programs target low-income families and have been shown to yield improvements in diet, food shopping and preparation, and nutrition knowledge (Joy, Pradhan, and Goldman 2006). Economic evaluations of these programs have been conducted in several states including Iowa (Wessman, Betterley, and Jensen 2000), California (Joy, Pradhan, and Goldman 2006), Tennessee (Burney and Houghton 2002), Oregon (Schuster et al. 2003), Virginia (Rajgopal et al. 2002), and New York (Dollahite, Kenkel, and Thompson 2008). All of these analyses have shown positive net benefits. The New York study followed all 5,730 adult graduates of that state's EFNEP program in fiscal year 2000. The costs estimated included the direct program costs, including staff, facilities, and equipment, and indirect costs, including the opportunity cost of participants' time and an estimate of the marginal excess burden of the taxes raised to finance the program. These costs came out to an average of $849 per graduate, of which $715 were direct costs. The benefits were calculated by measuring self-reported food and nutrition behaviors before and after participation in the education program, and then using pre-existing estimates to relate these behaviors to differences in disease incidence, including heart disease, stroke, hypertension, and foodborne illness. Outcomes were measured both as QALYs and in monetary terms. The cost-effectiveness was estimated to be $20,863/QALY, and the societal benefits were estimated to be $9.58 for every $1 spent.

These economic studies of EFNEP consistently show that the benefit of consumer education exceeded the cost of conducting the program, and illustrate the potential for other food education interventions. While having a preponderance of supportive economic analyses is reassuring, there are few instances in which policymakers have the luxury of such an evidence base, especially for food-related policies. It is perhaps worthwhile to reflect on why at least six formal evaluations of these programs exist. One aspect is certainly the methodological tractability. The format of an education intervention, where most costs are directly observable and participant testing can form the basis of outcome evaluation and benefit estimation, is certainly conducive to constructing defensible BCAs. It should also be noted that these studies were conducted by academic researchers who were presumably faced with incentives compatible with stakeholders' desires to have this sort of evaluation. In each case, there was funding available to support the research, and five of the six studies were published in peer-reviewed journals (albeit not in economics journals).

4   CONCLUSION: THE ACADEMIC (NON-) PRACTICE OF BENEFIT—COST ANALYSIS

The volume of evidence regarding EFNEP raises the question of whether conducting another study of that particular program would pass a BCA test itself. What is the optimal amount of BCA? There is a huge disconnect between the role that many economists wish formal economic analysis would take in public decision-making, and its status in peer-reviewed applied economic work. A search of *EconLit* suggests that only seven food-related articles with "benefit–cost analysis" (or "cost–benefit analysis") in the title have ever been published in the peer-reviewed journals indexed there. Indeed, the average number of peer-reviewed economics journal articles that refer to BCA in the title has been about one dozen per year over the past forty years (*Econlit* 2009). The publication of economic analyses by academics seems to find a home in applied health science journals, but not in the journals that are most important to a broader economic audience. If economists like BCA so much, why do we not conduct it more often?

Of course, at least part of this concern is no different from the bias toward methodological or theoretical innovation that pervades much of economic science. Yet we publish thousands of studies on policy effects each year. If BCA is first and foremost a "framework for organizing thoughts" that most economists agree can help achieve efficiency goals, why do we not adopt that framework more often in interpreting our own work? Relatively few academic studies that seek to estimate, for example, non-market benefits of a novel food attribute then go the next step to trying to fit the available evidence into a formal social welfare analysis framework. Doing so may be challenging and time-consuming to the researcher, but I suspect it would pass a potential compensation test with flying colors.

REFERENCES

Antle, J. M. 2001. "Economic Analysis of Food Safety." In B. Gardner and G. Rausser, eds, *Handbook of Agricultural Economics*, 1. Amsterdam: Elsevier Science.

Arrow, K. J., M. L. Cropper, G. C. Eads, R. W. Hahn, L. B. Lave, R. G. Noll, P. R. Portney, M. Russell, R. Schmalensee, V. K. Smith, and R. N. Stavins. 1996. "Is There a Role for Benefit–Cost Analysis in Environmental, Health, and Safety Regulation?" *Science* 272: 221–2.

Bergstrom, T. n.d. "Benefit–Cost Analysis." In Bergstrom, *Economics 230B: Theory of Public Goods and Externalities.* ⟨http://econ.ucsb.edu/~tedb/Courses/UCSBpf/econ230b.html⟩.

Bernheim, B. D., and A. Rangel. 2009. "Beyond Revealed Preference: Choice Theoretic Foundations for Behavioral Welfare Economics." *Quarterly Journal of Economics* 124: 51–104.

Boardman, A., D. Greenberg, A. Vining, and D. Weimer. 2005. *Cost Benefit Analysis: Concepts and Practice*, 3rd edn. Englewood Cliffs, NJ: Prentice-Hall.

Burney, J., and B. Houghton. 2002. "A Nutrition Education Program that Demonstrates Cost–Benefit." *Journal of the American Dietetic Association* 102: 39–45.

Chichilnisky, G. 1997. "The Costs and Benefits of Benefit–Cost Analysis." *Environment and Development Economics* 2: 202–5.

Clinton, W. J. 1993. Executive Order 12866. "Regulatory Planning and Review." *Federal Register* 58/190 (Oct. 4, 1993), as amended by EO 13258, *Federal Register* 67/40 (Feb. 28, 2002), and EO 13422, *Federal Register* 72/14 (Jan. 23, 2007).

Dollahite, J., D. Kenkel, and C. S. Thompson. 2008. "An Economic Evaluation of the Expanded Food and Nutrition Education Program." *Journal of Nutrition Education and Behavior* 40/3: 134–43.

Dupuit, J. 1844. "De la mesure de l'utilité des travaux publics." *Annales de Ponts et Chaussées*, 2nd ser., 8. Trans. as "On the Measurement of Utility of Public Works." *International Economic Papers* 2 (1952), 83–110. Trans. repr. in K. J. Arrow and T. Scitovsky, *Readings in Welfare Economics*. Homewood, IL: Richard D. Irwin, 1969.

EconLit. 2009. Ipswich, MA: EBSCO.

Freeman, A. M., III. 2003. *The Measurement of Environmental and Resource Values:Theory and Methods*, 2nd edn. Washington, DC: Resources for the Future.

Goodin, R. E. 1994. "Selling Environmental Indulgences." *Kyklos* 47/4: 573–96.

Gorman, W. M. 1955. "The Intransitivity of Certain Criteria Used in Welfare Economics." *Oxford Economic Papers*, new ser., 7/1: 25–35.

Graham, J. D. 2007. "The Evolving Regulatory Role of the U.S. Office of Management and Budget." *Review of Environmental Economics and Policy* 1/2: 171–91.

Gramlich, E. M. 1990. *A Guide to Benefit–Cost Analysis*, 2nd edn. Englewood Cliffs, NJ: Prentice-Hall.

Guevel, M. R., V. Sirot, J. L. Volatier, and J. C. Leblanc. 2008. "A Risk–Benefit Analysis of French High Fish Consumption: A QALY Approach." *Risk Analysis* 28/1: 37–48.

Hahn, R. W. 2000. *Reviving Regulatory Reform: A Global Perspective.* Washington, DC: AEI–Brookings Joint Center for Regulatory Studies.

——and P. M. Dudley. 2007. "How Well Does the U.S. Government Do Benefit–Cost Analysis?" *Review of Environmental Economics and Policy* 1/2: 192–211.

Hicks, J. R. 1939. "The Foundations of Welfare Economics." *Economic Journal* 49/196: 696–712.

Hoffman, S., and M. R. Taylor. 2005. *Toward Safer Food: Perspectives on Risk and Priority Setting.* Washington, DC: Resources for the Future.

Joy, A. B., V. Pradhan, and G. Goldman. 2006. "Cost–Benefit Analysis Conducted for Nutrition Education in California." *California Agriculture* 60/4: 185–91.

Just, R. E., D. L. Hueth, and A. Schmitz. 1982. *Applied Welfare Economics and Public Policy.* Englewood Cliffs, NJ: Prentice-Hall.

Just, R. E., D. L. Hueth, and A. Schmitz. 2004. *The Welfare Economics of Public Policy: A Practical Approach to Project and Policy Evaluation.* Cheltenham: Edward Elgar.

Kaldor, N. 1939. "Welfare Propositions of Economics and Interpersonal Comparisons of Uility." *Economic Journal* 49/195: 549–52.

Kenkel, D. 1997. "On Valuing Morbidity, Cost-Effectiveness Analysis, and Being Rude." *Journal of Health Economics* 16: 749–57.

Lincoln, A. 1989. *Speeches and Writings 1832–1858*, ed. D. E. Fehrenbacher. New York: Library of America.

Mangen, M. J., A. H. Havelaar, K. P. Poppe, and G. A. de Wit. 2007. "Cost–Utility Analysis to Control Campylobacter on Chicken Meat: Dealing with Data Limitations." *Risk Analysis* 27/4: 815–30.

Mas-Colell, A., M. D. Whinston, and J. R. Green. 1995. *Microeconomic Theory*. Oxford: Oxford University Press.

Nas, T. F. 1996. *Cost–Benefit Analysis: Theory and Application*. Thousand Oaks, CA: Sage.

Nussbaum, M. C. 2000. "The Costs of Tragedy: Some Moral Limits of Cost–Benefit Analysis." *Journal of Legal Studies* 29: 1005–36.

OMB (Office of Management and Budget). 1992. *Guidelines and Discount Rates for Benefit–Cost Analysis of Federal Programs*. Circular A-94. Washington, DC: OMB.

—— 2003. *Regulatory Analysis*. Circular A-4. Washington, DC: OMB.

Powell, L. M., M. C. Auld, F. J. Chaloupka, L. D. Johnston, and P. O'Malley. 2007. "Access to Fast Food and Food Prices: The Relationship with Fruit and Vegetable Consumption and Overweight Status among Adolescents." In K. Bolin and J. Cawley, eds, *Advances in Health Economics and Health Services Research*, 17: *The Economics of Obesity*. London: Elsevier.

Rajgopal, R., R. H. Cox, M. Lamburg, and E. C. Lewis. 2002. "Cost–Benefit Analysis Indicated the Positive Economic Benefits of the Expanded Food and Nutrition Education Program Related to Chronic Disease Prevention." *Journal of Nutrition Education and Behavior* 34: 26–37.

Reagan, R. 1981. Executive Order 12291: Federal Regulation. Public Papers of the Presidents. Washington, DC: General Printing Office.

Richardson, H. S. 2000. "The Stupidity of the Cost–Benefit Standard." *Journal of Legal Studies* 29: 971–1003.

Ruzante, J. M., V. J. Davidson, J. Caswell, A. Fazil, J. A. L. Cranfield, S. J. Henson, S. M. Anders, C. Schmidt, and J. M. Farber. 2010. "A Multifactorial Risk Prioritization Framework for Foodborne Pathogens." *Risk Analysis* 30: 724–42.

Schroeter, C., J. Lusk, and W. Tyner. 2008. "Determining the Impact of Food Price and Income Changes on Body Weight." *Journal of Health Economics* 27/1: 45–68.

Schuster, E., Z. L. Zimmerman, M. Engle, J. Smiley, E. Syversen, and J. Murray. 2003. "Investing in Oregon's Expanded Food and Nutrition Education Program (EFNEP): Documenting Costs and Benefits." *Journal of Nutrition Education and Behavior* 35/4: 200–6.

Scitovsky, T. 1941. "A Note on Welfare Propositions in Economics." *Review of Economic Studies* 9/1: 77–88.

Stokey, E., and R. Zeckhauser. 1978. *A Primer for Policy Analysis*. New York: W. W. Norton.

Sugden, R. 2009. "Market Simulation and the Provision of Public Goods: A Non-Paternalistic Response to Anomalies in Environmental Evaluation." *Journal of Environmental Economics and Management* 57: 87–103.

US FDA (United States Food and Drug Administration). 2003. "Food Labeling; Trans Fatty Acids in Nutrition Labeling; Consumer Research to Consider Nutrient Content and Health

Claims and Possible Footnote or Disclosure Statements. Final Rule and Proposed Rule." *Federal Register* 68/133 (July 11), 41433–506.

Wessman, C., C. Betterley, and H. Jensen. 2000. "An Evaluation of the Cost and Benefit of Iowa's Expanded Food and Nutrition Education Program (EFNEP): Final Report No. PM 1865. Ames: Iowa State University Extension.

Willig, R. D. 1976. "Consumer's Surplus without Apology." *American Economic Review* 66/4: 589–97.

Zerbe, R. O., and A. S. Bellas. 2005. *A Primer for Benefit–Cost Analysis*. Cheltenham: Edward Elgar.

PART III

TOPICS AND APPLICATIONS

CHAPTER 23

....

GLOBALIZATION AND TRENDS IN WORLD FOOD CONSUMPTION

....

JACINTO F. FABIOSA

A close examination of global food consumption trends from studies on food consumption over a long period of time and over a wide range of spatial coverage uncovers clear emerging patterns. The first pattern is in the "trading-up" consumption adjustment as consumers increase their income levels. That is, regardless of location, starting from a consumption basket that is primarily dominated by carbohydrate-rich staple grains such as rice or wheat, consumers increase their share of high-value animal-protein-rich meat and dairy products as their incomes rise. Second, their consumption shifts more toward convenience and variety expressed in the increase in the consumption share of food products with higher processed content such as ready-to-eat foods and/or an increase in away-from-home food consumption. Finally, consumers focus on specific product characteristics that are not traditionally considered as embodied in the food they consume. These include product characteristics such as food safety, impact on the environment, animal welfare, producer welfare, and a host of other considerations.

The second pattern is in the "convergence" consumption. That is, driven by higher income, the consumption pattern in low- to middle-income countries catches up or converges with the consumption pattern of high-income countries. This process is aided by general standardization of products moving within the value chain, and is further facilitated by the development of similar marketing and retail distribution systems across many countries. These systems are dominated by supermarkets and multinational hypermarkets that can put into place coordination mechanisms and incentive structures to deliver more sophisticated products in response to the specifications of consumers, on the one hand, but require adequate product volume movement to be profitable, on the other.[1]

The trading-up phenomenon and the convergence phenomenon are detailed in the rest of this chapter. First, the fundamental forces that drive the development of these patterns are identified. Second, specific country examples of these phenomena are given. Finally, some of the implications of this emerging consumption trend are explored, for example, resource requirements for production as well as health and other well-being outcomes.

1   THE EMERGING COMMON CONSUMPTION PATTERN AND THE TRADING-UP PHENOMENON

Let us start by first describing a big-picture landscape of food consumption in the world by reviewing the per capita consumption pattern of major agricultural commodities by country. To do this, we use consumption data published by the Food and Agricultural Policy Research Institute (FAPRI). Consumption is aggregated at the commodity level. For example, consumption of all wheat products (e.g., wheat flour) is aggregated and expressed in wheat grain equivalent. Also, consumption of all meat products (e.g., fresh beef, processed beef) is aggregated and expressed in carcass weight equivalent.

FAPRI maintains large econometric models covering major producing, consuming, and trading countries and regularly conducts an outlook of the world agricultural market including food consumption of major commodities projected over a ten-year period. For our own illustrative purposes, we select to report the per capita consumption of major feed grains including rice and wheat, major meat products including beef, pork, and poultry, and major vegetable oils including soybean oil, rapeseed oil, and sunflower oil. The data clearly show some strong regional consumption preferences for some commodities, while for other commodities it is more mixed. For example, as shown in Table 23.1, rice consumption is preferred mostly in Asia, with Myanmar and Vietnam posting the highest per capita rice consumption at 219 and 220 kilograms per person on average in the last five years. Some countries in Africa (e.g., Egypt, 43, Nigeria, 33, and Ivory Coast, 76 kg), South America (e.g., Brazil, 44, and Uruguay, 29 kg), and the Middle East (e.g., Iran, 48, and Iraq, 42 kg) also report modest per capita rice consumption. In contrast, rice is not popularly consumed in North America, with Mexico (7 kg), Canada (11 kg), and the United States (13 kg) having the lowest per capita

---

[1] The subject matter of this chapter closely shares common themes with the literature nutrition transition that refers to dietary and physical-activity changes and its accompanying nutritional-physical outcomes.

Table 23.1 Global per capita rice consumption, 1985–2018 (kg per person per year)

Regions	1985–9	1990–4	1995–9	2000–4	2005–9	2010–14	2015–18
European Union-27	4	4	5	5	6	6	6
Mexico	5	5	6	7	7	8	9
Argentina	6	6	6	9	8	8	8
Turkey	6	7	8	8	8	9	10
Canada	4	7	8	8	11	12	13
United States	10	12	13	13	13	14	14
Pakistan	20	19	19	17	14	14	13
Australia	7	15	17	19	17	17	18
South Africa	6	10	11	14	18	20	22
Uruguay	20	25	24	30	29	31	34
Nigeria	14	23	22	29	32	33	34
Iraq	33	28	38	46	42	44	45
Egypt	28	37	41	43	43	43	43
Brazil	50	50	47	47	44	46	47
Rest of world	34	32	35	41	44	45	50
Saudi Arabia	35	40	33	40	45	47	48
Hong Kong	66	62	49	46	46	46	46
Iran	37	39	44	46	48	52	54
Taiwan	87	74	62	52	50	51	49
Japan	80	77	73	67	64	65	64
World	63	65	65	65	64	64	64
Ivory Coast	54	50	56	65	76	82	86
India	80	87	84	79	79	81	81
China	96	99	96	96	89	89	86
Malaysia	90	87	89	89	91	89	89
South Korea	135	125	113	105	98	95	95
Philippines	99	96	105	113	132	139	139
Thailand	160	148	145	150	147	145	140
Indonesia	163	167	169	164	154	152	149
Bangladesh	155	161	167	192	201	201	199
Myanmar	176	199	215	222	219	222	226
Vietnam	170	185	202	218	220	219	219

Source: FAPRI.

rice consumption. On the other hand, as shown in Table 23.2, wheat consumption is a mostly European (Ukraine, 210 kg), North American (Canada, 134 kg), and North African (Egypt, 196 kg) commodity, while Latin America (Other Latin America, 52 kg) and Asia (Japan, 45 kg) have the lowest per capita wheat consumption.

A similar regional preference pattern is also evident in the case of meat consumption. In particular, as shown in Table 23.3, beef consumption is highest in the Americas—both in North America (United States, 41.6 kg) and South America

Table 23.2 Global per capita wheat consumption, 1985–2018 (kg per person per year)

Regions	1985–9	1990–4	1995–9	2000–4	2005–9	2010–14	2015–18
Other Asia	20	21	23	24	26	27	27
Japan	47	45	43	44	45	47	47
Taiwan	43	42	44	44	48	51	53
South Korea	50	47	47	50	50	52	52
Other Latin America	52	52	50	51	52	53	52
Brazil	n.a.	50	51	52	53	53	53
Other Africa/ Middle East	53	52	52	52	54	54	53
Mexico	46	51	51	55	56	59	60
India	62	63	70	66	66	68	68
China	88	86	84	77	74	72	70
Other eastern Europe	25	64	84	85	83	85	86
United States	91	98	100	95	93	94	94
Pakistan	131	141	146	125	129	130	130
Argentina	141	126	129	131	130	135	134
Australia	103	127	145	139	130	125	124
Canada	139	116	119	131	134	152	155
European Union	n.a.	n.a.	n.a.	130	136	147	151
Russia	99	159	157	162	164	168	168
Egypt	169	164	187	178	196	201	202
Morocco	202	195	183	194	209	218	219
Ukraine	123	203	205	206	210	219	225
Other Commonwealth of Independent States	n.a.	169	156	180	217	225	223
Iran	189	205	233	227	231	236	237
Algeria	203	200	206	211	235	245	247
Tunisia	208	242	239	252	276	303	307

Note: n.a. = not available.
Source: FAPRI.

(Argentina, 66.7 kg) where their land endowment (e.g., the Pampas in Argentina and Cerrado in Brazil) is suitable for cattle production. This is followed by some modest consumption in Europe (European Union, 17.5 kg), while Asia (Vietnam, 1.9 kg), which is most land-constrained, has the lowest per capita consumption.

Pork consumption is more spread out across different regions (Table 23.4), with countries in Asia (China, 34.0 kg), Europe (European Union, 42.7 kg), and North America (Canada, 29.8 kg) sharing in the high per capita consumption category, allowed by cheap labor in the case of Asia where small household-based production

Table 23.3 Global per capita beef and veal consumption, 1985–2018 (kg per person per year)

Regions	1985–9	1990–4	1995–9	2000–4	2005–9	2010–14	2015–18
India	1.92	1.46	1.15	1.41	1.55	1.60	1.64
Vietnam	n.a.	n.a.	n.a.	1.45	1.89	2.13	2.44
Indonesia	n.a.	1.61	1.71	1.73	2.03	2.10	2.38
Thailand	3.03	4.12	3.48	2.89	3.22	3.20	3.49
Philippines	1.88	2.34	3.05	4.28	3.92	3.91	4.11
Eastern Europe	n.a.	2.63	3.62	4.10	4.46	4.44	4.73
China	0.67	1.58	3.48	4.09	4.53	5.25	6.00
Taiwan	2.28	2.92	4.05	4.15	4.59	4.92	5.74
Egypt	10.12	8.96	8.86	8.38	8.18	7.48	7.90
Japan	7.17	9.90	11.79	10.67	9.32	10.27	10.89
South Korea	4.69	7.08	10.58	11.96	10.82	12.95	14.07
Ukraine	n.a.	27.49	15.96	10.77	11.06	11.21	11.60
South Africa	18.07	17.84	13.62	13.97	14.61	14.85	16.51
Hong Kong	14.39	15.20	12.45	13.55	15.68	16.96	18.12
Russia	n.a.	29.38	21.38	16.18	16.84	16.68	17.14
European Union	n.a.	n.a.	n.a.	17.19	17.54	17.50	17.15
Former Soviet Union countries	n.a.	13.36	18.80	15.90	18.41	19.27	19.83
Mexico	19.13	20.76	21.21	23.02	23.57	24.06	24.81
New Zealand	39.28	28.90	39.58	33.61	27.51	25.91	25.69
Paraguay	n.a.	n.a.	n.a.	34.46	32.59	31.86	31.76
Canada	38.81	33.49	31.02	31.64	32.62	32.22	32.17
Australia	40.89	37.74	39.02	37.23	35.50	33.71	33.74
Brazil	29.03	33.90	35.52	34.68	36.73	37.39	38.44
United States	n.a.	42.70	43.22	43.09	41.56	38.69	38.00
Argentina	76.49	66.29	63.87	65.10	66.73	66.64	66.56

Note: n.a. = not available.
Source: FAPRI.

Table 23.4 Global per capita pork consumption, 1985–2018 (kg per person per year)

Regions	1985–9	1990–4	1995–9	2000–4	2005–9	2010–14	2015–18
Indonesia	n.a.	3.18	2.92	2.25	2.47	2.47	2.54
Eastern Europe	n.a.	2.63	3.78	3.92	3.86	4.12	4.50
Argentina	n.a.	n.a.	n.a.	5.87	6.09	6.97	7.46
Brazil	7.61	7.46	9.13	10.65	11.60	12.97	13.44
New Zealand	n.a.	13.98	13.65	12.81	12.91	14.05	15.31
Philippines	8.41	10.23	11.80	13.17	13.25	13.63	14.34
Mexico	11.59	10.11	10.57	13.41	14.25	14.53	15.51
Paraguay	28.03	27.58	23.36	18.92	15.80	15.24	15.40
Japan	15.88	16.79	17.01	18.22	19.42	19.72	20.70
Australia	17.18	18.58	18.89	19.59	21.71	22.81	23.49
United States	n.a.	30.24	29.41	29.92	29.05	27.97	28.57
Canada	32.54	31.26	31.71	33.38	29.81	29.59	30.54
South Korea	11.97	16.28	19.63	25.54	29.99	33.27	35.96
China	17.02	22.62	29.42	32.18	34.05	37.07	40.90
European Union	n.a.	n.a.	10.57	41.90	42.71	42.92	43.54
Hong Kong	44.13	59.92	51.66	59.06	64.18	70.09	71.74

Note: n.a. = not available.
Source: FAPRI.

Table 23.5 Global per capita poultry consumption, 1985–2018 (kg per person per year)

Regions	1985–9	1990–4	1995–9	2000–4	2005–9	2010–14	2015–18
India	n.a.	0.50	0.71	1.32	2.00	2.38	2.43
Indonesia	n.a.	n.a.	2.25	2.73	3.28	3.69	4.04
Vietnam	n.a.	n.a.	1.29	4.15	3.83	3.95	4.31
Other eastern Europe	0.00	1.56	3.16	3.98	4.24	4.21	4.61
Former Soviet Union countries	n.a.	2.68	3.15	3.55	5.91	6.48	6.94
Paraguay	n.a.	n.a.	2.83	6.15	6.44	6.33	6.29
Egypt	5.81	4.01	6.04	6.40	6.47	6.82	7.18
Philippines	n.a.	n.a.	6.21	7.29	7.38	7.68	8.17
China	1.00	3.30	6.63	7.49	8.76	10.58	11.60
South Korea	n.a.	n.a.	9.02	10.39	12.31	15.10	16.06
Thailand	7.31	8.58	11.14	12.33	12.44	12.95	13.78
Ukraine	n.a.	1.93	1.73	4.22	13.83	19.93	22.63
Japan	12.41	13.08	13.68	14.08	15.12	15.60	15.75
European Union	0.00	0.00	3.78	15.85	16.73	17.57	17.92
Russia	n.a.	6.43	8.91	10.98	18.15	22.06	23.37
South Africa	12.33	13.88	16.68	18.56	25.15	28.20	31.35
Mexico	8.84	14.85	17.80	23.85	28.17	29.60	30.96
Taiwan	14.76	19.57	26.79	28.36	28.40	31.30	33.70
Argentina	10.75	15.93	22.45	20.87	29.87	35.41	36.81
Canada	20.60	22.90	25.67	29.36	30.28	31.65	32.56
Australia	21.20	23.15	26.23	30.53	33.49	33.07	34.34
New Zealand	12.32	18.14	24.80	33.38	35.44	34.95	36.70
Brazil	10.80	16.00	23.28	30.91	37.25	39.52	40.47
Hong Kong	22.81	38.65	42.13	34.62	37.43	37.75	38.95
United States	n.a.	34.30	37.51	42.22	44.94	44.74	45.44

Note: n.a. = not available.
Source: FAPRI.

is dominant, and cheap feed in the case of North America. South America (Argentina, 6.1 kg) is an exception, as pork consumption is not very popular there. Differences in income can largely explain the position of the remaining countries (e.g., Philippines, 13.2 kg). Per capita poultry consumption, like that of pork, is also more mixed in terms of the top consuming countries (Table 23.5).

Regional differences in preference are more pronounced in the case of dairy products consumption. Regions with climates that are suitable for more productive dairy breeds and with land resources to support pasture and feedgrains such as Oceania, Europe, and the Americas have higher per capita consumption of butter, cheese, and fluid milk, while countries in Asia that are constrained in both, have inadequate transport and refrigeration facilities, and whose population is more prone to lactose intolerance have the lowest per capita consumption (Tables 23.6–23.8). The exception is in milk powder (i.e., non-fat dry and whole milk powder), which can have extended shelf life even with lack of refrigeration, for which some Asian countries have high (e.g., Malaysia, 2.3 and 3.9 kg) to modest (e.g., Japan, 1.8, Thailand, 1.1, and the Philippines, 0.9 kg) per capita consumption levels (Tables 23.9 and 23.10).

Vegetable oil consumption is also more spread out, with the exception of Argentina, which has high per capita consumption of sunflower oil and peanut oil, and North America, which has high consumption of soybean oil (Tables 23.11–23.13).

Despite some regional differences in preference in some commodities, when consumption studies over a long period of time and over a wide range of spatial coverage are examined, it will become obvious that although consumers around the world have different tastes and preferences, there seems to be a similar path of trading-up adjustment in consumption as their incomes rise. Starting when households were still self-contained in terms of their production and consumption systems, households

Table 23.6 Global per capita butter consumption, 1985–2018 (kg per person per year)

Regions	1985–9	1990–4	1995–9	2000–4	2005–9	2010–14	2015–18
Peru	n.a.	n.a.	0.17	0.20	0.06	0.07	0.08
Vietnam	0.01	0.03	0.07	0.07	0.07	0.10	0.12
China	0.06	0.07	0.08	0.09	0.09	0.11	0.13
Indonesia	0.06	0.04	0.04	0.19	0.09	0.06	0.07
Philippines	0.12	0.15	0.15	0.12	0.11	0.12	0.12
Venezuela	0.32	0.11	0.09	0.11	0.13	0.15	0.18
Thailand	0.12	0.20	0.20	0.20	0.22	0.25	0.29
Brazil	0.54	0.49	0.47	0.44	0.41	0.42	0.42
Malaysia	0.09	0.13	0.28	0.41	0.41	0.48	0.53
Colombia	0.47	0.44	0.44	0.46	0.47	0.52	0.55
Egypt	0.90	0.99	0.82	0.81	0.66	0.75	0.78
Japan	0.69	0.71	0.72	0.69	0.69	0.69	0.70
Argentina	1.06	1.18	1.27	1.22	1.12	1.11	1.09
South Korea	0.69	1.03	1.14	1.20	1.12	0.99	0.97
Uruguay	1.40	1.11	1.11	1.21	1.41	2.08	2.30
Mexico	0.35	0.44	0.60	1.06	1.51	1.82	1.87
Ukraine	n.a.	1.11	2.39	2.30	2.01	1.71	2.01
United States	2.14	2.00	1.99	2.04	2.13	2.18	2.14
Canada	4.20	3.07	2.74	2.72	2.58	2.47	2.34
India	0.96	1.16	1.47	2.07	2.72	3.71	4.15
Russia	0.00	2.51	3.58	2.56	2.93	3.30	3.59
Australia	3.82	3.27	3.26	2.95	3.01	3.14	3.08
European Union	n.a.	n.a.	n.a.	3.94	4.02	3.95	3.83
Switzerland	6.84	6.23	6.24	5.88	5.95	6.23	5.96
New Zealand	13.43	15.16	10.01	6.94	6.13	5.59	5.31

Note: n.a. = not available.
Source: FAPRI.

Table 23.7 Global per capita cheese consumption, 1985–2018 (kg per person per year)

Regions	1985–9	1990–4	1995–9	2000–4	2005–9	2010–14	2015–18
Vietnam	n.a.	n.a.	0.01	0.01	0.01	0.02	0.02
Indonesia	0.01	0.02	0.03	0.03	0.03	0.04	0.05
Thailand	0.02	0.04	0.03	0.04	0.06	0.07	0.08
Philippines	n.a.	n.a.	n.a.	0.03	0.09	0.14	0.15
China	0.12	0.15	0.16	0.18	0.21	0.24	0.27
Malaysia	0.05	0.09	0.15	0.23	0.29	0.36	0.41
Peru	n.a.	n.a.	0.30	0.39	0.49	0.58	0.63
Colombia	1.65	1.52	1.39	1.27	1.29	1.37	1.49
South Korea	n.a.	n.a.	n.a.	1.01	1.49	1.85	2.04
Japan	0.91	1.22	1.55	1.84	2.01	2.26	2.47
Mexico	2.72	1.43	1.50	1.93	2.13	2.27	2.49
Brazil	1.93	1.94	2.54	2.60	2.81	3.58	3.89
Venezuela	4.53	4.31	3.18	2.84	2.81	3.02	3.27
Uruguay	3.15	3.07	3.52	3.12	2.84	3.81	4.21
Ukraine	n.a.	0.38	1.25	1.59	3.66	4.35	5.24
Russia	n.a.	0.87	2.30	2.58	4.40	5.12	5.69
Egypt	5.83	5.63	5.47	5.73	5.63	5.41	5.57
New Zealand	8.29	8.40	8.69	6.85	6.54	6.47	6.99
Canada	8.99	9.56	10.22	10.88	10.22	9.91	9.98
Argentina	7.84	8.63	10.60	10.39	10.46	14.05	16.00
Australia	8.10	8.62	9.79	11.09	10.75	10.73	11.28
European Union	n.a.	n.a.	n.a.	11.66	12.82	13.48	14.41
United States	10.43	11.36	12.34	13.59	14.58	15.03	15.44
Switzerland	13.62	14.42	15.80	20.46	18.96	19.97	19.94

Note: n.a. = not available.
Source: FAPRI.

tend to meet their basic energy and protein requirements for body maintenance and productive activities by producing food products with the least requirement of resources given their particular resource endowments (e.g., land) and production environments (e.g., temperature and precipitation patterns). For many countries around the world this means that consumers' consumption basket is first filled by carbohydrate-rich staple grains that can be easily and cheaply produced from the natural nutrients of the land. For example, wheat and potatoes are staples in Europe and the Americas, rice is a staple in Asia, and corn and tubers are staples in Africa. These staple grains are the cheapest sources of energy and nutrients. The price of wheat, for example, is only 9.6 percent of the price of meat products, and the price of rice is only 16.3 percent the price of meat products.[2] As households consume these products on a regular basis over

[2] Computed for the period 1999 to 2001 with the meat price derived as a simple average of the price of beef, pork, and poultry.

Table 23.8 Global per capita fluid milk consumption, 1985–2018 (kg per person per year)

Regions	1985–9	1990–4	1995–9	2000–4	2005–9	2010–14	2015–18
Philippines	n.a.	n.a.	n.a.	0.23	0.59	0.61	0.66
Indonesia	2.51	2.97	2.17	1.44	1.42	1.55	1.64
Vietnam	n.a.	0.86	0.83	1.24	1.76	2.32	2.68
Malaysia	n.a.	1.94	1.99	1.60	1.97	2.25	2.43
Venezuela	19.33	13.32	8.70	8.30	7.59	6.86	6.84
China	n.a.	1.79	1.93	4.64	8.44	12.29	16.77
Thailand	n.a.	n.a.	n.a.	9.10	12.35	14.97	20.51
Egypt	10.60	9.85	n.a.	n.a.	20.67	21.32	22.57
Peru	n.a.	n.a.	17.83	27.65	24.69	29.47	32.66
South Korea	n.a.	n.a.	n.a.	34.61	33.91	34.10	31.65
India	36.15	31.63	32.03	32.58	35.23	41.29	43.68
Japan	36.61	40.78	41.03	39.23	36.64	34.53	34.27
Mexico	56.30	36.74	36.34	39.69	39.94	36.13	37.57
Argentina	52.53	47.78	59.73	58.42	47.20	49.18	51.12
Brazil	50.07	52.20	67.29	69.92	63.58	60.83	69.97
European Union	n.a.	n.a.	n.a.	75.10	69.96	68.09	67.18
New Zealand	142.15	128.04	113.91	93.00	86.47	76.72	70.59
Russia		37.74	99.28	96.62	87.04	89.53	91.53
Canada	104.72	99.62	94.45	91.54	91.53	93.07	89.38
United States	n.a.	n.a.	n.a.	94.70	93.66	92.63	89.70
Uruguay	116.79	126.44	145.83	134.54	97.09	106.17	109.03
Colombia	n.a.	n.a.	100.12	107.18	97.85	103.39	109.13
Ukraine	0.00	15.03	63.58	65.78	98.71	61.32	92.81
Switzerland	128.95	114.88	100.86	89.63	100.40	97.89	94.16
Australia	106.05	105.13	105.26	102.27	104.99	106.64	105.76

Note: n.a. = not available.
Source: FAPRI.

an extended time period, they form consumption habits that make these products common staples.

There is overwhelming evidence in the literature that a substantial share of the consumer expenditure budget is allocated to staple crops in low-income countries (Meade and Rosen 1997; Regmi 2001; Seale, Regmi, and Bernstein 2003). Based on data from 114 countries, Seale, Regmi, and Bernstein (2003) estimated that the share of cereals (interchangeably referred to as staple grains) in total food expenditure is highest among eight food categories (beverages and tobacco, breads and cereals, meat, fish, dairy, fats and oils, fruits and vegetables, and other foods) in low-income countries.

The first major trading-up adjustment in consumption occurs as incomes of households increase, making their preference for better food product quality affordable and resulting in reallocation of food budgets and changes in food baskets represented by a shift from the consumption of carbohydrate-rich staple grains to high-value,

Table 23.9 Global per capita non–fat dry milk consumption, 1985–2018 (kg per person per year)

Regions	1985–9	1990–4	1995–9	2000–4	2005–9	2010–14	2015–18
China	n.a.	n.a.	0.04	0.07	0.08	0.09	0.12
Colombia	n.a.	n.a.	0.16	0.23	0.19	0.23	0.22
India	0.13	0.09	0.11	0.16	0.22	0.28	0.30
Peru	0.00	0.36	0.38	0.43	0.23	0.26	0.26
Vietnam	0.05	0.10	0.27	0.30	0.33	0.30	0.40
Argentina	0.46	0.68	0.53	0.54	0.34	0.30	0.34
Egypt	n.a.	n.a.	n.a.	n.a.	0.35	0.39	0.40
Venezuela	0.70	0.22	0.41	0.35	0.38	0.41	0.41
Ukraine	0.00	0.19	0.53	0.38	0.47	0.32	0.41
Indonesia	n.a.	n.a.	n.a.	0.35	0.58	0.63	0.69
South Korea	n.a.	n.a.	0.57	0.56	0.58	0.58	0.58
Brazil	0.71	0.56	0.64	0.62	0.64	0.78	0.90
Uruguay	0.82	0.33	0.82	0.65	0.74	1.49	1.55
Philippines	n.a.	n.a.	1.21	1.16	0.87	0.80	0.81
New Zealand	8.52	4.54	2.91	1.43	0.92	0.48	0.54
Russia	0.00	0.64	1.09	1.18	1.10	1.24	1.42
Thailand	n.a.	n.a.	n.a.	0.98	1.12	1.20	1.38
United States	1.12	1.16	1.56	1.38	1.56	1.51	1.41
Japan	2.20	2.28	2.20	1.79	1.76	1.61	1.55
Mexico	2.00	1.58	1.51	1.59	1.79	2.03	2.28
European Union	n.a.	n.a.	n.a.	2.14	1.83	1.68	1.51
Australia	3.13	2.29	2.26	1.69	1.89	2.33	2.22
Canada	2.15	1.58	1.09	1.35	2.00	2.11	2.22
Switzerland	3.51	2.93	3.27	1.99	2.14	2.27	2.29
Malaysia	2.00	3.30	3.58	2.68	2.34	2.43	2.72

Note: n.a. = not available.
Source: FAPRI.

animal-protein-rich meat and dairy products.[3] This adjustment is reflected in the changes in per capita consumption over the last decade whereby rice consumption declined by 0.28 percent annually while meat consumption increased by 1.6 percent, dairy products consumption increased by 1.8 percent, and vegetable oil consumption increased by 5.2 percent (FAPRI 2009). It is this same adjustment that explains why the proportion of total food expenditure on cereals in middle-income countries is

[3] The trading-up phenomenon and the convergence phenomenon were presented in broad strokes in earlier sections and may leave a partial impression that the progression of the consumption pattern in the world is uniform and linear. A few cases of variations and exceptions to the patterns described earlier can be cited. For example, in Pingali's (2004) Westernization of Asian diets, the trading-up adjustment is not directly from staple grains to meat and dairy products, but actually the substitution starts within the food grains, that is, from rice to wheat. This is also reported by Fabiosa (2006).

Table 23.10 Global per capita whole milk powder consumption, 1985–2018 (kg per person per year)

Regions	1985–9	1990–4	1995–9	2000–4	2005–9	2010–14	2015–18
Philippines	n.a.	n.a.	n.a.	0.45	0.12	0.17	0.23
South Korea	0.27	0.20	0.10	0.12	0.13	0.14	0.14
New Zealand	14.95	9.46	5.45	0.55	0.24	0.33	0.34
Ukraine	n.a.	n.a.	n.a.	0.17	0.26	0.41	0.47
Peru	0.00	0.69	1.55	0.75	0.30	0.55	0.61
Indonesia	n.a.	n.a.	n.a.	0.26	0.33	0.39	0.44
Egypt	0.31	0.43	0.33	0.50	0.45	0.52	0.58
Vietnam	n.a.	0.01	0.09	0.50	0.48	0.58	0.80
Thailand	n.a.	n.a.	n.a.	0.53	0.60	0.66	0.74
European Union	n.a.	n.a.	n.a.	0.85	0.79	0.80	0.73
Russia		0.40	0.88	0.76	0.80	1.00	1.04
Uruguay	0.08	0.72	0.85	1.02	1.13	1.90	1.96
Australia	3.71	1.72	1.11	1.20	1.28	1.60	1.65
Mexico	n.a.	0.90	1.47	1.44	1.33	1.36	1.48
Colombia	0.91	n.a.	1.17	1.40	1.47	1.68	1.88
Argentina	2.91	2.38	2.87	2.42	1.84	2.06	2.74
Brazil	1.00	1.25	1.97	2.25	2.50	2.83	2.91
Malaysia	2.94	1.94	1.26	2.50	3.88	4.01	4.18
Venezuela	8.15	6.34	4.30	4.47	4.62	4.46	4.20

Note: n.a. = not available.
Source: FAPRI.

Table 23.11 Global per capita soybean oil consumption, 1985–2018 (kg per person per year)

Regions	1985–9	1990–4	1995–9	2000–4	2005–9	2010–14	2015–18
Taiwan	n.a.	0.33	0.53	1.29	0.76	0.91	0.95
Japan	0.57	0.61	1.22	2.03	2.09	1.94	2.39
India	0.00	0.00	1.45	3.69	3.39	3.36	3.41
Argentina	n.a.	1.99	2.06	2.40	3.84	4.59	4.69
South Korea	5.60	5.32	5.32	5.48	4.48	4.43	4.44
European Union	0.83	1.13	2.34	4.39	6.85	8.62	10.66
Brazil	1.66	3.50	5.70	9.00	9.48	9.59	10.00
Commonwealth of Independent States	3.64	4.55	6.27	8.14	9.63	10.90	11.36
China	6.32	5.98	8.21	10.70	9.98	9.85	9.81
Canada	8.18	14.36	15.99	16.03	14.45	11.36	10.75
United States	14.68	18.74	17.85	18.30	17.55	18.36	19.62

Note: n.a. = not available.
Source: FAPRI.

Table 23.12 Global per capita rapeseed oil consumption, 1985–2018 (kg per person per year)

Regions	1985–9	1990–4	1995–9	2000–4	2005–9	2010–14	2015–18
Australia	0.34	0.35	0.34	0.39	0.38	0.38	0.39
United States	n.a.	0.23	0.49	0.25	0.63	0.85	0.86
Japan	1.48	1.88	1.77	1.63	1.79	1.66	1.67
European Union	1.70	2.12	2.79	3.30	3.35	3.50	3.62
India	n.a.	n.a.	3.24	5.76	5.20	4.97	5.02
Commonwealth of Independent States	5.51	6.21	6.57	7.22	7.48	8.28	8.69
Canada	1.71	3.81	4.35	6.80	8.22	8.13	7.83
China	11.52	16.44	17.17	13.66	11.45	12.09	12.12

Note: n.a. = not available.
Source: FAPRI.

Table 23.13 Global per capita sunflower oil consumption, 1985–2018 (kg per person per year)

Regions	1985–9	1990–4	1995–9	2000–4	2005–9	2010–14	2015–18
European Union	0.18	0.18	0.15	0.23	0.20	0.21	0.24
Commonwealth of Independent States	n.a.	n.a.	2.44	5.19	6.03	6.56	6.85
United States	n.a.	3.85	3.90	5.02	6.53	6.92	7.10
China	9.66	10.36	13.73	7.73	9.19	9.43	9.62
Argentina	20.15	22.06	24.53	26.25	23.18	21.12	20.85

Note: n.a. = not available.
Source: FAPRI.

33 percent less compared with that of low-income countries, and is 56 percent less for high-income countries compared to low-income countries.

The underlying preference structure of consumers that drives this adjustment is captured and measured by the differential responsiveness of different food categories to changes in income. The income elasticity estimates by Seale, Regmi, and Bernstein (2003) are reported in Table 23.14. They show that the income elasticity of cereals declines as income grows. The income elasticity of cereals for low-income countries is 0.53. The income elasticity of middle-income countries for cereals is only 71 percent that of the low-income countries, while cereals income elasticity for high-income countries is only 32 percent that of the low-income countries. In fact, some staple crops are already inferior goods (i.e., they have a negative income elasticity) for some countries. For example, the income elasticity of rice in mainland China is −0.07, −0.19 for Hong Kong, and −0.26 for Japan (FAPRI 2009).

Table 23.14 Income elasticity of cereals and meat–dairy products, by country income class

Income class	Cereals	Meat and dairy[a]
Low-income	0.527	0.808
Middle-income	0.373	0.661
High-income	0.170	0.365

[a]Weighted average based on expenditure share.
Source: Seale, Regmi, and Bernstein (2003).

In contrast, the income elasticity of meat and dairy products is high: 0.81 for low-income countries, 0.66 for middle-income countries, and 0.36 for high-income countries. Although low-income countries have the highest income elasticity for meat and dairy products, the ratio of the income elasticity of meat and diary products relative to the income elasticity of cereals is still highest in high-income countries at 2.15 times, compared with 1.77 for middle-income countries, and 1.53 for low-income countries. Hence, given an increase in household income, the rate of increase in the consumption of meat and dairy products is much higher than the rate of increase in the consumption of cereals. More specifically, the relative differential in the rates of increase is highest in high-income countries and lowest in low-income countries. Over time with sustained income growth, this trading-up consumption adjustment will result in a consumption basket with a high proportion of expenditure on meat and dairy products, likely overtaking the share of expenditure on cereals.

This trading-up phenomenon from staple grains to high-value meat and dairy products is evidenced in many countries. For example, Shapouri and Rosen (2007) report that in 1970 grains accounted for more than half of calories consumed in the United States. Sugar, the next-largest commodity group, had a 9 percent share. Both roots and vegetable oils held a 7.6 percent share, while meat accounted for 5.4 percent of the total. The second-highest growth was for meat, whose share exceeded 8 percent in 2005. This change represented an 80 percent increase in meat demand.

Also, the two largest emerging economies of India and China also clearly showed this trading-up pattern. Landes (2004) reported that consumption of fruits, vegetables, edible oils, and animal products was rising much faster than wheat and rice consumption, staple grains in the Indian diet. In particular, milk, eggs, and poultry meat are the most important animal products, and all are registering strong growth in production and consumption. In fact, the poultry sector is growing 10–15 percent per year, despite India's reputation as having a traditional vegetarian dietary preference.

Gale (2003) described the same trading-up adjustment in the case of China, in which Chinese households that gained greater spending power cut back on consumption of traditional staple grains—mostly rice and wheat—and increased their consumption of nearly every other food item. Purchases of dairy products, poultry, fish and other aquatic products, soft drinks, wine, and processed foods are all growing rapidly. Rice and wheat consumption leveled off in the last decade, but consumption of corn and soybeans has grown rapidly, reflecting the need for an expanding livestock herd to feed Chinese consumers' increasing demand for livestock products. This pattern is further corroborated by Zhang and Wang (2003), who reported a significant transition from staple foods such as rice and wheat to high-value products such as meats, aquatic products, vegetable oils, and dairy products in China. For example, per capita consumption of grains in urban China dropped steadily, from 135 kg in 1985 to 79 kg in 2001. On the other hand, urban per capita consumption of poultry increased from 3.2 kg to 5.3 kg over the same period.

The second major trading-up adjustment in consumption occurs as incomes of households increase, making their preference for more convenience and variety affordable, which results in food budget reallocation and change in consumption baskets represented by the increasing consumption of more processed food products such as ready-to-eat foods and increasing food-away-from-home (FAFH) consumption.

Regmi and Gehlhar (2005b) reported that processed food sales are a major component of global food markets and account for about three-fourths of total world food sales. Annual growth rates of retail sales of packaged food products in developing countries range from 7 percent in upper-middle-income countries to 28 percent in lower-middle-income countries, much higher than annual growth rates of 2–3 percent in developed countries. Also, it is reported that international commerce in processed foods substantially exceeds the value of unprocessed agricultural commodities and is expanding more rapidly. International trade in processed foods has been the most rapidly growing portion of world food and agricultural trade as early as the mid-1990s (Henderson, Handy, and Neff 1996). Price (1998) added that sales of meals and snacks away from home continue to increase and account for the largest and fastest-rising share of sales in the food service industry. In Japan, the food budget allocated to processed foods, including pizza and cheese-containing products, has risen from 20 percent in 1963 to 30 percent in 2003.

The emergence and growth of FAFH expenditure can be driven by many factors, including the greater proportion of women participating in the labor market, which raises the opportunity cost of home production of food (Nayga and Capps 1992). This is particularly true in societies in which food preparation is performed by the female members of the family. Another contributing factor is the demand for greater variety by consumers. In both cases, the growth in demand for FAFH is driven by increases in household income. It is for this reason that FAFH demand is usually associated with high responsiveness to income and, as a result, the rapid rise in the proportion of income that is spent on FAFH reported in many countries such as the United States (Lin, Guthrie, and Frazão 1999), China (Ma et al. 2006; Bai et al. 2008), Malaysia (Lee and Tan 2006), and Spain (Angulo, Gil, and Mur 2002).

In the United States, estimates suggest that in 2007, families spent nearly 42 percent of their food dollars on foods outside the home, up from 25 percent in 1970 (Clausen and Leibtag 2008, table 12). This also translates into an increasing proportion of caloric intake coming from FAFH. This increasing share of FAFH will continue over time as it is more responsive to changes in income than at-home foods. Davis and Stewart (2002) give an FAFH income elasticity of 0.46 compared to the 0.13 food-at-home income elasticity. Simulations by Stewart et al. (2004) indicate that per capita spending could rise by about 18 percent at full-service restaurants versus about a 6 percent increase for fast food between 2000 and 2020.

The trading-up consumption adjustment pattern for variety and convenience considerations is true not only in the United States but is also widely observed in many other countries. For example, Campo and Beghin (2005) report that in Japan the proportion of eating out in the household food budget increased from 7 percent in 1963 to 17 percent in 2003. For China, Gale (2005) reported that Chinese consumers are paying higher prices for meals in restaurants.

Many elasticity estimates suggest very responsive food expenditure for FAFH across many countries. For example, Ma et al. (2006) reported an FAFH consumption expenditure elasticity with respect to income for urban China of 0.21 to 0.77 for the conditional elasticity and 1.02 to 2.54 for the unconditional elasticity. Bai et al. (2008) reported a conditional elasticity of 1.38 and an unconditional elasticity of 2.33. Angulo, Gil, and Mur (2002) reported an unconditional elasticity of 0.80 for Spain. Stewart et al. (2004) reported a conditional elasticity of 0.64 for the United States.

Although FAFH is generally taken as a result of economic growth, it can also serve as a dynamic stimulant in the development of industries such as those related to hotels, restaurants, and other institutions in the food sector (Ma et al. 2006).

The third major trading-up adjustment in consumption occurs as incomes of households increase making affordable their preference for more specific product characteristics (e.g., food safety) and other new considerations, such as concern for the impact on the environment, welfare of animals, and welfare of producers.

At a high income level, consumers begin to look for specific product characteristics in the food items that they purchase. It can be a product characteristic that is an extension of the physical attribute of the product. For example, concern for food safety and health combined with a perception that poultry meat is a healthier meat product has increased the demand for poultry faster than can be explained by income growth alone. Regmi (2001) reported that in the United States, the red meat share of total meat consumption declined from 79 percent in 1970 to 62 percent thirty years later, while the poultry share increased from 21 percent to 38 percent during the same period. This change in consumption pattern is very evident, especially in the Americas, where beef used to be the dominant meat product in the consumption basket. But recently, per capita poultry consumption has exceeded beef consumption: in 2003 in the United States, in 2002 in Mexico, and in 2007 in Brazil. Taha (2003) reported that this preference for poultry meat over red meat due to health considerations is a worldwide phenomenon, with per capita poultry meat consumption growing faster than pork, bovine (beef and water buffalo), lamb, goat, and other meat consumption in all of the three income groups—low, middle, and high.

The growth of the organic food sector is another example of the trading-up consumption adjustment that is driven by the intersection of product safety considerations (e.g., less harmful chemical residues in food products) and the impact of production technology on the environment (e.g., less possible leaching of pollutants in the groundwater supply). Davis and Stewart (2002) reported that health-conscious consumers are driving increases in sales of organic and natural food products. The US Natural Marketing Institute reports that sales of organic foods increased by 20 percent between 1999 and 2000.

Even product characteristics that are not traditionally considered as part of the food products are now entering into the consumption decisions of consumers in high-income countries. For example, Codron et al. (2005) reported that demand patterns of European consumers are changing, with growing demand for food products with certain characteristics, such as products perceived to be safer, more healthful, or produced in ways that are more beneficial to the environment and that take animal welfare and equitable labor into consideration.

The growth in demand for these new considerations is driven both by demand-side factors, such as increases in consumer purchasing power, and by supply-side factors, such as new marketing and distribution methods that allow coordination mechanisms and incentive structures that enable the value chain to deliver the products with the characteristics desired by the consumers. This is largely made possible by improvements in information technologies that keep the costs of the marketing and distribution processes affordable.

2   CONVERGENCE TO THE EMERGING COMMON CONSUMPTION PATTERN

Given the common path of trading-up consumption adjustment that is repeated from country to country and over time, starting from a staple-grains-dominated consumption basket to adjustments driven by product quality, variety, and convenience, and other specific food product characteristics such as health, environment, and animal welfare, the next logical question is whether there is a tendency toward convergence in the consumption patterns across countries.

There is strong evidence presented in the literature that points to the convergence of consumption patterns. Pingali (2004) referred to homogenization of food tastes across the globe. Kónya and Ohashi (2004) provided statistical evidence of the convergence hypothesis suggesting a narrowing of differences in consumption pattern between countries. Pingali and Khwaja (2004) cited the globalization of Indian diets whereby households start to adopt food consumption patterns that differ from the traditional ones. In particular, they report that consumers exhibit strong preferences for meat or fish, temperate-zone foods such as apples, and highly processed convenience foods and drinks, all of which are readily available in the emerging supermarkets and fast food outlets. Fabiosa (2006) reported the Westernization of Indonesian diets with a marked substitution of wheat for rice in the Indonesian consumption basket, following the same pattern described by Pingali (2004) and Pingali and Khwaja (2004). Tokoyama et al. (2002) also talked about the Westernization of recent food consumption pattern of Japanese households. Specifically, they noted that the food consumption pattern of Japanese households is the use of more and more prepared foods and FAFH. The expenditure shares of both prepared foods and FAFH have doubled over the last thirty years.

There is a confluence of both demand-side and supply-side drivers in this convergence phenomenon. The primary driver on the demand side is the growth in income across many countries. Table 23.15 shows income growth rates in the last two decades. Emerging markets such as those of China and India and other developing countries show much higher rates of growth than those of the advanced economies. This allows low- to middle-income countries to catch up and converge with the consumption pattern of high-income countries because of their relatively higher income elasticities for high-value foods, processed foods, FAFH, and specific food product characteristics, on the one hand, and higher income growth, on the other. For example, as incomes of low-income countries improve, consumption of high-value products will increase faster than any increase in the consumption of high-value products in high-income countries, allowing these low-income countries to catch up in their consumption. Regmi, Takeshima, and Unnevehr (2008) observed significant convergence in consumption patterns for total food, cereals, meats, seafood, dairy, sugar and confectionery, caffeinated beverages, and soft drinks in forty-seven countries examined. They observed that convergence in total food expenditures, though, remains significant, particularly for meat, dairy, sugar, and caffeinated beverages.

Another significant driver is the widespread and increasing access to mass media—the Internet in particular—with many regular programs and advertisements having content with international scope, exposing consumers to lifestyles, including consumption patterns, and products from more developed countries. Exposure to these

Table 23.15 Global income growth rate, 1990–2018 (%)

Regions	1990	1993	1994–2000	2001	2004–7	2009	2011–18
World	3.0	1.7	3.2	1.5	3.8	0.2	3.6
OECD	3.0	1.1	3.0	1.1	2.8	−1.1	2.3
Non-OECD	2.7	4.8	4.2	3.4	7.6	3.6	5.9
Advanced economies	3.0	1.2	3.0	1.1	2.7	−1.2	2.3
Emerging markets	2.9	5.2	4.1	3.1	7.3	3.4	5.9
China	3.8	14.0	9.6	8.3	10.6	6.3	8.6
India	5.8	4.9	6.3	5.2	8.8	4.9	7.3
Developing countries	1.6	−0.7	3.0	3.5	6.6	2.9	4.5

Source: Global Insight.

experiences can lead to adaptation of lifestyles. The effectiveness of the mass media in creating desire among consumers along with rising purchasing power provides an effective combination of influence that can speed up the convergence phenomenon. Also, demographic changes, such as fast urbanization, open a host of factors that can lead to the convergence phenomenon. Migration to urban areas is often associated with increased income potential, increases exposure to mass media and their influence, and improves access to more food products and with wider variety selection.

From the supply side, trade liberalization agreements such as the Uruguay Round Agreement on Agriculture of the World Trade Organization, which commits contracting countries to reduction of their duties by 36 percent over a period of six years for developed countries and 24 percent over a period of ten years for developing countries, has opened markets. This improvement in market access has encouraged spatial movements of food products from surplus to deficit regions, introducing consumers to many affordable new products. Further deepening of market access would occur through substantial tariff reductions under consideration in the current Doha Round.

Related to this development is another specific factor cited as driving overall food expenditure convergence: the globalization of food processing, marketing, and distribution. This is particularly evident with the entrance of three types of institution and their increasing global reach and influence. The first are transnational food companies, which are locating their processing facilities in many countries, inserting and exerting strategic influence in the food value chain in these countries. Their greatest impact is in spreading access of standardized products to an ever-increasing consumer base across different countries. Second are international restaurants and fast-food chains (e.g., McDonalds), which exploit the increasing expenditures on FAFH in many countries. Third are modern foreign-owned supermarkets with global reach such as Wal-Mart, and Carrefour, which are now becoming dominant retail outlets in many countries. Regmi and Gehlhar (2005b) reported that in Latin America, from a 15 to a 30 percent share of national food sales before the 1980s, now supermarkets account for a 50–70 percent share. These supermarkets contribute to increasing standardization of packaged food product delivery at the retail level, which enhances convergence of consumption. Regmi and Unnevehr (2006) examined specific food-retailing and product introduction patterns for selected countries and found an increasing share of retail outlets selling standardized products.

3   POLICY IMPLICATIONS OF THE EMERGING AND CONVERGING CONSUMPTION PATTERNS

The policy implications of the emerging and converging consumption patterns are many, but two important ones deserve attention here. The first is food security. That is, if countries develop consumption patterns reflecting new appetites for products that they do not have adequate resources to produce, it may lead to the deterioration of the food security situation in many countries. This is particularly true since many of these food-importing countries are facing foreign exchange constraints. Moreover, world stocks of major commodities are declining relative to total use, making market adjustments to any shock more difficult. It is projected that wheat, rice, and corn stocks-to-use ratios in the next decade will be lower, by 12, 19, and 17 percentage points, respectively. A classic example is the Westernization of Indonesia's food consumption basket, whereby wheat is substituted for rice. Like many countries in South Asia, Indonesia does not produce any wheat, but at one point the country hosted the largest wheat milling (noodle) factory in the world, importing its entire wheat requirement. Any market interruptions in the wheat market, such as the one from 2006 to 2008 when the wheat price increased by 94.4 percent, would have serious repercussions on Indonesia's consumers. The second consideration is how this emerging consumption pattern will affect health outcomes. With diets rich in fat, sugar, and salt, but deficient in critical nutrients, Western societies are already facing negative diet-related health consequences such as obesity and all its attendant health issues. As developing countries tend to converge to the Western diet, increasing cases of obesity are already being reported even among developing countries (Popkin and Gordon-Larsen 2004). Given these countries' limited fiscal capacity in the public health sector, whether there should be any interventions to avoid the unintended health consequences becomes a legitimate policy question.

References

Angulo, A. M., J. M. Gil, and J. Mur. 2002. "Spanish Demand for Food Away From Home: A Panel Data Approach." Paper presented at the 10th European Association of Agricultural Economists Congress on Exploring Diversity in the European Agri-Food System, Zaragoza, Spain, Aug. 28–31. <http://ageconsearch.umn.edu/bitstream/24977/1/cp02fa31.pdf>.

Bai, J., T. I. Wahl, B. T. Lohmar, and J. Huang. 2008. "The Determinants of Consuming Food Away From Home in China: The Role of Hosted Meals." Paper presented at the Washington State University School of Economic Sciences Spring Seminar. <http://www.ses.wsu.edu/seminar/papers_Spring08/Bai_Role%20of%20hosted%20meals.pdf>.

Campo, I. S., and J. C. Beghin. 2005. Dairy Food Consumption, Production, and Policy in Japan. CARD Working Paper No. 05-WP-401. Ames: Center for Agricultural and Rural Development, Iowa State University. <http://ageconsearch.umn.edu/handle/18596>.

Clausen, A., and E. Leibtag. 2008. "Food CPI and Expenditures." Briefing Rooms, Economic Research Service, US Department of Agriculture. <http://www.ers.usda.gov/Briefing/CPIFoodAndExpenditures>.

Codron, J., K. Grunert, E. Giraud-Héraud, L. Soler, and A. Regmi. 2005. "Retail Sector Responses to Changing Consumer Preferences: The European Experience." In New Directions in Global Food Markets. AIB-794. Washington, DC: Economic Research Service, US Department of Agriculture. <http://www.ers.usda.gov/publications/aib794/aib794e.pdf>.

Davis, D. E., and H. Stewart. 2002. "Changing Consumer Demands Create Opportunities for U.S. Food System." *FoodReview* 25/1 (May), 19–23. <http://www.ers.usda.gov/publications/FoodReview/May2002/frvol25i1d.pdf>.

Fabiosa, J. F. 2006. *Westernization of the Asian Diet: The Case of Rising Wheat Consumption in Indonesia*. CARD Working Paper No. 06-WP 422. Ames: Center for Agricultural and Rural Development, Iowa State University.

FAPRI. 2009. *FAPRI 2009 U.S. and World Agricultural Outlook*. FAPRI Staff Report No. 09-FSR 1. Ames: Food and Agricultural Policy Research Institute, Iowa State University.

Gale, H. F. 2003. "China's Growing Affluence: How Food Markets Are Responding." *Amber Waves* 1/3 (June), 14–21. <http://www.ers.usda.gov/AmberWaves/June03/Features/ChinasGrowingAffluence.htm>.

—— 2006. "Trends in Chinese Food Demand and Trade Patterns." Paper presented at the USDA Agricultural Outlook Forum, Feb. 17, 2006. <http://ageconsearch.umn.edu/bitstream/33353/1/fo06ga30.pdf>.

Henderson, D. R., C. R. Handy, and S. A. Neff, eds. 1996. *Globalization of the Processed Foods Market*. Agricultural Economic Report No. 742. Washington, DC: Food and Consumer Economics Division, Economic Research Service, US Department of Agriculture. <http://www.ers.usda.gov/publications/aer742>.

Kónya, I., and H. Ohashi. 2004. *Globalisation and Consumption Patterns among the OECD Countries*. Working Paper. Boston, Lincs.: Boston College. <http://escholarship.bc.edu/econ_papers/20>.

Landes, M. R. 2004. "The Elephant Is Jogging: New Pressures for Agricultural Reform in India." *Amber Waves* 2/1(Feb.), 28–35. <http://www.ers.usda.gov/AmberWaves/February04/Features/ElephantJogs.htm>.

Lee, H., and A. Tan. 2006. "Determinants of Malaysian Household Expenditures of Food-Away-From-Home." Paper presented at the International Association of Agricultural Economists Conference, Gold Coast, Australia.

Lin, B.-H., J. Guthrie, and E. Frazão. 1999. "Nutrient Contribution of Food Away From Home." In E. Frazão, ed., *America's Eating Habits: Changes and Consequences*. Agriculture Information Bulletin No. 750. Washington, DC: Economic Research Service, US Department of Agriculture.

Ma, H., J. Huang, F. Fuller, and S. Rozelle. 2006. "Getting Rich and Eating Out: Consumption of Food Away From Home in Urban China." *Canadian Journal of Agricultural Economics* 54: 101–19.

Meade, B., and S. Rosen. 1997. "The Influence of Income on Global Food Spending." *Agricultural Outlook* (July). <http://www.ers.usda.gov/publications/agoutlook/jul1997/ao242e.pdf>.

Nayga, R. M., Jr., and O. Capps, Jr. 1992. "Analysis of Food Away From Home and Food At Home Consumption: A Systems Approach." *Journal of Food Distribution Research* 23/3: 1–10. <http://ageconsearch.umn.edu/handle/26649>.

Pingali, P. 2004. *Westernization of Asian Diets and the Transformation of Food Systems: Implications for Research and Policy*. ESA Working Paper No. 04-17. Washington, DC: Agriculture and Development Economics Division, Food and Agriculture Organization, United Nations. <http://ageconsearch.umn.edu/handle/23795>.

—— and Y. Khwaja. 2004. "Globalisation of Indian Diets and the Transformation of Food Supply Systems." Inaugural Keynote Address to the 17th Annual Conference of the Indian Society of Agricultural Marketing, Hyderabad, Feb. 5–7.

Popkin, B. M., and P. Gordon-Larsen 2004. "The Nutrition Transition: Worldwide Obesity Dynamics and their Determinants." *International Journal of Obesity* 28: S2–S9. <http://www.nature.com/ijo/journal/v28/n3s/pdf/0802804a.pdf>.

Price, C. C. 1998. "Sales of Meals and Snacks Away From Home Continue to Increase." *FoodReview* (Sept.–Dec.), 28–30. <http://www.ers.usda.gov/publications/foodreview/sep1998/frsept98f.pdf>.

Regmi, A., ed. 2001. *Changing Structure of Global Food Consumption and Trade.* Agriculture and Trade Report No. WRS01-1. Washington, DC: Market and Trade Economics Division, Economic Research Service, US Department of Agriculture. <http://www.ers.usda.gov/Publications/WRS011>.

—— and M. Gehlhar. 2005a. *New Directions in Global Food Markets.* Agriculture Information Bulletin No. 794. Washington, DC: Economic Research Service, US Department of Agriculture, Feb. <http://www.ers.usda.gov/publications/AIB794>.

—— ——. 2005b. "Processed Food Trade Pressured by Evolving Global Supply Chains." *Amber Waves* 3/1 (Feb.), 12–19. <http://www.ers.usda.gov/AmberWaves/February05/Features/ProcessedFood.htm>.

—— and L. Unnevehr. 2006. "Are Diets Converging Globally? A Comparison of Trends across Selected Countries." *Journal of Food Distribution Research* 37/1: 20–7. <http://ageconsearch.umn.edu/handle/8573>.

——, H. Takeshima, and L. Unnevehr. 2008. *Convergence in Global Food Demand and Delivery.* Economic Research Report No. ERR-56. Washington, DC: Economic Research Service, US Department of Agriculture. <http://www.ers.usda.gov/Publications/ERR56>.

Seale, J., A. Regmi, and J. Bernstein. 2003. *International Evidence on Food Consumption Patterns.* Technical Bulletin No. TB-1904. Washington, DC: Economic Research Service, US Department of Agriculture. <http://www.ers.usda.gov/publications/tb1904>.

Shapouri, S., and S. Rosen. 2007. *Global Diet Composition: Factors behind the Changes and Implications of the New Trends.* Food Security Assessment No. GFA-19. Washington, DC: Economic Research Service, US Department of Agriculture. <http://www.ers.usda.gov/Publications/GFA19/GFA19b.pdf>.

Stewart, H., N. Blisard, S. Bhuyan, and R. M. Nayga, Jr. 2004. *The Demand for Food Away From Home: Full-Service or Fast Food?* Economic Research Brief No. 829. Washington, DC: Economic Research Service, US Department of Agriculture. <http://www.ers.usda.gov/publications/AER829/aer829researchbrief.pdf>.

Taha, F. 2003. *Patterns of World Poultry Consumption and Production.* Outlook Report No. WRS03-02. Washington, DC: Economic Research Service, US Department of Agriculture.

Tokoyama, Y., S. Takagi, K. Ishibashi, and W. S. Chern. 2002. "Recent Food Consumption Pattern of Japanese Households: Driving Forces behind Westernization." Selected Paper presented at the Annual Meeting of the American Agricultural Economics Association, Long Beach, CA, July 28–31. <http://ageconsearch.umn.edu/handle/19712>.

Zhang, W., and Q. Wang. 2003. "Changes in China's Urban Food Consumption and Implications for Trade." Selected Paper presented at the Annual Meeting of the American Agricultural Economics Association, Montreal, July 27–30. <http://ageconsearch.umn.edu/handle/21986>.

CHAPTER 24

INCREASING AND MORE VOLATILE FOOD PRICES AND THE CONSUMER

JOACHIM VON BRAUN

1 INTRODUCTION

Consumers play an increasingly important role in shaping food prices and transforming the world food system through growing demand and shifting preferences. The food price hike in 2007–8 was partly caused by rising consumer demand due to population and income growth, coupled with factors such as high and variable energy prices, rise in use of grain for biofuels, slow agricultural supply response, and malfunctioning financial system and commodities markets (von Braun 2008). These causes can be broadly separated into slow-onset forces, such as population growth, consumption change, and resource scarcity, on the one hand, and fast-onset forces, such as acute production shocks or trade disruptions, on the other hand. The predictable slow-onset forces can reach tipping points when they transform in interactions with fast-onset forces into unpredictable market and food security crisis effects. The diversification of the world food system toward high-value products has been driven by shifting consumption away from grains and other staples to vegetables, fruits, meat, dairy, and fish, all of which are more resource-intensive, thereby increasing land and water scarcity and related resource costs and thus implicitly also staple food prices. Consumers have been negatively affected by the recent food price hikes and increased price volatility. Poor consumers in developing countries were especially hard-hit as high food prices, not matched by equivalent increases in income, undermined their food security and threatened their livelihoods.

Increasing and volatile food prices in developing countries are not a new phenomenon. After the global food price crisis in 1973–4, local prices have spiked often at times when global prices have not been affected. Cereal prices in the 1980s and early 1990s, for example in famine-prone areas in Africa, increased between two and five times in the course of a crisis year (von Braun, Teklu, and Webb 1998). Significant increases in the prices of certain commodities have also occurred owing to public policies. The rice price increase in Indonesia following the import ban introduced in 2004 harmed a large majority of consumers and particularly the poor (McCulloch 2008).

The fundamental policy dilemma around food prices remains as relevant today as in past decades. Policymakers are torn between high food prices, which encourage agricultural production, and low food prices, which benefit poor buyers of food. Within this dilemma, there are multiple objectives that policymakers try to meet with food price policy, including:

- raising production and productivity of agriculture at lowest costs,
- economic growth through balanced growth of agriculture, manufacturing, and services,
- multiple social objectives including reduction of hunger and poverty,
- ensuring national food security, and
- political objectives including social and political stability (Streeten 1987).

Meeting these multiple objectives requires careful analysis of the design, implementation, and impacts of alternative policy instruments.

Understanding the food demand structure is essential for food policy analysis at the broader macroeconomic level. Changes in consumer demand drive changes in market prices in the very short run, when food production is fixed, and are crucial for modeling of price formation in the medium and long run (Sadoulet and de Janvry 1995). Conceptually, however, the study of high and volatile food prices should be based on a comprehensive analysis of both demand- and supply-side causes and effects. A framework that assesses the relationship between increasing and volatile food prices and consumers examines only one side of the market, in which prices drive consumption, and consumption drives prices. To provide insights for policymaking, such a framework must implicitly include supply-side effects and responses to agricultural prices as well (for analysis of supply-side issues, see Mellor and Ahmed 1988).

Focusing on the relationship between consumers and food prices, this chapter addresses two main issues: (1) increases in food price levels and volatility caused by changes in consumption volumes and structure, and (2) changes in consumption caused by increases in food price levels and volatility. After a brief discussion of some relevant theoretical and conceptual issues, changes in food consumption will be addressed within a broad discussion of the patterns and determinants of high and volatile food prices. Next, consumer responses and impacts in the context of high and volatile food prices will be examined with a focus on poor consumers in developing countries. These consumer–price issues will be connected to the recent food price crisis in 2007–8, as well as to the fundamental issues underlying the food price sensitivity of the poor discussed in earlier literature. The supply side of increasing and volatile prices will be kept in the background of the discussion. The chapter will conclude with a brief discussion of existing and desired policy responses to stabilize consumption through price policy, stocks, and trade, as well as mitigation of negative effects on the most vulnerable through subsidies and social protection. To strengthen the design and implementation of these policies, the overarching actions needed in the areas of institutions and information will also be addressed briefly.

2   THEORETICAL AND CONCEPTUAL ISSUES RELATING TO PRICES AND CONSUMERS

As this volume addresses the theory of price formation and consumer behavior in other chapters, only brief references are made here to theoretical issues related to the linkages between increasing and volatile food prices and consumer welfare and implications for policy. Basic theory explains how a rational consumer makes consumption choices with regard to different prices and budget constraints. However, agents do not always have complete information about prices and do not always make rational choices. The theory of price formation under asymmetric information and uncertainty of actors is by now well developed (e.g., Grossman and Stiglitz 1980; Glosten and Milgrom 1985; Jackson and Peck 1999). In countries with market failures such as information deficiencies, high switching costs, and missing markets, the classical paradigm of the Law of One Price[1] and standard space determination models are far from applicable. High transaction costs arising from failings such as poor transportation or communication infrastructure result in incomplete price transmission to economic agents and suboptimal decisions contributing to inefficient outcomes (Rapsomanikis, Hallam, and Conforti 2006). Price volatility brings further impediments to market efficiency.

In broad terms, the sources of price volatility can be linked to variability in supply and demand, arbitrage, and speculation, as well as changes in government actions (Newbery and Stiglitz 1981). Demand variability can be due to systematic factors such as income variability, and non-systematic factors such as changes in tastes. Supply variability can be attributed to systematic factors such as weather and transport costs and non-systematic factors such as technical innovation. Price volatility is often perceived to be caused by arbitrage and speculation, but price volatility itself can cause a rise in arbitrage and speculation as well as overreactions and hysteria and drive prices further up.

Low-income consumers are extremely sensitive to high and variable food prices since a large proportion of their income is spent on food, as expressed in fundamental Engel's Law relationships. Poor people's responsiveness is also linked to liquidity and credit constraints as well as limited capacity to cope with shocks. Not only are low-income consumers more sensitive to high food prices; they also pay higher prices on per unit basis compared to high-income consumers. This "poverty penalty" effect is

---

[1] Assuming zero transaction costs and perfect information, the Law of One Price states that a homogeneous good trades at one price no matter who the buyer and seller are.

due not only to market failures but also to other factors such as "store effect" and "size effect" (e.g., Caplovitz 1963; Goodman 1968; Frankel and Gould 2001). Poor consumers tend to shop at smaller stores, which sell items at higher prices, and purchase items of smaller quantity, which have higher price per unit.

In discussions and analyses of the impacts of high food prices, "consumers" should not be treated as a uniform group. Many of the world's poor and the overwhelming majority of the urban poor are *net* food consumers, who often also engage in small-scale agriculture production. In rural areas, food production is often one of the strategies for increasing household food security and complementing earnings from low-skilled wage labor. Thus, when food prices rise, poor rural households are both winners and losers, who experience impacts diverse in nature and size.

3   DETERMINANTS AND PATTERNS OF INCREASING AND VOLATILE FOOD PRICES

The factors that caused the food price spike in 2007–8 are multiple and complex. These include simultaneous changes on both the demand and the supply side of the world food equation, as well as changes in markets and trade (Table 24.1). Although the power of formal economic tools for determining the partial causalities is limited in a complex crisis context of multiple factors at work, a mix of theory, reasoning, history, and statistical analysis can lead to a fuller picture of the causes of the price spike (Heady and Fan 2008).

Table 24.1 Factors driving the food price spike in 2007–8

Demand side	= ?	Supply side
Income growth		Underinvestment in agricultural technology
Population growth		Underinvestment in agricultural infrastructure
High and variable energy prices		Land and water constraints
Biofuel subsidies and mandates		Rising costs of inputs and transport
Income inequality		Weather variability and climate change
Changing consumer preferences		
	Trade and markets	
	US dollar depreciation	
	Stock depletion	
	Trade controls and protectionism	
	Speculation and expectations	

On the demand side, rising consumer incomes and population growth were among the long-run drivers that led to the increase in food prices. Developing countries in Asia grew at 10 percent and in Africa at 6 percent a year on average in 2005–7, and continued to grow at 6 percent and 4 percent respectively in 2008–9 despite the global recession (IMF 2009a). World population grew by 78 million per year in 2005–9, reaching 6.8 billion in 2009 (UN 2009). Also on the demand side, high energy prices and government biofuel subsidies and mandates have increased demand for biofuel feedstock. Biofuel production has been estimated to trigger a 30 percent increase of weighted average international grain prices from 2000 to 2007 (Rosegrant 2008). Through the stronger food–energy link, the volatility of energy prices now causes increased volatility in food prices. Because of simultaneity of effects and changing weights of factors at the margin at different price levels in the buildup of a price spike, the question of which factors were most important can hardly be determined with certainty at a global level.

Increased food demand has been accompanied by changes in its structure. Rising incomes, urbanization, and globalization have led to dietary transition away from grains and other staples to vegetables, fruits, meat, dairy, and fish. Demand for ready-to-cook and ready-to-eat foods has also been on the rise. Consumers, especially in the cities, are also being exposed to non-traditional foods. The consumption of wheat and wheat-based products, temperate zone vegetables, and dairy products in Asia has substantially increased (Pingali 2006). With annual growth of incomes of 10 percent per year, purchased quantities of fresh fruits and vegetables per capita in a country like Vietnam are expected to grow about ten to thirteen times from 2005 to 2015 (Mergenthaler, Weinberger, and Qaim 2009). These factors will still be in place in the future as annual incomes and population continue to grow. Factors long taken for granted, such as globalization and urbanization, have been put to test as trade protectionism has risen, and reverse urbanization has been seen owing to the recession in some countries in 2008 and 2009.

On the supply side, long-lasting underinvestment in agricultural technology and infrastructure as well as increasing land and water constraints have led to low agricultural productivity and a slow production response to surging demand. Annual world cereal yield growth, for example, declined from about 3 percent in the 1960s and 1970s to less than 1 percent since 2000 (World Bank 2007). In addition, total factor productivity (derived from the ratio of total output growth to total input growth) in developing countries grew by an average of just 2.1 percent per year from 1992 to 2003 (von Braun, Fan, et al. 2008). While high prices and favorable weather spurred agricultural expansion in developed countries in 2007 and 2008, production response in developing countries remained low, with China and Brazil being notably positive with exceptions of global weight due to large research and development investments and agricultural supply enhancement actions. Cereal output grew by 11 percent in developed countries between 2007 and 2008 but by only 0.9 percent in developing countries (FAO 2008). If Brazil, China, and India are excluded, cereal production in the rest of the developing countries actually fell by 1.6 percent. Even before the crisis hit, global cereal stocks were at their lowest levels since the early 1980s, fostering nervousness in the markets.

Decrease in market stability and restrictions on trade openness compounded the effects of supply and demand and slowing productivity. To minimize the effects of higher prices on their populations, many governments resorted to ad hoc policy measures, such as export restrictions, export taxes, and price controls. These policies may have reduced domestic food prices in the short term, but they also made the global food market smaller and more volatile, and put additional upward pressure on food prices. Rising expectations, speculation, and efforts at hoarding—including at household level—in times of low stocks are among the additional factors that played a role in the increasing level and volatility of food prices. As the flow of speculative capital from financial investors into agricultural commodity markets increased significantly, it pushed up futures and spot prices above levels that can be explained by demand and supply. In the first quarter of 2008 alone, the volume of globally traded grain futures and options increased by 32 percent compared with the same period in 2007 at the Chicago Board of Trade.

The price of almost every food item sharply increased in 2007–8. At their peaks in the second quarter of 2008, world prices of wheat and maize were three times higher than at the beginning of 2003, and the price of rice was five times higher (Figure 24.1). Dairy products, meat, palm oil, and cassava also experienced sharp price hikes. The prices of butter and milk, for example, tripled between 2003 and 2008, and the prices of beef and poultry doubled. Prices have since dropped, mainly owing to slowing food demand with the global financial crisis and recession and favorable production, but remain high compared to prices three years ago.

From a long-term historical perspective, recent hikes in food prices are not exceptionally high if transformed by average consumer price deflators into real terms

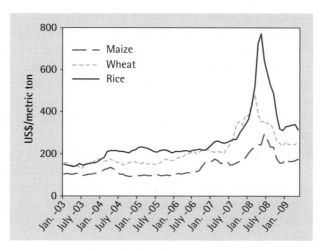

FIGURE 24.1 International grain prices, 2003–9

Sources: Date from FAO (2009).

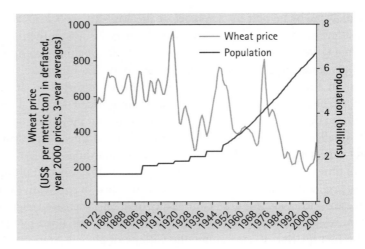

FIGURE 24.2 Food prices and population in history, 1872–2008

Sources: Data compiled and interpolated by the author from data from UN (1999, 2009); Godo (2001); OECD (2005); BLS (2008); NBER (2008); US Census Bureau (2008); FAO (2009).

(Figure 24.2). Setting aside the price spikes in the 1910s and 1940s, which occurred at a time of global warfare, the prices of major agricultural commodities at the beginning of 2008 were not even close to their peaks in 1973–4 (Piesse and Thirtle 2009). Applying average consumer price deflators, as is usually done, however, disregards the high food share in poor people's consumption basket. In view of the increased inequality in many countries, the recent international food price spike and the extent to which it was transmitted to local consumers may very well be on a historical high side for large shares of the world population. Overall, the challenge of feeding the world's growing population has greatly increased compared with past decades. Since the time of notoriously high food prices in the 1870s, world population has increased more than five times, raising neo-Malthusian concerns. The Green Revolution in Asia in the 1960s and 1970s has shown that rapid increases in agricultural production are possible with technological breakthroughs adopted on a large scale, and predictions of population growth outpacing agricultural production can be prevented. However, investment in agricultural science has been stagnating and the increase in agricultural productivity on the scale of the Green Revolution was never replicated in Africa, which poses a much more complex production environment.

The changes in global food prices are transmitted to different degrees to countries and communities owing to factors such as market structure and exchange rate dynamics. In Latin American countries there is strong evidence of cointegration between domestic and international food prices from 2002 to 2008 for almost all food items in Costa Rica, Honduras, Mexico, and Nicaragua. In other countries, such as the Dominican Republic, Ecuador, El Salvador, Guatemala, Panama, and Peru, however, there is evidence of cointegration just for one or two food products in the same period (Robles and Torero 2010). Since commodity markets in African coastal countries are in general well integrated with world markets (Abdulai 2006), global price shocks have been felt in most of the countries in the continent. Large countries in Asia, such as India and China, have managed to shield their consumers to a great extent from high global food prices, but countries such as Sri Lanka and Bangladesh were hard-hit by the food price shock.

4 CONSUMERS: RESPONSES AND IMPACTS

Consumption response to high food prices tends to be robust and predictable, with marked differences between rich and poor. Long before the 2007–8 prices hit, it was clear that the human costs of increasing and volatile food prices such as child malnutrition are high, and must be included in sound social costs and economic analysis of price volatility (Teklu, von Braun, and Zaki 1991).

Budget-schedule-derived estimates of price elasticities in 114 countries show that food demand in low-income countries is more responsive to changes in food prices compared to middle- and high-income countries, with price elasticity for food averaging −0.59 for low-income countries and −0.27 for high-income countries (Seale, Regmi, and Bernstein 2003). These estimates also show that consumption of staple food changes the least when prices change, while consumption of high-valued products such as beverages, meat, and dairy consumption change the most. Estimates of price elasticity which distinguish between income classes and characteristics of poverty establish even higher price elasticities for certain population groups in low-income countries, as shown in the example of Zambia (Table 24.2). The urban poor, however, tend to be less price-responsive than the rural poor in this example.

As a result of the recent price developments, it has become much more expensive to eat nutritious food. For example, in Guatemala, the price of a diet based on corn tortilla, vegetable oil, vegetables, beef, and beans—which supplies sufficient key recommended micronutrients—is almost twice as high as the price of a less nutritious diet based only on tortilla and vegetable oil (Figure 24.3). In fact, the cost of this balanced diet for just one person in 2008 was almost three-quarters of the total income of a poor person living on 1 dollar a day.

Poor communities and households are more sensitive to high food prices—not by choice, but by force. Since the poor already consume the lowest-quality and least diversified food and price increases occurred across all commodities, they have few options for substitution in their diets (Jensen and Miller 2008). Even when consumers are compensated for increases in food prices by increases in their income, evidence from Pakistan suggests that price elasticities drop only slightly (ul Haq, Nazli, and Meilke 2008).

To measure the responsiveness of nutrient consumption to such food price changes, price elasticity for micronutrient consumption can be calculated. Increases in maize prices in Malawi, for example, decrease the consumption of calories, protein, iron, zinc,

Table 24.2 Price elasticities of maize in Zambia per consumer group, 2002/3

	Maize price elasticity
North	
Commercial farm	−0.27
Small farm	−0.52
Rural non-farm	−0.59
Middle and urban rich	−0.45
Urban poor	−0.39
South	
Commercial farm	−0.25
Small farm	−0.33
Rural non-farm	−0.33
Middle and urban rich	−0.12
Urban poor	−0.18
National aggregate	−0.43

Source: Dorosh, Dradri, and Haggblade (2009); authors' "low" estimates of price elasticity used here.

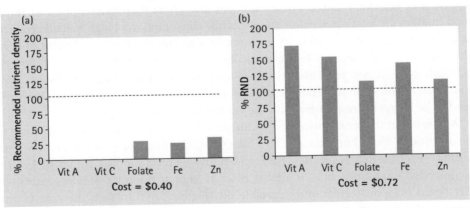

FIGURE 24.3 Costs per person per day of corn tortilla-based diets in Guatemala at different micronutrient levels
(a) Corn tortilla and vegetable oil.
(b) Corn tortilla, vegetable oil, carrots, orange, beef, spinach, and black beans.
Sources: Erick Boy, IFPRI, based on Guatemala city market prices in November 2008; and data from FAO/WHO 2002.

and vitamin B6 (Ecker 2009). In the case of Malawi, there are significant differences in the responsiveness to price changes of different nutrients and food items. The price elasticity for Vitamins A and C, for example, is higher since these vitamins are provided by relatively few and expensive food items, and it is more difficult for households to substitute them. Taking into account the complete diet, a 50 percent increase in the price of food in Bangladesh is estimated to raise the prevalence of iron deficiency among women and children by 25 percent (Bouis 2008).The resulting exacerbation of micronutrient deficiencies has negative consequences for nutrition and health, such as impaired cognitive development, lower resistance to disease, and increased risks during childbirth for both mothers and children.

Many poor households not only consume less food and shift to even less balanced diets, but also spend less on other goods and services that are essential for their short- and long-run health and welfare, such as clean water, sanitation, education, and health care. Coping capacity depends on the asset base of the household as well as on human resources and informal community networks. In response to the food price spike in 2007–8 a variety of other responses have been recorded. In Pakistan, for example, many parents have responded to high food prices in 2007–8 by taking children out of school, sending them to work, or switching them from private to cheaper public schools (UN Inter Agency Assessment Mission 2008). In Cambodia, many poor households have sold assets such as animals, and plan to sell land if they cannot cope with difficulties (CDRI 2008).The indebtedness of households also increased as a large share purchased food on credit. In response to food price volatility, small farmers increase their storage of food for their own consumption or for replanting in the next season. Other adaptation strategies to high food prices such as increased working times for women either in the labor market to receive more income, or in the house to process and cook cheaper, more starchy foods, add time burdens at the expense of child rearing and needed rest. All of these coping strategies have three general goals: "risk minimization," "risk absorption," and "risk taking to survive" (von Braun, Teklu, and Webb 1998). While these mechanisms could "buffer" the effect of shocks in the short run, this is more difficult to do in the long run (Jensen and Miller 2008). Strategies for risk minimization and especially for risk absorption and risk taking to survive can have irreversible negative effects on health, education, and assets, which might result in poverty traps.

The actual types and size of impacts of high food prices on consumers are radically different across households and individuals owing to different initial conditions and policy responses. At the household level, effects depend on a number of characteristics, including whether the household is a net food producer or consumer, the share of food in its expenditure, access to services and assets, and vulnerability due to non-price factors (Benson et al. 2008). Net food producers are likely to benefit from high food prices since the increase in their income will more than compensate for the increase in the food purchased. The majority of the population in developing countries, however, consists of net food consumers and they are negatively affected. Initial factors affecting the impact of high food prices, such as the share of food in household expenditure, show large regional, rural–urban, and income group differences within developing countries. In Ghana, for example, household expenditure on food varies between 41 percent in the urban coastal region, and 70 percent in the rural north savannah (Cudjoe, Breisinger, and Diao 2008). In Ethiopia, food in total daily expenditures is

41 percent in Addis Ababa, compared with 62 percent in the rural area of Dire Dawa (Ulimwengu, Workneh, and Paulos 2009).

In addition, effects of high food prices within the household vary, and depend on intra-household factors such as access to the household's resources and gender. Indeed, food crises tend to affect women more deeply and for longer because they more often lack the income and assets that could help them cope with the crisis than men (Quisumbing et al. 2008).

Cross-country evidence shows that poor consumers are affected much more than the rich and the combined effects of food price increases on poverty. The stylized distribution of gains and losses from a 10 percent rice price increase in Indonesia shows a pattern common in many low- and middle-income countries. In all income groups there are both winners and losers; for the poor, the monetary losses of the food price increase are greater than the gains (McCulloch 2008). For the rich, losses are the highest in absolute terms, but smaller in relative terms proportional to their high incomes. An eleven-country study of the impacts of high food prices shows that the poorest households are the worst affected overall, both in urban and in rural areas (Zezza et al. 2008).

An increase in the food prices often constitutes a transfer from the large majority of net consumers to a minority of net producers, and results in an overall increase of poverty. The domestic food price increase in 2007–8 in Pakistan is estimated to have increased poverty by 35–45 percent in urban areas and 33 percent in rural areas (ul Haq, Nazli, and Meilke 2008). Even in agricultural exporting countries, increases of food prices can lead to an increase in poverty. In Thailand, for example, the positive effects on poor food producers are smaller than the negative effects on poor food consumers (Warr 2008). Household data estimations on the effects of high food prices in nine low-income countries suggest that poverty increases are more common and larger than poverty reductions (Ivanic and Martin 2008). Dessus, Herrera, and de Hoyos (2008) show for a sample of seventy-three developing countries that the change in the cost of alleviating urban poverty brought about by the recent increase in food prices represents less than 0.1 percent of GDP, while in the most severely affected it may exceed 3 percent (Dessus, Herrera, and de Hoyos 2008). All of these studies, however, focus on the short-term impact of rising food prices only while the long-term implications through health add additional burden on the consequences of high food prices.

Panel surveys are an essential source for development policy analysis (Deaton 1997). Despite many improvements in data monitoring and analysis, many countries currently lack the capacity to provide timely and reliable data sets and carry out moderate and advanced data analyses. Relevant information is often outdated, spotty in coverage, and insufficiently disaggregated to local levels. Even information for basic and essential analysis such as up-to-date representative income and expenditure panel surveys are still scarce in developing countries. This information gap needs urgent correction to measure actual impacts of food price hikes on consumers and formulate appropriate policy responses.

5   Actions for Mitigation and Prevention of Adverse Effects

A long-standing set of government policies has tried to mitigate and prevent negative effects of high and volatile food prices. These polices include subsidies to mitigate the effects to consumers who cannot afford high food prices, and second, price stabilization to prevent adverse effects. Subsidies have traditionally been designed for two purposes: to ration food provided at specified minimum quantity, and to transfer income to certain populations (Pinstrup-Andersen and Alderman 1988). Many of these subsidies, however, have not been successful at reaching the intended beneficiaries owing to poor design and implementation. In India, for example, only 42 percent of subsidized grains reach the intended beneficiaries owing to leakages and diversions (Programme Evaluation Organisation 2005). Subsidies also have high fiscal costs and economic costs, especially when they are not targeted properly at the poor and not adjusted to price levels. The public distribution system in India covers about 600 million people, but this is done at a cost of $7 billion per year in recent years (Dorosh 2008). These subsidy policies popular in past decades have come back with a vengeance during the food price crisis in 2007–8, and countries that did not already have well-established targeting polices were confronted with large increases in food price subsidies for lack of alternative instruments on hand. The fiscal cost of poorly targeted, mainly in-kind food subsidies in Egypt, for example, grew from 1.3 percent of GDP in 2006/7 to 2.1 percent in 2008/9 (IMF 2009b).

The second long-standing set of government policies is that of instruments to stabilize food prices. The major mechanisms in developing countries are buffer stock agencies and trade-based stabilization instruments, which are often used simultaneously (McCulloch and Timmer 2008). Some of these policies and institutions that have been appropriate in past decades, however, have not proved so effective in the current environment. Agricultural parastatals, for example, are becoming increasingly expensive and inefficient and need to be replaced by alternative institutional mechanisms for achieving stability of food prices and food security (Rashid, Gulati, and Cummings 2008). One of the general lessons that can be drawn from the experiences of developing countries with food price stabilization is that large potential gains can be realized by relying on international trade and market mechanisms (Dorosh 2008). However, policies contradictory to this lesson have often been deployed during and in the aftermath of the 2007–8 price spike. Even though many countries had reduced their grain stocks prior to the 2007–8 food crisis and have been relying on market mechanisms, the accumulation of buffer stocks has also increased in major producers such as India and China. Doubts about market efficiency in times of rising price speculation have led to the occasional closure of trading grains commodity exchanges in India and China.

A sustainable solution to the food price crisis needs a holistic approach encompassing the whole agri-food system and even needs to go beyond agriculture with strengthening human capital and employment expansion in the non-farm economy. Interventions intended to mitigate adverse effects on consumers should be coupled with supply-side interventions intended to increase food production sustainably and to simultaneously implement policies preventing excessive price volatility, thereby serving consumers. Priorities for action include sound policies in three areas:

Promote pro-poor agricultural growth. To enhance agricultural productivity, investments should be scaled up in the areas of R & D, rural infrastructure, rural institutions, and information monitoring and sharing. Doubling investments in public agricultural research from the current about US$5 billion to US$10 billion from 2008 to 2013 would significantly increase agricultural output and millions of people would emerge from poverty. If these R & D investments are targeted at the poor regions of the world—sub-Saharan Africa and South Asia—overall agricultural output growth would increase by 1.1 percentage points a year and lift about 282 million people out of poverty by 2020 through income and consumption effects (von Braun et al. 2008).

Reduce extreme market volatility. Two global collective actions for food security are needed to reduce extreme market volatility: first, a small, independent physical reserve should be established exclusively for emergency response and humanitarian assistance; second, a virtual reserve, i.e., a financial fund and intervention mechanism, should be created to help avoid price spikes. The organizational design of the virtual reserve would include a high-level technical commission that would have the capacity to intervene in futures markets and a global intelligence unit that would signal when prices head toward a spike (von Braun and Torero 2009).

Expand social protection and child nutrition action. To protect the basic nutrition of the most vulnerable and improve food security, agricultural growth and reducing market volatility must be accompanied by social protection and nutrition actions. *Protective actions* are needed to mitigate short-term risks (including conditional cash transfers, pension systems, and employment programs), and *preventive actions* are needed to avoid long-term negative consequences (including preventive health and nutrition interventions such as school feeding and programs for improved early childhood nutrition and strengthened and expanded to ensure universal coverage). Safety nets are needed not only to transfer income to the most vulnerable, but also to insure against consumption of deficient diets and stabilize their asset base. Such safety nets need to have a counter-cyclical budget and target transitory correlates of poverty (Alderman and Haque 2006).

Sound institutions (laws and regulations, as well as organizations) have crucial roles to play in boosting agricultural and economy-wide growth, coping with and recovering from the recent world food crisis, as well as preventing similar crises in the future. Special attention needs to be paid to institutions that define scale in farming and food industries; contract and cooperation choices; roles of public and private sectors along the food value chains; market and trade arrangements; taxation, subsidies, and pricing;

and public sector functions in agriculture at central versus local government levels. Institutional innovations can play important roles in strengthening markets for commodities produced, bought, and sold by smallholders by reducing transaction costs, managing risk, building social capital, enabling collective action, and redressing missing markets.

REFERENCES

Abdulai, A. 2006. "Spatial Integration and Price Transmission in Agricultural Commodity Markets in Sub-Saharan Africa." In A. Sarris and D. Hallam, eds., *Agricultural Commodity Markets and Trade: New Approaches to Analyzing Market Structure and Instability.* Cheltenham: Edward Elgar; Northampton, MA: Food and Agriculture Organization of the United Nations.

Alderman, H., and T. Haque. 2006. "Countercyclical Safety Nets for the Poor and Vulnerable." *Food Policy* 31: 372–83.

Benson, T., N. Minot, J. Pender, M. Robles, and J. von Braun. 2008. *Global Food Crises: Monitoring and Assessing Impact to Inform Policy Responses.* Food Policy Report. Washington, DC: International Food Policy Research Institute.

BLS (Bureau of Labor Statistics). 2008. *BLS CPI (Consumer Price Index) Database.* <http://www.bls.gov/cpi/#data>.

Bouis, H. 2008. *Rising Food Prices Will Result in Severe Declines in Mineral and Vitamin Intakes of the Poor.* Washington, DC: HarvestPlus.

Caplovitz, D. 1963. *The Poor Pay More: Consumer Practices in Low-Income Families.* Toronto: Free Press of Glencoe.

CDRI (Cambodia Development Resource Institute). 2008. *Impact of High Food Prices in Cambodia.* Survey Report. <http://home.wfp.org/stellent/groups/public/documents/ena/wfp189739.pdf>.

Cudjoe, G., C. Breisinger, and X. Diao. 2008. *Local Impacts of a Global Crisis: Food Price Transmission and Poverty Impacts in Ghana.* Discussion Paper No. 00842. Washington, DC: International Food Policy Research Institute.

Deaton, A. 1997. *The Analysis of Household Surveys: A Microeconomic Approach to Development Policy.* Baltimore: Johns Hopkins University Press for the World Bank.

Dessus, S., S. Herrera, and R. de Hoyos. 2008. "The Impact of Food Inflation on Urban Poverty and its Monetary Cost: Some Back of the Envelope Calculations." *Agricultural Economics* 39: 417–29.

Dorosh, P. A. 2008. "Food Price Stabilisation and Food Security: International Experience." *Bulletin of Indonesian Economic Studies* 44: 93–114.

——, S. Dradri, and S. Haggblade. 2009. "Regional Trade, Government Policy and Food Security: Recent Evidence from Zambia." *Food Policy* 34/4: 350–66.

Ecker, O. 2009. *Economics of Micronutrient Malnutrition: The Demand for Nutrients in Sub-Saharan Africa.* Diss. University of Hohenheim.

FAO (Food and Agriculture Organization of the United Nations). 2008. *Food Outlook.* Rome: Food and Agriculture Organization of the United Nations.

—— 2009. *International Commodity Prices Database.* <http://www.fao.org/es/esc/prices/PricesServlet.jsp?lang=en>.

Frankel, D., and E. Gould. 2001. "The Retail Price of Inequality." *Journal of Urban Economics* 49: 219–39.

Glosten, L. R., and P. R. Milgrom. 1985. "Bid, Ask and Transaction Prices in a Specialist Market with Heterogeneously Informed Traders." *Journal of Financial Economics* 14: 1127–61.

Godo, Y. 2001. *Estimation of Average Years of Schooling by Levels of Education for Japan and the United States, 1890–1990.* FASID (Foundation for Advanced Studies on International Development) database, Japan. <http://www.fasid.or.jp/english/surveys/research/program/research/pdf/database/2001-001.pdf>.

Goodman, C. S. 1968. "Do the Poor Pay More?" *Journal of Marketing* 32: 18–24.

Grossman, S., and J. Stiglitz. 1980. "On the Impossibility of Informationally Efficient Markets." *American Economic Review* 70: 393–408.

Heady, D., and S. Fan. 2008. "Anatomy of a Crisis: The Causes and Consequences of Surging Food Prices." *Agricultural Economics* 39: 375–91.

IMF (International Monetary Fund). 2009a. *World Economic Outlook Database.* <http://www.imf.org/external/pubs/ft/weo/2009/01/weodata/index.aspx>.

—— 2009b. *Arab Republic of Egypt: 2008 Article IV Consultation.* IMF Country Report No. 09/25. Washington, DC: International Monetary Fund. <http://www.imf.org/external/pubs/ft/scr/2009/cr0925.pdf>.

Ivanic, M., and W. Martin. 2008. "Implications of Higher Global Food Prices on Poverty in Low-Income Countries." *Agricultural Economics* 39: 405–16.

Jackson, M., and J. Peck. 1999. "Asymmetric Information in a Competitive Market Game: Reexamining the Implications of Rational Expectations." *Economic Theory* 13: 603–28.

Jensen, R. T., and N. H. Miller. 2008. "The Impact of Food Price Increases on Caloric Intake in China." *Agricultural Economics* 39: 465–76.

McCulloch, N. 2008. "Rice Prices and Poverty in Indonesia." *Bulletin of Indonesian Economic Studies* 44: 45–63.

—— and P. C. Timmer. 2008. "Rice Policy in Indonesia: A Special Issue." *Bulletin of Indonesian EconomicStudies* 44: 33–44.

Mellor, J. W., and R. Ahmed. 1988. *Agricultural Price Policy in Developing Countries.* Baltimore: Johns Hopkins University Press for the International Food Policy Research Institute.

Mergenthaler, M., K. Weinberger, and M. Qaim. 2009. "The Food System Transformation in Developing Countries: A Disaggregate Demand Analysis for Fruits and Vegetables in Vietnam." *Food Policy* 34/5: 426–36.

NBER (National Bureau of Economic Research). 2008. *NBER Macrohistory Database.* <http://www.nber.org/databases/macrohistory/contents>.

Newbery, D., and J. Stiglitz. 1981. *The Theory of Commodity Price Stabilization: A Study in the Economics of Risk.* Oxford: Clarendon Press.

OECD (Organisation for Economic Co-operation and Development). 2005. *2005 OECD Agricultural Outlook Tables, 1970–2014.* <http://www.oecd.org/dataoecd/55/44/32980897.xls>.

Piesse, J., and C. Thirtle. 2009. "Three Bubbles and a Panic: An Explanatory Review of Recent Food Commodity Price Events." *Food Policy* 34: 119–29.

Pingali, P. 2006. "Westernization of Asian Diets and the Transformation of Food Systems: Implications for Research and Policy." *Food Policy* 32: 281–98.

Pinstrup-Andersen, P., and H. Alderman. 1988. "The Effectiveness of Consumer-Oriented Food Subsidies in Reaching Rationing and Income-Transfer Goals." In P. Pinstrup-Andersen, ed.,

Food Subsidies in Developing Countries: Costs, Benefits and Policy Options. Baltimore: Johns Hopkins University Press for the International Food Policy Research Institute.

Programme Evaluation Organisation. 2005. *Performance Evaluation of Targeted Public Distribution System.* New Delhi: Planning Commission, Government of India.

Quisumbing, A., R. Meinzen-Dick, L. Bassett, M. Usnick, L. Pandolfelli, C. Morden, and H. Alderman. 2008. *Helping Women Respond to the Global Food Price Crisis.* IFPRI Policy Brief No. 7. Washington, DC: International Food Policy Research Institute.

Rapsomanikis, G., D. Hallam, and P. Conforti. 2006. "Market Integration and Price Transmission in Selected Food and Cash Crop Markets of Developing Countries: Review and Applications." In A. Sarris and D. Hallam, eds., *Agricultural Commodity Markets and Trade: New Approaches to Analyzing Market Structure and Instability.* Cheltenham: Edward Elgar; Northampton, MA: Food and Agriculture Organization of the United Nations.

Rashid, S., A. Gulati, and R. Cummings, Jr. 2008. "Times Have Changed: Learning New Ways of Doing Business." In Rashid, Gulati, and Cummings, eds, *From Parastatals to Private Trade: Lessons from Asian Agriculture.* Baltimore: Johns Hopkins University Press for the International Food Policy Research Institute.

Robles, M., and M. Torero. 2010. "Assessing Impact of Increased Global Food Prices on the Poor in Selected Latin American Countries." *Economica* 10/2 (Spring), 117–64.

Rosegrant, M. W. 2008. "Biofuels and Grain Prices: Impacts and Policy Responses." Unpublished paper. Washington, DC: International Food Policy Research Institute, May 7.

Sadoulet, E., and A. de Janvry. 1995. *Quantitative Development Policy Analysis.* Baltimore: Johns Hopkins University Press.

Seale, J., A. Regmi, and J. Bernstein. 2003. *International Evidence on Food Consumption Patterns.* Technical Bulletin No. 1904. Washington, DC: US Department of Agriculture.

Streeten, P. 1987. *What Price Food? Agricultural Price Policies in Developing Countries.* Ithaca, NY: Cornell University Press.

Teklu, T., J. von Braun, and E. Zaki. 1991. *Drought and Famine Relationships in Sudan: Policy Implications.* Research Report No. 88. Washington, DC: International Food Policy Research Institute.

ul Haq, Z., H. Nazli, and K. Meilke. 2008. "Implications of High Food Prices for Poverty in Pakistan." *Agricultural Economics* 39: 477–84.

Ulimwengu, J. M., S. Workneh, and Z. Paulos. 2009. *Impact of Soaring Food Price in Ethiopia: Does Location Matter?* IFPRI Discussion Paper No. 846. Washington, DC: International Food Policy Research Institute.

UN (United Nations). 1999. *The World at Six Billion.* New York.

——2009. *World Population Prospects: The 2008 Revision. Highlights.* New York: United Nations.

UN (United Nations) Inter Agency Assessment Mission. 2008. *High Food Prices in Pakistan: Impact Assessment and the Way Forward.* <http://www.fao.org/GIEWS/ENGLISH/otherpub/PakistanImpactAssessment.pdf>.

US Census Bureau. 2008. *International Database.* <http://www.census.gov/ipc/www/idb>.

von Braun, J. 2008. *Food and Financial Crises: Implications for Agriculture and the Poor.* Food Policy Report. Washington, DC: International Food Policy Research Institute.

——and M. Torero. 2009. *Implementing Physical and Virtual Food Reserves to Protect the Poor and Prevent Market Failure.* Policy Brief No. 10. Washington, DC: International Food Policy Research Institute.

von Braun, J., S. Fan, R. Meinzen-Dick, M. W. Rosegrant, and A. Nin Pratt. 2008. *International Agricultural Research for Food Security, Poverty Reduction, and the Environment: What to Expect from Scaling up CGIAR Investments and "Best Bet" Programs.* Washington, DC: International Food Policy Research Institute.

——, T. Teklu, and P. Webb. 1998. *Famine in Africa: Causes, Responses, and Prevention.* Baltimore: Johns Hopkins University Press for the International Food Policy Research Institute.

Warr, P. 2008. "World Food Prices and Poverty Incidence in a Food Exporting Country: A Multi Household General Equilibrium Analysis for Thailand." *Agricultural Economics* 39: 525–37.

World Bank. 2007. *World Development Report 2008: Agriculture for Development.* Washington, DC: World Bank.

Zezza, A., B. Davis, C. Azzarri, K. Covarrubias, L. Tasciotti, and G. Anriquez. 2008. *The Impact of Rising Food Prices on the Poor.* ESA Working Paper No. 08-07. Washington, DC: Food and Agriculture Organization of the United Nations. <ftp://ftp.fao.org/docrep/fao/011/aj284e/aj284e00.pdf>.

CHAPTER 25

....

CHANGING NUTRITIONAL CONTENT OF FOOD

....

HELEN H. JENSEN

1 INTRODUCTION

....

Evidence is mounting that the quality of a population's diet has long-term consequences for its health. With rapidly diffusing technologies and information, and increased urbanization, dietary trends in developed nations have spread quickly to countries with lower per capita income. Diets are shifting from those high in complex carbohydrates to those that are more varied but that include relatively more sugars, fats, and oils. Accompanying the changes are problems of increased obesity and overweight worldwide. At the same time, deficiencies in micronutrients persist among the poor (WHO 2002). Although a variety of foods can offer nutrients that meet the needs of most healthy individuals, factors such as low income, poor access to some foods, processing, and packaging and delivery technologies have all influenced the nutritional content and availability of the food supply. This chapter addresses the changes in the nutritional content of foods across time and the factors that influence differences in the availability and access to nutrients.

Why is the nutritional content of food important to studies of food consumption? Although there is only mixed evidence that demand for nutrients themselves drives demand for food, the availability of nutrients in food is critically important to the design of food programs and policies and to the health of the population. Planning for targeted food assistance is based on assessment of the adequacy of diets in providing priority nutrients and effective, food-based approaches to designing food programs. When a nutrient is in short supply in the diet, planners consider efforts through income or in-kind transfer, nutrition information and education, or modification of foods themselves to improve the quality of diets. In evaluating marketing and health promotion efforts, understanding consumer responses to attributes in foods and the value of changing the nutritional profile of foods is also important to the food industry and policymakers. This chapter provides an overview of the changes in nutrient content of the food supply in the United States and then describes core concepts used in assessment of the adequacy of (or excess in) diets. Factors that affect nutrient availability in the food supply—such as the convergence of dietary patterns and food production and processing and distribution technologies—affect nutrient content. Although much of the evidence is drawn from the United States, the trends in other higher-income countries are similar. Fortification of food products is an extension of the discussion of technological interventions to change nutritional content of available foods and has important implications for health. Finally, the contribution of economics is considered in providing a better understanding of the factors that affect demand for foods and related nutrients.

2   Trends in Nutrient Intake

The nutrient content of the food supply has changed dramatically during the last century. The changes reflect underlying changes in the foods consumed, the effect of income and development, changes in dietary guidance, and changes in processing technology, as well as enrichment and fortification standards. A compilation of data on the nutrient content of the US food supply shows the important contribution of changing levels of food intakes as well as nutrient composition of the foods (see Table 25.1). By the turn of the twenty-first century, per capita food energy levels in the United States had reached an all-time high, a level of 4,000 kilocalories (kcal) in 2001 based on food availability, or "disappearance" estimates (Hiza and Bente 2007). More recent data confirm this trend (USDA ERS 2010). When these estimates are adjusted for food loss (food spoilage, plate waste, and other losses), the estimated food availability was 2,717 kcal per capita in 2000, and down slightly to 2,673 kcal per capita in 2008. At the same time, changes in global food consumption show an increase in calorie consumption as well as a shift from carbohydrate-rich staple grains to more protein-rich food sources in meat and dairy and to other more varied products. Fabiosa (Chapter 23 in this volume) reviews the global trends and the shift from staple crops to protein-rich foods and to more convenient and varied foods as consumers adjust consumption to reflect their higher income.

2.1   Macronutrients

Carbohydrates, protein, and fat (and alcohol) are the macronutrients that supply energy in the diet. In the United States and in most high-income countries, the share of energy supplied by fat has increased while the share from carbohydrates has fallen during the last century. Carbohydrates come from plant sources, and historically grains

Table 25.1 US food supply: selected nutrients contributed from major food groups, per capita per day, 1970 and 2004 (% of total nutrient)

Food group	Food energy (kcal)	Food energy (%)	Protein (%)	Fat (%)	Saturated fat (%)	Vitamin A (%)	Vitamin C (%)	Folate (DFE) (%)	Calcium (%)	Iron (%)	Zinc (%)	Sodium (%)
Meat, poultry, and fish												
1970	579.2	18.1	39.7	31.9	34.9	35.6	2.4	9.6	2.7	22.4	46.1	17.5
2004	522.6	13.4	40.3	20.3	22.5	32.0	2.3	2.8	3.4	15.7	37.2	16.5
Dairy products[a]												
1970	361.6	11.3	22.3	13.3	23.6	21.5	4.2	9.2	76.3	2.5	19.5	28.9
2004	335.4	8.6	19.0	10.4	20.8	17.5	2.5	2.6	71.7	1.9	16.3	34.7
Eggs												
1970	64.0	2.0	5.5	3.0	2.6	6.7	0.0	6.8	2.2	3.9	3.8	4.3
2004	54.6	1.4	4.0	2.0	2.0	6.4	0.0	1.9	1.8	2.2	2.6	3.7
Fats and oils[b]												
1970	576.0	18.0	0.2	45.1	34.8	11.4	0.0	0.1	0.6	0.1	0.1	14.3
2004	932.1	23.9	0.1	59.0	49.1	8.2	0.0	0.0	0.3	0.1	0.0	9.0
Fruits[c]												
1970	96.0	3.0	1.2	0.4	0.2	1.9	39.2	9.0	2.3	3.0	1.2	1.6
2004	120.9	3.1	1.2	0.5	0.3	2.4	40.7	4.7	2.6	2.5	1.2	2.0
Citrus												
1970	28.8	0.9	0.5	0.1	0.0	0.3	24.9	6.4	1.2	0.6	0.3	0.0
2004	35.1	0.9	0.5	0.0	0.0	0.4	27.6	3.4	1.2	0.4	0.3	0.1
Non-citrus												
1970	67.2	2.1	0.7	0.3	0.2	1.5	24.9	2.6	1.1	2.4	0.9	1.5
2004	85.8	2.2	0.7	0.5	0.3	2.0	27.6	1.3	1.4	2.1	0.9	1.9
Legumes, nuts, and soy												
1970	96.0	3.0	5.3	3.7	2.0	0.0	0.0	19.0	3.5	9.2	5.8	0.2
2004	120.9	3.1	6.1	4.1	2.4	0.0	0.1	7.0	4.3	7.4	5.7	0.3
Vegetables[d]												
1970	179.2	5.6	6.0	0.5	0.2	17.6	49.6	29.1	6.2	14.0	7.7	29.9
2004	18.3.3	4.7	5.5	0.5	0.2	26.8	48.8	10.0	7.0	10.1	6.4	28.9

(continued)

Table 25.1 Continued

Food group	Food energy (kcal)	Food energy (%)	Protein (%)	Fat (%)	Saturated fat (%)	Vitamin A (%)	Vitamin C (%)	Folate (DFE) (%)	Calcium (%)	Iron (%)	Zinc (%)	Sodium (%)
White potatoes												
1970	89.6	2.8	2.4	0.1	0.1	0.0	18.2	5.3	0.9	4.8	3.0	3.0
2004	93.6	2.4	2.2	0.1	0.1	0.0	15.5	1.7	0.9	3.4	2.3	3.2
Dark green, deep yellow												
1970	12.8	0.4	0.4	0.0	0.0	13.6	6.6	3.0	1.0	1.3	0.6	1.3
2004	15.6	0.4	0.5	0.1	0.0	22.2	13.0	1.8	1.4	1.2	0.6	1.2
Other vegetables												
1970	76.8	2.4	3.2	0.4	0.1	4.0	24.8	20.7	4.4	8.0	4.1	25.6
2004	78.0	2.0	2.7	0.3	0.1	4.7	20.3	6.4	4.8	5.4	3.3	24.5
Grain products												
1970	630.4	19.7	18.2	1.4	0.7	0.2	0.0	15.0	3.3	35.9	11.7	0.6
2004	916.5	23.5	21.8	2.3	1.5	5.0	4.6	69.9	4.9	51.2	25.8	1.0
Sugars and sweeteners												
1970	588.8	18.4	0.0	0.0	0.0	0.0	0.0	0.0	0.6	1.1	0.5	2.3
2004	674.7	17.3	0.0	0.0	0.0	0.0	0.0	0.0	0.6	0.8	0.4	3.4
Miscellaneous[d]												
1970	25.6	0.8	1.7	0.8	0.9	5.1	4.4	2.3	2.3	7.8	3.6	0.4
2004	35.1	0.9	2.0	1.0	1.3	1.7	1.0	1.1	3.3	8.1	4.4	0.5
TOTAL (RATIO OF CHANGE 1970/2004)												
1970	3,200.0	1.22[e]	1.15[e]	1.23[e]	1.10[e]	0.87[e]	1.12[e]	2.99[e]	1.01[e]	1.47[e]	1.21[e]	0.98[e]
2004	3,900.0											

Note: Percentages for food groups are based on aggregate nutrient data.
[a] Excl. butter.
[b] Incl. butter.
[c] Totals may not add owing to rounding.
[d] Coffee, tea, spices, chocolate liquor equivalent cocoa beans, and fortification not assigned to a particular group.
[e] These values are ratios of the values for energy, Protein, etc—not percentages.
Source: USDA Center for Nutrition Policy and Promotion, Feb. 27, 2009, based on data from the Food Availability Per Capita Data Sets; USDA ERS <http://www.ers.usda.gov/Data/FoodConsumption/#table>.

and vegetables (including potatoes) have been the major sources. In many countries with relatively low per capita income, wheat, rice, and maize are the staple crops that provide the carbohydrates. In high-income countries, nearly equally important in terms of energy is the contribution of sugars and sweeteners. In the US diet, the level of carbohydrate availability has increased by about 100 grams per capita per day since 1970 (to 481 grams per capita in 2004), with grain products contributing nearly 40 percent and sugars and sweeteners contributing 37 percent of the total.

Protein is available from both plant and animal sources. In the United States, total protein available for consumption has increased since the 1970s, up from levels near 98 grams per capita per day to 113 grams in 2004. Animal sources of protein are most important in the US diet. Meat, poultry, and fish contribute about 40 percent of total protein, and grain products contribute nearly 22 percent. Although the absolute level of protein from dairy products remains at the 1970 level, the relative contribution to total protein from dairy products has fallen below that of grain products, to 19 percent of the total. Protein from legumes, nuts, and soy has increased to 6 percent of the total protein in 2004. In other countries, the total protein available from the food supply increases with level of income and the shift in diet to animal protein sources. The animal-based protein sources themselves (dairy products, beef and veal, poultry, pork, and fish) vary with a country's natural endowment and cultural preferences.

In contrast to other macronutrients, the availability of fat in the food supply has increased throughout the world and reveals a shift in the structure of the food supply. The shift toward more fat in the diet now occurs at lower levels of per capita income than before, in large part because of the increased global availability of relatively inexpensive vegetable oils. Cheaper vegetable sources of fat, along with increased urbanization, have led to diets now higher in fat at all levels of income and a convergence of diets to a relatively higher share of calories from fat than existed earlier (Drewnowski and Popkin 1997). Larger supplies of domestic and imported oilseeds and vegetable oils have increased the supply of vegetable sources of fat globally. At the same time, higher income continues to be associated with an increased share of calories from animal fat.

In the US food supply, the total amount of fat has increased relatively steadily over the last century from 122 grams per capita per day in 1909 to 179 grams per capita in 2004. By 2004 the contribution of calories from fat had reached a level of 41 percent of total calories from energy, up from 31 percent at the beginning of the twentieth century (USDA ERS 2010). Although the percentage of calories from fat has not changed much since 1970, the amount of fat increased over 23 percent, from 145 to 179 grams, while the sources of fat have changed. During the period between 1970 and 2004, the share of total fat from meat, poultry, and fish decreased (from 31.9 to 20.3 percent) and the share from dairy also decreased (from 13.3 to 10.4 percent). At the same time, the share of fat from fats and oils increased sharply (from 45.1 to 59.0 percent). Fat from fats and oils is consumed directly through products such as salad oils, as well as consumed in processed products and used in preparing foods.

In the United States, dietary cholesterol consumption reached a peak in the late 1940s of 540 milligrams per capita. Since that time, intake has fallen, and since the mid-1970s it has ranged from 400 to 430 milligrams. Major food sources are eggs and meat, followed by dairy products. The amount of cholesterol in the diet reflects consumption of foods from these groups, as well as shifts within the groups (e.g., types of meat and even cuts of meat).

2.2   Micronutrients and Minerals

The overall diet and food variety contribute to the availability of micronutrients and minerals from food sources. Micronutrients include vitamins, such as vitamins A, C, and E, and the B vitamins (B6 and B12); folic acid; niacin and riboflavin; as well as other nutrients, such as choline. Minerals in the diet include calcium, iodine, iron, magnesium, phosphorus, potassium, sodium, and zinc, among others. In most high-income countries, micronutrients and minerals are widely available in the diet and have increased because of the greater availability of food, changes in dietary intakes, as well as enrichment and fortification regulations. Animal-based food sources are good sources of niacin, B6, B12, phosphorus, iron, and zinc in addition to protein. Although the diet provides adequate supplies of most nutrients, some nutrients are consumed at levels below those recommended and at levels identified as "of concern." Recent dietary guidance in the United States (Dietary Guidelines Advisory Committee 2010) notes concern for low levels of intake of vitamin D, calcium, potassium, and dietary fiber in general; low levels of folate and iron for women of reproductive age; and low levels of vitamin B12 for older individuals. Nutrients of concern for excessive intake include sodium, saturated fat, and added sugar.

Changes in food sources are important to explaining changes in availability over time. Vitamin A is a good example. Vitamin A (measured in Retinol Activity Equivalents, RAE) contributes to good vision, promotes growth and bone development, and supports the immune system. Animal products are an important source, and relatively high amounts of vitamin A are found in organ meats. In the United States, with the decline in consumption of organ meats in the last twenty-five years, the share contributed by other food sources has increased (see Table 25.1). Dark green and deep yellow vegetables and dairy products are now especially important sources. However, fortification of low-fat and skim milk with vitamin A has increased the availability of this vitamin, despite a shift from the naturally occurring sources in whole milk and butter and some meats.

Vitamin C is another example of a micronutrient with changes in availability that reflect shifts in the food supply as well as fortification. Fruits and vegetables are the primary sources of vitamin C, with about half of the vitamin coming from citrus products. White potatoes have traditionally been a good vegetable source in the past. Although still true today, dark green and deep yellow vegetables and other vegetables have become increasingly important sources. And grain products, which include the fortified ready-to-eat cereals, now contribute nearly 5 percent of vitamin C. In 1970 grains contributed only negligible vitamin C in the diet.

Enrichment of flour in the United States beginning in the 1940s, along with increased nutrient fortification of ready-to-eat breakfast cereals in 1974, had a significant influence in changing sources of the micronutrients thiamin, riboflavin, and niacin (Gerrior, Bente, and Hiza 2004). Today, these nutrients are consumed at levels that pose little risk of inadequacy in the diet. With enrichment and fortification of the breakfast cereals, grains have become leading sources for all three of the nutrients. Before enrichment, meat, poultry, and fish supplied the largest share of thiamin.

3   ASSESSING THE ADEQUACY OF NUTRIENT INTAKE AND DIETARY RECOMMENDATIONS

New scientific knowledge about nutrient requirements and methods of dietary assessment began to come to light in the mid-1980s, and this culminated in a set of new dietary reference standards called the Dietary Reference Intakes (DRIs) (Carriquiry 1999; IOM 2000, 2006). The DRIs replaced the previously used Recommended Dietary Allowances (RDAs) as the appropriate standard to use in determining whether diets are nutritionally adequate without being excessive. The DRI values have been established based on available scientific evidence by committees of the Institute of Medicine (IOM) since 1997 with the release of DRIs for calcium, phosphorus, magnesium, vitamin D, and fluoride. The IOM recommendations, as well as other sources, are considered by countries' policymakers in setting recommended levels and assessing the adequacy of dietary intakes (e.g., Rieken and Gedrich 2007).

For micronutrients, the DRIs include four reference standards: the Estimated Average Requirement, the Recommended Dietary Allowance, the Adequate Intake, and the Tolerable Upper Intake Level (IOM 2000).

- The Estimated Average Requirement (EAR) is an average daily nutrient intake value that is estimated to meet the requirement, as defined by the specified indicator of adequacy, of half of the healthy individuals in the specified life stage and gender group. At this level of intake, the other half of the healthy individuals in the specified group would not have their nutrient needs met. Thus, an EAR is the estimated midpoint (i.e., N, median) of the distribution of the nutrient requirements for the population in question.
- The Recommended Dietary Allowance (RDA) is an average daily dietary nutrient intake level that is sufficient to meet the nutrient requirement of nearly all (97–8 percent) of healthy individuals in the specified life stage and gender group.
- The Adequate Intake (AI) is used when available scientific evidence is not sufficient to determine the EAR (and thus also the RDA cannot be determined). The AI is the recommended average daily nutrient intake value based on experimentally derived intake levels or approximations of the mean nutrient intakes by a

group of apparently healthy people who are maintaining a defined nutritional state or criterion of adequacy.

- The Tolerable Upper Intake Level (UL) is the highest average daily nutrient intake level that is likely to pose no risk of adverse health effects to almost all individuals in the specified life stage and gender group. As intakes increase above the UL, the potential of adverse effects increases.

The EAR, UL, and, as appropriate, the AI are used in assessing the nutrient intakes of population subgroups to determine if the dietary intakes are adequate. The RDA is intended to be used as a goal for daily intakes of individuals and is not intended to be used in assessing group intakes (IOM 2000, 2006).

For macronutrients, such as energy, protein, and fat, different sets of DRIs have been developed. For energy, the dietary requirements are expressed in terms of Estimated Energy Requirements (EER), which sets levels of dietary energy intake needed to maintain energy balance in a healthy adult of a given age, gender, weight, height, and level of physical activity; and for infants and children, the EER also accounts for an allowance of energy needed to maintain normal growth and development. For fat, protein, and carbohydrates, the DRIs include an Acceptable Macronutrient Distribution Range (AMDR) for intakes as a percentage of dietary energy intakes.

The DRIs can be used to assess the prevalence of inadequate (or excessive) nutrient intakes for groups or populations (Carriquiry 1999; IOM 2000), and are now generally used in reporting the adequacy of nutrient intake in a population or population group. In the assessments, the DRIs are combined with estimates of the usual dietary intake distributions for micro- and macronutrients to address questions such as, what is the prevalence of inadequate intakes of particular nutrients of interest in the population, or, what is the prevalence of excessive intakes of particular nutrients? The use of estimated usual nutrient intake distributions and DRIs for assessment of dietary intakes has marked a significant shift in the approach to assessing the adequacy of nutrient intakes (Hoffmann et al. 2002). These methods are being used in many countries to weigh and assess standards for fortification in order to avoid excessive intakes by some population groups as well as enrich the diets of others.

4   CHANGES IN SUPPLY: FACTORS AFFECTING NUTRIENT AVAILABILITY

4.1   Food Supply

The available food supply is closely linked to the nutrients available for consumption. Increasing global trade, as well as shifts in domestic production, have influenced the structure of diets, and hence of available nutrients. As shown in Table 25.1, the dietary sources of nutrients have changed with changes in the food supply. As an example, in the United States, the share of saturated fat in the diet decreased from meat, poultry, and fish (from 35 percent down to 22 percent of the total) but increased from fats and oils consumption, including butter and other vegetable fat sources (up from 35 to 49 percent of the total).

Fruits and vegetables provide the bulk of vitamin C in the US diet, and imports of fruits and vegetables rank at a relatively high level among imported consumed foods. The import share of fruits has increased from 6 percent in 1980 to 22 percent in 2000 in the United States, and the types of imported fruits are much more diverse today than twenty years ago (Jerardo 2008). Fresh and frozen vegetables have also increased in import share, and these foods contribute to the more diverse consumption of fruits and vegetables and associated nutrients.

The variety of food available in most countries, and hence the sources of nutrients in the diet, has increased with trade. Increased income and urbanization explain much of the shift in food variety available, including in China and other countries in Asia (Drewnowski and Popkin 1997). As suggested by Fabiosa (Chapter 23 in this volume), a "trading up" has occurred in food consumption patterns with lower- and middle-income countries moving toward those of higher-income countries. Sugar intake and sweetener intake per capita have been increasing throughout the world but much more rapidly in developing countries than in the developed world (Beghin and Jensen 2008). Sweetener consumption on a per capita basis during the period 1999–2003 was 38 percent higher in developing countries and relatively unchanged in developed countries in comparison to the period 1970–5.

In addition to change induced by higher income and urbanization, convergence of dietary preferences—or homogenization of preferences—has also been proposed to explain the shift in global food consumption toward a more common pattern, especially for meats, seafood, dairy, sugar and confectionery, caffeinated beverages, and soft drinks and fruit ($p = 0.10$) (Fabiosa, Chapter 23 in this volume; Regmi, Takeshima, and Unnevehr 2008). Consumers in middle-income countries, in particular, exhibit strong responses to product labeling with information on healthful nutritional content.

In addition to increased fat and oils in diets at all income levels, globalization has also brought greater dietary diversity with increased availability of high-quality protein (meat, seafood, dairy), and shifts away from staple cereal grains. A shift to animal-sourced foods (meats and dairy sources) means that diets now provide good sources of protein, saturated fat, iron, vitamin B12 and B6, calcium, phosphorus, zinc, and niacin. It is important to recognize that with more processing, many of these animal source foods are converted to forms with different nutrient profiles (for example, whole milk turns into products with a higher concentration of saturated fat such as in cheese or ice cream, as well as products with lower saturated fat, such as skim milk). That is, the source of food is further processed to final consumption as foods. These foods as consumed will vary in nutrient content.

4.2   Food Processing, Packaging, and Technology

Higher income leads to shifts in food preparation and processing (packaging, flavoring, in forms ready for eating or quick cooking). Cutler, Glaeser, and Shapiro (2003) argue that the new technologies have lowered the time consumers spend on food preparation and, through making food more easily and readily accessible, contribute to overconsumption of calories. However, policies themselves can affect the use of food production and processing technologies and influence the available supply of nutrients in foods. For example, marketing orders and administrative milk pricing in the United States and Canada have favored the production of milk with higher butterfat content. Mandated labeling of trans fats in processed foods in the United States, or banning trans fats in Denmark, has reduced the availability of this form of fat in the food supply and shifted fat sources toward other ingredients. Dietary recommendations for increased whole-grain consumption have led to a rapidly expanded array of whole grain products available in the US market (Golan and Unnevehr 2008; Mancino, Kuchler, and Leibtag 2008; Unnevehr and Jagmanaite 2008).

Modifications of production and processing technologies in response to policies have led to changes in supply, sometimes without consumers knowing the difference in the products. In the United States, public support for research and development of corn production over that of sugar has favored the substitution of high fructose corn syrup (HFCS) for sugar as a lower-cost food ingredient in sweetened products (Beghin and Jensen 2008; Hailu, Cranfield, and Thangaraj 2010). In the case of trans fats, new labeling requirements, legal actions against firms, and local regulations limiting the amount of trans fats in foods have led to major changes in the food industry. The changes include substitution of frying oils used in food preparation in the food service industry, reformulation of packaged foods, and the development of alternative oil crops with an improved oil profile that has desirable manufacturing properties but reduces trans fat (Unnevehr and Jagmanaite 2008).

In countries with more traditional, less developed marketing systems, rising consumer income, urbanization, and more modern processing, packaging, procurement, and marketing systems have led to an increasing amount of foods supplied through formal market channels. Across countries ranked by income, an increasing share of food expenditures comes through packaged foods and foods sold through supermarkets at the higher income levels (Minten and Reardon 2008; Regmi, Takeshima, and Unnevehr 2008). These changes provide consumers with foods that are often higher-quality and cheaper, and foods promoted with improved nutritional content and enhancement. For example, improved milling of maize by large processors may remove micronutrients, yet the processors also have the ability to easily fortify the product destined for sale in packaged form.

5 FORTIFICATION

Food industries add vitamins and minerals to food products for several reasons. Micronutrients are often lost in food processing and added back to the final product to restore some of the values lost or to make the final product equivalent to the natural one (e.g., nutrients lost and restored to make refined grains equivalent to whole grains). In addition, products may be enriched, or fortified, with micronutrients that enhance the nutrient content beyond that in the natural product. The World Health Organization (WHO 2006) has identified iodine, iron, and vitamin A as the micronutrients with most widespread deficiencies throughout the world, and these nutrients are the target of fortification efforts, especially in lower-income countries. Others high on the list of risk of deficiencies include zinc, folate, and vitamin D.

Mass fortification is one type of fortification that uses widely consumed foods, such as staples or condiments, as the vehicle for the nutrient being supplied through fortification (Mertz 1997; WHO 2006). This type of fortification can be an efficient means of delivering the micronutrient to a large share of the targeted population, as it usually does not require a change in consumption habits or distribution networks (WHO 2006). Staple foods are often selected because they reach lower-income consumers. Examples include enrichment of refined flour with thiamin, riboflavin, niacin, and zinc; fortification of flour with iron or folic acid; iodine fortification of salt; and sugar fortification with vitamin A, as is done in Central America. Governments or industry groups often set the standards for product fortification levels. Although mass fortification of products can often be done at relatively low cost, possible risks include the fact that the fortificant is not well targeted and some groups may have intakes that are close to or exceed the UL (Sacco and Tarasuk 2009). Also, fortifying products at high levels may produce off flavors or undesired changes in other organoleptic properties of the final food product. Cost is also a limiting factor.

Switzerland and the United States began providing iodized salt in the 1920s in response to evidence that treatment with iodine was effective in preventing goiter. Today, although salt is fortified with iodine, consumers do have a choice, and salt is also offered in the market without fortification. In the 1930s, research on the benefits of vitamin D for health led to fortification of margarine and milk in the United States. By the 1940s, the United States began to fortify refined flour, and shortly after, bread and other bakery products, pasta, and rice, with niacin, thiamin, and riboflavin. In 1973, after further review and recognition of continuing iron deficiency, the United States added iron to the list of nutrients used in fortification of cereal grain products. Although countries vary considerably in their use of fortification as a means of addressing nutrient deficiencies, many higher-income countries maintain some mass fortification standards for foods or use publicly supported supplementation (Mertz 1997).

More targeted fortification efforts, directed to specific population groups, may use foods consumed by those groups or foods that are easily identified with special labeling or in targeted markets. Examples include infant formula, the addition of vitamin D to milk, which helps in absorption of calcium, or foods targeted to women or older people. Also, some food manufacturers fortify products in a market-driven effort to attract consumers. Examples include breakfast cereals fortified with an array of vitamins and minerals; fruit juices fortified with vitamin C, calcium, or vitamin D; and sports drinks. Although historically micronutrient fortification efforts have used the addition of fortificants in processing to achieve the fortification levels, recent efforts have also focused on biofortification through traditional breeding or genetic modification (Nestel et al. 2006). In tracking or analyzing nutrient intake over time, it is important to have access to food composition data that indicate the amount of nutrients in foods currently available to consumers, and inclusive of fortification levels available in the food supply.

Are fortification efforts effective at reducing micronutrient deficiencies? Hoffmann (2009) provides a review of several fortification efforts that have been successful at decreasing micronutrient deficiencies and improving health, including iodinization of salt in the United States, iron fortification and supplementation in several developing countries, and vitamin A fortification and supplementation. Although the studies show that fortification is an effective means to address micronutrient deficiencies, maintaining consistent supply in the market and effective demand in developing countries may be challenging.

Evidence from various countries and regions in the world indicates that fortification of foods is a cost-effective way to address micronutrient deficiencies and likely to be a method of choice for some nutrients, especially those for which there is large-scale central processing and either there is widespread deficiency or other ways of addressing the effects of deficiency are very costly (Horton 2006). Fortification of grain products with folic acid has significantly changed the food sources of folate in the food supply in the United States (from 15 percent of the total folate in 1970 to nearly 70 percent of the total intake in 2004) (see Table 25.1) and has been shown to be effective in reducing congenital heart disease (Ionescu-Ittu et al. 2009).

There is less evidence available on the effectiveness of biofortification at improving targeted micronutrient deficiencies. One complication is that often the crop that is biofortified most often has no superior production attributes, so adoption of the seed or plant by farmers depends on acceptance of information about improved product for home consumption or assurance of market channels for the improved product to be sold in the market. Studies on biofortification efforts have shown the positive effect of introduction of quality protein maize on the rate of growth in height and weight of infants and children in selected developing countries (Gunaratna, De Groote, and McCabe 2008); benefits of β-carotene in sweet potatoes (van Jaarsveld et al. 2005); and *ex ante* benefits from rice biofortified with vitamin A (Dawe, Robertson, and Unnevehr 2002; Zimmermann and Qaim 2004). Key challenges remain for biofortification efforts in surmounting the technical challenges of getting levels of fortification (e.g., vitamin A) sufficiently high to make a difference in outcome, and of achieving the change while maintaining consumer acceptance. Preference for white, not "golden," product means that there is limited acceptance of both biofortified rice and maize (Wansink 2005; De Groote, Kimenju, and Morawetz 2010). In spite of these challenges, Meenakshi et al. (2007) conclude that biofortification is a cost-effective technology within a wide range of interventions considered with expected levels of vitamin enhancement. If adopted and maintained in market channels, this offers prospects of a sustainable intervention available in very low-income countries to enhance the available nutrient content of the food supply.

6 ECONOMIC FACTORS

Economic factors play an important role in determining the available nutrients in the food supply. Despite Stigler's proposal that a minimum-cost diet could be achieved with little variety or concern with palatability (Stigler 1945), consumers prefer more variety and varied food attributes in their diets. This is because higher income supports demand for more nutritious foods (including fortification), and also because a diet that moves away from staple grains toward greater variety and more animal products provides a wider range of nutrients (Drewnowski and Popkin 1997). Studies of household food expenditures and consumer dietary choices show increasing food variety and related nutrient intakes with higher levels of income (see Unnevehr et al. 2010 and Weiss, Chapter 27 in this volume, for a review).

Figure 25.1 shows the positive relationship, though at a declining rate, between income and animal sources of protein across countries. Although natural endowment and cultural preferences do influence the transition, as countries achieve higher levels of income their dietary choices include more animal sources for foods. And, this transition indicates increasing levels of nutrients associated with animal products: protein, saturated fat, and animal-sourced nutrients and minerals.

Modeling traditional demand parameters of price and income is done either directly as nutrients (with an estimated nutrient price) or indirectly through food demand (LaFrance 2008). Beatty and LaFrance (2005) take the indirect approach and model nutrients as a linear function of food quantities. Following Beatty and LaFrance's notation,

$$Z = Nq$$

where Z is a vector of nutrients, N is a matrix of the nutrient composition of food, and q is a vector of food quantities. The nutrient price elasticities are expressed as

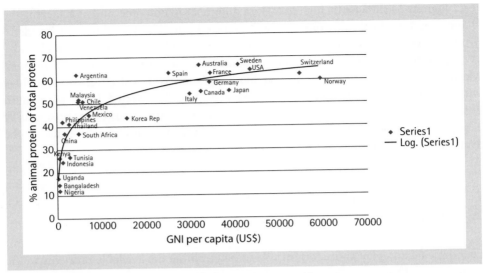

FIGURE 25.1 The share of animal protein in total protein shows a positive trend but at a declining rate, 2005

$$\varepsilon_{pk}^{Zi} = \sum_{j=1}^{nq} s_{ij}\, \varepsilon_{pk}^{qi}, \, i=1, \ldots, n_z$$

where ε_{pk}^{Zi} is the price elasticity of demand for nutrient i with respect to food k, price ε_{pk}^{qi} is the price elasticity for food j with respect to price k, and s_{ij} is the proportion of nutrient i contributed by food item j.

The nutrient income elasticities are expressed as

$$\varepsilon_{m}^{Zi} = \sum_{j=1}^{nq} s_{ij}\, \varepsilon_{m}^{qi}, \, i=1, \ldots, n_z$$

where ε_{m}^{Zi} is the income elasticity of demand for nutrient i, and ε_{m}^{qi} is the income elasticity of demand for food j.

With such a model, Beatty and LaFrance estimate food consumption in the United States with aggregate data (annual per capita) for food and nutrients for 1919–2000, excluding 1942–6 to account for the war period. The twenty-one food items cover all major food sources and were available in food quantities as well as nutrient components (seventeen nutrients including energy, protein, total fat, carbohydrates, total cholesterol, selected micronutrients, and minerals). The demand system model allows the estimation of price and income elasticities for both the food items as well as the seventeen nutrients. Their results show all foods except butter to be normal goods with respect to income or to be independent of income. Almost all of the price elasticities are negative and less than one (absolute value).

Estimates for the nutrients show all nutrient responses with respect to income are positive. The trend for nutrient income elasticities is positive starting with the 1950s. The greatest increases (and currently highest values) for nutrient income elasticities are for micronutrients associated with fruits and vegetables. However, all responses with respect to price are small. These estimates show support for the strong role of income in nutrient demand over time, and a relatively smaller role for prices. The small nutrient price response is likely due to the widely varied food supply and sources of nutrients, and, as Beatty and LaFrance note, suggests that policies designed to change nutrient intake by taxing selected foods (such as a "fat-tax" policy) may have little effect on the nutrient intake.

In contrast to the relatively small role of price on nutrient demand, there is evidence that nutritional information, campaigns, and education can influence demand for nutrients and other food components over time (Jensen, Kesavan, and Johnson 1992; Wansink 2005). Brown and Schrader (1990) created an index to measure the availability of information about cholesterol. The index was based on counts of medical journal articles with positive or negative information about cholesterol and human health. Increased information about cholesterol lowered demand for shell eggs with some lag. Furthermore, the information dampened the response to income and prices. Other studies have shown that information has an effect on demand for "healthier" products (e.g., lower fat), but results vary across the studies and products (Teisl, Bockstael, and Levy 2001; Mancino, Kuchler, and Leibtag 2008). Evidence from other studies suggests that the role of information and awareness on demand for nutrition and food components is likely to be complex. Consumer awareness of the health benefits of fortified (and biofortified) staple products in developing countries may show a positive effect in the short run, but sustained, longer-term changes are difficult to observe (Hoffmann 2009).

7   IMPLICATIONS

Consumers demand food that includes attributes related to source, location, method of production, and healthfulness. At the same time, nutrient content is tied inherently to food. Although only some nutrients seem to influence consumers' choice of foods, many of those that do influence demand are those that consumers try to limit. That is, consumers often choose products lower in cholesterol or saturated fat. Such changes can drive food formulations to offer lower-fat or lower-cholesterol products. New recommendations to reduce sodium are leading to industry efforts to reformulate products that use less sodium while still meeting consumer taste preferences. As markets and technologies evolve, consumers are also choosing foods with enhanced vitamin content. Such market-driven preferences, as well as mandated changes, can affect the available food supply and the nutrient profile of some of the traditional food groups. Understanding the strength of consumer preference, and changes in preference across income levels, offers the opportunity to tie foods more closely to health outcomes.

References

Beatty, T. K. M., and J. T. LaFrance. 2005. "United States Demand for Food and Nutrition in the Twentieth Century." *American Journal of Agricultural Economics* 87/5: 1159–66.

Beghin, J., and H. H. Jensen. 2008. "Farm Policies and Added Sugars in US Diets." *Food Policy* 33: 480–8.

Brown, D. J., and L. F. Schrader. 1990. "Cholesterol Information and Shell Egg Consumption." *American Journal of Agricultural Economics* 72/3 (Aug.), 548–55.

Carriquiry, A. L. 1999. "Assessing the Prevalence of Nutrient Inadequacy." *Public Health Nutrition* 2: 23–33.

Cutler, D. M., E. L. Glaeser, and J. M. Shapiro. 2003. "Why Have Americans Become More Obese?" *Journal of Economic Perspectives* 17/3: 93–118.

Dawe, D., R. Robertson, and L. Unnevehr. 2002. "Golden Rice: What Role Could It Play in Alleviation of Vitamin A Deficiency?" *Food Policy* 27: 541–60.

De Groote, H., S. C. Kimenju, and U. B. Morawetz. 2010. "Estimating Consumer Willingness to Pay for Food Quality with Experimental Auctions: The Case of Yellow versus Fortified Maize Meal in Kenya." *Agricultural Economics* 42/1: 1–16.

Dietary Guidelines Advisory Committee. 2010. *Report of the Dietary Guidelines Advisory Committee on the Dietary Guidelines for Americans.* <http://www.cnpp.usda.gov/DGAs2010-DGACReport.htm>.

Drewnowski, A., and B. M. Popkin. 1997. "The Nutrition Transition: New Trends in the Global Diet." *Nutrition Reviews* 55/2: 31–43.

Gerrior, S., L. Bente, and H. Hiza. 2004. *Nutrient Content of the U.S. Food Supply, 1901–2000.* Home Economics Research Report No. 56. Washington, DC: US Department of Agriculture, Center for Nutrition Policy and Promotion.

Golan, E., and L. Unnevehr. 2008. "Food Product Composition, Consumer Health, and Public Policy: Introduction and Overview of Special Section." *Food Policy* 33: 465–9.

Gunaratna, N. S., H. de Groote, and G. P. McCabe. 2008. "Evaluating the Impact of Biofortification: A Meta-Analysis of Community-Level Studies on Quality Protein Maize (QPM)." Paper presented to the European Association of Agricultural Economists 2008 International Congress, Ghent, Aug. 26–9.

Hailu, G., J. Cranfield, and R. Thangaraj. 2010. "Do U.S. Food Processors Respond to Sweetener-Related Health Information?" *Agribusiness* 26/3: 348–68.

Hiza, H. A. B., and L. Bente. 2007. *Nutrient Content of the U.S. Food Supply, 1909–2004: A Summary Report.* Home Economics Research Report No. 57. Washington, DC: Center for Nutrition Policy and Promotion, United States Department of Agriculture, Feb.

Hoffmann, K., H. Boeing, A. Dufour, J. L. Volatier, J. Telman, M. Virtanen, W. Becker, and S. Henauw. 2002. "Estimating the Distribution of Usual Dietary Intake by Short-Term Measurements." *European Journal of Clinical Nutrition* 56, suppl. 2: 53–62.

Hoffmann, V. 2009. "What You Don't Know Can Hurt You: Micronutrient Content and Fungal Contamination of Foods in Developing Countries." *Agricultural and Resource Economics Review* 38/2: 100–8.

Horton, S. 2006. "The Economics of Food Fortification." *Journal of Nutrition* 136: 1068–71.

IOM (Institute of Medicine). 2000. *Dietary Reference Intakes: Applications in Dietary Assessment.* Washington, DC: National Academy Press.

—— 2006. *Dietary Reference Intakes: The Essential Guide to Nutrient Requirements*, ed. J. J. Otten, J. P. Hellwig, and L. D. Meyers. Washington, DC: National Academy Press.

Ionescu-Ittu, R., A. J. Marelli, A. S. Mackie, and L. Pilote. 2009. "Prevalence of Severe Congenital Heart Disease after Folic Acid Fortification of Grain Products: Time Trend Analysis in Quebec, Canada." *British Medical Journal* 338 (May 12), b1673.

Jensen, H. H., T. Kesavan, and S. R. Johnson. 1992. "Measuring the Impact of Health Awareness on Food Demand." *Review of Agricultural Economics* 14/2 (July), 299–312.

Jerardo, A. 2008. "What Share of US Consumed Food Is Imported?" *Amber Waves* (Feb.). <http://www.ers.usda.gov/amberwaves/february08/datafeature>.

LaFrance, J. T. 2008. "The Structure of US Food Demand." *Journal of Econometrics* 147: 336–49.

Mancino, L., F. Kuchler, and E. Leibtag. 2008. "Getting Consumers to Eat More Whole-Grains: The Role of Policy, Information, and Food Manufacturers." *Food Policy* 33: 489–96.

Meenakshi, J. V., N. Johnson, V. M. Manyong, H. de Groote, J. Javelosa, D. Yanggen, F. Naher, C. Gonzalez, J. Garcia, and E. Meng. 2007. *How Cost-Effective Is Biofortification in Combating Micronutrient Malnutrition? An Ex-Ante Assessment.* HarvestPlus Working Paper No. 2. Washington, DC: HarvestPlus, Aug.

Mertz, W. 1997. "Food Fortification in the United States." *Nutrition Reviews* 55/2: 44–9.

Minten, B., and T. Reardon. 2008. "Food Prices, Quality, and Quality's Pricing in Super-markets versus Traditional Markets in Developing Countries." *Review of Agricultural Economics* 30/3: 480–90.

Nestel, P., H. E. Bouis, J. V. Meenakshi, and W. Pfeiffer. 2006. "Biofortification of Staple Food Crops." *Journal of Nutrition* 136: 1064–7.

Regmi, A., H. Takeshima, and L. Unnevehr. 2008. *Convergence in Global Food Demand and Delivery.* Economic Research Report No. ERR-56. Washington, DC: Economic Research Service, US Department of Agriculture, Mar. <http://www.ers.usda.gov/publications/ERR56>.

Rieken, K., and K. Gedrich. 2007. *Similarities and Dissimilarities of National and International Energy and Nutrient Intake Recommendations.* HECTOR Working Paper Part 1. Working Paper prepared in the context of the HECTOR Coordination Action (Milestone M4.1, Part 1), Freising.

Sacco, J. E., and V. Tarasuk. 2009. "Health Canada's Proposed Discretionary Fortification Policy Is Misaligned with the Nutritional Needs of Canadians." *Journal of Nutrition* 139: 1980–6.

Stigler, G. J. 1945. "The Cost of Subsistence." *Journal of Farm Economics* 37: 303–14.

Teisl, M. F., N. E. Bockstael, and A. Levy. 2001. "Measuring the Welfare Effects of Nutrition Information." *American Journal of Agricultural Economics* 83: 133–49.

Unnevehr, L. J., and E. Jagmanaite. 2008. "Getting Rid of Trans Fats in the US Diet: Policies, Incentives and Progress." *Food Policy* 33: 497–503.

——, J. Eales, H. Jensen, J. Lusk, J. McCluskey, and J. Kinsey. 2010. "Food and Consumer Economics." *American Journal of Agricultural Economics* 92/2: 506–21.

USDA ERS (Economic Research Service, United States Department of Agriculture). 2010. "Food Availability (Per Capita) Data System." *Data Sets.* <http://www.ers.usda.gov/Data/FoodConsumption>.

van Jaarsveld, P. J., M. Faber, S. Z. Tanumihardjo, P. Nestel, C. J. Lombard, and A. J. Spinnler Benade. 2005. "β-Carotene-Rich Orange-Fleshed Sweet Potato Improves the Vitamin A Status of Primary School Children Assessed with Modified-Relative-Dose-Response Test." *American Journal of Clinical Nutrition* 81: 1080–7.

Wansink, B. 2005. *Marketing Nutrition: Soy, Functional Foods, Biotechnology and Obesity*. Urbana: University of Illinois Press.

WHO (World Health Organization). 2002. *The World Health Report: Reducing Risk, Promoting Healthy Life. Overview*. Geneva: World Health Organization.

—— 2006. *Guidelines on Food Fortification with Micronutrients*, ed. L. Allen, B. de Benoist, O. Dary, and R. Hurrell. Geneva: World Health Organization and Food and Agricultural Organization of the United Nations.

Zimmermann, R., and M. Qaim. 2004. "Potential Health Benefits of Golden Rice: A Philippine Case Study." *Food Policy* 29: 147–68.

CHAPTER 26

....

FOOD AWAY FROM HOME

....

HAYDEN STEWART[*]

Among major developments to occur in food consumption in modern history is the growing popularity of away-from-home foods. Households in the United States and many other countries are increasingly turning to restaurants and other types of food service facilities to acquire a greater variety of foods and dining amenities than the households might otherwise be able to prepare for themselves. By eating out, households may also save time otherwise spent on food preparation and clean-up.

Food away from home can be defined to include restaurant foods as well as foods provided by other types of facility for on-premise or immediate consumption. Notably, restaurant foods can be considered away-from-home foods even if sold for carryout. Thus, this category of food can be defined by where the meals and snacks are prepared, not by where they are eaten. Foods prepared in a consumer's kitchen are at-home foods even if eaten outdoors, such as at a picnic, for example.

This chapter focuses on food away from home in the United States, changes in this market over time, and how these changes raise questions for policymakers and others concerned about both agriculture and diet quality. Because Americans are purchasing more of their foods away from home, trends in this market are ever more important to agricultural producers. Shifts in where people eat can affect the underlying demand for commodities like potatoes and dairy products. Changes in what people eat can also affect nutrient intake and overall health. Much research has been conducted on conditions in the United States, and, though important dfferences exist between conditions in the United States and elsewhere, trends in the American market may help researchers and others to understand and forecast changes elsewhere.

* I thank Anita Regmi for help with data on food service in countries other than the United States, Technomic Inc. for providing data on chain restaurants, Jayson Lusk for helpful comments, and Wallace Huffman for providing an advance draft of his contribution to this volume. The views and opinions expressed in this chapter do not necessarily reflect those of the Economic Research Service, US Department of Agriculture.

1   A LARGE AND GROWING MARKET

Away-from-home foods account for almost half of total food expenditures. According to the US Department of Agriculture's Economic Research Service (ERS), expenditures on away-from-home foods reached $565 billion in 2008, or, equivalently, 48.5 percent of total food expenditures, which were $1.17 trillion. By contrast, the food service share of total food expenditures was 45.4 percent in 1988, 33.1 percent in 1968, and 25.2 percent in 1958 (Figure 26.1). Clearly, expenditures on food away from home have been growing more rapidly than total food expenditures. However, the away-from-home share of total food expenditures has also been increasing more slowly since the mid-1980s.

Food expenditure statistics provided by the ERS are comprehensive. They account not only for the foods households purchase but also for the value of foods provided through governments, businesses, and non-profit organizations. For example, they include the value of foods purchased by the US government for domestic military personnel and the value of "free" and "reduced-price" meals provided through the National School Lunch and School Breakfast programs.

Unlike the ERS data series, the Consumer Expenditure Survey (CE) focuses exclusively on what consumers spend. The CE has two separate components through which participating households report their expenditures on goods and services—an interview and a diary survey. For the diary survey, households keep a record of their food expenditures over a two-week period. In this diary, households further distinguish between spending at full-service restaurants, fast-food places, and other types of food service facilities. The CE is published annually by the US Department of Commerce's Bureau of Labor Statistics (BLS). Comparable data are available for each year since 1984. According to the CE, US households devoted about 42 percent of their total food budget to away-from-home foods in 2008, 44 percent in 2005, 42 percent in 1998, and 40 percent in 1984.

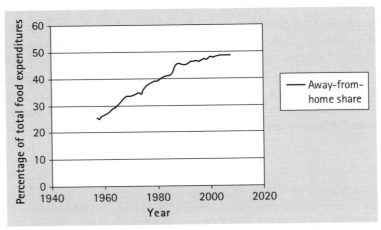

FIGURE 26.1 Food away from home growing as a share of total food expenditures
Source: Economic Research Service, US Department of Agriculture, *Food Expenditure Tables.*

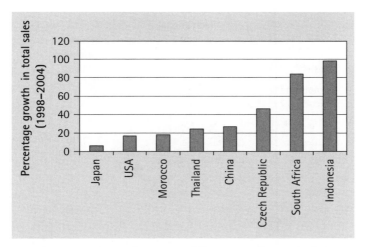

FIGURE 26.2 Food service growing faster in middle-income than in high-income countries, inflation-adjusted, total sales

Source: Euromonitor.

Still other surveys reveal away-from-home foods to account for a growing share of the average American's diet. Data on food consumption measure the physical quantities of foods eaten as opposed to expenditures on those foods. One way to measure physical quantities is by the amount of nutrients consumed. Lin, Guthrie, and Frazão (1999) use data collected by the US Department of Agriculture to compare the shares of calories and other nutrients that individuals obtain at home and away from home. These data include the 1977–8 and 1987–8 Nationwide Food Consumption Survey (NFCS) as well as the 1989–91 and 1994–5 Continuing Survey of Food Intake by Individuals (CSFII). Away-from-home foods are found to have grown from about 18 percent of daily caloric intake in 1977–8 to 34 percent in 1995.

The United States is not the only country in which the market for food away from home is growing. Indeed, spending on food away from home is expanding much more quickly in middle-income and lower-middle-income countries, such as China, than it is in the United States and other high-income countries (Figure 26.2). These differences in growth rates around the world suggest a convergence in food expenditure patterns among households in different countries, according to Regmi, Takeshima, and Unnevehr (2008).

2 EATING OUT AND THE THEORY OF HOUSEHOLD PRODUCTION

Becker's (1965) model of household production provides a theoretical framework within which researchers can analyze the demand for food away from home. This

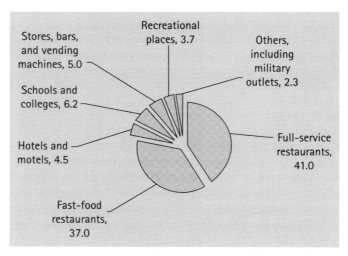

FIGURE 26.3 Away-from-home market composed of diverse segments, share of total sales by segment, 2008

Sales data are not as comprehensive as expenditure data; omitted from sales data are the value of some foods provided by facilities for which payment is not made.

Source: Economic Research Service, US Department of Agriculture, *Food Expenditure Tables*.

theory extends the classical model of demand to account for the value of time. Becker (1965) hypothesizes that households do not derive utility from pure market goods; rather, they produce the commodities that generate utility using both market goods and their own time as inputs. The "full price" of a commodity is likewise the sum of the value of the market goods bought and the value of the time used up.

At-home foods can be a relatively time-intensive commodity to consume. In general, these foods are produced from store-bought foods with households further devoting time to cooking and cleaning up as well as to eating.

The commodity, eating away from home, may generate different amounts of utility than eating at home. Indeed, it may allow households to enjoy amenities and types of foods that they cannot otherwise produce on their own. For example, the household may try specialty foods or enjoy a night of entertainment outside the home.

Consuming restaurant foods may or may not require as much of a household's time as eating at home. By definition, households outsource preparation and clean-up when eating out. This may create additional time for other leisurely activities or for earning wages. But time saved may also be spent socializing over a meal. And time spent traveling to a restaurant also needs to be factored in.

Of course, not all types of food away from home are the same; rather the food service industry is comprised of diverse segments (Figure 26.3). And firms in each segment offer a different mix of foods and services. As the name suggests, full-service restaurants, defined as establishments with waitstaff, tend to offer more varied menus and dining amenities. Fast-food outlets, by contrast, are also known as "limited-service" or "quick-service" restaurants. They have no waitstaff and customers pay prior to eating.

Menus also tend to be limited and dining amenities comparatively sparse; rather, they tend to emphasize convenience.

Becker (1965) demonstrates how changes in unearned income and full prices influence household behavior. Applying his model to the demand for food away from home, we expect households with more unearned income to demand more normal commodities, including, possibly, more dining amenities and a greater variety of foods. Indeed, some households may consider dining at a restaurant to be a special occasion during which they can have fun and indulge. Demand at full-service restaurants may increase most as this type of restaurant tends to offer a greater variety of foods and services.

Becker's (1965) model also suggests how a change in earned income (wages) could affect the demand for away-from-home foods. An increase in wages brings about an income effect—households with higher wages have more total resources. However, it also increases the value of time. For example, the more a homemaker can earn in wages outside the home, the greater is his or her household's opportunity cost of commodities like home-cooked meals. The household may substitute hours of work in the labor force for time previously spent on such time-intensive commodities. Prepared foods and restaurant foods may become relatively more economical. The consumption of fast food may increase most because this type of restaurant tends to emphasize convenience.

Household production theory also predicts how demand will change with the other determinants of full prices. Along with the value of a household's time, the prices of market-sourced inputs and the amount of time needed to consume a commodity also determine its full price. As an example, Becker (1965) discusses shaving. He argues that the introduction of home safety and electric razors reduced the full price of shaving. It no longer required a trip to a barber shop nor waiting time at the shop. By his model, households would demand more shaves and free up time for other activities. It can similarly be argued that innovations in food service might both stimulate demand and help households to create time for other activities. These innovations may include restaurant formats that offer faster service and home delivery, for example.

3   EMPIRICAL RESEARCH ON THE DEMAND FOR FOOD AWAY FROM HOME

The demand for food away from home is also the subject of a growing body of empirical research. Most studies invoke Becker's (1965) model. However, given the data available for empirical analysis, few attempt to estimate a complete Beckerian model as in Huffman (Chapter 2 in this volume); rather, existing studies tend to focus on the association between expenditures or consumption and a household's total income (unearned income and wages combined), employment outside the home, and, perhaps, other proxies for full prices. Empirical studies further extend theoretical results by demonstrating the importance of a household's demographic characteristics and by showing how demands vary by market segment.

Most empirical studies of the demand for away-from-home foods rely on survey data such as the CE, CSFII, or the National Health and Nutrition Examination Survey (NHANES).[1] These data include information on a household's income and demographic characteristics. Households participating in one of these surveys are further asked to report their food expenditures or consumption over a finite amount of time, such as a few days or a few weeks. However, it is generally the case that some households exhibited no demand over the survey period. These households are believed to eat out less frequently. Thus, when working with such data, researchers model a household's demand as a function of its income, proxies for its value of time, and other factors using a procedure that allows for a censoring of demand at zero. Some relatively recent studies of US households include McCracken and Brandt (1987), Yen (1993), Nayga and Capps (1994), Byrne, Capps, and Saha (1996), Byrne, Capps, and Saha (1998), Stewart et al. (2004, 2005), Stewart and Yen (2004), You and Nayga (2005), and Binkley (2006), among others.

Unfortunately, surveys like the CE or the NHANES that collect data on a household's food expenditures or consumption include little information about the determinants of Becker's (1965) full prices. Many empirical studies include a measure of the earnings or employment status of household members also responsible for food preparation. After that, it is generally assumed that households face the same market prices and need the same amount of time to consume food away from home. Indicator variables may account for the region of the United States where a household resides. This approach allows for some further differences in full prices between, say, the west and east.

Among the studies to account more explicitly for prices are Nayga and Capps (1992) and Reed, Levedahl, and Hallahan (2005), who include a measure of market prices in their models. Jekanowski, Binkley, and Eales (2001) further account for the amount of time needed to consume food away from home. That study uses market-level data as opposed to household survey data. Specifically, Jekanowski, Binkley, and Eales (2001) examine per capita fast-food consumption across eighty-five metropolitan statistical areas (MSAs). Included among the explanatory variables in their model are proxies to capture the income and the value of time of the residents of each MSA. To account for full prices in a manner consistent with Becker's (1965) model, they also include proxies for market prices as well as the number of fast-food outlets per 100 square miles. As household production theory suggests, the time costs for eating fast food depend upon how long consumers must travel to a restaurant. If driving to an outlet takes longer than cooking food at home, time is not saved. Conversely, the closer outlets are located to where people live, work, and shop, travel times are less, on average. Indeed,

---

[1] The CSFII and the NHANES were integrated in 2002. Participants in the integrated NHANES report their food intake on two non-consecutive days. This component of the NHANES is known as What We Eat in America. It is conducted as a partnership between the US Department of Agriculture and the US Department of Health and Human Services. Data are released every two years.

Jekanowski, Binkley, and Eales (2001) find that fast-food outlet density is positively associated with consumption, and market prices charged for fast food are negatively associated with consumption. Thus, in total, the lower is the full price of consumption, the greater is the quantity demanded.

In addition to accounting for variables explicitly motivated by Becker's (1965) model, empirical research also demonstrates the importance of a household's demographic characteristics. Important characteristics include age, household size, education, and race and ethnicity, among others. These characteristics may capture differences across households in preferences as well as variation in costs for consuming food at home relative to food away from home. Some of the more recent analyses further consider a person's desire for health and/or awareness of the link between diet quality and health (e.g., Stewart et al. 2005; Binkley 2006).

Many empirical studies further report results by market segment. They show how factors like income influence demand in particular market segments, such as for fast food or for meals at full-service restaurants. These include, but are not limited to, McCracken and Brandt (1987), Byrne, Capps, and Saha (1998), Jekanowski, Binkley, and Eales (2001), Stewart and Yen (2004), Stewart et al. (2005), and Binkley (2006).

There has also been interest in what drives the demand for meals and snacks at large chain restaurants as opposed to demand at small chains and independent restaurants. For example, many researchers focus on large chains in their analyses of fast-food advertising (e.g., Chou, Rashad, and Grossman 2008), how fast-food expenditures affect the health of children (e.g., You and Nayga 2005), and whether fast-food restaurants sell menu items with potentially addictive ingredients at lower prices in order to build a base of repeat customers (e.g., Richards, Patterson, and Hamilton 2007).

Of course, much research also examines the demand for food away from home outside of the United States, including in China (e.g., Ma et al. 2006), Greece (e.g., Mihalopoulos and Demoussis 2001), Ireland (e.g., Keelan, Henchion, and Newman 2007), Malaysia (e.g., Heng and Guan 2007), Spain (e.g., Angulo, Gil, and Mur 2007), Turkey (e.g., Akbay, Tiryaki, and Gul 2007), and the United Kingdom (e.g., Lund 1998), among other countries.

4   WHAT IS DRIVING THE GROWTH OF THE MARKET?

Household production theory and empirical studies suggest how the size of the market for food away from home could change over time. Indeed, it is often argued that the growth of the market, as shown in Figure 26.1, reflects long-run trends in demand determinants and in supply. Significant developments in the United States include changes in income and time use, especially the time of females, as more women are working outside their homes for wages. There have also been demographic developments such as aging, increased levels of educational attainment, and decreased household sizes. Restaurant foods have likely become more convenient to consume as well.

4.1   Growth in Income

Household income in the United States has been growing despite fluctuations that correspond to business cycles. For example, according to the March Income Supplement to the Current Population Survey (CPS), an annual assessment of household incomes conducted by the US Census Bureau, the median household had an annual income of $50,303 in 2008.[2] In real terms, this is less money than what the median household earned in 1998, but still greater than what it earned in 1988. The median household had an inflation-adjusted income of $51,295 in 1998 and $47,614 in 1988.[3] Other research by the Census Bureau further shows median annual household income to have expanded by 17 percent between 1967 and 1997 in real terms (Census Bureau 1998).

Changes in household income have likely contributed to the long-run expansion of the away-from-home market as well as to fluctuations that coincide with business cycles. Empirical studies show that demand at both fast-food and full-service restaurants increases with income, but demand at full-service restaurants is relatively more responsive (e.g., McCracken and Brandt 1987; Byrne, Capps, and Saha 1998).

4.2   Trends in the Rate of Female Labor Force Participation

The rate of female participation in the labor force rose quickly for several decades but has remained level since then. Time once available for cooking is now being spent working outside of the home for wages. Labor force statistics collected through the CPS and published by the BLS show that the rate of female participation in the civilian labor force began to increase before 1950 and continued to rise through the 1980s. However, it expanded little during the 1990s and did not change much in the 2000s. The BLS reports that about 37 percent of women worked for wages in 1958. That share rose to approximately 50 percent by 1978 and 60 percent by 1999. In 2009 it was still about 59 percent.

Changes in the rate of female participation in the labor force have likely been contributing to changes in the market for away-from-home foods. Fast-food operators may be most affected. Controlling for income, McCracken and Brandt (1987) find that a household's demand for fast food increases with the potential earnings of the head of household who is responsible for food preparation. The demand for food at full-service restaurants is less responsive. In later work, Byrne, Capps, and Saha (1998) replaced the potential earnings of the head of household responsible for food preparation, used in

---

[2] The CPS is a monthly survey of households conducted by the US Census Bureau. It collects data on the characteristics of the labor force, including employment and labor force participation. The March Income Supplement to the CPS further collects data on the annual income of individuals and families. Since March 1968 it has also collected data on the income of households in general.

[3] All figures are in real, 2008 dollars.

McCracken and Brandt's (1987) specification, with the number of hours worked by this person in the labor force. Despite using a different specification, they too find that the demand for fast food is more sensitive to changes in the value of time than is the demand for foods at full-service restaurants.

Together, trends in income and time use have led some researchers and policy advocates to speculate that the popularity of fast food is due in part to time-pressed households who have experienced little or no growth in real income.[4] Say Chou, Grossman, and Saffer (2004: 568), the prevalence of fast food partly reflects "labor market developments since 1970 that have witnessed declines or slow growth in real income of certain groups and increases in hours of work and labor force participation rates by most groups, especially women."

4.3   Importance of Demographic Trends

Demographic trends in the population are also contributing to changes in demand. One of these trends is the decreasing size of households. In the United States, the average household contained 2.8 persons in 1980, 2.5 persons in 2000, and could fall to just 2.4 persons by 2020 (Cromartie 2002). This may increase the demand for away-from-home foods because, as households have fewer members, they are less able to exploit economies of scale associated with meal preparation at home. And eating out becomes a relatively more cost-competitive choice for them.[5] Given a 10 percent decrease in size, Stewart and Yen (2004) predict that a household's per capita weekly spending at fast-food restaurants would grow about 1.4 percent and that at full-service restaurants would expand by 1.5 percent.

Also important to demand may be a trend toward higher levels of educational achievement. According to Cromartie (2002), the proportion of Americans with a bachelor's degree or higher level of education was 17 percent in 1980, 23.5 percent in 2000, and should reach 26.4 percent by 2020. Having a higher level of education is likely to be associated with a higher potential wage rate and, in turn, a higher opportunity cost of time for cooking at home. However, education may also be associated with a person's awareness of health and nutrition issues, which can further affect food choices. Stewart and Yen (2004) report that, if a head of household has a college education, then

---

[4] US households have not benefited equally from income growth. The March Income Supplement to the CPS shows a steady increase in income inequality as measured by the Gini coefficient. The Gini coefficient ranges from zero to one with larger values denoting more inequality. The Gini coefficient for annual household income in the United States rose from 0.386 in 1968 to 0.426 in 1988 and reached 0.466 in 2008.

[5] The time spent preparing food for each family member may decrease as the size of a family increases. For example, it might take thirty minutes to prepare a meal for four and twenty minutes to prepare a meal for one. The monetary costs for preparing meals are also likely to decrease on a per person basis as household size increases. Larger households may be better able to take advantage of larger package sizes with lower per unit costs.

that household can be expected to spend about $2.06 more per person each week at full-service restaurants. It can also be expected to spend more on fast food, but the effect is smaller in this segment of the market, an increase of $0.62.

Not all trends in the population support the expansion of the food service industry. The aging of the population is one such trend. Arguably, younger people may place more value on eating at restaurants in order to socialize or enjoy a variety of foods without needing to acquire specialized cooking skills. At the same time, if learning improves upon one's efficiency at preparing food at home, households with older managers may be better able to cook quickly and well. The proportion of the population aged 20 to 44 was 37.1 percent in 1980 and 37 percent in 2000, according to Cromartie (2002), who further estimates that this percentage will fall to 32.5 percent by 2020. Aging may have a negative impact on the demand for fast food. Stewart and Yen (2004) find that a 10 percent increase in the age of a household manager is associated with an 11 percent decrease in the household's per capita weekly spending for fast food. The same household's expenditures at full-service restaurants would not be affected much.

However, differences in dining out preferences across generations may prove to be a more important determinant of away-from-home food consumption than aging. As discussed above, past consumption patterns suggest that an individual's away-from home food expenditures decrease as the individual ages. However, these patterns may not apply to future generations of aging Americans, particularly baby boomers. Baby boomers may continue to prefer dining out, counteracting the traditional age effect that predicts a decline in away-from-home food expenditures. As baby boomers are making up a large and increasing share of the overall population, their future dining habits will have a significant effect on the food service industry.

4.4   Increasing Convenience of Food Away From Home

It also appears that market prices have increased little in inflation-adjusted terms, while restaurant foods have become much more convenient to consume. In 2009 the Consumer Price Index (CPI) was 214.5 for all items, 215.1 for food at home, and 223.3 for food away from home.[6] Thus, between 2009 and the CPI's base period of 1982–4, relative prices had changed little. On the other hand, the amount of time needed for consuming food away from home has decreased. One reason is that there are increasingly more restaurants in operation. According to data from the Economic Census, conducted every five years by the Census Bureau, the number of full-service restaurants nearly doubled between 1972 and 2007, while the number of fast-food outlets more than tripled (Table 26.1). This growth should translate into shorter travel times for households, on average, and, in turn, lower overall time costs for consumption.

---

[6] CPI reported by the BLS. All indices are US city average (1982–4 = 100).

Table 26.1 Growing number of restaurants in operation across the United States, 1972–2007

Year	Full-service restaurants	Fast-food restaurants
1972	112,656	72,850
1977	118,896	92,357
1982	122,851	109,353
1987	154,721	138,104
1992	170,183	164,341
1997	191,245	214,774
2002	195,659	228,789
2007	217,282	266,534

Note: Data for 1972–92 are based on the Standard Industrial Classification (SIC) system. Under SIC, fast-food restaurants were classified as "refreshment places" while full-service restaurants were classified as "restaurants and lunchrooms." Both are subcategories of SIC Code 58: Eating and Drinking Places. Data for 1997–2007 are based on the North American Industry Classification System (NAICS). Under NAICS, fast-food restaurants are classified as "limited-service eating places" while full-service restaurants are classified as "full-service restaurants." Both are subcategories of NAICS Code 72: Accommodation and Food Services. Differences in how data are reported for the period 1972–92 and the years 1997–2007 may affect comparisons over time. Figures include only establishments with payroll.

Source: US Census Bureau data for 1972, 1977, 1982, 1987, and 1992 are from the Economic Census: Retail Trade. Data for 1997, 2002, and 2007 are from the Economic Census: Accommodation and Food Services, <http://www.census.gov>.

Firms in particular segments of the restaurant industry have also done much to bring down other time costs associated with eating out such as developing restaurant concepts that offer faster service and shorter wait times. Some of these changes are described below along with growth in the away-from-home market by segment.

5   CHANGES IN MARKET COMPOSITION

Full-service and fast-food eateries account for the bulk of the away-from-home market, while other types of facilities, such as hotels and motels, schools and colleges, and retail stores, make up the balance (Figure 26.3). Aggregation over each of these segments allows one to estimate the overall market's size as in Figure 26.1. However, much information is also lost when aggregating, such as evidence on which segments of the market are growing most quickly. For several decades, the market for fast food grew much more quickly than did the market for food at full-service restaurants. That may now be changing. In recent years, sales at full-service restaurants have been growing as quickly as have sales of fast food (Figure 26.4).

During the second half of the twentieth century, fast-food restaurants not only benefited from the increasing rate of female participation in the labor force and

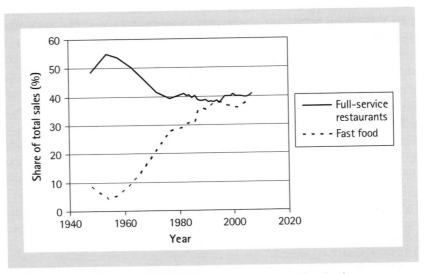

FIGURE 26.4 Share of away-from-home sales, full-service versus fast food
Sales data are not as comprehensive as expenditure data; omitted from sales data are the value of
some foods provided by facilities for which payment is not made.

Source: Economic Research Service, US Department of Agriculture, *Food Expenditure Tables.*

other trends discussed above, but they were leaders in developing new products and
services. Love (1986) credits McDonald's, in particular, with pioneering many of these
innovations in the 1940s and 1950s. As chronicled in his book *McDonald's: Behind the
Arches*, this company's first restaurant began as a drive-in with carhops and a menu of
twenty-five items including beef and pork sandwiches, among other things. The owners, Richard and Maurice McDonald, then reorganized their restaurant, bringing
assembly line techniques to food service. They invested in specialized cooking equipment and reduced their menu to only nine items. These changes meant that relatively
unskilled workers could be hired and trained to focus on specialized tasks. The brothers
also eliminated waitstaff. Patrons would thereafter order from a counter. They even
eliminated the need for a dishwasher by replacing all cutlery and dishware with paper
bags, wrappers, and cups. What customers lost in services and variety of foods,
however, they made up for in cost and convenience. The new "Speedy Service System"
reduced waiting times. The McDonald brothers were also able to reduce their prices
because of their lower unit costs. This appealed to families. Says Love (1986: 16),
"Working class families could finally afford to feed their kids restaurant food."

Since the 1960s and 1970s, fast-food companies have also added many more outlets
than have operators of full-service restaurants (Table 26.1). Indeed, the ongoing spread
of fast food can be seen in gas stations and in retail stores, such as Wal-Mart and
Target, who are now hosting food service chains like Pizza Hut and Taco Bell.
However, as Jekanowski, Binkely, and Eales (2001) note, the ubiquity of fast food raises
questions about whether the industry is reaching a saturation point. Though these
researchers find no evidence of such a point having been reached during the period

covered by their data, 1982–92, it is unclear whether the market has since neared a saturation point.

Future growth in the away-from-home market may depend primarily on how trends in the population further affect demand, especially if enough fast-food restaurants are already located in key markets so that opening new outlets would not significantly further reduce households' costs for travel. Rising incomes, aging, and now slowing growth in the rate of female labor force participation are unlikely to affect equally the demand for fast food and full-service restaurant foods. Stewart and Yen (2004) conclude that, on net, current trends are likely to support the expansion of the full-service segment relative to fast food.

Changes in demand might lead to changes in the mix of foods and services offered by restaurants. Stewart and Yen (2004) argue that any shift in demand between fast-food and full-service restaurants could influence the strategies of restaurants in both segments. For example, if trends favor full-service restaurants, the market could shift to include more full-service restaurants offering a wider range of menu items and dining amenities. In response, fast-food restaurants might introduce comparable foods and services. One example has been a move by fast-food chains to allow customers to pay by credit and debit card, which few accepted until the 2000s. Restaurants such as McDonald's have also diversified their menus to include vegetable salads, a fruit and yogurt parfait, and sliced apples, among other items.

6   GROWTH OF CHAIN RESTAURANTS

Another key change in the restaurant industry to accompany rising demand has been the rapid growth of large chain restaurants relative to smaller chains and independent restaurants. Indeed, the largest 100 chains now account for more than half of total restaurant industry sales. Data from Technomic, a Chicago-based consulting firm, show that the top 100 chains captured 50.1 percent of the market in 1997, up from 41 percent in 1982. That share had further increased to almost 53 percent by 2007 (Table 26.2).

The growing market share of very large chains raises questions about whether these restaurant companies can better provide what consumers demand than smaller firms can. Paul (1994), for one, lists some of the advantages that very large chains may enjoy, including advantages in both cost control and marketing activities, including an acceptance among consumers of chain restaurant foods as branded products.

Economies of scale help very large chain restaurants to reduce unit costs for developing new products and services. If a restaurant wishes to expand its menu, for example, it is likely to incur costs for developing new foods. Or, if the restaurant wants to provide consumers with information about the nutrient content of existing foods, it may likewise incur costs for conducting the necessary research. In both cases, many of these costs are likely to be fixed costs. And, compared with the largest chains, other restaurants can only spread any fixed costs over a small number of patrons. Barber and

Table 26.2 Largest restaurant chains expanding market share, sales (millions of dollars)

Year	Total restaurant sales	Top 100 restaurant chain sales	All other chains and independent restaurant sales	Top 100 share (%)
1982	88,392	36,225	52,167	41.0
1987	131,992	61,386	70,606	46.5
1992	172,781	82,533	90,248	47.8
1997	218,517	109,476	109,041	50.1
2002	278,969	143,055	135,914	51.3
2007	364,056	192,626	171,430	52.9

Source: Technomic, Inc., Chicago.

Byrne (1997), using annual reports and other sources of data on public companies, confirm that some very large chain restaurants do enjoy scale efficiencies.

Very large chains commonly advertise on television and in print media as well. Schlosser (2001) describes how fast-food chains, in particular, not only have used these traditional approaches but have further forged links with toy and entertainment companies. Says he, McDonald's is a large operator of playgrounds, a major distributor of toys, has staged promotions with the National Basketball Association and the Olympics, and has had exclusive contracts with the Walt Disney Company.

Advertising and marketing not only convey information about a restaurant's foods and, perhaps, generate excitement among consumers, but may also encourage households to accept these foods as branded products. Information economics suggests that consumers do not have full knowledge about the quality of products sold by different restaurants. Restaurants know relatively more about the quality of their foods. In a market with imperfect and asymmetric information, Erdem and Swait (1998) show that branding can be an effective signaling device if the brand is credible. What, then, determines the credibility of a brand? Erdem and Swait (1998) argue that firms can invest in their brands, such as through advertisements, which are essentially sunk costs. If a firm fails to keep its promises, the expected return on these investments will be lost. Potential losses serve to discourage cheating and give consumers confidence that firms will deliver what their brands promise. In turn, inexperienced consumers may perceive branded products to be less risky and initially try a branded product. If a consumer then has a positive experience with the good, he or she may continue to buy that particular brand owing to its now even lower perceived risk. However, in the restaurant industry, smaller chains and independent restaurants may have fewer resources available for supporting their brands than the largest chain restaurants have. Applying Erdem and Swait's (1998) result, it follows that consumers may not perceive brands supported by smaller companies as being as credible as brands maintained by larger chain restaurants. Indeed, in an experiment by Robinson and Matheson (2009), young children were given two pieces of hamburger, two chicken nuggets, two sets of french fries, two beverages, and two sets of baby carrots. The children were told that one of each type of food was from McDonald's. The children reported preferring the taste of the foods they thought were from McDonald's to the otherwise identical, non-branded food.

7   AN IMPORTANT MARKET FOR AGRICULTURAL GOODS

Shifts in where people eat can affect what they consume. As such, farmers could be affected by the growing size of the away-from-home market as well as by trends in the kinds of restaurants in operation. Nagengast and Appleton (1994: 133), for one, argue that the growth of large fast-food chains has had "far-reaching effects" on markets for commodities like potatoes, dairy products, and poultry. For instance, they credit large fast-food chains for having made frozen potato products more popular than fresh potatoes. The researchers also examine the significance of this development for agriculture. Growing the types of potato demanded by fast-food chains requires larger investments in land, seed, chemicals, irrigation water, and fertilizer than does producing other crops. In response, according to Nagengast and Appleton (1994), larger, more sophisticated potato farms have emerged and the amount of coordination between potato growers and processors has also increased, including, in some cases, the use of annual contracts between them.

Unfortunately, the growth of chain restaurants may also limit opportunities for small and medium-sized farmers who wish to engage in direct marketing. A report on direct marketing by a US Department of Agriculture-funded information center for sustainable agriculture acknowledges that chain restaurants typically centralize procurement and require prohibitively large volumes (Adam, Balasubrahmanyam, and Born 1999: 17). However, it "is still possible . . . to find an individually operated restaurant buying some food locally."

8   IMPACT ON CONSUMER HEALTH

Changes in where people eat can also affect the quality of their diets. It is therefore ominous that, when eating out, Americans do not typically make as nutritious food choices as when eating at home. Away-from-home foods are generally higher in calories and tend to provide a less healthful combination of nutrients, according to Lin, Guthrie, and Frazao (1999), Mancino, Todd, and Lin (2009), and Todd, Mancino, and Lin (2010), among other studies.

A growing body of research further suggests a relationship between eating out and health status. Binkley, Eales, and Jekanowski (2000), for one, find that consuming more restaurant foods is correlated with having a higher body mass index (BMI). Using the

1994–6 CSFII, a positive association is found among men between BMI and the share of one's total food intake that is acquired away from home. However, among women, this association is significant only for fast food. Binkley (2008) later examines the same set of data. In this later study, he finds that fast-food meals often contain fewer calories than what people eat at full-service establishments. The problem, Binkley (2008) suggests, is that some people are less likely to compensate for having eaten fast food by consuming less of other foods during the rest of the day.[7]

Still other studies suggest a link between the health status of individuals and the full price of restaurant foods. Chou, Grossman, and Saffer (2004), for one, use data collected between 1984 and 1999 on individuals and their BMI. They find that lower market prices for restaurant foods are associated with a higher BMI and an increased likelihood of obesity. By contrast, the number of restaurants per 10,000 persons in an individual's state of residence is positively associated with both BMI and the probability of obesity. As discussed above, the more restaurants are located in a community, the shorter will be travel times and the lower will be the full price of restaurant foods. The researchers conclude that "A literal interpretation of this result implicates fast-food and full-service restaurants as culprits in undesirable weight outcomes. But a very different interpretation emerges if one recognizes that the growth in these restaurants, and especially fast-food restaurants, is to a large extent a response to the increasing scarcity and increasing value of household or non-market time" (Chou, Grossman, and Saffer 2004: 584). Other studies to investigate the accessibility of restaurant foods and weight status include Mehta and Chang (2008) and Currie et al. (2009).

That people tend to eat less healthfully away from home has caused some health policy advocates and members of the media to scrutinize the restaurant industry. Many focus on large fast-food chains. One such critique is Schlosser's (2001) book *Fast Food Nation*. Though he acknowledges their efforts to introduce healthy dishes, Schlosser (2001: 241) also alleges that many fast-food chains continue to "heavily" promote high-fat foods: "the major chains have apparently decided that it's much easier and much more profitable to increase the size and the fat content of their portions than to battle eating habits largely formed by years of their own mass marketing."

The good news is that restaurants are providing more information about the nutritional content of foods. Subway, for instance, began voluntarily to list the caloric content of selected sandwiches on drink containers and compare it to that of competing products sold by Burger King and McDonald's. Similar information from these latter two companies was being provided through pamphlets and on their corporate websites. Since then, many state and municipal governments, including New York City,

---

[7] While Binkley, Eales, and Jekanowski (2000) and Binkley (2008) consider adults and all types of restaurant food, many other studies focus on fast food and the health of children. French et al. (2001), for one, survey children about how often they consume fast food, the quality of their diets, and a variety of environmental, personal, and behavioral factors that may be correlated with diet quality. Among their results, children who consume fast food more often are found to eat fewer fruits and vegetables, spend more time watching television, and be less concerned about diet and health.

have passed laws requiring chain restaurants to provide calorie and other nutritional information at the point of sale. In 2010 the Federal government moved to establish a uniform, national standard. When the new regulations take effect, restaurants that are part of a chain with twenty or more locations doing business under the same name will be required to disclose the number of calories in standard menu items in a clear and conspicuous manner. They will also provide upon request other nutritional information.

Patrons may also find more healthy foods choices on restaurant menus. Glanz et al. (2007) surveyed restaurant companies about menu trends, factors that influence their decisions to introduce and continue new menu items, and barriers to adding more healthy foods. Many reported having added healthy items. And most predicted that chain restaurants will be offering even more healthy items in the future. One reason is what restaurants call the "veto vote." That is, within a group of diners, there may be one or two people to whom healthier fare is important. The restaurants do not want these few people to dissuade an entire group of customers from patronizing their restaurant. However, many chains also felt that there was not a broader demand for healthier foods and, as such, what consumers demand will continue to constrain their ability to offer healthy menu items.

It remains to be seen whether recent efforts by restaurants to add more healthy menu items and other developments, such as nutrition labeling, will improve on the quality of what Americans eat out versus at home. Todd, Mancino, and Lin (2010) compare results using the 1994–6 CSFII and the 2003–4 NHANES. They find evidence of small improvements. For example, eating breakfast away from home had a less adverse impact on whole-grain intake in 2003–4 than it did in 1994–6. Similarly, in 2003–4, eating dinner away from home caused an increase in the share of total calories to come from solid fat, alcohol, and added sugars, but the size of the increase was less than in 1994–6.

9   CHANGES IN THE AWAY-FROM-HOME MARKET STIMULATE NEW RESEARCH QUESTIONS

The growing popularity of food away from home suggests that this market will be ever more important to the welfare of both consumers and agriculture. Policymakers, health policy advocates, and other parties are therefore likely to remain interested in the food service industry. Indeed, the questions and concerns of these parties are already motivating much new research.

New research on food service is being conducted to support farmers. Glanz et al. (2007), for one, focus on how fruit and vegetable growers might get more of their produce onto restaurants' menus. Maynard, Burdine, and Meyer (2003) examine whether restaurants are a good market for "locally produced" meats. In general, it is likely that groups with ties to agriculture will be interested in knowing more about how they can expand sales to the increasingly important away-from-home market.

Much new research is also being conducted out of a concern for diet and health. For example, Harnack and French (2008) examine whether providing point-of-purchase information on the calorie content of foods is likely to affect demand at restaurants and cafeterias. Chou, Rashad, and Grossman (2008) examine whether restrictions should be placed on television advertising by fast-food companies. And Schroeter, Lusk, and Tyner (2008) examine how market interventions, such as taxes and subsidies, could affect body weights. Contrary to intuition, they find that imposing a tax on restaurant foods could lead to further weight gain by encouraging Americans to increase their consumption of at-home foods that are similarly high in calories. This finding underscores the need for careful economic modeling when developing policies.

References

Adam, K., R. Balasubrahmanyam, and H. Born. 1999. *Direct Marketing*. Publication No. IP113. Fayetteville, AZ: National Sustainable Agriculture Information Service.

Akbay, C., G. Tiryaki, and A. Gul. 2007. "Consumer Characteristics Influencing Fast Food Consumption in Turkey." *Food Control* 18/8: 904–13.

Angulo, A., J. Gil, and J. Mur. 2007. "Spanish Demand for Food Away From Home: Analysis of Panel Data." *Journal of Agricultural Economics* 58/2: 289–307.

Barber, D., and P. Byrne. 1997. "U.S. Chain Restaurant Efficiency." *Journal of Food Distribution Research* 28/3: 54–62.

Becker, G. 1965. "A Theory of the Allocation of Time." *Economic Journal* 75/299: 493–517.

Binkley, J. 2006. "The Effect of Demographic, Economic, and Nutrition Factors on the Frequency of Food Away From Home." *Journal of Consumer Affairs* 40/2: 372–91.

——— 2008. "Calorie and Gram Differences between Meals at Fast Food and Table Service Restaurants." *Review of Agricultural Economics* 30/4: 750–63.

———, J. Eales, and M. Jekanowski. 2000. "The Relation between Dietary Change and Rising U.S. Obesity." *International Journal of Obesity* 24/8: 1032–9.

Byrne, P., O. Capps, Jr., and A. Saha. 1996. "Analysis of Food-Away-From-Home Expenditure Patterns for U.S. Households, 1982–89." *American Journal of Agricultural Economics* 78/3: 614–27.

——— ——— ———. 1998. "Analysis of Quick-Serve, Mid-Scale, and Up-Scale Food Away From Home Expenditures." *International Food and Agribusiness Management Review* 1/1: 51–72.

Chou, S., M. Grossman, and H. Saffer. 2004. "An Economic Analysis of Adult Obesity: Results from the Behavioral Risk Factor Surveillance System." *Journal of Health Economics* 23/3: 565–87.

———, I. Rashad, and M. Grossman. 2008. "Fast-Food Restaurant Advertising on Television and its Influence on Childhood Obesity." *Journal of Law and Economics* 51/4: 599–618.

Cromartie, J. 2002. "Population Growth and Demographic Change, 1980–2020." *FoodReview* 25/1: 10–12.

Currie, J., S. DellaVigna, E. Moretti, and V. Pathania. 2009. *The Effect of Fast Food Restaurants on Obesity*. Working Paper No. 14721. Cambridge, MA: National Bureau of Economic Research.

Erdem, T., and J. Swait. 1998. "Brand Equity as a Signaling Phenomenon." *Journal of Consumer Psychology* 7/2: 131–57.

French, S., M. Story, D. Neumark-Sztainer, J. Fulkerson, and P. Hannan. 2001. "Fast Food Restaurant Use among Adolescents: Associations with Nutrient Intake, Food Choices and Behavioral and Psychosocial Variables." *International Journal of Obesity* 25/12: 1823–33.

Glanz, K., K. Resnicow, J. Seymour, K. Hoy, H. Stewart, M. Lyons, and J. Goldberg. 2007. "How Major Restaurant Chains Plan their Menus: The Role of Profit, Demand, and Health." *American Journal of Preventive Medicine* 32/5: 383–8.

Harnack, L., and S. French. 2008. "Effect of Point-of-Purchase Calorie Labeling on Restaurant and Cafeteria Food Choices: A Review of the Literature." *International Journal of Behavioral Nutrition and Physical Activity* 5 (Oct.), 1–6.

Heng, H., and A. Guan. 2007. "Examining Malaysian Household Expenditure Patterns on Food-Away-From-Home." *Asian Journal of Agriculture and Development* 4/1: 11–24.

Jekanowski, M., J. Binkley, and J. Eales. 2001. "Convenience, Accessibility, and the Demand for Fast Food." *Journal of Agricultural and Resource Economics* 26/1: 58–74.

Keelan, C., M. Henchion, and C. Newman. 2007 "Quick-Service Expenditure in Ireland: Parametric vs. Semiparametric Analysis." *Applied Economics* 40/20: 2659–69.

Lin, B., J. Guthrie, and E. Frazão. 1999. *Away-From-Home Foods Increasingly Important to Quality of American Diet*. Agricultural Information Bulletin No. 749. Washington, DC: Economic Research Service, US Department of Agriculture.

Love, J. 1986. *McDonald's: Behind the Arches*. Toronto: Bantam Books.

Lund, P. 1998. "Eating Out: Statistics and Society Presidential Address." *Journal of Agricultural Economics* 49/3: 279–93.

Ma, H., J. Huang, F. Fuller, and S. Rozelle. 2006. "Getting Rich and Eating Out: Consumption of Food Away From Home in Urban China." *Canadian Journal of Agricultural Economics* 54/1: 101–19.

McCracken, V., and J. Brandt. 1987. "Household Consumption of Food Away From Home: Total Expenditure and by Type of Food Facility." *American Journal of Agricultural Economics* 69/2: 274–84.

Mancino, L., J. Todd, and B.-H. Lin. 2009. "Separating What We Eat from Where: Measuring the Effect of Food Away From Home on Diet Quality." *Food Policy* 34/6: 557–62.

Maynard, L., K. Burdine, and A. Meyer. 2003. "Market Potential for Locally Produced Meat Products." *Journal of Food Distribution Research* 34/2: 26–37.

Mehta, N., and V. Chang. 2008. "Weight Status and Restaurant Availability: A Multilevel Analysis." *American Journal of Preventive Medicine* 34/2: 127–33.

Mihalopoulos, V., and M. Demoussis. 2001. "Greek Household Consumption of Food Away From Home: A Microeconometric Approach." *European Review of Agriculture Economics* 28/4: 421–32.

Nagengast, Z., and C. Appleton. 1994. "The Quick Service Restaurant Industry." In L. Schertz and L. Daft, eds, *Food and Agricultural Markets: The Quiet Revolution*. Washington, DC: National Planning Association.

Nayga, R. M., Jr., and O. Capps, Jr. 1992. "Analysis of Food Away From Home and Food At Home Consumption: A Systems Approach." *Journal of Food Distribution Research* 23/3: 1–10.

——————. 1994. "Impact of Socio-Economic and Demographic Factors on Food Away From Home Consumption: Number of Meals and by Type of Facility." *Journal of Restaurant and Foodservice Marketing* 1/2: 45–69.

Paul, R. 1994. "Status and Outlook of the Chain-Restaurant Industry." *Cornell Hotel and Restaurant Administration Quarterly* 35/3: 23–6.

Reed, A., J. Levedahl, and C. Hallahan. 2005. "The Generalized Composite Commodity Theorem and Food Demand Estimation." *American Journal of Agricultural Economics* 87/1: 28–37.

Regmi, A., H. Takeshima, and L. Unnevehr. 2008. *Convergence in Global Food Demand and Delivery.* Economic Research Report No. 56. Washington, DC: Economic Research Service, US Department of Agriculture.

Richards, T., P. Patterson, and S. Hamilton. 2007. "Fast Food, Addiction, and Market Power." *Journal of Agricultural and Resource Economics* 32/3: 425–47.

Robinson, T., and D. Matheson. 2009. "Effects of Fast Food Branding on Young Children's Taste Preferences." *Archives Pediatrics and Adolescent Medicine* 161/8: 792–7.

Schlosser, E. 2001. *Fast Food Nation: The Dark Side of the All-American Meal.* Boston: Houghton Mifflin.

Schroeter, C., J. Lusk, and W. Tyner. 2008. "Determining the Impact of Food Price and Income Changes on Body Weight." *Journal of Health Economics* 27/1: 45–68.

Stewart, H., and S. Yen. 2004. "Changing Household Characteristics and the Away-From-Home Food Market: A Censored Equation System Approach." *Food Policy* 29/6: 643–58.

——, N. Blisard, S. Bhuyan, and R. M. Nayga, Jr. 2004. *The Demand for Food Away From Home: Full-Service or Fast Food?* Agricultural Economic Report No. 829. Washington, DC: Economic Research Service, US Department of Agriculture.

——————, D. Jolliffe, and S. Bhuyan. 2005. "The Demand for Food Away From Home: Do Other Preferences Compete with Our Desire to Eat Healthfully?" *Journal of Agricultural and Resource Economics* 30/3: 520–36.

Todd, J., L. Mancino, and B.-H. Lin. 2010. *The Impact of Food Away From Home on Adult Diet Quality.* Economic Research Report No. 90. Washington, DC: Economic Research Service, US Department of Agriculture.

US Census Bureau. 1998. *Measuring 50 Years of Economic Change Using the March Current Population Survey.* Current Population Reports No. P60–203. Washington, DC: US Census Bureau.

USDA ERS (Economic Research Service, US Department of Agriculture). *Food CPI and Expenditures: Food Expenditure Tables.* <http://www.ers.usda.gov/Briefing/CPIFoodAnd Expenditures/Data>.

Yen, S. 1993. "Working Wives and Food Away From Home: The Box–Cox Double Hurdle Model." *American Journal of Agricultural Economics* 75/4: 884–95.

You, W., and R. M. Nayga, Jr. 2005. "Household Fast Food Expenditures and Children's Television Viewing: Can They Really Significantly Influence Children's Dietary Quality?" *Journal of Agricultural and Resource Economics* 30/2: 302–14.

CHAPTER 27

CONSUMER DEMAND FOR FOOD VARIETY

CHRISTOPH R. WEISS*

1 INTRODUCTION

The idea that individuals demand variety certainly is not new. It was recognized by early philosophers and poets, is expressed concisely in Cicero's well-known phrase *variatio delectat*, and also found its way into the writings of classical economists. Referring to Nassau Senior's "law of variety,"[1] Jevons (1871) was among the first to stress the insatiability of consumers' taste for variety and to explore its implications in various fields of life:

> The necessaries of life are so few and simple, that a man is soon satisfied in regard to these, and desires to extend his range of enjoyment. His first object is to vary his food; but there soon arises the desire of variety and elegance in dress; and to this succeeds the desire to build, to ornament, and to furnish tastes which, where they exist, are absolutely insatiable, and seem to increase with every improvement in civilization. (Jevons 1871: 11)

Variety in (food) consumption is an issue that deserves attention for a number of reasons. First, food variety can be important for nutrition and in protecting against chronic diseases, obesity, diabetes, and cardiovascular risk factors (Temple 2006).[2] Nutritionists generally believe that the key to an optimal diet is to eat a variety of foods.

* I wish to thank Larissa Drescher as well as an anonymous referee for valuable comments on a previous draft of this chapter.

[1] In his "law of variety" the nineteenth-century British economist Walter Senior states that "It is obvious that our desires do not aim so much at quantity as at diversity" (Senior 1836: 11–12).

[2] The relationship between diversity and health outcomes seems to be a promising area of research in nutritional epidemiology: "Although the issues of dietary variety and nutrient adequacy have been addressed previously, nutrition research has only recently explored the issue of diet quality and begun to

On this account, variety in food consumption is included as a desirable component in the Healthy Eating Index developed by the US Department of Agriculture.

In addition to the beneficial instrumental effects of food variety on consumers' health, variety seems to have a positive direct effect on utility. The extent to which a nation's citizens consume a diversity of goods has been linked to the economic well-being of a country (Theil and Finke 1983). Recent work in urban economics suggests that product variety is one of several consumption amenities driving people to live in cities (Glaeser, Kolko, and Saiz 2001).

In the area of economics, product variety has played a central role in models of trade since the seminal work of Krugman (1979). Countries gain from trade through the import of new varieties. From a macroeconomic point of view, the expanding variety of consumption plays an important role in the process of long-run growth and development. This literature takes up the idea that in the process of growth, consumption is expanded along the hierarchy of wants.

Industrial Organization theory focuses on product differentiation as a way to increase profits due to economies of scope, an increase in consumer demand (by offering the consumer more varieties to choose from), and/or by differentiating their products strategically from those of their competitors to reduce the degree of price competition or to prevent entry of new competitors. The American food industry, for example, considers increasing demand for food diversity as one of its most important consumer trends (Connor and Schiek 1997; Blisard et al. 2002), driving production, processing, and distribution of many products in other countries as well.

Studying variety in the consumption of different food products may also reveal consumption patterns useful for marketing (van Trijp and Steenkamp 1992). Knowledge of consumer preferences on variety may serve as a criterion for market segmentation, may assist firms in adapting marketing strategies more effectively to consumers' needs, and has implications for retailer assortment and pricing policy.[3]

It is beyond the scope of this chapter to summarize the literature on (food) variety in these diverse areas of research. The focus is on one particular dimension of this literature only: the economics of consumer demand for food variety. More specifically, we aim at summarizing stylized facts emanating from the existing literature on the impact of various demographic and socioeconomic characteristics of households and consumers on their demand for food variety. We thus do not attempt to review studies on the supply of variety systematically (such as strategic product line decisions in management and the optimal degree of product differentiation in industrial

---

devise new methods for assessing healthful eating patterns" (Drewnowski et al. 1997: 664). The authors also refer to recent studies addressing this issue in more detail.

[3] If consumers value variety, a retailer with lower variety must compensate consumers in some other way, such as by lowering prices, for example. The strategic interaction of pricing and product line decisions made by retailers is studied in detail by Richards and Hamilton (2006).

organization or the macroeconomic consequences of these decisions for international trade and economic growth).[4]

Despite the fact that the supply of variety is not at the core of our investigation, supply-side issues often interfere with attempts to analyze consumer demand for variety. As Lancaster (1990) has pointed out, variety within a product group is determined by the interplay of supply and demand factors in a market economy. The observation that a particular household consumes a variety of different products, for example, does not necessarily imply a preference for variety but could result from the fact that the brand usually purchased is out of stock, that a competing brand currently is on sale, or that different household members prefer different products. The recent literature on the demand for variety recognizes the importance of these supply-side issues.

The following section will briefly review the different theoretical approaches that have been put forward to relate a preference for variety (a specific feature of the utility function) to an individual's purchasing and consumption behavior. Section 3 reviews the existing empirical evidence on the demand for variety by discussing various ways to measure variety in food consumption (Section 3.1) and summarizes a few stylized facts (Section 3.2) emanating from this literature. Section 4 finally addresses some issues that have been neglected in the economic analysis of the demand for food variety.

2   THEORIES ON DEMAND FOR VARIETY

Economic models to explain consumers' demand for variety are grounded in the economics of product differentiation. Conceptually, one can distinguish two different approaches that provide different explanations as to why consumers purchase a variety of products: "representative consumer models" and "characteristics models."[5]

In the "representative consumer approach," consumers are assumed identical (are characterized by identical preferences and resources) and can thus be represented by a

---

[4] The interested reader is referred to Ch. 5, by Adamowicz and Swait, and Ch. 10, by Mérel and Sexton, in this volume, for example. In studying the economics of variety Gronau and Hamermesh (2008) claim that economists have devoted substantial attention to the supply of variety while consumer demand for variety is typically taken as given. According to the authors, the reason for neglecting demand issues in studying variety has to do with the difficulties of measuring characteristics of products: "To analyze product variety one has to define the nature of the product, something most economists tend to shy away from" (Gronau and Hamermesh 2008: 562). The following sections, however, will refer to some recent studies trying to measure the characteristics of products as the "true source of product differentiation" (Pofahl and Richards 2009: 403) empirically.

[5] Different names are used for the two approaches: the "representative consumer model" is also known as Chamberlin's "model of monopolistic competition." Some authors refer to "characteristics models" as "attribute-based models," "address models," or "spatial models of product differentiation." For a detailed discussion on the economics of product differentiation, see Ch. 10 in this volume, by Mérel and Sexton.

single (representative) consumer. Demand for variety arises in a market because each individual consumer has a taste for variety and prefers to purchase a number of different products.

In "characteristic models," on the other hand, consumers are assumed to have different preferences (or "ideal locations" of a product in the space of product characteristics). Each consumer typically buys only a single product, the one that best fits his preferences. Firms differentiate their products because increased variety taps consumers in new segments of the market.

Whereas the "representative consumer model" derives a demand for variety at the level of each individual consumer, "characteristics models" typically explain a demand for variety at the aggregate (market) level only. This reduces the attractiveness of the "characteristics approach" as a basis for empirical studies to explain a varied consumption behavior at a disaggregate (individual consumer) level.

In reviewing the existing theoretical literature it is also helpful to distinguish between situations where an individual has a preference for purchasing different products at one point in time and situations where an individual switches between purchasing different products at different points in time. Marketing scientists and consumer behaviorists tend to make the distinction between "structural variety" and "temporal variety" (Pessemier 1985). The first case characterizes a consumer who derives utility from the fact that he can choose among a large number of similar products (substitutes) and may decide to purchase a smaller quantity from each of the different products instead of purchasing a large quantity from only one product. In this case, we argue that a consumer has a preference for variety. The second (related) stream of literature investigates consumers' purchases over time. Whereas loyal consumers repeatedly purchase the same product, other consumers might derive utility from switching between different products. This sort of behavior is analyzed in the literature on switching costs, brand loyalty, and variety-seeking behavior.

The following section (2.1) focuses on the demand for variety from the perspective of the traditional "representative consumer model." Attempts to incorporate product characteristics and combine features of the two types of model (representative consumer and characteristics model) are described in Section 2.2. Note that economic models typically focus on the effects of prices and income to explain changes in individual behavior. Relatively little attention is devoted to the analysis of preferences.[6] The parsimony of this paradigm has been criticized by psychologists and consumer behaviorists, who argue that an individual's "preferences" include many different dimensions of the desire for variety. The variety-seeking literature, which will be discussed in Section 2.3, focuses on preferences in explaining differences in individual behavior. Finally, Section 2.4 introduces an additional approach to understanding consumers' demand for variety which is based on the theory of household production.

---

[6] Becker and Stigler (1977), for example, claim that "all changes in behavior are explained by changes in prices and income" (Becker and Stigler 1977: 77). The title of their paper expresses the relative neglect of preferences in economics very clearly: "De Gustibus Non Est Disputandum."

2.1 Demand for Variety in the Representative Consumer Approach

Assume that consumer preferences are represented by a single "representative consumer" who derives utility from consuming two groups of products: one product group is composed of n differentiated products (q_j with $j = 1, \ldots, n$), the second product group is a composite product (q_0), which includes all other products in the economy. The utility function is assumed to be separable between the two groups: $U = U\left[V_n(q_j), q_0\right]$. An important assumption typically made concerning preferences is that $V_n(q_j)$ is symmetric in its arguments: all products are equally good substitutes for each other ("dispersed product rivalry"). By implication, any price change (or the introduction of a new product) will have an impact on all products in the group: product attributes do not matter!

Within this framework, different specifications of the sub-utility function $V_n(q_j)$ are used in the literature. The "standard models" of consumer choice, based on strictly quasi-concave preferences (smooth indifference curves convex to the origin), exhibit only interior solutions and imply an inherent preference for variety. There is a combination of n goods that is preferred to any combination of fewer goods that costs no more. Differences in the preference for variety are reflected in the curvature of the consumers' indifference curves and are expressed in terms of the relative quantity of each product in the consumption basket. In the two-product case, for example, variety in consumption will be larger if the household spends 50 percent of total expenditure on each product, as opposed to 99 percent on the first and 1 percent on the second.

The most popular specification is the constant elasticity of substitution (CES) function, $V_n(q_j) = \left(\sum_{j=1}^{n} q_j^{\theta}\right)^{1/\theta}$, $0 < \theta < 1$, where the elasticity of substitution between the different products is $\sigma = \frac{1}{\theta - 1}$. Following Benassy's (1996) definition of a preference for variety, one can show that the "taste for variety" (η) in the case of a CES utility function is directly proportional to the elasticity of substitution:[7] $\eta = \frac{1}{\theta} - 1 = -\frac{1}{1+\sigma}$. Figure 27.1 illustrates the preference for variety for a representative consumer for the two-product case.

With a given budget (y_0) and product prices (p_1 and p_2), the representative consumer could, for example, choose between the consumption bundles A, B, and C. Bundle A

---

[7] Assuming a constant elasticity of substitution of products (σ) has the property that, for given prices and income, the consumer is always better off spending $1/n$ of his budget on each of the n goods than spending $1/(n-1)$ of the budget on each of n-1 goods. This implies an insatiable taste for variety. Benassy (1996) defines a function $v(n) = \frac{V_n(q, \ldots, q)}{V_1(nq)} = \frac{V_n(1, \ldots, 1)}{V_1(n)}$ that depicts the utility gain derived from spreading a certain amount of production between n different products instead of concentrating it on a single variety. The "taste for variety" (the marginal taste for an additional variety) is then defined in terms of an elasticity: $\eta = \frac{\partial v(n)}{\partial n} \frac{n}{v(n)}$

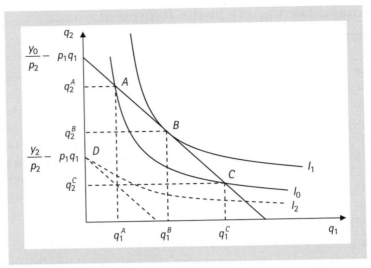

FIGURE 27.1 The preference for variety for a "representative consumer"

(C) is composed primarily of product 2 (product 1), whereas bundle B has a more balanced composition of the two products. The additional utility derived from a more balanced bundle (indifference curve I_1 implies a higher level of utility than I_0) represents the taste for variety. One can easily see from Figure 27.1 that consumers' preferences for variety are reflected by the curvature of the household's indifference curves for the two products.

The representative consumer approach has been criticized on several counts. When applied literally, the model predicts that all individuals will always consume all available products (Lancaster 1990).[8] The preference structure typically assumed in "representative consumer" models implies that the representative consumer buys some of every variant and is at an interior solution (corner solutions, such as the consumption bundle D chosen by a low-income (y_2) household, are not considered). To the extent that the representative consumer's behavior should describe the aggregate market, such a result in fact is plausible since in the aggregate, individuals necessarily consume all variants actually sold. As a description of individual consumption behavior, however, this implication is implausible since individual consumers tend to purchase only a few of the variants offered but not all of them. The standard representative consumer model thus is inappropriate for understanding situations where individual consumers are faced with the "pick k of n" assortment choice.

A more appropriate framework for modeling demand for variety, where some but not all varieties are chosen, was suggested by Jackson (1984). Jackson characterizes a

---

[8] Pettengill (1979) criticizes the representative consumer model of Dixit and Stiglitz (1977) on the ground that consumers in real markets do not consume a small proportion of each variant of a differentiated product.

class—called hierarchic demand systems—for which only a subset of commodities is in the purchased set.[9] Analytically, a hierarchy of purchases is introduced by specifically focusing on the non-negativity constraints in a demand system. At low levels of income, only a small fraction of all goods available is actually consumed. At certain levels of incomes, non-necessities sequentially enter the consumption bundle. This implies a non-linear Engel curve and a systematic relationship between consumers' income and the variety of consumed products. Incorporating corner solutions, however, is mathematically more demanding and models quickly become very complex, which reduces their applicability for empirical research.[10]

A second, and more fundamental, point of criticism on the traditional representative consumer model refers to the fact that characteristics of products do not matter. The assumption of "dispersed product rivalry" (all products are equally good substitutes for each other) is unrealistic and ignores an important dimension of the demand for variety. A consumption bundle (menu) with five different brands of pizza clearly is characterized by less variety than a bundle that consists of French, Italian, Chinese, Mexican, and Austrian cuisine. The attributes of the individual products consumed certainly matter in understanding consumer demand for variety.

2.2   Product Characteristics and the Demand for Variety

In "characteristic models" (or location or address models), consumers are assumed to have different preferences or "ideal locations" in the space of product characteristics. *Ceteris paribus*, they purchase the product that most closely matches their preferences in terms of product characteristics (Salop 1979).

Hart (1985) and Perloff and Salop (1985) have developed models of consumer behavior that combine elements of the representative consumer approach and the characteristics model. A representative consumer's utility function, which is consistent with the discrete choice framework of characteristics models, is given by

---

[9] A hierarchic model of consumer demand has been outlined more recently by Chattopadhyay, Majumder, and Coondoo (2009). For related approaches in the marketing literature, see (Kim, Allenby, and Rossi 2002).

[10] To keep those models tractable analytically, authors assume relatively simple utility functions. Preferences in Kim, Allenby, and Rossi (2002), for example, are characterized by an additive utility structure, which implies that marginal utility gained from one variety is independent of the consumption of other varieties. The authors argue that this assumption is plausible for different products within a product category that are close substitutes "because the offerings under consideration are not jointly consumed and, hence, the utility gained from one variety is unaffected by the consumption of others" (2002: 231). The fact, however, that two products are not jointly consumed suggests that there is some interdependence in consumption. The marginal utility of consuming yogurt with strawberry flavor will be influenced (most likely reduced) if the individual has just consumed yogurt with blueberry flavor.

$$U(q_1, \ldots, q_n) = \begin{cases} \sum_{j=1}^{n} a_j q_j - \mu \sum_{j=1}^{n} q_j \ln(q_j/Q) + q_0 & \text{if } \sum_{j=1}^{n} q_j = Q, \\ -\infty & \text{otherwise} \end{cases}$$

where $j = 1, \ldots, n$ are variants of a differentiated product, commodity o is an outside (composite) good. Demand for commodity j is q_j; aggregate demand for the differentiated product Q is assumed exogenously given; a_j and μ are non-negative scalars.[11]

This utility function has three terms. The first captures the effect of product characteristics a_j on consumers' utility. A preference for variety of the representative consumer is explicitly introduced in the second term of the utility function (Anderson, de Palma, and Thisse 1992). Note that $\sum_{j=1}^{n} q_j \ln(q_j/Q)$ is closely related to the entropy measure of diversity which is frequently used in empirical research to measure variety (Section 3.1). *Ceteris paribus*, the larger is μ, the greater is the preference for variety. When $\mu \to 0$, variety is not valued per se and the consumer buys solely the variant with the largest net surplus, $a_j - p_j$. When $\mu \to \infty$, consumption is divided equally among all available variants. The third part captures the utility derived from an outside good q_0. Anderson, de Palma, and Thisse (1992: 80ff.) provide an extensive discussion of this model including the calculation of the optimal number of products purchased by the consumer.

2.3   Variety Seeking and Temporal Variety

The economic models described so far are best interpreted as focusing on the decision of an individual to purchase one or many different brands of a particular product at a particular point in time ("structural variety"). Despite the fact that much progress has been made in improving our understanding of the demand for variety, such models rely on the assumption of stable preferences and do not capture an important dimension of variety seeking that is related to the temporal variety in consumer behavior.

The variety-seeking literature stresses temporal variety in consumer behavior.[12] "An individual exhibits varied consumption behavior by making choices that differ from one occasion to the next in the same class of potential substitutes" (Pessemier and Handelsman 1984: 435). This literature argues that individuals do not care only about

---

[11] Anderson, de Palma, and Thisse (1992: 78) show that this utility function is consistent with a multinomial logit demand model, which is widely used in empirical research.

[12] Some authors define "variety seeking" more broadly such that it also includes "structural variety." Others (such as Pessemier and Handelsman 1984 as well as Kahn, Kalwani, and Morrison 1986) equate "variety-seeking behavior" with temporal variety: "we view variety-seeking as the deliberate tendency to switch away from the brand purchased on the last one or more occasions" (Kahn et al. 1986: 90). McAlister and Pessemier (1982) offer a taxonomy of explanations for varied behavior and discuss the different motivations in more detail. An extensive review of the literature on variety-seeking behavior is also available in Khan (1995) and van Trijp (1995).

the physical characteristics of the different products; varied consumption behavior is pursued because "novelty," "unexpectedness," and "change" are inherently satisfying. This is expressed clearly in Givon (1984), for example, who defines variety-seeking behavior as "the phenomenon of an individual consumer switching brands (or repeat buying) induced by the utility (or disutility) she derives from the change itself, irrespective of the brands she switches to or from" (Givon 1984: 2–3). The observed consumption behavior is a result of the utilities derived from consuming a particular brand as well as from switching between brands.

Different motivations for this argument have been proposed (Kahn, Ratner, and Kahnemann 1997). A number of studies in marketing refer to psychological theories, where the concept of an "optimal level of stimulation" is central to explain variety-seeking tendencies in consumers (Scitovsky 1976). Individuals are assumed to select that collection of items that will provide just the right amount of stimulation. When stimulation is too high, consumers try to reduce the complexities in the situation by routinizing their buying decisions. Choosing to remain loyal to a specific item or brand may be regarded as one of the routinizing methods. Routinization, however, may eventually lead to feelings of monotony and boredom. Consumers may then try to increase stimulation by switching to a different product.

Substantial progress has been made in the literature on modeling consumer choice dynamics and temporal variety. McAlister (1982) develops a "dynamic attribute satiation model" in which the consumption history of an individual is represented by the accumulated attributes of past consumption activities (or attribute inventories) it generates.[13] The stock of attribute inventory increases each time an item containing that attribute is consumed and declines continually over time through psychological processing or forgetting (discounting of older consumption experiences). The configuration of attribute inventories can change considerably as the consumption history evolves, which generates shifts in preferences among choice alternatives. This explains, for example, why an individual consumes a cola at times (when the inventory of caffeine or sugar is low and the marginal utility of adding to that inventory is high) and prefers mineral water at other times (when the inventory of caffeine and sugar is high, implying that additions will have a small marginal impact on utility). Consumer preferences for particular attributes and products change over time. Changing preferences generate variety in consumption (Simonson 1990).

McAlister and Pessemier (1982) extend this model by introducing an additional term to the utility function, which represents the stimulation contribution to preference to account for the effect of new experiences. The authors further argue that behavioral patterns are typically influenced by those of one's peers.[14] A desire for uniqueness, the

---

[13] Jeuland (1978) develops a similar model in which inventories of items are accumulated instead of inventories of attributes.

[14] Pessemier (1985) distinguishes between "interpersonal" and "intrapersonal" variety. The notion of "interpersonal" variety represents an individual's need for group affiliation and/or personal identity. The importance of interpersonal mechanisms of the variety-seeking tendency is also documented in the

possession of commodities that are scarce or that are unavailable to others, would account for the varied behavior stimulated by fashion, for example. The importance of being affiliated with a group, on the other hand, may lead to following the new lifestyles of valued peers.

An "attribute-based" dynamic model, where consumers' preferences for brand attributes are assumed to depend on the attributes of the brand bought on the previous purchase occasion, has been introduced by Erdem (1996). Habit persistence (or positive state dependence) is characterized by a situation where consumer utility increases through successive purchases of products with similar attributes. Variety-seeking behavior (or negative state dependence) corresponds to a situation where consumer utility increases in the differences of the attribute levels consumed over past purchase occasions (a detailed review of the empirical literature on habit formation in food consumption is available in Chapter 31 in this volume, by Daunfeldt, Nordström, and Thunström).

Common to these explanations (as well as to those presented in Sections 2.1 and 2.2) is the idea that increased product variety is good for consumers: with more choices available, consumers can adjust their purchasing behavior if a consumption bundle yielding higher utility becomes available. However, a number of recent studies in marketing, psychology, and behavioral economics challenge this notion by suggesting that greater product variety can lower the utility experienced from consumption of the chosen good (Iyengar and Lepper 2000; Schwartz et al. 2002).

Different explanations for this "excessive-choice effect" (ECE) have been offered. If agents have self-control problems, for example, more choice provides additional opportunity for self-damaging behavior (Gul and Pesendorfer 2001). Based upon Schwartz (2004), Irons and Hepburn (2007) investigate a situation where individuals desire to avoid consequences in which they appear *ex post* to have made the wrong decision, even if the decision maximized expected utility *ex ante* ("regret theory"). They demonstrate that if agents suffer regret from unsearched options that turn out to be better than their choice, and anticipate this regret, an increase in the choice set can reduce consumer welfare.

Norwood (2006) and Kuksov and Villas-Boas (2010) argue that search/evaluation costs can explain the existence of an ECE. When too many alternatives are offered, the consumer may have to engage in many searches/evaluations to find a satisfactory fit. If the consumer considers this too costly, she might avoid making a choice altogether. The authors argue that the preference for smaller choice sets should be strongest for consumers with "mainstream tastes" since they believe that they can find a good fit even from smaller choice sets because sellers are motivated to cater to their "mainstream tastes."

experimental study of Ratner and Khan (2002) and Choi et al. (2006). Ratner and Khan (2002) demonstrate that individuals believe that others would seek more variety than they themselves would seek. Similarly, Choi et al. (2006) find that the variety-seeking tendency is greater in choices for others than in choices for self.

Empirical evidence on the ECE, which typically is based on experiments, is mixed. A recent study conducting four experiments using food items concludes: "although the ECE can arise, it seems to be the exception rather than the rule" (Arunachalam et al. 2009: 824).[15]

The last years have seen an extremely dynamic development of studies in the area of behavioral economics and the interface between economics and psychology (see also Chapter 4 in this volume, by Just). We may hope to gain further new and important insights on the demand for food variety from this research in the near future.

2.4   Demand for Variety from a Household Production Perspective

In the representative consumer approach as well as in characteristic models, all consumers face the same money prices, and the burden of explaining differences in consumption diversity mainly lies with income and preferences. Based on Becker's (1965) theory of household production, Gronau and Hamermesh (2008) develop a new approach that traces differences in the demand for variety to differences in opportunity costs of activities (the price of time). This approach emphasizes the price mechanism and explains why the demand for variety differs systematically with characteristics of the individual consumer.[16]

In contrast to traditional demand models, where utility is derived directly from goods purchased in the market, the theory of household production assumes that goods (together with time) are inputs in the production of commodities and provide utility indirectly. Following Becker (1991), assume that n different commodities (z_j, with $j = 1, \ldots, n$) are produced by using market purchases (x_j) and time t_j: it takes time to purchase food in the market, prepare, and finally consume the meal. The production

---

[15] Kuksov and Villas-Boas (2010) report some anecdotal evidence on the "excessive-choice effect" from the *New York Times*: "As a neophyte shoe salesman, I was told never to show customers more than three pairs of shoes. If they saw more, they would not be able to decide on any of them" (*New York Times*, Jan. 26, 2004, quoted in Kuksov and Villas-Boas 2010: 507).

[16] The authors also find empirical support for some of the models' implications by exploring data on the time allocation of individuals from time budget surveys for different countries. In different versions of the model, the authors apply the household production framework to studying the trade-off between the positive and negative effects of temporal variety/temporal routine ("Routine is productive, in that it enables the producer/consumer to mechanize decisions about when and how to engage in each activity, thus allowing her to produce/consume more of each commodity" (Gronau and Hamermesh 2008: 31–2). At the same time, temporal routine—maintaining the same schedule from day to day, is boring and inherently undesirable. Note that much earlier work by Shonkwiler, Lee, and Taylor (1987) also uses a household production framework when analyzing the demand for a varied diet. The household is assumed to minimize the expenditures necessary to achieve a given level and variety of food consumption. Shadow prices of food varieties are calculated from the cost function, which are then used in the utility maximization problem of the household to determine the optimal level and variety of food consumption.

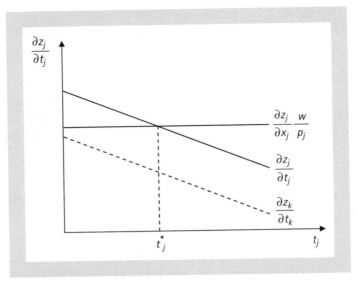

FIGURE 27.2. Time allocation in the household production model

function for commodities is $z_j = z_j(x_j, t_j)$ with $\frac{\partial z_j}{\partial x_j}, \frac{\partial z_j}{\partial t_j} > 0$; $\frac{\partial^2 z_j}{\partial x_j^2}, \frac{\partial^2 z_j}{\partial t_j^2} < 0$; $\frac{\partial^2 z_j}{\partial x_j \partial t_j} = 0$. Further assume that an individual derives utility (U) from different commodities according to the utility function $U = U(z_j)$.[17] The individual aims at maximizing utility subject to a budget as well as a time constraint. Total expenditures on market purchases may not exceed wage and property income $wl + v = \sum_{j=1}^{n} p_j x_j$, where p_j are exogenous prices of market purchases, w are exogenous earnings per hour of work, and v is property income. The time constraint states that total available time ($\bar{t}$) is divided among labor time (l) and time for producing the different activities (t_j): $\bar{t} = \sum_{j=1}^{n} t_j + l$. The maximization problem is represented by the following equation (Lagrange function):

$$\max_{x_j, t_j, l} \quad L = U\left[z_j(x_j, t_j)\right] + \lambda\left(\bar{t} - \sum_{j=1}^{n} t_j - l\right) + \mu\left(wl + v - \sum_{j=1}^{n} p_j x_j\right).$$

Figure 27.2 illustrates the solution to the optimal time allocation problem for an individual household. The formal model is presented in an appendix (which is available from the author upon request).

In allocating the available time to the difference activities, the household weights the (time) costs associated with producing commodities (inverse of $\frac{\partial z_j}{\partial t_j}$) against the opportunity costs of time in the labor market, which expands his ability to purchase inputs for producing commodities $\frac{\partial z_j}{\partial x_j}\frac{\partial x_j}{\partial t_j} = \frac{\partial z_j}{\partial x_j}\frac{w}{p_j}$. An individual will consume those commodities only for which the following condition holds: $\frac{\partial z_j}{\partial t_j} \geq \frac{\partial z_j}{\partial x_j}\frac{w}{p_j}$. Commodity k in Figure 27.2, for example, would not be produced.

---

17   For simplicity we assume that labor time does not enter the utility function.

Improvements in the efficiency of household production $(\frac{\partial z_j}{\partial t_j})$ allows the individual to economize on the direct time inputs going into the production of each commodity which increases as well as the number of commodities produced and consumed.[18]

An increase in non-labor income (v) softens the individual's budget constraint. Assuming that the marginal utility of additional income (μ) is decreasing, we would expect a positive effect of v on the number of commodities consumed (demand variety) since a decrease in $\mu = \frac{\partial U}{\partial z_j} \frac{\partial z_j}{\partial x_j} \frac{1}{p_j}$ shifts the horizontal $\frac{\partial z_j}{\partial x_j} \frac{w}{p_j}$ curve downwards, *ceteris paribus*. This implies a positive income effect for the demand for product variety.

An increase in wages will also soften the budget constraint and should thus initiate a positive income effect.[19] But at the same time, an increase in wages raises the opportunity costs of time devoted to the production of commodities (the pure price effect would shift the $\frac{\partial z_j}{\partial x_j} \frac{w}{p_j}$ −curve upwards).

The effect of schooling on demand for variety in the household production model is more complex. First, wages should increase with additional schooling, the consequences of which have just been discussed. Second, Michael (1973) has argued that schooling contributes to productivity at home. If more educated household members are planning and carrying out their activities more effectively, the marginal productivity of time $(\frac{\partial z_j}{\partial t_j})$ increases. This would imply a positive effect on the number of commodities produced and consumed at home.

The novel contribution of this approach is that the demand for diversity arises not only from the dispersion in preferences and income but also from the dispersion of individuals' opportunity costs of time. Differences in marginal time costs between individuals, but also changes in opportunity costs over time (due to rising wages and salaries and/or an increasing participation of women in the labor force), explain differences and changes in the demand for variety. Depending on the time-intensiveness of consumption, a household's time constraint will be relevant for consumption decisions for some (but not for all) products. The empirical evidence on the demand for food diversity to be discussed in the following section shows that household characteristics are of key importance for explaining observed differences in consumption behavior. Many of the effects observed are consistent with the household production approach.

---

[18] Cutler, Glaeser, and Shapiro (2003) argue that 57 percent of the total costs of food in 1960 in the United States were preparation and clean-up time. Married working (non-working) females on average spent 84.8 (137.7) minutes per day on food preparation and clean-up. Between 1965 and 1995 this number declined about 50 percent for both groups. The authors further argue that this reduction in the time cost of food contributes to the observed increase in food consumption variety (as well as quantity and the associated increase in obesity) over time.

[19] For a given marginal utility of "effective time" (λ), an increase in w corresponds to a decrease in μ. Assuming labor supply to be exogenous, an increase in the wage rate has a pure income effect: demand for variety increases with wages.

3   EMPIRICAL EVIDENCE ON THE DEMAND
FOR VARIETY

The empirical analysis of the demand for variety has started relatively early in the area of marketing (variety-seeking behavior) and only much later found the attention of (food and agricultural) economists. Different methodological approaches are applied in these areas. Ideally, a researcher would like to explore an individual's utility function and thus his preference for variety as directly as possible by measuring the change in "well-being" associated with any change in his choice set such as an increase in variety. In the area of marketing, researchers typically aim at isolating this intrinsic (or direct) motivation for consuming a variety of products. To measure the intrinsic motivation, researchers typically rely on direct measures (questionnaires). Van Trijp and Steenkamp (1992), for example, claim that "as many different consumer motivations may underlie observed variation in behavior, consumers' variety seeking tendency cannot be validly measured with measures of observed variation in consumer behavior. Consumers' variety seeking tendency should be measured directly" (van Trijp and Steenkamp 1992: 182). From an individual's response to a variety of items (such as "I like to buy new and different things"; McCarthy et al. 2007: 55), researchers aim at categorizing consumers into different groups according to their degree of variety-seeking tendency. The advantage of this direct approach is that the preference for variety can be studied in isolation; the effects of restrictions are not considered.

In economics, an indirect approach is more commonly applied: based on theoretical models to bridge the gap between observed purchasing behavior and a consumer's preference for variety, the actual consumption behavior of individuals is analyzed to derive information about a taste for variety from observed behavior. Observed consumer behavior, however, is not only determined by preferences; a number of additional factors will be important. The fact that a particular household purchases a number of different brands of wine, for example, might be due to the fact that different members of the household prefer different sorts of wine. The different brands of wine might also be used for different purposes (drinking versus cooking). The fact that (a) consumption behavior of the shopper typically reflects demand for the entire household and (b) the shopper must make multiple decisions in anticipation of the various future consumption occasions is difficult to integrate into theoretical and empirical research (Dube 2004).

Further, changes in the consumption behavior of a household over time might also be related to changes in the feasible set of products, e.g., the product that is typically purchased is out of stock or a competing product is on sale. Finally, changes in income and time restrictions will determine consumers' actual behavior. Considering the combined impact of these factors as well as an individual's inherent preference for variety is required in order to understand observed purchase decisions.[20] The point of departure of empirical studies of observed purchase decisions is to measure actual variety of consumption.

3.1 Measuring Food Variety

Research on variety in food consumption has used different measures.[21] The number of food items actually consumed in a given time period has been used in Jackson (1984), Lee (1987), Shonkwiler, Lee, and Taylor (1987), as well as a number of studies in the area of nutrition (Temple 2006). This index, although easy to interpret, has the disadvantage that it does not consider information on the distribution of individual food quantities consumed. If an individual consumes some of each product, then maximum variety is realized. In the two-product case, the consumer would move from no food variety to maximum food variety, if in fact the consumption bundle changed only marginally (from spending 100 percent of all expenditures on one product to spending 99 percent on one and 1 percent on the second product, for example). Substantial changes in consumption behavior, on the other hand, would not be represented in this measure (if, for example, the share of one product changes from 99 to 50 percent in the two-product case). A more appropriate alternative is the Berry index (Berry 1971), which is defined as $BI_i = 1 - H_i = \sum_{j=1}^{n} s_{i,j}^2$ where H_i is the well-known Herfindahl index for household i and $s_{i,j}$ is the share of product j in the total expenditures for food.

Another frequently used measure of diversity is the entropy index, which places greater weight on smaller shares and thus is especially sensitive to differences in the number of minor commodities in the consumption basket. It is defined as $EI_i = \sum_{j=1}^{n} s_j \log (1/s_j)$. The maximum of the entropy index is $\ln(1/n)$. The entropy index and the Berry index are closely related.[22]

---

[20] Distinguishing between these factors and the consumers' inherent preference for variety ("direct" and "derived" motivations in consumers' observed behavior) is a difficult task. Menon and Kahn (1995), for example, show that consumers' preference for variety is influenced by the choice context (i.e., supply conditions influence preferences). In assessing the relative importance of intrinsically and extrinsically motivated factors, Tang and Chin (2007) conclude: "the present results suggest that consumers' intrinsic desire for variety plays a minor role in brand-choice behavior, relative to other product-specific and behavior characteristics" (2007: 22).

[21] Literature in the area of nutrition typically focuses on the relationship between dietary diversity and health outcomes. Developing an adequate measure of diversity from a nutritional perspective is even more demanding since the "health value" of individual products has to be reflected in this index (Drescher, Thiele, and Mensink 2007). In principle, there is no guarantee that economic indicators of diversity and health (or medical) indicators of diversity point in the same direction. This study mainly focuses on economic aspects of food variety.

[22] The Berry index is also known as the Simpson index and the entropy measure is sometimes referred to as the Shannon index (Patil and Taillie 1982). A good discussion of the properties of the entropy and the Berry index is available in Gollop and Monahan (1991).

These indices are frequently used to measure "structural variety" in consumption where consumers have a preference for purchasing different products during a particular period of time. Temporal variety, on the other hand, where consumers express their demand for variety by switching between different products over time, is rarely addressed and measured in the empirical literature on food variety. An exception is Tang and Chin (2007), who use a simple measure of temporal variety. If the brand purchased on occasion t is the same as on occasion $t - 1$, the transaction is recorded as a repeat purchase and a dummy variable for brand switching is set equal to zero (otherwise the dummy variable for brand switching is set equal to one). Note the close relationship between temporal variety and the issue of brand loyalty, which has received considerable attention in the area of marketing. Reviewing this large literature clearly is beyond the scope of the present chapter. The interested reader is referred to Mellens, Dekimpe, and Steenkamp (1996).

It is also important to note that by using measures such as the "share of purchases going to the most frequently purchased brand" or "degree to which purchases are concentrated," an investigator loses information about the dissimilarity of brands chosen by an individual.[23] Pessemier and Handelsman (1984) develop an index of variety (ITV) which aims at capturing temporal variety as well as the similarity (or dissimilarity) of brands. The degree of dissimilarity between individual products (PRD, which is the "percentage of realized dissimilarity") is measured by the Euclidean distance along each defining attribute.[24] Temporal variety is captured by an index of "relative non-bunching" (RNB), which counts the number of contiguous changes between brands in a sequence of purchases: temporal variety is reduced when the same brand is chosen on consecutive occasions. The aggregate index of variety (ITV) developed in Pessemier and Handelsman (1984) is the weighted sum of an entropy measure (PRE) and the two measures just described: $ITV = w_1 PRD + w_2 PRE + w_3 RNB$, where w_1, w_2, and w_3 are weights assigned to the three elements in the equation.[25]

Gollop and Monahan (1991) generalize the Herfindal index of diversity to make it sensitive to product heterogeneity. Their "generalized index of diversification" combines different dimensions of variety (number, distribution, and heterogeneity): $D = \frac{1}{n}\left[\left(1 - \frac{1}{n}\right) + \sum_{j=1}^{n}\left(\frac{1}{n^2} - s_i^2\right) + \sum_{j=1}^{n}\sum_{k\neq j}^{n}s_j s_k \sigma_{jk}\right]$. The first term in brackets captures an increase in diversity as the number of products within the consumption basket increases. The second component measures the effects of the distribution of individual products in the consumption basket. The dissimilarity of products finally is accounted for in the third term in brackets, where σ_{jk} represents a measure of dissimilarity

---

[23] In the context of diversification of industries in Canada, Pomfret and Shapiro (1980) are the first to address this issue. They introduce a diversification measure that includes the degree of heterogeneity between industries.

[24] The attribute distance from product i to product j is $d_{ij} = \left(\sum_{k=1}^{K}\left(x_{ki} - x_{kj}\right)^2\right)^{1/2}$ where x_{kj} is the level of product i on attribute k. The measure of PRD, the "percentage of realized dissimilarity," is computed by dividing the total distance between all pairs of the m purchased brands by the maximum distance between brands. For a detailed discussion, see also Pessemier (1985).

[25] In their empirical analysis, the authors set $w_1 = w_2 = w_3 = 1$.

between product j and k.[26] However, this measure has not been used in the empirical studies on variety in food consumption so far.

The most elaborate approach to measure differences between products in attribute space is the distance metric (DM) demand model introduced by Pinkse, Slade, and Brett (2002) and Pinkse and Slade (2004). Each product in a category is viewed as a unique combination of characteristics and the degree of differentiation between products is determined by their relative proximity within this multidimensional characteristic space. Pinkse and Slade (2004) and Rojas and Peterson (2008) apply the DM approach to the beer market in the United Kingdom and the United States; Pofahl and Richards (2009) as well as Pofahl (2009) analyze consumer demand for shelf-stable juice products in the United States; and Gulseven and Wohlgenant (2010) investigate retail demand for fluid milk products in the United States. For continuous attributes x (such as sugar and juice content in the case of juice products), Pofahl and Richards (2009) use the following measure of attribute proximity between product i and j (which is very similar to the measure used in Pessemier and Handelsman 1984): $d_{ij}^c = \left(1 + 2\left[\sum_k \left(x_{ik} - x_{jk}\right)^2\right]^{1/2}\right)^{-1}$, where k is the number of different attributes. Discrete measures of distance (like flavor and brand of the products) can also be combined with this continuous measure.

3.2   Actual Consumption Behavior and the Demand for Variety

Much of the existing empirical literature on the demand for variety[27] focuses on the relationship between income and diversity. Whether or not income influences the demand for variety depends on specific characteristics of the underlying utility function. Assuming homothetic preferences for the representative consumer, for example, would imply that an increase in income raises expenditures for all products in fixed proportions and thus has no impact on the structure of consumption (variety). If, on the other hand, consumption expands in a hierarchical way (as in Jackson 1984, for example), then the range of products consumed by rich individuals will be larger than the range of products consumed by the poor. Food diversity would be positively correlated with income and this corresponds well to the results of empirical studies.

3.2.1 *The Effect of Household Income (and Wealth)*

In a cross-section of thirty countries, Theil and Finke (1983) report an increasing diversity (measured inversely by the Herfindahl index as well as the entropy index

---

[26] In an empirical application to measure diversification in US manufacturing, the definition of σ_{ik} is based on a vector of input cost shares for each product. Two products requiring the same inputs in identical proportions can be considered more homogeneous that two products having significantly dissimilar input requirements.

[27] A systematic summary of the empirical literature is available in the Appendix to this chapter (available from the author on request).

for broad commodity aggregates) with countries' per capita real income. Behrman and Deolalikar (1989) study the demand for variety in a sample of thirty-four countries in 1975 and sixty countries in 1980. Their estimates of elasticities of substitution between nine different food products are consistent with the idea that the demand for variety increases with the countries' per capita GDP. In a more detailed empirical analysis on the basis of data for ninety-one consumption items in fifty-seven countries, Falkinger and Zweimüller (1996) also find that the number of goods consumed (count index of variety) increases, and the concentration of expenditure (Herfindahl index) decreases with income per head. Income distribution within a country is found to be significantly related to the count index; no significant effect is observed for the Herfindahl index of consumption. More recently, Jekanowski and Binkley (2000) examine the factors that affect the variety of food purchases as reflected in aggregate sales shares across US markets. Using data for 484 products in fifty-four market areas in 1990, the authors show that the diversity of expenditures decreases as the proportion of low-income consumers in the market increases. In addition, they also find significant effects of racial diversity as well as of the average store size.

Jackson (1984) is among the first to study the demand for variety in a cross-section of households. Examining published data for 304 expenditure categories from the Consumer Expenditure Survey conducted in 1972–3 in the United States, Jackson reports a significant and positive relationship between the number of commodities purchased and household income. This result is confirmed by the study of Shonkwiler, Lee, and Taylor (1987), who explore cross-sectional differences in food consumption expenditures and food prices on the basis of the 1977–8 Survey of Household Food Consumption in the United States. From the estimation of a translog cost function on household expenditures, the authors find that the number of individual food products purchased significantly increases with household expenditures on all foods. A positive relationship between income (total expenditures) and variety is also reported in Lee and Brown (1989), Thiele and Weiss (2003), Stewart and Harris (2005), Temple (2006), and Drescher and Goddard (2008). Temple (2006) further observes a positive relationship between diversity and wealth (as measured by ownership of a dwelling). Owning a house frees up expenditures on rents and mortgages, enabling a greater proportion of income to be devoted to food. A positive effect of wealth on consumption diversity is also consistent with the theory of household production discussed in Section 2.4.

Note, however, that some of these studies focus on small subsamples of the whole population[28] and it is doubtful that the results can be generalized for a larger population since the characteristics of the individuals and households investigated typically influence their consumption behavior. In particular, the theory of household production suggests that an individual's opportunity cost of time determines her demand for variety. Further, note that data on consumption behavior typically are available at the

---

[28] Shonkwiler, Lee, and Taylor (1987) explicitly point to the fact that their analysis is restricted to childless households that have one male and one female member each between 23 and 51 years of age. Temple (2006) uses observation for households headed by adults aged 55 years and over.

household level (and not at the level of the individual consumer). If consumers have different preferences for food products, larger households (composed of many different individuals) *ceteris paribus* will purchase a larger variety of products than smaller households.[29]

3.2.2 *The Effect of Household Size and Structure*

Lee and Brown (1989) analyze data for 1,061 (urban) households from the 1981 consumer expenditure survey in the northeastern region of the United States. In addition to a significant and positive impact of total food expenditure on their measure of diversity, they also find that the demand for a diverse diet is positively related to the number of household members in different age and sex groups. Demand increases at a decreasing rate as household size increases. Similar results have been obtained for other US states (Lee 1987, as well as Stewart and Harris 2005), Germany (Thiele and Weiss 2003), Canada (Drescher and Goddard 2008), and Australia (Temple 2006). The observation that household size and consumption diversity are positively correlated could be explained by the existence of diseconomies of scale that occur when living alone. A large household can share fixed costs (housing bill) and each individual household member will devote a smaller income share to these expenses before allocating money to food. The variety-seeking literature explains this relationship with the fact that larger household will *ceteris paribus* be more diverse and thus will purchase a larger variety of products.[30] A positive relationship between variety and household size also is consistent with "characteristics models" (see Section 2.2). Lee (1987) suggests that an increase in household size by adding a female member has a greater impact on the number of different food items consumed at home than does the addition of a male member of the same age group. Similar results are reported in Thiele and Weiss (2003) and Tang and Chin (2007).

3.2.3 *The Effect of Age, Education, and Labor Market Participation*

Empirical studies find a significant relationship between the demand for diversity and household members' age. Thiele and Weiss (2003) suggest a non-linear relationship: food diversity decreases with age, reaches its minimum if the housekeeping person is 46 years, and then increases moderately again. This result corresponds to Lee (1987) and Lee and Brown (1989), who also report a similar non-linear impact of the age of family members. Investigating the food-purchasing behavior of 1,898 households headed by Australians aged 55 years and above, Temple (2006) finds a negative impact of age on

---

[29] This is the basic message of "address models." The distinction between "direct" and "derived" motives for food diversity is also stressed in McAlister and Pessemier (1982) and van Trijp and Steenkamp (1992). Whereas direct motives are related to the preference for variety, derived motives are "external or internal forces that have nothing to do with a preference for change in and of itself" (McAlister and Pessemier 1982: 313).

[30] "Multiple users refers to those cases in which different members of a household prefer different objects. This heterogeneity of preferences within the household leads to the selection of multiple objects even if each member uses only a single object" (McAlister and Pessemier 1982: 313).

food diversity. Assuming that the opportunity costs of an individual's time increases with age up to retirement, the pattern in the demand for variety corresponds to predictions derived from the theory of household production (Section 2.4.). However, this negative (or U-shaped) impact of age on the demand for variety is not undisputed. Drescher and Goddard (2008) observe a positive association between age and variety on the basis of Canadian data. Pessemier and Handelsman (1984) report similar results for liquid household cleaners but find no significant age effect for other product groups. They suggest "that the characteristics of 'variety seekers' will differ from one type of product to another" (Pessemier and Handelsman 1984: 440).[31] The effects of age on consumption behavior could be explained by different nutritional demands between young and old consumers, a different amount of information (education and experience), as well as different magnitude of opportunity costs of time.

Moon et al. (2002) expect education and the demand for food variety to be positively correlated: "Highly educated consumers likely have been exposed to information about potential benefits and detriments of eating various types of foods and have consumed many different products" (2002: 576).

Lee (1987) and Stewart and Harris (2005) also find a significant and positive impact of education. In contrast, the relationship between schooling and the demand for variety does not come out strongly in Thiele and Weiss (2003). Most of the dummy variables included in their econometric model are found to have a parameter estimate that is not significantly different from zero. Education not only improves a consumer's information but also influences her opportunity costs of time (wages in the labor market) as well as her productivity at home (Michael 1973).

Further, food diversity is found to be significantly lower if the housekeeping person is pursuing a full-time job in Lee (1987), Thiele and Weiss (2003), as well as Stewart and Harris (2005). This relationship is less pronounced when part-time work is considered.[32] Obviously, a full-time job leaves less time for preparation of a broad range of different meals (increases the opportunity costs of time) and thereby significantly reduces the variety of food products demanded.[33]

---

[31] Significant differences in the degree of variety seeking between products are also found in Erdem (1996), Helmig (1997), Meixner (2005), and Tang and Chin (2007). Tang and Chin (2007) find that variety seeking is particularly important for food products. The authors also explore the implications of differences across product categories for the decision-making of product-level marketing strategies.

[32] Temple (2006) does not find a significant relationship between the labor force status and consumption variety. It should be noted, however, that the empirical analysis in Temple (2006) is restricted to households that are headed by individuals aged 55 years and above. This truncation of the distribution reduces the variance in the labor force participation status, which might explain the insignificant impact of this variable in his paper.

[33] This is consistent with studies reporting the demand for prepared foods to increase with the number of wage earners in the household (Nayga 1998). The more earners there are in a household, the higher will be the opportunity cost of time of household members, which translates into a higher consumption of time-saving goods like prepared foods.

3.2.4 *Willingness to Pay for Variety*

The primary focus of the empirical literature mentioned so far is to investigate the relationship between a demand for variety as expressed in actual food consumption behavior and some individual and household characteristics. Drescher, Thiele, and Weiss (2008) follow a different approach and derive a hedonic price function for a household's consumption bundle. Regressions of prices on characteristics of the consumption bundle (including a measure of variety) yield gradients that estimate the buyer's marginal willingness to pay for each attribute. Assuming that an individual maximizes her utility (represented by the utility function shown in Section 2.2) under a budget constraint by choosing the quantity of each product within the consumption bundle, the authors derive the following equation: $P = A + \mu E + \lambda_1 - \mu$, where $P = \sum_{j=1}^{n} p_j s_j$ is the unit price of the consumption bundle for each household, $s_j = q_j/Q$ is the share of product j in aggregate household consumption (Q), and $E = -\sum_{j=1}^{n} \frac{q_j}{Q} \ln s_j = -\sum_{j=1}^{n} s_j \ln(s_j)$ is the entropy index of product diversity. The value of the consumption bundle per unit (P) depends on the characteristics of the products purchased (the physical attributes that are attached to the consumption bundle: $A = \sum_{j=1}^{n} a_j s_j$) as well as on the diversity of the consumption bundle (E). If households have a preference for variety, a significant relationship between the unit price the household pays for a bundle of products and the entropy measure for variety should be observed. [34]

The empirical analysis in Drescher, Thiele, and Weiss (2008) is conducted for 3,240 German households and their expenditure on 182 different soft drinks over a six-month period. Consumers are found to have a preference for variety in food consumption, *ceteris paribus*. The parameter estimate of the entropy measure ($\ln(E)$) is positive and significantly different from zero. The magnitude of the effects, however, turns out to be relatively small.[35] Note that only a very small segment of the food market is analyzed in Drescher, Thiele, and Weiss (2008), which brings us to mention some of the weaknesses of this as well as other empirical studies on the demand for food variety.

4 LIMITATIONS OF EXISTING STUDIES AND SUGGESTIONS FOR FUTURE RESEARCH

The first type of comment on existing studies can be summarized as "Better data are warranted." A second type of comment refers to (unexplored) linkages with related areas of research.

---

[34] A detailed discussion on the value attached to product characteristics using hedonic analysis is available in Costanigro and McCluskey, Ch. 6 in this volume.

[35] The parameter estimates reported suggest that a representative household would be willing to pay an additional 1.95 percent for a 50 percent increase in variety, *ceteris paribus*. This implicit price of variety does not decrease with variety; estimation results in Drescher, Thiele, and Weiss (2008) do not support a significant non-linear impact of the entropy measure.

Despite the fact that the quality of data available for empirical research has improved considerably, an adequate analysis of the demand for variety is still restricted owing to data limitations. Empirical estimates on the demand for variety in economics are typically conducted on the basis of observed purchase behavior. This approach, however, underestimates the "true" value of variety since (potentially) important dimensions of a demand for variety are ignored. Variety might have a value on its own, irrespective of the actual consumer's choice. Even if an individual in the end would decide to consume the same meal in two restaurants, she might prefer the restaurant that offers a larger variety of meals to choose from. Since actual food consumption decisions are often exclusive, empirical studies carried out on the basis of actual consumption behavior will underestimate the demand for variety.

The small value attached to variety in Drescher, Thiele, and Weiss (2008), for example, might further be related to the fact that only structural variety for a small group of rather homogeneous products is analyzed. Measuring and aggregating physical attributes of a large number of very different food products in the households' consumption bundle is far more demanding. Although empirical studies on the demand for variety have been conducted for different groups of products, none of the existing studies considers possible interaction effects between product groups. The demand for variety within one particular group of products might be small if the individual consumes a variety of products within another product category (Menon and Kahn 1995). Further, the product categories analyzed in empirical studies typically are not representative of the full domain of products available, which limits the validity and generalization of the findings.

Second, the relationship between temporal and structural variety is neglected in empirical studies. However, food consumption decisions are often exclusive: choosing one option (a particular menu at a restaurant, for example) rules out the possibility of choosing another one at the same time. In analyzing the demand for varied diet in an economy in transition (Bulgaria) on the basis of food intake survey data, Moon et al. (2002) report daily, weekly, and monthly consumption frequencies and find (among other things) that the length of time allowed for consumption is an important element in measuring the demand for food variety. Further, temporal and structural variety might be regarded as substitutes from the perspective of consumers, which would lead to an underestimation of the demand for variety in empirical studies focusing on one dimension of the demand for variety only.

Empirical studies can further be improved, with more substantial data on consumer purchase histories of actual purchases so that the effect of purchase history can be more fully examined and tested. Assessing the relative importance of different explanatory factors in explaining variety-seeking behavior, Tang and Chin (2007) suggest purchase history to be among the most important determinants. They find "that variety-seeking behavior is more likely to occur when the previous purchase transaction was a brand switch" (2007: 22).

Thirdly, we need more accurate data on *individual food consumption instead of household food purchases*. Because the consumption occasions are not observed in the purchase data, we are not able to analyze the precise context in which food products are actually consumed. The distinction between food purchases and food consumption has become more important over time, a trend that most likely will continue in the near future (Senauer 2001). The household (or family) is no longer the key decision-making unit in terms of food consumption. More and more meals are eaten away from home (or prepared from home[36]) and even for many at-home meal occasions, family members eat very differently. Data on food purchases at the household level increasingly become an inadequate measure of individual food consumption behavior.

Explicitly considering out-of-home food consumption is important for understanding the demand for food variety for two additional reasons. First, demand for variety in food products acquired for in-home food consumption will be influenced by expenditures for out-of-home food consumption behavior. Consumers enjoying a large variety of foods at restaurants *ceteris paribus* will demand less variety in food consumption at home. Second, demand for variety in out-of-home food consumption is an interesting topic per se. Schiff (2009) investigates a unique data set of 81,000 restaurants across sixty-three US cities differentiating between sixty-eight cuisines. The author finds that the demand for variety in restaurants is significantly related to characteristics of the city (population, demographics, land area). Median household income does not seem to be an important determinant of variety in the restaurant industry.[37]

By differentiating between a large number of cuisines from various countries, Schiff (2009) also highlights the impact of globalization on consumer demand for food. The fact that goods are differentiated by country of origin has been neglected in the above-mentioned empirical studies on the demand for variety, but is a topic that has received some attention in the recent trade literature. Opening up trade between hitherto isolated product markets increases the variety available to consumers *within* each country. When defining a variety as the import of a particular good from a particular country, Broda and Weinstein (2006), for example, suggest that the number of varieties available for US consumers rose by 212 percent between 1972 and 2001.[38] They estimate

---

[36] Senauer (2001) reports that the share of income spent for food at home fell from about 14 percent in 1960 to only 6.6 percent in 1997 in the United States, whereas the share spent on food away from home rose from about 3.5 to 4.1 percent over the same time period.

[37] Interestingly, the author also provides some first empirical evidence on the hierarchical structure of restaurants in cities. The null hypothesis of no hierarchical structure would imply that a city with just one type of cuisine should be no more likely to have a Chinese restaurant than an Afghani restaurant; i.e., the probability of selecting a particular cuisine for a city with n different cuisines should be identical for each of the n cuisines. The null hypothesis is clearly rejected. Further, Schiff finds that the probability of finding a particular cuisine in a given city increases with the number of cities in which a cuisine is found (this measure of "commonality" is inversely related to "rarity"). This is consistent with the idea that rarer cuisines are only found in bigger, denser cities and suggests a fairly consistent ordering of tastes across cities.

[38] The importance of variety growth through trade has already been noted in Hicks (1969). "The extension of trade does not primarily imply more goods . . . the variety of goods available is (also) increased, with all the widening of life that that entails. There can be little doubt that the main advantage that will accrue to those with whom our merchants are trading is a gain of precisely this kind" (Hicks

that consumers are willing to pay 0.1 percent of their income each year to have access to the new varieties created that year. This implies that "globalization had had substantial impacts on welfare through the import of new varieties. U.S. welfare is 2.6 percent higher due to gains accruing from the import of new varieties" (Broda and Weinstein 2006: 582).

Globalization, on the other hand, has been found to reduce the variety of food consumption *between* countries. The global expansion of multinational retail and food service chains has begun to standardize the manner in which food is produced, delivered, and consumed around the world (Regmi and Unnevehr 2006; Fabiosa, Chapter 23 in this volume). The implications of this globalization in food markets for consumer behavior and in particular the demand for variety are unclear. By exploring some of these issues in future research we may hope to find out more about the "spice of life," which is variety.

References

Anderson, S. P., A. de Palma, and J. F. Thisse. 1992. *Discrete Choice Theory of Product Differentiation*. Cambridge, MA: MIT Press.

Arunachalam, B., S. R. Henneberry, J. L. Lusk, and F. B. Norwood. 2009. "An Empirical Investigation into the Excessive-Choice Effect." *American Journal of Agricultural Economics* 91/3: 810–25.

Becker, G. S. 1965. "A Theory of the Allocation of Time." *Economic Journal* 75: 493–517.

—— 1991. *A Treatise on the Family*, enlarged edn. Cambridge, MA: Harvard University Press.

—— and G. J. Stigler. 1977. "De Gustibus Non Est Disputandum." *American Economic Review* 67: 76–90.

Behrman, J. R., and A. Deolalikar. 1989. "Is Variety the Spice of Life? Implications for Calorie Intake." *Review of Economics and Statistics* 71: 666–72.

Benassy, J.-P. 1996. "Taste for Variety and Optimum Production Patterns in Monopoly Competition." *Economics Letters* 52: 41–7.

Berry, C. H. 1971. "Corporate Growth and Diversification." *Journal of Law and Economics* 14: 371–83.

Blisard, N., B.-H. Lin, J. Cromartie, and N. Ballenger. 2002. "America's Changing Appetite: Food Consumption and Spending to 2020." *Food Review* 25/1: 2–9.

Broda, C., and D. E. Weinstein. 2006. "Globalization and the Gains from Variety." *Quarterly Journal of Economics* 121: 541–85.

Chattopadhyay, N., A. Majumder, and D. Coondoo. 2009. "Demand Threshold, Zero Expenditure and Hierarchical Model of Consumer Demand." *Metronomica* 60/1: 91–118.

Choi, J., B. K. Kim, I. Choi, and Y. Yi. 2006. "Variety-Seeking Tendency in Choice for Others: Interpersonal and Intrapersonal Causes." *Journal of Consumer Research* 32: 590–5.

Connor, J., and W. Schiek. 1997. *Food Processing: An Industrial Powerhouse in Transition*, 2nd edn. New York: Wiley.

1969: 56). An empirical analysis of the increasing variety of food products (cheese and fruits) is available in Mitchell (2006).

Cutler, D. M., E. L. Glaeser, and J. M. Shapiro. 2003. *Why Have Americans Become More Obese?* Discussion Paper No. 1994. Cambridge, MA: Harvard Institute of Economic Research.

Dixit, A., and J. Stiglitz. 1977. "Monopolistic Competition and Optimal Product Diversity." *American Economic Review* 67: 297–308.

Drescher, L. S., and E. Goddard. 2008. "Observing Changes in Canadian Demand for Food Diversity over Time." Paper presented at the Annual Meeting of the American Agricultural Economics Association, Orlando, FL, July 27–9. <http://purl.umn.edu/6357>.

——, S. Thiele, and G. B. M. Mensink. 2007. "A New Index to Measure Healthy Food Diversity Better Reflects a Healthy Diet than Traditional Measures." *Journal of Nutrition* 137: 647–51.

——, and C. R. Weiss. 2008. "The Taste for Variety: A Hedonic Analysis." *Economics Letters* 101: 66–8.

Drewnowski, A., A. S. Henderson, A. Driscoll, and B. J. Rolls. 1997. "The Dietary Variety Score: Associating Diet Quality in Healthy Young and Older Adults." *Journal of the American Dietetic Association* 97: 266–71.

Dube, J.-P. 2004. "Multiple Discreteness and Product Differentiation: Demand for Carbonated Soft Drinks." *Marketing Science* 23/1: 66–81.

Erdem, T. 1996. "A Dynamic Analysis of Market Structure Based on Panel Data." *Marketing Science* 15/4: 359–78.

Falkinger, J., and J. Zweimüller. 1996. "The Cross-Country Engle Curve for Product Diversification." *Structural Change and Economic Dynamics* 7: 79–97.

Givon, M. 1984. "Variety Seeking through Brand Switching." *Marketing Science* 3/1: 1–22.

Glaeser, E. L., J. Kolko, and A. Saiz. 2001. "Consumer City." *Journal of Economic Geography* 1: 27–50.

Gollop, F. M., and J. L. Monahan. 1991. "A Generalized Index of Diversification: Trends in U.S. Manufacturing." *Review of Economics and Statistics* 73: 318–30.

Gronau, R., and D. S. Hamermesh. 2008. "The Demand for Variety: A Household Production Perspective." *Review of Economics and Statistics* 90/3: 562–72.

Gul, F., and W. Pesendorfer. 2001. "Temptation and Self-Control." *Econometrica* 69/6: 1403–35.

Gulseven, O., and M. Wohlgenant. 2010. "A Hedonic Metric Approach to Estimating the Demand for Differentiated Products: An Application to Retail Milk Demand." Paper presented at the 84th Annual Conference of the American Agricultural Economics Society, Edinburgh, Mar. 29–31.

Hart, O. D. 1985. "Monopolistic Competition in the Spirit of Chamberlin: A General Model." *Review of Economic Studies* 52: 529–46.

Helmig, B. 1997. *Variety-Seeking-Behaviour im Konsumgüterbereich.* Wiesbaden: Gabler.

Hicks, J. R. 1969. *A Theory of Economic History.* Oxford: Clarendon Press.

Irons, B., and C. Hepburn. 2007. "Regret Theory and the Tyranny of Choice." *Economic Record* 83: 191–203.

Iyengar, S. S., and M. R. Lepper. 2000. "When Choice Is Demotivating: Can One Desire Too Much of a Good Thing?" *Journal of Personality and Social Psychology* 76: 995–1006.

Jackson, L. F. 1984. "Hierarchic Demand and the Engel Curve for Variety." *Review of Economics and Statistics* 66: 8–15.

Jekanowski, M. D., and J. K. Binkley. 2000. "Food Purchase Diversity across U.S. Markets." *Agribusiness* 16: 417–33.

Jeuland, A. P. 1978. "Brand Preferences over Time: A Partially Deterministic Operationaliza-
tion of the Notion of Variety Seeking." In S. Jain, ed., *Research Frontiers in Marketing:
Dialogues and Directions: 1978 Educators' Conference Proceedings*. American Marketing
Association No. 43. Chicago: American Marketing Association.

Jevons, W. S. 1871. *The Theory of Political Economy*. London: Macmillan.

Kahn, B. E. 1995. "Consumer Variety-Seeking among Goods and Services." *Journal of Consumer Retailer Services* 2/3: 139–48.

——, M. U. Kalwani, and D. G. Morrison. 1986. "Measuring Variety-Seeking and Reinforce-
ment Behaviors Using Panel Data." *Journal of Marketing Research* 23/2: 89–100.

——, R. Ratner, and D. Kahnemann. 1997. "Patterns of Hedonic Consumption over Time."
Marketing Letters 8/1: 85–96.

Kim, J., G. M. Allenby, and P. E. Rossi. 2002. "Modeling Consumer Demand for Variety."
Marketing Science 21/3: 229–50.

Krugman, P. 1979. "Increasing Returns, Monopolistic Competition, and International Trade."
Journal of International Economics 9: 469–79.

Kuksov, D., and J. M. Villas-Boas. 2010. "When More Alternatives Lead to Less Choice."
Marketing Science 29/3: 507–24.

Lancaster, K. 1990. "The Economics of Product Variety: A Survey." *Marketing Science* 9:
189–206.

Lee, J. 1987. "The Demand for Varied Diet with Econometric Models for Count Data."
American Journal of Agricultural Economics 69: 687–92.

——and M. Brown. 1989. "Consumer Demand for Food Diversity." *Southern Journal of
Agricultural Economics* 21: 47–53.

McAlister, L. 1982. "A Dynamic Attribute Satiation Model of Variety-Seeking Behavior."
Journal of Consumer Research 9: 141–50.

——and E. Pessemier. 1982. "Variety Seeking Behavior: An Interdisciplinary Review." *Journal of Consumer Research* 9: 311–22.

McCarthy, J. A., M. I. Horn, M. K. Szenasy, J. Feintuch. 2007. "An Exploratory Study of
Consumer Style: Country Differences and International Segments." *Journal of Consumer
Behaviour* 6: 48–59.

Meixner, O. 2005. "Variety Seeking Behaviour: Ein kausales Erklärungsmodell zum Marken-
wechselverhalten der Konsumenten im Lebensmittelbereich." *Jahrbuch der Österrei-
chischen Gesellschaft für Agrarökonomie* 10: 47–57 (with Eng. summary).

Mellens, M., M. G. Dekimpe, and J.-B. E. M. Steenkamp. 1996. "A Review of Brand-Loyalty
Measures in Marketing." *Tijdschrift voor Economie en Management* 16/4: 507–33.

Menon, S., and B. E. Kahn. 1995. "The Impact of Context on Variety Seeking in Product
Choices." *Journal of Consumer Research* 22: 285–95.

Michael, R. 1973. "Education and Nonmarket Production." *Journal of Political Economy* 81:
306–27.

Mitchell, L. 2006. "Variety, Agricultural Trade and Income." Paper presented at the Annual
Meeting of the American Agricultural Economics Association, Long Beach, CA, July 23–6.
<http://purl.umn.edu/21246>.

Moon, W., W. J. Florkowski, L. R. Beuchat, A. V. Resurreccion, P. Paraskova, J. Jordanov, and
M. S. Chinnan. 2002. "Demand for Food Variety in an Emerging Market Economy."
Applied Economics 34: 573–81.

Nayga, R. M., Jr. 1998. "A Sample-Selection Model for Prepared Food Expenditures." *Applied
Economics* 30: 345–52.

Norwood, F. B. 2006. "Less Choice Is Better, Sometimes." *Journal of Agricultural and Food Industrial Organization* 4/1, art. 3. <http://www.bepress.com/jafio/vol4/iss1/art3>.

Patil, G. P., and C. Taillie. 1982. "Diversity as a Concept and its Measurement." *Journal of the American Statistical Association* 77: 548–61.

Perloff, J. M., and S. C. Salop. 1985. "Equilibrium with Product Differentiation." *Review of Economic Studies* 52: 529–46.

Pessemier, E., and M. Handelsman. 1984. "Temporal Variety in Consumer Behavior." *Journal of Marketing Research* 21: 435–44.

Pessemier, J. S. 1985. "Varied Individual Behaviour: Some Theories, Measurement and Models." *Multivariate Behavioral Research* 20: 69–94.

Pettengill, J. S. 1979. "Monopolistic Competition and Optimum Product Diversity: Comment." *American Economic Review* 69/5: 957–60.

Pinkse, J., and M. Slade. 2004. "Mergers, Brand Competition, and the Price of a Pint." *European Economic Review* 48: 617–43.

————, and C. Brett. 2002. "Spatial Price Competition: A Semiparametric Approach." *Econometrica* 70/3: 1111–53.

Pofahl, G. M. 2009. "Merger Simulation in the Presence of Large Choice Sets and Consumer Stockpiling: The Case of the Bottled Juice Industry." *Review of Industrial Organization* 34: 245–66.

————, and T. J. Richards. 2009. "Valuation of New Products in Attribute Space." *American Journal of Agricultural Economics* 91/2: 402–15.

Pomfret, R., and D. Shapiro. 1980. "Firm Size, Diversification, and Profitability of Large Corporations in Canada." *Journal of Economic Studies* 7/3: 140–50.

Ratner, R. K., and B. E. Khan. 2002. "The Impact of Private vs. Public Consumption on Variety-Seeking Behavior." *Journal of Consumer Research* 29: 246–57.

Regmi, A., and L. Unnevehr. 2006. "Are Diets Converging Globally? A Comparison of Trends across Selected Countries." *Journal of Food Distribution Research* 37/1: 14–21.

Richards, T. J., and S. F. Hamilton. 2006. "Rivalry in Price and Variety among Supermarket Retailers." *American Journal of Agricultural Economics* 88/3: 710–26.

Rojas, C., and E. B. Peterson. 2008. "Demand for Differentiated Products: Price and Advertising Evidence from the U.S. Beer Market." *International Journal of Industrial Organization* 26: 288–307.

Salop, S. C. 1979. "Monopolistic Competition with Outside Goods." *Bell Journal of Economics* 10/1: 141–56.

Schiff, N. 2009. "Cities and Product Variety in the Restaurant Industry." Paper presented at the 7th International Industrial Organization Conference, Boston, Apr. 3–5.

Schwartz, B. 2004. *The Paradox of Choice: Why More Is Less.* New York: HarperCollins.

————, A. Ward, J. Monteroso, S. Lyubomirsky, K. White, and D. R. Lehmann. 2002. "Maximizing versus Satisficing: Happiness Is a Matter of Choice." *Journal of Personality and Social Psychology* 83/5: 1178–97.

Scitovsky, T. 1976. *The Joyless Economy.* Oxford: Oxford University Press.

Senauer, B. 2001. *The Food Consumer in the 21st Century: New Research Perspectives.* Working Paper No. 01-03. St Paul: Food Industry Center, University of Minnesota. <http://purl.umn.edu/14346>.

Senior, N. 1836. *An Outline of the Science of Political Economy.* London: Encyclopaedia Metropolitana.

Shonkwiler, J., J. Lee, and T. Taylor. 1987. "An Empirical Model for the Demand for a Varied Diet." *Applied Economics* 19: 1403–10.

Simonson, I. 1990. "The Effect of Purchase Quantity and Timing on Variety-Seeking Behavior." *Journal of Marketing Research* 27/2: 150–62.

Stewart, H., and J. M. Harris. 2005. "Obstacles to Overcome in Promoting Dietary Variety: The Case of Vegetables." *Review of Agricultural Economics* 27/1: 21–36.

Tang, E. P. Y., and I. O. K. Chin. 2007. "Analyzing Variety Seeking Behavior Using Panel Data." *Journal of International Consumer Marketing* 19/4: 7–31.

Temple, J. B. 2006. "Household Factors Associated with Older Austrians' Purchasing a Varied Diet: Results from Household Expenditure Data." *Nutrition and Dietetics* 63: 28–35.

Theil, H., and R. Finke. 1983. "The Consumer's Demand for Diversity." *European Economic Review* 23: 395–400.

Thiele, S., and C. R. Weiss. 2003. "Consumer Demand for Food Diversity: Evidence for Germany." *Food Policy* 28: 99–115.

van Trijp, H. J. C. M. 1995. *Variety-Seeking in Product Choice Behavior: Theory with Applications in the Food Domain.* Mansholt Series 1. Wageningen: Wageningen University.

—— and Steenkamp, J.-B. E. M. 1992. "Consumers' Variety Seeking Tendency with Respect to Foods: Measurement and Managerial Implications." *European Review of Agricultural Economics* 19: 181–95.

CHAPTER 28

....

EFFECTS OF GENERIC ADVERTISING ON FOOD DEMAND

....

HARRY M. KAISER

Most agricultural products produced in the United States have collective marketing programs aimed at increasing overall market demand (both domestic and foreign) and enhancing producer revenues. These programs, which are sometimes referred to as "check-off programs," are funded through assessments on producers in the industry. The assessments are usually mandatory for all producers after a majority of producers approve the check-off in a referendum, but there are also a couple of programs that are voluntary. The revenue raised by check-off programs is invested in a variety of marketing and research activities, and varies by commodity. The main activity used by the majority of check-off programs is generic advertising. More popular examples include: "Got milk?"; "Beef: it's what's for dinner"; "The incredible edible egg"; "Pork: the other white meat"; "Milk mustache"; and the "dancing raisins."

Generic advertising is "the cooperative effort among producers of a nearly homogeneous product to disseminate information about the underlying attributes of the product to existing and potential consumers for the purpose of strengthening demand for the commodity" (Forker and Ward 1993). Generic advertising differs from the much more common brand advertising in a number of ways. First, generic advertising is a collective effort by all or most producers within an industry and does not refer to any brand name, while brand advertising is done by an individual producer and has a brand name associated with it. Second, generic advertising is designed to increase overall market demand, while brand advertising is aimed at increasing the producer's market share. Finally, generic advertising works best for commodities that are relatively homogeneous as opposed to brand advertising, which works better for differentiable products. There have been volumes of research done to evaluate the economic impacts of generic advertising, and most have found small positive, but statistically significant, impacts on market demand (Ferrero et al 1996; Alston, Crespi, et al. 2007).

The purpose of this chapter is to examine the effects that generic advertising have on the demand for food and on nutrition in the United States. The chapter begins with an overview of generic advertising programs in the United States. This is followed by a conceptual discussion of the economic impacts of these programs on consumers and producers. Next, the methods economists use to examine the effects of generic advertising on food demand are reviewed. This is followed by a discussion of the results of selected studies with a particular focus on demand impacts. Next, the impact of generic advertising on obesity and poor nutrition is examined. The chapter concludes with a conclusion of findings.

1   GENERIC ADVERTISING PROGRAMS

Most generic food advertising programs were established after the early 1980s, but some have their roots in organizations that date all the way back to the early 1900s. For example, the earliest example of collective marketing efforts is local dairy associations that sponsored local promotions such as dairy princess competitions, June dairy month events, and country and state fair promotions. These programs have evolved in two fundamental ways over time. First, like the evolution of food markets, generic advertising programs have evolved from local and regional to national in scope. Today, the majority of generic food advertising is conducted nationally. Second, these programs have evolved from voluntary to mandatory participation. The reason for the switch is that voluntary programs, while generally successful immediately after the programs are established, have been plagued by free-rider problems over time (Messer, Schmit, and Kaiser 2005; Messer, Kaiser, and Schulze 2008). For this reason, today all but a handful of programs are mandatory and contain no refund provision. Two exceptions include generic sugar advertising and cut flowers.

Mandatory check-off programs are usually implemented through the introduction or modification of a marketing order at the federal or state level. The process for enacting such a program has differed for each commodity and may vary according to whether it is a state or federal program. The following gives a general overview of the process that is typically followed from start to finish in creating a mandatory check-off program.

Check-off programs are viewed as industry "self-help" programs, but the government is needed to create and provide oversight for the program. The process usually starts with industry leaders discussing the possibility of a program, and obtaining a rough gauge of whether a significant number of producers in the industry would favor a mandatory program. Assuming there is legitimate interest, industry leaders (e.g., frequently one or a number of large cooperatives in the industry) will approach the government and inform them that the industry would like to pursue the creation of a program. If it is a federal program, contact is made with the US Department of Agriculture's Agricultural Marketing Service, which is responsible for all agricultural check-off programs. If it is a state program, contact is made with the respective State Department of Agriculture. One of the first questions the governmental agency will want to answer is whether there is sufficient interest in a mandatory program by the industry in question. To do this, the government usually holds a series of informational meetings throughout the industry to hear the opinions of producers. If the government determines that there is a legitimate amount of interest by producers in the industry, the next step is to promulgate the check-off program for the referendum.

Mandatory check-off programs have uniform assessment rates on producers within the industry, and they are generally levied on the same unit basis as the price. For example, dairy farmers are assessed $0.15 per hundred pounds of milk that is sold. These assessments are almost always set at a level that is less than 1 percent of the price received by producers paying the assessment, which is a substantially lower advertising intensity[1] than most brand products such as Coke, Pepsi, Frito Lay, and Kraft Cheese. The determination of the assessment is one of the most critical aspects of formulating the check-off program. The assessment can be set on an *ad valorem* (percentage) basis (e.g., 0.5 percent of the market price received by the producer) or on a fixed rate, per unit amount (e.g., $1 per head of cattle). Some mandatory programs will exempt segments of the industry from having to contribute. For example, the dairy industry now exempts organic dairy farmers from their mandatory assessment. The egg industry and the fluid milk processors exempt the smallest producers from paying their assessment. Determining who, if anyone, will be exempt is therefore another key decision that must be made in crafting the mandatory program. There are many other decisions that need to be made in promulgating the check-off program such as determining who and how many people will be on the board of directors, what the focus of check-off activities will be (e.g., advertising versus research versus public relations), how the referendum will work (e.g., will it be a simple majority or something higher than 50 percent?), and other issues. During this phase, the government assists the industry in formulating the mandatory check-off program. Lawyers who are experts in check-off programs are involved with the industry as well at this stage of the process.

The government has followed two different approaches in the check-off process once a draft set of rules and regulations has been established. The traditional approach was to hold a number of hearings to get the opinions on the draft check-off from producers within the industry. At these hearings, expert witnesses and industry leaders can testify to give their opinions on various aspects of the proposed program. Both proponents and opponents of the proposed check-off program participate at these hearings. Based on these hearings, the government may make modifications in the rules and regulations of the mandatory check-off, and subsequently conduct the referendum.

Alternatively, a more recent approach that has been used for some commodities is actually to implement the draft check-off program prior to the referendum for a trial

---

[1] Advertising intensity is defined as total advertising expenditures divided by total gross revenue.

period, e.g., eighteen months. The idea here is that producers in the industry will be best informed about whether the program is good or not by actually living under it for a period of time. The government also usually stipulates that an economic evaluation of the program be performed by an independent economist, and the results disseminated prior to the referendum. The check-off program for cut flowers, which was a mandatory federal program, followed this approach.

If the program passes the referendum, everyone covered by the program is required to pay the assessment. This feature of mandatory programs is very controversial because not all producers support mandatory check-off programs, but they are still forced to contribute if the program passes the referendum. Despite an abundance of economic studies that suggest generic promotion[2] programs are generally beneficial to producers (Ferrero et al. 1996; Alston, Crespi, et al. 2007; and Table 28.1), a vocal minority of producers oppose these mandatory programs for various reasons. For example, many organic producers oppose paying for the promotions of conventionally produced commodities because they believe that this undermines their efforts to differentiate their own production methods. Also, some large producers maintain that they would be better off marketing their commodities on their own rather than collectively via a generic advertising campaign. Because of these and other concerns, there have been numerous legal challenges to these programs, with three cases heard by the US Supreme Court in the last decade. The diverse challenges led to a variety of decisions handed down by the Court. In 1997 the Court ruled that the California peaches, plums, and nectarines check-off program did not violate the plaintiff's rights to free speech since generic advertising was part of a larger set of regulations designed to help producers (*Glickman* v. *Wileman Brothers & Elliot, Inc.* 1997). In 2001 the Court ruled the mushroom check-off program unconstitutional because it was a stand-alone check-off advertising program and not part of a broader set of economic regulations (*United States* v. *United Foods* 2001). In 2005 the Court ruled the beef advertising check-off program constitutional because the advertising was considered "government speech" and hence protected from First Amendment challenges (*Johanns* v. *Livestock Marketing Association et al.* 2005). While it currently looks like the Court interprets these programs as "government speech," it is worth noting that two of the justices that voted in favor of them, Rehnquist and O'Connor, are no longer on the Court. Hence, future legal challenges to mandatory programs will likely continue in the future.

One of the main reasons why these programs have come under attack in the last decade is that the agricultural and food industry is becoming much more heterogeneous and fragmented over time. Mandatory check-off programs are designed to work

---

[2] While the terms generic "promotion" and "advertising" are used interchangeably throughout this chapter, they do have different meanings in marketing. Advertising refers to conveying a message about a product through media outlets such as television, radio, print, outdoor, and web advertisements. Promotion refers to marketing activities other than advertising that are designed to boost demand, such as price promotions, coupons, and in-store demonstrations. While most larger commodity check-off programs do both advertising and promotions, some of the smaller programs do not do much advertising as it is generally more expensive.

Table 28.1 Estimated generic promotion elasticities and benefit–cost ratios for selected commodities from single equation studies

Author(s)	Commodity	Promotion elasticity	Average benefit–cost ratio	Marginal benefit–cost ratio
Alston, Carman, et al. (1998)	California dried plums	0.050	n.a.	2.7
Alston, Chalfant, et al. (1997)	California table grapes	0.160	44.9	38.8
Capps and Williams (2008)	Lamb	0.044	n.a.	44.5
Carman and Craft (2005)	California avocados	0.130[a]	5.0	1.7
Carter, Chalfant, and Goodhue (2005)	California strawberries	0.160[a]	n.a.	44.0
Crespi and Sexton (2005)	California almonds	0.130	n.a.	6.2
Davis et al. (2000)	Pork	0.110	n.a.	16.0
Kaiser (1997)	All dairy products	0.016–0.021	3.4	n.a.
Kaiser (2005a)	Walnuts	0.005	1.65–9.72	n.a.
Kaiser (2005b)	Blueberries	0.043	4.46–13.22	n.a.
Kaiser, Liu, and Consignado (2003)	Raisins	0.029–0.133	5.1–15.3	0.42–3.19
Murray et al. (2001)	Cotton	0.022	3.2–6.0	n.a.
Richards and Patterson (2007)	Potatoes	0.013–.0464	6.5	n.a.
Schmit and Kaiser (1998)	Eggs	0.006	n.a.	0.54–6.33
Schmit and Kaiser (2004)	Fluid milk	0.040	n.a.	n.a.
Schmit, Rebert, and Kaiser (1997)	California eggs	0.130[a]	n.a.	6.9
Ward (1996)	Beef	0.028	5.7	5.7–9.7
Ward (2008a)	Honey	0.082	6.02–7.91	n.a.
Ward (2008b)	Watermelons	0.165	10.6	n.a.
Williams (1999)	Soybeans	0.0156–0.073	1.7–7.9	n.a.
Williams, Capps, and Bressler (2004)	Florida orange juice	0.127–0.428	2.9–7.0	NA
Median		0.045	6.0	6.3
Average		0.096	8.6	13.3

[a]Price flexibility coefficients not included in the mean and median calculations.
Note: n.a. = not available.

well for industries that produce a highly homogeneous commodity that has little ability for product differentiation among producers. In addition, these programs are designed for groups that share common goals. As even agricultural commodities have become less homogeneous over time (e.g., today there are many varieties of table grapes as opposed to fifteen years ago), this creates incentives for some individual producers to want to opt out of the collective program and market their own, differentiated product. Consequently, as agricultural commodities become more differentiable, the use of a collective approach to market an industry's product generically becomes less popular. Relatedly, in industries that are fragmented and do not share common goals, mandatory programs are difficult to establish, and if they are in place, become difficult to maintain owing to inherent disagreement among the groups participating in the program.

For example, about ten years ago, some leaders in the thoroughbred horse industry were interested in creating a mandatory check-off program to promote horse racing in the United States. The program would have included a group of disparate parties linked to this industry, including horse breeders, veterinarians, pet food companies, feed dealers, and race tracks. Given the fragmented nature of the groups involved, this program never got off the ground. Trying to get the various groups comprising this industry to agree on a common set of goals, and methods to achieve these goals, seemed to be an impossible task.

Nevertheless, today there are seventeen federal programs and numerous state check-off programs in existence (over fifty in California alone). The budgets for these programs total about $1 billion annually in the agricultural sector (Forker and Ward 1993). Economic studies evaluating commodity check-off programs show substantial net benefits. For example, Table 28.1 lists twenty-one selected studies of federal and state generic promotion programs. The median benefit–cost ratio (BCR) for these twenty-one studies was 6.0, indicating that average benefits were six times larger than the costs, and none of these studies had an average BCR that was below 1.0.[3]

2   A CONCEPTUAL MODEL OF ECONOMIC IMPACTS OF GENERIC ADVERTISING

Conceptually, the economic impacts of generic advertising can be well depicted within a supply and demand framework, as illustrated in Figure 28.1. In this figure, let D_0 and S_0 denote market demand and supply, respectively, without a mandatory generic advertising program, and P_0 and Q_0 be the initial equilibrium levels for price and quantity. The introduction of a mandatory generic advertising program impacts market demand by shifting the demand curve to the right, to D_1, assuming advertising is effective, which reflects an increase in consumers' willingness to pay for the commodity by k per unit for any quantity. Since producers must pay a tax of t per unit, the mandatory generic advertising program also shifts the supply curve to the left, to S_1, because it is now more expensive to produce each unit of the commodity. Hence, the impact of introducing generic advertising on the market is to raise the equilibrium price from P_0 to P_1, with consumers paying P_1 and sellers receiving a net price of P_1–t.

---

[3] Two studies in Table 28.1 have marginal BCRs that are below 1. A marginal BCR measures how much benefits increase given an extra dollar of advertising at the margin. As such, they are useful in determining whether the current level of advertising expenditures is optimal (BCR = 1), overallocated (BCR < 1), or underallocated (BCR > 1).

The impact on equilibrium quantity depends upon the relative magnitude of shifts in supply versus demand. If the shifts are equal, there is no impact on quantity; if demand increases more than supply decreases, then quantity increases; and if supply decreases more than demand increases, then quantity decreases. In Figure 28.1 it is assumed that demand increases by more than the decrease in supply; hence, equilibrium quantity increases from Q_0 to Q_1. In this case, the market impact of mandatory generic advertising is to raise equilibrium quantity and price (both consumer and net seller price) in the market.

One can evaluate welfare impacts of generic advertising by assuming Harberger's three postulates of applied welfare economics: (1) the area under the market demand curve represents total consumer benefits from consuming the commodity; (2) the area under the market supply curve corresponds to total variable costs of production; and (3) consumer and producer benefits and costs can be summed. Total generic advertising expenditures are equal to the area tQ_1 assuming an instantaneous shift in supply and demand) in Figure 28.1. Producer net welfare can be measured by the additional producer surplus associated with the increase in production from Q_0 to Q_1 measured along the supply curve that includes the check-off, S_1, which is equal to the trapezoidal area $GCBP_1$. Some studies have assumed that the consumer benefits generated by

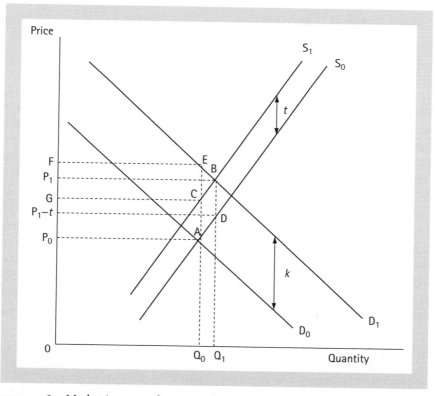

FIGURE 28.1 Market impacts of generic advertising

generic advertising can be approximated by changes in the standard measure of consumer surplus (Alston, Freebairn, and James 2003). Using this assumption, net consumer welfare can be measured by the change in consumer surplus associated with the increase in consumption from Q_0 to Q_1 measured along the final demand curve, D_1, which is equal to the trapezoidal area P_1BEF. Finally, combining the producer and consumer benefits yields an estimate of net national benefits from check-off-funded promotion programs compared with an absence of those programs, which is equal to the area GCBEF in Figure 28.1.

In practice, most empirical studies have focused on the benefits and costs of the check-off program to the producer. Consumer benefits and costs are rarely computed. Producer BCRs are required by law for all federal check-off programs, and many state programs have done studies to compute BCRs as well.[4] Costs are generally measured as actual program costs, but some studies have also used producer incidence of the check-off tax.

3   EMPIRICAL ANALYSIS OF GENERIC ADVERTISING IMPACTS ON FOOD DEMAND

There have been volumes of studies investigating the impacts of generic advertising on the demand for US agricultural commodities (for a thorough review, see Ferrero et al. 1996; Alston, Crespi, et al. 2007). The econometric approach used in these studies can be broadly classified into two categories: (1) single-equation demand functions, and (2) demand systems.

Most past studies have estimated single-equation demand models, usually using linear, square root, or double logarithmic functional form. Quantity-dependent and price-inverse demand specifications have been used. While specifications have varied, and have been ad hoc, single-equation demand models generally include the following explanatory variables in addition to the dependent variable (either quantity or own-price): prices of substitutes and complements, income, population demographics, own-advertising expenditures, advertising expenditures of competing commodities, and brand advertising. Since the majority of studies have relied on time-series data as the basis for the statistical model, the impacts of inflation on all variables measured in monetary terms need to be accounted for. Nominal prices, for example, are usually converted to real dollars by deflating the nominal prices by the Consumer Price Index for all items, or some other deflator. Similar techniques have been used to convert nominal income and promotion expenditures into real terms. Because inflation in

---

[4] Previous studies have computed both average and marginal producer BCRs. Average BCRs, which are computed as the difference in producer welfare with and without generic advertising, are most useful for evaluating the overall impact of the program. Marginal BCRs, which are computed as the difference in producer welfare from a marginal change in generic advertising, are most useful for evaluating optimal spending levels.

media costs is usually significantly higher than in the overall inflation rate, many studies have deflated advertising expenditures by a computed media cost index.

While the majority of studies have measured advertising effort as expenditures on media advertising, there have been several studies that have used measures of advertising exposure, such as gross rating points, which is a measure of the number of people exposed to the advertisement. The level of aggregation of the advertising variable has varied across studies. Some researchers have aggregated all demand-enhancing activities into one variable, which may include all forms of media advertising, public relations, sponsorships, retail programs, and promotional activities. This highly aggregated approach may be advantageous in saving degrees of freedom for the regression analysis, but can also suffer from aggregation bias. At the other end, there have been highly disaggregated studies as well, such as disaggregating generic advertising expenditures into separate variables for television, radio, print, and outdoor expenditures. One problem with this approach is that many check-off programs have such small marketing budgets that it may be difficult to find a positive demand effect when the level of disaggregation results in activities with minimal expenditure levels.

Since there can be a carry-over effect of advertising, most studies have incorporated this dynamic effect explicitly into the demand model. The carry-over effect can be captured by using a variety of techniques, but all use some sort of lag structure, i.e., current and lagged advertising expenditures are included. Several popular examples of lag specifications include: polynomial distributed lag models, polynomial inverse lag models, and unstructured lag models. In these cases, both a short- and long-term promotion effect can be calculated. Other studies have not lagged the advertising variable, but have lagged the dependent variable. These studies, which assume that advertising has a geometrically declining effect on demand over time, also permit the calculation of short- and long-run advertising elasticities.

The key elasticity that researchers are interested in in advertising studies is the advertising elasticity. Therefore, one of the key hypotheses that researchers test is whether the estimated advertising elasticity is positive and statistically significantly different from zero. If it is, this provides empirical evidence that generic advertising has a positive impact on food demand.

The majority of studies have used time-series data to estimate the demand equation, including annual, quarterly, and monthly models. A few studies have also used cross-sectional data based mainly on scanner data (e.g., Capps, Seo, and Nichols 1997). Finally, pooled cross-sectional and time-series data have been used in several studies to estimate advertising impacts (e.g., Schmit, Dong, et al. 2002; Schmit, Gould, et al. 2003).

Davis (2005) suggests an alternative method for measuring promotion effectiveness, which is a reduced-form equation approach. Under this approach, rather than estimating a structural demand equation, a reduced-form profit equation is estimated that includes generic promotion as one of the independent variables in addition to other demand and price variables. This approach is potentially beneficial because generic advertising impacts are larger on producer profits than on demand because profit includes both demand and price effects, and therefore it is possible that generic advertising may have an insignificant impact on demand, but a significant impact on profits. In such a case, looking only at demand will yield erroneous conclusions regarding the effectiveness of generic advertising.

The second major category of studies has used demand systems models to evaluate the impacts of generic advertising. Various systems models have been used, including the almost ideal demand systems model (AIDS) and its linear approximation (LA/AIDS), the Rotterdam model, translog, and the double logarithmic model. One advantage of the demand systems approach is that it explicitly captures "spillover" effects of generic advertising on competing commodities. For instance, while generic beef advertising may have a direct impact on beef demand, it is also likely to have a spillover effect on the demand for other meats such as pork, lamb, chicken, and fish. Failure to take into account spillover effects, especially for commodities that have a lot of close substitutes such as meat, may cause an upward bias in computing the BCR because second-round and feedback effects are not considered (Kinnucan and Zheng 2005). One advantage of the single-equation approach is that more elaborate structures can be included in the analysis such as detailed industry models, time-varying parameter specifications, and complex lag models. As a general rule, a demand systems approach is more appropriate for commodities that have very close substitutes such as beef, pork, lamb, and chicken in order to capture the spillover effects of advertising. The single-equation models are best used on commodities that do not have a lot of strong substitutes, e.g., cheese, and one can capture spillover effects through inclusion of prices and advertising of competing commodities in the single-equation demand model.

In terms of impact on demand, the most important hypothesis examined in empirical studies is whether generic advertising has a positive and statistically significant impact on demand. In studies using demand systems models, an auxiliary hypothesis is whether generic advertising has statistically significant cross (spillover) effects. The overwhelming empirical evidence is that these programs do have statistically significant positive impacts on own demand, and, in some cases, important spillover effects on the demand for other commodities.

Consider the twenty-one studies listed in Table 28.1. All of these twenty-one studies reported positive and statistically significant (at the 10 percent level or better) generic promotion elasticities. The median and average elasticities from these studies are 0.045 and 0.096, respectively, i.e., a 1 percent increase in generic promotion expenditures results in a 0.045 and 0.096 percent increase in demand for the commodity when holding all other demand determinants constant. The spread in promotion elasticities in these twenty-one studies ranges from a low of 0.005 to a high of 0.428. While statistically different from zero, it is clear that the typical impact of these programs on commodity demand is quite small. Indeed, in the majority of these studies, generic promotion is the least important of all demand determinants such as own-price, income, population demographics, and other commodity prices. A plausible reason why these programs have small impacts on demand is that the level of generic advertising is quite small, especially when compared with brand advertising. All of the mandatory generic advertising check-offs are smaller, in some cases much smaller, than 1 percent of the price received by producers. Hence, the advertising intensity ratios (advertising expenditures to total revenue) are tiny. Hence, it is not surprising that generic advertising has a small but positive impact on food demand.

Many of the studies that have used demand systems have also shown that the cross-advertising elasticities are significant, and some times even larger than the own elasticities. Consider, for example, the six demand system studies presented in Table 28.2. The median and average own-advertising elasticities from these studies

Table 28.2 Estimated generic promotion elasticities for selected commodities from demand system studies

Author(s)	Commodities	Own advertising elasticity	Significant cross-elasticities	Model/ period
Boetel and Liu (2003)	Beef	0.0000	0.0094, 0.0098	LA/AIDS
	Pork	0.0067[a]		1976–2000
	Fish	−0.0009		Quarterly
Brester and Schroeder (1995)	Beef	0.0060		Rotterdam
	Pork	−0.0005		1970–93
Kinnucan, Miao, et al. (2004)	Milk	0.0028	0.0277, 0.1780	Rotterdam
	Juice	0.1358[a]	0.0497, 0.2266	1970–94
	Soft drinks	−0.0999[a]	0.0930, 0.0394	Annual
	Coffee/tea	0.0016	0.2803, 0.3181	
Kinnucan, Xiao, et al. (1997)	Beef	0.0011	0.0073	Rotterdam
	Pork	0.0000		1976–93
	Fish	0.0001		Quarterly
Rusmevichientong and Kaiser (2009)	Rice	0.1860[a]	0.1740, 0.1720	LA/AIDS
	Wheat	0.2870[a]	0.2020, 0.0520	1975–2005
	Sorghum	0.1480[a]	0.0570, 0.1150	Annual
Zheng and Kaiser (2008)	Milk	0.0240[a]	0.049, 0.156, 0.023	LA/AIDS
	Juice	−0.0130	0.1150, 0.075, 0.098	1974–2005
	Soft drinks	0.0600[a]	0.0530, 0.253, 0.071	Quarterly
	Bottle water	0.0400	0.2580	
	Coffee/tea	0.1380[a]		
Median		0.0067	0.0084	
Average		0.0671	0.0610	

[a] Statistically significant.

Note: The statistically significant cross-advertising elasticities are presented in absolute values in order to get an accurate magnitude calculation for the median and average statistics. The median and average values for the cross-elasticities include the twenty-five non-significant values (treated as 0) not listed.

are 0.0067 and 0.0671, which is substantially lower than the estimates from single-equation (almost seven-times lower for the median measure). Kinnucan and Zheng (2005) point out that single-equation studies likely overstate the true own-advertising elasticitiy because they omit important spillover and second-round effects, and this may be the cause of the disparity between demand system and single-equation estimates. The other interesting observation from the six demand system studies is that the median and average cross-advertising effects are as large as the own-advertising effects. The median and average cross-advertising elasticities in Table 28.2 are 0.0084 and 0.0610, which is comparable in magnitude to the own-advertising elasticities.

These cross-advertising effects also have important implications for optimal advertising levels for competing commodities such as in the meat industry. Alston, Freebairn, and James (2001) simulate a cooperative strategy between competing commodity promotion programs where advertising expenditures are set collectively to maximize total combined profit of the industries versus a non-cooperative strategy where the competing industries independently set advertising levels to maximize their own profits. Using the US beef and pork promotion programs as an example, the authors find that the non-cooperative strategy leads to three times the level of combined advertising compared with the cooperative strategy, implying an overinvestment in advertising by the beef and pork industries. Consequently, when cross-effects are taken into consideration, it is possible that the competing industries would be better off to coordinate advertising levels so that producers from each industry were better off.

Almost all promotion evaluation studies provide a measure of the benefits and costs of these programs from a producer standpoint. In order to measure the benefits, the econometric model can be simulated within the data sample under at least two scenarios: (1) the baseline scenario where all exogenous demand variables are set at actual levels, and (2) the counterfactual scenario reflecting no generic promotion, which is the same as the baseline except generic promotion is set to zero or a small number. The difference in equilibrium prices and quantities between scenarios provides an empirical measure of the impacts of generic promotion. In order to conduct this simulation, the supply as well as demand side of the market must be taken into account. Previous researchers have accounted for producer supply response by either econometrically estimating a market supply equation, using previous estimates of own-price supply elasticities, or assuming various values for supply response. Once supply response is taken into account, the benefits and costs of the program can be empirically measured by comparing the two equilibrium outcomes of the two simulated scenarios.

The empirical evidence from past studies is that the average benefits of generic promotion are much larger than the costs (Table 28.1). These large estimates often prompt questions regarding the validity of the BCRs in economic evaluations of commodity check-off programs. BCRs are generally large because advertising and promotion expenditures are very small *relative* to product value, and therefore only a small demand and price effect is needed to generate positive and large returns. Advertising expenditures, for example, tend to be tiny (typically less than 0.5 percent) in comparison to producer total revenues. Also, since supply response for most agricultural commodities tends to be highly price-inelastic, even a small positive increase in demand due to generic advertising results in an amplified price effect. Hence, small demand increases due to advertising tend to cause net revenue (i.e., producer surplus) increases that are quite large *relative* to the costs of the programs.

Because of the vastly different methods and data sets used in the volumes of studies conducted on the impact of generic advertising, it is difficult to make accurate comparisons among studies on the various commodities. This is especially true in trying to compare specific advertising elasticity estimates and benefit–cost ratios among studies. Nevertheless, it is possible to make several generalizable conclusions from these studies.

First, the overwhelming bulk of empirical evidence supports the notion that generic advertising has a positive and statistically significant, but relatively small, impact on own demand for agricultural commodities. As noted earlier, all single-equation studies in Table 28.1, and eight out of twenty own-advertising elasticities from Table 28.2, support this conclusion.

Second, own-advertising effects tend to be higher from the single-equation than demand system models. Unlike demand system models, which explicitly measure potential spillover effects, single-equation models do not. Therefore, if the advertising of one product, X, decreases not only the demand but also the price of a substitute product, Y, the demand for X will be negatively impacted in second round effects from the lowered price of product Y which are ignored in single equation, but not demand system models. Not controlling for these feedback impacts may result in upward bias in both advertising elasticities and benefit cost ratios. Kinnucan and Zheng (2005) point out that "this is especially true in a situation where supplies are fixed . . . as then the price effects of advertising-induced demand shifts are magnified."

Third, generic advertising has potentially important cross-effects on competing commodities. Beef advertising not only impacts beef demand, but also pork, fish, lamb, and poultry demand. Generally, generic advertising has a negative impact on competing products, but sometimes it can also have significant complementary effects such as wine and nuts. As illustrated already in Table 28.2, these indirect effects can be as important as the own-advertising effects.

Fourth, there are substantial benefits to producers from these programs net of costs. Recall that the median average BCR for the twenty-one studies in Table 28.1 was 6.0, indicating the average benefits were six times larger than the costs. None of these studies had a BCR that was below 1.0.

Finally, generic advertising programs tend to be underfunded from a perspective of maximizing producer returns. This is evident from examining the marginal BCRs listed in Table 28.1. The median and mean marginal BCRs from these studies was 6.3 and 13.3, respectively. Moreover, eight out of ten studies had marginal BCRs larger than 1.0, and the remaining two had a range that included both less than and greater than 1.0. These results suggest that producers should increase the assessments and promote their commodities with higher intensity.

4   IMPACT OF GENERIC ADVERTISING ON OBESITY

With the trend toward increasing obesity in the United States, some nutritional researchers have blamed agricultural check-off programs for at least some of the problem. Critics point out that the rise in check-off programs and obesity has occurred in roughly the same time period. They also suggest that while promoting increased consumption of healthy foods such as fresh fruits and vegetables is worthwhile, the largest bulk of generic advertising comes from high-fat products such as fluid milk, dairy, and meat products, which account for over 60 percent of all check-off revenues in the United States. For instance, Sims (1998) notes that most generic promotion programs are "an anathema to most nutritionists and health professionals," and Nestle (2002) argues that they "promote products high in fat, saturated fat, and cholesterol, and the funds are used to influence food and nutritional policies favorable to industry."

Some economists have also been highly critical of generic promotion programs for food. For example, in a blog in Food Policy, Wilde (2008) referred to a study Messer, Kaiser, and Schulze (2008) conducted on designing voluntary agricultural check-off programs that sustain high levels of participation. In particular, Wilde was very critical of the following paragraph from that study that defended these programs:

> One might question the social importance and magnitude of under-provision of advertising for generic commodities. However, contrast the public health impacts from the types of foods associated with the majority of branded advertising, such as soda, beer, chips, and candy, to the types of foods that now benefit from mandatory generic advertising, such as fruits, vegetables, nuts, chicken, pork, beef, and milk. Not only do the generic commodities comprise the key nutritional elements of the United States Department of Agriculture food pyramid but these commodities also tend to be low in fat and salt (in comparison to branded snack foods and restaurant meals) and represent the bulk of what might be called the components of a healthy diet. If generic advertising for agricultural commodities collapses because mandatory programs are declared unconstitutional, the "Dancing Raisins" will be gone and the vast majority of ads for snacks will be for chips, cookies, and candy. Given important health problems such as obesity, juvenile diabetes, and osteoporosis, the under-funding of generic commodity advertising has serious public health consequences.

Wilde (2008) strongly condemned Messer, Kaiser, and Schulze's (2008) defense of generic advertising for agricultural commodities, arguing:

> Years of previous coverage here cast doubt on the claim that checkoff advertising is largely consistent with federal dietary guidance. The dancing raisins comparison is misleading, since a tiny fraction of checkoff advertising is for fruits and vegetables, while much of the funding is for high fat beef and pork and cheese . . . If you believe that the checkoff programs are mostly about skim milk, not cheese, you've been hoodwinked by the public relations. I am not sure where the "low fat" comment came from—federal dietary guidance gives greatest importance to saturated fat

rather than total fat, and the products covered by checkoff programs are dispro-portionally high contributors to saturated fat in U.S. diets, compared to foods not covered by checkoff programs. And, how could lower checkoff advertising possibly lead to obesity? This is a very, very bad paragraph.

While the intention of this chapter is not to defend these programs, an examination of time-series data on caloric intake in the United States reveals that generic advertising has not caused the obesity problem in the United States. In fact, to the extent that generic advertising has lessened the consumption of snacks, sugar, and junk food, it has actually combated the obesity problem. Consider, for instance, a recent study that indicates that per capita daily caloric intake in the United States has increased by a significant amount (523 calories per person) since 1970 (Farah and Buzby 2005). This substantial increase in caloric intake has certainly exacerbated the obesity problem.

However, when you examine the breakdown of changes in specific categories of foods consumed, which is provided in Table 28.3, it becomes clear that there is virtually no link between the introduction of generic food advertising and obesity. Wilde (2008) correctly points out that a sizable proportion of generic food advertising is for fluid milk, cheese, beef, and pork, but caloric intake for these foods has not increased since 1970. Calories from dairy consumption are actually down 11 calories per person per day, and meat, eggs, and nuts have increased by only 24 calories. Moreover, over this time period, there has been a general shift in meat consumption from less healthy (e.g., red meats) to healthier products such as poultry.

It appears from Table 28.3 that the main cause of higher incidences of obesity is the substantial rise in consumption of fat and oils, which increased by 216 calories since 1970. There is no significant generic advertising for fats and oils (the dairy industry use to conduct a small amount of butter advertising, but ceased doing so in the late 1980s).

Table 28.3 Changes in caloric intake by major food groups, 1970–2003

Commodity group	Per capita consumption			
	1970 (pounds)	2003 (pounds)	Increase in pounds, 1970–2003 (%)	Increase in daily calories, 1970–2003 (no.)
Fats and oils	53	86	63	216
Grains	136	194	43	188
Sugar and sweeteners	119	142	19	76
Meat, eggs, and nuts	226	242	7	24
Vegetables	337	418	24	16
Fruits	242	275	12	14
Dairy	564	594	5	−11
total	1,675	1,950	16	523

Note: US Department of Agriculture Economic Research Service per capita data represent the amount of food and calories available for consumption after adjusting for spoilage, plate waste, and other losses in the home or marketing system.

The caloric intake of sugar and sweeteners in the United States also increased a sizable 76 calories over this period, and while there is a voluntary generic sugar advertising program, it is very small, and probably had little to no impact on this increase. It is likely that most of the increase in sugar, fats, and oils calories is due to the population consuming a lot more sweets, junk food, and fast food than was consumed in 1970. A major contributor to this is the huge amount of brand advertising for these items, which completely overshadows the amount of generic food advertising.

How could a decrease in generic advertising possibly lead to obesity? Generic advertising of agricultural commodities has basically been a defensive strategy by agricultural producers to stabilize losses in market share to soda, chips, candy, and fast-food consumption. For example, one of the major reasons dairy farmers initiated generic milk advertising in the mid-1980s was to combat huge losses in market share to Coca-Cola, Pepsi-Cola, and other soda companies that were outspending the American Dairy Association by a ratio of 16 to 1 (Leading National Advertisers 1980–4). From 1970 to 2001, annual per capita soda consumption more than doubled, increasing from 21.9 gallons in 1970 to 54.3 gallons in 1999 (Beverage Marketing 2006). Over that same time period, annual per capita consumption of fluid milk products decreased over threefold from 25 to 8 gallons (Putnam and Allshouse 2003). Much of the loss in milk consumption over this period was the result of aggressive advertising by soda companies, which continue to outspend milk advertising by a substantial amount. For example, in 2003, even with a mandatory program, total soda advertising ($1.25 billion) was still 6.5 times the combined amount spent by dairy farmers and milk processors ($193 million) (Leading National Advertisers 2003).

Finally, it is hard to blame generic commodity advertising for significantly changing consumer demand since most estimates find these programs to have relatively small impacts on increasing overall consumption. Generic promotion of agricultural commodities has had only a minor impact on increasing caloric intake in the United States since 1970s, and a substantially larger cause has been the increasing trend toward away-from-home eating (especially fast food) and the increased consumption in high-fat and high-sugar junk foods, whose branded advertising dwarfs generic agricultural advertising.

While it is unlikely that these programs have been a major cause in the rise of obesity in the United States, there could certainly be nutritional improvements in mandatory generic advertising programs for food. More emphasis should be given to healthy foods such as fruits and vegetables and lower-fat products. There has been some progress in this area over the last ten years. There are now more generic advertising programs for fruits and vegetables than there were in the past. There is also discussion among fruit and vegetable industry leaders on enacting a broad-based generic advertising program to increase consumption.

In the past, generic milk advertising did not differentiate among whole, reduced-fat, low-fat, and skim milk, and now we are seeing more examples of skim and low-fat milk mustache advertisements. At the same time, there are some examples of promotional efforts that are not consistent with nutrition guidelines, but these activities are more exceptions than the rule.

5   CONCLUSIONS

Almost all agricultural products produced in the United States have collective marketing programs aimed at increasing overall market demand (both domestic and foreign) and enhancing producer revenues. The main activity used by the majority of these check-off programs is generic advertising. This chapter examined the impacts that generic advertising have on the demand for food and on nutrition in the United States.

The chapter began with an overview of generic advertising programs in the United States. There are currently seventeen federal programs and over fifty state check-off programs in existence. The budgets for these programs total about $1 billion annually in the agricultural sector (Forker and Ward 1993). These programs have evolved over time from being mainly state or regional to national in scope, and from being voluntary to mandatory. The vast majority of economic studies evaluating generic advertising show substantial net benefits, e.g., BCRs in the 6 to 1 neighborhood.

A conceptual supply and demand model was presented to illustrate, conceptually, the economic impacts of generic advertising on consumers and producers. The impacts of generic advertising depend critically on two factors. The first is the impact of generic advertising on increasing the demand curve; the more successful the advertising, the larger the demand increase. The second is the degree of industry supply response to the demand-increase-induced price increase. Producers will benefit more from generic advertising the lower the degree of supply response since price will increase more. Indeed, in the extreme case of a perfectly elastic supply, producers will not benefit at all from an advertising-induced demand increase. The welfare effects on consumers and producers were illustrated graphically as changes in consumer and producer surplus associated with the introduction of generic advertising.

The empirical methods economists use to examine the effects of generic advertising on food demand were discussed. Economists generally use two approaches: (1) single-equation demand models, and (2) demand systems models. An advantage of the demand systems approach is that it explicitly captures "spillover" effects of generic advertising on competing commodities. An advantage of the single-equation approach is that more elaborate structures can be included in the analysis such as detailed industry models, time-varying parameter specifications, and complex lag models. As a general rule, a demand systems approach is more appropriate for commodities that have very close substitutes such as beef, port, lamb, and chicken in order to capture the spillover effects of advertising. The single-equation models are best used on commodities that do not have a lot of strong substitutes, e.g., cheese, and one can capture spillover effects through inclusion of prices and advertising of competing commodities in the single-equation demand model.

The sizable empirical literature was reviewed, and several conclusions from these studies were noted. First, the bulk of empirical evidence supports the notion that generic advertising has a positive and statistically significant, but relatively small impact on own demand for agricultural commodities. Second, own-advertising effects tend to be higher from the single equation model that ignores spillover and second-round effects than demand system models that explicitly consider them. Third, generic advertising has potentially important cross-effects on competing commodities that are in some cases even more important than own effects. Fourth, there are substantial benefits to producers from these programs net of costs. Finally, and without exception, generic advertising programs are underfunded from an optimal perspective.

This chapter concluded with a discussion concerning the impacts of generic advertising on obesity and poor nutrition in the United States. Some nutritionists and economists have been highly critical of generic advertising, and have linked the rise in these programs to the increasing trend in obesity in the United States. However, it was argued that generic food advertising has not caused the obesity problem in the United States. In fact, to the extent that generic advertising has lessened the consumption of snacks, sugar, and junk food, it has actually combated the obesity problem.

REFERENCES

Alston, J. M., H. F. Carman, J. A. Chalfant, J. M. Crespi, R. J. Sexton, and R. J. Venner. 1998. *The California Prune Board's Promotion Program: An Evaluation*. Giannini Foundation Research Report No. 11926. Davis: University of California.

——, J. A. Chalfant, J. E. Christian, E. Meng, and N. E. Piggott. 1997. *The California Table Grape Commission's Promotion Program: An Evaluation*. Giannini Foundation Monograph No. 11932. Davis: University of California.

——, J. M. Crespi, H. M. Kaiser, and R. J. Sexton. 2007. "An Evaluation of California's Mandated Commodity Promotion Programs." *Review of Agricultural Economics* 29: 40–63.

——, J. W. Freebairn, and J. S. James. 2001. "Beggar-Thy-Neighbor Advertising: Theory and Application to Generic Commodity Promotion Programs." *American Journal of Agricultural Economics* 83: 888–902.

————. 2003. "Distributional Issues in Check-Off Funded Programs." *Agribusiness* 19/3: 277–88.

Beverage Marketing. 2006. *Carbonated Soft Drinks in the United States*. New York: Beverage Marketing.

Boetel, B. L., and D. J. Liu. 2003. "Evaluating the Effect of Generic Advertising and Food Health Information within a Meat Demand System." *Agribusiness* 19/3: 345–54.

Brester, G. W., and T. C. Schroeder. 1995. "The Impacts of Brand and Generic Advertising on Meat Demand." *American Journal of Agricultural Economics* 77/4: 969–79.

Capps, O., Jr., and G. W. Williams. 2008. *Is Lamb Promotion Still Working?* Report to the American Lamb Board. Aug. <http://www.lambcheckoff.com/Portals/30/Is%20the%20Lamb%20Checkoff%20Still%20Working%20Report%20to%20ALB.pdf>.

——, S. C. Seo, and J. P. Nichols. 1997. "On the Estimation of Advertising Effects for Branded Products: An Application to Spaghetti Sauces." *Journal of Agricultural and Applied Economics* 2: 291–302.

Carman, H. F., and R. K. Craft. 2005. "Evaluation of Avocado Promotion by the California Avocado Commission." In H. M. Kaiser, J. M. Alston, J. M. Crespi, and R. J. Sexton, eds, *Commodity Promotion: Lessons from California*. New York: Peter Lang.

Carter, C. A., J. Chalfant, and R. E. Goodhue. 2005. "The Red Edge: Demand-Enhancing Strategies for California Strawberries." In H. M. Kaiser, J. M. Alston, J. M. Crespi, and R. J. Sexton, eds., *Commodity Promotion: Lessons from California*. New York: Peter Lang.

Crespi, J. M., and R. J. Sexton. 2005. "Evaluating the Effectiveness of California Almond Promotion: How Much Did the Litigation Cost Producers?" In H. M. Kaiser, J. M. Alston, J. M. Crespi, and R. J. Sexton, eds., *Commodity Promotion: Lessons from California*. New York: Peter Lang.

Davis, G. C. 2005. "The Significance and Insignificance of Demand Analysis in Evaluating Promotion Programs." *American Journal of Agricultural Economics* 87: 673–88.

——, O. Capps, Jr., D. A. Bessler, J. H. Leigh, J. P. Nichols, and E. Goddard. 2000. *An Economic Evaluation of the Pork Checkoff Program*. College Station: Texas A & M University.

Farah, H., and J. Buzby. 2005. "U.S. Food Consumption Up 16 Percent since 1970." *Amber Waves* 3/5. <http://www.ers.usda.gov/AmberWaves/November05/findings/usfoodconsumption.htm>.

Ferrero, J., L. Boon, H. M. Kaiser, and O. D. Forker. 1996. *Annotated Bibliography of Generic Commodity Promotion Research (Revised)*. Ithaca, NY: National Institute for Commodity Promotion Research and Evaluation, Department of Agricultural, Resource, and Managerial Economics, Cornell University.

Forker, O. D., and R. W. Ward. 1993. *Commodity Advertising: The Economics and Measurement of Generic Programs*. New York: Lexington Books.

Glickman v. *Wileman Brothers & Elliott, Inc.* 521 U.S. 457 (1997).

Johanns v. *Livestock Marketing Association et al.* 544 U.S. 550 (2005).

Kaiser, H. M. 1997. "Impact of National Dairy Advertising on Dairy Markets, 1984–95." *Journal of Agricultural and Applied Economics* 29: 303–14.

—— 2005a. "An Economic Analysis of Domestic Impacts of the Walnut Marketing Board's Marketing Programs." In H. M. Kaiser, J. M. Alston, J. M. Crespi, and R. J. Sexton, eds, *Commodity Promotion: Lessons from California*. New York: Peter Lang.

—— 2005b. *An Economic Analysis of Domestic Market Impacts of the U.S. Highbush Blueberry Council*. Report Prepared for the US Highbush Blueberry Council. Ithaca, NY: Peter Lang.

——, D. J. Liu, and T. Consignado. 2003. "An Economic Analysis of California Raisin Export Promotion." *Agribusiness* 19: 189–202.

Kinnucan, H., and Y. Zheng. 2005. "National Benefit–Cost Estimates for the Dairy, Beef, Pork, and Cotton Promotion Programs: A Synthesis and Critique." In H. M. Kaiser, J. M. Alston, J. M. Crespi, and R. J. Sexton, eds, *Commodity Promotion: Lessons from California*. New York: Peter Lang.

——, Y. Miao, H. Xiao, and H. M. Kaiser. 2004. "Effects of Advertising on U.S. Non-Alcoholic Beverage Demand: Evidence from a Two-Stage Rotterdam Model." In M. R. Baye and J. P. Nelson, eds, *Advances in Applied Microeconomics*, 10. Amsterdam: Elsevier Science.

——, H. Xiao, C.-J. Hsia, and J. D. Jackson. 1997. "Effects of Health Information and Generic Advertising on U.S. Meat Demand." *American Journal of Agricultural Economics* 79/1 (Feb.), 13–23.

Leading National Advertisers. 1980–4, 2003. *AD & Summary*. New York: Leading National Advertisers.

Messer, K., H. M. Kaiser, and W. Schulze. 2008. "The Problem with Generic Advertising: Parallelism and Possible Solutions from the Lab." *American Journal of Agricultural Economics* 90: 540–52.

——, T. Schmit, and H. M. Kaiser. 2005. "Optimal Institutional Mechanisms for Funding Generic Advertising: An Experimental Analysis." *American Journal of Agricultural Economics* 87: 1046–60.

Murray, B. C., R. H. Beach, W. J. White, C. Viator, N. Piggott, and M. Wohlgenant. 2001. *An Economic Analysis of the Cotton Research and Promotion Programs*. Raleigh, NC: Research Triangle Institute.

Nestle, M. 2002. *Food Politics*. Berkeley: University of California Press.

Putnam, J., and J. Allshouse. 2003. "Trends in U.S. Per Capita Consumption of Dairy Products, 1909–2003." *Amber Waves* 12/3. <http://151.121.68.30/Amberwaves/june03/pdf/awjune2003datafeature.pdf>.

Richards, T. J., and P. M. Patterson. 2007. "Evaluation of Grower-Funded Value-Added Activities by the United States Potato Board." Unpublished Report prepared for the United States Potato Board.

Rusmevichientong, P., and H. M. Kaiser. 2009. "Are There Halo Effects of U.S. Grain Export Promotion?" *Applied Economics* 41: 1466–83.

Schmit, T. M., and H. M. Kaiser. 1998. "Egg Advertising, Dietary Cholesterol Concerns, and U. S. Consumer Demand." *Agricultural and Resource Economics Review* 27: 43–52.

——. 2004. "Decomposing the Variation in Generic Advertising Response over Time." *American Journal of Agricultural Economics* 86: 139–53.

——, D. Dong, C. Chung, H. M. Kaiser, and B. W. Gould. 2002. "Identifying the Effects of Generic Advertising on Household Demand for Fluid Milk and Cheese: A Two-Step Panel Data Approach." *Journal of Agricultural and Resource Economics* 27: 165–86.

——, B. W. Gould, D. Dong, H. M. Kaiser, and C. Chung. 2003. "The Impact of Generic Advertising on U.S. Household Cheese Purchases: A Censored Autocorrelated Regression Approach." *Canadian Journal of Agricultural Economics* 27: 15–37.

——, J. C. Reberte, and H. M. Kaiser. 1997. "An Economic Analysis of Generic Egg Advertising in California, 1985–95." *Agribusiness* 13: 365–73.

Sims, L. S. 1998. *The Politics of Fat*. Armonk, NY: M. E. Sharpe.

United States v. *United Foods, Inc.* 533 U.S. 405 (2001).

Ward, R. W. 1996. *The Beef Checkoff Impact on U.S. Beef Demand*. Gainesville, FL: Department of Agricultural Economics, University of Florida.

——2008a. "Measuring the Impact from Generic Promotions on the Demand for Honey." Unpublished Report prepared for the National Honey Board.

——2008b. "The National Watermelon Board: An Evaluation of their Program Impact on the Demand for Watermelons." Unpublished Report prepared for the National Watermelon Promotion Board.

Wilde, P. 2008. "What if Checkoff Programs Were Voluntary?" *U.S. Food Policy* (Mar. 17). <http://usfoodpolicy.blogspot.com/2008/10/what-if-checkoff-programs-were.html>.

Williams, G. W. 1999. "Commodity Checkoff Programs as Alternative Producer Investment Opportunities: The Case of Soybeans." *Agribusiness* 15: 539–52.

——, O. Capps, Jr., and D. A. Bressler. 2004. *Florida Orange Grower Returns from Orange Juice Advertising*. TAMRC Consumer and Product Research Report No. CP-01-04. College Station: Department of Agricultural Economics, Texas A & M University.

Zheng, Y., and H. M. Kaiser. 2008. "Advertising and U.S. Nonalcoholic Beverage Demand." *Agricultural and Resource Economics Review* 37: 147–59.

CHAPTER 29

....

FOOD CONSUMPTION
AND HEALTH

....

FABRICE ETILÉ[*]

While food security and food safety have historically been the main concerns of public food policies, over the past few decades trends in consumption have been associated with an increase in food-related chronic diseases (FRCD), such as obesity, cancer, and coronary heart disease. Food affluence poses new challenges to public health authorities, in essentially all developed countries, but also in a number of developing countries.

Official reports started to recommend nutritional guidelines to prevent FRCD in the late 1970s and the 1980s, starting in the United States, where the Surgeon General set out disease-prevention objectives related to nutrition in 1977. In the same year, a Senate Select Committee on Nutrition and Human Needs proposed "Dietary Goals for the United States," which called on Americans to reduce their consumption of red meat and dairy products, a recommendation that encountered strong opposition from the agro-industrial lobby. Instead of targeting specific food products, later reports were more focused on the promotion of medical norms with respect to nutrient intakes, and issued guidelines for a well-balanced diet that did not exclude the consumption of specific products. In the ensuing period, US and European food industries have put a great deal of effort into re-engineering and redesigning a number of processed food products, and developing new varieties under the broad label of "functional food." This category includes all foods claimed to have a health-promoting or disease-preventing property, such as high-fiber cereals, low-fat yogurts, or eggs enriched with omega 3 fatty acid. Health claims are now a key way of differentiating between food products. Yet, this market response to rising concerns about the health effects of overconsumption has apparently been insufficient to stop the "obesity epidemic" and, from the beginning of the 1990s onwards, prominent nutritionists and policymakers in the

* I should like to thank Olivier Allais, Jayson Lusk, and one anonymous referee for their comments and suggestions. I am deeply indebted to Andrew Clark, who devoted his time and labor to help me produce a vivid account of the economics of food and health.

United States and other countries have called for more active regulation of the food market, especially via nutritional taxes (see, for instance, Brownell 1994 for the United States; Marshall 2000 for the United Kingdom).

In this context, this chapter reviews the economic literature on the causes and consequences of current trends in FRCD from a policy evaluation viewpoint. It focuses on policy interventions on the consumer side in developed countries.[1] Bibliographical choices have been made on the basis of two criteria: most references outside the economic literature have been ignored, and empirical work has been included according to the robustness of the econometric analysis, and in particular the validity of the assumptions ensuring the identification of causal effects. This aspect of the chapter reflects not only my familiarity with econometrics, but is also important for deciding whether the research can inform policymaking or not.

The first section recalls some key facts regarding historical trends in nutrition and FRCD, and Section 2 highlights individual heterogeneity that is hidden behind aggregate trends. Some estimates of the medical and human capital costs of FRCD are provided in Section 3. The fourth section then considers the normative rationales for public intervention: (1) market failures, such as the presence of externalities, the *ex ante* moral hazard for health insurance systems, and imperfect information; and (2) failures of consumer rationality. Sections 5 and 6 bring together some of the available empirical evidence regarding price and information policies. Last, Section 7 concludes and proposes some directions for future research.

1   TRENDS AND PATTERNS IN NUTRITION AND FOOD-RELATED CHRONIC DISEASE

1.1   The Nutritional Transition

One of the most spectacular correlates of the economic growth of most Western countries in the nineteenth and twentieth centuries was the epidemiological transition from infectious diseases and premature death to chronic diseases and long lives. As emphasized by Fogel (2004), historical positive trends in anthropometric sizes, especially weight and height, show that better health went hand in hand with improvements in the quantity, quality, and safety of food supply. The nutritional transition that accompanied this epidemiological transition was marked by two key facts. First, the level of available calories per capita steadily increased throughout the nineteenth century and the first part of the twentieth century. The daily caloric supply per capita was around 3,050 in France in 1960, 3,280 in Great Britain, and 2,960 in Germany, as

---

[1] Competition on the food market, organization of the food chain, agricultural policies, or liability regimes may also interact with consumer-oriented health policies. These issues are treated in other chapters of this volume.

compared to only 1,850, 2,350, and 2,210 respectively in 1800 (Grigg 1995). Second, while cereals provided two-thirds or more of calories up to the middle of the nineteenth century, the consumption of meat, dairy products, sugar, fruit, vegetables, and oils increased, with concomitant positive effects on vitamin and mineral intake.

After the Second World War, industrialized countries entered the second stage of the transition, with the development of processed foods. Daily calories per capita continued to increase in these countries, from 2,947 in the mid-1960s to 3,380 in the late 1990s, and are expected to reach 3,500 around 2030. The average diet has become low in fiber and high in saturated fats, sugar, and sodium, which are commonly used as taste-enhancing additives. The share of dietary energy supplied by carbohydrates is around 30–40 percent, which is below the recommended 55 percent. The share supplied by fats is moving toward 40–45 percent, above the maximum recommended level of 30 percent, with one-fifth contributed by saturated fatty acids. Around 300 grams per capita per day of fruits and vegetables are consumed in developed countries, while the recommended intake is 400 grams (FAO 2002).

Diets high in fat (especially saturated fats), sugar, and sodium, and low in fiber, are considered to be risk factors for hypertension, cardiovascular diseases, diabetes, breast, colon, rectum, and prostate cancer, and obesity (WHO 2003). The latter is both a consequence of energy intake in excess of energy expenditure, and a risk factor in itself for a wide range of medical conditions, from diabetes and cancer to musculoskeletal impairments. Hence, secular trends in height and weight, which were associated with better health, are being replaced by an upward shift in the Body Mass Index (BMI) distribution that is associated with higher mortality risks (Komlos and Baur 2004; Sunder 2005).

1.2   Cross- and Within-Country Comparisons

Table 29.1 illustrates these facts for eleven OECD countries.[2] The prevalence of adult obesity, adult overweight (excluding obesity), child overweight, and diabetes are presented, as well as the mortality rates from acute myocardial infarction in some OECD countries.[3] The last four columns provide information on changes in the average daily calorie supply per capita, and the proportion coming from fat. At the beginning of the 1980s, the prevalence of adult obesity was low in all countries for which figures are

---

[2] The data are drawn from various sources including OECD Health Data 2009 and FAO Statistical databases, as indicated at the foot of the table. Hence, we should be cautious not to overinterpret cross-country differences.

[3] Following World Health Organization standards, adult obesity and overweight are measured by means of BMI, which is given by weight in kilograms divided by height in meters squared. An adult is strictly overweight if his/her BMI falls between 25 and 30, and obese above 30. The prevalence rates in Table 29.1 are generally based on self-reported weight and height data in national surveys. Since individuals tend to overestimate their height and underestimate their weight, the obesity and overweight rates presented here are lower bounds for actual prevalence. Child overweight is computed from weight and height adjusted for gender and age (see Cole et al. 2000).

Table 29.1 Some aggregate food and health statistics for selected countries and years

Country	Obese adults %		Overweight and not obese adults %		Overweight or obese children aged 7–11 yrs %	Mortality rates from acute myocardial infarction [a] (per 100,000)			Adults with diabetes (%)	Calorie supply (kCal/capita/day)	% from fat	Calorie supply (kCal/capita/day)	% from fat
Year	1980	2006	1980	2006	2000	1980	2006	Average yearly change (%)	2000	1980	1980	2005	2005
Australia	8.3	18.7	28.0	34.4	26.2	177.5	44.7	−5.6	6.8	3,051	33	3,084	39.1
Canada	13.8	23.1	35.4	36.1	25.1	139.9	41.5	−4.9	8.8	2,946	37	3,552	37.1
France	6.5	11.5	26.9	31.5	19.0	58.2	19.5	−4.1	3.9	3,376	39	3,603	40.7
Germany	—	13.6	—	36.0	16.0	105.7	44.2	−3.3	4.1	3,338	37	3,510	35.9
Greece	—	16.4	—	41.3	31.0	65.3	45.8	−1.4	10.3	3,216	35	3,700	35.7
Italy	7.1	10.2	27.4	35.0	36.0	64.7	28.2	−3.1	9.2	3,589	32	3,685	38.4
Japan	2.0	3.4	15.6	21.8	17.8	30.0	17.3	−2.1	6.7	2,720	23	2,743	28.0
Netherlands	5.1	11.3	28.2	35.2	12.0	139.0	36.6	−5.0	3.5	3,071	38	3,240	38.2
Norway	—	9.0	—	34.0	18.5	132.5	46.0	−5.2	3.9	3,350	40	3,478	37.4
UK	7.0	24.0	29.0	38.0	20.0	175.5	40.5	−5.5	3.9	3,159	39	3,421	36.5
USA	15.0	34.3	32.4	33.0	15.2	128.1	37.9	−4.8	8.8	3,155	36	3,855	39.4

[a] All rates are given for 1980 and 2006, except Australia (1980, 2004), Canada (1980, 2004) and the USA (1986, 2005).

Sources: Obese and overweight adults: OECD Health Data 2009 for Australia (1980); Canada (1980); Germany (2005); Greece (2006); Italy (2006); Japan (1980, 2006); Netherlands (1981, 2006); Norway (2005); UK (1980, 2006); USA (1978, 2006); except Australia (2004: National Health Survey); Canada (1978, 2004: <http://www.statcan.gc.ca/pub/82-620-m/2005001/t/adults-adultes/4053589-eng.htm>); France (1981, 2003: author's treatment of National Health Surveys "Enquête Santé"); Italy (1983: <http://www.ncbi.nlm.nih.gov/pmc/articles/PMC1381181/pdf/amjph00510–0119.pdf>).

Overweight children: Lobstein and Frelut (2003); except Australia (NSW schoolchildren aged 7–11) from <http://www.aph.gov.au/library/INTGUIDE/sp/obesity.htm>; Canada (children aged 7–11) and USA (children aged 6–11) from Bray et al. (2004); Japan (children aged 9–11) from Matsushita et al. (2004); Norway (4th graders) from Andersen et al. (2005).

Mortality acute myocardial infarction: OECD Health Data 2009.

Diabetes: Wild et al. (2004).

Calorie and fat supply: FAO statistics 2005, Food Balance Sheets.

available, apart from the United States and Canada. By the beginning of the twenty-first century, obesity had increased substantially, with notable differences between countries. Anglo-Saxon countries have the highest obesity rates, together with Greece, with an obesity prevalence of between 15 and 30 percent. In France, Germany, Italy, the Netherlands, and Norway the increase has been much less spectacular, with rates of around 10 percent. Last, Japan lies far behind other countries, with prevalence of obesity of around 5 percent. It is tempting to link this country ranking to differences in national eating patterns. From this perspective, overweight and obesity in Anglo-Saxon countries would be a consequence of their widespread use of refined and processed food, and adult populations in most continental European countries would have resisted the obesity epidemic thanks to their strong culinary traditions, while greater consumption of seafood would have protected Japan. However, these stereotypes fail to account for the greater prevalence of adult obesity in Greece, the 30 percent of overweight children in Italy, and the rise in overweight children observed in Japan. Diabetes is as high in Mediterranean countries as in Canada and the United States. The mortality rate from acute myocardial infarction has fallen in all countries, but this drop is mainly due to medical progress and smoking decline. This rate remains higher in Anglo-Saxon countries, Germany, Greece, and Norway than in Italy, France, or Japan. The relationship between cross-country variations in calorie and fat supply, on the one hand, and FRCD, on the other, is not straightforward. France has a higher level of calorie and fat supply (3,603 kilocalories, 40.7 percent of which from fat in 2000) than Australia (3,084 kilocalories, 39.1 percent from fat), but lower obesity and overweight rates. There is thus no clear deterministic pattern in the cross-country comparisons.

Within-country trends show that calorie supply and the proportion of calories coming from fat have increased in most countries over the past few decades, and it seems logical to link the time trend in calorie availability to that in FRCD. However, most medical diseases are produced at the individual level by the interaction of a number of factors: lifestyle behaviors (e.g., smoking, drinking, physical activity, use of health care services, and nutrition), environment (e.g., pollution, provision of health care services), and genes (with genetic pools potentially differing between countries). Loureiro and Nayga (2005) illustrate this point by the *multivariate* analysis of cross-country time-series data on obesity and overweight rates in OECD countries between 1990 and 2002. While these rates are positively related to calorie supply, as expected, they are also positively correlated with the per capita kilometers driven in private vehicles. As upward movements in the latter are likely to imply less physical activity, this suggests that car use has played some role in the obesity epidemic. Bleich et al. (2008) go further by constructing measures of average calorie intake *and* expenditure by country. They then use the energy balance equation to identify the relative contributions of changes in calorie intake and expenditure to the rise in obesity.[4] They conclude that increasing calorie intake explains more than 80 percent of the variation

---

[4] The energy balance equation states that calorie intake in excess of expenditure is stocked in fat cells, which implies a gain in body weight.

in obesity rates. However, the correlation between aggregate trends in food intake and medical conditions is not helpful for policymaking, since it ignores both individual heterogeneity and the likely behavioral response of consumers or household meal planners to changes in public policy.

2 THE MULTIFACTORIAL ETIOLOGY OF FOOD-RELATED CHRONIC DISEASES: ECONOMIC ASPECTS

....

Within a country, the risks of FRCD differ between individuals according to their socioeconomic background, their environment, and their genes. These factors are briefly reviewed in this section. The rest of the chapter, especially Sections 5 and 6, will emphasize food prices and information.

2.1 Socioeconomic Determinants

There is a social gradient in FRCD, which is correlated with social differences in food and lifestyle behaviors. In developed countries, lower socioeconomic groups tend to have diets that are richer in animal products, fat, and sugar, and poorer in fruit and vegetables (Robertson, Brunner, and Sheiham 2004). Among the variables that determine the social gradient, and which may affect the relative risk of FRCD, economists have been particularly interested in income, which determines the budget constraint together with relative prices, and education, which affects the way in which individuals process and use information. Income and education affect the slope of the relationship between policy variables (prices and information) and food-related health outcomes. Policymaking therefore has to address equity issues, as will be seen in Section 5.

2.2 Environmental Influences

Environments have been blamed by the public health sector for being *obesogenic*, in the sense that people face strong incentives to gain weight in order to adapt to exogenous changes in their environmental setting. This "obesogenic" label points to a number of different lines of research.

The quality of the urban environment (e.g., the supply of public transport, sports facilities, etc.) may affect physical activity, and therefore FRCD. Without developing this point any further, it is worth noting that the associated empirical evidence is mixed. For instance, there is a positive correlation between obesity and urban sprawl, which favors the use of cars and therefore reduces physical activity (Lopez 2004). However, this may merely reflect the self-selection of those who are more likely to be or become obese into neighborhoods with more sprawl (Eid et al. 2008).

The health consequences of food choices depend on exposure to acute and chronic social stress (Marmot 2004, chs 5 and 6). It has been shown in animal studies of groups of monkeys that the lower the status in the hierarchy, the greater the stress and the higher the probability of developing atherosclerosis for a given diet will be. The pathway from social rank and social instability to atherosclerosis, high blood pressure, and inflammation of abdominal fat tissue transmits via biological stress. The latter is a response to acute chronic threats that imply long-term changes in hormone levels (Kyrou, Chrousos, and Tsigos 2006). Since hormones are involved in the homeostatic regulation of satiety, hunger, and storage in fat cells, biological stress links environmental life conditions—in particular job security and social status—to the development of FRCD, *everything else equal*. The social gradient may have a direct biological impact on the relative risk of FRCD, beyond its indirect impact through the budget constraint or the ability to process and use information.

There is also some evidence from research in biology that synthetic chemicals can induce obesity by changing hormone levels or altering gene expression (see, e.g., Irigaray et al. 2007; Grün and Blumberg 2007). Hence, the increasing use of artificial additives in processed foods, and more generally increasing environmental pollution by synthetic chemicals, may affect both food behaviors and their health consequences. MacInnis and Rausser (2005) use a sample of American children from the Continuing Surveys of Food Intakes by Individuals (waves 1994–6, 1998) to estimate the impact of the amount of unidentified residuals, including food additives, in processed food on their BMI. Controlling for energy intake, fat intake, hours of TV, food stamp participation, income, age, and gender, they find a positive correlation between residuals and BMI, especially in overweight and obese children. This result raises issues of nutritional labeling that will be explored in Section 6.

There are spatial differences in the quality and quantity of food supplied that are not explained by cultural differences. They are likely to affect diet choices. This issue has fostered research on the role of "food deserts"—the absence of food shops in some areas—in the etiology of obesity (White 2007).

Last, the impact of food marketing on choices has been the subject of extensive debate over the past few decades. Section 6 will present some empirical evidence on the role of advertising in FRCD.

2.3   Genetic Factors

A number of genes have been linked to FRCD in the biomedical literature. With respect to obesity, differences in genes may explain up to 70 percent of the between-individual variance in BMI (Stunkard et al. 1990; Cutler and Glaeser 2005). Although changes in the gene pool are too slow to explain the recent rise in obesity (Philipson 2001), there is ample evidence that gene expression—the way genes affect biological processes—is involved in the development of obesity. As a result, faced with rapid changes in the environment, some individuals may be more able to adapt than others, i.e., to avoid gaining weight in the presence of energy imbalances. This is the "thrifty gene" hypothesis.[5]

3 THE ECONOMIC CONSEQUENCES OF FRCD

3.1 Medical Costs

Available data suggest that FRCD generate substantial growing medical costs, although health care costs are less well documented for FRCD other than for obesity (Lopez et al. 2006). Finkelstein, Fiebelkorn, and Wang (2004) estimate that, for the United States in 1998, obesity and overweight alone are associated with $78.5 billion of medical spending, representing 9.1 percent of national medical expenditures, half of which was financed by Medicare and Medicaid. The yearly medical overspending of obese adults, compared to adults with BMIs of under 25, was around $732. Emery et al. (2007) find similar results for France in 2003, with overspending of about €500–600 per year per obese individual. The total cost of obesity and overweight to the French public health insurance is estimated at €4.2 billion in 2003, i.e., 3.1 percent of annual public health expenditures. In the United Kingdom, the total medical cost of obesity is estimated at £1.1 billion in 2002, which represents 2.5 percent of total net National Health Service expenditures (McCormick and Stone 2007).

The burden of many FRCD, in particular diabetes and obesity, will likely mechanically increase in coming years, even if their prevalence remains stable, as a consequence of progress in medical technology, increases in life expectancy, and the aging of the ill population. The fraction of old-age activity limitations and cancers attributable to excess weight will become considerably higher.

As noted by Mazzocchi, Traill, and Shogren (2009), the literature on medical costs generally proposes biased estimates of the effect of changes in food choices on health

---

[5] Richards and Patterson (2006) propose a test of this hypothesis. They consider that genetic predisposition does not affect preferences but rather affects the expected budget constraint through variations in the perceptions of risk of food shortage. For Native American societies, scarcity is defined in terms of hunting and therefore shortage of protein. The "thrifty gene" specific to Native Americans assigns a greater probability to food shortages and therefore a higher shadow value to protein. Richards and Patterson estimate the shadow value of protein, fat, and carbohydrates for Native and non-Native Americans, and find that the former value protein much more than the latter, while the reverse holds for fat and carbohydrates. They interpret this as evidence in favor of the thrifty gene theory. However, it can be argued that African and European Americans are also likely to possess such a thrifty gene (European immigrants and African slaves often came from countries with recurrent food shortages), and their empirical finding is also consistent with pure anthropological taste variations.

care costs, as they treat FRCD as exogenous, and adjust for a limited set of confounders and control variables (usually age, sex, and smoking). Hence, omitted risk factors that are correlated with FRCD, and unobserved genetic, psychological, or socioeconomic factors that simultaneously affect the risk of FRCD and the use of health care services, may bias these estimates. Epidemiological studies of the food–health relationship are prone to the same bias.[6] Hence, these estimates must be used cautiously in the evaluation of the health and monetary benefits from nutritional policies.

The interactions between FRCD and health insurance also have economic consequences. While individuals with FRCD certainly cost the health insurance system more, they may also face different costs of being insured, and have different behavioral reactions to health insurance schemes. Bhattacharya and Bundorf (2009) find evidence that in the United States the medical costs of obesity are passed on to obese workers with employer-sponsored health insurance in the form of lower cash wages, while obese workers in firms without employer-sponsored insurance do not have lower wages relative to their non-obese peers. Using a structural approach to obesity and health insurance, Bhattacharya and Sood (2007) show, however, that the pooling of individuals with different weight statuses in a single risk pool by public and private insurers produces a welfare loss of $150 per US insured person per year. This loss is proportional to the medical cost of obesity and the elasticity of changes in body weight with respect to the health insurance subsidy induced by pooling. This elasticity reflects the extent of the *ex ante* moral hazard problem faced by health insurers, when they cannot discriminate between "healthy" and "unhealthy" eaters: insurance is not fully able to take into account the impact of pooling on food behaviors. This market failure is one rationale for regulation (see Section 4.2).

3.2   Human Capital Costs

The economic cost of FRCD is not limited to health care. Some work has uncovered empirical evidence of a negative impact of BMI on direct measures of welfare, such as life satisfaction or subjective well-being in UK and German data (Oswald and Powdthavee 2007; Blanchflower, Oswald, and van Landeghem 2009). The empirical analysis of obesity has also addressed labor market outcomes and children's performance at school. While the correlation between past or current BMI and employment,

---

[6] Chen et al. (2002) illustrate this point by showing that the effect of nutrient intake, exercise, and medication on blood pressure is greatly affected when these inputs of the "blood pressure production function" are instrumented. Using food prices, wages, and non-labor income as instruments, they find, for instance, that the effect of sodium on blood pressure, which is positive in the ordinary least squares (OLS) regression, becomes significantly negative in the instrumental variable (IV) regression. Unfortunately their instruments are weak, as the F-statistic for the instruments in the instrumental equation is less than 10. The negative IV effect of sodium is biased in the same direction as the OLS effect. Sodium intake may indeed have a large *positive* impact on blood pressure if the OLS effects are biased downward.

wages, or schooling is in general negative, this may not reflect a causal effect. Genetic and non-genetic factors simultaneously affect obesity risk and the outcome of interest. The main empirical difficulty is to find an exogenous source of variation in BMI, an instrument that can be argued not to affect the outcome. Instrumental variable or difference-in-difference strategies can then be implemented. Early work on obesity generally appealed to weak instruments or implausible identifying restrictions, and found negative human capital effects of obesity.[7] To date, the most promising instruments are genetic markers that are sometimes collected in large-scale surveys. The paradigm underlying this approach is called Mendelian Randomization, i.e., the random assignment of genotypes when passed from parents to offspring. Genes can be used as instruments under two conditions: (1) they must be known to be correlated with BMI, through food intake regulation processes (e.g., feelings of satiety/hunger) or metabolic processes (e.g., fat storage); and (2) they must not have an impact on the behavior we wish to explain. Both Norton and Han (2008) and Scholder et al. (2010) show that genetic markers are strong instruments, and therefore yield robust causal estimates. The former find no significant effect of lagged obesity on labor market outcomes in the United States; the latter show that the negative fatness–academic performance correlation found in UK children disappears once fatness is instrumented. These results imply that the economic cost of overweight and obesity in terms of human capital losses might well have been overestimated in previous work.

FRCD generates medical costs and, perhaps, human capital costs. Is this enough to justify costly public policies? The next section considers this question.

4   RATIONALES FOR PUBLIC POLICY

4.1   The Neoclassical Approach to Food and Health

The neoclassical model of consumer choice provides a normative standard for judging the relevance of public policy. There are two key building blocks in the neoclassical

---

[7] For instance, Averett and Korenman (1996) appeal to variations over time in the BMI difference between siblings to identify the causal effect of BMI on wages in the United States. This strategy assumes that genetic and non-genetic factors that are not shared by siblings randomize BMI between siblings, *but not their wages*. They find a wage penalty for white American women. Cawley (2004) uses a sibling's weight as an instrument for one's own weight in a wage equation. As the model is just identified, the restriction that the sibling's weight has no direct effect on the individual's own wage is not testable. He finds a negative effect of obesity on wages for white US women only. Morris (2006, 2007) uses area-level instruments, such as the mean proportion of adults classified as obese, to estimate the effect of BMI on employment and earnings in England. The model is just identified. The IV results are too imprecise to reject the null of no significant effect and the exogeneity of BMI, which has a negative effect. The area level of obesity is not a credible instrument because it is correlated with area characteristics (lack of health care, unemployment, etc.) that have a direct effect on individual labor market chances.

approach to the food–health relationship: the household production theory of consumer choice, on the one hand, and the demand-for-health model, on the other.

First, food consumption decisions are taken in order to maximize utility, subject to the individual's income and the prices that they face. Individuals do not enjoy utility from food purchases per se, but rather from a composite commodity called a "meal," which is produced by the combination of food products and the time required for cooking, cleaning, etc.[8] Since individuals have to allocate time between home cooking and working, the trade-off between home cooking and the reliance on ready meals and food away from home (FAFH) does not depend on income per se, but rather on the wage rate prevailing on the labor market, and the relative market price of food at home (FAH) and FAFH. Cutler, Glaeser, and Shapiro (2003) emphasize that since 1970 technological progress in the mass production of food has lowered the time cost of meal preparation for American families. The reduction of fixed costs of meal preparation helps to explain the increase in the number of meals consumed per day by Americans, i.e., snacking. The opportunity cost of home cooking has also risen and, especially for women, working in the labor market has become more attractive. This would explain why the reduction in time spent preparing meals is greater among married women than among any other demographic group, and equally why obesity has increased relatively more in this group.

Second, Grossman (1972) underlines individuals' intentional management of their health over time. There is a demand for health because it is a direct source of satisfaction for consumers, and it is used in combination with time and other goods to produce commodities. Health also determines individual wages through its effect on productivity. Health capital can also be produced by the purchase of medical goods and services, and by lifestyle choices that are themselves produced by combining time and goods. These inputs of the health production function are investments whose optimal level is fixed so as to set equal the marginal expected future benefits in terms of longevity and quality of life and the marginal opportunity costs in terms of forgone pleasure today.

When we combine these two theoretical blocks, food choices by neoclassical consumers have two key motivations: the maximization of immediate satisfaction from eating, at the lowest cost in terms of time and money; and eating in a way that is likely to preserve their health capital. Immediate pleasures and costs are weighted against future rewards and pain via a discount factor, in such a way that behaviors are time-consistent.[9] Some individuals will prefer junk food to fruit and vegetables, up to the point where the marginal satisfaction of eating junk food is equal to the discounted marginal disutility of worse future health (Levy 2002). Other motivations are sometimes introduced in the literature, such as aesthetic concerns regarding BMI.

---

[8] See Becker (1965) and Huffman, Ch. 2 in this volume, for more details.

[9] In intertemporal decision problems, individuals are time-consistent when, in the absence of shocks, they carry out at time t the action they decided on at time $t-1$ for period t. When the intertemporal utility function is separable, time consistency requires exponential discounting.

Individuals may have an incentive to stick to a social norm of beauty (an ideal BMI), where the latter is likely to differ from medical norms regarding BMI (Etilé 2007; Blanchflower, Oswald, and van Landeghem 2009).[10]

A natural implication of neoclassical models is that the reduction in the price of "unhealthy food" relative to "healthy food" over the past forty years has increased the marginal utility of the former relative to the latter. Price changes thus explain the development of FRCD in the population. However, when individuals eat unhealthy food, their health tends to deteriorate and they experience the unpleasant consequences of being above their ideal weight, having high cholesterol, and so on. Hence, the value of weight and diet control behavior increases, which raises the demand for exercise, functional food, and dieticians. In this setup, FRCD are only private health problems and, a priori, the market will be efficient at supplying health inputs, be they junk food or diets.

4.2 Market Failures as Rationales for Regulation

However, as noted in Section 3, FRCD generates externalities, which take the form of medical and human capital costs. As noted by Strnad (2005), these externalities have to be weighted against the benefits that unhealthy eating generates, in terms of jobs and profits in the food sector and fiscal revenues for governments. Externalities on their own may be insufficient to justify government intervention. However, in countries where individuals with FRCD are covered by public insurance, as in most European countries or for Medicare/Medicaid beneficiaries in the United States, an *ex ante* moral hazard problem arises as the consequence of the inability of public insurance to charge individuals fairly (see Section 3.1).[11] There is a market failure, and the usual remedy would be to adjust the premiums to reflect excess weight. This is not feasible in the context of public insurance (Schmidhuber 2004). Taxing unhealthy food will then be welfare-enhancing when the pre-policy welfare cost, which is only due to moral hazard on the insurance market, is higher than the post-policy welfare cost, which is the sum of the residual costs of *ex ante* moral hazard and consumer losses due to prices differing from marginal production costs. To reduce the latter, subsidizing healthy food is in general required (Arnott and Stiglitz 1986). Governments can therefore implement price policies, based on taxes and subsidies. The empirical aspects of the latter are detailed in Section 5.[12]

---

[10] Rosin (2008) provides an excellent survey of models of weight management, with formal analysis.

[11] Taxpayers may also have social preferences that favor the public coverage of health risks. For instance, Cawley (2008) finds that Americans would be willing to pay $47 more in taxes every year for a 50 percent reduction in childhood obesity.

[12] If obesity were the only problem, Grossman and Rashad (2004) suggest that subsidizing exercise would be more efficient as it would harm no one and would be more feasible than taxing excess weight.

As noted by Blaylock et al. (1999), consumers are often misinformed and misguided about the exact nutritional content of processed food, or possess nutritional knowledge that is limited in the light of the technical complexity of the food–health relationship. This situation produces a role for information policies that respect the neoclassical principle of "consumer sovereignty." These information policies are explored in Section 6.

4.3   Failures of Rationality as a Rationale for Regulation

The behavioral approach to economic decisions considers the rationality failures that cause choice outcomes to deviate from the predictions of neoclassical theory. Behavioral theories provide additional rationales for government intervention. It is wise to be cautious, however, in labeling behaviors as "irrational."

For instance, addiction to unhealthy food, i.e., the persistence of consumption despite detrimental health consequences, has been blamed for the obesity epidemic. However, Becker and Murphy (1988) have shown that neoclassical consumers can become rational addicts. They maintain their consumption as long as the current marginal benefit it produces is equal to or greater than its full price, which accounts for discounted future health and addiction costs that are perfectly anticipated. Addiction becomes a problem when the consumer does not recognize that higher levels of consumption now will lower the marginal utility of consumption in the future. There is ample evidence that high-fat, high-carbohydrate food has greater activation power on "brain rewards circuitry through faster sensory inputs and slower post-ingestive consequences" than fruit and vegetables. "The repeated physiological stimulation of reward pathways . . . triggers neurobiological adaptation," as in the case of drugs (Volkow and Wise 2005).[13] As most consumers are probably unaware of these mechanisms, they are likely to consume more than they would have done had they been rational addicts. This is a case of "naive" habit formation, which justifies either the diffusion of generic information about the dangers of specific foodstuffs, or their taxation to render consumption decisions closer to those of rational addicts.

Dieting behaviors also challenge neoclassical analysis. As failure is more common than success, dieting seems to be a self-defeating rather than a rational behavior. Cognitive restriction of food intake, i.e., the rational choice of dieting, entails metabolic and psychological costs. Hence, the marginal cost of weight loss around habitual weight is much larger (in absolute terms) than the marginal utility of a small weight gain.[14]

[13] In hedonic rating tests, the combination of fat and sugar is preferred and is related to the activation of endorphins. The latter are known to play a central role in behaviors characterized by a lack of self-control: craving, binge eating, bulimia-nervosa, etc. (see Miljkovic, Nganje, and de Chastenet 2008 and the references therein).

[14] Habitual weight corresponds to what physiologists call the body weight set-point. Various physiological systems regulate body weight and can maintain it, for relatively long periods, at a stable

Hence, as noted by Suranovic and Goldfarb (2007), dieting entails asymmetric adjustment costs. They propose a model wherein dieting costs take the form of increasing convex utility losses as the individual starts to lose weight around their habitual weight. Dieting arises because exogenous factors such as aging, or changes in prices or energy expenditures, reduce the marginal utility of staying at habitual weight, with this marginal utility now being smaller than the marginal disutility of dieting. Owing to the convexity of adjustment costs, the utility function is not concave around habitual weight, and dieting takes the form of sudden cuts in calorie intake, followed by an increase in the utility of gaining weight, and a slow return to almost the original habitual weight. The adjustment-costs hypothesis does not imply per se that individuals are irrational, but it explains the demand for dieting help. Whether such assistance should be publicly provided, at least for low-income individuals, depends on its costs and benefits. Regarding the latter, weight loss and weight loss maintenance interventions evaluated by randomized controlled trials produce only limited results in the long run (Strychar 2006).

Weakness of will in dieters also suggests the existence of self-control problems, which can be modeled in two distinct ways. A first approach is to assume that individuals do not discount the future exponentially, as in neoclassical theory, but quasi-hyperbolically.[15] The utility of the current period then has particular salience, and is overvalued relative to all future periods, so that decisions are dynamically inconsistent: when today comes, it is always optimal to postpone the dieting plan made yesterday (Laibson 1997). Hyperbolic discounting can explain why people employ pre-commitment devices, such as joining Weight Watchers (Scharff 2009). Hyperbolic discounting also implies that individuals do not receive in the long run the utility they would have received if they were to have been consistent. This concern justifies paternalistic interventions, which can take the form of a tax limiting consumption behaviors. We can easily imagine that a tax on junk food would hit individuals with self-control problems relatively hard. If the tax revenue is redistributed equally to the population, then income will be naturally redistributed from individuals with self-control problems to those without such problems. Such a "sin tax" may therefore correspond to a Pareto improvement as it would be beneficial to everyone (O'Donoghue and Rabin 2003, 2005).[16] Absent good measures of time preferences in a large-scale food survey, hyperbolic discounting models are not yet testable.[17]

---

level: the set-point (Cabanac 2001). For instance, in the case of caloric restriction, there is a reduction in resting energy expenditure that is greater than that expected from the loss of metabolic active tissues.

[15] The marginal rate of substitution between consumption at two future periods is constant, and greater than that between today and tomorrow.

[16] However, the sin tax does not always correspond to a Pareto improvement as it may restrict the choice set of future selves. In this case, the theory suggests that allowing individuals to purchase sin licenses, e.g., the right to consume junk food, would be preferable (Bhattacharya and Lakdawalla 2004; O'Donoghue and Rabin 2005). This is clearly unfeasible.

[17] Is there any empirical evidence that dynamic inconsistency might explain the rise in FRCD? Smith, Bogin, and Bishai (2005) find that the BMI of black and Hispanic men and black women in the United

A second approach to self-control problems, which is far less developed, posits that environmental cues trigger uncontrollable shifts in preferences. For instance, the smell of cakes and pastries when passing a bakery will instantaneously increase the marginal utility of a croissant. Past associations between cues and rewards (eating) are likely to elevate the triggering power of a cue (Laibson 2001). Evidence from research on dieting behavior reveals that controlling cues is important for the success of a diet. Signals from the body can trump the determined resolution to restrain intake. This is due to limits on cognitive resources, which favor the breakdown of dietary restraints when, for instance, dieters divide their attention between several cues, e.g., watching TV and resisting hunger (Herman and Polivy 2003). One important consequence of the cue theory of consumption is that cue-based strategies that firms use to encourage consumers' purchases have negative externalities: they lead to overconsumption and favor addiction (Smith 2004). As advertisements convey cues as well as information, the question of their regulation is an issue, and is explored in Section 6.

In the end, both the neoclassical and the behavioral approaches to food and health provide rationales for government interventions via prices and the information available to consumers, but they are likely to differ in their recommendations regarding the intensity and design of the policies. While testing behavioral explanations is certainly one of the most promising avenues of research, the neoclassical model still provides a normative target for public policies: they must leave consumer decisions as close as possible to the choices that would be made in the absence of market and rationality failures. Sections 5 and 6 now take a more pragmatic viewpoint, and present empirical evidence about food price and information policies.

5   PRICE POLICIES

In 1994 Kelly Brownell proposed that junk food be taxed to subsidize healthier foods and nutrition education programs. Since then, a part of the public health sector has seen taxes and subsidies as an appropriate tool for intervention in nutritional choices. Section 4 presented the main normative goals for price policies: (1) solving the *ex ante* hazard moral problem faced by public insurance; and (2) committing consumers to rational choices if they have self-control problems or are "naively addicted" to food. This section presents some empirical evidence about the effectiveness and the equity effects of price policies.

States is correlated with some proxies for dynamic inconsistency, such as dissaving. It is unclear that this relationship is causal. Borghans and Golsteyn (2006) find similar results for Dutch adults observed over the 1995–2004 period. In particular, BMI is inversely related to difficulty in managing spending. However, changes in these variables are uncorrelated with changes in BMI.

5.1   Food Prices and Health Outcomes

Price policies use tax and subsidies to alter relative prices. They may focus on the nutritional content of each product, or on specific food groups. Leicester and Wind-meijer (2004) argue that taxing nutrients would be very costly in terms of monitoring because the recipes of food producers change constantly. Moreover, human nutritional requirements vary by age, gender, and health, and a tax could have adverse health effects on at-risk groups in the population. As such, considering taxes or subsidies on product categories is more interesting. Specific taxes on confectionery, fizzy drinks, or snacks already exist in a number of US states, although not for nutritional reasons (Jacobson and Brownell 2000).

Price policies are of interest only if food prices have significant effects on the prevalence of FRCD. Empirical evidence on the long-term food price–health relation-ship is relatively scarce, and is available for the United States only.[18] Using time and regional variations in food taxes in the United States, Lakdawalla and Philipson (2002) find that the fall in the aggregate price of FAH explains 41 percent of the growth in BMI between 1981 and 1994. Chou, Grossman, and Saffer (2004) also report a negative and significant correlation between the price of food and BMI in repeated cross-sections from the 1984–99 Behavioral Risk Factor Surveillance System.[19]

Beyond aggregate food prices, the decline in the price of unhealthy food relative to the price of healthy food may explain the substitution of the former for the latter, and thus trends in FRCD. In the empirical literature, fruit and vegetables often represent healthy food, while the price of unhealthy food is proxied by fast-food prices. Sturm and Datar (2005) find, for instance, that observed spatial variations in fruit and vegetable prices can produce up to a 0.49 BMI units difference in the rise in body weight between the kindergarten and the third grade for American children. Fast-food prices have no significant effect. Using seven repeated cross-sections of the Monitoring the Future survey (1997–2003), Powell et al. (2007) report positive, albeit insignificant, estimates of the effect of the price of fruit and vegetables on the BMI of American adolescents. A 10 percent increase in the price of fast-food meals led to a 0.4 percent decline in BMI and a 5.9 percent fall in the probability of overweight.

These studies cannot, however, inform the construction of price policies because they do not consider the whole pattern of substitution between products. As shown by Schroeter, Lusk, and Tyner (2008), the effect of a change in the price of one product is determined by both the own- and the cross-price elasticities of consumption, and by

---

[18] Estimates for other countries are either not available or are not robust, for at least two reasons. First, there is a lack of panel data with information on food-related health outcomes and socioeconomic characteristics. Second, when food prices are available, they often do not display enough spatial variation. In this case, price effects are identified only parametrically, from time variations, through the non-linearity with respect to other time-varying variables.

[19] Chou, Grossman, and Saffer (2004) provide an additional result: the elasticities of BMI or obesity prevalence to the prices of FAH, full-service restaurants, and fast-food restaurants are the same.

the relative share of each product in nutrient intakes.[20] Hence, the effectiveness of price policy depends crucially on the choice of products whose prices are targeted. Suppose, for instance, that we want to reduce calorie intake by taxing "junk food." Energy-dense products that may then be substituted for the latter should not be left outside the tax base. As the degree of substitutability between products varies from one country to another, depending on food habits, the optimal tax base will be country-specific. The role of FAFH has also to be carefully considered in countries where snacking and the poor nutritional quality of FAFH is held responsible for FRCD, as is the case in the United States (Lin, Guthrie, and Frazão 1999; Cutler, Glaeser, and Shapiro 2003).[21]

5.2   Exogenous Constraints on Food Choices and Equity Issues

In addition to food habits, exogenous constraints can limit behavioral changes. This raises equity issues.

From the theory of household production, time constraints are likely to play an important role. There is evidence for the United States of a link between the increase in women's labor supply and the rise in the mass preparation of food. Technological innovations in the preparation and conservation of food and the decline in the full price of a meal have favored women's increasing participation in the labor market (Cutler, Glaeser, and Shapiro 2003). Working wives have a more positive attitude toward eating out and convenience food as they have a greater valuation of their time- and energy-saving aspects (Scholderer and Grunert 2005). However, most people are unable to measure the nutritional quality of prepared meals and processed foods (Blaylock et al. 1999). It is therefore unsurprising that obesity has increased to a much greater extent among married women than for other demographic groups (Cutler, Glaeser, and Shapiro 2003), and that maternal employment has a positive impact on children's overweight risk (Anderson, Butcher, and Levine 2003). Hence, taxing prepared food may be a policy to consider. However, for those individuals who cannot adjust their working hours in order to cook at home more, increasing the price of prepared food may be ineffective and have substantial welfare costs.

Individuals also have energy requirements that depend on characteristics that are to an extent not under their control: age, gender, health, and occupation. Darmon,

---

[20] Substitution between food and tobacco may also reduce the public health benefits of price policies. However, evidence on the effect of cigarette prices on BMI is mixed (see Cawley, Markowitz, and Tauras 2004; Chou, Grossman, and Saffer 2004; Gruber and Frakes 2006).

[21] The role of snacking in the obesity epidemic is not proven for all countries. In France, for instance, cohort studies show that snacking has a detrimental effect on diet quality only for individuals who are already obese (Bellisle 2004). We can also imagine that hyperbolic discounters only develop bad snacking habits when confronted with an increase in the supply of snacks. Hence, the positive snacking–obesity relationship may reflect inverse causality or a selection effect.

Ferguson, and Briend (2002) use linear programming techniques to identify the food choices that are the closest to the average French diet under three constraints: a given budget, limited portion sizes, and minimum energy intakes. Unsurprisingly, as the budget falls, so does the consumption of fruit and vegetables and meat and dairy products, while the proportion from cereals, sweets, and added fats rises. As individuals increase their consumption of energy-dense food in order to maintain their energy intake, there is a significant decline in micronutrient intake. Hence, a tax on energy-dense food would be regressive and have adverse effects in lower socioeconomic groups.

Last, food choices depend on available food supply. If local shops offer junk food rather than fruit and vegetables, then consumers will not be able to substitute the former for the latter, even if relative prices change. Work on "food deserts" has suggested that such barriers to healthy eating may have a particularly large effect on low-income households, single parents with children, the elderly, and those with mobility problems. However, they fail to establish a causal relationship between the presence or absence of stores and eating patterns (Cummins and Macintyre 2006).

These exogenous constraints limit individuals' ability to adjust their food choices when prices change, even if they have *ex ante* the same budget constraint. As such, price policies may raise problems of horizontal equity. Paternalists may also consider that vertical equity is violated as low-income individuals consume more unhealthy food and, as shown above, face more constraints when making their food choices: taxes are likely to be regressive.[22]

5.3   In Search of an Optimal Price Policy

The search for an optimal tax brings up both efficiency and equity issues. Using a food demand system approach, it is possible to evaluate the *ex ante* effects of taxes on nutrient intake and consumer welfare. The latter can be used to assess the short-term equity of a given policy.[23]

In this perspective, Chouinard et al. (2007) estimate an incomplete demand system to identify the impact of a "fat tax" on dairy products. They find that this policy would raise revenue but would not reduce fat intake from dairy products. The tax would also be regressive as the welfare losses would be higher for the poor. More generally, evidence on the effectiveness of price policies is mixed. Most work finds that price

---

[22] In the neoclassical approach, the regressive nature of taxes on "sin" goods is less of a concern than the distortions taxes create by redistributing income between individuals. This problem is mitigated if a portion of tax revenues is earmarked for expenditures that are designed to aid poorer members of society.

[23] The basic idea is to estimate food demand systems. Then, assuming that the nutritional composition of products is unaffected by price changes, the impact of prices on food quantities and therefore nutrient intakes can be simulated (Beatty and LaFrance 2005). The compensating variations associated with price changes measure their welfare effects. The evaluation of long-term welfare effects has to take into account the benefit of weight reduction in terms of well-being.

changes have only little effect on nutrient intake. For instance, using an incomplete demand system for snack food, Kuchler, Tegene, and Harris (2005) show that taxing salty snack foods would be ineffective in reducing their consumption. Huang (1996) estimates a complete demand system and finds in US data that increasing the price of beef would reduce cholesterol intake. However, this would also reduce calcium intake. Allais, Bertail, and Nichèle (2010) and Nordström and Thunström (2009) also find, in French and Swedish data respectively, that tax reforms require very large price changes to be efficient and have unintended consequences on the consumption of some healthy nutrients.[24] Last, tax regressivity and the lower responsiveness of lower social classes, which are more at risk of FRCD, likely limit the scope of price policies (Yen, Lin, and Smallwood 2003; Smed, Jensen, and Denver 2007).

The empirical analysis of the relationship between food prices and BMI and empirical evidence on the "demand for nutrients" based on food demand systems suggests that taxes are not an effective means of enhancing public health. As elasticities are small, taxes should be very large to have a significant impact on public health. There is thus contradictory evidence regarding the effectiveness of price policies. Nevertheless, if the only goal of a tax on unhealthy food is to solve the *ex ante* moral hazard problem faced by the public insurance system (see Section 4), then a smaller elasticity of consumption and nutrient intake is desirable. Following the Ramsey rule, this minimizes distortions in consumer choice. A lower elasticity also ensures a stable flow of revenue, which is important if the latter is earmarked for financing information policies. This viewpoint has been defended by prominent members of the public health community (e.g., Jacobson and Brownell 2000; Caraher and Cowburn 2005). Yet, what do we know about the effectiveness of information policies?

6   INFORMATION POLICIES

Information policies can be sorted into three distinct types of action: health education,[25] which takes the form of public information campaigns and nutritional education; the nutritional labeling of food products and restaurant menus; and advertising regulation.

---

[24] A number of studies also use pre-existing estimates of price elasticities to simulate the effects of price policies on food consumption and health outcomes (see, *inter alia*, Marshall 2000; Cash et al. 2005). They suggest that price policies have important benefits in terms of life saved. However, they use estimates of the food–health relationship that are likely to be biased (see Section 3.1).

[25] According to the American Joint Committee on Health Education and Promotion Terminology (2001), health education is "any combination of planned learning experiences based on sound theories that provide individuals, groups, and communities the opportunity to acquire information and the skills needed to make quality health decisions."

6.1 Health Education

With respect to health education, economists have mainly focused their attention on public information campaigns, which aim to inform consumers about the generic health consequences of their food choices.[26] In the neoclassical perspective, this is justified by the requirement that consumers be perfectly informed in order to maximize their well-being effectively, whatever the healthiness of the diet they choose. Ignorance has a cost in terms of well-being, and information policies are valuable if the cost of ignorance is higher than the cost of providing information. For the public health sector, information campaigns should also promote awareness of health risks in order to help bring about changes in food behaviors when desired by consumers.

Earlier empirical work examined the impact of generic information regarding cholesterol risk. This latter is measured by time-varying information indices constructed from counts of Medline or newspaper publications about the link between cholesterol and heart disease. Although these indices do not vary across individuals, they are introduced as covariates to explain the individual demand for products that are rich in cholesterol, such as meat or dairy products. This idea was originally proposed by Brown and Schrader (1990), who find a negative correlation between their index (based on Medline counts) and egg consumption in the United States. Chern and Rickertsen (2003) apply this method to a number of different countries and products. It is now, however, acknowledged that this method has some significant limitations. It does not identify the causal effect of information as it relies on particular assumptions regarding trends in other unobserved time-varying factors, and individual knowledge remains unobserved. Hence, the pathways from scientific publications or newspaper articles to changes in food behavior remain in a black box. We may indeed wonder whether publications affect consumers because they enhance their health knowledge or because they change social norms, first among the better-educated and better-off social groups, and then by contagion in the rest of society.

A second set of work goes one step further and examines the effect of individual information on knowledge, and the way in which it affects food consumption.[27] Using American data from the 1994–6 Continuing Survey of Food Intakes by Individuals, Kan and Yen (2003) find a positive correlation between "having heard information about health problems caused by eating too much cholesterol" (information) and deciding that it is "important to choose a diet low in cholesterol" (knowledge). Those who have more knowledge are less likely to consume eggs, but once the decision to consume eggs is made, knowledge does not affect the level of

---

[26] Regarding the effectiveness of targeted interventions based on nutritional education, see the associated literature in nutrition and health education.

[27] This literature sometimes uses the concepts of health awareness instead of health knowledge. The latter refers to very specific knowledge, such as the recommended percentage of calories that should come from fat or the nutrient content of a food (Blaylock et al. 1999).

consumption. Income, age, education, and being female are also positively correlated with knowledge, and the latter is in general positively related to healthy consumption (Carlson and Gould 1994; Variyam, Blaylock, and Smallwood 1996; Blaylock et al. 1999; Kan and Yen 2003). The education effect can be interpreted as reflecting a better ability to understand information. The richer and the better educated also have more incentives to accumulate knowledge as they face greater opportunity costs of unhealthy eating in terms of potential earnings losses (Grossman 2000). This is also the case for the elderly, whose mortality risks are higher. Last, in most households, women are the meal planners, and are therefore more exposed to information. The involvement of women in meal planning explains why mothers' nutritional knowledge is also positively correlated with children's dietary intake (Variyam, Blaylock, Lin, et al. 1999). Kan and Tsai (2004) focus more directly on the knowledge–BMI relationship. Perhaps surprisingly, quantile regression results show that more knowledge leads to a higher BMI for men who are neither overweight nor obese. The effect becomes significantly negative in obese men only.

However, these estimates again fail to identify causal information effects as this would require that the endogeneity of information and knowledge be treated via the use of plausible identifying assumptions. Consumer theory does not propose credible instruments, i.e., variables that strongly affect the search for information and the formation of knowledge but are uncorrelated with food choices (Park and Davis 2001).[28] Hence, the only way of evaluating the benefits of information policies is to use changes in information supply that are arguably exogenous. It is often difficult to find instrumental variables that exogenously shift the supply of information.[29]

To sum up, there are doubts about the effectiveness of public information campaigns. Natural, field, or laboratory experiments could provide more robust evidence, although their external validity is questionable.[30]

[28] Following Hirshleifer and Riley (1979), a rational consumer chooses to search for information if the search costs are smaller than the expected benefits in terms of the utility derived from consumption. Hence, the determinants of consumption and information demand are similar.

[29] For instance, Loureiro and Nayga (2006) estimate the effect of a doctor's advice regarding weight loss on the probability of individuals' eating fewer calories and less fat, and on physical activity, in data from the Behavioral Risk Factor Surveillance System. Doctors' advice is implemented according to whether or not the individual has a health plan and a regular doctor. Their identifying assumption is thus that unobserved heterogeneity such as time preferences do not simultaneously affect the demand for health care services, BMI, and health behaviors.

[30] One example is Roosen et al. (2009), who conducted a field experiment in France to evaluate the impact of health warnings about the risk of methyl mercury contamination on fish consumption. A sample of households from the city of Nantes on the Atlantic coast was randomized into treatment and control groups. The treatment group received health warnings, and both groups were followed over five months. A difference-in-difference estimation reveals that health warnings have only small effects on consumption. But is this result valid for individuals who do not live on the Atlantic coast and have different food habits?

6.2   Nutritional Labeling

For the public health sector, labels can be a way of helping consumers to discriminate between products according to their nutritional quality. For firms, they are a way of fostering differentiation between products. This strategic value for firms is exemplified by the use of health claims in the growing functional-food market.

Drichoutis, Lazaridis, and Nayga (2009) review the sociodemographic determinants of individual differences in label use. Women, households with young children, and those who have more time to shop are more likely to use labels. A positive correlation is also found with health awareness, nutritional knowledge, and education, but this relationship may not be causal. The sign and significance of the correlations with income, age, and occupation are more variable. Consumer use and understanding of labels also depend on their format. It is clear that consumers prefer color-based systems (e.g., traffic lights) to information about daily values for nutrients, even if use of the latter tends to produce better nutritional results.

Although a number of empirical studies have uncovered evidence of a positive relationship between label use and nutritional choices, they fail to identify causal effects.[31] Some authors, however, propose causal evidence based on exogenous variations in label regulation. The implementation of the US Nutritional Labeling and Education Act (NLEA) has been used by Mathios (2000) to analyze the impact of mandatory labeling on product choices in the salad-dressing market. Using a simple before–after framework, he shows that the NLEA caused a significant decline in the share of higher-fat dressings. Variyam (2008) exploits the NLEA's exemption of FAFH sources from labeling requirement. Assuming that individual heterogeneity has the same effect on FAH and FAFH consumption, he assesses the effect of mandatory labeling for label users by estimating the difference between label users and non-label users in the difference in intakes from FAH and FAFH. He detects no effect of label use and mandatory labeling. Last, Teisl, Bockstael, and Levy (2001) use data from a field experiment to evaluate the impact of nutritional shelf labeling in supermarket stores. They follow monthly scanner data in twenty-five stores between 1985 and 1988. From 1986 to 1988 stores were randomly assigned to a treatment or a control group, and treatment stores exhibited shelf tags augmented with nutrition information. Estimates reveal that nutritional shelf labeling has had mixed effects. Purchases of healthy products increased in some food categories, but not all.[32] While providing information does not always lead consumers to substitute healthy products for unhealthy products,

---

[31] Either the endogeneity of label use is not treated, or the identification strategy uses weak instruments or instrumental variables that are arguably correlated with the behavioral outcome of interest.

[32] In a similar but more recent field experiment, Kiesel and Villas-Boas (forthcoming) find that the "low-calorie" label has had a positive effect on sales, while the "low-fat" label has had a negative impact.

it has had clear reallocation effects that are associated with welfare gains.[33] Hence, mandatory labeling policies benefit consumers in the short term, even when there are few long-term benefits in terms of better health.

Health claims are now widely used by the food industry as a means of differentiation. They differ from standard nutritional labeling in that producers *choose* the nutritional attributes they want to label. Their regulation by food agencies is an important issue as false claims can misguide the consumer. There is little causal evidence about true claims because they are not exogenously provided by firms. One interesting exception is Ippolito and Mathios (1990), who use the suspension of the US bans on health claims at the end of 1984 after the Kellogg company began a campaign about the benefits of fiber to prevent cancer. This discontinuity in the provision of information revealed the impact of health claims on the ready-to-eat cereals market. They find that health claims were associated with an increase in the consumption of fiber cereals and led to product innovations. Their results also suggest that advertising reduced the differences in the probability of purchasing fiber cereals across consumers because it lowered the costs of information search. One implication is that the development of health claims and functional food may be more effective at changing consumer choices than public information campaigns. However, claims also have unintended consequences because they create a "halo" effect (Roe, Levy, and Derby 1999). Consumers focus their attention on the positive health attributes and make less use of other nutritional information or give less weight to the other negative health attributes. This may explain the current absence of empirical evidence in favor of health claims as a means of preventing or curing FRCD.

6.3   Restrictions to Advertising

The public health sector advocates regulation on advertising targeting children, while the industry contends that advertising simply affects market share but not the overall volume of sales.[34] Empirical evidence about the impact of advertising tends to show that it plays a minor but significant role in children's diet and obesity (Hastings et al. 2003). Chou, Rashad, and Grossman (2008) estimate, for instance, the effect of television fast-food restaurant advertising on the BMI of American children and teenagers by using spatial variations in television networks. They find that a ban on these

---

[33] The basic idea is that purchase behaviors after the treatment reveal the true preferences of consumers. Hence, differences in choices made before and after the treatment necessarily imply welfare gains. These correspond to the cost of ignorance borne by consumers before the treatment.

[34] The economic debate on advertising is based on other arguments. Following Becker and Murphy (1993), one may argue that some advertising is informative, some is uninformative, but in both cases they do not shift consumer tastes. In this view, consumers choose to buy advertised food because advertisements themselves are a good, which is complementary with food in the production of utility. Then, assuming perfect market competition, the equilibrium provision of advertising by firms maximizes social welfare. An alternative view is that advertising is used by firms to shift tastes and, as a consequence, the equilibrium level of advertising may be socially excessive (Dixit and Norman 1978).

advertisements would reduce the prevalence of overweight by about 10 percent. Should policymakers also ban part of food advertising directed at adults? The increasing amount of R & D expenditures in neurosciences by communication agencies indeed gives credence to the arguments from behavioral economics that advertising may also shift adults' tastes. This research question clearly requires further investigations.[35]

6   Concluding Remarks

Economic research on food and health has offered important rationales for public health policies. However, it has been less successful in answering policy questions about the effectiveness of price and information policies. In this perspective, I now present some avenues for future research.

Empirical evidence about price policies is mixed. *Ex ante* evaluations based on food demand systems or direct estimates of the food–BMI relationship reveal that feasible price policies would generate very small change in nutrient intakes or in the prevalence of overweight and obesity. One limitation of current works is that econometric models do not treat simultaneously, in a structural manner, demand for food and demand for health. Conditioning food demand by health outcomes, or health outcomes by food demand, should produce more consistent results. Proponents of price policies generally consider that tax and subsidies (e.g., VAT modulation) can be used to modify the pattern of relative food prices in favor of healthier food. However, there is little evaluation of the way tax hikes or subsidies could be transmitted to consumer prices. We may further imagine that producers and retailers will supply food at a lower cost, by lowering its nutritional quality. A structural approach to the market equilibrium effects of price policies can inform public policymaking. A related issue is whether public health policies should be focused on consumer choices or on producer supply of quality and quantity. Producer supply of quality could also be influenced by liability policies, which may be an interesting substitute for price policies (Coestier, Gozland, and Marette 2005).

A politically central issue is whether advertising, and more generally food marketing, increases consumption, and whether advertisement bans decrease it. Survey-based evidence on this question is scarce, in part because it is difficult to measure exposure to advertising and how it potentially affects tastes. However, there is a growing interest in environmental interventions to promote healthier choices. Experimental evidence from marketing, psychology, and behavioral economics show that food behaviors are influenced by environmental factors outside of conscious awareness, such as the

---

[35] For instance, it has been argued that allowing advertising for positive nutritional attributes only (i.e., health claims) would give a competitive advantage to producers of healthy products (Ippolito and Pappalardo 2002). However, as exposed above, health claims do not appear to favor significantly substitutions toward healthier products.

portion sizes offered in fast foods, the place where tempting foods are stored in the house, or the package size of products sold in supermarkets (see, e.g., Wansink, Just, and Payne 2009). Redesigning the food environment could help consumers to make healthier choices without constraining consumer sovereignty. However, it may require new regulations on food marketing.

There is an ongoing debate in economics about the role of contagion effects in the spread of obesity. While Christakis and Fowler (2007) and Fowler and Christakis (2008) argue that the positive correlation in obesity found in social networks of adults and adolescents is due to peer effects, Cohen-Cole and Fletcher (2008, 2009) uncover convincing evidence that this is due to contextual effects, i.e., changes in unobserved environmental factors. Identifying social interaction effects is an important issue because they increase the impact of changes in price and information, and can therefore multiply the effectiveness of public policies.

Last, although the empirical analysis of the food–health relationship can play an important role in guiding the construction of public health policy, we must keep in mind some essential limits of food policies: the risk of FRCD depends on a number of factors that are mediators and/or confounders of the impact of nutritional choices. These factors include, in particular, income shocks, economic insecurity, changes in the labor market, and other lifestyle factors.

REFERENCES

Allais, O., P. Bertail, and V. Nichèle. 2010. "The Effects of a Fat Tax on French Households' Purchases: A Nutritional Approach." *American Journal of Agricultural Economics* 92/1: 228–45.

American Joint Committee on Health Education and Promotion Terminology. 2001. "Report of the 2000 Joint Committee on Health Education and Promotion Terminology." *American Journal of Health Education* 32/2: 89–103.

Andersen, L. F., I. T. Lillegaard, N. Overby, L. Lytle, K. I. Klepp, and L. Johansson. 2005. "Overweight and Obesity among Norwegian Schoolchildren: Changes from 1993 to 2000." *Scandinavian Journal of Public Health* 33/2: 99–106.

Anderson, P. M., K. F. Butcher, and P. B. Levine. 2003. "Maternal Employment and Overweight Children." *Journal of Health Economics* 22/3: 477–504.

Arnott, R., and J. E. Stiglitz. 1986. "Moral Hazard and Optimal Commodity Taxation." *Journal of Public Economics* 29/1: 1–24.

Averett, S., and S. Korenman. 1996. "The Economic Reality of the Beauty Myth." *Journal of Human Resources* 31/2: 304–30.

Beatty, T. K., and J. LaFrance. 2005. "United States Demand for Food and Nutrition in the Twentieth Century." *American Journal of Agricultural Economics* 87/5: 1159–66.

Becker, G. S. 1965. "A Theory of the Allocation of Time." *Economic Journal* 75/299: 493–517.

Becker, G. S., and K. M. Murphy. 1988. "A Theory of Rational Addiction." *Journal of Political Economy* 96: 675–700.

———. 1993. "A Simple Theory of Advertising as a Good or Bad." *Quarterly Journal of Economics* 108/4: 941–94.

Bellisle, F. 2004. "Impact of the Daily Meal Pattern on Energy Balance." *Scandinavian Journal of Food and Nutrition* 48/3: 114–18.

Bhattacharya, J., and K. M. Bundorf. 2009. "The Incidence of the Healthcare Costs of Obesity." *Journal of Health Economics* 28/3: 649–58.

——and D. Lakdawalla. 2004. *Time-Inconsistency and Welfare*. NBER Working Paper No. 10345. Cambridge, MA: National Bureau of Economic Research.

Bhattacharya, J., and N. Sood. 2007. "Health Insurance and the Obesity Externality." In K. Bolin and J. Cawley, eds, *Advances in Health Economics and Health Services Research*, 17: *The Economics of Obesity*. London: Elsevier.

Blanchflower, D. G., A. J. Oswald, and B. van Landeghem. 2009. "Imitative Obesity and Relative Utility." *Journal of the European Economic Association* 7/2-3: 528–38.

Blaylock, J., D. Smallwood, K. Kassel, J. Variyam, and L. Aldrich. 1999. "Economics, Food Choices, and Nutrition." *Food Policy* 24/2-3: 269–86.

Bleich, S. N., D. Cutler, C. Murray, and A. Adams. 2008. "Why Is the Developed World Obese?" *Annual Review of Public Health* 29/1: 273–95.

Borghans, L., and B. H. H. Golsteyn. 2006. "Time Discounting and the Body Mass Index: Evidence from the Netherlands." *Economics and Human Biology* 4/1: 39–61.

Bray, G. A., C. Bouchard, and M. Dekker. 2004. *Handbook of Obesity, Etiology and Pathophysiology*, 2nd edn. Toronto: CRC Press.

Brown, D. J., and L. F. Schrader. 1990. "Cholesterol Information and Shell Egg Consumption." *American Journal of Agricultural Economics* 72/3: 548–55.

Brownell, K. D. 1994. "Get Slim with Higher Taxes." *New York Times*, Dec. 15: A-29.

Cabanac, M. 2001. "Regulation and the Ponderostat." *International Journal of Obesity* 25, suppl. 5: S7–S12.

Caraher, M., and G. Cowburn. 2005. "Taxing Food: Implications for Public Health Nutrition." *Public Health Nutrition* 8/8: 1242–9.

Carlson, K. A., and B. W. Gould. 1994. "The Role of Health Knowledge in Determining Dietary Fat Intake." *Review of Agricultural Economics* 16/3: 373–86.

Cash, S. B., D. L. Sunding, and D. Zilberman. 2005. "Fat Taxes and Thin Subsidies: Prices, Diet, and Health Outcomes." *Food Economics: Acta Agriculturae Scandinavica C* 2/3-4: 167–74.

Cawley, J. 2004. "The Impact of Obesity on Wages." *Journal of Human Resources* 39/2: 451–74.

——2008. "Contingent Valuation Analysis of Willingness to Pay to Reduce Childhood Obesity." *Economics and Human Biology* 6/2: 281–92.

——, S. Markowitz, and J. Tauras. 2004. "Lighting Up and Slimming Down: The Effects of Body Weight and Cigarette Prices on Smoking Initiation." *Journal of Health Economics* 23/2: 293–311.

Chen, S. N., J. F. Shogren, P. F. Orazem, and T. D. Crocker. 2002. "Prices and Health: Identifying the Effects of Nutrition, Exercise, and Medication Choices on Blood Pressure." *American Journal of Agricultural Economics* 84/4: 990–1002.

Chern, W. S., and K. Rickertsen. 2003. *Health, Nutrition and Food Demand*. Cambridge, MA: CABI.

Chou, S.-Y., M. Grossman, and H. Saffer. 2004. "An Economic Analysis of Adult Obesity: Results from the Behavioral Risk Factor Surveillance System." *Journal of Health Economics* 23/3: 565–87.

——, I. Rashad, and M. Grossman. 2008. "Fast-Food Restaurant Advertising on Television and its Influence on Childhood Obesity." *Journal of Law and Economics* 51/4: 599–618.

Chouinard, H., D. E. Davis, J. T. LaFrance, and J. M. Perloff. 2007. "Fat Taxes: Big Money for Small Change." *Forum for Health Economics and Policy* 10/2, art. 2. <http://www.bepress.com/fhep/10/2/2>.

Christakis, N. A., and J. H. Fowler. 2007. "The Spread of Obesity in a Large Social Network over 32 Years." *New England Journal of Medicine* 357/4: 370–9.

Coestier, B., E. Gozlan, and S. Marette. 2005. "On Food Companies Liability for Obesity." *American Journal of Agricultural Economics* 87/1: 1–14.

Cohen-Cole, E., and J. M. Fletcher. 2008. "Is Obesity Contagious? Social Networks vs. Environmental Factors in the Obesity Epidemic." *Journal of Health Economics* 27/5: 1382–7.

————. 2009. "Detecting Implausible Social Network Effects in Acne, Height, and Headaches: Longitudinal Analysis." *British Medical Journal* 337: a2533.

Cole, T. J., M. C. Bellizzi, K. M. Flegal, and W. H. Dietz. 2000. "Establishing a Standard Definition for Child Overweight and Obesity Worldwide: International Survey." *British Medical Journal* 320: 1240.

Cummins, S., and S. Macintyre. 2006. "Food Environments and Obesity: Neighbourhood or Nation?" *International Journal of Epidemiology* 35/1: 100–4.

Cutler, D. M., and E. Glaeser. 2005. "What Explains Differences in Smoking, Drinking, and Other Health Related Behaviors?" *American Economic Review* 95/2: 238–42.

————, and J. M. Shapiro. 2003. "Why Have Americans Become More Obese?" *Journal of Economic Perspectives* 17/3: 93–118.

Darmon, N., E. L. Ferguson, and A. Briend. 2002. "A Cost Constraint Alone Has Adverse Effects on Food Selection and Nutrient Density: An Analysis of Human Diets by Linear Programming." *Journal of Nutrition* 132: 3764–71.

Dixit, A., and V. Norman. 1978. "Advertising and Welfare." *Bell Journal of Economics* 9/1: 1–17.

Drichoutis, A. C., P. Lazaridis, and R. M. Nayga, Jr. 2009. "Consumers' Use of Nutritional Labels: A Review of Research Studies and Issues." *Academy of Marketing Science Review* 9. <http://www.amsreview.org/articles/drichoutis09-2006.pdf>.

Eid, J., H. G. Overman, D. Puga, and M. A. Turner. 2008. "Fat City: Questioning the Relationship between Urban Sprawl and Obesity." *Journal of Urban Economics* 63/2: 385–404.

Emery, C., J. Dinet, A. Lafuma, C. Sermet, B. Khoshnood, and F. Fagnagni. 2007. "Évaluation du coût associé à l'obésité en France." *La Presse Médicale* 36/6: 832–40.

Etilé, F. 2007. "Social Norms, Ideal Body Weight and Food Attitudes." *Health Economics* 16/9: 945–66.

FAO (Food and Agriculture Organization). 2002. *World Agriculture: Towards 2015/2030. Summary Report*. Rome: Food and Agriculture Organization of the United Nations.

Finkelstein, E. A., I. C. Fiebelkorn, and G. J. Wang. 2004. "State-Level Estimate of Annual Medical Expenditures Attributable to Obesity." *Obesity Research* 12/1: 18–24.

Fogel, R. W. 2004. *The Escape from Hunger and Premature Death, 1700–2100: Europe, America, and the Third World*. Cambridge: Cambridge University Press.

Fowler, J. H., and N. A. Christakis. 2008. "Estimating Peer Effects on Health in Social Networks: A Response to Cohen-Cole and Fletcher; and Trogdon, Nonnemaker, and Pais." *Journal of Health Economics* 27/5: 1400–5.

Grigg, D. 1995. "The Nutritional Transition in Western Europe." *Journal of Historical Geography* 21/3: 247–61.

Grossman, M. 1972. "On the Concept of Health Capital and the Demand for Health." *Journal of Political Economy* 80/2: 223–55.

—— 2000. "The Human Capital Model." In A. J. Culyer and J. P. Newhouse, eds, *Handbook of Health Economics*, edn 1, vol. 1. London: Elsevier.

—— and I. Rashad. 2004. "The Economics of Obesity." *Public Interest* 156: 104–12.

Gruber, J., and M. Frakes. 2006. "Does Falling Smoking Lead to Rising Obesity?" *Journal of Health Economics* 25/2: 183–97.

Grün, F., and B. Blumberg. 2006. "Environmental Obesogens: Organotins and Endocrine Disruption via Nuclear Receptor Signaling." *Endocrinology* 147/6: 50–5.

Hastings, G., M. Stead, L. McDermott, A. Forsyth, A. M. MacKintosh, M. Rayner, C. Godfrey, M. Caraher, and K. Angus. 2003. *Review of Research on the Effects of Food Promotion to Children: Final Report to the UK Food Standard Agency*. Strathclyde: Centre for Social Marketing, University of Strathclyde.

Herman, C. P., and J. Polivy. 2003. "Dieting as an Exercise in Behavioral Economics." In G. Loewenstein, D. Read, and R. F. Baumeister, eds, *Time and Decision*. New York: Russell Sage Foundation.

Hirshleifer, J., and J. G. Riley. 1979. "The Analytics of Uncertainty and Information." *Journal of Economic Literature* 17/4: 1375–1421.

Huang, K. S. 1996. "Nutrient Elasticities in a Complete Food Demand System." *American Journal of Agricultural Economics* 78/1: 21–9.

Ippolito, P. M., and A. D. Mathios. 1990. "Information, Advertising and Health Choices: A Study of the Cereal Market." *RAND Journal of Economics* 21/3: 459–80.

—— and J. K. Pappalardo. 2002. *Advertising, Nutrition and Health: Evidence from Food and Advertising 1977–1997*. Staff Report. Washington, DC: Federal Trade Commission Bureau of Economics.

Irigaray, P., J. A. Newby, S. Lacomme, and D. Belpomme. 2007. "Overweight/Obesity and Cancer Genesis: More than a Biological Link." *Biomedicine and Pharmacotherapy* 61/10: 665–78.

Jacobson, M. F., and K. Brownell. 2000. "Small Taxes on Soft Drinks and Snack Foods to Promote Health." *American Journal of Public Health* 90/6: 854–7.

Kan, K., and W.-D. Tsai. 2004. "Obesity and Risk Knowledge in Taiwan: A Quantile Regression Analysis." *Journal of Health Economics* 23/5: 907–34.

—— and S. T. Yen. 2003. "A Sample Selection Model with Endogenous Health Knowledge: Egg Consumption in the United States." In W. S. Chern and K. Rickertsen, eds, *Health, Nutrition and Food Demand*. Cambridge, MA: CABI.

Kiesel, K., and S. B. Villas-Boas. Forthcoming. "Can Information Costs Affect Consumer Choice? Nutritional Labels in a Supermarket Experiment." *International Journal of Industrial Organization*.

Komlos, J., and M. Baur. 2004. "From the Tallest to (One of) the Fattest: The Enigmatic Fate of the American Population in the 20th Century." *Economics and Human Biology* 2/1: 57–74.

Kuchler, F., A. Tegene, and J. M. Harris. 2005. "Taxing Snack Foods: Manipulating Diet Quality or Financing Information Programs?" *Review of Agricultural Economics* 27/1: 4–20.

Kyrou, I., G. P. Chrousos, and C. Tsigos. 2006. "Stress, Visceral Obesity, and Metabolic Complications." *Annals of the New York Academy of Sciences* 1083, Special Issue: *Stress, Obesity and Metabolic Syndrome*, 77–110.

Laibson, D. 1997. "Golden Egg and Hyperbolic Discounting." *Quarterly Journal of Economics* 112/2: 443–77.

—— 2001. "A Cue-Theory of Consumption." *Quarterly Journal of Economics* 116/1: 81–119.

Lakdawalla, D., and T. Philipson. 2002. *The Growth of Obesity and Technological Change: A Theoretical and Empirical Examination.* NBER Working Paper No. 8946. Cambridge, MA: National Bureau of Economic Research.

Leicester, A., and F. Windmeijer. 2004. *The "Fat Tax": Economic Incentives to Reduce Obesity.* Briefing Note No. 49. London: Institute for Fiscal Studies.

Levy, A. 2002. "Rational Eating: Can it Lead to Overweightness or Underweightness?" *Journal of Health Economics* 21/5: 887–99.

Lin, B.-H., J. Guthrie, and E. Frazão. 1999. "Nutrient Contribution of Food Away From Home." In E. Frazão, ed., *America's Eating Habits: Changes and Consequences.* Agriculture Information Bulletin No. 750. Washington, DC: Economic Research Service, US Department of Agriculture.

Lobstein, T., and M.-L. Frelut. 2003. "Prevalence of Overweight among Children in Europe." *Obesity Reviews* 4/4: 195–200.

Lopez, A. D., C. D. Mathers, M. Ezzati, D. T. Jamison, and C. J. L. Murray. 2006. *Global Burden of Disease and Risk Factors.* Washington, DC: World Bank; Oxford: Oxford University Press.

Lopez, R. 2004. "Urban Sprawl and Risk for Being Overweight or Obese." *American Journal of Public Health* 94/9: 1574–9.

Loureiro, M. L., and R. M. Nayga, Jr. 2005. "International Dimensions of Obesity and Overweight Related Problems: An Economics Perspective." *American Journal of Agricultural Economics* 87/5: 1147–53.

————. 2006. "Obesity, Weight Loss and Physician's Advice." *Social Science and Medicine* 62/10: 2458–2568.

McCormick, B., and I. Stone. 2007. "Economic Costs of Obesity and the Case for Government Intervention." *Obesity Reviews* 8, suppl. 1: 161–4.

MacInnis, B., and G. Rausser. 2005. "Does Food Processing Contribute to Childhood Obesity Disparities?" *American Journal of Agricultural Economics* 87/5: 1154–8.

Marmot, M. G. 2004. *The Status Syndrome: How Social Standing Affects Our Health and Longevity.* London: Bloomsbury.

Marshall, T. 2000. "Exploring a Fiscal Food Policy: The Case of Diet and Ischaemic Heart Disease." *British Medical Journal* 320: 301–5.

Mathios, A. D. 2000. "The Impact of Mandatory Disclosure Laws on Product Choices: An Analysis of the Salad Dressing Market." *Journal of Law and Economics* 43/2: 651–77.

Matsushita, Y., N. Yoshiike, F. Kaneda, K. Yoshita, and H. Takimoto. 2004. "Trends in Childhood Obesity in Japan over the Last 25 Years from the National Nutrition Survey." *Obesity* 12/2: 205–14. http://www.nature.com/oby/journal/v12/n2/full/oby200427a.html - affi

Mazzocchi, M., W. B. Traill, and J. F. Shogren. 2009. *Fat Economics.* Oxford: Oxford University Press.

Miljkovic, D., W. Nganje, and H. de Chastenet. 2008. "Economic Factors Affecting the Increase in Obesity in the United States: Differential Response to Price." *Food Policy* 33/1: 48–60.

Morris, S. 2006. "Body Mass Index and Occupational Attainment." *Journal of Health Economics* 25/2: 347–64.

—— 2007. "The Impact of Obesity on Employment." *Labour Economics* 14/3: 413–33.

Nordström, J., and L. Thunström. 2009. "The Impact of Tax Reforms Designed to Encourage Healthier Grain Consumption." *Journal of Health Economics* 28/3: 622–34.

Norton, E. C., and E. Han. 2008. "Genetic Information, Obesity and Labor Market Outcomes." *Health Economics* 17/9: 1089–1104.

O'Donoghue, T., and M. Rabin. 2003. "Studying Optimal Paternalism, Illustrated by a Model of Sin Taxes." *American Economic Review* 93/2: 186–91.

————. 2005. "Optimal Tax for Sin Goods." *Swedish Economic Policy Review* 12: 7–39.

Oswald, A., and N. Powdthavee. 2007. "Obesity, Unhappiness, and *The Challenge of Affluence*: Theory and Evidence." *Economic Journal* 117/521: F441–F454.

Park, J., and G. C. Davis. 2001. "The Theory and Econometrics of Health Information in Cross-Sectional Nutrient Demand Analysis." *American Journal of Agricultural Economics* 83/4: 840–51.

Philipson, T. 2001. "The World-Wide Growth in Obesity: An Economic Research Agenda." *Health Economics* 10/1: 1–7.

Powell, L. M., M. C. Auld, F. J. Chaloupka, L. D. Johnston, and P. O'Malley. 2007. "Access to Fast Food and Food Prices: The Relationship with Fruit and Vegetable Consumption and Overweight Status among Adolescents." In K. Bolin and J. Cawley, eds, *Advances in Health Economics and Health Services Research*, 17: *The Economics of Obesity*. London: Elsevier.

Richards, T. J., and P. M. Patterson. 2006. "Native American Obesity: An Economic Model of the 'Thrifty Gene' Theory." *American Journal of Agricultural Economics* 88/3: 542–60.

Robertson, A., E. Brunner, and A. Sheiham. 2004. "Food Is a Political Issue." In M. Marmot and R. Wilkinson, eds, *Social Determinants of Health*. Oxford: Oxford University Press.

Roe, B., A. S. Levy, and B. M. Derby. 1999. "The Impact of Health Claims on Consumer Search and Product Evaluation Outcomes: Results from FDA Experimental Data." *Journal of Public Policy and Marketing* 18/1: 89–105.

Roosen, J., S. Marette, S. Blanchemanche, and P. Verger. 2009. "Does Health Information Matter for Modifying Consumption? A Field Experiment Measuring the Impact of Risk Information on Fish Consumption." *Review of Agricultural Economics* 31/1: 2–20.

Rosin, O. 2008. "The Economic Causes of Obesity: A Survey." *Journal of Economic Surveys* 22/4: 617–47.

Scharff, R. L. 2009. "Obesity and Hyperbolic Discounting: Evidence and Implications." *Journal of Consumer Policy* 32/1: 3–21.

Schmidhuber, J. 2004. "The Growing Global Obesity Problem: Some Policy Options to Address It." *electronic Journal of Agricultural and Development Economics* 1/2: 272–90. <ftp://ftp.fao.org/docrep/fao/007/ae228e/ae228e00.pdf>.

Scholder, S. von H. K., C. Propper, D. A. Lawlor, F. Windmeijer, and G. Davey Smith. 2010. *Genetic Markers as Instrumental Variables: An Application to Child Fat Mass and Academic Achievement.* Imperial College Business School Working Paper. <http://hdl.handle.net/10044/1/5772>.

Scholderer, J., and K. G. Grunert. 2005. "Consumers, Food and Convenience: The Long Way from Resource Constraints to Actual Consumption Patterns." *Journal of Economic Psychology* 26/1: 105–28.

Schroeter, C., J. Lusk, and W. Tyner. 2008. "Determining the Impact of Food Price and Income Changes on Body Weight." *Journal of Health Economics* 27/1: 45–68.

Smed, S., J. D. Jensen, and S. Denver. 2007. "Socio-economic Characteristics and the Effect of Taxation as a Health Policy Instrument." *Food Policy* 32/5–6: 624–39.

Smith, P. K., B. Bogin, and D. Bishai. 2005. "Are Time Preference and Body Mass Index Associated? Evidence from the National Longitudinal Survey of Youth." *Economics and Human Biology* 3/2: 259–70.

Smith, T. G. 2004. "The McDonald's Equilibrium: Advertising, Empty Calories, and the Endogenous Determination of Dietary Preferences." *Social Choice and Welfare* 23/3: 383–413.

Strnad, J. 2005. "Conceptualizing the 'Fat Tax': The Role of Food Taxes in Developed Economies." *Southern California Law Review* 78: 1221–1326.

Strychar, I. 2006. "Diet in the Management of Weight Loss." *CMAJ* 174/1: 56–63.

Stunkard, A. J., J. R. Harris, N. L. Pederson, and G. E. McClearn. 1990. "The Body Mass Index of Twins Who Have Been Reared Apart." *New England Journal of Medicine* 322/21: 1483–7.

Sturm, R., and A. Datar. 2005. "Body Mass Index in Elementary School Children, Metropolitan Area Food Prices and Food Outlet Density." *Public Health* 119/12: 1059–68.

Sunder, M. 2005. "Toward Generation XL: Anthropometrics of Longevity in Late 20th-Century United States." *Economics and Human Biology* 3/2: 271–95.

Suranovic, S. M., and R. S. Goldfarb. 2007. "A Behavioral Model of Cyclical Dieting." In K. Bolin and J. Cawley, eds, *Advances in Health Economics and Health Services Research*, 17: *The Economics of Obesity*. London: Elsevier.

Teisl, M. F., N. E. Bockstael, and A. Levy. 2001. "Measuring the Welfare Effects of Nutrition Information." *American Journal of Agricultural Economics* 83/1: 133–49.

Variyam, J. N. 2008. "Do Nutrition Labels Improve Dietary Outcomes?" *Health Economics* 17/6: 695–708.

——, J. Blaylock, B.-H. Lin, K. Ralston, and D. Smallwood. 1999. "Mother's Nutrition Knowledge and Children's Dietary Intakes." *American Journal of Agricultural Economics* 81/2: 373–84.

—— ——, and D. Smallwood. 1996. "A Probit Latent Variable Model of Nutrition Information and Dietary Fiber Intake." *American Journal of Agricultural Economics* 78: 628–39.

Volkow, N. D., and R. A. Wise. 2005. "How Can Drug Addiction Help Us Understand Obesity." *Nature Neuroscience* 8/5: 555–60.

Wansink, B., D. R. Just, and C. R. Payne. 2009. "Mindless Eating and Healthy Heuristics for the Irrational." *American Economic Review* 99/2: 165–9.

White, M. 2007. "Food Access and Obesity." *Obesity Reviews* 8, suppl. 1: 99–107.

WHO (World Health Organization). 2003. *Diet, Nutrition and the Prevention of Chronic Diseases*. Report of a WHO Consultation: WHO Technical Reports Series No. 916. Geneva: World Health Organization.

Wild, S., G. Roglic, A. Green, R. Sicree, and H. King. 2004. "Global Prevalence of Diabetes." *Diabetes Care* 27/5: 1047–53.

Yen, S. T., B.-H. Lin, and D. M. Smallwood. 2003. "Quasi- and Simulated-Likelihood Approaches to Censored Demand Systems: Food Consumption by Food Stamp Recipients in the United States." *American Journal of Agricultural Economics* 85/2: 458–78.

CHAPTER 30

··

DEMOGRAPHICS AND FOOD CONSUMPTION: EMPIRICAL EVIDENCE

··

LUIS MIGUEL ALBISU, AZUCENA GRACIA, AND ANA ISABEL SANJUÁN

1 INTRODUCTION

··

Demography is the scientific and statistical study of populations. Demographic statistics characterizing human populations can also be associated with social and economic features besides the most common variables, which are currently considered on food consumption surveys. Demographics include all personal defining characteristics such as age, gender, income, education, race/ethnicity, household size and composition, geographical distribution of population, and living place. In this chapter all of them are considered, although sometimes the terms sociodemographics and socioeconomics are also used to reproduce terms used in the original works.

Pioneer empirical studies on food consumption were inspired by neoclassical consumer demand theory, and made use of aggregated time-series data to estimate the effect of price and income on food demand. However, as cross-section data became available (such as consumer expenditure surveys), food demand analysis was extended to include the impact of household characteristics (demographics) as additional explanatory factors of food consumption.

The inclusion of household characteristics on traditional food demand has been done in different ways (e.g., equivalence scales) (Deaton and Muellbauer 1980). However, these approaches explain only a small proportion of the actual heterogeneity in food consumption patterns observed in reality. Moreover, as food products became more differentiated, economic variables were no longer enough to explain consumers' choices fully and new theories and methods needed to be adopted (Unnevehr et al.

2010). In particular, the random preferences approach introduced by McFadden (1974) has been widely used. In this approach, assumptions about aggregation and regarding representative consumers or homogeneous preferences are relaxed and consumer responses to prices and non-price characteristics can be incorporated in the same model (Adamowicz and Swait, Chapter 5 in this volume). Moreover, the methods used to analyze food consumption have moved from the traditional estimation of demand systems to new procedures such as experimental methods (choice experiment, auctions) and scanner data analysis. The first chapters of the book revise an array of different models and approaches available to analyze food consumption.

This chapter reviews only those empirical works that report results on the influence of sociodemographic factors on food consumption, using any of the models and methods mentioned in the first chapters of the book, and published since 2000. The chapter does not intend to present an exhaustive review of the literature, but at least highlight those recent papers that can be helpful to the interested reader as a base to explore further aspects of demographics and food consumption. Reviewed empirical studies analyze the influence of demographics on food consumption following either of the two following approaches: the first one includes the household (or individual) sociodemographic characteristics as explanatory variables in a model aiming at explaining food consumption; and the second approach consists of identifying different consumer segments in terms of preferences or food consumption patterns, and then characterizes the demographic profile of each segment. Likewise, some of the papers reviewed combine both approaches.

We limit our explanations of the different reviewed papers to the issue of this chapter, demographics and food consumption, leaving the other aspects of the papers to be explained in the corresponding specific chapters of this book.

The next section presents the main demographic trends in developed countries. The following section gathers empirical evidence about the effect of demographic factors on food consumers' preferences for different food attributes, classified for pedagogical purposes in the following categories: ethics (organics, fair trade, and animal welfare), food safety and health (food safety, healthy diets, genetic modification, and irradiation), local and typical produce, ethnicity, and convenience. Finally, there is a section with some concluding remarks and comments about emerging trends for future research.

2   DEMOGRAPHIC TRENDS

While population growth may explain an increase in the demand for food in global quantitative terms, it is the structure of this population that can exert a greater influence on the patterns and composition of food demand. Developed countries are facing major changes in their population structures, mainly related to low fertility rates, long life expectancy, and large immigration flows, that are depicting an aging and multicultural society. Besides, socioeconomic changes such as the increase in average disposable income, education, and the participation of women in the workforce are contributing significantly to the demand for food diversity and value-added food products that incorporate some desirable quality attributes and convenience.

Population in developed countries is growing at a slow pace, and in some countries natural change (difference between births and deaths) has already become negative (European Commission 2009). The postponement of the decision of childbearing has led to fertility rates that demographers consider to be under the generation replacement threshold. Under these circumstances, net migration has become the main component of demographic growth. Improvements in income, education, and advances in medicine, on the other hand, have contributed significantly to elongate life expectancy. Finally, migration flows have added to the already existing patchwork of national minorities, enlarging the ethnic and cultural diversity. In the European Union, first-generation immigrants account for 7 percent of the total population (European Commission 2009), and ethnic minorities, which currently account for one third of the US population, are expected to grow to 54 percent by 2050 (US Census Bureau 2011).

The aging of population has implications on the type and quantity of food demanded and also where food is consumed. Physical constraints but also health concerns explain that older consumers tend to reduce energy intake, consuming smaller quantities than younger people and by replacing fats by fruits and vegetables. On the other hand, several studies show a tendency among older consumers to reject innovations in food and incorporate new items in their diet, as well as to eat less away from home. Besides, the average disposable income of elderly people is lower than in middle age, and the combined effect of income and age may become an important limitation on pursuing specific high-value-added food consumption patterns. Nevertheless, in order to forecast food demand in relation to age it is important to discern which influences are lifecycle and which are cohort effects. In other words, will current younger generations adopt the food demand patterns of current older generations when they achieve that age or, on the contrary, will keep their own habits when they get older? These issues have been examined by, among others, Harris and Blisard (2001), Wendt and Kinsey (2007), and Stewart and Blisard (2008) in the United States, and Mori and Clason (2004) in Japan. Patterns of drinks consumption in relation to lifecycle and cohort effects have also been investigated by Gustavsen and Rickertsen (2009) in Norway and Aristei, Perali, and Pieroni (2008) in Italy.

Ethnic diversity has brought about a blend of new cuisines, in which familiar and unfamiliar ingredients are mixed in a particular way, providing final dishes with ethnic identity that have crossed the cultural boundaries to reach mainstream consumers searching for new flavors and culinary experiences. Besides, ethnic identification has become an important sociodemographic variable aimed at explaining food dietary patterns and purchasing habits.

Household structure is also changing. The number of childless and single-person households is increasing, while large families are declining. More than a quarter of the households in the United States and the European Union are now composed of a single person, and an important share of them is headed by pensioners; in about half of the households in the United States, there are no children, while in one-fifth there is only one child (European Commission 2009; US Census Bureau 2011). These changes have favored eating out more, and the development of smaller food portions and individual ready meals. Furthermore, in the study conducted by Kalwij and Salverda (2007) across three decades in the Netherlands, it is found that moving away from the traditional one-earner family with children to more diverse household composition (single-person households; two-earner households; single parents; etc.) accounted for about one-third of the decrease in the household budget share of food and beverages.

The participation of women in the workforce has constituted a significant social and economic change in developed countries, and it is still expected to grow from the current 55 percent to 65 percent in 2025 (European Commission 2009). More income flowing into the household and less time available has encouraged the demand for convenience in purchasing, preparing, and eating food. Despite this, women are still the main meal planners in the household, and, therefore, their attitudes and behavior affect the food consumption of the whole family.

Although in the last decades there has been a substantial improvement in the general level of education attained by citizens of the OECD countries, the proportion of the adult population with tertiary education has started to decline in the European Union, while figures for the United States and Canada remain the highest (around 37 percent) (European Commission 2009). To the extent that education may promote awareness of new products, as well as health and ethical implications of food choice, a decline in education could lead to an inflection point in the new food trends. The relation between income and food demand is synthesized in Engle's Law. As average income grows, the budget share on food gets smaller, but also a diversification from staples to higher-value-added food is forecast. Developed societies have experienced significant increases in average disposable income, although this masks a skewed distribution.

3   EMPIRICAL EVIDENCE ON THE EFFECT OF DEMOGRAPHICS ON FOOD CONSUMPTION

The number of studies conducted from the year 2000 that have analyzed the effect of sociodemographic factors using traditional food demand systems has been small. Moro and Sckokai (2000) emphasized that changes in the sociodemographic structure of the population needed to be taken into account in order to avoid significant biases in longitudinal studies. Furthermore, the authors found different food expenditure shares and income elasticities across different income and age groups. Thus, the higher the income and the older the household members, the lower the proportion of food expenditures and the income elasticity, with the exception of the highest-income group, where income elasticity is higher.

Angulo and Gil (2006) found that the elasticities of the probability of participation in meat demand were positive with respect to the size of the household for all meat products in Spain, when nutrient contents were taken into consideration. Elasticities of family composition and education were different depending on the meat. Household meat expenditure was analyzed by Newman, Henchion, and Matthews (2001) in Ireland and results showed that households with specific characteristics—namely, young, with all adults employed, in an urban location, and having a higher professional social status—had an overall negative effect on meat expenditure. Age, education, and household composition were significant variables to explain demand for selected food nutrients in Greece but there were diverse responses (Fousekis and Lazaridis 2005).

However, much of the recent literature on food consumption has focused on the analysis of consumer preferences. An array of attributes are examined in the next sections using different and alternative methods to the more traditional food demand systems.

3.1   Ethics

Ethical issues are gaining relevance in the explanation of consumers' food choices. Beyond the nutritional aspect of food, consumers get indirect satisfaction from the benefit to society or the environment that derive from their decisions. This change of attitude has favored increasing growth rates in the market for organic and fair trade food products, and it has promoted an increasing demand for animal-welfare-enhancing practices. In this respect, Chapter 35 in this volume, by Loureiro, provides an exhaustive review of papers dealing with ethical issues and food demand.

3.1.1 Organics

The market for organic food has grown significantly in recent years, especially in the United States and central and northern countries in the European Union, to satisfy an increasing demand for healthy, tasty, and nutritious food that complies with higher environmental care standards. The economic literature highlights the linkage between health, environmental concerns (Durham 2007; Chen 2007), and personal values and emotions (Verhoef 2005) and consumers' willingness to buy and pay a premium for organic food. See Teisl, Chapter 34 in this volume, for further reading on the demand for organic food.

Empirical studies carried out in the 1990s, mainly based on stated preferences and purchase intentions, do not offer a unique sociodemographic profile of organic consumers (Dettmann 2008; Wier et al. 2008, provide exhaustive reviews). The results seem to be specific to the product(s) considered, the country where the study was conducted, and the methodology applied, and generalizations are difficult to draw. The demographic characteristics that are more prevalent as descriptors of the organic consumer in the European Union are to be female, young, to live in a major city, and to enjoy a higher education and income (Torjusen et al. 2004). Some of these characteristics, such as higher income and education, and younger age, are also supported by American studies (Loureiro and Hine 2002). Interestingly, though, the influence of such characteristics, in particular income, may be a result of better access to the organic distribution channels in more affluent neighborhoods (Zepeda and Li 2007). This point is also raised in studies conducted in the United States, where African Americans are found to have a lesser propensity to purchase organic (Dettmann 2008). The presence of young children has an ambiguous impact. On the one hand, when a positive effect is found, this is usually ascribed to a greater concern about health (Durham 2007), while when negative (Loureiro and Hine 2002), a possible association with less disposable income is claimed.

Several studies stress that different variables may explain the decision to enter the market or willingness to purchase, and the intensity of or commitment to that decision, measured either by means of the premium that the consumer is willing to pay, the frequency of consumption, or the percentage of the food budget devoted to organic food. Nevertheless, there is no consensus on which are the main sociodemographic determinants at each stage. For instance, younger age (Grannis and Thilmany 2002; Durham 2007; Zepeda and Li 2007), having young children, or a lower level of education (Zepeda and Li 2007) are found to affect negatively the decision to enter the market, while income becomes a more important restriction in the intensity of the commitment to organic food (Grannis and Thilmany 2002). Alternative results for the influence of education and having children are reported by Durham (2007).

More recent empirical studies employ actual consumers' purchase information and provide a more precise picture of actual behavior. Wier et al. (2008) found significant associations between an array of sociodemographics and the relative expenditure weight of organic produce in the food basket in mature markets such as Denmark and the United Kingdom. Thus, the budget devoted to organic food is larger in households with higher income and education, and higher social status, as well as in those located in urban areas. The presence of children reduces the propensity to buy organic, unless they are under 14 years old and the number of children is less than two. Households where the main shopper is of middle age are the most intensive organic buyers. In Denmark, the propensity to buy organic continues to increase with older age, while there is a reversion in the United Kingdom. However, no reference to the influence of gender of the main shopper is provided. An interesting point raised by the authors is a change in the pattern of organic purchases over the three years of the study (2001–3). Some households moved to higher levels of organic consumption, but in other households the opposite occurred. It is also claimed that, in the early stages of the development of the organic market, younger consumers are more receptive, while older people adopt tendencies already consolidated. Dettmann (2008) also provided support for the positive influence of education and income on the propensity to buy organic vegetables in the United States, with a subtle difference: while income positively affects the probability of entering the organic market, consumers with more income spend a smaller proportion of their budget, while consumers with higher education consistently devote a bigger share of their budget to purchase organic vegetables.

An interesting avenue of research investigates the trade-off between organic production methods and cosmetic damage (Yue, Alfnes, and Jensen 2009; Thompson and Kidwell 1998). Yue et al. (2009) found that higher-income consumers not only were willing to pay more for organic fresh apples, but also showed more tolerance for surface imperfections. Females, on the other hand, were less tolerant regarding blemishes. The authors also contribute to the overwhelming evidence on environmental concerns as more determinant in willingness to pay for organic food than sociodemographic variables.

Although most studies deal with fresh produce, where the organic attribute is either present or not, recent empirical investigation extends to multi-ingredient processed food, and certification schemes on gradations of organic content. Batte et al. (2007) conclude that there is a market for intermediate contents, and in particular, there is a segment composed of consumers with children, females, older people, and with higher personal income who are willing to pay more across categories.

In general, sociodemographic variables explain marginally and not always in a consistent way consumers' choice of organic food, and this applies to mature markets, such as the United States and northern EU countries in 2000s, but also to southern European countries (e.g., Krystallis and Chryssochoidis 2005; Gracia and de Magistris 2008).

3.1.2 Fair Trade

Fair trade (FT) labels guarantee that imported food products from developing countries satisfy economic, social, and environmental requirements in the production process. FT aims at improving the socioeconomic development of producing communities by providing a fair price for their products and facilitating their access to developed markets.

The growth of FT sales has stimulated research on consumers' motivations to buy FT products (De Pelsmacker, Driesen, and Rayp 2005; Ferran and Grunert 2005), on personal values that influence consumers' FT choices (De Pelsmacker et al. 2006; Doran 2009), and on willingness to pay (WTP) for FT labels. Although there are some papers focusing on the profile of the ethical consumer in general, there is still a dearth of equivalent research in the narrower context of FT and food products, in particular. When food is considered, coffee is usually chosen because of its relevance in the FT portfolio of merchandise. Most of the empirical literature agrees on the fact that WTP for the FT label is positively related to education and inversely related to age (De Pelsmacker, Driesen, and Rayp 2005; Loureiro and Lotade 2005), while being a woman and enjoying higher income levels are also reported as positive influences (Loureiro and Lotade 2005). However, there are exceptions. Arnot, Boxall, and Cash (2006) conducted a revealed preference experiment in order to explain consumers' choice of FT coffee, and found that gender did not exert any influence. Likewise, Doran (2009) did not find any significant association between an array of sociodemographic variables (gender, age, race, marital status, and education) and the probability of being a regular, intermittent, or non-consumer of FT products (mostly food but also crafted goods).

Becchetti and Rosati (2007) distinguished between direct and indirect effects of income and age on the demand for FT products (food and crafts): consumers with higher income and of older age spent more on FT products. However, income and age also exerted a negative influence through reduced awareness of criteria endorsed by the FT movement (fair and stable price, pre-financing schemes for producers, care for working and environmental conditions, long-run relationships with producers, informational transparency). In the authors' view the age effect was a cohort effect provided that the knowledge of FT was more widespread among the young and that FT itself was a recent phenomenon. Therefore, the authors foresee that when the younger generation gets older and wealthier, the demand for FT will expand. Becchetti and Huybrechts (2007) considered that different retail outlets serve a distinct profile of FT consumers. Thus, consumers purchasing FT products at specific FT outlets ("world shops" run by alternative trading organizations) were more educated and aware of pernicious working and social conditions in developing countries, and were mainly moved by ethical considerations.

3.1.3 *Animal Welfare*

Consumers show an increasing interest on the production process of food, and in particular, how animals are treated in the farm, transportation, and slaughter stages. This concern may respond to an altruistic sentiment for the well-being of animals, or an ethical commitment to the handling of animals in a humane way, but also to the perceived link between animal welfare and food safety and quality. These concerns have prompted legislative initiatives to mitigate and/or eliminate some of the unfriendly practices in the United States and the European Union.

From a research point of view, interest has focused on the viability of such initiatives, by studying the compatibility between the cost induced by such adjustments and the benefits generated to consumers. For this purpose, several studies have investigated consumers' WTP for animal-welfare-enhancing practices. The precision on the definition of such animal welfare measures varies across papers.

Only a few papers, however, report any influence of sociodemographics on preferences with respect to compliance with animal welfare issues. Urban and younger consumers are found to be more concerned (Verbeke and Viane 2000; Bernués, Olaizola, and Corcoran 2003). However, when investigation on the influence of habitat and age is conducted with respect to WTP, no significant effect is found (Lagerkvist, Carlsson, and Viske 2006).

Different studies report a distinct pattern of influence of gender on WTP. Lagerkvist, Carlsson, and Viske (2006) found that women get less utility from animal-welfare-enhancing measures in indoor pig production, such as providing pigs with more straw and allowing them to go outdoors, as well as avoiding long periods of restraint of sows to avoid their injuring the piglets. Results for the same country (Sweden) by Liljenstolpe (2008) also indicated that men got higher utility from the use of animal welfare practices in pig production, including, among others, rearing (stock size, housing systems, availability of straw, the use of anesthesia in castration) and transportation considerations (the use of mobile abattoirs, and limits on time and distance). In a more general setting, Verbeke and Viane (2000) also reported that males assigned more importance to animal-friendly production systems. In contrast, in the pan-European study conducted by Nocella, Hubbard, and Scarpa (2010), females manifested higher WTP for certification on compliance with an array of animal well-being practices related to animal handling during rearing and transport (provision of sufficient space and a balanced diet, use of qualified staff, specially equipped vehicles). Nevertheless, this result is confined to the Italian sample.

Support for a positive impact of income on WTP for animal-welfare-enhancing measures was found by Bennet and Blaney (2003) in the particular case of the elimination of keeping laying hens in battery cages; and Nocella, Hubbard, and Scarpa (2010) for a variety of relief practices. In contrast, Liljenstolpe (2008) found an inverse relationship.

Although additional variables, such as household size and composition, and education, have been used in the empirical literature to gain insight into possible sociodemographic drivers of consumers' preferences for animal welfare practices, no significant influences have been detected. Preference heterogeneity is pointed out by some authors, but sociodemographic variables fail to explain a significant part of this heterogeneity.

Nevertheless, the lack of significance and unanimity of results may be related more to the specificity of the problem dealt, which evokes different reactions among different sociodemographic segments of the population, than to a general trend in the direction of influence of each descriptor. In this sense, Carlsson, Frykblom, and Lagerkvist (2005) found that WTP for identical animal welfare attributes varied across products, revealing that consumers' preferences are animal-specific.

3.2 Food Safety and Health

Consumers are increasingly demanding food products that ensure that their health is not damaged or, on the contrary, can be improved, leading to a demand for safer and healthier food products. Thus, several empirical papers can be found on the impact of sociodemographics on consumers' demand for these two attributes. However, a larger number of papers have dealt with the analysis of consumers' aversion to some product characteristics perceived to be less or more safe, genetic modification, and irradiation.

3.2.1 *Food Safety*

The number of papers analyzing the demand for food products with enhanced food safety has been small, and they have focused on assessing WTP for food products with improved food safety (McCluskey et al. 2005; Tonsor et al. 2007). Moreover, effects of consumers' sociodemographic characteristics on these WTP were rather limited, but, interestingly, females and older people were more willing to pay for food safety improvements.

A few papers have also analyzed the issue of traceability, assessing willingness to pay for it, but only Dickinson and von Bailey (2002) and Lichtenberg, Heidecke, and Becker (2008) found that some sociodemographic characteristics influence WTP for traceability. In particular, less-educated people were willing to pay the highest premium for traceability and food safety for ham. Moreover, male consumers, consumers aged 46–55, retired people, consumers with a monthly income of $2,600–4,500, and families with two children were willing to pay a price premium for traceability in pork and turkey.

3.2.2 *Healthy Diet*

Two main changes in consumers' food choices show an increasing search for healthier diets; first, in the trend among consumers to shift from unhealthy to healthy diets, and second, in the increasing demand for food products with some specific enhanced nutritional properties (e.g., functional foods). The first consumers' trend has not been analyzed in depth, mainly because of a lack of the necessary information. Kim, Nayga, and Capps (2000, 2001) and Variyam (2008), using the same databases (the US Continuing Survey of Food Intakes for Individuals and the accompanying Diet and Health Knowledge Survey), attempted to analyze the factors affecting healthy food choices.

Kim, Nayga, and Capps (2000) examined the impact of different consumers' characteristics on selected nutrient intakes. They found that age and gender affected the intake of calories from total fat and cholesterol, indicating that older people and males tried to follow healthier diets. On the other hand, black people consumed more calories from total fat and cholesterol, following less healthy diets. The higher the education level, the lower the intake of saturated fat and cholesterol and the higher the intake of fiber. Employed people consumed more calories from total fat and sodium, and consumers living in central cities consumed fewer calories from total fat and more fiber.

Kim, Nayga, and Capps (2001) analyzed the impact of different factors on healthier food choices, using the concept of diet quality as measured by the Healthy Eating Index (HEI). They found that the income and age of consumers positively influenced the HEI, indicating an improvement in the overall quality of consumer diets. Moreover, male consumers, people with at least some college education, living in central cities, and Africans Americans had a higher-quality diet (HEI).

Variyam (2008) found that gender and income were not statistically significant to explain dietary outcomes, while age and education were. Older consumers tended to reduce the intake of added sugar, calcium, iron, and vitamin C, and increased the intake of fiber and protein. Consumers with a higher education tended to reduce the intake of total fat and cholesterol.

The empirical papers that have analyzed the intention to purchase functional foods with different nutritional and health properties showed that age and gender were the key sociodemographic characteristics (Bhaskaran and Hardley 2002; Verbeke 2006; Lyly et al. 2007; Henson, Masakure, and Cranfield 2008; Ares, Giménez, and Gámbaro 2009). They found that older consumers and women were more willing to purchase functional foods. Finally, only Teratanavat and Hooker (2006) suggested that women, younger, more educated, and higher-income consumers were more willing to pay for functional benefits.

3.2.3 *Genetic Modification*

Several papers have studied WTP to avoid GM content or the discount consumers needed to accept purchasing genetic modified (GM) food. The demographic factors that mainly affect consumers' WTP are age, education, and income, although gender and the presence of children in the household have been found significant in some cases. Hu, Hünnemeyer, et al. (2004) indicated that younger respondents are less likely to purchase GM food. According to Bernard, Zhang, and Gifford (2006), older people are more willing to pay for non-GM food and Hu, Adamovicz, and Veeman (2006) indicated that the discount needed to purchase GM food increases with age. McCluskey et al. (2003) stated that the discount needed to purchase GM food increases with higher education. In accordance with previous research findings, Kaneko and Chern (2005) and Bernard, Zhang, and Gifford (2006) found, respectively, that people with college education expressed higher WTP to avoid GM food and had a higher WTP for conventional and non-GM food. Loureiro and Hine (2002) found that upper-class households expressed higher WTP for genetically modified organisms-free food products. In the same way, Hu, Adamovicz, and Veeman (2006) also indicated that higher family incomes increase utility for consumers when GM ingredients are not present in bread. McCluskey et al. (2003) and Rousu et al. (2007) suggested that higher income increases the discount needed to purchase GM food. Finally, females and households with children under 17 expressed higher WTP to avoid GM food (Hu, Veeman, et al. 2006; Kaneko and Chern 2005).

3.2.4 *Irradiation*

Finally, some papers have assessed WTP for irradiated food products. They found that gender was the most important determinant of WTP for irradiated food, and females were willing to pay more for irradiated food (Nayga, Poghosyan, and Nichols 2004). Other sociodemographic factors influencing the purchase of irradiated food were income, the presence of children in the household, age, and education. Nayga, Aiew, and Nichols (2004) found that consumers with high school education were less likely to buy irradiated ground beef while middle-aged and lower-income consumers were more likely to buy them.

3.3 Local and Typical Produce

The physical proximity between producers and consumers is an essential characteristic in the definition of local and typical food as well as for the so-called food miles concept. The term "local product" is widely used all over the world, although it can be interpreted quite differently as a product coming from either the same area where food consumption is occurring or from the region or administrative district or even larger geographical areas. "Local" can also refer to products sold at farmers' markets or through distribution channels in the producing region or nearby. Freshness is the most relevant product attribute related to local food products. Moreover, local food products are related to environmental issues since they travel shorter distances, which requires less energy and produces fewer air pollutants (Teisl, Chapter 34 in this volume).

Typical products usually imply more than distance because tradition is also considered as a strong food attribute. Geographical indication labels enter this category whether they refer to a country, region, or town.

The concept "food miles" encompasses several approaches, and it is mostly related to environmental concerns and damage caused as a result of the miles the food has to be transported. It is important to distinguish those different situations because the consumers' sociodemographic characteristics could differ. It can be said that local and typical products benefit from the food miles concept although consumers might not relate to both when deciding to buy local produce (Sirieix, Grolleau, and Schaer 2007).

It was found that in United States whites were more likely to prefer to purchase directly but occasionally on local markets than other ethnic groups, and consumers' income was not a determining factor. Overall demographics are not important explanatory factors of the probability to purchase fresh produce at farmers' markets.

According to findings in a farmers' market located in California, purchasers differed from non-purchasers (Wolf and Berrenson 2003). In another study carried out in Alabama (Onianwa, Mojica, and Wheelock 2006), the authors found that shoppers were, on average, 41 years old, mostly men, and around 50 percent whites; 80 percent had above high school education and 90 percent had an income above $25,000. Another survey carried out in Florida (Adams and Adams 2008) described the most important sociodemographic profile of visitors to a farmers' market as females (60 percent), younger adults—under 25 (55 percent), with a university degree (56 percent), with no children (84 percent), whites (80 percent), and with incomes below $20,000. The authors stated that those profiles were not representative of Florida state, but it corresponded to Gainesville, home to the University of Florida. Zepeda and Li (2006) found that demographic variables were not significant when behaviors and attitudes were taken into account. Gender, age, education, race, and religion had no significant impact on the probability of buying local food. None of the economic variables (income or food expenditures) significantly affected the probability of buying locally. Gandee, Brown, and D'Souza (2003) analyzed direct farm marketing and found that there was a positive impact of income and the educational variables on buying probability, especially for those with a higher degree.

3.4   Ethnicity

Immigration in developed countries is giving societies an increasingly multicultural profile. The diversity of ethnic groups is becoming not only a marketing challenge for food supply chain agents but also an issue to address in food and health policies.

Ethnic groups demand specific food products that are traditional in their diets that may not be available in the host countries. This has favored the development of specialized ethnic food distribution channels, such as grocery stores and restaurants. Some papers have aimed at evaluating opportunities for processors and retailers, identifying food categories demanded by specific ethnic groups for which there is lack of supply (e.g., Salvadoreans in the United States, Batres-Marquez, Jensen, and Brester 2003; Latin Americans in Belgium, Verbeke and Poquiviqui López 2005). Additionally, recent literature aims at explaining the role of ethnic identity and perceived norms in the purchase of ethnic food by specific ethnic groups (e.g., Carrus, Nenci, and Caddeo 2009).

As a consequence of this ethnic diversity and market dynamics, the host population is increasingly exposed to other food experiences, even if they have never travelled abroad. The economic literature on drivers of ethnic food choices among the host citizens is scarce, and there are very few references to sociodemographic variables. One exception is Verbeke and Poquiviqui López (2005), who found that consumption of ethnic food was positively affected by the level of education and by inhabiting big cities, and negatively affected by age; that is, older consumers were more reluctant to try ethnic food. Gender and income, however, were not found to be significant.

Normally, empirical investigations on food choice and demand include ethnicity as an additional sociodemographic variable to capture cultural-specific behaviors (there are a few examples throughout this chapter). In contrast, there is an avenue of research focused on the specificity of food consumption patterns by ethnic groups. Lanfranco, Ames, and Huang (2002) calculated that in the United States, the Hispanic population spent a higher proportion of their budget on food, and proportionally more on consuming at home, than African Americans and non-Hispanic whites. Likewise, the authors showed that the demand for different food categories varied significantly across ethnic groups in the United States with different tastes and gastronomic cultures, leading to significant differences in price, cross-price, and income elasticities that might even turn out to be of the opposite sign. Ethnicity also becomes central in policy-oriented papers, mainly based in the United States, evaluating the effectiveness of food and income transfer programs targeted at specific ethnic minorities and aimed at promoting diversified diets and nutrient intake (Lanfranco et al. 2001).

Nevertheless, ethnicity plays a central role in other disciplines. There is an abundant literature on nutrition and medicine that warns how the adoption of a more Westernized lifestyle and diet by ethnic minorities in developed countries is likely to replace some healthy components of their traditional diets and habits, which have contributed to a lower incidence of diseases more frequent in the mainstream population (e.g., obesity, hypertension, cardiovascular diseases). In this sense, several studies have focused on the effects of acculturation (proxied by the number of years that the immigrant has been living in the host country, the command of its language, as well as belonging to the second (or later) generation of immigrants) on the modification of eating patterns, which, depending on the ethnic group, may have a positive or negative effect.

3.5   Convenience

Reduced time and effort are the two main reasons for consumers to purchase convenience foods and to eat out of the home. Convenience or prepared food has different definitions but the common concept is that it minimizes food selection, purchase, preparation, cooking, or cleaning time. Ready meals are good examples of convenience food products, whether they are fully prepared ready to eat or they have to be mixed with other ingredients but still avoid time and effort in comparison to other normal products. Scholderer and Grunert (2005) tried to reconcile two approaches that had been used to explain consumers' tendency toward effort and time saving in food shopping and meal preparation: the household production approach, or Beckers' model (Becker 1965), and the convenience orientation approach (Candel 2001). Senauer (2001) stated that the most fundamental segmentation of food consumption and shopping patterns could differentiate consumers into those who were price-conscious with lower incomes and those who were convenience/quality-oriented with higher incomes. An income increase is generally linked to an increase in spending on convenience food products. According to Newman, Henchion, and Matthews (2003), as household income increased, expenditure on convenience food also increased but at a decreasing rate. They also found that, for Irish consumers, the responsiveness of household expenditure on convenience or prepared meals to changes in income was declining from 1987 to 1994. The increase in two-earner households and smaller households has encouraged the consumption of convenience food. Nevertheless, according to Botonaki, Natos, and Mattas (2009), income was found to affect perceived budget significantly, but it was not found to affect behavior.

Both approaches, Becker's model and the convenience orientation, consider that demographic household characteristics, such as the participation of women in the labor force, have a positive impact, but not all findings have been homogeneous. A plausible explanation is that households with more income have a tendency to eat out more. For example, there was no evidence that working wives purchased more convenience food products (Botonaki, Natos, and Mattas 2009), and for Harris and Shiptsova (2007), the number of wage earners in the households was not found to explain differences in expenditures with respect to food convenience. The effect of the number of wage earners on expenditure dedicated to food convenience products is insignificant, and the same is true in regard to the number of hours worked, as perceived time pressure is probably more important than the actual number of working hours.

However, it is clear that households with children and especially single-person households are more motivated by convenience food. In general, single-person households are likely to purchase convenience food more than married-couple households, and urban/suburban dwellers more than consumers living in rural areas, as groups willing to buy more convenience food have a tendency to devote more attention to leisure time. More education leads to less convenience consumption, as consumers may be more concerned about healthy food or probably eat out more often; households with children have a positive effect, but, on an adult equivalent basis, they consume less per head because they require smaller portions.

According to Harris and Shiptsova (2007), there was a negative effect related to age, which means that expenditure on convenience food declined with age of the head of the household; and the same results were reported by Newman, Henchion, and Matthews (2003). Olsen (2003) found that there was evidence of a negative relationship between age and convenience seafood consumption.

Race or ethnic differences show a different impact on consumption of convenience food, and this is clearer in US studies, where ethnic groups have a greater impact on society. The increase in individual choice when eating in family gatherings and social groups, with more individualistic behavior as a result of less structured households, has a positive effect on convenience consumption. Most of the surveys interviewed the main purchaser in the household, but the proportion of food purchased by other household members has been increasing, with more snacking and grazing. Consumers in general may be behaving in a more convenience manner than the main household purchaser (Buckley et al. 2005).

The growing of food away from home (FAFH) consumption is one of the major developments observed in food markets in modern history (see Stewart, Chapter 26 in this volume).

Most analyses dealing with FAFH consumption introduce the influence of socio-demographic variables, among other elements. Common findings in most studies show that, as income increases, there is a positive influence on FAFH consumption, although the magnitude differs among countries, cultures, and whether consumers live in rural or urban areas (Mutlu and Gracia 2004). Nevertheless, Mihalopoulos and Demoussis (2001) found that the relationship between eating out and household income was particularly important for low-income households. The opportunity cost of women or main meals planners' time, age, number of people in the household, and gender also play a primary role in FAFH consumption, although results are not homogeneous across studies.

The variable age has been considered at different disaggregation levels under different circumstances. Older individuals, women, households with adults without children living at home, and those with young children appear to display reduced levels of FAFH expenditure. Most commonly, as household size increases, there is less tendency to eat out, reflecting the scale economies and cost opportunity achieved through household meal buying and preparation (Mutlu and Gracia 2004). Single households, as well as those households with members with full working schedules and more hours worked during the week, have a tendency to eat out more often. Angulo, Gil, and Mur (2007) considered that for single-person households between 36 and 55 years old, employed, and living in large towns, FAFH had become a necessity.

Education had a positive effect on the level of expenditure dedicated to eating out (Mihalopoulos and Demoussis 2001 and other studies), without differentiating restaurant type. It may be that the close relationship between education and income reinforces their influence on FAFH. Ethnicity is included in most studies undertaken in the United States because of the multiplicity of ethnic groups living in that country. There were different reactions depending on the type of restaurant, and this was also related to income and education level. The differences were particularly important in relation to fast-food restaurants (Jekanowski, Binkley, and Eales 2001).

Some studies become involved in more disaggregated evaluations, for example Stewart et al. (2005), who made the distinction between the frequency that people go to so-called full- or table service restaurants with waitstaff and fast-food restaurants, and the reasons for going to either of those places. Income had a positive impact on visiting table service restaurants but not fast-food restaurants (Binkley 2006).

It is expected that the increasing proportion of households containing a single person or multiple adults, without children living at home, will cause spending per person to rise on full-service more than on fast-food restaurants, and the aging of the population will decrease spending on fast food (Stewart and Yen 2004; Stewart et al. 2005).

Fast-food restaurants are more often attended by young people, while older people tend to go to full-service restaurants. Educated people have a greater tendency to go to table service restaurants. Years of education had a positive effect on visits to table service restaurants but not on fast-food restaurants. Rural consumers were less likely to use fast food than those in suburban areas, while urban consumers were likely to make greater use of table service restaurants. Finally, Mutlu and Gracia 2006 analyzed the relationship between FAFH by type of meal (breakfast, lunch, dinner, and snacking) and sociodemographic characteristics for Spanish consumers. They found that the food-purchasing behavior of Spanish consumers differs by type of meals away from home. However, results suggest that income, the opportunity cost of women's time, and household size are the common factors explaining these three types of expenditure pattern.

4   Concluding Remarks

This chapter has reviewed the influence of demographics on food consumption. A section has presented the main demographic trends in developed countries. However, most of the chapter has been dedicated to showing significant empirical findings related to specific headings, such as ethics, food safety and health, local and typical produce, ethnicity, and convenience.

The scientific published literature shows that there are a great number of works dealing with food consumption but demographics are not included in their analyses. Their approaches try to get responses for all consumers without breaking them into groups according to their demographics. However, there are a reasonable number of published articles that include demographic variables, and it is on those that we have concentrated. For each subject, a good sample of works has been selected in order to understand the main results. Although sometimes contradictory, these results may still help readers to follow up on specific issues.

It has being claimed by some authors that demographics were not important determinants of food consumption, and other variables were becoming more significant. This chapter provides evidence that demographics still play an important role in many issues related to food consumption, especially in explaining heterogeneous preferences. Food consumption and food choice are becoming more complex, and the market is split into many different segments. Each segment has some demographic particularities, with distinguishing traits, but it requires a detailed analysis, which is rarely undertaken. Food firms are willing to use that information for marketing purposes, but policymakers are not so interested in disaggregated analyses.

There are some demographics that seem to be more discriminatory than others, but not across all subjects as in each case there are different responses. It is claimed that income does not play such an important role as it used to, but many details are lacking, as, for example, the frequency with which consumers buy food products and not only the quantity purchased. As income increases, its influence on food expenditure decisions does not always decline in importance. Understanding the factors shaping expenditure decisions becomes increasingly important with increasing income levels. Age and income together have an impact on food consumption behavior.

Health and food safety are key issues for consumers, with women and old people more sensitive to incorporating them into their food habits. There are significant differences between urban and rural dwellers, especially as concerns the use of time, and the same is true among ethnic groups, but this is probably the result of a combination of different income and education levels plus well-established habits. Some issues have more recently been introduced into society, and it is normal that they have a greater influence on younger people as they react more rapidly and incorporate them into their decision-making processes.

There are many issues that could be of interest for future research. Consumers' groups differentiated by their demographics have different reactions in the food consumption decision-making process. We need more insights into the linkage between those reactions and actual consumption patterns. There are many interactions among demographic characteristics that are not well known, in both static and dynamic processes that culminate in food consumption decisions. Food markets and consumers' reactions are quite different from place to place; thus, generalizations about demographics should be avoided, and there should be thorough investigation in order to draw accurate conclusions.

Modeling is in constant evolution, and analysis of the influence of demographics on food consumption should benefit from it. In particular, there are two approaches that may add more insights than others, i.e., structural equations and choice experiments modeling. Both could be particularized for consumers' segments with specific demographics.

To sum up, there is evidence that demographics differentiate consumers' food consumption behavior and choice, and this is a field that should receive more attention, in line with micromarketing activities that aim increasingly to differentiate consumers' targets. Any opportunity should be taken to use new conceptual and methodological approaches to help further research.

References

Adams, D., and A. E. Adams. 2008. "Availability, Attitudes and Willingness to Pay for Local Foods: Results of a Preliminary Survey." Selected Paper prepared for the Annual Meeting of the American Agricultural Economics Association, Orlando, FL, July 27–9.

Angulo, A. M., and J. M. Gil. 2006. "Incorporating Nutrients into Meat Demand Analysis Using Household Budgets Data." *Agricultural Economics* 35: 131–44.

——————, and J. Mur 2007. "Spanish Demand for Food Away From Home: Analysis of Panel Data." *Journal of Agricultural Economics* 58/2: 289–307.

Ares, G., A. Giménez, and A. Gámbaro. 2009. "Consumer Perceived Healthiness and Willingness to Try Functional Milk Desserts: Influence of Ingredient, Ingredient Name and Health Claim." *Food Quality and Preference* 20: 50–6.

Aristei, D., F. Perali, and L. Pieroni. 2008. "Cohort, Age and Time Effects in Alcohol Consumption by Italian Households: A Double-Hurdle Approach." *Empirical Economics* 35/1: 29–61.

Arnot, C., P. C. Boxall, and S. B. Cash. 2006. "Do Ethical Consumes Care about Price? A Revealed Preference Analysis of Fair Trade Coffee Purchases." *Canadian Journal of Agricultural Economics* 54: 555–65.

Batres-Marquez, S. P., H. H. Jensen, and G. W. Brester. 2003. "Salvadoran Consumption of Ethnic Foods in the United States." *Journal of Food Distribution Research* 34: 1–16.

Batte, M. T., N. H. Hooker, T. C. Haab, and J. Beaverson. 2007. "Putting Their Money Where Their Mouths Are: Consumers' Willingness to Pay for Multi-Ingredient, Processed Organic Food Products." *Food Policy* 32: 145–59.

Becchetti, L., and B. Huybrechts. 2007. "The Dynamics of Fair Trade as a Mixed-Form Market." *Journal of Business Ethics* 81: 733–50.

—— and F. C. Rosati. 2007. "Global Social Preferences and the Demand for Socially Responsible Products: Empirical Evidence from a Pilot Study on Fair Trade Consumers." *World Economy* 30/5: 807–36.

Becker, G. S. 1965. "A Theory of Allocation of Time." *Economic Journal* 75: 493–508.

Bennet, R. M., and R. J. P. Blaney. 2003. "Estimating the Benefits of Farm Animal Welfare Legislation Using the Contingent Valuation Method." *Agricultural Economics* 29: 85–98.

Bernard, J. C., C. Zhang, and K. Gifford. 2006. "An Experimental Investigation of Consumer Willingness to Pay for Non-GM Foods when an Organic Option Is Present." *Agricultural and Resource Economics Review* 35/2: 374–85.

Bernués, A., A. Olaizola, and K. Corcoran. 2003. "Extrinsic Attributes of Red Meat as Indicators of Quality in Europe: An Application for Market Segmentation." *Food Quality and Preference* 14: 265–76.

Bhaskaran, S., and F. Hardley. 2002. "Buyer Beliefs, Attitudes and Behaviour: Foods with Therapeutic Claims." *Journal of Consumer Marketing* 19/7: 591–606.

Binkley, J. K. 2006. "The Effect of Demographic, Economic, and Nutrition Factors on the Frequency of Food Away From Home." *Journal of Consumer Affairs* 40/2: 372–91.

Botonaki, A., D. Natos, and K. Mattas. 2009. "Exploring Convenience Food Consumption through a Structural Equation Model." *Journal of Food Products Marketing* 15/1: 64–79.

Buckley, M., C. Cowan, M. McCarthy, and C. O'Sullivan. 2005. "The Convenience Consumer and Food-Related Lifestyles in Great Britain." *Journal of Food Products Marketing* 11/3: 3–25.

Calvet, L., and E. Comon. 2003. "Behavioural Heterogeneity and the Income Effect." *Review of Economics and Statistics* 85/3: 653–69.

Candel, M. J. 2001. "Consumers' Convenience Orientation towards Meal Preparation: Conceptualization and Measurement." *Appetite* 36: 15–28.

Carlsson, F., P. Frykblom, and C. J. Lagerkvist. 2005. "Consumer Preferences for Food Product Quality Attributes from Swedish Agriculture." *Ambio* 34: 4–5.

Carrus, G., A. M. Nenci, and P. Caddeo. 2009. "The Role of Ethnic Identity and Perceived Ethnic Norms in the Purchase of Ethnical Food Products." *Appetite* 52: 65–71.

Chen, M. F. 2007. "Consumer Attitudes and Purchase Intentions in Relation to Organic Foods in Taiwan: Moderating Effects of Food-Related Personality Traits." *Food Quality and Preference* 18: 1008–21.

Deaton, A., and J. Muellbauer. 1980. *Economics and Consumer Behaviour*. New York: Cambridge University Press.

De Pelsmacker, P., L. Driesen, and G. Rayp. 2005. "Do Consumers Care about Ethics? Willingness to Pay for Fair-Trade Coffee." *Journal of Consumer Affairs* 39: 363–85.

——, W. Janssens, E. Sterckx, and C. Mielants. 2006. "Fair-Trade Beliefs, Attitudes and Buying Behaviour of Belgian Consumers." *International Journal of Nonprofit and Voluntary Sector Marketing* 11: 125–38.

Dettmann, R. L. 2008. "Organic Produce: Who's Eating It? A Demographic Profile of Organic Produce Consumers." Selected Paper prepared for the Annual Meeting of the American Agricultural Economics Association, Orlando, FL, July 27–9.

Dickinson, D. L., and D. von Bailey. 2002. "Meat Traceability: Are U.S. Consumers Willing to Pay for It?" *Journal of Agricultural and Resource Economics* 27/2: 348–64.

Doran, C. J. 2009. "The Role of Personal Values in Fair Trade Consumption." *Journal of Business Ethics* 84: 549–63.

Durham, C. A. 2007. "The Impact of Environmental and Health Motivations on the Organic Share of Produce Purchases." *Agricultural and Resource Economics Review* 36/2: 304–20.

European Commission. 2009. *Demographic Trends, Socio-economic Impacts and Policy Implications in the European Union 2008.* Monitoring Report prepared by the European Observatory on the Social Situation—Demography Network. Brussels: Directorate-General for Employment, Social Affairs and Equal Opportunities, European Commission.

Ferran, F., and K. G. Grunert. 2005. "French Fair Trade Coffee Buyers' Purchasing Motives: An Exploratory Study Using Means–End Chains Analysis." *Food Quality and Preference* 18: 218–29.

Fousekis, P., and P. Lazaridis. 2005. "The Demand for Selected Nutrients by Greek Households: An Empirical Analysis with Quantile Regressions." *Agricultural Economics* 32: 267–79.

Gandee, J. E., C. Brown, and G. E. D'Souza. 2003. "The Role of Spatial and Demographic Characteristics in Direct Farm Marketing: An Econometric Approach." Paper presented to the Annual Meeting of the American Agricultural Economics Association, Montreal, July 27–30.

Gracia, A., and T. de Magistris. 2008. "The Demand for Organic Foods in the South of Italy: A Discrete Choice Model." *Food Policy* 33/5: 386–96.

Grannis, J., and D. D. Thilmany. 2002. "Marketing Natural Pork: An Empirical Analysis of Consumers in the Mountain Region." *Agribusiness* 18/4: 475–89.

Gustavsen, G. W., and K. Rickertsen. 2009. "Consumer Cohorts and Demand Systems." Contributed Paper presented at the Conference of the International Association of Agricultural Economists, Beijing, Aug. 16–22.

Harris, J. M., and N. Blisard. 2001. "Analyzing the Impact of Generational Effects on Consumer Expenditures for Meats: A Cohort Approach." *Journal of Food Distribution Research* 32/1: 64–73.

——and R. Shiptsova 2007. "Consumer Demand for Convenience Foods: Demographics and Expenditures." *Journal of Food Distribution Research* 38/3: 22–36.

Henson, S., O. Masakure, and J. Cranfield. 2008. "The Propensity for Consumers to Offset Health Risks through the Use of Functional Foods and Nutraceuticals: The Case of Lycopene." *Food Quality and Preference* 19/4: 395–406.

Hu, W., A. Hünnemeyer, M. Veeman, W. Adamovicz, and L. Srivastava. 2004. "Trading Off Health, Environmental and Genetic Modification Attributes in Food." *European Review of Agricultural Economics* 31/3: 389–408.

——W. L. Adamovicz, and M. Veeman. 2006. "Labeling Context and Reference Point Effects in Models of Food Attribute Demand." *American Journal of Agricultural Economics* 88/4: 1034–49.

——, M. Veeman, W. Adamowicz, and G. Gao. 2006. "Consumers' Food Choices with Voluntary Access to Genetic Modification Information." *Canadian Journal of Agricultural Economics* 54: 585–604.

Jekanowski, M. D., J. K. Binkley, and J. Eales. 2001. "Convenience, Accessibility and the Demand for Fast Food." *Journal of Agricultural and Resource Economics* 26/1: 58–74.

Kalwij, A., and W. Salverda. 2007. "The Effects of Changes in Household Demographics and Employment on Consumer Demand Patterns." *Applied Economics* 39/11: 1447–60.

Kaneko, N., and W. S. Chern. 2005. "Willingness to Pay for Genetically Modified Oil, Cornflakes, and Salmon: Evidence from a U.S. Telephone Survey." *Journal of Agricultural and Applied Economics* 37/3: 701–19.

Kim, S.-Y. K., R. M. Nayga, Jr., and O. Capps, Jr. 2000. "The Effect of Food Label Use on Nutrient Intakes: An Endogenous Switching Regression Analysis." *Journal of Agricultural and Resource Economics* 25/1: 215–31.

———————. 2001. "Food Label Use, Self-Selectivity, and Diet Quality." *Journal of Consumer Affairs* 35/2: 346–63.

Krystallis, A., and G. Chryssochoidis. 2005. "Consumers' Willingness to Pay for Organic Food: Factors That Affect It and Variation Per Organic Product Type." *British Food Journal* 107/5: 320–43.

Lagerkvist, C. J., F. Carlsson, and D. Viske. 2006. "Swedish Consumer Preferences for Animal Welfare and Biotech: A Choice Experiment." *AgBio Forum* 9/1: 51–8.

Lanfranco, B. A., G. C. W. Ames, and C. L. Huang. 2002. "Comparison of Hispanic Households' Demand for Meats with Other Ethnic Groups." *Journal of Food Distribution Research* 33/1: 92–101.

———————, and F. Stegelin. 2001. "WIC and the Demand for Food by the Hispanic Community in the United States." *Journal of Food Distribution Research* 32/1: 85–96.

Lichtenberg, L., S.-J. Heidecke, and T. Becker. 2008. "Traceability of Meat: Consumers' Associations and their Willingness-to-Pay." Paper presented at the International Congress of the European Association of Agricultural Economists, Ghent, Aug. 26–9.

Liljenstolpe, C. 2008. "Evaluating Animal Welfare with Choice Experiments: An Application to Swedish Pig Production." *Agribusiness* 24: 67–84.

Loureiro, M. L., and S. Hine. 2002. "Discovering Niche Markets: A Comparison of Consumer Willingness to Pay for a Local (Colorado-Grown), Organic, and GMO-Free Product." *Journal of Agricultural and Applied Economics* 34/3: 477–87.

——and J. Lotade. 2005. "Do Fair Trade and Eco-Labels in Coffee Wake Up the Consumer Conscience?" *Ecological Economics* 53: 129–38.

Lyly, M., K. Roininen, K. Honkapää, K. Poutanen, and L. Lähteenmäki. 2007. "Factors Influencing Consumers' Willingness to Use Beverages and Ready-to-Eat Frozen Soups Containing Oat β-Glucan in Finland, France and Sweden." *Food Quality and Preference* 18: 242–55.

McCluskey, J. J., K. M. Grimsrud, H. Ouchi, and T. I. Wahl. 2003. "Consumer Response to Genetically Modified Food Products in Japan." *Agricultural and Resource Economics Review* 32/2: 222–31.

———————. 2005. "Bovine Spongiform Encephalopathy in Japan: Consumers' Food Safety Perceptions and Willingness to Pay for Tested Beef." *Australian Journal of Agricultural and Resource Economics* 49: 197–209.

McFadden, D. 1974. "Conditional Logit Analysis of Qualitative Choice Behaviour." In P. Zarembka, ed., *Frontiers in Econometrics*. New York: Academic Press.

Mihalopoulos, V. G., and M. Demoussis. 2001. "Greek Household Consumption of Food Away From Home: A Microeconometric Approach." *European Review of Agricultural Economics* 28/4: 421–32.

Mori, H., and D. L. Clason. 2004. "A Cohort Approach for Predicting Future Eating Habits: The Case of At-Home Consumption of Fresh Fish and Meat in an Aging Japanese Society." *International Food and Agribusiness Management Review* 7/1: 22–41.

Moro, D., and P. Sckokai. 2000. "Heterogeneous Preferences in Household Food Consumption in Italy." *European Review of Agricultural Economics* 27/3: 305–23.

Mutlu, S., and A. Gracia. 2004. "Food Consumption Away From Home in Spain." *Journal of Food Products Marketing* 10/2: 1–16.

——. 2006. "Spanish Food Expenditure Away From Home (FAFH): By Type of Meal." *Applied Economics* 38/9: 1037–47.

Nayga, R. M., Jr., W. Aiew, and J. P. Nichols. 2004. "Information Effects on Consumers' Willingness to Purchase Irradiated Food Products." *Review of Agricultural Economics* 27/1: 37–48.

——, A. Poghosyan, and J. P. Nichols. 2004. "Will Consumers Accept Irradiated Food Products?" *International Journal of Consumer Studies* 28/2: 178–85.

Newman, C., M. Henchion, and A. Matthews. 2001. "Infrequency of Purchase and Double-Hurdle Models of Irish Households' Meat." *European Review of Agricultural Economics* 28/4: 393–412.

——. 2003. "A Double-Hurdle Model of Irish Household Expenditure on Prepared Meals." *Applied Economics* 35/9: 1053–61.

Nocella, G., L. Hubbard, and R. Scarpa. 2010. "Farm Animal Welfare, Consumers Willing to Pay, and Trust: Results of a Cross-National Survey." *Applied Economics Perspectives and Policies* 32/2: 275–97.

Olsen, S. O. 2003. "Understanding the Relationship between Age and Seafood Consumption: The Mediating Role of Attitude, Health and Convenience." *Food Quality and Preference* 14/3: 199–209.

Onianwa, O., M. Mojica, and G. Wheelock. 2006. "Consumer Characteristics and Views regarding Farmers Markets: An Examination of On-Site Survey Data of Alabama Consumers." *Journal of Food Distribution Research* 37/1: 119–25.

Rousu, M., W. E. Huffman, J. F. Shogren, and A. Tegene. 2007. "Effects and Value of Verifiable Information in a Controversial Market: Evidence from Lab Auctions of Genetically Modified Food." *Economic Inquiry* 45/3: 409–32.

Scholderer, J., and K. G. Grunert. 2005. "Consumers, Food and Convenience: The Long Way from Resource Constraints to Actual Consumption Patterns." *Journal of Economic Psychology* 26: 105–28.

Senauer, B. 2001. *The Food Consumer in the 21st Century: New Research Perspectives.* Working Paper No. 01-03. St Paul: Food Industry Center, University of Minnesota.

Sirieix, L., G. Grolleau, and B. Schaer. 2007. *Consumers and Food Miles.* Working Paper No. 3/2007. Montpellier: UMR MOISA.

Stewart, H., and N. Blisard. 2008. "Are Younger Cohorts Demanding Less Fresh Vegetables?" *Review of Agricultural Economics* 30/1: 43–59.

—— and S. T. Yen. 2004. "Changing Household Characteristics and the Away-From-Home Food Market: A Censored Equation System Approach." *Food Policy* 29/6: 643–58.

——, N. Blisard, D. Jolliffe, and S. Bhuyan. 2005. "The Demand for Food Away From Home: Do Other Preferences Compete with Our Desire to Eat Healthfully?" *Journal of Agricultural and Resource Economics* 30/3: 520–36.

Teratanavat, R., and N. H. Hooker. 2006. "Consumer Valuations and Preference Heterogeneity for a Novel Functional Food." *Journal of Food Science* 71/7: 533–41.

Thompson, G. D., and J. Kidwell. 1998. "Explaining the Choice of Organic Produce: Cosmetic Defects, Prices, and Consumer Preferences." *American Journal of Agricultural Economics* 80/2: 277–87.

Tonsor, G. T., T. C. Schroeder, J. M. E. Pennings, and J. Mintert. 2007. *Consumers Valuations and Choice Processes of Food Safety Enhancement Attributes: An International Study of Beef Consumers*. Working Paper prepared for the Annual Meeting of the American Agricultural Economics Association, Portland, OR, July 30–Aug. 1.

Torjusen, H., L. Sangstad, K. O'Doherty Jensen, and U. Kjærnes. 2004. *European Consumers' Conceptions of Organic Food: A Review of Available Research*. Professional Report No. 4. Oslo: National Institute for Consumer Research.

Unnevehr, L., J. Eales, H. Jensen, J. Lusk, J. McCluskey, and J. Kinsey. 2010. "Food and Consumer Economics." *American Journal of Agricultural Economics* 92/2: 506–21.

US Census Bureau. 2011. *The 2011 Statistical Abstract*. <http://www.census.gov/compendia/statab/cats/population.html>.

Variyam, J. N. 2008. "Do Nutrition Labels Improve Dietary Outcomes?" *Health Economics* 17: 695–708.

Verbeke, W. 2006. "Functional Foods: Consumer Willingness to Compromise on Taste for Health?" *Food Quality and Preference* 17: 126–31.

——and G. Poquiviqui López. 2005. "Ethnic Food Attitudes and Behaviour among Belgians and Hispanics Living in Belgium." *British Food Journal* 107: 823–40.

——and J. Viane. 2000. "Ethical Challenges for Livestock Production: Meeting Consumer Concern about Meat Safety and Animal Welfare." *Journal of Agricultural and Environmental Ethics* 12: 141–51.

Verhoef, P. C. 2005. "Explaining Purchases of Organic Meat by Dutch Consumers." *European Review of Agricultural Economics* 32/2: 245–67.

Wendt, M., and J. Kinsey. 2007. *Do Eating Patterns Follow a Cohort or Change over a Lifetime? Answers Emerging from the Literature*. Working Paper No. 2007-01. St Paul: Food Industry Center, University of Minnesota.

Wier, M., J. K. O'Doherty, L. M. Andersen, and K. Millock. 2008. "The Character of Demand in Mature Organic Food Markets: Great Britain and Denmark Compared." *Food Policy* 33: 406–21.

Wolf, M. M., and E. Berrenson. 2003. "A Comparison of Purchasing Behaviors and Consumer Profiles at San Luis Obispo's Thursday Night Farmers' Market: A Case Study." *Journal of Food Distribution Research* 34/1: 107–22.

Yue, C., F. Alfnes, and H. H. Jensen. 2009. "Discounting Spotted Apples: Investigating Consumers' Willingness to Accept Cosmetic Damage in an Organic Product." *Journal of Agricultural and Applied Economics* 41/1: 29–46.

Zepeda, L., and J. Li. 2006. "Who Buys Local Food?" *Journal of Food Distribution Research* 37/3: 1–11.

————. 2007. "Characteristics of Organic Food Shoppers." *Journal of Agricultural and Applied Economics* 39/1: 17–28.

CHAPTER 31

HABIT FORMATION IN FOOD CONSUMPTION

SVEN-OLOV DAUNFELDT, JONAS NORDSTRÖM,
AND LINDA THUNSTRÖM

1 INTRODUCTION

Pollak (1970) states that consumption of a good is habit-forming if current preferences depend on past consumption. Thus, habit formation means that past consumption reinforces the propensity to consume the same good over time.

Habit formation in food has implications for public policies and marketing campaigns. Firms or public authorities might want to influence consumption of a specific food product or type (e.g., healthy or organic food) through price, availability, or information. If there is habit formation in consumption, consumption will be sticky in the short run—i.e., short- and long-term responses to price and income changes, as well as information, will differ. Further, if habit formation is strong, information campaigns will need to be more forceful (and therefore more costly) to change consumption patterns, and price changes will have little effect in the short run compared to cases where habit formation is weak.

In this chapter we summarize the empirical literature on habit formation in food consumption in order to analyze the hypothesis that food consumption is habit-forming. It should be stressed that not all of the studies included in the review focus solely on habit formation in food; on the contrary, often food is just one consumption category, or habit formation just one aspect of food choices analyzed in the studies.

We also describe the most commonly used demand models. In doing so, we depart from the static version of the models and describe how these models can be extended to dynamic versions incorporating habit formation. The focus is on the functional form of the models rather than estimation. Chapter 1 of this volume, by Piggott and Marsh, considers demand system estimation. For the specific econometric issues related to estimation of dynamic models, we refer the reader to the standard econometric literature in this field. An excellent description of the estimation of discrete choice models can be found in Train (2003).

The empirical studies reviewed in this chapter generally find habit formation in food consumption, implying that dynamics is an important factor in food demand analysis. However, the evidence of habit formation in food seems to vary across data sets and methods used in the analysis. Studies based on macro-data generally find habit formation in food consumption. In studies based on micro-data using continuous demand models, habit formation in food is generally found, but the results are more mixed. The studies reviewed here, based on micro-data that apply discrete choice models (both economics and marketing studies), all find evidence of habit formation. In addition, the strength of habit formation seems to vary across food categories.

In this chapter, we use "habit formation" as a collective term to include "habit persistence" and "state dependence." Most of the economics studies use the term "habit formation."[1]

In the following section, we review the main econometric models used to study habits in food consumption. Section 3 summarizes and comments on the results. Section 4 concludes the chapter and discusses fruitful areas for future research.

2 EMPIRICAL MODELS

Various models and data sets have been used to study habit formation in food consumption. In this section, we focus on the most commonly used models in more recent studies.

The most commonly used models are dynamic versions of the linear expenditure system (Klein and Rubin 1947–8; Stone 1954b), the translog model (Christensen, Jorgenson, and Lau 1975), and the almost ideal demand system (Deaton and Muellbauer 1980a). A number of studies have also applied models based on a single equation, or single demand functions, and recently also discrete choice models. In this section, therefore, we provide brief descriptions of the following empirical models:

(a) Single demand functions
(b) Linear expenditure systems (LESs)
(c) Almost ideal demand system (AIDS)
(d) Translog demand systems
(e) Discrete choice models.

An overview of all reviewed studies on food consumption and habit formation, sorted by their choice of empirical model, is given in Table 31.1.

---

[1] Even if we treat the terms as synonymous, note that state dependence might be explained by factors other than habit persistence (when consuming a product enhances the taste for that product), such as learning combined with risk. Consuming a product might provide the consumer with knowledge of the product attributes and therefore reduce the risk of choosing the same product in the future.

Table 31.1 Summary of studies on food consumption and habit formation, sorted by their choice of empirical model

Study	Country	Model	Period	Data	Products	Habit formation
Chang (1977)	USA	Single demand function	1935–41, 1948–74	Macro	Meat	Yes
Pope, Green, and Eales (1980)	USA	Single demand function	1950–75	Macro	Beef, pork, poultry, fish	Yes
Okunade (1992)	USA	Single demand function	1957–87	Macro	Coffee	Yes
Naik and Moore (1996)	USA	Single consumption function	1977–87	Micro	Aggregate food	Yes
Pollak and Wales (1969)	USA	Linear expenditure system	1929–65	Macro	Aggregate food	Mixed
McFall Lamm (1982)	USA	Linear expenditure system	1947–78	Macro	31 different food groups	Yes
Darrough, Pollak, and Wales (1983)	Japan	Quadratic expenditure system	1953–77	Grouped household data	Aggregate food	Yes
Heien and Durham (1991)	UK USA	Quadratic expenditure system	1966–72 1980–1	Micro	Food consumed at home and outside the home	Yes
Khare and Inman (2006)	USA	Hierarchical linear model	2 weeks in 1998 and 1999	Micro	Mix of nutrients consumed each meal	Yes
Blanciforti and Green (1983)	USA	AIDS	1948–78	Macro	Aggregate food, and meats, fruits, vegetables, bakery, cereal products	Yes
Pashardes (1986)	UK	AIDS	1947–80	Macro	Aggregate food	Yes
Alessie and Kapteyn (1991)	Netherlands	AIDS	1980–1	Micro	Aggregate food	No

Study	Country	Model	Data period	Data type	Food groups	Separability
Edgerton et al. (1996)	Denmark, Finland, Norway, Sweden	AIDS	1953–90, 1960–90, 1962–88, 1963–89	Macro	Various food groups	Mixed
Holt and Goodwin (1997)	USA	Inverse AIDS	1960–93	Macro	Beef, pork, chicken, turkey	Yes
Rickertsen (1998)	Norway	AIDS	1962–91	Macro	Various foods consumed at home and outside the home	Yes
Guha (2004)	India	AIDS	1972–3, 1977–8, 1983–4, 1987–8	Micro	Cereal, milk products, oil, meat, eggs, fish, other foods	Mixed
Browning and Collado (2007)	Spain	AIDS	1985–96	Micro	Food consumed at home, and outside the home	Mixed
Liao and Chern (2007)	China	AIDS	2002–3	Micro	Grain, oil, eggs, meat, poultry, fish, fresh vegetables, fresh fruit	Mixed
Manser (1976)	USA	Indirect translog demand system	1948–72	Macro	Meats, fruit and vegetables, cereal and bakery products, miscellaneous food	Yes
Menkhaus, St Clair, and Hallingbye (1985)	USA	Translog demand system	1965–81	Macro	Meat	No
Meghir and Weber (1996)	USA	Translog demand system	1980–91	Micro	Food at home	No
Carrasco, Labeaga, and Lopez-Salido (2005)	Spain	Translog demand system	1985–95	Micro	Food at home	Yes
Wohlgenant and Zhen (2006)	USA	Translog demand system	1980–2004	Macro	Meat	Mixed
Guadagni and Little (1983)	USA	Discrete choice	1978–80	Micro	Coffee	Yes
Chintagunta (1993)	USA	Discrete choice	1985–8	Micro	Yogurt	Yes
Erdem (1996)	USA	Discrete choice	1986–8	Micro	Margarine, peanut butter, yogurt	Yes
Keane (1997)	USA	Discrete choice	1987–8	Micro	Ketchup	Yes
Ailawadi and Neslin (1998)	USA	Discrete choice	1986–8	Micro	Yogurt and ketchup	Yes

(continued)

Table 31.1 Continued

Study	Country	Model	Period	Data	Products	Habit formation
Seetharaman, Ainslie, and Chintagunta (1999)	USA	Discrete choice	1985–8	Micro	Ketchup, peanut butter, stick margarine, canned tuna	Yes
Seetharaman (2004)	USA	Discrete choice	1985–7	Micro	Ketchup	Yes
Richards, Patterson, and Tegene (2007)	USA	Discrete choice	1998–2001	Micro	Snack food	Yes
Arnade, Gopinath, and Pick (2008)	USA	Discrete choice	1998–2003	Micro	Cheese	Yes
Thunström (2010)	Sweden	Discrete choice	2003	Micro	Breakfast cereals	Yes
Dynan (2000)	USA	Lifecycle consumption model	1974–87	Micro	Aggregate food	No
Price and Gislason (2001)	Japan	State adjustment model	1963–91	Macro	Seafood, meat, cereal, vegetables, fruit	Mixed
Flavin and Nakagawa (2004)	USA	Separate Engle curves	1975–85	Macro	Aggregate food	No

2.1   Single Demand Functions

A number of studies analyze food demand using a single demand equation approach. The most commonly used functional forms are linear specifications, where quantity demanded is assumed to be a linear function of the explanatory variables, and the double logarithmic specification $\log x_{i,t} = \alpha_i + \sum_{k=1}^{n} \varphi_{ik} \log p_{k,t} + \delta_i \log m_t$, where $x_{i,t}$ is the quantity demanded of product i (of in total n goods) in period t, p_k is the price of the kth good, and m is total expenditure on the n goods. In the double logarithmic model, the parameter estimate δ_i is the expenditure elasticity, and φ_{ik} is the cross-price elasticity of the kth price on the ith demand. Dynamics can be added to the model by including consumption in the previous period, $x_{i,t-1}$, as an explanatory variable.

Dynamic specifications have been used in estimation of food demand by Chang (1977), Pope, Green, and Eales (1980), Okunade (1992), and Naik and Moore (1996). Naik and Moore (1996) use household panel data on aggregate food to analyze habit formation. In their model specification, aggregate food consumption depends linearly on aggregate food consumption in the previous time period. The choice of functional form is, however, not given a priori and can be varied. A more general functional form is provided by the Box–Cox transformation, where both the linear and the logarithmic specifications are embedded as special cases.[2] Chang (1977) and Pope, Green, and Eales (1980) apply the Box–Cox transformation to dynamic models analyzing US demand for meat in general, as well as separately for beef, pork, poultry, and fish. Okunade (1992) apply the Box–Cox transformation to analyze habit effects in US demand for coffee.

The single demand functions approach is a convenient way of modeling demand for an individual good, with the advantage of flexibility in the choice of functional form. However, the main disadvantage of the approach is that it relies on very restrictive assumptions of separability between demand for the (single) food analyzed and other types of food or consumption. To include more food groups and allow for substitution with other consumption, researchers therefore often turn to demand systems. In addition, when applying complete systems of demand equations, economic theory becomes much more relevant. As far as theory is concerned, only the homogeneity restriction has implications for the single equation approach.

---

[2] The transformation developed by Box and Cox is of the functional form $q_{i,t}^{*} = (q_{i,t}^{\lambda} - 1)/\lambda$, where $q_{i,t}$ is the tth observation of a variable i, and λ represents a transformation parameter to be determined. Applying the Box–Cox transformation to the single-equation demand specification, the static model becomes $x_{i,t}^{*} = \alpha_i + \sum_{k=1}^{n} \varphi_{ik} p_{k,t}^{*} + \delta_i m_t^{*}$. This equation reduces to the linear form when λ equals one. If λ approaches zero, the model approaches the double log demand specification. By relaxing the assumption that all the λs are the same for each variable, the semilog and log-inverse functional forms can be obtained.

2.2   Linear Expenditure Systems

Demand systems that consider the allocation of expenditures among a number of goods are referred to as expenditure systems. Linear expenditure systems (LESs) that allow for habit formation in food consumption have been used by Pollak and Wales (1969) and McFall Lamm (1982). Both studies analyze habit formation using US macrodata. Pollak and Wales analyze habit formation in aggregate food consumption, whereas McFall Lamm analyzes habit formation in a wide range of food groups.

For LES, the direct utility function, $U(X)$, is assumed to have the form

$$U(X) = \sum_{i=1}^{n} a_i \log (x_i - b_i), a_i > 0 \forall i, (x_i - b_i) > 0 \forall i, \sum_{i=1}^{n} a_i = 1, \tag{1}$$

where x_i denotes the quantity of good i and n the number of goods. To derive the demand function, the direct utility function (1) is maximized subject to the budget constraint

$$\sum_{i=1}^{n} p_i x_i = m \tag{2}$$

where p_i is the price for the ith good and m is total expenditure on the n goods. The resulting ordinary (i.e., Marshallian) demand function is

$$x_i = b_i - \frac{a_i}{p_i} \sum_{k=1}^{n} p_k b_k + \frac{a_i}{p_i} m. \tag{3}$$

A demand system consistent with utility maximization is said to be "theoretically plausible." The LES is the only theoretically plausible demand system for which expenditure on each good is a linear function of all prices and expenditure.[3] The LES is transparent in the sense that its parameters have simple behavioral interpretations. In this model, a household is often described as first purchasing "necessary" or "committed" quantities of each good $(b_1, \ldots, b_n)$, and then dividing its remaining expenditure, $(m - \sum p_i b_i)$, among the goods in fixed proportions $(a_1, \ldots, a_n)$. Thus, the quantities $(b_1, \ldots, b_n)$ can be interpreted as a "necessary basket."[4]

Pollak and Wales (1969) extend the LES by adding dynamics. Dynamics are obtained in the model by allowing the bs in the direct utility function (1) to be functions of past consumption. Pollak and Wales suggest a variety of functional forms, where one of the

---

[3] In expenditure form the LES is given by $p_i x_i = p_i b_i + a_i(m - \sum_{k=1}^{n} p_k b_k)$. Indeed, the LES owes its name to the fact that expenditure on each good is a linear function of all prices and expenditure. The equation for the budget share, w_i, devoted to good i can be written as $w_i = p_i b_i / m + a_i(1 - \sum_{k=1}^{n} p_k b_k / m)$.

[4] An often criticized shortcoming of the LSE, especially when applied to household budget data, is its property of expenditure proportionality. In the case of expenditure proportionality, marginal budget shares are independent of the level of expenditure, implying that rich and poor households spend the same fraction of an extra dollar on each good. For the LES the marginal budget shares are equal to the as.

simplest assumptions is that b_i in period t, i.e., b_{it}, is a linear function of consumption of the ith good in the previous period, $x_{i,t-1}$, namely:

$$b_{it} = \bar{b}_i + \beta_i x_{i,t-1}. \tag{4}$$

β_i is a *habit-forming coefficient*, which is positive if habit formation is present. A more general specification would be, for instance, to allow b_{it} to depend linearly on the consumption of all the n goods in the previous period, e.g., $b_{it} = f(x_{i,t-1}, \ldots, x_{n,t-1})$. If all goods are subject to habit formation of the type described by (4), then the utility function becomes

$$U(X_t; X_{t-1}) = \sum_{i=1}^{n} a_i \log (x_{i,t} - \bar{b}_i - \beta_i x_{i,t-1}), \tag{5}$$

with the corresponding short-run demand function

$$x_{i,t} = \bar{b}_i + \beta_i x_{i,t-1} - \frac{a_i}{p_{i,t}} \sum_{k=1}^{n} p_{kt} \beta_k x_{k,t-1} - \frac{a_i}{p_{i,t}} \sum_{k=1}^{n} p_{k,t} \bar{b}_k + \frac{a_i}{b_i} m. \tag{6}$$

The semicolon separating X_t and X_{t-1} in (5) indicates that the preference ordering over current consumption X_t is conditional on past consumption, X_{t-1}. These short-run demand functions, like their static counterparts (3), are locally linear in expenditure. By modifying the $b_{i,t}$ function, it is easy to extend the LES to depend on consumption in the more distant past rather than the immediately preceding period.

The LES is a special case of the more general quadratic expenditure system (QES), a functional form where the demand equations are quadratic in expenditure.[5] Darrough, Pollak, and Wales (1983) and Heien and Durham (1991) apply the QES to analyze habit formation in household food consumption by British and Japanese, and US households, respectively.

2.3   The Almost Ideal Demand System

The restrictions embedded in the expenditure systems (such as expenditure proportionality; see also Christensen, Jorgenson, and Lau 1975 and Deaton and Muellbauer 1980b: 64–7) have prompted the development of other models. A number of researchers approximate the direct utility function, the indirect utility function, or the cost function by some specific functional form that has sufficient parameters to be regarded as a reasonable approximation of whatever the true unknown function may be. In the empirical analysis of food habit formation, the most commonly used model is the dynamic versions of the almost ideal demand system (AIDS), which incorporates a flexible functional form of the cost function.

---

[5] For a thorough description of the QES, see Pollak and Wales (1978).

Blanciforti and Green (1983), Pashardes (1986), Alessie and Kapteyn (1991), Ingco (1991), Holt and Goodwin (1997), Rickertsen (1998), Guha (2004), and Liao and Chern (2007) apply dynamic AIDS in their analyses of food demand. Blanciforti and Green analyze US macro-data on aggregate food consumption and several more specific food categories. Pashardes (1986) and Alessie and Kapteyn (1991) analyze aggregate food consumption in the United Kingdom and the Netherlands, respectively. Ingco analyzes consumption of several food groups in the Philippines. Holt and Goodwin use an inverse dynamic AIDS to analyze US demand for meats, chicken, and turkey. Rickertsen studies the demand for food and beverages in Norway. And Guha (2004) and Liao and Chern (2007) analyze demand for various food groups in rural India and China, respectively.

The almost ideal demand system is derived from a flexible form of the household's cost function $\log c(u, p) = \alpha_0 + \sum_k \alpha_k \log p_k + \frac{1}{2} \sum_k \sum_j \gamma_{kj} \log p_k p_j + u\beta_0 \prod_k p_k^{\beta_k}$, where u is utility. In budget share form, the static demand function is given by

$$w_i = \alpha_i + \sum_j \gamma_{ij} \log p_j + \beta_i \log (m/P) \tag{7}$$

where P is a price index defined by $\log P = \alpha_0 + \sum_k \alpha_k \log p_k + \frac{1}{2} \sum_j \sum_k \gamma_{jk} \log p_k \log p_j$. In applied work this price index is often approximated by Stone's (1954a) index $\log P = \sum_k w_k \log p_k$. Blanciforti and Green (1983) pioneer in adding dynamics to Deaton and Muellbauer's AIDS model. They express α_i, in equation (7), as a linear function of previous consumption levels.[6] In a later study, Alessie and Kapteyn (1991) specify a dynamic AIDS by expressing α_i as a linear function of previous consumption, in budget share form, lagged one period.[7] Their version of the dynamic AIDS can then be written as

$$w_{it} = \bar{\alpha}_i + \sum_{j=1}^n \varphi_{ij} w_{j,t-1} + \sum_{j=1}^n \gamma_{ij} \log p_{jt} + \beta_i \log (m/P), \tag{8}$$

where P is defined by $\log P = \alpha_0 + \sum_{k=1}^n (\bar{\alpha}_k + \sum_{k=1}^n \varphi_{kj} w_{j,t-1}) \log p_{k,t} + \frac{1}{2} \sum_{k=1}^n \sum_{j=1}^n \gamma_{kj} \log p_{kt} \ln p_{jt}$.

2.4   Translog Demand Systems

Translog utility functions offer flexible functional forms of the utility function. They have been used to analyze dynamics in food demand by Manser (1976), Menkhaus,

---

[6] Although this specification introduces dynamics to the demand function in a simple way, it does not satisfy adding up unless one is willing to impose the additional restriction that the parameter of the lagged budget share is the same in all equations.

[7] To obtain a dynamic consumption system consistent with cost minimization, Ray (1984) and Blanciforti, Green, and King (1986) adapt the expenditure function to allow for adjustment costs. The resulting demand equations contain more parameters than the demand equations presented in equation (8).

St Clair, and Hallingbye (1985), Meghir and Weber (1996), Carrasco, Labeaga, and Lopez-Salido (2005), and Zhen and Wohlgenant (2006).

The *indirect translog utility function*, introduced by Christensen, Jorgenson, and Law (1975), approximates the indirect utility function by a quadratic form in the logarithms of the price-to-expenditure ratios, i.e., the specification provides a local second-order approximation to any indirect utility function, and is given by

$$V(p,m) = -\sum \alpha_k \log \frac{p_k}{m} - \frac{1}{2} \sum\sum \beta_{kj} \log \frac{p_k}{m} \log \frac{p_j}{m}, \beta_{ij} = \beta_{ji}, \sum \alpha_k = 1. \tag{9}$$

Applying the logarithmic form of Roy's Identity (see e.g., Christensen, Jorgenson, and Law 1975), the budget share, w_i, equations are given by

$$w_i = \frac{\alpha_i + \sum_j \beta_{ij} \log (p_j/m)}{1 + \sum\sum \beta_{kj}(p_j/m)}. \tag{10}$$

In a dynamic specification of the model, Manser (1976) allows α_k in (9) to depend linearly on consumption in the previous period by the function $\alpha_{k,t} = \bar{\alpha}_k + \delta_k x_{k,t-1}$, resulting in a dynamic budget share equation of the form

$$w_i = \frac{\bar{\alpha}_i + \delta_i x_{i,t-1} + \sum_j \beta_{ij} \log (p_j/m)}{1 + \sum \delta_i x_{i,t-1} + \sum\sum \beta_{kj}(p_j/m)}. \tag{11}$$

Menkhaus, St Clair, and Hallingbye (1985) use the same specification to analyze demand for beef, pork, and chicken.

The *direct translog utility function* is given by a function quadratic in the logarithms of the quantities consumed:

$$U(X) = \sum a_k \log x_k + \frac{1}{2} \sum\sum b_{kj} \log x_k \log x_j, b_{ij} = b_{ji}, \sum a_k = 1. \tag{12}$$

A dynamic version of the direct translog model is presented in Meghir and Weber (1996), where (12) is augmented by the expression $\sum_{k=1}^{n} \gamma_k \log x_{k,t} \log x_{k,t-1}$, i.e., $x_{k,t}$ is allowed to interact with the lagged value of itself $x_{k,t-1}$ but not with lagged values of other goods. The same model is used by Carrasco, Labeaga, and Lopez-Salido (2005), who analyze habit formation in consumption of food at home. Zhen and Wohlgenant (2006) also apply a direct translog utility function in their analysis of meat demand under rational habit formation.

2.5 Discrete Choice Models

Discrete choice models are advantageous when treating products as bundles of characteristics, i.e., moving from product space to characteristics space (see Lancaster 1971). Like the above models, discrete choice models are based on assumptions of utility-maximizing consumers. The parameter estimates provided by these models are therefore assumed to represent optimal economic decisions.

Several marketing studies on brand choice apply discrete choice models that include dynamics represented by brand loyalty (see Guadagni and Little 1983; Chintagunta 1993; Erdem 1996; Keane 1997; Ailawadi and Neslin 1998; Seetharaman, Ainslie, and Chintagunta 1999; Seetharaman 2004). Recently, a few economics studies using discrete choice models to analyze dynamics have emerged. Richards, Patterson, and Tegene (2007) use a mixed multinomial logit model (MMNL) to analyze rational addiction associated with food nutrients; Arnade, Gopinath, and Pick (2008) use a dynamic probit model to analyze demand for cheese; and Thunström (2010) uses an MMNL to analyze habit formation in breakfast cereal consumption.

Here we focus on providing an overview of the application of dynamic multinomial logit models. The most general discrete choice model is the MMNL, also referred to as the random coefficients logit model, random parameter logit, the hybrid logit, or the mixed logit model.[8]

The random utility model provides the theoretical foundation for multinomial logit models. In the random utility model, utility of a choice alternative, j (for instance, a specific commodity, brand, or nutrient), for household n in period t, is determined by factors observed by the researcher, x_{njt}, and factors unobserved by the researcher, ε_{njt}, i.e., $V_{njt} = \beta' x_{jnt} + \varepsilon_{njt}$. The unobserved part of utility, ε_{njt}, is a random variable. The household chooses the alternative j (of J possible choices) that yields the highest utility.

In the multinomial logit (MNL) model, the unobserved part of the utility is assumed to be extreme value as well as identically and independently distributed (iid), i.e., error terms are uncorrelated over time and alternatives. The iid assumption gives rise to the independence of irrelevant alternatives (IIA) property, a property that often imposes unrealistic restrictions on substitution patterns between alternatives (see Train 2002; Hensher, Rose, and Greene 2005). The MMNL relaxes the iid assumption and hence does not have the restrictions imposed by the IIA property.

The MNL can capture the dynamics of repeated choice if unobserved factors are independent over time in repeated choice situations. The MMNL, however, allows for unobserved heterogeneity in preferences across consumers.[9] This feature of the MMNL may be particularly helpful when analyzing habit formation. Heckman (1981) notes that observed choice persistence may be a result of both habit formation and preference heterogeneity. Specific characteristics (for instance, being diabetic) may result in a consumer repeatedly choosing non-sweetened yogurts over other types of yogurt, for example. In this case, the choice of non-sweetened yogurt is not reinforced by

---

[8] The MMNL can approximate any discrete choice model (McFadden and Train 2000). For instance, an MMNL with fixed parameters collapses to a multinomial logit model (MNL) and an MMNL with heterogeneity in the alternative specific intercepts approximates a nested logit model (Hensher, Rose, and Greene 2008).

[9] The MNL can represent heterogeneity in preferences, or taste, relating to characteristics observed by the researcher, but not random taste variation, i.e., differences in taste that cannot be linked to observed characteristics.

previous choices (habit formation) but is merely a result of consumer preferences. If heterogeneity is present in the true model but ignored, the degree of habit formation tends to be overestimated.

A general form of the MMNL may be described as follows. Household n's indirect utility of choosing product j at time t is defined as

$$V_{njt} = \beta'_n x_{njt} + \varepsilon_{njt} = (\bar{\beta}' + \mu'_n) x_{njt} + \varepsilon_{njt} = \bar{\beta}' x_{njt} + \mu'_n x_{njt} + \varepsilon_{njt} \tag{13}$$

where the parameter vector β_n consists of two parts: $\bar{\beta}$, which is common to all households and equal to the mean of the distribution of all individual β_n s, and a household-specific error term, μ_n, with zero mean (i.e., preferences may be heterogeneous across individuals).[10] The parameter β_n is distributed in the population with density $f(\beta_n \mid \theta)$, where θ represents the parameters of the distribution for β_n (i.e., the mean and the variance). The functional form, $f(\tilde{n})$, is specified by the researcher. In the MMNL, the unobserved part of utility consists of $\xi_{njt} = \mu'_n x_{njt} + \varepsilon_{njt}$. As in the MNL, the error term ε_{jnt} is assumed to be iid extreme value. The distribution of μ_n differs from the iid extreme value distribution, however.

If household n faces a sequence of T repeated choices over time, it can be shown that the unconditional choice probability of the household making the observed choice sequence is

$$P(y_n \mid x, \theta) = \int_{\beta_n} \prod_{t=1}^{T} \left(\frac{e^{\beta'_n x_{nit}}}{\sum_j e^{\beta'_n x_{njt}}} \right) f(\beta_n \mid \theta) d\beta_n = \int_{\beta_n} \prod_{t=1}^{T} L_{nit}(\beta_n) f(\beta_n \mid \theta) d\beta_n. \tag{14}$$

Exact maximum likelihood estimation of (14) is not possible since the integral cannot be calculated analytically. Simulation-based estimation techniques are therefore used. For excellent descriptions of the estimation procedure and properties of the simulated choice probabilities, see, e.g., Revelt and Train (1998), Hensher and Greene (2003), and Hensher, Rose, and Greene (2005). Train (2003) shows that lagged dependent variables may enter the model without revising the estimation procedure.

None of the models presented above can be said a priori to be superior—it depends on the analysis and the type of data available. While the LES has also been used because of easy interpretation of parameters, it has been criticized for its restrictive functional form describing individual preferences. The translog models and the AIDS apply less restrictive functional forms on the individual preferences. The disadvantage of both models is that they are non-linear in the variables, which can complicate estimation. However, in the AIDS it is the price index P alone that gives rise to non-linearity. Linearity can therefore be achieved by applying Stone's price index to the model, which may facilitate estimation. Some of the reviewed studies adapt the direct or indirect utility function or the expenditure function to account for habit formation

[10] β_n can also be allowed to vary over time, and may be either alternative-specific or generic across alternatives, i.e., the strength of state dependence may, for instance, be the same for all alternatives, or vary across products.

or adjustment costs. However, a relatively large proportion of the studies adjust the demand functions directly to account for habit formation. This is usually done by adding previous consumption levels or budget shares to the demand equation.

The discrete choice models are particularly well suited for analyses of demand for certain attributes in food. However, the flexible structure of the most general discrete choice mode, the MMNL, may result in empirical identification problems of the parameters (see, e.g., Cherchi and Ortúzar 2008; Revelt and Train 1998 n. 8).

3   RESULTS

Empirical studies on habit formation in food consumption can be classified into two broad categories: macro-data time-series studies and micro-data (household/individual panel data) studies. Table 31.2 provides a summary of the results from these studies, and includes information on food categories studied, type of data, choice of country, and whether habit formation is found or not found, or if the results are mixed. An overview of all reviewed studies on food consumption and habit formation is given in Table 31.1.

Habit formation has been analyzed for a wide variety of food consumption, from aggregate food consumption to specific food categories, products, brand choices, and, recently, even nutrients. Table 31.2 shows that studies analyzing habit formation in aggregate food consumption (based on macro- or micro-data) come to mixed conclusions: some find habit formation in aggregate food consumption (Darrough, Pollak, and Wales 1983; Pashardes 1986; Naik and Moore 1996) and others do not (Alessie and Kapteyn 1991; Dynan 2000; Flavin and Nakagawa 2004). One study (Pollak and Wales 1969) finds mixed evidence of habit formation in aggregate food consumption.

A clear majority of macro- or micro-data-based studies analyzing more disaggregated data (e.g., different food categories, brands, or nutrients) do find habit formation in consumption of the food analyzed. However, the conclusions depend on the data and methods used. The micro-data-based studies that apply discrete choice models reviewed here all find habit formation in food consumption. The results are more mixed in micro-data-based studies that apply continuous demand models to study habit formation in broader food categories.

The results of studies analyzing habit formation in various food categories imply that the strength of habit formation varies across different types of food. For instance, Price and Gislason (2001) used annual retail-level Japanese data for five commodities (meat, cereals, fruits, vegetables, and seafood) for the period 1963–91. Their results suggest that consumption of meat and cereals is characterized by habit formation, whereas consumption of fruit and vegetables does not seem to be enhanced by habit. Some household panel data studies (e.g., Guha 2004; Khare and Inman 2006; Liao and Chern 2007) have also found mixed evidence of habit formation, i.e., that some food consumption is characterized by habit formation while other food consumption is not. In addition, even where habit formation is found to be associated with consumption of

Table 31.2 Summary of results: reports if habit formation is found (Yes), not found (No), or whether results are mixed (Mixed)[a]

Study	Micro-data			Macro-data			N
	Yes	No	Mixed	Yes	No	Mixed	
Food category							
Aggregate	4	4	0	3	1	1	13
Bakery and cereal	4	0	1	3	0	0	8
Coffee	1	0	0	1	0	0	2
Dairy	4	1	1	0	0	0	6
Fish	2	0	0	1	1	0	4
Fruit and vegetables	1	0	1	2	1	0	5
Ketchup	4	0	0	0	0	0	4
Meats	1	0	1	6	1	1	10
Nutrients	1	0	0	0	0	0	1
Oil	1	0	1	0	0	0	2
Snack food	1	0	0	0	0	0	1
Other	0	0	1	0	0	0	1
Method							
Single demand	1	0	0	3	0	0	4
Linear expenditure	2	0	0	1	0	1	4
AIDS	0	2	2	4	0	0	8
Translog demand	1	1	0	1	1	1	5
Discrete choice	10	0	0	0	0	0	10
Other	1	1	0	0	1	1	4
Country							
China	0	0	1	0	0	0	1
India[b]	0	0	1	0	0	0	1
Japan	1	0	0	0	0	1	2
Netherlands	0	1	0	0	0	0	1
Spain	1	1	0	0	0	0	2
Sweden	1	0	0	0	0	0	1
UK	1	0	0	1	0	0	2
USA	12	2	0	5	2	2	23

[a] All studies in Table 31.1, except McFall Lamm (1982) and Edgerton et al. (1996), are summarized in this table.
[b] This study focuses on the presence of habit formation in the regions of Tamil Nadu, Punjab, West Bengal, and Gujarat. Habit formation is in all regions found for some food categories but not for others.

virtually all foods analyzed, there may be considerable variation in the strength of habit formation across different types of food (see, e.g., McFall Lamm 1982). Thus, when aggregating consumption of food categories associated with varying degrees of habit formation, statistically significant habit effects that are present in a disaggregated analysis might be lost (or vice versa).

Micro-data studies using discrete choice models are most often marketing studies on brand choice. It should be noted that these studies do not focus explicitly on habit formation; however, they include lagged dependent variables in their analyses and thus contain measures of habit formation. All these studies find evidence of habit formation in product choice. For example, Guadagni and Little (1983), Chintagunta (1993), Erdem (1996), Keane (1997), Ailawadi and Neslin (1998), Seetharaman, Ainslie, and Chintagunta (1999), and Seetharaman (2004) all report significant effects of previous brand choices on current brand choice, suggesting that selection of a particular brand is reinforced by having chosen the same brand previously. It is noteworthy, however, that many of these studies use similar empirical models and partly or fully the same micro-level data set, which is likely to explain much of the similar findings in the influence of lagged brand choice. Economics studies analyzing habit formation using highly dis-aggregated data include Richards, Patterson, and Tegene (2007), Arnade, Gopinath, and Pick (2008), and Thunström (2010). These apply discrete choice models to data on snack foods, cheese, and breakfast cereals, respectively. All three studies find evidence of habit formation in food product choice.

Aggregation of products is only a problem if we wish to generalize results on habit formation across food categories. A perhaps more important data aggregation problem is the one associated with aggregation across households. As Heckman (1981) notes, to identify true habit formation, the researcher needs to control for individual (or household) heterogeneity in preferences. Regardless of the food category analyzed, or the level of product aggregation, studies based on macro-data (and therefore unable to control for household-specific preferences) are likely to overestimate habit formation.

The bias resulting from aggregating data across households has been analyzed by, for instance, Heien and Durham (1991) and Naik and Moore (1996), who use US household panel data to analyze habit formation in food consumed at home and outside the home, and aggregate food consumption, respectively. Both studies confirm Heckman's results and find that controlling for preference heterogeneity substantially reduces the estimated effect of habit formation. To enable identification of true habit formation, it is therefore necessary to use individual (or household) panel data. All the studies applying discrete choice models mentioned above use household panel data. In addition, an increasing number of studies based on continuous demand models (Alessie and Kapteyn 1991; Naik and Moore 1996; Meghir and Weber 1996; Dynan 2000; Guha 2004; Carrasco, Labeaga, and Lopez-Salido 2005; Khare and Inman 2006; Browning and Collado 2007; Liao and Chern 2007) use household panel data. The relatively limited number of studies based on household panel data can be explained by the lack of access to household-level data (Carrasco, Labeaga, and Lopez-Salido 2005; Browning and Collado 2007).

A majority of the studies applying household panel data to continuous demand models find that food consumption is habit-forming. However, a few studies based on household panel data find no evidence of habit formation: Alessie and Kapteyn (1991), who analyze habit formation in Dutch aggregate food consumption using household expenditure data from 1980–1; Meghir and Weber (1996), who analyze habit formation in US food consumed at home using household expenditure data from 1980–91; and Dynan (2000), who analyzes habit formation in total US food consumption using household expenditure data from 1974–87. Dynan (2000: 392) concludes that "habit formation has at most an extremely limited influence on consumers' behavior."

As noted by Carrasco, Labeaga, and Lopez-Salido (2005), many early household panel data studies on habit formation in food consumption (e.g., Meghir and Weber 1996; Naik and Moore 1996; Dynan 2000) did not control for potential endogeneity and/or time-invariant unobserved heterogeneity across households. Using Spanish household panel data on expenditures for up to eight consecutive quarters, Carrasco, Labeaga, and Lopez-Salido (2005) estimate Euler equations and the within-period marginal rate of substitution between commodities, controlling for time-invariant unobserved heterogeneity across households and using lagged values of the variables as instruments. The authors find evidence of habit formation in food consumed at home when they control for unobserved heterogeneity and use adequate instruments; however, when they do not control for unobserved heterogeneity, they find no evidence of habit formation.

Browning and Collado (2007) used the same expenditure survey as Carrasco, Labeaga, and Lopez-Salido (2005) to analyze habit formation. They estimate a dynamic AIDS model[11] and come to different conclusions. Browning and Collado, who also apply an instrumental variable approach and allow for unobserved correlated heterogeneity across households, find no evidence of habit formation in food consumed at home, but they do find evidence of habit formation in food consumed outside the home. This seems to indicate that the choice of method and selection of sample also influence the results.

Another aspect that might influence the finding of habit formation is the frequency of the data or the length of the period analyzed. For instance, preferences and habits may change over time. Regarding the studies using micro-data, the length of the period analyzed does not seem to have a clear influence on the finding of habit formation. However, for the studies based on macro-data, those with the shortest time-series (Menkhaus, St Clair, and Hallingbye 1985, who use a sample covering sixteen years, and Flavin and Nakagawa 2004, who use a sample covering ten years) find no significant effect of habit formation, whereas the other macro-data-based studies (with an average sample length of 29.4 years—min. 24, max. 37 years) either find habit formation in all food consumption or report mixed results.

As shown by Table 31.2, the great majority of studies on habit formation in food consumption analyze habit formation either in aggregate groups of food or in specific food products. Khare and Inman (2006) and Richards, Patterson, and Tegene (2007) are notable by taking a different approach, analyzing habit formation in consumption of food nutrients. Richards, Patterson, and Tegene (2007) apply a discrete choice model to US household panel data on snack consumption and analyze rational addiction in the consumption of food nutrients associated with obesity. Their results suggest that,

---

[11] Browning and Collado (2007) use time dummies instead of prices in the demand functions, estimating each demand equation separately.

apart from sodium, consumption of all nutrients is addictive, i.e., associated with habit formation, and that addiction to carbohydrates is stronger than addiction to other nutrients. Khare and Inman (2006) analyze habit formation in nutrient consumption across meals during the day, applying a hierarchical linear model to US panel data on individual meal consumption. They find habit formation in the consumption of all nutrients analyzed. Their results also imply that consumption of nutrients is more habitual within meals (e.g., the impact of yesterday's breakfast on today's breakfast) than across meals.

Note, finally, that a vast majority of the studies summarized in Table 31.2 are based on US data, suggesting that there are many markets that are not covered by the literature on habit formation in food.

4   CONCLUDING REMARKS

The purpose of this chapter is to summarize and analyze the empirical literature on food consumption and habit formation, as well as to give an overview of the most commonly used methods in analyses of habit formation. This is an important research area since the question of habit formation in food consumption has strong implications for food policy. For instance, if food consumption is characterized by a high level of habit formation, information campaigns and taxes will have little effect on demand in the short term compared to cases where habit formation is weak. In addition, if habit formation in food consumption is present but ignored in empirical models of food demand, the model will yield biased results.

The results of empirical studies analyzing habit formation in food consumption can be summarized as follows:

- A majority of the empirical studies find that food consumption is characterized by habit formation. It thus seems that current preferences depend on past consumption and that past consumption reinforces the propensity to consume the same good over time, suggesting that dynamics are a crucial component of models of food demand. If dynamics are omitted from the empirical analysis, and habit formation is present, parameter estimates for food consumption are very likely to be biased. However, some of the studies that find evidence of habit formation are based on macro-data that tend to overestimate habit effects and others are based on brand choices that do not explicitly focus on habit formation.
- The results seem to depend on the data sets and empirical methods. All micro-data studies reviewed here that apply discrete choice models to analyze brand choices find evidence of habit formation, whereas the results are more mixed in macro-data studies and in micro-data studies using continuous demand models. In addition, habit formation is more often found in studies using highly disaggregated product data.

- Many early studies on habit formation in food use macro-data. They are therefore unable to distinguish between preference heterogeneity and habit formation. Habit effects tend to be overestimated if preference heterogeneity is not controlled for. To be able to distinguish between habit formation and preference heterogeneity, it is necessary to use micro-level panel data.
- The degree of habit formation in food consumption appears to vary across food commodities. If the researcher is interested in the strength of habit formation for certain types of food, it is therefore important to use disaggregated data in the analysis. For example, if one is interested in the effect of campaigns targeted toward motivating people to consume a healthier diet, one has to consider the degree of habit formation of wholesome (and less wholesome) food.

An increasing number of studies have investigated whether habits influence food consumption choices. However, a number of important research questions concerning habit formation remain unanswered and constitute fruitful areas for future research.

Most empirical studies are based on US data. The lack of studies covering other markets is a significant gap in the research, since studies suggest that there are regional and/or cultural differences in the strength of habit formation associated with food consumption. For instance, Guha (2004) finds regional differences in the strength of habit formation in consumption of various foods in rural India, and Edgerton et al. (1996) find differences in the strength of habit formation of food across the Nordic countries.

Further, the difference in the strength of habit formation across different types of food constitutes an interesting research area. For instance, is consumption of organic foods associated with stronger or weaker habit formation than consumption of their conventional substitutes?

Another interesting question for future research is whether the degree of habit formation varies by household type. Few studies have analyzed such variations and the results of those that have are mixed. Seetharaman, Ainslie, and Chintagunta (1999) find no differences across households in the strength of habit formation for ketchup, peanut butter, margarine, or tuna, whereas Thunström (2010) finds evidence of variations across households in the strength of habit formation associated with breakfast cereal consumption.

Another interesting question to examine is whether habit formation is affected by the frequency that consumers purchase a certain food category; i.e., is consumption of food that households purchase frequently associated with stronger habit formation than food purchased less often? For instance, Seetharaman, Ainslie, and Chintagunta (1999) find that the strength of brand loyalty (habit formation) diminishes with the time elapsed since the previous purchase.

Price variations in survey-based panel data (or scanner data) are often relatively small, especially if the period covered by the data is short. As noted above, if food consumption is associated with habit formation, increases in the relative price of food will not immediately result in consumer adjustments of consumption. Field experiments where prices are changed more dramatically would therefore be of interest. This could be useful in analyses both of the strength of habit formation and of the rate at which adjustment occurs for different types of food.

To summarize, considerable ground on how habits influence food consumption has been covered in the literature, but many important questions remain to be addressed. It is therefore likely that a literature review in ten years' time will reveal new research findings that increase our understanding of how habits are related to food consumption choices.

REFERENCES

Ailawadi, K. L., and S. A. Neslin. 1998. "The Effect of Promotion on Consumption: Buying More and Consuming it Faster." *Journal of Marketing Research* 35: 390–8.

Alessie, R., and A. Kapteyn. 1991. "Habit Formation, Interdependent Preferences and Demographic Effects in the Almost Ideal Demand System." *Economic Journal* 101/406: 404–19.

Arnade, C., M. Gopinath, and D. Pick. 2008. "Brand Inertia in U.S. Household Cheese Consumption." *American Journal of Agricultural Economics* 90/3: 813–26.

Blanciforti, L., and R. Green. 1983. "An Almost Ideal Demand System Incorporating Habits: An Analysis of Expenditures on Food and Aggregate Commodity Groups." *Review of Economics and Statistics* 65: 511–15.

————, and G. King. 1986. *U.S. Consumer Behaviour over the Postwar Period: An Almost Ideal Demand System Analysis*. Davis: Giannini Foundation of Agricultural Economics, University of California. <http://escholarship.org/uc/item/3zh108k2>.

Browning, M., and D. M. Collado. 2007. "Habits and Heterogeneity in Demands: A Panel Data Analysis." *Journal of Applied Econometrics* 22/3: 625–40.

Carrasco, R., J. M. Labeaga, and J. D. Lopez-Salido. 2005. "Consumption and Habits: Evidence from Panel Data." *Economic Journal* 115/1: 144–65.

Chang, H. 1977. "Functional Forms and the Demand for Meat in the United States." *Review of Economics and Statistics* 59/3: 355–9.

Cherchi, E., and J. de D. Ortúzar. 2008. "Empirical Identification in the Mixed Logit Model: Analysing the Effect of Data Richness." *Networks and Spatial Economics* 8: 109–24.

Chintagunta, P. K. 1993. "Investigating Purchase Incidence, Brand Choice and Purchase Quantity Decisions of Households." *Marketing Science* 12/2: 184–208.

Christensen, L. R., D. W. Jorgenson, and L. J. Lau. 1975. "Transcendental Logarithmic Utility Functions." *American Economic Review* 65: 367–83.

Darrough, M. N., R. A. Pollak, and T. J. Wales. 1983. "Dynamic and Stochastic Structure: An Analysis of Three Time Series of Household Budget Studies." *Review of Economics and Statistics* 65: 274–81.

Deaton, A., and J. Muellbauer. 1980a. "An Almost Ideal Demand System." *American Economic Review* 70: 312–26.

————. 1980b. *Economic and Consumer Behavior*. Cambridge: Cambridge University Press.

Dynan, K. E. 2000. "Habit Formation in Consumer Preferences: Evidence from Panel Data." *American Economic Review* 90/3: 391–406.

Edgerton, D. L., B. Assarsson, A. Hummelmose, I. P. Laurila, K. Rickertsen, and P. H. Vale. 1996. *The Econometrics of Demand Systems: With Applications to Food Demand in the Nordic Countries*. Dordrecht: Kluwer Academic Publishers.

Erdem, T. 1996. "A Dynamic Analysis of Market Structure Based Panel Data." *Marketing Science* 15/4: 359–78.

Flavin, M., and S. Nakagawa. 2004. *A Model of Housing in the Presence of Adjustment Costs: A Structural Interpretation of Habit Persistence*. NBER Working Paper No. 10458. Cambridge, MA: National Bureau of Economic Research.

Guadagni, P. M., and J. D. Little. 1983. "A Logit Model of Brand Choice Calibrated on Scanner Data." *Marketing Science* 2/3: 203–38.

Guha, P. 2004. *Habit Formation in Consumption: A Case Study of Rural India*. EconWPA, Econometrics No. 0412012. <http://129.3.20.41/eps/em/papers/0412/0412012.pdf>.

Heckman, J. J. 1981. "Heterogeneity and State Dependence." In S. Rosen, ed., *Studies in Labor Markets*. Chicago: University of Chicago Press.

Heien, D., and C. Durham. 1991. "A Test of the Habit Formation Hypothesis Using Household Data." *Review of Economics and Statistics* 2: 189–99.

Hensher, D. A., and W. H. Greene. 2003. "The Mixed Logit Model: The State of Practice." *Transportation* 30: 133–76.

Hensher, D. A., J. M. Rose, and W. H. Greene. 2005. *Applied Choice Analysis*. Cambridge: Cambridge University Press.

———————. 2008. "Combining RP and SP Data: Biases in Using the Nested Logit 'Trick'—Contrasts with Flexible Mixed Logit Incorporating Panel and Scale Effects." *Journal of Transport Geography* 16/2: 126–33.

Holt, M. T., and B. K. Goodwin. 1997. "Generalized Habit Formation in an Inverse Almost Ideal Demand System: An Application to Meat Expenditures in the U.S." *Empirical Economics* 22: 293–320.

Ingco, M. D. 1991. *Is Rice Becoming an Inferior Good? Food Demand in the Philippines*. Working Paper Series 722. Washington, DC: International Economics Department, World Bank.

Keane, M. P. 1997. "Modeling Heterogeneity and State Dependence in Consumer Choice Behavior." *Journal of Business and Economic Statistics* 15/3: 310–27.

Khare, A., and J. J. Inman. 2006. "Habitual Behavior in American Eating Patterns: The Role of Meal Occasions." *Journal of Consumer Research* 32: 567–75.

Klein, L. R., and H. Rubin. 1947–8. "A Constant-Utility Index of the Cost of Living." *Review of Economic Studies* 15: 84–7.

Lancaster, K. 1971. *Consumer Demand: A New Approach*. New York: Columbia University Press.

Liao, H., and W. S. Chern. 2007. "A Dynamic Analysis of Food Demand Patterns in Urban China." Selected Paper prepared for the Annual Meeting of the American Agricultural Economics Association, Portland, OR, July 29–Aug. 1.

McFadden, D., and K. Train. 2000. "Mixed MNL Models for Discrete Response." *Journal of Applied Econometrics* 15: 447–70.

McFall Lamm, R. 1982. "A System of Dynamic Demand Functions for Food." *Applied Economics* 14: 375–89.

Manser, M. 1976. "Elasticities of Demand for Food: An Analysis Using Non-Additive Utility Functions Allowing for Habit Formation." *Southern Economic Journal* 43: 879–91.

Meghir, C., and G. Weber. 1996. "Intertemporal Nonseparability or Borrowing Restrictions? A Disaggregate Analysis Using a U.S. Consumption Panel." *Econometrica* 64/5: 1151–81.

Menkhaus, D. J., J. S. St Clair, and S. Hallingbye. 1985. "A Reexamination of Consumer Buying Behavior for Beef, Pork and Chicken." *Western Journal of Agricultural Economics* 10/1: 116–25.

Naik, Y. N., and M. J. Moore. 1996. "Habit Formation and Intertemporal Substitution in Individual Food Consumption." *Review of Economics and Statistics* 78/2: 321–8.

Okunade, A. A. 1992. "Functional Forms and Habit Effects in the US Demand for Coffee." *Applied Economics* 24: 1203–12.

Pashardes, P. 1986. "Myopic and Forward Looking Behavior in a Dynamic Demand System." *International Economic Review* 27/2: 387–97.

Pollak, R. A. 1970. "Habit Formation and Dynamic Demand Functions." *Journal of Political Economy* 78: 745–63.

——— and T. J. Wales. 1969. "Estimation of the Linear Expenditure System." *Econometrica* 37: 629–750.

———. 1978. "Estimation of Complete Demand Systems from Household Budget Data: The Linear and Quadratic Expenditure Systems." *American Economic Review* 68: 348–59.

Pope, R., R. Green, and J. Eales. 1980. "Testing for Homogeneity and Habit Formation in a Flexible Demand Specification of U.S. Meat Consumption." *American Journal of Agricultural Economics* 62: 778–84.

Price, D. W., and C. Gislason. 2001. "Identification of Habit in Japanese Food Consumption." *Agricultural Economics* 24: 289–95.

Ray, R. 1984. "A Dynamic Generalisation of the Almost Ideal Demand System." *Economic Letters* 14: 235–9.

Revelt, D., and K. Train. 1998. "Mixed Logit with Repeated Choices: Households' Choices of Appliance Efficiency Level." *Review of Economics and Statistics* 80: 1–11.

Richards, T. J., P. M. Patterson, and A. Tegene. 2007. "Obesity and Nutrient Consumption: A Rational Addiction?" *Contemporary Economic Policy* 25/3: 309–24.

Rickertsen, K. 1998. "The Demand for Food and Beverages in Norway." *Agricultural Economics* 18: 89–100.

Seetharaman, P. B. 2004. "Modeling Multiple Sources of State Dependence in Random Utility Models: A Distributed Lag Approach." *Marketing Science* 23/2: 263–71.

———, A. Ainslie, and P. K. Chintagunta. 1999. "Investigating Household State Dependence Effects across Categories." *Journal of Marketing Research* 36 (Nov.), 488–500.

Stone, J. R. N. 1954a. *The Measurement of Consumers' Expenditure and Behaviour in the United Kingdom, 1920–1938*, 1. London: Cambridge University Press.

———1954b. "Linear Expenditure Systems and Demand Analysis: An Application to the Pattern of British Demand." *Economic Journal* 64: 511–27.

Thunström, L. 2010. "Preference Heterogeneity and Habit Persistence: The Case of Breakfast Cereal Consumption." *Journal of Agricultural Economics* 61/1: 76–96.

Train, K. 2003. *Discrete Choice Methods with Simulation*. Cambridge: Cambridge University Press.

Zhen, C., and M. K. Wohlgenant. 2006. "Food Safety and Habits in U.S. Demand under Rational Expectations." Paper presented at the Annual Meeting of the American Agricultural Economics Association, Long Beach, CA, July 23–6.

CHAPTER 32

....

DEMAND FOR MEAT QUALITY ATTRIBUTES

....

TED C. SCHROEDER AND GLYNN T. TONSOR*

1 INTRODUCTION

Consumer demand for meat is constantly changing and agricultural economists have been prolifically researching this change for more than twenty years. A web search of the phrase *meat demand change* using Google Scholar conducted during December 2009 resulted in 368,000 articles, of which 65 percent were published since 1990 and 35 percent since 2000. This large body of literature is rationalized by the global economic importance of meat in overall food consumption and the myriad of factors associated with changing consumer meat demand. Meat demand is complex and multifaceted and despite the massive literature agricultural economists still do not fully understand it, we do not have demand methodology mastered, and data shortcomings are pervasive.

The drivers of meat demand are numerous and aligned with evolving consumer preferences associated with changing lifestyles and available information. Among important changes in consumer preferences for meat products is evolving demand for broadly defined meat quality attributes. "Meat quality attributes" is a broad term encompassing a large array of desired product characteristics. The purpose of this chapter is to give an overview of demand for meat quality attributes and to discuss implications for industry stakeholders and policymakers. Discussion will focus especially on demand for red meat quality attributes by consumers in the United States and Europe.

Demand for meat quality attributes in the United States and Europe is a timely topic. The European Commission and United States signed a landmark Memorandum of Understanding in May 2009 attempting to reduce the long-standing beef trade dispute between the two major economic powers. Although under the specifications of this

* We gratefully acknowledge helpful comments and suggestions provided by Jayson Lusk.

agreement red meat markets across the nations involved will still not be highly integrated with each other, this agreement will serve as a catalyst for more red meat trade between Europe and the United States. The trade agreement, together with the long-standing limited access of US-raised beef in Europe, exemplifies the role government trade policies play in market access. Of course, trade policies are ultimately driven by domestic consumer demands as well as industry lobby efforts and political motivations.

2   Meat Demand Structural Change: Cause of Constant Research

Changes in price and income were once considered sufficient for explaining changes in demand over time. Much of demand theory and empirical work completed prior to the 1990s surrounded traditional demand determinants and model structure. However, traditional demand determinants have lost their ability to explain changes in per capita meat demand over time. For instance, Tonsor and Marsh (2007) estimate that approximately three-fourths of variability over time in US consumer beef and pork demand is driven by factors other than income and meat prices. Declining importance of income and prices in explaining meat demand corresponds with the declining proportion of total expenditures US and European consumers have allocated to all food products over the last couple decades (European Commission 2008; USDA ERS 2009).

Inability to explain demand with traditional model specifications prompted a huge body of research on the topic of structural change in meat demand. A Google Scholar search for the words *meat demand structural change* completed in December 2009 resulted in 73,600 articles. The essence of the problem was that meat demand model parameter estimates were changing over time. As a result, econometric models estimated using historical time-series data generated unstable parameter estimates. Furthermore, meat demand models were progressively less able to explain consumer demand changes using traditional determinants.

Tomek (1985) recognized the problem twenty-five years ago when he determined, using US meat demand data:

> Clearly the conventional models fit the recent period less well than they fit the earlier period and the deterioration in explanatory power is worse for beef than pork.... The poorer fit of the beef model is consistent with the hypothesis that new demand shifters are at work or that structural changes have occurred. (1985: 908–9)

Purcell (1998) found that even more pronounced beef demand structural changes were unexplainable by traditional demand determinants, prompting his conclusion:

> there is something acting on demand for beef and prompting prices to go down over time over and above the influence from changes in the level of beef quantity,

the impact of meat substitutes, changes in consumers' incomes, and any regular and rhythmic seasonal pattern in beef prices. (1998: 13)

In Europe, Bansback (1995) drew the same conclusions; the explanatory power of price and income effects on beef, pork, and lamb demand declined substantially relative to non-traditional factors affecting demand for meat. Why were traditional econometric demand models no longer working? Model misspecification was the culprit. Specifically, omission of evolving relevant demand shifters was a substantial part of the misspecification problem.

Traditional demand drivers are important to include in aggregate consumer demand analysis (Tonsor, Mintert, and Schroeder 2009). However, a host of demand shifters that used to be ignored have become progressively more important meat demand determinants. As a result, the omission of evolving demand shifters in traditional demand models results in biased, unreliable, and unstable parameter estimates and associated elasticities. Over time, in addition to traditional demand determinants, consumer demand for particular red meat product quality attributes has become more prominent in demand modeling. The increased importance of red meat quality attributes in demand is especially apparent in relatively affluent regions of the world such as the United States and European Union countries. This is because economic affluence is generally a prerequisite to being able to afford product quality attributes important to US and European consumers. Thus, properly specified meat demand models require variables capturing changing consumer lifestyles and preferences for specific meat quality attributes if models are to be of value in understanding consumer behavior.

3   DEMAND TRENDS

Before detailing the complexity of product quality factors affecting red meat demand, of interest is overall patterns in meat demand. Measuring changes in meat demand over time is not a trivial exercise as the precise data needed to determine consumer demand accurately do not exist. For example, nearly one-half of beef and pork consumed in the United States is at food service establishments. No price data exist for what consumers pay for meat products at food service. Without price data, one cannot determine demand. Many data challenges exist with respect to retail meat prices as well (Lensing and Purcell 2006). With data limitations in mind, US annual beef and pork retail demand indexes have been constructed to provide an estimate of consumer demand changes over time.

The US beef and pork demand indexes used here are calculated by Schroeder (2010) at Kansas State University. They are calculated by assuming constant own-price demand elasticities of −0.67 for beef and −0.69 for pork (based on a synthesis of several published studies). The demand index is calculated in the following way. First, inflation-adjusted retail price and per capita quantity consumed each year are collected. Given the per capita quantity consumed and the demand elasticity, the inflation-adjusted price that would have been present if the demand curve was the same as it was in 1980 is calculated (see Schroeder 2010 for a link to a spreadsheet containing formulae for this calculation). The demand index is then calculated as the price that would have been present without any demand curve shift as a percentage of the 1980 base year price. For example, a demand index value of 61 percent for beef in 2005 means that if the same quantity of beef per person were available in 2005 as in the base year of 1980, the inflation-adjusted retail beef price in 2005 would have only been 61 percent of the 1980 real price to clear the market.

Demand indexes calculated in this way provide a broad barometer of how demand is changing over time. However, several weaknesses and limitations surround demand indexes. Weaknesses include: (1) Only retail price is used, ignoring food service prices, which is important given the increasing prominence of food service. The challenge is that a representative food service price series does not exist. (2) A constant demand elasticity is assumed over time, which may not be reasonable. However, the demand indexes are not highly sensitive to reasonable elasticity changes. (3) The demand indexes include only domestic price and per capita consumption, ignoring export markets. Domestic price and consumption is affected by export markets, but a separate index for export market demand may be worth developing for industry to monitor in addition to domestic demand. (4) The index can be unstable and unable to be calculated if per capita consumption increases by a very large amount. For example, per capita consumption can expand so rapidly that on the base year demand curve, to get consumers to consume the amount of product they consumed, price would have to be zero or negative. This occurs with broilers and turkeys in the United States where consumption expanded so rapidly that starting with a base year of 1980, the index cannot be calculated by 1998 (see Schroeder 2010, for example, of how and why this occurs). (5) Finally, the demand index only reveals the demand pattern and provides no information about why demand shifted. Demand modeling must be completed to identify determinants of change.

The US retail beef demand index is presented in Figure 32.1. Striking is the decline in beef demand for eighteen consecutive years from 1980 to 1998. Also, the magnitude of beef demand decline is dramatic, reaching an index of 51 percent in 1998. That means that to get consumers to consume the same amount of beef per person in 1998 as they did in 1980, the real retail beef price would have to have been about half of what it was in 1980. After 1998 beef demand increased to 63 percent in 2004 and since then has weakened again, being 56 percent in 2008, and likely declined a small amount in 2009.

The US retail pork index is shown in Figure 32.2. Pork demand has bounced around without a marked trend over the 1998–2008 period. The retail pork demand index has remained primarily in the 70 percent to 80 percent range (relative to 1980) since 1992. In 2008 the index was at 67 percent and will likely end up being at a similar level in 2009.

The demand indexes, together with the fact that traditional demand drivers do a poor job of explaining demand changes, suggest that the beef industry in particular has not provided the meat product quality demanded by consumers relative to competing meats. That is, the dramatic decline in the US beef retail demand index means that beef

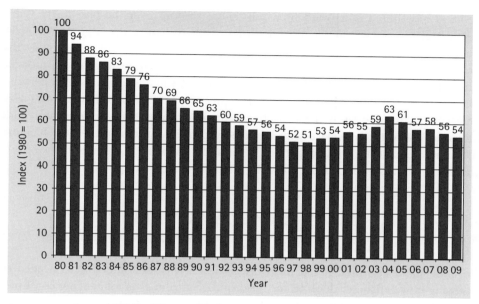

FIGURE 32.1 Annual US Beef Demand Index, 1980–2009 (Preliminary), 1980=100

Source: T. Schroeder, Kansas State University, Oct. 2009. <http://www.NAIBER.org>.

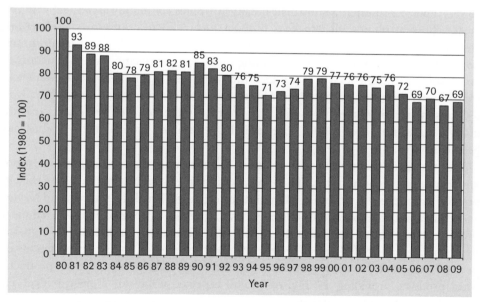

FIGURE 32.2 Annual US Pork Demand Index, 1980–2009 (Preliminary), 1980=100

Source: T. Schroeder, Kansas State University, Oct. 2009. <http://www.NAIBER.org>.

demand has shifted downward by a substantial amount over the past thirty years. Relative prices and consumer income do not explain these shifts (e.g., Tomek 1985; Purcell 1998). Thus, the implication is that the beef industry did not provide the product quality attributes consumers wanted relative to competing meat products. The pork industry has fared better than the beef industry in meeting consumer demand for quality, but even pork has lost demand relative to what it enjoyed in the early 1980s. One could conclude from the collective demand analyses that the beef and pork industries have not kept pace with competing protein sources relative to changing consumer demand for meat quality. This naturally leads us to the next focus of this chapter to discuss meat product characteristics consumers want.

4   MEAT QUALITY ATTRIBUTES

To understand and predict red meat demand better, careful attention is needed in assessing how consumer demand for meat quality attributes is influencing consumer meat purchasing decisions. Meat product quality is a broad term encompassing an array of product characteristics. Meat product characteristics can be broadly categorized as *extrinsic* and *intrinsic* (Bernués, Olaizola, and Corcoran 2003).

Intrinsic quality attributes refer to physical performance, product composition, and process-focused meat product attributes (Caswell, Noelke, and Mojduszka 2002; Gao 2007). Table 32.1 summarizes intrinsic quality attributes commonly associated with red meat. These attributes include how product form matches consumer preferences, pleasure associated with the eating experience, innate food safety and health/nutritional attributes associated with consuming meat, and provenance and production or processing characteristics of the product. Many intrinsic attributes are also characterized as *experience* product quality attributes, meaning they can be discerned or judged by consumers when they consume the product. Other quality traits are *credence attributes*, meaning they cannot necessarily be determined even after the product has been consumed.

Intrinsic meat quality is not known prior to consuming the product, and often not known even after consumption. Therefore, *extrinsic* meat product attributes are used to provide signal cues to consumers about intrinsic quality (Brucks, Zeithaml, and Naylor 2000; Miyazaki, Grewal, and Goodstein 2005). Examples of specific extrinsic red meat product attributes are summarized in Table 32.2. Consumers synthesize cues signaled by extrinsic product attributes, together with past experience, to form expectations or perceptions about the utility of purchasing and consuming particular meat products. Meat products providing the highest overall expected utility for a given budget are those the consumer will purchase.

Table 32.1 Intrinsic quality attributes of red meat products

Performance	Composition	Process focused
Sensory/organoleptic	Food safety	Provenance/process
Flavor[a]	Food-borne pathogens[b]	Animal welfare[b]
Tenderness[a]	Pesticide or drug residues[b]	Origin[b]
Color[a]	Toxins or contaminants[b]	Traceability[b]
Freshness[b]	Food additives[b]	Natural[b]
Aroma[a]	Spoilage[a]	Organic[b]
Purge[a]	Physical hazards[a]	Biotechnology[b]
Blemishes[a]		Environmental[b]
		Growth hormones[b]
Value/function	Nutrition/health	
Product form[a]	Calories[b]	
Meat cut[a]	Cholesterol[b]	
Convenience[a]	Fat content/type[b]	
Freshness[b]	Carbohydrates[b]	
Size[a]	Sodium[b]	
	Protein[b]	
	Iron[b]	
	Zinc[b]	

[a] Experience product attribute.
[b] Credence product attribute.
Source: Adapted from Gao (2007).

Table 32.2 Extrinsic quality attributes of red meat products

Cues	Tests and measurements
Price	Certification
Brand	Labeling
Co-brand	Inspection stamps
Store reputation	Quality assurances
Past purchase experience	Production/genetic information
Product packaging	Government regulations
Product presentation	
Advertising	
Media information	

Source: Adapted from Gao (2007).

5 CONSUMERS REVEAL PREFERENCES

Researchers realized that traditional demand models were not working. Previously ignored changes in consumer lifestyles, information, and evolving preferences were becoming highly relevant in understanding and in modeling meat demand. As such, new theories and methods to discern intrinsic product quality attributes and related consumer perceptions were developed and a new paradigm in consumer meat demand research evolved. Research identifying, quantifying, and measuring consumer perceptions about, and determining how consumers value, extrinsic and intrinsic meat quality characteristics exploded. A Google Scholar search for "willingness to pay meat" completed in December 2009 revealed 61,600 articles, about half of which have been published since 1995. What has research about consumer demand for intrinsic meat quality attributes revealed? Too much to detail in this chapter. However, we generalize what we have learned about consumer demand for meat quality attributes.

The body of research on consumer valuation of intrinsic meat quality attributes reveals that many consumers demand more than competitively priced generic unlabeled meat products. Numerous economic experiments and surveys reveal that consumers are willing to pay more for products they perceive possess intrinsic quality attributes they want.[1]

5.1 Sensory

Consumers expect meat products to possess certain attributes when they make a purchase that depends on the use of the product. For example, leanness of ground beef is a quality trait consumers consider and value when making purchase decisions (Brester et al. 1993). In contrast, when purchasing beef steaks, tenderness is an economically important product quality characteristic. Lusk, Fox, et al. (2001) found that when consumers were provided information regarding steak tenderness together with completing a taste test, 90 percent preferred a steak known to be tender relative to a tough steak. Furthermore, 51 percent were willing to pay an average premium of $1.84 per pound for a tender relative to tough steak. Similar results have been found in pork that consumers are willing to pay for sensory attributes of the product (Melton et al. 1996).

5.2 Food Safety

Numerous studies demonstrate that consumers are concerned with a variety of aspects of food safety for meat products. Consumers often perceive food safety concerns that may

---

[1] A large body of research exists on the appropriate methodology to use to estimate reliable consumer valuations of food product attributes in economic experiments. We largely ignore this important methodology-focused literature here and encourage interested readers to see Part I of this volume.

not be actual hazards, and food safety concerns have affected consumer demand for meat products (Schroeder, Tonsor, Pennings, and Mintert 2007; Schroeder, Tonsor, Mintert, and Pennings 2006). In addition, many consumers are willing to pay economically important premiums for food products possessing food safety assurances (Caswell and Siny 2007; Tonsor, Schroeder, Pennings, and Mintert 2009).

In Europe, concerns with bovine spongiform encephalopathy (BSE) and suspected transmission to humans in the form of new-variant Creutzfedt–Jakob disease had a dramatic impact on meat demand (e.g., Burton and Young 1996; Setbon et al. 2005). In the United States research has been conducted analyzing impacts of food safety media information and meat product food safety recalls on meat demand (Marsh, Schroeder, and Mintert 2004; Piggott and Marsh 2004; Tonsor, Mintert, and Schroeder 2009). These studies find economically small, but statistically significant, effects of food safety events on meat demand.

An example of influential food safety perceptions with no scientifically known threat is biotechnology adoption by agricultural producers. Some consumers view adoption of biotechnology as a food safety threat. Lusk et al. (2005) completed a meta-analysis of twenty-five published studies estimating consumer willingness to pay for food products produced without use of genetically modified organisms (non-GM food). Consumers were willing to pay a 23 percent weighted-average premium for non-GM food products (excluding one outlier study). In addition, European consumers had a 29 percent larger willingness to pay premium than US consumers for non-GM food. A large body of literature examines consumer concerns with foods produced using genetically modified foods, despite there being no scientifically documented health risks from GM-produced foods.

Another example of influential food safety perceptions is use of growth hormones in livestock production. European consumers are notably less accepting of meat produced using growth hormones than US consumers (Lusk, Roosen, and Fox 2003; Tonsor, Schroeder, Fox, and Biere 2005). However, preferences are heterogeneous within each country. In a study of Norwegian consumers, Alfnes and Rickertsen (2003) found 25 percent unwilling to purchase US hormone-treated beef while 28 percent preferred US hormone-treated to US hormone-free beef. Moreover, trade impacts of policies reflecting consumer perceptions and preferences are notable (Bureau, Marette, and Schiavina 1998). Combined, these examples of GM and hormone use demonstrate how important consumer perceptions are as demand drivers.

5.3   Provenance

Country-of-origin and related product cue labeling has received considerable attention in the literature. One comprehensive meta-analysis study of country-of-origin labeling was that completed by Verlegh and Steenkamp (1999). Their analysis of forty-one published articles revealed, "the country-of-origin effect can be classified as a substantial factor in product evaluations" (1999: 538). They concluded that country of origin had a strong link with perceived product quality, performance, and consumer satisfaction. Country of origin is complex because it conjures a large number of varied perceptions about the product that may include quality attributes as well as normative judgments about the product. Umberger et al. (2003) concluded that US consumers viewed country-of-origin labels on beef as cues for food safety, health, and product freshness, as well as providing a feeling that they were supporting local producers.

5.4   Nutrition and Health

Consumers respond to nutritional and health information. Miljkovic and Mostad (2005) found that media attention to low-carbohydrate diets had longer-lasting impacts on beef demand than media articles regarding low-fat/low-cholesterol diets. Brown and Schrader (1990), Capps and Schmitz (1991), and Kinnucan et al. (1997), found statistically significant effects from cholesterol information on US meat and egg demand. Adhikari et al. (2006) found that cholesterol information reduced US demand for beef and pork and increased demand for chicken. Rickertsen, Kristofersson, and Lothe (2003) concluded that chicken demand in Finland, Norway, and Sweden increased as information about cholesterol was more widely disseminated.

Tonsor, Mintert, and Schroeder (2009) concluded: "New information available to consumers regarding how meat consumption impacts human health provides an important set of demand determinants. Links among fat, cholesterol, heart disease, or arteriosclerosis; iron, zinc, or protein and meat consumption; Atkins, high protein, or low carbohydrates and human diets all have significant impacts on meat demand" (2009: 21).

5.5   Production Practices

Consumers are increasingly interested in knowing how their food is produced. Two issues that are rapidly increasing in importance are consumer concern over how animals are cared for and the impact of livestock production on the environment. Several recent studies have examined how consumers value meat products carrying "animal-friendly" labels (e.g., Carlsson, Frykblom, and Lagerkvist 2007a, b; Lusk, Nilsson, and Foster 2007). An increasing number of US and European consumers are willing to pay premiums for meat produced using production methods consumers view as improving animal livelihood. Moreover, recent research suggests that consumers reveal these preferences through both their purchases and their voting behavior on legislation regulating livestock production practices (Tonsor, Olynk, and Wolf 2009; Tonsor, Wolf, and Olynk 2009).

Similarly, consumers in the US and Europe are increasingly demanding meat products originating from farms adopting "environmentally friendly" production practices. Nilsson, Foster, and Lusk (2006) found US consumers willing to pay premiums for pork chops certified to be produced using environmentally friendly methods. Verhoef (2005) found that Dutch consumers purchase organic meat partially because of the associated environmental impacts of organic production methods.

5.6   Price

Despite all of the discussion here about non-price product attributes, price is a very important meat consumption determinant (Tonsor, Mintert, and Schroeder 2009). In surveys of consumers in the United States, Canada, Japan, and Mexico, Schroeder, Tonsor, Mintert, and Pennings (2006) found price to be among the top three ranked product attributes consumers in each country considered when they made beef purchase decisions. Freshness was the top-rated attribute in each of the four countries. Strong demand exists for low-priced generic products in the retail grocery food market for a significant segment of society, suggesting that consumers are price-sensitive (Szymanski and Busch 1987).

6   INDUSTRY RESPONSE

Substantial declines in red meat demand make the prosperity of producers and processors in these industries challenging. Production and processing for both beef and pork are industries fraught with capital-intensive, illiquid, fixed investments that are uniquely suited to production in that industry. Many assets in red meat production have twenty-year or longer useful lives. Moreover, livestock production is inherently characterized by lengthy biological lags. Thus, when consumer demand declines, producers and processors suffer financial losses because they cannot quickly adjust supply in response to declining prices. Over time, the overall red meat industry eventually shrinks in size in response to perpetual demand decline. The US beef cattle herd is indicative of this response, shrinking from 37.1 million head in 1980 to 31.6 million head in 2009, a 15 percent decline.

In response to demand challenges and the need to meet consumer demand for meat quality attributes, the red meat industries are in the midst of major redesign and paradigm shifts. That is, these industries, both through their own initiatives, as well as through policy-driven changes, are adopting new practices and technology to address consumer concerns regarding the broad array of meat quality. We highlight a few of the industry efforts to address consumer demands for quality.

6.1   Alliances and Vertical Market Coordination

Beef producers, processors, and retailers have designed marketing alliances to provide stronger value–quality signals and incentives in the vertical market chain (Schroeder and Kovanda 2003). Certified Angus Beef (CAB) is one of the well-known and highly successful beef alliances. For beef to qualify as Certified Angus Beef it must come from fed cattle that are at least 51 percent Angus breed, all black-hided, "A" maturity (meaning typically less than 30 months of age), and of modest or higher level of marbling, in addition to other requirements. Beef carcasses that qualify for CAB can realize $2–5 per hundred weight premiums when cattle are sold on a carcass quality and yield grade grid. CAB "is the largest, most successful brand of beef and is a symbol of excellence to consumers at more than 15,000 businesses in 46 countries. More than 1.7 million pounds are sold daily through foodservice and grocery channels, generating an estimated $2.7 billion in consumer sales annually" (Certified Angus Beef 2009). Numerous other beef alliances with quite different structures and designs from that of CAB are also operating with varying degrees of success.

In the pork industry, vertical integration through processors owning or contracting hogs, owning genetics, and managing production has been much of the effort to improve vertical market coordination. In 1994, 62 percent of market hogs in the United States were sold on a negotiated spot-market basis; by 2009 only 8 percent were negotiated spot sales (Grimes and Plain 2009). The goals of increased vertical market coordination strategies in the red meat production and processing industries are generally to improve and/or assure many of the intrinsic red meat product quality attributes presented in Table 32.1. Different vertical coordination methods address most intensively different subsets of intrinsic quality attributes, but nearly all of them target at least a set of the intrinsic quality attributes. As vertical coordination plans are enacted, differentiated and branded retail and wholesale meat products are the main mechanisms used to send signals to consumers about improved quality.

6.2   Value-Based Pricing

Value-based pricing mechanisms of livestock (rather than meat) have become more prevalent in recent years (USDA GIPSA 1998, 2003). In both beef and pork complexes, these changes have been spurred by increasing consumer preferences for lean meat. In the cattle sector this is referred to as grid pricing; in the pork complex this is referred to as carcass lean pricing, both of which displaced average live-weight pricing. In both cattle and hog industries, the move away from live pricing has led to animals being evaluated and priced on individual carcass bases rather than in groups or lots.

In cattle, grid evaluation considers characteristics such as carcass quality grade, red meat yield estimates, carcass weight, animal source and age verification, and blemishes or other undesirable carcass traits. In hogs, evaluated traits include loin area and back fat depth (Schroeder, Mintert, and Berg 2004). Producers who adopt grid pricing realize stronger pricing signals and gain from more detailed information about the quality of each carcass they produce (Schroeder, Ward, et al. 2002; Riley et al. 2009).

Despite the fact that grid pricing was designed to provide incentives to producers to encourage production of animals yielding higher-quality meat products, there is scant evidence that expansion of grids has appreciably improved overall meat quality or translated into stronger meat demand. A comprehensive discussion describing why this is the case is beyond the scope of this chapter. However, the main reason why meat quality has not appreciably improved is because the dominant driver of revenue under grid pricing is carcass weight and not meat quality premiums (Johnson and Ward 2005). Certified premium programs using pricing grids, such as CAB, have grown over time, suggesting the success of some grid programs in establishing a stronger market presence and enhanced demand. In addition, increased grid pricing has paralleled increased retail product branding, especially in beef. This suggests that grid pricing has increased the ability of processors to influence the mixture of carcass and meat attributes they procure from producers.

6.3   Process Certification

Third party process certification and verification programs have become common red meat industry production strategies. For example, the US Department of Agriculture (USDA) has Process Verified programs that use the International Organization for Standardization's ISO 9000 standards for documented quality management. About thirty livestock producer, processor, service provider, or breed association companies have approved Process Verified programs that are audited by USDA (USDA AMS 2009a). USDA has also introduced new livestock marketing claims standards. For example, USDA has recently developed and approved age verification, hormone-free, grass-fed, naturally raised, tenderness, traceable to farm of origin, and grain-fed marketing claims standards that can be used to assure certain production or processing practices (USDA AMS 2009b).

6.4   Animal Identification

Increasing interest exists in animal identification and movement tracing. In the United States, the cattle industry has a limited amount of animal traceability as many animals change hands multiple times and are commingled from many different herds in the production process. Efforts to develop national animal identification systems similar to those operating in Canada and Australia have met with resistance from some producer organizations. The United States hog industry has adopted animal group movement tracking, which is much easier and lower-cost than in the beef industry because hogs typically are owned by only one or two producers, stay in the same groups throughout their lives, and move in groups to processors (NAIS Benefit–Cost Research Team 2009). Estimates suggest that as much as 80 percent of hogs currently produced in the United States have group traceability (Webb 2008).

Interest in and adoption of animal identification systems varies notably across countries. The European Union has a mandatory animal identification system comprised of paper passports being assigned to each animal (Souza-Monteiro and Caswell 2004). Internationally, most existing national systems are generally "birth to slaughter" systems that do not match retail meat products with live animals via a "birth to retail" system.

Animal identification and movement tracking has potentially large economic impacts that are well recognized in the global red meat industry (NAIS Benefit–Cost Research Team 2009). Based on interviews with CEOs and directors of food companies located in several European countries, Knight, Holdsworth, and Mather (2007) concluded, "Our study indicates that, in the eyes of the food channel members interviewed, New Zealand is in the fortunate position of being perceived as 'less risky' than many other countries, as a direct result of the efforts that have been made to institute the best quality control and traceability systems and technology available" (2007: 121).

A large and growing body of research suggests that consumers value traceability or attributes made available through traceability of food products. In the United States, Dickinson and Bailey (2002) conducted binding experiments using beef and pork sandwiches with base prices of $3 and actual dollar exchange to determine consumer willingness to pay for traceability. Participants were willing to pay on average $0.23 more for traceability to the farm for beef and $0.50 for pork. Other studies find similar support for US consumers demanding animal and meat traceability (e.g., Loureiro and Umberger 2004; Ward, Bailey, and Jensen 2005). International consumers have also demonstrated demand for traceability and/or product attributes that traceability enhances the feasibility of providing (e.g., Hobbs 1996; Buhr 2003; Gracia and Zeballos 2005; Hobbs et al. 2005; Tonsor, Schroeder, Fox, and Biere 2005; Schroeder, Tonsor, Mintert, and Pennings 2006; Cuthbertson and Marks 2008). Dickinson and Bailey (2005) concluded that consumers in Japan, Canada, the United States, and the United Kingdom were willing to pay on average 7–25 percent more for beef and pork sandwiches containing traceable meat.

Traceability alone is less valuable than what traceability better enables the food supply chain to deliver in regard to food safety assurances, enhanced product quality, origin labeling, and related product credence characteristics (Hobbs et al. 2005; Schroeder, Tonsor, Mintert, and Pennings 2006; Verbeke and Ward 2006). Mennecke et al. (2007) conducted a national survey of 1,171 consumers in addition to surveys of seventy-six business and animal science students and 221 other students about beef steak attribute preferences. They concluded, "Our results clearly indicate that information about the region of origin, the use or nonuse of growth promoters, guaranteed tenderness, and traceability could all be critical elements of consumer decision making" (2007: 2653).

7   FUTURE DIRECTIONS

Researchers will certainly continue to evaluate consumer demand for meat quality attributes. Accordingly, it is useful to outline several meat demand analysis arenas rising in importance in the coming years. The paths can be split into either methodological or subject-focus categories.

Methodologically, the selection of quantity and price data to be used in meat demand empirical modeling will be more intensely evaluated. Lensing and Purcell (2006) noted that most work to date has used simple average as opposed to purchase-volume-weighted average price data, which may be problematic. Volume-weighted average retail meat prices are different from simple average posted store prices. If price data used in demand estimation do not reflect actual prices consumers paid, resulting elasticity estimates are likely wrong. Future research needs to examine use of quantity-weighted price data in meat demand evaluations to reflect retail sales at discounted prices accurately.

Future work will also be characterized by expanded use of product-level scanner data that is increasingly available. In particular, most existing research has used either aggregate, commodity-level disappearance data or product-level consumer-survey-obtained data. Future research will expand on this by better leveraging rich panel data sets containing consumer demographics and real-world consumption decisions of specific meat products.

In addition to methodological evaluations, a range of additional subjects are ripe for future research. Investigating impacts of changing population demographics in the United States and Europe, exploring differential demands of meat purchasing at food service and at-home-meal-preparing consumers, and evaluating impacts of consumers being presented with increasing volumes of information on quality aspects of their food are noteworthy examples of rich areas for future research. Moreover, future work will examine the impact of consumers wanting to know more about how their food was produced; with particular focus on how this information is conveyed to consumers and how consumers motivate this information provision through purchasing and voting behavior.

Of considerable ongoing interest is how livestock producers, meat processors, and food preparers can efficiently adopt production, food safety, and marketing protocols that provide what consumers want. The ability to accomplish this depends largely upon new technology and especially information technology. Furthermore, vertical coordination and information flow between production, processing, and marketing segments of the livestock and meat market system is crucial for the red meat industry to be able to respond to consumer demand for meat quality. Research is needed to determine ways the beef sector especially, but the pork sector as well, can improve vertical coordination to meet the needs of modern consumers.

REFERENCES

Adhikari, M., L. Paudel, J. Houston, K. P. Paudel, and J. Bukenya. 2006. "The Impact of Cholesterol Information on Meat Demand: Application of an Updated Cholesterol Index." *Journal of Food Distribution Research* 37: 60–9.

Alfnes, F., and K. Rickertsen. 2003. "European Consumers' Willingness to Pay for U.S. Beef in Experimental Auction Markets." *American Journal of Agricultural Economics* 85: 396–405.

Bansback, B. 1995. "Towards a Broader Understanding of Meat Demand: Presidential Address." *Journal of Agricultural Economics* 46: 287–308.

Bernués, A., A. Olaizola, and K. Corcoran. 2003. "Extrinsic Attributes of Red Meat as Indicators of Quality in Europe: An Application for Market Segmentation." *Food Quality and Preference* 14: 265–76.

Brester, G. W., P. Lhermite, B. K. Goodwin, and M. C. Hunt. 1993. "Quantifying the Effects of New Product Development: The Case of Low-Fat Ground Beef." *Journal of Agricultural and Resource Economics* 18: 239–50.

Brown, D. J., and L. F. Schrader. 1990. "Cholesterol Information and Shell Egg Consumption." *American Journal of Agricultural Economics* 72: 548–55.

Brucks, M., V. A. Zeithaml, and G. Naylor. 2000. "Price and Brand Names as Indicators of Quality Dimensions for Consumer Durables." *Journal of the Academy of Marketing Science* 28: 359–74.

Buhr, B. L. 2003. *Traceability, Trade and COOL: Lessons from the EU Meat and Poultry Industry*. International Agricultural Trade Research Consortium Working Paper No. 03-5. St Paul: Department of Applied Economics, University of Minnesota, Apr.

Bureau, J., S. Marette, and A. Schiavina. 1998. "Non-Tariff Trade Barriers and Consumers' Information: The Case of the EU–US Trade Dispute over Beef." *European Review of Agricultural Economics* 25: 437–62.

Burton, M., and T. Young. 1996. "The Impact of BSE on the Demand for Beef and Other Meats in Great Britain." *Applied Economics* 28: 687–93.

Capps, O., Jr., and J. D. Schmitz. 1991. "A Recognition of Health and Nutrition Factors in Food Demand Analysis." *Western Journal of Agricultural Economics* 16/1: 21–35.

Carlsson, F., P. Frykblom, and C. J. Lagerkvist. 2007a. "Consumer Willingness to Pay for Farm Animal Welfare: Mobile Abattoirs versus Transportation to Slaughter." *European Review of Agricultural Economics* 34: 321–44.

————————. 2007b. "Farm Animal Welfare: Testing for Market Failure." *Journal of Agricultural and Applied Economics* 39: 61–73.

Caswell, J. A., and J. Siny. 2007. *Consumer Demand for Quality: Major Determinant for Agricultural and Food Trade in the Future?* Department of Resource Economics Working Paper No. 2007-4. Amherst: University of Massachusetts.

——, C. M. Noelke, and E. M. Mojduszka. 2002. "Unifying Two Frameworks for Analyzing Quality and Quality Assurance for Food Products." In B. Krissoff, M. Bohman, and J. A. Caswell, eds, *Global Food Trade and Consumer Demand for Quality*. New York: Kluwer Academic Publishers.

Certified Angus Beef. 2009. <http://www.certifiedangusbeef.com>.

Cuthbertson, B., and N. Marks. 2008. "Beyond Credence: Emerging Consumer Trends in International Markets." Paper presented to the Australian Agricultural and Resource Economics Society Conference, Canberra, Feb. 5–8.

Dickinson, D. L., and D. Bailey. 2002. "Meat Traceability: Are U.S. Consumers Willing to Pay for It?" *Journal of Agricultural and Resource Economics* 27/2: 348–64.

————. 2005. "Experimental Evidence on Willingness to Pay for Red Meat Traceability in the United States, Canada, United Kingdom, and Japan." *Journal of Agricultural and Applied Economics* 37/3: 537–48.

European Commission. 2008. *Food: From Farm to Fork Statistics.* <http://epp.eurostat.ec.europa.eu/cache/ITY_OFFPUB/KS-30-08-339/EN/KS-30-08-339-EN.PDF>.

Gao, Z. 2007. "Effect of Additional Quality Attributes on Consumer Willingness-to-Pay for Food Labels." Ph.D. diss. Kansas State University.

Gracia, A., and G. Zeballos. 2005. "Attitudes of Retailers and Consumers toward the EU Traceability and Labeling System for Beef." *Journal of Food Distribution Research* 36/3: 45–56.

Grimes, G., and R. Plain. 2009. *U.S. Hog Marketing Contract Study.* Department of Agricultural Economics Working Paper No. AEWP 2009-1. <http://agebb.missouri.edu/mkt/vertstud09.htm>.

Hobbs, J. E. 1996. "A Transaction Cost Analysis of Quality, Traceability and Animal Welfare Issues in UK Beef Retailing." *British Food Journal* 98/6: 16–26.

——, D. Bailey, D. L. Dickinson, and M. Haghiri. 2005. "Traceability in the Canadian Red Meat Sector: Do Consumers Care?" *Canadian Journal of Agricultural Economics* 53: 47–65.

Johnson, H. C., and C. E. Ward. 2005. "Market Signals Transmitted by Grid Pricing." *Journal of Agricultural and Resource Economics* 30/3: 561–79.

Kinnucan, H. W., H. Xiao, C. Hsia, and J. D. Jackson. 1997. "Effects of Health Information and Generic Advertising on US Meat Demand." *American Journal of Agricultural Economics* 79: 13–23.

Knight, J. G., D. K. Holdsworth, and D. W. Mather. 2007. "Country-of-Origin and Choice of Food Imports: An In-Depth Study of European Distribution Channel Gatekeepers." *Journal of International Business Studies* 38: 107–25.

Lensing, C., and W. Purcell. 2006. "Impact of Mandatory Price Reporting Requirements on the Level, Variability, and Elasticity Parameter Estimates for Retail Beef Prices." *Review of Agricultural Economics* 28: 229–39.

Loureiro, M. L., and W. J. Umberger. 2004. "A Choice Experiment Model for Beef Attributes: What Consumer Preferences Tell Us." Selected Paper presented at the Annual Meeting of the American Agricultural Economics Association, Denver, CO, Aug. 1–4.

Lusk, J. L., J. A. Fox, T. C. Schroeder, J. Mintert, and M. Koohmaraie. 2001. "In-Store Valuation of Steak Tenderness." *American Journal of Agricultural Economics* 83: 539–50.

——, J. Roosen, and J. Fox. 2003. "Demand for Beef from Cattle Administered Growth Hormones or Fed Genetically Modified Corn: A Comparison of Consumers in France, Germany, the United Kingdom, and the United States." *American Journal of Agricultural Economics* 85: 16–29.

——, M. Jamal, L. Kurlander, M. Roucan, and L. Taulman. 2005. "A Meta-Analysis of Genetically Modified Food Valuation Studies." *Journal of Agricultural and Resource Economics* 30: 28–44.

——, T. Nilsson, and K. Foster. 2007. "Public Preferences and Private Choices: Effect of Altruism and Free Riding on Demand for Environmentally Certified Pork." *Environmental and Resource Economics* 36/4: 499–521.

Marsh, T. L., T. C. Schroeder, and J. Mintert. 2004. "Impacts of Meat Product Recalls on Consumer Demand in the USA." *Applied Economics* 36: 897–909.

Melton, B. E., W. E. Huffman, J. F. Shogren, and J. A. Fox. 1996. "Consumer Preferences for Fresh Food Items with Multiple Quality Attributes: Evidence from an Experimental Auction of Pork Chops." *American Journal of Agricultural Economics* 78: 916–23.

Mennecke, B., A. M. Townsend, D. J. Hayes, and S. M. Lonergan. 2007. "A Study of the Factors that Influence Consumer Attitudes toward Beef Products Using the Conjoint Market Analysis Tool." *Journal of Animal Science* 85/10: 2639–59.

Miljkovic, D., and D. Mostad. 2005. "Impacts of Changes in Dietary Preferences on U.S. Retail Demand for Beef: Health Concerns and the Role of Media." *Journal of Agribusiness* 23: 183–98.

Miyazaki, A. D., D. Grewal, and R. C. Goodstein. 2005. "The Effect of Multiple Extrinsic Cues on Quality Perceptions: A Matter of Consistency." *Journal of Consumer Research* 32: 146–53.

NAIS Benefit–Cost Research Team. 2009. *Benefit–Cost Analysis of the National Animal Identification System.* Final Research Report Submitted to the US Department of Agriculture, Animal and Plant Health Inspection Service. Jan. <http://www.agmanager.info/livestock/marketing/NAIS/BC_Analysis_NAIS.pdf>. <http://www.aphis.usda.gov/traceability/downloads/Benefit_Cost_Analysis.pdf>.

Nilsson, T., K. Foster, and J. L. Lusk. 2006. "Marketing Opportunities for Certified Pork Chops." *Canadian Journal of Agricultural Economics* 54: 567–83.

Piggott, N. E., and T. L. Marsh. 2004. "Does Food Safety Information Impact US Meat Demand?" *American Journal of Agricultural Economics* 86: 154–74.

Purcell, W. D. 1998. *Measures of Changes in Demand for Beef, Pork, and Chicken, 1975–1998.* Blacksburg, VA: Research Institute on Livestock Pricing, Oct. <http://naiber.org/Publications/RILP/demandchanges.pdf>.

Rickertsen, K., D. Kristofersson, and S. Lothe. 2003. "Effects of Health Information on Nordic Meat and Fish Demand." *Empirical Economics* 28: 249–73.

Riley, J. M., T. C. Schroeder, T. L. Wheeler, S. D. Shackleford, and M. Koohmaraie. 2009. "Valuing Fed Cattle Using Objective Tenderness Measures." *Journal of Agricultural and Applied Economics* 41: 163–75.

Schroeder, T. C. 2010. *Beef Demand Index.* <http://www.naiber.org/beefdemandindex.html>.

——— and J. Kovanda. 2003. "Beef Alliances: Motivations, Extent, and Future Prospects." *Veterinary Clinics of North America Food Animal Practice* 19: 397–417.

———, J. Mintert, and E. P. Berg. 2004. *Valuing Market Hogs: Information and Pricing Issues.* Marketing Fact Sheet MF-2644. Manhattan: Kansas State University , Jan.

———, G. Tonsor, J. Mintert, and J. M. E. Pennings. 2006. *Consumer Risk Perceptions and Attitudes about Beef Food Safety: Implications for Improving Supply Chain Management.* Manhattan: Agricultural Experiment Station and Cooperative Extension Service, Kansas State University, Nov. <http://naiber.org/Publications/NAIBER/Consumer.Perceptions.Final.pdf>.

Schroeder, T. C., G. Tonsor, J. M. E. Pennings, and J. Mintert. 2007. "Consumer Food Safety Risk Perceptions and Attitudes: Impacts on Beef Consumption across Countries." *B. E. Journal of Economic Analysis and Policy Contributions* 7: 1–29.

———, C. E. Ward, J. Lawrence, and D. M. Feuz. 2002. *Fed Cattle Marketing Trends and Concerns: Cattle Feeder Survey Results.* Marketing Fact Sheet MF-2561. Manhattan: Agricultural Experiment Station and Cooperative Extension, Kansas State University, June. <http://www.agmanager.info/livestock/marketing/bulletins_2/marketing/fed_cattle/mf2561.pdf>.

Setbon, M., J. Raude, C. Fischler, and A. Flahault. 2005. "Risk Perception of the 'Mad Cow Disease' in France: Determinants and Consequences." *Risk Analysis* 25: 813–26.

Souza-Monteiro, D. M., and J. A. Caswell. 2004. *The Economics of Implementing Traceability in Beef Supply Chains: Trends in Major Producing and Trading Countries.* Working Paper No. 2004-6. Amherst: Department of Resource Economics, University of Massachusetts.

Szymanski, D. M., and P. S. Busch. 1987. "Identifying the Generics-Prone Consumer: A Meta-Analysis." *Journal of Marketing Research* 24: 425–31.

Tomek, W. G. 1985. "Limits on Price Analysis." *American Journal of Agricultural Economics* 67: 905–15.

Tonsor, G. T., and T. L. Marsh. 2007. "Comparing Heterogeneous Consumption in US and Japanese Meat and Fish Demand." *Agricultural Economics* 37/1 (July), 81–91.

——, J. Mintert, and T. C. Schroeder. 2009. "U.S. Meat Demand: Household Dynamics and Media Information Impacts." Unpublished Working Paper, Dec.

——, N. Olynk, and C. Wolf. 2009. "Consumer Preferences for Animal Welfare Attributes: The Case of Gestation Crates." *Journal of Agricultural and Applied Economics* 41: 713–30.

——, T. C. Schroeder, J. A. Fox, and A. Biere. 2005. "European Preferences for Beef Steak Attributes." *Journal of Agricultural and Resource Economics* 30: 367–80.

————, J. M. E. Pennings, and J. Mintert. 2009. "Consumer Valuations of Beef Steak Food Safety Enhancements in Canada, Japan, Mexico, and the United States." *Canadian Journal of Agricultural Economics* 57: 395–416.

——, C. Wolf, and N. Olynk. 2009. "Consumer Voting and Demand Behavior regarding Swine Gestation Crates." *Food Policy* 34: 492–98.

Umberger, W. J., D. M. Feuz, C. R. Calkins, and B. M. Sitz. 2003. "Country-of-Origin Labeling of Beef Products: U.S. Consumers' Perceptions." *Journal of Food Distribution Research* 34/3: 103–16.

USDA AMS (Agricultural Marketing Service, US Department of Agriculture). 2009a. *Official Listing of Approved USDA Process Verified Programs.* <http://www.ams.usda.gov/AMSv1.0/getfile?dDocName=STELPRD3320450>.

—— 2009b. *Grading, Certification, and Verification.* <http://www.ams.usda.gov/AMSv1.0/ams.fetchTemplateData.do?template=TemplateL&navID=MarketingClaimStandards&rightNav1=MarketingClaimStandards&topNav=&leftNav=GradingCertificationandVerfication&page=PublicationsProposedMarketingClaimsRulemaking&resultType=&acct= lsstd>.

USDA ERS (Economic Research Service, United States Department of Agriculture). 2009. *Food CPI, Prices and Expenditures: Food Expenditure Tables.* <http://www.ers.usda.gov/Briefing/CPIFoodAndExpenditures/Data>.

USDA GIPSA (Grain Inspection, Packers and Stockyards Administration, United States Department of Agriculture). 1998. *Packers and Stockyards Statistical Report: 1996 Reporting Year.* Washington, DC: GIPSA, Oct.

—— 2003. *Packers and Stockyards Statistical Report: 2001 Reporting Year.* Washington, DC: GIPSA, Sept.

Verbeke, W., and R. W. Ward. 2006. "Consumer Interest in Information Cues Denoting Quality, Traceability and Origin: An Application of Ordered Probit Models to Beef Labels." *Food Quality and Preference* 17: 453–67.

Verhoef, P. C. 2005. "Explaining Purchases of Organic Meat by Dutch Consumers." *European Review of Agricultural Economics* 32: 245–67.

Verlegh, P. W. J., and J.-B. E. M. Steenkamp. 1999. "A Review and Meta-Analysis of Country-of-Origin Research." *Journal of Economic Psychology* 20/5: 512–46.

Ward, R., D. Bailey, and R. Jensen. 2005. "An American BSE Crisis: Has it Affected the Value of Traceability and Country-of-Origin Certifications for US and Canadian Beef?" *International Food and Agribusiness Management Review* 8/2: 92–114.

Webb, P. 2008. Director, Swine Health Programs, National Pork Board, Des Moines, IA. Personal conversation. Feb. 1.

CHAPTER 33

....

GEOGRAPHICALLY DIFFERENTIATED PRODUCTS

....

ROLAND HERRMANN AND RAMONA TEUBER[*]

1 INTRODUCTION

....

Origin-based marketing strategies for foods and agricultural products have a long history, and some of the most renowned agri-food products in the world have built up their reputation based on their geographical origin. Prominent examples are Parmigiano-Reggiano and Champagne. However, product differentiation based on geographical origin has gained markedly in importance in recent years. This is reflected in the steadily growing number of foods marketed with an origin-linked quality label. The increasing interest in origin labeling is not restricted to European countries: a growing number of geographically differentiated products can also be observed for non-European countries as the examples of Washington apples, Darjeeling tea, and Café de Colombia illustrate (Fink and Maskus 2006). Moreover, product differentiation based on origin can be observed across all product categories, and even in markets traditionally considered to be homogeneous, "decommodification" has evolved as a strategy. This development is especially apparent in international agricultural trade, where trade in differentiated high-value agri-food products is becoming increasingly important (World Bank 2007).

The reasons for this surge of origin-labeled products are manifold. First, owing to rising income, increasing concerns about food quality and food safety issues, and a growing desire for variety, consumers' demand for high-quality and regional specialty products has risen (Bramley, Biénabe, and Kirsten 2009). A growing number of

* This chapter was written while both authors were with the Institute of Agricultural Policy and Market Research, Justus-Liebig University Giessen.

consumers place value on the traceability of the foods they eat and, in addition, origin-labeled foods are considered to be a counter-movement against the increasing globalization of food chains with international brands (Broude 2005). Authenticity and cultural heritage have become important product characteristics in food demand, at least for certain consumer segments. Second, the gradually changing pattern in governmental agricultural policy from direct commodity support to support of farmers through payments that are coupled to food safety and food quality standards has fuelled the interest in geographical indications for agricultural products. Particularly in the European Union, high-quality products with a strong link to a certain geographical region are considered useful tools in rising farmers' income and fostering rural development, especially in less favored production areas (Josling 2006).

However, geographical indications (GIs) are not without controversy.[1] This is mainly due to the fact that geographical indications are both an agricultural policy instrument as well as an intellectual property right (van Caenegem 2004). In general, GIs are protected at the level of national jurisdictions and these jurisdictions differ quite remarkably across countries. Countries with a more lenient approach to protect GIs, such as the United States and Australia, fear that countries with a rather strict approach, particularly the European Union, could use GIs as non-tariff trade barriers at the international level (Fink and Maskus 2006). The debate on GIs is not just a debate on differing laws and regulations. To some extent it is a difference in paradigms with respect to which functions geographical indications should fulfill in the marketplace.

Given this background, the economics of geographically differentiated products will be summarized and surveyed in this chapter. The rationale for regulation will be presented and the likely economic implications of regulation on geographical indications will be elaborated by use of various theoretical approaches. Furthermore, we will survey and assess the broad empirical literature on consumer preferences for geographically differentiated products and on the socioeconomic impacts of geographical indications. The chapter is organized as follows. Section 2 will define the concepts of geographically differentiated products and geographical indications and outline briefly the different legal regulations in force. Thereafter, the economic rationale for establishing and protecting GIs as well as the different paradigms prevailing in the European Union and the United States are presented and discussed in Section 3. Moreover, economic impacts of protecting and promoting GIs are analyzed theoretically. Section 4 reviews and synthesizes the available empirical evidence on consumers' willingness to pay (WTP) for origin labels and the socioeconomic impacts of GIs. The analyses comprise a large number of different approaches and case studies reflecting the array of research questions arising out of geographically differentiated products. Section 5 concludes and provides an outlook on future research.

---

[1] In this chapter the term "geographically differentiated products" will be used to refer to all products that are differentiated based on their geographical origin, whereas the term "geographical indication" is used to refer to products that possess a certain quality–origin link (see Section 2 for more details).

2   GEOGRAPHICALLY DIFFERENTIATED PRODUCTS: DEFINITIONS AND REGULATIONS

The term "geographically differentiated products" is rather self-explanatory. It refers to products that are differentiated from other products based on their origin. However, looking at this term in more detail, it turns out that there is no single widely accepted definition of geographically differentiated products. In the literature we find numerous terms for these products that are used more or less interchangeably: origin-labeled products, origin-based products, country brands, geographical indications, regional specialties, regionally differentiated products, regionally denominated products. Another closely related term is "local foods." Local foods are mostly marketed and promoted by their geographical origin and, thus, can be classified as geographically differentiated products. Geographically differentiated products, however, are not necessarily local foods. Café de Colombia and Parma ham are definitely geographically differentiated products but, given the large export share of these products, they will not be perceived as local foods by consumers.

If we apply a broad definition of geographically differentiated products, all products that are differentiated based on their origin are covered by this term. Such a broad definition encompasses all labeling and branding schemes referring to the geographical origin, such as the well-known "Made in . . . " labels. These labels do not usually require any specific link between the geographical origin and the product's quality. However, there are examples where country-of-origin labels are used to create country brands, as in the case of New Zealand lamb (Clemens and Babcock 2004). A country brand, like any other brand, tries to signal a constant and high quality to consumers, and it is therefore often coupled to certain quality standards. Consequently, a quality–origin link is established. This is much in line with the definition of geographical indications in the Agreement on Trade-Related Aspects of Intellectual Property Rights (TRIPS),[2] which came into force in 1995. Article 22 of TRIPS defines GIs as follows: "Geographical indications are indications which identify a good originating in the territory of a Member, or a region or locality in that territory, where a given quality, reputation or other characteristic of the good is essentially attributable to its geographical origin." Accordingly, products labeled with a GI have one important feature in common: there must be a specific link between the place of production and the product's quality, characteristics, or reputation. This quality–origin nexus is sometimes referred to with the French term *terroir*. The *terroir* concept is based on the idea that special geographical microclimates yield food products with a unique flavor profile that cannot be replicated elsewhere (Barham 2003; Raustiala and Munzer 2007). In a narrow sense, *terroir* refers to a physical environment including soil, elevation, climate, and related

---

[2] The TRIPS agreement is not the first international agreement on GIs, but the most important one. For an overview about the historical development of GI protection, see Mosoti and Gobena (2007, ch. 5).

factors only. In a broader sense, it also includes the human environment, that is, traditional knowledge, local skills, and processing practices (Broude 2005).

Although the TRIPS agreement provides a general framework for the protection of geographical indications, it does not provide details on how each member country should implement its GI system. Essentially, two alternative regulation approaches can be observed across countries. The first one protects GIs within the common trademark law, whereas the second one provides protection through a *sui generis* system, which is a system especially designed for protecting geographical indications (Lovenworth and Shiner 2008; Bramley, Biénabe, and Kirsten 2009).

In most countries that follow the first approach, for example the United States, Canada, Australia, and South Africa, geographical terms are protected as certification marks and less frequently as collective marks or trademarks. A certification mark refers to a "word, symbol, name or device" used by someone other than the owner of the certification mark to certify certain product characteristics, such as the geographical origin or certain processing practices. Certification marks are typically owned by governmental institutions.

Sui generis systems were originally developed in Roman law countries (i.e., France, Italy, and Spain) and are currently in force in the European Union (EU Regulation No. 510/2006) and in several Asian and Latin American countries (WIPO 2007).[3] The registration of a product under a *sui generis* system requires that a specific link between the product's quality and its geographical origin must be proven, accompanied by a code of practice that specifies the way the product has to be produced. Once the product name is protected, it cannot be used by any other producer who is not located inside the specific region and who does not produce according to the registered product specification. On the other hand, any producer located in the specific area and whose products comply with the defined product standards cannot be excluded from using the label.

However, national regulations do not offer protection against fraud in foreign markets. In order to protect a GI in foreign markets, producer groups have to apply for registration and protection in each export market separately. In some cases, bilateral and multilateral agreements are in force covering the protection of certain geographical names (WTO 2004).[4]

The interrelation between the different concepts we shall cover in this chapter is illustrated in Figure 33.1. The broadest concept is geographically differentiated products. A subgroup are GI products, which are products that possess a certain quality–origin nexus, and among these products we speak of protected GI products if these products are protected through one of the above-presented legal systems.

---

[3] Examples are Vietnam, Mongolia, Colombia, and Costa Rica.

[4] One prominent example is the bilateral agreement between the European Commission and Australia on trade in wine, in which both parties agreed to protect each other's geographical indications. Consequently, Australian producers had to stop using terms such as "Burgundy," "Champagne," and "port" for their wines.

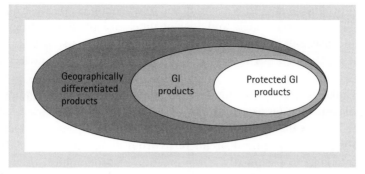

FIGURE 33.1 Taxonomy and interrelation between different types of product linked to geographical origin

In reality the classification of a product either as a geographically differentiated product or a geographical indication is not always as straightforward and clear-cut as in theory. The definition of GIs and the underlying *terroir* concept has been questioned by several researchers and it is still a widely debated topic (e.g., Raustiala and Munzer 2007; Gergaud and Ginsburgh 2008; Teil 2009). The discussion centers on the question whether natural conditions or whether human skills and established quality standards that are transferable to other regions are the important factors in determining product quality. Moreover, in this context subjective quality, that is, perceived quality by consumers, is a major point. Even if there is no detectable quality–origin link from an expert's point of view, consumers can still perceive the product as a higher-quality product owing to its geographical origin.[5]

3   POLICIES TOWARD GEOGRAPHICALLY DIFFERENTIATED PRODUCTS: RATIONALE, OPTIONS, IMPACTS

3.1   Rationale for Regulation

How can it be justified that geographical names are given legal protection? The main economic rationale is that consumers may suffer from quality uncertainty in an unregulated market. Consumers are typically less informed about the quality of a

---

[5] We shall elaborate on this point in Sections 3.3.3 and 4.1.2, where we present the theoretical framework and empirical evidence with respect to consumers' preferences for geographically differentiated products.

product than producers and, thus, asymmetric information on product quality arises. In an unregulated market, high and low qualities are often indistinguishable for consumers and may sell at the same price. Akerlof (1970) has shown in his "lemon" example that under such circumstances high qualities may be crowded out by low qualities.

If a higher quality of a good is due to its geographical origin, the legal protection of the geographical indication as a distinctive sign may avoid this market failure. Consumers of the high-quality good may gain from regulation: by legal protection and an associated label, the geographical origin turns from a credence characteristic into a search characteristic. Consequently, the protection of geographical-origin labels will reduce consumers' search costs and may raise consumers' welfare.

This argument is also taken up in the EU regulation on GIs, where it is stated that "in view of the wide variety of products marketed and abundance of product information provided, the consumer should, in order to be able to make the best choices, be given clear and succinct information regarding the product origin" (European Commission 2006, L 93/12). As far as quality information for consumers raises demand for high-quality foods, prices will increase and producer welfare will improve as well.

Apart from these primary effects of better information for consumers, producers of the high-quality good will benefit from the intellectual property right that is introduced to protect the origin–quality link against misuse by non-original producers (Fink and Maskus 2006). Producers' collective reputation is secured against counterfeiting and the issue of high quality being crowded out by low quality in the sense of Akerlof may be avoided. Owing to the intellectual property right, demand for high-quality food is kept above the level of a hypothetical, unregulated market on which low-quality imitations would erode the price premium and the average product quality would fall. In the European Union, additional agricultural and rural policy objectives are attributed to these medium-run implications of GI regulation. The preamble of the EU regulation on geographical indications states that "the promotion of products having certain characteristics could be of considerable benefit to the rural economy, particularly to less favored and remote areas, by improving the incomes of farmers and by retaining the rural population in these areas" (European Commission 2006, L 93/12).

Further policy goals pursued by the protection of geographical indications are the conservation of biodiversity, which includes the protection of animal breeds, plant varieties, and landscapes, and cultural diversity, which refers to traditional knowledge, skills, and practices (Broude 2005; Bérard and Marchenay 2006). The policy objectives of protecting diversity and fostering rural development are considered to be especially relevant for developing countries. In these countries biological and cultural diversity is assumed to be endangered by globalization processes, and small-scale farmers often lack the resources to establish other distinctive signs to differentiate and promote their products (Addor, Thumm, and Grazioli 2003).

3.2   Different Paradigms on Regulation

Very different paradigms on regulation do exist, with the European and the American positions being most controversial. The different paradigms on policies toward geographical indications have been discussed extensively from an economic point of view (Bureau and Valceschini 2003; Josling 2006; Becker 2009) and from an international law point of view (Geuze 2009; Ibele 2009).

In Europe, especially in the Mediterranean countries, small-scale production is still common and there is a strong identification between foods and the place of production. In these countries geographical indications are considered to protect traditional production methods and support rural economies while at the same time ensuring high-quality production. Thus, in the European Union the protection of GI products is viewed as a means of providing credible quality information to consumers in increasingly globalized markets, on the one hand, and of supporting high-quality producers for whom the geographical origin is the key to the quality of the product, on the other hand. Consequently, the regulation on GIs has become a major pillar of the European Union's food quality policies besides organic certification and food quality assurance systems (Becker 2009). The US position is quite different. Geographical indications are not considered as a special class of intellectual property rights and protection is granted within the existing trademark law. Trademarks are seen as an effective and sufficient instrument to protect intellectual property rights for geographic names.

The "war on terroir," as Josling (2006) puts it, is consistent with differential views toward agriculture and agricultural policy in the United States and in Europe. Josling (2002) distinguished four different agricultural policy paradigms in industrialized countries: (1) the dependent agriculture paradigm; (2) the competitive agriculture paradigm; (3) the multifunctional agriculture paradigm, and (4) the global agriculture paradigm. Moreover, he identified shifts away from the dependent agriculture paradigm, according to which structural disadvantages of agriculture compared to the non-farm sector had been stressed as well as the need for political support to agriculture. The United States moved toward the competitive agriculture paradigm claiming that agriculture is and should be able to compete on unregulated markets without governmental support. Consequently, the US point of view on GIs is fully consistent with this orientation. In the European Union, however, the multifunctional agriculture paradigm came to the fore. Within a more differentiated view on policy, agriculture is supposed to provide public goods for the society, like preservation of the countryside, rural development, and social and economic cohesion. This development explains why the protection of GIs has become a central part of the European Union's food quality policy.

3.3   Impacts of Regulation: Theoretical Approaches and Results

Geographically differentiated products have been analyzed within a rather large number of different disciplines such as law, sociology, marketing, and economics. For an economic assessment of policies toward these products, three methodological approaches and branches of the literature are particularly relevant: (1) price and welfare analyses based on market models of origin-labeled products; (2) welfare analyses of GI regulations within models of vertical product differentiation; (3) consumer studies on attitudes toward geographically differentiated products.

3.3.1 *Market, Price, and Welfare Effects of Regulation*

It is straightforward to think about economic implications of regulations on geographical indications in terms of their price, market, and welfare impacts. Consequently, quite a number of studies, such as those on the economics of commodity promotion (Alston, Freebairn, and James 2003; Alston et al. 2005; Kaiser et al. 2005), have utilized the standard supply-and-demand and welfare framework. In studies on labeling and quality information policy (Foster and Just 1989; Just, Hueth, and Schmitz 2007, ch. 11; Kaiser, Chapter 28 in this volume), this framework has been extended by findings from the economics of advertising and information (Dixit and Norman 1970; Nelson 1974; Becker and Stigler 1977; Becker and Murphy 1993; Ackerberg 2001) when analyzing policy impacts on consumer welfare and consumer preferences. Also relevant is the literature on the economics of trademarks and intellectual property rights (Landes and Posner 1987; Barnes 2006), the economics of labeling (Marette and Roosen, Chapter 19 in this volume; Drichoutis, Nayga, and Lazaridis, Chapter 20 in this volume) and the literature on reputation (Shapiro 1983; Grossman and Shapiro 1988; Tirole 1996; Winfree and McCluskey 2005).

Figure 33.2 illustrates market and welfare impacts of a regional-origin label that provides credible information to consumers on the origin–quality link. A competitive market is posited for the GI product.

Suppose that a GI product faces a demand curve D in the initial situation without regulation. The supply curve for the GI product is S and the equilibrium price and equilibrium quantity are p_0 and q_0, respectively. Now the geographical indication is protected by either of the legal means presented in Section 2. We posit further that the club of producers supports the label by informative advertising, which is financed by the club in the form of a check-off system. The demand curve for the GI product shifts from D to D' if protection and promotion are effective. At the same time, the costs of GI producers rise owing to compliance with quality standards as well as additional certification and promotion costs. Hence, the supply curve shifts from S to S'. In the new market equilibrium, the S' curve and the D' curve intersect at a new price, p_c, and a new quantity, q_1. The price p_c is the consumer price of the protected GI product. The producer price p_p is the net price that ranges by the marginal costs of participating in the collective production and marketing of the GI product, i.e. k, below the consumer price p_c.

Figure 33.2 reveals first the price premium arising from GI regulation. This is a key concept for deriving the consequential welfare impacts. It can be seen that the shift of the demand curve exceeds the shift of the supply curve. This is a necessary condition for the producer club to gain from the protection and promotion of the geographical

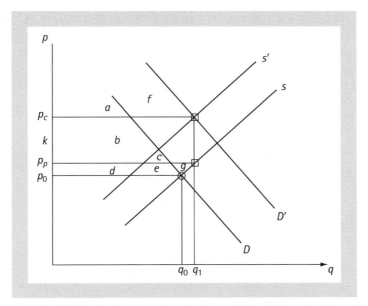

FIGURE 33.2 Price and welfare implications of labeling and protection of a geographical indication

origin. Given the assumptions of credible quality information for consumers and a competitive market, the price premium due to GI regulation is $(p_p - p_0)$. It is based on the comparison of producer prices with and without regulation.

It should be noted here that the concept outlined above has rarely been applied consistently in the empirical literature on GI products. In most cases, the observed situation with GI regulation was not compared with a hypothetical and modeled situation without GI regulation. Other, more pragmatic benchmark situations have typically been used and results have to be interpreted with care. Sometimes, the situations before and after GI registration were compared. In the before–after approach, the *ceteris paribus* condition is typically not fulfilled as other price determinants apart from regulation will have changed over time, too. In other cases, a price premium was derived by contrasting the price of the origin-labeled good with that of its generic counterpart. Although such comparisons have been categorized as with-and-without approaches (Reviron, Thevenod-Mottet, and El Benni 2009), they are not. Observed prices for two different markets, namely the regulated and the unregulated markets, are utilized when computing the price premium rather than prices in one market with and without regulation. The computed price premium in such pragmatic approaches may be very different from that outlined in Figure 33.2. They also suffer from the fact that GI regulation will typically affect the price ratio between the origin-labeled and the generic product (Anders, Thompson, and Herrmann 2009).

Apart from the price premium, welfare impacts of the described GI regulation on the market of the high-quality product may be derived. The implications of quality information on consumer welfare in particular are non-trivial. It has been shown in the economics of information that welfare impacts of quality information on consumers depend on whether (1) the information provided is true or false; (2) consumers' perceptions on quality were true or false prior to the information provided; (3) preferences change owing to quality information or not (Just, Hueth, and Schmitz 2004, ch. 11).

If the provided information on the origin–quality link is fully credible and quality uncertainty is present in the situation without this information, it can be posited that GI regulation shifts demand for the GI product from D to D'. D' represents planned demand if correct information is provided by the GI regulation. The following welfare effects for consumers will arise. At any price, consumers would have been at a suboptimal level of consumption without the quality information: i.e., on D rather than D'. With the move from the old to the new equilibrium, quality information raises consumption to the optimum level, which means from q_0 to q_1. Given Marshallian demand functions, the net welfare effect on consumers can be derived if consumer surplus with protected geographical indications, $(a + f)$, is compared with consumer surplus in the situation without regulation, $(a + b + c + d + e)$. The change in consumer surplus is $(f - b - c - d - e)$. There are two components of the net welfare effect on consumers. First, there is a welfare gain by raising consumption at the new price p_c to the optimal level. This additional consumer surplus illustrated by area f is the value of quality information for consumers at the new equilibrium price. It can also be interpreted as consumers' welfare gain due to a reduction in search costs. Second, as the price rises from p_0 to p_c, a price-induced loss of consumer surplus by $(b + c + d + e)$ arises. Consequently, consumers can experience a net gain if the reduction in search costs overcompensates the loss due to the price increase, that is, if $f > (b + c + d + e)$.

The impact of quality information on producer welfare is a function of the price premium producers receive. Producers will gain area $(d + e + g)$ in Figure 33.2 as their net price increases owing to protection and promotion of the geographical indication. As far as the supply shift, that is, the additional costs of participating in the labeling system, is lower than the demand shift, the welfare effect on producers will remain positive.

If we aggregate welfare impacts on consumers and producers, the welfare impact of a GI regulation is $(f + g - b - c)$. This aggregate welfare impact will be positive, as $f > (b + c)$ under the assumptions given. If the supply shift exceeds the demand shift and a negative price premium arises, the aggregate welfare impact will turn negative.

Real-world protection may now deviate from the benchmark scenario presented in Figure 33.2 in many ways and in some cases to a significant extent:

i. Quality information may become persuasive rather than informative. In this case, additional rents for producers arise but aggregate welfare impacts of GI regulation may become more negative since consumption will exceed the socially optimal level.

ii. Protection of geographical indications may occur on a market segment where the producer club already exerts market power or the regulation leads to market power in an otherwise competitive market. The price premium as well as the redistributive and allocative implications of regulations would then differ from the competitive case.

iii. There is a major discussion in the economics of information whether consumer preferences will actually change owing to additional information (Becker and Stigler 1977). If they do, the welfare consequences of GI regulation will be different from those in Figure 33.2. It is necessary then to evaluate the welfare implications for consumers either on the basis of *ex ante* or *ex post* preferences (Dixit and Norman 1970). With true information, a change in preferences as outlined by the shift from *D* to *D'*, and on the basis of *ex post* preferences, implications for consumer and aggregate welfare will deteriorate compared to the benchmark situation above.

iv. The market and welfare effects in Figure 33.2 still exclude the linkages between the market segment of the GI product and its substitutes. The analysis needs to be extended in order to take Akerlof's lemon case fully into account. In a partially eroded market, where the high-quality good has in part been crowded out by a low-quality good and both goods sell at a uniform price, producers and consumers of the high- and low-quality good have to be distinguished in order to derive comprehensive results on welfare and redistributive effects of GI regulation. This distinction is also crucial for the analysis of trade impacts by GI regulation.

It is particularly the last point that has been addressed in the theoretical literature on GIs applying models of vertical product differentiation, to which we turn next.

3.3.2 *Welfare Analysis of Geographical Indication Regulation in Vertically Differentiated Markets*

An increasing number of studies have addressed GIs from an economic welfare perspective by using models of vertical product differentiation of the Mussa–Rosen (1978) type[6] (Zago and Pick 2004; Lence et al. 2007; Langinier and Babcock 2008; Moschini, Menapace, and Pick 2008). This methodological framework makes it possible to account for the existence of heterogeneous consumers and to analyze different institutional arrangements of GI regulation on the supply side. It has been used to study equilibrium prices and quantities, market shares, and the welfare of the interest groups involved under alternative market structures. In all contributions two quality levels are modeled: the GI product as the high-quality good and the generic one as the low-quality good. There are *N* consumers in the market and each consumer buys either one or zero units of the good. Consumers derive utility according to

---

[6] For a detailed analysis of these models, see Giannakas (Chapter 9 in this volume).

$$U = \theta q - p(q)$$

where $q \in \mathfrak{R}^+$ represents the quality of the product, $\theta \in \mathfrak{R}^+$ indexes consumer types, and $p \in \mathfrak{R}^{++}$ is the price of the good of quality q. The parameter θ can be interpreted as either a measure of consumers' intensity of preference for quality or the inverse marginal rate of substitution between income and quality for consumers who have an identical intensity of preferences for quality but differ in terms of income. Hence, the WTP for the quality attribute varies across consumers. Figure 33.3 illustrates the market equilibria in the situations with and without regulation in force.

Without regulation products are differentiated but consumers are not able to distinguish between the different qualities. Hence, a pooled equilibrium with an expected quality level of $\bar{q}$ sold at $\bar{p}$ will evolve. The net utility consumers derive in such a situation is $U_{without}$. If a credible GI regulation is implemented, consumers are able to distinguish between the low- and the high-quality product. Since it is assumed that it is costlier to produce the GI product than the generic counterpart because of stricter production standards, the GI product must sell at higher prices (i.e., $p_H > p_L$).[7]

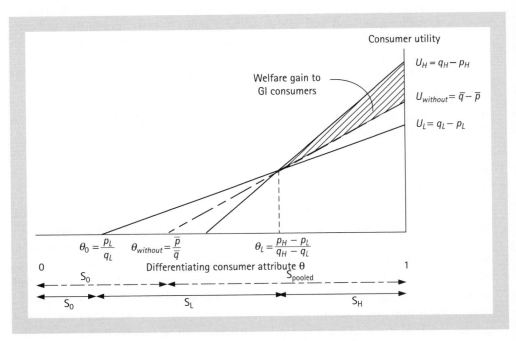

FIGURE 33.3 Consumer welfare in situations with and without regulation

The greater is θ, the more a consumer values quality differences and the greater is his WTP for this quality difference. This is depicted in Figure 33.3, where the utility of purchasing quality q at price p is a function of θ, which is normalized to the interval $[0, 1]$. The consumer who is indifferent between buying the low-quality good at price p_L and purchasing the high-quality good at price p_H is denoted by θ_L. Thus, consumers with a high income or a strong preference for quality (i.e., consumers with $\theta \in (\theta_L, 1)$) purchase the high-quality good, whereas consumers with $\theta \in (\theta_0, \theta_L)$ purchase the low-quality good and consumers with $\theta \in (0, \theta_0)$ purchase nothing at all. The indifferent consumers determine the market demand, whereby s_0 represents the share of consumers not buying anything, and $s_L(s_H)$ is the share of consumers purchasing the low-quality (high-quality) good. Without regulation in force there is only one indifferent consumer, $\theta_{without}$, who is indifferent between buying the good of expected quality $\bar{q}$ and buying nothing at all.

Despite these similarities, the available studies on GI regulation differ in some important points. Zago and Pick (2004) and Langinier and Babcock (2006) assume that the supply of the quality attribute is exogenous. This implies that product quality is determined by *terroir* and producers are *ex ante* identified as either high- or low-quality producers. On the other hand, Moschini, Menapace, and Pick (2008) assume that entry into the high-quality market is endogenous, that is, producers are free to produce either the low- or the high-quality good. Based on these assumptions, the studies derive the following welfare effects of implementing a credible GI regulation. Zago and Pick (2004) conclude that high-quality consumers gain whereas low-quality consumers lose owing to the fact that these consumers benefited from a higher average quality sold in the unregulated market. In the scenario chosen by Moschini, Menapace, and Pick (2008) without regulation only the low quality is produced and sold. Accordingly, low-quality consumers are unaffected by the regulation. However, all studies conclude that the main beneficiaries of the regulation are consumers of the GI good. This welfare gain is also illustrated in Figure 33.3, whereby its size depends on cost and quality differences between the low- and the high-quality good and on the distribution of θ. Welfare gains to GI consumers are higher, the higher are quality differences, the lower are cost differences, and the more the distribution of θ is skewed toward 1.

With respect to welfare effects on producers and implications for government intervention, the study results also differ. However, they all share the conclusion that under some circumstances government intervention policies, either by subsidizing certification or by allowing collusion among producers, are welfare-enhancing. Lence et al. (2007) argue that allowing producers to collude can be welfare-enhancing if fixed costs of developing the geographically differentiated high-quality product, typically certification costs, are too high to be developed under perfect competition. Consequently, even if the intervention policy itself induces welfare losses, total social welfare can increase owing to the welfare gains that arise from the consumption of the high-quality product that would have been non-existent in the market without government intervention. Zago and Pick (2004) elaborate further that besides producers' ability to exercise market power (e.g., via land restrictions), the level of administrative costs and quality differences determine total welfare effects. If administrative costs of regulation are high and quality differences are low, the effect on total welfare may be negative. Hence, a GI regulation will not always have the positive welfare impacts that, for example, the European Union stresses in its food quality policy.

One important limitation of the available theoretical literature is that only two different quality levels are considered and a vertically differentiated demand structure is assumed. It could be argued that the GI product and the non-labeled product are not vertically but horizontally or even both vertically and horizontally differentiated. This seems to be highly relevant for product markets with a high density of GI products such as the wine or cheese market. Although it has been demonstrated that models of horizontal and vertical product differentiation are closely connected, they do not yield the same theoretical results in any given case (Cremer and Thisse 1991). Moreover, these models are all one-dimensional models of unit demand, meaning that the characteristics space is one-dimensional (high- versus low-quality) and consumers buy only one unit of the product. Real purchase decisions, in which consumers face a large number of product cues, differ clearly from such a scenario. Therefore, understanding which factors determine consumers' purchase decisions is of great importance. The next section will cover the theoretical background on the determinants of consumers' purchase decisions with respect to geographically differentiated products.

3.3.3 *Consumer Preferences for Geographically Differentiated Products: Theoretical Considerations*

As discussed above, it is crucial for the determination of price and welfare effects how strongly demand shifts owing to GI regulation, which means how consumers react to additional information on the geographical origin of a product. Without explicitly stressing this link to the economic theory of GIs, a large number of studies have investigated consumer perceptions and the willingness to buy (WTB) and WTP for certain products. Most of these studies are embedded in marketing research.

There is a large body of literature on consumers' perceptions of country- and region-of-origin labels (among others Verlegh and Steenkamp 1999; van der Lans et al. 2001; van Ittersum et al. 2007). Main conclusions that can be drawn from this literature are that consumers use the information on product origin as an extrinsic quality cue and that this cue influences consumers' purchase decisions in multiple ways.[8] First, if the consumer connects a special image with the production region, this image can be used to form a quality evaluation of the product. This effect can be either positive or negative. Second, the origin label can be used during repeat purchases to reidentify a product. If the consumer was satisfied with the product the first time, it is likely that he will buy the same product again or at least another product from that specific region (Grunert 2005). Besides this cognitive mechanism of an origin label, that is, origin as

---

[8] A product cue is classified as extrinsic if variations in the product cue do not alter the physical state of the product.

a cue for product quality, the origin can also have an effect on consumer demand through affective and normative mechanisms. In the former case consumer demand is influenced by symbolic and emotional associations evoked by the product origin; in the latter case a certain origin is preferred because of social and personal norms (Verlegh and Steenkamp 1999).

Van Ittersum, Candel, and Meulenberg (2003) point out that region-of-origin labels differ from country-of-origin labels in some important aspects. A more consistent image is attributed to region-of-origin compared to country-of-origin labels, since regions are far more homogeneous than countries, for example, in terms of natural conditions. Moreover, region-of-origin labels offer the opportunity to differentiate the product from both foreign and domestic competitors. The proposed theoretical model to capture the effect of a regional image on product preferences is presented in Figure 33.4.

The model states that differences in product preference for regionally differentiated products can be explained by differences in *product-attribute perception, attitude toward the region*, and *product-specific regional image*. The attitude toward the region captures the general image consumers relate to the specific region. This general image of a region influences the product preference directly and indirectly by influencing both the product-specific regional image and the product attribute perception. The authors stress that one important success factor is the positive product-specific regional image. This implies that empirical research should always deal with a specific product–region combination, since a positive or negative image of a region is always closely connected with a certain product. Parma is perceived by consumers as a region well suited for producing high-quality ham. However, this does not mean that producers located in Parma starting to produce wine would also benefit from a positive product-specific regional image. Results from several focus group discussions indicate that a

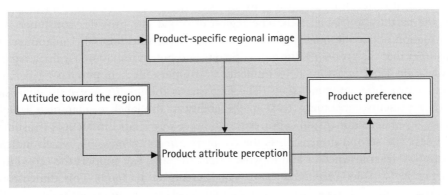

FIGURE 33.4 Theoretical model of the effect of the region-of-origin cue on the preference for a product

Source: Modified presentation on the basis of van Ittersum, Candel, and Meulenberg (2003).

product-specific regional image consists of two dimensions, a human and a natural environment factor (van Ittersum, Candel, and Meulenberg 2003). The human factor refers to the expertise present in the region to produce a certain good, and the natural environment factor refers to agro-ecological conditions. These two dimensions reflect the already mentioned *terroir* concept.

The model presented in Figure 33.4 does not capture the effect of an origin label itself. An augmented model used by van Ittersum et al. (2007) on regional certification labels integrates this aspect. It is presented in Figure 33.5.

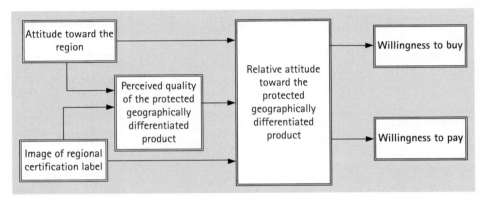

FIGURE 33.5 Conceptual model of the influence of regional certification labels on consumers' willingness to buy and willings to pay for a protected regional product

Source: Modified presentation on the basis of van Ittersum et al. (2007).

In studies dealing with the influence of regional labels on consumers' product evaluation it is necessary to distinguish between the effect of the region-of-origin cue and the certification label itself. The region-of-origin cue provides consumers with information about the quality of the product. The certification label guarantees the consumer that the product is the authentic one and not an imitation. Again, a regional certification label is assumed to influence consumers in their purchasing behavior through two different dimensions. The first one is the *quality warranty dimension*, which represents consumers' trust in the ability of the label to guarantee a higher quality level. This dimension captures the indirect way a label influences consumers' attitudes. The second dimension is the *economic support dimension*, which indicates consumers' trust in whether and to what extent the label can support the economy in that region (van der Lans et al. 2001; van Ittersum et al. 2007). This dimension is responsible for the direct effect of a certification label on consumers' attitudes. The first dimension is relevant for all consumers of the product, the second one predominantly for consumers located inside the production area.

4   EMPIRICAL EVIDENCE ON CONSUMER ATTITUDES TOWARD ORIGIN LABELS AND THE IMPACTS OF GEOGRAPHICAL INDICATIONS

Empirical studies analyzing geographically differentiated products cover a wide range of different research questions and applied methodologies. The following section will review the main empirical findings by highlighting the chosen approaches and discussing the obtained results. The findings will be synthesized in order to draw some general conclusions and to point out which questions need to be addressed in future research. Given the different paradigms with regard to geographical indications and the various policy approaches toward these products, it is no surprise that most of the empirical evidence comes from Europe.

4.1   Consumer Studies: Willingness to Pay for and Perceptions of Geographical Indications

One of the earliest studies focusing explicitly on consumer perceptions and awareness of protected regional foods was carried out by Tregear, Kuznesof, and Moxey (1998). Its main finding is that perceived authenticity is the essential determinant of whether a food is considered as being truly regional. Perceived authenticity in turn depends on a range of factors including personal factors (e.g., knowledge), product-related factors (e.g., label or packaging), and situational factors (e.g., retail outlet). Furthermore, the study highlights that most consumers are not aware of the official EU certification scheme on geographical indications. A low level of awareness and knowledge of European Regulation EC No. 510/2006 was also found in more recent studies, in which less than 10 percent of the respondents claimed to know the labeling scheme (Fotopoulos and Krystallis 2000; Teuber 2011).

Nevertheless, consumers are aware of traditional products or products protected under the regulation. The products are most often well known, at least in the region of production. However, most consumers do not recognize the official EU logos and have no, or very limited, knowledge concerning the requirements involved.

As stated in Section 3.3, a crucial assumption in all theoretical models on geographically differentiated products is the presence of a consumer segment valuing the origin attribute. The following research questions are typically addressed in empirical consumer studies. First, are there consumers in the marketplace who are willing to pay a premium for the differentiated product? Second, how large is their WTP for the GI attribute? Third, is it possible to classify consumer segments according to their WTP based on sociodemographic or psychographic factors?

WTB and WTP studies can be based both on revealed-preference and on stated-preference data. In the latter case, methods such as contingent valuation, experimental auctions, and conjoint analysis are used to collect data (Grunert 2005). In the former case, most often the hedonic pricing methodology is applied.[9] This method has been used quite frequently for analyzing price differences and reputation effects in the wine market. Results for wine indicate that regions having established a collective reputation can achieve higher prices even after controlling for current quality differences (Landon and Smith 1997; Angulo et al. 2000; Schamel 2006). Similar results were found for the high-quality coffee market, where certain countries and regions can realize higher prices owing to reputational effects (Donnet, Weatherspoon, and Hoehn 2008; Teuber 2010). The origin cue seems to be an important price determinant in these markets. Consumers were found to pay higher prices for wine and coffee from countries or regions they perceive as very suitable for producing these products.

However, the underlying factors that motivate consumers to buy products from a certain origin cannot be elaborated within hedonic analyses. This research question is typically addressed in consumer studies using methods like contingent valuation or discrete choice modeling. There is a large body of literature on consumers' attitudes toward country-of-origin labeling and Pharr (2005) even concludes that such labeling is the most widely researched aspect in marketing and consumer behavior. Although most of the studies deal with manufactured products, there are also several studies investigating country-of-origin label effects for foods (e.g., Juric and Worsley 1998; Hoffmann 2000; Loureiro and Umberger 2003, 2005, 2007; Ehmke, Lusk, and Tyner 2008).

Besides the country-of-origin labeling literature there is also a growing empirical literature on consumer attitudes toward regional certification labels. The most comprehensive study is the one by van Ittersum et al. (2007), to which we referred in Section 3.3.3. The theoretical framework presented in Section 3.3.3 was tested in a study with 1,200 consumers from three different European countries. The obtained results confirm that consumers' perceptions of regional certification labels consist of two dimensions: the quality warranty and the economic support dimension. The quality warranty dimension was found to influence the WTB and WTP indirectly through the perceived quality of the protected product, whereas the economic support dimension directly affects the relative attitude toward the protected product. Most important among all determinants in consumers' WTB and WTP, and therefore the main factor of success for an origin-based differentiation strategy, is the perceived higher quality. This finding is consistent with other consumer studies in the field of origin labeling and certification (McCluskey and Loureiro 2003).

---

[9] For more detailed information on these methodologies, see the chapters in this volume by Adamowicz and Swait (Ch. 5), Costanigro and McCluskey (Ch. 6), Carlsson (Ch. 7), and Alfnes and Rickertsen (Ch. 8).

Table 33.1 summarizes results on the WTB and WTP for geographically differentiated foods, on the role of psychographic and sociodemographic factors, and possible interactions between different product attributes. The latter aspect captures how regional certification labels interact with other labels and brands, and is especially interesting given the background of a steadily increasing label proliferation.

The results provide no uniform pattern on how certain psychographic and sociodemographic characteristics affect attitudes toward geographically differentiated products. There is one hypothesis, however, that was confirmed in all studies and that is a clear ethnocentric behavior among consumers. Ethnocentric behavior, also known as "home bias" in the trade literature, refers to the fact that consumers with a close proximity to the producing region exhibit a higher WTB and WTP than consumers not located in the region of origin (Scarpa, Philippidis, and Spalatro 2005).

The results with respect to the interaction effects of region-of-origin cues and brands suggest that weak brands seem to benefit relatively more from a region-of-origin label than strong brands (Hassan and Monier-Dilhan 2006; Profeta, Enneking, and Balling 2008).[10] In other words, the label itself is more favorable for producers who have not yet established a strong reputation in the marketplace. Another important aspect is the relative importance of the country-of-origin cue compared to other product cues such as price, brand, or a certain production process. Ehmke, Lusk, and Tyner (2008) conducted conjoint experiments in four different countries, namely China, France, Niger, and the United States, to investigate the relative importance of the origin cue compared to the product attributes GMO- and pesticide-free. The results indicate that the origin was in most cases the least important attribute among the three investigated.

Generally, the results document that in the analysis of origin labels it is indispensable to rely on multiple-cue study designs. Such a study design makes it possible to incorporate interaction effects among product attributes that can alter results from single-cue studies substantially. The results concerning preference heterogeneity are mixed and provide no clear pattern in terms of consumer segmentation. Moreover, all studies investigated the WTP of domestic consumers. It is most likely that results will differ for foreign consumers, since the economic support dimension was in most cases a strong WTP determinant for domestic consumers. Foreign consumers' preferences are of special importance for GIs in less developed countries, since products such as coffee, tea, or cocoa are typically exported.

---

[10] This is in line with findings by Crespi and Marette (2002) and Crespi (2007) on the effects of generic advertising on individual producers. They point out that if generic advertising diminishes product differentiation, it is possible that low-quality producers can increase their market shares at the expense of high-quality producers.

Table 33.1 Willingness to buy (WTB) and willingness to pay (WTP) for geographically differentiated products

Author	Product	Data and methodology	Results
Influence of psychographic and sociodemographic characteristics			
Fotopoulos and Krystallis (2000)	Zagora apples (Greece)	Consumer survey, SP, Conjoint analysis	GI label seems to be important for only ⅓ of buyers. WTP of ~20% of product value. Cluster "indication-of-origin fans": mainly female, close proximity to the producing region, higher income.
Skuras and Vakrou (2002)	Moschofilero wine (Greece)	Consumer survey, SP, CVM	Higher educated consumers and consumers that are stronger associated with the region of origin exhibit a higher WTP.
Scarpa and Del Giudice (2004)	Olive oil (Italy)	Consumer survey, SP, Ranked choice experiment	Home bias is found in all three samples; preference intensity for the GI attribute always dominates preference for organic production.
Scarpa, Philippidus, and Spalatro (2005)	Oranges, table grapes, olive oil (Italy)	Consumer survey, SP, Conjoint analysis	Home bias is prevalent for all three products, but most dominant in the case of olive oil. Only limited evidence of national preference heterogeneity conditional on socioeconomic characteristics.
Interaction with brands			
Bonnet and Simioni (2001)	Camembert cheese (France)	Scanner data, RP, MMNL	Brand appears to be more important than the GI label; most consumers attach a negative value to the GI label.
Loureiro and McCluskey (2000)	Galician veal (Spain)	Spanish HH data, RP, Hedonic analysis	GI label leads to a significantly positive effect on the price for intermediate quality meat, the label is not significant for either quality extreme.
Hassan and Monier-Dilhan (2006)	Camembert cheese (France) Dry cured ham (France)	French HH data, RP, Hedonic analysis	GI label yields a significantly by positive effect on the price. Interaction effect with strong brands is negative, but with weak brands it is positive. Weak brands extract more value from the GI label.
Profeta, Enneking, and Balling (2008)	Bavarian Beer (Germany)	Consumer survey, SP, Conjoint analysis	Weak beer brands benefit more from region-of-origin label than strong beer brands.

Interaction with other product attributes			
Loureiro and Umberger (2007)	Beef	Consumer survey, SP, Choice experiment	Food safety certification is the most important product attribute, followed by the country-of-origin label, a traceability cue and guaranteed tenderness.
Ehmke, Lusk, and Tyner (2008)	Onions	Consumer survey, SP, Conjoint analysis	Consumers in all four countries prefer domestic food. Origin is less important to consumers than the attributes GMO- and pesticide-free.

Note: CVM = contingent valuation method; GI = geographical indication; GMO = genetically modified organism; MMNL = mixed multinomial logit model; RP = revealed-preference data; SP = stated-preference data.

4.2   Price and Welfare Impacts of Geographically Differentiated Products

4.2.1   *Cost–Benefit Analyses*

One of the most comprehensive studies in this field was conducted within an EU-financed pilot project on the economics of food quality assurance and certification schemes. Within this project, four different GI products were analyzed with respect to their economic performance (ETEPS 2006). The following points were addressed in detail: farmer participation, market shares and their evolution over time, costs and benefits for all actors involved, and price formation, i.e., price premiums and price differentials. The investigated production systems were Parmigiano-Reggiano cheese, Comté cheese, Dehesa de Extremadura ham, and Baena olive oil.

The findings with respect to costs and benefits can be summarized as follows. Direct costs such as certification costs, membership fees, and control costs do usually not exceed 1–3 percent of total costs. In most cases indirect costs are much more important. Indirect costs are costs that arise from specific production and processing requirements such as restrictions on animal feed, herd density, or processing technologies. Table 33.2 presents a short overview of the direct and indirect costs identified for each case study.

Stringent production requirements exist in all analyzed production chains. In the case of Dehesa de Extremadura ham, for example, the pigs must be fed solely with acorns. Such strict production rules are assumed to have a much higher cost impact compared to the direct costs of certification. However, quantifying these indirect costs is a difficult task. The additional costs due to the product and process restrictions established within the certification scheme have to be disentangled from production costs in the absence of certification. Hence, quantitative estimations of the cost impact of product and process requirements are not presented in the EU study.

Table 33.2 Costs in four GI supply chains

Case study	Costs	
	Direct costs	Indirect costs
Baena olive oil (Spain)	Farmers: fee equivalent to 0.3% of the average production value/ha. Milling industry: tax of 1.25% of its sales price. Bottling industry: tax for labeling.	Only local varieties can be used. Higher labour costs due to prescribed period of harvesting (less flexibility to spread harvesting through time).
Comté cheese (France)	Production quota fee of 10 cents per kg Comté cheese. Fee of €2/kg for production above set quota. In addition, a contribution of €3/ton cheese to INAO, which controls the Comté GI.	Restrictions on animal feed, breed, and herd density. Transportation of milk is limited.
Dehesa de Extremadura ham (Spain)	Frequent controls at all stages of the production and processing process. Registered farms pay a fee to the Ruling Council of €5/pig. In addition, the processing industry pays a fee that is calculated according to the number of hams and shoulders sent to the market. No precise figure given.	Very extensive pig raising based on acorns only. No additional feeding allowed. Processing according to strict rules. Processing industries are required to specialize in Dehesa de Extremadura ham.
Parmigiano-Reggiano cheese (Italy)	€6 per wheel of cheese at the time of certification after 12 months, or 17–18 cents per kg of Parmigiano-Reggiano cheese sold.	Restrictions on animal feed, breed, herd density, transportation of milk, processing of milk.

Source: ETEPS (2006: 25).

On the other hand, higher prices paid by processors were identified as the main benefit for producers. It was analyzed from the individual producer's point of view whether it is more favorable to produce the GI product compared to the non-GI product that is a close substitute in production. Table 33.3 presents the main results with respect to market structure, reference products, and achieved price differentials for three analyzed GI products.

In nearly all cases the GI product achieves a higher price compared to the non-GI product. Only in the case of Baena olive oil do olive growers receive an undifferentiated price. The price differentiation takes place further downstream, at the bottling stage. However, since the processing stage is dominated by farmer cooperatives, it is argued that the price differential achieved at the bottling stage is passed on to farmers through a higher undifferentiated price for crude olives (ETEPS 2006).

These findings are confirmed by a study on the French Brie cheese industry. Bouamra-Mechemache and Chaaban (2010) investigated the cost and production structure of Brie de Meaux and Brie de Melun, two French cheeses protected as GIs,

Table 33.3 Market structure and price differentials for three GI products

	Baena olive oil (Spain)	Comté cheese (France)	Dehesa de Extremadura ham (Spain)
Market structure	Perfect competition	Monopolistic competition/Oligopoly	Oligopoly
Market share	2.3% of Spanish olive oil production. 1.4% of Spanish consumption.	4% of French cheese production.	3% of Spanish ham production. 2% of national consumption.
Reference product	Olive oil without a GI	French Emmental	Iberian ham without a GI
Price differences			
Farm-level	No difference	+26%	+29%
Processing stage	No difference +9%/+30%[a]	+22%	+21%
Retail-level	+22%	+41%	+6%

[a] No price difference at the pressing stage, but considerable price differences at the bottling stage (bulk and bottled).

Source: ETEPS (2006).

and compared these with non-GI Brie producers. Their results point out that the GI technology results on average in 40 percent higher variable production costs owing to strict production requirements, especially the use of unpasteurized milk and labor-intensive techniques. However, this cost disadvantage is compensated by higher retail prices.

Other studies point out that benefits to producers can accrue to the lowering of transaction costs, increasing turnover in existing marketing channels and the ability to enter new marketing channels (Barjolle and Chappuis 2000; Belletti et al. 2009). Canada and Vazquez (2005) found that in the case of Spanish olive oil protected as a GI, the GI label serves as a quality assurance system for distributors, especially for the retailing industry located outside Spain. This argument is also put forward in a study by Belletti et al. (2009) on the role of GIs in the internationalization process of agri-food products. Based on a survey carried out on four products from Tuscany (Italy) they conclude that the GI label acts as quality standard, especially for professional operators, enabling small and medium enterprises to enter new distribution channels. However, they also highlight the importance of collective promotional activities for entering successfully new markets.

It was also found that higher prices do not necessarily lead to an agricultural income that is above average. In the case of Comté cheese, producing milk is costlier than in other parts of France because of difficult agro-ecological conditions.[11] Indeed, owing to

[11] The Comté area is located for the most part in mountainous areas.

a lower labor efficiency in this region, the income per family worker is even lower than in other milk-producing regions in France. Therefore, the higher prices paid for milk used for Comté production compensate for higher production costs. These findings suggest that the production system of Comté is a positive example in terms of the explicitly stated goal of regulation EC No. 510/2006 to support less favored regions.

The presented results for European products indicate that pursuing an origin-based differentiation strategy was in most cases favorable for the actors involved, but there are differences in the degree of success quantified in price differentials and income effects. One of the major success factors seems to be a well-established reputation in the marketplace, as the cases of Comté and Parmigiano-Reggiano cheese illustrate. However, reputation is not built overnight; both products have been in the marketplace for decades and can be considered mature systems.[12] Another crucial success factor seems to be promotional activity. The ETEPS (2006) study states that in the cases of Comté and Parmigiano-Reggiano considerable sums are spent on advertising and promotion. These are important points to be considered while analyzing recently established geographical indications that target mainly export markets.

It should be noted that the presented case studies concentrate on the likely costs of and benefits for producers supplying the geographically differentiated product. They do not cover a comprehensive cost–benefit analysis as suggested in Section 3.3.1. The price impacts of GI regulation are not modeled explicitly and there is no aggregate welfare analysis covering all producers and consumers of the product, and its major substitutes.

4.2.2 *Coordination and Competition*

In order to establish a geographically differentiated product, the actors in the supply chain are required to cooperate, either horizontally, vertically, or both. This collective action, which is one of the main features of geographical indications, raises concerns about possible anti-competitive practices, particularly the risk of monopolistic cartels and unjustified barriers to entry (Lucatelli 2000). On the other hand, collective action at upstream stages of the marketing chain can also be seen as an attempt to countervail the increasing market power by downstream actors such as retailers. Additionally, as argued by one strand of the theoretical literature (see Section 3.3.2), supply control can be a necessary precondition for the creation of the differentiated product if fixed costs of the implementation are high.

Questions with respect to possible welfare losses due to collective action and market power were addressed in several studies in some detail (Lucatelli 2000; Carter, Krissoff, and Zwane 2006; ETEPS 2006; Hayes, Lence, and Stoppa 2004; Mérel 2009).

The study by Lucatelli (2000) lists several antitrust cases against European GI products. The cases presented comprise French and Italian products for which producer groups or consortia had implemented measures to control total supply. One of

---

[12] The tradition of Parmigiano-Reggiano production dates back to the thirteenth century (de Roest and Menghi 2000).

the main arguments put forward for these arrangements was that supply control is essential for quality control. For each product an antitrust case was enforced but with different outcomes. In the case of Parma and San Daniele ham, the argumentation to implement a quota system in order to secure the high quality of the product was temporarily accepted, whereas for Parmigiano-Reggiano and Grana Padano cheese this line of argument was rejected. It is interesting to note that in neither of the case studies does the area limitation itself restrict total output. However, in most cases it is assumed that the strict production standards limit total output (ETEPS 2006).

More advanced market power studies in the context of geographically differentiated products are rare. One exemption is the study by Mérel (2009) on Comté cheese. In this study a new empirical industrial organization approach is applied to investigate econometrically whether the vertically integrated Comté production sector is able to exercise market power. The estimate of the market power coefficient is small and statistically insignificant, leading to the conclusion that the supply control scheme has no significant effect on consumer prices and, thus, social welfare is not harmed by the supply control scheme in place. According to the author, a possible explanation for this result could be the fact that the production plan must be approved yearly by government agencies, preventing the vertically integrated producer association of Comté to restrict supply far from competitive levels. Another aspect not taken up by the studies presented so far is that most GI products face a large number of substitutes limiting the ability to exercise market power. This point is of great importance while analyzing the welfare impacts of GIs. It is true that geographical indications grant a legal name monopoly. However, this name monopoly does not necessarily lead to an economic monopoly.

To sum up, all these findings support the statement by Bureau and Valceschini (2003: 74) that "there is a fine line between the organized cartelization in the public interest and undue barriers to entry set by a small group of producers." Hence, the question whether regulations on geographical indications can lead to negative welfare effects owing to legally granted market power needs to be addressed with a case-by-case approach.

4.3   Social and Environmental Impacts

Certification schemes for geographical indications are often designed with the aim of maintaining or promoting rural development. GIs are assumed to incorporate and valorize many local assets with special or immobile characteristics linked to the area (Tregear et al. 2007). Barjolle and Sylvander (1999) call the expected impacts of GIs on the rural economy the "social success."

Tregear et al. (2007) investigated the impacts of the European GI scheme on rural development by analyzing three different case studies. The findings point out that even under the same certification scheme, in this case EC Regulation No. 510/2006, very distinct socioeconomic outcomes can be observed. The involvement and motivations of the supply chain actors, as well as the strategy pursued, differed remarkably. Given the obtained mixed results, the authors point out that collective action, the degree of economic and cultural significance of the product for the whole region, and the access to and visibility of the product in the region are major determinants of the rural development impact of a regional certification strategy.

Other case studies report very mixed results, too. Whereas de Roest and Menghi (2000) find very positive impacts on rural development in the production system of Parmigiano-Reggiano, the results by Bowen and Valenzuela Zapata (2009) for the production system of tequila are negative. In the case study on Parmigiano-Reggiano the main benefits in terms of rural development are higher levels of employment both in agriculture and in upstream and downstream activities. These higher employment effects are due to the traditional and, hence, more labor-intensive techniques used at all stages of the production process.[13] The results obtained by Bowen and Valenzuela Zapata (2009) indicate the opposite. The authors claim that the establishment of a geographical indication for tequila has largely failed to benefit the local population. This is noteworthy given the economic success of this GI. Tequila, a protected GI since 1974, is considered to be the oldest non-European GI. Its reputation and market share has grown substantially over the last fifteen years and the quality level could be improved significantly (Bowen and Valenzuela Zapata 2009). Based on these developments tequila is often recognized as one of the most successful GIs outside of Europe. Nevertheless, Bowen and Valenzuela Zapata (2009) argue that the social success is quite different. Traditional agave cultivation techniques have been replaced by more mechanized, chemically intensive systems leading to negative environmental effects and a marginalization of small farmers. The authors attribute this development to the missing link between the *terroir* and the product. Despite the fact that the Mexican legislation on GIs explicitly requires this link, it is not enforced in practice.

The empirical evidence suggests that the rural development impact of a regional certification scheme strongly depends on the design and enforcement of the national regulation in place and the ability of the different actors in the supply chain to cooperate and set up a coherent strategy of collective action. Moreover, as the results for tequila and other products highlight, many GI products are no longer as artisanal and traditional as their image suggests (Broude 2005).[14]

---

[13] The benchmark scenario is the industrial dairy system in the Parmigiano-Reggiano region, since this is the alternative market for liquid milk in that area (de Roest and Menghi 2000).

[14] Riccheri et al. (2006) conducted a comprehensive study for eight different GI products on the environmental impacts of GI protection. The results indicate in most cases a positive impact on biodiversity conservation and maintenance of cultural landscapes. However, they did also observe intensification processes with negative environmental impacts leading to the conclusion that GIs have a more or less neutral impact on the environment.

5 CONCLUDING REMARKS

The number of geographically differentiated products is steadily increasing, as is the number of foods with a protected geographical origin. Consequently, the success of origin-labeled foods and market regulation for geographical indications has gained strong and increasing interest in the theoretical and empirical literature. This chapter has shown that a wide variety of empirical results have been elaborated with very different methodological approaches. Some questions can be answered unambiguously, but many queries remain with regard to the role of public policy and the impacts of regulation for consumers, producers, and the society as a whole.

Geographically differentiated products can create economic value if the origin is valued by consumers. Empirical studies clearly confirm that there are consumers who appreciate information on the geographical origin of foods (1) as a quality cue, and (2) because of ethnocentric tendencies. Therefore, there are incentives for private firms to differentiate their products in terms of origin. However, the empirical evidence has also highlighted that geographically differentiated products are by no means a self-runner. The most successful GI products such as Parmigiano-Reggiano or Parma ham are managed like international brands, and advertising and promotion play a crucial role.

Origin labeling, however, is susceptible to imitation, and market failure may occur owing to quality uncertainty by consumers. A case for market regulation, information, policy, and protected geographical indications can be made. It is exactly at this point where many questions remain unanswered in the literature. In the large number of empirical case studies, the welfare impacts of regulation on consumers have typically been excluded. Most often, the impacts of protected geographical indications on prices, overall welfare for producers, as well as the redistributive consequences in the marketing chain, have also not been modeled. Studies are needed that apply theoretical cost–benefit approaches encompassing all affected groups to empirical case studies of GI regulation. It is also important to integrate more findings from consumer studies and welfare economics in the analysis of geographically differentiated products. If ethnocentrism is important, as consumer studies claim, new policy implications might arise with regard to the trade and welfare impacts of GI regulation. It could be much more difficult than previously expected to correct for market failure arising from quality uncertainty in the sense of Akerlof. If consumers react not only to origin labels as they provide a quality cue but also for ethnocentric motivations, a targeted policy to correct for market imperfections may overshoot and raise demand for the geographically differentiated product above the socially optimal level. The home bias of domestic consumers may then cause trade distortions even if GI regulation aims at the correction of market failure alone.

References

Ackerberg, D. A. 2001. "Empirically Distinguishing Informative and Prestige Effects of Advertising." *RAND Journal of Economics* 32/2: 316–33.

Addor, F., N. Thumm, and A. Grazioli. 2003. "Geographical Indications: Important Issues for Industrialized and Developing Countries." *IPTS Report* 74: 24–31.

Akerlof, G. 1970. "The Market for 'Lemons': Quality Uncertainty and the Market Mechanism." *Quarterly Journal of Economics* 84/3: 488–500.

Alston, J. M., J. M. Crespi, H. M. Kaiser, and R. Sexton. 2005. "Introduction to the Economics of Commodity Promotion Programs." In Kaiser et al. (2005).

——, J. W. Freebairn, and J. S. James. 2003. "Distributional Issues in Check-Off Funded Programs." *Agribusiness*, Special Issue: *Distribution of Benefits and Costs of Commodity Checkoff Programs* 19/3: 277–87.

Anders, S., S. Thompson, and R. Herrmann. 2009. "Markets Segmented by Regional-Origin Labelling with Quality Control." *Applied Economics* 41/3: 311–21.

Angulo, A. M., J. M. Gil, A. Gracia, and M. Sanchez. 2000. "Hedonic Prices for Spanish Red Quality Wine." *British Food Journal* 102/7: 481–93.

Barham, E. 2003. "Translating *Terroir*: The Global Challenge of French AOC Labeling." *Journal of Rural Studies* 19/1: 127–38.

Barjolle, D., and J.-M. Chappuis. 2000. "Transaction Costs and Artisanal Food Products." Paper presented at the 4th Annual Conference of the International Society for New Institutional Economics, Tuebingen, Germany, September 22–24.

—— and B. Sylvander. 1999. "Some Factors of Success for Origin Labelled Products in Agri-Food Supply Chains in Europe: Market, Internal Resources and Institutions." Paper presented at the 67th European Association of Agricultural Economists Seminar, "The Socio-Economics of Origin Labelled Products in Agrifood Supply Chains," Le Mans, Oct. 28–30.

Barnes, D. W. 2006. "A New Economics of Trademarks." *Northwestern Journal of Technology and Intellectual Property* 5/1: 22–67.

Becker, G. S., and K. M. Murphy. 1993. "A Simple Theory of Advertising as a Good or Bad." *Quarterly Journal of Economics* 108/4: 941–64.

—— and G. J. Stigler. 1977. "De Gustibus Non Est Disputandum." *American Economic Review* 67/2: 76–90.

Becker, T. 2009. "European Food Quality Policy: The Importance of Geographical Indications, Organic Certification and Food Quality Assurance Schemes in European Countries." *Estey Centre Journal International Law and Trade Policy* 10/1: 111–30.

Belletti, G., A. Marescotti, T. Burgassi, E. Manco, A. Marescotti, A. Pacciani, and S. Scaramuzzi. 2009. "The Role of Geographical Indications in the Internationalisation Process of Agri-Food Products." In M. Canavari, N. Cantore, A. Castellini, E. Pignatti, and R. Spadoni, eds, *International Marketing and Trade of Quality Food Products*. Wageningen: Wageningen Academic Publishers.

Bérard, L., and P. Marchenay. 2006. "Local Products and Geographical Indications: Taking Account of Local Knowledge and Biodiversity." *International Social Science Journal* 187/1: 109–16.

Bonnet, C., and M. Simioni. 2001. "Assessing Consumer Response to Protected Designation of Origin Labeling: A Mixed Multinomial Logit Approach." *European Review of Agricultural Economics* 28: 433–49.

Bouamra-Mechemache, Z., and J. Chaaban. 2010. "Determinants of Adoption of Protected Designation of Origin Label: Evidence from the French Brie Cheese Industry." *Journal of Agricultural Economics* 61/2: 225–39.

Bowen, S., and A. Valenzuela Zapata. 2009. "Geographical Indications, *Terroir*, and Socioeconomic and Ecological Sustainability: The Case of Tequila." *Journal of Rural Studies* 25/1: 108–19.

Bramley, C., E. Biénabe, and J. Kirsten. 2009. "The Economics of Geographical Indications: Towards a Conceptual Framework for Geographical Indication Research in Developing Countries." In WIPO, *The Economics of Intellectual Property: Suggestions for Further Research in Developing Countries and Countries with Economies in Transition*. Geneva: World Intellectual Property Organization.

Broude, T. 2005. "Taking 'Trade and Culture' Seriously: Geographical Indications and Cultural Protection in WTO Law." *Journal of International Economic Law* 26/4: 633–92.

Bureau, J.-C., and E. Valceschini. 2003. "European Food-Labeling Policy: Successes and Limitations." *Journal of Food Distribution Research* 34/3: 70–6.

Canada, J. S., and A. M. Vázquez. 2005. "Quality Certification, Institutions and Innovation in Local Agro-Food Systems: Protected Designations of Origin of Olive Oil in Spain." *Journal of Rural Studies* 21/4: 475–86.

Carter, C., B. Krissoff, and A. P. Zwane. 2006. "Can Country-of-Origin Labeling Succeed as a Marketing Tool for Produce? Lessons from Three Case Studies." *Canadian Journal of Agricultural Economics* 54: 513–30.

Clemens, R., and B. Babcock. 2004. *Country of Origin as a Brand: The Case of New Zealand Lamb*. MATRIC Briefing Paper No. 04-MBP 9. Ames: Iowa State University.

Cremer, H., and J.-F. Thisse. 1991. "Location Models of Horizontal Differentiation: A Special Case of Vertical Differentiation Models." *Journal of Industrial Economics* 39/4: 383–90.

Crespi, J. M. 2007. "Generic Advertising and Product Differentiation Revisited." *Journal of Agricultural and Food Industrial Organization* 5/1: 691–701.

——and S. Marette. 2002. "Generic Advertising and Product Differentiation." *American Journal of Agricultural Economics* 84/3: 691–701.

de Roest, K., and A. Menghi. 2000. "Reconsidering 'Traditional' Food: The Case of Parmigiano Reggiano Cheese." *Sociologia Ruralis* 40/4: 439–51.

Dixit, A., and V. Norman 1970. "Advertising and Welfare." *Bell Journal of Economics* 9/1: 1–17.

Donnet, L., D. Weatherspoon, and J. P. Hoehn. 2008. "Price Determinants in Top Quality E-Auctioned Specialty Coffees." *Agricultural Economics* 38/3: 267–76.

Ehmke, M. D., J. L. Lusk, and W. Tyner. 2008. "Measuring the Relative Importance of Preferences for Country of Origin in China, France, Niger and the United States." *Agricultural Economics* 38/3: 277–85.

ETEPS (ETEPS AISBL and JRC-IPST). 2006. *Economics of Food Quality, Assurance and Certification Schemes Managed within an Integrated Supply Chain. Final Report*. Brussels: European Commission.

European Commission. 2006. Council Regulation No. 510/2006 of 20 March 2006 on the Protection of Geographical Indications and Designations of Origin for Agricultural Products and Foodstuffs. *Official Journal of the European Union* (Mar. 31), L 93/12–L 93/25.

Fink, C., and K. E. Maskus. 2006. "The Debate on Geographical Indications in the WTO." In R. Newfarmer, ed., *Trade, Doha and Development: A Window into the Issue*. Washington, DC: World Bank.

Foster, W. G., and R. E. Just. 1989. "Measuring Welfare Effects of Product Contermination with Consumer Uncertainty." *Journal of Environmental Economics and Management* 17/3: 266–83.

Fotopoulos, C., and A. Krystallis. 2000. "Quality Labels as a Marketing Advantage: The Case of the 'PDO Zagora' Apples in the Greek Market." *European Journal of Marketing* 37/10: 1350–74.

Gergaud, O., and V. Ginsburgh. 2008. "Natural Endowment, Production Technologies and the Quality of Wines in Bordeaux. Does *Terroir* Matter?" *Economic Journal* 118/529: 142–57.

Geuze, M. 2009. "The Provisions on Geographical Indications in the TRIPS Agreement." *Estey Centre Journal of International Law and Trade Policy* 10/1: 50–64.

Grossman, G. M., and C. Shapiro. 1988. "Counterfeit-Product Trade." *American Economic Review* 78/1: 59–75.

Grunert, K. G. 2005. "Food Quality and Safety: Consumer Perception and Demand." *European Review of Agricultural Economics* 32/3: 369–91.

Hassan, D., and S. Monier-Dilhan. 2006. "National Brands and Store Brands: Competition through Public Quality Labels." *Agribusiness* 22/1: 21–30.

Hayes, D. J., S. H. Lence, and A. Stoppa. 2004. "Farmer-Owned Brands?" *Agribusiness* 20/3: 269–85.

Hoffmann, R. 2000. "Country of Origin: A Consumer Perception Perspective of Fresh Meat." *British Food Journal* 102/3: 211–29.

Ibele, E. W. 2009. "The Nature and Function of Geographical Indications in Law." *Estey Centre Journal of International Law and Trade Policy* 10/1: 36–49.

Josling, T. 2002. "Competing Paradigms in the OECD and their Impact on the WTO Agricultural Talks." In L. Tweeten and S. R. Thompson, eds, *Agricultural Policy for the 21st Century*. Ames: Iowa State University Press.

——2006. "The War on *Terroir*: Geographical Indications as a Transatlantic Trade Conflict." *Journal of Agricultural Economics* 57/3: 337–63.

Juric, B., and A. Worsley. 1998. "Consumers' Attitudes toward Imported Food Products." *Food Quality and Preference* 9/6: 431–41.

Just, R. E., D. L. Hueth, and A. Schmitz. 2004. *The Welfare Economics of Public Policy: A Practical Approach to Project and Policy Evaluation*. Cheltenham: Edward Elgar.

Kaiser, H. M., J. M. Alston, J. M. Crespi, and R. Sexton, eds. 2005. *The Economics of Commodity Promotion: Lessons from California*. New York: Peter Lang.

Landes, W. M., and R. A. Posner. 1987. "Trademark Law: An Economic Perspective." *Journal of Law and Economics* 30/2: 265–309.

Landon, S., and C. E. Smith. 1997. "The Use of Quality and Reputation Indicators by Consumers: The Case of Bordeaux Wine." *Journal of Consumer Policy* 20/3: 289–323.

Langinier, C., and B. A. Babcock. 2008. "Agricultural Production Clubs: Viability and Welfare Implications." *Journal of Agricultural and Food Industrial Organization* 6/1: 1–29.

Lence, S. H., S. Marette, D. J. Hayes, and W. Foster. 2007. "Collective Marketing Arrangements for Geographically Differentiated Agricultural Products: Welfare Impacts and Policy Implications." *American Journal of Agricultural Economics* 89/4: 947–63.

Loureiro, M. L., and J. J. McCluskey. 2000. "Assessing Consumer Response to Protected Geographical Indication Labeling." *Agribusiness* 16/3: 309–20.

——and W. J. Umberger. 2003. "Consumer Response to the Country-of-Origin Labeling Program in the Context of Heterogeneous Preferences." Paper prepared for presentation at the American Agricultural Economics Association Annual Meeting, Montreal, July 27–30.

————. 2005. "Assessing Consumer Preferences for Country-of-Origin Labeling." *Journal of Agricultural and Applied Economics* 37/1: 49–63.

————. 2007. "A Choice Experiment Model for Beef: What US Consumer Responses Tell Us about Relative Preferences for Food Safety, Country-of-Origin Labeling and Traceability." *Food Policy* 32/4: 496–514.

Lovenworth, S. J., and M. Shiner. 2008. "Protecting Geographically Unique Products." *New York Law Journal* (Jan. 22).

Lucatelli, S. 2000. *Appellations of Origin and Geographical Indication in OECD Member Countries: Economic and Legal Implications.* AGR/CA/APM/TD/WP (2000)15/Final. Paris: OECD.

McCluskey, J. J., and M. L. Loureiro. 2003. "Consumer Preferences and Willingness to Pay for Food Labeling: A Discussion of Empirical Results." *Journal of Food Distribution Research* 34/3: 95–102.

Mérel, P. 2009. "Measuring Market Power in the French Comté Cheese Market." *European Review of Agricultural Economics* 36/1: 31–51.

Moschini, G., L. Menapace, and D. Pick. 2008. "Geographical Indications and the Competitive Provision of Quality in Agricultural Markets." *American Journal of Agricultural Economics* 90/3: 794–812.

Mosoti, V., and A. Gobena. 2007. *International Trade Rules and the Agricultural Sector: Selected Implementation Issues.* FAO Legislative Study No. 98. Rome: FAO.

Mussa, M., and S. Rosen. 1978. "Monopoly and Product Quality." *Journal of Economic Theory* 18/2: 301–17.

Nelson, P. 1974. "Advertising as Information." *Journal of Political Economy* 82/2: 729–54.

Pharr, J. M. 2005. "Synthesizing Country-of-Origin Research from the Last Decade: Is the Concept Still Salient in an Era of Global Brands?" *Journal of Marketing Theory and Practice* 13/4: 34–45.

Profeta, A., U. Enneking, and R. Balling. 2008. "Interactions between Brands and CO Labels: The Case of 'Bavarian Beef' and 'Munich Beer.' Application of a Conditional Logit Model." *Journal of International Food and Agribusiness Marketing* 20/3: 73–89.

Raustiala, K., and S. R. Munzer. 2007. "The Global Struggle over Geographical Indications." *European Journal of International Law* 18/29: 337–65.

Reviron, S., with E. Thevenod-Mottet and N. El Benni. 2009. *Geographical Indications: Creation and Distribution of Economic Value in Developing Countries.* NCCR Trade Working Paper No. 2009/14. Institute for Environmental Decisions, ETH Zurich. <http://phase1.nccr-trade.org/images/stories/publications/IP5/report_IP5_GI_Value_2009.pdf>.

Riccheri, M., B. Görlach, S. Schlegel, H. Keefe, and A. Leipprand. 2006. *Assessing the Applicability of Geographical Indications as a Means to Improve Environmental Quality in Affected Ecosystems and the Competitiveness of Agricultural Products. Final Report.* Impacts of the IPR Rules on Sustainable Development, Contract No. SCS8-CT-2004-503613. <http://www.underutilized-species.org/Documents/PUBLICATIONS/wp3_final_report.pdf>.

Scarpa, R., and T. Del Giudice. 2004. "Market Segmentation via Mixed Logit: Extra Virgin Olive Oil in Urban Italy." *Journal of Agricultural and Food Industrial Organization* 2/1, art. 7G.

————, Philippidis, and F. Spalatro. 2005. "Product-Country Images and Preference Heterogeneity for Mediterranean Food Products: A Discrete-Choice Framework." *Agribusiness* 21/3: 329–49.

Schamel, G. 2006. "Geography versus Brand in a Global Wine Market." *Agribusiness* 22/3: 363–74.

Shapiro, C. 1983. "Premiums for High Quality Products as Returns to Reputations." *Quarterly Journal of Economics* 89/4: 659–80.

Skuras, D., and A. Vakrou. 2002. "Consumers' Willingness to Pay for Origin Labelled Wine: A Greek Case Study." *British Food Journal* 104/11: 898–912.

Teil, G. 2009. "The French Wine 'Appellations d'Origine Contrôlée' and the Virtues of Suspicion." *Journal of World Intellectual Property* 13/2: 253–74.

Teuber, R. 2010. "Geographical Indications of Origin as a Tool of Product Differentiation: The Case of Coffee." *Journal of International Food and Agribusiness Marketing* 22/3–4: 277–98.

—— 2011. "Consumers' and Producers' Expectations towards Geographical Indications: Empirical Evidence for a German Case Study." *British Food Journal* 113/7, in press.

Tirole, J. 1996. "A Theory of Collective Reputation." *Review of Economic Studies* 63/1: 1–22.

Tregear, A., F. Arfini, G. Belletti, and A. Marescotti. 2007. "Regional Foods and Rural Development: The Role of Product Qualification." *Journal of Rural Studies* 23: 12–22.

——, S. Kuznesof, and A. Moxey. 1998. "Policy Initiatives for Regional Foods: Some Insights from Consumer Research." *Food Policy* 23/5: 383–94.

van Caenegem, W. 2004. "Registered GIs: Intellectual Property, Agricultural Policy and International Trade." *European Intellectual Property Review* 26/4: 170–81.

van der Lans, I. A., K. van Ittersum, A. De Cicco, and M. Loseby. 2001. "The Role of the Region of Origin and EU Certificates of Origin in Consumer Evaluation of Food Products." *European Review of Agricultural Economics* 28/4: 451–77.

van Ittersum, K., M. J. J. M. Candel, and M. T. G. Meulenberg. 2003. "The Influence of the Image of a Product's Region of Origin on Product Evaluation." *Journal of Business Research* 56/3: 215–26.

——, M. T. G. Meulenberg, H. C. M. van Trijp, and M. J. J. M. Candel. 2007. "Consumers' Appreciation of Regional Certification Labels: A Pan-European Study." *Journal of Agricultural Economics* 58/1: 1–23.

Verlegh, P., and J.-B. Steenkamp. 1999. "A Review and Meta-Analysis of Country-of-Origin Research." *Journal of Economic Psychology* 20/5: 521–46.

Winfree, J. A., and J. J. McCluskey. 2005. "Collective Reputation and Quality." *American Journal of Agricultural Economics* 87/1: 206–13.

WIPO (World Intellectual Property Organization). 2007. *Perspectives for Geographical Indications.* WIPO/GEO/BEI/07. Presentation by Mrs Ester Olivas Cáceres, Secretary General of OriGIn, Alicante, Spain, International Symposium on Geographical Indications, Beijing, June 26–8.

World Bank. 2007. *World Development Report 2008: Agriculture for Development.* Washington, DC: World Bank.

WTO (World Trade Organization). 2004. *World Trade Report 2004.* Geneva: World Trade Organization.

Zago, A. M., and D. Pick. 2004. "Labeling Policies in Food Markets: Private Incentives, Public Intervention and Welfare Effects." *Journal of Agricultural and Resource Economics* 29/1: 150–65.

CHAPTER 34

....

ENVIRONMENTAL CONCERNS IN FOOD CONSUMPTION

....

MARIO F. TEISL[*]

This chapter outlines the major environmental issues related to food consumption, which encompass not only the impacts caused by the production of food, but also those generated by food transport, processing, packaging, consumption, and disposal. That is, the environmental impacts related to food consumption are directly and indirectly related to consumers' food choices, the way they shop, handle, and cook food, and how they handle food waste. Food choices are intertwined with production decisions all along the food supply chain, so food choices are not just a choice of one attribute over another. For example, the selection of a tomato and its associated environmental impacts could be examined by the production methods (organic versus conventional), the locality and seasonality of production (local stored versus non-local fresh), the transport used (ship versus air), the packaging (none versus cello-wrapped on a polystyrene tray), etc. As a result, although this chapter is divided into several sections, the divisions are somewhat arbitrary. Lastly, this chapter reviews a large amount of literature with some commentary but necessarily ends up ignoring much more.

The topic is important as the food consumption system directly or indirectly contributes to many environmental problems, e.g., greenhouse gas emissions, energy, water, and land use (Nijdam et al. 2005). For example, 20 percent of the total energy use in Sweden (SEPA 1997a, cited by Davis and Sonesson 2008) and over 70 percent of the world's use of water (World Resource Institute 2006) can be attributed to the food system, and 50 percent of all eutrophic emissions come from agriculture (SEPA 1997b, c, d, all cited by Davis and Sonesson 2008). Food production and consumption is

* Funding for this chapter was provided in part by the Maine Sustainability Solutions Initiative, National Science Foundation Grant EPS-0904155 to Maine EPSCoR at the University of Maine. Maine Agricultural and Forest Experiment Station No. 3191.

responsible for global deforestation, loss of biodiversity (Massari 2003), topsoil erosion, and desertification (Goodland 1997). Food processing and packaging use large amounts of energy and water, and produce greenhouse gas emissions as well as liquid and solid waste (Pack 2006). Food retailers generate greenhouse gas emissions through transport and refrigeration. Transportation is also a large environmental contributor as food and raw materials are transported throughout the food system. Finally, households impact the environment by transporting, washing, storing, and cooking food[1] and through food and food packaging waste disposal (Payer, Burger, and Lorek 2000); Tukker et al. (2005) estimate that about one-third of a household's environmental impact is related to food consumption.

Although the total amount of food per capita has not changed much over time, the types of foods consumed has changed (WHO 2003; Fabiosa, Chapter 23 in this volume; Stewart, Chapter 26 in this volume) in many different dimensions; e.g., daily per capita energy consumption has increased, consumption has shifted away from starches to animal products and fats, and more consumption occurs outside the home. In addition, fresh fruit/vegetable and meat availability has grown significantly, especially in the developing world (e.g., China's consumption of meat has increased 500 percent since 1980). As will be discussed later, these foods differ in how they affect the environment. For example, meat is generally more energy-intensive to produce and some animal feeding operations can lead to extreme local water pollution problems; however, fresh produce is often transported global distances (owing to seasonality of production) and generates global warming gases through this transport.

Fresh produce and minimally processed meat is the predominant food form (Birkett and Patel 2008), but increasingly more foods are processed, which entails additional energy and resource use in processing, transportation, and packaging, but may garner significant energy savings at the consumer level. Convenience foods are also garnering an increased share of the food consumption pie (Birkett and Patel 2008), often requiring refrigeration or freezing. Some of the drivers of these food consumption changes include: increased household incomes, decreased household size, increased participation of women in the workforce, increased health-related food concerns, increased urbanization (Birkett and Patel 2008), and increased age and education (Pack 2006). Many of these trends (e.g., the desire for variety, prepared, and convenience foods) are expected to continue (Blisard et al. 2002; Kristensen 2004).

Of course, the current food production system also generates vast benefits to society. Although the distribution of these benefits varies by geography, it is clear that the current food system allows people to consume more, and a greater variety of, foods. Many of these foods have improved safety and convenience characteristics while also being lower in price. From an economic viewpoint, the environmental costs of modern food production, increased food transport, refrigeration, and processing must be balanced against these social benefits. For example, the author, who lives in a place

---

[1] Refrigeration, cooking, and washing food account for about 10 percent of a household's energy use (OECD 2001).

known for its cold winters, enjoys the benefit of having a banana (grown and transported from Ecuador) and yogurt (from Canada) along with toasted bread (no doubt made from wheat grown with pesticides and containing additives to protect its freshness/lengthen its shelf life) while drinking coffee (shipped from Papua New Guinea). Further, production efficiencies make fruits and vegetables relatively cheaper, allowing me to consume more of them in my diet, which may reduce my risk of some cancers.

Before proceeding, I want to point out that much of the literature cited here uses product- or process-based lifecycle analysis (LCA), also known as lifecycle assessment or ecobalance analysis. LCA is a physical science approach, combining engineering and environmental science to examine the flows of environmental resources used, and the emissions generated, by product production and/or consumption.[2] Thus, these analyses are limited to identifying relative changes to environmental parameters caused by the production and/or consumption of specific products or the use of specific processes, and they do not examine changes in social welfare (i.e., LCA is not an economic approach as it ignores any consumption or production benefits—e.g., the joy I experience while drinking my imported coffee). Nevertheless, LCA is important as it is the standard environmental measurement approach recognized by the International Organization for Standardization (ISO) 14000 (environmental management) standards, is the basis for certain types of eco-labeling (see ISO 14020), and could be used as an input into a cost–benefit analysis.

LCAs are quite data-intensive and rigorous, and theoretically form the basis for environmentally comparing products and processes; however, the results of many LCAs are not easily compared. One reason is that there is no agreed framework for LCAs. Further, LCAs, like most empirical research, require the analyst to make specific assumptions. One such assumption is determining the technical scope of analysis (called drawing the system boundary); that is, what parts of the lifecycle are included (e.g., cradle to farm gate, cradle to plate, cradle to grave) and what inputs (e.g., energy, land) or outputs (air emissions, water emissions) are included in the analysis. Differences in the way studies determine and define the geographical boundaries of the analysis also lead to potential differences across studies (e.g., what is meant by "local"), as does the choice of measurement units and differences in the quality of available data and calculation methods. As a result, LCA is a useful tool because it can illuminate potential technical and environmental trade-offs in consumption, and highlight factors influencing these trade-offs; however, it can "rarely point unambiguously at the 'best' technological choice" (Ayres 1995: 201), much less the choice that it most valued. In turn, most of the comparisons in the next section are meant to be qualitatively illustrative and should not be seen as definitive. Interested readers should examine the source materials directly; for a good review of some of the issues related to LCA, see Ayres (1995) and Roy et al. (2009).

---

[2] A broader approach links LCA with economic input output analysis (Rebitzer, Loerincik, and Jolliet 2002).

1   CHOICES, CHOICES, TOO MANY CHOICES?

Blair and Sobal (2006) define Luxus Consumption as food being produced but not used or needed; that is, the food is either lost as waste (waste is used here in the technical, not economic sense) or is consumed beyond what is needed for good health.[3] Food is lost throughout the food supply and consumption chain; e.g., meat is trimmed, and blemished or undersized fruit and vegetables are removed from sale (Griffin, Sobal, and Lyson 2009), and consumers waste food through poor handling and planning; all of this edible food ends up as waste. The factors encouraging food waste are varied: from farm subsidies that promote overproduction (Poppendieck 1986) to poor storage, spillage, or pest damage at the farm (Kantor et al. 1997), to plate scraps from food service establishments (often not salvaged owing to food safety regulations), to consumers discarding blemished but edible food (Munro 1995). The low cost of food is also a culprit, as it encourages wasteful behaviors (Harrison et al. 1975).

The food waste issue is non-trivial (Gallo 1980; Sobal and Nelson 2003; Griffin, Sobal, and Lyson 2009). For example, about a quarter to a third of the fresh produce grown ends up as waste (see Kantor et al. 1997; Putnam and Allshouse 1999; Blair and Sobal 2006; Garnett 2006). Griffin, Sobal, and Lyson (2009) examined the waste stream in a US county and estimate that 20 percent of food waste was from the production stage, another 20 percent from processing and distribution, and 60 percent was generated by consumers; a vast majority of this food waste (72 percent) was landfilled. In addition to solid waste, the food system generates large amounts of liquid waste with high organic content (UNEP 1995).

In the United Kingdom, about a third of the food bought by consumers is thrown out (WRAP 2008), which caused 18 million tons of CO_2 emissions during 2007. Notably, the authors indicate that two-thirds of this waste (and presumably the CO_2 emissions) could have been avoided with better shopping and meal planning. In addition to global warming gases, food waste harms the environment owing to an overuse of inputs (e.g., land, energy, pesticides), leading to increased air and water pollution (Griffin, Sobal, and Lyson 2009) and increased use of landfill space (Blair and Sobal 2006). Although Griffin, Sobal, and Lyson (2009) note that much of the consumer-based food waste is preventable, most consumers would rather throw leftover items away than have to consume them again, store them for a future meal, or compost them—highlighting the difference in the technical versus economic vision of "wasting" food.

Any food wasted after the farm gate means more food has to be produced, leading to higher environmental impacts (Davis and Sonesson 2008). In addition, the

---

[3] Note this assumes a very restrictive utility function, ignoring things like variety, taste, and convenience (see, e.g., Weiss, Ch. 27 in this volume)—and it would be the "height of absurdity" (see Stigler 1945 for his analysis related to a low-cost diet) to assume it reflects most consumers.

environmental impact of waste becomes worse as it occurs further along the supply chain because, as food moves up the supply chain, it carries with it all of the energy and resources used to produce it to that stage (Davis and Sonesson 2008). Thus, very modest reductions in consumer and industrial food waste can make significant reductions in environmental impacts in the production stage (Davis and Sonesson 2008).

Given the above, the environmental impacts of the food system can be reduced with improved waste management. For example, to reduce the scale of water pollution, highly polluted wastewater can be separated from the large volume of relatively unpolluted wastewater (Ramjeawon 2000). Industrial food waste can also be used as animal feed, thus reducing the environmental impact of the initial food production and of the secondary production. Muñoz et al. (2004) and Lundie and Peters (2005) indicate that composting food waste can lower the environmental impact of the food system and that home composting is better than centralized composting (owing to the additional environmental impacts of transport and handing). The environmental impacts of other waste management options vary; e.g., if the option includes material recycling (Nyland et al. 2003), waste reduction (McComas and McKinley 2008), or incineration with energy or heat recovery (Hirai et al. 2000; Bovea and Powell 2005). In general, integrated waste management systems are better performers (Roy et al. 2009).

The environmental impacts of overeating, the other component of Luxus consumption, has been estimated by Blair and Sobal (2006). They note that the age-adjusted incidence of obesity and overweight in the United States grew by 36 percent from the late 1970s to the late 1990s, so that currently the average person in the United States carries an extra 4.5 kilograms of fat. Mokdad et al. (1999, 2001, 2003) state higher values. Some of this weight is likely due to increased incomes, increased consumption of meat, and an increase in portion sizes (American Dietetic Association 2001; Engstrom and Carlsson-Kanyama 2004). This translates into an increased use of 3.1 percent of the total US energy consumption and of 100.6 million hectares of land just in the farm production phase. In addition, there are the other associated environmental costs due to excess production (e.g., pesticides, fertilizers, diversion of water for irrigation, soil erosion) as well as the costs of excess transportation, storage, processing, etc. Of course, more eating leads to more toilet-borne wastes, which can lead to eutrophication issues and requires energy and water to treat (Tidaker et al. 2006).

Another component of Luxus consumption is the consumption of resources to provide non-nutritive beverages (Blair and Sobal 2006). Although increasing social welfare, diet soft drinks, and, one could argue, bottled water provide no calories but require energy and resources to manufacture the containers (Blair and Sobal 2006), and for the transport, storage, and refrigeration of the product, as well as managing the container waste. Many of these costs are reduced if the containers are recycled. Similarly, there are additional environmental burdens of manufacturing low-fat products; e.g., the fat in dairy products needs to be separated and replaced by fat substitutes, which involves a greater use of energy and water, and leads to some waste (Dewick, Foster, and Green 2007).

2   FOOD MILES ANYONE?

A recent issue to emerge that is related to the environmental impacts of food consumption is the concept of food miles; i.e., the environmental costs related to transportation of food from the farm or production facility to the retail store (Frith 2005; Smith et al. 2005; Hamilton 2006; Weber and Matthews 2008). This concern stems from the increasingly international nature of food; for example, fruit and vegetable trade increased by over 150 percent in the 1980s and 1990s (Diop and Jaffe 2005). This internationalization of food is due to changing consumer tastes and preferences,[4] and increased incomes (Desrochers and Shimizu 2008); improvements in transportation, IT, and food storage technologies (Desrochers and Shimizu 2008; Smith et al. 2005); and reductions in trade barriers (Smith et al. 2005). For example, much food is now transported across the world instead of being grown locally because the real cost of sea freight has declined by 70 percent in the last two decades (Smith et al. 2005) and the cost of air freight has declined as well (Smith et al. 2005). In addition, the increased consumption of more highly processed or exotic foods (Smith et al. 2005) means more ingredients are being transported across production facilities (Boge 1995; Smith et al. 2005). Indeed, numerous private and public advocacy groups (see, e.g., Jones 2002; NRDC 2009) and consumers (termed "locavores") have been touting the environmental benefits of buying local food (Morgan, Marsden, and Murdoch 2006); however, as Edward-Jones et al. (2008) indicate, "local" remains relatively undefined.

Although the distance traveled by food has many real and perceived (La Trobe 2001; Draper and Green 2002; Weatherell, Tregear, and Allinson 2003) quality implications (e.g., nutrition, freshness, taste, support for local economic development), I shall focus only on the environmental characteristics of the food miles debate. Although food production, processing, and transport contribute to several environmental issues,[5] the focus of this debate has primarily centered on the climate change (carbon footprint[6]) aspects. The premise is that local foods are environmentally preferred since they travel shorter distances, which requires less energy and produces fewer air pollutants. Indeed, some have advocated the labeling of foods with a food miles label (Desrochers and Shimizu 2008).

The food miles concept appears to be a simple way of indicating the environmental impacts of food consumption, but the reality is much more complex. For example, the

---

[4] For example, Smith et al. (2005) claims UK consumers prefer sweeter apples such as Braeburns, which are not grown in the United Kingdom.

[5] Other environmental impacts of food production include emissions related to pesticides (Havlikova and Kroeze 2006; Almasri and Kaluarachchi 2007; Powers 2007; Edwards-Jones et al. 2008), soil erosion (Van Oost et al. 2006), and biodiversity (Butler, Vickery, and Norris 2007). All these impacts could vary by locality (Edwards-Jones et al. 2008).

[6] However, most of a food's climate impact is due to non-CO_2 gases, like methane (CH_4) and nitrous oxide (N_2O), emissions (Weber and Matthews 2008).

food miles idea only examines the distance the food has traveled, without any consideration of the form of transportation used; but, transport mode makes a difference (Smith et al. 2005). For instance, shipping food by air[7] has a relatively high global warming impact per ton kilometer (the impact of moving 1 ton of goods a distance of 1 kilometer), while ocean shipping is relatively efficient (Smith et al. 2005). This means that one mile of air transport could produce many times the global warming effect of one mile of sea transport. Even within a transportation mode, there are differences in transportation efficiency related to vehicle size and type of distribution network (Smith et al. 2005).

Because of large differences in energy intensity across modes (Weber and Matthews 2008), food miles do not correlate well with the environmental impacts of transportation (Smith et al. 2005). For example, although sea transport accounts for a majority (65 percent) of the United Kingdom's food miles (measured in ton kilometers) (Desrochers and Shimizu 2008), it only accounts for 12 percent of CO_2 emissions (Smith et al. 2005). In fact, local road transport accounts for over 78 percent of CO_2 emissions from food-related transport, most of this (83 percent) accounted for by heavy and light goods vehicles (large and small trucks) with the remaining accounted for by personal vehicles.[8] Consumer food shopping trips, being relatively inefficient (Desrochers and Shimizu 2008), have a higher global warming impact than those generated by food shipping. Desrochers and Shimizu (2008: 9) states that a "UK consumer driving six miles to buy green beans air freighted from Kenya may emit more CO_2 per bean than the air transport from Kenya to the UK." Thus, at least in the United Kingdom the use of cars for food shopping, and the distances driven, have increased (Smith et al. 2005; DETR 1999). This increase is both a cause and effect of the closing of small local stores and the rise of large out-of-town stores (Raven et al. 1995). Further, transportation throughout the supply chain is responsible for only about 10 percent of the global warming impact of food consumption (only 4 percent occurs during final delivery— the food miles concept); over 80 percent is at the farm level (Engelhaupt 2008), which indicates that the food miles concept would need to be broadened to include all food supply transportation (Weber and Matthews 2008).

Since food production has such a large share of the global warming impact of food consumption, it should not be surprising that any environmental benefits of local food could be reduced or even eliminated by differences between the local and non-local food production systems. For example, Smith et al. (2005) show that it could be environmentally better to ship fresh produce (e.g., tomatoes) from a warmer country than to produce them locally in heated greenhouses. In addition, Saunders, Barber, and

---

[7] The environmental concerns related to air freight induced large food retailers like Tesco (Leahy 2007; Desrochers and Shimizu 2008) and Marks and Spencer (Desrochers and Shimizu 2008) to begin labeling foods with an "air freighted" label.

[8] To capture size economies and improve supply management, the commercial food system increasingly relies on spatial specialization and concentration of farms, storage and processing units (e.g., warehouses), distribution and retail centers, which increases the amount of miles a food may be transported, even locally (Smith et al. 2005).

Taylor (2006) and Milà i Canals et al. (2007) show that the environmental impacts of consumption can depend on the length of storage between production and consumption. For example, an apple produced and transported from New Zealand in August could have less of an environmental impact than a UK (local) apple that was produced in the preceding year and stored. In this way, the food miles concept ignores one of the standard economic arguments for trade—that there exist potential comparative advantages (e.g., seasonality: Milà i Canals et al. 2007; Desrochers and Shimizu 2008) across countries.

Other differences in farm production across localities have been cited as a critique of the food miles concept. For example, it may be environmentally better to import organic foods rather than grow non-organic foods locally (Smith et al. 2005), since the manufacture and use of fertilizers is energy-intensive and has a large environmental impact (Roelandt, van Wesemael, and Rounsevell 2005). Again, this result depends upon the mode and distance of transportation. For example, producing and shipping organic wheat from the United States to the United Kingdom has a lower environmental impact than growing conventional UK wheat. In contrast, producing and trucking Italian organic wheat to the United Kingdom by truck does not (Smith et al. 2005).

The scale of production efficiency may also matter; Schlich and Fleissner (2005) suggest larger producers, because they are more energy-efficient, can transport food longer distances and still have a smaller environmental impact than smaller, local producers. In studying bread production, Sundkvist, Jansson, and Larsson (2001) come to a similar conclusion in terms of energy efficiency, but Andersson and Ohlsson (1999) find lower emissions per kilogram of bread in smaller bread-making facilities.

Given all of the above arguments, "it is currently impossible to state categorically whether or not local food systems emit fewer GHGs [greenhouse gases] than non-local food systems" (Edward-Jones et al. 2008: 270).

3   TO MEAT OR NOT TO MEAT...IS THAT THE QUESTION?

Several studies (Goodland and Pimentel 2000; Steinfeld et al. 2006; Weber and Matthews 2008) have indicated large differences in the environmental impacts of a vegetarian versus non-vegetarian diet; and between a strict vegetarian (vegan) diet and a lacto-ovo vegetarian diet. The results have led some to call for consumers to shift toward such diets (Eshel and Martin 2006), but convincing people to reduce or eliminate meat consumption is difficult as it lowers gustatory pleasure or interferes with cultural values (Davis and Sonesson 2008). In fact, in the United States, meat is the most highly valued food category (Lusk and Norwood 2009).

In terms of greenhouse gas emissions, red meat production is more intensive than all other forms of food, producing about 10.8 grams of CO_2 per kilocalorie of meat, with dairy products being second, producing about 5.3 grams of CO_2 per kilocalorie (Weber and Matthews 2008). In addition to greenhouse gas emissions, van der Pijl and Krutwagen (2001, cited in Reijnders and Sore 2003) did a cradle-to-grave assessment of the environmental benefits (e.g., changes in land use, acidification, and eutrophication of water) of replacing a meat with a vegetarian alternative (using soybean protein-based product), and found that the vegetarian meal had half the impact.

Reijnders and Sore (2003) summarize a series of comparisons between meat- and soy-based protein. Given that different types of meat have different vegetable-to-meat protein conversion rates, 18 percent for chicken, 9 percent for pork, and 6 percent for beef (Pimentel and Pimentel 1982), the environmental impacts are stated in ranges. Meat protein production requires about six to seventeen times more land; twenty-six times more water (Reijnders 2001); and six to twenty times more fossil fuel (Uhlin 1998; Reijnders 2001). In terms of inputs, the meat production requires seven times more phosphate, which can cause water eutrophication (Reijnders and Sore 2003); seven times (Reijnders 2001) more acidifying compounds, e.g., sulfur and nitrogen oxides, and ammonia, which can cause detrimental effects on biodiversity and on water quality (Bleken and Bakken 1997; Reijnders 2001); six times (Reijnders 2001) more use of biocides (e.g., disinfectants and pesticides), which can harm human and ecosystem health (Reijnders 2001; Tilman et al. 2001).

The above comparisons are not cradle-to-grave. Including post farm-gate activities (e.g., transport, processing, and storage) reduces the scale of some differences (Reijnders and Sore 2003). For example, vegetables that are air-freighted (especially if they are exotic; Carlsson-Kanyama 1998), grown in heated greenhouses, or deep-frozen may be more harmful than local organic meat production (Jungbluth, Tietje, and Scholz 2000). However, in general replacing meat with plant-based foods could reduce the environmental impacts of food consumption (Goodland and Pimentel 2000). In reference to the debate about food miles, Weber and Matthews (2008) indicate that even a small shift away from meat consumption (i.e., eliminating meat one day a week) would have the same global warming benefit as buying only local food. Also note that in the above studies, the vegetarian diet is assumed as full vegetarian—no eggs or dairy. Kytzia, Faist, and Baccini (2004) state that the environmental benefits of a lacto-ovo vegetarian diet over a meat diet are relatively smaller since the lacto-ovo vegetarian leads to an increased production of meat, as cows need to bear calves to produce milk.

In addition, since chicken production has a relatively lower environmental impact compared to the production of other meats (Davis and Sonesson 2008), all else equal, replacing beef with chicken decreases the environmental impacts. Alternatively, Gerbens-Leenes, Nonhebel, and Ivens (2002) indicate that beef production is twice as land-intensive than pork production, partially owing to the fact that half of the energy in pig fodder is derived from food industry waste.[9] The authors indicate how sensitive

---

[9] The availability and quality of food waste for animal feed is a byproduct of the increased consumption of preprocessed foods—which moved some food waste away from the consumer and to the processor (Elferink, Nonhebel, and Moll 2008).

land use is to even small changes in food choices. For example, replacing one mouthful of meat with potatoes per capita per day would reduce annual land use by over 100 square meters per household.

Well, if land-based meat is bad then what about fish; and what type of fish—caught or farmed? There are not many studies examining the lifecycle of fish products but Ellingsen and Aanondsen (2006) did an environmental comparison of Norwegian cod fishing, salmon farming, and chicken farming. They did not examine all of the environmental impacts (e.g., disposal of pesticides and escapes of farmed salmon are excluded) but provide a good comparison of many of them. For example, they include a variety of impacts like land use in the production of feed (for both chicken and salmon farming), the energy use for fish capture and initial processing, and potential copper pollution due to the use of antifouling paint on boats and fish cages.[10] They found that most of the environmental impacts were related to the production phase, farming of salmon and chicken (including the farming necessary in the provision of feed), and capture for cod (including damage from bottom trawling).[11] The most important environmental impacts were related to energy use and emissions of NO_x (from both types of fish production) and ammonia (from chicken farming). In general, chicken production uses the least amount of energy, followed by salmon farming and cod capture. Part of the reason why salmon farming is relatively energy-intensive is that a major constituent of its feed is wild-caught fish; replacing this fish-based feed with vegetarian feed (e.g., grains) makes salmon farming less energy-intensive than chicken farming since salmon are relatively more efficient than chickens in converting feed to meat (Ellingsen and Aanondsen 2006). One aspect that would need to be studied is how salmon that are genetically modified to have a higher feed-to-meat conversion ratio compare in terms of the environmental impacts.

4   "Cooking Should be a Carefully Balanced Reflection of All the Good Things of the Earth"[12]

The environmental impact of food consumption is also related to if, how, or where the food is cooked (Garnett 2006). Foods that are more highly processed are increasingly common (Davis and Sonesson 2008); for example, about one-third of hot meals in Norway are pre-prepared (Kjærnes 2001, cited by Ahlgren, Gustafsson, and Hall 2004). In some cases this processing adds environmental impacts (additional water and

---

[10] Every year the Norwegian aquaculture industry places about 200 tons of copper into local waters (Vannebo et al. 2000, cited by Ellingsen and Aanondsen 2006).

[11] Fosså (2000, cited by Ellingsen and Aanondsen 2006) estimates bottom trawls have damaged almost half of the coral reefs in the northeast Atlantic.

[12] Jean and Pierre Troisgros.

energy use[13]) by changing the food (e.g., conversion of milk to yogurt; Feitz et al. 2005; Dewick, Foster, and Green 2007) without any major changes to consumer-level impacts. In other cases the pre-processing of the food includes pre-cooking, adding increased energy use at the processing level but with a potential energy savings at the consumption level since the food only needs reheating (Heller and Keoleian 2000).

In general, more processing or more cooking entails more environmental impacts; e.g., apples are usually consumed raw but potatoes are rarely eaten raw, which means that most of the energy and CO_2 emissions are related to home cooking (Mattson and Wallén 2003). Some argue that processed, ready-to-eat foods use less energy than home cooking of unprocessed foods (Smith et al. 2005), while early studies indicate that 30–40 percent of the energy used in the food chain is by household cooking, storage, and transportation (Uhlin 1997, cited in Carlsson-Kanyama and Boström-Carlsson 2001).

Carlsson-Kanyama and Boström-Carlsson (2001) made a comparison between the energy used in industrial processing and in home cooking and found relatively small differences in energy use. Because of the potentially large impact generated by household cooking, they went on to examine the amount of electricity needed to cook various foods (wheat, spaghetti, pasta, barley, rice, potatoes, couscous, and mashed potatoes from powdered potatoes) using various methods. They found that per portion energy use was minimized when larger meals were prepared in the home; the per portion energy use was two to four times higher when cooking single portions. The type of appliance and how it was used also made large energy differences. For example, using a microwave oven to bake potatoes used a tenth of the energy used by a conventional oven, but using a microwave to simmer rice used much more energy than using a hot plate (Carlsson-Kanyama and Boström-Carlsson 2001). Energy use is high when cooking items that traditionally require boiling a lot of water (e.g., pasta); it may be that recipes need to be adjusted to minimize the water used.

Davis and Sonesson (2008) studied the environmental impacts of two different chicken meals (home-made and semi-prepared). In addition to comparing the two types of meal in terms of energy use and environmental impacts, they also examined ways to make each meal more environmentally friendly (reducing energy consumption in transport, industrial processing, retailing, and home cooking, reducing waste and packaging in industry, reducing consumer shopping frequency and food waste). They show that most of the energy used for each meal occurred after the farm gate—about 65 percent for the homemade meal and as much as 75 percent for the semi-prepared meal (in addition to higher energy used in the processing, part of the higher energy cost of the semi-prepared meal is the freezer storage at the retail and consumer level). Less consumer transport, more efficient household cooking appliances, and a reduction in packaging lowered the home-made meal's energy requirement by about 15 percent and,

[13] Yogurt uses six times the electricity of raw milk production (Feitz et al. 2005).

along with industry-level savings, the semi-prepared meal by more than 20 percent, indicating the importance of consumer actions.

In summary, home cooking can be a significant portion of the energy used in a food product's lifecycle, and consumers can minimize its environmental impacts by proper use of appliances and ingredients (Carlsson-Kanyama and Boström-Carlsson 2001).

5   WOULD YOU LIKE PAPER OR PLASTIC?

Although much food processing is driven by consumers' demand for convenience, some processing is related to increasing the variety of foods available. Dewick, Foster, and Green (2007) indicate that yogurt used to be a basic product with no added flavors or colors, often sold in larger containers. In time, yogurt manufacturers began adding both, along with fruit, nuts, candy pieces, etc. With this diversification came smaller individualized containers and a significant change in how yogurt was processed (continuous runs versus batch processing). Several environmental costs come with this increased variety; e.g., increased use of packaging, increased consumption of water (associated with the added cleaning needed for the production of more product varieties), increased levels of effluent, and increased transportation. Increased variety could also increase waste at the consumer level (Berlin, Sonnesson, and Tillman 2007) and reduce the efficiencies or "ecologies of scale" associated with mass production (Dewick, Foster, and Green 2007).

A benefit of food processing and packaging is improved food safety characteristics. The traditional methods of food processing for safety include, among others: pickling, salting, air or smoke curing, and thermal methods. Since methods like pickling or smoke curing impact food flavors, which may be undesirable for many products, thermal methods are often used. Note, however, that thermal processes, e.g., sterilization of the bottles used in pickling, is still used in parts of these other food preservation systems. Further, newer technologies, like irradiation (electron beam processing), can be used to improve the food safety characteristics of raw food and foods that cannot withstand high temperatures, such as cheeses.

These thermal approaches can be very energy-intensive and generate large amounts of greenhouse gases. Irradiation can provide the same level of food safety while decreasing energy and water consumption, and reducing air emissions. Martin et al. (2000) and Tyson et al. (2008) indicate energy reductions of up to 90 percent compared to conventional pasteurization. Icke (2008) compares electron beam processing versus traditional methods (using heat and chemicals) to sterilize PET bottles to provide aseptic packaging. The electron beam process has environmental advantages including eliminating water and chemicals in the sterilization process, and allowing for thinner-walled, lighter-weight bottles (which reduces transportation-related energy). Based on his results, the electron beam process could save 175 million liters of water, 2 million kilowatts of electricity, and over 300,000 liters of chemicals annually in a PET bottling plant. However, most major food companies avoid use of this technology since it is viewed in a negative light by some consumers (Skerret and Bartlett 1997).

Although packaging plays a critical role in food safety, storage, and transport (Roy et al. 2009), packaging waste is a growing component of the total mass of municipal waste; for example, in Italy, packaging waste represents 35 percent in weight and 50 percent in volume of total municipal waste (Fasoli 1997, cited in Monte, Padoano, and Pozzeto 2005). As a result, packaging can impose some significant environmental burdens (Sonesson and Berlin 2003; Hospido, Moreira, and Feijoo 2005), such as acidification, smog, heavy metal, and carcinogenic generation (Zabaniotou and Kassidi 2003). However, as Roy et al. (2009) point out, packaging choice needs to balance packing waste generation against food losses generated by inferior packaging. Further, refrigeration adds to the environmental burden of food consumption. One way to reduce this burden is through aseptic packaging. For example, milk in the European Union is often processed this way, which may be more energy-intensive in the processing stage but eliminates the need for refrigeration during the transport, storage, and retail phases.

One method of reducing the environmental impacts of packaging is through recycling and the adoption of more environmentally friendly packaging; e.g., reducing the wall thickness of plastic bottles (Dewick, Foster, and Green 2007) or using packaging that is reusable (Ekvall et al. 1998). Zufia and Arana (2008) indicate that products' environmental burdens could be reduced at the development and design phase, because it is at this stage that many choices that affect the environment are made. The improvements could include design to reduce the use of packaging materials, using more environmentally benign packaging materials, and improving transport and storage efficiency. For example, the authors studied the redesign of a tuna product. They found significant environmental benefits by changing the type of cardboard used (reducing cardboard use by 18 percent) and more efficient trimming of the cardboard packing (reducing cardboard use by 10 percent). This redesign of the packaging led to an increase in the number of packages that fit in a shipping box (reducing cardboard use by 15 percent). In addition, the package size was increased,[14] the food tray redesigned, and the type of plastic changed, reducing tray weight by 40 percent, water use by 10 percent, and electricity use by 5 percent (per kilogram of product). The redesigned packaging also reduced distribution effort (owing to the optimization of cargo space), reducing transport effort by 10 percent (kilometers per kilogram).

To reduce environmental impacts, industry could invest in packaging that is more easily recycled and municipal waste management systems could expand the availability of recycling programs. Although there are potentially large resource reductions when

---

[14] Larger packages generally provide the smallest environmental impact (e.g., see De Monte, Padoano, and Pozzetto 2005); however, depending upon the product, larger packages may lead to increased food waste or increased refrigeration costs at the consumer level.

packaging materials are redesigned to be more recyclable,[15] it is still contingent on the consumer actively participating in recycling programs (De Monte, Padoano, and Pozzetto 2005). However, recyclability is not a panacea; for example, non-recyclable plastic pouches use less energy, and produce less air, water, and solid waste pollution relative to recyclable bottles since they use less material in production (EUROPEN 1999). Similarly, De Monte, Padoano, and Pozzetto (2005) indicate that polylaminate bags can be environmentally better than metal cans even though this does not favor material recycling (producing metal cans involves the generation of heavy metals, acidification, greenhouse gases, and carcinogens). Another potential alternative to recycling is to develop and use biodegradable/renewable materials (e.g., potatoes to plastics); however, the end biodegradability of these materials depends upon how the waste is disposed of (i.e., some biodegradable materials need air or sunlight to degrade—items in short supply within a landfill).

6   BETTER FARMING THROUGH TECHNOLOGY... BUT WHICH ONE?

For various reasons, e.g., perceived environmental, nutrition, health or taste improvements (Teisl, Fein, and Levy 2009), consumers have increased their purchases of organic foods (ERS 2003; Greene 2004). A key question is whether this shift toward organic consumption leads to a real improvement in environmental outcomes. This is particularly important as modern agriculture is seen to be a major threat to biodiversity (Tilman et al. 2001; Hole et al. 2005), water quality (USGS 2001), fisheries (Frankenberger and Turco 2003), and soil erosion (Pimentel et al. 2005). These negative effects of modern farming methods may expand given the growth in the population, resulting in an additional billion hectares of land being converted to agriculture, which could lead to a twofold increase in nitrogen, phosphorus, and water use, and threefold increase in pesticide use (Hole et al. 2005).

With respect to biodiversity,[16] Hole et al. (2005) provide some answers by reviewing seventy-six studies comparing organic versus conventional agriculture. Of ninety-nine species comparisons, they find organic farming is significantly better than conventional farming in sixty-six; eight showed some negative effects and twenty-five had mixed or no impacts. The positive effects include: increased bacterial and fungal abundance/ activity; increased nematode abundance, increased earthworm, spider, and beetle abundance, and species diversity. Studies also indicate an increased level of small

---

[15] Mourad et al. (2008) indicate that higher recycling rates can lead to lower energy, water, wood, and land use and lower levels of greenhouse gases.

[16] The comparisons made in this section between organic and conventional farming primarily relate to horticulture; several studies indicate few differences in organic versus conventional management of pasture lands.

mammal (e.g., mice, voles, and bats) and bird activity. Although Hole et al. (2005) emphasize that the methodological differences across studies limit their comparability, the general trend in the literature supports the notion that organic farming is more likely to support biodiversity. However, they also note that the positive effects may not be supported on all types of organic farm, as organic farming is increasingly becoming larger and more commercial.

The above studies do not generally take into account that more land may need to be cultivated under an organic system (Kytzia, Faist, and Baccini 2004) since organic yields tend to be lower (Renagold et al. 2001; Andrews, Karlen, and Mitchell 2002). This increased conversion of land to agriculture could have negative impacts on biodiversity. However, Pimentel et al. (2005) suggest that organic yields are lower only in the short run and that after a few years organic yields are comparable to conventional farm yields. In addition, on average, organic lands suffer about 15 percent less erosion compared to conventional agriculture (Auerswald, Kainz, and Fiener 2003) and have better soil characteristics, e.g., in terms of soil organic matter, soil structure, aggregate stability (Brown, Cook, and Lee 2000; Pulleman et al. 2005), air, and available water capacity (Brown, Cook, and Lee 2000), and carbon and nitrogen mineralization (Pulleman et al. 2005).[17] Organic farming can also be less energy-intensive since it does not require the additional energy needs associated with fertilizer production. For example, Pimentel et al. (2005) indicate that energy use for organic corn production was about 30 percent less than conventional production, although there was no difference in energy use between organic and conventional soybean production.

In the comparisons above, the definition of conventional farming is not entirely clear. For example, it is not clear whether any of the corn farming analyses included the use of genetically modified corn, which allows for no-till farming (Fawcett and Towery 2002), thus lowering some of the environmental impacts (e.g., soil erosion). Also of interest is whether the studies include new precision agriculture methods, which can lower farming's environmental impacts (Bongiovanni and Lowenberg-Deboer 2004). Finally, Trewavas (2004) suggests that many of the environmental benefits associated with organic relative to conventional farming are not due to the use of organic methods per se, but are because organic farmers tend to be better managers.

Although the environmental problems associated with "conventional" agriculture has led some consumers to back less technological production practices (like organic production), an alternative strategy would be to seek out food produced with the use of more technological production methods; e.g., foods derived from biotechnology. Indeed, there have been several studies indicating that genetically modified (GM) foods can reduce specific environmental impacts. For example, GM crops have been shown to increase yields (Peng et al. 1999; Taylor et al. 2001; Regierer et al. 2002), meaning less land needs to be used for food production, preserving land for other uses. Similarly, technological inputs in livestock-based food production (e.g., the use of recombinant

---

[17] Although some of these differences are small (e.g., Pulleman et al. 2005).

bovine somatotropin in dairy production) have been indicated to provide significant environmental benefits, such as reduced use of inputs (water, fossil fuels, and land) and reduced negative outputs (lower levels of nitrogen excretion and greenhouse gas emissions) (Capper et al. 2008).

Some scientists and consumers fear that the true environmental costs of new technologies have not yet been realized. Concerns[18] related to the use of GM include: potential transfer of genetic material into wild plant populations (e.g., leading to the development of "superweeds"), adverse impacts on non-target organisms, or the development of pesticide resistance in targeted pest populations (Thies and Devare 2007). Thies and Devare (2007) indicate that gene flow potential has already been observed, and in some cases non-targeted insects have been adversely affected. For example, in investigating the abundance of wild bees and their effect on pollination activity around organic, conventional, and GM fields, Morandin and Winston (2005) find that bee abundance was greatest in organic fields and lowest in GM fields; this led to pollination deficits in conventional and GM fields relative to the organic fields.

Ammann (2005) points out that tillage practices used in conventional agriculture can degrade the soil (through erosion, nutrient loss, and biological deterioration). Although the benefits of reduced tillage have been known, farmers have been reluctant to adopt this practice because it increases the amount of effort needed for weed control (Ammann 2005). The development of biotech crops that are tolerant to herbicides has increased the adoption of conservation tillage and no-till practices (Fawcett and Towery 2002). For example, the adoption of cotton genetically engineered to be herbicide-tolerant decreased the amount of tillage passes (National Cotton Council of America 2008), which farmers say increased soil fertility. Reduced tillage leads to improvements in soil organic matter, structure, and water retention characteristics (Thies and Devare 2007) and results in decreased soil erosion, pesticide runoff, and improved air quality (Carpenter et al. 2002).

Numerous studies indicate that the use of GM crops (soybean, rape, cotton, and maize) has reduced pesticide use (Benedict and Altman 2001; Carpenter and Gianessi 2001; Phipps and Park 2002), and in the United States has led to an average decrease of 10 (Hin, Schenkelaars, and Pak 2001) to 14 percent (Gianessi and Carpenter 2001), while in China, reductions are estimated to be more than 70 percent (Huang et al. 2003). This is important since pesticide use is implicated in bird population declines (Krebs et al. 1999; Paoletti and Pimental 2000); for example, Paoletti and Pimental (2000) argue that pesticide use leads to about 70 million bird deaths annually in the United States. The use of GM crops also seems to have led to reductions in herbicide use (Phipps and Park 2002) and to a switch toward the use of the herbicide glyphosate and away from more environmentally harmful alternatives (Nelson, Bullock, and Nitsi 2001; Phipps and Park 2002). Bennett, Phipps, and Strange (2006) estimate the environmental benefits of GM corn production over conventional corn includes reductions in global warming

---

[18] I only highlight some of the environmental concerns; there are moral and other concerns as well.

potential (13.5 percent reduction), stratospheric ozone depletion (16.7 percent), and freshwater eco-toxicity (12.6 percent). Finally, farmers using GM crops use less fuel owing to reductions (Gianessi and Carpenter 2001 estimate a 22 percent reduction) in some field operations leading to reduced greenhouse gas emissions (Phipps and Park 2002). It is estimated that if the European Union replaced half of their corn, cotton, oil seed rape, and sugar beet crops with GM varieties, they could reduce carbon emissions by 73,000 tons per year (Phipps and Park 2002).

Since both organic and GM crop systems have been compared to conventional cropping and found, on at least some metrics, to be environmentally superior, one question is why few have made comparisons in the environmental impacts between organic and GM cropping.[19]

7   CONCLUSIONS

This chapter has provided a background on many, but nowhere near all, of the environmental impacts of food consumption. Regulations can be used to minimize these impacts (e.g., the US Environmental Protection Agency's 2008 regulations on Concentrated Animal Feeding Operations[20]). Alternatively, consumers can be provided information, through labeling or advertising, about a food's environmental impacts. Indeed, some of this labeling already occurs; e.g., the US Department of Agriculture's organic labeling program.[21] However, as this chapter has tried to emphasize, labeling of farm practices (e.g., organic) or other isolated food supply processes (e.g., air miles) is not likely to properly convey the environmental impacts of food consumption. In fact, focusing on one segment of the supply chain, or focusing on processes over outcomes, is just as likely to make things worse rather than better. Further, this emphasis is more likely to confuse consumers and lead to disruptive behaviors across production entities (e.g., between one type of farmer versus another).

Ultimately, all forms of food production, transport, storage, and handling are environmentally disruptive on some scale or metric and it is counter-productive and false to claim one process is always better than another. Use of lifecycle analyses that focus on input use and output generation seems to be a promising path. However, this approach will be more useful once there is a more consistent, agreed upon set of metrics and procedures. It is then that these metrics could be consistently used as an input into cost–benefit analyses and that foods could begin to be labeled according to these metrics (or some simplification of these metrics) to assist consumers. Consumers will also need to be informed and educated about these metrics; otherwise there is

---

[19] This question is posed but not answered by Dale, Clarke, and Fontes (2002).

[20] See <http://www.epa.gov/guide/cafo>.

[21] The organic label is not strictly speaking an environmental label; the label conveys positive perceptions of food safety, nutrition, and taste (Teisl, Fein, and Levy 2009).

a good chance that the labels will be ignored or misinterpreted, and choices consumers make will not reflect their values.

However, labeling will only go so far since much of the environmental impact of food consumption occurs at the consumer level through their choices of how they handle, store, and process the food, and how they handle wastes (both food and food packaging). Consumers will also need to be educated about how their household production decisions affect the environment. In addition, municipal waste management may need to allow for more waste recycling and recovery.

REFERENCES

Ahlgren, M., I. Gustafsson, and G. Hall. 2004. "Attitudes and Beliefs Directed towards Ready-Meal Consumption." *Food Service Technology* 4/4: 159–69.

Almasri, M. N., and J. J. Kaluarachchi. 2007. "Modelling Nitrate Contamination of Groundwater in Agricultural Watersheds." *Journal of Hydrology* 343/3–4: 211–29.

American Dietetic Association. 2001. "Position of the American Dietetic Association: Dietetics Professionals Can Implement Practices to Conserve Natural Resources and Protect the Environment." *Journal of the American Dietetic Association* 101/10: 1221–7.

Ammann, K. 2005. "Effects of Biotechnology on Biodiversity: Herbicide Tolerant and Insect Resistant GM Crops." *TRENDS in Biotechnology* 23/8: 388–94.

Andersson, K., and T. Ohlsson. 1999. "Life Cycle Assessment of Bread Produced on Different Scales." *International Journal of Life Cycle Assessment* 4/1: 25–40.

Andrews, S. S., D. L. Karlen, and J. P. Mitchell. 2002. "A Comparison of Soil Quality Indexing Methods for Vegetable Production Systems in Northern California." *Agriculture, Ecosystems and Environment* 90: 25–45.

Auerswald, K., M. Kainz, and P. Fiener. 2003. "Soil Erosion Potential of Organic versus Conventional Farming Evaluated by USLE Modelling of Cropping Statistics for Agricultural Districts in Bavaria." *Soil Use and Management* 19: 305–11.

Ayres, R. U. 1995. "Life Cycle Analysis: A Critique." *Resources, Conservation and Recycling* 14: 199–223.

Benedict, J. H., and D. W. Altman. 2001. "Commercialisation of Transgenic Cotton Expressing Insecticidal Crystal Protein." In J. J. Jenkins and S. Saha, eds, *Genetic Improvement of Cotton: Emerging Technologies*. Enfield, NH: Science Publishers.

Bennett, R. M., R. H. Phipps, and A. M. Strange. 2006. "The Use of Life Cycle Assessment to Compare the Environmental Impact of Production and Feeding of Conventional and Genetically Modified Maize for Broiler Production in Argentina." *Journal of Animal and Feed Sciences* 15: 71–82.

Berlin, J., U. Sonnesson, and A. Tillman. 2007. "A Life Cycle Based Method to Minimise Environmental Impact of Dairy Production through Product Sequencing." *Journal of Cleaner Production* 15/4: 303–84.

Betz, F. S., B. G. Hammond, and R. L. Fuchs. 2000. "Safety and Advantages of *Bacillus thuringiensis*-Protected Plants to Control Insect Pests." *Regulatory Toxicology and Pharmacology* 32/2: 156–73.

Birkett, D., and M. K. Patel. 2008. *The Effect of Food Consumption and Production Trends on Energy, Greenhouse Gas Emissions and Land Use*. Utrecht: Department of Science, Technology and Society, Utrecht University, 15 Aug.

Blair, D., and J. Sobal. 2006. "Luxus Consumption: Wasting Food Resources through Overeating." *Agriculture and Human Values* 23: 63–74.

Bleken, M., and L. R. Bakken. 1997. "The Nitrogen Cost of Food Production: Norwegian Society." *Ambio* 26: 134–9.

Blisard, N., B.-H. Lin, J. Cromartie, and N. Ballenger. 2002. "America's Changing Appetite: Food Consumption and Spending to 2020." *FoodReview* 25/1: 1–8.

Boge, S. 1995. "The Well Travelled Yoghurt Pot." *World Transport Policy and Practice* 1/1: 7–11.

Bongiovanni, R., and J. Lowenberg Deboer. 2004. "Precision Agriculture and Sustainability." *Precision Agriculture* 5/4: 1385–2256.

Bovea, M. D., and J. C. Powell. 2005. "Alternative Scenarios to Meet the Demands of Sustainable Waste Management." *Journal of Environmental Management* 79: 115–32.

Brown, S. M., H. F. Cook, and H. C. Lee. 2000. "Topsoil Characteristics from a Paired Farm Survey of Organic versus Conventional Farming in Southern England." *Biological Agriculture and Horticulture* 18/1: 37–54.

Butler, S. J., J. A. Vickery, and K. Norris. 2007. "Farmland Biodiversity and the Footprint of Agriculture." *Science* 315/5810: 381–4.

Capper, J. L., E. Castañeda Gutiérrez, R. A. Cady, and D. E. Bauman. 2008. "The Environmental Impact of Recombinant Bovine Somatotropin (rbST) Use in Dairy Production." *Proceedings of the National Academy of Sciences* 105/28: 9668–73.

Carlsson-Kanyama, A. 1998. "Climate Change and Dietary Choices: How Can Emissions of Greenhouse Gases from Food Consumption Be Reduced?" *Food Policy* 23: 277–93.

—— and K. Boström-Carlsson. 2001. *Energy Use for Cooking and Other Stages in the Life Cycle of Food: A Study of Wheat, Spaghetti, Pasta, Barley, Rice, Potatoes, Couscous and Mashed Potatoes*. FMS Report No. 160. Stockholm: Stockholm University, Jan.

Carpenter, J. E., and L. P. Gianessi. 2001. *Agricultural Biotechnology: Updated Benefit Estimates*. Washington, DC: National Center for Food and Agriculture Policy. <http://www.ncfap.org/documents/updatedbenefits.pdf>.

——, A. Felsot, T. Goode, M. Hammig, D. Onstad, and S. Sankula. 2002. *Comparative Environmental Impacts of Biotechnology-Derived and Traditional Soybean, Corn, and Cotton Crops*. Ames, IA: Council for Agricultural Science and Technology. <http://www.soyconnection.com/soybean_oil/pdf/EnvironmentalImpactStudy-English.pdf>.

Dale, P. J., B. Clarke, and E. M. G. Fontes. 2002. "Potential for the Environmental Impact of Transgenic Crops." *Nature Biotechnology* 20: 567–74.

Davis, J., and U. Sonesson. 2008. "Life Cycle Assessment of Integrated Food Chain: A Swedish Case Study of Two Chicken Meals." *International Journal of Life Cycle Assessment* 13: 574–84.

De Monte, M., E. Padoano, and D. Pozzetto. 2005. "Alternative Coffee Packaging: An Analysis from a Life Cycle Point of View." *Journal of Food Engineering* 66: 405–11.

Desrochers, P., and H. Shimizu. 2008. *Yes, We Have No Bananas: A Critique of the "Food Miles" Perspective*. Mercatus Policy Series, Policy Primer No. 8. Arlington, VA: Mercatus Center, George Mason University, Oct.

DETR (Department of the Environment, Transport and the Regions). 1999. *Transport Statistics Great Britain*. London: HMSO.

Dewick, P., C. Foster, and K. Green. 2007. "Technological Change and the Environmental Impacts of Food Production and Consumption: The Case of the UK Yogurt Industry." *Journal of Industrial Ecology* 11/3: 133–46.

Diop, N., and S. M. Jaffe. 2005. "Fruit and Vegetables: Global Trade and Competition in Fresh and Processed Product Markets." In M. A. Aksoy and J. C. Beghin, eds, *Global Agricultural Trade and Developing Countries*. Washington, DC: World Bank.

Draper, A., and J. Green. 2002. "Food Safety and Consumers: Constructions of Choice and Risk." *Social Policy and Administration* 36/6: 610–25.

Edwards-Jones, G., L. Milà i Canals, N. Hounsome, M. Truninger, G. Koerber, B. Hounsome, P. Cross, E. H. York, A. Hospido, K. Plassmann, I. M. Harris, R. T. Edwards, G. A. S. Day, A. D. Tomos, S. J. Cowell, and D. L. Jones. 2008. "Testing the Assertion that 'Local Food Is Best': The Challenges of an Evidence Based Approach." *Trends in Food Science and Technology* 19: 265–74.

Ekvall, T., L. Person, A. Ryberg, J. Widheden, N. Frees, P. H. Nielsen, and M. S. Wesnas. 1998. *Life Cycle Assessment on Packaging Systems for Beer and Soft Drinks*. Environmental Project No. 399. Copenhagen: Danish Environmental Protection Agency, Ministry of Environment and Energy.

Elferink, E. V., S. Nonhebel, and H. C. Moll. 2008. "Feeding Livestock Food Residue and the Consequences for the Environmental Impact of Meat." *Journal of Cleaner Production* 16: 1227–33.

Ellingsen, H., and S. A. Aanondsen. 2006. "Environmental Impacts of Wild Caught Cod and Farmed Salmon: A Comparison with Chicken." *International Journal of Life Cycle Assessment* 1/1: 60–5.

Engelhaupt, E. 2008. "Do Food Miles Matter?" *Environmental Science and Technology* 42/10: 3482.

Engstrom, R., and A. Carlsson-Kanyama. 2004. "Food Losses in Food Service Institutions: Examples from Sweden." *Food Policy* 29: 203–13.

ERS (Economic Research Service, US Department of Agriculture). 2003. *Organic Production*. Washington, DC: US Department of Agriculture.

Eshel, G., and P. A. Martin. 2006. "Diet, Energy, and Global Warming." *Earth Interactions* 10/9: 1–17.

Europen. 1999. *Use of Life Cycle Assessment (LCA) as a Policy Tool in the Field of Sustainable Packaging Waste Management*. Discussion Paper. Brussels: EUROPEN. <http://www.europen.be/download_protected_file.php?file=48>.

Fasoli, D. 1997. "Rifiuti: Questi 'trasformisti.'" In *Proceedings of the Meeting: Environment and Communication—Wastes—a Challenge for the 21st Century and the Role of Communication*, Monza, Italy, Oct. 31. <http://www.see.it/agam/rifiuti.html>.

Fawcett, R., and D. Towery. 2002. *Conservation Tillage and Plant Biotechnology: How New Technologies Can Improve the Environment by Reducing the Need to Plow*. West Lafayette, IN: Purdue University.

Feitz, A., S. Lundie, G. Dennien, M. Morain, and M. Jones. 2005. "Allocating Intra Industry Material and Energy Flows Using Physio Chemical Allocation Matrices: Application to the Australian Dairy Industry." Paper presented at the Fourth Australian Life Cycle Assessment Conference, Sydney, 23–5 Feb.

Fosså, J. H. 2000. *Sluttrapport: Effekter av fiske på korallrev på den norske kontinentalsokkelen*. NFR prosjekt 121 122/122.

Frankenberger, R., and R. Turco. 2003. *Hypoxia in the Gulf of Mexico: A Reason to Improve Nitrogen Management.* Purdue Animal Issues Briefing No. AI-6. <http://www.ansc.purdue.edu/anissue/AI6.pdf>.

Frith, M. 2005. "How Far Has Your Christmas Dinner Travelled?" *The Independent*, Dec. 24. <http://news.independent.co.uk/uk/this_britain/article335011.ece>.

Gallo, A. E. 1980. "Consumer Food Waste in the United States." *National Food Review* (Fall), 13–16.

Garnett, T. 2006. *Fruit and Vegetables and UK Greenhouse Gas Emissions: Exploring the Relationship.* Working Paper. Guildford: Food Climate Research Network.

Gerbens-Leenes, P. W., S. Nonhebel, and W. P. M. F. Ivens. 2002. "A Method to Determine Land Requirements relating to Food Consumption Patterns." *Agriculture, Ecosystems and Environment* 90: 47–58.

Gianessi, L. P., and J. E. Carpenter. 2000. *Agricultural Biotechnology: Benefits of Transgenic Soybeans.* Washington, DC: National Center for Food and Agricultural Policy.

Goodland, R. 1997. "Environmental Sustainability in Agriculture: Diet Matters." *Ecological Economics* 23/3: 189–200.

—— and D. S. Pimentel. 2000. "Environmental Sustainability and Integrity in the Agriculture Sector." In D. S. Pimentel, L. Westra, and R. F. Noss, eds, *Ecological Integrity: Integrating Environment, Conservation, and Health.* Washington, DC: Island Press.

Greene, C. 2004. *Data Sets:Organic Production.* Washington, DC: Economic Research Service, US Department of Agriculture. <http://www.ers.usda.gov/Data/organic>.

Griffin, M., J. Sobal, and T. A. Lyson. 2009. "An Analysis of a Community Food Waste Stream." *Agriculture and Human Values* 26: 67–81.

Hamilton, A. 2006. "Christmas Lunch Will Fly 84,000 Miles to your Table." *The Times*, Nov. 20. <http://www.timesonline.co.uk/tol/news/uk/article642552.ece>.

Harrison, G. G., W. L. Rathje, and W. W. Hughes. 1975. "Waste Behavior in an Urban Population." *Journal of Nutrition Education* 7/1: 13–16.

Havlikova, M., and C. Kroeze. 2006. "Evaluation of Methods for Quantifying Agricultural Emissions of Air, Water and Soil Pollutants." *Science of the Total Environment* 372/1: 133–47.

Heller, M. A., and G. A. Keoleian. 2000. *Life Cycle Based Sustainability Indicators for Assessment of the U.S. Food System.* Center for Sustainability Systems Report No. CSS00-04. Ann Arbor: University of Michigan, Dec.

Hin, C. J. A., P. Schenkelaars, and G. A. Pak. 2001. *Agronomic and Environmental Impacts of Commercial Cultivation of Glyphosate Tolerant Soybean in the USA.* Utrecht: Centre for Agriculture and Environment.

Hirai, Y., M. Murata, S. Sakai, and H. Takatsuki. 2000. "Life Cycle Assessment for Foodwaste Recycling and Management." In *Proceedings of the Fourth International Conference on EcoBalance*, Tsukuba, Japan, Oct. 31–Nov. 2. <http://homepage1.nifty.com/eco/pdf/ecobalanceE.pdf>.

Hole, D. G., A. J. Perkins, J. D. Wilson, I. H. Alexander, P. V. Grice, and A. D. Evans. 2005. "Does Organic Farming Benefit Biodiversity?" *Biological Conservation* 122: 113–30.

Hospido, A., M. T. Moreira, and G. Feijoo. 2005. "Environmental Analysis of Beer Production." *International Journal of Agricultural Resources, Governance and Ecology* 4/2: 152–62.

Huang, J., R. Hu, C. Pray, F. Quiao, and S. Rozelle. 2003. "Biotechnology as an Alternative to Chemical Pesticides: A Case Study of Bt Cotton in China." *Agricultural Economics* 29: 55–67.

Icke, D. 2008. *Benefits of Compact Electron Beam Adoption in Industrial Processes*. Presentation at CTSI, Boston, June 3. <http://www.aeb.com/Default.aspx?app=LeadgenDownload&shortpath=docs%2fAEB+CSI+presentation.pdf>.

Jones, A. 2002. "An Environmental Assessment of Food Supply Chains: A Case Study on Dessert Apples." *Environmental Management* 30/4: 560–76.

Jungbluth N., O. Tietje, and R. W. Scholz. 2000. "Food Purchases: Impacts from the Consumers' Point of View Investigated with a Modular LCA." *International Journal Life Cycle Assessment* 5: 134–42.

Kantor, L. S., K. Lipton, A. Manchester, and V. Oliveira. 1997. "Estimating and Addressing America's Food Losses." *Food Review* 20/1: 2–12.

Kjærnes, U. 2001. "Discussion and Conclusions." In Kjærnes, ed., *Eating Patterns: A Day in the Lives of Nordic Peoples*. Report No. 7. Lysaker: SIFO.

Krebs, J. R, J. D. Wilson, R. B. Bradbury, and G. M. Sirwardena. 1999. "The Second Silent Spring." *Nature* 400: 611–12.

Kristensen, P. 2004. *Household Consumption of Food and Drinks*. Background Paper for the European Environment Agency Report on Household Consumption and the Environment. Roskilde: National Environmental Research Institute.

Kytzia, S., M. Faist, and P. Baccini. 2004. "Economically Extended—MFA: A Material Flow Approach for a Better Understanding of Food Production Chain." *Journal of Cleaner Production* 12: 877–89.

La Trobe, H. 2001. "Farmers' Markets: Consuming Local Produce." *International Journal of Consumer Culture* 25/3: 181–92.

Leahy, T. 2007. *Tesco, Carbon and the Consumer*. Speech given by Sir Terry Leahy to invited stakeholders at a joint Forum for the Future and Tesco event in central London, Jan. 18.

Lundie, S., and G. M. Peters. 2005. "Life Cycle Assessment of Food Waste Management Options." *Journal of Cleaner Production* 13/3: 275–86.

Lusk, J. L., and F. B. Norwood. 2009. "Some Economic Benefits and Costs of Vegetarianism." *Agricultural and Resource Economics Review* 38: 83–92.

McComas, C., and D. McKinley. 2008. "Reduction of Phosphorus and Other Pollutants from Industrial Dischargers Using Pollution Prevention." *Journal of Cleaner Production* 16/6: 727–33.

Martin, N., E. Worrell, M. Ruth, L. Price, R. N. Elliott, A. M. Shipley, and J. Thorne. 2000. *Emerging Energy Efficient Industrial Technologies*. Berkeley: Environmental Energy Technologies Division, Ernest Orlando Lawrence Berkeley National Laboratory, Oct.

Massari, S. 2003. *Current Food Consumption Patterns and Global Sustainability*. United Nations Environment Programme Discussion Paper. <http://www.agrifood forum.net/issues/consumption/doc/agriconsumption.pdf> (no longer available).

Mattson, B., and E. Wallén. 2003. "Environmental Life Cycle Assessment (LCA) of Organic Potatoes." *Acta Horticulturae* 619: 427–35.

Milà i Canals, L., S. Cowell, S. Sim, and L. Basson. 2007. "Comparing Local versus Imported Apples: A Focus on Energy Use." *Environmental Science and Pollution Research* 14: 276–82.

Mokdad, A. H., B. A. Bowman, E. S. Ford, F. Vinicor, J. S. Marks, and J. P. Koplan. 2001. "The Continuing Epidemics of Obesity and Diabetes in the United States." *Journal of the American Medical Association* 286: 1195–1200.

——, E. S. Ford, B. A. Bowman, W. H. Dietz, F. Vinicor, V. S. Bales, and J. S. Marks. 2003. "Prevalence of Obesity, Diabetes, and Obesity Related Health Risk Factors, 2001." *Journal of the American Medical Association* 289: 76–9.

——, M. K. Serdula, W. H. Dietz, B. A. Bowman, J. S. Marks, and J. P. Koplan. 1999. "The Spread of the Obesity Epidemic in the United States, 1991–1998." *Journal of the American Medical Association* 282/16: 1519–22.

Morandin, L. A., and M. L. Winston. 2005. "Wild Bee Abundance and Seed Production in Conventional, Organic, and Genetically Modified Canola." *Ecological Applications* 15/3: 871–81.

Morgan, K., T. Marsden, and J. Murdoch. 2006. *Worlds of Food: Place, Power and Provenance in the Food Chain.* Oxford: Oxford University Press.

Mourad, A. L., E. E. S. Garcia, G. B. Vilela, and F. von Zuben. 2008. "Environmental Effects from a Recycling Rate Increase of Cardboard of Aseptic Packaging System for Milk Using Life Cycle Approach." *International Journal of Life Cycle Assessment* 13/2: 140–6.

Muñoz, P., A. Antón, J. I. Montero, and F. Castells. 2004. "Using LCA for the Improvement of Waste Management in Greenhouse Tomato Production." In *Proceedings from the Fourth International Conference on Life Cycle Assessment in the Agri-Food Sector.* Bygholm, Denmark, Oct. 6–8. Tjele: Danish Institute of Agricultural Sciences. <http://www.lcafood.dk/lca_conf/DJFrapport_paper_2_poster.pdf>.

Munro, R. 1995. "The Disposal of the Meal." In D. Marshall, ed., *Food Choice and the Consumer.* New York: Blackie Academic and Professional.

National Cotton Council of America. 2008. "Study Shows Biotech Is Key Factor in Move to Conservation Tillage in Cotton." Feb. 8. <http://www.cotton.org/news/releases/2003/tillage-survey.cfm>.

Nelson, G. C., D. Bullock, and E. Nitsi. 2001. "Environmental Effects of GMOs: Evidence from the Use of Glyphosate Resistant Soybeans." Paper presented at the 5th International Consortium on Agricultural Biotechnology Research, Ravello, Italy, June 15–18. Abstract. <http://www.economia.uniroma2.it/conferenze/icabro1/nontechabsrtact 2001/Nelson.htm>.

Nijdam, D. S., H. C. Wilting, M. J. Goedkoop, and J. Madsen. 2005. "Environmental Load from Dutch Private Consumption: How Much Damage Takes Place Abroad?" *Journal of Industrial Ecology* 9/1–2: 147–68.

NRDC (Natural Resources Defense Council). 2009. *Eat Local: Does Your Food Travel More Than You Do?* <http://www.nrdc.org/health/foodmiles>.

Nyland, C. A., I. S. Modahl, H. L. Raadal, and O. J. Hanssen. 2003. "Application of LCA as a Decision Making Tool for Waste Management Systems." *International Journal of Life Cycle Assessment* 8/6: 331–6.

OECD (Organisation for Economic Co-operation and Development). 2001. *Household Food Consumption: Trends, Environmental Impacts and Policy Responses.* Sustainable Consumption: Sector Case Study Series. Paris: Organisation for Economic Co-operation and Development.

Pack, A. 2006. *The Environmental Sustainability of Household Food Consumption in Austria: A Socio-economic Analysis.* Scientific Report No. 17. Graz: Wegener Center for Climate and Global Change, University of Graz, July.

Paoletti, M. G., and D. S. Pimentel. 2000. "Environmental Risks of Pesticides versus Genetic Engineering for Agricultural Pest Control." *Journal of Agricultural and Environmental Ethics* 12/3: 279–303.

Payer, H., P. Burger, and S. Lorek. 2000. *Food Consumption in Austria: Driving Forces and Environmental Impacts.* National Case Study for the OECD Programme on Sustainable

Consumption. Vienna: Federal Ministry of Agriculture, Forestry, Environment and Water Management.

Peng, J., E. Richards, N. M. Hartley, G. P. Murphy, K. M. Devos, J. E. Flintham, J. Beales, L. J. Fish, A. J. Worland, F. Pelica, D. Sudhakar, P. Christou, J. W. Snape, M. D. Gale, and N. P. Harberd. 1999. "'Green Revolution' Genes Encode Mutant Gibberellin Response Modulators." *Nature* 400: 256–61.

Phipps, R. H., and J. R. Park. 2002. "Environmental Benefits of Genetically Modified Crops: Global and European Perspectives on their Ability to Reduce Pesticide Use." *Journal of Animal and Feed Sciences* 11: 1–18.

Pimentel, D. S., and M. Pimentel. 1982. *Food Energy and Society.* London: Edward Arnold.

——, P. Hepperly, J. Hanson, D. Douds, and R. Seidel. 2005. "Environmental, Energetic, and Economic Comparisons of Organic and Conventional Farming Systems." *BioScience* 55/7: 573–82.

Poppendieck, J. 1986. *Sweet Charity: Emergency Food and the End of Entitlement.* New York: Viking Press.

Powers, S. E. 2007. "Nutrient Loads to Surface Water from Row Crop Production." *International Journal of Life Cycle Assessment* 12/6: 399–407.

Pulleman, M. M., J. Six, N. van Breemen, and A. G. Jongmans. 2005. "Soil Organic Matter Distribution and Microaggregate Characteristics as Affected by Agricultural Management and Earthworm Activity." *European Journal of Soil Science* 56/4: 453–67.

Putnam, J. J., and J. E. Allshouse. 1999. *Food Consumption, Prices and Expenditures: 1970–1997.* Statistical Bulletin No. 965. Washington, DC: Food and Rural Economics Division, Economic Research Service, US Department of Agriculture. <http://www.ers.usda.gov/publications/sb965>.

Ramjeawon, T. 2000. "Cleaner Production in Mauritian Cane Sugar Factories." *Journal of Cleaner Production* 8/6: 503–10.

Raven, H., T. Lang, and C. Dumonteil. 1995. *Off Our Trolleys: Food Retailing and the Hypermarket Economy.* London: Institute of Public Policy Research.

Rebitzer, G., Y. Loerincik, and O. Jolliet. 2002. "Input Output Life Cycle Assessment: From Theory to Applications." *International Journal of Life Cycle Assessment* 7/3: 174–6.

Regierer, B., A. R. Fernie, F. Springer, A. Perez Melis, A. Leisse, K. Koehl, L. Willmitzer, P. Geigenberger, and J. Kossman. 2002. "Starch Content and Yield Increase as a Result of Altering Adenylate Pools in Transgenic Plants." *Nature Biotechnology* 20: 1256–60.

Reijnders, L. 2001. "Environmental Aspects of Meat Production and Vegetarianism." In J. Sabaté, ed., *Vegetarian Nutrition.* Boca Raton, FL: CRC Press.

—— and S. Sore. 2003. "Quantification of the Environmental Impact of Different Dietary Protein Choices." *American Journal of Clinical Nutrition* 78, suppl., 664S–668S.

Renagold, J. P., J. D. Glover, P. K. Andrews, and H. R. Hinman. 2001. "Sustainability of Three Apple Production Systems." *Nature* 410: 926–30.

Roelandt, C., B. van Wesemael, and M. Rounsevell. 2005. "Estimating Annual N_2O Emissions from Agricultural Soils in Temperate Climates." *Global Change Biology* 11: 1701–11.

Roy, P., N. Daisuke, O. Takahiro, Q. Xu, H. Okadome, N. Nakamura, and T. Shiina. 2009. "A Review of Life Cycle Assessment (LCA) on Some Food Products." *Journal of Food Engineering* 90: 1–10.

Saunders, C., A. Barber, and G. Taylor. 2006. *Food Miles: Comparative Energy/Emissions Performance of New Zealand's Agriculture Industry.* Research Report No. 285. Christchurch, New Zealand: Agribusiness and Economics Research Unit, Lincoln University.

Schlich, E. H., and U. Fleissner. 2005. "The Ecology of Scale: Assessment of Regional Energy Turnover and Comparison with Global Food." *International Journal of Life Cycle Assessment* 10: 219–23.

SEPA (Swedish Environmental Protection Agency). 1997a. *Att äta för en bättre miljö* [Eating for a Better Environment]. Report No. 4830. Stockholm: Swedish Environmental Protection Agency.

—— 1997b. *Fosfor: Livsnödvändigt, ändligt och ett miljöproblem* [Phosphorous: Essential, Limited, and an Environmental Problem]. Report No. 4730. Stockholm: Swedish Environmental Protection Agency.

—— 1997c. *Kväve från land till hav* [Nitrogen from Land to Sea]. Report No. 4735. Stockholm: Swedish Environmental Protection Agency.

—— 1997d. *Kväveläckage från svensk åkermark* [Nitrogen Leakage from Swedish Agricultural Land]. Report No. 4741. Stockholm: Swedish Environmental Protection Agency.

Skerrett, P. J., and H. Bartlett. 1997. "Will it Keep the Doctors Away?" *MIT's Technology Review* 100/8: 28. <http://www.technologyreview.com/biomedicine/11621>.

Smith, A., P. Watkiss, G. Tweddle, A. McKinnon, M. Browne, and A. Hunt. 2005. *The Validity of Food Miles as an Indicator of Sustainable Development*. Report No. ED50254. Didcot: Department for Environment, Health and Rural Affairs. <http://www.wildchicken.com/grow/defra%20foodmiles%20execsumm.pdf>.

Sobal, J., and M. Nelson. 2003. "Food Waste." In S. H. Katz, ed., *Encyclopedia of Food and Culture*, 1. New York: Charles Scribner's Sons.

Sonesson, U., and J. Berlin. 2003. "Environmental Impact of Future Milk Supply Chains in Sweden: A Scenario Study." *Journal of Cleaner Production* 11/3: 253–66.

Steinfeld, H., P. Gerber, T. Wassenaar, V. Castel, M. Rosales, and C. de Haan. 2006. *Livestock's Long Shadow: Environmental Issues and Options*. Rome: Food and Agriculture Organization of the United Nations.

Stigler, G. J. 1945. "The Cost of Subsistence." *Journal of Farm Economics* 27/2: 303–14.

Sundkvist, A., A. M. Jansson, and P. Larsson. 2001. "Strengths and Limitations of Localizing Food Production as a Sustainability-Building Strategy: An Analysis of Bread Production on the Island of Gotland, Sweden" *Ecological Economics* 37: 217–27.

Taylor, D. C., V. Katavic, J. Zou, S. L. MacKenzie, W. A. Keller, J. An, W. Friesen, D. L. Barton, K. K. Pedersen, M. E. Giblin, Y. Ge, M. Dauk, C. Sonntag, T. Luciw, and D. Males. 2001. "Field Testing of Transgenic Rapeseed cv. Hero Transformed with a Yeast *sn*-2 Acyltransferase Results in Increased Oil Content, Erucic Acid Content and Seed Yield." *Molecular Breeding* 8: 317–22.

Teisl, M. F., S. B. Fein, and A. S. Levy. 2009. "Information Effects on Consumer Attitudes toward Three Food Technologies: Organic Production, Biotechnology, and Irradiation." *Food Quality and Preference* 20: 586–96.

Thies, J. E., and M. H. Devare. 2007. "An Ecological Assessment of Transgenic Crops." *Journal of Development Studies* 43/1: 97–129.

Tidaker, P., E. Karrman, A. Baky, and H. Jonsson. 2006. "Wastewater Management Integrated with Farming: An Environmental Systems Analysis of a Swedish Country Town." *Resources, Conservation and Recycling* 47: 295–315.

Tilman, D., J. Fargione, B. Wolff, C. D'Antonio, A. Dobson, R. Howarth, D. Schindler, W. H. Schlesinger, D. Simberloff, and D. Swackhamer. 2001. "Forecasting Agriculturally Driven Global Environmental Change." *Science* 292/5515: 281–4.

Trewavas, A. 2004. "A Critical Assessment of Organic Farming and Food Assertions with particular respect to the UK and the Potential Environmental Benefits of No Till Agriculture." *Crop Protection* 23: 757–81.

Tukker, A., G. Huppes, T. Geerken, and P. Nielsen. 2005. *Environmental Impact of Products (EIPRO)*. Draft Report of the Institute for Prospective Technological Studies (IPTS) and the European Science and Technology Observatory (ESTO), Brussels: IPTS/ESTO.

Tyson, M., M. Rutherford, A. Testoni, and J. Epstein. 2008. "Benefits of Compact Electron Beam Adoption in Industrial Processes: Case Studies on Energy and Water Savings and Reduced Pollution Output and Chemical Use." In *Technical Proceedings of the 2008 Clean Technology Conference and Trade Show*. Cambridge, MA: Clean Technology and Sustainable Industries Organization/CRC Press. <http://www.ct-si.org/publications/proceedings/procs/Cleantech2008/6/70236>.

Uhlin, H. E. 1997. *Energiflöden i livsmedelskedjan*. Report No. 4732. Stockholm: Swedish Environmental Protection Agency.

—— 1998. "Why Energy Productivity Is Increasing: An I-O Analysis of Swedish Agriculture." *Agricultural Systems* 56/4: 443–65.

UNEP (United Nations Environment Programme). 1995. "Food Processing and the Environment." *Industry and Environment* 18/1: 3.

USGS (US Geological Survey). 2001. *Selected Findings and Current Perspectives on Urban and Agricultural Water Quality by the National Water Quality Assessment Program*. Washington, DC: US Geological Survey, US Department of the Interior.

van der Pijl, S., and B. Krutwagen. 2001. *Domeinverkenning Voeden* [Exploration of the Food Domain]. The Hague: Schuttelaar.

Vannebo, H., B. Aalvik, S. O. Rabben, and T. Olafsen. 2000. *Handlingsplan for redusert utslipp av kobber fra norsk oppdrettsnæring* [Action Plan for Reducing Emissions of Copper from the Norwegian Aquaculture Industry]. Oslo: Fishery and Aquaculture Industry Association.

van Oost, K., G. Govers, S. de Alba, and T. A. Quine. 2006. "Tillage Erosion: A Review of Controlling Factors and Implications for Soil Quality." *Progress in Physical Geography* 30/4: 443–66.

Weatherell, C., A. Tregear, and J. Allinson. 2003. "In Search of the Concerned Consumer: UK Public Perception of Food, Farming and Buying Local." *Journal of Rural Studies* 19: 233–44.

Weber, C. L., and H. S. Matthews. 2008. "Food-Miles and the Relative Climate Impacts of Food Choices in the United States." *Environmental Science and Technology* 42/10: 3508–13.

WHO (World Health Organization). 2003. *Diet, Nutrition and the Prevention of Chronic Diseases: Report of a Joint World Health Organization/Food and Agriculture Organization Expert Consultation*. WHO Technical Report No. 916. Geneva: World Health Organization.

World Resource Institute. 2006. *Water Withdrawals: Percent Used for Agricultural Purposes*. <http://earthtrends.wri.org/searchable_db/index.php?theme=2>.

WRAP (Waste and Resources Action Programme). 2008. *The Food We Waste: A Study of the Amount, Types and Nature of the Food We Throw Away in UK Households*. <http://wrap.s3.amazonaws.com/the-food-we-waste-executive-summary.pdf>.

Zabaniotou, A., and E. Kassidi. 2003. "Life Cycle Assessment Applied to Egg Packaging Made from Polystyrene and Recycled Paper." *Journal of Cleaner Production* 11/5: 549–59.

Zufia, J., and L. Arana. 2008. "Life Cycle Assessment to Eco-Design Food Products: Industrial Cooked Dish Case Study." *Journal of Cleaner Production* 16: 1915–21.

CHAPTER 35

....

ETHICAL CONSIDERATIONS AND FOOD DEMAND

....

MARIA L. LOUREIRO*

1 INTRODUCTION

....

Ethical issues related to food production and distribution became predominant after the Second War World. During the 1960s ethical aspects linked to food production and distribution, proper pricing, and unequal consumption opportunities were predominant in the mass media. However, since the 1980s all these earlier concerns have been accompanied by others related to the increasing gap between producers and consumers, the heavy industrialization process, and concentration of power in the marketplace. Korthals (2010) suggests three main types of ethical concern nowadays that are common to many countries: the first type covers substantial issues like animal welfare and fair trade practices, the second covers concerns related to access to reliable information, and the third covers involvement and participation in the food chain. As a consequence, food is becoming more and more an item on the political agenda around the world. In order to satisfy these various demands, producers provide a large array of goods and services manufactured under ethical guidelines. Such ethical guidelines may require minimal harm to animals, proper labor conditions, or good environmental conditions, among others. Ethical consumption is also at times exercised by excluding particular products and services from the food basket, using, for example, consumer boycotts against disrespectful practices.

In recent years, ethical claims have been increasing in the marketplace worldwide, and this movement contributes to market differentiation and product proliferation.

* This chapter was written while the author had a research appointment at the Norwegian Agricultural Economics Research Institute, Oslo, and all materials employed in this chapter were provided by the funding of the research project "Food Labelling and Quality" funded by the Norwegian Research Council.

Such a trend is evidenced by the large or substantial market shares achieved by many of these ethically sound products around the world. For example, recent statistics have shown that ethical consumerism has increased at an average rate of 15 percent per annum since 2002 in the UK (Co-operative Bank 2008). Similar data have shown a growth in ethical consumption in the United States for fair trade certified products. In particular, consumers' knowledge of fair trade products has also increased to 28 percent between 2003 and 2007, while sales have increased by 46 percent with respect to 2006 (TransFair USA 2007). However, the choices involved in being an ethical consumer are becoming more complex and sophisticated, with many conflicts and paradoxes. Yet this ethical movement is not exclusive to the food sector, and nowadays there is almost no economic sector that is not devoted to promoting ethical claims (the financial and housing sectors, transportation, etc.).

In the food economics and demand literature, multiple studies on the various aspects of ethical consumption have documented the importance of ethical attributes in current consumption patterns. Most of these analyses are based on stated preference studies, which rely on direct elicitation of data. However, there are also a few revealed preference studies conducted with direct retail data, including Teisl and Roe (2002) and Dhar and Foltz (2005), among others. Revealed preference studies are expected to be more accurate than stated preference ones, although at times, and owing to the lack of market data, researchers must rely on the analysis of stated preferences. In their work, Teisl and Roe (2002) use an almost ideal demand system (AIDS) model to assess the impact of the dolphin-safe tuna on consumer behavior using supermarket data. Their results show that consumers respond to environmentally friendly labels, increasing the market share for canned tuna. Using the same methodology, Dhar and Foltz (2005) look at the impact of the introduction of rBST-free and organic milk in the US milk market. They find significant consumer benefits linked to the introduction of organic milk, and also to some extent from rBST-free milk.

However, as stated previously, most studies are based on the analysis of consumers' stated preferences, which are not exempt from biases and accuracy concerns. Stated preference studies rely on survey opinions or other hypothetical methods rather than actual consumer behavior. The fact that such elicited data may not fully represent consumer behavior has always been a major concern in this type of literature. Furthermore, the obtained results may not be fully comparable across studies, owing to methodological or geographical differences, and consequently, any benefit transfer exercise may suffer from various biases or a general lack of accuracy. An additional aspect that may not help us in generalizing the findings provided by these studies is that contributions to this abundant literature are scattered throughout multiple outlets at the international level. Because of all the above issues, it has become quite difficult to gather conclusions with respect to the assessment of the multiple ethical claims available in the food market.

In this context, the objectives of this chapter are twofold: first, to provide some background information to contextualize the multiple ethical claims according to different underlying economic and physiological theories; and second, to assess the marginal value of each of the main ethical food claims present nowadays in the marketplace. Specifically, the question related to what ethical claims consumers value most is one of the most important ones that are answered in the following exercise. In order to conduct such an analysis, an extensive literature review was compiled to estimate a meta-analytical regression at the international level. Results with respect to the relative preferences toward the various ethical claims are described and discussed. Overall, the obtained meta-analytical results show that there are clear differences between the valuations achieved by the different ethically sound claims. With respect to consumers' preferences toward ethical claims, genetically modified (GM)-free claims are the most valued ones in the marketplace worldwide. Implications of this result are discussed.

2 BACKGROUND ON ETHICAL VALUES

Maslow's hierarchy of needs (Maslow 1943) is very applicable to understanding the growth in ethical food demand. Maslow describes how people's needs move from basic hunger satiety through several stages to self-actualization as their wealth increases. Therefore, this theoretical framework helps us understand the desires of wealthier people to express and differentiate themselves through their market choices. Consequently, as societies become wealthier, consumers may move from satisfying basic hunger needs to purchasing ethical foods carrying other personal ideals and messages.

From an economic viewpoint, multiple theories have tried to explain the growth of ethical behavior. For example, such concerns may be behind an altruistic feeling (Andreoni and Miller 2002), or reciprocity, or concerns for inequality (Fehr and Schmidt 1999). Other theories have looked at the effect of social norms or conformity according to which people care about their behavior relative to the behavior of others (Bernheim 1994). Thus, multiple motives (and not only the availability of higher income shares) may lead to ethical consumerism. These findings from the economic literature have encouraged the inclusion of additional variables reflecting concerns for others into the traditional demand function solely based on consumers' own utility. Multiple recent economic experiments try to shed light on the explanatory power of these new theoretical predictions by understanding direct motivations of people's preferences when making choices (see List 2006).

Given that ethical concerns are widely spread in the marketplace, a single classification of ethically sound products is complex owing to the multiple messages that may be conveyed by a single claim. However, there are previous attempts that may help us to provide a classification of these various ethical messages. For example, Lusk and Briggeman (2009) present a very useful classification of food values that may be offered as a basic reference for the present study. In their application, the importance of eleven different food values is measured, including price, safety, nutrition, taste, naturalness, convenience, appearance, environment, fairness, tradition, and origin. They find that measured values were significantly related to revealed and stated preferences for organic food. Therefore, based on the list of values previously assessed in the literature, this chapter focuses on those with a strong ethical content, excluding from the analysis others that may be classified as general characteristics of the product (such as taste, convenience, and appearance).

In the empirical analysis that follows, the theory behind Maslow's hierarchy of needs is employed as a general framework for classification of ethical concerns as constructs of analysis. Such a classification is also influenced by the kind of empirical studies available and, as indicated, by the stage of development of the literature in this area. Thus, in order to arrange the available data in a sensible way that may allow us to conduct an empirical analysis, claims were classified into various large groups, including environmentally related concerns, welfare concerns, GM-free claims, and others (including origin, tradition, and food safety) that are explicitly considered in the analysis. Such a classification of claims resembles that employed by Lusk and Briggeman (2009) and is also based on reflections in Korthals (2010). Similar classifications were also provided by Jones, Haenfler, and Johnson (2007). Environmental and welfare concerns are cornerstones of ethical marketing, and more recently, the genetic modification of animals and plants is also attracting much concern. Thompson (2010) analyzes the ethical perspective of food biotechnology, addressing various concerns, including food safety issues and the need for provision of information in order to make responsible decisions, religious dimensions of the various food manipulations, and the moral status of animals, among others.

In order to respond to the question of what ethical claims consumers value most, and given the large amount of valuation studies analyzing consumer preferences for ethically sound attributes and the difficulty of gathering conclusions in regard to the assessment of the multiple ethical claims worldwide, a meta-analytical regression model is used. This analysis allows us to understand not only consumer preferences, but also the differential effects carried out by the various geographical areas and valuation methods. In the next section, I describe the methodology employed, as well as the criteria for selecting studies for inclusion in the analysis. The empirical model is presented, as well as the main results and conclusions.

3 DATA

An extensive search of published articles related to consumer valuation studies for ethical claims has been conducted in AgEconSearch, *Econlit*, Business Source Premier, and Google Scholar, among others. This initial compilation resulted in a database containing more than 200 different studies. However, several criteria had to be employed in order to determine whether each particular study ought to be included into the data set of analysis. Given the large variety of products carrying ethical claims, I selected only those related to food and beverages, excluding all studies of forest-related products, clothing, energy, and other goods and services. Based on the interest in food products exclusively, the next step required a selection of the studies that contained all required explanatory variables. Of particular interest is the dependent variable of the regression, the mean willingness to pay (WTP) for a pound of a food product carrying ethical claims. Such WTP was mainly expressed in monetary values or price premiums over the original price. The international studies in which WTP was presented in any currency were all converted to the same monetary unit (US$ 2008). This was done utilizing the exchange rate of the different countries published by the Penn World Table (CIC 2008). Then, the dollar price of the year of reference was converted into 2008 dollars employing the consumer price index of the United States. Thus, all monetary values are expressed in US$ 2008, independently of the currency and year of study. This facilitated the inclusion of many international studies, although all those in which the physical weight of the product was not included were excluded from the sample (for example, a box of cereals, a loaf of bread, etc.).

Another difficulty found in regard to the inclusion of other studies was that a large number of analyses reported only the additional percentages individuals were willing to pay for the particular ethical food product, without including the reference price; owing to that, these were excluded from the final analysis because of the difficulty of transferring the valuation into meaningful economic estimates. Once this collection of studies was selected, the next step was to find a set of explanatory variables that determined the different valuations. In this respect, a series of variables were collected, such as: (a) description of the study itself, including the author, place, and time when the study was undertaken; (b) other methodological variables that defined the types of technique employed in the valuation exercise (experimental auctions, contingent valuation, or choice experiments), as well as variables related to the sample size of participants and the response or participation rate (when described) and the frequency of payment; (c) other variables related to the type of good being valued. The final sample contains a total of 138 observations from thirty-four studies. Table 35.1 offers a summary and basic description of the studies included. As noted, a large variety of valuations have been undertaken, with different elicitation techniques.

As indicated in Table 35.2, most of the studies correspond with choice experiment applications (49.8 percent) and contingent valuation analyses (27.4 percent), whereas experimental auctions were used in 25.4 percent of the studies analyzed. In regard to the geographical area where the study took place, 53.4 percent of the data come from studies conducted in North America, and 36.3 percent in Europe, whereas 10.3 percent are from the rest of the world. About 64 percent of the studies contained in the database are related to consumer preferences toward GM-free food. Green claims are also predominant (including organic foods, pesticide-free, and eco-labeled products) summing up to 21.9 percent of the observations. Other claims concerning food products relating to animal welfare standards and fair trade practices are also contained in the data set, representing in total 4.8 percent. Finally, claims related to country-of-origin labeling, denominations of origin, and other food safety standards represent nearly 8.21 percent of the studies. Unfortunately, and in order not to reduce any further the

Table 35.1 Data sources

Author	Source	Country
Aldanondo-Ochoa and Almansa-Sáez (2009)	*Land Use Policy*	Spain
Bazoche, Deola, and Soler (2008)	12th Congress of the European Association of Agricultural Economists	France
Bernard and Gifford (2006)	*Consumer Interests Annual*	United States
Bukenya and Wright (2007)	*Agribusiness*	United States
Carlsson, Frykblom, and Lagerkvist (2005)	*Ambio*	Sweden
Carlsson, Frykblom, and Lagerkvist (2007)	*American Journal of Agricultural Economics*	Sweden
Chen and Chern (2002)	Annual Meeting of the American Agricultural Economics Association	United States
Chern et al. (2002)	*AgBioForum*	United States, Norway
Christoph, Roosen, and Bruhn (2006)	American Agricultural Economics Association Annual Meeting	Germany
Corsi and Novelli (2003)	*Proceedings of the 25th International Conference of Agricultural Economists*	Italy
Ehmke, Lusk, and Tyner (2006)	International Association of Agricultural Economists Conference	China, United States, France, Niger
Grannis and Thilmany (2002)	*Agribusiness*	United States
Howard and Allen (2008)	*Renewable Agriculture and Food Systems*	United States
Hu (2006)	*Empirical Economics*	China
Kaneko and Chern (2004)	American Agricultural Economics Association Annual Meeting	Japan
Kaneko and Chern (2005)	*Journal of Agricultural and Applied Economics*	United States
Kimenju and De Groote (2008)	*Agricultural Economics*	Kenya
Krystallis, Fotopoulos, and Zotos (2006)	*Journal of International Consumer Marketing*	Greece
Liljenstolpe (2008)	*Agribusiness*	United States
Loureiro and Bugbee (2005)	*Journal of Consumer Affairs*	United States
Loureiro and Hine (2002)	*Journal of Agricultural and Resource Economics*	United States
Loureiro and Lotade (2005)	*Ecological Economics*	United States
Loureiro, McCluskey, and Mittelhammer (2002)	*Journal of Consumer Affairs*	United States
Lusk (2003)	*American Journal of Agricultural Economics*	United States
Lusk, Daniel, et al. (2001)	*Journal of Agricultural and Resource Economics*	United States
Lusk, Morrow, et al. (2002)	*International Food and Agribusiness Management Review*	United States

Lusk, Roosen, and Fox (2003)	*American Journal of Agricultural Economics*	France, Germany, United Kingdom, United States
Lusk, Nilsson, and Foster (2007)	*Environmental and Resource Economics*	United States
Mabiso et al. (2005)	American Agricultural Economics Association Annual Meeting	United States
Rousu et al. (2003)	Working Paper, RTI International, Raleigh, NC, Jan. 2003	United States
Tonsor and Schroeder (2003)	American Agricultural Economics Association Annual Meeting	United Kingdom, Germany
Tonsor and Schroeder (2003)	American Agricultural Economics Association Annual Meeting	France, United Kingdom, Germany
Wachenheim and van Wechel (2004)	*Journal of Food Distribution Research*	United States
Wessells, Johnston, and Donath (1999)	*American Journal of Agricultural Economics*	United States
West et al. (2002)	*Canadian Journal of Agricultural Economics*	Canada

Table 35.2 Summary of explanatory variables

Variable name	Definition	Mean	Standard deviation
WTP	US$ willingness to pay extra per pound	7.933	26.394
CV	Contingent valuation study = 1; 0 otherwise	0.274	0.447
CE	Choice experiment = 1; 0 otherwise	0.562	0.498
Auction	Experimental auction = 1; 0 otherwise	0.178	0.383
NorthAmerica	Study conducted in North America = 1; 0 otherwise	0.534	0.500
Europe	Study conducted in Europe = 1; 0 otherwise	0.3630	0.4825
Restworld	Restworld = 1 if study not conducted in North America or Europe; 0 otherwise	0.1027	0.30466
GMFree-Food	Gm_Free_Food = 1 if food product carries GM-free food label; 0 otherwise	0.644	0.480
Green-Food	Green claim (organic product, co-labeled) = 1 if food grown according to environmental standards; 0 otherwise	0.219	0.415
Welfare-Food	Welfare claim = 1 if food product considered fair trade or animal welfare practices; 0 otherwise	0.048	0.214
Other	Other labeling schemes = 1 if food label is a local denomination of origin, food safety standards; 0 otherwise	0.0821	0.2756
Household	Respondent belongs to a household or acts in representation of one = 1; 0 otherwise	0.609	0.489
Consumer	Participant is a consumer = 1; 0 otherwise	0.198	0.400
Other-participant	Participant is a student, farmer, or other type = 1; 0 otherwise	0.0273	0.163
SampleSize	Number of participants in study	839.123	1309.27
Inperson	Data were collected in person, 0	0.212	0.410

sample of study, it was not possible to collect the socioeconomic characteristics of each particular study in this selected data set based on the corresponding samples. This was due to the large heterogeneity present when reporting crucial variables such as income, education, and age.

To identify the effects of all the aforementioned variables on the premium for ethical food claims, a linear regression model is used, where the dependent variable is the price premium or WTP for the particular ethical product expressed in US$ 2008 (US cents per pound), with robust standard errors obtained by clustering the observations by study. In addition to the mean WTP modeled here, it is necessary to highlight the need to look at the median and dispersion measures. Unfortunately, most studies reported just one welfare estimate (mean or median) and very few construct confidence intervals around them. This is the main reason to select the mean WTP as the dependent variable in the following estimation.

4 METHODOLOGY AND MODEL SPECIFICATION

As is well known, a meta-analysis approach can be defined as the study of studies. It refers to the statistical analysis of a large collection of results from individual studies for the purpose of integrating the main findings (Glass, McGaw, and Smith 1981). Proponents of meta-analysis maintain that the valuable aspects of narrative reviews can be communicated in such studies, and are in fact extended with quantitative features (Rosenthal and Di Matteo 2001). Recent meta-analyses have been conducted in the field of economic valuation of environmental resources, impacts, and services (Brander, Florax, and Vermaat 2006; Ojea and Loureiro 2011). However, the meta-analysis conducted by Lusk, Jamal, et al. (2005) to assess preferences for GM foods is of particular interest for the objectives of the current study.

The dependent variable in our meta-regression equation is a vector of WTP values, denoted as y. Following Brander, Florax, and Vermaat (2006), the explanatory variables are grouped into three different categories that include the study characteristics in X_s, the product ethical characteristics in X_p, and the socioeconomic and participants' characteristics in X_e. The empirical estimation is undertaken with an ordinary linear regression model, which corresponds with the following empirical equation:

$$y = \beta_0 + \beta_1 Green\_Food + \beta_2 Welfare\_Food + \beta_3 GMFree\_Food$$
$$+ \beta_4 Inperson + \beta_5 SampleSize + \beta_6 CV + \beta_7 CE + \beta_8 NorthAmerica$$
$$+ \beta_9 Europe + \beta_{10} Households + \beta_{11} Consumers + \varepsilon$$

The dependent variable (y) in our regression equation is a vector of WTP values. The first group of explanatory variables is the product's characteristics, including whether the product has been produced following environmental standards (*Green_Food*), welfare and social considerations (*Welfare_Food*), or GM-free processes

(*GMFree_Food*), omitting the variable *others*, which contains food safety studies and others related to designation of origin.

Additional variables are related to the study's characteristics, including whether the observations were elicited in person (*Inperson*), the sample size of participants (*SampleSize*), the elicitation method employed to collect the data, explicitly considering contingent valuation (*CV*) and choice experiments (*CE*), while *Experimental Auctions* is the omitted variable. Additional information includes the indicator variable denoting whether the study was conducted in European countries (*Europe*), in North America (*NorthAmerica*), or in the rest of the world (*rw*, omitted).

5 Results

Table 35.3 presents the results of this analysis. Results are reported presenting the implicit valuations of the three main ethical claims (Table 35.3), including *GMFree-Food*, *Green-Food*, and *Welfare-Food*, in regard to the omitted variable (*Others*). With respect to the types of ethical claim, the results obtained from this meta-analysis allow us to conclude that GM-free is the most valuable ethical claim worldwide, when compared with the implicit valuations of animal welfare, green certification schemes, and others. In particular, the results show that food products with a GM-free label carry on average a price premium of about 20 cents over the original price. This encouraging result is followed by the price premium gathered by ethical claims, which is statistically significant at the threshold level of 10 percent. Additionally, other results indicate that claims denoting that a product is green do not impact the valuation of the product in any statistically significant way.

Table 35.3 Meta-analytical regression (N = 138)

Variable	Coefficient	Robust standard error	T-statics	p-value
Green-Food	8.797	7.802	1.13	0.268
Welfare-Food	15.421	9.178	1.68	0.102
GMFree-Food	20.277	10.114	2.00	0.053
Inperson	−8.426	11.822	−0.71	0.481
SampleSize	0.001	0.001	0.59	0.559
CV	−5.948	6.124	−0.97	0.339
CE	−6.911	5.520	−1.25	0.219
NorthAmerica	−37.643	22.100	−1.70	0.098
Europe	−23.900	20.438	−1.17	0.251
Household	9.466	4.742	2.00	0.054
Consumer	33.937	11.055	3.07	0.004
Constant	15.168	11.055	3.07	0.004
R-squared	0.392			

In regard to the *CV* and *CE* variables, results seem to indicate that studies using *CV* or *CE* procedures were not necessarily more likely to provide higher WTP values than experimental auctions. This may be explained by the fact that experimental auctions can also be hypothetical, and, owing to the small sample size, there is no differentiation between real and experimental auctions. In regard to other methodological variables, we find that participants belonging to a household or acting on behalf of a household, or consumers from a convenient sample, increase the elicited value significantly in regard to other groups made up of students, visitors, farmers, or occasional shoppers. Some significant differences seem to emerge from the different geographical areas in which the studies were conducted. In this respect, the indicator variable denoting that the study was conducted in North America is negative and statistically significant. In regard to the general model fitting, the adjusted R^2 is 0.39, which is comparable to other published meta-analysis in environmental economics using cross-sectional studies (see Brander, Florax, and Vermaat 2006). The F-test is 10.63, with an associated *p*-value of 0.000, denoting the overall significance of the included variables.

6 Conclusions

Although a large body of literature is growing in regard to the valuation of ethical claims, so far no study has tried to gather international evidence and findings extracted from the analysis of a wide variety of studies. In this chapter, a database is collected at international level, compiling studies published in the area of food valuation in different continents across different years. The usefulness of the findings presented here goes beyond the previous results and can be used to design future studies carefully, mainly in two directions. In general, the predictive capacity of the present model can also be used to obtain starting point bids useful for designing a survey instrument or experimental auction.

Other implications derived from the previous findings are related to the policy recommendations based on the statistical significance of the GM-free product, which may be associated with current international consumer concerns related to food safety scares and food manipulation. This significant preference for GM-free technologies may have to be properly handled by governments and interested parties owing to the current GM proliferation. Additionally, the lack of statistical significance of the various green claims may show a need to communicate the content of such environmentally friendly products better. Overall, the current findings are useful in terms of future design of other studies, and also to recommend current actions to inform policymakers properly of the importance and preferences linked with the claims.

References

Aldanondo-Ochoa, M. A., and C. Almansa-Sáez. 2009. "The Private Provision of Public Environment: Consumer Preferences for Organic Production Systems." *Land Use Policy* 26/3: 669–82.

Andreoni, J., and J. H. Miller. 2002. "Giving According to GARP: An Experimental Test of the Consistency of Preferences for Altruism." *Econometrica* 70/2: 737–53.

Bazoche, P., C. Deola, and L. G. Soler. 2008. "An Experimental Study of Wine Consumers' Willingness to Pay for Environmental Characteristics." Paper presented at the 12th Congress of the European Association of Agricultural Economists, Ghent, Aug. 26–9.

Bernard, J. C., and K. Gifford. 2006. "Consumer Willingness to Pay Premiums for Non-GM and Organic Foods." *Consumer Interests Annual* 52: 343–54.

Bernheim, B. D. 1994. "A Theory of Conformity." *Journal of Political Economy* 102/5: 841–77.

Brander, L., R. Florax, and J. Vermaat. 2006. "The Empirics of Wetland Valuation: A Comprehensive Summary and a Meta-Analysis of the Literature." *Environmental and Resource Economics* 33: 223–50.

Bukenya, J. O., and N. R. Wright. 2007. "Determinants of Consumer Attitudes and Purchase Intentions with regard to Genetically Modified Tomatoes." *Agribusiness* 23/1: 117–30.

Carlsson, F., P. Frykblom, and C. J. Lagerkvist. 2005. "Consumer Preferences for Food Product Quality Attributes from Swedish Agriculture." *Ambio* 34: 366–70.

——————. 2007. "Consumer Benefits of Labels and Bans on GM Foods: Choice Experiments with Swedish Consumers." *American Journal of Agricultural Economics* 89: 152–61.

Chen, H., and W. S. Chern. 2002. "Consumer Acceptance of Genetically Modified Foods." Paper prepared for the Annual Meeting of the American Agricultural Economics Association, Long Beach, CA, July 28–31.

Chern, W. S., K. Rickertsen, N. Tsuboi, and T. Fu. 2002. "Consumer Acceptance and Willingness to Pay for Genetically Modified Vegetable Oil and Salmon: A Multiple-Country Assessment." *AgBioForum* 5/3: 105–12.

Christoph, I. B., J. Roosen, and M. Bruhn. 2006. "Willingness to Pay for Genetically Modified Food and Non-Food Products." Selected Paper prepared for the Annual Meeting of the American Agricultural Economics Association, Long Beach, CA, July 23–6.

CIC (Center for International Comparisons of Production, Income and Prices). 2008. *Penn World Table 2008.* <http://pwt.econ.upenn.edu>.

Co-operative Bank. 2008. *The Ethical Consumerism Report, 2007.* <http://www.co-operative bank.co.uk/images/pdf/ethical_consumer_report_2007.pdf>.

Corsi, A., and S. Novelli. 2003. *Measuring Quantity-Constrained and Maximum Prices Consumers Are Willing to Pay for Quality Improvements: The Case of Organic Beef Meat.* Department of Economics Working Papers No. 200207. Turin: University of Turin.

Dhar, T., and J. D. Foltz. 2005. "Milk by Any Other Name . . . Consumer Benefits from Labeled Milk." *American Journal of Agricultural Economics* 87/1: 214–28.

Ehmke, M. T., J. L. Lusk, and W. Tyner. 2006. "The Relative Importance of Preferences for Country-of-Origin in China, France, Niger and the United States." Contributed Paper prepared for the International Association of Agricultural Economists' Conference, Gold Coast, Australia, Aug. 12–18.

Fehr, E., and K. M. Schmidt. 1999. "A Theory of Fairness, Competition, and Cooperation." *Quarterly Journal of Economics* 114/3: 817–68.

Glass, G., B. McGaw, and M. L. Smith. 1981. *Meta-Analysis in Social Research.* Beverly Hills, CA: Sage.

Grannis, J., and D. Thilmany. 2002. "Marketing Natural Pork: An Empirical Analysis of Consumers in the Mountain Region." *Agribusiness* 18/4: 475–89.

Howard, P. H., and P. Allen. 2008. "Consumer Willingness to Pay for Domestic 'Fair Trade': Evidence from the United States." *Renewable Agriculture and Food Systems* 23/3: 235–42.

Hu, W. 2006. "Comparing Consumers' Preferences and Willingness to Pay for Non-GM Oil Using a Contingent Valuation Approach." *Empirical Economics* 31: 143–50.

Jones, E., R. Haenfler, and B. Johnson. 2007. *The Better World Handbook: Small Changes that Make a Big Difference.* <http://www.betterworldhandbook.com/2nd/index.html>.

Kaneko, N. 2005. "Three Essays on Economic Valuation of Consumer Preferences on Genetically Modified Foods." Ph.D. diss. Ohio State University.

——and W. S. Chern. 2004. "Willingness to Pay for Non-Genetically Modified Food: Evidence of Hypothetical Bias from an Auction Experiment in Japan." Paper presented at the Annual Meeting of the American Agricultural Economics Association, Denver, 1–4 Aug.

——2005. "Willingness to Pay for Genetically Modified Oil, Cornflakes, and Salmon: Evidence from a U.S. Telephone Survey." *Journal of Agricultural and Applied Economics* 37/3: 701–19.

Kimenju, S. C., and H. De Groote. 2008. "Consumer Willingness to Pay for Genetically Modified Food in Kenya." *Agricultural Economics* 38: 35–46.

Korthals, M. 2010. "Ethics of Food Production and Consumption." Department of Social Science, Wageningen University. <http://www.app.wur.nl/NR/rdonlyres/E96C8F3F-A0A4-48C3-956C-355C676B1836/24283/MichielKorthalsEthicsofFoodProductionandConsumptio.doc>.

Krystallis, A., C. Fotopoulos, and Y. Zotos. 2006. "Organic Consumers' Profile and their Willingness to Pay (WTP) for Selected Organic Food Products in Greece." *Journal of International Consumer Marketing* 19/1: 81–106.

Liljenstolpe, C. 2008. "Evaluating Animal Welfare with Choice Experiments: An Application to Swedish Pig Production." *Agribusiness* 24/1: 67–84.

List, J. A. 2006. "'Friend or Foe?' A Natural Experiment of the Prisoner's Dilemma." *Review of Economics and Statistics* 88/3: 463–71.

Loureiro, M. L., and M. Bugbee. 2005. "Enhanced GM Foods: Are Consumers Ready to Pay for the Potential Benefits of Biotechnology?" *Journal of Consumer Affairs* 39/1: 52–70.

——, J. J. McCluskey, and R. C. Mittelhammer. 2002. "Will Consumers Pay a Premium for Eco-Labeled Apples?" *Journal of Consumer Affairs* 36/2: 203–19.

——and S. Hine. 2002. "Discovering Niche Markets: A Comparison of Consumer Willingness to Pay for Local (Colorado-Grown), Organic, and GMO-Free Products." *Journal of Agricultural and Applied Economics* 34/3: 477–87.

——and J. Lotade. 2005. "Do Fair Trade and Eco-Labels in Coffee Wake Up the Consumer Conscience?" *Ecological Economics* 53: 129–38.

Lusk, J.L. 2003. "Effects of Cheap Talk on Consumer Willingness-to-Pay for Golden Rice." *American Journal of Agricultural Economics* 85/4: 840–56.

——and B. C. Briggeman. 2009. "Food Values." *American Journal of Agricultural Economics* 91/1: 184–96.

——, M. S. Daniel, D. R. Mark, and C. L. Lusk. 2001. "Alternative Calibration and Auction Institutions for Predicting Consumer Willingness to Pay for Non-Genetically Modified Corn Chips." *Journal of Agricultural and Resource Economics* 26: 40–57.

——, M. Jamal, L. Kurlander, M. Roucan, and L. Taulman. 2005. "A Meta-Analysis of Genetically Modified Food Valuation Studies." *Journal of Agricultural and Resource Economics* 30/1: 28–44.

——, M. Moore, L. House, and B. Morrow. 2002. "Influence of Brand Name and Type of Modification on Consumer Acceptance of Genetically Engineered Corn Chips: A Preliminary Analysis." *International Food and Agribusiness Management Review* 4: 373–83.

——, T. Nilsson, and K. Foster. 2007. "Public Preferences and Private Choices: Effect of Altruism and Free Riding on Demand for Environmentally Certified Pork." *Environmental and Resource Economics* 36/4: 499–521.

——, J. Roosen, and J. A. Fox. 2003. "Demand for Beef from Cattle Administered Growth Hormones or Fed Genetically Modified Corn: A Comparison of Consumers in France, Germany, the United Kingdom, and the United States." *American Journal of Agricultural Economics* 85: 16–29.

Mabiso, A., J. Sterns, L. House, and A. Wysocki. 2005. "Estimating Consumers' Willingness to Pay for Country of Origin Labels in Fresh Apples and Tomatoes: A Double-Hurdle Probit Analysis of American Data Using Factor Scores." Paper presented at the Annual Meeting of the American Agricultural Economics Association, Providence, RI, 24–7 July.

Maslow, A. 1943. "A Theory of Human Motivation." *Psychological Review* 50: 370–96.

Ojea, E., and M. L. Loureiro. 2011. "Identifying the Scope Effect on a Meta-Analysis of Biodiversity Valuation Studies. *Resource Energy and Economics*. <http://www.sciencedirect.com/science?_ob=ArticleURL&_udi=B6VFJ-52BGCPJ-2&_user=2345338&_coverDate= 03%2F08% 2F2011 &_rdoc=1&_fmt=high&_orig= gateway&_origin=gateway&_sort=d&_do canchor= & view= c&_searchStrId=1737900256&_rerunOrigin=google&_acct=C000057006&_version=1&_url Version=0&_userid=2345338&md5=d5bd92a4da400b5b56b7b66e46103a6d&searchtype=a>.

Rosenthal, R., and M. R. DiMatteo. 2001. "Meta-Analysis: Recent Developments in Quantitative Methods for Literature Reviews." *Annual Review of Psychology* 52: 69–82.

Rousu, M., W. E. Huffman, J. F. Shogren, and A. Tegene. 2003. *Should the United States Regulate Mandatory Labeling for Genetically Modified Foods? Evidence from Experimental Auctions*. Working Paper. Raleigh, NC: RTI International, Jan.

Teisl, M. F., B. Roe, and R. L. Hicks. 2002. "Can Eco-Labels Tune a Market? Evidence from Dolphin-Safe Labeling." *Journal of Economics and Management* 43: 339–59.

Thompson, P. B. 2010. *Food Biotechnology in Ethical Perspective*, 2nd edn. International Library of Environmental Agricultural and Food Ethics, 10. Dordrecht: Springer.

Tonsor, G., and T. Schroeder. 2003. "European Consumer Preferences for U.S. and Domestic Beef: Willingness to Pay for Source Verification, Hormone-Free, and Genetically Modified Organism-Free Beef." Selected Paper presented at the Annual Meeting of the American Agricultural Economics Association, Montreal, July 27–30.

TransFair USA. 2007. *Annual Report 2007*. <http://www.transfairusa.org/sites/default/files/2007%20Annual%20Report.pdf>.

Wachenheim, C. J., and T. van Wechel. 2004. "The Influence of Environmental-Impact Information on Consumer Willingness to Pay for Products Labeled as Free of Genetically Modified Ingredients." *Journal of Food Distribution Research* 35: 1–13.

Wessells, C. R., R. J. Johnston, and H. Donath. 1999. "Assessing Consumer Preferences for Ecolabeled Seafood: The Influence of Species, Certifier and Household Attributes." *American Journal of Agricultural Economics* 81/5: 1084–9.

West, G., B. Larue, C. Gendron, and R. Lambert. 2002. "Consumers' Valuation of Functional Properties of Foods: Results from a Canada-Wide Survey." *Canadian Journal of Agricultural Economics* 50/4: 541–58.

INDEX